1302490

Handbook of Research on Reading Comprehension

DI024646

"The Handbook—this term connotes a touchstone across disciplines and areas, whose function is to capture a field, past, present, and future. The result of an enormous effort, a handbook provides a benchmark at a particular point in time.... Two ingredients are of foundational importance for a well-built handbook: the structure and the writers. The editors of this Handbook have assembled an extraordinary assemblage of authors, each distinguished in his or her own right, but a group that is exceptional for the breadth and comprehensiveness of perspectives that they bring to bear.... This Handbook provides an excellent snapshot of the field."

Robert C. Calfee, From the Foreword

The *Handbook of Research on Reading Comprehension* assembles researchers of reading comprehension, literacy, educational psychology, psychology, and neuroscience to document the most recent research on the topic. It summarizes the current body of research on theory, methods, instruction, and assessment, including coverage of landmark studies. Designed to deepen understanding of how past research can be applied and has influenced the present, and to stimulate new thinking about reading comprehension, the volume is organized around seven themes:

- Historical perspectives on reading comprehension
- Theoretical perspectives
- Changing views of text
- Elements of reading comprehension
- Assessing and teaching reading comprehension
- Cultural impact on reading comprehension
- Where to from here?

This is an essential reference volume for the international community of reading researchers, reading psychologists, graduate students, and professionals working in the area of reading and literacy.

Susan E. Israel, Author and Literacy Consultant

Gerald G. Duffy, University of North Carolina at Greensboro, USA

Handbook of Research on Reading Comprehension

Edited by

Susan E. Israel
Author and Literacy Consultant

Gerald G. Duffy
University of North Carolina at Greensboro, USA

Routledge
Taylor & Francis Group

NEW YORK AND LONDON

First published 2009
by Routledge
270 Madison Ave, New York, NY 10016

Simultaneously published in the UK
by Routledge
2 Park Square, Milton Park, Abingdon, Oxon OX14 4RN

Routledge is an imprint of the Taylor & Francis Group, an informa business

© 2009 Taylor & Francis

Typeset in Sabon by EvS Communication Networx, Inc.
Printed and bound in the United States of America on acid-free paper by Sheridan Books, Inc.

All rights reserved. No part of this book may be reprinted or reproduced or utilised in any form or by any electronic, mechanical, or other means, now known or hereafter invented, including photocopying and recording, or in any information storage or retrieval system, without permission in writing from the publishers.

Trademark Notice: Product or corporate names may be trademarks or registered trademarks, and are used only for identification and explanation without intent to infringe.

Library of Congress Cataloging in Publication Data
Handbook of research on reading comprehension / edited by Susan E. Israel and Gerald G. Duffy.
p. cm.
Includes bibliographical references and index.
1. Reading comprehension—Handbooks, manuals, etc. I. Israel, Susan E. II. Duffy, Gerald G.
LB1050.45.H365 2008
428.4'3072—dc22
2007037175

ISBN 10: 0-805-86200-5 (hbk)
ISBN 10: 0-805-86201-3 (pbk)
ISBN 10: 1-410-61585-5 (ebk)

ISBN 13: 978-0-805-86200-3 (hbk)
ISBN 13: 978-0-805-86201-0 (pbk)
ISBN 13: 978-1-410-61585-5 (ebk)

In Memory of Michael Pressley
A scholar
A colleague
A mentor
Our friend

Contents

Foreword

Robert C. Calfee

Constructing a handbook for a field of study is a daunting task, especially for an area as changeable as reading and reading comprehension. The present volume emerges as we end the first decade of the 21st century. Imagine its form if it had been conceived during each of the past several decades, beginning in the 1950s. What were the seminal events and critical issues?

1950s—the postwar era, the Cold War, Sputnik, the publication by Flesch (1955) of *Why Johnny can't read*, which bewailed the proliferation of look-say approaches in early reading instruction.

1960s—the appearance of Jeanne Chall's (1967) landmark volume, *Learning to read: The great debate*, often viewed as concluding that systematic phonics was the essential prerequisite for literacy, but which more importantly led to her formulation of the "stage" model of reading acquisition; the First-grade Reading Studies (Bond & Dykstra, 1967), which suggested that direct instruction in systematic phonics produced higher test scores, but also showed that teacher-within-program variance was substantial, and later revealed the "poop-out" effect; and *Project Literacy* (reported in Gibson & Levin, 1975), which convened interdisciplinary groups to build a broad-based agenda for literacy research.

1970s—the National Institute of Education established a panel headed by George Miller (1973) to advise on a research center focused on reading comprehension, taking advantage of emerging findings in psycholinguistics and cognition; the appearance of Resnick and Weaver's (1979) three-volume work, an extension by LRDC of the *Project Literacy* effort; along with calls for major school improvement.

1980s—establishment of the Center for the Study of Reading (Anderson, 1985) and later the Center for the Study of Writing, which worked from different conceptual models and methodologies to explore the "worlds beyond the basics;" the appearance of *Nation at risk* (National Commission on Excellence in Education, 1983), which called into question the competence of the entire educational establishment.

1990s—the rise and fall of other "reading centers," of the Whole Language movement, and of reform movements (ranging from Slavin to Accelerated Schools to Comer). A time of political change and uncertainty in education generally and for literacy in particular. The earlier hopes for quick and easy fixes began to fade.

2000s—The *No Child Left Behind* Act and then *Reading First*; the National Reading Panel Report (NICHD, 2000) and a return to the basics (primarily phonics); randomized field trials as the methodological gold standard (in many

Support provided by U.S. Department of Education Institute for Education Sciences Grant No. R305G50069.

respects a replay of the First-grade Reading Studies); and a sense that many educators are holding their breaths (and raising their thumbs) in anticipation of the sea changes that may be ahead.

This brief survey portrays pendulum swings, to be sure, but the appearance of this Handbook suggests that, despite a history of to-and-fro events, an optimistic observer can find signs of progress here and there. On the one hand, the chapters document the substantial progress achieved in recent decades. In 1968, Kolers' introduction to Huey's (1908/1968) classic *The psychology and pedagogy of reading* found few breakthroughs in theory and research on the "basics" of reading (decoding and phonics), but commented that Huey was at a loss to deal with comprehension: "The brilliance of Huey's observation and insight [about the word recognition aspects of reading] dims at the mares-nest of 'meaning...,' [but] he does make some very useful points" (pp. xxix–xxx). Most of these points centered around word-level understanding, and the interplay of audition and imagery. But Huey also offered words of advice related to comprehension that, while not supported by empirical research, strike a resonant chord in today's classroom practices: "School readers, especially primers, should largely disappear, except as they may be competent editings of real literature, presented in literary wholes, or as records of the children's own experiences or thoughts.... Children should learn to read books, papers, records, letters, etc., as need arises in their lives, just as adults do, and they should be trained to do such reading effectively. They should from the first read as fast as the nature of the matter read and their purpose with it will permit, but without *hurry*" (p. 381). The implication is that students should read things that matter, and that they should take time to study what they read, both of which relate far more to comprehension than to word recognition.

I was not around during the Huey days, of course, but my career does span much of the past several decades, sometimes an observer and sometimes a participant, sometimes in research and sometimes in practice. These experiences lead me now to venture a few thoughts about literacy, about comprehension, and about building a handbook on these topics.

Literacy—as a result of hard fought battles across these decades, the field now possesses models and evidence to support the advantages of a balanced view of literacy (Pressley, 2005), an enormous data base for shaping practice that is cogently presented in this volume. The evidence is based in part on negative findings; a failure to attend systematically to the development of skill and knowledge about English orthography leaves many students in a lurch, and likewise for a failure to attend systematically to the development of skill and knowledge about comprehension and vocabulary. To be sure, the difficult tasks of engineering an appropriate balance remain to be tackled. In addition, these findings are often disregarded in practice, but one can find elements incorporated in basal readers where the rubber hits the road. Unfortunately, today's teachers, working under the pressures of test-driven accountability, often follow the basic strands, and spend little time on the boxed asides about meta-cognitive questions and the like.

In particular, development and learning pathways remain largely unexplored territory (Resnick & Weaver, 1979). Chall's "stages" provide the map most often used in practice, one that meshes well with the "simple" view of reading that Duffy and Israel see as pervasive throughout this volume. Teach young children to decode with fluency, and then move them toward comprehension, where they can rely upon established oral language capacity. This model seems to me to go awry in various ways, of which I will mention two. First, studies of academic language (Wong-Fillmore & Snow, 2000) show quite clearly the need to guide all students toward the formal language register that is essential for success in school—and beyond. Much of this handbook centers around the notion of comprehension as deep understanding of "text," requiring skill and will, explicitness, strategy and purpose, the essence of academic language.

Second, the notion of a linear progression from letters to sounds to words to sentences and finally to sentences seems fundamentally flawed. As an aside, it is certainly not the model followed by middle-class parents, who instead immerse their children in a broad array of literate activities virtually from conception onward. But more to the point, waiting for children to acquire fluency with the print system before engaging them in other aspects of language development can waste years of opportunities that may be especially valuable for those from homes where academic language is not the norm. It also means that these children do not see the purpose in what is too often a struggle to learn that alphabetic squiggles can be translated into "texts" with little to comprehend and even less to provide interest. Rather than a linear progression from bits and pieces to the "good stuff," imagine instead the learning of literacy as a braid stretching from the earliest encounter with schooling onward, in which decoding is interwoven with vocabulary, with literary narratives, and with expository reports, where comprehension and composition receive equal attention. While the child is working to comprehend orthography (and I use "comprehend" intentionally), oral language and figural graphics support the other areas. A young student may struggle with vowel digraphs, but that is no reason to deny him or her access to dinosaurs and Tyrannosaurus Rex, nor dissuade him or her from reporting reactions to these beasts of long ago. An echo of Huey, including the connection to writing.

Orchestrating the weaving of this braid during a school year and across the years requires a high degree of professional skill on the part of teachers. Instructional tools (e.g., basal readers, along with other technologies) might play an important role—they would require considerable redesign to support the braid concept. But it is, as the teacher assesses and guides learning, that the braid is woven and the strands shaped. Balance in this model requires a continual analysis of the numerous braids that make up a class of students at any point in time, and a continual eye for problems and opportunities.

Comprehension—as a first definition, let me suggest "the strategic reconstruction of a text toward a particular purpose." Each of these terms, but especially "text," requires explication—much of this volume is dedicated to this task. "Purpose" may seem out of place, but let me suggest that it plays an important role in the move from a natural to formal language register. Before a child becomes literate, purpose remains implicit and often undetected. When Johnny says, "I didn't hear you," he often means "I see no point in attending to what you were saying."

Success in school tasks requires students to create a sense of purpose in situations that have no immediate interest and no obvious long-term value. They are asked to engage in strategic activities that at first seem quite unnatural and unnecessarily demanding. The Latin root suggests that to "comprehend" is to "wrestle with something." For both individual reflection and action by the teacher, explicitness—the capacity to explain one's thinking—is critically important. And explicitness depends upon possession of a shared vocabulary of key terms and relations. Hence, the importance of "meta-comprehension" in the development of comprehension.

Two terms have emerged as keystones for comprehension instruction: *genre* and *structure*. Genre has evolved from the classical rhetoric in recent decades to take on new socio-cultural meanings (Schleppegrel, 2004), but many of the traditional concepts and contrasts serve quite well across the grades: the contrast between narration and exposition, and the functions of informing, persuading, and explaining. These labels may not be easy words for kindergartners, but the concepts are both teachable and learnable, and they can be translated. Text structures (Chambliss & Calfee, 1998), especially for explicating comprehension schemata, were a major contribution from the 1980s, and possess substantial potential for reconstructing and constructing texts, and for the interplay between the two. Again, for kindergartners the structures chosen to begin with may be simple, but they provide prototypes for grander constructions in later grades.

The *handbook*—the term connotes a touchstone across disciplines and areas, whose function is to capture a field, past, present and future. Building a handbook is necessarily a dynamic enterprise. The result of enormous effort, a handbook provides a benchmark at a particular point in time, one that is outdated virtually almost as soon as it is published. A handbook is clearly a labor of love—I have yet to meet with an editorial team who did it for money, nor even for fame.

Two ingredients are of foundational importance for a well-built handbook: the structure and the writers. The editors of this volume have assembled an extraordinary collection of authors, each distinguished in his or her own right, but a group that is exceptional for the breadth and comprehensiveness of perspectives that they bring to bear. Although admittedly heavy in the educational psychology arena, the authors include representatives from linguistics, anthropology, and the curriculum-instruction arenas. The volume encompasses a broad range of experience, including contributors from my generation (I was pleased to find chapters by the Goodmans and Harste, among the first to call for more attention to the importance of comprehension in the early grades), along with a sprinkling of graduate student co-authors. The reader will find hard-nosed empirical scholars (I would place Paris and Alexander in this category) along with strong-voiced advocates (certainly the Goodmans and Harste, but also Tierney and Allington; this aside is admittedly an oversimplification, because all of the contributors bring a range of talents and commitments to the task, but it points out the political aspects of reading comprehension).

I have read only selected chapters at the time of this writing but will conclude with a few thoughts about content and organization as I await the final version. The volume appears to have touched all the bases that I mentioned earlier, and provides an excellent snapshot of the field. When I receive the book, I will be interested in looking at connections among certain key elements: theory and process; instruction and assessment; development (spread over a couple of sections) and learning (what is it that needs to be learned); cultural and linguistic; teachers and home/family. Of particular importance will be the treatment of discourse, including variation in language registers (natural vs. academic language), the contrasts between narrative and expository texts, and the interplay of comprehension and composition. These queries are really meant to help set the stage for the editors of the second edition, who will probably want to give more attention to the teacher's role in promoting comprehension, and in the intertwining braid of learning from early childhood through the young adult years. To be sure, the passage of time changes our perspectives. The handbook published in 2017 will undoubtedly surface a different set of issues, but it will find in this volume a solid foundation for advancing the field. We can only hope that the political context will provide the understanding to support these advances.

REFERENCES

Anderson, R. C. (1985). *Becoming a nation of readers*. Urbana, IL: National Council of Teachers of English.
Bond, G. L., & Dykstra, R. (1967). The cooperative research program in first-grade reading instruction. *Reading Research Quarterly, 2* (Whole No. 4).
Chall, J. S. (1967). *Learning to read: The great debate*. New York: McGraw-Hill.
Chambliss, M. J., & Calfee, R. C. (1998). *Textbooks for learning: Nurturing children's minds*. Oxford, UK: Blackwell.
Flesch, R. (1955). *Why Johnny can't read*. New York: Harper.
Gibson, E. J., & Levin, H. (1975). *The psychology of reading*. Cambridge, MA: MIT Press.
Huey, E. B. (1968). *The psychology and pedagogy of reading*. Cambridge, MA: MIT Press. (Original work published 1908)

Miller, G. A. (Ed.). (1973). *Linguistic communication: Perspectives for research* (Report of the Study Group on Linguistic Communication to the National Institute of Education). Newark, DE: International Reading Association.

National Commission on Excellence in Education (1983). *A nation at risk*. Washington, DC: U. S. Government Printing Office.

NICHD (2000). *Report of the National Reading Panel: Teaching children to read.* (NIH Publication No. 00-4709). Washington, DC: U. S. Government Printing Office.

Pressley, M. (2005). *Reading instruction that works: The case for balanced teaching,* Revised Ed. New York: Guilford.

Resnick, L. B., & Weaver, P. A. (1979). (Eds.). *Theory and practice of early reading,* Vols 1–3. Hillsdale, NJ: Erlbaum.

Schleppegrel, M. (2004). *The language of schooling.* Mahwah, NJ: Erlbaum.

Wong-Fillmore, L., & Snow, C. (2000). *What reading teachers need to know about the English language.* Washington, DC: Center for Applied Linguistics.

Preface

Men must keep thinking; and the data assumed by psychology, just like those assumed by physics and the other natural sciences, must some time be overhauled. The effort to overhaul them clearly and thoroughly is metaphysics; but metaphysics can only perform her task well when distinctly conscious of its great extent.

William James (1971, p. xiv)

The editors and contributors of this volume realize the importance of reading comprehension acquisition and the role of effective instruction in the future of reading achievement and literacy development. Through a lifetime of literacy research, some longer than others, we have spent our careers thinking, reading, and analyzing reading research in order to discover the very best methods of teaching reading and reading comprehension. One editor of this volume, while serving as a classroom teacher, discovered *Mosaic of Thought* (Keene & Zimmermann, 1997), a book that raised her curiosity about how best to teach reading comprehension. Similar to William James' thought noted above, Keene and Zimmermann believed that thought is about revisiting the "myriad of ways in which we construct meaning as we read."

> This book is about having a conversation with ourselves and with children. It is about revisiting the myriad ways in which we construct meaning as we read. It is about lively talk in classrooms and what happens when children develop an awareness of their thought processes as they read. It is about explicit comprehension instruction that is rich and deep and invites children to contribute significantly to the conversation about the mental journey we take when we read. (p. 11)

Delivery of effective reading comprehension depends on research. Communicating this research is the main goal of the editors and contributors of this volume.

DESIGN OF THE VOLUME

The Handbook of Research on Reading Comprehension disseminates the research on reading comprehension to date. This book is not an attempt to replace two exceptional books on comprehension instruction: *Comprehension Instruction: Research-based Best Practices* edited by Block and Pressley (2002) or *Improving Comprehension Instruction: Rethinking Research, Theory, and Classroom Practice* edited by Block, Gambrell, and Pressley (2002). Both are excellent resources. However, *The Handbook of Research on Reading Comprehension* is unique in that it assembles researchers of reading comprehension, psychology, educational psychology, neuroscience, and literacy to document the most recent research on the topic.

OVERVIEW OF MAJOR THEMES

This volume is organized into seven major parts representative of the major bodies of research in reading comprehension. Part I places the volume in the historical aspects of reading comprehension. Part II explores the theoretical perspectives on the comprehension processes that provide the foundation for the research on reading comprehension. Part III, Changing Views of Text, summarizes new and changing domains of reading comprehension. Part IV, Elements of Reading Comprehension, focuses on the developmental aspects of reading comprehension, as well as metacognitive and self-regulated strategies. Part V, Assessing and Teaching Reading Comprehension, presents research in the area of assessing reading comprehension, comprehension instruction, and intervention practices that influence reading comprehension. Part VI, Cultural Impact on Reading Comprehension, focuses on the field's new advances on how to address student diversity in our changing society. Part VII, Where to from Here?, summarizes the current situation from the perspective of teacher education and of policy and summarizes the questions raised and themes presented throughout the volume.

Our goal is that this book will help you deepen your understanding of how past comprehension research can be applied and has influenced the present in the area of reading comprehension. We also hope this volume will stimulate continued thinking, reflecting, and studying of reading comprehension.

On behalf of the editors and contributors, a portion of the royalties of this book are being contributed to scholarship funds set up in memory of Michael Pressley at the University of Notre Dame and at Michigan State University.

REFERENCES

Block, C. C., & Pressley, M. (2002). *Comprehension instruction: Research-based best practices.* New York: Guilford.

Block, C.C., Gambrell, L. B., & Pressley, M. (2002). *Improving comprehension instruction: Rethinking research, theory, and classroom practice.* San Francisco, CA: Jossey-Bass and Newark, DE: International Reading Association.

James, W. (1971). *The principles of psychology.* William Benton, Publisher: Encyclopedia Britannica. (Original work published 1952)

Keene, E. O., & Zimmermann, S. (1997). *Mosaic of thought: Teaching comprehension in a reader's workshop.* Portsmouth, NH: Heinemann.

Acknowledgments

First, we want to acknowledge the contributors who worked diligently in meeting our deadlines, revising their chapters as requested, and working in a collegial manner at all times. The contributors accepted with enthusiasm the responsibility for writing the chapters that focused on their area of expertise. In addition, they made our job as editors extremely easy by working with us throughout the editing process of their chapters, as well as providing us with suggestions on how to restructure the contents. For their scholarship and dedication to the field of reading, we are extremely grateful.

We would also like to thank our editor, Naomi Silverman, who believed in the value of publishing this volume.

We would like to acknowledge the assistance of Katie Cosgrove and Sara Roscoe, graduate students at the University of North Carolina – Greensboro. Their hard work is much appreciated.

Finally, I, Susan E. Israel, wish to express my gratitude to my coeditor, Gerry Duffy. As a senior scholar in the area of literacy, Gerry accepted the invitation to be my co-editor, and he provided the level of expertise necessary to produce a volume of the highest quality. However, Gerry provided more than expertise; he provided mentorship and leadership. Gerry, if this is your swan song, then I am feeling extremely privileged to have worked with you. Thank you.

About the Editors

Susan E. Israel, PhD, is currently a literary consultant. She taught at the University of Notre Dame for the Alliance for Catholic Education summer program. Her research agenda focuses on reading comprehension and child-mind development as it relates to literacy processes in reading and writing. Dr. Israel was awarded the 2005 Panhellenic Council Outstanding Professor Award at the University of Dayton. She was the 1998 recipient of the teacher-researcher grant from the International Reading Association where she has served and been a member for over a decade. Currently, she is exploring publishing opportunities in the area of children's literature and young adult fiction and nonfiction. She is also studying the effectiveness of undergraduate student-faculty research collaboratives. She works primarily with literacy professional development in Catholic schools. She recently published two books with the International Reading Association: an edited volume with Michelle M. Israel titled, *Poetic Possibilities: Poems to Enhance Literacy Learning* (2006), which features poems from the *Reading Teacher,* and an edited volume with E. Jennifer Monaghan titled, *Shaping the Reading Field: The Impact of Early Reading Pioneers on Scientific-research and Progressive Education.* Dr. Israel would enjoy hearing from those who have found this volume useful. She may be contacted at sueisrael@insightbb.com.

Gerald G. Duffy, EdD, is the William E. Moran Distinguished Professor of Reading and Literacy at the University of North Carolina at Greensboro. He is also Professor Emeritus at Michigan State University where he served for 25 years as a faculty member and as a Senior Researcher for the Institute of Research on Teaching. He is a past president of the National Reading Conference and a Member of the Reading Hall of Fame. His research has utilized both qualitative and quantitative designs in studying effective reading strategy instruction and teacher development in naturalist classroom-based and field-based settings. He has published over 150 journal articles, chapters, and research monographs, and has written or edited five books, most recently *Explaining Reading* published by Guilford (2003). His teaching and service includes developing and teaching a variety of innovative teacher education programs, conducting short and long-term field-based literacy workshops, teaching undergraduate and graduate literacy classes at university and school sites throughout North America, Asia, and Europe, and mentoring doctoral students. His work at Greensboro focuses on studying the intersection of teacher effectiveness in literacy and the effectiveness of teacher preparation programs. Dr. Duffy may be contacted at ggduffy@aol.com.

Contributors

Peter Afflerbach, University of Maryland, College Park, MD

Patricia A. Alexander, University of Maryland, College Park, MD

Richard L. Allington, University of Tennessee, Knoxville, TN

Janice F. Almasi, University of Kentucky, Lexington, KY

Kathryn H. Au, University of Hawai'i, Honolulu, HA

Linda Baker, University of Maryland, Baltimore, MD

James F. Baumann, University of Dayton, Dayton, OH

Lisa Carter Beall, University of Maryland, Baltimore, MD

Cathy Collins Block, Texas Christian University, Fort Worth, YX

Patrick Bresnahan, University of Illinois, Chicago, IL

JoAnne Caldwell, Cardinal Stritch University Random Lake, WI

Robert C. Calfee, University of California, Riverside, CA

Gerald Campano, Indiana University, Bloomington, IN

Kelly B. Cartwright, Christopher Newport University, Newport News, VA

Byeoung-Young Cho, University of Maryland, College Park, MD

Helen Kim Chou, Stanford University, Stanford, CA

Mark W. Conley, Michigan State, East Lansing, MI

Jewell E. Cooper, University of North Caroline – Greensboro, NC

James S. Damico, Indiana University, Bloomington, IN

Stephanie G. Davis, University of North Carolina – Greensboro, NC

Janice A., Dole, University of Utah, Salt Lake City, UT

Kathryn K. Doyle, University of North Carolina – Greensboro, NC

Dina Drits, University of Utah, Salt Lake City, UT

Patricia A. Edwards, Michigan State University, East Lansing, MI

Colleen M. Fairbanks, University of North Carolina – Greensboro, NC

Beverly Faircloth, University of North Carolina – Greensboro, NC

Emily Fox, University of Maryland, College Park, MD

James Gavelek, University of Illinois, Chicago, IL

Karen W. Gavigan, University of North Carolina – Greensboro, NC

MariAnne George, University of Illinois, Chicago, IL

Kenneth S. Goodman, University of Arizona, Tucson, AZ

Yetta M. Goodman, University of Arizona, Tucson, AZ

Erika Swarts Gray, University of North Carolina – Greensboro, NC

Ellen E. Hamilton, University of Michigan, Ann Arbor, MI

Jerome C. Harste, Indiana University, Bloomington, IN

James V. Hoffman, University of Texas-Austin, TX

George G. Hruby, Utah State University, Logan, UT

Angela Gating Jones, University of North Carolina – Greensboro, NC

Michael L. Kamil, Stanford University, Stanford, CA

Julie Kaomea, University of Hawai'i-Manoa, Manoa, HA

Kathryn A. Kear, University of North Carolina – Greensboro, NC

Jan Lacina, Texas Christian University, Fort Worth, TX

Lauren Leslie, Marquette University, Milwaukee, WI

Penny Mason, University of North Carolina – Greensboro, NC

Dixie D. Massey, University of Puget Sound, Orting, WA

Lynn Masteson, University of Texas at Austin, TX

Anne McGill-Franzen, University of Tennessee, Knoxville, TN

Samuel D. Miller, University of North Carolina – Greensboro, NC

Abigail Nies, University of Illinois, Chicago, IL

Jeffery Nokes, Brigham Young University, Provo, UT

Scott G. Paris, University of Michigan, Ann Arbor, MI

Seth A. Parsons, University of North Carolina – Greensboro, NC

P. David Pearson, University of California, Berkeley, CA

Kathryn Prater, University of North Carolina – Greensboro, NC

Roya Qualls, University of North Carolina-Greensboro, NC

Taffy E. Raphael, University of Illinois, Chicago, IL

Cathy Roller, International Reading Association, Washington, DC

Misty Sailors, University of Texas-San Antonio, TX

Cynthia Shanahan, University of Illinois, Chicago, IL

Katherine A. Dougherty Stahl, New York University, New York, NY

Shannon Swiger, University of New Hampshire, Durham, NH

Robert Tierney, University of British Columbia, Vancouver, BC

Jennifer D. Turner, University of Maryland, College Park, MD

Sandra M. Webb, University of North Carolina – Greensboro, NC

Catherine M. Weber, University of Illinois, Chicago, IL

Ruth Wharton-McDonald, University of New Hampshire, Durham, NH

Baxter Williams, University of North Carolina – Greensboro, NC

Keli Garas-York, Buffalo State College, Buffalo, NY

Part I

Historical Perspectives on Reading Comprehension

1 The Roots of Reading Comprehension Instruction*

P. David Pearson

University of California, Berkeley

This volume is a watershed in the field of reading. That we have reached the point in our history when an entire handbook could be devoted to the topic of reading comprehension is gratifying, especially for those (many of whom are authors in the volume) who have worked across the last 40 years to ensure that reading comprehension has a home in the field's portfolio of theory, research, curriculum, and assessment. Lest we dwell too long in celebratory mode, we would do well to remind ourselves that it has not been easy to secure a foothold for reading comprehension in these conversations about reading, especially around the question of early reading pedagogy. As I will document in this chapter, it was not until the 1980s that it really started to take hold especially as a fact of everyday classroom instruction informed by theory and research. And then suddenly, after 15 years of prominence in conversations of theory, research, and practice—and for a host of reasons, many having to do with curricular politics (Pearson, 2004, 2007), reading comprehension was placed on a back burner from the mid-1990s to the mid-2000s. It is time it returned to a central role in discussions of reading pedagogy. To assure its return, we will have to give it our rapt and collective attention.

Reading comprehension, both its instruction and its assessment, is arguably the most important outcome of reform movements designed to improve reading curriculum and instruction—or at least it ought to be. The trends over the past 5 or 6 years are encouraging (e.g., this volume; Snow, 2003). The emphasis on comprehension has been reinforced by attention to the plight of older readers, for whom comprehension is the both the central goal and barrier (Biancarosa & Snow, 2006). The time is right to undertake a new initiative in the area of reading comprehension, and this volume marks our professional commitment to do so. By taking stock of our past and present, we pave the way for future lines of inquiry, curriculum, and professional development to make sure we will all keep comprehension in clear professional focus.

The process of text comprehension has always provoked exasperated but nonetheless enthusiastic inquiry within the research community. Comprehension, or "understanding", by its very nature, is a phenomenon that can only be observed *indirectly* (Pearson & Johnson, 1978; Johnston, 1984). We talk about the "click" of comprehension that propels a reader through a text, yet we never see it directly. We can only rely on indirect symptoms and artifacts of its occurrence. People tell us that they understood, or were puzzled by, or enjoyed, or were upset by a text. Or, more commonly, we quiz them on "the text" in some way—requiring them to recall its gist or its major details, asking specific questions about its content and purpose, or insisting on an interpretation

---

*Many of the concepts in this chapter first appeared in other works, such as Pearson and Stephens (1993), Pearson (2000), or Pearson (2004).

and critique of its message. All of these tasks, however challenging or engaging they might be, are little more than the residue of the comprehension process itself. Like it or not, it is precisely this residue that scholars of comprehension and comprehension assessment must work with in order to improve our understanding of the construct. The transparency of the act of comprehension is not much better for instruction than assessment. We talk about activities that foster reading comprehension and those that allow students to monitor their comprehension (Palincsar & Brown, 1984), we teach skills and strategies explicitly (Afflerbach, Pearson, & Paris, 2008), and we engage in rich talk about text (Nystrand, Gamoran, Kachur, & Prendergast, 1997; Nystrand, Wu, Gamoran, Zeiser, & Long, 2003), but we are seldom privy to the "aha!" that occurs when there is a "meeting of the minds" between author and reader (King, 2000).

Most of this chapter is history—a history that attempts to weave together threads from research, theory, and curricular practice for the expressed purpose of understanding what we do inside schools and classrooms to support and promote reading comprehension. But in an introductory chapter, all I can do is to highlight themes, trends, and insights with the broadest of brush strokes. The real history, enlivened by all of the excruciating detail of research studies and deep analyses of theory, comes in the remainder of the volume. In the pages that follow, I try to provide a systematic unpacking of those themes, trends, and insights. My goal is to provide sufficient detail to bring you to the brink of the current era, roughly, the latest turn of the century, as a way of providing a baseline for what comes in the rest of the volume. I have divided the world of reading comprehension instruction into three periods with decidedly and admittedly overlapping boundaries; the one observation I am sure of is that any divisions made in the historical timeline are doomed to misrepresentation. Ideas and practices come with ancestors and precedents, even when they appear to emerge suddenly, and they persist long after their theoretical and research foundations appear to have been overturned. But some rough divisions are helpful, even if they obscure some of the truth. The first period tracks the evolution of reading comprehension instruction before the beginning of the revolution in cognitive psychology that led to a paradigm shift in how we think about comprehension and its instruction—roughly the first 75 years of the 20th century. The second period is a short 15 years, from 1975 to the early 1990s; it examines the theoretical and research bases of the instructional activities and routines spawned by the cognitive revolution. The last period is even shorter, from the early 1990s, but with strong roots in the 1980s and even the 1970s, to the end of the century, spilling over into the early years of the 21st century.

READING COMPREHENSION INSTRUCTION BEFORE 1975

Reading comprehension has been a part of classrooms as long as there have been schools, texts, students who desire (or are required) to read them, and teachers wanting to both promote and assess their understanding. Throughout the history of reading instruction, every assignment given by a teacher, every book report or chapter summary, and every conversation about a book, story, article, or chapter has provided an opportunity promoting comprehension. However, it was not until well into the 20th century that comprehension arrived as a modal index of reading competence and performance. There are two plausible explanations for the relatively late arrival of comprehension as an indicator of reading accomplishment. First, the default indicator of reading prowess in the 17th to19th centuries was definitely oral capacity, indexed either by accuracy or by expressive fluency, in the tradition of declamation and oratory (see Smith & Miller, 1966, or Mathews, 1966, for accounts of this emphasis). Second, within ecclesiastical circles, comprehension, at least in the sense of personal understanding, was not truly valued; if it mattered, it mattered largely as a stepping stone to the more valued commodity of text memorization.

An indirect look inside classrooms   To get a handle on how reading comprehension was "taught" in classrooms in the early half of the 20th century, one can examine what is asked of students in their reading anthologies, which date back to the 1840s, by the way, and what is suggested to teachers in training manuals and textbooks. Given the emphasis on accuracy and expressive fluency, the answer, "not much," is not surprising. But there were some consistent threads. Dating back to late 1890s, basal authors included right in the student books (at the end of each selection) several types of "study aids" for students: words to study, phrases to study, and questions to use in preparing for a discussion and/or quiz (Elson & Keck, 1911; Gates & Ayer, 1933). As early as 1912, Longmans Green & Co published a separate book of *Daily Lesson Plans* with suggested vocabulary and comprehension probes to use in introducing and discussing selections. Scott Foresman, the publisher of the Elson Readers from 1909 through the 1930s, also published teacher manuals with answers to the questions in the student books. They added William S. Gray, who made his mark in the field with one of the earliest standardized tests, the Gray Oral Reading Test (Thorndike, 1914), to the roster in the 1920s. The Gray-Elson collaboration resulted in the *Curriculum Foundation Series*, most famous, of course, for Dick and Jane (who were actually Elson's creation, not Gray's), but even more influential in shaping the course of reading instruction over four decades from the early 1930s through the late 1960s. By the 1940s (Gray, Arbuthnot, et al., 1940–1948; Gray, Arbuthnot, Artley, Monroe, et al., 1951–1958), after Elson's death, Gray became the driving force in this influential series. An examination of the manuals (e.g., 1946–47) during this period is instructive because it is clear that the implicit theory behind promoting comprehension (as well as response to literature) was to have the teacher use a range of questions to guide students in conversation during page-by-page guided reading and in a post-reading discussion.

Testing as a catalyst for comprehension   The scientific movement and the changing demographic patterns of schooling in the United States conspired, albeit inadvertently, to bring reading comprehension into instructional focus in the first third of the 20th century. Schools had to accommodate to rapid increases in enrollment due to waves of immigration, a rapidly industrializing society, the prohibition of child labor, and mandatory school attendance laws. The spike in school enrollment, coupled with a population of students with dubious literacy skills, dramatically increased the need for a cheap, efficient screening device to determine students' levels of literacy. During this same period, psychology struggled to gain the status of a "science" by employing the methods that governed physical sciences and research. In the United States, the behaviorist schools of thought, with their focus on measurable outcomes, strongly influenced the field of psychology (Johnston, 1984; Resnick, 1982; Pearson, 2000); quantification and objectivity were the two hallmarks to which educational "science" aspired. Thus, when psychologists with their newfound scientific lenses were put to work creating cheap and efficient tests for beleaguered schools, the course of reading assessment was set. More efficient, group administered, multiple-choice, standardized tests would be the inevitable result. And while there were curricular forces campaigning for a shift away from skills, phonics and oral reading, the need for efficiency certainly served as a catalyst for accelerating the move to more silent reading in our classrooms. Unlike oral reading, which had to be tested individually and required that teachers judge the quality of responses, silent reading comprehension (and rate) could be tested in group settings and scored without recourse to professional judgment; only stop watches and multiple choice questions were needed. In modern parlance, we would say that they moved from a "high inference" assessment tool (oral reading and retelling) to a "low inference" tool (multiple choice tests or timed readings). Thus, it fit the demands for efficiency (spawned by the move toward more universal education for all students) and objectivity (part of the emerging scientism of the period). The practice proved remarkably persistent for at least another 50 or 60 years. And, of course, just like in today's world, if a phenomenon can be assessed, then curriculum and pedagogy to teach it will soon follow.

Early forays into theorizing comprehension   Both Edmund Burke Huey (1908) and Edward Thorndike (1917) undertook early efforts to understand the comprehension process. Huey, a theorist, researcher, and practitioner anticipated constructivist views of reading development (the reader creates the meaning from the traces left on the page by the author) but regarded comprehension as a somewhat mysterious, unapproachable phenomenon, suggesting (1908, p. 163) that

> The consciousness of meaning itself belongs in the main to that group of mental states, the feelings, which I regard with Wundt as unanalyzables, or at lest as having a large unanalyzable core or body.

Huey also foreshadowed the constructivist turn in psychology, literary theory, and pedagogy that would come in the 1970s and 1980s, arguing for a model of sense-making rather than accurate rendition as the hallmark of expert reading:

> And even if the child substitutes words of his own for some that are on the page, provided that these express the meaning, it is an encouraging sign that the reading has been real, and recognition of details will come as it is needed. (Huey, 1908, p. 349)

Huey went on to argue that teachers need to rid themselves of the false ideal that had taken over reading pedagogy: "that to read is to say just what is upon the page, instead of to think, each in his own way, the meaning that the page suggests" (Huey, 1908, p. 349).

Thorndike was probably the first educational psychologist to try to launch inquiry into the complex thought processes associated with comprehension. He regarded reading "as reasoning," suggesting there are many factors that comprise it: "elements in a sentence, their organization…proper relations, selection of certain connotations and the rejection of others, and the cooperation of many forces" (Thorndike, 1917, p. 323). He proposed ideas about what should occur during "correct reading," claiming that a great many misreadings of questions and passages are produced because of under- or over-potency of individual words, thus violating his "correct weighting" principle:

> Understanding a paragraph is like solving a problem in mathematics. It consists in selecting the right elements in the situation and putting them together in the right relations, and also with the right amount of weight or influence or force of each." (Thorndike, 1917, p. 329)

Of course, Thorndike assumed that there are such things as "correct" readings. He argued further that in the act of reading, the mind must organize and analyze ideas from the text. "The vice of the poor reader is to say the words to himself without actively making judgments concerning what they reveal" (Thorndike, 1917, p. 332). Clearly for Thorndike, reading was an active and complex cognitive process. Thorndike's account of reading as meaning making, like Huey's epic treatment of all aspects of reading (1908), is best viewed as an interesting and curious anomaly. It did not become domi-

nant in this early period, either for the field or for Thorndike, but it certainly anticipated, as did Huey's account, the highly active view of the reader that would become
prominent during the cognitive revolution of the 1970s.[1]

Text difficulty and readability   Text difficulty, codified as readability, emerged as an
important research area and curricular concept in the first half of the 20th century.
Unlike the developments in testing, which were grounded in the scientific movement in
psychology, readability was grounded in child-centered views of pedagogy dating back
to theorists such as Pestalozzi, Froebel, and Herbart and championed by the developmental psychology emerging in the 1920s and 1930s.[2] The motive in developing readability formulas was to screen texts so that they could be matched students' interests
and developmental capacities rather than to baffle them with abridged versions of adult
texts. The first readability formula, created to gauge the grade placement of texts,
appeared in 1923 (Lively & Pressey), and it was followed by some 80 additional formulas over the next 40 years until the enterprise drew to at least a temporary close in the
late 1960s.[3] Irrespective of particular twists in individual formulas, each more or less
boiled down to a sentence difficulty factor, typically instantiated as average sentence
length, and a word factor, typically codified as word frequency. These formulas were
critical in the production of commercial reading materials from the 1920s through the
1980s. For reasons that will become apparent later in this chapter, readability formulas
did not survive the cognitive revolution in reading instruction in the 1970s and 1980s,
although there are signs of their recovery in the last decade.[4]

Reading skills   The most influential construct influencing the comprehension curriculum of schools in this period was the "reading skill"—that discrete unit of the
curriculum that ought to be learned by students and taught by teachers. It is hard to
fix the precise genesis of the "reading skill," but it is clearly and hopelessly confounded
with the testing movement. Tests had to measure something, and the something they
measured looked a lot like skills that were a part of the basal reading programs for
elementary and secondary schools of the period. As an example of this relationship,
consider the groundbreaking psychometric work of Frederick Davis (1944) to establish an infrastructure of reading comprehension skills (see Leslie, chapter 19, this
volume, for a more extensive treatment of Davis' work). He was able to develop test
items for nine separate categories, which, when he examined the degree of interrelat-
edness among them reduced to two—a word factor (something like vocabulary) and a
reasoning factor (something like drawing inferences between the text and knowledge).
But the key question is, where did those nine candidate skills come from? The answer
is straightforward: he reviewed the literature describing reading comprehension as
a construct and commonly used elementary and high school curricula of the times.
He found literally hundreds of labels to name the skills, but they all reduced to these
nine conceptual categories (see Table 1.1) that he felt constituted conceptually distinct
groups; from these, as I indicated, he deduced two independent factors—word knowledge and reasoning.

Table 1.1   Davis' Nine Potential Factors

1. Word meanings	6. Text based questions with paraphrase
2. Word meanings in context	7. Draw inferences about content
3. Follow passage organization	8. Literary devices
4. Main thought	9. Author's purpose
5. Answer specific text-based questions	

While we cannot be sure where the skills came from, for either instruction or assessment, it is clear that both domains were using the same infrastructure of tasks; clearly, what happened in either domain influenced the other. These tasks/labels—finding main ideas, noting important details, determining sequence of events, cause-effect relations, comparing and contrasting, and drawing conclusions—are noteworthy for their persistence for they are all a part of current curricula and assessments in the early part of the 21st century.

An important related construct was the notion of a scope and sequence of skills, a linear outline of skills that if taught properly ought to lead to skilled reading. While skills have always been a part of reading instruction (witness all the bits and pieces of letter sounds and syllables in the alphabetic approach), the skill as a fundamental unit of curriculum and the scope and sequence chart as a way of organizing skills that extend across the elementary grades are 20th-century phenomena

The basal experience with skills led quite directly to two additional curriculum mainstays—the teachers manual and the workbook.[5] Throughout the 19th century and at least up through the first three decades of the 20th century, basal programs consisted almost entirely of a set of student books. Teachers relied on experience, or perhaps normal school education, to supply the pedagogy used to teach lessons with the materials. Occasionally, for students who had progressed beyond the primer to one of the more advanced readers, questions were provided to test understanding of the stories in the readers. In the early 1900s, publishers of basals began to include supplementary teaching suggestions, typically a separate section at the front or back of each book with a page or two of suggestions to accompany each selection. In one common practice of the period, publishers provided a model lesson plan for two or three stories; for later stories, they referred the teacher back to one of the models with the suggestion that they adapt it for the new story. By the 1930s, the teachers' manuals had expanded to several pages per selection.[6] The other significant development in the 1930s was the workbook, often marketed with titles like *My Think and Do Book* or *Work Play Books*.[7]

Both of these developments were symptomatic of the expansion of scope and sequence efforts: the more skills included, the more complicated the instructional routines and the greater the need for explicit directives to teachers and opportunities for students to practice the skills. From the 1930s until at least the 1980s, this approach to skills development increased in intensity and scope. It was gradually extended beyond phonics to include comprehension, vocabulary, and study skills.[8] As I indicated earlier, the comprehension skills that made their way into basal workbooks and scope and sequence charts were virtually identical to those used to create comprehension tests. The trend toward heftier and more complex manuals and workbooks for teachers has continued virtually unchecked since it began in the 1930s until today, when the manual for each grade consists of a small library rather than a single book.

Theory and professional thinking were not divorced from this expansion of the skills in basals and on tests. The practice in each succeeding generation is mirrored by research-based accounts of reading curricula in influential yearbooks published by the National Society for Studies in Education; in this series, reading research and curriculum is synthesized every decade or so. So, for example, in the 24th Yearbook of the Society (1925), William S. Gray's chapter on objectives for teaching reading included both simple and complex "interpretation habits." Among the simple were:

- Concentrating attention on the content
- Associating meanings with symbols
- Anticipating the sequence of ideas
- Associating ideas together accurately
- Recalling related experiences

- Recognizing the important elements of meaning
- Deriving meanings from the context and from pictures (Gray, 1925, p. 14)

Among the more complex were these:

- Analyzing or selecting meanings;
  - To select important points and supporting details
  - To find answers to questions ...
- Associating and organizing meanings; for example,
  - To grasp the author's organization
  - To associate what is read with previous experience
  - To prepare an organization of what has been read
- Evaluating meanings; for example,
  - To appraise the value or significance of statements
  - To compare facts read with items of information from other sources
  - To weigh evidence presented
  - To interpret critically
- Retaining meanings; for example,
  - To reproduce for others
  - To use in specific ways (Gray, 1925, pp. 14–15)

Durrell (1949), writing the first chapter devoted exclusively to comprehension in any NSSE Yearbook (by that time 10 yearbooks had been partially or exclusively devoted to reading) provided a perspective that focused on skills but acknowledged that reader knowledge, motivation, and attention would exert strong influences on comprehension. He outlined the following general characteristics of a skills program in reading comprehension:

- Selection of essential skills to be observed and taught
- Analysis of difficulties of those skills
- Intensive teaching of those skills through graded exercises in suitable material
- A motivation program which shows the child the importance of those skills and enables him to see his progress in them. (Durrell, 1949, p. 200)

Durrell never outlined the specific skills with the detail and precision provided in the 1920s by Gray, but it is clear that an approach that decomposed comprehension into a set of teachable skills was assumed in his general approach. As close as he comes to defining skills (pp. 200–202) is in discussing the difficulties in text at the word (vocabulary and word meaning), sentence (overcoming the barriers of complex syntax by careful analysis), and paragraph and passage (discovering the often implicit organization of ideas) levels that teachers must attend to in diagnosing and remediating students' problems in comprehension. He also pointed to the importance of a solid program in decoding and fluency as a firm basis for comprehending, implying, of course, that he believed, at least in part, in the simple view of reading—that decoding words to an auditory code would enable oral language competence to enact text comprehension (i.e., that reading comprehension is the product of decoding and listening comprehension).

McKee (1949) in the chapter on reading in grades 4–8 for the same 48th Yearbook, also mentioned "comprehension" fostering activities, although he used the word comprehension only once in his 20-page chapter. In discussing what students needed to become independent readers who could cope with difficulty on their own, he mentioned knowing lots of word meanings (including navigating multiple meanings), using context to infer word meanings, figurative language, using syntax to relate ideas to one another in a sentence, linking ideas across sentences, and distinguishing emotive from informative expressions (p. 135). He also acknowledged—and this is the first mention of it I can find in any of the NSSE volumes up until that time—the role of text discussion as contributing to understanding; interestingly, he pled for open rather than closed conversations about text:

> The discussion which follows the reading of a given selection should be, not a quizzing activity in which the teacher tests the pupil's retention of what has been read, but rather an informal conversation in which pupils make comments and raise queries about the selection, just as an individual and his friends discuss a book they have read or a movie they have seen.

In 1968, just on the cusp of the cognitive revolution in psychology that would spawn a paradigm shift in our views of comprehension, the NSSE Yearbook on reading would have a different character. What is most striking in the chapter most clearly related to comprehension (Clymer, 1968) is how much the development of theory over the 1950s and 1960s had altered the views of comprehension presented. Clymer cited the empirical theories of scholars such as Holmes (sub-strata factor theory), the emerging cognitive work in Project Literacy at Cornell, and the instructional framework of Barrett to ponder the question, What is reading? In privileging the emerging work of Barrett, he placed comprehension at the center of the answer to that question. He also provided some indirect evidence that Gray was moving toward a more comprehension-centric view of reading processes.

The centerpiece of Clymer's chapter is Barrett's taxonomy, which is loosely coupled to Bloom's (1956) Taxonomy of Educational Objectives. Essentially, he borrowed liberally, whenever there was a comfortable fit, from Bloom's constructs of knowledge, comprehension, application, analysis, synthesis, and evaluation, as well as from the key descriptors Bloom used to "enact" those basic constructs—words like recall, recognize, infer, and summarize. Perhaps even more important, he used the taxonomic frame established by Bloom to unpack his infrastructure for reading comprehension. According to Clymer, "The type of comprehension demanded and the difficulty of the task is a product of (a) the selection, (b) the questions, and (c) the reader's background" (p. 19). Barrett then embedded some familiar terms into his taxonomy—popular standards such as main idea, sequence, comparison, cause-effect relationships, and character traits. While he did not choose a tabular format for presenting, three of the major categories certainly invite a matrix presentation, as depicted in Table 1.2.

His other categories—Reorganization, Judgment, Evaluation, and Appreciation—are idiosyncratic in nature. But Barrett's taxonomy and Clymer's treatment of it and other conceptions of reading are notable not so much for their particular content as for

Table 1.2   A Tabular Account of a Part of Barrett's Taxonomy

	Literal Comprehension		Inferential Comprehension
	Recognition	*Recall*	
Main Ideas	√	√	√
Supporting Details	√	√	√
Sequence	√	√	√
Comparison	√	√	√
Cause Effect	v	√	√
Character Traits	√	√	√

serving as harbingers of things to come a half decade later with the onset of the cognitive revolution and a major paradigm shift in comprehension.

A portend of things to come: psycholinguistics   Beginning in the late 1950s, and marked most vividly by the publication of Chomsky's groundbreaking work in linguistics (1957) and critique of behaviorist views of language, psycholinguistics had tremendous appeal for three reasons. Part of its appeal stemmed from the feeling that it would constitute a paradigm shift. Based upon studies like that of Gough (1965), there was a genuine feeling that behavioristic views of language development and processing would have to be supplanted with views that were both nativistic (people are born with a genetic capability to learn language) and cognitive (something really does go on inside that black box) in orientation. Furthermore, these research studies seemed to suggest that the transformational generative grammar created by Chomsky (1957, 1965) might actually serve as a model of human language processing. Thus, there was a ready-made theory waiting to be applied to reading comprehension. Psycholinguistics was also appealing to educational scholars because it commanded academic respectability. There was something appealing about standing on the shoulders of the new psychology, working within a paradigm for which there was a model that made fairly precise predictions and thus had testable hypotheses.

Hence it was that beginning in the late 1960s and extending into the mid-1970s, considerable empirical and theoretical work was completed within the psycholinguistic tradition. The influence of psycholinguistics on reading is nowhere better demonstrated than in the work of Kenneth Goodman (1965) and Frank Smith (1971). For both Goodman and Smith, looking at reading from a psycholinguistic perspective meant looking at reading in its natural state, as an application of a person's general cognitive and linguistic competence. It seems odd even to mention their names in discussing the influence of psycholinguistics on comprehension research because neither Goodman nor Smith distinguishes between reading and reading comprehension. Their failure to make the distinction is deliberate, for they would argue that reading is comprehending (or that reading without comprehending is not reading). A distinction between word identification and comprehension would seem arbitrary to them. For others, the influence of the psycholinguistic tradition (particularly the use of transformational-generative grammar as a psychological model) on views of reading comprehension was quite direct. The work of Bormuth (1966), Bormuth, Manning, Carr, and Pearson (1971), Fagan (1971), and Pearson (1974–75) reveals a rather direct use of psycholinguistic notions in studying reading comprehension. Such was the scene in the early seventies. The conventional modes of research, while still strong, were being challenged by a new interloper from the world of linguistic research—psycholinguistics.

Several points about the teaching and learning of reading comprehension during the 75 years of the century seem warranted from this perspectives presented thus far:

1. Whatever theorizing about reading comprehension might have been done by a few early scholars and by psycholinguistics very late in the period, the bulk of the writing and activity focus on comprehension focus comprehension skills as a way of organizing curriculum (what gets taught) and assessment (what gets tested).
2. Most scholars thought that comprehension skill resulted from practicing separable skills within a balanced scope and sequence. The most common criterion for sequencing comprehension skill was from literal to inferential to some beyond the text activity, such as creative, aesthetic, or critical.
3. Curriculum and assessment were tightly bound together, so much so that they present a classic chicken and egg problem.

4. Notably absent in discussions of curriculum was any advice about pedagogy supporting the development of these skills.[9]
5. The role of discussion and questions about text were not well-represented in the professional literature on comprehension, but questions and talk about text were ubiquitous in the materials throughout this period. Thus an implicit theory, evident in practice is that the ability to answer questions was considered to be the most basic piece of evidence that students could comprehend, and asking them to practice answering lots of questions was thought by many to be the best path to nurturing comprehension
6. Implicit in much of the presentation of comprehension (save Huey's account) was an assumption that the simple view of reading (RC = Dec * LC) is accurate, so that if we can get those lower order skills in place and provide students with lots of opportunity to practice skills in text discussions and workbooks, reading comprehension will take care of itself.

READING COMPREHENSION INSTRUCTION AFTER THE COGNITIVE REVOLUTION: 1975–1990

The cognitive turn in psychology

In comparison to what happened in the space of 5 years from roughly 1975 to 1980, the sum total of developments in the first 75 years of the 20th century pale. Rooted, as suggested, in the Chomskian revolution in linguistics (Chomsky, 1957, 1959, 1965) and experiencing a trial run in the young field of psycholinguistics in the late 1960s, the cognitive perspective allowed psychologists to re-embrace[10] and extend constructs such as human purpose, intention, and motivation to a greater range of psychological phenomena, including perception, attention, comprehension, learning, memory, and executive control or "metacognition" of all cognitive process. All of these would have important consequences in reading pedagogy.

The most notable change within psychology was that it became fashionable for psychologists, for the first time since the early part of the century, to study complex phenomena such as language and reading.[11] And in the decade of the 1970s, works by psychologists flooded the literature on basic processes in reading. One group focused on characteristics of the text and a second on the nature of the knowledge students bought to the reading task. Those who privileged text comprehension tried to explain how readers come to understand the underlying structure of texts. They offered story grammars—structural accounts of the nature of narratives, complete with predictions about how those structures impede and enhance story understanding and memory (Rumelhart, 1977; Stein & Glenn, 1977). Others chose to focus on the expository tradition in text (e.g., Kintsch, 1974; Meyer, 1975). Like their colleagues interested in story comprehension, they believed that structural accounts of the nature of expository (informational) texts would provide valid and useful models for human text comprehension. And in a sense, both of these efforts worked. Story grammars did provide explanations for story comprehension. Analyses of the structural relations among ideas in an informational piece also provided explanations for expository text comprehension (see Pearson & Camparell, 1981). But neither text-analysis tradition really tackled the relationship between the knowledge of the world that readers bring to text and comprehension of those texts. In other words, by focusing on structural rather than the ideational, or content, characteristics of texts, they failed to get to the heart of comprehension. That task, as it turned out, fell to one of the most popular and influential movements of the 1970s, schema theory.

The emergence of schema theory   The most prevalent metaphor to emerge from this revolutionary period was the "reader as builder"—an active meaning constructor (Anderson, 1977; Collins, Brown, & Larkin, 1980), an aggressive processor of language and information who filters the raw materials of reading (the clues left by the author on the printed page) through her vast reservoir of knowledge to continuously revise a dynamic, ever-emerging model of text meaning. The reader assumed greater importance in the period, and the text assumed less: the builder became more important than the materials used to do the building. This is not to say that text was neither appreciated nor studied during this period; what occurred is better characterized as a shift in emphasis from the dominance of text variables in the reading models leading into 1970s.

Schema theory (see Anderson & Pearson, 1984; Rumelhart, 1981) is not a theory of reading comprehension but rather a theory about the structure of human knowledge as it is represented in memory. In our memory, schemata are like little containers into which we deposit the particular traces of particular experiences as well as the "ideas" that derive from those experiences. So, if we see a chair, we store that visual experience in our "chair schema." If we go to a restaurant, we store that experience in our "restaurant schema," if we attend a party, our "party schema," and so on.

Even so, schema theory was readily appropriated to provide a credible account of reading comprehension, which probably, more than any of its other features, accounted for its popularity within the reading field in the 1970s and 1980s. Schema theory struck a sympathetic note with researchers as well as practitioners. It provided a rich and detailed theoretical account of the everyday intuition that we understand and learn what is new in terms of what we already know. It also accounted for the everyday phenomenon of disagreements in interpreting stories, movies, and news events—we disagree with one another because we approach the phenomenon with very different background experiences and knowledge. Anderson (1984) provided us with the most elaborate account of the uses that we, as readers, can make of schemata:

a. Schemata provide ideational scaffolding for assimilating text information. Schemata have slots that readers expect to be filled with information in a text. Information that fills those slots is easily learned and remembered.
b. Schemata facilitate the selective allocation of attention. Put simply, schemata guide our search for what is important in a text, allowing us to separate the wheat from the chaff.
c. Schemata enable inferential elaboration. No text is ever fully explicit. Schemata allow us to make educated guesses about how certain slots must have been filled.
d. Schemata allow for orderly searches of memory. For example, suppose a person is asked to remember what he did at a recent cocktail party. He can use his cocktail party schema, a specification of what usually happens at cocktail parties, to recall what he ate, what he drank, who he talked to, and so on.
e. Schemata facilitate editing and summarizing. By definition, any schema possesses its own criteria of what is important. These can be used to create summaries of text that focus on important information.
f. Schemata permit inferential reconstruction. If readers have a gap in their memory, they can use a schema, in conjunction with the information recalled, to generate hypotheses about missing information. If they can recall, for example, that the entree was beef, they can infer that the beverage was likely to have been red wine.

So powerful was the influence of prior knowledge on comprehension that Johnston and Pearson (1982; see also, Johnston, 1984) found that prior knowledge of topic was a better predictor of comprehension than either an intelligence test score or a reading achievement test score.

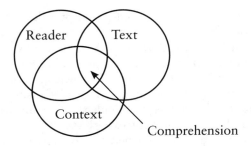

Figure 1.1 Comprehension occurs at the intersection of reader, text, and context.

With respect to reading comprehension, schema theory did not ignore text. Instead, it encouraged educators to examine texts from the perspective of the knowledge and cultural backgrounds of students in order to evaluate the likely connections that they would be able to make between ideas inscribed[12] in the text and the schema that they would bring to the reading task. Schema theory also promoted a constructivist view of comprehension; all readers, at every moment in the reading process, construct the most coherent model of meaning for the texts they read.[13] Perhaps the most important legacy of this constructivist perspective was that it introduced ambiguity about the question of where meaning resides. Does it reside in the text? In the author's mind as she sets pen to paper? In the mind of each reader as she builds a model of meaning unique to her experience and reading? In the interaction between reader and text? Schema theory raised, but did not settle these questions. But it did privilege the interaction metaphor in suggesting that comprehension occurs at the intersection of reader, text, and context (see Figure 1.1).

Metacognition   Nearly as popular as the builder was the metaphor of the "fixer"—the problem solver who can repair virtually any comprehension failure with her toolbox of strategies.[14] Most commonly referred to as the strategic reader (Paris, Lipson, & Wixson, 1983), she is a paragon of adaptability and flexibility. She immediately sizes up the potential influence of relevant factors in the reading environment (particular attributes of the text, the situation, which can be construed to include other learners, and the self) and then selects, from among a healthy repertoire of strategies that enable and repair comprehension, exactly that strategy or set of strategies that will maximize comprehension of the text at hand.

Sometime during the late 1970s, this new interloper burst onto the research stage, bearing the cumbersome but intellectually appealing label of metacognition. It seemed a logical extension of the rapidly developing work on both schema theory and text analysis. These latter two traditions emphasized declarative knowledge, knowing that X or Y or Z is true, but were scant on specifying procedural knowledge, knowing how to engage a strategy for comprehension or memory. This is precisely the kind of knowledge that metacognitive research has emphasized. The key phrases associated with metacognition reveal its emphasis: awareness, monitoring, control, and evaluation. Two parallel strands of research dominated the early work in metacognition. The first, metamemory research, is most typically associated with Flavell and his associates at Stanford. They discovered that along with the capacity to remember more information, human beings develop tacit and explicit strategies for remembering. The second line of research, meta-comprehension, was more typically associated with Brown and Campione and their colleagues at Illinois, and with Paris at Michigan. It emphasized the strategies that readers use on-line in monitoring, evaluating and repairing their comprehension of written text (see Paris, Lipson, & Wixson, 1983; also Baker & Beall, chapter 17, this volume).

The metacognitive turn helped us understand that reading involves many different kinds of knowledge (Paris, Lipson, & Wixson, 1983). First, declarative knowledge, knowing *that*, includes our knowledge of the world at large and our knowledge of the world of text (prototypical structures and authorial devices). Procedural knowledge, knowing *how*, includes all of the strategies we use to become aware of, monitor, evaluate, and repair our comprehension. To these more transparent sources of knowledge, Paris, Lipson, and Wixson (1983; also Paris & Hamilton, chapter 2, this volume) argued convincingly that we should add conditional knowledge, knowing *when* and *why* we would call up a particular strategy (in preference to others) to aid our comprehension. The real contribution was helping us understand that we cannot characterize comprehension or comprehension instruction without including all of these kinds of knowledge.

From process to pedagogy: the impact of cognitive research on reading comprehension instruction

Research on reading comprehension instruction in the 15 years following the onset of the revolution tended to fall into one of two categories (see Pearson & Gallagher, 1983)—descriptions and interventions. Some studies attempted to describe what is going on in the name of reading comprehension, either in our schools or our textbooks. Other studies attempted to try out different ways of teaching or allowing students to practice reading comprehension strategies or activities. They represent what we might call pedagogical experiments; their goal was (and is) to evaluate competing practices over relatively short but intensive treatment periods (1–10 weeks). A few, very few, of these experiments had more of a program evaluation flavor and examined a practice or set of practices embedded into a larger curriculum and usually for a longer period of time.

Descriptions   The descriptions in this period taught us more about what is not being done than what is. The landmark study in the period was Durkin's (1978–79) documentation of the paucity of instruction inside classrooms and a follow-up (1981) examination of the comprehension instruction pedagogy recommended in teacher manuals. In short, she found very little direct instruction of comprehension in intermediate grade classrooms (1978–79) or suggested in teacher manuals (1981). Instead of offering students advice about how to employ reading skills, teachers and manuals tend to assess comprehension by asking or suggesting many questions about the selections students read and by providing enormous quantities of practice materials in the form of worksheets and workbooks. Sometimes, teachers or manuals "mention," or say just enough about the skill so that students understand the formal requirements of the task. Rarely do teachers or manuals require application of the skill to reading real texts. Even more rarely do they discuss the kind of conditional knowledge suggested by Paris, et al. (1983). Durkin (1981) found that teachers rarely use that section of the teachers' manual suggesting background knowledge activities but rarely skip the story questions or skillsheet activities.

Beck and her colleagues at Pittsburgh (Beck, McKeown, McCaslin, & Burkes, 1979) have found several features of commercial reading programs that may adversely affect comprehension. Among them are the use of indirect language (using high frequency words such as "this" or "him" instead of lower frequency but more image-evoking words like garbage can or Mr. Gonzalez), elaborate but misleading pictures, inappropriate story divisions, misleading prior knowledge and vocabulary instruction, and questions that focus on unimportant aspects of the stories students read.

Other descriptive studies of the era concentrated more on pupil texts than on teacher manuals or classroom instruction. For example, Davison and Kantor (1982) studied the kinds of adaptations publishers make when they rewrite an adult article for students in order to meet readability guidelines. They found a number of examples of practices that may actually make passages harder rather than easier to understand: (a) reducing sentence length by destroying interclausally explicit connectives, (b) selecting simpler but less descriptive vocabulary, (c) altering the flow of topic and comment relations in paragraphs, and (d) eliminating qualifying statements that specify the conditions under which generalizations are thought to hold. Anderson and Armbruster (Armbruster & Anderson, 1981, 1982, 1984; Anderson, Armbruster, & Kantor, 1980) examined a number of dimensions of student text material in social studies and science that may cause unintentional difficulty. Among their observations are that content area texts often (a) fail to structure the information within a predictable and recurrent frame (like a schema for text), (b) use subheadings that do not reveal the macrostructure of the topic, (c) avoid using visual displays of information, particularly to summarize information presented textually, (d) use obscure pronoun references, and (e) fail to use obvious connectives, such as because, since, before, after, etc., when they clearly fit. To make the picture even drearier, Bruce (1984) compared basal stories to those found in trade books and concluded that basal stories avoid features commonly found in stories, such as inside view, internal conflict, and embedded narratorship. An apt summary of the descriptive research of this period is pretty dismal: texts with counterproductive features, teacher manuals with scant, misleading, or unhelpful suggestions, teachers who do not teach comprehension skills and strategies in any explicit way.

Experiments   The experimental work was more encouraging (see Pearson & Fielding, 1991; or Tierney & Cunningham, 1991 for elaborate summaries of this work). More comprehension instruction research was conducted between 1980 and 1990 than in all of the previous history of reading research. Examined in the broadest strokes, this body of work was strongly supportive of instructional applications of schema theory and the new work on metacognitive development.

1. Whether it comes packaged as a set of questions, a text summary, a story line, or a visual display of key ideas, students of all ages and abilities benefit from conscious attempts by teachers to focus attention either on the structure of the text to be read or the structure of the knowledge domain to which the text is related (see Pearson & Camparell, 1981).
2. Students' disposition to draw inferences or make predictions improves when they and their teachers make a conscious effort to draw relationships between text content and background knowledge. (Hansen, 1981; Hansen & Pearson, 1983).
3. When students learn how to monitor their reading to make sure it makes sense to them, their comprehension skill improves (Palincsar & Brown, 1984; Paris, Cross, & Lipson, 1984). This third generalization is predictable from the first two because the only criterion readers can use to evaluate the "sense" of the model of meaning they are building is their own knowledge.
4. When strategies are taught in explicit, transparent ways, students can learn to apply them in ways that improve both their comprehension of the texts in which they are embedded and texts they have yet to encounter

Taken together, these general findings supported instruction that is based upon the driving metaphors of the new comprehension paradigm—the reader as builder and the reader as fixer; these findings are support a "generative" view of comprehension and learning (Wittrock, 1992), a view that in which comprehension is facilitated by the transformation of ideas from one form into another. It may be in this transformation process that what began as the author's ideas become the reader's ideas (Pearson & Fielding, 1991).

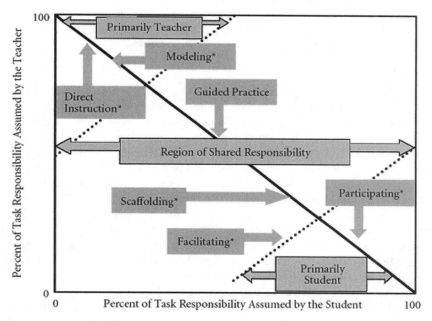

Percent of Task Responsibility Assumed by the Teacher

Percent of Task Responsibility Assumed by the Student

Figure 1.2 Updated gradual release of responsibility model.

Another outcome of these early pedagogical experiments was the evolution of an instructional model that has persisted from the early 1980s. The model, which defines the dynamic role of the teacher as instruction ensues, was implicit in virtually all of the research evaluating the explicit teaching of strategies, but was first made explicit by Pearson and Gallagher (1983)[15] as a tool for explaining commonalities across a range of research efforts from the late 1970s and early 1980s. Dubbed the gradual release of responsibility model, the idea is that as teachers move from the teacher roles of modeling and direct instruction to scaffolding and guided practice and onto facilitation and participation, they release more and more responsibility to students for completing key tasks. An updated version reprinted here (Figure 1.2) is an adaptation of the original Pearson and Gallagher graphic from Duke and Pearson (2002).

FROM REVOLUTION TO RECONTEXTUALIZATION AND REVISIONISM: THE 1990S

The impact of schema theory and metacognition on pedagogy continued into at least the middle 1990s. But it did begin to lose its hold as the dominant theory of comprehension processing. It was not as though schema theory died, but it is probably best to regard the decade from of the 1990s as the era in which reading, including schema theory, was recontextualized as a process that is intimately related to its sibling linguistic processes of writing, listening, and speaking and to the social and cultural contexts underlying.[16] In fact, it became increasingly common for scholars to refer to *literacy* research rather than either reading or writing research. A telling example of this change in perspective occurred in the latter part of the decade when the National Reading Conference changed the name of its journal from the *Journal of Reading Behavior* to *JRB: A journal of literacy.*[17] Conferences and edited volumes of the period also revealed these trends toward contextualizing reading. We moved from conferences about reading or writing to conferences about the dynamics of language learning, the contexts of school-based literacy, and multidisciplinary perspectives on literacy research. In the eighties we were arguing for integration; in the 1990s, we were assuming it.

Advances in research on comprehension processes

Cognitive shifts   If schema theory (see Anderson & Pearson, 1984), with its twin emphases on the importance of knowledge in determining comprehension and the central role of inference in helping to build complete models of text meaning was the conventional wisdom leading us into this post-paradigm shift period, beginning in the mid-1980s, then the rest of the decade, and indeed most of the following decade, is best viewed as a series of attempts to account for weaknesses attributed to schema-theoretic accounts of reading comprehension. In fact, the theme of this period might be labeled, moving beyond schema theory.

The more general notion of building mental models (see McNamara, Miller, & Bransford, 1991 for a summary of this work has characterized basic research on comprehension processes completed by the cognitive science community in the latter part of the decade. Mental models, which appear to be more spatial, episodic, and almost cinematic in character, as least when compared to abstract, semantically-based schemata, provide readers with alternatives to propositional and schema models for representing emerging models of text meaning. The purported advantage (Johnson-Laird, 1983) of mental models over schema models is that they can handle both heavily scripted events like going to a restaurant or a movie, which schema models also handle quite well, and unique, unscripted activities, which schema models can accommodate only with great strain. The comprehension research evaluating the efficacy of mental models (see McNamara et al., 1991) suggests that they are quite useful in accounting for the dynamic course of comprehension during reading. For example, the mental models approach is quite sensitive to subtle shifts in comprehension focus (e.g., when a reader shifts from an hypothesis that character A rather than character B is the likely candidate for protagonist). This work on mental models reached its zenith in the middle 1990s in the work of Kintsch, fully summarized in his 1998 book on comprehension and featuring his highly influential constructs of the text base and the situation model. The text base is a largely veridical map of the key ideas in the text that is hammered out with deliberate bottom-up processes that involve decoding in a central way. The situation model is akin to the model of meaning put forward in the early 1980s by that ever evolving, always elusive model built at the intersection of prior knowledge and the text base and providing the momentarily best account

Another attempt to accommodate for problems with schema theory came from the work of Spiro and his colleagues (Spiro, Vispoel, Schmitz, Smarapungavan, & Boerger, 1987). Operating out of a Wittgensteinian perspective, Spiro argued that the schema model of comprehension so dominant in prior period runs the risk of seducing us into oversimplified notions of comprehension and learning by implying that schema have a fixed, static character. According to Spiro's Cognitive Flexibility Theory, we need to expand schema theory to account for the dynamic nature of comprehension and learning, especially in domains of knowledge that have an ill-structured character, where the category distinctions are fuzzy and the operational rules have numerous exceptions. We need to view the development of these fundamental cognitive processes from multiple perspectives. It is not enough to facilitate the understanding of a text, for example, by helping readers adopt the most appropriate schema for understanding it. Instead, we must encourage learners to approach the comprehension of a text and the learning of a new domain of knowledge by examining each from as many perspectives as possible. Spiro is wary of the process of schema selection, or activation. Consistent with his preference for multiple perspectives, Spiro prefers to talk about *assembling* schemata to fully comprehend a specific text, topic or situation rather than *selecting* a particular schema to do the job.

Working simultaneously in a wide range of domains of knowledge, Spiro and his colleagues were able to demonstrate the constricting, oversimplifying, and conceptually misleading effects of singular perspectives, including simplifying analogies, when students try to understand or learn information in a complex, ill-structured domain of inquiry. In arguing for multi-perspectival approaches to learning and comprehension, Spiro takes a "case well-studied" approach. To that end, he uses the Wittgensteinian metaphor of criss-crossing a landscape from many directions in order to achieve an understanding and appreciation of it. For example, in examining the ways in which medical students acquire (or fail to acquire) knowledge about the heart and what causes heart attacks, Spiro and his colleagues have found that students develop misconceptions whenever they cling to a single concept, analogy, or model. In order to overcome misconceptions, students must confront multiple models and analogies, even though they may sometimes logically contradict one another. In learning about heart muscles, part of the truth is captured by the "crew analogy"—a bunch of rowers all pulling and relaxing in unison, while part of the truth is captured by the "turnbuckle" analogy—tension from within creates external stretching. And to counteract the unison and synchrony implied by the crew analogy, a Roman galley ship analogy, with more emphasis on the voluntary, and hence asynchronous (maybe even chaotic), actions of individual oars, must be provided. According to Spiro and his colleagues, it is only when a single, complex construct is informed by these multiple, sometimes contradictory, perspectives that adequate comprehension and learning can occur.

A third initiative, dubbed situated cognition, with strong roots in the Vygotskian tradition of learning theory (see Gavalek & Bresnahan, chapter 7, this volume) emerged from the work of Brown, Collins and Duguid (1989). They argued that our approaches to nurturing cognitive development are so abstract and divorced from the "authentic activity" that they are designed to nurture, that they cannot and do not promote adequate comprehension of either a particular text or the more general topic exemplified by a particular text. Even an inherently abstract domain such as mathematics has a specific context of application and "practice." In our zeal to develop context-free, transferable concepts and skills, we have inadvertently and inappropriately focused upon the teaching and learning of explicit but abstract rules and conceptual features. What we need, they argued, is a "situated" view of cognition and epistemology. If cognition, including comprehension and learning, is regarded as a situated phenomenon, then we will accept and take advantage of the fact that most events and concepts derive most of what we regard as meaning from the contexts in which we encounter them. Meaning is as much "indexical" (i.e., contextually bound) as it is conceptual. Notice that while the rationale for moving beyond schema theory is different from that proposed by Spiro and his colleagues, the final recommendation for "teaching" is quite similar: in order to help learners develop useful models of meaning for text or experience, teachers need to design work that situates students in the specific rather than the abstract. In the end, both of these positions argue, we are faced with the paradox that in order to learn what is abstract, general, and context-free, we have to behave as though understanding phenomena as they exist within their natural context is all that mattered.

The social turn   Perhaps the most important development in this period was the increased prominence of a range of social perspectives on reading and learning more general; they came with a range of hyphenated names, such as socio-cultural, social-historical, and even soci-psycholinguistic. These scholars (e.g., Harste, Burke, & Woodward, 1984) provided more socially oriented critiques, with constructs like the social construction of reality imported from sociology. They also provided new research methodologies that emphasized the social and cultural and even political contexts of teaching, learning, and understanding (see Pearson & Stephens, 1993), but that most interesting and controversial topic is beyond the scope of this analysis. Suffice it to say that the shift in methods used by doctoral students and presented at national conferences in this era revealed a marked trend toward understanding understanding in its highly contextualize, situated, and particular aspect.

The rediscovery of the Russian psychologist Vygotsky (1978) alluded to earlier and the Russian literary theorist Bakhtin (1981) provided even more ammunition for socially based views of cognition, learning, and development. From Vygotsky (see Gavalek & Besnahan, chapter 17, this volume) reading researchers fixed their attention on the social nature of learning and the key role that teachers and peers play in facilitating individual learning. Vygotsky's "zone of proximal development," that range defined by the difference between the learning a child can accomplish on her own and what she can accomplish with the assistance of someone else (a teacher, a mentor, a parent, or a knowledgeable peer), may be the most popular learning construct of the 1980s. From Bakhtin's dialogical perspective, scholars forged a preview of coming attractions in what is destined to become a classic perspective of the future—an intertextual view of reading comprehension and the basic premise that we understand each new "text"—be it written, oral, or experiential—in relation to all the previous "texts" we have experienced (see Hartman, 1995). While some observers have questioned whether these more socially driven views of cognition represent a substantial departure from schema theory, they nonetheless shifted the attention of reading researchers from the individual and the text to the situational context surrounding the act of reading.

But one cannot understand the changes in pedagogy that occurred in the late 1980s and early 1990s without understanding the impact of literary theory, particularly reader response theory. From literary theory came the reincarnation of Rosenblatt's (1978) Deweyian-inspired transactional view of the relationship between reader and writer and Bleich's (1988) concept of the intersubjective negotiation of meaning; these constructs were eagerly and readily repositioned in pedagogical language and activity (e.g., Langer, 1990). In our secondary schools, the various traditions of literary criticism have always had a voice in the curriculum, especially in guiding discussions of classic literary works. Until the middle 1980s, the "New Criticism" (Richards, 1929) that began its ascendancy in the depression era dominated the interpretation of text for several decades. It had sent teachers and students on a search for the one "true" meaning in each text they encountered.[18] With the emergence (some would argue the re-emergence) of reader response theories, all of which gave as much authority to the reader as to either the text or the author, theoretical perspectives, along with classroom practices, changed dramatically. The basals that had been so skill-oriented in the 1970s and so comprehension oriented in the 1980s, became decidedly literature-based in the late 1980s and early 1990s. Comprehension gave way to readers' response to literature. Reader response emphasized affect and feeling that can either augment or replace cognitive responses to the content. To use the terminology of the most influential figure in the period, Louise Rosenblatt (1978), the field moved from efferent to aesthetic response to literature. And a "transactive model" replaced the "interactive model" of reading championed by the cognitive views of the 1980s. According to Rosenblatt, meaning is created in the transaction between reader and text. This meaning, which she refers to as the "poem," is a new entity that resides above the reader-text interaction. Meaning is therefore, neither subject nor object nor the interaction of the two. Instead it is transaction, something new and different from any of its inputs and influences.[19]

In the most fully articulated version of this perspective, Smagorinsky (2001) borrowed heavily from the reader response theory of Rosenblatt (1978) and the activity theories emanating from the Vygotskian tradition (e.g., Wertsch, 1993) to create what he called a cultural model of reading, in which he argued that the meaning in understanding resides not within the text or within the reader but within that transactional (borrowing from Louise Rosenblatt) zone it which reader, text, and context meet and become something more than their sums or products. The fundamental argument in Smagorinsky's model is that readers quite literally compose new texts in response to texts they read; their recompositions are based upon the evocations (links to prior texts and experiences) that occur during the act of reading within a context that also shapes the type and manner of interpretations they make. These evocations hearken back to both Bakhtin's notion of intertextuality (for they are, even in a literal sense, connections to other texts), the cultural practices notions of writers such as Wertsch (1993) and Gee (1992), and the reading as writing models of the middle 1980s (e.g., Tierney & Pearson, 1983).

Developments in comprehension instruction

A new generation of strategy instruction research Gathering momentum from landmark studies (e.g., Palincsar & Brown, 1984; Hansen, 1981; or Paris, Cross, & Lipson, 1984) early in the 1980s, strategy instruction expanded rapidly over the next 15 years, so rapidly indeed that it was the frequent object of review throughout the 1990s and into the early part of the 21st century (e.g., Dole, et al., 1991; Duke & Pearson, 2002; NICHD, 2000; Pearson & Fielding, 1991; Pressley, 2000; Pressley et al., 1994; Rosenshine & Meister, 1994; Rosenshine, Meister, & Chapman, 1996).[20] Two basic findings, also present in the earlier iteration of strategy instruction research were these: (a) when students are taught to apply strategies to text, their comprehension of those texts improves, and (b) often their comprehension of new texts (transfer tasks) in which they are required to apply the strategies, also improves. A major question in strategy instruction research is whether strategies should be taught as singletons, one by one, until many are acquired (this is the logic of the approach taken by Ellen Keane in her very popular book, *Mosaic of Thought* (1997) or as a "suite" of strategies from which a reader select the strategy most appropriate to a problem confronting them, which is the underlying logic of two of the most popular and well-studied approaches to strategy instruction—reciprocal teaching (RT; see Rosenshine & Meister for an extensive review of studies on RT) and transactional strategies instruction (Pressley et al., 1994).[21] Of all the approaches to strategy instruction that emerged in the 1980s and 1990s, none has had more direct impact than Reciprocal Teaching, mainly because it has been appropriated and adapted by a number of instructional researchers for a variety of pedagogical contexts (virtually all subject areas) and ages (from kindergarten through community college (see Rosenshine and colleagues, 1994, 1996). The line of work on Transactional Strategies Instruction is noteworthy for two reasons. First, it was created as a collaboration between university researchers (i.e., Michael Pressley and his colleagues at the University of Maryland) and a host of teachers from Montgomery County Maryland; hence it embodied the connection between theories of metacognition and comprehension processes and the problems of practice and implementation. Second, it surrounded the four strategies of Reciprocal Teaching with a few more cognitive strategies (text and story structure analysis) and a host of interpretive strategies that were closely allied with literary analysis—character development, figurative language, point of view, personal connections, thematic analysis, intertextual connections, and a range of literary elements. The inclusion of the interpretive strategies was a brilliant stroke because its literary patina softened what might otherwise have been construed as a highly cognitive and routinized approach, and directly appealed to teachers who were adopting literature-based reading approaches in the late 1980s and early 1990s.

The Achilles heel for strategy instruction, both in this period and even today, is finding a way to make it a part of "daily life" in classrooms. It is one thing to implement strategy instruction for a certain number of minutes each day for the ten weeks of a pedagogical experiment, but it is quite another to sustain a strategy emphasis over an entire school year (see Hacker & Tenent, 2002). In short, it is easy to teach strategies in short spurts, but it is hard to curricularize them. Should a teacher have students use the four strategies of RT every day? For every text segment they read? Or should they encourage students to "select" the optimal strategy for a particular situation or problem? And if a teacher encourages such flexible use, how will she make sure students select useful strategies, i.e., strategies that actually solve their problems. Even so, the consistent pattern of findings favoring the explicit teaching of strategies over a period of 15 years virtually guaranteed them a place in the curriculum of the early to mid 1990s.

Literature-based reading   Even though selections from both classical and contemporary children's literature have always been a staple of basal selections dating back to the 19th century (especially after grade 2 when the need for strict vocabulary control diminished), literature virtually exploded into the curriculum in the late 1980s and early 1990s. Beyond basals, children's literature has played an important supplementary role in the classrooms of teachers who believed that they must engage their students in a strong parallel independent reading program. Often this has taken the form of each child selecting books to be read individually and later discussed with the teacher in a weekly one-on-one conference. And even as far back as the 1960s, there were a few programs which turned this individualized reading component into the main reading program.[22]

But in the late 1980s and early 1990s, literature was dramatically repositioned. Several factors converged to pave the way for a groundswell in the role of literature in elementary reading. Surely the resurgence of reader response theory as presented by Rosenblatt was important, as was the compatibility of the reader response theory and its emphasis on interpretation with the constructivism that characterized both cognitive and sociolinguistic perspectives. Research also played a role; in 1985, for example, in the watershed publication of the Center for the Study of Reading, *Becoming a Nation of Readers*, Richard Anderson and his colleagues documented the importance of "just plain reading" as a critical component of any and all elementary reading programs.[23] But perhaps most influential were the perspectives of practitioners who championed literature. And no one was more influential than Nancie Atwell, who, with the publication of her influential book In the Middle (1987), brought many teachers into the world of literature in their classrooms. In her account she laid out her story, as a middle school teacher, of how she invited readers, some of whom were quite reluctant, into a world of books and reading. The credibility of her experience and the power of her prose were persuasive in convincing thousands of classroom teachers that they could use existing literature and "reading workshops" to accomplish anything that a basal program could accomplish in skill development while gaining remarkable advantages in students' literary experience.

In terms of policy and curriculum, the most significant event in promoting literature-based reading was the 1987 California Reading Framework. The framework called for reading materials which contained much more challenging texts at all levels. More important, it mandated the use of genuine literature, not the dumbed-down adaptations and excerpts from children's literature that had been the staple of basal programs for decades. Publishers responded to the call of California's framework and produced a remarkably different product in the late 1980s and early 1990s than had ever appeared before on the basal market.[24] Gone were excerpts and adaptations, and with them almost any traces of vocabulary control. Skills that had been front and center in the basals of the 1970s and 1980s were relegated to appendix-like status. Comprehension questions were replaced by more interpretive, impressionistic response to literature activities. All this was done in the name of providing children with authentic literature and authentic activities to accompany it. The logic was that if we could provide students with real literature and real motivations for reading it, much of what is arduous about skill teaching and learning will take care of itself.

Book Clubs and literature circles are the most visible instantiations of the literature based reading movement.[25] The underlying logic of Book Clubs is the need to engage children in the reading of literature in the same way as adults engage one another in voluntary reading circles. Such voluntary structures are likely to elicit greater participation, motivation, appreciation, and understanding on the part of students. Teachers are encouraged to establish a set of "cultural practices" (ways of interacting and supporting one another) in their classrooms to support students as they make their way into the world of children's literature. These cultural practices offer students both the opportunity to engage in literature and the skills to ensure that they can negotiate and avail themselves of that opportunity.

Integrated instruction   Integrated instruction has been a much-discussed but seldom enacted part of the thinking about elementary reading curriculum.[26] There was much talk of it during the early progressive period, but until the late 1980s, integration of the language arts curriculum assumed a minor role in American reading instruction. In basal manuals, for example, integration was portrayed almost as an afterthought until the late 1980s; it appeared in the part of the lesson that follows the guided reading and skills instruction sections, signaling that these are things that a teacher can get to "if time permits." Things changed in the late 1980s and early 1990s. For one, integrated curriculum fit the sociolinguistic emphasis on language in use—the idea that language, including reading, is best taught and learned when it is put to work in the service of other purposes, activities, and learning efforts. Similarly, with the increase in importance of writing, especially early writing of the sort discussed by Graves and his colleagues,[27] it was tempting to champion the idea of integrated language arts instruction; after all, reading and writing were both acts of construction (remember the builder metaphor). In fact, the constructivist metaphor is nowhere played out as vividly and transparently as in writing, leading many scholars to use writing as a model for the sort of constructive approach they wanted to promote in readers. The notion was that we needed to help students learn to "read like a writer."[28]

Whole language   One might plausibly argue that whole language brought together all of the constructivist and progressive trends of the post revolution period—comprehension, literature-based reading, integrated instruction and even process writing—by incorporating them into its fundamental set of principles and practices. It is also fair to argue that whole language owed its essential character and key principles to the insights that came from all of the linguistic, psycholinguistic, cognitive, sociolinguistic, and literary theoretic research that was played out from the late 1960s through the early 1990s. That said, the Whole Language movement has always had a strained and strange relationship with reading comprehension, particularly comprehension instruction. With the strong emphasis on authenticity in of the texts and tasks we ask students to engage in and the equally strong disdain for skills instruction (see Pearson, 2004, for an extended analysis), comprehension that emerges from rich, authentic encounters from text in a meaning-making community of readers is preferred to explicit instruction in skills, strategies, or vocabulary, which have an excessive didactic emphasis that is inconsistent with the strong child-centered philosophy underlying Whole Language. So, to the degree that comprehension was emphasized in Whole Language, it was largely through classroom, preferably small group, conversations about texts that students read together—with an occasional mini-lesson on a particular meaning making (e.g., making predictions) or repair (e.g., clarifying unknown words through contextual analysis) strategy offered when the situation called for it. For these very reasons, the pedagogical premises of literature-based instruction were a very comfortable fit for Whole Language.

This then was the set of instructional options available to teachers in the early to middle 1990s—elaborate strategy instruction, rich conversations about literature, a yearning for more integrated instruction, and an umbrella pedagogy in which to embed it all. No matter how different the approaches were in implementation, there were several underlying commonalities—a commitment to reading as the construction of meaning in response to text; a dynamic view of the teacher involving roles as one who moves from modeling and explicit teaching, to scaffolding and coaching, to facilitating and participating as students develop greater competence, confidence, and independence; and a general commitment to student rather than teacher centered practices.

THE CURRENT CONTEXT FOR THIS VOLUME

The stage is nearly set for the unfolding of all the glorious detail in the chapters of this volume, save for a commentary on the political context in which we have been foundering for the past decade. For a host of reasons that go beyond the scope of this introductory chapter, much of this momentum toward reading as a meaning-making process was reached in the last few years of the 20th century and the first few years of the 21st. Suffice it to say that several forces conspired to create a movement that took us back to the basics—a kind of "first things first" reform movement that created fuel for its mission by arguing that the lack of attention given to fundamental skills in the constructivist pedagogies of the previous 20 years was responsible for what has often, and unfairly, been characterized as the awful performance of students on important outcome measures.[29] And while there has been nothing in these reforms to suggest that comprehension instruction should be suspended, there is a subtle repositioning. In the reforms ushered in with the critique of constructivist practices, comprehension has become the natural consequence of teaching the code well in the early stages of instruction instead of the primary goal and focus of attention from the very beginning of a child's instructional lives in school. This is a return to the simple view of reading that formed the basis of pedagogy prior to the paradigm shift of the 1970s: reading comprehension is the product of listening comprehension and decoding (see Hoffman, chapter 3, this volume).

But some recent signs point in a more positive direction. First, there is the important work of the Rand Study Group (Snow, 2002), outlining an agenda for future work on reading comprehension, including the much neglected topic of assessment (see Pearson & Hamm, 2005; Leslie & Caldwell, chapter 19, this volume). Second, the Carnegie Report, *Reading Next* (Biancarosa & Snow, 2006), focuses our attention on older struggling readers, students for whom comprehension, especially of content area materials, is an alarming problem. Third, we have relatively recent movements that hold promise for moving comprehension into different domains, domains that both challenge and excite students. The first is the domain of new literacies, including those emanating from technological advances (see the chapters by Kamil & Chou (chapter 13) and by Tierney (chapter 12), both in this volume) and those that reside in spaces outside of schools (Alvermann & Xu, 2003; Moje, 2004; Hull & Schultz, 2002). The second is a renewed interest in the role of conversations about text (see Almasi & York, chapter 22, this volume); more important, we seem to have much more intellectual and methodological muscle available to examine the issues than in previous eras. The third is a rejuvenation of content area reading (see Conley, chapter 25, this volume), particularly for secondary students. The trends within that field seem particularly promising include (a) research in which reading and writing are put to work in the service of acquiring knowledge and skill in the disciplines (Guthrie et al., 2004; Cervetti Pearson, Barber, Hiebert, & Bravo, 2006; Sutherland et al., in press), and (b) research that attempts to understand the discursive and social practices of disciplinary learning in school settings (Moje et al., 2004).

So, there are signs of both concern and hope in the current professional and policy context. With any luck, the very existence of this volume will, as the ideas it brings to field get played out in classrooms, schools, and community contexts, actually alter the context in ways that will create more space for teachers and students to focus on what really matters in reading—understanding, insight, and learning—the very things that are both the cause and consequence of comprehension.

Notes

1. It is somewhat ironic that the sort of thinking exhibited in this piece did not become dominant view in the teens and twenties. Unquestionably, Thorndike was the pre-eminent educational psychologist of his time. Further, his work in the psychology of learning (the law of effect and the law of contiguity) became the basis of the behaviorism that dominated educational psychology and pedagogy during this period, and his work in assessment led was highly influential in developing the components of classical measurement theory (reliability and validity). Somehow this more cognitively oriented side of his work was less influential, at least in the period in which it was written.

2. See Smith (1986), American Reading Instruction, 259–262, for an account of the emergence of child-centered reading pedagogy. Foundational thinkers for this movement were Pestalozzi (1898), Froebel, (1887), and Herbart (1901).

3. Ironically, it was the field's most ambitious effort in readability by Bormuth in 1966 that provided the closing parenthesis on this 40-year enterprise.

4. The very latest iterations of readability take the form of tools to place students in books by putting student test scores and text readability on the same scale. Lexiles (Stenner & Burdick, 1997; Stenner et al., 1987) are the most common tool in the current educational marketplace. But the readability architecture underlying Lexile scaling is measuring average sentence length and average word length.

5. Smith (1986) documents the growth in size and changes in emphases of these two mainstays in each of the chapters detailing 20th century reading instruction.

6. Smith (1986) suggests that by the 1940s, teacher editions had expanded to more than 500 pages per student book.

7. See Smith (1986), pages 208–229; Gates and Humber, 1930.

8. See Smith (1986), pages 231–239.

9. This absence would prove prophetic some 30 years later when Dolores Durkin (1978) conducted her infamous "where is the comprehension instruction" study.

10. The term re-embrace is used intentionally to capture the fact that intellectual ancestors from the early part of the 20th century, scholars such as Huey, talked of these constructs freely in the days before behaviorism took hold in the field. Even the early Thorndike of the 1917 piece on reading as reasoning was a very different psychologist from the one who developed the laws of effect and contiguity.

11. During this period, great homage was paid to intellectual ancestors such as Edmund Burke Huey, who as early as 1908 recognized the cognitive complexity of reading. Voices such as Huey's, unfortunately, were not heard during the period from 1915 to 1965 when behaviorism dominated psychology and education.

12. Smagorinsky (2001) uses the phrase "inscribed" in the text as a way of indicating that the author of the text has some specific intentions when he or she set pen to paper, thereby avoiding the thorny question of whether meaning exists "out there" outside of the minds of readers. We use the term here to avoid the very same question.

13. Most coherent model is the model that provides the best account of the "facts" of the text uncovered at a given point in time by the reader in relation to the schemata instantiated at that same point in time. This is very much akin to Kintsch's construct of situation model, which Kintsch defines as the reader's current best fit between the facts of the text (coming from the text base) and relevant concepts from prior knowledge. Both Kintsch and

the schema theorists viewed this best fit as a dynamic phenomenon that gets updated as new information emerges from the text and triggers (instantiates is the operative word in schema theory) the activation of relevant schemata from memory.

14. See Baker and Beall, chapter 17, this volume, for an extended treatment of metacognition, both its history and current instantiation.

15. The original version of the model actually emerged from many conversations between Pearson and Joe Campione and Ann Brown at the Center for the Study of Reading in the early 1980s, and was heavily influenced by the scaffolding metaphor from Wood, Bruner, and Ross (1976), the dynamic assessment work of Feuerstein and colleagues (1979), and then emerging zone of proximal development construct of Vygotsky (1978).

16. See Pearson and Stephens (1992) for an account of the forces that led to these shifts; see also McVee, Dunsmore, & Gavalek (2005) for a more analytic treatment of the shortcomings of schema theory and the tensions between it and more socioculturally grounded conceptions of comprehension.

17. By the mid-1990s, the transformation was complete, and NRC had the *Journal of Literacy Research*. No reading. Ironically, the organization kept its name, creating an emblematic disconnect between the name of the organization and the name of the journal.

18. It is most interesting that the ultimate psychometrician, Frederick Davis (e.g., 1944), was fond of referencing the New Criticism of I. A. Richards (1929) in his essays and investigations about comprehension.

19. Rosenblatt credited the idea of transaction to John Dewey, who discussed it in many texts, including *Experience and Education* (1938).

20. See Dole, Nokes, and Drits, chapter 16, this volume, for a thorough treatment of the entire line of strategy instruction research, including work extending into the 21st century.

21. Even though it was conducted well after the end date (roughly 2002) for this chapter, it is worth noting that Reutzel and his colleagues (2005) found that one menu approache of TSI's suite was more effective in promoting understanding of science texts with young readers.

22. It is undoubtedly Jeanette Veatch (1959) who served as the most vocal spokesperson for individualized reading. She published professional textbooks describing how to implement the program in one's class in the middle 1960s.

23. Anderson and his colleagues (1984) reported several studies documenting the impact of book reading on children's achievement gains.

24. Hoffman and his colleagues (1994) painstakingly documented these sorts of changes in the early 90s basals.

25. For a complete account of the Book Club movement, see McMahon and Raphael (1997).

26. Perhaps the most complete current reference on integrated curriculum is a chapter by Gavelek and his colleagues in the 2000 *Handbook of Reading Research*. It is also interesting to note that in chapter 10 of Huey's 1908 book on reading, two such programs, one at Columbia and one at the University of Chicago, were described in rich detail. It is Dewey's insistence that pedagogy be grounded in the individual and collective experiences of learners that is typically cited when scholars invoke his name to support integrated curriculum.

27. See Graves (1983) for an explication of his views on writing.

28. STierney and Pearson (1983) carried this metaphor to the extreme, using the reading "like a writer" metaphor to emphasize the constructivist nature of reading.

29. Accusations of this sort are curious at best in light of 30 years of remarkably level performance on the National Assessment of Educational Progress. A better argument for a crisis would be our inability to close the remarkably persistent achievement gap between rich and poor or majority and minority students. Some would argue (e.g., Pearson, 2004) that the use of achievement levels in NAEP (basic, proficient, and advanced) with rigid cut scores is the perfect policy tool for fomenting a crisis because it allows policy makers to make arguments of the ilk, "Forty percent of America's fourth graders read below basic!" Such accusations fail to admit the obvious—that given the current standards and cut scores, 40% of America's fourth graders have read below basic for the last 30 years. In short, there is little compelling evidence to fix the blame for the achievement of America's students on any particular curricular movement or practice.

References

Afflerbach, P., Pearson, P. D., & Paris, S. (2008). Clarifying differences between reading skills and reading strategies. *The Reading Teacher, 61,* 364–373.

Alvermann, D. E., & Xu, S. H. (2003). Children's everyday literacies: Intersections of popular culture and language arts instruction across the curriculum. *Language Art, 81,* 145–154.

Anderson, R. C. (1977). The notion of schemata and the educational enterprise: General discussion of the conference. In R. Anderson, R. Spiro, & M. Montague (Eds.), *Schooling and the acquisitioning of knowledge.* Hillsdale, NJ: Erlbaum.

Anderson, R. C. (1984). Role of readers' schema in comprehension, learning and memory. In R. Anderson, J. Osbourne, & R. Tierney (Eds.), *Learning to read in American schools: Basal readers and content text.* Hillsdale, NJ: Erlbaum.

Anderson, R. C., Hiebert, E., Scott, J., & Wilkinson, I. (1984). *Becoming a nation of readers.* Champaign, IL: Center for the Study of Reading.

Anderson, R. C., & Pearson, P. D. (1984). A schema-theoretic view of basic processes in reading comprehension. In P.D. Pearson, R. Barr, M. L. Kamil, & P. Mosenthal (Eds), *Handbook of reading research.* New York: Longman.

Anderson, T. H., Armbruster, B. B., & Kantor, R. N. (1983). *How clearly written are children's textbooks? Or, of bladderworts and alfa* (Reading Education Rep. No. 16). Urbana: University of Illinois, Center for the Study of Reading.

Armbruster, B. B., & Anderson, T. H. (1981). *Content area textbooks* (Reading Education Rep. No. 23). Urbana: University of Illinois, Center for the Study of Reading.

Armbruster, B. B., & Anderson, T. H. (1982). *Structures for explanations in history textbooks, or so what if Governor Stanford missed the spike and hit the rail?* (Tech. Rep. No. 252). Urbana: University of Illinois, Center for the Study of Reading.

Armbruster, B. B., & Anderson, T. H. (1984). *Producing considerate expository text: Or easy reading is damned hard writing* (Reading Education Rep. No. 46). Urbana: University of Illinois, Center for the Study of Reading.

Atwell, N. (1987). *In the middle: Writing, reading, and learning with adolescents.* Portsmouth, NH: Heinemann.

Bakhtin, M. M. (1981). *The dialogic imagination.* Austin, TX: University of Austin Press.

Beck, I. L., McKeown, M. G., McCaslin, E. S., & Burkes, A. M. (1979). *Instructional dimensions that may affect reading comprehension: Examples from two commercial reading programs.* Pittsburgh: University of Pittsburgh, Learning Research and Development Center.

Biancarosa, C., & Snow, C. E. (2006). *Reading next—A vision for action and research in middle and high school literacy: A report to Carnegie Corporation of New York* (2nd ed.). Washington, DC: Alliance for Excellent Education.

Bleich, D. (1988). *The double perspective: Language, literacy, and social relations.* New York: Oxford University Press.

Bloom, B.S. (1956). Taxonomy of educational objectives. *Handbook 1: Cognitve Domain.* New York: McKay.

Bormuth, J. R. (1966). Reading: A new approach. *Reading Research Quarterly, 1,* 79–132.

Bormuth, J. R., Manning, J. C., Carr, J. W., & Pearson, P. D. (1971). Children's comprehension of between- and within-sentence syntactic structures. *Journal of Educational Psychology, 61,* 349–357.

Brown, J., Collins, A., & Duguid, P. (1989). Situated cognition of learning. *Educational Researcher, 18,* 32–42.

Bruce, C. (1984). A new point of view on children's stories. In R. Anderson, J. Osbourne, & R. Tierney (Eds.), *Learning to read in American schools: Basal readers and content readers* (pp. 153–174). Hillsdale, NJ: Erlbaum.

California Department of Education (1987). *English-Language Arts Framework for California Public Schools, K–12.* Sacramento, CA: California Department of Education.

Cervetti, G., Pearson, P. D., Barber, J., Hiebert, E., & Bravo, M. (2006). Integrating literacy and science: The research we have, the research we need. In M. Pressley, A. K. Billman, K. Perry, K. Refitt & J. Reynolds (Eds.), *Shaping literacy achievement* (pp. 157–174). New York: Guilford Press.

Chomsky, N. (1957). *Syntactic structures.* The Hague: Mouton.

Chomsky, N. (1959). A review of B. F. Skinner's *Verbal Behavior. Language,* 35(1), 26–58.

Collins, A., Brown, J. S., & Larkin, K. M. (1980). Inference in text understanding. In R. J. Spiro, B. C. Bruce, & W. F. Brewer (Eds.), Theoretical issues in reading comprehension. Hillsdale, NJ: Erlbaum.

Clymer, T. (1968). What is "reading"? Some current concepts. In H. Richie & H. Robinson (Eds.), *Innovation and change in reading instruction* (pp. 7–29). Chicago: National Society for the Study of Education.

Davis, F. B. (1944). Fundamental factors of comprehension of reading. *Psychometrika, 9,* 185–197.

Davison, A., & Kantor, R. N. (1982). On the failure of readability formulas to define readable texts: A case study from adaptations. *Reading Research Quarterly, 18*, 187–209.

Dewey, J. (1938). *Experience and education*. New York: Simon and Schuster.

Dole, J. A., Duffy, G. G., Roehler, L. R., & Pearson, P. D. (1991). Moving from the old to the new: Research on reading comprehension instruction. *Review of Educational Research, 61*, 239–264.

Duke, N., & Pearson, P. D. (2002). Effective practices for developing reading comprehension. In A. Farstrup & J. Sameuls (Eds.), *What research has to say about reading instruction*, 3rd ed. (pp. 205–242). Newark, DE: International Reading Association.

Durkin, D. (1978–79). What classroom observations reveal about reading comprehension instruction. *Reading Research Quarterly, 14*, 481–533.

Durkin, D. (1981). Reading comprehension instruction in five basal reader series. *Reading Research Quarterly, 16*(4) 515–544.

Durrell, D. D. (1949). The development of comprehension and interpretation. In N. B. Henry & A. I. Gates (Eds.), *Reading in the elementary school* (pp. 193–204). Chicago: National Society for Studies in Education.

Elson, W. H., & Gray, W. S. (1936). *Elson-Gray basic readers: Curriculum foundation series*. Chicago: Scott, Foresman.

Elson, W. H., & Keck, C. M. (1911). *The Elson readers, Book 5*. Chicago: Scott, Foresman.

Fagan, W. T. (1971). Transformations and comprehension. The Reading Teacher, 169–172.

Feuerstein, R., Rand, Y., & Hoffman, M. (1979). *Dynamic assessment of the retarded performer*. Baltimore, MD: University Park Press.

Froebel, F. *The education of man*. New York: D. Appleton and Company.

Gates, A. I., & Huber, M. H. (1930). *The work-play books*. New York: Macmillan.

Gates, A. I., & Ayer, J. Y. (1933). *Golden leaves*. New York: Macmillan.

Gee, J. (1992). *The social mind*. Westport, CT: Bergin & Garvey.

Goodman, K. G. (1965) A linguistic study of cues and miscues in reading. *Elementary English, 42*, 639–643.

Graves, D. (1983). *Writing: Teachers and children at work*. Portsmouth, NH: Heinemann.

Gray, W. S. (1925) Essential objectives of instruction in reading. In G. M. Whipple (Ed.), *Twenty-fourth yearbook of the National Society for Studies in Education: Report of the National Committee on Reading* (vol. 24(1), pp. 9–19). Chicago, IL: National Society for Studies in Education.

Gray, W. S., Arbuthnot, M. H., et al. (1940–1948). *Basic readers: Curriculum foundation series*. Chicago: Scott, Foresman.

Gray, W. S., Arbuthnot, M. H., Artley, S. A., Monroe, M., et al. (1951–1957). *New basic readers: Curriculum foundation series*. Chicago: Scott, Foresman.

Guthrie, J. T., Wigfield, A., Barbosa, P., Perencevich, K. C., Taboada, A., Davis, M. H., Scafiddi, N. T., & Tonks, S. (2004). Increasing reading comprehension and engagement through Concept-Oriented Reading Instruction. *Journal of Educational Psychology, 96*, 403–423.

Hacker, D. J., & Tenent, A. (2002). Implementing reciprocal teaching in the classroom: Overcoming obstacles and making modifications. *Journal of Educational Psychology, 94*(4), 699-718.

Hansen, J. (1981). The effects of inference training and practice on young children's reading comprehension. *Reading Research Quarterly, 17*, 391– 417.

Hansen, J., & Pearson, P. D. (1983). An instructional study: Improving the inferential comprehension of fourth grade good and poor readers. *Journal of Educational Psychology, 71*, 821–829.

Harste, J., Burke, C., & Woodward, V. (1984). *Language stories and literacy lessons*. Portsmouth, NH: Heinemann.

Hartman, D. K. (1995). Eight readers reading: The intertextual links of proficient readers reading multiple passages. *Reading Research Quarterly, 30*(3), 520–561.

Herbart, J. F. (1901). *Outlines of educational doctrine*. New York: Macmillan.

Hoffman, J. V., McCarthey, S. J., Abbott, J., Christian, C., Corman, L., Dressman, M., Elliot, B., Matheme, D., & Stahle, D. (1994) So what's new in the "new" basals. *Journal of Reading Behavior, 26*, 47–73.

Huey, E. B. (1908). *The psychology and pedagogy of reading*. New York: Macmillan.

Hull, G. & Schultz, K. (Eds) (2002). *School's out! Bridging out-of-school literacies with classroom practice*. New York: Teachers College Press

Johnston, P. H. (1984) Assessment in reading. In P. D. Pearson, R. Barr, M. Kamil, & P. Mosenthal (Eds.), *Handbook of reading research* (pp. 147–182). New York: Longman.

Johnston, P., & Pearson, P. D. (1982, June). *Prior knowledge, connectivity, and the assessment of reading comprehension* (Tech. Rep. No. 245). Urbana: University of Illinois, Center for the Study of Reading.

Keane, E., & Zimmerman, S. (1997). *Mosaic of thought: Teaching comprehension in a readers' workshop*. Portsmouth, NH: Heinemann.

Kintsch, W. (1974). *The representation of meaning in memory*. Hillsdale, NJ: Erlbaum.

Langer, J. A. (1990) The process of understanding: Reading for literary and informative purposes. *Research in the teaching of English, 24*(3), 229–260.

Lively. B. A., & Pressey, S. L. (1923). A method for measuring the vocabulary burden of textbooks. *Educational Administration and Supervision, 9,* 389–398.

Matthews, M. (1966). *Teaching to read*. Chicago: University of Chicago Press.

McKee, P. (1949). Reading programs in grades IV through VIII. In N. B. Henry & A. I. Gates (Eds.), *Reading in the elementary school* (pp. 127–146). Chicago: National Society for Studies in Education.

McMahon, S. I., Raphael, T. E., with Goatley, V., & Pardo, L. (1997). *The Book Club connection*. New York: Teachers College Press.

McNamara, T. P., Miller, D. L., & Bransford, J. D. (1991). Mental models and reading comprehension. In R. Barr, M. Kamil, P. Mosenthal, & P. D. Pearson (Eds.), *Handbook of reading research, vol. 2* (pp. 490–511). New York: Longman.

McVee, M. B., Dunsmore, K., & Gavalek, J. R. (2005). *Review of Educational Research, 75*(4), 531–566.

Meyer, B. J. F. (1975). *The organization of prose and its effects on memory*. Amsterdam: North Holland Publishing.

Moje, E. B., Peek-Brown, D., Sutherland, L. M., Marx, R. W., Blumenfeld, P., Krajcik, J. (2004). Explaining explanations: Developing scientific literacy in middle-school project-based science reforms. In D. Strickland & D. E. Alvermann, (Eds.), *Bridging the gap: Improving literacy learning for preadolescent and adolescent learners in grades 4–12* (pp. 227–251). New York: Teachers College Press.

National Institute of Child Health and Human Development. (2000). Report of the National Reading Panel. Teaching children to read: an evidence-based assessment of the scientific research literature on reading and its implications for reading instruction: Reports of the subgroups (NIH Publication No. 00-4754). Washington, DC: U.S. Government Printing Office.

Nystrand, M., Gamoran, A. Kachur, R., & Prendergast, C. (1997). *Opening dialogue: Understanding the dynamics of language and learning in the English classroom*. New York: Teachers College Press.

Nystrand, M., Wu, L., Gamoran, A., Zeiser, S., & Long, D. (2003). Questions in time: Investigating the structure and dynamics of unfolding classroom discourse. *Discourse Processes, 35,* 135–196.

Palincsar, A. M., & Brown, A. L. (1984). Reciprocal teaching of comprehension-fostering and comprehension-monitoring activities. *Cognition and Instruction,* 117–175.

Paris, S., Lipson, M., & Wixson, K. (1983). *Becoming a strategic reader.*

Paris, S. G., Cross, D. R., & Lipson, M.Y. (1984). Informed strategies for learning: A program to improve children's reading awareness and comprehension. *Journal of Educational Psychology, 76*(6), 1239–1252.

Pearson, P. D. (1974–75). The effects of grammatical complexity on children's comprehension, recall, and conception of certain semantic relations. *Reading Research Quarterly, 10,* 155–192.

Pearson, P. D. (2000). Reading in the 20th century. In T. Good (Ed.), *American education: Yesterday, today, and tomorrow. Yearbook of the National Society for the Study of Education* (pp. 152–208). Chicago: University of Chicago Press

Pearson, P. D. (2004). The reading wars: The politics of reading research and policy: 1988 through 2003. *Educational Policy, 18*(1), 215–252.

Pearson, P. D. (2007). An endangered species act for literacy education. *Journal of Literacy Research, 39,* 145–162.

Pearson, P. D., & Camparell, K. (1981). Comprehension of text structures. In J. Guthrie (Ed.), *Comprehension and teaching* (pp. 27–54). Newark DE: International Reading Association

Pearson, P. D., & Fielding (1991). Comprehension instruction. In R. Barr, M. Kamil, P. Mosenthal, & P. D. Pearson (Eds.), *Handbook of reading research* (Vol. 2). New York: Longman.

Pearson, P. D., & Gallagher, M. C. (1983). The instruction of reading comprehension. *Contemporary Educational Psychology, 8,* 317–344.

Pearson, P. D., & Hamm, D. N. (2005). The assessment of reading comprehension: A review of practices: Past, present, and future. In S. G. Paris & S. A. Stahl (Eds.), Children's reading comprehension and assessment (pp. 13–69). Mahwah, NJ: Erlbaum.

Pearson, P. D., & Johnson, D.D. (1978). *Teaching reading comprehension*. New York: Holt, Rinehart, and Winston.

Pearson, P. D., & Stephens, D. (1993). Learning about literacy: A 30-year journey. In C. J. Gordon, G. D. Labercane & W. R. McEachern (Eds.), *Elementary reading: Process and practice* (pp. 4–18). Boston: Ginn Press.

Pestalozzi, J. (1898) *How Gertrude Teaches Her Children*. Syracuse, New York: C. W. Barden Publisher.

Pressley, M. (2000). What should comprehension instruction be the instruction of? In M. Kamil, Mosenthal, P., Pearson, P. D., & Barr, R. *Handbook of reading research* (Vol 3). Hillsdale, NJ: Erlbaum.

Pressley, M., Almasi, J., Schuder, T., Bergman, J., Hite, S., El-Dinary, P. B., & Brown, R. (1994). Transactional instruction of comprehension strategies: The Montgomery County, Maryland, SAIL Program. *Reading and Writing Quarterly: Overcoming Learning Difficulties, 10,* 5–19.

Resnick, D. P. (1982). History of educational testing. In A. K. Wigdor & W. R. Garner (Eds.), *Ability testing: Uses, consequences, and controversies* (Part 2). Washington, D.C.: National Academy Press.

Reutzel, R. D., Smith, J. A., & Fawson, P. C. (2005). An evaluation of two approaches for teaching reading comprehension strategies in the primary years using science information texts. *Early Childhood Research Quarterly, 20*(3), 276–305.

Richards, I. A. (1929). *Practical criticism*. New York: Harcourt, Brace.

Rosenblatt, L. M. (1978). *The reader, the text, the poem: The transactional theory of the literary work*. Carbondale: Southern Illinois University Press.

Rosenshine, B., & Meister, C. (1994). Reciprocal teaching: A review of research. *Review of Educational Research, 64,* 479–530.

Rosenshine, B., Meister, C., & Chapman, S. (1996). Teaching students to generate questions: A review of the intervention studies. *Review of Educational Research, 66,* 181–221.

Rumelhart, D. E. (1977). Understanding and summarizing brief stories. In D. LaBerge & J. Samuels (Eds.), *Basic processes in reading perception and comprehension*. Hillsdale, NJ: Erlbaum

Rumelhart, D. E. (1981). Schemata: The building blocks of cognition. In J. T. Guthrie (Ed.), *Comprehension in teaching* (pp. 3–26). Newark, DE: International Reading Association.

Smagorinsky, P. (2001). If meaning is constructed, what is it made from? Toward a cultural theory of reading. *Review of Educational Research, 71*(2), 133–169.

Smith, F. (1971). *Understanding reading: A psycholinguistic analysis of reading and learning to read*. New York: Holt, Rinehart, & Winston.

Smith, F., & Miller, G. A. (Eds.) (1966).*The genesis of language: A psychology approach*. Cambridge: M.I.T. Press, 1966.

Smith, N. B. (1986). *American reading instruction*. Newark, DE: International Reading Association. (Original published 1966)

Snow, C. (2003). Reading for Understanding: Toward an R&D Program in Reading Comprehension. Santa Monica, CA: Rand.

Spiro, R. J., Vispoel, W., Schmitz, W., Samarapungavan, A., Boerger, A. (1987). Knowledge acquisition for application: Cognitive flexibility and transfer in complex content domains. In B. C. Britton & S. Glynn (Eds.), *Executive control processes*. Hillsdale, NJ: Erlbaum.

Stein, N., & Glenn, C. G. (1977). An analysis of story comprehension in elementary school children. In R. Freedle (Ed.), *Discourse production and comprehension* (Vol. 1). Norwood, NJ: Ablex.

Stenner, A. J., & Burdick, (1997). *The objective measurement of reading comprehension*. Durham, NC: MetaMetrics, Inc.

Stenner, A. J., Smith, D. R., Horabin, I., & Smith, M. (1987). *Fit of the Lexile Theory to item difficulties on fourteen standardized reading comprehension tests*. Durham, NC: MetaMetrics Inc.

Sutherland, L. M., Meriweather, A., Rucker, S., Sarratt, P., Hale, Y., Krajcik, J., Moje, E. B. (in press). *More emphasis on scientific explanation: Developing conceptual understanding while developing scientific literacy*. Washington, DC: NSTA.

Thorndike, E. L. (1914). The measurement of ability in reading: Preliminary scales and tests: Introduction. *Teachers College Record, 15*(4), 1–2.

Thorndike, E. L. (1917). Reading as reasoning: A study of mistakes in paragraph reading. *Journal of Educational Psychology, 8,* 323–332.

Tierney, R. & Cunningham, J. (1991). Research on teaching reading and comprehension. In R. Barr, M. Kamil, P. Mosenthal, & P. D. Pearson (Eds.), *Handbook of Reading Research* (Vol. 2, pp. 609–655). Mahwah, NJ: Erlbaum.

Tierney, R. J., & Pearson, P. D. (1983). Toward a composing model of reading. *Language Arts, 60,* 568–580.

Veatch, J. (1959). *Individualizing your reading program.* New York: G. P. Putnam's Sons.

Vygotsky, L. S. (1978). *Mind in society.* Cambridge, MA: Harvard University Press.

Wertsch, J. (1993). *Voices of the mind: A sociocultural approach to mediated action.* Cambridge, MA: Harvard University Press.

Wittrock, M. (1992). Generative process of the brain. *Educational Psychologist, 27,* 531–541.

Wood, D., Bruner, J. S., & Ross, G. (1976). The role of tutoring in problem solving. *Journal of Psychology and Psychiatry. 17,* 89–100.

2 The Development of Children's Reading Comprehension

Scott G. Paris and Ellen E. Hamilton

University of Michigan

Understanding the meanings of printed words and texts is the core function of literacy that enables people to communicate messages across time and distance, express themselves beyond gestures, and create and share ideas. Without comprehension, reading words is reduced to mimicking the sounds of language, repeating text is nothing more than memorization and oral drill, and writing letters and characters is simply copying or scribbling. Making sense of printed words and communicating through shared texts with interpretive, constructive, and critical thinking is perhaps the central task of formal schooling around the world. Given the importance of reading comprehension for children's literacy and learning, it is surprising that there are so few theories about it.

Although researchers have made considerable progress in identifying and addressing children's early decoding difficulties (Snow, Burns, & Griffin, 1998), less attention has been given to children's comprehension skills (RAND Reading Study Group, 2001). Hence, there is little agreement about the developmental course of reading comprehension, the precursors of good comprehension, effective assessments of comprehension, and practical interventions that promote children's comprehension (Pearson & Hamm, 2005). The purpose of this chapter is to summarize the prevailing views of children's reading comprehension, to highlight key developmental issues and unsolved problems, and to propose a new way to think about the developing skills that enable children to comprehend text.

DEFINING COMPREHENSION

There are many definitions of comprehension, but little consensus, perhaps because the boundaries of the topic are so broad and so poorly marked. Reading comprehension is only a subset of an ill-defined larger set of knowledge that reflects the communicative interactions among the intentions of the author/speaker, the content of the text/message, the abilities and purposes of the reader/listener, and the context/situation of the interaction. Early definitions of reading comprehension focused on thinking and reasoning about text (e.g., Thorndike, 1917) whereas recent national reports have emphasized the constructive and interactive processes of reading comprehension. For example, the RAND report (2001) defines comprehension as, "The process of simultaneously extracting and constructing meaning through interaction and involvement with written language" (p. 11). The NAEP (2009) Reading Framework Committee defines reading comprehension as ..."an active and complex process that involves understanding written text, developing and interpreting meaning, and using meaning as appropriate to type of text, purpose and situation (National Center for Educational Statistics, 2005, p. 2).

The broad and inclusive definitions of reading comprehension present problems for specifying what, how, and when various components develop. Consequently, educational approaches to assessment and instruction of reading comprehension often take a practical but piecemeal approach that emphasize various components of comprehension, for example, fluent oral reading, making inferences, connecting text to background knowledge, or asking and answering questions. Although these pragmatic approaches to promote comprehension have been numerous and diverse, they have shown that there are multiple pedagogical strategies for helping students understand what they read. In the next section, we review some prevailing views of reading comprehension in order to identify the usefulness of each view for understanding how children's reading comprehension develops.

VIEWS OF SKILLED READING COMPREHENSION

Information processing models

Information processing models of reading describe the mental operations applied by readers to the text (input) that yield comprehension (output). Learning to read makes the component processes automatic (i.e., faster and more accurate). For example, LaBerge and Samuels (1974; Samuels & LaBerge, 1983) describe children as "reading factories" where raw materials (texts) are processed by four production machines (visual memory, phonological memory, semantic memory, and situated memory). The production foreman is attention, and it determines the allocation of finite cognitive resources to the reading task. The initial work is decoding the text. If the text is difficult, the majority of attention is given to decoding. It is through the automation of decoding that additional cognitive resources become available for comprehension. Developing automatic word recognition and decoding is the primary focus of early instruction in this reading model because comprehension is derived from word recognition. Indeed, LaBerge and Samuels (1974) provide little description of cognitive processes involved in comprehension because they treat it as an automatic consequence of decoding words quickly.

Although, there is an obvious relation between decoding abilities and reading comprehension, one does not guarantee the other. Correlations between decoding and comprehension (among older readers) range from $r = .3 - .7$ (Juel, Griffith, & Gough, 1986; Yuill & Oakhill, 1991). Many of the low correlations are evident for a specific subset of children who show strong decoding skills and low comprehension skills. Studies comparing readers with good and poor comprehension do not show differences between groups in word reading speed, automatic decoding, and accuracy of non-word reading (Cain & Oakhill, 2003). Likewise, there has been little evidence of phonological deficits causing comprehension impairment (Cain, Oakhill, & Bryant, 2000; Stothard & Hulme, 1995). Thus, decoding is necessary but not sufficient for comprehension.

A second type of information processing model describes reading as the interaction of bottom-up and top-down processes. Rummelhart (1994) and Stanovich (1980) propose that readers construct meaning from text using multiple tools. Bottom-up processing is focused on decoding and understanding words. Top-down processing involves the integration of background knowledge with the text. The system is compensatory because readers are believed to use strong skills to compensate for weak skills. Researchers have shown how component skills interact, for example, phonemic awareness and orthographic knowledge in beginning word identification (Ehri, 1995), but it is difficult to identify the reciprocal and compensatory relations among comprehension components at different levels of proficiency. Perfetti, Landi, and Oakhill

(2005) suggest that reading comprehension and listening comprehension influence each other but not always equally. Likewise, knowledge of word meanings and comprehension develop interactively. They suggest that word identification sets a limit on comprehension, especially during beginning reading acquisition. Thus, interactive process models are beginning to specify how some component processes limit, enable, or bootstrap comprehension development.

The simple view

Gough and Tunmer (1986) suggest a "simple view of reading" in which reading (and reading comprehension) is a function of the interaction between two factors: (1) the ability to decode words (D) and (2) language comprehension (LC). The former is mostly bottom-up and the latter is mostly top-down processing. The relation can be expressed in an equation as ($R = D \times LC$). When decoding is slow, laborious, and inaccurate, reading comprehension is suppressed because the person does not know the words and has few cognitive resources left to apply to language comprehension. When decoding skills are automatic, comprehension is easier, but is influenced by a variety of language factors. The simple view is an extension of the model proposed by LaBerge and Samuels (1974) in which comprehension is the result of the efficiency of decoding. Both are consistent with a layperson's view of reading comprehension that distinguishes deciphering print from reasoning about meaning. The simple view is evident in many theories that differentiate word identification skills from linguistic and cognitive processes in reading (e.g., Athey & Singer, 1987; Perfetti, Landi, & Oakhill, 2005). The simple model is appealing because it is both parsimonious and comprehensive in the isolation of code-breaking skills from meaning-making skills. However, it is worth unpacking the two factors in the simple model to identify some hidden problems.

The simple view treats D and LC as equally weighted variables across time, texts, and contexts. That seems wrong from a developmental view because skills related to D (such as letter knowledge, phonemic awareness, phonics, spelling, and concepts about print) are constrained (cf., Paris, 2005) because they are usually learned relatively quickly and to asymptotic levels of performance by 8 to 9 years of age. Skills related to LC, in contrast, are unconstrained and develop from infancy through adulthood. The simple view asserts that when D is zero or slight, comprehension is negligible. That is almost tautological. After D is near 100%, then LC factors are mainly responsible for changes in comprehension. The simple view fails to articulate the developmental trajectories of D and LC and how their interactions vary across developing proficiency. Skills related to LC always influence comprehension whereas skills related to D influence comprehension most when decoding is being learned and automated (i.e., at about 8 to 9 years of age).

Decoding skills enable comprehension but they do not insure it. This necessary but insufficient causal relation is obscured in the simple view. We return to it later and propose that decoding sets a threshold that permits reading comprehension. The causal relation in the simple view is disguised because it is really the lack of decoding that causes poor comprehension. Indeed, when the words cannot be deciphered, recognized, or spoken, language comprehension is prevented. It is easy to see the causal relation when decoding is near zero, just as there is no causal relation when the decoding is near 100%; so the empirical question boils down to how much decoding accuracy is necessary to permit adequate comprehension of text. Determining this threshold value is difficult because it varies according to context, familiarity, and all the other skills involved in LC.

Stahl and Hiebert (2005) criticize the simple model for a different reason. They claim that word recognition (decoding) is influenced by a person's knowledge of words and language. For example, words are recognized faster in meaningful sentence contexts than in isolation (Adams, 1990). Stahl and Hiebert (2005) believe that children's emerging understanding of vocabulary is more important than automatic word recognition alone. They also maintain that as children learn to read, their miscues become more based on meaning than on graphic similarity (Biemiller, 1970) so that fluent reading becomes "language like" in accuracy, rate, and intonation—all processes that are far more complex than automatic recognition of words. Stahl, Kuhn, and Pickle (1999) claim that the simple view contradicts their clinical experiences because they have seen young children with adequate language abilities who can decode automatically yet still exhibit problems comprehending text. Their research suggests that children with poor comprehension but with adequate language skills may have impairments in the strategic control of reading, a factor not included in the simple view.

Thus, the simple view fails to identify the developmental relations between D and LC, and the equation reduces to two simple claims: 1) comprehension is minimal when decoding is low, and 2) when decoding is very good, comprehension is a function of LC skills. In addition, the simple view implies that comprehension increases continuously with decoding skill. For example, as a reader's decoding improves from 10% to 50% to 90% of the words on a page (and LC remains constant or improves), then reading (and comprehension) should also increase at least 10%, 50%, and 90%, respectively. This is simply not true because comprehension is severely limited or nil until most words can be decoded (and most word meanings are known). The discontinuous relation between decoding and comprehension is not captured in the simple view.

A CONSTRUCTION-INTEGRATION MODEL

A model of reading comprehension proposed by Kintsch (1998) called the construction-integration (CI) model is perhaps the most popular model of adult reading comprehension processes. Kintsch (1998) proposed that readers construct simultaneously a model of the literal text and an elaborated model of the situation implied by the text. These two representations of text are constructed through re-reading and thinking about meaning in cyclical ways so they mutually reinforce each other. The construction of a text base depends on the reader's ability to construct the relations in both the microstructure and macrostructure of the text, two levels of propositional relations according to Kintsch and Kintsch (2005). The construction of the situation model reflects the reader's ability to make inferences that go beyond the text base and connect it to previous experience and other knowledge. Reconciling the successive inferences and unfolding relations in text in coherent representations is the integration part of the model.

The CI model is a bottom-up model because it begins with decoding the literal text, and it is a top-down model because the situation model depends on prior knowledge, vocabulary, and the activation of relevant schemata (Anderson & Pearson, 1984; Langer, 1984). As readers engage text, they proceed through two stages. First, they construct meaning from the text to produce a network of activated mental concepts. This may be represented as a set of hierarchical propositions varying in importance (Kintsch & van Dijk, 1978) or as a network of propositions. In the second stage, readers integrate the network concepts that are compatible with the implied situation, while concepts that are not compatible with the context are de-activated. Without adequate background knowledge, the text will predominate in the comprehension process so readers may be required to connect many disconnected facts and details. Without adequate knowledge of the actual text, the representation would rely more heavily on the reader's prior knowledge and experiences so it might distort the intended text meaning. When the two models are coherent, readers use each to constrain the other and produce a cohesive interpretation of the text.

It is unclear how children develop skills needed to construct text base and situation models and how to integrate their previous knowledge with the constructed representation. Are the processes constrained by working memory, lack of attention resources, lack of monitoring strategies, lack of knowledge, or something else? What is required for children to construct meaning from text beyond fluent decoding? How do children learn to revise their comprehension in an iterative manner, through re-reading and re-thinking? The transaction between a reader and a text is the focus of the next approach to comprehension.

Comprehension as envisionment through stances

Sociocultural and sociohistorical research during the past 30 years has highlighted the transaction between life experiences and comprehension, a view consistent with the constructivist approaches of reading as a meaning-making activity. Literacy was regarded as "situated cognition," i.e., the development of rule-governed representations by an individual in a particular context, with a particular background, and at a particular time (Langer & Flihan, 2000). Judith Langer's approach to comprehension emphasizes the contribution of a variety of macrostructure factors in the transaction between reader and text. To capture the recursive growth of comprehension, Langer proposes the idea of envisionment building (e.g., Langer, 1989, 2004). While reading, individuals create schemata or envisionments capturing at that particular moment, what they understand, predictions about what is going to occur, emotional responses to characters and situations that are occurring as they read (Langer, 2004). These envisionments, or text worlds, are a product of one's experience, what one knows about the topic and the situation and one's objectives in the reading process. However, these envisionments change as each new event, situation, character, or fact from the text changes the representation slightly and resonates with different background factors within the individual. Thus, throughout the reading process, the individual produces a series of envisionments that change and develop with further reading (Langer, 1989).

Because of the transactions between text and reader, Langer advocates for research that captures the process not just the end product of comprehension. Langer (1989) analyzed think-aloud protocols from seventh and eleventh graders' online processing of 24 different types of text and identified four critical stances to describe how readers reacted to the text over time. The first stance, labeled the "Being Out and Stepping Into an Envisionment" is described as the process whereby the reader makes initial contact with the genre, content, structure, and language of the text, and superficially applies prior knowledge and experiences to begin the construction of an envisionment. The second stance, "Being In and Moving Through an Envisionment," builds from the first and captures the process whereby readers extend their envisionments. The latter two stances, "Stepping Back and Rethinking What One Knows" and "Stepping Out and Objectifying the Experience," capture the processes whereby the text influences the reader's knowledge. In the "Stepping Back" stance, readers apply their newly formed envisionments to restructure their previous knowledge, and in the "Stepping Out" stance, they distance themselves from the text and react to the text as an objective observer independent of the social context.

Likewise, the NAEP reading framework for 1992–1998 assessed readers' abilities to understand text from four stances or orientations. The first stance is initial understanding and the second is developing an interpretation, both close to the text base in propositional meanings. The third stance is a personal response and the fourth is a critical stance that examines the author's style and craft. Comprehension is viewed as multi-faceted, recursive, and contextualized in approaches that emphasize stances and envisionments. More broadly, sociocultural and constructivist approaches to comprehension emphasize how the unique history, background, abilities, situation, purpose, and knowledge of readers influence the processes as well as the products of comprehension of text.

CHILDREN'S DEVELOPING READING COMPREHENSION

Researchers have proposed both stage and information processing models of children's reading development. We consider some examples in the following sections.

A stage model of reading development

Jeanne Chall (1967, 1996) proposed a six-stage developmental model of reading in which readers acquire skills in a linear and sequential manner starting with pre-reading skills then decoding skills and then comprehension of complex text. In the first stage, the pre/emergent reader is learning important skills for later independent reading. These skills include concepts of print, letter knowledge, phonemic awareness, and book-handling skills. The second stage usually occurs during grades 1 and 2, and it is the beginning of conventional reading when early readers develop decoding skills such as letter/word recognition and letter/sound correspondence.

Other models of reading acquisition describe similar serial sequences in more detail. For example, a model proposed by Ehri and Wilce (1980) and Ehri, (1995) postulated four stages of decoding skills in reading development. The first stage is non-reading context decoding in which children are unable to read any words, yet understand that the text has meaning. The second stage is visual-cue decoding where children use the shapes of letters in a word as a clue to what the word could be. Early readers in this stage are limited because they do not know many letters, but they understand that the letters provide some clues to meaning. The third stage of decoding corresponds to phonetic cues. Children at this stage have some letter recognition and phonological awareness. In the fourth stage of the model, children begin systematic phonemic decoding of words. The children know that the letters in print are associated with specific sounds of oral language. They are proficient decoders who are developing automatic decoding. Children pass through four phases of word recognition according to Ehri (1995); pre-alphabetic, partial alphabetic, full alphabetic, and consolidated alphabetic word recognition.

In the third stage of Chall's model (about grades 2–3), readers consolidate their decoding skills, build their sight word vocabularies, and increase their reading fluency. The increased sight word vocabulary improves reading accuracy and children begin to attend to the prosodic aspects of text. The fourth stage occurs in grades 4–8 and is marked by a pronounced shift from "learning to read" to "reading to learn". There is a corresponding shift in the classroom from an emphasis on narrative stories to expository passages as the subject of reading becomes more integrated into content area reading. The fifth and sixth stages focus on increasing comprehension of more complex text. Children in stage five can read about different views on the same subject, but they are unable to synthesize these views coherently like a stage six child.

Chall's stage theory was proposed in an era when Piaget's stage theory of cognitive development was popular so sequential stages of literacy development seemed plausible. However, Chall's theory suffered from the same criticisms leveled against other stage models, namely, not all children went through the stages in the prescribed order and the stages seemed to under-estimate children's emerging knowledge and control. For example, Chall claims that children focus on decoding words in grades 1 and 2 and do not focus on "reading to learn" until fourth grade are contradicted by children's accomplishments at earlier ages. Development beyond grade 4 also seems inadequately described, as most students in grades 4–8 can read and discuss text from different perspectives. Thus, the development of comprehension skills are not identified and explained according to the developing competencies of the child or the increasing complexity of texts and uses of reading in school.

MULTI-COMPONENT MODELS OF COMPREHENSION

Many current approaches are eclectic rather than theoretical because of the limitations identified with stage models, information processing models, and the simple view of reading. Instead, researchers often regard proficient reading as the assembly, coordination, and automatic use of multiple component processes (Adams, 1990; Stanovich, 2000). The processes include a variety of knowledge and skills, some specific to print and some not, that develop into a coordinated activity of skilled reading, usually during childhood. For example, Rathvon (2004) lists 10 components of reading that predict reading acquisition or diagnose reading problems; phonological processing, rapid letter naming, orthographic processing, oral language, print awareness and concept of word, alphabet knowledge, single word reading, oral reading in context, reading comprehension, and written language. The National Reading Panel (2000) identified a list of five essential components of early reading that included the alphabetic principle, phonemic awareness, oral reading fluency, vocabulary, and comprehension. Researchers and educators generally regard the acquisition and integration of these components to be essential for reading development.

To our knowledge, no one has suggested a specific list of attributes essential for reading comprehension that is different than the list of components necessary for proficient reading. However, there is a growing body of research examining cognitive and linguistic skills that affect the ability to construct integrated and stable meaning representations (e.g., Graesser, Singer, & Trabasso, 1994; Oakhill & Cain, 2003). Comprehension demands integration of meaning across words, sentences and passages, and relies on component skills at each of these levels for the construction of meaning. Next, we examine component processes of comprehension by level of analysis.

Word-level   Given the tight coupling between word meaning and comprehension, vocabulary has long been believed to be an important, if not, historically, the most important component of comprehension (see Perfetti, 1994, for reviews). Research has supported a relation between verbal IQ (often measured by vocabulary) and comprehension in adults and children (e.g., Sternberg & Powell, 1983). Children who have poor comprehension have lower verbal IQ scores than do children who have good comprehension (e.g., Stothard & Hulme, 1996). Tentative support for the causal importance of vocabulary is evident in training studies that demonstrated improved comprehension as a result of training in word meanings (e.g., Beck, McKeown, & Omanson, 1987), and longitudinal studies that demonstrate a unique contribution of vocabulary to individual differences in comprehension (Muter et al., 2004; Seigneuric & Ehrlich, 2005). However, vocabulary is only one component, and it is a necessary but not a sufficient skill to ensure good comprehension (e.g., Cain, Oakhill, & Lemmon, 2004).

Sentence-level   Comprehension of a sentence requires the processing, storage, and integration of a variety of syntactic and semantic information. Syntactic knowledge may help bootstrap labored decoding and ambiguous semantic information, or it may aid in detection of reading errors (Tunmer & Hoover, 1992). The relation between syntactic ability and comprehension may change with development. Oakhill, Cain, and Bryant (2004) found that syntactic ability did not predict concurrent comprehension for 7- to 8-

year-olds, but it did predict comprehension one year later. Detecting inconsistencies in both semantics and syntax is related to comprehension ability. Yuill, Oakhill, and Parkin (1989) found that good comprehenders are better at identifying and resolving internal consistencies in sentences and paragraphs than less-skilled comprehenders although the two groups show similar verbatim memory. This performance differential increased dramatically when the distance in text between inconsistencies was increased.

Text-level At the level of the text, research has identified two fundamental components in children's developing comprehension that appear crucial for establishing coherence, inference-making and comprehension-monitoring (e.g., Cain, Oakhill, & Bryant, 2004). Research has shown developmental improvements in children's inferences from text (e.g., Paris & Upton, 1976; Trabasso & Suh, 1993). Age-related improvements are evident for connecting information from different parts of text and for inferences involving textual coherence such as themes and main ideas. What's more, less-skilled readers show deficits in producing both local and global coherence while reading text (Cain & Oakhill, 1999, 2003; Oakhill, 1982, 1984). Studies using comprehension age-match (e.g., Cain & Oakhill, 1999) and training studies (e.g., Yuill & Joscelyne, 1988) have suggested that inadequate inference-making abilities may cause poor comprehension.

Similarly, as children get older, they are more proficient at identifying text inconsistencies that are either internal (where portions of the text are contradictory) or external (where there are conflicts between what one reads and what one knows) (Baker, 1984). In addition, skilled comprehenders are more proficient at paragraph-level detection of anomalies than less-skilled comprehenders after controlling for vocabularly and decoding differences (Oakhill, Hartt, & Samols, 2005). Overall, inference-making and comprehension-monitoring abilities may be causally related to differences in comprehension. In a longitudinal analysis, 102 seven- to eight-year-old children were assessed on a battery of reading-related measures (decoding, vocabulary, verbal ability, working memory, inference-making skill, comprehension monitoring, and knowledge of story structure) in order to determine the relations among subcomponents of comprehension (Cain, Oakhill, & Bryant, 2004). Inference-making and comprehension monitoring were the only two independent variables to contribute unique variance to comprehension after removing the effects of decoding skill, verbal ability, and working memory (Cain, Oakhill, & Bryant, 2004).

Multi-component views are open-ended because any linguistic, cognitive, or social skill might potentially influence comprehension. The breadth of a multi-component model is appealing on the one hand, but, on the other hand, the lack of boundaries, explanatory power, and developmental sequences limit the usefulness of an expansive approach. In particular, multi-component models need to distinguish the different developmental trajectories of various skills because they vary widely in age of onset, duration and rate of learning, and level of proficiency or mastery. Some knowledge and skills influence emerging literacy, some shape literacy among older readers, and some function across the lifespan.

Another problem with multi-component models concerns the statistical models used to assess the influence of various components. The usual analytical procedures of factor analyses, multivariate analyses of variance, correlations and regressions, path analyses, and HLM treat the components equally. Yet, we know that the components influence comprehension in different ways and to different degrees according to the skills and ages of readers, the difficulty and familiarity of texts, and the purposes of reading. Multi-component models make no assumptions about the relative importance of various components and let the empirical data describe the patterns among them. Unfortunately, the variations in texts, readers, and purposes of reading interact with developmental proficiencies so there are often wide differences among empirical findings that remain ambiguous and prevent clear demonstrations of developing comprehension abilities.

Our brief review of six prominent views of reading comprehension has revealed some heuristic features and some gaps in the models for understanding how children develop deeper, richer understanding. The review has also shown that part of the difficulty in defining comprehension is due to three problems. First, reading comprehension is not a static or uniform outcome; it varies widely across people reading the same text and within the same person reading the text as each new reading, stance, or recursive thinking about text may lead to new envisionments, new inferences, and new ideas. Second, comprehension is often defined by (a) successive depths of processing, (b) increasing numbers of ideas, inferences, or connections, or (c) larger units of coherence or more structured models of the text base and situation, but there are few operational measures of comprehension depth and thoroughness. Third, developmental changes in reading comprehension are evident in the quality and quantity of ideas as outcomes, but underlying these changes are important cognitive processes such as better working memory, more automatic and fluent reading, and greater use of strategies and self-control over skills that enhance comprehension. Thus, the development of reading comprehension is inter-related with the development of knowledge and reasoning over a longer period of time than the development of decoding skills. Next, we examine a few key issues regarding the development of comprehension.

Key issue #1: How is comprehension affected by changes in working memory?

Research has demonstrated the importance of working memory in decoding and comprehension, but little research has explored the reciprocal relations between developmental changes in working memory and reading (e.g., Seigneuric & Ehrlich, 2005). Until adolescence, children show poorer performance on memory processing tasks than adults. One hypothesis is that the actual storage space in memory increases with age. An alternative hypothesis is that the total processing space is constant over development, and thus age-related differences are related to the trade-off between operating space and storage space during processing (Case, 1995). Little research has explored the implication of these results for reading comprehension. Are improvements in comprehension with age and skill due to increases in working memory capacity and processing efficiency?

Because reading comprehension requires integration of meaning across words, sentences, and passages, there are demands on working memory (a) at the individual word-level (recall and retention of semantic meaning), (b) the sentence-level (merging of the syntactic and semantic cues to create a proposition), and (c) the text-level (synthesizing propositions into a coherent idea). Research has shown a strong and consistent relation between measures of working memory and comprehension (e.g., Gathercole, Pickering, Ambridge, & Wearing, 2004). In a meta-analysis of 77 studies of memory and cognition, Daneman and Merikle (1996) found that the correlation between reading span, a standard measure of working memory (Daneman & Carpenter, 1980), and comprehension was $r = .41$.

Skilled readers appear to construct integrated and cohesive text comprehension with little effort. However, less-skilled readers appear to exhibit specific and consistent impairments in the components required to build these cohesive representations, leading to the hypothesis that impairment in working memory may underlie problems in comprehension. Many task designs have revealed a processing-load differential between skilled and less-skilled comprehenders in conditions taxing verbal working memory (e.g., Oakhill, Cain, & Bryant, 2004; Seigneuric, Ehrlich, Oakhill, Yuill, 2000) but not visual-spatial memory (e.g., Nation, Adams, Bowyer-Crane, & Snowling, 1999;

Seigneuric et al., 2000). Furthermore, performance differences at the word-, sentence-, and text-level all appear to be exacerbated if the demands on working memory are increased.

Research has highlighted the importance of working memory for explaining differences in developing readers' comprehension. Several longitudinal studies have revealed a strong relation between measures of verbal working memory and comprehension in children even when controlling for other literacy-related skills such as phonological awareness, verbal IQ, and vocabulary (Oakhill, Cain, & Bryant, 2004; Oakhill, Hartt, & Samols, 2005). In a 3-year longitudinal study, 56 seven-year-olds were tested on a large battery of tests measuring phonological ability, vocabulary, working memory, and comprehension (reading, sentences, and text) in first, second, and third grade (Seigneuric & Ehrlich, 2005). Vocabulary emerged as a direct predictor of comprehension at all three time points, whereas working memory only predicted comprehension in third grade. Interestingly, when the autoregressive effect was added, vocabulary in grade 1 and working memory in grade 2 both explained unique variance in comprehension at grade 3, suggesting that these variables may become stronger predictors of comprehension with age. These findings suggest different developmental relations of vocabulary and working memory with comprehension.

A further complication is that differences in working memory may underlie the relations among word, sentence, and even text-level components and comprehension. For example, some research has suggested that working memory may mediate the strong, and sometimes hypothesized causal, relation between vocabulary and comprehension. Vocabulary and working memory are highly correlated with comprehension, and working memory and vocabulary are also highly correlated (Adams & Gathercole, 1996, 2000; Gathercole, Service, Hitch, Adams, & Martin, 1999).

Perhaps improvements in working memory mediate improvements in comprehension partly through automatic access to vocabulary or richer semantic representations. Less-skilled comprehenders may have more shallow representations or representations that are more susceptible to interference. In support of this hypothesis, research has shown that less-skilled comprehenders recall equal numbers of concrete nouns, but fewer abstract nouns (Nation, Adams, Bowyer-Crane, & Snowling, 1999). They also generate fewer examples of category members than skilled readers in a semantic fluency test (Nation & Snowling, 1998), although not when matched for decoding ability (Cain, Oakhill, & Lemmon, 2004).

Alternatively, the shared resource aspect of storage *and* processing in working memory may suggest that with heavier processing loads, there is less efficient encoding or transfer of lexical representations to long-term memory (Daneman, 1988). Learning new words, particularly when relying on context, puts heavy demands on the simultaneous storage of the word and the accretion of contextual clues used to derive meaning. Research has shown that performance gets worse, particularly for less-skilled comprehenders, with increasing distance between the novel word and the supporting contextual knowledge (Oakhill, Hart, & Samols, 2005).

Cain, Oakhill, and Lemmon (2004) provided clarification of the relations among working memory, vocabulary, and comprehension measures. Three groups of 9- to 10-year-olds were tested on their ability to learn novel words in context. One group was skilled and another group was less skilled on comprehension measures, and they were matched on decoding and vocabulary. A third group of less-skilled comprehenders had weak vocabulary scores but was matched on comprehension scores to the other less-skilled group. Both groups of poor comprehenders had more difficulty understanding the meanings of novel vocabulary words from context than the skilled comprehenders. The degree of difficulty was magnified by the distance between the novel word and the supporting context clues suggesting that a major source of difficulty is the processing load of maintaining information over time for integration into lexical representations. Interestingly, an important distinction appeared between the two groups of the less-skilled comprehenders. The group with the weak vocabulary showed additional difficulty in learning new words through direct instruction, requiring more instructional sessions in order to reach criterion whereas the less-skilled comprehenders matched for vocabulary to the skilled comprehenders, showed no difference. More research is needed to explore the changing contribution of working memory to comprehension and the pattern of components of comprehension with developing age and proficiency.

Key issue #2: How are changes in oral reading fluency related to comprehension?

Intuitively, oral reading fluency, however it is assessed, should be related positively to comprehension. However, different theories imply that there are occasions, based on emerging skill proficiency or text difficulty, in which oral reading fluency and comprehension may not be related strongly (Kuhn & Stahl, 2003). The relation between fluency and comprehension has important implications because many early reading assessments assume that fluency measures predict comprehension well so fluency, particularly reading rate, is assessed instead of comprehension. One of the reasons is that reading rate can be assessed more quickly and easily than comprehension, but the liability is the assumption that fluency is a good indicator of comprehension across age and skill levels.

Chall's model of reading acquisition (1967, 1996) asserted that readers move from pre-reading skills to decoding to constructing their own understanding of text. Some "bottom-up" processing models assert that breaking the code is the necessary and sufficient condition for text comprehension. Other reading theories suggest a different relation between oral reading and comprehension. For example, LaBerge and Samuels (1974; Samuels & LaBerge, 1983) argued that as word recognition becomes automatic, there are more cognitive resources available for comprehension. There is a period when reading is accurate but not automatic, before attention shifts to the semantic processor for comprehension. Students at this phase of reading would display highly accurate readings of text but not good comprehension. However, as readers become more proficient in word recognition, one would expect the additional resources devoted to comprehension to result in better understanding of the text. This model of developing automaticity predicts low correlations between fluency and comprehension initially that increase with automatic decoding.

In contrast, Goodman (1976) suggested that students may be better at comprehending text than reading aloud accurately. He theorized that reading involves continual hypothesis testing whereby the reader looks for confirmation of hypothesized meaning from the text. The reader uses context and the least possible input to judge the validity of the initial hypothesis. More proficient readers make better initial hypotheses and require less text input to analyze the veracity of their hypotheses. They do not decode every word to construct meaning; instead meaning is accepted or rejected based on the confirmation of the hypothesis with some words in the text. This "top-down" approach implies a low correlation between oral reading accuracy and comprehension, at least for some readers on some occasions.

Recent studies suggest that the overall significant correlations between oral reading fluency and comprehension measures may mask an important developmental shift in the relation (Paris, Carpenter, Paris, & Hamilton, 2005; Stahl & Hiebert, 2005). There appears to be developmental disjunction between oral reading fluency and comprehension because the relation is strongest for beginning and struggling readers. With increasing age and reading skill, older children and better readers exhibit more variable relations between oral reading fluency and comprehension. The variable patterns include children who are skilled word callers or skilled gap fillers in addition to children who are high or low on both fluency and comprehension. It is the numbers of subjects in the discordant cells (i.e., word callers and gap fillers) that attenuate the intuitively expected positive correlations between oral reading fluency and comprehension. Paris, and colleagues (2005) found the developmental disjunction of fluency and comprehension in studies with different subjects, different passages, and different components of fluency and comprehension. The correlations between fluent oral reading and comprehension of the same passages declined with increasing age and decoding skill. The same patterns were evident with each component of oral reading and the results were similar when examined by raw scores, factor scores, or IRT-scaled scores.

The findings are consistent with an interactive-compensatory model of reading (e.g., Stanovich, 1980) because gap fillers and word callers exemplify different profiles of skill proficiencies. Children use their strongest skills when asked to read a passage for accuracy and meaning, and it seems plausible that some children use more "top-down" context-driven strategies to fill in meaning while others focus on saying the words quickly and accurately. These groups of readers will display negative correlations between fluency and comprehension measures that attenuate the positive correlations evident among children who are either high or low in both fluency and comprehension. Thus, the pattern of disjunction depends on the relative numbers of gap fillers and word callers in a sample, which in turn will influence the strength of the correlation observed between fluency and comprehension in any particular sample.

The developmental aspect of the disjunction is due to the greater range of skill proficiencies and the greater diversity of skill profiles that are evident among older children and more skilled readers. The studies suggest that by the time children can read passages at a third-grade level, the diversity of skill profiles may attenuate the correlations between fluency and comprehension in a group analysis (Riddle-Buly & Valencia, 2002). Fuchs, Fuchs, Hosp, and Jenkins (2001) noted the same decline in the importance of oral reading fluency with increasing age. They said, "Research …suggests that the typical developmental trajectory of oral reading fluency involves the greatest growth in the primary grades, with a negatively accelerating curve through the intermediate grades and perhaps into junior high school" (p. 242).

How can we reconcile the developing disjunction with previous research that has reported a strong relation between oral reading fluency and comprehension (e.g., Good, Simmons, & Kame'enui, 2001)? The positive relations in previous studies are found when the data are summed across age, ability, and passage difficulty, and importantly, when the data for oral reading and comprehension are collected from different tasks and texts. Thus, the positive correlations between oral reading fluency and comprehension may be evident in cross-sectional but not longitudinal studies and in cross-task but not within-task correlations. Failure to analyze the relation within-passages may have led to exaggerated claims about the relation of fluency to comprehension in children's reading. Indeed, it is likely that the strong correlations between oral reading fluency and standardized test scores reflect general developmental differences among good and poor readers rather than a causal connection between oral reading fluency and comprehension. In this view, reading rate is a proxy measure for many concurrent developmental differences including automatic word recognition, vocabulary knowledge, content knowledge, motivation, test-taking skills, intelligence, and so forth. Slow readers in first and second grade differ from fast readers on many dimensions, and their oral reading rate is only a proxy for many between-subjects differences that actually mediate reading comprehension. Of course, labored decoding among beginning readers also overloads working memory and disallows comprehension strategies so the higher correlations between fluency and comprehension are evident for struggling readers.

We have also argued for caution in interpreting correlations between fluency and comprehension. To our knowledge, there are no experimental studies within-subjects to show that making children read faster improves their understanding of the same text. Indeed, given the speed-accuracy trade-off in most skilled performance, it seems unlikely that making children or adults read faster when reading aloud would improve their comprehension, especially if the baseline is their preferred rate of reading. Faster reading, and better accuracy and prosody too, might be consequences of practice, automatic word recognition, and repeated reading, but they are not likely to be the cause of better reading comprehension. Thus, oral reading fluency is more prudently interpreted as a proxy variable for many other developmental accomplishments such as automatic word recognition. The correlations between fluency and comprehension may only be artifacts of the inter-correlations among many early reading skills and literacy experiences. It is the complex relations among these variables that change with age and render oral reading fluency less correlated with comprehension among older and more skilled readers.

Key issue #3: Developing self-regulated reading comprehension

If reading comprehension involves construction of meaning and integration of models of text, prior knowledge, and situations implied by text, then readers can vary in the effort, thoroughness, efficiency, and accuracy of their constructed meanings. These changes reflect cognitive development, learning, and motivation. We summarize these multiple accomplishments in terms of children's developing abilities to regulate their own reading behaviors and cognitive resources toward goals of understanding. Changes in metacognition, cognitive strategies, and motivation combine to promote self-regulated reading comprehension.

Children become aware of conventions in language and text as they begin to read. Children develop early awareness of the dimensions of reading from their early exposure to print, usually in joint book reading activities with adults (Snow & Ninio, 1986). These scaffolded interactions provide crucial opportunities for learning initial concepts about print. Between the ages of 3 and 5 years, children improve dramatically in their ability to identify and name letters and to discriminate the visual and auditory aspects of print (Adams, 1990). Lomax and McGee (1987) studied children's awareness of different aspects of reading from three to seven years and found a dramatic increase in metacognition between three and four year olds. Lomax and McGee proposed that the early concepts about print form a foundation for subsequent reading development.

Clay (1979) found that beginning readers often did not understand that print rather than pictures tell the story and they were confused about the direction that one reads print on the page. Weintraub and Denney (1965) found that only 20% of first graders understand that reading is a cognitive activity that helps learning. Many children think that reading is simply saying the words on the page (Bondy, 1990). Children need to become aware of the nature and purposes for reading as well as concepts about print. Acquiring new vocabulary permits the young child to talk and think about the activity of reading itself. Becoming aware of the units of distinct phonemes, letters, words, and sentences requires a level of linguistic awareness that helps children reflect on their own reading and writing (Adams, 1990).

Children also develop metacognition about strategies that foster comprehension. Beginning readers often show little comprehension monitoring (Baker and Beall, chapter 17, this volume); they may skip words, guess, or fabricate interpretations of text rather than re-read to repair comprehension failures. Young children focus on decoding words rather than assessing their understanding of the micro and macrostructure of text as they read (e.g., Johnston & Afflerbach, 1985), perhaps because they have only a modest understanding of the variety of reading strategies that they might use before, during, and after reading (Paris, Wasik, & Turner, 1990). They have difficulty identifying main ideas, rarely look back in text, and summarize sequential bits of information in text rather than overarching concepts, propositional relations, and themes (Brown & Day, 1983; Garner, 1987).

Strategies for monitoring and improving comprehension develop throughout K–12 schooling, and they benefit from direct, explicit instruction (Block, 2003). For example, Paris, Cross, and Lipson (1984) used classroom discussions about strategies to promote understanding among third and fifth graders. Palincsar and Brown (1984) taught junior high students to work in pairs as they applied reading strategies through reciprocal teaching. Pressley, Almasi, Schuder, Bergman, Hite, El-Dinar, and Brown (1994) developed transactional strategy instruction to teach children how to apply comprehension strategies. Liang and Dole (2006) summarized five less-known instructional frameworks that have been shown in research studies to improve children's comprehension. Two methods focus on teaching the content, two focus on teaching comprehension strategies, and one combines both foci. For example, "scaffolded reading experiences" (Tierney & Readance, 2005) and "questioning the author" (McKeown & Beck, 2004) provide interactive experiences as students read (such as questions and discussion) that promote deeper engagement with the ideas in text. The discussions about the text content can occur before, during, or after reading the text and can take place in small or large group instruction. Methods that focus on teaching specific comprehension strategies include "collaborative strategic reading" (Klinger, Vaughn, & Schumm, 1998) and "peer-assisted learning strategies" (Mathes, Howard, Allen, & Fuchs, 1998). The first method uses four cards and specific strategy routines to help students preview the text, monitor comprehension, identify main ideas, and summarize the text. The second method requires students to alternate roles as "coach" and "reader" as they use strategies to observe and personalize text, search and retrieve information, comprehend and integrate information, and summarize and present information to others.

The final method is "concept-oriented reading instruction" (Guthrie et al., 1996) that includes explicit instruction about text content and strategies with activities that foster student engagement. The methods are similar to strategy instruction developed by Palincsar, Paris, Pressley, and others in the 1980s in four key ways. First, they provide metacognitive discussions about effective comprehension strategies. Second, the methods provide socially-supported practice applying the strategies. Third, the methods provide motivating activities to learn about strategies. Fourth, the methods emphasize the importance of personal agency and control so that students take responsibility for using strategies. The historical changes in research from promoting metacognition to teaching strategy use to fostering control of strategies reflect recognition that deep, rich reading comprehension depends on the coordination of learning strategies, motivational orientations, and interactive discussions about the content of text. This is the same developmental competency emphasized by Clay (1991) as the development of "inner control" of reading skills.

A NEW APPROACH TO UNDERSTANDING CHILDREN'S READING COMPREHENSION

As more researchers and policymakers turn their attention to improving students' reading comprehension, there is an increasing need for new theories, research methods, interventions, and assessments. In this chapter we have highlighted prevailing theories and problems for understanding how children develop thorough comprehension skills. Although there are many potential new approaches to studying the development of comprehension, we will outline one approach that extends the distinction between constrained and unconstrained reading skills (Paris, 2005). The basic notion is that the multiple components involved in reading comprehension interact in different and non-linear ways according to the proficiency of the reader and the characteristics of the text. We introduce the notion of skill thresholds to characterize the interactions among various developmental trajectories and suggest directions for future research.

Consider the simple case of reading and understanding the word "cat." A child may be able to guess the word correctly, if the initial and final consonants can be read, by saying (vocally or subvocally) various iterations such as cit, cot, cet, and cat, especially if there are pictures in text or reference in a previous context to associate the word with the animal. Whether or not the word is read (or guessed) correctly depends on exceeding a threshold of letter and phoneme recognition that is high but less than 100%. This description is consistent with an interactive-compensatory view of reading (e.g., Rumelhart, 1994; Stanovich, 1980), but it adds the notion of thresholds to letter and phoneme recognition. A threshold enables decoding to occur. Likewise, a threshold of vocabulary knowledge is necessary to allow understanding of the meaning of the word "cat" because even a narrow familiarity with the animal would allow literal comprehension of the word.

Thresholds suggest that comprehension does not occur below certain skill levels, but it does not mean that comprehension is either present or absent all the time. People can comprehend in different ways and to different degrees, but only after the thresholds have been met. We suggest that the lack of comprehension is a categorical state that is evident when skill thresholds are not met. In contrast, comprehension can be multifac-eted and differ in depth after the thresholds are exceeded. Certainly comprehension of words, sentences, and texts can yield graded levels, depths, or thoroughness of comprehension, as evident in recursive envisionments and successively deeper, more integrated, and more coherent comprehension with repeated reading and thinking about text. When the thresholds of letter knowledge, phonemic recognition, and vocabulary knowledge are met, the reader constructs a minimal interpretation of the sentence that is based on word meanings and the microstrucure of text. If these thresholds are not met, comprehension cannot occur and is essentially zero or erroneous. Thresholds become graduated as comprehension exceeds the minimal interpretation of words.

In the multiple component model of comprehension, each component must meet a threshold value for minimal comprehension to occur. However, the various components, such as decoding, vocabulary, and fluency, do not have to be 100% accurate to enable some comprehension to occur. Fr exlm!p, y7u can raed th;is snetcne evn tuohg* the wrds r msiplld. Likewise, you can read and understand (to a degree) the words in the previous sentence. Why? Because skilled readers can recognize approximated spellings of real words, they can slow their reading rate to hypothesize literal interpretations, they can rearrange the order of words to create a propositional meaning, and they can fill in gaps with their vocabulary knowledge. Less-skilled readers use similar interactive-compensatory processes, but if any of their skills do not meet a high threshold, then comprehension may fail.

The longitudinal importance of thresholds is evident for a variety of constrained skills that develop quickly with beginning reading. For example, learning the names and sounds of letters in the alphabet and learning basic concepts about print are constrained skills that are learned to a very high asymptote by beginning readers, and each one must be learned to a high threshold before decoding is enabled which in turn enables comprehension. Parenthetically, the serial contingencies or bootstrapping relations are important and simply not captured by multivariate techniques that treat all variables as equivalent at any given point in time. We might speculate that beginning readers need to know 90% of the 26 alphabet letters and 90% of the basic 44 English phonemes to decode a modest variety of decodable texts. Knowing 90% of Clay's concepts of print might also be a threshold for beginning readers to decode text. When readers meet these threshold values, and the vocabulary words are appropriate for the readers' age and experiences, comprehension is possible but not guaranteed.

One value of the notion of thresholds is that they represent the interaction between the reader's skills and the characteristics of the text. Comprehension is enabled when thresholds are exceeded. So, a child who knows only a few letters of the alphabet may read, write, and comprehend the letter string or sentence approximation, "ilovmumy," but the same child may fail to read and comprehend simple sentences with the same letters such as, "Mom likes me" because the phonemes are not decoded properly. Thus, thresholds take into account the interactions between text features, such as difficulty and familiarity, and the reader's emerging skills, such as decoding and vocabulary. Comprehension, at least at a minimal level, is enabled when the component skill thresholds are met for a specific text. This view situates comprehension in the interactions among the individual, text, and context.

A second value of thresholds is that they re-define comprehension as both categorical and continuous. Failures to comprehend text may occur when any of the component skills do not meet threshold values so lack of comprehension has many contributing factors and can occur even when some skills exceed thresholds (e.g., when a reader can decode all the words or knows the meanings of nearly all the words in text). For example, "Colorless green ideas sleep furiously" is decodable but meaningless for most readers. Thus, comprehension below combined thresholds is nil and is common for young readers who may encounter difficulty meeting a minimum threshold for phonemes, vocabulary, syntax, and general knowledge. In contrast, comprehension beyond thresholds may be continuous in gradations because the minimal interpretation can be embellished in many ways. Metaphors of richer, deeper, and layered comprehension convey a graded variety of meanings that can be constructed for text. In the same manner, comprehension from different perspectives or stances, like critical and deconstructed meanings, have continuous nuances or levels. (It is also possible to conceptualize multiple stances or understandings as different categories or types or understanding rather than graduated on a single scale of meaning, but the heuristic value of thresholds is clear in either view.)

Third, thresholds help to re-interpret developing relations among skills. Comprehension among beginning readers depends almost entirely on components of decoding (e.g., phonemic awareness, letter knowledge, concepts about print) and vocabulary knowledge, just as the simple view of reading suggests. However, by grades 2 to 3, there is an increasing developmental disjunction between fluency and comprehension as fluency rate exceeds 100 wpm and accuracy exceeds 90% correct. These thresholds appear adequate for minimal comprehension of text, as long as vocabulary and prior knowledge also meet acceptable thresholds. However, some good decoders have poor comprehension, and some struggling decoders are able to achieve good comprehension of text. The reason may be that decoding enables but does not assure comprehension so it acts as a threshold rather than a cause of comprehension. For skilled readers who engage complex text, thresholds of strategy use, such as monitoring and enriching comprehension while reading and studying, may be required in order to stimulate thorough comprehension.

There are also problems with the notion of thresholds of comprehension. One obvious problem is how to determine threshold values of component skills. We suggest that 90% accuracy of component skills necessary for a given text (e.g., letter knowledge, phoneme recognition, concepts of print, genre structure, vocabulary) may be a good approximation until empirical research establishes better standards. Current practices with informal reading inventories usually describe 90% accuracy as the minimum level to avoid frustration. Fluency rates may have a lower threshold, but it really depends on the memory load and processing rate of the specific text. Oral reading rates approach asymptote (at 50th percentiles) for grades 4–8 at about 150 wpm. In our experience, an oral reading rate of 90–100 wpm appears to be a minimum threshold value that reflects automatic word identification among young readers. This level of oral reading fluency permits readers to apply cognitive resources to comprehension in addition to decoding.

Thresholds present challenges for measurement and data analyses because thresholds introduce nonlinear growth and discontinuous relations among variables over the course of reading development. Developmental step functions like thresholds cannot be tested in correlational or traditional designs. It may be a virtue in one sense because thresholds help distinguish constrained skills that have rapid and asymptotic growth from unconstrained skills that develop over longer time periods. However, thresholds are challenging because new data analyses are needed that allow contingency analyses, step functions, conditional probabilities, nonlinear growth trajectories, and other methods to predicate comprehension on the levels of component skills. Despite the mix of benefits, problems, and challenges, we think new conceptualizations of comprehension development are needed to overcome the limitations of traditional theories such as stage models and component assembly models that treat all variables as equivalent in multivariate statistical analyses.

IMPLICATIONS AND CONCLUSIONS

How to conceptualize, assess, and improve reading comprehension are enormous problems that are made even more complex when we add developmental questions such as what develops—when and how—and what kinds of instruction foster better reading comprehension. Simple models of reading comprehension that posit automatic understanding as a consequence of decoding are inadequate to answer these questions. Likewise, we think that additive (e.g., Decoding + Vocabulary = Comprehension) and multiplicative models (e.g., D × LC = C) that predict linear and monotonic improvements in comprehension with improving decoding and vocabulary are inadequate too. The value of threshold models of comprehension is that they predict little or no comprehension until the reader meets acceptable threshold values of decoding, vocabulary, working memory, prior knowledge, and so forth.

Skeptics may say that there may be many potential variables in a threshold model, and they may question how the threshold values are determined. In order to avoid tautological arguments that thresholds predict comprehension but only comprehension can establish threshold values, researchers need to devise empirical methods to determine which variables ought to be included in a model and how the thresholds can be determined. Both issues can be resolved through empirical research. Threshold models recognize that comprehension is contingent on many component processes so these kinds of models are consistent with multi-component models of reading development. Threshold models can also be consistent with stage models, construction-integration, and envisionment models, but there are extra demands to identify which variables must be developed to what minimum levels in order to enable comprehension. Threshold models can be thought of as enabling, bootstrapping, step-wise, or contingency models—all non-linear models—that are distinctly different from additive or multiplicative component models.

Once threshold values for decoding are met, readers must do the hard cognitive work of constructing models of the text and situation, integrate those models with prior knowledge, and operate recursively on the representations to monitor and revise them. Each of these processes improves with age, working memory, fluent decoding, and cognitive abilities so we can expect wide variation in the depth and quality of understanding a text beyond a minimal level of literal comprehension. These are developmental changes in reasoning rather than decoding and reveal that instruction may foster comprehension among beginning readers for two different reasons. First, instruction that promotes learning constrained skills and decoding fluency enables basic reading comprehension, and the jump between no understanding and basic comprehension should be dramatic as constrained skills are learned to a minimum threshold level. Second, instruction that improves cognitive strategies, inferences, monitoring, and recursive envisionments is more relevant to thinking about the content of text in elaborated models of the text and situation, and it may be revealed in more graduated and gradual differences between texts and readers because it is based on continuous processes.

One implication of this difference is that early learning and instruction of constrained skills may be more rapid and the consequences for comprehension may be more evident than instruction on vocabulary, general knowledge, comprehension strategies, or metacognition. These latter, unconstrained skills may develop more slowly and continuously with subtle and gradual effects on comprehension, whether learned through practice or direct instruction. Both constrained and unconstrained reading skills must be learned in order to comprehend text thoroughly so the issue is not which type of learning or instruction is more important. The issue instead is to develop theories of different growth trajectories and to understand that instructional effects will vary by skill and age. Teachers should emphasize and teach constrained and unconstrained reading skills equally for beginning readers without privileging one over the other, an error made in the "reading wars" (i.e., the rift over priority of decoding vs. meaning-based approaches to reading instruction).

So what should teachers and parents do to help young readers develop good comprehension? Here are some general guidelines based on the research reviewed in this chapter. First, teach background knowledge about concepts and themes that are relevant for the texts children use to learn to read. Children need to understand the situations, contexts, facts, words, and ideas in their own language and in their own words to provide a foundation for understanding text about the same ideas. Comprehension precedes reading comprehension and helps children map words onto their knowledge in the same way they map language development on to their understanding of the world. Second, build automatic word identification through practice, modeling, and repeated reading. These experiences will help children translate graphemes to phonemes quickly and reduce the load on working memory. Third, develop oral reading fluency as a way to practice prosodic reading, increase decoding speed, and develop habits of re-reading for understanding. Fourth, teach vocabulary in texts as part of larger units of ideas, themes, and concepts so that children see the relations among words and ideas. They need to produce as well as recognize vocabulary so instruction that builds speaking and listening skills can enhance comprehension. Fifth, teach specific comprehension strategies, even with young readers, so they understand what main ideas are, how to skim, why to re-read, and so forth (Block, 2004). These are the declarative, procedural, and conditional aspects of metacognition about reading that are important (Paris, Wasik, & Turner, 1990). Sixth, the heart of reading comprehension is learning so instruction on reading comprehension cannot be divorced from the motivating activities used to increase learning about new topics. During the past 20 years, researchers have shown that comprehension can be increased significantly when it is taught explicitly, when it is intertwined with engaging activities, when it is focused on learning new content, and when it is assessed and re-taught to a deep level of new understanding. In this view, enhancing children's reading comprehension is synonymous with teaching children to be thoughtful, strategic, and independent learners.

REFERENCES

Adams, M. J. (1990). *Beginning to read: Thinking and learning about print.* Cambridge, MA: MIT Press.

Adams, A-M., & Gathercole, S. (1995). Phonological working memory and speech production in preschool children. *Journal of Speech and Hearing Research, 38,* 403–414.

Adams, A-M., & Gathercole, S. (1996). Phonological working memory and spoken language development in young children. *The Quarterly Journal of Experimental Psychology A: Human Experimental Psychology, 49A*(1), 216–233.

Adams, A-M., & Gathercole, S. (2000). Limitations in working memory: Implications for language development. *International Journal of Language & Communication Disorders, 35,* 95–116.

Anderson, R. C., & Pearson, P. D. (1984). A schema-theoretic view of basic processes in reading comprehension. In P. D. Pearson, R. Barr, M. Kamil, & P. Mosenthal (Eds.), *Handbook of reading research* (pp. 255–291). New York: Longman.

Athey, I., & Singer, H. (1987). Developing the nation's reading potential for a technological era. *Harvard Educational Review, 57*(1), 84–93.

Baker, L. (1984). Spontaneous versus instructed use of multiple standards for evaluating comprehension: Effects of age, reading proficiency, and type of standard. *Journal of Experimental Child Psychology, 38,* 289–311.

Beck, I., McKeown, M., & Omanson, R. (1987). The effects and uses of diverse vocabulary instruction techniques. In M. McKeown & M. Curtis (Eds.), *The nature of vocabulary acquisition* (pp. 147–163). Hillsdale, NJ: Erlbaum.

Biemiller, A. (1970). The development of the use of graphic and contextual information as children learn to read. *Reading Research Quarterly, 6,* 75–96.

Block, C.C. (2003). *Teaching comprehension: The comprehension process approach.* Boston: Allyn & Bacon.

Bondy, E. (1990). Seeing it their way: What children's definitions of reading tell us about improving teacher education. *Journal of Teacher Education, 41,* 33–45.

Brown, A., & Day, J. (1983). Macrorules for summarizing text: The development of expertise. *Journal of Verbal Learning and Verbal Behavior, 22,* 1–14.

Cain, K., & Oakhill, J.V. (1999). Inference making ability and its relation to comprehension failure in young children. *Reading and Writing: An Interdisciplinary Journal, 11,* 489–503.

Cain, K., & Oakhill, J.V. (2003). Reading comprehension difficulties. In T. Nunes & T. Bryant (Eds.), *Handbook of children's literacy* (pp. 313–338). Dordrecht: Kluwer Academic Publishers.

Cain, K., Oakhill, J. V., & Bryant, P. (2000). Investigating the causes of reading comprehension failure: The comprehension-age match design. *Reading & Writing: An Interdisciplinary Journal, 12,* 31–40.

Cain, K., Oakhill, J. V., & Bryant, P. (2004). Children's reading comprehension ability: Concurrent prediction by working memory, verbal ability, and component skills. *Journal of Educational Psychology, 96*(1), 31–42.

Cain, K., Oakhill, J. V., & Lemmon, K. (2004). Individual differences in the inference of word meanings from context: The influence of reading comprehension, vocabulary knowledge, and memory capacity. *Journal of Educational Psychology, 96*(4), 671–681.

Case, R. (1995). Capacity-based explanations of working memory growth: A brief history and reevaluation. *Memory Performance and Competencies: Issues in growth and development,* (pp. 23–44). Mahwah, NJ: Erlbaum.

Chall, J. S. (1967). *Learning to read: The great debate.* New York: McGraw Hill.

Chall, J. S. (1996). *Stages of reading development, 2nd edition.* Orlando, FL: Harcourt Brace & Company.

Clay, M. M. (1979). *Reading: The patterning of complex behavior* (2nd ed.). Auckland: Heinemann Publishers.

Clay, M. M. (1991). *Becoming literate: The construction of inner control.* Portsmouth, NH: Heinemann.

Daneman, M. (1988). Word knowledge and reading skill. In M. Daneman, G. MacKinnon, & T. G. Waller (Eds.), *Reading research: Advances in theory and practice, Vol. 6* (pp. 145–175). San Diego, CA: Academic Press.

Daneman, M., & Carpenter, P. A. (1980). Individual differences in working memory and reading. *Journal of Verbal Learning and Verbal Behavior, 19,* 450–466.

Daneman, M., & Merikle, P. (1996). Working memory and language comprehension: A meta-analysis. *Psychonomic Bulletin & Review, 3,* 422–433.

Ehri, L.C. (1995). Development of the ability to read words. In R. Barr, M. Kamil, P. Mosenthal, & P. Pearson (Eds.), *Handbook of reading research* (Vol. 2, pp. 383–417). Hillsdale, NJ: Erlbaum.

Ehri, L. C. (1995). Phases of development in learning to read words by sight. *Journal of Research in Reading, 18,* 116–125.

Ehri, L. C., & Wilce, L. S. (1980). The influence of orthography on readers' conceptualization of the phonemic structure of words. *Applied Psycholinguistics, 1,* 371–385.

Fuchs, L. S., Fuchs, D., Hosp, M. K., & Jenkins, J. R. (2001). Oral reading fluency as an indicator of reading competence: A theoretical, empirical, and historical analysis. *Scientific Studies of Reading, 5*(3), 241–258.

Garner, R. (1987). *Metacognition and reading comprehension.* Norwood, NJ: Ablex.

Gathercole, S., Pickering, S., Ambridge, B., & Wearing, H. (2004). The structure of working memory from 4 to 15 years of age. *Developmental Psychology, 40,* 177–190.

Gathercole, S., Service, E., Hitch, G., Adams, A-M., & Martin, A. (1999). Phonological short-term memory and vocabulary development: Further evidence on the nature of the relationship. *Applied Cognitive Psychology, 13,* 65–77.

Good, R. H., Simmons, D. C., & Kame'enui, E. J. (2001). The importance and decision-making utility of a continuum of fluency-based indicators of foundational reading skills for third-grade high-stakes outcomes. *Scientific Studies of Reading, 5*(3), 257–288.

Goodman, K. S. (1976). Reading: A psycholinguistic guessing game. In H. Singer & R. B. Ruddell (Eds.), *Theoretical Models and Processes of Reading.* Newark, DE: International Reading Association.

Gough, P. B., & Tunmer, W. E. (1986). Decoding, reading, and reading disability. *Remedial and Special Education, 7*(1), 6–10.

Graesser, A. C., Singer, M., & Trabasso, T. (1994). Constructing inferences during narrative text comprehension. *Psychological Review, 101*(3), 371–395.

Guthrie, J. T., Van Meter, P., McCann, A. D., Wigfield, A., Bennett, L., Poundstone, C. C., et al. (1996). Growth of literacy engagement: Changes in motivations and strategies during concept-oriented reading instruction. *Reading Research Quarterly, 31,* 306–332.

Johnston, P., & Afflerbach, P. (1985). The process of constructing main ideas from text. *Cognition & Instruction, 2,* 207–232.

Juel, C., Griffith, P. L., & Gough, P. B. (1986). Acquisition of literacy: A longtiduinal study of children in 1st grade and 2nd grade. *Journal of Educational Psychology, 78*(4), 243–255.

Kintsch, W. (1998). *Comprehension: A paradigm for cognition.* New York: Cambridge University Press.

Kintsch, W., & Kintsch, E. (2005). Comprehension. In S. Paris & S.Stahl (Eds.), *Children's reading comprehension and assessment* (pp. 71–92). Mahwah, NJ: Erlbaum.

Kintsch, W., & van Dijk, T. A. (1978). Towards a model of text comprehension and production. *Psychological Review, 85,* 363–394.

Klinger, J. K., Vaughn, S., & Schumm, J. S. (1998). Collaborative strategic reading during social studies in heterogeneous fourth-grade classrooms. *The Elementary School Journal, 99,* 3–23.

Kuhn, M. R., & Stahl, S. A. (2003). Fluency: A review of developmental and remedial practices. *Journal of Educational Psychology, 95*(1), 3–21.

LaBerge, D., & Samuels, S. J., (1974). Toward a theory of automatic information processing in reading. *Cognitive Psychology, 6,* 293–323.

Langer, J. A. (1984). Examining background knowledge and text comprehension. *Reading Research Quarterly, 19*(4), 468–481.

Langer, J. A. (1989). *The process of understanding literature* (Center for Learning and Teaching of Literature Research Monograph, 2.1). Albany, NY: SUNY Albany.

Langer, J. A. (2004, May). Developing the literate mind. Paper presented at the meeting of the International Reading Association, San Diego, CA.

Langer, J. A., & Flihan, S. (2000). Writing and reading relationships: Constructive tasks. In R. Indrisano & J. R. Squire (Eds.), *Writing: Research/theory/practice* (pp. 112–139), Newark: DE: International Reading Association.

Liang, L. A., & Dole, J. A. (2006). Help with teaching reading comprehension: Comprehension instructional frameworks. *The Reading Teacher, 59,* 742–753.

Lomax, R. G., & McGee, L. M. (1987). Young children's concepts about print and reading: Toward a model of word reading acquisition. *Reading Research Quarterly, 22,* 237–256.

Mathes, P. G., Howard, J. K., Allen, S. H., & Fuchs, D. (1998). Peer-assisted learning strategies for first-grade readers: Responding to the needs of diverse learners. *Reading Research Quarterly, 33,* 62–94.

McKeown, M. G., & Beck, I. L. (2004). Transforming knowledge into professional development resources: Six teachers implement a model of teaching for understanding text. *The Elementary School Journal, 104*, 391–408.

Muter, V., Hulme, C., Snowling, M., & Stevenson, J. (2004). Phonemes, rimes, vocabulary, and grammatical skills as foundations of early reading development: Evidence from a longitudinal study. *Developmental Psychology, 40*, 665–681.

Nation, K., Adams, J. W., Bowyer-Crane, C. A., & Snowling, M. J. (1999). Working memory deficits in poor comprehenders reflect underlying language impairments. *Journal of Experimental Child Psychology, 73*, 139–158.

Nation, K., & Snowling, M. J. (1998). Semantic processing and the development of word recognition skills: Evidence from children with reading comprehension difficulties. *Journal of Memory and Language, 39*, 85–101.

National Center for Educational Statistics. (2005). *2009 NAEP reading framework*. Washington DC: Author.

National Reading Panel (NRP) (2000). *Teaching children to read: An evidence-based assessment of the scientific research literature on reading and its implications for reading instruction: Reports of the subgroups*. Bethesda, MD: NICHD.

Oakhill, J. V. (1982). Constructive processes in skilled and less skilled comprehenders' memory for sentences. *British Journal of Psychology, 73*(1), 13–20.

Oakhill, J. V. (1984). Inferential and Memory Skills in Children's Comprehension of Stories. *British Journal of Educational Psychology, 54*(1), 31–39.

Oakhill, J. V., & Cain, K. (2003). The development of comprehension skills. In T. Nunes & T. Bryant (Eds.), *Handbook of children's literacy* (pp. 155–180). Dordrecht: Kluwer Academic Publishers.

Oakhill, J. V., Cain, K., & Bryant, P. E. (2004). The dissociation of word reading and text comprehension: Evidence from component skills. *Language and Cognitive Processes, 18*(4), 443–468.

Oakhill, J. V., Hart, J., & Samols, D. (2005). Levels of comprehension monitoring and working memory in good and poor comprehenders. *Reading & Writing, 18*, 657–686.

Palincsar, A. S., & Brown, A. (1984). Reciprocal teaching of comprehension-fostering and comprehension-monitoring activities. *Cognition and Instruction, 1*, 117–175.

Paris, S. G. (2005). Re-interpreting the development of reading skills. *Reading Research Quarterly, 40*(2), 184–202.

Paris, S. G., Carpenter, R. D., Paris, A. H., & Hamilton, E. E. (2005). Spurious and genuine correlates of children's reading comprehension. In S. G. Paris & S. A. Stahl (Eds.), *Children's reading comprehension and assessment* (pp. 131–160). Mahwah, NJ: Erlbaum.

Paris, S. G., Cross, D. R., & Lipson, M. Y. (1984). Informed strategies for learning: A program to improve children's reading awareness and comprehension. *Journal of Educational Psychology, 76*, 1239–1252.

Paris, S. G., Wasik, B. A., & Turner, J. C. (1990). The development of strategic readers. In R. Barr, M. Kamil, P. Mosenthal, & P. D. Pearson (Eds.), *Handbook of reading research* (2nd ed., pp. 609–640). New York: Longman.

Paris, S. G., & Upton, L. R. (1976). Children's memory for inferential relationships in prose. *Child Development, 47*, 660–668.

Pearson, P. D., & Hamm, D. N. (2005). The assessment of reading comprehension: A review of practices — past, present, and future. In S. Paris & S. Stahl (Eds.), *Children's reading comprehension and assesment* (pp. 13–69). Mahwah, NJ: Erlbaum.

Perfetti, C. A. (1994). Psycholinguistics and reading ability. In M. Gernsbacher (Ed.), *Handbook of psycholinguistics* (pp. 849–894). San Diego, CA: Academic.

Perfetti, C. A., Landi, N., & Oakhill, J. (2005). The acquisition of reading comprehension skill. In M. J. Snowling & C. Hulme (Eds.), *The science of reading: A handbook* (pp. 227–247). Malden, MA: Blackwell Publishing.

Pressley, M., Almasi, J., Schuder, T., Bergman, J., Hite, S., El-Dinar, P. B., & Brown, R. (1994). Transactional instruction of comprehension strategies: The Montgomery County, Maryland, SAIL program. *Reading and Writing Quarterly: Overcoming Learning Difficulties, 10*, 5–19.

RAND Reading Study Group. (2001). Reading for understanding: Towards an R&D program in reading comprehension. Report prepared for OERI.

Rathvon, N. (2004). *Early reading assessment: A practitioner's handbook*. New York: Guilford Press.

Riddle-Buly, M., & Valencia, S. W. (2002). Below the bar: Profiles of students who fail state reading assessments. *Educational Evaluation and Policy Analyses, 24*, 219–239.

Rumelhart, D. E. (1994). Toward an interactive model of reading. In R. B Ruddell, M. Rapp-Ruddell, & H. Singer (Eds.), *Theoretical models and processes of reading, 4th ed.* (pp. 864–894). Newark, DE: International Reading Association.

Samuels, S. J., & LaBerge, D. (1983). A critique of, 'A Theory of Automaticity in Reading': Looking back: A retrospective analysis of the LaBerge-Samuels reading model. In L. M. Gentile, M. L. Kamil, & J. S. Blanchard (Eds.), *Reading Research Revisited*. Columbus, OH: Charles E. Merrill publishing Company.

Seigneuric, A., & Ehrlich, M-F. (2005). Contribution of working memory capacity to children's reading comprehension: A longitudinal investigation. *Reading and Writing, 18,* 617–656.

Seigneuric, A., Ehrlich, M.-F., Oakhill, J. V., & Yuill, N. M. (2000). Working memory reseources and children's reading comprehension. *Reading and Writing, 13,* 81–103.

Snow, C. E., & Ninio, A. (1986). The contracts of literacy: What children learn from learning to read books. In W. H. Teale & E. Sulzby (Eds.), *Emergent literacy: Writing and reading* (pp. 116–138). Norwood, NJ: Ablex.

Snow, C. E., Burns, M. S., & Griffin, P. (1998). *Preventing reading difficulties in young children.* Washington, DC: National Academy Press.

Stahl, S. A., & Hiebert, E. H. (2005). The "word factors": A problem for reading comprehension assessments. In S. G. Paris & S. A. Stahl (Eds.), *Current issues in reading comprehension and assessment* (pp. 161–186). Mahwah, NJ: Erlbaum.

Stahl, S. A., Kuhn, M. R., & Pickle, J. M. (1999). An educational model of assessment and targeted instruction for children with reading problems. In D. Evenson & P. Mosenthal (Eds.), *Reconsidering the role of the reading clinic in a new age of literacy* (pp. 249–272). Greenwich, CT: JAI Press.

Stanovich, K. (1980). Toward an interactive-compensatory model of individual differences in the development of reading fluency. *Reading Research Quarterly, 16* (1), 32–71.

Stanovich, K. E. (2000). *Progress in understanding reading: Scientific foundations and new frontiers.* New York: Guilford.

Sternberg, R. J., & Powell, J. S. (1983). Comprehending verbal comprehension. *American Psychologist, 38,* 878–893.

Stothard, S. E., & Hulme, C. (1995). A comparison of phonological skills in children with reading comprehension difficulties and children with word reading difficulties. *Journal of Child Psychology and Child Psychiatry, 36,* 399–408.

Stothard, S. E., & Hulme, C. (1996). A comparison of reading comprehension and decoding difficulties in children.

Thorndike, L. (1917). Reading as reasoning. *Journal of Educational Psychology, 8*(6), 323–332.

Tierney, R. J., & Readance, J. E. (2005). *Reading strategies and practices: A compendium* (6th ed.). Boston: Allyn & Bacon.

Trabasso, T., & Suh, S. (1993). Understanding text: Achieving explanatory coherence through online inferences and mental operations in working memory. *Discourse Processes, 16,* 3–34.

Tunmer, W. E., & Hoover, W. A. (1992). Cognitive and linguistic factors in learning to read. In P. Gough, L. Ehri, & R. Treiman (Eds.), *Reading acquisition* (pp. 175–214). Hillsdale, NJ: Erlbaum.

Weintraub, S., & Denney, P. T. (1965). What do beginning first graders say about reading? *Childhood Education, 41,* 326–327.

Yuill, N., & Joscelyne, T. (1988). Effect of organizational cues and strategies on good and poor comprehenders' story understanding. *Journal of Educational Psychology, 80,* 152–158.

Yuill, N., & Oakhill, J. (1991). *Children's problems in text comprehension: An experimental investigation.* Cambridge: Cambridge University Press.

Yuill, N., Oakhill, J., & Parkin, A. (1989). Working memory, comprehension ability, and the resolution of text anomaly. *British Journal of Psychology, 80,* 351–361.

3   In Search of the "Simple View" of Reading Comprehension

James V. Hoffman

The University of Texas at Austin

> For every complex problem, there is a solution that is simple, neat, and wrong.
>
> *H.L. Mencken (1880–1956)*

Recently, Levitz (2006) reported the findings of an experimental study in which he compared the growth in reading achievement for second grade students under several different conditions. The teachers in the primary experimental intervention followed a scripted, systematic and sequential program of instruction focused on rapid decoding of nonsense words. Students in classrooms who participated in this primary treatment condition demonstrated significant improvement in the reading of real and nonsense words on the DIBELS. Students in the primary experimental condition also showed growth in reading comprehension at statistically significant levels higher than students in the comparison group that was offered "wide reading" and a traditional control group that received no special instruction outside the regular curriculum. The findings, with respect to the improvement in reading comprehension, are explained with reference to the "simple view." The intervention study was conducted in schools serving low-income communities with the required time for teacher training to implement the program at less than 4 hours. A school-board trustee, concerned with low-performing schools in the district, puts this study as a discussion agenda item for the next meeting. A member of the state legislature, who serves as the chair on the education task force for raising reading scores, sends all members a copy of the study and requires that it be read in preparation for the next meting. The commercial publisher of the intervention program promotes the program at state and national conferences as a "proven" intervention to raise reading comprehension scores. The author of the report is an author of the program. The report of the study is published in a national, refereed journal and gains an award from a national literacy organization. The US Secretary of Education mandates that the program must be used in all programs that draw on federal support. The Minister of Education in Peru is presented with the findings from this report and subsequently accepts support from the USAID to develop assessment tools for improving reading rate among primary grade, Quetchua speaking learners in the high Andes. The Minister of education of South Africa submits a proposal to the European Economic Union (EEU) for support of implementing a similar program in rural schools serving black, multi-lingual learners.

At what point in reading the opening paragraph did you begin to suspect that this description is invented? Or, did you ever? It is.

However, I will argue that the "sense" of what is described in this scenario is easy to accept if not as a reality today then at least as an envisioned future—including the reference to educational reform in developing countries. The simple view of reading comprehension (Gough & Tunmer, 1986; Hoover & Gough, 1990; Gough, Hoover,

54

& Peterson, 1996) and its close corollary the simple reading fluency model (Schwanen-flugel et al., 2006) are at the heart of this vision. Wren (2006) regards the simple view of reading as "one of the most widely accepted models of the reading process." There is some evidence in support of this assertion given the citation rates in the professional literature. The *Web of Science Citation Index* identifies 243 citations of the seminal Gough and Tunmer (1986) report through March, 2007. Citation rates, however, can be misleading as evidence of support. The contents of this volume are prima facie evidence that the simple view may not be as widely influential within the scholarly community as Wren suggests. Most of the researchers writing in this volume ignore the simple view entirely, whereas the authors represented here have chosen to engage with and explore the complexity of the reading comprehension process. Textbooks on the teaching of reading comprehension (e.g., Irwin, 2007) often do not mention the simple view but offer guidance on teaching that reflects a complex, socioconstructivist view of reading comprehension. The National Reading Panel Report (2000) describes comprehension as a complex process and reviews literature that subscribes to this perspective.

However, ignoring the simple view is not a fair examination of its merits and under-estimates the substantial impact of the simple view at the level of policy and practice. The simple view has received positive attention in the policy community and is finding its way into programs, instructional materials and teacher training curricula both in the United States and in the U.K. (Chew, 2006; Ross Report, 2006). In this review I will consider research and theory related to the simple view of reading comprehension. I will pose the question: What is new in the simple view? I will then consider the research literature in search of the contributions, the shortcomings, and even the dangers of adopting the simple view to inform theory, practice and policy. Finally, I will make recommendations for future research.

BACKGROUND

According to the simple view, reading comprehension is portrayed as an outcome of development in two basic areas: decoding skills and listening comprehension (Gough & Tunmer, 1986; Hoover & Gough, 1990). Growth in reading comprehension is explained primarily by increases in the automaticity of decoding accompanied by increases in general cognitive and language abilities. Once decoding reaches an automatic level then there is little to distinguish listening comprehension from reading comprehension. While the labeling of the "simple view" is just a little over two decades old, the roots of the simple view reach back at least two decades earlier.

Auding, reading, and rauding

The late 1960s and the early 1970s were a time of exciting research in the field of psychology in general and in the area of language processes in particular (Bruner, 1990). The Chomsky revolution in linguistics toppled existing psychological models of language acquisition rooted in Skinnerian behaviorism. Psycholinguistics emerged as a discipline of inquiry focused on issues of language processing, language production and language development. While the early models of language processes growing out of constructivism were focused on the development of oracy skills, attention eventually focused on the relationships between the development of and relationship between oracy and literacy processes (see Kavanagh & Mattingly, 1972).

Sticht and colleagues were among the first literacy scholars to explore closely the relationship between the processes of auding (active listening) and reading as language comprehension processes (see Sticht et al., 1974). Sticht explored rates of processing language and the success in language comprehension. He theorized that auding and reading are closely interrelated. He hypothesized that auding and reading comprehension would become the same as the learner acquired basic reading skills (of word recognition). Sticht conducted an extensive review of research focuses on four major hypotheses.

1. Performance on measures of ability to comprehend language by auding will surpass performance on measures of ability to comprehend language by reading during the early years of schooling until the reading skill is learned, at which time ability to comprehend by auding and reading will become equal.
2. Performance on measures of ability to comprehend language by auding will be predictive of performance on measures of ability to comprehend language by reading *after* the decoding skills of reading have been mastered.
3. Performance on measures of rate of auding and rate of reading will show comparable maximal rates of languaging and conceptualizing for both processes, assuming fully developed reading decoding skills.
4. Training in comprehending by auding of a particular genre (e.g., "listening for the main idea") will transfer to reading when that skill is acquired. Conversely, once reading skill is acquired, new cognitive content learned by reading will be accessible by auding. Again, this reflects the model's position that reading and auding simply represent alternative in-roads to shared languaging competencies and cognitive content. Thus, additions to this content become equally accessible by auding and reading, once the latter is acquired (p. 2).

The research reviewed by Sticht offered support for the first three hypotheses with some limited evidence in support of the fourth. Sticht argued that "languaging" is the underlying ability that links the different forms of production and reception. Consistent with the emerging constructivist views, he regarded all languaging processes as highly active and purposeful. Sticht also seemed to align with the view that oracy is the primary basis for language, at least from a developmental perspective, with the acquisition of literacy as derivative.

Carver, similarly, was interested in the relationship between auding and reading Carver focused the bulk of his research on the process of "rauding" (summarized in Carver, 1990). Rauding is the parallel construct to "auding" only in the reading mode. Rauding is defined by Carver as "typical" reading where the reader focuses on almost every word in the text, moves in a linear mode through the text, with the goal of understanding all of the ideas presented by the author (p. 1). Rauding is the process that "operates normally." Carver contrasted rauding with several other forms of reading: scanning, skimming, learning and memorizing. The bulk of Carver's research, however, focused on the qualities of rauding as the "most important of the reading processes because it is the essence of most people's daily reading" (p. 142). Carver offered evidence to support his theory that reading rate is fairly constant for the individual reader regardless of the difficulty level of the material. He challenged the traditional notion of flexibility that portrays the reader adjusting rate to purpose (p. 185). Across numerous studies, Carver amassed empirical data supporting the close link between auding and reading processes. Research on auding, following the work of Sticht cited earlier, seemed to suggest that the rates of listening are constant for the listener when the input is calculated in terms of syllables rather than words. According to rauding theory, at any point in development, the reader has an optimal rate for rauding text. The optimal rate maximizes the reader's efficiency of comprehension of the text. Carver measured rate in "standard words" (defined as six characters in length) and found that rate did not vary for the reader in easy or more difficult text as long as the reader was engaged in text that was at or below their level of ability. Reading level was rooted in two variables: word recognition (decoding ability) and listening comprehension. Additional constructs influencing the rauding process are cognitive power and cognitive speed (p. 167).

Carver recognized the limitations of rauding theory in two ways. First, the theory did not explain reading behaviors that were outside of the rauding mode. The reader might choose, for example, to engage with text in a scanning, or skimming, or learning, or memorizing mode. Or, the reader might be forced out of the rauding mode because the material has become too difficult for the reader (p. 329). The challenge could come at the conceptual level or at the decoding level. The mathematical models in support of rauding theory were not valid when the reader engaged with text that was above their current skill level. Carver never referred to his theory as a "simple view." In fact, those who have engaged deeply with this theory recognize its complexity.

Automaticity and fluency

LaBerge and Samuels' (1974) work examined automaticity in the development of reading abilities. While their work did not focus specifically on the relationship between listening comprehension and reading comprehension in the same ways as Sticht and Carver did, Laberge and Samuels did examine the relationship between the development of automaticity and comprehension. Adopting a "cognitive attention" hypothesis, LaBerge and Samuels argued that readers who had to devote considerable effort to the decoding challenges of text have less opportunity to engage with text at the meaning level. Conversely, readers who were more automatic in their decoding abilities could engage more directly with the "ideas" in a text. Automaticity is defined as processing without attention. Automaticity is relevant to any skilled activity but in reading it is most often referenced to decoding processes. LaBerge and Samuels and others (e.g., Dahl, 1979; Dowhower, 1987) demonstrated through several studies the ways in which an increase in automaticity led to an increase in comprehension of text. At the experimental level, interventions that focused on word recognition led to increased comprehension—without any specific attention to comprehension processes.

The "simple view" labeled

Gough and Tunmer (1986) and Hoover and Gough (1990) were the first to assign the term "simple view" to the existing notions found in the seminal work of Sticht, Carver, and Laberge and Samuels. In the simple view, reading comprehension is explained by the interaction of two variables: automaticity of decoding and listening comprehension. The simple view is represented in the formula: $R = D \times C$. In the formula, R stands for reading comprehension, D stands for decoding ability, and C stands for language comprehension (listening ability). Improvement in decoding or in listening comprehension will result in an increase in reading comprehension. A student who has decoding levels of zero will comprehend nothing regardless of his listening ability. Similarly, a reader with outstanding decoding skills will comprehend little if listening comprehension levels are low.

The simple view asserts that difficulties with reading comprehension are invariably caused by deficits in language comprehension or decoding skill, and often by some combination of the two. Reading difficulties or comprehension difficulties are either rooted in poor decoding or in limited listening comprehension abilities. According to Hoover and Gough (2000), there are three basic types of reading disorder (ranked in order from least common to most common):

Hyperlexia, which is characterized by the ability to rapidly and easily decode text without understanding what is being read (very rare).

True dyslexia, or the ability to understand spoken language but an inability to decode text (less rare).

Garden-variety reading disorder, which characteristically involves a difficulty decoding text *and* a difficulty understanding spoken language (relatively common).

There have been numerous attempts in the research literature to gather empirical data to support the simple view (e.g., Chen & Vallutino, 1997). The findings from this research suggest that the two major variables in the model (decoding ability and listening comprehension) contribute significantly to the prediction of reading comprehension. In some cases, the word recognition component of the simple view has been measured by the decoding of nonsense words (e.g., Hoover & Gough, 1990; Joshi & Aaron, 2000). In other cases this component has been measured with the reading of real words (e.g., Dreyer & Katz, 1992). And in some instances the measure has been a combination of the two (e.g., Adolph, Catts, & Little, 2006). The prediction models tend to account for between 50% and 60% of the variance—a strong prediction but still leaving substantial variance unaccounted for in the reading comprehension process. Some researchers (e.g., Joshi & Aaron, 2000) have suggested that there should be a third part of the prediction equation that relates to "speed of processing." Joshi and Aaron found that reading correlated more highly with processing speed added to the product of decoding and listening comprehension (.76) than with just the product of decoding and listening comprehension (.69). They found that the inclusion of this predictor added an additional 10% to the prediction.

What's new in the simple view?

It is difficult to identify any significant contribution of the simple view to theory beyond the earlier work of Sticht, Carver, and those who have studied automaticty and fluency. If anything, the simple view ignores elements (e.g., attention to speed of processing), conditions (e.g., the challenge level of the tasks and the mode of reading), and text features (e.g., Carver's assessments of text difficulty) that were well established prior to the labeling of the simple view (see Carver, 1993, for a complete discussion of this argument). Perhaps the only element that is new within the simple view is the representation of three kinds of reading problems—although, here again, the notions of dyslexia and hyperlexia have a long history in the field of reading and special education. Again, though, these are labels within the simple view and not deeply developed models of disability. The appeal of the simple view outside of theory appears tied to its label and its simplicity. It is just that simple. The basic argument is made that reading comprehension is influenced by decoding and listening comprehension (primarily) and if you want to help readers (struggling or not) then you must focus your assessments and your instructional interventions on either or both of these elements.

What's troubling in the simple view?

The simple view might be ideal if individuals, the reading process, and the teaching of reading were not so complex. The reality is that there is complexity and variation in each of these. I will offer several different points of concern regarding the simple view: (1) Theory—What does the simple view explain and what does it ignore? (2) Fluency—How is prosody ignored as a mediating process between decoding and comprehension? (3) Flexibility—What happens when the reader chooses to or is forced to deal with challenging texts? (4) Text Structures—How do "new literacies" fit into the simple view? (5) Pedagogy—What does "simple" comprehension instruction look like? (6) Disability—What is a reading difficulty? (7) Policy—What are the dangers associated with the policy mandates tied to the simple view?

Theory

What does the simple view explain and what does it ignore? Clearly, decoding abilities and listening comprehension contribute to reading comprehension. This assertion is beyond dispute. However, it is not as clear in the arguments made for the simple view what model or theory of comprehension processes explains how listening processes work and under what conditions. Is it constructivist? Socio-constructivist? Is it amenable to a social practice perspective? These questions are typically ignored in the discussions of the simple view. Rather, it seems sufficient to say that what happens in reading comprehension is "whatever takes place in listening." Hoover and Gough draw on Fries (1963) in support of their arguments for the link between reading and listening. Fries notes that while reading certainly does involve (a) host of higher mental processes.... "every one of the abilities (observed in reading comprehension)...may be developed and has been achieved by persons who could not read...(as) they are all matters of the uses of language and are not limited to the uses of reading" (p. 118). This interpretation falls short in explaining strategic reading behaviors on the part of the reader—in particular the strategic reading behaviors that are not available in the auding mode. Further, how does the simple view, as a theory, explain the fact that general cognitive abilities and language abilities in particular are enhanced through engagement with texts (e.g., Storch & Whitehurst, 2002). This is clearly the case in the development of vocabulary. Many of the new words encountered come through print sources and not an oral medium. Even at the emergent level, the texts that surround the learner offer constant mediation for the development of new concepts (e.g., to suggest that listening comprehension is the key variable is to ignore that text experiences inform language development and listening comprehension abilities).

Fluency

How is prosody ignored as a mediating process between decoding and comprehension? The term "fluency" is used by different groups to mean quite different things (Hoffman, Sailors, & May, in press). For some, fluency is attentive to accuracy and rate of processing. The rate of processing may consider the rate of reading of connected text or may simply refer to the speed of word identification (e.g., word naming). For others, the term fluency is considerate of accuracy, rate and prosody. The first version of fluency (i.e., without attention to prosody) might be termed the simple view of fluency. Schwanenflugel et al. (2006) recently published a study that examined the relationship between automaticity and fluency. The findings from the research supported what they refer to as a "Simple Reading Fluency Model." They found that performance on comprehension measures was strongly predicted by word level automaticity measures (speed and accuracy). They found no significant contribution to these prediction models for measures related to fluency of reading connected text. They found no evidence to suggest that readers "utilize text fluency-related skills such as sentence-parsing skills...and the contextual activation of word meanings...to aid in the comprehension of text once their basic word reading is automatic enough to free up cognitive resources" (pp. 516–517). This view is closely aligned with the simple view of reading. Swanenflugel et al. found no effect for fluency measures of connected reading of text over the speed of word identification of isolated words on comprehension. However, as the authors recognize, they did not measure prosody directly in their study of fluency and this may explain, in part, the absence of findings related to connected reading and comprehension. Adolf, Catts, and Little (2006) measured rate and accuracy (a simple view of fluency without attention to prosody) and found no additional contribution to the prediction of reading comprehension beyond oral language/listening measures and decoding. measures. The more complex notion of fluency suggests that prosody operates as a process to assist the reader in constructing the sense of (the meaning of) the text (Allington, 1983; Rasinski, Blachowicz, & Lems, 2006; Rasinski & Hoffman, 2005; Schrieber, 1980, 1987). The developing reader in this view uses their knowledge of the prosodic elements of language to support the construction of the meaning of a text. "Reading with expression" is more than just an outcome of the development of automaticity, as suggested by Chard (2006). Rather it is an active strategy the reader uses to construct the meaning of a text (Hoffman, Sailors, & May, in press).

Flexibility

What happens when the reader chooses to or is forced to deal with challenging texts? While this consideration is part of the early work of Sticht and Carver, it is not addressed in the simple view. As mentioned, Carver was careful to focus on the efficiency of rauding in text that was relatively easy for the reader in the same way that Sticht focused on auding of material that was easy for the listener. Under these conditions, the predictors used by Sticht and Carver fit the outcomes they observed. But is this "typical" reading as Carver has argued? Most educators would argue that instruction (from a Vygotskian, zone of proximal development perspective) is offered in tasks (through texts) that challenge the reader beyond what they already know. Readers become strategic as they engage with these materials and teachers scaffold the learners toward strategies that empower them as independent learners. Most of the studies of the simple view do not examine readers as they move from text that is at their independent level to text that is instructional or even frustrational. Indeed, few of the researchers actually examine the predictions of reading comprehension of specific texts that have been read. Following Carver, if they did, they might discover that the predictions of comprehension are enhanced with a consideration of strategic comprehension behaviors along with fluency strategies that rely on prosody. This is speculation at this point because researchers have not conducted these kinds of studies.

Text structure

How do "new literacies" fit into the simple view? Hoover and Gough argue that reading is an exclusively linguistic act. They question or dismiss the notion that literacy tasks such as how to carry out arithmetic operations or how to "read" a map are acts of reading (p. 30). This narrow interpretation of literacy is one of the foundational assumptions of the simple view and is at odds with most current representations of reading activity found in the professional literature (e.g., Kellner, 2001; Street, 2005). Adults actively engage with all kinds of texts (including electronic texts that offer the reader opportunities to manipulate the text) to achieve purposes. The work of Guthrie and colleagues (e.g., Guthrie, Britten, & Barker, 1991; Kirsch & Guthrie, 1984) revealed the ways in which learners actively use text search strategies to construct the meaning of text. Readers vary in this skill and this influences comprehension of these texts. Leu, Kinzer, Coiro, and Cammack (2004) and many others (see Coiro, Knobel, Lankshear, & Leu, 2007) are currently investigating the reading and learning associated with electronic texts. These texts are not constructed in as linear a fashion as traditional text and readers who demonstrate flexibility are the ones who succeed in learning through texts.

Pedagogy

What does "simple" comprehension instruction look like? Pressley et al. (in press) worry that the simple view offers a rationale for more of the same for struggling readers (drill on decoding) and less of explicit comprehension instruction. Perhaps the best insight into the kind of instruction that is aligned with the simple view is through consideration of the assessment tools. The DIBELS (Dynamic Indicators of Basic Early Literacy Skills) assessment plan offers the most radical version of instruction inside the simple view (Goodman, 2006). Assessment with DIBELS is focused on accuracy and rate. It does not matter that the "fluency" with reading is even done with real words—nonsense words may actually offer a more pure mode of assessment. Instruction that is dependent on these outcome measures reflects the assessment itself. The learner is expected to practice automatic recognition of nonsense words and real words. Comprehension is assessed through DIBELS by asking the reader repeat what they have just read and then to calculate a comprehension score based on the number of words said by the learner (see Pressley, Hilden, & Shankland, 2005, for a critique of this measure of comprehension). In some instances, such as with the PALS assessment, comprehension is not even assessed at the early grade levels because: "PALS does not consider reading comprehension scores in calculating functional reading levels because students' reading comprehension should be commensurate with their ability to comprehend spoken language. Decoding is the principal focus for the early reader as decoding is the strongest predictor of reading comprehension at this level" (Invernizzi, 2003, p. 2).

Proponents of the simple view would likely argue that the learner should be actively engaged in the development of general language abilities as decoding becomes more automatic. The presumption here is that this instruction would be offered absent of text and absent of the support for the reader to develop comprehension strategies for engaging with challenging texts. This view reflects the same kind of flaw that was revealed in phonemic awareness training. Phonemic awareness was viewed as an insight about oral language that supports the development of decoding. In the early stages of this work, phonemic awareness training was conducted without text. What was soon learned through research is that the engagement with text (in particular through writing) supported developing readers' insights into oral language and the parsing of words into sounds (e.g., Ehri et al., 2001).

Storch and Whitehurst (2002) suggest the importance of the interactive quality of oral language and print in their longitudinal study of language development. Evidence is also found in the work of Dickenson et al. (2003). A more complex view of comprehension supports models of teaching that include attention to all language systems. Duke, Purcell-Gates, Hall, and Tower (2007), for example, argue for the role of "authentic literacy activities" to support the development of comprehension abilities. Authentic literacy activities stress the importance of real purposes and functions for reading as well as contexts for tasks that link in school and out of school reading. There is a heavy emphasis in the use of informational and procedural texts. Authentic literacy activities have a writer and a reader—"a writer who is writing to a real reader and a reader who is reading what the writer wrote" (p. 346).

The greatest concern with pedagogy and the simple view is the role of the teacher. If there is no attempt to challenge the learner with texts that require the development and use of new strategies, what happens to the important role of the teacher to scaffold learning? There is none. It is as if the best instruction would be for the learner to just read (practice) in easy text to increase automaticity. Comprehension will come along with growth in general language ability. But should instruction in general language ability be offered without text? Why should that be?

Disability

What is a reading difficulty? The simple view posits two kinds of reading disability. One source of disability is poor decoding with a learner that has strong language comprehension (dyslexia). The other source of disability is for the learner that has poor decoding skills and low general language ability. This second type of disability is labeled as "garden variety." Setting aside the derogatory connotations for this label, what is suggested for the teacher in working with children so labeled? Is there an unspoken reference here to role of intelligence in determining the capacity for literate activity? Does the theory suggest anything beyond what any other learner might be offered in the way of instruction? It is as easy to read into "garden variety" as "they are what they are" as it is to assume a different stance toward support. Here, the simple view not only falls short in terms of offering direction, it may even lead to an acceptance of the status quo. As Pressley et al. (in press) argue:

> It should not be surprising that, as we write this chapter, we are frustrated with the over-attention to sound-, letter-, and word-level processing that characterizes instruction for many struggling readers, given the evidence that progress often boils down to a little progress in learning how to sound out words and only small improvement in comprehension. This is not to say we believe phonics instruction is not necessary for many struggling readers, but that it is not sufficient. (p. 4)

Policy

What are the dangers associated with the policy mandates tied to the simple view? If the simple view were a pure academic debate, it would be one thing. It would provide a foil for complex representation of reading comprehension. There would be no harm here and perhaps even some valuable basis for scholarly inquiry. But, the academic debates over reading and reading instruction are often and quickly polarized and politicized. Policy makers are not particularly concerned about theory. Policy makers want results (the quicker the better and the cheaper the better). They are also responsive to representations that they can convey to their constituents in familiar terms. "Just read more" became the cure for reading in California in the literature-based movement. Policy makers jumped on the band-wagon and all but pushed "teaching" out of the literacy curriculum. The same is occurring today with respect to the simple view. Proponents for the simple view of reading comprehension among scholars are few but they have achieved broad support within the policy community based on the promise of quick, cheap results in terms they understand. The legislative requirements of programs like No Child Left Behind and Reading First weigh heavy on teachers as they reflect this simple view. Teachers who are in close contact with learners are severely limited in the ways in which they can be responsive to learner needs.

The alternative

Reading is a complex act that rests on the motivation (desire) to learn and the application of strategic behaviors to achieve purposes. The effective reader is active, strategic, flexible and self-regulating. The effective reader develops efficiency in decoding (automaticity) and fluency as the result of frequent engagement with texts (Duffy, 2003a,

2003b, 2003c). The effective reader, even in early emergent stages of reading development, uses encounters with texts to enhance their overall language abilities (including listening comprehension). This complex view of reading comprehension, widely supported in the research literature, informs a complex model of reading comprehension instruction. The teacher of reading comprehension must model, explicate, and adapt strategies with the reader to promote independence.

Gough and Tunmer claim that, while bottom-up models of reading have been proven wrong, the bottom-up model is true in relation to fluent reading… "a strong, empirically supported argument can be made that during normal reading, the more proficient the reader, the less the reliance on context…In short, fluent reading may best be characterized as a bottom-up process" (p. 4). The same argument can be made for the simple view. That is, during normal reading (i.e., a "rauding" mode) in texts that are not challenging for the reader (i.e., a skilled reader in relation to text demands) the elements of the simple view predict a large portion of the variance in the outcome (i.e., reading comprehension). The bottom-up version of reading (i.e., the version that diminishes the role of context and the active application of strategies for word recognition) is of little use to educators who work with learners (not just struggling readers but all readers) to develop self-generating strategies (Pinnell, 1985) as they engage with challenging texts. Similarly, the simple view of reading is of little use to educators who work with learners in a variety of different kinds of texts that challenge the reader (beyond their current levels of understanding) to develop strategies that will support the student as an independent learner.

Needed research

Those who advocate for the simple view must provide research evidence of the relative predictive power of the two components (decoding ability and listening comprehension) as readers move from easy to challenging texts; studies of readers as they move from texts that are appropriate to a "rauding" mode vs. texts that are less linear in structure; and studies that explore variations of readers' purposes as they interact with different text structures. These kinds of studies might begin to study variance in reader strategies in relation to these different conditions. There are some first steps along this path to be found in the work of Walczyk and Griffith-Ross (2007). They frame their research with a simple view but move on to explore what they call "compensatory" strategies that readers use to support their comprehension of texts. While the framework assumes a somewhat "deficit" perspective, it still represents the beginning of a strategic view of reading in relation to the simple view.

SUMMARY

This review of the reading comprehension literature suggests that the simple view of reading and reading comprehension is inadequate as a theoretical framework for understanding reading, inadequate as a useful guide for the design of curriculum, inadequate in its power to guide instruction, and inadequate in the way it is being used to shape educational policy. The simple view inflames the political climate for teachers and literacy instruction and discourages thoughtful research and reflective practice. In promising so much for so little, the simple view appeals to the policy community and marginalizes more complex representations of comprehension that could better guide instructional innovations. At best, the simple view offers an empirical account for a substantial portion of the variance in comprehension as long as the reader is skilled with respect to the challenges of the text and engaged in a "typical" reading (rauding) mode. But, most educators are working with learners for whom this is not the case, and most readers engage in reading tasks inside and outside of school that do not reflect these conditions.

I opened this chapter with a hypothetical in which the simple view was being imported into literacy instruction in developing countries where schools serve impoverished communities. I confess that this is not totally hypothetical (see, for example, Abadzi et al., 2005). I work in schools in developing countries. I work to support teachers in helping students develop literacy under the most challenging of circumstances. But this kind of thoughtful support for teachers is not always valued in the developing world. I have observed the adaptation of the DIBELS instruments to be used to assess learners in home languages in South Africa. I have seen the plans to use these assessments to build national standards for reading. I know how this will play out for learners in schools and for the teachers in developing countries. I know because I have seen the same scenario played out in the schools that serve the most impoverished communities in the United States. Certainly, our theories can offer more to these educators and these learners. I do not question the motivations of those who advocate for the simple view. I believe they have the best intentions in mind toward improving reading achievement. But they are wrong, and the simple view is the wrong approach to take in promoting the development of strategic readers. The issues of reading comprehension are complex. The field cannot be seduced into simple ways of thinking because the alternative is challenging. We must strive to construct models that resonate with both theoretical frames and instructional frames.

REFERENCES

Abadzi, H., Crouch, L., Echegaray, M., Pasco, C., & Sampe, J. (2005). Monitoring basic skills acquisition through rapid learning assessments: A Case Study. *Prospects, 35*(2), 137–156.

Adolf, S. M., Catts, H. W., & Little, T. D. (2006). Should the simple view of reading include a fluency component? *Reading and Writing, 19*, (9), 457–468.

Allington, R. L. (1983). Fluency: The neglected reading goal. *The Reading Teacher, 37*, 556–561.

Bruner, J. (1990). *Acts of meaning.* Cambridge, MA: Harvard University Press.

Carver, R. P. (1990). *Reading rate: A review of research and theory.* San Diego, CA: Academic Press.

Carver, R. P. (1993). Merging the simple view of reading with Rauding Theory. *Journal of Reading Behavior, 25*(4), 439–455.

Chard, D. (2006). *Using core instruction to meet the needs of diverse learners.* Retrieved November 22, 2006, from: http://216.239.51.104/search?q=cache:-W0QnjrFHGkJ:www.edina. k12.mn.us/creekvalley/staffdev/Chard%2520Differentiation%2520of%2520Instruction. ppt+david+chard+fluency+pikulski&hl=en&gl=us&ct=clnk&cd=10&client=safari.

Chen, R. S., & Vallutino, F. R. (1997). Prediction of reading ability: A cross-validation study of the simple view of reading. *Journal of Literacy Research, 29*(1), 1–24.

Chew., J. (2006). New Literacy Framework: http://www.teachingtimes.co.uk/index. php?option=com_content&task=view&id=116&Itemid=56

Coiro, J., Knobel, M., Lankshear, C., & Leu, D. J. (2007). *Handbook of research on new literacies.* Mahwah, NJ: Erlbaum.

Dahl, P. R. (1979). An experimental program for teaching high speed word recognition and comprehension skills. In J. E. Button, T. Lovitt, & T. Rowland (Eds.), *Communications research in learning disabilities and mental retardation* (pp. 33–65). Baltimore, MD: University Park Press.

Dickenson, D., McCabe, A., Anastasopoulos, L., Peisner-Feinberg, E. S., & Poe, M. D. (2003). The comprehensive language approach to early literacy: The interrelationships among vocabulary, phonological sensitivity, and print knowledge among preschool-aged children. *Journal of Educational Psychology, 95*(2), 465–481.

Dowhower, S. L. (1987). Effects of repeated reading on second-grade transitional readers' fluency and comprehension. *Reading Research Quarterly, 22*, 389–406.

Dreyer, L. G., & Katz, L. (1992). An examination of "the simple view of reading". *National Reading Conference Yearbook, 41*, 169–175.

Duffy, G. (2003a). *Explaining reading: A teacher's resource for teaching concepts, Skills and strategies.* New York: Guilford.

Duffy, G. (Ed.) (2003b). *Improving comprehension: Ten research-based principles.* Washington, DC: National Education Association.

Duffy, G. (2003c). Teachers who improve reading achievement: What they do and how to develop them. In D. Strickland & M. Kamil (Eds.), *Improving reading achievement through professional development.* New York: Christopher-Gordon.

Duke, N. K., Purcell-Gates, V., Hall, L. A., & Tower, C. (2007). Authentic literacy activities for developing comprehension and writing. *Reading Teacher, 60*(4), pp 344–355.

Ehri, L. C., Nunes, S R., Willows, D. M., Schuster, B., Yaghoub-Zadeh, Z., & Shanahan, T. (2001). Phonemic awareness instruction helps children learn to read: Evidence from the National Reading Panel's Meta-Analysis. *Reading Research Quarterly, 36*(3), 250–287.

Fries, C. (1963). *Linguistics and reading.* New York: Holt, Rinehart, & Winston.

Goodman, (2006). *Examining DIBELS: What is it and what it does.* Brandon, VT: Vermont Society for the study of education.

Gough, P. B., Hoover, W. A., & Peterson, C. L. (1996). Some observations on a simple view of reading. In C. Cornoldi & J. Oakhill (Eds.), *Reading comprehension difficulties: Process and intervention* (pp. 1–13). Mahwah, NJ: Erlbaum.

Gough, P. B., & Tunmer, W. (1986). Decoding, reading, and reading disability. *Remedial and Special Education, 7,* 6–10.

Guthrie, J. T., Britten, T. K., & Barker, G. (1991). Roles of Document Structure, Cognitive Strategy, and Awareness in Searching for Information. *Reading Research Quarterly, 26*(3), 300–324.

Hoffman, J. V., Sailors, M., & May, L. (in press). Reading fluency: Neglected or abducted? *Yearbook of the National Reading Conference.*

Hoover, W. A., & Gough P. B. (1990). The simple view of reading. *Reading and writing: An interdisciplinary journal, 2,*127–160.

Hoover, W. A., & Gough, P. B. (2000). The reading acquisition framework - An overview by Wesley A. Hoover and Philip B. Gough. Retrieved February, 27, 2007, from http://www.sedl.org/reading/framework/overview.html

Invernizzi, M. (2003). PALS comprehension scores and instructional reading levels. University of Virginia. http://readingfirst.virginia.edu/pdfs/comp_white_paper.pdf

Irwin, J. W. (2007). *Teaching reading comprehension processes* (3rd ed.) Boston, MA: Pearson.

Joshi, R., & Aaron, P. G. (2000). The component model of reading: Simple view of reading made a little more complex. *Reading Psychology, 21,* 85–97.

Kavanagh, J. F., & Mattingly, I. G. (1972). *Language by ear and by eye; the relationships between speech and reading.* Cambridge, MA: MIT Press.

Kellner, K. (2001). New technologies/new literacies: Reconstructing education in the new millennium. *International Journal of Technology and Design Education, 11,* 67–81.

Kirsch, J. T., & Guthrie, J. T. (1984). Prose Comprehension and Text Search as a Function of Reading Volume. *Reading Research Quarterly, 19*(3), 331–342.

LaBerge, D., & Samuels, S. J. (1974). Toward a theory of automatic information processing in reading. *Cognitive Psychology, 6,* 293–323.

Leu, D. J., Kinzer, C. K., Coiro, J. L., & Cammack, D. W. (2004). Toward a theory of new literacies emerging from the internet and other information and communication technologies. In R. Ruddell & N. Unrau (Eds.), *Theoretical models and processes of reading* (5th ed., 125–138). Newark, DE: International Reading Association.

National Reading Panel (2000). *Teaching children to read: An Evidence-Based assessment of the scientific research literature on reading and its implications for reading instruction.* Retrieved February 26, 2007, from http://www.nichd.nih.gov/publications/nrp/upload/report_pdf

Pinnell, G. S. (1985). Helping teachers help children at risk: Insights from the Reading Recovery Program. *Peabody Journal of Education, 62*(3), 70–85.

Pressley, M., Duke, N. K., Gaskins, I. W., Fingeret, L., Halladay, J., Hilden, K., Park, Y., Zhang, S., Mohan, L., Reffitt, K., Bogaert, L. R., Reynolds, J., Golos, D., Solic, K., & Collins, S. (in press). Working with struggling readers: Why we must get beyond the simple view of reading and visions of how it might be done. In T. Gutkin & C. R. Reynolds (Eds.), *The handbook of school psychology, fourth edition.* New York: Wiley.

Pressley, M., Hilden, K., & Shankland, R. (2005). *An evaluation of End-Grade 3Dynamic Indicators of Basic Early Literacy Skills (DIBELS): Speed reading without comprehension, predicting little.*

Rasinski, T., Blachowicz, C., & Lems, K. (2006). *Fluency Instruction: Research-based best practices.* New York: Guilford.

Rasinski, T., & Hoffman, J.V. (2005). Theory and research into practice: Oral reading in the school literacy Curriculum. *Reading Research Quarterly, 11,* 65–73.

Ross Report. (2006). *The new conceptual framework for teaching reading: the 'simple view of reading' — overview for literacy leaders and managers in schools and Early Years settings.* http://www.standards.dfes.gov.uk/primaryframeworks/downloads/PDF/Paper_on_searchlights_model.pdf

Schreiber, P. A. (1980). On the acquisition of reading fluency. *Journal of Reading Behavior, 12,* 177–186.

Schreiber, P. A. (1987). Prosody and structure in children's syntactic processing. In R. Horowitz & S. J. Samuels (Eds.), *Comprehending oral and written language* (pp. 243–270). New York: Academic Press.

Schwanenflugel, E. B., Meisinger, E. B., Wisenbaker, J. M., Kuhn, R. R., Strauss, G. P., & Morris, R. D. (2006). Becoming a fluent and automatic reader in the early elementary years. *Reading Research Quarterly, 41*(4), 496–522.

Sticht, T. G., Beck, L. J., Hauke, R. N., Kleiman, G. M., & James, J. H. (1974). *Auding and Reading: A Developmental Model.* Alexandria, VA: Human Resources Research Organization (HumRRO).

Storch, S. A., & Whitehurst, G. J. (2002). Oral language and code-related precursors to reading: Evidence from a longitudinal structural model. *Developmental Psychology, 38,* 934–947.

Street, B. (2006). *Literacies across educational contexts: Mediating learning and teaching.* Philadelphia: Casion.

Walczyk, J. J., & Griffith-Ross D. A. (2007). How important is reading skill fluency for comprehension? *Reading Teacher, 60*(6), 560.

Wren, S. A. (2006). The Simple view of reading: R = D × C. Retrieved March 2007, from http://www.balancedreading.com/simple.html.

Part II
Theoretical Perspectives

4 Identifying and Describing Constructively Responsive Comprehension Strategies in New and Traditional Forms of Reading

Peter Afflerbach and Byeong-Young Cho

University of Maryland

OUR GOALS FOR THE CHAPTER

We begin this chapter with a definition of constructively responsive reading comprehension strategies. We then describe the theoretical and practical significance of the investigation of strategies. Next, we consider the means to investigate these strategies, noting recent developments in new and mixed methodologies that help us catalog and describe the diverse constructively responsive reading comprehension strategies and their uses. We describe strategies of reading comprehension, with a focus on recent research of the strategies involved in reading multiple documents and in Internet and hypertext reading. We conclude by proposing future directions for research of the constructively reading comprehension strategies and for the methodologies that enable this inquiry.

A DEFINITION OF CONSTRUCTIVELY RESPONSIVE READING COMPREHENSION STRATEGIES

Reading comprehension strategies involve mindful plans that demand reader attention and resources, and are focused on the goal of constructing meaning (Kintsch, 1998). More specifically, reading strategies are "the reader's deliberate, goal-directed attempts to control and modify their efforts to decode text, understand words, and construct meanings of text." (Afflerbach, Pearson, & Paris, in press). Strategies figure largely when an elementary student effectively searches the Internet for information on the Nez Perce, and reads and understands text to learn new information that is used to help construct a diorama for a class project. The strategies help a middle school student reading two original source texts of the Boston Massacre, one each from newspapers in London and Boston, and analyzing and critically interpreting the texts for their provenance and accuracy. Strategies are essential for the high school student reading and studying for a unit test, realizing that little has been understood and remembered, and deciding to more carefully read the previous three pages. Strategies figure largely in an adult reading two opposing editorials on the war in Iraq to help shape a personal stance towards each editorial and towards the war itself.

Strategies are notable for their intentionality: the goal-directed and resourceful application of strategies distinguishes them from other reading processes, which can include perceiving of visual information from the page through the eye to the brain (McConkie, 1997) and the automatic retrieval of meaning from well-learned and rehearsed sight word vocabularies (Perfetti, 1985). Strategies vary in form and function. As well, they differ in the attention they demand of readers, highly practiced, oftentimes near automatic and operating at the edge of consciousness, while at other times deliberate and resource consuming. Thus, particular reading strategies are most often surrounded by reading skills and other, related reading strategies, making the delineation and nature of each strategy an important research goal.

Strategies are developmental in nature: they may, in a reader's initial uses, demand the reader's full attention for successful implementation, and then require less attention as they are practiced and mastered. Thus, strategies can be "skills under consideration" (Paris, Lipson, & Wixson, 1983). Strategies are related to skills in that particular reading strategies, with practice, may become skills: those operations that are conducted by the reader without attention, and automatically. In challenging reading situations, strategies may morph from the quick and effortless use to the thoughtful and effortful application that characterize skill and strategy, respectively. The nature of a strategy is contextually determined in relation to the familiarity of the text topic, the genre of text, and the nature of the reading and reading-related tasks (e.g., read a chapter and answer a theme question). We may experience such a range of strategy use within one reading event, as when we effortlessly process known words, increase the time and attention given to summarizing text, and grind to a slow pace when trying to determine the meaning of unknown words.

Consider the following passage, taken from Afflerbach (1990), which when read silently helps us become reacquainted with some of those strategies that are raised to consciousness when the construction of even a literal meaning is challenging:

> It is legitimate to further characterize the broadpoint appearance as a major archeological horizon marker for the eastern seaboard. In the terms of Willey and Phillips, a horizon is "a primarily spatial continuity represented by cultural traits and assemblages whose nature and mode of occurrence permit the assumption of a broad and rapid spread." That a quick expansion of the broadpoint-using peoples took place is indicated by the narrow range of available radiocarbon dates, along with a correspondingly wide areal distribution of components. Once established, the broadpoint horizon developed as a "whole cultural pattern or tradition" in its own right by persisting and evolving over an expansive region for 500 to 1000 years. (Turnbaugh, 1975)

Attempts to understand the above text typically evoke constructively responsive reading comprehension strategies. These may include efforts to identify key vocabulary (e.g., broadpoint), to note the novel use of other vocabulary (e.g., horizon) and to engage appropriate prior knowledge (What do I know about radiocarbon dating?). These strategies are coordinated and used in conjunction with metacognitive strategies that include comprehension monitoring (realized in relation to re-reading and varying the rate of reading to accommodate the degree of comprehension) and parsing sentences in an attempt to make them more manageable for processing, as readers seek to construct meaning. We note that the text, which focuses on Native American broadpoint arrowheads, has been modified to eliminate some of the cues that readers typically use to help build meaning, including a title or topic sentence. This renders reading more difficult and helps bring cognitive strategies to the surface, allowing us to focus on and perhaps, scrutinize them. We believe that reading the above text excerpt illustrates well the fact that while we are talented and opportunistic strategy users, we may not always (or even frequently) be aware of the strategies we employ. Challenging reading can remind us of the sometimes arduous nature of strategy use.

Strategy use is a central feature of constructively responsive reading (Pressley & Afflerbach, 1995) in which successful readers

> know and use many different procedures (strategies) in coming to terms with text: They proceed generally from front to back of documents when reading. Good read-

ers are selectively attentive. They sometimes make notes. They predict, paraphrase, and back up when confused. They try to make inferences to fill in the gaps in text and in their understanding of what they have read. Good readers intentionally attempt to integrate across the text. They do not settle for literal meanings but rather interpret what they have read, sometimes constructing images, other times identifying categories of information in text, and on still other occasions engaging in arguments with themselves about what a reading might mean. After making their way through text, they have a variety of ways of firming up their understanding and memory of the messages in the text, from explicitly attempting to summarize to self-questioning about the text to rereading and reflecting. The many procedures used by skilled readers are appropriately and opportunistically coordinated, with the reader using the processes needed to meet current reading goals, confronting the demands of reading at the moment, and preparing for demands that are likely in the future (e.g., the need to recall text content for a test). (pp. 79–80)

To summarize, constructively responsive reading comprehension strategies are used with effort and attention, in relation to a reader's goals and abilities. These strategies are developmental in nature, learned and then practiced by increasingly accomplished readers until fluency of strategy use is achieved. This creates the paradox in which the more successful we become with the use of particular reading strategies, the less aware we may be that we are using them. This should not belie the fact of reading strategies' importance to successful reading and the challenge they may present to developing readers. Strategies play a central role in traditional and recent contexts of literacy, and their use and effectiveness is determined always in relation to the complexity of the reading task.

THE VALUE OF STUDYING CONSTRUCTIVELY RESPONSIVE READING COMPREHENSION STRATEGIES

The past three decades have seen copious research on reading comprehension and the constructive nature of reading (Coiro & Dobler, 2007; Lorch & van den Broek, 1997; Pressley & Afflerbach, 1995; Snow, 2002; van Dijk & Kintsch, 1983). Our conceptualization of constructive reading comprehension strategies is always subject to modification and revision, evolving as our understanding of cognition, literacies and the contexts in which they operate contribute new information. There is much understood and agreed upon when it comes to conceptualizing and categorizing these strategies, yet the field will benefit from continuing efforts to further describe reading comprehension strategies, especially those involved in historically recent forms of reading.

Why study constructively responsive reading comprehension strategies? Beyond reminding us of the considerable achievement that reading represents (Huey, 1908), the continued study and explication of reading strategies has important theoretical and practical outcomes. Research on how people use strategies to construct meaning and how they use what is understood from reading can make ongoing contributions to theories of cognitive processes, strategy use in reading and the relation of strategy to other factors, such as readers' prior knowledge and affect in reading. Establishing this depth and breadth of knowledge helps us better understand these intricate workings of mind. The new information serves to replenish and extend our knowledge of the construct of reading. In turn, the refined understanding of basic psychological processes and the contexts in which constructively responsive reading strategies operate should have positive implications for how we conceptualize and foster students' reading development.

Knowledge of reading comprehension strategies, gathered through research, informs successful reading comprehension instruction programs (Pressley, 2000). This knowledge helps us conduct task analyses of the things we would teach related to strategic reading and informs the manner in which we present and portray strategy use for students (Kucan & Beck, 1997). Further, clear understanding of these processes allows us to gauge comprehension instruction to readers' developmental levels, as along a novice-to-expert continuum. New knowledge helps us develop detailed approaches to teaching reading strategies that can include modeling, explanation and thinking aloud, as students engage in traditional and new forms of reading.

An overview of the methodologies of inquiry into reading comprehension strategies and their relation to theories of mind

There is an important relationship between the conception of mind and the means of inquiry used to investigate mind. With a historical perspective we can understand how behaviorists might describe thinking in terms of stimuli and response; under such a view reading involves a text and a reader's reaction to it. Information processing advocates could describe reading as the moving of considerable amounts of data from the text through the eye to the brain, with important text contents identified, learned and stored. And cognitive psychologists might consider these accounts as parts (and partial explanation) of the elaborate strategies that accomplished readers use to meld text with prior knowledge in the construction of meaning in relation to goals. Accompanying each of these perspectives are chosen methodologies, believed to be most appropriate for investigating particular phenomena.

The investigation of reading strategies (or mental operations, or moves, or processes) is influenced by contemporary conceptions of mind and accomplished through particular means of inquiry. In turn, investigations of psychological phenomena provide data, new information, that can change our conception of mind and suggest new areas and means of inquiry. Conception of mind and the characterization of readers as active processors, complex reactants, or absorbing sponges will, of course, influence our inquiry into their reading. For example, the idea that reading is enabled by sets of cognitive strategies and skills can be complemented by experimental methodologies that seek to identify individual strategies and skills, describe them in detail, chart their interrelationships and describe their workings in different contexts. Reading research has made considerable contribution to the first two areas, and is making inroads in the latter two. We note the reciprocity and recursivity of the paradigm-methodology dynamic: appropriate methodologies can provide data that contribute to paradigm revision and change, and this change can inform the future use of appropriate methodologies.

Reading comprehension strategies are invisible, and methodologies to investigate them must be designed to give us appropriate information from which we make inferences and hypotheses about strategy use and development. Across the centuries, we can trace efforts to better know what is going on in the human mind. Aristotle and Plato both encouraged colleagues to discuss their thinking. James (1890) and Wundt (1896–97) sought to determine and describe thinking and reading. A century ago, Thorndike (1912) produced descriptions of readers' comprehension processes that have considerable goodness of fit with contemporary narratives of reading and understanding. The dynamic nature of reading was explored using subjects' introspective reports (Huey, 1908; McCallister, 1930; Piekarz, 1954), despite the reign of behaviorism and the theoretical exclusion of verbalizations as data (Watson, 1913, 1920). Eye movement studies examined reading by collecting data on where readers' eyes tracked while reading (McConkie, 1997). Information processing models (LaBerge & Samuels, 1974) were applied to reading and research, along with ideas of the nature of working and long term memory. Problem-solving aspects of human cognition (Newell & Simon, 1972) were detailed, which contributed to the conception of reading as strategic problem-solving

(Olshavsky, 1976–1977). The role of reading strategies in processing text information was described in considerable detail by van Dijk and Kinstch (1983). Interest in metacognition (Brown, 1980; Flavell, 1979) further raised the need for online data (Ericsson & Simon, 1980) that helps describe how readers know their own thinking and in what way they control their mindful processes (Paris & Flukes, 2005; Veenman, VanHout-Wolters, & Afflerbach, 2006). Most recently, inquiry into Internet reading comprehension strategies uses method that yields "a real-time movie of all online actions on the screen as well as an audio recording of verbal think-aloud data" (Leu et al, 2008).

One result of the past century's work to describe reading is the robust accounting of reading strategies. This work suggests that reading behaviors are of notable consistency; it is the interpretive frameworks that we use to describe and define reading activity that change. Thus, we can review a century of reading research and interpret it according to salient paradigms and their accompanying research methods. We can consider periods including behaviorism, information processing and cognition, review this work and, based on our appraisal of the conditions and design under which data were gathered, recast findings in relation to our most recent understandings of reading.

Efforts to describe and detail the strategic work of reading often focus on accomplished readers, and this preference is intentional. More accomplished readers often are of higher verbal ability, they are more often successful in choosing and using reading strategies and they may use more diverse reading comprehension strategies. Thus, these readers may be better able to describe and account for their strategies (when subjects are interviewed or asked to provide verbal reports), more efficient with strategy use (our models of reading comprehension assume success) and more diverse in the strategies they use (as we describe reading we attempt to be comprehensive and inclusive of successful strategy use). An ongoing focus on accomplished and expert reading can benefit developing readers. That is, as cognitive strategy research is charting the territories of expert performance, related efforts may inform approaches to teaching developing readers, in relation to the novice-expert paradigm. Here, the characterization of fledgling and accomplished reading can be used to so designate particular readers and then to speculate on the space between the two (Bruner, 1985). Determining this space is akin to identifying successive zones of proximal development (Vygotsky, 1979) for readers and considering appropriate strategy instruction in relation to this development.

SPECIFIC METHODOLOGICAL APPROACHES TO INVESTIGATING READING COMPREHENSION STRATEGIES

To date, researchers have used a variety of methods and data sources, including verbal reports and protocol analysis, theoretical task analyses, eye movements, protocol logs, observation of readers as they read and readers' self-reports to examine reading comprehension strategies. Each of these methodologies and approaches is accompanied with contingent advantages and concerns. As important, each particular methodology may be used in relation to others, providing complementary accounts of reading comprehension strategy use and triangulating information so that our inferences about readers' strategies may be bolstered. In this section we overview these different approaches and the manner in which they provide information about constructive reading comprehension strategies.

Verbal reports and protocol analysis

Verbal reports are spoken records of things that readers do and think related to their reading. Protocol analysis is the examination of verbal reports that allows us to describe reader behaviors, specifically their strategies, plans and goals. Protocol analysis as methodology was systematically reviewed and carefully advocated by Ericsson and Simon (1980, 1993). They described the use of protocol analysis to explore information processing and cognition, and provided substantial evidence to support their claims of validity of the method. Afflerbach and his colleagues (Afflerbach, 2000; Afflerbach & Johnston, 1984; Pressley & Afflerbach, 1995) elaborated potential strengths of protocol analysis for describing readers' comprehension strategies, as well as caveats related to the methodology in reading inquiry. We believe that the verbal reporting approach to describing conscious processes in reading is best characterized as a maturing methodology, one which has demonstrated clearly its worth. The continued inquiry into strategic text processing with protocol analysis is enhanced by the rigor of methodological application (Veenman, VanHout-Wolters, & Afflerbach, 2006).

We are encouraged by the use of the verbal reporting methodology to explore newer literacies, including strategic processing in Internet and hypertext environments (Castek et al., 2008; Coiro & Dobler, 2007; Leu et al., 2008; Yang, 2003), the effect of epistemological understanding on metacognitive processes during online searching (Hofer, 2004), the influence of understanding diagrams on text comprehension processes (Butcher, 2006), and patterns of strategic processes when reading multiple documents (Wolfe & Goldman, 2005). Verbal reporting and protocol analysis are the source of considerable data that describes constructively responsive reading comprehension strategies. The methodology is well-suited to the task of providing descriptions of strategies of traditional reader-text interactions as well as more recently investigated acts of literacy involving readers with multiple texts and readers reading in Internet environments.

Theoretical task analyses of reading comprehension strategies

Theoretical analyses of reading comprehension strategies can help us predict what strategies readers will use in particular reading situations, as well as when and how readers will use the strategies. Task analysis should be conducted in relation to well-defined and detailed theories of reading comprehension. Cogent task analysis demands researchers to use state of the art knowledge about reading strategies, combined with our understanding of situational factors (including reader ability and affect, text components, and related task demands) to predict or infer readers' strategies, moves, and events. Diverse theories associated with individual differences, structures, and contents of materials, contextual factors surrounding subjects as well as target strategies should be comprehensively examined as a theoretical analysis is conducted. This will allow for the scaffolding of new understandings about reading strategies from the existing knowledge base. In either case, the triangulation provided by different data sources can provide information for which we have high faith, and this can be used to verify, revise, or amend our particular understandings of the nature of strategies.

Magliano and Graesser (1991) suggested a coordinated, three-pronged procedure that employs the theoretical task analysis of the readers' comprehension strategies, such as making inferences during comprehension. Also involved are the analyses of verbal protocols gathered online as subjects read, combined with data from offline measures such as readers' free recall of text and sentence reading times. Together, these data can be used to build more detailed accounts of reading strategy use and to provide evidence from each of the methodologies that is mutually supportive. Or, particular data may serve as the foil, disconfirming a hypothesis of reading comprehension strategy, based on conflicting information from the different methodologies. Each of the components in this three-pronged approach can play explorative, predictive, disputative, or confirmative roles in helping us understand constructively responsive reading strategies. Particularly, Magliano and Graesser emphasize that a finely detailed and well supported theory of text comprehension helps explain the missing or unclear information in analysis of verbal reports and behavioral tasks. In other words, the role of theoretical task analysis in studies on reading comprehension is to fill in gaps from experimental data with clearly specified theory of what may be occurring, while building an inferential bridge between real mental processes performed and verbal report data produced during the reading. Thus, a particular aspect of Magliano and Graesser's approach is the anticipatory role that theoretical analysis can play in reading strategy specification.

Eye movement data and reading comprehension strategies

Studies of readers' eye movements provide detailed information about reading as information processing (McConkie, 1997; Rayner, 1978, 1998; Rayner & Sereno, 1994). This research focuses on the behavior of the eye and allows inferences about readers' strategies related to these behaviors. Rayner (1997) describes important eye movements that include *fixations* (where the reader's eyes fix when reading), *fixation durations* (how long eyes remain fixed), *saccades* (the reader's eye movement from fixation to fixation), and *regressions* (backward eye movements). Eye movements represent a mechanical and measurable aspect of reading from which inferences can be made about ongoing mental processes during reading (Just & Carpenter, 1980). Eye movement research provides data that can inform our descriptions of reading strategies. For example, eye-movement research provides an account of the physical moves of the eye when readers encounter and respond to new or inconsistent information in text (Hyona, 1995; Rayner, Chace, Slattery, & Ashby, 2006; Vauras, Hyona, & Niemi, 1992), when readers judge the relevance of text information (Rothkopf & Billington, 1979; Kaakinen, Hyona, & Keenan, 2002), and individual differences in strategy use (Hyona, Lorch, & Kaakinen, 2002).

Eye-movement research helps identify when and where accomplished readers consciously regulate their information processing, as when they regress in text to re-read. While eye-movement data may be less informative about the details and complexity of mental events during reading, they allow us to literally fixate on the places in text and time where readers "are." With such information we may be in the position to make more informed inferences about reading comprehension strategies. Ongoing development with the eye movement methodology focuses on what may be more ecologically valid reading task situations, as when eye movements are examined in the reading of entire texts, as opposed to classic eye movement laboratory approaches in which readers read a series of single words or sentences (Hyona, Lorch, & Kaakinen, 2002; Hyona, Lorch, & Rinck, 2003).

Eye movements during the performance of mental tasks like reading are sometimes difficult to predict, and may be characterized by huge variability across readers. For example, the nature of eye regressions "has an infinite number of forms" (Paulson, 2005, p. 344). This may discourage researchers from predicting accurately the path of eye movements and at the same time qualify interpretations in relation to their specificity and explanatory power. Although eye movements in reading are useful indicators, particularly, in understanding the "where" in multimedia text processing (Kamil, 2004), the quantitative nature of the measurement limits the ability to address the qualitative questions of "how" and "why" processing and comprehension occur. Eye movement data are a potentially rich means of triangulating other reading process data. For example, combined with verbal reports, reading eye movement data can provide evidence of where readers' eyes are, when they are there and how they operate in concert with readers' reported strategies.

Self-reports of reading strategies: Process logs, interviews, questionnaires, and retrospective reporting

An entire class of data gathering processes involves readers' reflective self-reports of strategy use. The assumption with such methodologies is that readers have access to knowledge of their strategy use and can reliably report their strategies. Although these approaches are subject to considerable skepticism (Veenman, 2005), they may provide useful information that helps us better understand the nature of strategic reading. Strategy process logs feature in writing research (Segev-Miller, 2007); they are typically used by writers as they reflect on the processes they use to create their texts. The use of process logs to study reading strategies involves readers reporting on the strategies they are aware of and remember using. As with verbal reports, readers' verbal ability is implicated as reflective accounts demand from readers descriptive competence, to the point that accounts are helpful to the researcher. A further concern is the grain size of detail. That is, how and what is reported in a process log may vary in attention to detail and allegiance to the time frame in which self-reported strategies actually occurred. Finally, the retrospective nature of process logs can lead to memory influences on what is recorded and described.

Like process logs, interviews with readers and self-report questionnaires may provide information that is helpful in describing and conceptualizing reader strategies. Both interviews and questionnaires must be used and interpreted with care, as they often lack reliability. For example, in commenting on the relationship between self-reports of strategies and actual strategy use, Veenman (2005) found that readers "simply don't do what they say they do." Readers often fail to exhibit the strategies that they report they will use in prospective questionnaires and their performances often lack the breadth and frequency of the strategies claimed in retrospective questionnaires.

Whatever the insights provided by data from a particular methodology, they represent a single view to the complexity of accomplished reading strategy use, a view that should be complemented with data from other methodologies. Combined, different methodologies can assist us in developing highly refined interpretations of data and related models of readers' cognitive strategies. While we have learned much about cognitive strategies in the last 30 years, we need still more rigorous interpretations to describe the complexity of reading strategies and the influence of contextual variables on them. For example, Kaakinen and Hyona (2005) experimented on the possibility of triangulation of verbal reports, eye-movement patterns, and recall rates to examine the effect of readers' perspectives on comprehending relevant and irrelevant information from expository text. In this study, verbal reports help describe how readers deploy deeper processing strategies when reading a perspective-relevant sentence, and these conscious processes were substantiated by the measures of eye movements and recall rates. Leu et al. (2008) use Camtasia, a system that allows for videotaping readers as they interact with Internet texts while recording their think-aloud verbalizations. This information can be compared with records of students Internet navigation to create a thick description of strategies and the specific text environments in which they are used.

RECENT RESEARCH THAT DESCRIBES CONSTRUCTIVELY RESPONSIVE READING

The investigation of reading is almost as old as the field of psychology (Huey, 1908; James, 1890; Thorndike, 1917). An observation of a talented reader can reveal that there is something startlingly complex when the eye meets the page, and research increasingly informs us as to the inner workings of this impressive human accomplishment. Currently, two complementary forces guide our investigations of reading comprehension strategies: one focuses on describing in increasing detail the cognitive strategies that readers use to construct meaning. The other seeks to contextualize this cognition in relation to the situations in which readers do their work.

Pressley and Afflerbach (1995) conducted a meta-analysis of research that uses think-aloud protocol data and created a comprehensive catalog of the strategies that readers use when reading conventional text. They analyzed 63 published research studies, synthesized findings across the studies, and developed a detailed description of constructively responsive reading. A thumbnail sketch of constructively responsive reading is presented in Table 4.1.

Pressley and Afflerbach (1995) characterized constructively responsive reading as expert and accomplished, involving three broad areas of strategy use: identifying and remembering important information, monitoring, and evaluating. For example, explicitly looking for related words, concepts and ideas in text and using them to construct a main idea or summary statement is a strategy for identifying and remembering important information in text. Determining that a word is unknown and then re-reading to try to establish the word's meaning is an example of a monitoring strategy. Analyzing the nature of an author's claim and judging that the text provides sufficient evidence to support the claim is an evaluation strategy.

We do not intend to review Pressley and Afflerbach's (1995) work in this chapter. Rather, we aim to describe the research done since the publication of their book, examining especially acts of reading that are the focus of recent research. These include the reading strategies that may be specific to particular content domains, the reading of multiple documents, and reading with Internet and hypertexts. We replicated the

Table 4.1 A Thumbnail Sketch of Constructively Responsive Reading Strategies

- Overviewing before reading (determining what is there and deciding which parts to process).
- Looking for important information in text and paying greater attention to it than other information (e.g., adjusting reading speed and concentration depending on the perceived importance of text to reading goals).
- Attempting to relate important points in text to one another in order to understand the text as a whole.
- Activating and using prior knowledge to interpret text (generating hypotheses about text, predicting text content).
- Relating text content to prior knowledge, especially as part of constructing interpretations of text.
- Reconsidering and/or revising hypotheses about the meaning of text based on text content.
- Reconsidering and/or revising prior knowledge based on text content.
- Attempting to infer information not explicitly stated in text when the information is critical to comprehension of the text.
- Attempting to determine the meaning of words not understood or recognized, especially when a word seems critical to meaning construction.
- Using strategies to remember text (underlining, repetition, making notes, visualizing, summarizing, paraphrasing, self-questioning, etc.).
- Changing reading strategies when comprehension is perceived not to be proceeding smoothly.
- Evaluating the qualities of text, with these evaluations in part affecting whether text has impact on reader's knowledge, attitudes, behavior, and so on.
- Reflecting on and processing text additionally after a part of text has been read or after a reading is completed (reviewing, questioning, summarizing, attempting to interpret, evaluating, considering alternative interpretations and possibly deciding between them, considering how to process the text additionally if there is a feeling it has not been understood as much as it needs to be understood, accepting one's understanding of the text, rejecting one's understanding of a text).
- Carrying on responsive conversation with the author.
- Anticipating or planning for the use of knowledge gained from reading.

Note. From *Verbal protocols of reading: The nature of constructively responsive reading* (p. 105), by M. Pressley and P. Afflerbach, 1995, Hillside, NJ: Erlbaum. Copyright 1995 by Lawrence Erlbaum Associates, Inc. Reprinted with permission.

methods of Pressley and Afflerbach, identifying research studies in reading, psychology, computer literacy, and related fields that examined reading strategies specific to a particular content domain, reading multiple texts and Internet and hypertext reading. Our synthesis of this research yields narrative descriptions of each of the above categories. As well, our synthesis is presented in Tables 4.2 and 4.3. To test the integrity of our meta-analysis and synthesis, we randomly selected research studies, isolated reported reading strategies and assigned them to the strategy categories listed in the two tables. These tests were successful, resulting in our confidence that the tables represent a comprehensive summary of reading in multiple text and Internet/hypertext environments.

Readers' strategies in different content areas and knowledge domains

In spite of our considerable knowledge of individual reading strategies, we can benefit from more detailed understanding of how individual reading strategies are employed in the real-time of a reading event, and how domain knowledge and situational contexts influence reading strategy selection, use and success. Contextual variables that include task, reader ability, time, resources available, and present and anticipated human interactions may influence a reader's choice of reading strategies and relative success in using them. An example comes from research on how readers employ strategies when reading history texts, one area of content-domain reading that has been relatively well-researched (VanSledright, 2002; Wineburg, 1998). General accounts of readers' strategies include identifying and remembering important information in text, monitoring progress and accomplishment while reading and evaluating various aspects of the act of reading (Pressley & Afflerbach, 1995). For example, identifying and remembering important information in text includes using prior knowledge of language, content area and text structure as a filter for focusing on particular parts of text. We do not focus on articles (e.g., "the," "an") when we read a history text, just as we may not focus on a detailed explanation of the Boston Massacre if we believe that we already have an adequate understanding of it. However, history requires of readers special, domain-specific reading strategies that help them read like historians. To read like a historian is to understand the text *and* to construct meaning about when the text was written, who wrote it, and under what circumstances. This latter information, a type of subtext, is used by the historian to render judgments on the trustworthiness and reliability of the text and author. In addition, historians seek to identify text status. Thus, the history readers' strategies may include searching for cues (including archaic vocabulary or syntax, text attribution, or author voice; Afflerbach & VanSledright, 2001) to determine if a text is a primary source text or a secondary source text. And this determination may then be used in developing an understanding of the trustworthiness of the author, the accuracy of the information, and the suitability of the resources used.

Each of the historian's reading strategies relates to a more general characterization. For example, the strategies listed in the above paragraph, such as determining where information comes from and the trustworthiness of the information, fit easily within a category of critical and evaluative reading strategies (Pressley & Afflerbach, 1995). A concern is that these more general characterizations of reading strategy lack explanatory power because they are removed from the contexts and goals of history reading. Nevertheless, we do well to note commonalities of text structure and author approach and the readers' strategies related to them. For example, the historian reads to find cues to determine whether he or she is reading a primary or secondary source text, and then makes a judgment about the accuracy of the author's portrayal, the truthfulness of the claims in relation to the historic record. Readers in science may search texts for evidence that serves to support an author's claim (in the form of scientific explanation) of why the moon looks larger when it is closer to the horizon. The reader who understands what strategies to use to locate a claim in text, to search for evidence that supports the claims and then to render judgment on the suitability of the evidence for supporting the claim may do well not only when reading history and science, but also when reading advertisements, political campaign material and other propaganda. To summarize, the strategies used by readers in particular content domains appear to be a combination of unique strategies with instantiations of more general strategies. Attention to how reading comprehension strategies are used in content domains can inform our ideas about families of strategies that cross content domains and reading tasks, and those iterations of strategy that are particular to specific domain reading.

Reading comprehension strategies for multiple texts

In many reading situations, readers read sets of texts. They do so to compare and contrast author perspectives, to increase the depth and breadth of their knowledge, to write reports or to prepare for exams. How do readers comprehend more than one text and what strategies do they deploy? In relation to this question, research has identified multiple-document reading strategies. Readers of multiple documents are required to solve the problems related to processing not only within a single text, but processing between two or more texts to understand the whole set of documents meaningfully. As Perfetti, Rouet, and Britt (1999) noted, in order for successful reading of multiple documents, readers must use strategies to construct *the document model*, which comes from the interaction between *the situation model* representing situated meaning from the texts and *the intertext model* made of the connections among the different texts as well as any additional information on the source, content, and goal of the texts.

Research exploring multiple-text reading demonstrates that a global understanding (representing intertextual meaning across the different texts) is constructed by linking activities which can be explained as comparing, contrasting, relating, and differentiating information contained in each single text. For example, the strategic connecting processes serve diverse sub-goals for learning from documents. Proficient readers relate the currently read text to previous texts, extract related information by referencing, assemble the different ideas into globally coherent meaning (Hartman, 1995) and continuously elaborate a cross-textual mental model by deploying linking strategies (Wolfe & Goldman, 2005). Effortful strategies to piece together information from each text contribute to the integrated understanding of all texts, and help readers monitor their own comprehension strategies when attempting a particular reading task (Braten & Stromso, 2003; Stromso & Braten, 2002; Stromso, Braten, & Samuelstuen, 2003). Based on the links that they make across different texts, talented readers are able to not only build an argument model of multiple sources and contents, but they also employ the model to judge the usefulness and trustworthiness of the individual documents (Rouet, Britt, Mason, & Perfetti, 1996; Rouet, Favart, Britt, & Perfetti, 1997; Wineburg, 1998). Even some fifth graders can evaluate reliability and validity of texts by employing an event model structured in relation to the historical events described in different texts (Afflerbach & VanSledright, 2001; VanSledright & Kelly, 1998).

Reading multiple documents is the process of "deconstruction *and* reconstruction of links among textual resources" (Hartman, 1995, p. 556), portrayed as a zigzagged weave between one text and other texts or readers' knowledge and text contents (Wineberg, 1998). At the beginning of reading several documents, readers may concentrate on the current, single text whose reading will contribute to an initial, global representation. This representation may be referenced and revised in relation to the constructed meaning of subsequent texts. Accomplished readers can rearrange their reading foci and place increased attention on assembling meaning in different texts, and then attempt to draw a mental bird's eye view reflecting the global meaning structure across the texts as they proceed to the subsequent readings. However, when readers lack prior knowledge and possess insufficient understanding of a previous or current text, they may reserve judgment of text contents and later try to solve the problem in the broad context constructed with intertextual connections (Wineburg, 1998). Consequently, linking strategies during the reading of multiple texts can serve to both revise and enhance meaning construction in a manner related to (and different from) single text comprehension.

Linking strategies are pivotal for understanding multiple texts, and constructively responsive reading strategies contribute to meaning construction, monitoring comprehension, and evaluating texts at the cross-textual level of reading. Based on work that classified reading strategies in broad groups (i.e., identifying and remembering important information, monitoring, evaluating; Pressley & Afflerbach, 1995), Table 4.2 extends that earlier work and contributes new information on reading strategies used with multiple texts.

Table 4.2 Constructively Responsive Reading Comprehension Strategies Used In Reading Multiple Texts[1]

1. Identifying and learning important information
   A. Reading and relating the current text to recently read (prior) texts
   B. Predicting contents of current text based on understanding of previously understood text
   C. Comparing and contrasting the content of the text being read with the content of related texts to develop a coherent account of cross-textual contents
   D. Generating causal inferences by searching for relationships between texts and connecting information from current text with previous text contents
   E. Elaborating with information from current act of reading (of two or more texts) to understand text contents by connecting ideas between texts
   F. Identifying a theme or topic across multiple texts
   G. Attending to an identified theme or topic across two or more texts to organize and remember this information
   H. Organizing related information across texts by using related strategies (e.g., concept mapping, outlining, summarizing)
   I. Activating knowledge acquired in previous readings to augment comprehension of the current text
   J. Noting tentative meaning of texts and searching for information in other texts to reduce the ambiguity in this tentative meaning
   K. Reading sections of different texts recursively, as required to solve problems across multiple texts
   L. Building increased understanding of topic by re-reading the information contained in two or more texts
   M. Using the increased understanding (new insights) to further learn from multiple texts
   N. Taking notes to record information from current text and connect it to related information from previous texts
   O. Focusing on gist information across multiple texts to recursively construct meaning
   P. Rereading and linking text segments that were previously regarded as unrelated to finalize cross-textual meaning structures
   Q. Identifying the unique and shared contributions of information to the constructed meaning of 2 or more texts
2. Monitoring
   A. Managing the local processing in one or multiple texts (e.g., constructing meaning from a paragraph) and the global processing in one or multiple texts (e.g., managing the synthesis of the constructed meaning of the paragraph with all related paragraphs to account for the entire reading)
   B. Detecting a comprehension problem with a particular text and trying to solve the detected problem by searching for clarifying information in other available texts
   C. Changing strategic processing foci from understanding within-text meaning to integrating across-text meaning by utilizing domain knowledge increased due to previous readings, during the sequential readings (i.e., decreasing links to primary endogenous resources and increasing connections to secondary endogenous resources when moving through the passages)

    D. Monitoring comprehension strategies and meaning construction with current text in relation to constructed meanings of other relevant texts

    E. Monitoring degree and nature of comprehension of a current passage by referencing exogenous sources, using knowledge established previously (beyond the current set of documents)

    F. Regulating meaning construction strategies according to original task and goal and revised task and goal

    G. Perceiving that multiple texts related to the same topic can provide diverse views about the topic, complementary information about the topic, or both

    H. Managing meaning construction through understanding that different types of texts can contribute different types of knowledge to that meaning construction (i.e., in history, primary and secondary source texts may make different contributions to the construction of meaning)

    I. Determining that existing content domain knowledge or expertise, including specific strategies and knowledge, can be used when studying multiple texts in a specific domain

3. Evaluating

    A. Using information about the source of each text to evaluate and interpret text contents

    B. Perceiving and distinguishing the characteristics of different texts (e.g., text types, age, author, prose styles) and evaluating texts' accuracy

    C. Perceiving and distinguishing the characteristics of different texts (e.g., text types, age, author, prose styles) and evaluating texts' trustworthiness based on these features

    D. Perceiving and distinguishing the characteristics of different texts (e.g., text types, age, author, prose styles) and evaluating their usefulness for constructing meaning based on these features

    E. Gestalt evaluation of text, employing a variety of criteria, to decide if text is useful in constructing overall meaning from several texts

    F. Critically evaluating validity and reliability of texts by criteria of text contents, author's point of view, and context, using a cumulative representation of a whole document set

    G. Conduct a text to text evaluation using a gestalt impression of each text

    H. Evaluate one text in relation to another, using specific information in each text (e.g., comparing claim and evidence in two or more texts)

    I. Judging usefulness of information provided by a single text in relation to other text

    J. Evaluate contribution of single text to proximal and distal reading and task goals

---

Reading comprehension strategies for Internet and hypertext

Internet and hypertext reading are historically new forms of literacy, forms that are the focus of a considerable amount of research (Castek et al., 2008; Coiro & Dobler, 2007; Yang, 1997). For this aspect of our investigation, we use what we believe to be an inclusive and general definition of hypertext:

> Hypertext is made of blocks of text—in the form of written text, pictures, video and sound, chained together by electronic links. (Rasmussen, 2007)

This definition allows us to combine the work done in both Internet reading situations and other hypertext environments. We believe that hypertext and Internet reading represents a fundamental change in the architecture of acts of reading. With what can be called traditional reading, a reader interacts with a single text, applying strategies and skills with prior knowledge to construct text meaning. This construction of meaning occurs with in a problem space that allows for different single reader-single text interactions, but that is nevertheless bounded by the fact of the single text . Compare this with hypertext and Internet reading in which the same reader will face a series of unknowns related to possible links, possible texts, possible decisions and possible interactions. While readers can apply the strategies that work for traditional forms of reading, in hypertext, the reader-text(s) interactions may be more complex and demanding.

    Hypertext reading presents particular challenges and students with fewer reading strategies (or less well-developed strategies) encounter difficulties when reading in hypermedia environments. For example, searching for and locating information in hypertext challenges many readers' self-regulatory processes (Azevedo, Guthrie, & Seibert, 2004). In fact, a significant proportion of some students' cognitive capacity may be consumed by attempts to not get lost in the complex information structure of the World Wide Web (Eveland & Dunwoody, 2000). Hypertext introduces the need for readers to control uncertainty, as they move from a currently displayed text into a series of unknowns, encountering texts that may be both unhelpful and unnecessary to the task at hand. Further, readers must be strategic in maintaining a focus on the task at hand in a hypertext environment that may often distract.

As readers begin reading in hypertext environments, they must initiate a process that we characterize as realizing and constructing potential texts to read. By this, we mean that the rules of reading change: no longer is there one text, a given, for the reader. The reader must work to identify a series of links and texts that helps the reader move towards the particular goal attainment that is set prior to the commencement of reading. There is the potential for much uncertainty, given the ephemeral nature of reader choice, the degree of preciseness of search engines and strategies, and the universe of possible links to what may be related (or unrelated) texts.

Hypertext has the structure in which information units are multiply networked, and this feature demands readers' strategies for the processing of relationships among information (Alexander, Kulikowich, & Jetton, 1994; Balcytiene, 1999; Eveland & Dunwoody, 2000; Tremayne & Dunwoody, 2001; Yang, 1997; Wenger & Payne, 1996). Wenger and Payne (1996) demonstrated that for the effective learning from hypertext, readers need to attend to deciding and predicting connections that *may* exist between sites and their related information. In effect, inferences are educated guesses about unknowns that can include particular links, texts and solution paths. Readers must be able to anticipate and then contend with the reading space and path represented by hypertexts, and not just their content.

Alexander, Kulikowich, and Jetton's (1994) finding supports that hypertext readers tend to focus on how to access and relate textual information at the level of macroprocessing, in contrast to readers with linear text who attend to the processing of information at the micro-level. That is, during the hypertext reading, comprehenders use diverse linking activities for the construction of global meaning across networked-information in hypertext. Balcytiene (1999) observed that readers who have high metacognitive skills are able to allocate their cognition to construct a global mental model presented in hypertext structure, extracting the entire information and elaborating the mental representation in the relationships among sources. In this aspect, the reading of hypertext and multiple-texts are related in the use of strategies for relating information scattered in a complex reading environment.

While there are related strategies for multiple-document reading and hypertext reading, the latter may require particular metacognitive strategies to control the reading process (Eveland & Dunwoody, 2000; Tremayne & Dunwoody, 2001; Yang, 1997). This is because hypertext structure can have the characteristics of flexibility and complexity, simultaneously. With hypertext, reading text is a given, but *what* text is not. The possible flexibility of hypertext allows for readers to make particular choices on the path to constructing meaning, but this characteristic requires that readers not lose their way in a complex context in which a variety of irrelevant or seductive information may be linked, accessed, and therefore, presented.

Research shows that the product and process of comprehension with hypertext or the Web are influenced by text features, such as the internal information structure (McNamara & Shapiro, 2005; Salmeron, Canas, Kintsch, & Fajardo, 2005; Schwartz, Anderson, Hong, Howard, & McGee, 2004; Shapiro, 1998, 1999) and the visualized functional structure or text format (Chen & Rada, 1996; Dee-Lucas & Larkin, 1995;

Hofman & van Oostendorp, 1999; Lee & Tedder, 2004), as well as interaction of these features with readers' background knowledge or differences of cognitive processing styles (Balcytiene, 1999; Dunser & Jirasko, 2005). The structural uniqueness of hypertext requires specific, probably unique types of reading comprehension strategies when compared with more traditional text reading.

As Alexander et al. (1994) noted, dynamic information-presentation patterns in hypertext impose on readers a two-fold responsibility, which is to construct meaning and reduce the cognitive load. Skilled readers focus on constructing meaning in reading hypertext as long as few comprehension problems are detected. In contrast, as readers perceive a disorientation or that they are running askance of their plan, they allocate the cognitive resources to minimize the risk of hindering their comprehension, and becoming detached from the reading planned originally. In other words, hypertext readers need to draw on strategies for managing the information load to prevent disorientation (Tremayne & Dunwoody, 2001; Yang, 1997). Cognitive strategies for orienting one's self in hypertext reading compete for cognitive capacity that might otherwise be devoted to comprehension of text information (Eveland & Dunwoody, 2000). Skilled readers are able to balance both demands for comprehending and orienting in hypertext. Recently, Leu et al. (2008) examined the strategies of Internet readers and proposed distinct families of strategy: Identifying a question of defining a problem, using the Internet to locate an information resource, critically evaluating information, and integrating information from multiple resources. They also examined the strategies used by readers related to communicating to share responses. Table 4.3 summarizes the constructive reading comprehension strategies used by readers during Internet and hypertext reading.

Table 4.3   Constructively Responsive Reading Comprehension Strategies Used during Internet Hypertext Reading[2, 3]

1. Realizing and constructing potential texts to read
   A. Searching for relevant Web sites or information retrieval systems to access and overview possible target information
   B. Reducing the range of possible information to be encountered by generating key words related to topic and focus of a particular task
   C. Scrutinizing Internet hypertextual links to anticipate and judge the usefulness and significance of the information before accessing it, based on specific reading goals
   D. Exploring and sampling goal-related information in Internet hypertexts at the initial stage of reading to establish a dynamic plan to achieve one's own goal
   E. Predicting utility of a link within Internet text when confronted with more than one hypertext link
   F. Generating inferences about the relevance (or goodness of fit) of at least some of the other links on the pages visited prior to main act of reading
   G. Choosing and sequencing the reading order by accessing links based on the criteria of coherence among links and relevance to situational interests
   H. Conducting complementary searches with modified or revised keywords in order to better clarify suitability of links and potential reading path
2. Identifying and learning important information
   A. Using navigation functions to select, structure, and create environments to assist in constructing text meaning
   B. Using Web site structures to help construct meaning
   C. Using Web site search engines to help construct meaning
   D. Searching in Internet hypertext environments for information related to already established meaning
   E. Linking to additional Internet sites to obtain more information that is related to but beyond the original goal (e.g., linking to Google and then to a listed Google website and then to subsidiary websites while searching for information because the links appear promising)
   F. Using multilayered inferences across the three-dimensional space of Internet hypertext to anticipate meaning of texts that are hidden from view, or to be encountered

(*continued*)

Table 4.3   Continued

G. Retaining information (e.g., cutting and pasting or highlighting important information) using computer and software tools

H. Backlinking and revisiting pages to revise constructed meaning

I. Revising reading goals based on experiences and progress on hypertext path to resolution

J. Combining disparate forms of information to construct meaning, including text, graphics, illustrations, embedded video

3. Monitoring

A. Determining that an aspect of Internet hypertext reading needs attention

B. Determining that an alternative way to navigate Internet hypertext is needed because the current means of navigation is ineffective

C. Changing search engine to navigate Internet hypertext

D. Changing search strategy to navigate Internet hypertext

E. Determining that found Internet sites are not helpful to task or goal

F. Determining that Internet hypertext content is not comprehensible due to form, structure, new information, or combination of these

G. Noting disorientation due to difficulty in locating specific information in Internet hypertext

H. Noting disorientation due to problems using the application functions in Internet hypertext

I. Perceiving meaning construction problems due to diversity of information encountered

J. Perceiving meaning construction problems due to volume of information encountered

K. Perceiving meaning construction problems due to managing information overload

L. Noting problems while searching for information that is expected/anticipated and perceived to be valuable but is not found or available

M. Managing disorientation by increasing memory allocation to solve the problem of disorientation

N. Managing disorientation to refocus on original search plan and goal(s)

O. Realizing that original goal for reading needs revision based on Internet hypertext-reader interaction to current point in reading

4. Evaluating

A. Evaluating the possible paths through Internet hypertext to successful completion of task(s), using standards of breadth and depth

B. Assessing relevance and usefulness of information, in relation to the tentative meaning constructed through the initial and ongoing exploration

C. Assessing credibility of information found in Internet hypertext environment

D. Assessing the clarity of information found in Internet hypertext environment

E. Evaluating the Internet hypertext links that the reader accesses in relation to an imagined or proposed solution path to achieve goals, using an anticipatory "goodness of fit"

F. Assessing relative value of websites and web pages that are determined to have related information

G. Evaluating URL of website to make determination of usefulness, suitability or trustworthiness of information

H. Evaluating entry shorthand (e.g., 10 sites per page listed by Google) to make determination of usefulness, suitability or trustworthiness

I. Evaluating nature, tone or feel of Website and deciding to use (or not use)

J. Evaluating the result of search or move in Internet hypertext

We end this section with the observation that Internet and hypertext readers appear to use strategies that address the considerable task of reducing unknowns as they read. In contrast to more traditional one reader/one text interactions, these readers must work to identify and move through a universe of many possible texts. They must ignore distractions, anticipate and predict meaningful moves with minimal text information. We believe that Internet and hypertext reading include a new generation of reading strategies that clearly reflect the role of the reader in the new architecture of reading.

CONCLUSIONS

Our investigation demonstrates that knowledge of reading strategies in "traditional" reading situations has considerable application to new and more recently researched forms of reading. Thus, our understanding of constructively responsive reading can be regularly revisited and updated. While the evolution of understanding reading strategies continues apace, we acknowledge that there continues the need to conduct research in areas that are underspecified by research. These include reading strategies in particular content domains, reading strategies when reading multiple texts and hypertext reading environments. A synthesis of reading strategy research can help guide this inquiry into "new" literacies. The collection and interpretation of reader strategy data is not without challenges, but ongoing research experiences can provide good models of questions to ask and methodologies best suited to answering the questions. The challenge to describe reading strategies is met, in part, by the methodological tools used to reliably gather data and provide triangulation of information. There are numerous approaches to reading strategy data collection and it is important to consider the unique contributions that particular methodologies can make, as well as combinations of methodologies that can provide rich data sets, strengthen our inferences and bolster our confidence that data are describing true phenomena.

The studies synthesized here provide glimpses of new frontiers in reading and new takes on known constructively responsive reading strategies. Investigations of constructively responsive reading strategies will be well-situated when they reference the existing and considerable catalog of reading strategies for guidance on strategy categorization while simultaneously focusing on the novel or hybrid strategies that new reading situations create. We believe that Table 4.2 and Table 4.3 demonstrate this operational dynamic. Research of reading in new and varied formats provides the opportunity to toggle back and forth between precedent and novelty as we examine strategies.

FUTURE DIRECTIONS FOR RESEARCH ON CONSTRUCTIVELY RESPONSIVE READING COMPREHENSION STRATEGIES

In this chapter we identified three areas in which we expect ongoing, productive research: investigations of reading strategies particular to specific content domains (VanSledright, 2002), the reading strategies used when reading two or more texts (Hartmann, 1995), and the reading strategies involved in navigating and comprehending within hypertext environments (Leu et al., 2008). Each of these areas is worthy of extensive investigation that provides new information and connects results to existing research and knowledge. We also expect that important research will continue to describe the general classes of reading strategy, identifying and remembering important text information, monitoring reading and evaluating reading, as proposed by Pressley and Afflerbach (1995).

Future research on constructively responsive reading strategies should focus on the contextual influences on reading. We have some work in this area, but needed is more comprehensive approach to study of reading strategy use in traditional learning domains, including school content areas, and research in hybrid areas. This will help us examine the legitimacy of claims regarding general reading strategies and those strategies that appear to be unique for certain reader-text(s)-task(s)-context(s) combinations. Also needed is research that describes the extent and orchestration of constructively responsive reading strategies across entire acts of reading. Research that focuses on particular types of strategies such as prediction or summarization can provide valuable information on such strategies. Yet, it may miss the big picture of how accomplished readers coordinate their strategies, or how they negotiate an entire text (or texts) in relation to task demands. Needed is focused work on reading strategies from the start to finish of acts of reading.

A valuable precedent of previous reading strategy research is the attention to translating research on readers' strategies to inform instruction so that developing readers become highly strategic (Kucan & Beck, 1997; Pressley, 2000). The connection between success in life and individual's developed literacies is apparent, and students must be competent at reading complex text, understanding and comparing the content of several texts and comprehending well in hypertext environments. As well, they must learn the special strategies that mark accomplished reading in particular content domains, including history and science.

The literature we reviewed emanates from different traditions and interest groups, including literacy research, cognitive psychology, information systems research, web design research and library sciences research. It is not surprising that these groups are asking related questions and generating important results, but it is perhaps disappointing that so many efforts focused on related topics may not bear the full fruit of labor. We need to work to bring together these literatures, continue the synthesis of the important work from each tradition, building understanding across traditions of inquiry while maintaining the particular perspectives that the efforts represent. Research on constructively responsive reading strategies will help us address the issue of how new "new" literacy strategies are, or whether or not they are novel variations on a theme. This will carry on the strong tradition of conducting research to inform models of reading and thinking.

We are hopeful that the methodological choices made by researchers will reflect the best combination of means for inquiry into reading strategy use. Just as we learn more about strategies, we should learn about the appropriateness of methodology to assist us in answering our research questions.

NOTES

1. Research contributing to this inventory: Afflerbach & VanSledright, (2001); Braten & Stromso (2003); Hartman (1995); Leinhardt & Young (1996); Rouet, Britt, Mason, & Perfetti (1996); Rouet, Favart, Britt, & Perfetti (1997); Stahl, Hynd, Britton, McNish, & Bosquet, D. (1996); Stromso & Braten (2002); Stromso, Braten, & Samuelstuen (2003); VanSledright (2002); VanSledright & Kelly (1998); Wineburg (1991, 1998); Wolfe & Goldman (2005).
2. We note that hypertext and Internet reading often involve more than one text, document or page. Thus, strategies listed in Table 4.2 may be applicable to certain Internet hypertext reading situations.
3. The literature contributing to this inventory: Azevedo et al., (2004); Balcytiene, (1999); Castek et al., (in press); Charney (1987); Coiro (2003); Coiro & Dobler, (2007); Duke, Schmar-Dobler & Zhang (2006); Eveland & Dunwoody (2000); Henry (2005, 2006); Hill & Hannafin (1997); Lacroix (1999); Lawless, Brown, Mills, & Mayall (2003); Leu et al., (2008); Leu, Kinzer, Coiro, & Cammack (2004); McEneany (1998); Protopsaltis and Bouki (2005; 2006); Puntambekar & Stylianou (2005); Ricardo (1998); Rouet (1992); Rouet & Passerault (1999); Salmeron, Kintsch, & Canas (2006); Salmeron, Canas, & Fajardo (2005); Salmeron, Canas, Kintsch, & Fajardo (2005); Schmar (2002); Sutherland-Smith (2002); Tabatabai & Shore (2005); Tosca (2000); Tremayne & Dunwoody (2001); Wenger & Payne (1996); Yang (1997).

REFERENCES

Afflerbach, P. P. (1990). The influence of prior knowledge on expert readers' main idea construction strategies. *Reading Research Quarterly, 25,* 31–46.

Afflerbach, P. (2000). Verbal reports and protocol analysis. In M. Kamil, P. Mosenthal, P. Pearson, & R. Barr (Eds.), *Handbook of reading research* (Vol. 3, pp. 163–179). Mahwah, NJ: Erlbaum.

Afflerbach, P., & Johnston, P. (1984). On the use of verbal reports in reading research. *Journal of Reading Behavior, 16,* 307–322.

Afflerbach, P., Pearson, P., & Paris, S. (in press). How distinctions between reading skills and strategies can improve instruction. *The Reading Teacher.*

Afflerbach, P., & VanSledright, B. (2001). Hath? Doth? What! The challenges middle school students face when reading innovative history text. *Journal of Adolescent and Adult Literacy, 44,* 696–707.

Alexander, P., Kulikowich, J., & Jetton, T. (1994). The role of subject-matter knowledge and interest in the processing of linear and nonlinear texts. *Review of Educational Research, 64,* 201–252.

Azevedo, R., Guthrie, J. T., & Seibert, D. (2004). The role of self-regulated learning in fostering students' conceptual understanding of complex systems with hypermedia. *Journal of Educational Computing Research, 30,* 87–111.

Balcytiene, A. (1999). Exploring individual processes of knowledge construction with hypertext. *Instructional Science, 27,* 303–328.

Braten, I., & Stromso, H. (2003). A longitudinal think-aloud study of spontaneous strategic processing during the reading of multiple expository texts. *Reading and Writing: An Interdisciplinary Journal, 16,* 195–218.

Britt, M. A., & Aglinskas, C. (2002). Improving students' ability to identify and use source information. *Cognition and Instruction, 20,* 485–522.

Brown, A. L. (1980). Metacognitive development and reading. In R. J. Spiro, B. C. Bruce, & W. F. Brewer (Eds.), *Theoretical issues in reading comprehension: Perspectives and cognitive psychology, linguistics, artificial intelligence, and education* (pp. 453–481). Hillsdale, NJ: Erlbaum.

Bruner, J. (1985). Models of the learner. *Educational Researcher, 14,* 5–8.

Butcher, K. R. (2006). Learning from text with diagrams: Promoting mental model development and inference generation. *Journal of Educational Psychology, 98,* 182–197.

Castek, J., Leu, D. J., Jr., Coiro, J., Gort, M., Henry, L. A., & Lima, C. (2008). Developing new literacies among multilingual learners in the elementary grades. In L. Parker (Ed.), *Technology-based learning environments for young English learners: Connections in and out of school.* Mahwah, NJ: Erlbaum.

Charney, D. (1987). Comprehending non-linear text: The role of discourse cues and reading strategies. Paper presented at the Hypertext'87, Chapel Hill, North Carolina.

Chen, C., & Rada, R. (1996). Interacting with hypertext: A meta-analysis of experimental studies. *Human-Computer Interaction, 11,* 125–156.

Coiro, J. (2003). Exploring literacy on the Internet. *The Reading Teacher, 56,* 458–464.

Coiro, J., & Dobler, B. (2007). Exploring the online comprehension strategies used by sixth-grade skilled readers to search for and locate information on the Internet. *Reading Research Quarterly, 42,* 214–257.

Dee-Lucas, D., & Larkin, J. (1995). Learning from electronic texts: Effects of interactive overviews for information access. *Cognition and Instruction, 13,* 431–468.

Dreher, M. & Guthrie, J. (1990). Cognitive processes in textbook chapter search tasks. *Reading Research Quarterly, 25,* 323–339.

Duke, N. K., Schmar-Dobler, E., & Zhang, S. (2006). Comprehension and technology. In M. C. McKenna, L. D. Labbo, R. D. Kieffer, & D. Reinking (Eds.), *International handbook of literacy and technology* (Vol. II). Mahwah, NJ: Erlbaum.

Dunser, A., & Jirasko, M. (2005). Interaction of hypertext forms and global versus sequential learning styles. *Journal of Educational Computing Research, 32,* 79–91.

Ericsson, K., & Simon, H. (1980). Verbal reports as data. *Psychological Review, 87,* 215–253.

Ericsson, K., & Simon, H. (1993). *Protocol analysis: Verbal reports as data.* Cambridge, MA: MIT Press. (Original work published 1984)

Eveland, W., & Dunwoody, S. (2000). Examining information processing on the World Wide Web using think-aloud protocols. *Mediapsychology, 2,* 219–244.

Flavell, J. (1979). Metacognition and cognitive monitoring: A new area of cognitive developmental inquiry. *American Psychologist, 34,* 906–911.

Hartman, D. (1995). Eight readers reading: The intertextual links of proficient readers reading multiple passages. *Reading Research Quarterly, 30,* 520–561.

Henry, L. (2005). Information search strategies on the Internet: A critical component of new literacies. *Webology, 2,* Article 9.

Henry, L. (2006). SEARCHing for an answer: The critical role of new literacies while reading on the Internet. *The Reading Teacher, 59,* 614–627.

Hill, J. R., & Hannafin, M. J. (1997). Cognitive strategies and learning from the World Wide Web. *Educational Technology Research and Development, 45,* 37–64.

Hofer, B. (2004). Epistemological understanding as a metacognitive process: Thinking aloud during online searching. *Educational Psychologist, 39,* 43–55.

Hofman, R., & van Oostendorp, H. (1999). Cognitive effects of a structural overview in a hypertext. *British Journal of Educational Technology, 30*, 129–140.

Huey, E. (1908). *The psychology and pedagogy of reading*. Cambridge, MA: MIT Press.

Hyona, J. (1995). An eye movement analysis of topic-shift effect during repeated reading. *Journal of Experimental Psychology: Learning, Memory, and Cognition, 21*, 1365–1373.

Hyona, J., Lorch, R., & Kaakinen, J. (2002). Individual differences in reading to summarize expository text: Evidence from eye fixation patterns. *Journal of Educational Psychology, 94*, 44–55.

Hyona, J., Lorch, R., & Rinck, M. (2003). Eye movement measures to study global text processing. In J. Hyona, R. Radach, & H. Deubel (Eds.), *The mind's eye: Cognitive and applied aspects of eye movement research* (pp. 313–334), Amsterdam, The Netherlands: Elsevier.

James, W. (1890). *The principles of psychology*. New York: Holt.

Just, M., & Carpenter, P. (1980). A theory of reading: From eye fixations to comprehension. *Psychological Review, 87*, 329–354.

Kaakinen, J., & Hyona, J. (2005). Perspective effects on expository text comprehension: Evidence from think-aloud protocols, eyetracking, and recall. *Discourse Processes, 40*, 239–257.

Kaakinen, J., Hyona, J., & Keenan, J. (2002). Perspective effects on online text processing. *Discourse Processes, 33*, 159–173.

Kamil, M. (2004). The current state of quantitative research. *Reading Research Quarterly, 39*, 100–107.

Kintsch, W. (1998). *Comprehension: A paradigm for cognition*. Cambridge: Cambridge University Press.

Kucan, L., & Beck, I. (1997). Thinking aloud and reading comprehension research: Inquiry, instruction, and social interaction. *Review of Educational Research, 67*, 271–299.

LaBerge, D., & Samuels, S. J. (1974). Toward a theory of automatic information processing in reading. *Cognitive Psychology, 6*, 293–323.

Lacrolx, N. (1999). Macrostructure construction and organization in the processing of multiple text passages. *Instructional Science, 27*, 221–233.

Lawless, K. A., Brown, S. W., Mills, R., & Mayall, H. J. (2003). Knowledge, interest, recall and navigation: A look at hypertext processing. *Journal of Literacy Research, 35*, 911–934.

Lee, M., & Tedder, M. (2004). Introducing expanding hypertext based on working memory capacity and the feeling of disorientation: Tailored communication through effective hypertext design. *Journal of Educational Computing Research, 30*, 171–195.

Leinhardt, G., & Young, K. M. (1996). Tow texts, three readers: Distance and expertise in reading history. *Cognition and Instruction, 14*, 441–486.

Leu, D. J., Kinzer, C. K., Coiro, J. L., & Cammack, D. W. (2004). Toward a theory of new literacies emerging from the Internet and other information and communication technologies. In R. B. Ruddell & N. J. Unrau (Eds.), *Theoretical models and processes of reading* (5th ed., pp. 1570-1613). Newark, DE: International Reading Association.

Leu, D., Zawilinski, L., Castek, J., Banerjee, M., Housand, B., Liu, Y., et al. (2008). What is new about the new literacies of online reading comprehension? In L. S. Rush, A. J. Eakle, & A. Berger (Eds), *Secondary school literacy: What research reveals for classroom practices* (pp. 37–68). Urbana, IL: NCTE/NCRLL.

Lorch, R., & van den Broek, P. (1997). Understanding reading comprehension: Current and future contribution of cognitive science. *Contemporary Educational Psychology, 22*, 213–246.

Magliano, J., & Graesser, A. (1991). A three-pronged method for studying inference generation in literacy text. *Poetics, 20*, 193–232.

McCallister, J. (1930). Reading difficulties in studying content subjects. *Elementary School Journal, 31*, 191–201.

McConkie, G. W. (1997). Eye movement contingent display control: Personal reflections and comments, *Scientific Studies of Reading, 4*, 303–316.

McEneaney, J. E. (2000). Navigational correlates of comprehension in hypertext. Paper presented at the Hypertext 2000, San Antonio, TX.

McNamara, D., & Shapiro, A. (2005). Multimedia and hypermedia solutions for promoting metacognitive engagement, coherence, and learning. *Journal of Educational Computing Research, 33*, 1–29.

Newell, A., & Simon, H. (1972). *Human problem solving*. Englewood Cliffs, NJ: Prentice Hall.

Olshavsky, J. (1976–1977). Reading as problem solving: An investigation of strategies. *Reading Research Quarterly, 12*, 654–674.

Paris, S., & Flukes, J. (2005). Assessing children's metacognition about strategic reading. In S. E. Israel, C. C. Block, K. L. Bauserman, & K. Kinnucan-Welsch (Eds.), *Metacognition in literacy learning: Theory, assessment, instruction, and professional development* (pp. 121–139). Mahwah, NJ: Erlbaum.

Paris, S. G., Lipson, M. Y., & Wixson, K. (1983). Becoming a strategic reader. *Contemporary Educational Psychology, 8*, 293–316.

Paulson, E. (2005). Viewing eye movements during reading through the lens of chaos theory: How reading is like the weather. *Reading Research Quarterly, 40*, 338–358.

Perfetti, C., Rouet, J-F., & Britt, M. (1999). Toward a theory of documents representation. In H. van Oostendorp & S. R. Goldman (Eds.), *The construction of mental representations during reading* (pp. 99–122). Mahwah, NJ: Erlbaum.

Perfetti, C. (1985). *Reading ability*. New York: Oxford Press.

Piekarz, J. (1954). *Individual responses in interpretive responses in reading*. Unpublished doctoral dissertation, University of Chicago.

Pressley, M. (2000). What should comprehension instruction be the instruction of? In M. Kamil, P. Mosenthal, P. D. Pearson, & R. Barr (Eds.), *Handbook of reading research* (Vol 3). Hillsdale, NJ: Erlbaum.

Pressley, M., & Afflerbach, P. (1995). *Verbal protocols of reading: The nature of constructively responsive reading*. Hillsdale, NJ: Erlbaum.

Protopsaltis, A., & Bouki, V. (2005). Towards a hypertext reading/comprehension model. Paper presented at the SIGDOC'05, Coventry, UK.

Protopsaltis, A., & Bouki, V. (2006). The effects of reading goals in hypertext reading. Paper presented at the SIGDOC'06, Myrtle Beach, SC.

Puntambekar, S., & Stylianou, A. (2005). Designing navigation support in hypertext systems based on navigational patterns. *Instructional Science, 33*, 451–481.

Rasmussen, T. (2007). Hypertext reading as practical action-notes on technology, objectivation and knowledge. Retrieved April 15, 2007, from: http://www.w3.org/People/howcome/p/telektronikk-4-93/Rasmussen_T.html

Rayner, K. (1978). Eye movements in reading and information processing. *Psychological Bulletin, 85*, 618–660.

Rayner, K. (1997). Understanding eye movements in reading. *Scientific Studies of Reading, 1*, 317–339.

Rayner, K. (1998). Eye movements in reading and information processing: 20 years of research. *Psychological Bulletin, 124*, 372–422.

Rayner, K., & Sereno, S. (1994). Eye movements in reading: Psycholinguistic studies. In M. A. Gernsbacher (Ed.), *Handbook of psycholinguistics* (pp. 57–81). San Diego, CA: Academic.

Rayner, K., Chace, K., Slattery, T., & Ashby, J. (2006). Eye movements as reflections of comprehension processes in reading. *Scientific Studies of Reading, 10*, 241–255.

Ricardo, F. J. (1998). Stalking the paratext: Speculations on hypertext links as a second order text. Paper presented at the Hypertext'98, Pittsburgh, PA.

Rothkopf, E. Z., & Billington, M. J. (1979). Goal-guided learning from text: Inferring a descriptive processing model from inspection times and eye movements. *Journal of Educational Psychology, 71*, 310–327.

Rouet, J-F. (1992). Cognitive processing of hyperdocuments: When does nonlinear help? Paper presented at the ACM ECHT conference, Milano, Italy.

Rouet, J-F., Britt, M. A., Mason, R. A., & Perfetti, C. A. (1996). Using multiple sources of evidence to reason about history. *Journal of Educational Psychology, 88*, 478–493.

Rouet, J-F., Favart, M., Britt, M., & Perfetti, C. (1997). Studying and using multiple documents in history: Effects of discipline expertise. *Cognition and Instruction, 15*, 85–106.

Rouet, J-F., & Passerault, J-M. (1999). Analyzing learner-hypermedia interaction: An overview of online methods. *Instructional Science, 27*, 201–219.

Salmeron, L., Canas, J. J., & Fajardo, I. (2005). Are experts users always better searchers? Interaction of expertise and semantic grouping in hypertext search tasks. *Behavior & Information Technology, 24*(6), 471–475.

Salmeron, L., Canas, J., Kintsch, W., & Fajardo, I. (2005). Reading strategies and hypertext comprehension. *Discourse Processes, 40*, 171–191.

Schmar, E. S. (2002). A collective case study of reading strategies used by skilled fifth graders reading on the Internet. (Doctoral Dissertation, Kansas State University). *Dissertation Abstracts International, 63*, 4227.

Schwartz, N., Andersen, C., Hong, N., Howard, B., & McGee, S. (2004). The influence of metacognitive skills on learners' memory of information in a hypermedia environment. *Journal of Educational Computing Research, 31*, 77–93.

Segev-Miller, R. (2007). Cognitive processes in discourse synthesis: The case of intertextual processing strategies. In D. Galbraith, M. Torrance, & L. van Waes (Eds.), *Writing and cognition* (4th ed., 231–250). Oxford: Elsevier.

Shapiro, A. (1998). Promoting active learning: The role of system structure in learning from hypertext. *Human-Computer Interaction, 13*, 1–35.

Shapiro, A. (1999). The relevance of hierarchies to learning biology from hypertext. *The Journal of the Learning Sciences, 8*, 215–243.

Slameron, L., Kintsch, W., & Canas, J. J. (2006). Reading strategies and prior knowledge in learning from hypertext. *Memory & Cognition, 34*, 1157–1171.

Snow, C. (2002). *Reading for understanding: Toward a R&D program in reading comprehension.* Santa Monica, CA: RAND Education.

Stahl, S., Hynd, C., Britton, B., McNish, M., & Bosquet, D. (1996). What happens when students read multiple source documents in history? *Reading Research Quarterly, 31*, 430–456.

Stromso, H., & Braten, I. (2002). Norwegian law students' use of multiple sources while reading expository texts. *Reading Research Quarterly, 37*, 208–227.

Stromso, H., Braten, I., & Samuelstuen, M. (2003). Students' strategic use of multiple sources during expository text reading: A longitudinal think-aloud study. *Cognition and Instruction, 21*, 113–147.

Sutherland-Smith, W. (2002). Weaving the literacy Web: Changes in reading from page to screen. *The Reading Teacher, 55*, 662–669.

Tabatabai, D., & Shore, B. M. (2005). How experts and novices search the Web. *Library & Information Science Research, 27*, 222–248.

Thorndike, E. L. (1912). *Education: A first book.* New York: Macmillan.

Thorndike, E. L. (1917). Reading as reasoning: A study of mistakes in paragraph reading. *Journal of Educational Psychology, 8*, 323–332.

Tosca, S. P. (2000). A pragmatics of links. Paper presented at the Hypertext 2000, San Antonio.

Turnbaugh, W. (1975). Toward an explanation of the broadpoint dispersal in eastern North American prehistory. *Journal of Anthropological Research, 31*, 51–68.

Tremayne, M., & Dunwoody, S. (2001). Interactivity, information processing, and learning on the World Wide Web. *Science Communication, 23*, 111–134.

VanDijk, T., & Kintsch, W. (1983). *Strategies for discourse comprehension.* New York: Academic Press.

VanSledright, B. (2002). *In search of America's past: Learning to read history in elementary school.* New York: Teachers College Press.

VanSledright, B., & Kelly, C. (1998). Reading American history: The influence of multiple sources on six fifth graders. *The Elementary School Journal, 98*, 239–265.

Vauras, M., Hyona, J., & Niemi, P. (1992). Comprehending coherent and incoherent text: Evidence from eye movement patterns and recall performance. *Journal of Research in Reading, 15*, 39–54.

Veenman, M. (2005). The assessment of metacognitive skills: What can be learned from multi-method designs? In C. Artelt & B. Moschner (Eds.), *Lernstrategien und metakognition: Implikationen fur forshcung und praxis.* (pp. 77–99). Munster, Germany: Waxmann.

Veenman, M., VanHout-Wolters, B., & Afflerbach, P. (2006). Metacognition and learning: Conceptual and methodological considerations. *Metacognition Learning, 1*, 3–14.

Vygotsky, L. S. (1979). *Mind in society: The development of higher psychological processes.* Cambridge, MA: Harvard University Press.

Watson, J. (1913). Psychology as the behaviorist views it. *Psychological Review, 20*, 158–177.

Watson, J. (1920). Is thinking merely the action of language mechanism? *British Journal of Psychology, 11*, 87–104.

Wenger, M. J., & Payne, D. (1996). Comprehension and retention of nonlinear text: Consideration of working memory and material-appropriate processing. *American Journal of Psychology, 109*, 93–130.

Wineburg, S. S. (1991). Historical problem solving: A study of the cognitive processes used in the evaluation of documentary and pictorial evidence. *Journal of Educational Psychology, 83*, 73–87.

Wineburg, S. (1998). Reading Abraham Lincoln: An expert/expert study in the interpretation of historical texts. *Cognitive Science, 22*, 319–346.

Wolfe, M., & Goldman, S. (2005). Relations between adolescents' text processing and reasoning. *Cognition and Instruction, 23*, 467–502.

Wundt, W. M. (1896–97). *Outlines of psychology* (Charles Hubbard Judd, Trans.). Online extracts maintained by Christopher D. Green. Retrieved on December 10, 2006, from: http://www.hyorku.ca/dept/psych/classics/Wundt/Outlines/

Yang, S. (1997). Information seeking as problem-solving using a qualitative approach to uncover the novice learners' information-seeking processes in a Perseus Hypertext System. *Library & Information Science Research, 19*, 71–92.

Yang, S. (2003). Reconceptualizing think-aloud methodology: Refining the encoding and categorizing techniques via contextualized perspectives. *Computers in Human Behavior, 19*, 95–115.

5 Helping Readers Make Sense of Print
Research that Supports a Whole Language Pedagogy

Kenneth S. Goodman and Yetta M. Goodman

University of Arizona

In our research, over several decades, we have attempted to understand reading as a receptive language process. Our research is based on the assumption that comprehension, the construction of meaning, is the essence of reading and that everything that happens in reading is directed toward comprehension (Flurkey & Xu, 2003; Wilde, 1996).

From early on, we became aware that what was reported in the professional literature as reading research focused on three very different though interdependent phenomena. The first is research on the process of reading. **The question being asked is: how do people make sense of print?** To answer this question our primary research was on miscues readers make in oral reading of whole real texts (K. Goodman & Burke, 1973; K. Goodman & Y. Goodman, 1978). We defined miscues as events in oral reading where the observed response to the text did not match the expected response. More recently, we have used an eye tracking machine to study how the eye is used in making sense of print. With colleagues and former students we developed a combined research, Eye Movement Miscue Analysis (EMMA) which combined eye tracking with oral miscue analysis (Duckett, 2003; Paulson & Freeman, 2003; Paulson, 2007).

The second focus is on how reading is learned. **The question is: how do people learn to make sense of print?** Our research and that of our colleagues and students looked at how beginning readers responded to print awareness and other reading tasks and how their writing developed (Goodman & Martens, 2007).

And the third focus is on how reading is most effectively taught. **The question asked is: how does instruction most effectively support the learning of reading?** In collaboration with teachers, the pedagogy that came to be known as *whole language* developed. This built on the understandings of the reading process and how it is learned and developed a strong instructional focus on supporting developing readers in making sense of whole real texts (K. Goodman, 1986).

These three questions are interdependent. In understanding *how reading is learned* we need to understand *what is being learned*. And in understanding *how best to teach reading* we need to understand *how the process of making sense of print is developed*.

But these very different questions asked in "reading research" are often treated as a single phenomenon without separating teaching from learning from process. And often research that compares methods of teaching reading is nothing more than trial and error with no support in research on how readers make sense of print or how they learn to do so. In fact, assumptions are made about how sense is made of print or how reading is learned with no support in research.

So, we have organized this chapter to focus on each of these three ways of looking at reading. We discuss each separately, but refer to their relationship in our explanation of whole language reading comprehension instruction. We draw on our own research but also build on the research of many others in developing a holistic pedagogy. In the early 1980s we were commissioned by the National Institute of Education to write a position paper (K. Goodman & Y. Goodman, 1981, p. 1). In it we stated:

> Research has demonstrated the universal language learning strength present among people of all backgrounds, including those who already speak two or more languages when they come to school and those whose home dialect is different from the teachers. In the whole-language, comprehension-centered pedagogy, literacy—reading and writing—is regarded as a natural extension of human language development. It is based on developmental psycholinguistic research and on theories of language development, language processes and language learning including research on reading and writing.

In whole language, the role of the teacher and the role of the learner are valued. Learners learn written language in much the way they learn oral language. Teachers organize learning to provide opportunities for students to use their language learning ability and what they have already learned in developing literacy (M. Taylor, 2007).

In whole language research, there are no experiments that reduce the reading process to non reading experiences. Research takes place in homes and schools analyzing individual cases of readers and reading development over time (Whitmore, Martens, Goodman, & Owocki, 2004); it takes into consideration the great variety of written texts that humans use daily in their literacy engagements.

Most of our own research has been in the reading of English, but the theory of reading comprehension we have developed supports a view that there is a universal reading process but a universal that is strongly constrained by the language, the text, the reader and the reading within a culture and across domains. Therefore we have to take into account research in other languages. That includes the Piagetian research of Ferriero and Teberosky (1982), Tolchinsky (2003), and others on reading and writing and literacy development that is linguistically and culturally specific in Spanish, French, Italian, Portuguese, and Hebrew. It also includes miscue research on reading alphabetically written languages, syllabic languages such as Hebrew and Arabic, and ideographic languages including Chinese, Japanese, and Korean (Korean can be written in Chinese characters or in a syllabic orthography unique to Korean) (Brown, K. Goodman, & Marek, 1996; Xu, 1998; Hung, 2000; Wang, 2006).

GUIDING PRINCIPLES

The research on which whole language is based involves some guiding principles that both guide the pedagogy and the interpretation of the research it is based on.

A. *There is no reading without comprehension.* The study of reading is the study of reading comprehension. Learning to read is learning to make sense of written language and teaching reading is supporting the development of comprehension.
B. *Everything necessary to the development of reading comprehension is learned in the process of using written language to make sense.* There are no skills to be learned prior to reading real meaningful texts. Vocabulary is built in the process of reading just as oral vocabulary is learned from oral communication.
C. *Nothing needs to be learned prior to using meaningful authentic texts in instruction.* There is no sequence of skills or sub skills that must be learned prior to reading for comprehension. Reading is learned from whole to part and not part to whole.

D. *Learners need access to authentic written materials appropriate to their language, interests and experiences.* Materials for reading instruction do not need to be built according to controlled phonics rules, word frequency or any other criteria. Written texts must be authentic and comprehensible. Krashen's (2004) hypothesis about comprehensible input applies to written as well as to oral language. Miscue analysis starts with real reading of a real text (not any artificially constructed one).

Miscue analysis and related research have as their underlying paradigm, scientific realism. Unlike the experimental paradigm that relies on statistical probabilities of cause–effect relationships in controlled experiments, scientific realism looks for the underlying structures and processes of any aspect of reality (Flurkey, Paulson, & K. Goodman, 2007). Like other forms of realism, it assumes that the real world exists independent of our experiencing it. Scientific realism has as its goal the construction of models or theories of reality which can explain its structures and processes.

Whole language is based on theory, but the theory is derived through scientific research.

ASPECTS OF A REALIST'S VIEW OF SCIENCE

The task of science is to invent theory   In the case of reading comprehension the purpose of research is to produce an increasingly sophisticated theory of how readers make sense of print.

Science determines structures and processes to explain how entities act, which is always in terms of tendencies and probabilities   The research always involves real acts of reading. The analysis of the miscues that are produced reveals how the structures and processes are involved in the reader making sense of print.

Events are the outcomes of complex causal configurations which sometimes cancel each other out   There is no simple single cause of each act of reading. Rather, in a real context, the language cuing systems are all involved.

Facts are theory-laden   The motto of experimental researchers is, "I only know what I see." The scientific realist says, "I only see what I know." The former confines research to what the researcher experiences. In scientific realism, developing theory is used in analyzing actual reading. So, the facts are rooted in the theory.

Knowledge is a social and historical product   Since meaning is constructed we are always constructing what we know on the basis of what was previously known.

The real world is complex and stratified   Explorations at one level lead to discovery of deeper levels to be explained. The more we understand of reading comprehension the more we realize that there is still more to understand.

These principles apply equally to research on the reading process, on how reading is learned and how best to teach reading.

HOW READERS MAKE SENSE OF PRINT

Early in the 1960s, K. Goodman began to study reading as a language process using principles of linguistics that were developed in the study of oral language (Goodman,

1965). He began using the research techniques of descriptive linguistics developed by Charles Fries (1952) and other linguists. Much of the study of language prior to that time was prescriptive. It was assumed that the role of grammarians was to prescribe how language should be used though even educated people often deviated from the rules the grammarians laid out. Descriptive linguists believed that the role of the linguist was to describe the living language. Grammar, to them, was the system of the language as they found it in use.

K. Goodman had readers read whole real stories of the type they were asked to read in the basal reading programs of the time. He found among his first subjects (a range of first, second, and third graders) that they all produced unexpected oral responses to the text. Research prior to that time had assumed that reading should be accurate and treated these unexpected responses as errors to be eliminated. K. Goodman called these unexpected responses miscues on the premise that they were produced in response to the same linguistic cues that produced expected responses. The miscues provided a window into how the readers were making sense of print.

Over time, miscue analysis drew on the linguistic theories of Noam Chomsky (1957) and the generative transformational linguists and subsequently the functional systemic theories of Michael Halliday (1985) and others. In 1967, K. Goodman published an article titled *Reading: A Psycholinguistic Guessing Game* in which he rejected the common view of reading as accurate sequential word recognition and laid out a theory of reading as meaning construction. A series of funded research studies built a taxonomy of reading miscues which moved beyond the view of reading as a linguistic process to a view of reading as psycholinguistic (K. Goodman, 1969). Studies of readers who spoke several different dialects of English revealed that reading is a socio-psycholinguistic process. Language is both personal and social (K. Goodman & Y. Goodman, 1978).

The research of Jean Piaget (1977) and Lev Vygotsky (Cole, John-Steiner, Scribner, & Souberman, 1978) supported the understanding of how miscues revealed how readers make sense of print. The psycholinguist Tom Bever (in progress) calls this view of constructing meaning "analysis by synthesis" and suggests that it applies equally to making sense of oral language. In oral and written language the brain works in highly related and similar ways to make sense. Recent brain research indicates that human intelligence involves the brain predicting what the senses provide based on memory (Hawkins, 2004). Reading comprehension is therefore an instance of all comprehension. The brain makes use of prior knowledge and experience to comprehend new experiences and to build new strategies for making sense of the world.

Here is a summary of the view of how the reading process works which underlies whole language (K. Goodman, 1996).

Language strata or cuing systems

What K. Goodman called the three cuing systems readers use in making sense of print are what linguist Halliday (1985) calls language strata.

The Signal level is the observable level that includes the phonology, the orthography and the phonic relationships between them in alphabetically written language (K. Goodman, 1993).

The lexico-grammatical level includes both the wording and grammar of the language. The choice of words made in the text depends on the grammar structures and these are dependent on the choice of words.

And the third level is *the semantic or meaning level*. Readers comprehend written language using cues from these three language levels at the same time.

Psycholinguistic strategies

Making sense of print involves a set of psycholinguistic strategies for using information in reading from these three levels.

Sampling and selecting: Readers sample the input the senses provide selecting the most useful input.

Predictions and inferences: This sampling is done on the basis of predictions and inferences the brain makes.

Confirming and disconfirming: In making sense of print, the reader is tentative, using subsequent input to confirm and disconfirm the meaning being constructed. If necessary, corrections are made either by regressing to gather more input or reprocessing the input to make sense.

CYCLES IN READING

Reading is cyclical involving a sequence of cycles.

The visual cycle   The eye is an optical instrument. Light bounces off the page to the reader's eyes but the brain only gets useful visual input as the eye fixates, that is it stops and focuses. Eye movement research has shown that when a fixation occurs only a small area of print, the fovea, an area of about half a dozen letters, is in sharp focus depending on font size. Around that area, is the parafovea where what is seen is fuzzy and beyond that there is a peripheral visual field in which little can be identified other than movement.

The perceptual cycle   What is seen is less important than what we think we see. The brain forms perceptual images by sampling from the visual input on the basis of what it expects to see and the meaning it is constructing. Eye movement studies demonstrate that readers only fixate on about 70% of words and only half as many function words (prepositions, determiners, conjunctions, etc.) are fixated as content words (nouns, verbs, adjectives, and adverbs). During oral reading, the mouth is reporting the text the brain has constructed and often not in the order the eye has sent it to the brain.

The lexico grammatical cycle   As the perceptions are formed, the reader assigns a grammatical pattern and specific wording to construct a sensible text. In miscue analysis this is obvious from the reader's oral intonation patterns which reveal that the reader is predicting a question, a statement, a command, a dependent clause, etc. The choice of words and the form of words are also apparent in this cycle. For example tense, person, number and syntax etc. determine word form.

The semantic cycle   Since the goal of reading is always comprehension, once the meaning is constructed the reader has a sense that all the available information has been used even though the eye movements make clear that it has not and in fact the information used is not processed sequentially. So, reading involves a sequence of cycles from visual to perceptual to lexicogrammatical and to meaning. Each cycle follows but also precedes the others as the reader progresses through the text, always with the brain's goal of making sense.

To illustrate how miscues reveal readers' meaning construction, Figure 5.1 shows one sentence out of the reading of *Little Brown Hen* by a fourth-grade African American nine-year-old in rural Mississippi (Flurkey, Paulson, & K. Goodman, 2007). She made three miscues.

```
Mr.                    his
Mrs. Johnson opened the screen door, smoothing


                                        $axt
her blue apron, "How are you? Willie" she asked.
```

Miscue: Reader says Mr. where text says Mrs.

Miscue: Reader says his where text says the

Miscue: Reader says $axt where text says asked.

Figure 5.1 Miscues in one sentence.

The first miscue is her substitution of Mr. for Mrs. Mr. and Mrs. have letters in common. An unusual historical language convention has resulted in the written forms being an abbreviation of the oral forms, Mister and Missus, so they violate spelling conventions. But Mr. and Mrs. have sounds in common. Both are titles of respect to be used in proper names of people so they fit both the syntax of the sentence and the semantic requirement of using such a title before a last name. Furthermore, in the southern community of this reader, Willie, a child character in the story, would be quite likely to use such a polite form in addressing an adult. Such social constraints are part of the pragmatics of language. To summarize, Mr. and Mrs. look similar, sound similar, share semantic features, have the same syntactic function and fit the culture of the community.

However, substituting Mr. for Mrs. does change the meaning of the text. Mr. Johnson has already appeared in the story and Mrs. Johnson has not, so it is likely that the miscue is influenced by the reader's prior knowledge and expectations. That hunch is supported by the miscue which follows. Having read Mr. Johnson, the reader substitutes *his* for *the*. What the reader has done is attributed the door to Mr. Johnson. This substitution of the possessive pronoun is a common miscue. In English, definite nouns require the determiner *the*. But possessives subsume that function. However the shift to *his* creates an inconsistency since the possessive in the next noun phrase *her blue apron* is feminine. This is a point where the reader might have corrected but she didn't, at least not overtly.

The final miscue, *$axt* for *asked*, is marked with a dollar sign indicating we're spelling it the way the reader said it. This is not really a miscue. She read the word *asked* the way she and other members of her dialect community say the word.

Several aspects of miscue analysis are illustrated in this short sequence. We start from the premise that the reader is transacting with the text. Miscues, like expected responses result from that transaction. Each miscue is not random but is the result of complex causal configurations in the text, in the reader and in the transactions of the reader with the text. We cannot know exactly why a single miscue occurs but we can consider the tendencies and probabilities that are revealed in the patterns of such miscues and come up with probable explanations for the miscues. At the same time, what we have learned from miscue analysis entitles us to reject alternative explanations: that any of these miscues are random or the result of careless reading, that saying *$axt* for *asked* affects the comprehension of the story and that miscues indicate ineffective reading. All these miscues show a reader actively engaged in meaning construction.

Effective reading is successful comprehension. Efficient reading is comprehending with the minimum of input, effort, and energy. So, reading is a guessing game in which meaning is constructed using cues from the text and efficient and effective strategies through the cycles from vision to meaning. In fact, the reader is not making sense of the printed text directly. The reader is constructing a text parallel to the printed text and it is that text which is comprehended or understood by the reader.

ACCURACY, AMBIGUITY, AND REDUNDANCY IN LANGUAGE

It has always been puzzling to linguists that language is both ambiguous and redundant at all levels. To those who have not studied language in depth, it seems logical that language should be precise and that readers and listeners must be accurate for language to work. Yet, no two speakers sound alike, and, in fact, language would be impossible if it required all speakers to sound the same. Obviously, there are limits on how much our speech can vary before the difference would cause problems. On the other hand, being exact is at least as much of a problem. Language is also always changing. It has to change or it would be unable to express new ideas and new experiences. Dialects grow apart, new registers develop to deal with new areas of knowledge. And personal meanings always influence each person's interpretation of a text.

Every language has words that sound the same but mean different things and words that sound different but mean the same thing. Grammatical rules are necessary for users of the language to share meanings but the rules are never perfect or exact.

What makes language work at all is that human beings have a set for ambiguity. We can tolerate the ambiguities in language and still comprehend. One major reason is that language is also redundant—it usually provides more than one cue to the meaning. In a sentence like *The boys ate their lunches,* for example, there are several cues that the subject is plural. Information from the three cuing system creates a context that not only resolves much of the ambiguity but usually makes the reader unaware that there was any ambiguity.

No writing system fully represents the sound features of oral language in its written form. In Hebrew and Arabic vowels are only minimally represented in print. That means that much of the grammar is also not directly represented since much of it depends on vowel affixes. But the syntax disambiguates what looks visually the same.

A single Chinese character may represent many different words with different meanings and/or sounds. Conversely several different characters may represent the same sound or meaning. The context disambiguates the meaning. The system works and has for centuries.

Simply speaking both oral and written language are constructive processes. Meaning is not built letter by letter, word by word, and character by character. Speakers and writers construct texts which more or less represent meaning. Readers and writers construct meaningful texts parallel to the speaker's or writer's text. And comprehension is always relative. There may be a high degree of agreement between the reader and the writer on the meaning or not depending on what each brings to the transactions. No matter how skillfully a writer constructs a text or how well the writer knows the readers, there are always differences in what is understood. And, no matter how skillfully the reader reads, there are always misunderstandings.

HOW READING IS LEARNED

If reading is making sense of written language, then learning to read is learning to make sense of written language. Whole language pedagogy is based in constructivist views of learning (Bruner, 1966; Piaget, 1977; Cole, John-Steiner, Scribner, &

Souberman, 1978; Ferriero & Teberosky, 1982). In these views, humans construct their own knowledge. Their personal literacy constructions are highly influenced by conventions about literacy held by the people in the communities most closely associated with the learners. Learning is both social and personal. Learners construct their own knowledge. Teaching can support or disrupt learners in their meaning construction but there is no simple one to one correspondence between what teachers teach and what students learn.

Researchers interested in the learning of young children began to carefully observe, in depth, behaviors of young children in order to understand what writing concepts children were developing about their world (Burrows, 1959). Early childhood researchers were learning to carefully document young children's knowledge construction about literacy in a range of social contexts. In the 1970 and 1980s, researchers were reporting the novel constructions of young children's individual responses to print as well as their responses to literacy events in social settings in homes and school contexts (Read, 1971; Clay, 1975; Ferriero & Teberosky, 1982; Harste, Woodward, & Burke, 1984; Teale & Sulzby, 1986). Yetta Goodman popularized the term *kid-watching* to describe this type of depth analysis of children's behavior within classroom contexts (Owocki & Y. Goodman, 2002; Wilde, 1996).

The developing constructions of young children do not match adult concepts of literacy but show clearly that children are building their knowledge from their experiences with reading and writing in their world. One such example is three- and four- year-olds beliefs that word length should be proportional to the size of objects in the environment (Ferriero & Teberosky, 1982). The word for a rooster should be longer than the word for a hen and chick should have only a few letters. The children talk about their concepts of written language by showing their developing awareness of the phonological, orthographic, and font systems of their language.

Emilia Ferreiro (2003) expresses the excitement of early literacy researchers during the last century.

> These children, four to six years old, helped us to argue that reading was not equivalent to decoding, that to be literate was not the same as "knowing the alphabet," that cognitive difficulties with understanding a particular way of representing language (writing) had nothing to do with difficulties acquiring one or another technology of writing. These children, four to six years old, obliged us researchers to assign new meaning to the relationship between writing and language, to apply all levels of linguistic analysis in order to understand reading behavior... (p. 52)

> ... Once upon a time there was a child, who was accompanied by an adult, and the adult had a book and the adult read. And the child, fascinated, listened to how oral language became written language. Fascinated precisely with how something known turned into something unknown, which is the perfect place for taking up the challenge of knowing and growing. (p. 56)

Early literacy researchers studied children's literacy development as they held books, responded to print in their environment, transacted with print with teachers, parents, siblings, and other adults in their communities, composed texts, retold narratives, played at literacy, and talked and thought about how literacy worked. The analyses of their writing and reading productions and oral responses to the literacy events in which they participated provide a rich array of knowledge about how children learn about literacy in their own language. This large body of research continues to grow and informs whole language teachers and researchers about what happens during and as a result of engaging in human literacy practices in different settings, with different literacy artifacts, with people of different ages and abilities (Gregory, Long, & Volk, 2004; Whitmore et al., 2004; Y. Goodman, & Martens, 2007).

Following young readers' and writers' changes longitudinally provides evidence of children's literacy development. Writing research, for example, not only shows changes in children's invented spellings but demonstrates how children develop knowledge about character development, use dialogue, and develop themes in their compositions. They show how children reflect their cultural communities as they participate in writing communities (Dyson, 2003). And it is obvious from the earliest interactions that children know that the functions of producing and receiving literacy events always involves comprehension and serves purposes important to their lives. As literacy events make sense, children become curious about how they make sense and invent ways to do so as they move toward the literacy conventions of society. A key aspect of reading development and learning is this tension between *individual invention* and *social convention.*

Halliday states that as people use language they are engaged in learning language, learning through language and learning about language. Language learning in Halliday's view is learning how to mean- to express meaning comprehensibly and to comprehend what others are saying (Halliday, 2003a).

One of the major principles and conclusions that result from research on young children is that children learn to read by reading and learn to write by writing. It is, as Dewey said, learning by doing. In summary, these are the key concepts on how literacy develops that are foundational to whole language instruction:

A. Written language is learned in the same way and for the same reasons as oral language: to construct meaning—to comprehend.
B. Reading and writing are learned best in the context of their use for real purposes.
C. Young children become aware of and respond early to print in their environment. They observe how written language is used in their homes and communities and begin to play at these social uses.
D. Children invent written language and move toward the conventions of the written language in use around them.
E. Young learners use what they have learned in oral language development in their literacy development.

RESEARCH ABOUT READING INSTRUCTION THAT FOCUSES ON WHOLE LANGUAGE COMPREHENSION

John Dewey (1915) advised teachers to start where the learners are. So, whole language teachers are aware that their pupils already make sense of oral language and that many have begun to make sense of print as well. Whole language theorists take into consideration Dewey's concept of curriculum that includes all the experiences in which the students are learning by doing, engaged in inquiry and involved in self-reflection.

To "start where they are" teachers who have a whole language philosophy often engage in their own classroom research. They are skillful kid-watchers informed and knowledgeable about teaching, learning, curriculum, language (including literacy), and the social community. They know the research on how reading works and how it is learned. While the learners are focused on using language for a variety of purposes and functions to solve problems and to learn, whole language teachers are monitoring and documenting oral and written language development. Teachers analyze literacy artifacts and activities as the students are actively exploring and learning. Teachers use the results of their kid-watching to direct learners' attention to aspects of language in the contexts of their authentic use and to plan for maximum literacy development in their students. Therefore, whole language is not simply a method of teaching reading (and writing) but the use of holistic principles to develop a curriculum that engages students in a wide range of learning.

Whole language teachers see reading as one of the key tools needed to participate in a language-centered curriculum. In this sense, reading and writing development are incidental to the curriculum but central to learning. Reading and writing are mediators through which learning occurs (Y. Goodman & K. Goodman, 1992). A whole language view of instruction is supported by Paolo Freire's view that humans read the world and the word (Freire & Macedo, 1987). Therefore to explore reading comprehension in a whole language classroom, it is necessary to seriously consider what we know about the role of classroom organization, the role of the teachers, the uses of language across the curriculum as well as the specific lessons planned for teaching about language.

Organizing the classroom: Immersion in whole language

We use the terms "holistic learning" and "whole language" synonymously. We believe that many programs that use terms such as balanced or integrated instruction include principles that are whole language in nature. The notion disseminated by some detractors that whole language teachers do not directly teach aspects of language such as phonics, spelling, vocabulary or grammar is a myth. There is always a double agenda in whole language classrooms. The class is organized so that while learners are immersed in using language to solve problems and ask new questions, teachers are monitoring oral and written language development as students actively participate in science, social studies, math, art, music, and other learning experiences.

Holistic literacy instruction begins where it ends, with whole language (reading, writing, speaking, and listening) in all its varieties: mundane, useful, relevant, interesting, social, personal, and functional. It involves symbol systems that interrelate with written language—technology, drama, music, art, oral language and the structures of reading and writing specific to math, science and the social sciences. Opportunities to use and work within these systems and materials have comprehension or meaning making as a central goal.

Whole language teachers use real and authentic literacy materials. Fiction and non-fiction is available in school and classroom libraries. Materials are easily accessible so that students have planned and spontaneous opportunities to compose and construct meaning through reading and writing. Organizing materials for accessibility is part of the curriculum as students alphabetize, categorize, label, and develop criteria for use, and care of texts. Print in the classroom involves captions, labels and naming that serves real purposes. There are places to listen to books on tapes, to compose by hand or on computers, to participate in computer games and gather information, and to play at reading and writing. Students come to know themselves as literate members of a learning community immersed in an environment they helped to organize that is dripping with print. Frank Smith (1987) calls this inviting learners to join the literacy club.

There are changes in materials and classroom spaces on a regular basis to relate to changes in students' interests: the focus is on the knowledge they are exploring, the places they need to learn and the objectives of the curriculum. Teachers group students in a variety of ways to provide interactions that promote comprehension. Small group discussions, buddy reading, listening to teachers and others read aloud help students comprehend and build comprehension strategies. Reading is both personal and social and whole language instruction is organized to provide opportunities to read alone and with others and to discuss and share their understanding of their reading and writing (Mooney, 1990).

At all levels, whole language teachers shape the classroom organization to be compatible with students' interests and development and to fit the content to be taught. Students participate in these changes as they are involved in organizing study projects, theme cycles, displays, art galleries, bulletin boards, libraries and work spaces. They set up and use technology appropriate to their learning. The variety of reading and writing contexts and learning opportunities result in students who continue to build flexibility in their comprehension of multiple texts.

The role of the knowledgeable and experienced teacher

There has been a tendency for university reading researchers to look at the relationship between researcher and teacher as a one way street: researchers study how reading is or should be taught and tell teachers what to do in their classrooms as a result of their findings. In this view, teachers are considered *only* consumers of research.

In a whole language perspective, the relationship between researchers and teachers is reciprocal. Teachers are considered knowledgeable and their professional experiences and judgments are valued and used to inform the work of university researchers and other teacher educators. Experienced whole language teachers are consciously aware of their research capabilities. They understand that careful observation and documentation of what their children do in their classrooms is research that informs their curriculum development.

Organizing the classroom to engage students in learning builds an environment in which reading comprehension is expected. During the 1980s and 1990s as whole language was being discussed seriously in schools and professional organizations, classroom teachers authored books and articles describing their research in their own classrooms through their teacher lens. Although these carefully documented descriptions focused on the learning, teaching, and curriculum experiences in their classrooms, the teaching of literacy was often a rich part of the classroom description. Comprehension of oral and written language was highlighted as the authors described the conditions of learning (Cambourne, 1993, 2003) in their classrooms. Their focus was on the discourse used, the ideas their students explored and the experiences they had as they provided classroom discussions, small group and individual conversations, responses to literature and content and explained the samples of students' writing that demonstrated their students' development as reader and writers. Because whole language teachers know their students well, there are in depth descriptions of students in these classrooms and the help they received based on written assessments that built on their strengths and supported their needs (D. Taylor, 1993).

These classroom narratives tell the stories of the multiple learning pathways teachers provide as they encourage inquiry, self-reflection and active participation. The classroom stories specify the learning that takes place in the classroom for a range of student with diverse abilities. The teachers describe how they help students build confidence in their own capabilities as students and learn math, social studies, and science in theme cycles in a community of learners. They describe the ways in which author's chairs, reading and writing workshops and conferences and children's and adolescent literature are incorporated into daily classroom experiences. The portraits provide insights into the abilities of whole language teachers to organize their classrooms to participate in ongoing assessment through thoughtful interactions, careful observations and analyses of students' works. We reference a few of the teachers who write about their classrooms to represent a range of ages and proficiencies of their students. Many of these books continue to be used in teacher education courses and are bought by teachers. Some have recently been rewritten and updated (Atwell, 1998; Avery, 2002; Barbieri, 1995;

Christensen, 2000; Cole, 2003; Fisher, 1998; D. Goodman, 1999; Harvey & Goudois, 2007; Harwayne, 2001).

In addition to teacher researchers in the classroom, a range of university researchers, doctoral students and teacher educators collaborate with teachers to do research as a team in their classrooms (Michalove, Allen, & Shockley, 1993; Casey, 1997; Clyde, Barber, Hogue, & Wasz, 2006; Graves, 1983; Kucer, Silva, & Delgado-Larocco, 1995; Moll, Amanti, Neff, & Gonzalez, 1992; Short, Harste, & Burke, 1996; Short & Pierce, 1990; Whitmore & Crowell, 1994. Publishers such as Stenhouse, Heinemann, and Richard C. Owen continue to support classroom and teacher research publications because of their use by teachers, teacher education programs and literacy researchers to inform classroom practices.

There are also researchers, critical of whole language, who collaborate with teachers and work directly in classrooms. Their conclusions also reveal the importance of authentic literacy experiences in student's motivation and learning. They describe characteristics of teaching practices that are not in conflict with conclusions by whole language teacher researchers. Pressley and colleagues, for example, report that successful literacy teachers engage their students in reading authentic materials, writing meaningful compositions and letters, and involve their students in integrating their content studies with literacy experiences (Pressle, Warton-McDonald, Mistretta-Hampston, & Echevarria 1998). Bogner, Raphael, and Pressley (2002) conclude that "Literacy is blended with content learning virtually all day" (p. 162).

These works on classroom research are often not considered in the discussion of research on comprehension because those who report such studies tend to see the teaching of reading and the development of comprehension as separate from ongoing and daily classroom engagements. A careful meta-analysis of the rich literature by teacher researchers and their university collaborators would yield important information to help literacy professionals understand the role of the teacher in the overall curriculum on the development of reading comprehension. The field would also benefit from additional rich descriptions of reports of the development of reading (and writing) in classroom settings during authentic learning experiences.

Studies by Linda Darling-Hammond (2006) make clear that the quality of teachers is key to student achievement. For many political reasons such research on teachers has been ignored in discussions of what is effective reading instruction yet the conclusions are quite clear that the role of knowledgeable and experienced teachers is of prime importance to reading achievement.

KNOWING READERS (AND WRITERS): KID-WATCHING AND ONGOING EVALUATION

Teachers use their knowledge about the readers and writers in classrooms to motivate them as they carefully observe what engages students in learning and what is easy or challenging to them. Research on young children's writing has provided a range of new insights about how children learn to use written language (Burrows, 1959; Dyson, 1989, 2003; Clay, 1975; Ferriero & Teberosky, 1982; Tolchinsky, 2003). The careful analysis of the writing of older students in classrooms is also part of this research base (Romano, 1987; Rief, 1991).

Miscue analysis, originally a research tool, has become an important tool for teaching and evaluating readers' comprehension. The most important role that miscue analysis plays for the classroom teacher and literacy instruction is insight into the strengths and needs of their students (Y. Goodman & K. Goodman, 2004). Teachers report that once they have completed miscue analysis on only a few of their students, they listen to their students' reading with new understandings.

A wide range of miscue analysis studies that began in 1963 and continue to this day involve close observation of readers by analyzing the relationship between what is printed in the text and what a reader reads orally and is able to retell following the reading (Brown, K. Goodman, & Marek, 1996). Miscue analysis is qualitative and quantitative. It analyzes a single oral reading of a complete story or article which yields numbers and percentages and provides a micro-analysis of a reader's response to a text (both reading and retelling).

The degree to which miscues result in sentences that are semantically or syntactically acceptable results in a comprehending score. Comprehending reveals the readers' concerns for understanding the text during the reading itself. Percentages also show the degree to which reader's miscues look or sound like the expected response providing insight into the readers' knowledge of phonics and orthography. The rate of a reader's reading and the number of miscues per 100 words are also quantitative and the retelling provides a score that shows what the reader chooses to tell about what he/she has read following the reading (Y. Goodman, Watson, & Burke, 2005).

Miscues are also examined for their qualitative changes to the text. Miscues are considered high quality when they support the meaning of the text with synonym substitutions, omissions of redundant words or phrases, insertions of words and shifts of intonation patterns that enhance the text's meaning. When readers correct miscues that disrupt meaning, it is evidence that they are monitoring their reading in order to make sense. Teachers competent in miscue analysis make use of the quantitative and qualitative analysis to develop reading strategy lessons for students (see below). They also develop sessions that involve students in evaluating and becoming consciously aware of their own miscues to understand the role of miscues in comprehension. This conversation with readers is called retrospective miscue analysis (RMA) and results in readers revaluing themselves (see below).

With knowledge about miscue analysis, teachers engage students in over the shoulder miscues (Davenport, 2002; Flurkey, 2007). These are direct teaching strategies that involve students as they read individually or in small groups to talk and think about the language cueing systems and their reading strategies. These are critical teaching moments during which teachers focus readers on comprehension. A teacher with a background in miscue analysis uses a variety of evaluative techniques ranging from making mental or quickly written notes as a learner reads orally to analyzing a complete reading as described in the Reading Miscue Inventory (Y. Goodman, Watson, & Burke, 2005). Through miscue analysis, teachers discover a variety of miscue patterns such as students who are able to read with few miscues but do not fully comprehend what they have read in contrast to readers who have many miscues but understand the text very well. Such information provides teachers with information to plan specific reading strategy instruction (see below).

Miscue studies have been done with readers who speak different languages and dialects, and with readers who represent a range of proficiencies, grade levels, ages, and background knowledge (Brown, K. Goodman, & Marek, 1996).

In the last 10 years, miscue analysis research has been combined with eye movement studies to discover how eye movements relate to miscues (Paulson, 2007). This combined research methodology has supported conclusions of miscue analysis and also extended our knowledge about the reading process especially in relation to readers' perceptions. One example is learning that the eye is ahead of the mouth during oral reading. This suggests that teachers need to be careful when they ask readers to attend to specific letters or words as they read. The reader's eye may be fixating at the end of a sentence while they are orally reading a phrase closer to the beginning of the sentence. The students may as a result be confused about what words or letters the teacher is asking them to attend.

The following conclusions from miscue analysis and eye movement research are especially relevant for teachers as they plan comprehension instruction.

A. Comprehension is central to the reading process.
B. Accuracy in reading is not necessary for comprehension.
C. All readers make miscues.
D. Readers do not process meaningful text letter by letter, word by word, or character by character.
E. The brain directs the eye and the mouth to do different but related activities during reading.
F. Prediction and confirmation are strategies employed by readers to comprehend text.
G. Syntactic, semantic, and graphophonic knowledge are used by readers selectively and simultaneously to comprehend text.
H. Proficient readers are more flexible in their use of language knowledge and reading strategies than less proficient readers.

Whole language teachers help less proficient readers to understand that all readers struggle with texts to varying degrees especially when they are unfamiliar with the content and help them understand that the more they read the more flexible they will become. Teachers can minimize methods that focus struggling readers to use narrow strategies of sounding out and reading word by word. They help readers avoid becoming instructional dependent personalities, caught up in the mechanical use of what they've been taught to do rather than focusing on making sense.

Building on miscue research, whole language teachers encourage lots of reading, help readers understand the role of predicting, self-correcting, and informed guessing, and plan for opportunities for oral discussions and writing as part of literacy discussion. They help proficient readers to expand on their developing reading abilities by encouraging them to choose to read more varied and challenging texts.

In addition to knowing the specific reading and writing behaviors of their students, whole language teachers seek to know their students' homes and communities. They use the funds of knowledge they learn about, to support curriculum development and to develop learning experiences that connect to their students' lives and to bring parents into a home-school collaboration that benefits students' learning (Moll, Amanti, Neff, & Gonzalez, 1992). Teachers use the understandings they develop about their students' backgrounds and their meaning making processes through their kid-watching to develop a rich literacy curriculum always with the focus on comprehension (Owocki & Y. Goodman, 2002).

LANGUAGE ACROSS THE CURRICULUM: READING, WRITING, AND ORAL LANGUAGE

Whole language teachers develop curriculum *with their students* who are part of deciding what they want to learn based on examining what they already know and the questions they have. Commercial text books may be used selectively to support the curriculum but such programs do not control it.

Dewey's notion that education "is a process of living not a preparation for future living" (Dewey, 1897, p. 78) is a central theoretical construct. Teachers don't spend classroom time getting kids ready to read, they immerse them in real reading experiences. The teachers make sure they achieve the goals of state and district guidelines. But the real curriculum is shaped by the students' questions and their problem posing (Harste, Short, & Burke, 1995). These ideas go back to the curricular studies of Hilda Taba (1962) and John Dewey (1915) and have been researched for well over a century. When teachers engage learners in curriculum, they support literacy learning.

Language is learned most easily when it is relevant, functional, useful, interesting, and valued within the cultural community of the learner—both the home and the school. Such learning is self-motivating and therefore whole language is sensitive to assuring that the texts which are being used in instruction meet these criteria. The curriculum builds on and accepts differences in language and culture. Books and other literacy artifacts in the various languages and dialects are part of libraries and displays in the schools and classrooms. A wide range of materials reflects an understanding of individual differences that values the diversity in students' interests, questions, and backgrounds. Whole language teachers are always ready for the student who doesn't want to read Harry Potter.

LOTS TO READ PROMOTES READING COMPREHENSION

Whole language educators believe that people learn to read by reading. So, there is a lot to read in whole language classrooms. And reading opportunities are embedded in a range of writing opportunities. Krashen (1988, 2004) researched the role of library use and participation in lots of reading that support his comprehensible input hypothesis: that people learn to read by reading. Elley (1991, 1998), building on the New Zealand concept of the importance of lots of self-selected reading of authentic books, developed a book flood concept that resulted in English reading achievement with second language learners in developing South Pacific nations.

The characteristics of authentic materials include real and functional language. Their focus is on knowledge and enjoyment in a range of literacy genres. Materials in books, newspapers, magazines, computers, iPods, etc. often include unusual but naturally occurring features or complex syntax. Encouraging students to struggle with new and unfamiliar texts helps readers develop flexible use of their reading strategies and language cuing systems. On the other hand, much of the material is familiar and predictable. Reading materials are hard or easy depending on how predictable and familiar they are for individual readers.

Margaret Meek (1988) demonstrated that texts themselves teach. As readers transact with texts, the texts become mediators that build and expand readers' comprehension. Readers learn about the structure of the text, the grammar of the language and the ideas, vocabulary and meanings and authors' styles in different ways from different texts. Miscue research shows clearly that readers learn to treat texts differently based on their grammatical structure and content. Readers develop concepts of the phrases and words in a text based on the richness of the text in the context of the whole.

Students' flexibility in their writing and reading are supported by opportunities for self-selection of materials based on their interests and questions. The importance of the role of the text in developing comprehension, suggests that teachers must know a great deal about children's and adolescent literature to help students select materials that are easy for them to read but also to explore more challenging materials to extend reader's flexibility.

READER RESPONSE AND LITERATURE DISCUSSIONS PROMOTE READING COMPREHENSION

The role of talking and thinking by students about language, literature, and learning is another important aspect of whole language environments. There has been a wide body of research that focuses on reading comprehension based on analysis of classroom conversations, literature discussions and readers' responses to texts they read. These studies show how comprehension is mediated by the text and context of literacy events. Growth in oral language, grammatical and vocabulary development are a result of these discussions. Often this research has a basis in anthropological or sociolinguistic research which seeks to understand how readers make sense of a printed text and the context in which it exists. The New Literacies researchers in Europe have looked at literacy practices outside of school as well as in school to see how different kinds of literacy are used and comprehended (Street, 2005).

Nystrand (2006) provides an overview of how classroom discourse influences and promotes reading comprehension. His analysis of classroom discourse focuses on reciprocal teaching, transactional strategy instruction, questioning the author and elaborative interrogation involving students in making connections to their own experiences and knowledge development. These studies explore the language that teachers and students use that influences the development of comprehension.

Whole language teachers have always used the power of classroom discussions throughout the curriculum. They make use of the research on classroom discourse to consider ways to interact with their students to highlight comprehension. And they are aware of the importance of organizing classrooms so such discussions are central to reading instruction and take place regularly. VanDeWeghe (2007) states: "...teachers who lead learners in a discussion of a text are teaching reading: they help students to make sense of literary (and nonliterary) texts, they invite students to deepen their understanding of literature, and they challenge or refine students' interpretations—all with the effect of improving achievement in reading comprehension" (p. 86).

There is also a rich body of research on literature discussions in response to reading self-selected children's literature (Martinez-Roldan, 2003; Peterson & Eeds, 2007; Short & Pierce, 1990). Much of the research takes place with narrative although there is growing research involving texts that focus on thematic explorations in different subject matter areas. Talking about books provides students with language to use as they explore their own responses to what they read.

WRITING AND OTHER MEDIA PROMOTE READING COMPREHENSION

In addition to encouraging reading a range of genre and content written for children and adolescents, whole language teachers plan for continuous opportunities for students to compose through writing. Readers and writers learn to write by writing (Smith, 1982). They produce books, magazines, and newsletters. They write letters to pen pals and organize post offices in their schools. They develop Web sites and computer programs. And all of this writing involves reading and talk.

READING AND WRITING AS RECIPROCAL AND SUPPORTIVE PROCESSES

Reading provides writing models and writing provides models for reading. Years of research on the writing process extends this notion (Dyson, 1989, 2003; Graves, 1983;

Smith, 1982). As a result, whole language curriculum includes all kinds of writing. Because of the reciprocal and symbiotic relations between reading and writing, the term "literacy programs" or "literacy curriculum" is often used instead of planning for separate reading and writing courses.

Many whole language instructional practices include both reading and writing. An example is written conversations where the teacher starts writing a personal text to the reader such as: My name is Yetta. What is your name? The teacher may start by reading the written sentences to the student while she is writing and encouraging the reader/writer to talk aloud as he/she writes. This way both the learner and the teacher know what the other is writing. Eventually, the written conversation continues without oral support. This is also a way to evaluate the degree to which adult learners are able to manage English literacy. Text messaging would be an interesting extension of written conversations in classrooms particularly for adolescents.

Language Experience (Lameroux & Lee, 1943; Van Allen & Van Allen, 1982) is another practice that involves reading and writing in authentic settings. Language experience advocates believe that "what I can say, I can write and what I can write, I can read." But they also make clear that the power of language experience is using written language as a tool to explore and record *experience*. It provides opportunities to extend vocabulary and grammatical patterns into written language. For example, the children in a primary classroom have taken a field trip or experienced a new pet such as a gerbil in the classroom. The teacher asks the children to write the experience for purposes of a newsletter to share with their parents. Early on, the teacher may act as a scribe and take the children's dictation as the whole class or a small group observes the teacher writing but eventually the children write about the experience individually. These language experiences become reading experiences as the children put them together as books or magazines to share with their classmates.

Books, journals, and newsletters are published in whole language classrooms. Based on the reading of a rich diet of children or adolescent literature, the students are encouraged to write their own narratives and reports. Students' interests in science or social studies projects may conclude with content focused pamphlets or newsletters. These written works become part of the classroom or school library. Student-authored works are enjoyed greatly by their classmates and there are research possibilities to discover the ways in which students respond to the published writing of their peers.

READING STRATEGY INSTRUCTION

We have made clear that every engaging experience that learners have with authentic written language results in expanding their comprehension strategies. We also believe that there are times in the daily schedule in which teachers organize individual, small groups and sometimes the whole class to focus on learning about language as an object of study. We've said previously that Halliday conceives of learning about language as a result of language use. He documents that whenever learners use language, they learn language, learn through language and learn about language (Halliday, 2003b). For whole language educators, learning about language involves planning lessons with students that include talking and thinking about language as it is being used. In this way students become consciously aware of the social and personal uses of language in order to make sense of the world. Some scholars call such discussions metalingusitic and metacognitive awareness. For us, the focus is talking and thinking about how language is used and how it works. In a curriculum that focuses on language study, teachers find many opportunities spontaneously and during planned experiences for students to consider language knowledge itself as important and interesting (Y. Goodman, 2003).

We call the organization and planning for opportunities and experiences to study about written language, reading strategy lessons (Y. Goodman, Watson, & Burke, 1987). Those who are involved in writing process research and teaching use the term mini lessons which we consider a synonymous term. These are the times in the language arts curriculum set aside to examine language with students to inquire into its history, its use, its structure, its variety, its purposes and functions (Y. Goodman, 2003). We don't ignore phonics or grammar as some claim, rather we look at language as a field of study where knowing grammar and the relations between how oral and written language relate are part of exploring language use (including reading and writing). Language study includes critical moment teaching, strategy lessons and theme cycle studies. Our previous discussion on the relation between literacy learning and content focuses on the importance of studying language (oral and written) across the curriculum. In this section, we focus on paying close attention to language through critical moment teaching and strategy lessons.

Strategy lessons or mini lessons relate to the language knowledge students need to think and wonder about. Students ask: "I wonder what this means?"; "How can we say this so it's clear to others?"; "Why does language work this way?" Whole language teachers check in with students and interact with them as they work on individual or small group projects. In such settings, teachers join their students in exploring meanings of words or concepts and engage students in discussions of their questions about language as they are reading and writing. Such spontaneous and continuous interactions with students are aspects of "critical moment teaching" where teachers take advantage of students' disequilibrium as they wonder about the best strategies to use in specific language contexts. Often strategy lessons take place as a result of spontaneous interactions between the teacher and the students. "Did you know that 'going home' and 'coming home' can mean the same thing?" asked one fourth grader. That started a useful discussion.

Don Howard, an elementary school teacher (Y. Goodman & Marek, 1996), talks about sending children off on a language safari to study a particular language issue. For example, his second graders wondered why *cord* and *word* didn't rhyme and he sent them out on an "ord" safari. They watched for a few weeks and kept lists to document how "ord" occurred in different language settings. They interviewed teachers and parents to consider what they thought about this discrepancy and after a few weeks of collecting data they decided that the "wo" seemed to control the shift in the vowel sound.

Strategy lessons are planned lessons about language organized similar to guided or directed teaching lessons (Y. Goodman, D. Watson, & Burke, 1987). For example, teachers select a predictable book that has a grammatical sequence that seems to trouble a small group of students. They talk with their students about the various reading strategies to use to work out the problem. Or teachers prepare worksheets that they know will cause discussion about interpretations and understandings of a specific text. Grammar and phonics lessons are highlighted as children need them. But these lessons are not presented as didactic. Rather the teacher involves the students in inquiries about specific language units. They consider how these linguistic units work when they are reading on their own, in small groups and in other curricular areas. Any study of language outside of the context of its use, is put back into a familiar context to help the student make appropriate connections to real language use.

One such example includes group cloze procedure worksheets. The teacher selects specific words or phrases which cause the students problems to be replaced with blanks. The teacher asks two or three students to read and fill in the blanks together to decide what words are possible in the selected slots. They wonder together about why they choose one over the other, and how the context of the language surrounding the blanks helps them understand. They discuss grammatical features of the language and explore the predicting and confirming strategies that helped them make decisions.

Although the focus is on the direct teaching of linguistic concepts, how function words, nouns or verbs are used in English, for example, students are encouraged to talk about why and how such phenomena occur. The focus is inquiry into language structure not simply memorizing abstract rules. In fact, rules are often placed on the board and deconstructed over time to discover the degree of regularity in real language use.

In such lessons students' attention toward language structure is not on abstract study of small units of language but toward how language is organized in its authentic use. Fragmented exercises which turn real language into abstract bits and pieces and require unquestioning memorization have no place in whole language reading programs.

Another reading strategy involves students in *directed reading thinking activities*. Based on Stauffer's (1976) view that reading is thinking, teachers stop students at selected points in a text and invite them to consider what will happen next. They talk about what cues in the language helped them make good guesses and the importance of their background knowledge and predication strategies in this process.

Another major type of strategy lesson that has a large research base is *retrospective miscue analysis* (RMA) (Y. Goodman & Marek, 1996; Moore & Gilles, 2005). During RMA lessons, readers reflect on and evaluate their reading by analyzing their own or a classmate's oral reading miscues. Involving readers in evaluating their miscues is supported by a knowledgeable teacher or researcher who holds a sociopycholingusitic view of reading. Such lessons are organized to support readers towards developing a holistic view of the reading process. The aim of reading instruction is not to eliminate miscues since all readers make miscues. Rather the aim of the instruction is to help readers understand that miscues provide a wealth of information about the reading process in action and about individual readers' strengths and weaknesses. As a result, readers build confidence in their own reading strengths and come to *revalue* themselves as readers and to demystify the reading process.

As a result of RMA, readers become aware that reading is not simply being able to sound out and recognize what every word means. It is not being able to read "without messing up" or remembering everything they read as so many struggling readers report. Rather, readers discover that reading is "making sense" for their own purposes and their miscues and retellings are based on their own interpretations. They discover that this is legitimate behavior for all good readers: that all readers use reading strategies such as predicting, inferring, selecting, confirming, and disconfirming informed by their own personal background knowledge. They become aware that they use the language cuing systems—graphophonics, syntax, and semantics to make sense.

Research on retrospective miscue analysis over several decades demonstrates that as readers' personal models of reading shift from text reproductive models of reading toward meaning construction models, their reading strategies reflect an increase in miscues that are syntactically and semantically acceptable in the whole text and do not disrupt meaning. At the same time, their total number of miscues tends to diminish. RMA involves readers in self-reflection and self-study as they inquire into their own reading behavior. They take into consideration their attitudes and emotions toward reading. They become aware that proficient readers are risk takers who are flexible, leap to meanings, and check out their comprehension by reading ahead or rereading specific portions of a text.

CONCLUDING REMARKS AND FURTHER RESEARCH

Reading professionals need to honor research that documents reading comprehension in the environments in which it is used. What students do on tests of reading comprehension or narrowly conceived responses to short readings and recall questions do little to reveal how well students comprehend written texts in the real world. Research that looks only at disembodied responses to narrowly conceived test items reduces reading to disembodied responses. For whole language purposes, however, reading research needs to be conducted with authentic materials being read by students for real and functional purposes.

The influences of reading outside of the school environment in the home and community needs to be studied to learn about how reading in the home and community supports reading development in school. Many students report reading experiences outside of school, but they do not believe that this is appropriate reading for academic purposes. They do not make connections between their everyday personal reading and reading in school and as a result they do not have the confidence to be challenged by school literacy opportunities. We've reported on research that examines the experiences in homes and communities and more needs to be done to understand reading comprehension during engagements with literacy experiences in real world settings in and out of school.

Whole language researchers will continue to consider questions that concern the learner, the teacher and the text. Here are a few such questions:

How do students' views of themselves as literate beings influence (expand or narrow) their reading experiences in the classroom and their comprehension of school or academic materials?

How do emotional and attitudinal views of themselves as literate members of society support or interfere with their reading of materials?

How do students' affective and emotional responses impact reading comprehension?

How do students' interests impact comprehension of texts?

What are the features of texts that influence reader's comprehension?

Are there changes in the orthography of the text and how it is organized that could support greater comprehension?

What are the features of non-fiction texts that help or hinder reader's comprehension?

Are there texts that are difficult for proficient readers?

How do proficient readers develop the flexibility they need to attend to the variations in texts?

Reading researchers in the United States would do well to be more knowledgeable about research on reading comprehension in other countries and in languages other than English. Much of what is known about reading in the United States is based on research in English and the alphabetic writing system. In research on nonalphabetic languages and alphabets other than the Roman alphabet, the model of English phonics, grammar, and meaning development is often imposed. We need to broaden our understandings of how languages and cultures differ and how such differences influence the writing systems of these languages as well as the writing of the texts and reading comprehension.

We need to continue to document the ways in which reading to learn and learning to read are reciprocal. Given the influence of print in the world of students, the myth about learning to read as a prerequisite to reading to learn needs to be carefully documented and the results disseminated.

Whole language is a pedagogical theory that sees the classroom as an environment that invites and engages learners in becoming literate members of their communities with a focus on social justice and democracy (Edelsky, 1999; Rosenblatt, 1978).

Whole language teachers and researchers are aware of the importance of taking into account the ecology of the whole classroom including the knowledge and beliefs teachers hold about teaching, learning, curriculum, language, and the influences of the social community. They understand that emotions and attitudes about schooling and literacy influence students' views about becoming literate members of society. Literacy never occurs in a vacuum apart from its use nor apart from a social context. Literacy uses, practices, and proficiencies always depend on context. Using reading and writing lessons outside of authentic texts prompts learners to believe they are not literate because literacy in school is esoteric and what they learn about reading and writing in classrooms is not relevant to their lives.

Throughout this discussion of research on comprehension instruction in a whole language context, we argue that reading—making sense of printed text—is one of the many tools learners use to expand on their knowledge of the world. And readers must come to understand the importance of this statement in order to appreciate themselves as capable of reading comprehension.

REFERENCES

Atwell, N. (1998). *In the Middle: New understandings about writing, reading and learning.* Portsmouth, NH: Boynton Cook.

Avery, C. (2002). *And with a light touch: Learning about reading, writing and teaching with first graders.* Portsmouth, NH: Heinemann.

Barbieri, M. (1995). *Sounds from the heart: Learning to listen to girls.* Portsmouth, NH: Heinemann.

Bever, T. (in progress). All language understanding is a psycholinguistic guessing game. In P. Anders et al. (Eds.), *Defying convention,: inventing the future in literacy research and practice: Festschrift for Kenneth and Yetta Goodman.* New York: Erlbaum.

Bogner, K., Raphael, L., & Pressley, M. (2002). *Scientific studies of reading, 6*(2), 135–165.

Brown, J., Goodman, K., & Marek, A. (1996). *Studies in miscue analysis: An annotated bibliography.* Newark, DE: International Reading Association.

Bruner, J. (1966). *Toward a theory of instruction.* Cambridge, MA: Harvard University Press.

Burrows, A. (1959). *Teaching composition: What research says to the classroom teacher.* Washington, D.C. National Education Association.

Cambourne, B. (1993). *The whole story: Natural learning and the acquisition of literacy in the classroom.* New York: Scholastic.

Cambourne, B. (September, 2003). Connecting Brian Cambourne's conditions of learning theory to brain/ mind principles: Implications for early childhood educators. *Early Childhood Education Journal, 31*(1), 123–139.

Casey, J. (1997). *Early literacy: The empowerment of technology.* Westport, CT: Libraries Unlimited.

Chomsky, N. (1957). *Syntactic structures.* New York: Mouton de Gruyter

Christensen, L. (2000). *Reading, writing and rising up: Teaching about social justice and the power of the written word.* Milwaukee, WI: Rethinking Schools.

Clay, M. (1975). *What did I write?* Exeter, NH: Heinemann.

Clyde L., Barber, S., Hogue, S., & Wasz, L. (2006*). Breakthrough to meaning: Helping your kids become better readers, writers and thinkers.* Portsmouth, NH: Heinemann.

Cole, A. (2003). *Knee to knee, eye to eye: Circling in on comprehension.* Portsmouth, NH: Heinemann.

Cole, M., John-Steiner, V., Scribner, S., Souberman, E. (1978). *Vygotsky: Mind in society.* Cambridge, MA: Harvard University Press.

Darling-Hammond, L. (2006). *Powerful teacher education.* Hoboken, NJ: Jossey-Bass.

Davenport, R. (2002). *Miscues, not mistakes. Reading assessment in the classroom.* Portsmouth, NH: Heinemann.

Dewey, J. (1897). My pedagogic creed. *The School Journal, 54*(3), 77–80.

Dewey, J. (1915). *The school and society & the child and the curriculum.* Chicago: University of Chicago Press.

Duckett, P. (2003). Envisioning story: The eye movements of beginning readers. *Literacy Teaching and Learning: An International Journal of Early Reading and Writing, 7*(1–2), 77–89.

Dyson, A. (1989). *Multiple worlds of child writers.* New York: Teachers College Press.

Dyson, A. (2003). *The brothers and sisters learn to write: Popular literacies in childhood and school cultures.* New York: Teachers College Press.

Edelsky, C. (1999). *Making justice our project: Teachers working toward critical whole language practice.* Urbana, IL: National Council of Teachers of English.

Elley, W. (1991). Acquiring literacy in a second language: The effect of book-based programs. *Language Learning, 41,* 371–411.

Elley.W. (1998). *Raising literacy levels in third world countries: A method that works.* Culver City, CA: Language Education Associates.

Ferreiro, E. (2003). *Past and present of the verbs to read and to write.* Toronto, Ontario: Douglas and McIntire.

Ferreiro, E., & Teberosky, A. (1982). *Literacy before schooling* (Karen, trans.). Goodman Portsmouth, NH: Heinemann.

Fisher, B. (1998). *Joyful learning in kindergarten.* Portsmouth, NH: Heinemann.

Flurkey, A., Paulson, E., & Goodman, K. (Eds.) (2007). *Scientific realism in studies of reading.* New York: Erlbaum.

Flurkey, A., & Xu, J., (Eds.) (2003). *On the revolution of reading: The selected writings of Kenneth S. Goodman.* Portsmouth, NH. Heinemann.

Freire, P., & Macedo, M. (1987). *Literacy: Reading the world and the word.* South Hadley, MA: Bergin and Garvey.

Fries, C., (1952). *The structure of English.* New York: Harcourt, Brace.

Goodman, D. (1999). *The reading detective club: Solving the mysteries of reading.* Portsmouth, NH: Heinemann.

Goodman, K. (Oct. 1965). A linguistic study of cues and miscues in reading. *Elementary English, 42*(6), 639–643.

Goodman, K. (1967). Reading: A psycholinguistic guessing game. *Journal of the Reading Specialist, 6,* 126–135.

Goodman, K. (Fall, 1969). Analysis of oral reading miscues: Applied psycholinguistics. *Reading Research Quarterly, 9*–30.

Goodman, K. (1986). *What's whole in whole language.* Portsmouth, NH: Heinemann.

Goodman, K. (1993). *Phonics phacts.* Richmond Hill: Ontario, CA: Scholastic Canada.

Goodman, K. (1996). *On reading.* Portsmouth, NH: Heinemann.

Goodman, K., (2007). Miscue analysis as scientific realism. In Flurkey, A., Paulson, E., & Goodman, K. (Eds), *Scientific realism in studies of reading.* New York: Erlbaum.

Goodman, K., & Burke, C. (1973). *Theoretically based studies of patterns of miscues in oral reading performance* (Grant No. OEG-0-0-32-374-4269). Washington, D.C.: U.S. Department of Health, Education & Welfare.

Goodman, K., & Goodman, Y. (1978). *Reading of American children whose language is a stable rural dialect of English or a language other than English* (Contract No. NIE-C-00-3-0087). Washington, D.C.: National Institute of Education.

Goodman, K., & Goodman, Y. (1981). *A whole language comprehension centered view of reading development.* Tucson: University of Arizona, College of Education, Language, Reading and Culture, No. 1.

Goodman, Y. (2003). *Valuing language study: Inquiry into language for elementary and middle schools.* Urbana, IL: National Council of Teachers of English.

Goodman, Y., & Goodman, K. (1992). Vygotsky in a whole-language perspective. In L. Moll (Ed.), *Vygotsky and education: Instructional implications and applications of sociohistorical psychology* (pp. 223–250). New York: Cambridge University Press.

Goodman, Y., & Goodman K. (2004). To err is human: Learning about language processes by analyzing miscues. In R. Ruddell & N. Unrau (Eds.), *Theoretical models and processes of reading, fifth edition* (pp. 620–639). Newark, DE: International Reading Association.

Goodman, Y., & Marek A. (1996). *Retrospective miscue analysis: Revaluing Readers and Reading.* Katonah, NY: Richard C. Owen Publishers.

Goodman, Y., & Martens, P. (2007). *Critical issues in early literacy development.* New York: Erlbaum.

Goodman, Y., Watson, D., & Burke, C., (1987). *Reading strategies: Focus on comprehension.* Katonah, NY: Richard C. Owen Publishers.

Goodman, Y., Watson, D., & Burke, C., (2005). *Reading miscue inventory: From evaluation to Instruction.* Katonah, NY: Richard C. Owen, Publishers.

Graves, D. (1983). *Writing: Teachers and children at work.* Exeter, NH: Heinemann.

Gregory, E., Long, S., & Volk, D. (Eds.). (2004). *Many pathways to literacy: Young children learning with siblings, grandparents, peers and communities.* New York and London: Routledge-Falmer.

Halliday, M. (1985). *An introduction to functional grammar.* London: Edward Arnold

Halliday, M. (2003a). Learning how to mean (1975). In Webster, J. (Ed.), *The language of early childhood, Volume 4: The collected works of M.A.K. Halliday* (pp. 6–89). London: Continuum.

Halliday, M. (2003b). Three aspects of children's language development: Learning language, learning through language, learning about language (1980). In J. Webster (Ed.), *The language of early childhood, Volume 4: The collected works of M.A.K. Halliday* (pp. 308–326). London: Continuum.

Harste, J., Short, K., & Burke, C., (1995). Creating classrooms for authors & inquirers. Portsmouth, NH: Heinemann.

Harste, J., Woodward, V., & Burke, C. (1984). *Language stories and literacy lessons.* Portsmouth, NH: Heinemann.

Harvey, S., & Goudois, A. (2007). *Strategies that work: Teaching Comprehension.* Portland, ME: Stenhouse Publishing.

Harwayne, S. (2001). *Writing through childhood: Rethinking process and product.* Portsmouth, NH: Heinemann.

Hawkins, J. (with Blakeslee, S.). (2004). *On intelligence.* New York: Henry Holt.

Hung, Y. (2000). What is writing and what is Chinese writing: A historical, linguistic and social Literacies Perspective. Unpublished doctoral dissertation, University of Arizona, Tucson.

Krashen, S. (1988). Do we learn to read by reading? The relationship between free reading and reading ability. In D. Tannen (Ed.), *Linguistics in context: Connecting observation and understanding* (pp. 269–298). Norwood, NJ: Ablex.

Krashen, S. (2004). *The power of reading: Insights from research.* Portsmouth, NH: Heinemann.

Kucer, S., Silva, S., & Delgado-Larocco, E. (1995). *Curriculum conversations.* Portland, ME: Stenhouse Publishers.

Lamoreaux, L., & Lee, D. (1943). *Learning to read through experience.* New York: D. Appleton-Century.

Martin, N., & Lightfoot, M. (Eds.). *The word for teaching is learning: Essays for James Britton.* Portsmouth, NH: Heinemann.

Martinez-Roldan, C. (2003). Building worlds and identities: A case study of the role of narratives in bilingual literature discussions, *Research in the reaching of English, 37*(4), 491–526.

Meek, M. (1988). *How texts teach what readers learn.* Great Britain: Thimble Press.

Michalove, B., Allen, J., & Shockley, B. (1993). *Engaging children: Community and chaos in the lives of young literacy learners.* Portsmouth, NH: Heinemann.

Moll, L., Amanti, X., Neff, X., & Gonzalez, V. (1992). Funds of knowledge for teaching: Using a qualitative approach to connect homes and classrooms. *Theory into practice, 31*(2), 132–141.

Mooney, M. (1990). *Reading to, with and by children.* Katonah, NY: Richard C. Owen Publishers.

Moore, R., & Gilles, C. (2005). *Reading conversations: Retrospective miscue analysis with struggling readers, grades 4–12.* Portsmouth, NH: Heinemann

Nystrand, M. (April, 2006). Research on the role of classroom discourse as it affects reading comprehension. *Research in the Teaching of English, 20,* 392–412.

Owocki, G., & Goodman, Y. (2002). *Kidwatching: Documenting children's literacy development.* Portsmouth, NH: Heinemann.

Paulson, E. (2007). Eye movements in miscue analysis: Functions of comprehension. In A. Flurkey, E. Paulson, & K. Goodman (Eds.), *Scientific realism in studies of reading.* Mahway, NJ: Erlbaum.

Paulson, E., & Freeman, A. (2003) *Insight from the eyes: The science of effective reading instruction.* Porstmouth, NH: Heinemann

Peterson, R., & Eeds, M. (2007). *Grand conversations: Literature Groups in action (Grades 2-6).* New York: Scholastic–TAB Publications Teaching Resources.

Piaget, J. (1977). *The development of thought: Equilibration of cognitive structures* (A. Rosin, trans.). New York: Viking Press.

Pressley, M., Wharton-McDonald, R., Mistretta-Hampston, J., & Echevarria, M. (1998) Literacy instruction in 10 fourth- and fifth-grade classrooms in upstate New York. *Scientific Studies of Reading, 2*(2), 157–194

Read, C. (1971). Preschool Children's Knowledge of English Phonology. *Harvard Educational Review 41*(1),1–34,

Rief, L. (1991). *Seeking diversity: Language arts with adolescents.* Portsmouth, NH: Heinemann.

Romano, T. (1987). *Clearing the way: Working with teenage writers.* Portsmouth, NH: Heinemann.

Rosenblatt, L. (1978). *The reader, the text, the poem: The transactional theory of literary work.* Carbondale, IL: University Press.

Short, K., Harste, J., & Burke, C. (1996). *Creating classrooms for authors and inquirers.* Portsmouth, NH: Heinemann.

Short, K., & Pierce, C. (1990). *Talking about books: Creating literate communities.* Portsmouth, NH: Heinemann.

Smith, F., (1982). *Writing and the writer.* New York: Holt, Rinehart & Winston.

Smith, F., (1987). *Joining the literacy club: Further essays into education.* Portsmouth, NH: Heinemann.

Stauffer, R. (1976). *Teaching reading as a thinking process.* New York: Harper.

Street, B. (2005). *Literacy across educational contexts: Mediating learning and teaching.* Philadelphia: Caslon Publishers.

Taba, H. (1962). *Curriculum development: Theory and practice.* New York: Harcourt Brace and World.

Taylor, D. (1993). *From the child's point of view.* Portsmouth, NH: Heinemann.

Taylor, M. (Ed.) (2007). *Whole language teaching, Whole-hearted practice: Looking back, looking forward.* New York: Peter Lang.

Teale W., & Sulzby, E. (Eds.) (1986). *Emergent literacy: Writing and reading.* Norwood, NJ: Ablex.

Tolchinsky, L. (2003). *The cradle of culture and what children know about writing and numbers before being taught.* Mahway, NJ: Erlbaum.

Van Allen, R., & Van Allen, C. (1982). *Language experience activities.* Boston: Houghton Mifflin.

VanDeWeghe, R. (Jan. 2007). What kinds of classroom discussion promote reading comprehension? *English Journal, 3,* 86–90.

Wang, S. (2006). A socio-psycholinguistic study on L2 Chinese readers' behavior while reading orally. Unpublished doctoral dissertation, University of Arizona, Tucson.

Whitmore, K., & Crowell, C. (1994). *Inventing a classroom. Life in a bilingual whole language learning community.* Portland, ME: M.E. Stenhouse Publishers.

Whitmore, K., Martens, P., Goodman, Y., & Owocki, G. (Eds.) (2004). Critical lessons from the transactional perspective on early literacy research. *Journal of Early Childhood Literacy, 4*(3), 291–325.

Wilde, S. (Ed.) (1996). *Notes from a kidwatcher: Selected writings of Yetta M. Goodman.* Portsmouth, NH: Heinemann.

Xu, J. (1998). A study of the reading process in Chinese through detecting errors in a meaningful text. Unpublished Doctoral Dissertation, University of Arizona.

6 The Role of Cognitive Flexibility in Reading Comprehension
Past, Present, and Future

Kelly B. Cartwright

Christopher Newport University

Reading comprehension is a complex accomplishment that requires readers to coordinate multiple features of text—seamlessly and fluidly—for optimal performance. As early as 1917, Thorndike characterized reading comprehension as "an elaborate procedure...involving many elements" (p. 323). Forty years later Gray and Reese (1957) wrote that "comprehension, if its multiple and complex role is thoughtfully considered, is little short of a miracle." Comprehension certainly seems miraculous, especially when one considers the myriad features that must be processed for skilled reading (e.g., phonological, orthographic, morphological, syntactic, semantic, metacognitive, and strategic) as well as the relative inflexibility of beginning and struggling readers, who often focus on graphophonological features of print to the exclusion of meaning (Bialystok & Niccols, 1989; Clay, 2001; Dewitz & Dewitz, 2003; Gaskins & Gaskins, 1997; Oakhill, 1993; Oakhill & Yuill, 1996; Pressley, 2006; Schwartz & Stanovich, 1981).

Put another way, skilled reading comprehension requires the simultaneous, flexible consideration, or mental representation, of multiple elements (Cartwright, 2008). Pressley and colleagues aptly characterized this phenomenon as "cognitive juggling," arguing that such juggling is essential to skilled reading (Pressley, Duke, Gaskins, Fingeret, Halladay, Hilden, et al., in press). It should be noted that the mental representations juggled by skilled readers may or may not be consciously accessible (Forguson & Gopnik, 1988; Masson, 1987). For example, even though phonological processes ordinarily operate below the level of conscious awareness in both child and adult skilled readers, these processes still interact with semantic processes (Crain-Thoreson, 1996; Luo, Johnson, & Gallo, 1998; McCutchen & Crain-Thoreson, 1994; McCutchen, Dibble, & Blount, 1994; Van Orden, 1987).

Theories of reading have consistently emphasized the multiplicity, complexity, and simultaneity inherent in skilled reading, whether at the word level or at higher levels of semantic processing (e.g., Adams, 1990, 2004; Adams & Collins, 1985; Anderson & Pearson, 1984; Ehri, 1991, 1992; Graesser, Singer, & Trabasso, 1994; Just & Carpenter, 1980; Kintsch, 1988; Kintsch & van Dijk, 1978; Perfetti, 1985, 1992; also see Paris and Hamilton's discussion of multi-component models, chapter 2, this volume). Thus, the literature provides a rich theoretical foundation for considering the multiple processes involved in reading comprehension. However, much less work has focused on the cognitive skills necessary for coordinating the multiple mental representations required for reading tasks, and even less work has investigated the development of such cognitive coordination. Contemporary work in cognitive development has focused on *cognitive flexibility*, an aspect of executive control that involves the ability to coordinate simultaneously, and access flexibly, multiple features of cognitively complex tasks. Although this work has important implications for further informing our understanding of reading comprehension, little work has bridged these areas of research. This is not surprising, as the fields of developmental and educational research have typically operated independently (Sternberg, 2000; Sternberg & Lyon, 2002).

In this chapter I will argue that cognitive flexibility, especially as construed by contemporary perspectives in cognitive development, has important implications for informing understanding of reading comprehension. As reviewers of my work have noted, flexibility is not a new concept in the reading literature. Thus, after describing contemporary perspectives on cognitive flexibility from the cognitive development literature, I will provide an overview of past work on flexibility in reading, and then review empirical work that points to the important role of cognitive flexibility in skilled reading comprehension.

CONTEMPORARY PERSPECTIVES ON COGNITIVE DEVELOPMENT AND THE DEVELOPMENT OF COGNITIVE FLEXIBILITY

Piaget's theory of cognitive development provided the foundation for contemporary perspectives on the development of thinking and representational abilities, especially his observation that children gradually improve in the ability to handle flexibly multiple perspectives on, or elements of, various kinds of tasks (Inhelder & Piaget, 1964; Piaget & Inhelder, 1969). After Piaget's ideas were introduced in the United States in the late 1950s and 1960s, many researchers examined the relation between academic skills and performance on general Piagetian measures of flexible thinking (e.g., Piagetian conservation, seriation, and classification tasks all require children to attend to multiple aspects of a problem or stimulus). And, not surprisingly, several researchers found that reading skill was significantly related to these general measures of cognitive flexibility (Althouse, 1985; Arlin, 1981; Briggs & Elkind, 1973; Canter, 1975; Elkind, Larson, & Van Doorninck, 1965). Additionally, training on general measures of flexibility produced improvements in reading skill (Cohen, Hyman, & Battistini, 1983). However, these studies did not indicate the precise relation of developing representational ability to skilled reading.

Contemporary perspectives on cognitive development have expanded on Piaget's original ideas in at least three important ways, by emphasizing representational complexity, revealing domain-specificity in cognitive development, and demonstrating that cognitive development continues across the lifespan into adulthood. Each of these aspects of contemporary cognitive developmental theory will be described in the following paragraphs with particular emphasis on what these concepts can offer for better understanding reading comprehension.

A focus on cognitive complexity

Contemporary cognitive developmental work has focused in particular on cognitive complexity, and that a number of elements or representations must be considered when engaging in cognitively complex tasks, like reading. This work has revealed important insights about children's and adults' thinking that may inform our understanding of skilled reading processes. The Cognitive Complexity and Control Theory, for example, proposes children have difficulty conceptualizing complex cognitive tasks in multiple ways, which prevents them from considering flexibly the multiple aspects of complex tasks (Frye, Zelazo, & Burack, 1998; Frye, Zelazo, & Palfai, 1995; Jacques & Zelazo, 2001; Zelazo & Frye, 1998; Zelazo, Müller, Frye, & Marcovitch, 2003; also see Andrews & Halford, 2002; Perner & Lang, 1999). Others have described this development by suggesting children have difficulty holding multiple, competing representations about objects or learning "to think about one object in different ways" (Kloo &

Perner, 2005, p.53; also see Kloo & Perner, 2003). This notion is consistent with what is known about beginning and struggling readers, children we might label "word callers." For these children, print is the "object" of consideration, and they tend inflexibly to consider only one aspect of print, usually graphophonological information, while not attending to other important aspects like meaning (Bialystok & Niccols, 1989; Clay, 2001; Dewitz & Dewitz, 2003; Gaskins & Gaskins, 1997; Oakhill, 1993; Oakhill & Yuill, 1996; Pressley, 2006; Schwartz & Stanovich, 1981).

Cognitive flexibility, the ability to consider flexibly multiple mental representations, improves with age (e.g., Inhelder & Piaget, 1964), support (Kirkham, Cruess, & Diamond, 2003; Kloo & Perner, 2003), and practice (e.g., Bigler & Liben, 1992). Knowledge of children's developing representational abilities has informed understanding of many other developments in children's thinking (see Flavell, 1988 for a review), such as language skill (e.g., Deák, 2003; Jacques & Zelazo, 2005); understanding of the representational nature of pictures and models (e.g., DeLoache, 1991); understanding the differences between appearance and reality (e.g., Flavell, Green, & Flavell, 1986); and theory of mind, or the understanding of one's own and others' mental states (e.g., Astington, Harris, & Olson, 1988; Perner & Lang, 1999). Despite the utility of considering applications of developing representational ability for understanding these various aspects of children's thinking, relatively little work has explored specific applications of cognitive flexibility to reading skill.

Emphasis on domain-specificity

This last point is particularly important, given that contemporary work indicates cognitive development is domain-specific (e.g., see Alexander, 1998; Alexander, Jetton, & Kulikowich, 1995; Alexander, Sperl, Buehl, Fives, & Chiu, 2004; Case, 1992; Case & Okamoto, 1996; Flavell, 1992; Karmiloff-Smith, 1991; Sinnott, 1998). In other words, cognitive development proceeds differently in different kinds of thinking tasks, depending on experience. Thus, although Piaget originally described general, rather homogeneous changes in thinking across childhood that affected all kinds of thinking tasks (Piaget & Inhelder, 1969), recent work shows cognitive development is more heterogeneous, with children and adults exhibiting higher levels of cognitive development in domains in which they have more knowledge or experience. In fact, in the later years of his career Piaget acknowledged the role of experience in producing cognitive change (Piaget, 1972).

An example may be useful for illustrating the importance of domain-specificity for attempting to assess or improve flexibility in cognitive processing. Classification tasks are often used to measure the ability to consider flexibly multiple aspects of stimuli at once (e.g., see Bialystock, 1989; Bigler & Liben, 1992; Frye, Zelazo, & Palfai, 1995; Inhelder & Piaget, 1964; Jacques & Zelazo, 2001; Kloo & Perner, 2003, 2005; Zelazo, Müller, Frye, & Marcovitch, 2003), though other tasks known to tap multiple representational ability, like theory of mind tasks, are also used for this purpose. Classification tasks that tap cognitive flexibility may require successive sorts of objects along different dimensions (e.g., sorting pictures first by color and then sorting them by shape) or simultaneous sorts of objects along multiple dimensions at once (e.g., sorting pictures by color and shape at the same time). Bigler and Liben (1992) adapted the multiple classification task to teach children to think more flexibly about gender roles (e.g., that both men and women can be doctors or nurses), training some children with a general flexibility task (e.g., simultaneous sorting of pictures by color and shape) and training other children with a social-specific flexibility task (e.g., simultaneous sorting of pictures of men and women into stereotypical and counter-stereotypical occupations). Only children who experienced the gender-role-specific training showed improvements in flexible thinking about gender roles. These findings and others like them suggest cognitive flexibility in particular domains, like reading, should be assessed with domain-specific measures, rather than general measures (Cartwright, Bock, Guiffré, & Montaño, in press). In support of this claim, Cartwright (2002) demonstrated training with a reading-specific flexibility task (e.g., sorting printed words by graphophonological and semantic features) produced significant improvements in reading comprehension, while training with a general flexibility task did not. These examples illustrate two important points regarding applications of work in cognitive flexibility for understanding reading comprehension. First, flexible thinking *can be taught*. However, reading-specific tasks should be used to do that teaching.

A lifespan perspective

Finally, in contrast to Piaget's classic work that focused on children (Piaget & Inhelder, 1969), contemporary work has shown that cognitive development occurs across childhood and into adulthood (Andrews & Halford, 2002; Labouvie-Vief, 1990, 1992; Luna, Garver, Urban, Lazar, & Sweeney, 2004; Sinnott, 1998). Further, although adults are certainly capable of considering flexibly multiple aspects of cognitively complex tasks, Zelazo et al. (2003) suggest that we do not always do so, and even adults vary in the ability to coordinate flexibly multiple mental representations (Diamond & Kirkham, 2005; Kuhn & Pease, 2006; Miller, 2006). These findings imply that even though adults are skilled readers, adults should vary in the flexibility with which they can handle the various representations required for skilled reading. Cartwright (2007; also see Cartwright, Isaac, & Dandy, 2006) demonstrated that this is the case, with reading-specific flexibility contributing significant unique variance to adults' reading comprehension, even when other variables were controlled.

COGNITIVE PROCESSES RELATED TO FLEXIBILITY

Cognitive flexibility as described in this chapter is certainly related to other cognitive abilities that have received more attention in the reading research literature, such as metacognition, metalinguistic abilities, executive control, and even working memory. According to the Cognitive Complexity and Control theory of cognitive development, flexibility is an important aspect of executive control that involves the ability to conceptualize a task or situation in multiple ways and flexibly switch between those conceptualizations (Zelazo & Frye, 1998). Others have characterized this aspect of executive control as the ability to "simultaneously maintain dual representations...[that can be] attended to flexibly" (Kuhn & Pease, 2006, p. 289), or, more simply, attentional flexibility (Miller, 2006). It should be noted that individuals' conscious access to their mental representations improves with age and experience (Inhelder & Piaget, 1964; Karmiloff-Smith, 1991), even in adults (Sinnott, 1998). Thus, as cognitive flexibility develops, individuals may or may not be consciously aware of the representations that are flexibly coordinated when performing a task like reading (Forguson & Gopnik, 1988; Masson, 1987).

This contrasts with metacognition, which by definition requires conscious access to representations. Metacognition involves knowledge about cognition and cognitive processes (Baker & Brown, 1984/2002; Flavell, 1977, 1979) that develops with age (e.g., Flavell, Friedrichs, & Hoyt, 1970), while executive control involves the ability to control one's cognitive processes and allocate resources to handle cognitive tasks (Britton & Glynn, 1987; Garner, 1994). Metalinguistic abilities are a special case of metacognition involving reflection on one's linguistic processes, and include such things as phonological awareness, morphological awareness, and syntactic awareness (Nagy, 2007). Because metacognitive activities require that one consider multiple mental representations (e.g., phonological awareness requires that one consider words as wholes and as made up of individual phonemes), metacognition seems to require cognitive flexibility. In fact, in longitudinal studies Tunmer and colleagues (Tunmer, Herriman, & Nesdale, 1988; Tunmer & Hoover, 1992) found that cognitive flexibility in pre-readers (assessed with classic Piagetian tasks) was a necessary precursor to children's metalinguistic abilities. Further support for this notion comes from Farrar, Ashwell, and Maag (2005; also see Farrar & Ashwell, 2008) who found cognitive flexibility (assessed with theory of mind tasks) predicted unique variance in phonological awareness even when age, vocabulary, and working memory were controlled.

These findings bring up the question of working memory and its relation to cognitive flexibility. Working memory involves keeping task elements in mind while processing other elements, or "actively combining...processing and storage operations" (Bayliss, Jarrold, Baddeley, & Leigh, 2005, p. 77). Holding a number of task elements in mind, however, does not ensure that one can shift attention flexibly between those elements, and Farrar and colleagues' work suggests that working memory and cognitive flexibility are not synonymous. Guajardo, Parker, and Turley-Ames (2007) recently found that working memory, assessed with multiple measures (backward word, backward digit, and counting and labeling), was moderately correlated with general cognitive flexibility, but a Cronbach's alpha across the three measures of working memory and the measure of general cognitive flexibility was low (.44) and jumped to .76 when flexibility was removed (also see Deák, 2003, who reviewed research indicating cognitive flexibility and working memory are different constructs). Recently, Munakata and colleagues have argued cognitive flexibility is an aspect of working memory (e.g., Brace, Morton, & Munakata, 2006; Stedron, Sahni, & Munakata, 2005); but future work is necessary to determine precisely how these variables are related. What seems evident at this point is that cognitive flexibility cannot simply be explained in terms of working memory capacity.

HISTORY OF FLEXIBILITY IN READING

As noted in the introduction to the chapter, flexibility is not a new concept in the reading literature. This section highlights some of the most prominent perspectives on flexibility in reading that have emerged over the past 70 years. Each of the viewpoints presented here is consistent with the position taken in this paper, namely that reading requires individuals to deal simultaneously and flexibly with multiple mental representations. However, none of these perspectives provides the theoretical foundation for the current perspective, nor are they situated in a common theoretical base. So, what do these perspectives offer contemporary reading researchers? They each point to the importance of cognitive flexibility in reading processes. What is missing? Each perspective offers an incomplete account of how cognitive flexibility might be related to skilled reading. Moreover, none offer insight into the development of such flexibility as clearly as current perspectives from the cognitive developmental literature, which provide a theoretical framework that captures these early notions of flexibility and extends them in empirically testable ways.

Early perspectives on flexibility in reading

Some of the earliest work on flexibility in reading focused on the ability to vary reading rate and attentional focus, according to the readers' purpose. According to Fry (1978,

p. 11), "One sign of a good reader is flexibility. Good readers are able to adapt their reading skills to meet the demands of the material they wish to cover." This perspective appeared in the literature as early as the 1940s and remained the dominant perspective on flexibility in reading into the 1980s (Carillo & Sheldon, 1952; DiStefano, Noe, & Valencia, 1981; McDonald, 1965). Blommers and Lindquist (1944), for example, assessed good and poor comprehenders' reading rates across the same passages. Good comprehenders were significantly more likely to purposefully vary reading rate depending on the difficulty of the passages (also see Dowdy, Crump, & Welch, 1982, who presented similar findings). Further work showed this kind of flexibility develops with age (Ramsel & Grabe, 1983), and can be taught, resulting in improvements in comprehension (Berger, 1967; Braam, 1963). This perspective is certainly consistent with current conceptions of cognitive flexibility, as monitoring one's own understanding of a text, adjusting reading rate to maintain understanding, and simultaneously attending to the text's meaning require flexible attention to multiple factors.

More recent perspectives on flexibility in reading

Around the late 1970s and into the 1980s, theorists began to turn their attention more fully to the notion of flexibility as an important component of skilled reading. Four perspectives will be reviewed in this section, which were offered by Marie Clay, Ken Goodman, Rand Spiro and colleagues, and Wagner and Sternberg. Each of these perspectives offers a slightly different conceptualization of flexibility in reading processes, while all are consistent with current cognitive developmental perspectives.

Marie Clay[1]   Marie Clay was trained in developmental psychology, and she has focused on the child's developing control over reading processes. Clay's work (1969, 1985, 1991, 2001) has consistently emphasized the importance of teaching children to use multiple cues for reading, such as meaning, sentence structure, order cues, size cues, and sounds. She argued that "reading for meaning involves the monitoring of cues from all these sources" (Clay, 1985, p. 7), a notion that is clearly consistent with contemporary perspectives on cognitive development. In the 1991 revision of her ideas, she maintained a focus on flexibility, defining "reading as a message-getting, problem-solving activity which increases in power and flexibility the more that it is practiced" (1991, p. 6).

Her most recent theoretical work (Clay, 2001) provides a much more explicit emphasis on the importance of flexibility to the reading process, describing it in terms that are remarkably similar to ideas presented in the contemporary cognitive developmental literature. In that work, Clay focused in particular on children's increasing flexible control of a complex system of information, observing that beginning readers seem to be "limited to one task at a time" (p. 56), while more proficient readers use "several sources of information" (p. 57). Even in some of her earlier work, Clay (1985) noted the inflexibility that is often evident in less-skilled readers' processing. In her observations of struggling readers, she found that "[i]t is not uncommon for children to find it easy to attend to separate aspects of reading and writing tasks but quite difficult to bring two aspects together" (Clay, 2001, p. 61). She argued that proficient readers manage several kinds of information when they read, as though they are "juggling many things simultaneously" (p. 92). Clay's successful Reading Recovery® program teaches children how to use multiple cues and strategies simultaneously when engaged in reading tasks and has produced significant improvements in children's reading comprehension (see D'Agostino & Murphy, 2004, for a meta-analysis).

Ken Goodman   Like Clay, Goodman's (1973) work on miscue analysis emphasized the importance of multiple cues, such as graphophonological, semantic, and syntactic cues, for skilled reading. Working from a psycholinguistic perspective, Goodman argued that inefficient readers focus rather inflexibly on graphophonological information, while skilled readers rely much less on graphophonological information, instead utilizing information from multiple text sources. In later work Goodman (1976, 1994) continued to emphasize the importance of flexibility, arguing that in addition to flexibly using various text cues, readers must also be prepared to apply strategies differently in different types of texts and be flexible in the way reading processes are applied to meet various goals. Like Clay's perspective, Goodman's view is consistent with contemporary cognitive developmental work on cognitive flexibility, but Goodman's view is less transparent about ways flexibility develops and can be improved.

Rand Spiro   Around the same time that Clay and Goodman were emphasizing the importance of flexibility in application of decoding strategies for skilled reading, Spiro and his colleagues were emphasizing the importance of flexibility in semantic processing. In an early study, for example, Spiro and Tirre (1980) found individuals who were more flexible in considering multiple aspects of a task, assessed with an Embedded Figures Test, demonstrated significantly better recall on a task that required the coordination of prior knowledge (schemas) and text-based information. Drawing from research on expert cognitive processing, Spiro and colleagues (Spiro, Coulson, Feltovich, & Anderson, 1994/1988; Spiro, Vispoel, Schmitz, Samarapungavan, & Boerger, 1987; Spiro, 2004) developed Cognitive Flexibility Theory, arguing that in complex knowledge domains like reading, skilled performance is characterized by flexibility in knowledge representation as well as the ability to connect or recombine components of one's knowledge. They emphasized the importance of the "ability to adopt multiple perspectives and frames of reference" (Feltovich, Spiro, & Coulson, 1997, p. 138), an assertion consistent with the view presented in this chapter. Further, Spiro and colleagues suggested traditional educational techniques often oversimplify the presentation of knowledge in ways that hinder subsequent ability to use knowledge flexibly, and argued that instruction must present information in multiple ways to foster flexible thinking, a method they called "criss-crossing the landscape" (Spiro, 2004; Spiro et al., 1987). Given their emphasis on the necessity for coordinating different sources of knowledge and understanding multiple connections between types of knowledge, Spiro and colleagues' ideas are consistent with contemporary cognitive developmental perspectives on cognitive flexibility. However, their perspective is less clear about the manner in which cognitive flexibility develops or ways such flexibility might be improved other than flexible instruction.

Wagner and Sternberg   At about the same time that Spiro and colleagues offered their Cognitive Flexibility Theory, Wagner and Sternberg (1987) linked the notion of flexibility in reading to executive control and metacognitive processes, thus linking flexibility to an information-processing perspective. They argued that the best readers are able to adjust reading rate and attentional focus according to task demands and reading goals (similar to the earliest definitions of flexibility reviewed above), which is evidence of flexibility in cognitive monitoring and control. In a review of research on children's cognitive monitoring abilities, they noted children are often unable to monitor the difficulty level of tasks, monitor changes in levels of task difficulty, monitor their own understanding, allocate appropriate levels of attention to tasks, and predict their own performance. Wagner and Sternberg then presented data from two studies with adult readers, which confirmed that skilled adult readers monitor their own reading processes and determine how and what to read, depending on their reading goals. Flexible attention to multiple aspects of reading tasks, as described by Wagner and Sternberg (1987), is consistent with the contemporary cognitive developmental perspective presented in this chapter. However, like the other perspectives that emerged around this time, Wagner and Sternberg's description of flexibility in reading did not clearly indicate how such flexibility developed or could be improved.

LANDMARK STUDIES THAT PROVIDE EVIDENCE FOR COGNITIVE FLEXIBILITY IN READING COMPREHENSION

This section reviews work situated in contemporary cognitive developmental perspectives that provides evidence for the important role of cognitive flexibility in reading comprehension. The introduction to this chapter highlighted three important features of contemporary cognitive developmental work: a focus on cognitive complexity, the importance of domain-specificity in cognitive development, and a lifespan perspective on cognitive change.

Cartwright's research program has applied these features of contemporary cognitive developmental work to better understand the processes underlying reading comprehension (see Cartwright, Hodgkiss, & Isaac, 2008, for a review). As noted previously, reading is cognitively complex and requires attention to multiple elements, but beginning and struggling readers typically focus inflexibly on phonological features of print to the exclusion of meaning. Cartwright hypothesized that cognitive inflexibility might prevent struggling readers from attending to semantic features of print in addition to phonological features, thus preventing comprehension.

To test this hypothesis, she adapted the multiple classification task, a classic task used to assess cognitive flexibility, to tap individuals' flexibility in thinking about phonological and semantic aspects of print (Cartwright, 2002). The reading-specific flexibility task required individuals to sort printed words on graphophonological and semantic dimensions (by initial phoneme and word meaning), indicating individuals' ability to consider flexibly both of these aspects of printed words. Graphophonological-semantic flexibility contributed unique variance to second to fourth graders' reading comprehension, beyond age, general flexibility, semantic, and phonological processing (Cartwright, 2002), and these results were replicated in samples of first and second graders (Cartwright, Marshall, Dandy, & Isaac, 2007) and adults (Cartwright, 2007). Further, a cross-sectional comparison of second graders, fourth graders, and adults demonstrated graphophonological-semantic flexibility improves across the lifespan (Cartwright, Isaac, & Dandy, 2006). Taken together, these results indicate the important independent contribution of reading-specific flexibility to reading comprehension in beginning and skilled readers beyond general flexibility, even when participants' independent processing of the two dimensions coordinated in the reading-specific flexibility task (semantic and phonological) was controlled. These results are consistent with contemporary cognitive developmental perspectives, as they indicate cognitive flexibility's contribution to reading comprehension is domain-specific and occurs across the lifespan.

Moreover, an experimental study showed individually-administered graphophonological-semantic flexibility training (15 minutes per day, over 5 days) produced significant improvements in second to fourth grade children's reading comprehension, while general flexibility training did not (Cartwright, 2002, 2006), further confirming the domain-specific role of cognitive flexibility in reading comprehension. An adaptation of this intervention for small group administration by reading teachers also produced significant improvements in children's reading comprehension on both researcher- and school-administered measures (Cartwright, Schmidt, Clause, Price, & Thomas, 2007). These findings confirm that reading-specific cognitive flexibility can be taught, resulting in improved reading comprehension.

This body of work confirms the important contribution of reading-specific cognitive flexibility for reading comprehension across the lifespan. Further, this work points to the domain-specific nature of cognitive development, as only reading-specific cognitive flexibility training produced improvements in comprehension (Cartwright, 2002, 2006; Cartwright et al., 2007), and reading-specific flexibility contributed to reading comprehension beyond general flexibility in children and adults, even when the individual components of the reading-specific flexibility task (phonological and semantic processing) were controlled (Cartwright, 2002, 2007; Cartwright, Marshall, et al, 2007).

Recently, Rong and Guo-liang (2006) extended Cartwright's work to a sample of Chinese children and examined the role of cognitive flexibility in reading comprehension for reading-disabled and non-reading-disabled students. Rong and Guo-liang assessed cognitive flexibility with a domain-general flexibility task, and found significant relations between cognitive flexibility, language knowledge, and reading comprehension. Further, reading-disabled students were significantly less cognitively flexible than their more able peers. Although Rong and Guo-liang did not use a reading-specific measure of cognitive flexibility in their work, they suggested that reading-specific flexibility tasks might produce more improvement in reading-disabled students' comprehension than general flexibility tasks. These results extend work on cognitive flexibility in reading to a Chinese-speaking sample and provide further evidence for the important role of cognitive flexibility in reading comprehension.

Nicola Yuill's research program has also examined the relation between readers' ability to deal flexibly with multiple aspects of literacy tasks and reading comprehension. In particular, she has focused on uses of language that require individuals to construct simultaneous, conflicting mental representations, thus requiring cognitive flexibility (e.g., Yuill, 1996; Yuill & Oakhill, 1991). For example, Yuill has examined children's understanding of jokes and riddles that rely on verbal ambiguity and the relation of that understanding to reading comprehension. Jokes and riddles involve cognitive flexibility because they rely on multiple, simultaneous interpretations of text. For example, the classic riddle "What's black and white and red all over?" relies on this kind of ambiguity, as the listener must be able to interpret the word "red" in two ways: as the color red and as the homonymous word "read."

Yuill and Oakhill (1991) compared skilled and unskilled comprehenders who were matched on age-appropriate decoding skills, and found that the less-skilled comprehenders had difficulty understanding ambiguous jokes that required simultaneous, conflicting interpretations. Further, less-skilled comprehenders defined skilled reading rather inflexibly in terms of decoding skill (much like Gaskins and Gaskins's [1997] struggling readers at Benchmark School). However, when less-skilled comprehenders were trained to recognize verbal ambiguity in riddles, forcing them to consider multiple interpretations of text, their reading comprehension improved (Yuill, 1996). Yuill speculated that riddles provide a "decentered awareness of language" (p. 218), as they require "verbatim recall and simultaneous reinterpretation" (p. 219). That is, they require cognitive flexibility.

More recently, Yuill's work has focused on collaborative discussion as a way to promote children's practice coordinating multiple mental representations involved in literacy tasks. For example, she implemented a training study involving poor comprehenders' collaborative discussion of the verbal ambiguity in jokes and riddles. Children's discussion and explanations required conscious reflection on the multiple meanings inherent in the jokes and riddles, and trained children demonstrated improved reading comprehension (Yuill, in press a, in press b). In other work, Yuill and colleagues have adapted Cartwright's reading-specific cognitive flexibility task for administration in a collaborative computerized framework. Children had to work together to sort words on surface and semantic features, and trained children showed significant improvement in reading-specific cognitive flexibility (Yuill, Kerawalla, Pearce, Luckin, & Harris, 2008). From informal observations of children's discussions during the study, Yuill et al. suggested the collaborative computerized task may be a promising avenue for improving reading comprehension (in addition to reading-specific cognitive flexibility), and they have work underway to investigate this possibility (Yuill, personal communication, March 22, 2007).

RESEARCH THAT INDICATES COGNITIVE FLEXIBILITY IN SKILLED COMPREHENSION

This section includes work that demonstrates skilled comprehension requires individuals to coordinate flexibly multiple mental representations, whether they are text features, reader knowledge, or strategic processes. Although the research reviewed here is not derived from contemporary cognitive developmental work, the findings are consistent with the perspective presented in this chapter and point to potentially fruitful directions for future research. The following review focuses in particular on three kinds of flexible coordination of elements in reading tasks: coordinating semantic propositions within texts to detect inconsistencies; linking semantic propositions within texts, across texts, and with prior knowledge to make inferences; and managing text content alongside metacognitive and strategic processes. In addition, though semantic processes are typically the focus in analyses of reading comprehension processes, cognitive flexibility is also evident in word-level processes, and that research will be briefly reviewed. Finally, much work on reading comprehension processes has focused on less-skilled readers who provide an incomplete picture of optimal comprehension processes. Much less work has investigated the nature of highly skilled readers' cognitive processes, although such work may provide a more complete picture of the nature of cognitive processing, and the role of cognitive flexibility, in optimal reading comprehension. Thus, this section closes with a review of work on expert readers, as expert readers provide a picture of the best possible processing in reading comprehension, which is typically characterized by tremendous flexibility.

Coordinating semantic features within and across texts

Often, skilled reading comprehension requires individuals to make cognitive connections between various semantic aspects of text. Sometimes these elements may be inconsistent with one another, and the inconsistency must be noted and resolved. In other cases semantic features of text must be used together, often combined with readers' prior knowledge, to produce inferences about text meaning. Although inconsistencies typically require longer processing times than integration of consistent information (Hakala & O'Brien, 1995), in each of these cases, skilled readers must coordinate flexibly multiple mental representations in order to produce an accurate understanding of a text. The sections that follow review work on resolving inconsistencies and making inferences (within and across texts) as these comprehension processes appear to require cognitive flexibility.

Resolving inconsistencies

The ability to notice and resolve inconsistencies in reading tasks requires that readers be able to hold and coordinate information from two different locations in text. That is, they must be able to consider flexibly multiple text features. Although children are capable of detecting logical inconsistency in individuals' verbal utterances at about age 6 (Ruffman, 1999), detecting logical inconsistency in text seems to appear later. Similar to the development of cognitive flexibility, the ability to detect inconsistencies in text develops with age across the elementary school years. For example, Markman (1979) demonstrated children's detection of text inconsistencies improved from third to sixth grades. She noted that to detect inconsistencies children must maintain conflicting representations in memory and compare them: a task which contemporary cognitive developmental work would suggest is difficult for children. Consistent with this notion, Markman found that third to sixth children's ability to detect inconsistencies was not reliable, even when the inconsistencies were made explicit.

Research comparing skilled and less-skilled comprehenders on the ability to detect inconsistencies in text shows a consistent pattern from childhood into adulthood. Across all age groups, less-skilled comprehenders show a marked difficulty detecting inconsistencies, indicating that they are less able to consider flexibly multiple text elements. For example, in a sample of fifth grade children, August, Flavell, and Clift (1984) found skilled comprehenders were better able to detect inconsistencies explicitly and implicitly than less-skilled comprehenders, a difference not mediated by decoding skill, intelligence, or memory for text information. In samples of fourth grade children, Ehrlich, Redmond, and Tardieu (1999) and Dash and Mohanty (1992) observed similar patterns of inconsistency detection across skilled and less-skilled comprehenders. Additionally, in a cross-sectional comparison of fourth-, fifth-, and sixth-grade children, Zabrucky and Moore (1989) compared skilled, average, and less-skilled readers on a variety of text comprehension measures, including inconsistency detection. Skilled readers were significantly better able to detect inconsistencies in text than average and less-skilled readers; and a similar pattern emerged across grade level.

As noted in the introduction to this chapter, work in cognitive development shows children must develop the ability to consider multiple aspects of stimuli, and Ruffman (1996) explained children's comprehension difficulties in these terms, noting that "children are predisposed to derive a single interpretation from a text" (p. 62). According to Ruffman, even when faced with inconsistent text information, children's inability to consider multiple features of texts leads them to select one interpretation over others (rather than considering and comparing alternative perspectives and then choosing the most appropriate one), resulting in poor text comprehension. Moreover, according to contemporary perspectives in cognitive development, even though adolescents and adults typically have less difficulty than elementary-aged children coordinating multiple elements of complex tasks, this ability still develops across the lifespan into adulthood. In support of this notion, less-skilled comprehenders' difficulties in detecting text inconsistencies are evident beyond childhood. For example, Garner and Kraus (1981) demonstrated such a difference in middle school students, and Zabrucky (1990) demonstrated similar differences in college students.

Although poor comprehenders have difficulty with inconsistency detection, indicating an apparent difficulty in coordinating text features, inconsistency detection can be trained, similar to work in cognitive flexibility. For example, Reis and Spekman (1983) trained comprehension monitoring in sxith and seventh grade less-killed comprehenders, resulting in significant improvement in inconsistency detection for trained children. In a younger sample of third-and sixth-grade students, Rubman and Waters (2000) used a storyboard training procedure, which provided an external representation of text elements, to teach children to detect inconsistencies in text. Training in using the storyboard resulted in improved comprehension, especially for the less-skilled readers in the study. Taken together, work on inconsistency detection is consistent with contemporary perspectives on cognitive flexibility, as the ability to consider flexibly multiple, inconsistent aspects of text is deficient in less-skilled readers, develops with age, and can be taught, leading to improved comprehension.

Making inferences

Like the detection of inconsistencies, inference making requires that readers consider multiple elements of text simultaneously and relate those text elements to prior knowledge. Thus, inference making clearly requires that readers consider simultaneously multiple mental representations. Keenan, Ruffman, and Olson (1994) have shown that children begin to understand logical inference as a potential source of information around 4 to 5 years of age (assessed with verbal tasks, not reading tasks). However, beginning and struggling readers vary in the degree to which they take advantage of logical inference as a source of information about texts' meanings. For example, Oakhill, Yuill, and Parkin (1986) compared inference making abilities of skilled and less-skilled 7- to 8-year-old comprehenders who did not differ on decoding skill or working memory, finding that less-skilled comprehenders were significantly less likely to make inferences from text. Cain and Oakhill (1999) reported similar findings, even when skilled and less-skilled comprehenders possessed the requisite prior knowledge to support inference generation (also see Oakhill, Cain, & Bryant, 2003, who reported similar findings in a 2-year longitudinal study, and Laing & Kamhi, 2002, who reported similar findings in third graders). These studies indicate struggling comprehenders across the elementary grades demonstrate particular difficulty with inference making and appear to be cognitively inflexible, as they are unable to coordinate features within texts with one another or with prior knowledge.

Because children's inflexibility in handling text features and prior knowledge appears to contribute to comprehension failure, it is reasonable to assume that training in inference making might produce improvements in comprehension, an assumption confirmed in several studies. For example, McGee and Johnson (2003) taught 6- to 9-year-old less-skilled comprehenders how to attend to multiple text features and use them to make inferences, resulting in significant improvements in comprehension compared to a control group who received "standard comprehension exercises." Yuill and Oakhill (1988) reported similar intervention effects for 7- to 8-year-old children. Further, Reutzel and Hollingsworth (1988) produced significant improvements in third graders' comprehension with an inference intervention that increased children's flexible attention to the multiple text elements necessary for inference making. Other work has demonstrated similar effects with older children. For example, Carr, Dewitz, and Patberg (1983) trained sixth-grade children to connect background knowledge to text information to generate inferences, which produced improvements in comprehension immediately and after a 6 week delay, especially for less-skilled comprehenders; and Dewitz, Carr, and Patberg (1987) reported similar results for an inference making intervention with fifth-grade students. Finally, in a sample of eighth-grade students, Vidal-Abarca, Martínez, and Gilabert (2000) developed a text elaboration procedure that supported students' inference making by drawing their attention to the relevant text features. Students who read the elaborated texts showed significant, positive effects on inferential learning, while students who read texts in which inference requirements were reduced and students who read unaltered texts did not. Thus, at least for elementary and middle school children, training in inference making improves comprehension. This research supports the notion that comprehension requires the flexible, simultaneous consideration of multiple elements, including text elements and prior knowledge. Moreover, the training studies suggest that students can be taught to attend flexibly to multiple text elements, and when they are comprehension improves.

Integrating information across texts in content areas

As children progress into the middle school, high school, and even college years, the need to integrate text information expands as students are faced with learning in content areas. In content area courses students are often expected to integrate information and make inferences from ideas across texts rather than just within texts. To do this, readers must be able to coordinate information from multiple, often conflicting, sources to arrive at a global understanding of content, and this presents a representational problem. For example, students have difficulty reconciling their prior beliefs about scientific concepts with contradictory information encountered in texts (e.g., Chinn & Brewer, 1993; Hynd, McWhorter, Phares, & Suttles, 1994; Hynd, 1998). Additionally, in domains such as history, students appear to treat different texts on the same topic as independent, often ignoring inconsistencies across texts (Hynd & Stahl, 1998; Wineburg, 1991). Even college students have difficulty learning how to reconcile different accounts of concepts encountered across texts, indicating that these students have difficulty considering flexibly multiple text perspectives (Hynd-Shanahan, Holschuh, & Hubbard, 2004). However, this work also showed that college students can be explicitly taught to integrate conflicting features of multiple texts (Hynd-Shanahan et al., 2004), and other work demonstrates similar success with fifth grade students (VanSledright, 2002) and middle school students (Wolfe & Goldman, 2005). Thus, it is clear that students must continue to develop cognitive flexibility in reading processes beyond the elementary years, in order to achieve optimal comprehension in content area reading tasks. This work demonstrates that to succeed in these tasks, students must flexibly consider multiple mental representations, including prior knowledge and multiple text perspectives, and this flexibility can be taught, consistent with current perspectives on cognitive flexibility.

Metacognitive and strategic processes

A great deal of research indicates readers' knowledge of their own cognitive processes, or metacognition, plays an important role in reading comprehension (Block & Pressley, 2001; Israel, Block, Kinnucan-Welsch, & Bauserman, 2005). In order to consider one's own thought processes while reading, however, a reader must be able simultaneously to reflect on thought processes while also attending to text features such as meaning. Thus, by its nature, metacognition involves cognitive flexibility, as it requires the simultaneous representation of multiple elements. According to Block, Schaller, Joy, and Gaine (2001), "Skilled readers process many thoughts as they read...and such complex cognitive, metacognitive, attentional, and emotional processes are difficult to negotiate" (p. 42).

Skilled readers use metacognitive comprehension strategies significantly more often than less-skilled readers (e.g., Israel, 2002, as cited in Israel & Massey, 2005; Israel, 2008; Myers & Paris, 1978; Paris & Myers, 1981; Sadoski, 1983). For example, Sadoski (1983) demonstrated the fifth-grade students who reported using imagery while reading had significantly higher levels of reading comprehension than their counterparts who did not use imagery. Israel (in press) demonstrated that middle school students who used metacognitive strategies which required multiple mental representation (e.g., using text features to determine word meaning, or using prior knowledge to support liberal interpretations of text) demonstrated better reading comprehension than middle school students who used a less cognitively flexible strategy (i.e., literal interpretation of text, which requires only one representation of text). Skilled comprehenders appear to be significantly better able to consider metacognitive information alongside text features, indicating that they are better able to consider flexibly multiple mental representations than their less-skilled counterparts.

In addition, research has demonstrated a causal role of metacognitive knowledge in reading comprehension (see Pressley, El-Dinary, Gaskins, Schuder, Bergman, Almasi, & Brown, 1992, for a review). These studies have involved instruction in single strategies, such as imagery (Borduin, Borduin, & Manley, 1994; Oakhill & Patel, 1991; Pressley, 1976), question generation (Davey & McBride, 1986), and recognition and summarization of text structure (Armbruster, Anderson, & Ostertag, 1987), all resulting in improvements in reading comprehension. Other work has focused on teaching a small repertoire of metacognitive comprehension strategies, such as summarizing, questioning, clarifying, predicting, and imagery (the specific combination of strategies has varied across studies), and this work has demonstrated improvements in reading comprehension across age groups: for second graders (Brown, Pressley, Van Meter, & Schuder, 1996), third graders (Duffy, Roehler, Sivan, Rackliffe, Book, Meloth, et al., 1987; also see Duffy, Roehler, & Herrmann, 1988), second to sixth graders (Block, 1993), and seventh graders (Palincsar & Brown, 1984). However, Willoughby, Porter, Belsito, and Yearsley (1999) found that across the elementary years children differ in the degree to which they can benefit from metacognitive strategies instruction. In their study second-, fourth-, and sixth-grade students were taught imagery and verbal elaboration strategies. All children benefited from the verbal elaboration strategy, while imagery was most effective for sixth-grade students, indicating that metacognitive strategies instruction should be monitored carefully for younger readers who may not yet be able to coordinate strategy use with text processing. In summary, this body of work supports the important role of cognitive flexibility in reading comprehension by demonstrating that skilled comprehension requires the simultaneous processing of multiple elements: text elements and information about individuals' own cognitive processes. Further, consistent with work on cognitive flexibility, the ability to consider flexibly metacognitive comprehension strategies alongside text content can be taught, producing improvements in comprehension.

Flexibility in word-level processes

Although word-level processes are typically not the focus in analyses of skilled reading comprehension, word-level processing occurs alongside the meaningful and metacognitive processes necessary for comprehension. In other words, in addition to strategic and semantic processes, readers must also handle decoding processes, which require additional cognitive flexibility, especially in English. For example Goswami and colleagues (Goswami, Ziegler, Dalton, & Schneider, 2001, 2003; Wimmer & Goswami, 1994; also see Brown & Deavers, 1999, and Simpson & Kang, 1994, for similar work) have compared decoding skills in German- and English-speaking children, as German has a regular orthography with transparent correspondences between graphemes and phonemes, while English has a less regular orthography with irregular, and sometimes unpredictable, correspondences between graphemes and phonemes. Successful readers of English orthographies must employ flexible decoding strategies, as they must consider single grapheme-phoneme relations in some cases, clusters of graphemes to be read by analogy in other cases, and irregular words to be read by sight in still other cases. Readers of German, on the other hand, need not employ such flexible strategy use to decode skillfully. Consistent with this notion, Nagy, Berninger, and colleagues (Nagy, Berninger, & Abbott, 2006; Nagy, Berninger, Abbott, Vaughan, & Vermeulen, 2003) have demonstrated children (reading English) must use flexibly orthographic, phonological, and morphological information, which contribute differentially to children's comprehension across the elementary years and into middle school; and they proposed Triple Word Form Theory to explain the flexibility with which children must learn to use these features to decode new words (Berninger & Nagy, in press).

The necessity for cognitive flexibility in decoding processes is most apparent in work in which such flexibility has been taught. For example, Gaskins and colleagues developed an incredibly effective word identification program at Benchmark School for struggling readers. This program was based on the premise that beginning and struggling readers need flexible access to their knowledge about word reading (like Spiro's notion of flexibility, above). Thus, they devised a method whereby students would learn to "fully analyze words" by processing multiple aspects of printed words and by using multiple decoding strategies. This program essentially improves children's cognitive flexibility in word reading, resulting in significant improvement in reading achievement for these students (Gaskins, 2004, 2005, 2008; Gaskins, Downer, Anderson, Cunningham, Gaskins, Schommer et al., 1988; Gaskins, Ehri, Cress, O'Hara, & Donnelly, 1996–97, 1997). Taken together, the work reviewed in this section indicates cognitive flexibility plays an additional role in reading comprehension through its influence in successful decoding processes.

Expert readers

Much of the work on reading comprehension processes has focused on less-skilled readers, the processes that are deficient in these readers, or the interventions that produce improvement in these readers. However, less-skilled readers provide an incomplete picture of optimal comprehension processes. Comparatively little work has investigated the nature of highly skilled readers' cognitive processes, although such work may provide a more complete picture of the nature of cognitive processing, and the role of cognitive flexibility, in optimal reading comprehension. Thus, this section closes with a brief review of work on expert readers, as expert readers provide a picture of the best possible comprehension processing, which may provide insight on the potential roles of cognitive flexibility in skilled reading comprehension.

Research on highly skilled readers shows that their reading processes are characterized by tremendous flexibility and coordination of multiple elements, including prior knowledge, text features, and metacognitive, strategic processes (e.g., Pressley & Afflerbach, 1995; Wyatt, Pressley, El-Dinary, Stein, Evans, & Brown, 1993). Recently, Pressley and Lundeberg (2008) offered a review of work on expert readers' cognitive processes, arguing that expert reading comprehension is "massively flexible" and "is an acquisition that involves many components and develops over an extended period of time, with the case made that a comprehensive theory of reading development and education must be one that includes many more components and many more years than the theories of reading development and instruction that we currently have" (p. 2). They concluded expert reading is planful, metacognitively reflective, informed by prior domain knowledge, and highly flexible. These characteristics are remarkably similar to those described by Feltovich, Prietula, and Ericsson (2006) in a recent review of the psychological literature on experts' cognitive processes. Feltovich et al. concluded, for example, that expertise is domain specific, experts are metacognitively reflective, and they are purposefully selective of relevant task features for processing (Feltovich, Prietula, & Ericsson, 2006). Further, they noted that expert cognitive processing involves "integrated representations of knowledge and coordination of initially separate tasks that make the fundamental information-processing limits inapplicable or substantially attenuated" (p. 59). The flexibility and coordination observed in experts' processing is consistent with the account of cognitive flexibility presented in this chapter. Additionally, such flexibility must necessarily develop over time, but relatively little work has investigated how expert reading processes develop. Contemporary work in cognitive development, especially research that focuses on the development of cognitive flexibility, may provide fruitful directions for better understanding how the development of highly flexible, expert comprehension develops.

WHERE ARE WE NOW, AND WHERE DO WE GO FROM HERE?

The purpose of this chapter was to demonstrate applications of contemporary cognitive developmental work on cognitive flexibility to research in reading comprehension. These perspectives offer much beyond classic (Piagetian) notions of cognitive change, including a focus on cognitive complexity, the notion of domain specificity in cognitive change, and a lifespan perspective. Cognitive flexibility, the ability to coordinate and attend flexibly to multiple task elements or mental representations, may help to explain how readers handle the complexities involved in reading tasks, how such cognitive coordination develops, and how it can be taught. To date, relatively little research on reading comprehension has been derived from contemporary work on cognitive flexibility, but recognition of the importance of flexibility to reading comprehension processes has been evident in the literature for almost a century. Historically, notions of flexibility, although slightly different in focus, have all had in common the assertion that readers must consider flexibly multiple elements, whether they are aspects of print, text propositions, metacognitive strategies, decoding strategies, or prior knowledge. Thus, each of the historical perspectives on flexibility is compatible with contemporary perspectives on cognitive flexibility. However, these perspectives were less clear regarding the mechanisms by which reading-specific cognitive flexibility develops across the lifespan and the mechanisms by which such flexibility can be taught.

Hence, much remains to be done in order to elucidate the nature of cognitive flexibility in skilled reading. Work on expert readers' comprehension processes may offer a model of optimal flexibility that can guide future research, but additional work is needed to clarify the precise nature and operation of cognitive flexibility in expert reading. Additionally, the development (or lack of development) of cognitive flexibility in reading processes across childhood should be examined. Further, what is the natural course of the development of reading-specific cognitive flexibility (i.e., what does it look like across the lifespan)? How do readers acquire the ability to coordinate text elements? These are questions that need answers to further inform our understanding of the role of cognitive flexibility in the development of comprehension.

Reading comprehension research clearly indicates that children can be taught to consider flexibly multiple features of reading tasks: graphophonological and semantic features; inconsistent propositions in text; text propositions and prior knowledge; metacognitive strategies and text content; and even multiple decoding strategies and meaning. Much of this research was not informed, however, by recent work on cognitive flexibility. Given that cognitive flexibility develops with domain-specific experience and is improved with domain-specific interventions, reading researchers may benefit from analyses of particular demands of reading tasks with which less-skilled readers demonstrate inflexibility. For example, beginning and struggling readers tend to focus inflexibly on graphophonological features of print to the exclusion of meaning (e.g., Dewitz & Dewitz, 2003; Gaskins & Gaskins, 1997; Yuill & Oakhill, 1991). By developing a task that forces readers to focus flexibly on both of these aspects of print, an effective intervention for improving reading comprehension emerged (Cartwright, 2002, 2006; Cartwright et al., 2007). Comparisons of highly skilled, expert readers to less-skilled readers may point to additional, task-specific opportunities for improving cognitive flexibility and comprehension.

In addition to investigating the natural course of developing flexibility and reading-specific opportunities for flexibility intervention, research must also examine the relative efficacy of different instructional approaches for fostering cognitive flexibility in reading. The Reading Wars in recent decades have centered on rather unitary approaches to reading instruction (either phonics or whole language, which emphasize graphophonemic or meaningful aspects of print, respectively). Recent analyses (e.g.,

Pressley, 2006) indicate neither extreme is optimal for student learning and that balanced, or integrated, instructional approaches produce optimal reading achievement. Perhaps a balanced perspective, which focuses on multiple elements of reading tasks, fosters the kind of cognitive flexibility essential for skilled reading that the more unitary approaches do not. This is a question that remains for future research.

Finally, the research reviewed in this chapter has important implications for theoretical conceptions of skilled reading. Many have argued that current conceptions of reading skill in the United States are too simple (e.g., Allington, 2002; Cartwright, 2007; Pressley, Duke et al., in press). However, the reading comprehension research reviewed here points to the complexity inherent in reading processes and the flexibility with which individuals must learn to process the many elements to be handled in reading tasks. These complexities must be understood and addressed in theoretical conceptions of reading comprehension, in research agendas, and in educational practice in order to foster optimal reading comprehension for all students. Integrating notions of cognitive flexibility into these arenas has the potential to move the field closer to that goal.

NOTE

1. I am indebted to Emily Rodgers who brought Clay's perspective on flexibility to my attention.

REFERENCES

Adams, M. J. (1990). *Beginning to read: Thinking and learning about print.* MIT Press: Cambridge, MA.

Adams, M. J. (2004). Modeling the connections between word recognition and reading. In R. B. Ruddell & N. J. Unrau (Eds.), *Theoretical models and processes of reading* (5th ed., pp. 1219–1243). Newark, DE: International Reading Association. Reprinted from R. B. Ruddell, M. R. Ruddell, & H. Singer (Eds.) (1994). *Theoretical models and processes of reading* (4th ed., pp. 838–863). Newark, DE: International Reading Association.

Adams, M. J., & Collins, A. (1985). A schema-theoretic view of reading. In H. Singer & R. B. Ruddell (Eds.), *Theoretical models and processes of reading* (3rd ed., pp. 404–425). International Reading Association.

Alexander, P. A. (1998). The nature of disciplinary and domain learning: The knowledge, interest, and strategic dimensions of learning from subject matter text. In C. R. Hynd (Ed.) *Learning from text across conceptual domains* (pp. 263–286). Mahwah, NJ: Erlbaum.

Alexander, P. A., Jetton, T. L., & Kulikowich, J. M. (1995). Interrelationship of knowledge, interest, and recall: Assessing a model of domain learning. *Journal of Educational Psychology, 87,* 559–575.

Alexander, P. A., Sperl, C. T., Buehl, M. M., Fives, H., & Chiu, S. (2004). Modeling domain learning: Profiles from the field of special education. *Journal of Educational Psychology, 96,* 545–557.

Allington, R. (2002). *Big brother and the national reading curriculum: How ideology trumped evidence.* Portsmouth, NH: Heinemann.

Althouse, R. (1985). The relationship between initial reading and performance on Piagetian tasks. *Reading Improvement, 22,* 21–28.

Anderson, R. C., & Pearson, P. D. (1984/2002). A schema-theoretic view of basic processes in reading comprehension. In P. D. Pearson (Ed.), *Handbook of Reading Research* (Vol. 1, pp. 255–291). Mahwah, NJ: Erlbaum.

Andrews, G., & Halford, G. S. (2002). A cognitive complexity metric applied to cognitive development. *Cognitive Psychology, 45,* 153–219.

Arlin, P. (1981). Piagetian tasks as predictors of reading and math readiness in Grades K–1. *Journal of Educational Psychology, 73,* 712–721.

Armburuster, B. B., Anderson, T. H., & Ostertag, J. (1987). Does text structure/summarization instruction facilitate learning from expository text? *Reading Research Quarterly, 22,* 331–346.

Astington, J. W., Harris, P. L., & Olson, D. R. (1988). *Developing theories of mind*. New York: Cambridge University Press.

August, D. L., Flavell, J. H., & Clift, R. (1984). Comparison of comprehension monitoring of skilled and less skilled readers. *Reading Research Quarterly, 20,* 39–53.

Baker, L. & Brown, A. L. (1984/2002). Metacognitive skills and reading. In P. D. Pearson (Ed.), *Handbook of reading research* (Vol. I, pp. 353–394). Mahwah, NJ: Erlbaum.

Bayliss, D. M., Jarrold, C., Baddeley, A. D., & Leigh, E. (2005). Differential constraints on the working memory and reading abilities of individuals with learning difficulties and typically developing children. *Journal of Experimental Child Psychology, 92,* 76–99.

Berger, A. (1967). Effectiveness of four methods of increasing reading rate, comprehension, and flexibility. *Perceptual & Motor Skills, 24,* 948–950.

Berninger, V. W., & Nagy, W. (in press). Flexibility in word reading: Multiple levels of representations, complex mappings, partial similarities, and cross-modality connections. In K. B. Cartwright (Ed.), *Flexibility in literacy processes and instructional practice: Implications of developing representational ability for literacy teaching and learning*. New York: Guilford.

Bialystok, E., & Niccols, A. (1989). Children's control over attention to phonological and semantic properties of words. *Journal of Psycholinguistic Research, 18,* 369–387.

Bigler, R. S., & Liben, L. (1992). Cognitive mechanisms in children's gender stereotyping: Theoretical and educational implications of a cognitive-based intervention. *Child Development, 63,* 1351–1363.

Block, C. C. (1993). Strategy instruction in a literature-based reading program. *The Elementary School Journal, 94,* 139–151.

Block, C. C., & Pressley, M. (2001). *Comprehension instruction: Research-based best practices*. New York: Guilford Press.

Block, C. C., Schaller, J. L., Joy, J. A., & Gaine, P. (2001). Process-based comprehension instruction. In C. C. Block & M. Pressley (Eds.), *Comprehension instruction: Research-based best practices* (chapter 4, pp. 42–61). New York: Guilford.

Blommers, P., & Lindquist, E. F. (1944). Rate of comprehension of reading: Its measurement and its relation to comprehension. *Journal of Educational Psychology, 35,* 449–473.

Borduin, B. J., Borduin, C. M., & Manley, C. M. (1994). The use of imagery training to improve reading comprehension of second graders. *Journal of Genetic Psychology, 155,* 115–118.

Braam, L. (1963). Developing and measuring flexibility in reading. *The Reading Teacher, 16,* 247–251.

Brace, J. J., Morton, J. B., & Munakata, Y. (2006). When actions speak louder than words: Improving children's flexibility in a card sorting task. *Psychological Science, 17,* 665–669.

Briggs, C., & Elkind, D. (1973). Cognitive development in early readers. *Developmental Psychology, 9,* 279–280.

Britton, B. K., & Glynn, S. M. (1987). *Executive control processes in reading*. Hillsdale, NJ: Erlbaum.

Brown, G. D. A., & Deavers, R. P. (1999). Units of analysis in nonword reading: Evidence from children and adults. *Journal of Experimental Child Psychology, 73,* 208–242.

Brown, R., Pressley, M., Van Meter, P., Schuder, T. (1996). A quasi-experimental validation of transactional strategies instruction with low-achieving second-grade readers. *Journal of Educational Psychology, 85,* 18–37.

Cain, K., & Oakhill, J. V. (1999). Inference making ability and its relation to comprehension failure. *Reading and Writing, 11,* 489–503.

Canter, A. (1975). *A developmental study of the relationships between cognitive abilities and early reading achievement*. Unpublished doctoral dissertation, University of Minnesota.

Carr, E. M., Dewitz, P., & Patberg, J. P. (1983). The effects of inference training on children's comprehension of expository text. *Journal of Reading Behavior, 15,* 1–18.

Carrillo, L. W., & Sheldon, W. D. (1952). The flexibility of reading rate. *Journal of Educational Psychology, 43,* 299–305.

Cartwright, K. B. (2002). Cognitive development and reading: The relation of reading-specific multiple classification skill to reading comprehension in elementary school children. *Journal of Educational Psychology, 94,* 56–63.

Cartwright, K. B. (2006). Fostering flexibility and comprehension in elementary students. *The Reading Teacher, 59,* 628–634.

Cartwright, K. B. (2007). The contribution of graphophonological-semantic flexibility to reading comprehension in college students: Implications for a less simple view of reading. *Journal of Literacy Research, 39,* 173–193.

Cartwright, K. B. (Ed.) (2008). *Literacy processes: Cognitive flexibility in learning and teaching*. New York: Guilford Press.

Cartwright, K. B., Bock, A., Guiffré, H., & Montaño, M. (2006). Using classification tasks to assess and improve reading-specific cognitive flexibility. *Cognitive Technology, 11*(2), 23–29.

Cartwright, K. B., Hodgkiss, M. D., & Isaac, M. C. (2008). Graphophonological-semantic flexibility: Contributions to skilled reading across the lifespan. In K. B. Cartwright (Ed.), *Literacy processes: Cognitive flexibility in learning and teaching*. New York: Guilford.

Cartwright, K. B., Isaac, M. C., & Dandy, K. L. (2006). The development of reading-specific representational flexibility: A cross-sectional comparison of second graders, fourth graders, and college students. In A.V. Mittel (Ed.), *Focus on educational psychology*. New York: Nova Science Publishers.

Cartwright, K. B, Marshall, T. R., Dandy, K. L., & Isaac, M. C. (2007). The development of graphophonological-semantic flexibility and its contribution to reading comprehension in beginning readers. Manuscript under review.

Cartwright, K. B., Schmidt, K., Clause, J., Price, G., & Thomas, S. (2007). Small group reading-specific flexibility intervention for struggling readers. Unpublished data.

Case, R. (1992). Neo-Piagetian theories of child development. In R. J. Sternberg & C. A. Berg (Eds.) *Intellectual development* (chapter 6, pp. 161–196). New York: Cambridge University Press.

Case, R., & Okamoto, Y. (1996). The role of central conceptual structures in the development of children's thought. *Monographs of the Society for Research in Child Development, 61*(1–2, Serial No. 246).

Chinn, C., & Brewer, W. F. (1993). The role of anomalous data in knowledge acquisition; a theoretical framework and implications for science instruction. *Review of Educational Research, 63*, 1–49.

Clay, M. M. (1969). Reading errors and self-correction behavior. *British Journal of Educational Psychology, 39*, 47–56.

Clay, M. M. (1985). *The early detection of reading difficulties* (3rd ed.). Portsmouth, NH: Heinemann.

Clay, M. M., (1991). *Becoming literate: The construction of inner control*. Portsmouth, NH: Heinemann.

Clay, M. M. (2001). *Change over time in children's literacy development*. Portsmouth, NH: Heinemann.

Cohen, S. A., Hyman, J. S., & Battistini, E. E. (1983). Effects of teaching Piagetian decentration upon learning to read. *Reading Improvement, 20*, 96–104.

Crain-Thoreson, C. (1996). Phonemic processes in children's listening and reading comprehension. *Applied Cognitive Psychology, 10*, 383–401.

D'Agostino, J. V., & Murphy, J. A. (2004). A meta-analysis of Reading Recovery in United States schools. *Educational Evaluation and Policy Analysis, 26*, 23–38.

Dash, U. N., & Mohanty, A. (1992). Relationship of reading comprehension with metalinguistic awareness. *Social Science International, 8*, 5–13.

Davey, B., & McBride, S. (1986). Effects of question-generation training on reading comprehension. *Journal of Educational Psychology, 78*, 256–262.

Deák, G. O. (2003). The development of cognitive flexibility and language abilities. In R. Kail (Ed.), *Advances in Child Development and Behavior* (pp. 271–327). San Diego, CA: Academic Press.

DeLoache, J. (1991). Symbolic functioning in very young children: Understanding of pictures and models. *Child Development, 62*, 736–752.

Dewitz, P., Carr, E. M., & Patberg, J. P. (1987). The effects of inference training on comprehension and comprehension monitoring. *Reading Research Quarterly, 22*, 99–121.

Dewitz, P., & Dewitz, P. K. (2003). They can read the words, but they can't understand. *The Reading Teacher, 56*, 422–435.

Diamond, A., Kirkham, N. (2005). Not quite as grown up as we like to think: Parallels between cognition in childhood and adulthood. *Psychological Science, 16*, 291–297.

DiStefano, P., Noe, M., & Valencia, S. (1981). Measurement of the effects of purpose and passage difficulty on reading flexibility. *Journal of Educational Psychology, 73*, 602–606.

Dowdy, C. A., Crump, W. D., & Welch, M. W. (1982). Reading flexibility of learning disabled and normal students at three grade levels. *Learning Disability Quarterly, 5*, 253–263.

Duffy, G. G., Roehler, L. R., & Herrmann, B. A. (1988). Modeling mental processes helps poor readers become strategic readers. *The Reading Teacher, 41*, 762–767.

Duffy, G. G., Roehler, L. R., Sivan, E., Rackcliffe, G., Book, C., Meloth, M. S., Vavrus, L. G., Wesselman, R., Putnam, J., & Bassiri, J. (1987). Effects of explaining the reasoning associated with using reading strategies. *Reading Research Quarterly, 22*, 347–368.

Ehri, L. (1991). Development of the ability to read words. In R. Barr, M. Kamil, P. Mosenthal, & P.D. Pearson (Eds.), *Handbook of reading research, Vol. II* (pp. 383–417). New York: Longman.

Ehri, L. C. (1992). Reconceptualizing the development of sight word reading and its relationship to recoding. In P. B. Gough, L. C. Ehri, & R. Treiman (Eds.), *Reading acquisition* (chapter 5, pp. 107–143). Hillsdale, NJ: Erlbaum.

Ehrlich, M., Remond, M., & Tardieu, H. (1999). Processing of anaphoric devices in young skilled and less skilled comprehenders: Differences in metacognitive monitoring. *Reading & Writing, 11*, 29–63.

Elkind, D., Larson, M., & Van Doorninck, W. (1965). Perceptual decentration learning and performance in slow and average readers. *Journal of Educational Psychology, 56*, 50–56.

Farrar, M. J., & Ashwell, S. (2008). The role of representational ability in the development of phonological awareness in preschool children. In K. B. Cartwright (Ed.), *Literacy processes: Cognitive flexibility in learning and teaching*. New York: Guilford.

Farrar, M. J., Ashwell, S., & Maag, L. (2005). The emergence of phonological awareness: Connections to language and theory of mind development. *First Language, 25*, 157–172.

Feltovich, P. J., Prietula, M. J., & Ericsson, K. A. (2006). Studies of expertise from psychological perspectives. In K. A. Ericsson, N. Charness, P. J. Feltovich, & R. R.Hoffman (Eds.) *The Cambridge handbook of expertise and expert performance* (pp. 41–67). New York: Cambridge University Press.

Feltovich, P. J., Spiro, R. J., & Coulson, R. L. (1997). Issues of expert flexibility in contexts characterized by complexity and change. In P. J. Feltovich, K. M. Ford, & R. R. Huffman (Eds.), *Expertise in context: Human and machine* (pp. 125–146). Cambridge, MA: MIT Press.

Flavell, J. H. (1977). *Cognitive development*. Prentice Hall.

Flavell, J. H. (1979). Metacognition and cognitive monitoring: A new area of cognitive-developmental inquiry. *American Psychologist, 34*, 906–911.

Flavell, J. H. (1988). The development of children's knowledge about the mind: From cognitive connections to mental representations. In J. W. Astington, P. L. Harris, & D. R. Olson (Eds.), *Developing theories of mind* (pp. 244–267). New York: Cambridge University Press.

Flavell, J. H. (1992). Cognitive development: Past, present, and future. *Developmental Psychology, 28*, 998–1005.

Flavell, J. H., Friedrichs, A. G., & Hoyt, J. D. (1970). Developmental changes in memorization processes. *Cognitive Psychology, 1*, 324–340.

Flavell, J. H., Green, F. L., & Flavell, E. R. (1986). Development of knowledge about the appearance-reality distinction. *Monographs of the Society for Research in Child Development, 51*(1, Serial No. 212).

Forguson, L., & Gopnik, A. (1988). The ontogeny of common sense. In J. W. Astington, P. L. Harris, & D. R. Olson (Eds.), *Developing theories of mind* (pp. 226–243). New York: Cambridge University Press.

Fry, E. B. (1978). *Skimming & scanning*. Providence, RI: Jamestown Publishers.

Frye, D., Zelazo, P. D., & Burack, J. A. (1998). Cognitive complexity and control I: Theory of mind in typical and atypical development. *Current Directions in Psychological Science, 7*, 116–121.

Frye, D., Zelazo, P. D., & Palfai, T. (1995). Theory of mind and rule-based reasoning. *Cognitive Development, 10*, 483–527.

Garner, R. (1994). Metacognition and executive control. In R. B. Ruddell, M. R. Ruddell, & H. Singer (Eds.), *Theoretical models and processes of reading* (4th ed., pp. 715–732). Newark, DE: International Reading Association.

Garner, R., & Kraus, C. (1981). Good and poor comprehender differences in knowing and regulating reading behaviors. *Educational Research Quarterly, 6*, 5–12.

Gaskins, I. (2004). Word detectives. *Educational Leadership, 61*, 70–73.

Gaskins, I. (2005). *Success with struggling readers: The Benchmark School approach*. New York: Guilford.

Gaskins, I. W. (2008). Developing cognitive flexibility in word reading among beginning and struggling readers. In K. B. Cartwright (Ed.), *Literacy processes: Cognitive flexibility in learning and teaching*. New York: Guilford.

Gaskins, I.W., Downer, M., Anderson, R., Cunningham, P., Gaskins, R., Schommer, M., & the Teachers of Benchmark School (1988). A metacognitive approach to phonics: Using what you know to decode what you don't know. *Remedial and Special Education, 9,* 36–41.

Gaskins, I. W., Ehri, L., Cress, C., O'Hara, C., & Donnelly, K. (1996–97). Procedures for word learning: Making discoveries about words. *The Reading Teacher, 50,* 312–327.

Gaskins, I. W., Ehri, L., Cress, C., O'Hara, C., & Donnelly, K. (1997). Analyzing words and making discoveries about the alphabetic system: Activities for beginning readers. *Language Arts, 74,* 172–184.

Gaskins, R. W., & Gaskins, I. W. (1997). Creating readers who read for meaning and love to read: The Benchmark School reading program. In S. A. Stahl & D. A. Hayes (Eds.), *Instructional models in reading* (chapter 6, pp. 131–159). Mahwah, NJ: Erlbaum.

Goodman, K. S. (1973). Miscues: Windows on the reading process. In K. S. Goodman (Ed.), *Miscue analysis: Applications to reading instruction.* Urbana, IL: ERIC Clearinghouse on Reading and Communication Skills.

Goodman, K. S. (1976). Behind the eye: What happens in reading. In H. Singer & R. B. Ruddell (Eds.), *Theoretical models and processes of reading* (2nd ed. pp. 470–496). Newark, DE: International Reading Association.

Goodman, K. S. (1994). Reading, writing, and written texts: A transactional sociopsycholinguistic view. In R. B. Ruddell, M. R. Ruddell, & H. Singer (Eds.), *Theoretical models and processes of reading* (4th ed., pp. 1093–1130).

Goswami, U., Ziegler, J. C., Dalton, L., & Schneider, W. (2001). Pseudohomophone effects and phonological recoding procedures in reading development in English and German. *Journal of Memory and Language, 45,* 648–664.

Goswami, U., Ziegler, J. C., Dalton, L., & Schneider, W. (2003). Nonword reading across orthographies: How flexible is the choice of reading units? *Applied Psycholinguistics, 24,* 235–247.

Graesser, A. C., Singer, M., & Trabasso, T. (1994). Constructing inferences during text comprehension. *Psychological Review, 101,* 371–395.

Gray, L., & Reese, D. (1957). *Teaching children to read.* New York: Ronald Press.

Guajardo, N. R., Parker, J., & Turley-Ames, K. J. (2007). Associations among false belief understanding, counterfactual reasoning, and information processing skills. Manuscript in preparation.

Hakala, C. M., & O'Brien, E. J. (1995). Strategies for resolving coherence breaks in reading. *Discourse Processes, 20,* 167–185.

Hynd, C. (1998). Conceptual change in a high school physics class. In B. Guzzetti and C. Hynd (Eds.), *Perspectives on conceptual change: Multiple ways to understand learning and knowledge in a complex world.* Mahwah, NJ: Erlbaum.

Hynd, C., McWhorter, Y., Phares, V., & Suttles, W. (1994). The role of instructional variables in conceptual change in high school physics students. *Journal of Research in Science Teaching, 31,* 933–946.

Hynd, C., & Stahl, S. (1998). What do we mean by knowledge and learning? In C. Hynd (Ed.), *Learning from text across conceptual domains* (pp. 15–44). Mahwah, NJ: Erlbaum.

Hynd-Shanahan, C., Holschuh, & Hubbard, B. P. (2004). Thinking like a historian: College students' reading of multiple historical documents. *Journal of Literacy Research, 36,* 141–176.

Inhelder, B., & Piaget, J. (1964). *The early growth of logic in the child* (E. A. Lunzer & D. Papert, Trans.). New York: Humanities Press.

Israel, S. E. (2008). Flexible use of comprehension monitoring strategies: Investigating what a complex reading framework might look like. In K. B. Cartwright (Ed.), *Literacy processes: Cognitive flexibility in learning and teaching.* New York: Guilford.

Israel, S. E., Block, C. C., Kinnucan-Welsch, K., & Bauserman, K. (2005). *Metacognition in literacy learning: Theory, assessment, instruction, and professional development.* Mahwah, NJ: Erlbaum.

Israel, S. E., & Massey, D. (2005). Metacognitive think-alouds: Using a gradual release model with middle school students. In S. E. Israel, C. C. Block, K. L. Bauserman, & K. Kinnucan-Welsch (Eds.), *Metacognition in literacy learning: Theory, assessment, instruction, and professional development* (chapter 10, pp. 183–198). Mahwah, NJ: Erlbaum.

Jacques, S., & Zelazo, P. D. (2001). The flexible item selection task (FIST): A measure of executive function in preschoolers. *Developmental Neuropsychology, 20,* 573–591.

Jacques, S., & Zelazo, P. D. (2005). Language and the development of cognitive flexibility: Implications for theory of mind. In J. W. Astington & J. A. Baird (Eds.), *Why language matters for theory of mind* (chapter 8, pp. 144–162). New York: Wiley.

Just, M. A., & Carpenter, P. A. (1980). A theory of reading: From eye fixations to comprehension. *Psychological Review, 87,* 329–354.

Karmiloff-Smith, A. (1991). Innate constraints and developmental change. In S. Carey & R. Gelman (Eds.), *The epigenesis of mind: Essays on biology and cognition* (pp. 171–197). Hillsdale NJ: Erlbaum.

Keenan, T., Ruffman, T., & Olson, D. R. (1994). When do children begin to understand logical inference as a source of knowledge? *Cognitive Development, 9,* 331–353.

Kintsch, W. (1988). The role of knowledge in discourse comprehension: A construction-integration model. *Psychological Review, 95,* 163–182.

Kintsch, W., & van Dijk, T. A. (1978). Toward a model of text comprehension and production. *Psychological Review, 85,* 363–394.

Kirkham, N. Z., Cruess, L., & Diamond, A. (2003). Helping children apply their knowledge to their behavior in a dimension-switching task. *Developmental Science, 6,* 449–476.

Kloo, D., & Perner, J. (2003). Training transfer between card sorting and false belief understanding: Helping children apply conflicting descriptions. *Child Development, 74,* 1823–1839.

Kloo, D., & Perner, J. (2005). Disentangling dimensions in the dimensional change card-sorting task. *Developmental Science, 8,* 44–56.

Kuhn, D., & Pease, M. (2006). Do children and adults learn differently? *Journal of Cognition and Development, 7,* 279–293.

Labouvie-Vief, G. (1990). Modes of knowledge and the organization of development. In M. L. Commons, C. Armon, L. Kohlberg, F. A. Richards, T. A. Grotzer, & J. D. Sinnott (Eds.), *Adult development, Volume 2: Models and methods in the study of adolescent and adult thought* (chapter 3, pp. 43–62). New York: Praeger.

Labouvie-Vief, G. (1992). A neo-Piagetian perspective on adult cognitive development. In R. J. Sternberg & C. A. Berg (Eds.), *Intellectual development* (chapter 7, pp. 197–228). New York: Cambridge University Press.

Laing, A. P., & Kamhi, A. G. (2002). The use of think-aloud protocols to compare inferencing abilities in average and below-average readers. *Journal of Learning Disabilities, 35,* 436–447.

Luna, B., Garver, K. E., Urban, T. A., Lazar, N. A., & Sweeney, J. A. (2004). Maturation of cognitive processes from late childhood to adulthood. *Child Development, 75,* 1357–1372.

Luo, C. R., Johnson, R. A., & Gallo, D. A. (1998). Automatic activation of phonological information in reading: Evidence from the semantic relatedness decision task. *Memory and Cognition, 26,* 833–843.

Markman, E. (1979). Realizing that you don't understand: Elementary school children's awareness of inconsistencies. *Child Development, 50,* 643–655.

Masson, M. E. (1987). Remembering reading operations with and without awareness. In B. K. Britton & S. M. Glynn (Eds.), *Executive control processes in reading* (pp. 253–277). Hillsdale, NJ: Erlbaum.

McCutchen, D., & Crain-Thoreson, C. (1994). Phonemic processes in children's reading comprehension. *Journal of Experimental Child Psychology, 58,* 69–87.

McCutchen, D., Dibble, E., & Blount, M. M. (1994). Phonemic effects in reading comprehension and text memory. *Applied Cognitive Psychology, 8,* 597–611.

McDonald, A. S. (1965). Research for the classroom: Rate and reading flexibility. *Journal of Reading, 8,* 187–191.

McGee, A., & Johnson, H. (2003). The effect of inference training on skilled and less skilled comprehenders. *Educational Psychology, 23,* 49–59.

Miller, P. H. (2006). A lot of knowledge is a dangerous thing: Learning in children and adults. *Journal of Cognition and Development, 7,* 305–308.

Myers, M., & Paris, S. G. (1978). Children's metacognitive knowledge about reading. *Journal of Educational Psychology, 70,* 680–690.

Nagy, W. (2007). Metalinguistic awareness and the vocabulary-comprehension connection. In R. K. Wagner, A. E. Muse, & K. R. Tannenbaum (Eds.), *Vocabulary acquisition: Implications for reading comprehension.* New York: Guilford.

Nagy, W., Berninger, V., & Abbott, R. (2006). Contributions of morphology beyond phonology to literacy outcomes of upper elementary and middle school students. *Journal of Educational Psychology, 98,* 134–147.

Nagy, W., Berninger, V., Abbott, R., Vaughan, K., & Vermeulen, K. (2003). Relationship of morphology and other language skills to literacy skills in at-risk second-grade readers and at-risk fourth-grade writers. *Journal of Educational Psychology, 95,* 730–742.

Oakhill, J. (1993). Children's difficulties in reading comprehension. *Educational Psychology Review, 5,* 223–237.

Oakhill, J. V., Cain, K., & Bryant, P. E. (2003). The dissociation of word reading and text comprehension: Evidence from component skills. *Language and Cognitive Processes, 18,* 443–468.

Oakhill, J., & Patel, S. (1991). Can imagery training help children who have comprehension problems? *Journal of Research in Reading, 14,* 106–115.

Oakhill, J., & Yuill, N. (1996). Higher order factors in comprehension disability: Processes and remediation. In C. Cornoldi & J. Oakhill (Eds.), *Reading comprehension difficulties: Processes and intervention* (pp. 69–92). Mahwah, NJ: Erlbaum.

Oakhill, J., Yuill, N., & Parkin, A. (1986). On the nature of the difference between skilled and less skilled comprehenders. *Journal of Research in Reading, 9,* 80–91.

Palinscar, A. S., & Brown, A. L. (1984). Reciprocal teaching of comprehension-fostering and comprehension-monitoring activities. *Cognition and Instruction, 1,* 117–175.

Paris, S. G., & Myers, M. (1981). Comprehension monitoring, memory, and study strategies of good and poor readers. *Journal of Reading Behavior, 13,* 5–22.

Perfetti, C. A. (1985). *Reading ability.* New York: Oxford University Press.

Perfetti, C. A. (1992). The representation problem in reading acquisition. In P. B. Gough, L. C. Ehri, & R. Treiman (Eds.), *Reading acquisition* (chapter 6, pp. 145–174). Hillsdale, NJ: Erlbaum.

Perner, J., & Lang, B. (1999). Development of theory of mind and executive control. *Trends in Cognitive Sciences, 3*(9), 337–344.

Piaget, J. (1972). Intellectual evolution from adolescence to adulthood. *Human Development, 15,* 1–12.

Piaget, J., & Inhelder, B. (1969). *The psychology of the child* (Helen Weaver, Trans.). New York: Basic Books. (Original work published 1966)

Pressley, M. (1976). Mental imagery helps eight-year-olds remember what they read. *Journal of Educational Psychology, 68,* 355–359.

Pressley, M. (2006). *Reading instruction that works: The case for balanced* teaching (3rd ed.). New York: Guilford.

Pressley, M., & Afflerbach, P. (1995). *Verbal protocols of reading: The nature of constructively responsive reading.* Mahwah, NJ: Erlbaum.

Pressley, M., Duke, N. K., Gaskins, I. W., Fingeret, L., Halladay, J., Hilden, K., Park, Y., Zhang, S., Mohan, L., Reffitt, K., Bogaert, L. R., Reynolds, J., Golos, D., Solic, K., & Collins, S. (in press). Working with struggling readers: Why we must get beyond the simple view of reading and visions of how it might be done. In T. Gutkin & C. R. Reynolds (Eds.), *Handbook of school psychology* (4th ed.). New York: Wiley.

Pressley, M., El-Dinary, P. B., Gaskins, I., Schuder, T., Bergman, J. L., Almasi, J., & Brown, R. (1992). Beyond direct explanation: Transactional instruction of reading comprehension strategies. *The Elementary School Journal, 92,* 513–555.

Pressley, M., & Lundeberg, M. (2008). An invitation to study professionals reading professional-level texts: A window on exceptionally complex, flexible reading. In K. B. Cartwright (Ed.), *Literacy processes: Cognitive flexibility in learning and teaching.* New York: Guilford.

Ramsel, D., & Grabe, M. (1983). Attention allocation and performance in goal-directed reading: Age difference in reading flexibility. *Journal of Reading Behavior, 15,* 55–65.

Reis, R., & Spekman, N. (1983). The detection of reader-based versus text-based inconsistencies and the effects of direct training of comprehension monitoring among upper-grade poor comprehenders. *Journal of Reading Behavior, 15,* 49–60.

Reutzel, D. R., & Hollingsworth, P. M. (1988). Highlighting key vocabulary: A generative-reciprocal procedure for teaching selected inference types. *Reading Research Quarterly, 23,* 358–378.

Rong, Y., & Guo-liang, Y. (2006). Cognitive flexibility of reading-disabled children: Development and characteristics. *Chinese Journal of Clinical Psychology, 14,* 33–35.

Rubman, C. N., & Waters, H. S. (2000). A, B seeing: The role of constructive processes in children's comprehension monitoring. *Journal of Educational Psychology, 92,* 503–514.

Ruffman, T. (1996). Reassessing children's comprehension-monitoring skills. In C. Cornoldi & J. Oakhill (Eds.), *Reading comprehension difficulties: Processes and intervention* (chapter 3, 33–67). Mahwah, NJ: Erlbaum.

Ruffman, T. (1999). Children's understanding of logical inconsistency. *Child Development, 70,* 872–886.

Sadoski, M. (1983). An exploratory study of the relationships between reported imagery and the comprehension and recall of a story. *Reading Research Quarterly, 19,* 110–123.

Schwartz, R. M., & Stanovich, K. E. (1981). Flexibility in the use of graphic and contextual information by good and poor readers. *Journal of Reading Behavior, 13,* 263–269.

Simpson, G. B, & Kang, H. (1994). The flexible use of phonological information in word recognition in Korean. *Journal of Memory & Language, 33,* 319–331.

Sinnott, J. D. (1998). *The development of logic in adulthood: Postformal thought and its applications.* New York: Plenum Press.

Spiro, R. J. (2004). Principled pluralism for adaptive flexibility in teaching and learning to read. In R. B. Ruddell & N. J. Unrau (Eds.), *Theoretical models and processes of reading* (5th ed., pp. 654–659). Reprinted from Flippo, R. F. (Ed.) (2000). *Reading researchers in search of common ground* (pp. 92–97). Newark, DE: International Reading Association.

Spiro, R. J., Coulson, R. L., Feltovich, P. J., & Anderson, D. K. (1994/1988). Cognitive flexibility theory: Advanced knowledge acquisition in ill-structured domains. In R. B. Ruddell, M. R. Ruddell, & H. Singer (Eds.), *Theoretical models and processes of reading* (4th ed., pp. 602–615). Newark, DE: International Reading Association (reprinted from *Tenth Annual Conference of the Cognitive Science Society Proceedings*).

Spiro, R. J., & Tirre, W. C. (1980). Individual differences in schema utilization during discourse processing. *Journal of Educational Psychology, 72,* 204–208.

Spiro, R. J., Vispoel, W. P., Schmitz, J. G., Samarapungavan, A., & Boerger, A. E. (1987). Knowledge acquisition for application: Cognitive flexibility and transfer in complex content domains. In B. K. Britton & S. M. Glynn (Eds.), *Executive control processes in reading* (pp. 177–199). Hillsdale, NJ: Erlbaum.

Stedron, J. M., Sahni, S. D., & Munakata, Y. (2005). Common mechanisms for working memory and attention: The case of perseveration with visible solutions. *Journal of Cognitive Neuroscience, 17,* 623–631.

Sternberg, R. J. (2000). The rebirth of children's learning. *Child Development, 71,* 26–35.

Sternberg, R. J., & Lyon, G. R. (2002). Making a difference in education: Will psychology pass up the chance? *Monitor on Psychology, 33*(7), 76.

Thorndike, E. L. (1917). Reading as reasoning: A study of mistakes in paragraph reading. *Journal of Educational Psychology, 8,* 323–332.

Tunmer, W. E., Herriman, M. L., & Nesdale, A. R. (1988). Metalinguistic abilities and beginning reading. *Reading Research Quarterly, 23,* 134–158.

Tunmer, W. E., & Hoover, W. A. (1992). Cognitive and linguistic factors in learning to read. In P. B. Gough, L. C. Ehri, & R. Treiman (Eds.), *Reading acquisition* (chapter 7, pp. 175–214). Hillsdale, NJ: Erlbaum.

Van Orden, G. C. (1987). A ROWS is a ROSE: Spelling, sound, and reading. *Memory and Cognition, 15,* 181–198.

VanSledright, B. (2002). Confronting history's interpretive paradox while teaching fifth graders to investigate the past. *American Educational Research Journal, 39,* 1089–1115.

Vidal-Abarca, E., Martínez, G., & Gilabert, R. (2000). Two procedures to improve instructional text: Effects on memory and learning. *Journal of Educational Psychology, 92,* 107–116.

Wagner, R. K., Sternberg, R. J. (1987). Executive control in reading comprehension. In B. K. Britton, & S. M. Glynn (Eds.), *Executive control processes in reading* (pp. 1–21). Hillsdale, NJ: Erlbaum.

Willoughby, T., Porter, L., Belsito, L., & Yearsley, T. (1999). Use of elaboration strategies by students in grades two, four, and six. *The Elementary School Journal, 99,* 221–231.

Wimmer, H., & Goswami, U. (1994). The influence of orthographic consistency on reading development: Word recognition in English and German. *Cognition, 51,* 91–103.

Wineburg, S. S. (1991). On the reading of historical texts: Notes on the breach between school and academy. *American Educational Research Journal, 28,* 495–519.

Wolfe, M. B. W., & Goldman, S. R. (2005). Relationships between adolescents' text processing and reasoning. *Cognition & Instruction, 23,* 467–502.

Wyatt, D., Pressley, M., El-Dinary, P. B., Stein, S., Evans, P., & Brown, R. (1993). Comprehension strategies, worth and credibility monitoring, and evaluations: Cold and hot cognition when experts read professional texts that are important to them. *Learning and Individual Differences, 5,* 49–72.

Yuill, N. (1996). A funny thing happened on the way to the classroom: Jokes, riddles, and metalinguistic awareness in understanding and improving poor comprehension in children. In C. Cornoldi & J. Oakhill (Eds.), *Reading comprehension difficulties: Processes and intervention* (chapter 9, 193–220). Mahwah, NJ: Erlbaum.

Yuill, N. (in press a). Visiting Joke City: How can talking about jokes foster metalinguistic awareness in poor comprehenders? In D. MacNamara (Ed.), *Reading comprehension strategies: theories, interventions and technologies.* Mahwah, NJ: Erlbaum.

Yuill, N. (in press b). The relation between ambiguity understanding and metalinguistic discussion of joking riddles in good and poor comprehenders: Potential for intervention and possible processes of change. *First Language.*

Yuill, N., Kerawalla, L., Pearce, D., Luckin, R., & Harris, A. (2008). Using technology to teach flexibility through peer discussion. In K. B. Cartwright (Ed.), *Literacy processes: Cognitive flexibility in learning and teaching.* New York: Guilford.

Yuill, N., & Oakhill, J. (1988). Effects of inference awareness training on poor reading comprehension. *Applied Cognitive Psychology, 2,* 33–45.

Yuill, N., & Oakhill, J. (1991). *Children's problems in text comprehension: An experimental investigation.* Cambridge: Cambridge University Press.

Zabrucky, K. (1990). Evaluation of understanding in college students: Effects of text structure and reading proficiency. *Reading Research and Instruction, 29,* 46–54.

Zabrucky, K., & Moore, D. (1989). Children's ability to use three standards to evaluate their comprehension of text. *Reading Research Quarterly, 24.* 336–352.

Zelazo, P. D., & Frye, D. (1998). Cognitive complexity and control II: The development of executive function in childhood. *Current Directions in Psychological Science, 7,* 121–126.

Zelazo, P. D., Müller, U., Frye, D., & Marcovitch, S. (2003). The development of executive function in early childhood. *Monographs of the Society for Research in Child Development, 68* (3, Serial No. 274).

7 Ways of Meaning Making
Sociocultural Perspectives on Reading Comprehension

James Gavelek and Patrick Bresnahan

University of Illinois at Chicago

> It is the theory that decides what we can observe.
>
> *Albert Einstein*

INTRODUCTION

Fostering the development of students' abilities to construct and communicate meaning represents a critical goal of education. And more often than not, it is the construction of symbolic meanings that is the coin of the realm in schools. Indeed, this verbocentrism has gone largely unquestioned in guiding how we think about and enact school instruction and assessment. It should come as no surprise, then, that reading comprehension—the construction of meaning from text—is one of the most important competencies that students can master. But to define reading comprehension as solely the construction of meaning from text glosses too much to usefully inform pedagogical practices that are educative. Such a definition leads to a conception of comprehension that is static, unidimensional, and one that obscures the often non-symbolic, sociocultural origins of meaning (Merrell, 1997).

As the quote at the beginning of this chapter suggests, theories serve as lenses drawing our attention of what to see. But if theories can direct us to what is important, they can also serve as a set of blinders leading us to ignore what would otherwise be important. We believe that a sociocultural framework provides the means to bring these nuanced dimensions of reading comprehension and their implications for instruction into far greater relief and it is to this end that this chapter is directed.

In what follows, we maintain that sociocultural theory is really a family of theoretical perspectives sharing common assumptions concerning the nature of mind and its development. And while our focus is mainly on the theory, research, and practices inspired by the seminal ideas of Vygotsky (1978, 1987), we draw upon other sociocultural perspectives (i.e., sociolinguistics, social semiotics, second generation cognitive science) in an effort to offer a more comprehensive and integrative conception of *comprehension* and its *instruction*. After reviewing these sociocultural perspectives, we problematize the very notion of comprehension, arguing that as a social construct, what it means to comprehend a text is dynamic, multidimensional, and contested. We then turn to sociocultural perspectives on comprehension instruction, reviewing illustrative studies that have contributed to our understanding of the role of instruction in comprehension.

Next, we critically discuss the implications of assuming a sociocultural perspective toward comprehension for practice, research and policy. We conclude with a sober appraisal of the challenges that we confront in facing an increasingly more complex global and technical world while truly leaving no child left behind.

SOCIOCULTURAL THEORY

Delineating sociocultural theory

In discussing the ways that sociocultural theory might inform our understanding of reading comprehension, it is first necessary that we make clear how we interpret the term *sociocultural*. In the literature, sociocultural is varyingly used to refer to a specific theoretical perspective and to a family of theoretical perspectives that share common metatheoretical assumptions concerning the nature of mind, the world, and the relationship between the two. In its former, more specific sense, sociocultural theory refers to the seminal ideas deriving from and informed by the original contributions of the Russian psychologist Lev Vygotsky (1962, 1978, 1987, 1997). When used more inclusively, the term *sociocultural* refers not only to those approaches originating directly from Vygotsky, but to a family of disciplinary perspectives including pragmatism, sociolinguistics, social semiotics, and second-generation cognitive science. In this chapter we use the term *sociocultural* in this more inclusive sense and, to avoid confusion, refer to cultural-historical theory when discussing those approaches originating from Vygotsky. While our focus in this chapter *is* on cultural-historical theory, we draw liberally on the scholarship from these other sociocultural perspectives to offer a more comprehensive and integrated conceptualization of comprehension and comprehension instruction.

CULTURAL-HISTORICAL THEORY

Vygotsky's life and times

To appreciate the contributions of Vygotsky it is necessary to understand the setting and times in which he developed his ideas. Born in 1896, Vygotsky's life was cut short by tuberculosis in 1934 prompting philosopher Stephen Toulmin (1978) to characterize him as the "Mozart of psychology." While Vygotsky lived through the Russian Revolution and was attempting to create a Marxist psychology, he was no party apparatchik. As a member of relatively well to do family, Vygotsky enjoyed a liberal European education that was to play an essential role in his thinking. With a deep and abiding love of the arts and letters, Vygotsky served as a theatre and literary critic, collaborated with the great cinematographer Eisenstein, often quoted poetry and was a serious student of the novel. Although considered one of the great developmental psychologists of the twentieth century, he, like Piaget, never had formal training in psychology. Instead, Vygotsky studied and received a degree in law while at the same time working toward his doctorate at a second university. His dissertation *The Psychology of Art* (1971) was a literary analysis of reader response to Shakespeare's *Hamlet*, this, more than a decade before Louise Rosenblatt completed her classic *Literature as Exploration* (1938) on reader response. He was a polymath of the first order.

In formulating his cultural-historical conception of mind, Vygotsky drew on the writings of prominent European (i.e., mainly German) intellectuals as well as those of John Dewey, William James, and James Mark Baldwin in the United States. Because of this cosmopolitanism, many of Vygotsky's ideas fell out of favor once Stalin came to power. His premature death meant that Vygotsky would never incur the wrath of Communist hardliners; however, his followers were faced with the prospect of toeing the party line or else. Vygotsky's texts were suppressed during the Stalinist era, not to be made available again until 1956. Vygotsky's classic *Thought and Language* was published in the United States in 1962 but devoid of the Marxist philosophy that informed the development of his cultural-historical theory. Vygotsky's influence was largely overshadowed by Piagetian theory until the late 1970s. The individualism and rationalism of the latter resonated more with the cognitive revolution that was then taking place. Moreover, early in his career, Vygotsky had used the language of behaviorism that led some to believe he was simply another contributor to what was becoming a refuted perspective. Nothing could have been further from the truth but it would not be until the early 1980s that the writings of Vygotsky began to enjoy a wider readership. As we shall see, however, the uptake by U.S. educators of Vygotsky's work has been an incomplete and misleading account of his theory.

Vygotsky's Marxist psychology

Vygotsky struggled with the same subject-object dualisms that continue to fragment psychology and the other social sciences today, specifically, how to resolve the disparity between idealist perspectives that depicted the individual as lost in thought or vulgar materialism that left the subject missing in action. Toward this end he set out to create a Marxist psychology but as suggested earlier his was by no means a knee-jerk reaction to the received Soviet interpretation of Marx. Indeed, his reluctance to uncritically adhere to party orthodoxy would be the source of conflict not only between Vygotsky and proponents of the official Soviet party, but also between Vygotsky and some of his followers. This would result in the creation of a separate Kharkov school and what eventually was to become cultural-historical *activity* theory discussed later in the chapter (Leont'ev, 1981; Gielen & Jeshmaridian, 1999).

Three themes in Vygotsky's cultural-historical theory

Three interrelated themes are commonly identified in characterizing Vygotsky's original cultural-historical theory: 1) the social origins of mind and knowledge; 2) the mediation of mind by tools and signs; and 3) the genetic or developmental analyses of mind (Wertsch, 1985).

Social origins of mind

Perhaps the central tenet of all sociocultural theories, cultural-historical and otherwise, is the assumption that mind emerges in our interaction with others. In his general genetic law of cultural development Vygotsky claimed:

> Every function in the child's cultural development appears twice: first, on the social level, and later on the individual level; first, between people (interpsychological), and then inside the child (intrapsycholgoical)... All the higher functions originate as relations between human individuals. (Vygotsky, 1978, p. 57)

While he cited the formation of concepts and logical memory as examples of these higher functions, Vygotsky could just as well have mentioned the processes involved in reading comprehension that, far from being natural, have their origins in an individual's interaction with knowledgeable others. The transition from adult mediation to child control of the reading process is depicted visually by means of a series of figures from Cole (1996, p. 273). Figure 7.1a represents adult mediation of child's interactions with the world. El'konin (1972) illustrates the extent to which the meaning of objects and events that as adults we take for granted but must be mediated for the developing child:

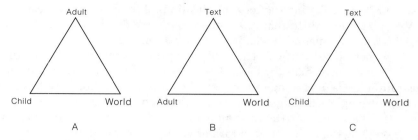

Figure 7.1 Three mediation triangles for reading instruction. Reprinted by permission of the publisher from *Cultural Psychology: A Once and Future Discipline* by Michael Cole, pp. 275, Cambridge, MA: The Belknap Press of Harvard University Press, copyright © 1996 by the President and Fellows of Harvard College.

> The system "child-thing' is in reality the system 'child-social object,' Socially evolved modes of action with these are not given immediately as physical properties of the objects. We do not find inscribed on the object where and how it originated, how we may operate on it, how we can reproduce it. Therefore, that object cannot be mastered through adaptation, through a mere 'accommodation' to its physical properties. This must take place internally; the child must go through a special process of learning the social modes of action with objects. In this process the physical properties of an object serve merely as referents for the child's orientation in his actions with that object. (El'konin, 1972, pp. 237–238)

The developing child's embodied participation in "socially evolved modes of action" (described above) is essential in grounding the text-based meanings that he or she eventually will be able to read and understand. Absent such groundings, words are simply empty vessels. Figure 7.1b represents the competent adult readers' ability to textually mediate their own understanding of the world with Figure 7.1c illustrating the goal of instruction—the child's textual understanding of the world. Finally, Figure 7.2 (from Cole, 1996, p. 276) captures this sequence of mediation by overlaying these three figures indicating how an adult reader is able to mediate text-world relationships in interaction with the developing reader.

Recognition of the essential role played by the more knowledgeable other gave rise to the construct most associated with Vygotsky's theory—the zone of proximal development (ZPD) which he defined as "the distance between the actual developmental level as determined by independent problem solving and the level of potential development as determined through adult guidance, or collaboration with more capable peers"

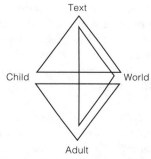

Figure 7.2 The three mediational systems combined to illustrate the relationship between the adult and the developing reader in which the adult assists the reader's meaning making with text. Reprinted by permission of the publisher from *Cultural Psychology: A Once and Future Discipline* by Michael Cole, pp. 275, Cambridge, MA: The Belknap Press of Harvard University Press, copyright © 1996 by the President and Fellows of Harvard College.

(Vygotsky, 1978, 86). The instructional implications of the ZPD are far-reaching (Miller, 2003). Vygotsky maintained that rather than *following* development, good instruction ought to *lead* development. He claimed, "what a child can do with assistance today she can do by herself tomorrow." The ZPD thus provides theoretical grounding for the longstanding distinction made by Betts (1946) between the instructional, independence, and frustration levels in reading instruction. The Russian term *obuchenie* captures this conjunction of taught learning leading to development in a way that no single English word is able. The zone construct also underscores the importance of dynamic assessment—the ongoing dialectic between formative assessment and instruction—a point to which we return later (Brown & Ferarra, 1985).

Mediation by signs and tools

The second major theme characterizing Vygotsky's original thinking is the importance that he attributed to the mediation of mind by tools and signs. In the Russian original of his classic *Myshlenie I Rech* (*Thinking and Speech*), Vygotsky quotes Sir Francis Bacon (1620) who claimed, "Neither the bare hand nor reason in and of themselves are capable of anything. They are completed only by tools and auxiliary means" (from Luria, 1982, p. 378). The position that tools play in Vygotsky's theory is a testament to both his commitment to Marxist philosophy and the enduring role that language and literature played in this thinking. On the one hand, he recognized the important role that the material tools of labor (e.g., a hammer) played in controlling the environment. On the other, he believed that signs, what he called "psychological tools," played a formative role in enabling individuals to bring their own behavior under control. Mere behavior could be transformed into purposive action. Material tools were thus outward oriented while psychological tools were inward. According to Vygotsky:

> The following can serve as examples of psychological tools and their complex systems: language; various systems of counting; mnemonic techniques; algebraic symbol systems; works of art; writing; schemes, diagrams, maps and mechanical drawings; all sorts of conventional signs, and so on. (from Wertsch 1985, p. 79)

While the above quote indicates that Vygotsky recognized the importance of semiotic processes other than language, it is, nonetheless, language that would be the focal point of his semiotic theory of mind. The importance that he attributed to language as a psychological tool closely parallels that of Dewey who characterized language as the "tool of all tools ... the cherishing mother of all significance" (Dewey, 1925).

Vygotsky (1978) further distinguished between what he called first-order and second order symbol systems. First-order symbol systems entailed an individuals' ability to speak and understand oral language while second-order symbol systems referred to an individual's understanding of written language. The initial acquisition of a written language required that an individual use an intermediate oral sign to understand the written word but once mastered the abilities to read and write enabled individuals to use language as a first-order system thus enabling the beginnings of the ability to think abstractly.

Vygotsky believed that competence in using written language has the potential to significantly enhance an individual's cognitive abilities. However, whether or not this potential is realized depends importantly on the uses to which reading and writing are put. The issue of whether or not there is a "great divide" bestowing unique cognitive abilities on those who are literate when compared to those who are not has long been debated. In a series of studies of the Vai, a West African people, described in their classic *Psychology of Literacy*, Scribner and Cole (1981) found that whether or not reading and writing enhanced individuals' cognitive abilities depended on the cultural practices in which these acts of literacy were embedded. Because the Vai learned and practiced their written script system independent of schooling, Scribner and Cole were able to assess the effects of this "literacy without education." They concluded that school-based literacy practices had the potential to enhance performance on school-like tasks but that in and of itself command of a written language didn't automatically bestow upon individuals any unique cognitive abilities. Parenthetically, Scribner and Cole's studies of the Vai stand as a model of methodological pluralism illustrating how both qualitative and quantitative methods could be used synergistically to study complex issues. Their study of the Vai also anticipated the now widely recognized situated nature of reading (Gee, 2001). Reading can no longer be treated as a generic process. We engage in different social practices, reading different texts for different purposes, and must be instructed accordingly.

Genetic (developmental) analyses

The third and final major theme characterizing Vygotsky's cultural-historical theory was the importance that he attributed to developmental or genetic analyses. He believed that to fully understand any psychological function such as the ability to comprehend text one must understand the origins of and processes by which that function develop. Toward this end Vygotsky identified four interrelated genetic domains or time scales.

Phylogenesis The first and most expansive domain is *phylogenesis* or what we commonly think of as evolution. Here it is the precursors to written language and comprehension that are most relevant. What do we know of the evolution of protolanguages and their critical role in what the evolutionary biologist Dobzhansky (1962) (as cited in Fischer, 1965) described as the emergence of culture, and with it the—"evolution of educability?" Psychologist and primatologist Michael Tomasello (1999) characterizes this evolutionary advance as "the ratchet effect." the capacity unique to humans to invent and communicate cultural knowledge and practices to successive generations such that each generation can build on the collective knowledge of its predecessor without having to start all over. It would be many millennia from the emergence of oral language to the invention of written language systems and with it the capacity to read. The development of written language did not replace but instead is closely linked to our capacity to comprehend orally communicated meanings.

Cultural history The above-described evolution of educability makes possible the second major genetic domain identified by Vygotsky—cultural history. Here, the focus is on those factors contributing to the culturally variable and historically changing nature of a given psychological function. Reading is not a natural act. Not all cultures have developed systems of reading and writing and even within those that have there still remains individuals who have not acquire the ability to read and write. What are the processes by which humans learn to comprehend text? How do these processes vary culturally? Scholarly treatments of the cultural history of reading have been the subject of numerous articles and books (Graff, 1982; Kaestle, 1991; Martin, 1988).

We have seen that from a cultural-historical perspective tools and signs (i.e., psychological tools) play a formative role in the development of mind. It follows that the cultural variability and historically changing nature of the tools and the social practices associated with literacy have the potential to transform the very nature of comprehension. Here a sampling of the range of these cultural achievements associated with the history of reading must suffice to give the reader an appreciation of the dynamic and variable nature of what it means to read.

The advent of the alphabet—what Cole and Griffin (1986) characterized as the bane of all school children—dates back almost five millennia and yet there continue languages (e.g., Chinese) that are today still logographic. Thus, while the arbitrary nature of alphabetic characters may make it more difficult to decode and create meaning, the task of eventually coming to comprehend the meaning of a large lexicon of word meanings is not nearly as daunting as that in Chinese. The invention of the computer, and with it the creation of word processing software, has necessitated the adaptation of non-alphabetic languages so that characters could be converted for the use on keyboards.

Toulmin (1979) suggests the very process of reading silently must be understood historically:

> The art of "reading to yourself," in our modern sense—reading at high speed without articulating the words even under your breath—is apparently an historical discovery or cultural invention and perhaps a quite recent one. This is a statement both about the historical development of culture and the psychological development of individuals. (p. 6)

While the notion that at one time the process of reading was only done aloud might seem counterintuitive, and yet the possibility that humans would have developed reading as a silent process from the very beginning seems even less plausible.

Vygotsky maintained, "If one changes the tools of thinking available to the child, his mind will have a radically different structure" (Vygotsky, 1978, p. 126). Interestingly, newly emerging digital tools now have the potential to restructure the development of an individual's thinking in ways that Vygotsky could not have anticipated. The advent of computer-based, hypertext and hypermedia has transformed reading comprehension from a linear, symbol-based process to one that is both multidirectional and multimodal (Kress, 2000, 2003; Hull & Nelson, 2005). In so doing, both material and psychological tools interact and have the potential to transform the very notion of what it means to comprehend at text. Burbules (1997) suggests that different individuals reading the "same" hypertext are literally in a position to author different readings depending upon the unique trajectory that they follow as they course through a hypertext. One can now read once conventional texts such as *Hamlet* or *Dante's Inferno* as hypertexts. While the digital revolution has spawned new genres with their associated social practices (e.g., email, blogs), with the wisdom of hindsight we can only imagine what a world minus poetry or the novel might have been like.

Finally, we are all acutely aware that what it means to read as instantiated in standardized tests of reading achievement has undergone significant change and can vary even across adjacent school districts. Reading is a historical, cultural, and social construct.

Ontogenesis   The genetic domain that we most commonly think of as "developmental" is ontogenesis, those changes that occur within the individual over the course of her lifetime or some period thereof (e.g., emergent or adolescent literacy). In terms of reading and comprehension, representative questions associated within this domain are likely to be: When and how does a child first learn how to comprehend text? What are the conditions that contribute to this learning, how does an individual eventually become able to read to learn, how does an individual come to read critically? These are questions that are the focus of a later section in this chapter.

Microgenesis   To more fully understand the ontogenesis of reading requires that we pursue a more detailed understanding or *microgenesis* of the processes by which comprehension develops. Where the time scale for phylogenesis is millennia, cultural history is generations, and ontogenesis is years, microgenesis describes developmental changes that occur over hours, minutes or even seconds. Examples in reading would be the initial understanding of a word's meaning or the acquisition of a comprehension related cognitive or metacognitive strategy. Children's in- and out-of-school text-based social interactions are replete with opportunities for such microgenetic developments which, when aggregated over time serve to describe their ontogenetic development. It is here where qualitative methodologies (ethnographies, discourse analyses) can reveal important insights concerning the origins and development of the processes of reading comprehension.

It is important to reiterate the dynamic and interactive nature of the above-defined genetic domains. Thus, while the microgenesis of a culturally given reading process (e.g., reading aloud) may reproduce that which has developed culturally, over time such processes may be transformed such that new comprehension-related, cultural practices can emerge that had not heretofore existed (e.g., reading silently).

In addition to understanding the affordances and constraints made possible by the development of contemporary reading-related cultural tools and practices, it is important that we be mindful of the cultural variability and historically changing nature of comprehension that should caution us against essentializing what it is that we take reading to be.

Summary of cultural-historical theory

We have seen the importance that Vygotsky attributed to semiotic mediation (mainly language) in the development of mind and that while this was partly a matter of a rich literary background that he was nonetheless striving to create a Marxist psychology. This notwithstanding, Vygotsky and some of his colleagues would come under increasing attack from Soviet ideologues for what the latter took to be their idealism. They had departed from Marxist dogma by not attributing greater importance to material action (i.e., labor) in conceptualizing the development of mind and in so doing had largely ignored more macro cultural-historical issues such as economics and class struggle.

In the last years of his life, Vygotsky would witness colleagues move away from his ideas, eventually forming the Kharkov school whose members would formulate cultural-historical *activity* theory (Gielen & Jeshmaridian, 1999). And, while it seems likely that the impetus for change by these breakaway Vygotskians was in part the result of a repressive Soviet state, their criticism were not without merit. While Vygotsky certainly recognized both the role of action in his semiotic approach to human development, he also recognized the importance of broader cultural-historical contexts and issues like class struggle. However, these ideas remained underdeveloped in his original cultural-historical theory.

One can only speculate what form Vygotsky's thinking might have taken had he lived longer. His writings and that of his close colleague Alexander Luria were banned for two decades, not emerging for wider audiences until after Stalin's death. But how Vygotsky would have responded to the newly developing activity strand of his original theory is unclear. What is clear is that the differences between this activity strand and Vygotsky's original semiotically oriented cultural-historical theory are more differences of emphases than of kind. Indeed, as we will suggest below, there is considerable overlap between the two. Nonetheless, we believe that there is value added to our understanding of reading comprehension by drawing upon cultural-historical *activity* theory.

Cultural-historical activity theory

Cultural-historical activity theory is an evolving theoretical framework that can be characterized as having three separate generations (Engeström, 1999). We describe each

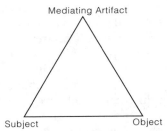

Figure 7.3 The basic mediational triangle. Reprinted by permission of the publisher from *Cultural Psychology: A Once and Future Discipline* by Michael Cole, pp. 119, Cambridge, MA: The Belknap Press of Harvard University Press, copyright © 1996 by the President and Fellows of Harvard College.

generation and how it informs our understanding of reading comprehension. Note that each generation provides the foundation for the successive one.

First generation activity theory

As stated above, first generation activity theory began in the 1930s with the inception of the Kharkov school. There, former students of Vygotsky conducted research aimed at understanding the relationship between thought and acivity. Despite this deliberate move away from semiotic mediation, members of the Kharkov school utilized Vygotsky's notion of mediated action for conducting research.

Within cultural-historical activity theory, the construct of mediation is depicted graphically through a triangle (Figure 7.3). Here, the triangle represents the structural relationship between the individual (subject), their environment (object), and cultural artifacts. The base of the triangle represents the natural or unmediated transaction between individual and their environment while the vertex of the triangle represents the mediated processes where the relation between subject and environment are linked through cultural artifacts that can be either material (e.g., a hammer) or ideal (e.g., language). From an activity theoretical perspective, the entire triangle captures the structural dimension of human activity in which the individual (subject) engages in a goal-directed activity (object) in order to meet a particular human need or want through the use of cultural artifacts. Thus, the interaction between the subject, object, and artifacts has a synergistic bond in which each component can mediate other components shaping the entire activity (Cole, 1996). Before moving on, it is important that we define what is meant by an activity. From an activity theoretical perspective, an activity involves doing something that is motivated by a biological need or by a culturally constructed need (e.g., to read different kinds of texts).

First generation activity theory provides a conceptual lens for a nuanced view of reading comprehension beyond the traditional rationalist and individualist perspectives that view comprehension as extracting meaning from text. Instead, activity theory provides a dynamic model for understanding and explaining comprehension by making visible the unmediated relationships between the reader and the world and the mediated relationship between reader and the text. In keying off the reader, we see the importance of reader's interactions with the world as an essential component in making sense (i.e., symbolic grounding) of the text. Comprehension is also mediated by the reader's use of various cultural artifacts: the material text (a configuration of signs and symbols), the lived experiences or representations that the student brings to the text, and finally the cultural-historical practices that guided the way we read the text (e.g., left to right or right to left).

Cultural artifacts play a pivotal role in activity theory and in reading comprehension and have been described in terms of three different levels (Wartofsky, 1973; Cole, 1996).

First level artifacts are material in nature and they are used directly in production. In literacy, examples of primary artifacts include words, books, writing instruments, and telecommunication networks. Second level artifacts consist of representations of primary artifacts and modes of actions for using primary artifacts. Secondary artifacts preserve and transmit modes of action and belief. Examples of these artifacts might include ways of thinking, talking, and reading within a particular discourse community. Third level, or tertiary artifacts, are imaginative in that they come to alter the way we see the "actual" world that provides the use with a tool for changing current praxis. Through the use of tertiary artifacts, traditional rules, conventions, and outcomes are called into question to the point where they no longer apply to practical activities. All cultural artifacts are constituted from the object of the activity. Therefore, cultural artifacts are simultaneously ideal (conceptual) and material in that their material form is shaped by their use in previous human activities as well as the way in which the artifacts mediate the present activity (Ilyenkov, 1977).

Second generation activity theory

The second generation of activity theory brings together Vygotsky's notion of mediated action with Leont'ev's notion of activity by emphasizing the motive or object behind mediated action, and in doing so, mediated action becomes tied to the larger category of practical human activity. Leont'ev (1981) was most instrumental in advancing a framework for analyzing activities. He distinguished between three separate levels of analysis in human activity: activity, action, and operation. Leont'ev claimed that activities could be distinguished by their object or purpose that guides and directs the actions of a collective group of individuals. Actions are the means by which activities are realized while operations are the performed action under certain conditions in response to a goal-directed task. If we apply Leont'ev's theory of activity to reading and comprehension, then reading is seen not as an isolated individual action, but an action that takes place within a larger collective activity under certain conditions that influences the individual's ability to making meaning from a text. Thus, the same act of reading (e.g., interpretation) can take place in very different activities (e.g., reading for pleasure, for learning, or as part of ones work) and in so doing be directed at very different objectives.

While Leont'ev identified the difference between individual action and collective activity, it was Engeström (1987) who graphically extended Vygotsky's basic mediational triangle to account for the complex interrelations between the individual subject and the collective activity system. Engeström proposed that an individual activity system (the original mediational triangle) is an integral part of a much larger collective activity system (see figure 7.4).

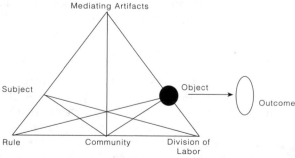

Figure 7.4 The basic mediational triangle expanded (after Engeström, 1987). Reprinted by permission of the publisher from *Cultural Psychology: A Once and Future Discipline* by Michael Cole, pp. 140, Cambridge, MA: The Belknap Press of Harvard University Press, copyright © 1996 by the President and Fellows of Harvard College.

Following Engeström (1987), the subject refers to the individual or collective group whose agency is the focus of analysis. The object refers to the problem space or the aim of the activity that is modeled and transformed into outcomes through the use of cultural artifacts (material and ideal). *Community* consists of multiple individuals and/or subgroups who share the same object (e.g., teacher and students). *Division of labor* signifies what each subject is doing toward realizing the object in terms of the horizontal division of tasks as well as the vertical division of power and status (e.g., teacher is the instructional leader and students follow). *Rules* refer to the explicit and implicit regulations, norms, and conventions that constrain actions and interactions within the activity system (classroom rules, grading policies, instructional practices).

Because second generation activity theory links the individual reader to the entire instructional environment, it allows researchers to analyze how different constituent components of the activity system influence comprehension. Moreover, analyses can take place on either a microsocial or macrosocial level. On the microsocial level, the researcher examines the social interaction among classroom participants to understand the relation between the social process and students psychological processes. Generally, U.S. literacy researchers have focused most of their attention on these microsocial interactions. On the macrosocial level, the researcher examines the relationship between structural factors (economic, social, institutional and cultural) and individual's psychological processes. Engeström (1987) observes that

> The behavioral and social sciences have cherished a division of labor that separates the study of socioeconomic structures from the study of individual behavior and human agency. In this traditional framework, the socioeconomic structures look stable, all-powerful, and self-sufficient. The individual may be seen as an acting subject who learns and develops, but somehow the actions of the individual do not seem to have any impact on the surrounding structures. (p. 19)

This incisive observation is especially pertinent when we seek to understand the relationship between the macro structures of reading (e.g., ideologies, institutions, policies) and the microsocial practices of instruction. It may seem that activity systems are static units, but they are dynamic systems always vacillating between equilibrium and disequilibrium. Different types of contradictions—conflict and discoordination—create dynamics within the activity system. Contradictions manifest themselves as problems, interruptions, and controversies that represent sources of transformation and expansion within the activity system (Engeström, 1987). A good example of a contradiction is the growing number of English language learners entering reading classrooms. This contradiction has disrupted traditional methods for teaching students how to read and thus, created innovative ways for teaching reading. From a reading and comprehension perspective, contradictions represent instructional impasses that must be resolved in order to advance students' reading and comprehension.

Third generation activity theory

The third generation of activity theory is a response to the criticism that second-generation activity theory showed no signs of cultural sensitivity (Cole, 1996; Ratner 1996, 1997). According to Engeström (2001), third generation activity theory represents the movement toward a theory of activity that develops the conceptual tools for understanding dialogue, multiple perspectives, and networks of interacting activity systems (see Figure 7.5). Third generation activity theorists use Bakhtian concepts of dialogicality and multi-voicedness to expand upon the second generation activity theory. Briefly, dialogicality refers to the interaction among interlocutors while multi-voicedness refers to the multiple perspectives, traditions, and interests that people bring to the activity.

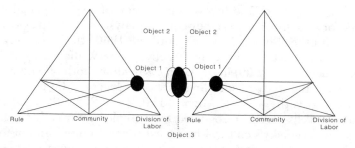

Figure 7.5 Two interacting activity systems as a model for third generation activity theory from Engeström, 2001.

In explaining this model, Engeström focuses on the movement and transformation of the object of the activity across multiple activity systems. Following Engeström (2001), the object moves from an initial state of self contained, situated problem space (object 1; e.g., a specific student entering into a classroom) to a collectively meaningful object constructed by the activity system (object 2; e.g., the student constructed as a subject of an academic institution through the teachers instantiation of the general object of schooling). As the student and teacher socially interact, there is potential for co-constructing the object (object 3; e.g., a collaboratively constructed understanding of the student's personal histories to develop an educational plan). In the third generation of activity theory, the object of the activity has a shifting quality, not reducible to a predetermined set of goals.

Third generation activity theory is only in its early stages of development, but Engeström cites the theoretical construct of a "third space" where the teacher script and the student script intermingle in meaningful and productive ways to co-construct new forms of knowledge (Gutierrez, Baquedo-López, & Tejeda, 1999) as opening the door to further development. However, thus far, the notion of a third space has only been confined to discourse and social process of a single classroom. We know nothing about how readers might construct a third space while they read a particular text nor do we know anything how authors afford and constraint the reader's ability to create a third space. These are all areas for future research.

Literacy researchers have documented a number of situations in which the educational activity has placed the student at a disadvantage (Moje, Ciechanowskiet, et al., 2004). In *Ways with Words*, Brice-Heath (1983) studied the literacy practices of minority families and how these literacy practices are not recognized in educational activities, in particular how reading places these students at a disadvantage.

OTHER SOCIOCULTURAL THEORETICAL PERSPECTIVES

While semiotic and activity strands of cultural-historical theory are the focus of this chapter, it is important to mention two related theoretical perspectives that make for a more comprehensive and integrative sociocultural understanding of reading comprehension and its instruction.

Sociolinguistics

Vygotsky's theorizing concerning the relationship between language and thought was for the most part limited to the analysis of word meaning. This should come as no surprise since the study of connected discourse during Vygotsky's lifetime was heavily dominated by formal linguistics fathered by Ferdinand de Saussure. Although Bakhtin

(1981, 1986), a contemporary and fellow countryman of Vygotsky, had begun laying the groundwork for sociolinguistics and discourse analysis there is no evidence that they were aware of each other's work. It wasn't until the 1960s that the study of sociolinguistics began in earnest. Major figures in this effort were William Labov (1972) in this country and Basil Bernstein (1990) in the United Kingdom, both of whom made significant contributions to the study of sociolinguistics in education. Of particular relevance in the present context is the work of Michael Halliday (1978, 1989, 1993) and James Gee (1990, 2000). Wells (1994) recognized the complementarity between Halliday's sociolinguistics and Vygotsky's cultural-historical conception of mind in formulating a language-based theory of language. He quotes Halliday who suggests,

> the distinctive characteristic of human learning is that it is a process of making meaning—a semiotic process; and the prototypical form of human semiotic is language." He continues by asserting that "Language is the essential condition of knowing, the process by which experience becomes knowledge. Learning is learning to mean, and to expand one's meaning potential. (1993, p. 93)

Halliday (1978, 1989, 1993) has made significant contributions to our understanding of comprehension by detailing how the grammatical structure of both oral and written language contributes to the resources available for the creation and communication of meaning at both the societal and individual levels. His systemic functional grammar has been used in the development of a multiliteracies curriculum designed to teach elementary and secondary youngsters how language works in the creation of meaning across the curriculum (Unsworth, 2001, 2002). Halliday's social semiotics were featured prominently in *A Pedagogy of Multiliteracies: Designing Social Futures* (1996) a manifesto proposed by *The New London Group* that consisted of influential sociolinguists and other language notables recommending changes in how we best think about language and literacy for the 21st century. Among their many recommendations were that we: a) conceptualize literacies as multimodal; b) teach students of all grade levels a metalanguage that empowers them to understand how language works in the creation of meaning across the curriculum; and c) incorporate these critical, multimodal curriculum literacies in a larger curricular framework that fosters students developing ability to engage in the processes of design.

James Gee, a sociolinguist and member of the *New London Group* (New London Group, 1996; Cope & Kalantzis, 2000) has also contributed significantly to our sociocultural understanding of the processes of reading comprehension (Gee, 2000, 2001, 2003). Gee (1996) draws the important distinction between an individual's primary and secondary discourses. An individual's primary Discourse refers to the unique ways that she has been apprenticed into making and communicating meanings—both verbal and non-verbal as part of her upbringing. A person is typically apprenticed into her primary Discourse early in life with it becoming an integral part of her identity. As she matures and participates in activities outside the home, she begins to acquire secondary Discourses—as disparate as one's church, a gang, a sports team, or school subjects. Knowledge of secondary Discourses enables us to communicate and be a part of different affiliation groups while the absence of such knowledge condemns us to the margins of such groups. Youngsters' acquisitions of the secondary discourses associated with schooling, both verbal and nonverbal, play no small role in their academic success.

Gee (2001) also argues that we best understand the processes of reading as situated and not some general purpose free-standing skill. Knowledge-able individuals must learn to read different texts in different ways for different purposes and should be taught accordingly. The situated nature of reading along with the different primary and secondary Discourses students often bring to the classroom place an substantial burden of proof on anyone who would defend the use of high stakes assessments while maintaining that all students have an equal opportunity to learn (Gee, 2003).

Second-generation cognitive science

Another prominent group of researchers, who have both drawn upon and contributed to our developing sociocultural understanding of language and the processes of comprehension, come from an area loosely known as second-generation cognitive science (Varela et al. 1991; Clark, 1997; Lakoff & Johnson, 1999; Keijzer, 2002, Sumara, 2003; Gibbs, 2006). The first generation cognitive scientists, architects of the cognitive revolution of mid twentieth century, have had the greatest impact on how we have come to think about reading comprehension and it instruction. Research on comprehension to date has been overwhelming cognitive (Pearson, Barr, et al., 1984; Barr, Kamil, et al., 1991; Kamil, Mosenthal, et al., 2000).

In certain respects, second-generation cognitive science may be understood as a reaction to what its proponents take to be the excesses of its progenitors. An important catalyst in this reassessment is Jerome Bruner, who was a major player in the original cognitive revolution. In his book, *Acts of Meaning* (1990), Bruner argues that many first generation proponents went awry in adopting the computer as the fundamental metaphor for conceptualizing and modeling mind. By substituting input and output for stimuli and responses, cognitive scientists were led away from what ought to have been the major focus of "the revolution"—the construction of meaning. Bruner argued further that human psychology is, or ought to be, a cultural psychology. His book would become a focal point of a major conference, *Reassessing the Cognitive, Revolution* (1993) attended by major contributors to cognitive science from around the world (Johnson & Erneling, 1997). Because it is far beyond the scope of this chapter to offer a detailed exposition of second-generation cognitive science, a discussion of some of the major principles and their relevance to understanding the processes of comprehension must suffice. Stated concisely, proponents of this reformed conception of mind argue that cognition is best thought of as social (and cultural-historical), situated, and embodied. On its surface, there may not appear to be anything unique about these assumptions—all have a long history of support. Upon closer scrutiny, however, the acknowledgement that cognition is social, situated, and embodied stands in marked contrast to the original and dominant first generation of cognitive science that has been individualistic, dispositional, and disembodied in its conception of mind (Gardner, 1987).

Moreover, many second-generation researchers now challenge the utility of postulating central cognitive structures (e.g., schemata, representations) in accounting for human action (Bickhard, 1994; Hutto, 1999; McVee et al., 2005). The importance of hypothesized cognitive structures has been a central organizing principle of research on reading. While cognitively oriented reading researchers have grudgingly acknowledged the social and situated nature of cognition, the notion that meaning might be embodied has gone largely ignored. Like cultural-historical activity theory, second generation cognitive scientists believe that the origins of human meaning are to be found in our embodiment (i.e., that the purchase on symbolic meanings is to be found in our perceptual-motor transactions with a material world).

PROBLEMATIZING COMPREHENSION

For all practical purposes, reading *is* comprehension. But from a sociocultural perspective what we take comprehension to mean is inherently problematic. What it means to read and comprehend a text is understood as culturally variable and historically chang-ing—it is a social construction. Thus while the received view in the reading research literature is that comprehension involves the *construction* of *meaning* from *text* (Alling-ton, 1983; Samuels, 1988; Schreiber, 1980), all three of the italicized terms have been contested and heatedly debated. What *is* the relationship between the word and the world (Freire & Macedo, 1987)? How are we to understand the processes of meaning making? What does it mean to *construct* meaning? Scholes (1989) distinguishes what he terms the "centripetal" from "centrifugal "readings of a text. Whose construction is to count? To what ends, to meet the author halfway, to interpret, to engage critically? What constitutes a text? How we understand the semiotics processes of comprehen-sion is linked to the material tools with which "textual signs" are communicated (e.g., graphic novels, computer-based hypertext/hypermedia). Increasingly, the act of reading is accomplished on computer screen involving not only the presentation of words but images and sound (Kress, 2003). Moreover, the manner in which one traverses through such texts need no longer be linear.

The problem of understanding comprehension is further complicated when we rec-ognize that while not reducibly so, the ability to read the word is inseparably yoked to our capacity to read the world (Freire & Macedo, 1987). What is often encapsulated in the term *background knowledge* in actuality can index anything ranging from super-ficial and disembodied declarative knowledge—what Whitehead (1929) called "inert knowledge"—to richly embodied, multimodal transactions with the world. Second gen-eration cognitive scientists have underscored the importance of understanding the *sym-bol grounding problem*—the processes involved in signification when a sign becomes linked to its referent (Harnad, 1990).

Implications for research and practice

Van der Veer & Valsiner (1991) make clear that Vygotsky believed that "Practice (praxis) is the strictest test for any theory" (p. 150). In the selective review that follows we are guided by a comprehensive and integrative sociocultural framework interweaving the implications for research and practice focusing on the processes of comprehension and comprehension instruction. We begin at the microsocial level with selective treatments of the role both of upbringing and instruction in fostering the development of compre-hension and move toward increasingly more macrosocial levels of analysis (i.e., teacher preparation and reading policies).

We've seen that Vygotsky believed that an individuals' upbringing and instruction plays a formative role in the development of mind. This notion is perhaps best cap-tured by the Russian term *obuchenie* that, roughly translated, means teaching leading to learning and development. We have also seen that Vygotsky distinguished between two important dimensions of individual human development—ontogenesis and micro-genesis. Ontogenesis refers to what is most commonly thought of as development—individual change over the course of a lifetime or some period thereof (e.g., emergent literacy). Here the concern is with how comprehension first emerges in young children and the various ways in which the processes of comprehension are refined such that she is eventually able to read independently. To fully understand an individual's ontoge-netic development however, requires more nuanced microgenetic analyses of the higher psychological processes of comprehension over a relatively short period of days or even minutes or seconds. How does a child acquire a concept with its associated word mean-ing? How does a child learn to monitor her own comprehension? In this section we review sociocultural research that focuses on the micro- and ontogenetic development of individual's ability to comprehend text.

UPBRINGING AND EARLY COMPREHENSION (OR PRE-SCHOOL COMPREHENSION "INSTRUCTION")

Intention reading and reading the world

While reading is not a natural act, what *is* natural is the potential that young biological humans have to acquire higher psychological (e.g., comprehension) processes in interaction with more knowledgeable others. In his book *The Cultural Origins of Human Cognition*, Tomasello (1999) suggests that it is the unique capability of humans to "understand conspecifics as intelligent agents like the self" that enables their imitative, instructed, and collaborative forms of learning. These forms of learning serve as a built in "ratchet" that prevents members of each subsequent generation of a culture from backsliding and having to begin the processes of knowledge creation all over again. This biologically based "ratchet effect" thus enables the cumulative nature of human cultural learning.

Tomasello (1999) identifies three social processes of "intention reading" that are critical to young children's acquisition of oral language and their subsequent ability to understand written symbols. The first of these social processes are young toddlers' abilities to engage jointly with adults in attending to some object or event in the immediate environment. Tomasello maintains that these joint attentional scenes constitute a middle ground of "socially shared reality between the larger perceptual world and smaller linguistic world." Such scenes are created through the triangulation of an adult, an entity of joint attention, and the child herself (see Figure 7.1a). Early on these entities of joint attention are likely to be objects and material practices with these objects thus enabling youngsters to acquire and ground symbolic meanings critical to the uses of spoken language (e.g., to understand that the word x refers to the object or experience of y). The importance that Tomasello attributes to joint attention between adult and child is relevant to understanding the processes of comprehension because it identifies mechanism by which symbolic meanings are initially grounded in a child's experience. It is in this sense that a child's developing ability to read the word is integrally related to her ability to read the world (Freire & Macedo, 1987).

A second social process enabling youngsters to comprehend the adult use of linguistic symbols is their developing understanding of the communicative intentions of others thus enabling them "to understand tool use or a symbolic practice—what it is "for," what "we," the users of this tool or symbol do with it." (p. 6). The third and final important social process essential to children's developing ability to understand oral and written language is their capacity to engage in role reversal. A child is able to use symbols toward adults in the same ways that adults use them toward her. Tomasello maintains that such a process is necessary if the developing child is to arrive at intersubjectively shared meanings with others. "It is the main cultural learning process by means of which children acquire the active use of linguistic symbols" (Tomasello, 1999, p. 96).

It is by means of children's first-order uses of language in which they are able to connect meaningful sounds to their embodied everyday experiences that they are eventually able to understand the second-order association between written symbols and these sound representations. This is no straightforward matter if the written language a child is attempting to learn is alphabetically based. Indeed, Cole characterizes the alphabet as the "bane of all schoolchildren" and that the necessity to understand the alphabetic principle (i.e., that letters have sounds that, in turn, are associated with word meaning) represents the one of the major challenges in the developing child's ability to read.

CLASSROOM INSTRUCTION AND SCHOOL ORGANIZATION

Most American literacy research and practice informed by Vygotskian perspectives has focused on social interaction in the classroom. In most respects, this can be understood as a direct offshoot of Vygotsky's general genetic law of cultural development described earlier. Not surprisingly, he assumed that instruction plays a central formative role in leading development. Davydov (1988; 1998), a student of Vygotsky's elaborates on this relationship between taught learning and development in what he describes as *developmental teaching*. In what follows, we first discuss the implications of sociocultural perspective for classroom-based, comprehension instruction. We then proceed to a consideration of the role of more macrosocial considerations ending with a discussion of implications for policy.

Classroom instruction

Overview

We believe that a cultural-historical activity theory provides a conceptual framework for expanding the notion of reading beyond the cognitive psychological (constructivist) dimensions that dominates the field of reading research to include the cultural-historical dimensions as well as the textual (semiotic) of reading and reading comprehension. Thus, we understand reading to be much more than a simple transmission of information from the text to the mind of the reader. Rather, reading is viewed as a social practice in which each act of reading requires the reader to engage in culturally defined ways of using text as they participate in meaningful cultural activity (Gee, 1999; Lee, 1995; Scribner & Cole, 1981). Moreover, texts are viewed as configurations of signs (Smagorinsky, 2001) in which signs are historically constituted through social interactions in culturally defined activities (Vygotsky, 1987; Wertsch, 1991, 1998), and thus, texts are the products of specific social languages. Additionally, the act of reading is influenced by the specific conditions in which reading occurs and the social and communicative functions that it serves (e.g., Courts, 1997; Schoenbach, Cziko, & Mueller, 2001; Scribner & Cole, 1981; Wineburg, 1991). In sum, making meaning from texts simply does not just happen—it occurs as a result of participation in a particular cultural-historical context (Cole, 1996). We divide our discussion of classroom instruction into several categories mindful of the overlap between them.

Classroom organization and instructional discourse

Classroom organization   While the role of social interaction is considered of crucial importance in the development of comprehension, the form that such interaction can take varies considerably. Different participation structures serve different instructional purposes. On the one hand, there are teacher mediated social relationships that can range from individual guidance (e.g., Reading Recovery) to small group (e.g., guided reading) and whole class instruction. Alternatively, reading instruction can be organized so that students interact with and learn from each other (e.g., reciprocal teaching, book clubs). When, where, and how a given participation structure is most likely to foster student learning is an important aspect of the effective teachers instructional decision making. Moreover, students must learn how to learn collaboratively and here the role of the teacher in scaffolding such collaboration is also essential.

Instructional discourse   The widely quoted aphorism by Dewey (1925/1958) that language is the "tool of all tools" must be qualified. To be sure, language *is* the major means by which instruction is carried out in the classroom (Wells, 1990); however, how one uses language, the specific social practices of a language, can determine whether students thrive and are academically successful or are marginalized and struggle to just keep up.

Earlier, in discussing Gee's contributions to a sociocultural perspective we introduce his distinction between primary and secondary Discourses. While individuals have only one primary Discourse, they participate in a number of different secondary Discourses both in and out of school. Gee maintains that it is essential students become conversant with school discourses if they are to succeed academically. Among the important secondary Discourses occurring in the classroom are those associated with specific content areas. One reads and discusses (and writes) history different than she does chemistry (Unsworth, 2001; Wyatt-Smith & Cumming, 2003). Moreover, as Gee conceptualizes the term, *Discourses* refer to more than how individuals engage in language practices but also include our embodied ways of acting within different contexts. Our doings as well as our sayings communicate meaning. Recent methodological developments and research findings in mediated discourse analysis testify to a growing recognition of the importance of embodied, multimodal dimensions of discourse (Norris & Jones, 2005).

Discourses are cultural as well as social (Hicks, 1995; Lee, 2000; Lee and Smagorinsky, 2000). A number of individuals have pointed to the difficulties that can follow when children confront secondary Discourses at school that contrast with the culturally based, primary Discourse that they've experienced at home. In her study of different participation structures used for creating reading groups with Hawaiian second graders, Au (1980) found those youngsters who were taught using talk-story, a participation structure more congruent with their cultural ways of communicating outside of school, showed the higher achievement gains in reading than those taught using traditional round-robin reading instruction. Similarly, Delpit (1988) has pointed to the home-school disparities that can exist when African American youngsters are taught utilizing white, middle-class indirect speech acts (e.g., request that students do something that in actuality is required). Wertsch (1985) suggests that children from middle-class families are more likely to be prepared for the sort of discourse that they encounter in school because their home discourse closely resembles the sort of questioning patterns that are found in the classroom.

Strategy instruction

Mindful of the importance of the instructional discourse and participation structures used in comprehension instruction another major line of reading research both informed by and in the spirit of sociocultural theory has focused on cognitive and metacognitive strategy instruction. A number of experimental studies in the 1980s and 1990s identified individual reading strategies found to be effective in fostering student's comprehension (see Raphael, George, Weber, & Nies, chapter 21, this volume).

Brown, Campione, and Day (1981) contrasted training studies in which the efficacy of a given comprehension strategy (e.g., summarization) was demonstrated through direct instruction by an experimenter with instructional research designed to teach students to engage in the self-regulation of the strategy. It is not enough that a strategy is shown to be efficacious in fostering comprehension. To be useful instructionally it must be demonstrated that teachers are able to mediate their students' acquisition of cognitive and metacognitive comprehension strategies such that her students are able to independently incorporate them in their reading.

Implicit in Vygotsky's assertion that higher psychological processes are social before they become individual is the notion that while social these processes are also public. We can distinguish a continuum with respect to how explicit or implicit a more knowledgeable individual is in making public the strategic knowledge necessary to enhance instruction (e.g., modeling, think-alouds, explanations). Kucan and Beck (1997) reviewed research examining the relationship of think-alouds and reading comprehension both as method of inquiry and also as means of facilitating student comprehension of text. Duffy, Roehler, et al. (1986a, 1986b) have stressed the importance of teacher explicitness in instruction and, specifically, the nature of the explanations that teachers are able to offer in relating strategic actions to reading comprehension.

Palincsar (1986) reviewed research on the role of dialogue in scaffolding of students' comprehension instruction. Although not a term used originally by Vygotsky, the concept of scaffolding as a source of instructional support that is gradual and temporary has been closely linked with Vygotsky's notion of the zone of proximal development. Vygotsky stressed the role of teacher-student and peer-peer interactions, it was Bakhtin (1981) who greatly elaborated the idea that thinking is fundamentally dialogic in nature (Wells, 2002).

While important in their own right, comprehension strategies have proven to be especially powerful when bundled into more systematic instructional approaches. One of the most widely cited multi-strategy interventions in the comprehension instruction literature is reciprocal teaching (Palincsar & Brown, 1984). In addition to including multiple strategies (questioning, predicting, summarizing and requesting clarity), embedded these strategies within an instructional format in which the role of teacher and student rotated among small groups of students. Thus, on one occasion a student who was previously asked to predict what was to occur text in a text passage might then assume the role of teacher in asking yet another student to summarize what she had read. Although designed originally for struggling readers, reciprocal teaching has been used successfully in enhancing reading achievement with a number of populations. Reciprocal teaching and other interactive participation structures have been frequently contrasted with the initiate-respond-evaluate (IRE) pattern of instruction often observed in classrooms (Cazden, 1988). Wertsch (1998) suggests that it is the agentive nature of such instruction (i.e., students assumed the role of teacher and are able to engage in dialogic interactions), which is as likely to facilitate comprehension as the specific strategies themselves. Instruction that encourages and supports the development of student agency underscores the importance motivational dimensions in instruction (McCaslin, 1989; Hickey & Zuiker, 2005).

Reading in the content areas: Curriculum literacies

As the child transitions from elementary school to middle school, they engage less and less in direct activities designed to teach them how to read. Instead, students participate in content area classrooms designed to teach them content area knowledge in literature, history/social studies, and science. Historically, content area classes have been organized around the textbook where reading represents the primary means (mediational) for constructing disciplinary knowledge. All too often the object of content area instruction is to read a text in order to memorize and recall information for the purposes of meeting course requirements (Fichtner, 1984; Mason, 2000).

One of the consequences of understanding reading as situated is that we can no longer think of reading as a generic process. Recognition of the need to think in terms of multiple literacies carries enormous implications for how we understand and foster the processes of reading in the content areas. Moreover, as suggested earlier these literacies are embodied and multimodal in nature (Siegel, 1995).

Word meaning and vocabulary   Vygotsky's distinction between everyday and scientific concepts is important in understanding the processes of meaning making in the content areas (van der Veer, 1998). Everyday concepts refer to the sort of meanings that individuals acquire in their interaction with social and nonsocial objects and events outside the contexts of formal schooling. On the other hand, scientific concepts refer to the sort of explicitly taught ways of organizing experience into knowledge in a given content domain. Thus, a child's everyday understanding of the concept of "dogs" is likely to be based upon her concrete experiences with specific instances of dogs. By contrast, the scientific understanding of dogs might refer to the systematically organized ways of classifying and understanding dogs of a zoologist or veterinarian. Several points regarding the everyday-scientific distinction are in order. First, Vygotsky considered both sorts of experience essential to an individual's genuine conceptual understanding. An individual's everyday understandings were grounded in her embodied material interactions with her environment. Absent these, opportunities for symbolically grounding her experience and any "scientific" understanding of a concept is inert and meaningless. Second, "scientific" concepts refer to disciplined, systematically ordered knowledge (e.g., history, literary theory) and are not limited to what we commonly think of as science. Third, while by definition the development of a child's everyday concepts are limited to her personal history; scientific concepts are cultural-historical in nature. How zoologists have classified dogs has changed historically. Finally, and perhaps most relevant in the present context, the distinction between everyday and scientific concepts and the importance of understanding their symbiotic relationship speaks to processes by which word meanings within different content areas come to be understood (Adam & Bullock, 1987). "Book learning" will take you only so far. One must have the everyday understandings that give symbolic sustenance to the words we read.

Curriculum discourses and genres   Earlier, the point was made that Vygotsky focused on the word as the fundamental "cell" for understanding meaning. Developments in sociolinguistics and the recognition of the importance of connected discourse in understanding and communicating meanings did not occur until a quarter century after his death. Recently, a number of individuals have argued for the importance of curriculum literacies in understanding and teaching in the content areas (Unsworth, 2001; Wyatt-Smith & Cumming, 2003). Not only do different content areas have unique concepts and vocabularies, but they are also characterized by different discursive practices and genres for communicating and comprehending their respective meanings (Berkenkotter & Huckin, 1993; Miller 1994; Gavelek & Raphael, 1996).

Teaching and learning these curriculum literacies is all the more challenging with the content-specific use of the technologies that are an increasingly integral role in their mastery. Just as it no longer suffices to think of reading comprehension in generic terms, so too students must be taught the specific use of literacy technologies (e.g., hypertexts and hypermedia, podcasts) in reading history, biology, or literature (Lemke, 1998). Recently, Mishra and Koehler (2006) argue for the importance of teachers' working understandings of *technological* pedagogical content knowledge.

While important, the ability to simply read, internalize, and reproduce the meanings of subject matter texts is not enough. In arguing for the importance of what he calls *textual powers,* Scholes (1985) suggests that it is necessary that students develop the ability to read, interpret, and criticize texts. In reading, individuals produce a text *within* a text; in interpretation, they produce a text *upon* a text; while in criticism they produce a text *against* a text. Our job, Scholes maintains, "is not to produce 'readings' for our students but to give them tools for producing their own" (p. 24).

Influenced originally by Dewey, Louise Rosenblatt (1994) further enriched her transactional theory of reading by recognizing the importance of Vygotsky's (1934/1987) distinction between meaning and sense. If one imagines an iceberg, then meaning is that part of the iceberg that is above water for others to see in common. On the other hand, the sense that individuals comes to attach to experience refers to all meaning—that which is public as well as beneath the surface—that individuals come to experience in their transactions with a text. The distinction between meaning and sense is closely akin to the distinction Rosenblatt made between efferent and aesthetic readings of a text. Rosenblatt argued that students bring a reservoir of meanings to the reading of literary texts but that it is efferent meanings that are privileged.

It is an all too common assumption that "factual" textbooks are beyond interpretation or criticism—that they invite only efferent meanings. de Castell (1990) questions why it is that so much time is spent analyzing the authors of fictional texts while so little time is devoted to considering how authors arrive at the facts that they include in their textbooks. Textbooks, she argues, "derive their authority from being authorized not from being authored." de Castell maintains that it is essential to fostering the development of students textual powers that they be taught documentary literacies in which text books are subject to criticism (see also Lewis & Moje, 2003).

Cultural-historical activity theory provides a tool for understanding how meanings are made from text and the potential to make meaning from text. According to Engeström (1987), in-school learning and reading leads to a reversal of object and artifact which means that the object of the activity is no longer constructing meaning for the text. Rather, it is to reproduce an exact mental representation of the textbook. Consequently, students are denied opportunities for interpreting and criticizing the text, and thus, limit the reader's overall meaning making potential. This occurs because in-school content area reading is isolated from other societal activities, especially its connection to its disciplinary community (Miettinen, 1999; Dewey & Childs, 1933).

To liberate content area readers from reproductive reading practices, we believe that the practice of reading should be situated within the disciplinary community (Moje, 2006). This means that students should engage in disciplinary specific tasks providing them with an opportunity to draw on the artifacts and practices that constitute the discipline. Here, reading is incorporated with other forms of literacy, such as, speaking, listening, thinking, writing, and interacting within the disciplinary community (e.g., Gee, 2001). For example, Wineburg (1991) argued that reading, in history, involves viewing texts as "speech acts" on paper that can be understood by trying to reconstruct the social interaction in which they occurred. By so doing, Wineburg found that historians employ three readings strategies as they read and made sense of the text—corroboration or comparing and contrasting documents with one another; sourcing or looking at the source of the document before reading to consider bias; contextualization or situating the text in a temporal and spatial context to consider the time and place in which the text was written. All three of these reading strategies represent conventionalized ways of reading in history that enable readers to make meaning within the discipline. In other words, disciplinary specific reading strategies represent essential cultural artifacts for meaning making in the discipline. This suggests that reading instruction should provide student with opportunities to practice the use of disciplinary specific reading practices in the context of disciplinary tasks, and thus, creating an activity system that expands the meaning making potential to enable readers to interpret and criticize different texts (Moje, 2006).

Re-mediating struggling readers

Historically, students, who struggle to develop as readers in regular educational classrooms, are labeled as learning disabled (LD) (Gindis, 1995). These students are entitled to receive remedial assistance from a certified special education teacher usually in an alternative setting outside the regular classroom. As a way of re-conceptualizing our current notion of pedagogical practices in special education, Michael Cole and Griffin (1986) introduced the notion of re-mediation (i.e., to mediate in a new way) that places emphasis not on the individual but the social interaction between students and teacher.

Cole (1996) stresses that reading requires the coordination of information from two different directions. The reader must see the world as refracted through the text as well as draw on their world-view. In doing so, the reader simultaneously connects their world view with the text—producing a new representation or expanded understanding. To assist struggling readers in this meaning making process, Cole and his colleagues combined the students' ability to mediate interactions with the world through adult assistance with the teacher's ability to use texts to mediate their interaction with world. This produced an activity system in which the teacher provided mediation by coordinating the entire act of reading for the student before they could accomplish this activity on their own. By emphasizing the re in re-mediation, Cole shows educators that instruction can lead development and thus emphasizing "the special role of the teacher in arranging the medium that coordinates preexisting systems of mediation in a single system of joint activity subordinating the goal of comprehension" (p. 285).

Biliteracy

As activity theory maintains, meaning making occurs through participation in cultural-historical activities that are constituted through macrosocial forces and microsocial interactions. Reading research has paid little attention to how macrosocial forces shape the reader's meaning making (John-Steiner, 1985). This is particularly problematic for English language learners. In this next section, we discuss the macrosocial factors and how these factors play out in the how English language learners develop as readers as well as how instruction affords and constraints the meaning making of these students.

Specificity concerning how reading is taught and acquired by English language learners is nearly impossible, but the macrosocial forces operating outside schools and classrooms have produced remarkably similar program across the United States. As of this writing, policymakers, in the United States, are pursuing a monolingual language policy that views national languages other than English as the root cause of underachievement by English language learners. Consequently, instruction ignores the linguistic and cultural resources of English language learners placing these students at a disadvantage when it comes to reading. These macrosocial factors shape both the social consciousness of teachers and students, and thereby, the microsocial interactions that place inside schools which ultimately affects how English language learners learn to read and make meanings.

Nowhere are these microsocial practices more harmful to students than in content area classrooms where students are expected to read the textbook to develop disciplinary understandings. Limited exposure to the cultural and linguistic resources that constitute a particular text affects the English language learner's potential to understand and interpret the textbook (Moll & Dworin, 1996). These texts assume that readers have both an extensive and varied literacy background as well as common cultural experiences. Moreover, in history, textbooks present the reader with an "inconsiderate" text, since it fails to present a coherent and comprehensible text that would enable the reader to construct an in-depth understanding of events in terms of people's motivations, actions, and consequences (e.g., Armbruster & Anderson, 1984; Beck, McKeown, Sinatra, & Loxterman, 1991; Beck & McKeown, 1991). Thus, when English language learners read textbooks to make meaning, they are denied an opportunity to draw on their meaning-making resources (logical reasoning, problem solving, and mathematical skills) because the activity system fails to utilize students' cultural and linguistic resources as assets for meaning making. Instead of considering the instructional approach, educators believe that students' struggle to read and make meaning are directly related to their limited English skills which shifts the focus from reading and making meaning in the content area to building fluency in English. Consequently, English language learners miss opportunities to acquire disciplinary literacies (analyzing and interpreting events) necessary for academic and economic advancement. In the end, students participate in instruction that forces them to memorize and recall existing forms of knowledge that reproduce the dominant culture's social and racial hierarchy (Gutierrez, Larson, & Kreuter, 1995; Fairclough, 1992; Gee, 1990; Delgado-Gaitan & Trueba, 1991).

Often times, educators misinterpret English language learners struggle with text. It is convenient to assume that the source of English language learners struggles to learn how to read and make meaning resides with their limited English proficiency. Educators, who subscribe to cognitive theories of reading, fail to recognize how different texts and sign socially position readers. For many English language learners, reading creates a situation in which they must negotiate between their culture and the dominate culture, but instruction rarely provides a space of students to negotiate with the text. As a result, students employ strategies of resistance in an attempt to transform the situation. These strategies may include refusing to participation in the social process of the activity and/or attempting to use alternative cultural artifacts that create a meaning consistent with the students' world view (Gutierrez, Baquedano-Lopez, & Larson, 1995). When English language learners employ these strategies to resist the meanings of the dominate culture, teachers interpret their actions as a language deficit because students struggle to express their world view in English and their interpretation does not mirror the official text. Thus, cultural-historical activity theory enables educators to understand the complexity of making meaning process for English language learners.

We believe that activity systems that only allow English language learners to read and make meaning in English and force students to reproduce existing forms of knowledge is not only unethical but creates a context for failure. We know that these students have limited experience in using English for academic purposes. We also know that readers make sense of texts based on their own situated meanings about the world and they also construct meanings congruent to their identity or social position in the world (Gee, 2001, 2003; Lantolf & Thorne, 2006). We further know that English language learners enter the classroom unfamiliar with the different types of texts, the issues and themes, certain practices inside the classroom and certain practices in society, and certain ways of talking, and ways of viewing the world (Gee, 1997). Yet, instruction expects English language learners to read texts without making explicit the context that affords meaning making or comprehension while expecting students to take up meanings that may well subordinate themselves and their families.

Assessment

Formative assessment and instruction constitute an inseparable and dialectical whole as conceived by Vygotsky in his notion of the zone of proximal development (Johnston, 1988). While most discussions of the ZPD tend to emphasize its importance in conceptualizing instruction, part and parcel of responsive instruction are teachers' abilities to engage in real-time assessments of where students are at within their respective zones. This is a knowledge-intensive endeavor involving teachers' abilities to integrate their knowledge of the specific cultural and developmental dynamics of the students that they teach along with an understanding of the reading process as it relates to the goals of the specific content and comprehension processes being taught. Stone and Wertsch (1984) and Stone (1994) have characterized this as a proleptic process in which teachers must keep one eye focused on the future (i.e., the goals of instruction) with the other attuned to where their students are presently functioning. In effect, teachers must seek to induce students understanding of how to comprehend difficult texts (i.e., texts at their instructional level) as a precondition for creating that understanding (Cole, 1996, p. 183). It is in this sense that Cazden (1988) suggests that in mastering complex cognitive tasks performance often precedes competence. In addition to mediating and monitoring students understanding of comprehension, teachers must also be able to frame reading activities in ways that are motivating. It involves the integration of teacher competencies that one observes when successfully engaged in the process of guided reading (Fountas & Pinell, 2001).

School organization and professional development

Daniels observes that "many post-Vygotskian studies ... fail to articulate a concern for the school as an organized institution" (Daniels, 2006, p. 517). While not sufficient, the existence of coherent school-wide instructional programs is now recognized as important to continuing student reading achievement (Newmann et al., 2001). All too often school reading programs are fragmented and short-lived with the result being incoherent experiences for students and teachers alike. Erickson and Schultz (1991) emphasized the importance of understanding the student's experience of the curriculum. We have little understanding of how students experience what Newman and his colleagues characterize as "Christmas tree" innovations of the reading curriculum.

More than a quarter century ago, Lortie (1975) documented the isolation of teachers and the cellular organization of schools. If teachers are to achieve both horizontal (i.e., within grade level) and vertical (i.e., across grade level) integration then there must be ample opportunity for continuing professional development (Tharp & Gallimore, 1988). Sociocultural perspectives view language as underdetermined in the communication of meaning. Just as meanings between teacher and students must be negotiated if they are to develop classroom communities of practice, so too must content and grade level teachers have opportunities to negotiate meanings in the service of literate school communities (Wells & Chang, 1990). Seymour and Osana (2003) demonstrated the problems teachers experience in achieving intersubjective agreement of what is involved in reciprocal teaching, and that there were differences between a teacher's verbalized understandings of reciprocal teaching and their actual practices.

In a widely cited book, Wenger (1998) details the conditions known to foster the establishment and maintainence of *communities of practice*. Wenger maintains that practice is always *social* practice and that:

> Such a concept of practice includes both the explicit and the tacit. It includes what is said and what is left unsaid; what is represented and what is assumed. It includes the language, tools, documents, images, symbols, well-defined roles, specified criteria, codified procedures, regulations, and contracts that various practices make explicit for a variety of purposes. But it also includes all of the implicit relations, tacit conventions, subtle cues, untold sensitivities, embodied understandings, underlying assumptions, and shared worldviews. (p. 47)

Clearly, if a school is to meet the rigorous conditions that Wenger sets forth for developing a community for practice then not only must there be frequent and sustained opportunities for professional development but there must also be instructional leaders who are able see to it that such conditions are satisfied. Moreover, while coherence may be necessary it is not sufficient in fostering the development of schools with high levels of reading achievement. Whether it be in the persons of principals and/or proven literacy teachers or coaches, there must be individuals who are able to select strong, evidence-based reading programs *and* see to it that such programs are implemented with fidelity.

TEACHER PREPARATION

Understood from a sociocultural perspective, comprehension instruction is both a knowledge and labor-intensive activity (Huizen, Oers et al., 2005, Smagorinsky, Cook, et al., 2003). Let us take stock.

- The origins and development of the ability to comprehend texts are to be found in individuals' interactions with more knowledgeable others—with teachers.
- In fulfilling this function, teachers must know when and how to orchestrate an array of participation structures that are geared to different instructional objectives.
- Part and parcel of this orchestration is the ability of teachers to engage in dynamic assessment enabling them to differentiate their instruction both in terms of culturally appropriate discursive practices and the strategic comprehension processes of instruction.
- If children are to learn from and with their peers, then they must be taught how to learn collaboratively.
- Because reading is a situated activity one cannot assume that the processes of comprehension are generalizable across content domains. A teacher must have the content and pedagogical content knowledge to teach these curriculum literacies.
- Since increasingly the means for comprehending text are multimodal, teachers must have a working knowledge of the full range of these semiotic domains—symbolic and non-symbolic.
- And because the "tools of the trade" now include computers, hypertext, and hypermedia teachers must have the technological pedagogical content knowledge to integrate the use of these tools in ways that are often situated in specific subject matter.

It is doubtful, under the presented conditions, whether we can reasonably expect to educate a critical mass of teachers who are prepared to engage youngsters in the sort of educative experiences described above.

Ours is not the intent to engage in teacher bashing. Teachers are confronted with an untenable situation in which they fail to receive in-depth, pre-service preparation in child and adolescent development (e.g., including cultural dimensions of such development), content and pedagogical content knowledge, and the semiotics and technological tools (symbolic and non-symbolic) geared to the populations and content areas that they teach.

Nor do we believe that sociocultural theories are to be faulted for articulating such a demanding job description for teachers. While there has been little research on teacher education informed by sociocultural theories, a number of researchers (Moll, 2001; Tharp & Gallimore, 1988; Seymour & Osana, 2003) have given us a glimpse of what such preparation might look like and not surprisingly the principles that underlie such a model closely resemble those for the students that they would teach. Like teaching itself, the preparation of teachers to teach is a labor-intensive undertaking requiring not only the detailed substantive knowledge discussed above, but also the knowledge-in-practice by which the former is instantiated. Apprenticeships in teaching take time and require that the sort of coherence discussed earlier occur in both teacher preparation programs and the school in which they are to be inducted.

Finally, when analyzed from a sociocultural perspective the demands of comprehension instruction require that we revisit the differential preparation of elementary and secondary teachers. We speak of an organizational structure that continues to prepare elementary school teachers who as *bricoleurs* are expected to incorporate the language arts into and across multiple subjects that they have relatively little content or pedagogical content knowledge about. In contrast, secondary school teachers may enjoy the luxury of focusing on a single subject area are nevertheless taught in manner and come to believe that it is not their responsibility to teach reading. In both instances, elementary and secondary teachers often have little working knowledge of culture and/or technology that they can integrate into their pedagogy. Such a separation of duties and powers between elementary and secondary teachers has created a rigid caste system in which the latter comes to look down on the former. Anybody who has spent enough time to become familiar with a universities culture soon learns that there is a pecking order that starts at the top in colleges of liberal arts and descends downward to early childhood education. What this often means is that liberal arts professors who teach "the disciplines" do not see it as part of their responsibility to use the semiotic tools (e.g., how to read) in their disciplines. This attitude is then passed on to prospective secondary teachers who are then resistant to anything that resembles what elementary teachers must do. The elementary-secondary divide in professional preparation of teachers must be broken if their respective students are to experience the kind of developmentally-informed, semiotically-mediated, deep and authentic content instruction that they all deserve.

If teachers are to be prepared to engage in comprehension instruction in a manner informed by sociocultural theory, then the onus for the above-described transformation rests ultimately within the arena of policy making at the district, state, and national levels.

READING POLICIES?

In a recent issue of *Time Magazine* (Willis & Steptoe, December, 10, 2006), a proverbial Rip Van Winkle awakens from a century long sleep and is amazed to see the how the world has changed—until he ventures into a schoolhouse.

The multiple meanings of the title for this penultimate section of our chapter are deliberate. How *are* we to comprehend reading comprehension policies? When understood from a sociocultural perspective we have a reasonably good working knowledge of best practices for what is conventionally understood to be comprehension. Seldom, however are these best practices enacted. There is a disjuncture between what we know about best practices and the policy context in which comprehension instruction occurs. Why then is Mr. Van Winkle likely to find so little has changed?

In this section we use a sociocultural framework in an attempt to analyze and understand this policy-practice disjuncture with the goal of offering a few suggestions of how it might be understood. The cognitive psychological approach that has dominated reading research has for the most part ceded policy matters to others. This is not to claim that cognitive psychologists have not influenced policy but rather to underscore the poverty of cognitivism as a philosophical and theoretical position for addressing anything social.

The (mis)appropriation of sociocultural theory?

As a family, sociocultural theories are unique in their potential to relate societal issues at the macro level with face-to-face, instructional interactions at a microsocial level, and ultimately relate the two in understanding the development of mind (Tudge & Scrimsher, 2003). And yet the interpretation and application of sociocultural theories to comprehension instruction by U.S. researchers and practitioners has focused for the most part on the classroom. In one sense, this is understandable; the interactive use of oral and written language played a central role in Vygotsky's original semiotically oriented theory. However, a number of individuals have taken U.S. educators to task for what they believe is the limited and limiting application of sociocultural theory (Daniels, 2001, 2006; Elhammoumi, 2002; Engeström, 1991; Tudge & Scrimsher, 2003). Consider the following quotes:

> In North America, however, the complexity of Vygotsky's theory has been for the most part ignored in favor of a reliance on a single concept, the zone of proximal development. Moreover, the concept itself has too often been viewed in a rather limited way that emphasizes the interpersonal at the expense of the individual and cultural-historical levels and treats them in a unidirectional fashion. (Tudge & Scrimsher, 2003, p. 211)

and

> Today many of the more pragmatically oriented American psychologists treat Vygotsky's work as a kind of psychological gold mind that exists to be plundered for nuggets of insight and wisdom and hints for new research. In contrast, they tend to pay insufficient attention to the question of how and for what purpose the gold mine came into being in the first place. (Gielen & Jeshmaridian, 1999, p. 275)

and finally

> a good deal of the post-Vygotskian research conducted in the West has focused exclusively on the effects of interaction at the interpersonal level, with insufficient attention paid to the interrelations between interpersonal and socio-cultural levels. (Daniels, 2006, p. 517)

In effect, most American literacy researchers and practitioners working from a sociocultural perspective have interpreted Vygotsky's cultural-historical theory ahistorically. And while there are those working in a Vygotskian tradition who have called for a more comprehensive understanding (e.g., Cole, 1996; Engestrom, 1999; Daniels, 2001; Rogoff, 2003) such calls have gone largely unheeded.

Ideology matters

How are we to make sense of so ironic an oversight? We believe that the irony is more apparent than real. Any comprehensive sociocultural conception of reading that seeks to relate public policy to classroom instruction must be interpreted with an eye to the ideological presuppositions that permeate a society. It is instructive to examine the prevailing ideology that undergirds American education and reading specifically.

When Vygotsky's *Thought and Language* was first published in 1962 it was devoid of reference to Marxist theory or the political context in which his theory had developed. Even today, Elhammoumi (2002) maintains, "the hostility of mainstream psychology toward Marxism has contributed to the widespread ignorance of the contributions of Marx's writings to the development of the human mind" (p. 98).

Ageyev (2003) a Russian émigré, Vygotskian scholar, and current U. S. university professor maintains that Vygotskian theory contradicts core values of American culture. One such value is the importance that Americans attribute to individualism. Ageyev suggests that American educators seek to interpret sociocultural concepts created from an ideology of collectivism with their own countervailing ideology that values individualism. He notes, "the very idea that human mind is so deeply shaped and formed by social interaction seems directly to contradict many prominent American values and ideals, such as individualism, independence, and self-reliance" (p. 435). One finds this individualism manifest in education in: a) the persistent belief on the part of many parents that teachers' uses of cooperative learning represents an abdication of their professional responsibility; b) an ethos of competition in which individual is pitted against individual; c) a tendency to blame the victim be she student or teacher for academic performance; d) the cellular organization of schools and lack of support for teachers professional development; and e) static conceptions of assessment in which the measure of a student's ability is based upon how she performs by herself.

At best, Americans have tended to view the role of social interaction as facilitative of already native potentials rather than formative in creating the sort of individual a person might become. Ageyev (2003) further suggests that Americans' impoverished view of the social carries over to how they think about culture. While the potential to create and communicate cultural practices to one's progeny and successive generations appears to be a biological universal (i.e., see earlier discussion of "ratchet effect"), the directions that a specific culture's development can take are multifarious. And yet, despite its cultural diversity, the press for cultural uniformity in American education is evinced in: a) a belief that the "same" instructional environment for children of different cultural backgrounds ensures equal opportunities to learn (Gee, 2003); b) an attitude that children should have to adapt to the educational system rather than vice versa (Deschenes, Cuban, & Tyack, 2001); or c) the belief that learning two or more languages is a problem rather than something to be fostered. Social practices are also cultural practices and the failure to recognize their constitutive functions in determining who we are and what we might become represents a major blind spot in our American ideology.

In a similar vein, Popkewitz (1998) maintains that current U.S. reform efforts built around constructivist teaching and learning have appropriated the ideas of Vygotsky and Dewey without understanding the broader cultural and historical context in which these ideas were developed. It is instead a constructivism emanating from cognitive psychology in which students are encouraged to "construct" knowledge that mirrors the logical structures of the disciplines but are excluded "from the recognition of the social and historical mooring of that knowledge" (p. 552).

Apprenticeships of observation

If they are to serve as more than mere abstractions, ideologies must assist us in understanding material human practices. An important nexus where ideology meets practice may be found in what Lortie (1975) identified as teachers' *apprenticeships of observation*. In his classic text *Schoolteacher*, Lortie documents the extent to which teachers must function in professional isolation. He further suggests that the prior beliefs that prospective teachers bring to their teacher preparation programs are often resistant to change and that once having completed their programs teachers will frequently revert back to practices consistent with the ways that they were taught as schoolchildren. Lortie explained these enduring beliefs in terms of teacher candidates' *apprenticeships of observation*. By virtue of having spent 12 years in their elementary and secondary educations, these individuals know all too well what teaching looks like. The problem is that while they have had an extensive history observing teaching—good and bad, they have little knowledge of *why* teachers did what they did. Once they have their own classroom, such teachers often revert back to the ways that they were taught in lieu of their formal professional preparation. The press to conform to the status quo and put aside what they've learned in teacher preparation programs is often reinforced once newly initiated teachers assume responsibility for their own classrooms and interact with experienced teachers who invoke their own "wisdom of practice" as a reason for staying the course.

In and of themselves, teachers' apprenticeships of observation are a recipe for a vicious circle (i.e., teachers teach students some of whom go on to become teachers themselves thus perpetuating similar apprenticeships of observation and related pedagogical practices). However, there is little reason to believe that these school-related, apprenticeships of practice are confined to teachers. The various publics who influence literacy policy either directly or indirectly (e.g., parents, school boards, politicians, and, increasingly, corporate heads) often draw upon their own experiences as students in justifying their beliefs concerning best practices and/or resisting innovations that depart from their experiences. Thus the circle remains unbroken and the call for "back to basics" continues unabated.

In assuming a dialectical relationship between policy and practice, sociocultural approaches have the potential to explicitly understand sort of disjunctions found between reading policy and comprehension instruction. In effect, the assumed dialectical relationship and contradiction between policy and practice becomes the engine for change. The direction that this change takes is what is at issue. Giddens (1984, 1986) *structuration theory* and Engeström's (1987, 1991, 1999) *theory of expansive learning* offer sociocultural frameworks in beginning to undertake such analyses.

In his structuration theory, Giddens maintains that we can best understand social problem by assuming a duality of structure between individual agency (e.g., teachers) and the structural contexts in which these agents must function. Cole (1996) depicts these structures as they relate to issues of reading instruction as set of nested contexts (see Figure 7.6) with the outermost structures referring to national and state reading polices and inner most circles addressing teachers in their reading related instructional interactions. Here the structure (rules, mandates) of reading instruction serve as both medium and outcome of reading practices. By engaging in these practices teachers reproduce and thus perpetuate the "existence" of the rules that that govern them. Giddens allows for the possibility that as agents (i.e., teachers and other actors) can transform the rules governing the reading process.

In his theory of *learning by expanding,* Engestrorm (1987) offers a similar analysis of the relationship between activity systems (e.g., policies) and actions (e.g., comprehension instruction). To understand Engestrom's treatment of these relationships the reader is referred back to Figures 7.4 and Figure 7.5. Figure 7.4 depicts what could be any system of comprehension instruction (e.g., instruction in critical reading). Such an activity occurs within a classroom community and a set of rules governing interactions between teachers and student and students with each other (e.g., one can criticize ideas but not persons). All of this occurs with the goal of instruction being teaching students to engage texts critically. Problems arise when the objects and intended outcomes of different activity systems (e.g., between teachers and administrators) come into conflict with each other (see Figure 7.5) forming what Gutierrez and Stone (2000) refer to as *third spaces*. The contradictions that occur in a third space create opportunities for expanded learning but can also lead to deleterious outcomes as well.

Within society, activity systems are hierarchically arranged such that macro-social activity systems push on local or microsocial activity systems in ways that shape the face-to-face interaction among people. While there are a multitude of macro-social activity systems (e.g., economic and political), we are concerned with the governmental educational polices that influence the microsocial activity systems of the classroom which profoundly shapes the meaning making potential of teachers and students.

We currently find ourselves in a political climate in which the federal government is exerting pressure on public schools through its No Child Left Behind educational reform policy. The policy is designed to improve the academic performance of all students by holding schools accountable for the academic performance through the use of standardized assessments. The policy has lead to changes at the microsocial level

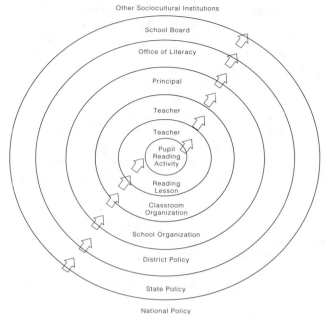

Other Sociocultural Institutions

School Board

Office of Literacy

Principal

Teacher

Teacher

Pupil
Reading
Activity

Reading
Lesson

Classroom
Organization

School Organization

District Policy

State Policy

National Policy

Figure 7.6 Concentric circles representing the notion of context "that which surrounds," with a reader at its center. Adapted by permission of the publisher from *Cultural Psychology: A Once and Future Discipline* by Michael Cole, pp. 275, Cambridge, MA: The Belknap Press of Harvard University Press, copyright © 1996 by the President and Fellows of Harvard College.

of the classroom, especially with respect to the poorer students and English language learners. Because a school's success is measured by the performance of their students on state assessments, administrators and teachers have been coerced into making the object of instruction preparing students for the assessments. Consequently, students are receiving an improvised curriculum in that instruction emphasizes on the acquisition of autonomous skills such as vocabulary, decoding, and phonics, rather than including these literacy skills in richer literacy program that would afford opportunities for making meaning in the context of disciplinary courses. As a result, students spend all day developing discrete literacy skills using texts that replicate state assessments. Thus, No Child Left Behind enables students to learn how to read and make meaning for the purposes of passing a standardized assessment that severely constrains their potential for making meanings in real world situations.

The problem confronting the sort of social analyses provided by both Giddens and Engeström is the multilayered, nested nature of structures that instructional agents (e.g., teachers, principals) must work within (again, see Figure 7.6). While not a solution to the sort of disjunctions between reading policies and instructional practices such analyses at least call attention to what the multiple nexuses are likely to be.

SYNTHESIS AND CRITIQUE

Is appropriation the sincerest form of flattery?

Sociocultural theory has served as a rich source of ideas in informing research on comprehension (e.g., reciprocal teaching) instruction as well as framing extant research (e.g., guided reading). This should come as no surprise since the notion that instruction plays a leading role in the intellectual development of individuals is central to Vygotsky cultural-historical theory. Recognition of the social mediation of cognition has been grudgingly assimilated by cognitively oriented researchers who now seem willing to concede that the mechanisms by which cognition are formed are social but once internalized these structures are then the purview of cognitive psychology. This concession hasn't come easily. Writing in his definitive history of cognitive science, *The Mind's New Science,* Gardner (1987) indicated as one of the five major features of cognitive science was:

> the deliberate decision to de-emphasize certain factors which may be important for cognitive functioning but whose inclusion at this point would unnecessarily complicate the cognitive-scientific enterprise.. These factors include the influence of affective factors or emotions, the contributions of historical and cultural factors, and the role of the background context in which particular actions or thoughts occur. (p. 6)

Whether the assimilation of sociocultural constructs by cognitively oriented, reading researchers is the sincerest form of flattery is doubtful. Most sociocultural theorists eschew the sort of cognitive structures postulated in cognitive science. Moreover, Vygotsky criticized this sort of eclecticism believing that once you borrow from other schools of thought that you also borrow the assumptions that underlie those ideas (Van der Veer & Valsiner, 1991).

> It is this feeling of a system, the sense of a (common) style, the understanding that each particular statement is linked with and dependent upon the central idea of the whole system of which it is a part, which is absent in the essentially eclectic attempts at combining parts of two or more systems that are heterogeneous and diverse in scientific origin and composition... Usually one gets a conglomerate of scientific theories, facts, etc. which have been squeezed into the framework of the unifying idea with horrible arbitrariness." (Vygotsky, p. 259)

Vygotsky was not a theoretical fundamentalist. He expected his theory to be superseded but believed that practice was to serve as the ultimate criterion by which to test and hold a theory accountable. For Vygotsky the pitfalls of eclecticism are likely to be visited on the practitioner as well as theoretician. Any teacher educator who has had the experience of introducing new concepts or strategies to teachers and has been greeted with the claim "I already do that" can readily appreciate the problem of communicating across belief systems.

Like most orthodoxies, current interpretations of sociocultural theory in the United States run the risk of becoming ossified. Recently, U.S. researchers working from a sociocultural perspective have been taken to task for their narrow and apolitical appropriation of Vygotsky's ideas (Daniels, 2006; Elhammoumi, 2002; Engestrom, 1991; Tudge, 2003). One needn't be a Marxist to recognize that macrosocial issues (e.g., the distribution of wealth, globalization) have consequences for what happens at microsocial levels (e.g., in the home or classroom).

CONCLUSIONS

In assessing the implications of an integrative and comprehensive sociocultural framework for understanding reading comprehension, we are led to several conclusions. In many respects, sociocultural theory has become the new orthodoxy in education and the study of reading comprehension. While sociocultural theories have has a significant impact on both the design and conduct of research on comprehension instruction and in organizing and make sense of extant research and practices, the real value of such a comprehensive and integrative conception of comprehension has hardly been mined. We speak of the potential of a sociocultural framework to connect what up until now has been an unbridgeable chasm—the relationships between macro-social structures & microsocial processes, between culturally variable and historically changing time and face-to-face social interactions, between policy and practice. These are no small matters. A comprehensive and integrative approach also has the potential to be reflexive and self-critical. Absent such a perspective, instructional researchers and practitioners will continue being relegated to the role of custodians of the status quo—practitioners of a form of technical rationality subservient to the whims of those who seek solutions to our current and future challenges by looking to what once was.

Perhaps the greatest obstacle to making these connections has been ideological. Ours has been an ideology that values individualism over social connectedness; that offers one-size fits all solutions to a richly multicultural citizenry; that seem intent on repeating history rather than learning from it; that labors with the belief that nothing is lost when one reduces complexity to simplicity; and in its search for the timeless and universal often fails to see and appreciate the local and situated.

The societal and global challenges that we face are of unparalleled complexity and gravity and include but are not limited to:

- Globalization and the need to remain economically competitive at a time of increasing interdependence between nations
- The digital revolution and proliferation of information requiring that citizens acquire the multiliteracies that enable them to critically assess
- The permeability of national borders and multiculturalism
- Global pollution and warming
- The potential for mass annihilation

While far from sufficient, the ability to read and read critically and constructively and then to act will be a necessary tool in the larger toolbox of multiliteracies important in addressing these challenges. Perhaps the greatest challenge, however, is whether we can begin addressing these pressing issues of the 21st century while truly leaving no child left behind.

REFERENCES

Adam, & Bullock, D. (1987). Apprenticeship in word use: Social convergence processes in learning categorically related nouns. In I. I. S. A. Kuczaj & M. D. Barrett (Eds.), *The development of word meaning* (pp.155–197). New York, Springer-Verlag.

Ageyev, V. S. (2003). Vygotsky in the mirror of cultural interpretations. In A. Kozulin, B. Gindis, V. S. Ageyev, & S. M. Miller (Eds.), *Vygotsky's educational theory in cultural context* (pp. 432–449). Cambridge, Cambridge University Press.

Allington, R. L. (1983). Fluency: The neglected reading goal. *The Reading Teacher, 37,* 556–561.

Armbruster, B. B., & Anderson, T. H. (1984). Structures of explanations in history textbooks or so what if Governor Stanford missed the spike and hit the rail? *Journal of Curriculum Studies, 16,* 247–274.

Au, K. H. (1980). Participation structures in a reading lesson with Hawaiian children: Analysis of a culturally appropriate instructional event. *Anthropology & Education Quarterly* 11(2), 91–115.

Bakhtin, M. M. (1981). *The dialogic imagination.* Austin, TX: University of Texas Press.

Bakhtin, M. M. (1986). *Speech genres & other late essays.* Austin, TX: University of Texas Press.

Barr, R., Kamil, M. L., et al. (Eds.). (1991). *Handbook of reading research* (Vol. 2). New York, Longman.

Beck, I. L., & McKeown, M. G. (1991). Social studies texts are hard to understand: Mediating some of the difficulties. *Language Arts, 68,* 482–490.

Beck, I., McKeown, M. Sinatra, G., & Loxterman, J. (1991). Revising social studies text from a text processing perspective: Evidence of improved comprehensibility. *Reading Research Quarterly, 26,* 251–276.

Berkenkotter, C., & Huckin, T. N. (1993). Rethinking genre from a sociocognitive perspective. *Written communication 10*(4), 475–509.

Bernstein, B. (1990). *The structure of pedagogic discourse: Class, codes and control.* London, Routledge.

Betts, E. A. (1946). *Foundations of reading instruction.* New York: American Book.

Bickhard, M. H. (1994). World mirroring versus world making: There's gotta be a better way. In L. P. Steffe & J. Gale (Eds.), *Constructivism in education.* Hillsdale, NJ, Erlbaum.

Brown, A. L., Campione, J. C., & Day, J. M. (1981). Learning to learn: On training students to learn from texts. *Educational Researcher 10,* 14–21.

Brown, A. L., & Ferrara, R. A. (1985). Diagnosing zones of proximal development. In J. V. Wertsch (Ed.), *Culture, communication and cognition* (pp. 273–305). New York: Cambridge University Press.

Bruner, J. (1990). *Acts of meaning,* Cambridge, MA: Harvard University Press.

Burbules, N. C. (1997). Rhetorics of the web: Hyperreading and critical literacy. In I. Snyder (Ed.), *From age to screen: Taking literacy into the electronic era* (pp. 102–122). Sydney: Allen & Unwin.

Cazden, C. B. (1988). *Classroom discourse.* Portsmouth, NH: Heinemann.

Clark, A. (1997). *Being there: Putting, brain, body, and the world together again.* Cambridge, MA: The MIT Press.

Cole, M. (1996). *Cultural psychology: A once and future discipline.* Cambridge: Harvard University Press.

Cole, M., & Griffin, M. (1986). A sociohistorical approach to remediation. In S. de Castell, A. Luke, & K. Egan (Eds.), *Literacy, society, and schooling* (pp. 110–131). New York: Cambridge University Press.

Cope, B., & Kalantzis, M. (2000). A of pedagogy of multiliteracies designing social futures. In B. Cope & M. Kalantzis (Eds.), *Multiliteracies: Literacy learning and the design of social futures* (pp. 9–37). London: Routldege.

Daniels, H. (2001). *Vygotsky and pedagogy.* New York: Routledge Falmer.

Daniels, H. (2006). The 'social' in post-Vygotskian theory. *Theory & Psychology 16*(1), 37.

Davydov, V. V. (1988). Problems of developmental teaching: The experience of psychological research Excerpts (Part II). *Soviet Education, XXX*(9), 3–83.

Davydov, V. V. (1998). The concept of developmental teaching. *Journal of Russian and East European Psychology 36*(4), 11–36.

de Castell, S. (1990). Teaching the Textbook: Teacher/Text Authority and the Problem of Interpretation. *Linguistics and Education 2,* 75–99.

Delgado-Gaitan, C., & Trueba, H. (1991). *Crossing cultural borders: Education for immigrant families in America.* London: Falmer Press.

Delpit, L. D. (1988). The silenced dialogue: Power and pedagogy in educating other people's children. *Harvard Educational Review 58*(3), 280–298.

Dewey, J. (1925/1958). *Experience and nature.* New York, Dover.

Dewey, J., & Childs, J. L. (1933). The social-economic situation and education. In W. H. Kilpatrick (Ed.), *The educational frontier* (pp. 32–72). New York: D. Appleton-Century.

Dobzhansky, T. (1962). *Mankind evolving.* New Haven, CT: Yale University Press.

Duffy, G. G., Roehler, L. R., et al. (1986a). The relationship between explicit verbal explanations during reading skill instruction and student awareness and achievement: A study of reading teacher effects. *Reading Research Quarterly 21*(3), 237–252.

Duffy, G. G., Roehler, L. R., et al. (1986b). How teachers' instructional talk influences students' understanding of lesson content. *The Elementary School Journal 8*(1), 3–16.

El'konin, D. B. (1972). Toward the problem of stages in the mental development of the child. *Soviet Psychology 10,* 225–251.

Elhammoumi, M. (2002). To create psychology's own capital. *Journal for the Theory of Social Behavior 32*(1), 89–104.

Engeström, Y. (1987). *Learning by expanding.* Helinskin: Orienta-Konsulit Oy.

Engeström, Y. (1991). *Non sclae sed vitae discimus:* Toward overcoming the encapsulation of school learning. *Learning and Instruction 1*(3), 243–259.

Engeström, Y. (1999). Activity theory and individual and social transformation. In Y. Engestrom, R. Miettinen, & R.-L. Punamaki (Eds.), *Perspectives on activity theory.* New York: Cambridge University Press.

Erickson, F., & Schultz, J. (1991). Students' experience of the curriculum. In P. W. Jackson (Ed.), *Handbook of Research on Curriculum* (pp. 465–485). New York: Macmillan.

Fairclough, N. (1992). *Discourse and social change*. Cambridge, UK: Blackwell Publishing.

Fichter, B. (1984). Co-ordination, co-operation and communication in the formation of theo-retical concepts in instruction. In M. Hedegaard, P. Hakkarainen, & Y. Engeström (Eds.), *Learning and teaching on a scientific basis: Methodological and epistemological aspects of the activity theory of learning and teaching*. Aarhus: Aarhus Universitet, Psychologisk Institut.

Fischer, J. L. (1965). Psychology and Anthropology. *Biennial Review of Anthropology 4*, 211–261.

Fountas, I. C., & Pinnell, G. S. (2001). *Guided Reading: Essential Elements: The Skillful Teacher*. A two-tape video set. Portsmouth, NH: Heinemann.

Freire, P., & Macedo, D. (1987). *Literacy: Reading the word and the world*. South Hadley, MA: Bergin & Garvey.

Gardner, H. (1987). *The mind's new science*, New York: Basic Books.

Gavelek, J. R., & Raphael, T. E. (1996). Changing talk about text: New roles for teachers and students. *Language Arts 73*(3), 182–192.

Gee, J. (1990). *Social linguistics and literacies: Ideology in discourses*. New York: Falmer Press.

Gee, J. P. (1991). What is literacy? In C. Mitchell & K. Weiler (Eds.), *Rewriting literacy: Culture and the discourse of the other* (pp. 3–11). New York: Bergin & Garvey.

Gee, J. P. (1997). Thinking, learning, and reading: The situated sociocultural mind. In D. Kir-shner & J. A. Whitson (Eds.), *Situated cognition: social, semiiotic, and psychological per-spectives* (pp. 235–259). Mahwah, NJ: Erlbaum.

Gee, J. P. (2000). Discourse and sociocultural studies in reading. In M. Kamil, P. Mosenthal, P. Pearson, & R. Barr (Eds.), *Handbook of reading research* (pp. 195–207). Mahwah, NJ: Erlbaum.

Gee, J. P. (2001). Reading as situated language: A sociocognitive perspective. *Journal of Adoles-cent & Adult Literacy 44*(8), 714–725.

Gee, J. P. (2003). Opportunity to learn: A language-based perspective on assessment. *Assess-ment in Education 10*(1), 27–46.

Gee, J. P. (2003). *What video games have to teach us about learning and literacy*. New York: Palgrave Macmillan.

Gibbs, R. L. (2006). *Embodiment and cognitive science*. Cambridge: Cambridge University Press.

Giddens, A. (1984). *The constitution of society*. Berkeley: University of California Press.

Giddens, A. (1986). Action, subjectivity, and the constitution of meaning. *Social Research 53*(3), 529–545.

Gielen, U. P., & Jeshmaridian, S. S. (1999). Lev S. Vygotsky: The man and the era. *International Journal of Group Tensions 28*(3/4), 273–300.

Gindis, B. (1995). Viewing the disabled child in the sociocultural mileiu. *School Psychology International 16*, 155–166.

Graff, H. J. (1982). The legacies of literacy. *Journal of Communication 32*(1), 12–26.

Greenleaf, C. L., Schoenbach R., et al. (2001). Apprenticing adolescent readers to academic lit-eracy. *Harvard Educational Review 71*(1), 79–129.

Gutierrez, K., Baquedano-Lopez, P., & Tejeda, C. (1999). Rethinking diversity: Hybridity and hybrid language practices in the third space. *Mind, Culture, & Activity: An International Journal 6*(4), 286–303.

Gutiérrez, K. D., & Stone, L. D. (2000). Synchronic and diachronic dimensions of social prac-tice: An emerging methodology for cultural-historical perspecitives on literacy learning. In C. D. Lee & P. Smagorinsky (Eds.), *Vygotskian perspectives on literacy research: Con-structing meaning through collaborative inquiry* (pp. 150–164). Cambridge: Cambridge University Press.

Halliday, M. A. K. (1978). *Language as social semiotic: The social interpretation of language and meaning*. London: Edward Arnold.

Halliday, M. A. K. (1989). *Spoken and written language*. Oxford,: Oxford University Press.

Halliday, M. A. K. (1993). Towards a language-based theory of learning. *Linguistics and Educa-tion 5*, 93–116.

Harnad, S. (1990). The symbol grounding problem. *Physica 42*, 335–346.

Heath, S. B. (1983). *Ways with words: Language, life, and work in communities and class-rooms*. Cambridge: Cambridge University Press.

Hickey, D., & Zuiker, S. (2005). Engaged participation: A sociocultural model for motivation with implications for educational assessment. *Educatonal Assessment 10*(3), 277–305.

Hicks, D. (1995). Discourse, learning, and teaching. *Review of Research in Education, 21,* 49–95. Washington: American Educational Research Association.

Huizen, P. V., Oers, B. V., et al. (2005). A Vygotskian perspective on teacher education. *Journal of Curriculum Studies* 37(3), 267.

Hull, G. A., & Nelson, M. E. (2005). Locating the semiotic power of multimodality. *Written Communication* 22(2), 224–261.

Hutto, D. D. (1999). Cognition without representation? In A. Riegler, M. Peschel, & A. v. Stein (Eds.), *Understanding representation in the cognitive sciences* (pp. 57–74). New York: Kluwer Academic/Plenum.

Ilyenkov, E. V. (1977). The problem of the ideal. *In Philosophy in the USSR: Problems of dialectical materialism.* Moscow: Progress.

John-Steiner, V. (1985). The road to competence in alien land: A Vygotskian perspective on bilingualism. In J. V. Wertsch (Eds.), *Culture, communication, and cognition: Vygotskian perspectives* (pp. 348–371). New York: Cambridge University Press.

Johnson, D. M., & Erneling, C. E. (Eds.). (1997). *The future of the cognitive revolution.* Oxford: Oxford University Press.

Johnston, P. (1984). Instruction and student independence. *The Elementary School Journal 84,* 338–344.

Johnston, P. H. (1988). A Vygotskian perspective on assessment of reading. In S. B. Sigmon (Ed.), *Critical voices on special education* (pp. 103–241). Albany, NY: SUNY Press.

Kaestle, C. F., Damon-Moore, H., Stedman, L. C., Tingsley, K., & Tollinger, W. V. (1991). *Literacy in the United States: Readers and reading since 1880.* New Haven, CT: Yale University Press.

Kamil, M. L., Mosenthal, P., et al. (Eds.) (2000). *Handbook of reading research (Vol. 3).* Mahwah, NJ: Erlbaum.

Keijzer, F. (2002). Representation in dynamical and embodied cognition. *Cognitive Systems Research 3,* 275–288.

Kress, G. (2000). Multimodality. In B. Cope & M. Kalantzis (Eds.), *Multiliteracies: Literacy learning and the design of social futures* (pp. 182–202). London: Routldege.

Kress, G. (2003). *Literacy in the new media age.* London: Routledge.

Kucan, L. , & Beck, I. L. (1997). Thinking Aloud and Reading Comprehension Research: Inquiry, Instruction, and Social Interaction. *Review of Educational Research 67*(3), 271–299.

Labov, W. (1972). *The transformation of experience in narrative: Language in the inner city.* Philadelphia: University of Pennsylvania Press.

Lakoff, G., & Johnson, M. (1999). *Philosophy in the flesh: The embodied mind and its challenge to Western thought.* New York: Basic Books.

Lantolf, J. P., & Thorne, S. L. (2006). *Sociocultural theory and the genesis of second language development.* Oxford: Oxford University Press.

Lee, C. D. (2000). Signifying in the zone or proximal development. In C. D. Lee & P. Smagorinsky (Eds.), *Vygotskian perspectives on literacy research: Constructing meaning through collaborative inquiry* (pp. 191–225). Cambridge: Cambridge University Press.

Lee, C. D., & Smagorinsky, P. (Eds.). (2000). *Vygotskian perspectives on literacy research: Constructing meaning through collaborative inquiry.* Cambridge: Cambridge University Press.

Lemke, J. L. (1998). Metamedia literacy: Transforming meanings and media. In D. Reinking, M. C. McKenna, L. D. Labbo, & R. D. Kieffer. *Handbook of literacy and technology: Transformations in a post-typographic world* (pp. 283–301). Mahwah, NJ: Erlbaum.

Leont'ev, A. N. (1981). *Problems of the development of the mind,* Moscow: Progress Publishers.

Lewis, C., & Moje, E. B. (2003). Sociocultural perspectives meet critical theories: Producing knowledge through multiple frameworks. *International Journal of Learning* 10, 1979–1995.

Lortie, D. C. (1975). *Schoolteacher.* Chicago: University of Chicago Press.

Luria, A. R. (1982). *Language and cognition,* New York: Wiley.

Martin, H. J. (1988). *The history and power of writing.* Chicago: The University of Chicago Press.

Mason, M. (2000). Teachers as critical mediators of knowledge. *Journal of Philosophy of Education. 34*(2), 343–352.

McCaslin, M. (1989). Self-regulated learning and academic achievement: A Vygotskian view. In B. Zimmerman & D. Schunk (Eds.), *Self-regulated learning and academic achievement: Theory, research and practice.* New York: Springer-Verlag.

McVee, M. B., Dunsmore, K., et al. (2005). Schema theory revisited. *Review of Educational Research, 75*(4), 531–566.

Merrell, F. (1997). *Peirce, signs, and meaning.* Toronto: University of Toronto Press.

Miettinen, R. (1999). Transcending traditional school learning: Teachers' work and networks of learning. In Y. Engeström, R. Miettinen, & R.-L. Punamaki (Eds.), *Perspectives on activity theory* (pp. 325–344). New York: Cambridge University Press.

Miller, C. R. (1994). Genre as Social Action. In A. Freedman & P. Medway (Eds.), *Genre and the New Rhetoric: Critical Perspectives on Literacy and Education* (pp. 23–42). Bristol: Taylor & Francis.

Miller, S. M. (2003). How literature discussion shapes thinking: ZPD's for teaching/learning habits of the heart and mind. In A. Kozulin, B. Gindis, V. S. Ageyev, & S. M. Miller (Eds.), *Vygotsky's educational theory in culturall context*. Cambridge: Cambridge University Press.

Mishra, P., & Koehler, M. J. (2006). Technological pedagogical content knowledge: A framework for teacher knowledge. *Teachers College Record, 108*(6), 1017–1054.

Moje, E. B. (2006). Developing socially just subject-matter instruction: A review of the literature on disciplinary literacy teaching. *Review of Research in Education 31*(1), 1–44.

Moje, E. B., Ciechanowski, K. M., et al. (2004). Working toward third space in content area literacy: An examination of everyday funds of knowledge and discourse. *Reading Research Quarterly, 39*(1), 38–70.

Moll, L. C. (2001). Through the mediation of others: Vygotskian research on teaching. *Handbook of research on teaching* (pp. 111–129). Washington, DC: American Educational Research Association.

Moll, L. C. and Dworin, J. E. (1996). Biliteracy development in classrooms: Social dynamics and cultural possibilities. In D. Hicks (Ed.), *Discourse, learning, and schooling* (pp. 221–246). Cambridge: Cambridge University Press.

Nelson, K. (2007). *Young minds in social worlds: Experience, meaning and memory*. Cambridge, MA: Harvard University Press.

Newmann, F. M., Smith, B. S., et al. (2001). Instructional program coherence: What it is and why it should guide school improvement policy? *Educational Evaluation and Policy Analysis, 23*(4), 297–321.

Norris, S., & Jones, R. H. (Eds.) (2005). *Discourse in action: Introducing mediated discourse analysis*. New York: Routledge.

Palincsar, A. S. (1986). The role of dialogue in providing scaffolded instruction. *Educational Psychologist, 21*(1 & 2), 73–98.

Palincsar, A. S., & Brown, A. L. (1984). Reciprocal teaching of comprehension-fostering and comprehension-monitoring activities. *Cognition and Instruction, 1*, 117–125.

Pearson, P. D., Barr, R. M., et al. (Eds.) (1984). *Handbook of reading research* (Vol.1). New York: Longman.

Popkewitz, T. S. (1998). Dewey, Vygotsky and the social administration of the individual: Constructivist pedagogy as systems of ideas in historical spaces. *American Educational Research Journal 35*(4), 535–570.

Ratner, C. (1996). Activity as a key concept for cultural psychology. *Culture & Psychology, 2*, 407–434.

Ratner, C. (1997). In defense of activity theory. *Culture & Psychology, 3*(2), 211–223.

Rogoff, B. (2003). *The cultural nature of human development*. New York, Oxford University Press.

Rosenblatt, L. M. (1994). The transactional theory of reading and writing. In R. B. Ruddell, M. R. Ruddell, & H. Singer (Eds.), *Theoretical models and processes or reading* (pp. 1057–1092). Newark, DE: International Reading Association.

Samuels, S. J. (1988). Decoding and automaticity: Helping poor readers become automatic at word recognition. *The Reading Teacher, 41*, 756–760.

Scholes, R. (1989). *Protocols of reading*. New Haven, CT: Yale University Press.

Scholes, R. E. (1985). *Textual power: Literary theory and the teaching of English*. New Haven, CT: Yale University Press.

Scribner, S. (1984). Literacy in three metaphors. *Journal of Education, 93*, 6–21.

Schreiber, P. A. (1980). On the acquisition of reading fluency. *Journal of Reading Behavior, 12*, 177–186.

Scribner, S., & Cole, M. (1981). *The psychology of literacy*. Cambridge: Harvard University Press.

Seymour, J. R., & Osana, H. P. (2003). Reciprocal teaching procedures and principles: Two teachers' developing understanding. *Teaching and Teacher Education, 19*, 325–344.

Siegel, M. (1995). More than words: The generative power of transmediation for learning. *Canadian Journal of Education, 20*(4), 455–475.

Smagorinsky, P. (2001). If meaning is constructed, what is it made from? Toward a cultural theory of reading. *Review of Educational Research, 71*(1), 133–169.

Smagorinsky, P., Cook, L. S., et al. (2003). The twisting path of concept development in learning to teach. *Teachers College Record, 105*(8), 1399–1436.

Snow, C. E. (2002). *Reading for understanding: Toward a research and development program in reading comprehension*. Arlington, VA: Office of Education Resarch and Improvement.

Stone, A., & Werstch, J. V. (1984). A social-interactional analysis of learning disabilities. *Journal of Learning Disabilities, 17*, 194–199.

Stone, C. A. (1993). What is missing in the metaphor of scaffolding? In E. A. Forman, N. Minnick, & C. A. Stone (Eds.), *Contexts for learning: Sociocultural dynamics in children's development*. New York: Oxford University Press.

Sumara, D. J. (2003). Toward a theory of embodied literary experience. *English Journal, 2*(2), 88–95.

Tharp, R. G., & Gallimore, R. (1988). *Rousing minds to life: Teaching, learning, and schooling in social context*. Cambridge: Cambridge University Press.

The New London Group (1996). A pedagogy of multiliteracies: Designing social futures. *Harvard Educational Review, 66*(1), 60–92.

Tomasello, M. (1999). *The cultural origins of human cognition*. Cambridge, MA, Harvard University Press.

Toulmin, S. (1978, September). The Mozart of psychology. *New York Review of Books*.

Toulmin, S. (1979). The inwardness of mental life. *Critical Inquiry, 6*, 1–16.

Tudge, J., & Scrimsher, S. (2003). Lev. S. Vygotsky: A cultural-historical, interpersonal, and individual approach to development. In B. J. Zimmerman & D. H. Schunk (Eds.), *Educational psychology: A century of contributions* (pp. 207–228). Mahwah, NJ: Erlbaum.

Unsworth, L. (2001). *Teaching multiliteracies across the curriculum: Changing contexts of text and image in classroom practice: Changing contexts of text and image in classroom practice*. Philadelphia: Open University Press.

Unsworth, L. (2002). Changing dimensions of school literacies. *The Australian Journal of Language and Literacy, 25*(1), 62–77.

van der Veer, R. (1998). From concept attainment to knowledge formation. *Mind, Culture, and Activity, 5*(2), 89–94.

Van der Veer, R., & Valsiner, J. (1991). *Understanding Vygotsky: A quest for synthesis*. Oxford: Blackwell.

Varela, F. J., Thompson, E., et al. (1991). *The embodied mind: Cognitive science and human experience*. Cambridge, MA: The MIT Press.

Vygotsky, L. S. (1962). *Thought and language*. Cambridge, MA: The M.I.T. Press.

Vygotsky, L. S. (1971). *The psychology of art*. Cambridge, MA: The M.I.T Press.

Vygotsky, L. S. (1978). *Mind in society*. Cambridge, MA: Harvard University Press.

Vygotsky, L. S. (1987). *The collected works of L. S. Vygotsky: Problems of general psychology*. New York: Plenum. (Original work published 1934)

Vygotsky, L. S. (1997). *The collected works of L. S. Vygotsky: Problems of theory and history of psychology*. New York: Plenum.

Wallis, C., & Steptoe, S. (2006, December, 10). How to bring our schools out of the 20th century. *Time Magazine*.

Wartofsky, M. (1973). *Models*. Dordrecht: D. Reidel.

Wells, G. (1990). Talk about text: Where literacy is learned and taught. *Curriculum Inquiry, 20*(4), 369–404.

Wells, G. (1994). The complementary contributions of Halliday and Vygotsky to a "language based theory of learning." *Linguistics and Education, 6*, 41–90.

Wells, G. (2002). The role of dialogue in activity theory. *Mind, Culture, and Activity, 9*(1).

Wells, G., Chang, L. M., et al. (1990). Creating classroom communities of literate thinkers. In S. Sharan (Ed.), *Cooperative learning: Theory and research*. New York, Praeger.

Wenger, E. (1998). *Communities of practice: Learning, meaning, and identity*. Cambridge, MA: Cambridge University Press.

Wertsch, J. V. (1985). *Vygotsky and the social formation of mind*, Cambridge, MA: Harvard University Press.

Wertsch, J. V. (1991). *Voices of the Mind*, Cambridge, MA: Harvard University Press.

Wertsch, J. V. (1998). *Mind as action*. Oxford: Oxford University Press.

Whitehead, A. N. (1929). *The aims of education*, New York: Macmillan.

Wineburg, S. S. (1991). Historical problem solving: A study of cognitive processes used in the evaluation of documentary and pictorial evidence. *Journal of Educational Psychology, 83*, 73–87.

Wyatt-Smith, C. M., & Cumming, J. J. (2003). Curriculum literacies: Expanding domains of assessment. *Assessment in Education, 10*(1), 47–59.

8 Transactional Theory and Critical Theory in Reading Comprehension

James S. Damico, Gerald Campano, and Jerome C. Harste

Indiana University, Bloomington

INTRODUCTION

The modifiers *transactional* and *critical* when used with the word 'theory' call attention to sets of sophisticated ideas and practices regarding the ways readers make meaning with different kinds of texts. In the context of education, transactional theory and critical theory have raised fundamental questions about the purposes and consequences of reading and schooling. Transactional theory, rooted in the work of Louise Rosenblatt (1938, 1978), has helped us better understand the ways individual readers actively construct meanings with texts, especially literary texts; while critical theory foregrounds issues of power, enabling us to see the ways that texts, contexts, and institutions inform, shape, and circumscribe meaning-making—how reading is shaped by structural forces, constraints, and contingencies. This chapter considers the import of transactional theory and critical theory to the field of literacy. After attending to some definitional issues, we situate the two theories historically, tracing theoretical developments and weaving in landmark studies of classroom practices. Toward this end we divide this section of the chapter into two periods, using the two seminal texts of Rosenblatt, *Literature as Exploration* (1938) and *The Reader, the Text, the Poem* (1978) and the work of the Frankfurt School (late 1930's) and Paulo Freire (beginning in 1970 with the publication of *Pedagogy of the Oppressed*), as markers for the beginning of each time period. This attention to history illuminates transactional theory as an increasingly vital perspective literacy researchers have used to frame and understand K–12 readers' relationships to texts, and critical theory as a vibrant set of perspectives to guide systemic, social critique yet more sparingly making inroads through empirical studies of readers working with texts in classrooms. The chapter also demonstrates transactional and critical theory working in complementary ways, beginning in the late 1930s and continuing today, to challenge the reign of positivism and instrumental rationality in schooling and, more specifically, in reading education. Transactional theory offers an antidote to prescriptive, pre-packaged curricula where meanings are viewed as pre-ordained. Critical theory offers tools to examine any forms of authoritarianism and routinization, especially forms being enacted in the current era of standardization and test-score accountability informed by "scientifically-based research." The chapter concludes with implications and new directions about collectivist forms of response in reader-text-context relationships. This leads to how we might envision and enact readings and responses that are *consequential* to living in a democratic society.

DEFINITIONAL ISSUES

In laying out her transactional theory of reading literature, Rosenblatt makes a distinction between an interaction and a transaction. Whereas an interaction model presupposes "separate, self-contained, and already different entities acting on one another," a transactional view entails "an ongoing process in which the elements or factors are... aspects of a total situation, each conditioned by and conditioning the other" (1978, p. 17). In this intersubjective process, the experiences, emotions, and attitudes of individual readers fuse with a text to evoke a "poem," what Rosenblatt defines as "an event in time...not an object or ideal entity [but] a coming-together, a compenetration, of a reader and a text" (p. 12). The idea of a literary transaction, where "the reader's creation of a poem out of text must be an active, self-ordering and self-corrective process" (Rosenblatt, 1978, p. 11), opened a pathway where a proliferation of meanings, rather than single or fixed meanings, could become a standard approach to literary interpretation or textual response.

From the perspective of critical theory, the production and dissemination of texts and all readings and responses to texts are ideological practices, deeply enmeshed in relationships of power. Understanding ideology as "a set of ideas that legitimize the benefits enjoyed by a particular group, religion or country, where those benefits are simply assumed as natural... or as deserved" (Werner, 2002, p. 420), critical theory is committed to the twin goals of critique and transformation: questioning and challenging ideological assumptions, conflicts and contradictions of the power-knowledge nexus (Apple, 1993; Freire & Macedo, 1987; Lankshear & McLaren, 1993; Morgan, 1997), especially as they are played out in and through a host of institutional structures; and working to create for people more socially just material conditions and lived experiences. Applied to reading, critical theory leads to questioning and challenging the ways authors and texts attempt to persuade, influence, and position readers as well as examining the values, experiences, and beliefs that readers bring to texts.

THEORETICAL DEVELOPMENTS AND CLASSROOM CONNECTIONS

Rosenblatt, the Frankfurt School, the reign of New Criticism

Seven decades ago, Louise Rosenblatt in her book, *Literature as Exploration* (1938), helped reconceptualize what counted as reader response by impugning the relatively undisputed belief that meanings were located in texts. Challenging the prevailing perspective of textual objectivity or textual autonomy, she instead maintained the interdependence of both text and reader, holding neither solely determinate of meaning. Rather than thinking of response as finding the "correct" meaning *in* the text, she described how a reader could draw upon a reservoir of experiences, emotions, and attitudes in response to a text, what she called "the lived-through process of building up the work under the guidance of the text" (1978, p. 69). Rosenblatt also challenged dualistic thinking in other ways. Her theory of reading literature emerged from her philosophy of teaching (Rosenblatt, 1995, p. xvi), thus disrupting the theory/practice dichotomy. Like Dewey, she eschewed a binary stance toward what counted as art and science, and she also worked to fracture the prevailing practice of dichotomizing cognition and emotion. Rosenblatt confronted this dualism, in part, by arguing that texts are first "aesthetically evoked" before becoming "the object of reflection and analysis" (Rosenblatt, 1995, p. 295).

At roughly the same time as the initial publication of *Literature as Exploration*, the Frankfurt School of Social Science—with leading figures Max Horkheimer, Theodor Adorno, Herbert Marcuse, and Jurgen Habermas—were explicating a set of ideas committed to the critique and transformation of society. Generated in response to the totalitarianism they were witnessing in Europe in general, and with Nazi Germany in particular, these ideas, which came to be known as critical theory or critical social theory, also leveled a critique against logical positivism (school of thought that championed the view that only certain mathematical and science procedures could lead to accurate determinations of truths and falsehoods) and instrumental rationality (the view that valorized finding cost-effective means toward particular ends without critical or reflective attention to why the ends are being sought), troubling the ways these perspectives disregarded the interests and needs of human beings. The Frankfurt School rejected the positivistic view of knowledge as value-neutral, objective, and independent of human intervention and interests (Cherryholmes, 1999) and instead placed "human subjectivity and social action at the center of history" in order to "reestablish the meaning of freedom based on human values, just social relations, and equality" (Shannon, 1990, p. 148).

With the postwar climate of the 1940s through McCarthyism and the post-Sputnik era consumed by a "narrow empiricism as behaviorism dominated psychology and logical positivism reigned in philosophy" (Rosenblatt, 1995, p. 290), the formalist tenets and practices of New Criticism (Brooks & Warren, 1938; Wellek & Warren, 1949) prevailed as the dominant way of thinking about reading and teaching literature. While New Criticism contributed a well-articulated vocabulary (e.g., ambiguity, paradox, irony, and coherence) toward "the study of literature as a coherent discipline" (McGillis, 1996, p. 10), what readers brought to each text—including thoughts and feelings—was deemed extraneous to meaning-making, what New Critics labeled the "affective fallacy." Theoretical work during this period relied heavily on revealing patterns, themes, and structures embedded in texts, while classroom instruction focused on finding these predetermined patterns, themes, and structures—what Booth (1995) describes as "delving endlessly for the gold: the one right reading" (p. ix).

During the 1940s and through much of the 1960s, New Criticism remained relatively unchallenged in theory and practice. There is not much research evidence of Rosenblatt's reader response perspective making many inroads in classrooms during this time. The focus was on the text, not the reader. Although empirical studies of critical theory applications in K–12 classrooms during this time remain mostly non-existent, there was some interesting curricular work being done, especially in the 1930s and into the 1940s. The critical theory connection to education and classrooms at this time came mostly from the social reconstructionist strand within the Progressive Education movement led by Theodore Brameld and George Counts. With goals of curriculum reform, the social reconstructionists argued that students should "directly study poverty, crime, political corruption, unemployment, and abuse of power as the themes that would prepare them for adult society" (Shannon, 1990, p. 13). A primary pedagogical goal of the social reconstructionists was critical reading of texts and contexts, as Shannon describes:

> No longer was it sufficient for the literate to read accurately or to write clearly and expressively. What was needed for the educational frontier was the ability to read beyond the text to understand how the author and the ideas connected with various political, economic, and social arguments concerning the future of America... [what was needed was] an expanding definition of literacy—one that encouraged readers and writers to see the ideological basis of any text. (1990, p. 97)

This view of reading remained intimately tied to the stance that schools needed to be committed to radical social change, as George Counts argued in likely his most famous paper, "Dare the School Build a New Social Order?" (1932). The curricular and pedagogical instantiation of these ideas is perhaps best represented in the work of Harold Rugg whose social studies textbooks found their way into a number of U.S. junior high and secondary classrooms (Tanner & Tanner, 1995) especially in the more politically palatable times for social reconstructionists during the 1930s and 1940s.

While the reign of New Criticism in U.S. classrooms continued relatively unabated through the middle and into the latter decades of the 20th century, it began to be challenged theoretically by the end of the 1960s as the confluence of other emerging or re-emerging philosophical stances began to alter ideas about what counted as response. Psychoanalytic-based literary theory, although initiated in the 1920s, resurfaced more widely during the 1960s and several studies explored the ways individual responses were influenced by unconscious as well as conscious processes (Holland, 1969; Purves & Rippere, 1968). This shift to focusing more on individual responses was further aided by studies in bibliotherapy, which considered the reader's personality when assessing responses to texts (Purves & Beach, 1972). Significant theoretical contributions in this area of experiential response also came from Stanley Fish and David Bleich. Fish (1980) and his concern for "affective stylistics" or the readers' moment to moment reactions and decisions as they negotiate the text sentence by sentence led him to argue that "meaning is not what one extracts from a poem but the experiences one has with the course of reading" (in Tompkins, 1980, p. xxii). Bleich (1978) described reading as a subjective process, shaped indelibly by a reader's personality, and he offered a "framework for the intermingling of the cognitive and the affective" thus making it possible "to conceptualize language as dialogical or interactional" (1978, p. 73).

These theoretical developments reached reading researchers who used different foci and employed a range of analytic frameworks, such as aesthetic responses, personality variables, psychoanalytic theory, affective concerns, among others (Squire, 1994), to broaden conceptions of response to include "cognition, perception, and some emotional or attitudinal reactions" (Purves & Beach, 1972, p. 178). Drawing upon Rosenblatt's notion of an efferent and aesthetic response continuum, some researchers considered how readers' stances could shape their responses (Hunt & Vipond, 1985; Many, 1994) as well as how these stances can blur and coexist. Other researchers have focused on emotional response as it related to the interpretation or the impact of readers' attitudes (see Beach & Hynds, 1990, for a list of these studies).

The next section continues the exploration of transactional theory and critical theory and connections to practice. With transactional theory, Rosenblatt's book, *The Reader, the Text, the Poem* (1978), provides a historical signpost, providing a through-line from this text to *Literature as Exploration* published four decades earlier. For critical theory, we mark the passage of time with attention to Paulo Freire because his scholarship, including *Pedagogy of the Oppressed* (1970), resonates with ideas developed by the Frankfurt School. Freire also has had a prodigious influence on the ways critical-minded educators have framed curricular and pedagogical decisions with their students.

Return to Rosenblatt, the influence of Paulo Freire

After developing a theory of reader response in *Literature as Exploration* (1938), Rosenblatt elaborated upon this theoretical work with what she called a *transactional theory* of reading literature in her book, *The Reader, The Text, The Poem: The Transactional Theory of the Literary Work* (1978). With this theory, which grew out of her own praxis as a literature professor at the university, she refused to dichotomize response and meanings as either existing in the text or in the reader. Coinciding with theoretical advances in the ways the literacy field began to understand reading as a constructive meaning-making process—e.g., with psycholinguistics (Goodman, 1965; Smith, 1971), cognitive psychology and schema theory (Anderson & Pearson, 1984), sociolinguistics (Bloome & Green, 1984; Labov, 1972), and semiotics (Eco, 1979)—many reading researchers began discovering (or re-discovering) Rosenblatt after the publication of *The Reader, the Text, the Poem* (Pearson & Stephens, 1994). Rosenblatt, throughout her work, established the understanding that the beliefs, attitudes, experiences, associations, and feelings of readers were pivotal to textual meaning-making. Rather than abandon this reservoir of resources (as the formalists and New Critics contended), readers need to access and mobilize relevant and meaningful personal experiences to foster deeper engagements with texts.

Paulo Freire theorized the relationship between readers (and what they bring to texts) and the sociohistorical contexts in which they read. With his groundbreaking book, *Pedagogy of the Oppressed* (1970), and throughout his work, Freire argued that the experiences and histories of marginalized and oppressed groups needed to be the launching point for critical inquiry. Children and adults learn to "read the word" through "reading the world" (Freire & Macedo, 1987), each "person learning words concomitantly engaged in a critical analysis of the social framework in which men [and women] exist" (Freire, 1985, p. 56). For Freire, the goals of reading, and education more generally, involve a two-fold process: gaining deeper levels of critical consciousness about the ways inequitable social conditions and structures are created and maintained; and engaging in transformative action against authoritarianism of any kind to alter these conditions through a humanist and liberating praxis. Pedagogically this involves dialogue with both teachers and students immersed in collaborative knowledge building.

We see these two scholars, Rosenblatt and Freire, as well as these two theories, transactional and critical, opening up spaces for a multiplicity of meanings and heightened levels of critical awareness: Rosenblatt continuing to promote the democratizing view that meaning construction is an intersubjective process between reader and text, where a proliferation of meanings are possible; Freire for the ways he links reading text to examining sociopolitical contexts and systemic injustices, and how he outlines and champions self and social critique as a pathway to transformation. Put another way, we see Rosenblatt's maxim that meaning-making is shaped by the experiences, attitudes, values and emotions that readers bring to texts intersecting with Freire's argument that readers situate their own readings within sociohistorical contexts rife with inequities. Rosenblatt and Freire also set the stage in this chapter for a closer consideration of how context and culture shape readers' relationships to texts. While Rosenblatt retained a theoretical emphasis on the reader and the text, she was well-aware of the role context plays in meaning-making, stating that the response process "does not occur in a vacuum but is deeply conditioned by the social context" (1978, p. 135). For Freire, "reading the world" involves developing critical understandings about the ways different contexts (cultural, political, social, economic, religious, etc. across local, regional, national and more global levels) engender more or less equitable and humane conditions for people to live and thrive.

The research in the following sections of this chapter draws on diverse and often multidisciplinary perspectives in making theoretical and empirical contributions to the field. Yet the sampling of scholarly work discussed can be viewed as aligned with transactional theory and sensitive to critical perspectives.

CONTEXT, CULTURE, AND RESPONSE

The knowledge base of reader response research has expanded significantly in the past 30 to 40 years (Beach & Hynds, 1991; Galda & Beach, 2001; Marshall, 2000; Martinez & Roser, 2003; Rogers, 1999; Sipe, 1999), an expansion led by conceptual advancements in the ways the field frames the impact of cultural and social factors on readers' transactions with literature—to the point where literature can be understood as "a number of ways in which people relate themselves to writing" (Eagleton, 1996, p. 8) and response itself is deemed "a cultural act" (Beach & Freedman, 1992). Considering culture has led to myriad new understandings and possibilities in the study and practice of response. The recognition that individual responses to texts are informed and shaped by social and cultural factors has engendered more analyses of what readers bring to texts, and the perspective that all texts reflect ideological assumptions and stances has opened spaces for critical investigations into the ways texts position readers to adopt particular views and subject positions and how readers might challenge or resist the ways texts are positioning them.

Cultural connections and dissonances

Some scholars working within sociocultural paradigms spotlight how cultural identities of readers transact with the cultural knowledge, values, and rhetorical patterns embedded in texts. Lee (1995), for example, used a culturally-based cognitive apprenticeship model to document the ways urban African American readers activated their tacit knowledge of *signifying*, a form of figurative oral language use in African American communities (e.g., playing "the dozens"), to enrich their comprehension and interpretations of sophisticated literary texts. Lee's research points to the benefits of using ethnically diverse literature in classrooms as she establishes the connection between the social practices of a community and the language conventions of literary texts, guiding us to understand an "aesthetic territory where oral and literate rhetorical patterns meet" (p. 627). Building on this work, Brooks (2006) forges a link between literary understanding and the cultural knowledge of readers in her study of a group of African American middle school students. After identifying three sets of African American textual features—*recurring cultural themes* (e.g., confronting and overcoming racism, discovering history as a source of pride), *linguistic patterns* (e.g., African American vernacular English, Southern rural dialect), and *ethnic group practices* (e.g., beliefs in supernatural, quilting, religion) in three "culturally conscious" African American texts (Sims, 1982), Brooks shows how the students developed literary understandings by tapping into their cultural knowledge and experiences of these themes, patterns and practices.

There are also cultural mismatches and disconnections and resistance as readers transact with texts. Sims (1983), for example, documented the cultural disconnect between a text and an African American girl's experiences and expectations while Moller and Allen (2000), in a study of the ways four fifth grade girls (one Latina and three African American) responded to Mildred Taylor's text, *The Friendship* (1987), describe the "engaged resisting" of the girls. With the following categories of "engaged resistance"—critiquing characters' actions, rewriting characters' actions, rewriting with own selves, predicting with less negative outcomes, and stating their own discomfort when transacting with the text (2000, p. 171)—Moller and Allen describe how the use of engaged resistance "grew out of deep engagement and identification with characters and their experiences or with textual events and the intercontextual connections these sparked in discussion" (p. 172). The researchers go on to point out that despite identifying strongly with story characters, readers can "resist the feelings of helplessness or danger that this arouses" (p. 172).

The concept of resistance engenders questions about the ways authors and texts position readers to transact with texts in particular ways. Based on the understanding that texts "do not *reflect* reality, they promote a certain *version* of reality, and they position their readers within a certain reality as well" (Apol, 1998, p. 34), readers are invited into a text, encouraged to embrace its storyline and corresponding sets of assumptions. Put another way, the text is playing a significant part in constructing or "forming" readers as particular subjects (Bennett, 1979) where "readers not only produce inter-pretations of texts but are produced as subjects by the texts they read" (Surber, 1998, p. 245). For educators who value critical orientations to texts, this places a pedagogical priority on issues of authorship as teachers help students to question the choices (and consequences of these choices) that authors make, guiding their students to understand the work that authors do. Because all texts embody values and agendas and thus can never be neutral, readers embody a healthy skepticism toward texts, asking questions such as what views of the world are promoted in texts and whether they should accept these views (McLaren, 1999). In this sense, readers are encouraged to analyze how texts offer and transport representations of the world because these representations have implications for how gender, class, race, ethnicity, nationality, individuality (among others) are viewed and, in turn, constructed. Texts embody certain assumptions about who readers are, and they also constitute readers who react in certain ways—whether it be to adopt political perspectives, purchase products, etc. Because all texts are medi-ated by and embedded in ideologies (Althusser, 1971; Eagleton, 1991), readers need to cultivate understandings of "how, why, and in whose interests particular texts might work" (Luke & Freebody, 1997, p. 218).

Literary theories

One approach to discern how texts work to "form readers" (Bennett, 1979) and to better understand the range of ways readers might transact with texts is to use literary theories as lenses. Literary theory, understood broadly as the analysis and interpreta-tion of literature, represents a wide and diverse array of perspectives that can be brought to bear on texts, including feminism and gender studies, Marxism and neo-Marxist approaches, new historicism, cultural studies, deconstruction, rhetorical studies, post-colonial criticism, among others. Applied to texts (as well as other objects, works of art, etc.), "literary theory is a tool we can use to help us determine the ideology—the cultural assumptions and unexamined messages—contained in texts" (Apol, 1998, p. 35). For example, feminist theories reveal patriarchal agendas and expectations in texts, supporting readers to resist rather than assent to what Fetterley (1978) has called "a series of designs on the female reader" while postcolonial perspectives challenge the ways that literature of colonizing powers can perpetuate problematic notions of colo-nized groups as subordinate or inferior. Sharra (2001) offers an example of postcolonial criticism as he surfaces a colonialist ideology at work in an award-winning book, *The Baboon King* (Quintana, 1982). Sharra elucidates how in this book "Western children rarely see anything that would provide them with a way to contextualize conditions in Africa; neither are they encouraged to consider how some problems are the direct result of the subjugations of the continent in the service of other international relationships and priorities" (2001, p. 97). As Sharra demonstrates, a postcolonial lens helps to his-toricize and contextualize events, making visible the obvious and more subtle ways that colonizing ideologies function in texts.

While offering a range of useful lenses to guide textual critique, literary theory has been located primarily in university English departments with scholars charting important conceptual terrain, such as the journey from formalism to poststructural-ism (Tompkins, 1980), yet leading to "very little data about how individual readers construct responses to literature" (Marshall, 2000, p. 388). Some scholars in the field of education, however, are working to forge connections between literary theory and readers' responses in K–12 classroom. This line of work often begins with the stance that when considering classroom implications of literary theories, it is perhaps more useful to think about theory not as "a machine for grinding out interpretations but a way of generating fruitful questions about texts" (Phelan, 1999, p. ix). Employing a set of literary theories to young adult literature with the goal of "raising more questions than answers," Soter (1999) applies critical perspectives as "exploratory" and "indicative of possibilities" rather than as definitive textual interpretations (p. 14). Apol (1998) adopts a similar approach, offering sets of guiding questions that teachers can use with students to investigate relationships among texts, authors, readers and the world (p. 38). Examples of these questions include: what does this text ask of you as a reader? What does it assume about your beliefs, values, and experiences? Are you as a reader willing to go along with those assumptions? Are there aspects of the text you wish or feel compelled to resist or refuse? What happens if various elements of the text—race, gender, and social class—are transposed? Whose voices are given prominence? What might the silent or silenced voices say? (p. 38). Discussing these kinds of questions can empower readers, as Comber notes: "it is in children's individual and collective interests to know that texts are questionable, [that] they are put together in particular ways by particular people hoping for particular effects, and they have particular consequences for their readers, producers, and users" (1999, p. 7). One promise of literary theory to classroom teaching and learning is for students to acquire or regain "textual power" where the role of teachers "is not to produce 'readings' for students but to give them the tools for producing their own" (Scholes, 1985, p. 24). This enables students to cultivate their critical and interpretive abilities and "tilt the asymmetries and inequalities between themselves and the text in their favor" (Cherryholmes, 1999, p. 66).

While literary theories primarily provide readers with tools to help determine ideological agendas and assumptions operating in texts, it bears mentioning that ideologies are not located solely in texts and transmitted to children "as if they were empty receptacles"; rather ideologies are "something which they already possess, having drawn it from a mass of experiences far more powerful than literature" (Hollindale, in McGillis, 1996, p. 125). As raced, classed, gendered, and religious beings, readers "accept, reinterpret, and reject what counts as legitimate knowledge selectively" (Apple, 1993, p. 61). Beach (1997), for example, documented the ways European American secondary school students resisted multicultural literature, expressing their resistance with denial, hostility and shame while Enciso (1994) discovered that a group of predominately White fourth and fifth grade students did not engage seriously with issues of race when responding to the contemporary realistic novel *Maniac Magee* (Spinelli, 1990).

NEW DIRECTIONS—COLLECTIVE AND CONSEQUENTIAL RESPONSE

Galda and Beach (2001) argue that sociocultural theories have complicated any tidy distinctions among readers, texts, and contexts and that the meanings of readers' responses are better understood as being grounded in cultural and historical worlds, activity systems, and tools where children and youth, for example, are engaged in the response practices of rewriting, parodying, and creating new texts (p. 70). Beach and Myers (2001) explore what this might mean as they reframe the English classroom with an emphasis on students' "social worlds"—both "lived" social worlds (actual school, family, peer worlds) and "represented" social worlds (texts such as literature and mass media that relate to or comment on students' lived experiences). Reminiscent of Freire, their approach involves readers in a two-fold process of consciousness raising and transformation. Beach and Myers argue that an inquiry approach into social worlds enables students to "become more conscious of how language, symbols, and actions create and maintain social worlds" as well as "increase their own agency to construct more equitable and just social worlds because they have a fuller understanding of how the values of a social world are generated and contested through social interaction and literacy practices" (p. 8).

An emphasis on readers engaged in collaborative inquiry into social worlds points to a promising direction for research related to transactional theory and critical theory. The empirical research continues to evolve with social and cultural identities of readers in the foreground along with more sophisticated understandings of how texts work and how readers might employ critical perspectives with texts. Yet there remains a relatively untapped area for research: collective response—how groups or communities of readers author responses to texts. Moving from a more traditional research on response paradigm where readers are regarded as "individuals, pursuing individual interests, perspectives, and practices" (Galda & Beach, 2001, p. 66), collective response conceptualizes readers through their group memberships, for example, being from migrant families or from working class backgrounds. This situates them within what MacDonald and Sanchez-Casal (2002) call "communities of meaning" (p. 3), communities that can provide the social support for students to come to consciousness about issues of power and inequality, which in turn influence how they respond to texts. For example, Vivian Vasquez (2004) describes her kindergartners coming together to collectively protest a policy which excludes them from a school function, and Campano & Damico (2007) analyze how grade five students draw on their shared family, cultural, and class-based experiences in order to take profound intellectual, ethical, and political stands in their responses to literature. Thus, one promising new direction for research would be to further examine collective response, and looking outside academic literature in education, where these types of responses are being theorized and enacted, might be a place to start. For example, we can learn the ways activists arrive at consensus about how they are going to write back to, disrupt, take direct action against, or otherwise respond to a text (e.g., a xenophobic editorial in a newspaper), and come to better understand how they are at once engaging in and self-reflecting on the process of collective response. In an age of "new literacies," many young people are also finding technological venues for response and composition that spill outside the bounds of the ideology of individual authorship (e.g., political blogs).

For us, the idea of collective response—groups of readers authoring responses to texts—points to questions about how we might conceptualize and cultivate response as *consequential*. Thinking of response in terms of consequences links to a core tenet of philosophical pragmatism where the meaning of a concept or an action is derived by "trac[ing] out in the imagination the conceivable practical consequences" of the particular concept or action (Peirce, 1905/1984, in Cherryholmes, 1999, p. 26). This invites educators to imagine the consequences of a response or set of responses in a classroom through grappling with a core question: *what work in the world does or can response do?* Rosenblatt offers one answer to this question by reminding us that literature response "helps readers develop the imaginative capacity to put themselves in the place of others—a capacity essential in a democracy, where we need to rise above narrow self-interest and envision the broader human consequences of political decisions" (Rosenblatt, 1999, p. 169). Transactional theory and critical theory compel us to address this core question and conceive of consequences through goals and lenses of democratic citizenship—cultivating opportunities for response where democratic deliberation across multiple perspectives can lead to humane, transformative social action.

CONCLUDING THOUGHTS

This chapter has explored transactional theory and critical theory with a focus on how these perspectives help us understand the ways readers respond to texts. In this conclusion we, in part, step outside of readers' relationships with texts in classrooms to consider how these two theoretical perspectives can be used to understand the ways current political forces are shaping how reading education is being framed.

186 *James S. Damico, Gerald Campano, and Jerome C. Harste*

From their inception, transactional and critical theories have challenged the reign of positivism (school of thought that promoted the view that only certain mathematical and science procedures could lead to accurate determinations of truths and falsehoods) and instrumental rationality (perspective that valorizes finding cost-effective means toward particular ends without critical or reflective attention to why the ends are being sought) in society, in schooling, and in reading education. At the society level, the Frankfurt School leveled a critique of instrumental rationality for the ways this can lead to dehumanizing conditions and consequences, including large-scale human suffering. At the school level, critical theory has helped reveal and problematize authoritarian structures and practices, such as the homogenization and rote standardization of curricula as well as positivistic assumptions undergirding much "scientifically-based research." Rosenblatt has based her critique of instrumental rationality on democratic principles, arguing that moving acritically toward ends in literature classrooms—such as, singular authoritative interpretations of text—is antithetical to living in a democracy, to "living into the experiences of others ... [whose] goals and aspirations ... [are] different from our own" (1938, p. 108).

Transactional theory and critical theory are perhaps more relevant than ever in this current era of educational accountability, where the means of teaching reading often become conflated with its ends through a type of tautological reasoning: Test preparation drives instruction because students have to take tests; Curricula are standardized because there are standards. Not valuing the meaning-rich, sophisticated ways individuals and communities transact with texts leads to instrumentalizing and routinizing reading and literature instruction through the increasing administrative surveillance of students and teachers. Pedagogy informed by transactional and critical perspectives, in contrast, invites teachers, students, and literacy researchers to view the ends of education and reading as an area for continued intellectual and ethical inquiry and as part of the democratic project, raising important questions about why we read as well as what kind of lives we wish to live and what kinds of people we wish to be.

REFERENCES

Althusser, L. (1971). *Lenin and philosophy* (B. Brewster, Trans.). London: New Left Books.
Anderson, R. C., & Pearson, P. D. (1984). A schema-theoretic view of basic processes in reading comprehension. In P. D. Pearson (Ed.), *Handbook of reading research* (pp. 255–291). White Plains, NY: Longman.
Apol, L. (1998). "But what does this have to do with kids?": Literary theory and children's literature in the teacher education classroom. *The New Advocate, 24*(2), 32–46.
Apple, M. (1993). *Official knowledge: Democratic education in a conservative age* (2nd ed.). New York: Routledge.
Beach, R. (1997). Students' resistance to engagement with multicultural literature. In T. Rogers & A.O. Soter (Eds.), *Reading across cultures: Teaching literature in a diverse society* (pp. 69–94). New York: Teachers College Press.
Beach, R., & Freedman, K. (1992). Responding as a cultural act: Adolescents' responses to magazine ads and short stories. In C. Cox & J. Many (Eds.), *Reader stance and literary understanding: Exploring the theories, research, and practice* (pp. 162–188). Norwood, NJ: Ablex.
Beach, R., & Hynds, S. (1990). Research in response to literature. In E. J. Farrell & J. R. Squire (Eds.), *Transactions with literature* (pp. 131–206). Urbana, IL: National Council of Teachers of English.
Beach, R., & Hynds, S. (1991). Research on response to literature. In R. Barr, M. L. Kamil, P. Rosenthal, & P. D. Pearson (Eds.), *Handbook of Reading Research* (Vol. II, pp. 453–489). New York: Longman.
Beach, R., & Myers, J. (2001). *Inquiry-based English instruction: Engaging students in life and literature*. New York: Teachers College Press.
Bennett, T. (1979). *Formalism and Marxism*. London: Methuen.

Bleich, D. (1978). *Subjective criticism.* Baltimore: Johns Hopkins University Press.

Bloome, D., & Green, J. (1984). Directions in the sociolinguistic study of reading. In P.D. Pearson (Ed.), *Handbook of reading research* (pp. 395–452). White Plains, NY: Longman.

Booth, W. (1995). Foreword, *Literature as exploration* (5th ed., pp. vi–xiv). New York: The Modern Language Association.

Brooks, W. (2006). Reading representations of themselves: Urban youth use culture and African American textual features to develop literary understandings. *Reading Research Quarterly, 41*(3), 372–392.

Brooks, C., & Warren, R.B. (1938). *Understanding poetry.* New York: Holt, Rinehart.

Campano, G., & Damico, J.S. (2007). Doing the work of social theorists: Children enacting epistemic privilege as literacy learners and teachers. In M. Blackburn & C. Clark (Eds.), *New directions in literacy research for Political action and social change* (pp. 219–233). New York: Peter Lang.

Cherryholmes, C. (1999). *Reading pragmatism.* New York: Teachers College Press.

Comber, B. (1999). Critical literacies: Negotiating powerful and pleasurable curricula—how do we foster critical literacy through English language arts? Paper presented at the National Conference of Teachers of English, Denver, CO.

Counts, G. (1932). *Dare the School Build a New Social Order?* Carbondale: Southern Illinois University Press.

Eagleton, T. (1991). *Ideology: An introduction.* London: Verso.

Eagleton, T. (1996). *Literary theory: An introduction* (2nd ed.). Minneapolis, MN: University of Minnesota Press.

Eco, U. (1979). *The role of the reader: Explorations in semiotics of text.* Bloomington: Indiana University Press.

Enciso, P. (1994). Cultural identity and response to literature: Running lessons from Maniac Magee. *Language Arts, 71,* 524–533.

Fetterley, J. (1978). *The resisting reader: A feminist approach to American fiction.* Bloomington: Indiana University Press.

Fish, S. (1980). Literature in the reader: Affective stylistics. In J. Tompkins (Ed.), *Reader-response criticism: From formalism to post-structuralism* (pp. 70–100). Baltimore: The Johns Hopkins University Press.

Freire, P. (1970). *Pedagogy of the oppressed.* New York: Continuum.

Freire, P. (1985). *The politics of education: Culture, power, and liberation.* New York: Bergin & Garvey.

Freire, P., & Macedo, D. (1987). *Literacy: Reading the word and the world.* South Hadley, MA: Bergin and Garvey.

Galda, L., & Beach, R. (2001). Response to literature as a cultural activity. *Reading Research Quarterly, 36*(1), 64–73.

Goodman, K. (1965). A Linguistic Study of Cues and Miscues in Reading. *Elementary English, 42*(6), pp. 639–643.

Holland, N. (1969). *The dynamics of literary response.* New York: Oxford University Press.

Hunt, R. A., & Vipond, D. (1985). Crash-testing a transactional model of literary learning. *Reader, 14,* 23–39.

Labov, W. (1972). *Language of the inner city.* Philadelphia: University of Pennsylvania Press.

Lankshear, C., & McLaren, P. (1993). *Critical literacy: Politics, praxis, and the postmodern.* Albany: State University of New York Press.

Lee, C. (1995). A culturally based cognitive apprenticeship: Teaching African American high school students' skills in literary interpretation. *Reading Research Quarterly, 30,* 608–630.

Luke, A., & Freebody, P. (1997). The social practices of reading. In S. Muspratt, A. Luke, & P. Freebody (Eds.), *Constructing critical literacies: Teaching and learning textual practice* (pp. 185–226). Cresskill, NJ: Hampton Press.

Macdonald, A., & Sanchez-Casal, S. (2002). *Twenty-first century feminist classrooms: Pedagogies of identity and difference.* New York: Palgrave-Macmillan.

Many, J. E. (1994). The effect of reader stance on students' personal understanding of literature. In R. B. Ruddell, M. R. Ruddell, & H. Singer (Eds.), *Theoretical models and processes of reading* (pp. 653–667). Newark: DE: International Reading Association.

Marshall, J. (2000). Research on response to literature. In M. L. Kamil, P. B. Rosenthal, P. D. Pearson, & R. Barr (Eds.), *Handbook of reading research* (Vol. III, pp. 381–402). Mahwah, NJ: Erlbaum.

Martinez, M., & Roser, N. (2003). Children's responses to literature. In J. Flood, D. Lapp, J. R. Squire, & J. M. Jensen (Eds.), *Handbook of research on teaching the English language arts* (2nd ed., pp. 799–813). Mahwah, NJ: Erlbaum.

McGillis, R. (1996). *The nimble reader: Literary theory and children's literature*. New York: Twayne.

McLaren, P. (1999). A pedagogy of possibility: Reflecting upon Paulo Freire's politics of education. *Educational Researcher, 28*(2), 49–54.

Moller, K., & Allen, J. (2000). Connecting, resisting, and searching for safer places: Students respond to Mildred Taylor's "The friendship." *Journal of Literacy Research, 32*(2), 145–186.

Morgan, W. (1997). *Critical literacy in the classroom: The art of the possible*. New York: Routledge.

Pearson, P. D., & Stephens, D. (1994). Learning about literacy: A 30-year journey. In R. Ruddell, M.R. Ruddell, & H. Singer (Eds.), *Theoretical models and processes of reading* (4th ed., pp. 22–43). Newark, DE: International Reading Association.

Phelan, J. (1999). Literary theory and YAL: Strange bedfellows or match made in heaven? Foreword. In A. O. Soter (Ed.), *Young adult literature and the new literary theories: Developing critical readers in middle school* (pp. ix–xi). New York: Teachers College Press.

Purves, A. C., & Beach, R. (1972). *Literature and the reader: Research in response to literature, reading interests, and the teaching of literature*. Urbana, IL: National Council of Teachers of English.

Purves, A. C., & Rippere, V. (1968). *Elements of writing about a literary work: A study of response to literature*. NCTE Research report (no. 9). Urbana, Illinois.

Quintana, A. (1982). *The Baboon King*. Netherlands: Dehavianenkonig (J. Nieuwenhuizen, trans., 1999). New York: Walker.

Rogers, T. (1999). Literary theory and children's literature: Interpreting ourselves and our world. *Theory into Practice, 38*(3), 138–146.

Rosenblatt, L. (1938). *Literature as exploration*. New York: D. Appleton-Century.

Rosenblatt, L. (1978). *The reader, the text, the poem*. London: Southern Illinois University Press.

Rosenblatt, L. (1995). *Literature as exploration* (5th ed.). New York: The Modern Language Association.

Rosenblatt, L. (1999). Theory and practice: An interview with Louise M. Rosenblatt. *Language Arts, 77*(2), 158–170.

Scholes, R. (1985). *Textual power: Literary theory and the teaching of English*. New Haven: Yale University Press.

Shannon, P. (1990). *The struggle to continue: Progressive reading instruction in the United States*. Portsmouth, NH: Heinemann.

Sharra, S. (2001). *The Baboon King*: Institutionalizing anti-African bias in children's literature. *Children's Literature Association Quarterly, 26*(2), 96–99.

Sims, R. (1982). *Shadow and substance*. Urbana, IL: National Council of Teachers of English.

Sims, R. (1983). Strong black girls: A ten-year old responds to fiction about Afro Americans. *Journal of Research and Development in Education, 16*, 21–28.

Sipe, L. (1999). Children's responses to literature: Author, text, reader, context. *Theory into Practice in Education, 38*(3), 120–129.

Smith, F. (1971). *Understanding reading: A psycholinguistic analysis of reading and learning to read*. New York: Holt, Rinehart.

Soter, A. O. (1999). *Young adult literature and the new literary theories: Developing critical readers in middle school*. New York: Teachers College Press.

Spinelli, G. (1990). *Maniac Magee*. Boston: Little Brown.

Squire, J. (1994). Research in reader response, naturally interdisciplinary. In R. B. Ruddell, M. R. Ruddell, & H. Singer (Eds.), *Theoretical models and processes of reading* (4th ed., pp. 637–652). Newark, DE: International Reading Association.

Surber, J. P. (1998). *Culture and critique: An introduction to the critical discourses of cultural studies*. Boulder, CO: Westview Press.

Tanner, D., & Tanner, L. (1995). *Curriculum development: Theory into practice* (3rd ed.). Englewood Cliffs, NJ: Merrill.

Taylor, M. (1987). *The friendship*. New York: Dial Books.

Tompkins, J. P. (Ed.). (1980). *Reader-response criticism: From formalism to post-structuralism*. Baltimore: The Johns Hopkins University Press.

Vasquez, V. (2004). *Negotiating critical literacies with young children*. Mahwah, NJ: Lawrence Erlbaum.

Wellek, R., & Warren, R. B. (1949). *Theory of literature*. New York: Harcourt Brace.

Werner, W. (2002). Reading visual texts. *Theory and Research in Social Education, 30*(3), 401–428.

9 Grounding Reading Comprehension in the Neuroscience Literatures

George G. Hruby

Utah State University

Neuroscience researchers study *the brain*, a shorthand signifier for the complex suite of anatomical structures and biological processes that allow neurologically endowed organisms to effectively regulate body states and negotiate environments. A reader of this volume may well wonder what such research could possibly say about reading comprehension. Upon further reflection, however, granting that language comprehension is a demonstrated capability of a particular species of biological organism, one that inhabits and negotiates, among other environments, symbolic environments of its own devising, a reader may wish to consider what empirical research on the biological processes underlying symbol use and language development might contribute to a comprehensive discussion of the nature of reading comprehension and its social augmentation.

I will address that question in this chapter, but I will require some patience from the reader. In order to review the various neuroscience literatures and the implications of this work for reading and literacy education scholarship, it will first be necessary to review several theoretical and methodological preliminaries. I will do this with deliberation because a failure to acknowledge the topical, paradigmatic, and philosophical differences between mainstream scholarship in reading and literacy education and the scholarship of the neurosciences will guarantee confusion and premature dismissal of the latter's potential value. As this chapter will indicate, neuroscientists researching reading comprehension processes (or language comprehension processes using written prompts) do not draw their inspiration or testable hypotheses from either the reading education literature, or the paradigmatic and philosophical orientations shared across educational and most social science research. There are good reasons for this, and researchers of reading comprehension might do well to reflect on these reasons as they readdress their need for comprehensive theory. More to the point, as other chapters in this volume will confirm, appropriate prior knowledge is crucial for adequate reading comprehension. Potentially incommensurate background knowledge and misleading if colorful assumptions about the neurosciences need to be interrogated before more compelling use can be made of this literature.

In keeping with the parallel structure of the many chapters in this volume, I will first review the theoretical and historical perspectives informing neuroscience research on reading comprehension, taking time to trace the theoretical assumptions underlying and vying for primacy in these literatures. I will then trace the landmark areas of study by reviewing the various techniques they employ, summarize what can be said about reading comprehension from their vantage point, analyze illustrative issues regarding appropriate research design involving these methods, and conclude with a brief discussion of future incorporation of this research into reading comprehension theory. I will maintain that the neurosciences can contribute to comprehensive reading comprehension theory by providing a naturalistic orientation at once empirically rich and theoretically profound.

THEORETICAL AND HISTORICAL PERSPECTIVES

In approaching the neuroscience literatures on reading, most literacy scholars probably assume a ready connection with cognitive science. After all, such a reader might ask, is it not the case that the mind in the brain? On behalf of this assumption, literacy scholars will likely parse neuroscience research by drawing on their background knowledge of the spirited debates about reading comprehension that have occurred over the decades, and the wealth of models and theories it has generated (e.g., Ruddell & Unrau, 2004). In addition, literacy scholars inadvertently may bring impressions shared by the general public gleaned from the mass media that typically convey neuroscience research with easily grasped but potentially misleading metaphors, such as that of the brain as a computer, or of the neuron as a wire, and similar idioms that enforce an information science rather than a life science view of the nervous system (e.g., Blum, 2006; Gorman, 2003).

Such assumptions will need correction before a reader can fully grasp the neurosciences and make useful connection between them and the domain of literacy education and reading comprehension. Scholars within various fields and disciplines often hold to favored metaphors to consolidate sets of assumptions about their targeted phenomena. Just as some cognitive reading researchers might refer to human beings as if they were information processing machines (Gough, 1972; Rumelhart, 1994), or as some sociolinguistic literacy scholars might posit signification as situated semiotic arbitraries bounding a cultural landscape (Leander & Rowe, 2006; Marsh, 2006), so, too, naturalistically-informed reading theorists would need have their preferred analogies. Generally, neuroscientists and literacy socionaturalists, if I may employ that neologism, assume that human beings are ecologically-situated biological kinds, and that this is theoretically significant (Bennett & Hacker, 2003; Millikan, 1984; Oyama, 2000).

Dynamics across scales of organization

One foundational issue to initially address is the relationship of biology to the cognitive and social domains, particularly the causative dynamics scholars in these domains presume. Most cognitive and socio-cognitive research seems to presume a unitary worldview, built upon a single plane, in which all components are operating at a similar scale of organization, although within different, possibly embedded, but isomorphic, categorical sets. Thus, a simple and direct relationship between discrete cognitive processes and equally discrete observable behaviors is typically posited. Certain cognitive neuroscientists would extend this two-dimensional plane further from discrete neural mechanisms, to discrete cognitive processes, and then to discrete behaviors. No distinction is made in these cases for differences of scale of organization. Some stuff is inside the head, in these models, and some stuff is outside the head, and some of the stuff gets transferred in between. As a result, such models suffer from metonymy, or the mereological fallacy (Bennet & Hacker, 2003), causatively ascribing to parts of an entity (such as the brain, or a specific area of the cortex) qualities or abilities only the entire entity *in situ* could possess.

By contrast, theory and research on the dynamics of living systems requires an understanding of the causative interrelationship between higher-order and lower-order phenomena at varying scales of spatial and temporal organization. This interrelationship extends from the low-end atomic, to the genetic, up through the proteomic (the biochemistry of proteins), to the cytological (cellular structure and function), to the intercellular (e.g., neural networks, signal factors), across the systemic (e.g., cortical, autonomic, endocrine), to the functional structure of the whole organism, and onward towards its behaviorally mediated relationship with still higher-order environmental, socioemotional, symbolic, cultural, and ecological scales of organization. This tiered view of process may prompt questions about bottom-up versus top-down effects, but it is important to understand that all levels are operating simultaneously and in transactive coordination with one another. The structures change over time on behalf of the functional co-regulation of the entire system (Thelen & Smith, 2006; Verela, Thompson, & Rosch, 1991; for theoretical application to biological development, see Gottlieb, Wahlsten, & Likliter, 2006). There is no transference of stuff (in the form of symbolic representations) across levels.

An inherent tension exists in this transactional view between reduction and emergence that needs to be appreciated. Lower-order phenomena make higher-order phenomena possible, but higher-order phenomena cannot be entirely reduced to lower-order phenomena. This is in part because higher-order phenomena orchestrate the structural interrelationship of their lower-order requisites (in some cases, the two may be inseparable). This generally occurs on behalf of more efficient or productive energy flow, with its redistribution going to support higher-order structure. This rechanneling of energy on behalf of higher-order structure makes for the "value-added" nature of systemic transactions, and makes transactive wholes seem more than the sum of their parts. Although these ideas are well employed in the disciplines of economics and ecology, they have only rarely been applied in education (but see Davis & Sumara, 1998, 2006; Fischer & Bidell, 2006; Jacobson & Wilensky, 2006). Nonetheless, system dynamics is sufficiently advanced as a theoretical orientation in neighboring disciplines to offer differing perspectives (Doyle & Csete, 2007), including theories of cognitive performance in living systems (Thelen & Smith, 2006; Van Orden, Holden, & Turvey, 2003).

For illustration, consider the simplified example of a classroom. Individual agency stands as a lower-order phenomenon; classroom activity stands as a higher-order phenomenon. Individual agency makes classroom activity possible, but classroom activity, by way of its intermediating protocols, constrains and directs individual agency more effectively toward the ends (such as comprehension) that identify the system as a classroom. Thus, classroom activity cannot be reduced to merely a lot of individual agency. A single student at a desk alone does not make for a fraction of a functioning classroom. A critical mass of such students organized by classroom protocol on behalf of classroom activity is required for classroom activity to occur.

However, the self-regulation of agents (teacher and students engaged in classroom activity) at a particular scale of organization is not the entire story. There are higher-order influences on classroom activity in the form of redirective social and cultural systems, and, pertinent to this chapter, lower-order influences on classroom activity from cognitive and neurological systems self-organizing into individual agency. These higher- and lower-order influences operate at different scales of organization and require scale-specific models of structure, process, and legacy that allow for systems effects. Thus, the notion of emergence cautions us against simple single-scale models of causative influence from the gene to the brain to the mind to behavior and thence to sociality and cultural forms such as literacy. The brain can make literacy possible, but literacy cannot be reduced to merely the workings of the brain.

Situating cognitive neuroscience

Beyond this concern for transactive dynamics, there is a need for clarity about interdisciplinary linkage between the neurosciences and educational research on reading. It has been compellingly argued that cognitive neuroscience is the neuroscience field most coherently accessible to education researchers (Ansari & Coch, 2006; Blakemore & Frith, 2000; Bruer, 1997, 2003). Though this may be persuasive advice, the following observations should be borne in mind: (1) the neurosciences are plural, and most of them are more situated in life science than in information science; (2) cognitive neuro-science is only one of the neurosciences, although well-recommended for educational scholars seeking insight into the nature of the underlying physiological processes of learning; (3) yet, cognitive neuroscience is not a seamlessly cohesive field of inquiry, but a hybrid domain struggling to bridge neuroscience's two potentially incommensurable orientations; (4) if literacy scholars are willing to broach paradigmatic schisms into exogenous fields, developmental neuroscience, social neuroscience, affective neurosci-ence, and system-based neuroscience could also stand as potential sources of coherent consideration; (5) in drawing from the neuroscience literatures (or, indeed, from any exogenous research base), it is crucial to mind the topical, thematic, and philosophical constraints by which such knowledge is generated and to have a rich grounding in the disciplinary background knowledge assumed in the domain.

The neurosciences are plural   Neuroscience research is pursued within several diverse fields. These fields, described in any introductory neuroscience text, include neuropsy-chology, psychobiology, genetic neuroscience, molecular neuroscience, neurocytology, neurology, neurosurgery, neuroendocrinology, psychopharmacology, the neuroscience of sensation and perception, behavioral neuroscience, developmental neuroscience, neu-ropediatrics, cognitive neuroscience, the neuroscience of affect, neuropsychiatry, social neuroscience, therapeutic neuroscience, computational neuroscience, systems-based neuroscience, and more. Current textbooks and journals cover each of these fields in detail. In addition, there is lively scholarship inspired by these empirical fields to be found in philosophy of mind, and of biology (e.g., Block, Flanagan, & Güzeldere, 1997; Petitot, Varela, Pachoud, & Roy, 1999; Sober 2000; Sterelney, 2003), and more recently within the philosophy of neuroscience including neuroethics (Bennett & Hacker, 2003; Brook & Akins, 2005; Illes, 2005; Spivey, 2006).

The Society for Neuroscience (SfN) offers a useful categorical schema in its multi-volume annual conference program for organizing the neurosciences. Currently, SfN arranges research papers and posters into 8 letter-coded themes: (A) Development, (B) Neural Excitability, Synapses, and Glia, Cellular Mechanisms, (C) Sensory and Motor Systems, (D) Homeostatic and Neuroendocrine Systems, (E) Cognition and Behavior, (F) Disorders of the Nervous System, (G) Techniques in Neuroscience, and (H) History and Teaching of Neuroscience (Society for Neuroscience, 2005). In short, it would be inaccu-rate to assume that neuroscience is a monolithic entity, or that its primary focus is simply the localization in the brain of cognitive processes responsible for human behaviors, as it is often presented in the media and in brain-based educational materials (e.g., Jensen, 1998; Milne, 2005; Ronis, 2007; Tate, 2005; Wolfe & Nevills, 2004). There are many lenses, foci, fields, and sub-disciplines by which to parse the reading brain.

Although readily accessible to many educational researchers, cognitive neuroscience is only one of the neurosciences   From the above it should be obvious that to equate cog-nitive neuroscience with all of the neurosciences is rather like equating reading research on phonological awareness with all of literacy education research. But such an error may be understandable given that, as with phonology in reading, cognitive neuroscience has received inordinate media attention, often being presented as neuroscience in its entirety. The neurosciences have grown over the past 30 years in part by technological advances for imaging correlates to brain function, but largely through basic biological research, some of which has had profound practical impact on psychopharmacology and neuropsychiatry.

Nonetheless, research on the biochemistry of the brain, though powerful, is unlikely to offer judicious inspiration to researchers and theorists in reading and literacy edu-cation. Therefore, a cogent argument has been advanced that the best way to inform and ground educational research with insights from the neurosciences is by way of the intermediary disciplines of cognitive psychology and cognitive neuroscience (Ansari & Coch, 2006; Bruer, 1997, 2003; Varma, Schwartz, & McCandliss, 2006). The central argument is that educational researchers and theorists are already well informed about cognitive psychology and its paradigmatic assumptions and constraints. Moreover, cognitive psychology's potential to promote effective instruction of students in classrooms has a proven track record. Thus, education scholars should avoid getting lost in the intricacies of the neurosciences (which are not, after all, about educational practice), but instead should concern themselves with advances in cognitive psychology informed by cognitive neuroscience. According to this view, attempts to connect education practice or research to the neurosciences directly would be crossing a "bridge too far" (Bruer, 1997).

Cognitive neuroscience has at least two orientations   Cognitive neuroscience is a hybrid field of inquiry, bringing together cognitive psychology with the neurosciences. The field includes both cognitive psychologists who test theories about the structure and function of the mind by way of techniques and technologies borrowed from brain research, and neurophysiologists who research brain states during putatively cognitive events as observed in behavior. But relating the mind and the brain—and the two orientations that study them—can be fraught with philosophical difficulties.

In spite of the obvious virtues of interdisciplinary collaboration, certain tensions are undeniable within cognitive neuroscience. Some cognitive scientists dismiss exploratory neuroanatomical imaging, insisting the only coherent use of such methods is for testing out theories of mental structure (Kosslyn, 1999). By contrast, some physiologists are dubious of the value of the mind as an ontological construct, at least as it has been typically described (Churchland, 2005; Gernsacher & Kaschak, 2003). For such researchers, models of mind are occasionally valuable only as heuristics, and do not actually indicate causative processes for thought or behavior. There are also debates about coherence in cognitive neuroscience research designs, appropriate use of the imaging technologies, and the necessary constraints within which data should be interpreted (discussed below).

Epistemology and ontology lurk just beneath the surface of such distinctions. The cognitive psychologists envision the mind/brain as an information processing system, which, of course, presumes that the world is made up of information ready to be processed. That information can take the form of symbolic representations, propositions, and category schemas. The neurophysiologists, by contrast, envision the brain as an evolved and developing biological system for actively negotiating actual environments (including symbolic ones). The neurological and systemic processes involved are constructive and ecologically responsive, and in so far as there is information to be processed in the form of symbolic representations, it is only known to exist in the conscious and cultural experience of a single species, homo sapiens. Although this species must necessarily use symbolic representations when scientifically investigating the world, it does not follow that the world being investigated is itself symbolic in nature. Believing so is to succumb to the notorious error of confusing the map with the territory (Bredo, 2006). Succinctly, we find here the broader interdisciplinary tensions in current efforts to reconcile the natural and social sciences. I will return to the issue of interdisciplinary reapproachment in the conclusion of the chapter.

Alternative sources of neuroscientific insight for literacy research exist   As the diversity of the neurosciences might suggest, to claim that educational researchers would do better to attend to neuroscience-informed models of mental process over the interactions of synaptic molecules is to offer a false choice. Three ancillary neuroscience fields for informing reading and literacy scholarship might be suggested: (1) developmental neuroscience (the study of change over time in neurologically-endowed living systems, as observed in neural networks, homeostatic systems, and behavior, including the developmental integration of neuroendocrinological self-regulation in children and adults), (2) social neuroscience (the study of self-regulating systems and how their environmentally-mediated development foster social interaction and hierarchy by way of cognition and affect, including through communication systems), and (3) supportive research in neuroendocrinology and neuropsychiatry on emotional self-regulation and identity development. Reading and literacy education researchers targeting similar topics (development, sociality, and identity, respectively) might find as much benefit in a familiarity with these literatures as in the research from neuropsycholinguistics reviewed in this chapter. Such ancillary sources of orientation do not yet offer a robust research base on reading comprehension *per se*, but they do offer insights into factors that support it.

Findings from the neurosciences need to be understood within their topical, thematic, and philosophical context   Given the focal diversity and philosophical tensions described above, it is important to situate any particular neuroscience study in context before appropriating findings and idioms for use in an exogenous field like reading education. I would suggest there are three conceptual contexts to consider in this regard: topical, thematic, and philosophical.

First, regarding topicality, it is important to keep disciplinary boundaries in mind when evaluating a research report. Disciplines and fields are defined by the topics or phenomena they study. To borrow insights from one field into another is to momentarily switch the focal topic. Therefore, borrowers must be clear about which phenomena particular disciplines do and do not study. Neuroscience research tells us something research-based about *the organic brain*. Cognitive research tells us something about *models of cognitive process*. Both of these literatures may inspire our thinking about learning and *effective classroom practice*. But only research on effective classroom practice can tell us anything research-based about effective classroom practice. It is incoherent to claim that findings about a phenomenon studied in one domain "prove" theories or assumptions about a different phenomenon studied in another domain, for application to a third phenomenon in yet another domain. This is the muddle too often found in the brain-based practitioner materials.

Readers should be cautious about claims drawn from supposed *neuroscience research on reading*. Brain research, by both literal and disciplinary definition, is not about reading but about the brain. Neurological studies wherein subjects are asked to read words or engage in behaviors presumed significant to a particular theory of reading process do not in fact test the reading behaviors or the reading theories employed for justification; rather, they test for functional brain states, typically as indicated by hemodynamic or electromagnetic correlations. Thus, findings about the brain in such studies do not, strictly speaking, prove anything about the experimental reading behaviors or theoretical assumptions about reading employed in the protocols. That is simply not what such studies are designed to demonstrate. What such studies can do is better describe the neurological subprocesses that make reading possible. But detailing these subprocesses no more describes reading than reciting a list of ingredients describes a soufflé. Moreover, and obviously, brain imaging technologies are no better suited for directly visualizing the floating signifier of reading comprehension than reading comprehension tests are suited for directly visualizing brains.

Therefore, to be adequately precise about topical boundaries, sojourning literacy scholars visiting other disciplines for inspiration need to be clear on what the research reports they survey are about. Neurochemistry? Neural networks? Cortical architecture? Cognitive process timing? Reading mind models? Reader response? Effective classrooms? The issue is not whether the phenomena underlying these research bases have anything to do with one another. It is not unreasonable to imagine they do. The problem is when *methodological reductionism* (recourse to lower-order phenomena to make sense of vexingly complex higher-order phenomena) permutes into *theoretical or eliminative reductionism* (explaining away higher-order phenomena as epiphenomenal by virtue of the existence of lower-order phenomena).

Whatever else readers are, they are most certainly biological entities with developing brains. Most neuroscience is about biology and the bio-ecological dynamics of development. But it does not follow that full understanding of how the brain functions during the comprehension of texts will explain the nature of comprehension in readers during classroom activities. To paraphrase a critique of neuro-reductionism often repeated in philosophy of mind (Chalmers, 1996; Searle, 1992), if all that reading comprehension was was the firing of particular networks of neurons, then that is all it would be and nothing more. But clearly we experience it as something more. And it is that something more that needs explaining. That being said, it is the assumption of this chapter that understanding the biological underpinnings of higher-order processes on behalf of a *comprehensive* theory of reading comprehension is a necessary endeavor.

Second, regarding the issue of thematic context, Ryle (1949) identified severe cases of phenomenal incommensurability as examples of category error. The mind and the brain cannot be coherently mapped onto one another, he maintained, because they are not merely two different entities, but inhabit *two different categories of entity*. To look for the mind in the brain, Ryle contended, is as confused as looking for team spirit in the rules of play in cricket. Philosophers and developmental psychologists have suggested that incommensurable categories of entity are identifiable though the operative metaphors commonly used to illuminate the phenomena under investigation (Lerner, 2002; Pepper, 1948; Reese & Overton, 1970). This is most typical when the phenomenon under investigation is not directly observable or readily describable in its own terms. Often the operative metaphor is said to inform an implicit but persistent *worldview* constraining how researchers envision the phenomena they investigate (Lerner, 2006). It could be argued that cognitive psychology finessed Ryle's concern with category error by employing the computer as a unifying metaphor, with the brain as the hardware and the mind as the software.

It is important that scholarly foragers distinguish such metaphor-based themes because of the assumptions about causation they imply. In fields like molecular biochemistry or cognitive neuroscience, mechanistic structure is often the guiding theme. The phenomenon under investigation is considered as if it were a simple machine, where structure is understood as being responsible for function. Alternatively, in fields such as developmental neuroscience or social neuroscience, organic systematicity is often the guiding theme. The phenomenon under investigation is approached as if it were a bio-ecological system, where structure and function are co-causative over time. Mechanical structure and organic systematicity are potentially complementary themes. However, they are not the same theme. The fundamental assumptions about causation contained in their metaphors and that distinguish them when considered individually are at odds. They may well be further at odds with the metaphorically-driven causative assumptions within certain veins of reading and literacy education scholarship.

Finally, there is the third issue of the philosophical context within which neuroscientists work, particularly the epistemological and ontological commitments they presume. Many neuroscientists are engaged in life science, hold to an empiricist epistemology (believe knowledge comes primarily from directed sensory observation, both as a research strategy and as a theory of biological process), and many, though not all, presume a materialist ontology (believe reality is made up of substance in the form of matter and energy). Others, such as certain cognitive neuroscientists, some social neuroscientists, and many computational neuroscientists, are better described as being engaged in information science, are epistemologically rationalist (believe knowledge comes primarily from reasoning, theory construction, or computation, again, both as a methodological and theoretical assumption), and may even be decidedly idealist in ontology (believe reality is a manifestation of ideas or information). As with focal and thematic contexts, it is not necessary that foraging scholars share these commitments to make sense of the findings they foster. But it is important that such scholars are aware of these distinctions and of the potential for confused interpretations stemming from unacknowledged incommensurabilities in the research they would borrow for inspiration.

On neurons as "wires," brains as "information processors," and knowing when a good metaphor is just a good metaphor

The science-inspired media are keen to present breakthroughs in the neurosciences by the light of operative metaphor, particularly those employed in cognitive neuroscience, but they do so with a great degree of poetic license and categorical conflation. They often breathlessly describe brains as wet computers of the utmost processing power, replete with visuals of circuit boards in the head (e.g., *Reader's Digest*, 2007). As with computers, the brain is said to crunch data and generate output. Its underlying program structure is signaled through hard-wired neural transistors, supposedly blueprinted in the genetic code, anatomical modules that are pictured through rainbow-colored advances in brain-imaging technology. In fairness to science reporters, these are indeed motifs commonly employed by certain cognitive and computational neurotheorists (Pinker, 1997; Fodor, 2000). In additional fairness, however, they are also motifs about which many neuroscientists and neurophilosophers are, at best, agnostic.

Metaphors are unquestionably important in human thought, including that of scientists. But ultimately, the psycholinguistic scaffold of a powerful metaphor needs to drop off the phenomenon under investigation, like a cast broken free from a newly minted bronze, revealing our best approximation of the phenomenon in its own terms. There comes a time when things should no longer be referenced as if they were something else when they are not. Obviously, neurons are not literally wires—their signaling is painfully slow compared to the flow of electrons in, say, a telephone line—and the kinds of signals neurons transport are clearly biochemical in nature and may well have no direct symbolic significance.

As to whether it is helpful to think of brains primarily as information processors—which is to say, as reshufflers of symbolic representations—this is a far from comprehensive metaphor for brains as most neuroscientists understand them, one that faces challenges from evolutionary theory and developmental science, and that grinds to a halt in the face of the sorts of phenomena that comprehension scholars wish to investigate. Computers do not make meaning, after all. They reshuffle symbolic representations into output that can potentially be made meaningful by meaning-makers such as human beings. Thus, computers do not stand as a useful analogy to human meaning-making or comprehension because their functions presume and precede it. From a neuroscientifically informed stance, we are thus left to ponder the question, what would a theory of meaning as an organic phenomenon look like?

LANDMARK AREAS OF STUDY

Neuroscience researchers not only variously rely on biological and informational metaphors, they literally bring together cutting-edge advances in biology and information technology. The result can seem foreign and perhaps even unpalatable to many scholars of literacy education. The terminology employed in these studies can be bewildering, particularly when multiple yet incommensurate systems of physiological identification and operational vocabulary make it difficult to relate findings across multiple studies. This is an acknowledged problem even for seasoned neuroscientists who would review the literature (Gernsacher & Kaschak, 2003; Osterhout, Kim, & Kuperberg, in press).

Determining landmark status of particular studies would be speculative at best. Studies in the neurosciences are relatively new, and their growth has been explosive. As an indication, Cabeza and Nyberg (2000) found fewer than 10 PET or fMRI studies on cognition of any sort to review in 1991. But by 1995, 73 such studies had been published (reviewed in Cabeza & Nyberg, 1997). During the 3 years that followed, over 200 more were published (reviewed in Cabeza & Nyberg, 2000). By 2003, Tootle, Tsao, and Vanduffel (2003) observed that studies on a wide range of topics employing fMRI alone were being published at a rate of 4 per working day (approximately 1000 per year). The total since can only be guessed.

In the course of this expansion, new technologies and refinements of older technologies have fostered challenges to previous findings and theoretical assertions. This in turn has led to a growing body of critical scholarship within the neurosciences (see Implications section). In this section, I will describe the major investigative techniques employed in neuroscience research on reading comprehension as landmark *areas* of research, as this distinction is commonly used to categorize the literature in neuroscience research reviews.

Neural activation (evoked potential) methods

Evoked potential methods measure electrical activity in the brain in response to experimental stimuli. This electrical activity is the result of the de- and re-polarization of a nerve cell's outer membrane in a physio-chemical cascade along the length of the cell. This cascade is known as an *action potential*. When the cascade reaches the axonal end of the neuron, its depolarization releases neurotransmitters into the synaptic gap between it and an adjacent neuron. The uptake of these neurotransmitters by the adjacent neuron (at a location known as the dendrite) can similarly depolarize the membrane of *that* neuron inciting a similar physio-chemical cascade down its length. In this way, action potentials are conducted from neuron to neuron (Purves, Augustine, Fitzpatrick, Hall, LaMantia, et al., 2007).

Action potentials, the fluctuation of ionic charge along a cell's membrane, are exhibited by many kinds of cells, even in some species of plant. But its specialized function in neurons inspires the common metaphor of nerve cells as wires, neuronal activation as electrical signaling, neural networks as circuits, and even of the brain as a computer-like information processor. But there is no evidence that action potentials are symbolic representations in and of themselves, signaling like Morse codes. Fluctuations in action potential rates in single neurons may have functional significance for neural assemblies and the emergence of higher-order levels of processing that do involve symbolic representation, but just how this might occur is a matter of on-going theoretical speculation. Nonetheless, action potential signatures are an unquestionable indication of neural activity and are thus of interest to neuroscientists.

Event-related potentials (ERPs) are averaged measures of neuronal activity (specifically of the coordinated spiking of action *potentials*) time-*related* to a particular cognitive or sensory *event*. ERPs can be tracked either in individual neurons (see next below), or in larger networks or assemblies. In the latter case, ERPs indicate the net electrical signature (or *field potential*) from the synchronous firing of action potentials at hundreds of thousands of dendrites. The resulting wave-form data indicate voltage changes measured at particular positions along the scalp. These data can be interpreted, relative to the wave-forms recorded by sensors placed elsewhere on the scalp, to indicate the timing and general location of neural processing related to the experimental event. (Wave-form data perhaps inspire the popular notion of "brain waves.") Because a scalp sensor will pick up a lot of noise during an experimental condition (other types of spontaneous and non-event-related neuronal firings), a single measurement is insufficient to demonstrate ERPs, and scores of event-related trials are required for averaging out the random firings not related to the experimental event.

ERPs are commonly measured by electroencephalography (EEG) or magnetoencephalography (MEG). Both methods measure the net effect of electrical activity at the dendrites of masses of neurons firing synchronously. EEG measures the net electrical signature of this activity; MEG measures the magnetic fields generated by such electrical activity. The use of 64 to 128 sensors spaced across and around the subject's head is typical in most EEG studies, although newer MEG technology allows for more. The data are often mapped onto head diagrams (the head is typically represented as a simple circle with ears and a nose for orientation purposes as viewed from above), and the activation differentials of each sensor at significant time frames are tonally segued across the diagram. Although the timing of ERPs can be focused to a matter of milliseconds, the localization of these events to specific physical locations is poor compared to that of hemodynamic methods (which in turn lack the temporal resolution of these ERP measures; see below). In addition, ERP methods have historically been limited to measurements close to the scalp; deep brain measurements of ERP have been complicated by a variety of physiological and technical challenges (Michel et al., 2004).

Just what wave-form patterns indicate about neural processing beyond their timing is unclear. Numerous neural networks would reside in any given sensor location, and which ones are firing, let alone how they are structured, or whether the result of the activation is excitatory or inhibitory, etc., cannot be determined. Nonetheless, wave-forms dependably demonstrate stereotypical responses to particular events. For instance, semantically anomalous words elicit an exaggerated N400 signature, a peaking of negative charge approximately 400 milliseconds after the lexical anomaly, in the central parietal region (Van Berkum, Hagoort, & Brown, 1999; see review in Kutas, Van Petten, & Kluender, in press). By contrast, anomalous syntactic structure elicits an abnormal early positive charge in the left anterior region, followed by an exaggerated P600 signature, a peaking of positive charge 600 milliseconds after onset, either, as with the N400, in the central parietal region (Friederici, & Kotz, 2003; Friederici, von Cramon, & Kotz, 1999) or in more anterior (i.e., frontal) areas of the brain (Osterhout, Kim, & Kuperberg, in press). These unique signatures suggest that semantic and syntactic processing are neurologically distinct operations. In spite of the uncertainties, timing of process is clearly of importance (Perfetti & Bolger, 2004), and when matched to more spatially precise imaging techniques, described below, ERP methods may give a persuasive indication of the order and structure of cortical processing of texts during comprehension (Heim, 2005).

In addition to ERPs, there are spontaneous and event-related wave form oscillations, measures of the rate of rhythmic change in electrical fields across the brain, that some scholars have suggested are the means by which individual neurons or neural networks are coordinated, and possibly how conscious awareness is orchestrated (see Fingelkurts & Fingelkurts, 2001; Nunez, 2006; for relation of this construct to language processing, see Bastiaansen & Hagoort, 2006; Karakas, Erzengin, & Basar, 2000). The phenomenon they trace is rather like the wave-like cascades of cicada chirps in summer trees. Some neurons chirp in response to the chirps of neighboring neurons, others chirp spontaneously, but the over-all result is wave-like. Again, just what this means for cortical processing is uncertain.

Single-neuron recording methods

There are invasive but precise means to measure the event-related activity of individual neurons using micro-electrode recordings in the brains of laboratory animals. These techniques are of no direct value for research on language or reading comprehension as they are too invasive to employ on healthy human subjects. However, they do provide a basis for mapping out neural activity in actual, functional cortical networks, as contrasted to the hypothesized distributed networks simulated on computers by information processing researchers and computational neuroscientists (see subsection below on computational modeling). In conjunction with neurocytological research and studies using newer imaging techniques for mapping deep white matter tracts in the brain (LeBihan et al., 2000), a firmer picture of the structure and variability of real neural tissue is emerging.

It should be understood that interconnectivity is extensive in neural tissue, with the average number of dendritic connections per cell being about 500, ranging from only a few to over 80,000 in purjinke cells in the cerebellum. As a result, there are hundreds of trillions of synapses connecting neurons in the human brain. Each synapse is a decision point. Each synapse harbors tens of thousands of receptor sites in dozens of chemical configurations. Each receptor site is, similarly, a decision point. Each dendrite leads to junctions with others as they approach the soma, or cell body, and each of these merging locations are a decision point, as is the soma itself, where the nerve cell calculates if accruing stimulation is sufficient to translate into a continuation of the action potential down the axon toward other downstream neurons (Purves et al., 2007).

But neural tissues are not undifferentiated webs of equipotentiation. Some neural tracts are physiologically dedicated, others develop through stimulation in use. There are many kinds of neurons in the brain with particular structures and dedicated functions. Pyramidal neurons trace through and interconnect layers of orthogonally structured nerve networks. Spindle neurons connect subcortical brain areas for the regulation of emotion and arousal to executive control areas in the frontal cortex. A neuron, by virtue of its axonal connection can serve different functions relative to the other neuron it enjoins (excitation, inhibition, confirmation, etc.). Some neurons fire when activated by other neurons or sensory stimuli, but others fire spontaneously. Empirical research on this complexity and its emergent and self-regulative dynamics is, at this stage, perhaps too speculative and technically arcane an endeavor for enlightening reading comprehension theory directly.

However, physiological, genetic, and biochemical research on actual cortical structure has recently lent weight to theories about the role of long-term potentiation (LTP) in hippocampal memory formation and retrieval (Malenka & Bear, 2004; Pastalkova et al., 2006). Rapid learning into long-term memory in the neocortex has also been observed (Tse et al., 2007). Single-neuron recording research on rats has also revealed single *place* neurons for recognizing locations (see review in Moita, Rosis, Zhou, LeDoux, & Blair, 2004), and, in primates, single *mirror* neurons for tracking intentional behaviors of conspecifics (Nelissen, Luppino, Vaanduffel, Rizzolatti, & Orban, 2005). This latter work has generated much theoretical speculation about the evolution of imitation, theory of mind, primate communication, and language (Gallese, Keysers, & Rizollatti, 2004; Ramachandran, 2000). Thus, surprising as it may seem, findings from research on single neurons in laboratory animals could arguably be germane for language and reading comprehension theory in the future (Rizzolatti & Arbib, 2002).

Computer simulation of neural processes

There are two noteworthy efforts to model neural dynamics: distributed network modeling and systems-based modeling (O'Reilly, 2006). The first approach models the structural dynamics of interconnecting array networks, using numerical value to crudely imitate the functionally developed interconnectedness of neurons in cortical tissue. The other approach models structural dynamics, typically within single neurons from the genetic to the network levels.

Distributed network models track the shifting of connection strengths or weights between value-holding nodes in a linked program array. This modeling supposedly mimics the way neurons function in neural networks (Plunkett & Sinha, 1992; Seidenberg & McClelland, 1989). The more a particular connection is used, the stronger it becomes (that is, the more easily it can transmit a signal). Those connections which are functional are presumed to be the ones that get the most use and thus are the ones to become most developed. Inspired by Hebbian cell theory and demonstrated with computer simulations, these networks employ the computed node values as a stand-in for the physiological changes actual neurons undergo in response to activation. The development of these functional networks through trials is not guided by a genetic blueprint, but by the dynamics of selective adaptation.

The results have been intriguing, mimicking some of the counterintuitive behavior of human language development (McClelland & Rogers, 2003; Plaut & Booth, 2000; Plaut, McClelland, Seidenberg, & Patterson, 1996; Plunket, 1993; Rumelhart & McClelland, 1992). However, these models may be of more use in information science than in the study of actual neural networks as the assumptions about neurons and networks designed into these models are too simplistic to capture the intricately varied structure and functioning of actual neurons *in vivo*. Nonetheless, connectionist theory has proven itself a robust inspiration for reading process theory (Adams, 1990; Kintsch, 1998; Rumelhart, 1994).

The second modeling approach attempts to address the complexity of neural dynamics and signal processing by aligning hypothetical systems more closely to what is known about actual neurons and neural networks. Rather than modeling neural network webs, single neurons are modeled at several distinct levels of complexity, including the neural mechanisms behind task-specific computations for discernible behaviors. In their brief review of this work, Herz, Gollish, Machens, and Jaeger (2006) note that the complex morphology of real neurons, the "composition of ionic conductances, and [the] distribution of synaptic inputs generate a plethora of dynamical phenomena [that] support various fundamental computations" (p. 80). Given the discovery of single neurons that fire in response to spatial location, location-emotion association, or recognition of intentional behavior, the modeling of intra-cellular (rather than inter-cellular) dynamics is appropriate and intriguing. Although this approach is more conceptually complex than neural network models, the models are not as demonstrationally robust. However, this work does underscore caution about the over-simplified neuron-as-wire analogy.

Lesion studies and other experiments-in-nature

Lesion studies correlate damage to particular areas of the brain from stroke, disease, trauma, surgery, or developmental malformation, with the disabling of particular functions. This approach, which originally advanced the 19th-century pseudo-science of phrenology, assumed that particular areas of the brain were discretely dedicated to particular functions. Today, neuroscientists have a more sophisticated understanding of the limitations of such lesion studies. Moreover, they often employ lesion data to illuminate the importance of individual developmental variation and plasticity in brain function (Jaillard, Martin, Garambois, LeBas, & Hommel, 2005; Johansson, 2000; Sanes & Donoghue, 2000; Soltesz, 2006). Lesion research data are most helpful when they confirm or challenge findings generated by other methods.

Lesion studies provided some of the earliest indication of specialization of brain regions for language processing (Broca, 1861, Wernicke, 1874). The idea that the left inferior frontal gyrus, known as Broca's area, was dedicated to language production, and the left superior temporal gyrus, known as Wernicke's area, was responsible for language reception was drawn from early lesion studies. Further analysis of the distinct aphasia's caused by damage to these areas led to the claim that Broca's area was responsible for syntactic processing, while Wernicke's area was responsible for semantic processing. Currently, research suggests these generalizations are much too simplistic (Müller & Basho, 2004; Stowe, Haverkort, & Zwarts, 2005; Zahn, Schwartz & Huber, 2006).

Lesions and other localized damage to the brain are difficult to analyze. It is not always clear how extensive the damage is, what particular neural networks have been damaged, or whether disruption of connections between intact areas is the cause of resulting dysfunction. It is therefore difficult to average across cases. In spite of this, the logic of localization informing this work is similar to that employed in interpreting hemodynamic brain images.

Vascular (hemodynamic) methods

Vascular methods trace changes in cerebral blood flow as an approximation of changes in neuronal activity. This activity is then correlated to experimental functions. The logic is simple. Neurons, like any living cell, require glucose and oxygen (and other resources) to function. The more active a neuron is, the more resources it needs. Resources reach the neurons through the bloodstream. Thus, increases in neuronal activity will require increases in blood flow to those areas of the brain that are most active. Imaging of changes in blood flow, therefore, can be employed as an approximation of neuronal activity. Although these methods for approximating neuronal activity are less direct and less temporally precise than methods for tracking action potentials described above, the anatomical specificity of this method is much greater (Gazzaniga, 2004).

The two best-known methods of measuring vascular response in the brain are positron emission tomography (PET), and functional magnetic resonance imaging (fMRI). Both methods require the subject to lie motionless in a large, closely encircling scanner. PET requires the injection of radioactive compounds into the subject's bloodstream. Typically, flurodeoxyglucose, a sugar with a radioactive florine isotope attached, is used in PET studies. As the isotope decays it emits sub-atomic particles that can be detected by the scanner indicating the compound's localization. Essentially, this method traces both blood flow and the uptake of glucose as proxies for neuronal activity. Other ligands can be bound with radioactive isotopes to allow the tracking of neurotransmitters as they are taken up in areas of the brain, expanding the use of this method to explore the physiological distribution of endocrinological and proteomic correlates to cognition, mood, and emotion.

Magnetic Resonance Imaging (MRI) visualizes the brain's folds (gyri) and fissures (sulci) with magnetic pulses to align the water molecules in brain tissues, creating an image of the morphology of the brain differentiated by water densities. This provides the map of the brain upon which activation data are overlaid. Comparison of blood flow between two conditions is a simple approach to detecting metabolic change and is known as *functional MRI* (fMRI). Advanced techniques such as Blood Oxygenation Level Dependent contrast (BOLD) differentiate between oxygenated and deoxygenated blood in fMRI, giving further focus to where oxygen is being consumed by brain tissue during functioning. Changes in blood flow and de-oxygenation are thus easily tracked, and recent advances can differentiate the blood flow in small capillaries from that in larger arteries, allowing closer imaging of neuronal metabolism.

Both PET and fMRI are highly technical and complex methods, and their successful use is fraught with procedural difficulties and study design challenges. To avoid spurious data and fanciful interpretations, careful research designs and well-constructed theories for testing are crucial (Caplan, 2004; Davidson & Irwin, 2002; see discussion in Implications section). Although technical advances allow for ever more precise physiological focus, the temporal precision of vascular imaging techniques is relatively poor, generating images over a period of seconds, rather than milliseconds as in EEG and MEG. An enormous amount of complex and potentially non-linear neural processing can transpire within the span of a few seconds.

The idea of matching complementary results from vascular methods such as fMRI and PET, with neuronal activation methods such as EEG, is intriguing (Perfetti & Bolger, 2004). However, recent studies indicate that fMRI may correlate more closely with general metabolic activity than with the spiking field potentials of interest to researchers seeking to demonstrate circuit models of brain function. It is worth noting that most of the cells in the brain are glial cells, not neurons. Glial cells are crucially important for brain function and similarly require glucose and oxygen, yet no one proposes that they are components of the signal circuit models of neural processing many neuroscientists advance. Further, shifts in blood flow may reflect changes in neurotransmitter concentrations rather than metabolic activity of neurons per se. This may explain why localizations of function in fMRI do not always match those indicated for the same event in EEG, the gentle boundaries of the latter images not withstanding.

The theoretical value of fMRI's spatial precision also is debatable. Much of the clean-cut boundaries visualized in fMRI charts are as much the result of subtractive designs, choice of base-line, setting of noise-signal thresholds, cleaning of data, and outlier selection, as they are of the underlying phenomenon being visualized— blood flow—which actually has no such neat boundaries. Hemodyamic brain charts that visualize neatly compartmentalized areas of brain function are perhaps enticing to advocates of modular processing models of cognition, but they are less useful for understanding the brain and its globally orchestrated development in its own terms (Hruby & Hynd, 2006).

Some reviewers describe vascular imaging studies as *neophrenological*, which is not a dismissal but merely a consideration of the value of structural research for the study of brain function (Thompson, Lutz, & Cosmelli, 2005). Where a process occurs in the brain is arguably not as significant as when it occurs, particularly given the functional plasticity and individual variability of brain morphology (Soltesz, 2006). Other scholars do dismiss the less careful vascular imaging work as "blobology" (Lieberman, 2006, p. 173), or worse. The nonspecialist may need to be reminded that, in spite of their vibrancy, rainbow-colored hemodynamic images are statistical charts about task-dependent blood flow in averaged subject populations, not photographs of a brain in action.

Experimental manipulation studies

Excision or lobotomy of live brains for experimental purposes is obviously inappropriate with human subjects. As a result, most research on brain structure and function in language processes is correlational in nature. However, temporary, non-invasive techniques such as transcranial magnetic stimulation (TMS) and repeated transcranial magnetic stimulation (rTMS) are being refined for experimental purposes. These methods fire a magnetic pulse into a highly focused area of the outer cortex. The magnetic pulse temporarily depolarizes the neurons in the area targeted, thereby either disabling or priming them. Researchers then observe the effect on subject performance of tasks they presume functionally centralized in the area.

SYNTHESIS

Because the technologies behind the rapid growth of neuroscience research are relatively new and continually advancing in sophistication, debates about validity, significance, appropriate research design, and the need for caution in interpretation have informed a healthy critical literature (e.g., Cacioppo et al., 2003; DeBot, 2006; Dobbs, 2005; Hagoort, 2006; Heeger & Rees, 2002; Mitchell et al., 2004; Picton et al., 2000; Uttal, 2001; Willingham & Dunn, 2003). However, these debates make fair evaluation of current studies difficult. The literature reviews included in individual neuroscience reports on reading comprehension subprocesses are often conflicting (Osterhout, Kim, & Kuperberg, in press). Reading and literacy scholars should therefore be particularly wary of neuroscience-based arguments flaunting only a handful of studies.

General reviews of neuroscience research on, or at least including, language and reading comprehension are only beginning to appear (Caplan, 2004; Gernsacher & Kaschak, 2003; Mar, 2004; Mody, 2004). Several are forthcoming and in-press as of this writing (several chapters in Gaskell, in press; Kutas, Van Petten, & Kluender, in press; Osterhout, Kim, & Kuperberg, in press). So far there have been few proper meta-analyses of the neuroscience research on reading comprehension or its subprocesses for technical reasons (but see Bolger, Perfetti, & Schneider, 2005; Ferstl, Neumann, Bolger, & von Cramon, 2007).

Published reviews of the literature

Previous reviews on the neuroscience of reading have largely ignored the issue of comprehension and focused instead on text decoding subprocesses and the differences found between dyslexic and typical readers. For instance, in their review on the neurobiology of reading and reading disorders, Shaywitz et al. (2000) make no mention of reading comprehension processes save for the use of presumed semantic processing tasks in subtraction designs to better distinguish phonological processing. Similarly, Papanicolaou, Pugh, Simos, and Mencl (2004) mention "meaning" (p. 406) only in reference to its relationship to orthographic and phonological processing. In their review of the research on educational neuroscience, subtitled, "the case of *literacy*" (italics added), Katzir and Paré-Blagoev (2006) described only 4 reading studies, all of them comparing decoding processes in dyslexic and normal subjects. In Berninger and Richards' otherwise commendable book-length treatment, *Brain literacy for educators and psychologists* (2002), the authors devoted a single, non-indexed paragraph to reading comprehension devoid of any citations of neuroscience research. In her review of language and reading impairments, Mody (2004) made brief mention of only a few fMRI studies on semantic and syntactic processing. The thoughtful special-issue review of reading comprehension neuroscience by Caplan (2004) focused chiefly on research design issues.

Studies of comprehension processes

The above reviews of the neuroscience research on reading emphasize visual, orthographic, phonological, or limited word form recognition subprocess research. Although such subprocesses are crucial to comprehension, they are not actually about comprehension per se, as reading theorists would typically describe it. Without the inclusion of robust neuroscience research on comprehension itself, presumed neurological correlates indicating the effect of comprehension processes on text decoding processes are difficult to assess (Sandak, Mencl, Frost, & Pugh, 2004). As the following illustrative review will show, research on reading comprehension does exist, but it tackles comprehension within several subprocess frames and at different scales of organization.

The various studies are not always confirmative, and attempts to localize discrete processing to match each category have generated overlapping results, possibly suggesting that these subprocess categories are inappropriate for bounding the neurological processing they require (Devlin et al., 2002; Mechelli, Gorno-Gorno-Tempini, & Price, 2003). The following summation is not by any means comprehensive, but it should give a sense of the sort of findings commonly acknowledged in the literature reviews of studies on particular subprocesses.

Word processing studies   The most basic level of single word processing involves the recognition of whether or not a letter string is in fact a word. Subjects are asked to identify real words in pairings that may contain real words, pseudo-words (contain language-possible but meaningless letter combinations), or nonwords (meaningless and unpronounceable letter strings, or strings of letter-like markings). Often this research is actually focused on orthographic or phonological processing, and employs lexical indexing comparisons to distinguish pure (i.e., nonsemantic) letter-to-word processing (for a review see Shaywitz et al., 2000; Papanicolaou et al., 2004).

Current theories suggest words are identified by letter sequence pattern identification, or through direct relation to phonological representation (so-called exception words). Words that are less common to the reader may require more effortful letter-by-letter translation into phonological form for identification (see review in Xu et al., 2001). Brain areas that relate to these processes include Wernicke's area, the left superior marginal gyrus, left angular gyrus, and other areas along the occipital and temporal lobe boundaries.

Subtractive design research on word recognition has given rise to the construct of the Visual Word Form Area (VWFA) for assembling an identifiable word form prior to lexical processing in the left midfusiform gyrus (McCandliss, Cohen, & Dehaene, 2003). The debate about the nature of the processing in the area has been notable (e.g., Binder, Medler, Westbury, Liebenthal, & Buchanan, 2006; Cohen et al., 2000; Devlin, Jamison, Gonnnerman, & Matthews, 2006; Hillis et al., 2005; Pammer et al., 2004; Price & Devlin, 2003; Vigneau, Jobard, Mazoyer, & Tzourio-Mazoyer, 2005).

Theories variously suggest the area is dedicated to recognizing word forms directly, to constructing word forms, recognizing orthographic patterns, or making pattern-to-gestalt comparisons, either to higher-order constraints such as phonological patterns or semantic structures. Researchers have also questioned whether a dedicated area is even necessary given that word-to-discourse levels of processing rely on extended and distributed areas of activation across the brain and word identification may thus be heavily context-driven (Chater & Manning, 2006; Xu, Kemeny, Park, Frattali, & Braun, 2005).

Like several other reputed language areas that share function with non-language processes (Maess, Koelsch, Gunter, & Friederici, 2001; Price, Thierry, & Griffiths, 2005; Stowe, Haverkort, & Zwarts, 2005), the VWFA is also implicated in processing for other kinds of tasks. Recognition of objects, faces, and colors elicits activation in the area, as does the reading of nonwords (Price & Devlin, 2003). What these cognitive processes might have in common at a neural level of processing is an open question, and there is the possibility that the area is merely a bottleneck for neural signaling between the occipital and temporal lobes.

Stewart, Myer, Frith, and Rothwell (2001) used rTMS to depolarize the posterior portion of Broadman's area (BA) 37, approximate to the VWFA, and found that only object recognition as indicated by picture matching tasks was affected. Such findings, in combination with the evidence for developmental plasticity in response to experience (Maguire, Spiers, Good, Hartley, Frackowiak, & Burgess, 2003), may cast doubt on assertions of inherent "wiring glitch[es]" (Shaywitz, 2003, p. 82) in the VWFA as the basis for higher-order neurological disabilities such as dyslexia (Shaywitz, Lyon, & Shaywitz, 2006).

Hickok and Poeppel (2004, 2007) have suggested a dual route phonology-to-lexical access model linking the area to more frontal areas of the brain that might account for double disassociations and inconsistent data on word form identification in the lesion literature, possibly supported by physiological studies (Borowski et al., 2006; Catani, Jones, & Ffytche, 2005; Mandonnet, Nouet, Gatignol, Capelle, & Daffau, 2007; Mechelli, et al., 2005). Other researchers suggest that the convergence of written and verbal words for comprehension may be located further upstream in the anterior and posterior poles of the temporal lobes (Dupont, 2002).

Word class identification is another focus of single word studies. ERP studies have examined how subjects' brains activate differently as they distinguish between open and closed class words (i.e., content vs. function words), degree of abstraction of words, imageability of words, or grammatical parts of speech (for a thorough review of field potential studies see Kutas, Van Petten, & Kluender, in press). These studies typically assume word class identification is crucial for the preliminary syntactic processing necessary in certain models of comprehension (e.g., Chomsky, 1986). However, word class studies involving semantic ambiguity show that separating word class from semantic content is not as simple as theory might suggest (Bedny & Thompson-Schill, 2006; Lee & Federmeier, 2006).

A third focus of word processing research studies how subjects process words for their semantic reference, including degree of familiarity, priming effects, length, and morphological complexity (Kutas, Van Petten, & Kluender, in press). This work may approximate neural subprocesses employed in sentence processing, and may indicate a foundational level of semantic processing. Other studies, mostly hemodynamic, have focused on vocabulary category. These studies identify the temporal lobes as contributing to the processing of word meaning. Collectively, these studies have been inconclusive regarding dedicated semantic maps in the temporal lobes for particular vocabulary, indicating either high individual variability or a reliance on semantic access (Binder et al., 2003). However there is at least some consistency in localization studies distinguishing processing of nouns regarding either natural or man-made objects (Devlin et al., 2002).

Word processing can also involve frontal areas of the brain, chiefly in cases of effortful semantic decisions during sentence or discourse processing (Scott, Leff, & Wise, 2003). These include the left inferior frontal gyrus (IFG) and associated areas that may variously be involved in phonological, syntactic, and semantic processing or word retrieval, production, or decision-making. It may be that the IFG area is not about those processes as they are typically defined, but instead is variously dedicated for construction and parsing of sequential patterns and so could be tapped or developmentally dedicated for both production and reception at multiple levels of organization (Vigneau et al., 2006). Additionally, it is possible that language production/reception and language comprehension-as-meaning-making are much more intertwined than presumed in some cognitive models (Coulson, 2006; Gernsbacher & Kaschak, 2003; Heim, 2005; Heim & Friederici, 2003; Lieberman, 2006).

Syntactic processing   As an extension upon the word class studies, examination of syntactic processing presumes separable syntactic and semantic processes identifiable at the neural level, with syntax being most dependably associated with the left frontal gyrus/Broca's area (Sakai, Noguchi, Takeuchi, & Wantanabe, 2002). As previously noted, ERP studies indicate different neural activation timing signatures for anomalous syntactic (P600) versus anomalous semantic (N400) indicators, but the research further suggests that typical processing is also similarly timed (Kaan, Harris, Gibson, & Holcomb, 2000). In other words, ERP studies indicate that on a word-by-word basis, early brain activation is for syntactic identification, followed at the N400 by semantic identification, followed at the P600 by a syntactic recheck (Friederici, & Kotz, 2003). Such findings are cited in support of linear theories of syntactic processing (e.g., Friederici, 2002), although alternative distributed processing theories have been suggested (e.g., Hagoort, 2003) and supported by studies (Cooke et al., 2006; Hald, Bastiaansen, & Hagoort, 2006).

Syntax-semantics coordination theories   As noted earlier, the traditional functional distinction between Broca's and Wernicke's area presumed the former was dedicated to language production and the latter to language processing. Subsequent analyses of the aphasias related to these areas and early imaging studies suggested that Broca's area processed syntax and Wernicke's area processed semantic information. But recent research has complicated that neat distinction, and there is now doubt whether syntactic or semantic processing can be strictly localized in those areas alone, or even disentangled (Dronkers, Plaisant, Iba-Zizen, & Cabanis, 2007; Dronkers, Wilkins, Van Valin, Redfern, & Jaeger, 2004; Heim & Friederici, 2003; Price, Thierry, Griffiths, 2005).

There are two major perspectives on the coordination of syntactic and semantic processes. One is the syntax-first view inspired by Chomsky (1986), and Fodor and Ferreira (1988). This view claims that words are parsed for their grammatical function without reference to their semantic content and that semantics and, subsequently, meaning are built upon this (see review in Cooke et al., 2006). The other is a family of constraint-based models that suppose interactive processing from early recognition of speech sounds or print words guided by anticipation of probability satisfaction employing accrued sentence and discourse semantic context as an engine for both anticipation and recheck (see review in Osterhout, Kim, & Kuperberg, in press). Priming effects studies support this possibility (e.g., DeLong, Urbach, & Kutas, 2005). Most research working from the latter models nonetheless assume that syntax drives comprehension of sentences unless the syntax is ambiguous or indeterminate.

But other studies suggest that semantics is equally important in driving sentence comprehension from the morpho-syntactic level on up (Kim & Osterhout, 2005; Müller & Hagoort, 2006). In this latter case, there may be an early, contextually constrained, tipping point for which of the two processes drives the initial construction of meaning. This approach, like most of the others, acknowledges subsequent process is mediated by accrued sentence structure and discourse context effects (Noppenny & Price, 2004; van den Brink & Hagoort, 2004). Most natural language, after all, is full of false starts, grammatical mismatches, and, in sophisticated texts, daunting embedding and recursion. In these instances, the brain requires a flexible processing approach as would be provided by multiple processing pathways making optimal use of linguistic affordance (Kaschak & Glenberg, 2000).

Hemodynamic imaging methods such as PET and fMRI have also suggested separable localization for syntactic and semantic processes (e.g., Newman, Pancheva, Ozawa, Neville, & Ullman, 2001). However, the terminology of these studies can be confusing. As Gernsbacher and Kaschak (2003) have noted, "...the labels attached to these tasks (e.g., 'semantic decision') are probably considered a convenient means of categorization. The labels are often so broad as to be next to useless in making generalizations across experiments" (p. 108). (For reviews of semantic organization models based in neuroscience research, see Hart & Kraut, 2007; Landauer, McNamara, Dennis, & Kintsch, 2007.) Taken together, the research on neural correlates of syntactic and semantic task processing presents a wide range of structures and processes in a "many-to-many mapping" (Gernsacher & Kaschak, 2003, p. 108) across the variously related neuroscience literatures.

Sentence processing Studies on sentence comprehension have typically presumed a unitary construct of what sentence comprehension entails. Attempts to tease out sentence comprehension components beyond those identified in single word studies (e.g., Cutting et al., 2006; Haller, Radue, Erb, Grodd, & Kircher, 2005), or attempts to identify loci for the integration of such components with lower level components (Hagoort, Hald, Bastiaansen, & Petersson, 2004; Spitsyna, Warren, Scott, Turkheimer, & Wise, 2006) lead to quite a lot of neural activation. Determining what it signifies requires comparison to the larger corpus of studies on language processing. The importance of context effects in sentence semantic processing is well established (DeLong, Urbach, & Kutas, 2005; Rodd, Davis, & Johnsrude, 2005; Vandenberghe, Nobre, & Price, 2002), yet some studies seem to presume that sentence comprehension is basically the accrual of individual word comprehension, and the studies are constructed accordingly, with individual words being presented in sequence, but at a very slow rate of delivery to allow the imaging technology to reset between words. Such an approach would possibly preclude some context and anticipation effects and strain short-term memory, thereby giving a truncated picture of sentence comprehension processing (Humphries, Binder, Medler, & Liebenthal, 2006; for additional methodological concerns see review in Osterhout, Kim, & Kuperberg, in press).

Areas of the left brain that are activated during sentence comprehension (and their probable function according to Gernsacher & Kaschak, 2003) include Wernicke's area (phonological processing and some word identification processing), the superior and middle temporal regions (lexical or vocabulary processing), Broca's area (syntactic analysis), additional areas in the inferior frontal gyrus (processing of sequences in phonology, syntax and semantics), middle and superior frontal regions (semantic analysis, the more so the more complex the sentence), and, in the right hemisphere, homologues to these areas, especially in cases where the sentence complexity is great, where references are less familiar or more abstract than the baseline, or where monitoring emotional intonation for prosody is necessary for clarifying meaning.

Discourse processing Processing of larger units of text, such as thematically unified passages or story narratives, tends to activate areas of the brain distinct from other language areas. Research suggests this activation is highly distributed in several areas across the right hemisphere, although also including bilateral activation of the anterior temporal poles (Dupont, 2002; Spitsyna, Warren, Scott, Turkheimer, & Wise, 2006). This activation would seem to be less about necessary language processing and more about use of conceptual representation (Bornkessel, Zysset, Friederici, von Cramon, & Schlesewsky, 2005; Grindrod & Baum, 2005). Given the number of anatomically distinct areas involved, subprocesses for this might include memory retrieval, concept integration, abstract or thematic relationship, story structure construction, and emotional valuation.

Robertson and colleagues (2000) found activation similar to story reading with picture stories requiring subjects to construct a narrative structure from the images. St. George and colleagues (1999) found a similar but greater effect in these right cortical areas when stories were presented without titles (i.e., with less context) than with. In conjunction with studies showing the activation of several of these same areas for more abstract word processing, prosody, or tasks of greater difficulty, interpretation, or novelty, this right hemisphere activation may only suggest the effortful construction of a novel narrative requires more neural processing capacity (Just & Carpenter, 1992). Although on the basis of ERP experiments, van Berkum, Hagoort, and Brown (1999) suggested there was no difference between sentence-level and discourse-level semantic integration, Gernsacher and Kaschak (2003) caution that it is not effort alone that requires this distribution of activity, but right-localized processes unique to narrative structure building and revision, as demonstrated in several studies (see review in Mar, 2004; Nieuwland & Van Berkum, 2006; Schmithorst, Holland, & Plante, 2006).

Second language studies   Though there is an increasing interest in bilingual language processing, questions about whether L1 and L2 are localized, structured or processed differently are clouded by a general lack of control for the degree and means of acquisition of L2. Work specifically on second language reading comprehension is rarer still, but the findings from related studies, such as those on discourse processing, give no reason to theorize a difference at that level. Whether L2 can be processed differently at a phonological, lexical, or syntactic level is a formative area of research (but see reviews and proposals in Birdsong, 2006; Davidson, 2006; Osterhout, McLaughlin, Pitkänen, Frenck-Mestre, & Molinaro, 2006; Watson-Gegeo, 2004).

Miscellaneous comprehension-related studies   Comprehension related neuroscience studies on imagery (Bedny & Thompson-Shill, 2006; Just, Newman, Keller, McEleney, & Carpenter, 2004), idioms (Oliveri, Romero, & Papagno, 2004), joking (Coulson & Williams, 2005), emotional valence (Beaucousin et al., 2007; Ferstl, Rinck, & von Cramon, 2005), prosody (Wartenburger et al., 2007), and plausibility (Waters, Caplan, Alpert, & Stanczak, 2003), add necessary complexity to our understanding of brain processes in comprehension. Additionally, studies of non-linguistic tasks processed in brain areas related to presumed language processing similarly provide depth to the picture we have of the comprehending brain, and give further reason for caution in assuming discrete categories of reading or language process disassociated from the embodied and situated states that correlate with meaning and meaningfulness (Barsalou, Simmons, Barbey, & Wilson, 2003; Borregine & Kaschak, 2006; Coulson, King, & Kutas, 1998; Gibbs, 2001; Glenberg, 2000, in press; Richardson, Spivey, Barsalou, & McRae, 2003; Scorolli & Borghi, 2007; Stowe, Paans, Wijers, & Zwarts, 2004; Wallentin, Østergard, Lund, Østergard, & Roepstorff, 2005).

Similarly, research on sub-cortical activity in language processing (e.g., Banai, Nicol, Zecker, & Kraus, 2005; Friederici, von Cramon, & Kotz, 1999; Longworth, Keenan, Barker, Marslen-Wilson, & Tyler, 2005) calls attention to the potential of theories less solely focused on the symbolic-cortical aspects of language, and more inclusive of the embodied and emotional associations in language processes and comprehension. When comprehension is embodied, its development is more easily merged with the development of anatomical structure and neuroendocrinological process and the behaviors these make possible (Dehaene-Lambertz et al., 2006; Hahne, Eckstein, & Friederici, 2004; Hruby, forthcoming; Uylings, 2006).

Putting it all together

Neuroscientists have begun to map out some very basic models of neurological subprocess for reading and language comprehension, but there is still much debate about these models because of the contradictions in the research base. Most literacy scholars would assume a ready distinction between such seemingly obvious categories as word class and word meaning, syntax and semantics, anticipation and confirmation, or language production and comprehension. Similarly, neuroscience researchers have assumed such distinctions when searching for their neurological correlates. And most published neuroscience research informed by these categories regularly contains claims regarding these distinctions. But general reviews of the research base paint a very different picture, one in which such distinctions are fuzzy at best and potentially misleading for understanding the neurological processes that subserve such distinctions in behavior (Price, Thierry, & Griffiths, 2005; Kaan & Swaab, 2002; Stowe, Haverkort, & Zwarts, 2005). Developing methods for comparing limited types of studies may produce more useful reviews and meta-analyses in the future (see Bolger, Perfetti, & Schneider, 2005; Ferstl et al., 2007, for examples of this).

It bears repeating that neuroscience on reading is actually neuroscience on the brain (while the subjects engage in some task deemed pertinent to reading). These studies generally are not designed to test the validity of the psycholinguistic and cognitive reading constructs they presume. If a temporal or physiological signature is correlationally associated with a given behavior, it does not necessarily follow (and may well be unlikely) that the time frame or area in question is solely dedicated to independently processing the behavior directly. Other areas may well be involved even though their activation is insufficient to significantly exceed the signal-noise ratio in a particular study. Therefore, to assert that such studies prove the constructs that constrain them is to make a claim beyond what the data can support, and may be a case of circular reasoning. On the other hand, repeated failure to dependably correlate a given category with discrete neurological signatures calls into question its validity for parsing neurological process.

Put another way, neuroscientists do not construct or test theories about reading comprehension per se, but about the brain processes that give rise to what we can observe or experience as reading comprehension. Such neurological processes occur at very different scales of temporal and spatial organization from that of direct human experience or abstract calculation. The debates surrounding these theories of neurological process are intriguing in their own right. But a few of the more noteworthy debates are analogous (or, if you allow for the universal influence of philosophy, homologous) to similar debates in literacy education practice, and may suggest useful constraints on theories of reading comprehension process and development.

Specifically, the modular vs. distributed cognition debates evident in both disciplines may, in the neurosciences, be heading for a resolution centered on developmental trade-off (e.g., McCandliss, Cohen, & Dehaene, 2003) and modality specificity (e.g., Barsalou, Simmons, Barbey, & Wilson, 2003). Also reminiscent of longstanding literacy education debates is the opposition of incremental, linear neural process models with the essentially constructivist neuroscience models emphasizing context effects in language comprehension. Again, similar neural architecture, such as that used to focus perception with attention (though not necessarily awareness, Lamme, 2004) (Barceló, Suwazono, & Knight, 2000), may account for discourse structure and world knowledge directing lower-order comprehension processes (Coulson, 2006). (For additional theoretical accounts on the role of neural architecture in context construction, cf. van der Velde & de Kamps, 2006 and Van Orden, Holden, & Turvey, 2003.)

In a general way, these biologically informed theoretical positions within the neurosciences are reminiscent of whole-theme educational theories (e.g., Iran-Nejad, 2000), and are as likely to lend credence to holistic theories of reading development as to more mechanistic models of cognitive process. It would be premature, however, to suggest anything like neuroscience evidence for such models of comprehension. If nothing else, these theoretical debates should inspire cautious reflection on the folk and formal categories employed in literacy education scholarship.

IMPLICATIONS FOR FUTURE RESEARCH

Although the research base is still very formative and explorative, the neuroscience research on reading comprehension is growing rapidly and greater theoretical maturity can be anticipated in the future. Reading and literacy education researchers need not take up the technologies of neuroscience inquiry to advance the knowledge base on effective reading instruction. However, appreciative understanding of literacy-related neuroscience investigations could well inspire better focused research in reading and literacy education using the techniques and methodologies that literacy researchers already have at their disposal.

Moreover, it is possible that loose reference to neuroscience research will continue to decorate the political rhetoric of literacy-focused educational reforms and the sales pitches of educational materials manufacturers. It is important, then, that reading and literacy scholars develop the ability to judge neuroscience research-based claims with more acuity than at present. Familiarity with the theoretical and methodological constraints on this kind of research may be increasingly necessary in this regard. For this reason, rather than anticipate future research directions in this section, I shall review several exemplary issues regarding the special challenges of research design in the neurosciences. These issues relate to the kind of neuroscience research on reading typically cited in so-called brain-based and early reading education or reading disabilities literatures, and similar careless regard in the area of reading comprehension is possible.

The challenge of solid research design in neuroscience

There are several commonly cited design challenges in constructing valid research studies in the neurosciences using the techniques described in previous sections of this chapter. Davidson and Irwin (2002) note four central issues in vascular image-based neuroscience research on emotion. With minor modifications, these four points are of equal importance in designs for reading comprehension study. (For ERP issues, see review in Kotchoubey, 2005; for review of problematic methodological assumptions regarding sentence comprehension research, see Osterhout, Kim, & Kuperberg, in press.) In addition, general cautions regarding the viability of testing traditional cognitive models of reading with brain imaging techniques are required.

First, the self-perception of comprehension by a subject should be distinguished from comprehension processes per se. This requires a theoretically clear distinction between self-monitoring processes and comprehension processes, otherwise subjects will be said to comprehend their perceptions of comprehension confounding identification of actual comprehension processing in the experimental condition. Research requiring metacognition for self-report purposes presents particular difficulty in this regard.

Second, there is no such thing as a true control condition for comparison in brain imaging research. Instead, two active conditions are compared, with the nonexperimental condition taken as a baseline for comparison purposes. To focus the result of a subtractive comparison design, it is important to select base-line/experimental condition distinctions that rule out as much extraneous (if necessary) processing as possible from the processing targeted in the investigation. Caplan (2004) argued that within-task parametric variation of sentence-level factors was the most easily interpretable approach to brain imaging studies of reading comprehension. In his review of this work, he noted:

> The issue is not the logic of subtraction or conjunction but its application in terms of tasks and stimuli. Comparisons of sentences against low-level baselines are inherently multidetermined; comparisons of similar structures across different tasks are often

hard to interpret; the use of unusual stimuli (ill-formed structures, jabberwocky) may lead to the use of unusual [neural] mechanisms. (Caplan, 2004, p. 237)

Nonetheless, he observed "…that even the narrowest comparisons leave room for multiple interpretations." (Caplan, 2004, p. 234)

Third, stimuli used to elicit comprehension processes in comparison conditions must be matched for conceptual complexity, topic familiarity, vocabulary level, and interest to subject, otherwise the result of the subtraction is as likely to indicate brain processes related to confusion or dissonance, effortful searching of background knowledge, or emotional arousal, in addition to comprehension processes. (Of course, it could be argued that such functions may in fact be integral to comprehension.) Similarly, varied experimental stimuli must be matched for surface features such as font, style, intonation, gender of speaker, etc., lest the activation of brain areas responsive to such factors be confused with processes unique to comprehension.

Fourth, claims of asymmetrical activation between brain areas, such as the left and right cortices, must be rigorously demonstrated. Typical analyses of fMRI or PET data often declare such asymmetries when an area in one hemisphere demonstrates activation above the statistical threshold while the same area in the opposite hemisphere does not. This only tests for main effect to the condition, however. To demonstrate an actual difference between the two hemispheres, it is necessary to test the Condition X Hemisphere, or Group X Hemisphere interaction, something often neglected. Such tests are necessary to demonstrate statistical asymmetry, and may also locate significant interactions where no significant main effect is indicated (Davidson & Irwin, 2002).

Fifth, when designing studies to test out models of cognitive process with brain imaging techniques, researchers must be mindful of the different scales of organization present (Poeppel, 1996). The scale of analysis employed in cognitive process research may be too great for identifying actual neural processes that realize the behaviors of interest. For instance, in behavioral observation we might report on a reader's *fluency*, as if it were a single process, although identified by three main characteristics (speed, accuracy, and prosody). Yet cognitive research demonstrates that fluency relies on several disassociable subprocesses (letter identification, phonemic processing, lexical access, syntactic and semantic processing on behalf of correct prosody, etc.). The behavioral category of fluency does not match one-on-one to the cognitive subprocesses that subserve it. Similarly, cognitive subprocesses may not match one-on-one to subserving neural subprocesses. Thus, imaging of neural processes may not generate anything recognizable to the categorical distinctions employed in cognitive models.

Additionally, to use the example of fluency again, lexical access is not just a subprocess important to fluency. It is also important to other reading skills, such as the integration of vocabulary knowledge in semantic processing. In the same fashion, neural subprocesses may subserve several distinct cognitive processes. And neural processes themselves operate on several scales of operation from the genetic to the cytological to the systemic level. In short, the dimensional flatness and grain of analysis of cognitive models of reading may be unsuitable to identify the multiple neural processes involved. In a nutshell, there may be necessary neural processes not anticipated in cognitive models, or cognitive functions that are not distinguishable by brain processes made manifest through visualization methods.

Sixth, a sensitivity to cortical bias in researchers' suppositions is in order. Until recently, it was not possible to calculate whole brain data sets. Thus, researchers tended to apply subtractive methods to locate activation within the specific areas of the brain they believed they had reason to examine. The value of these separable analyses for parsing whole brain activity has been debated, and it is clear that reading processes beyond word identification activate diverse areas across the brain. Moreover, cognitive researchers tend to exhibit a cortical bias, focusing their technologies on the "higher" processing centers in the cortex, because humans have more of such tissue than any other species. Because language and symbolic reasoning are capacities only possessed by humans, cognitive neuroscience researchers assumed they would find these capacities located in those areas of the brain unique to humans.

But, as noted, research has demonstrated that sub-cortical regions and pathways are also crucially active during language and reading processing, including comprehension processing. The assumption that higher-order phenomena unique to humans, such as attentive consciousness, symbol parsing, and comprehension, ought to be found in those areas of the brain of which humans have more than other species erroneously presumes that evolution proceeds on the basis of mutations for new structure fashioned on best-design principles. But evolution often proceeds by the readaptation of already existing structures for new purposes in the face of conditions different than those that originally fostered the structure. The rededication of structures results, as anyone with back problems can attest, in good-enough-on-average design, not best design. Intriguingly, geneticists have discovered that the chimpanzee genome holds more positively selected genetic changes since its divergence from the shared ancestor with human beings 6 million years ago than does the human genome (Bakewell, Shi, & Zhang, 2007, in Hopkin, 2007). As Bakewell, et al. observe, the increased neural capacity that makes language possible may have required far fewer genetic modifications than previously assumed.

Lastly, the conceptual categories with which psychologists carve nature at the joints into separable features or functions may be only heuristic conveniences and may not at all align with how nature has, by fortuitous evolutionary and developmental circumstance, assembled a functioning brain capable of reading or anything else.

> An obstacle to understanding neural processing may arise from the field's co-opting of cognitive psychological methods and metaphors. The information-processing model of cognition, which underlies much work in psycholinguistics, arose at a time when the neural operations involved in cognition could mainly be discussed metaphorically.... there is reason to suspect that nature has not cooperated by designing the brain to match our information-processing intuitions. This likely explains why we observe the many-to-many mapping of structures and putative processes across imaging studies. (Gernsbacher & Kaschak, 2003, pp. 109–110)

CONCLUDING THOUGHTS

For theoretical purposes, the open question remains, how can biological processes as studied in the neurosciences be related to cultural forms such as texts and literacy. Three possibilities come to mind. First, findings about neurological process may constrain our assumptions about plausibility regarding cognitive and phenomenological theories of comprehension process. Second, transactive dynamics between phenomena at different scales of organization may stand as a useful analogy to the co-regulation of behavior and sociality at the heart of much classroom-based literacy research. Taking this a step further, the multiple scales of organization studied in the neurosciences require dynamic corridors of effect across scales, giving rise to alternative vocabularies and conceptual systems for parsing embedded and intermediated behaviors education researchers commonly describe with less precise if comfortable folk terminology. In this way, the neurosciences may help reading and literacy scholars reconnect to current theory in developmental science. And last, the thematic and philosophical constraints of the neurosciences, and the life sciences more generally, may stand as a complimentary counter-stance to the information science and cultural context motifs currently advancing the fields of reading comprehension and literacy development (for a substantive and nuanced introduction to these concepts, see Thompson, 2007).

A paradigmatic example of how disciplines studying the natural and social world might be conceptually related for research purposes was proposed in the early 20th century by the physicist Schrödinger (1944/1992). Schrödinger took exception to vitalist explanations in turn-of-the-century biology that held that a life-force, or *élan vital*, must exist to account for the mysterious difference between living and inanimate entities. Schrödinger observed that although biological entities could not be reduced to mere chemicals in motion, they nonetheless were chemical and physical entities. Thus, any account of biological phenomena that violated what scientists knew with a fair degree of certainty about chemistry or physics could be dismissed as lacking much probability, especially if the explanation involved unobservable agents.

On the other hand, Schrödinger suggested that the dependence of biological phenomena on physics and chemistry usefully constrained questions about biology. Rather than unfocused speculation on the nature of life, Schrödinger suggested the real question was how biological entities—alone among chemical entities—managed to defy the second law of thermodynamics (the universal trend toward entropy). Rather than follow the flow of matter and energy to ever further homogenous dissipation, life systems develop and evolve toward ever more complex forms and ecosystems. He did not have an explanation for how this was possible, but 9 years later, Watson and Crick (1953) proposed a model for the structure of DNA that not only accounted for its chemical properties, but suggested the mechanism for the replication of traits with variation in organisms. As theorists combined Crick and Watson's model with Darwin's theory of natural selection and Mendel's theory of the gene, the answer to Schrödinger's reframed question emerged.

This same line of reasoning has been reprised by naturalists in regard to social phenomena. Humans are social, linguistic, and cultural beings, but just what this means and how it works has only recently been explored. Theories have been speculative, and are often not amenable to traditional research methods for determining causation. The standard social science model seems curiously disconnected from the natural world, as if society and culture were self-instantiating. Reapplying Schrödinger's paradigm, we might note that whatever else human beings are, they are most certainly biological beings. This in no way can lead one to reduce sociality, culture, or literacy to mere biology. Nonetheless, biology makes sociality, culture, and literacy possible. And that in turn places some foundational constraints on what can be considered a plausible theory of comprehension. Specifically, any theory of social phenomena that violates what we know with a fair degree of certainty about biological systems (or chemistry, or physics) can be dismissed as lacking much probability, especially if the explanation involves agents that cannot be directly observed. By this logic, one might discount Hegelian *Weltgeists*, or even cognitive models of non-conscious mental structure, to explain things like human sociality, abstract reasoning, or literacy practices. From this view, *Weltgeists* and computational mind structures are bad faith feints in response to wrong questions.

Given that the fundamental assumption within the neurosciences is that human beings (and human readers) are bio-ecological kinds and that this is significant, we may ask how is it that symbol-using species, such as human beings—alone among biological, and even social, species—are able to generate higher-order cultural forms such as literacy that can redirect biological development on behalf of language and thought in ways that make literacy behaviors not only possible but functionally distributable across social collectives with value added in the form of shared comprehension. Assuming this is the right question, reading and literacy scholars are already on to serviceable theories, as other chapters in this volume indicate.

Following Tinbergen (1963), the proximal and distal questions a literacy socionaturalist might ask specifically of reading processes include (1) what biological structures make literacy possible; (2) how and why do these structures develop as they do over time; (3) how is literacy functional for human beings and how does that functionality promote literate development; and (4) how has/does literacy evolve? (This last is not a purely genetic question, but would include the ecological effects of historically accrued cultural traditions, such as childrearing practices and education, for the epigenesis of literacy abilities and concomitant higher-order thinking skills, and their redounding effect back to shared cultural legacy.) From the standpoint of the neurosciences, the answer to the first question is in part found in functional neuroanatomy, to the second in developmental neuroscience, to the third in social neuroscience, and to the fourth in dynamical systems neuroscience.

Scholars of literacy would do well to consider all of these areas, particularly the dynamical systems orientation, to make sense of the biological requisites of reading comprehension on behalf of a comprehensive theory. Biological systems theory emphasizes that the evolution and development of organic complexity demonstrates legacies of functionality. Whether in the case of simple unicellular organisms, nervous systems, neurologically-endowed organisms—or even, it might be argued, human collectives—organic structures are not only multiply embedded and transactionally complex, they are also continuously changing over time. To persist over time, structural relationships between lower-order agents within such changing structures must also change, and in functional ways. This observation potentially addresses how a nonintelligent process could give rise to the emergence of organic intelligence. The evolutionary algorithm of adaptive selection based on multiplicity with variation could make possible the necessary neurological plasticity for learning. That is, to be adaptive in relation to indeterminably changing contexts, intelligent systems require a degree of variance among their constituting agents to provide structural options for adaptation or functional reorganization.

This would seem to be a good description of what nervous systems do indeed do as they learn through experience, even in animals with simple nervous systems (Striedter, 2005). The implications of neurologically plausible adaptive systems theory for educational psychology and literacy theory are only beginning to be articulated (Aaron & Joshi, 2006; Davis & Sumara, 2006; Hruby, 2001; Jordan et al., 2007; Plotkin, 2004). This functionalist insight into the dynamics of neurological structure hardly overturns traditional conjectures about the nature of meaning-making. But perceptual and constructive abilities are possibly both predicated on a highly fluid neural architecture that allows for functional plasticity—or, in other words—allows neurologically endowed organisms to wrap their nervous systems around their environment in highly individualized yet functional ways. Symbolic systems of communication, such as language, have apparently emerged upon this same set of neurological affordances, as perhaps have culturally-mediated technologies of symbolic representation (i.e., texts).

Of course, this is only a part of the story, albeit a fundamental part. As researchers across the life sciences have well observed, the structure of lower-order phenomena alone cannot provide a sufficient account of emergent higher-order phenomena. A host of other causative factors, from the impetus of functionality, to the dynamics of development, to the legacy of history, whether evolutionary or cultural—and their mutual co-regulation—are equally necessary for a comprehensive account (Hauser, Chomsky, & Fitch, 2002; Johnson, 2005; Munakata & Johnson, 2006). But as it is the case that such complex naturalistic accounts are currently being offered across the life and social sciences, their prospective value for parsing higher-order behaviors such as proficient reading comprehension and its effective facilitation in schools may be worth pursuing as a future contribution to the theoretical literature.

REFERENCES

Aaron, P. G., & Joshi, J. M. (2006). Written language is as natural as spoken language: A biolinguistic perspective. *Reading Psychology, 27,* 263–311.

Adams, M. J. (1990). *Beginning to read: Thinking and learning about print.* Cambridge, MA: MIT Press.

Ansari, D., & Coch, D. (2006). Bridges over troubled waters: Education and cognitive neuroscience. *Trends in Cognitive Science, 10,* 146–151.

Bakewell, M. A., Shi, P., & Zhang, J. (2007). More genes underwent positive selection in chimpanzee evolution than in human evolution. *PNAS,* April 20 [electronic publication ahead of print]. Retrieved April 27, 2007, from http://www.ncbi.nlm.nih.gov/entrez/query.fcgi?cmd=Retrieve&db=PubMed&list_uids=17449636&dopt=Citation

Banai, K., Nicol, T., Zecker, S. G., & Kraus, N. (2005). Brainstem timing: Implications for cortical processing and literacy. *The Journal of Neuroscience, 25,* 9850–9857.

Barceló, F., Suwazono, S., & Knight, R. T. (2000). Prefrontal modulation of visual processing in humans. *Nature Neuroscience, 3,* 399–403.

Barsalou, L. W., Simmons, W. K., Barbey, A. K., & Wilson, C. D. (2003). Grounding conceptual knowledge in modality-specific systems. *Trends in Cognitive Sciences, 7,* 84–91.

Bastiaansen, M., & Hagoort, P. (2006). Oscillatory neural dynamics during language comprehension. *Progress in Brain Research, 159,* 179–96

Beaucousin, V., Lacheret, A., Turbelin, M-R., Morel, M., Mazoyer, B., & Tzourio-Mazoyer, N. (2007). FMRI study of emotional speech comprehension. *Cerebral Cortex, 17,* 339–352.

Bedny, M., & Thompson-Shill, S. L. (2006). Neuroanatomically seperable effects of imageability and grammatical class during single-word comprehension. *Brain & Language, 98,* 127–139.

Bennet, M. R., & Hacker, P. M. S. (2003). *Philosophical foundations of neuroscience.* Oxford: Blackwell Publishing.

Berninger, V. W., & Richards, T. L. (2002). *Brain literacy for educators and psychologists.* New York: Academic.

Binder, J. R., McKiernan, K. A., Parsons, M. E., Westbury, C. F., Possing, E. T., Kaufman, J. N., & Buchanan, L. (2003). Neural correlates of lexical access during visual word recognition. *Journal of Cognitive Neuroscience, 15,* 372–393.

Binder, J. R., Medler, D. A., Westbury, C. F., Liebenthal, E., & Buchanan, L. (2006). Tuning of the human left fusiform gyrus to sublexical orthographic structure. *Neuroimage, 33,* 739–748.

Birdsong, D. (2006). Age and second language acquisition: A selective overview. *Language Learning, 56,* 9–49.

Blakemore, S., & Frith, U. (2000). *The implications of recent developments in neuroscience for research on teaching and learning.* London: Institute of Cognitive Neuroscience.

Block, N., Flanagan, O., & Güzeldere, G. (Eds.). (1997). *The nature of consciousness: Philosophical debates.* Cambridge, MA: MIT Press.

Blum, D. (2006, December 30). Ghosts in the machine. *New York Times.* Retrieved January 12, 2007, from http://select.nytimes.com/search/restricted/article?res=F30B16FF3D540C738FDDA

Bolger, D. J., Perfetti, C. A., & Schneider, W. (2005). Cross-cultural effect on the brain revisited: Universal structures plus writing system variation. *Human Brain Mapping, 25,* 92–104.

Bornkessel, I., Zysset, S., Friederici, A. D., von Cramon, D. Y., & Schlesewsky, M. (2005). Who did what to whom? The neural basis of argument hierarchies during language comprehension. *Neuroimage, 26,* 221–233.

Borowski, R., Cummine, J., Owen, W. J., Friesen, C. K., Shih, F., & Sarty, G. E. (2006). FMRI of ventral and dorsal processing streams in basic reading processes: Insular sensitivity to phonology. *Brain Topography, 18,* 233–239.

Borregine, K. L., & Kaschak, M. P. (2006). The action-sentence compatibility effect: It's all in the timing. *Cognitive Science, 30,* 1097–1112.

Bredo, E. (2006). Conceptual confusion and educational psychology. In P. A. Alexander, & P. H. Winne (Eds.), *Handbook of educational psychology* (2nd ed., pp. 43–57). Mahwah, NJ: Erlbaum Associates.

Broca, P. (1861). Remarques sur le egesiège de la faculté du langage articulé, suivies d'une observation d'aphémie (perte de la parole). *Bulletins et Mémoires de la Société Anatomique de Paris, 36,* 330–357.

Brook, A., & Akins, K. (2005). *Cognition and the brain: The philosophy and neuroscience movement.* New York: Cambridge University Press.

Bruer, J. T. (1997). Education and the brain: A bridge too far. *Educational Researcher, 26*(8), 4–16.

Bruer, J. T. (2003). Building bridges in neuroeducation. Address given at the 400th Anniversary Meeting of the Papal Academy of Science, Vatican City, November 7, 2003.

Cabeza, R., & Nyberg, L. (1997). Imaging cognition: An empirical review of PET studies with normal subjects. *Journal of Cognitive Neuroscience, 9*, 1–26.

Cabeza, R., & Nyberg, L. (2000). Imaging cognition II: An empirical review of 275 PET and fMRI studies. *Journal of Cognitive Neuroscience, 12*, 1–47.

Cacioppo, J. T., Bernston, G. G., Lorig, T. S., Norris, C. J., Rickett, E., & Nusbaum, H. (2003). Just because you're imaging the brain doesn't mean you can stop using your head: A primer and set of first principles. *Journal of Personality and Social Psychology, 85*, 650–661.

Caplan, D. (2004). Functional neuroimaging studies of written sentence comprehension. *Scientific Studies of Reading, 8*, 225–240.

Catani, M., Jones, D. K., & Ffytche, D. H. (2005). Perisylvian language networks of the human brain. *Annals of neurology, 57*, 8–16.

Chalmers, D. J. (1996). *The conscious mind: In search of a fundamental theory.* New York: Oxford Press.

Chater, N., & Manning, C. D. (2006). Probabilistic models of language processing and acquisition. *Trends in Cognitive Science, 10*, 335–344.

Chomsky, N. (1986). *Knowledge of language.* New York: Praeger.

Churchland, P. S. (2005). A neurophilosophical slant on consciousness research. *Progress in Brain Research, 149*, 285–293.

Cohen, L., Dehaene, S., Naccache, L., Lehéricy, S., Dehaene-Lambertz, G., Hénaff, M., & Michel, F. (2000). The visual word form area: Spatial and temporal characterization of an initial stage of reading in normal subjects and posterior split-brain patients. *Brain, 123*, 291–307.

Cooke, A., Grossman, M., DeVita, C., Gonzalez-Atavales, Moore, P., Chenc, W., Gee, J., & Detre, J. (2006). Large-scale neural network for sentence processing. *Brain and Language, 96*, 14–36.

Coulson, S. (2006). Constructing Meaning. *Metaphor & Symbol, 21*, 245–266.

Coulson, S., King, J. W., & Kutas, M. (1998). Expect the unexpected: Event-related brain responses to morphosyntactic violations. *Language and Cognitive Processes, 13*, 21–58.

Coulson, S., & Williams, R. F. (2005). Hemispheric asymmetries and joke comprehension. *Neuropsychologia, 43*, 128–141.

Cutting, L. E., Clements, A. M., Courtney, S., Rimrodt, S. L., Schafer, J. G. B., Bisesi, J., Pekar, J. J., & Pugh, K. R. (2006). Differential components of sentence comprehension: Beyond single word reading and memory. *Neuroimage, 29*, 429–438.

Davidson, D. (2006). Strategies for longitudinal neurophysiology: Commentary on Osterhout et al. *Language Learning, 56*, 231–234.

Davidson, R. J., & Irwin, W. (2002). The functional neuroanatomy of emotion and affective style. In J. T. Cacioppo, G. G. Bernston, R. Adolphs, C. S. Carter, R. J. Davidson, et al. (Eds.), *Foundations in social neuroscience* (pp. 473–490). Cambridge, MA: MIT Press.

Davis, B., & Sumara, D. (1998). Cognition, complexity, and teacher education. *Harvard Educational Review, 67*, 105–125.

Davis, B., & Sumara, D. (2006). Challenging images of knowing: Complexity science and educational research. *International Journal of Qualitative Studies in Education, 18*, 305–321.

De Bot, K. (2006). The plastic bilingual brain: Synaptic pruning or growth? Commentary on Green, et al. *Language Learning, 56*, 127–132.

Dehaene-Lambertz, G., Hertz-Pannier, L., Dubois, J., Meriaux, S., Roche, A., Sigman, M., & Dehaene, S. (2006). Functional organization of perisylvan activation during presentation of sentences in preverbal infants. *PNAS, 103*, 14240–14245.

DeLong, K. A., Urbach, T. P., & Kutas, M. (2005). Probabilistic word pre-activation during language comprehension inferred from electrical brain activity. *Nature Neuroscience, 8*, 1117–1121.

Devlin, J. T., Jamison, H. L., Gonnerman, L. M., & Matthews, P. M. (2006). The role of the posterior fusiform gyrus in reading. *The Journal of Cognitive Neuroscience, 18*, 911–922.

Devlin, J. T., Moore, C. J., Mummery C. J., Gorno-Tempini, M. L., Phillips, J. A., Noppeney, U., Frackowiak, R. S. J., Friston, K. J., & Price, C. J. (2002). Anatomic constraints on cognitive theories of category specificity. *Neuroimage, 15*, 675–685.

Dobbs, D. (2005). Fact or phrenology? *Scientific American Mind, 16*, 24–31.

Doyle, J., & Csete, M. (2007). Rules of engagement. *Nature, 446*, 860.

Dronkers, N. F., Plaisant, O., Iba-Zizen, M. T., & Cabanis, E. A. (2007). Paul Broca's historic cases: High resolution MR imaging of the brains of LeBorgne, and LeLong. *Brain, 130,* 1432–1441.

Dronkers, N. F., Wilkins, D. P., Van Valin Jr., R. D., Redfern, B. B., & Jaeger, J. J. (2004). Lesion analysis of the brain areas involved in language comprehension. *Cognition, 92,* 145–177.

Dupont, S. (2002). Investigating temporal pole function by functional imaging. *Epileptic Disorders, 4,* S17–S22.

Ferstl, E. C., Neumann, J., Bolger, C., & von Cramon, D. Y. (2007). The extended language network: A meta-analysis of neuroimaging studies on text comprehension. *Human Brain Mapping (Early View).* Published Online 7 June 2007. Retrieved October 11, 2007, from: www3.interscience.wiley.com/cgi-bin/fulltext/114277612/HTMLSTART

Ferstl, E. C., Rinck, M., & von Cramon, D. Y. (2005). Emotional and temporal aspects of situation model processing during text comprehension: An event-related fMRI study. *Journal of Cognitive Neuroscience, 17,* 724–739.

Fingelkurts, A., & Fingelkurts, A. (2001). Operational architectonics of the human brain biopotential field: Towards solving the mind-brain problem. *Brain and Mind, 2,* 261–296.

Fischer, K. W., & Bidell, T. R. (2006). Dynamic development of action, thought, and emotion. In R. M. Lerner (Ed.) & W. Damon (Series Ed.), *Handbook of child psychology: Vol. 1. Theoretical models of human development* (6th ed., pp. 313–399). New York: Wiley.

Fodor, J. (2000). *The mind doesn't work that way: The scope and the limits of computational psychology.* Cambridge, MA: MIT Press.

Fodor, J. D., & Ferreira, F. (1988). *Reanalysis in sentence processing.* Boston: Kluwer Academic.

Friederici, D. (2002). Towards a neural basis of auditory sentence processing. *Trends in Congitive Sciences, 6,* 78–84.

Friederici, D., & Kotz, S. A. (2003). The brain basis of syntactic processing: function imaging and lesion studies. *Neuroimage, 20,* S8–S17.

Friederici, D., von Cramon, Y., & Kotz, S. A. (1999). Language related brain potential in patients with cortical and subcortical left hemisphere lesions. *Brain, 122,* 1033–1047.

Gallese, V., Keysers, C., & Rizollatti, G. (2004). A unifying view of the basis for social cognition. *Trends in Cognitive Sciences, 8,* 396–403.

Gaskell, M. G. (Ed.). (in press). *Oxford handbook of psycholinguistics.* Oxford: Oxford University Press.

Gazzaniga, M. S. (2004). *The cognitive neurosciences III.* Cambridge, MA: MIT Press.

Gernsacher, M. A., & Kaschak, M. P. (2003). Neuroimaging studies of language production and comprehension. *Annual Review of Psychology, 54,* 91–114.

Gibbs, R. W. (2001). Embodied experience and linguistic meaning. *Brain and Language, 84,* 1–15.

Glenberg, A. M. (2000). Symbol grounding and meaning: A comparison of high-dimensional and embodied theories of meaning. *Journal of Memory and Language, 43,* 379–401.

Glenberg, A. M. (in press). Language and action: Creating sensible combinations of ideas. In M. G. Gaskill (Ed.), *The Oxford Handbook of Psycholinguistics.* Oxford: Oxford University Press.

Gorman, C. (2003, July 28). The new science of dyslexia. *Time,* 52–59.

Gottlieb, G., Wahlsten, D., & Likliter, R. (2006). The significance of biology for human development: A developmental psychobiological systems view. In R. M. Lerner (Ed.) & W. Damon (Series Ed.), *Handbook of child psychology: Vol. 1. Theoretical models of human development* (6th ed.; pp. 210–257). New York: Wiley.

Gough, P. B. (1972). One second of reading. In J. F. Kavanagh, & I. G. Mattingly (Eds.), *Language by ear and by eye: the relationships between speech and reading* (pp. 331–338). Cambridge, MA: MIT Press.

Grindrod, C., M., & Baum, S. R. (2005). Hemispheric contributions to lexical ambiguity resolution in a discourse context: Evidence from individuals with unilateral left and right hemisphere lesions. *Brain & Cognition, 57,* 70–83.

Hagoort, P. (2003). How the brain solves the binding problem for language: A neurocomputational model of syntactic processing. *Neuroimage, 20,* S18–S29.

Hagoort, P. (2006). What we cannot learn from neuroanatomy about language learning and language processing: Commentary on Uylings. *Language Learning, 56,* 91–97.

Hagoort, P., Hald, L., Bastiaansen, M., & Petersson, K. M. (2004). Integration of word meaning and world knowledge in language comprehension. *Science, 304,* 438–441.

Hahne, A., Eckstein, K., & Friederici, A. D. (2004). Brain signatures of syntactic and semantic processes during children's language development. *Journal of Cognitive Neuroscience, 16,* 1302–1318.

Hald, L. A., Bastiaansen, M. C. M., & Hagoort, P. (2005). EEG theta and gamma responses to semantic violations in online sentence processing. *Brain and Language, 96*, 90–105.

Haller, S., Radue, E. W., Erb, M., Grodd, W., & Kircher, T. (2005). Overt sentence production in event-related fMRI. *Neuropsychologia, 43*, 807–814.

Hart, J., & Kraut, M. A. (2007). *Neural Basis of Semantic Memory*. Cambridge: Cambridge University Press.

Hauser, M. D., Chomsky, N., & Fitch, W. T. (2002). The faculty of language: What is it, who has it, and how did it evolve? *Science, 298*, 1569–1579.

Heeger, D., & Rees, D. (2002). What does fMRI tell us about neuronal activity? *Nature Reviews/Neuroscience, 3*, 142–151.

Heim, S. (2005). The structure and dynamics of normal language processing: Insights from neuroimaging. *Acta Neurobiologiae Experimentalis, 65*, 95–116.

Heim, S., & Friederici, A. D. (2003). Phonological processing in language production: Time course of brain activity. *Neuroreport, 14*, 2031–3033.

Herz, A. V. M., Gollish, T., Machens, C. K., & Jaeger, D. (2006). Modeling single-neuron dynamics and computations: A balance of detail and abstraction. *Science, 314*, 80–85.

Hickok, G., & Poeppel, D. (2004). Dorsal and ventral streams: A framework for understanding aspects of the functional anatomy of language. *Cognition, 92*, 67–99.

Hickok, G., & Poeppel, D. (2007). The cortical organization of speech processing. *Nature Reviews Neuroscience, 8*, 393–402.

Hillis, A.E., Newhart, M., Heidler, J., Barker, P., Herskovits, E., & Degaonkar, M. (2005). The roles of the "visual word form area" in reading. *Neuroimage, 24*, 548–559.

Hopkin, M. (2007). Chimps lead evolutionary race. *Nature, 446*, 841.

Hruby, G. G. (2001). The descent of Internet publications: A review of literacy journals online. *Reading Research and Instruction, 40*, 243–252.

Hruby, G. G. (Forthcoming). *Reading comprehension and literacy development: The quest for a comprehensive theory*. Cambridge: Cambridge University Press.

Hruby, G. G., & Hynd, G. W. (2006). Decoding Shaywitz: The modular brain and its discontents. [Review of the book "Overcoming dyslexia: A new and complete science-based program for reading problems at any level."] *Reading Research Quarterly, 41*, 544–556.

Humphries, C., Binder, J. R., Medler, D. A., & Liebenthal, E. (2006). Syntactic and semantic modulation of neural activity during auditory sentence comprehension. *Journal of Cognitive Neuroscience, 18*, 665–679.

Illes, J. (Ed.). (2005). *Neuroethics: Defining the issues in theory, practice and policy*. Oxford: Oxford University Press.

Iran-Nejad, A. (2000). Brain, knowledge, and self-regulation. *The Journal of Mind and Behavior, 21*(1 & 2), entire special issue.

Jacobson, M. J., & Wilensky, U. (2006). Complex systems in education: Scientific and educational importance and implications for the learning sciences. *The Journal of Learning Sciences, 15*, 11–34.

Jaillard, A., Martin, C. D., Garambois, K., LeBas, J. F., & Hommel, M. (2005). Vicarious function within the human primary motor cortex? A longitudinal fMRI stroke study. *Brain, 128*, 1122–1138.

Jensen, E. (1998). *Teaching with the brain in mind*. Alexandria, VA: Association for Supervision and Curriculum Development.

Johansson, B. B. (2000). Brain plasticity and stroke rehabilitation. *Stroke, 31*, 223–230

Johnson, M. H. (2005). Developmental neuroscience, psychophysiology, and genetics. In M. H. Bornstein & M. E. Lamb (Eds.), *Developmental science: An advanced textbook* (5th ed.,pp. 187–222). Mahwah, NJ: Erlbaum.

Jordan, M. E., Schallert, D. L., Cheng, A., Park, Y., Lee, H., Chen, Y., Yang M., Chu, R., & Chang, Y. (2007). Seeking self-organization in classroom-mediated discussion through a complex adaptive systems lens. *The 56th Yearbook of the National Reading Conference*, 304–318.

Just, M. A., & Carpenter, P. A. (1992). A capacity theory of comprehension: individual differences in working memory. *Psychological Review, 99*, 122–149.

Just, M. A., Newman, S. D., Keller, T. A., McEleney, A., & Carpenter, P. A. (2004). Imagery in sentence comprehension: an fMRI study. *Neuroimage, 21*, 112–125.

Kaan, E., Harris, A., Gibson, E., & Holcomb, P. (2000). The P600 as an index of syntactic integration difficulty. *Language and Cognitive Processes, 15*, 159–201.

Kaan, E., & Swaab, T. Y. (2002). The brain circuitry of syntactic comprehension. *Trends in Cognitive Sciences, 6*, 350–356.

Karakas, S., Erzengin, Ö. U., & Basar, E. (2000). A new strategy involving multiple cognitive paradigms demonstrates that ERP components are determined by the superposition of oscillatory responses. *Clinical Neurophysiology, 111,* 1719–1732.

Kaschak, M. P., & Glenberg, A. M. (2000). Constructing meaning: The role of affordances and grammatical constructions in sentence comprehension. *Journal of Memory and Language, 43,* 508–529.

Katzir, T., & Paré-Blagoev, J. (2006). Applying cognitive neuroscience research to education: The case of literacy. *Educational Psychologist, 4,* 53–74.

Kim, A., & Osterhout, L. (2005). The independence of combinatory semantic processing: Evidence from event-related potentials. *Journal of Memory and Language, 52,* 205–225.

Kintsch, W. (1998). *Comprehension: A paradigm for cognition.* Cambridge: Cambridge University.

Kosslyn, S. M. (1999). If neuroimaging is the answer, what is the question? *Philosophical Transactions of Royal Society of London (Part B), 354,* 1283–1294.

Kotchoubey, B. (2005). Event-related potentials, cognition, and behavior: A biological approach. *Neuroscience and Biobehavioral Reviews, 30,* 42–65.

Kutas, M., Van Petten, C. K., & Kluender, R. (2006). Psycholinguistics Electrified II (1994–2005). In M. A. Gernsbacher & M. Traxler (Eds.), *Handbook of Psycholinguistics* (2nd ed.) (pp. 625–724). New York: Elsevier Press.

Lamme, V. A. F. (2004). Separate neural definitions of visual consciousness and visual attention: A case for phenomenal awareness. *Neural Networks, 17,* 861–872.

Landauer, T. K., McNamara, D. S., Dennis, S., & Kintsch, W. (Eds.). (2007). *Handbook of Latent Semantic Analysis.* Mahwah, NJ: Erlbaum.

Leander, K., & Rowe, D. W. (2006). Mapping literacy spaces in motion: A rhizomatic analysis of a classroom literacy performance. *Reading Research Quarterly, 41,* 428–461.

LeBihan, D., Mangin, J., Poupon, C., Clark, C. A., Pappata, S., Molko, N., & Chabriat, H. (2000). Diffusion tensor imaging: Concepts and applications. *Journal of Magnetic Resonance Imaging, 13,* 534–546.

Lee, C. L., & Federmeier, K. D. (2006). To mind the mind: An event-related potential study of word class and semantic ambiguity. *Brain Research, 1081,* 191–202.

Lerner, R. M. (2002). *Concepts and theories of human development* (3rd ed.). Mahwah, NJ: Erlbaum.

Lerner, R. M. (2006). Developmental science, developmental systems, and contemporary theories of human development. In R. M. Lerner (Ed.) & W. Damon (Series Ed.), *Handbook of child psychology: Vol. 1. Theoretical models of human development* (6th ed.; pp. 1–17). New York: Wiley.

Lieberman, P. (2006). *Toward an evolutionary biology of language.* Cambridge, MA: Belknap/Harvard.

Longworth, C. E., Keenan, S. E., Barker, R. A., Marslen-Wilson, & Tyler, L. K. (2005). The basal ganglia and rule-governed language use: Evidence from vascular and degenerative conditions. *Brain, 128,* 584–596.

Maess, B., Koelsch, S., Gunter, T. C., & Friederici, A. D. (2001). Musical syntax is processed in Broca's area: An MEG study. *Nature Neuroscience, 4,* 540–545.

Maguire, E., Spiers, H., Good, C., Hartley, T., Frackowiak, R., & Burgess, N. (2003). Navigation expertise and the human hippocampus: A structural brain imaging analysis. *Hippocampus, 13,* 250–259.

Malenka, R., & Bear, M. (2004). LTP and LTD: An embarrassment of riches. *Neuron, 44,* 5–21.

Mandonnet, E., Nouet, A., Gatignol, P., Capelle, L., & Daffau, H. (2007). Does the left inferior longitudinal fasciculus play a role in language? A brain stimulation study. *Brain, 130,* 623–629.

Mar, R. A. (2004). The neuropsychology of narrative: story comprehension, story production and their interrelation. *Neuropsychologia, 42,* 1414–1434.

Marsh, J. (2006). Popular culture in the literacy curriculum: A Bordieuan analysis. *Reading Research Quarterly, 41,* 160–175.

McCandliss, B. D., Cohen, L., & Dehaene, S. (2003). The visual word form area: Expertise for reading in the fusiform gyrus. *Trends in Cognitive Sciences, 7,* 293–299.

McClelland, J. L., & Rogers, T. T. (2003). The parallel distributed processing approach to semantic cognition. *Nature Reviews Neuroscience, 4,* 310–322.

Mechelli, A., Crinion, J. T., Long, S., Friston, K. J., Ralph, M. A. L., Patterson, K., McClelland, J. L., & Price, C. J. (2005). Dissassociating reading processes on the basis of neuronal interactions. *Journal of Cognitive Neuroscience, 17,* 1753–1765.

Mechelli, A., Gorno-Tempini, M. L., & Price, C. J. (2003). Neuroimaging studies of word and pseudo word reading: Consistencies, inconsistencies, and limitations. *Journal of Cognitive Neuroscience, 15*, 260–271.

Michel, C. M., Murray, M. M., Lantz, G., Gonzalez, S., Spinelli, L., & de Peralta, R. G. (2004). EEG source imaging. *Clinical Neurophysiology, 115*, 2195–2222.

Millikan, R. G. (1984). *Language, thought, and other biological categories: New foundations for realism.* Cambridge, MA: MIT Press.

Milne, D. (2005). *Teaching the brain to read.* Artarmon, Australia: SK Publishing.

Mitchell, T. M., Hutchinson, R., Niculescu, R. S., Pereira, F., Wang, X., Just, M., & Newman, S. (2004). Learning to decode cognitive states from brain images. *Machine Learning, 57*, 145–175.

Mody, M. (2004). Neurobiological correlates of language and reading impairments. In C. A. Stone, E. R. Silliman, B. J. Ehren, & K. Apel (Eds.), *Handbook of language and literacy: Development and disorders* (pp. 49–72). New York: Guilford.

Moita, M. A. P., Rosis, S., Zhou, Y., LeDoux, J. E., & Blair, H. T. (2004). Putting fear in its place: Remapping of hippocampal place cells during fear conditioning. *The Journal of Neuroscience, 24*, 7015–7023.

Müller, O., & Hagoort, P. (2006). Access to lexical information in language comprehension: Semantics before syntax. *Journal of Cognitive Neuroscience, 18*, 84–96.

Müller, R. A., & Basho, S. (2004). Are nonlinguistic functions in Broca's area prerequisites for language acquisition? fMRI findings from anontogenetic viewpoint. *Brain and Language, 89*, 329–336

Munakata, Y., & Johnson, M. (Eds.). (2006). *Processes of change in brain and cognitive development.* Oxford: Oxford University Press.

Nelissen, K., Luppino, G., Vanduffel, W., Rizzolatti, G., & Orban, G. A. (2005). Observing others: Multiple action representation in the frontal lobe. *Science, 310*, 332–336.

Newman, A. J., Pancheva, R., Ozawa, K., Neville, H. J., & Ullman, M. T. (2001). An event-related fMRI study of syntactic and semantic violations. *Journal of Psycholinguistic Research, 30*, 339–364.

Nieuwland, M. S., & Van Berkum, J. J. A. (2006). When peanuts fall in love: N400 evidence for the power of discourse. *Journal of Cognitive Neuroscience, 18*, 1098–1111.

Noppenny, U., & Price, C. J. (2004). An fMRI study of syntactic adaptation. *Journal of Cognitive Neuroscience, 16*, 702–713.

Nunez, P. L. (2006). *Electric fields of the brain: The neurophysics of EEG* (2nd ed.). Oxford: Oxford University Press.

O'Reilly, R. C. (2006). Biologically based computational models of high-level cognition. *Science, 314*, 91–94.

Oliveri, M., Romero, L., & Papagno, C. (2004). Left but not right temporal involvement in opaque idiom comprehension: A repetitive transcranial magnetic stimulation study. *Journal of Cognitive Neuroscience, 16*, 848–855.

Osterhout, L., Kim, A., & Kuperberg, G. (in press). The neurobiology of sentence comprehension. In M. Spivey, M. Joannisse, & K. McRae (eds.), *The Cambridge handbook of psycholinguistics.* Cambridge: Cambridge University Press.

Osterhout, L., McLaughlin, J., Pitkänen, I., Frenck-Mestre, C., & Molinaro, N. (2006). Novice learners, longitudinal designs, and event-related potentials: A means for exploring the neurocognition of second language processing. *Language Learning, 56*, 199–230.

Oyama, S. (2000). *The ontogeny of information: Developmental systems and evolution* (2nd ed.). Durham, NC: Duke University Press.

Pammer, K., Hansen, P. C., Kringelbach, M. L., Holliday, I., Barnes, G., Hillebrand, A., Singh, K. D., & Cornelissen, P. L. (2004). Visual word recognition: The first half second. *Neuroimage, 22*, 1819–1825.

Papanicolaou, A. C., Pugh, K. R., Simos, P.G., & Mencl, W. E. (2004). Neuroimaging and brain research. In P. McCardle and V. Chhabra (Eds.), *The voice of evidence in reading research* (pp. 385–416). Baltimore: Brookes.

Pastalkova, E., Serrano, P., Pinkhasova, D., Wallace, E., Fenton, A. A., & Sacktor, T. C. (2006). Storage of spatial information by maintenance mechanism of LTP. *Science, 313*, 1141–1144.

Pepper, S. C. (1948). *World hypotheses: A study in evidence.* Berkeley: University of California Press.

Perfetti, C. A., & Bolger, D. J. (2004). The brain might read that way. *Scientific Studies of Reading, 8*, 293–304.

Petitot, J., Varela, F. J., Pachoud, B., & Roy, J. (Eds.). (1999). *Naturalizing phenomenology: Issues in contemporary phenomenology and cognitive science.* Stanford, CA: Stanford University Press.

Picton, T. W., Bentin, S., Berg, P., Donchin, E., Hillyard, S.A., Johnson, Jr., R., Miller, G. A., Ritter, W., Ruchkin, D.S., Rugg, M. D., & Taylor, M. J. (2000). Guidelines for using human event-related potentials to study cognition: Recording standards and publication criteria. *Psychophysiology, 37,* 127–152.

Pinker, S. (1997). *How the mind works.* New York: Norton.

Plaut, D. C., & Booth, J. R. (2000). Individual and developmental differences in semantic priming: Empirical and computational support for a single-mechanism account of lexical processing. *Psychological Review, 107,* 786–823.

Plaut, D. C., McClelland, J. L., Seidenberg, M. S., & Patterson, K. (1996). Understanding normal and impaired word reading: Computational principles in quasi-regular domains. *Psychological Review, 103,* 56–115.

Plotkin, H. C. (2004). *Evolutionary thought in psychology: A brief history.* Malden, MA: Blackwell.

Plunkett, K. (1993). Lexical segmentation and vocabulary growth in early language acquisition. *Journal of Child Language, 20,* 43–60.

Plunkett, K., & Sinha, C. (1992). Connectionism and developmental theory. *British Journal of Developmental Psychology, 10,* 209–254.

Poeppel, D. (1996). A critical review of PET studies of phonological processing. *Brain and Language, 55,* 317–351.

Price, C. J., & Devlin, J. T. (2003). The myth of the visual word form area. *Neuroimage, 19,* 473–481.

Price, C. J., Thierry, G., & Griffiths, T. (2005). Speech-specific auditory processing: Where is it? *Trends in Cognitive Sciences, 9,* 271–276.

Purves, D., Augustine, G. J., Fitzpatrick, D., Hall, W. C., LaMantia, A., McNamara, J. O., & White, L. E. (2007). *Neuroscience* (4th ed.). Sunderland, MA: Sinauer Associates.

Ramachandran, V.S. (2000). Mirror Neurons and imitation learning as the driving force behind "the great leap forward" in human evolution. *Edge, 69,* May 29, 2000. Retrieved August 1, 2006, from www.edge.org/3rd_culture/ramachandran/ramachandran_p1.html

Reader's Digest. (2007, March). Front cover.

Reese, H.W., & Overton, W. F. (1970). Models of development and theories of development. In L. R. Goulet and P. B. Baltes (Eds.), *Life-span developmental psychology: Research and theory* (pp. 115–145). New York: Academic Press.

Richardson, D. C., Spivey, M. J., Barsalou, L. W., & McRae, K. (2003). Spatial representations activated during real-time comprehension of verbs. *Cognitive Science, 27,* 767–780.

Rizzolatti, G., & Arbib, M. A. (2002). Language within our grasp. In J. T. Cacioppo, G. G. Bernston, R. Adolphs, C. S. Carter, R. J. Davidson, et al. (Eds.), *Foundations in social neuroscience* (pp. 247–258). Cambridge, MA: MIT Press.

Robertson, D. A., Gernsbacher, M. A., Guidotti, S., Robertson, R., Irwin, W., Mock, B. J., & Campana, M. E. (2000). Functional neuroanatomy of the cognitive process of mapping during discourse comprehension. *Psychological Science, 11,* 255–260.

Rodd, J. M., Davis, M. H., & Johnsrude, I. S. (2005). The neural mechanisms of speech comprehension: fMRI studies of semantic ambiguity. *Cerebral Cortex, 15,* 1261–1269.

Ronis, D. L. (2007). *Brain-compatible assessments* (2nd ed.). Thousand Oaks, CA: Corwin Press.

Ruddell, R. B., & Unrau, N. J. (Eds.). (2004). *Theoretical models and processes of reading* (5th ed.). Newark, DE: International Reading Association.

Rumelhart, D. E. (1994). Toward an interactive model of reading. In R. B. Ruddell, M. R. Ruddell, & H. Singer (Eds.), *Theoretical models and processes of reading* (4th ed, pp. 864–894). Newark, DE: International Reading Association.

Rummelhart, D. E., & McClelland, J. L. (1992). An interactive activation model of context effects in letter perception: Part 2. The contextual enhancement effect and some tests and extensions of the model. *Psychological Review, 89,* 60–94.

Ryle, G. (1949). *The concept of mind.* London: Hutchinson's University Library.

Sakai, K. L., Noguchi, Y., Takeuchi, T., & Wantanabe, E. (2002). Selective priming of syntactic processing by event-related transcranial magnetic stimulation of Broca's area. *Neuron, 35,* 1177–1182.

Sandak, R., Mencl, W. E., Frost, S. J., & Pugh, K. R. (2004). The neurobiological basis of skilled and impaired reading: Recent findings and new directions. *Scientific Studies of Reading, 8,* 273–292.

Sanes, J. N., & Donoghue, J. P. (2000). Plasticity and primary motor cortex. *Annual Review of Neuroscience, 23,* 393–415.

Schmithorst, V. J., Holland, S. K., & Plante, E. (2006). Cognitive modules utilized for narrative comprehension in children: A functional magnetic resonance imaging study. *Neuroimage, 29,* 254–266.

Schrödinger, E. (1944/1992). *What is life?* With *Mind and matter* and *Autobiographical sketches.* Cambridge: Canto/Cambridge University.

Scorolli, C., & Borghi, A. M. (2007). Sentence comprehension and action: Effector specific modulation of the motor system. *Brain Research, 1130,* 119–124.

Scott, S. K., Leff, A. P., Wise, R. J. (2003). Going beyond the information given: A neural system supporting semantic interpretations. *Neuroimage, 19,* 870–876.

Searle, J. R. (1992). *The rediscovery of the mind.* Cambridge, MA: MIT Press.

Seidenberg, M. S., & McClelland, J. L. (1989). A distributed developmental model of visual word recognition and naming. *Psychological Review, 84,* 321–330.

Shaywitz, B. A., Pugh, K. R., Jenner, A. R., Fulbright, R. K., Fletcher, J. M., Gore, J. C., & Shaywitz, S.E. (2000). The neurobiology of reading and reading disability (dyslexia). In M. L. Kamil, P. B. Mosenthal, P. D. Pearson, & R. Barr (Eds.), *Handbook of reading research, volume III* (pp. 229–250). Mahwah, NJ: Erlbaum.

Shaywitz, B. A., Lyon, G. R., & Shawitz, S. E. (2006). The role of functional magnetic resonance imaging in understanding reading and dyslexia. *Developmental Neuropsychology, 30,* 613–632.

Shaywitz, S. (2003). *Overcoming dyslexia: A new and complete science-based program for reading problems at any level.* New York: Knopf.

Sober, E. (2000). *The philosophy of biology* (2nd ed.). Boulder, CO: Westview Press.

Society for Neuroscience. (2005). *Final Program, Neuroscience 2005, SfN 35th Annual Meeting.* Washington, DC: Author.

Soltesz, I. (2006). *Diversity in the neuronal machine.* Oxford: Oxford University Press.

Spitsyna, G., Warren, J. E., Scott, S. K., Turkheimer, F. E., & Wise, J. S. (2006). Converging language streams in the human temporal lobe. *The Journal of Neuroscience. 26,* 7328–7336.

Spivey, M. (2006). *The continuity of mind.* Oxford: Oxford University Press.

St. George, M., Kutas, M., Martinez, A., & Sereno, M. I. (1999). Semantic integration in reading: Engagement of the right hemisphere during discourse processing. *Brain, 122,* 1317–1325.

Sterelney, K. (2003). *Thought in a hostile world: The evolution of human cognition.* London: Blackwell.

Stewart, L., Meyer, B., Frith, U., & Rothwell, J. (2001). Left posterior BA37 is involved in object recognition: A TMS study. *Neuropsychologia, 39,* 1–6.

Stowe, L. A., Haverkort, M., & Zwarts, F. (2005). Rethinking the neurological basis of language. *Lingua, 115,* 997–1042.

Stowe, L. A., Paans, A. M. J., Wijers, A., & Zwarts, F. (2004). Activations of "motor" and other non-language structures during sentence comprehension. *Brain & Language, 89,* 290–299.

Striedter, G. F. (2005). *Principles of brain evolution.* Sunderland, MA: Sinauer Associates.

Tate, M. L. (2005). *Reading and language arts worksheets don't grow dendrites: 20 literacy strategies that engage the brain.* Thousand Oaks, CA: Corwin.

Thelen, E., & Smith, L. B. (2006). Dynamic systems theory. In R. M. Lerner (Ed.) & W. Damon (Series Ed.), *Handbook of child psychology: Vol. 1. Theoretical models of human development* (6th ed., pp. 258–312). New York: Wiley.

Thompson, E. (2007). *Mind in life: Biology, phenomeonology, and the sciences of mind.* Cambridge, MA: Belknap Harvard.

Thompson, E., Lutz, A., & Cosmelli, D. (2005). Neurophenomenology: An introduction for neurophilosophers. In A. Brook & K. Akins (eds.), *Cognition and the brain: The philosophy and neuroscience movement* (pp. 40–97). New York: Cambridge University Press.

Tinbergen, N. (1963). On the aims and methods of ethology. *Zeitschrift für Tierpsychologie, 20,* 410–429.

Tootle, R. B. H., Tsao, D., & Vanduffel, W. (2003). Neuroimaging weighs in: Humans meet macaques in "primate" visual cortex. *The Journal of Neuroscience, 23,* 3981–3989.

Tse, D., Langston, R. F., Kakeyamaa, M., Bethus, I., Spooner, P. A., Wood, E. R., Witter, M. P., & Morris, R. G. M. (2007). Schemas and memory consolidation. *Science, 316,* 76–82.

Uttal, W. R. (2001). *The new phrenology: The limits of localizing cognitive processes in the brain.* Cambridge, MA: MIT Press.

Uylings, H. B. M. (2006). Development of the human cortex and the concept of "critical" and "sensitive" periods. *Language Learning, 56,* 59–90.

Van Berkum, J. J. A., Hagoort, P., & Brown, C. M. (1999). Semantic integration in sentences and discourse: Evidence from the N400. *Journal of Cognitive Neuroscience, 11,* 657–671.

Van den Brink, D., & Hagoort, P. (2004). The influence of semantic and syntactic context constraints on lexical selection and integration in spoken-word comprehension as revealed by ERPs. *Journal of Cognitive Neuroscience, 16,* 1068–1084.

Van der Velde, F., & de Kamps, M. (2006). Neural blackboard architectures of combinatorial structures in cognition. *Behavioral and Brain Sciences, 29,* 37–108.

Van Orden, G. C., Holden, J. C., & Turvey, M. T. (2003). Self-organization of cognitive performance. *Journal of Experimental Psychology: General, 132,* 331–350.

Vandenberghe, R., Nobre, A. C., & Price, C. J. (2002). The response of left temporal cortex to sentences. *Journal of Cognitive Neuroscience, 14,* 550–560.

Varma, S., Schwartz, D. L., & McCandliss, B. (2006). Is neuroscience a learning science? In S. Barab, K. Hay, & D. Hickey (Chairs), Proceedings of the 7th International Conference on Learning Sciences. Retrieved February 2, 2007, from http://portal.acm.org/citation.cfm?id=1150034.1150149

Verela, F. J., Thompson, E., Rosch, E. (1991). *The embodied mind: Cognitive science and human experience.* Cambridge, MA: MIT Press.

Vigneau, M., Beaucousin, V., Herve, P. Y., Duffau, H., Crivello, F., Houde, O., Mazoyer, B., Tzourio-Mazoyer, N. (2006). Meta-analyzing left hemisphere language areas: Phonology, semantics, and sentence processing. *Neuroimage, 30,* 1414–1432.

Vigneau, M., Jobard, G., Mazoyer, B., & Tzourio-Mazoyer, N. (2005). Word and non-word reading: What role for the visual word for area? *Neuroimage, 27,* 694–705.

Wallentin, M., Østergaard, S., Lund, T.E., Østergaard, L., & Roepstorff, A. (2005). Concrete spatial language: See what I mean? *Brain & Language, 92,* 221–233.

Wartenburger, I., Steinbrink, J., Telkemeyer, S., Friedrich, M., Friederici, A. D., & Obrig, H. (2007). The processing of prosody: Evidence of interhemispheric specialization at the age of four. *Neuroimage, 34,* 416–425.

Waters, G., Caplan, D., Alpert, N., & Stanczak, L. (2003). Individual differences in rCBF correlates of syntactic processing in sentence comprehension: Effects of working memory and speed of processing. *Neuroimage, 19,* 101–112.

Watson, J. D., & Crick, F. H. C. (1953). Genetical implications of the structure of deoxyribonucleic acid. *Nature, 171,* 964–967.

Watson-Gegeo, K. A. (2004). Mind, language, and epistemology: Toward a language socialization paradigm for SLA. *The Modern Language Journal, 88,* 331–350.

Wernicke, C. (1874). *Der aphasische Symptomenkomplex. Eine psychologische Studie auf anatomischer Basis.* Breslau: Cohn and Weigart.

Willingham, D. T., & Dunn, E. W. (2003). What neuroimaging and brain localization can do, cannot do, and should not do for social psychology. *Journal of Personality and Social Psychology, 85,* 662–671.

Wolfe, P., & Nevills, P. (2004). *Building the reading brain, pre-K-3.* Thousand Oaks, CA: Corwin.

Xu, B., Grafman, J., Gaillard, W. D., Ishii, K., Vega-Bermudez, F., Pietrini, P., Reeves-Tyer, P, DiCamillo, P., & Theodore, W. (2001). Conjoint and extended neural networks for the computation of speech codes: The neural basis of selective impairment in reading words and pseudo words. *Cerebral Cortex, 11,* 267–277.

Xu, J., Kemeny, S., Park, G., Frattali, C., & Braun, A. (2005). Language in context: Emergent features of word, sentence, and narrative comprehension. *Neuroimage, 25,* 1002–1015.

Zahn, R., Schwartz, M., & Huber, W. (2006). Functional activation studies of word processing in the recovery from aphasia. *Journal of Physiology — Paris, 99,* 370–385.

Part III
Changing Views of Text

10 Text Comprehension
A Retrospective, Perspective, and Prospective

Emily Fox and Patricia A. Alexander

University of Maryland

Since reading first became recognized as a field of study in the early 20th century, understanding of written linguistic information or text comprehension has been a focus of attention (Pearson & Hamm, 2005). This attention has been manifest in some form regardless of the views toward schooling, learning, and literacy that have prevailed across reading's colorful and sometimes contentious history (Alexander & Fox, 2004, in press). Indeed, it is almost impossible to discuss reading without considering the traces that human encounters with text leave on the thoughts or behaviors of the individuals or groups engaged in that literacy act.

Perhaps because comprehension has been and remains such a centerpiece in reading, its very nature has to some degree escaped the level of scrutiny to which texts and pedagogical practices have been subjected over past decades. Certainly, there have been theories and models that have sought to capture the process by which individuals or groups extract or, alternatively, construct meaning from text—models we will consider herein. But within those theories or models, it may be less apparent how the very conception of comprehension has been adapted to conform to theoretical assumptions or to model parameters. Yet, is it conceivable that the forms of texts in postindustrial societies could be so markedly transformed in the past century, that the theoretical orientations toward reading could be so dramatically altered, the outcomes of reading so varied, or the character of reading instruction so repeatedly reformed, all without a concomitant shift in our understanding of what it means to comprehend? That is the central question we explore in this analysis of text comprehension.

As a means of addressing our guiding question, we examine text comprehension in three phases: retrospective, perspective, and prospective. First, we look back at reading's recent past and to the prevailing view of text comprehension indicative of that period. Our intention in this retrospective is to offer a generalized framework of text comprehension that is illustrative of the overall theoretical and empirical work of the time. To support that framework, we make reference to particular process models laid out in landmark publications that exemplify or typify the features we identify.

In the perspective phase, we reflect on the view of text comprehension that currently predominates in the research literature. Our goal in this analysis is to ascertain the state-of-the-state in the domain of reading and to consider the implications for how text comprehension is defined, modeled, investigated, and presented in the classroom. Here again, we focus on specific theoretical models and empirical works that underlie the characteristics of text comprehension that we discern.

Finally, we look ahead to the future of text comprehension research. Through this prospective, we attempt to articulate a hypothesized framework for text comprehension that is reflective of the emerging theory and research from various venues, including studies of hypermedia learning, expertise development, and discourse processing.

Although we attempted to be broad and encompassing in our analysis of the reading literature, there were certain assumptions about the nature of learning and about the reading process that guided our interpretations.

- Comprehending is a process that involves at least three elements: reader, text, and activity (RAND, 2002); that is, comprehension may result from the interaction of a person (reader) engaged with linguistic materials (text) for some given or self-generated purpose (activity). More recently, those three elements have been expanded to consider the time and place of such engagement (situation).
- Comprehension results in the formation of mental representations of some durability, although those representations can be short-lived, difficult to resurrect, or hard to communicate (Kintsch, 1986). There are presently theories of learning that do not acknowledge mental representations or structures as centerpieces of human cognition (Greeno & Moore, 1993). However, our examination is built on the assumption that text comprehension does require the internalization of thoughts, images, or conceptions that can be reflected upon and potentially shared with others.
- How the comprehension process unfolds and what readers build in terms of mental representations are reflective of the interaction between reader, text, activity, and situation (Jenkins, 1974). Specifically, characteristics of the reader (e.g., prior knowledge or motivations), text (e.g., familiarity and coherence), activity (e.g., locate details or evaluate arguments), or the situation (e.g., cooperative groups or high-stakes testing situation) significantly affect the process of comprehending and the internal representations formed.

With these guiding assumptions in place, let us now consider the prevailing framework for comprehension manifest in the research in the later half of the 20th century. We should note that the literature upon which we base our three-phase analysis has been predominately conducted within postindustrial societies, most notably the United States, and is most concerned with reading in school settings. Therefore, we do not claim that the insights we offer generalize to other venues (e.g., developing nations or on-the-job reading).

EXTRACTING AND ASSEMBLING THE MESSAGE: A RETROSPECTIVE

General models of text comprehension for any given period are necessarily bound up with considerations of the prevailing view of text, along with judgments as to what can be taken as a typical text and the reader's typical interaction with that text, situated within the typical instructional context. How would we typify the text, reader activity, and context within United States classrooms in the 1960s and 1970s, and how were those conditions mirrored in models of text comprehension?

As remains true in contemporary studies, the emphasis in the reading literature during this period was on younger children acquiring the fundamentals of text processing (Barr, 1984/2002). The first edition of *Theoretical Models and Processes of Reading* (Singer & Ruddell, 1970), which presented a representative sample of general models of the reading process prevalent at the time, was partially motivated and funded by the National Institute of Child Health and Human Development (NICHD) for its potential contribution to scientifically-based remediation of children's difficulties with acquiring these fundamentals.

There was a growing body of work on the diagnosis and treatment of those with reading problems, as well as consideration for linguistic diversity and the potential conflicts with school and everyday language (Shuy, 1981). Direct instruction (Osborn, 1968) and explicit teaching of strategies (Pearson & Gallagher, 1983) were seen as mechanisms for addressing the problems in comprehension that were documented among young and struggling readers. Further, with the increased presence of cognitive psychology, and the emergent interest in schema theory, there was a strong awareness that prior or background knowledge was likely to play a significant role in the understandings that would be reached in readers' encounters with text.

Even though more cognitive orientations to learning and literacy had begun to fill the pages of the research literature, schools of this period still reflected beliefs in the 3Rs: recitation, repetition, and replication. In effect, teachers frequently lectured and then questioned or interrogated their students over readings (i.e., recitation) with classroom discussion and cooperative learning models serving more as the exceptions than the pedagogical rule (Mehan, 1979). Reading lessons were focused on acquiring a carefully sequenced set of skills, and repeated skill practice (i.e., repetition) was seen as an essential ingredient in that skill development.

During reading instruction, students generally encountered a single purposefully-crafted text that was often part of a chosen basal program. Those texts were frequently crafted to control for certain linguistic elements (e.g., vocabulary, passage length, or sentence structure), and were accompanied by practice materials intended to test comprehension and reinforce target skills through a series of brief and often unrelated exercises. As Rosenblatt (1978/1994) suggested, it appeared that the text, as part of literacy instruction, was most often conceived as a means of transmitting particular factual or procedural information rather than as a literary work with multiple interpretations and the potential for an aesthetic response.

In keeping with these typical features, early models of comprehension explained reading comprehension as the extraction and assembly or reconstruction of a message contained in a text (e.g., Gibson & Levin, 1975; LaBerge & Samuels, 1974; Singer, 1969, 1970), with text seen as synonymous with the traditional written document (e.g., book, story, article; Alexander & Jetton, 2003). That extraction (i.e., replication) was to occur at the level of the individual reader working as an independent agent. While it might be expected that individuals would be more or less successful at uncovering the meaning of the given text as a consequence of their abilities or experiences, there was the presumption that arriving at the designated message in the text *was* the desired outcome. Even though much of the basal material used in the early grades was narrative in form, it often served an informational or efferent function (Rosenblatt, 1978/1994).

What was the model of comprehension that arose from the interaction of these reader, text, and activity elements? We would contend that the prevailing view of text comprehension from this period could be best captured by an *extraction and assembly model* (see Table 10.1). In essence, text comprehension involved the reader's assembly or other generation of an internal mental representation of the incoming or external text information, which was matched to or reconciled with existing or internal mental

Table 10.1   Elements of Text Comprehension in Extraction-Assembly Models

Element	Description
View of text	Static container or transmitter of message coded into written symbols
Typical text	Single unambiguous text often specifically crafted to convey a message or develop a skill (e.g., basal reader)
Reader's activity	Extracting and assembling or reconstructing information from the text, matching it to existing mental contents
Reader's product	Mental representation of the text information as matched with existing mental contents

contents (Gibson & Levin, 1975; Singer, 1969). Important text factors related to this view of comprehension included readability, text structure, concreteness, and typography (Gibson & Levin, 1975).

> How material is written and presented in text—its style, what content is included, what is excluded in relation to the topic, and even physical features of presentation—make a difference in the ease of the reader's comprehension and consequently what he can learn. (p. 414)

This prevailing orientation toward the reader and text interaction is well represented in the models collected in the first and second editions of *Theoretical Models and Processes of Reading* (Singer & Ruddell, 1970, 1976). These models of reading originated from a psycholinguistic (e.g., Goodman, 1970), information processing (e.g., LaBerge & Samuels, 1974), developmental (e.g., Singer, 1969, 1970), or affective orientation (e.g., Mathewson, 1976). Although originating from such different orientations, text comprehension in all of these models of reading was viewed as some form of extraction and assembly of meaning, where the reader's task was to "produce an oral language equivalent of the graphic input...and reconstruct the meaning of what he is reading" (Goodman, 1970, p. 265), as he "decodes the meaning of the reading selection" (Mathewson, 1976, p. 663), and engages in "organization of...word meanings" (LaBerge & Samuels, 1974) to develop a "reconstructed or transformed message" (Singer, 1969, p. 151).

Although comprehension was recognized as being critical, the bulk of the modeling and research attention at the time focused on the more or less effortful "extraction" of the encoded meaning in the written text via perceptual and word recognition processes (Samuels & Kamil, 1984/2002). How the reader assembled or reconstructed an understanding of the text from these meaning units was often glossed over or assumed to happen on its own, via overarching language processing capabilities.

By the early 1980s, however, a shift had begun to a more bidirectional view of text comprehension, one in which the reader's contribution in terms of constructive activity played a much more significant role, where a text might have more than one interpretation, and in which top-down integration as well as bottom-up assembly processes might be involved. Samuels (1983) captured the tenor of this shift in his discussion of inside- and outside-the-head factors influencing reading comprehension:

> No longer do we think of reading as a one-way street from writer to reader, with the reader's task being to render a literal interpretation of the text, and, in a classroom situation, come up with the "correct answer." Instead, today we think of reading as the active construction of a text's meaning, proceeding from an interaction between writer and reader. (p. 261)

THE-STATE-OF-THE-STATE: TEXT COMPREHENSION IN PERSPECTIVE

Over the course of the last 20 years, there have been major theoretical, empirical, and pedagogical shifts in perceptions of reading and what constitutes the typical reading situation. The dominant paradigm in recent years has been *constructive-integrative models* of comprehension that allow for the possibility of more individualized response, as each reader builds his or her own mental representation of what the text is saying and of what it means (RAND, 2002). The interaction of bottom-up and top-down processes during this constructive activity provides a role for the reader's knowledge and for the context in shaping the text's message (Goldman & Rakestraw, 2000; van den Broek, Young, Tzeng, & Linderholm, 1999).

Possible products of this constructive process include multiple levels of mental representation, such as the textbase and situation model levels outlined in Kintsch's highly influential construction-integration model (1998). Within this model, the textbase refers to "those propositions that are directly derived from the text," whereas the situation model consists of "propositions (this includes imagery and action, which we also represent as propositions) contributed from long-term memory" (p. 49).

The theoretical rationale and empirical support for the predominant models within the currently prevailing construction/integration orientation are well represented in the volume on *Models of Understanding Text*, edited by Britton and Graesser (1996), as well as in *The Construction of Mental Representations During Reading*, edited by van Oostendorp and Goldman (1999). The first of these works presents a variety of models of text understanding targeted at different levels of explanation and different types of reading situations. Graesser and Britton (1996) identify five metaphors for text understanding that they see as shared among all of the models offered, and from them derive a definition of text understanding that articulates an agenda for the investigation of what occurs in reading comprehension:

> Text understanding is the dynamic process of constructing coherent representations and inferences at multiple levels of text and context, within the bottleneck of a limited-capacity working memory. (p. 350)

The second work, *The Construction of Mental Representations During Reading* (van Oostendorp & Goldman, 1999), presents five models of processing and representation, along with discussions of specific processes and strategies associated with the construction of representations from text and with the monitoring and adaptation of representations during this construction process. Goldman and van Oostendorp (1999) identify a number of unresolved issues and challenges for research that arise from the way text comprehension is conceptualized and investigated, including when, why, and how readers update their representations, and how readers handle the integration of representations at different levels or from multiple sources and across multiple modalities.

Much of the research related to the construction/integration orientation has used narrative texts to explore readers' constructions, as being possibly more inference-driven and dependent on general world knowledge (e.g., Gernsbacher, Robertson, Palladino, & Werner, 2004; Graesser, Singer, & Trabasso, 1994; Graesser, Swamer, Baggett, & Sell, 1996; Zwaan, 1996; Zwaan & Radvansky, 1998; Zwaan, Magliano, & Graesser, 1995). Less often, contemporary research has focused on readers' constructive activity while reading expository or informational texts, and has explicitly considered readers' learning of new information (Goldman, Varma, & Coté, 1996); however, these expository texts are typically assumed to be credible and authoritative sources of information, often with an "invisible" author, as in a textbook (see Table 10.2).

Table 10.2 Elements of Text Comprehension in Constructive-Integrative Models

Element	Description
View of text	Static written presentation of propositional network
Typical text	Single, often narrative, text or an informational text from authoritative/invisible author (e.g., textbook)
Reader's activity	Constructing meaning from text and background knowledge, using integration, elaboration, interpretation
Reader's product	Mental representations of a text on a propositional level and as integrated with background knowledge – e.g., textbase and situation model

During the 1990s and even into the early 2000s (before the No Child Left Behind Act left its indelible mark on school curricula), the typical reading situation still entailed a reader encountering a single text. Moreover, in this theoretical iteration, the reader is still primarily engaged with grappling with the text *as given*, rather than the text as the product of an author or authors. Important text factors that were perceived as influential within this literature were genre, structure, coherence, complexity, and media form, such as textbook or electronic media (see RAND, 2002, for an overview of possible sources of variability related to text factors). In addition to those factors that are more or less inherent in the text itself, consideration has been given to the interaction of text and reader factors in regard to such aspects as demandingness of text, appropriateness or familiarity of content, and interest level (RAND, 2002).

As we move deeper into this new century, several trends are becoming more evident. For one, there is seemingly a growing disconnect between the nature of reading being espoused within the research community and the practice of reading being demanded by national mandates and carried out in classrooms—emphases that bear a striking resemblance to earlier decades (Pressley & Allington, 1999). For another, in the last decade there has been a rising interest in the way in which the social context and the human and non-human resources that are part of the overall learning environment shape the understandings constructed from reader and text interactions (Wade & Moje, 2000). Further, our understanding of typical reading situations is now broadening to include the reading of multiple informational texts (Afflerbach & VanSledright, 2001; Perfetti, Rouet, & Britt, 1999; Wineburg, 1991), texts needing evaluation for credibility or accuracy (Horowitz, 1994), argumentative, persuasive, or two-sided texts (Chambliss, 1995; Kardash & Howell, 2000; Kardash & Scholes, 1995), hypermedia (Goldman & Rakestraw, 2000; Leu, Kinzer, Coiro, & Cammack, 2004), blogs, and such ephemera as text messages (Carrington, 2005). Important factors associated with the emerging conception of text comprehension beyond those already discussed include:

- non-traditional forms of text, including oral discussions and graphic representations (Wade & Moje, 2000);
- text features only possible or only emphasized in electronic environments, such as use of color, interactivity, animations, and iconic cues indicating links (Leu et al., 2004);
- readers' capability to modify, enhance, program, link, collapse, and collaborate when using forms of electronic text (Anderson-Inman & Reinking, 1998);
- explicitness or directness of connections and the degree of congruence among multiple texts (Alexander & Jetton, 2003; Perfetti et al., 1999).

As a consequence of these emergent trends, models of comprehension have become strained, as researchers try to talk about what reading comprehension means across diverse contexts involving both traditional and alternative contexts. Primarily due to the expansion in what is now seen as text and what now qualifies as a reading situation, combined with the heightened role of the sociocultural context and social interactions, the call for a new and improved understanding of reading comprehension is being heard in the field (Coiro, 2003; Leu et al., 2004).

However, this concern has typically been approached in terms of adding on newly-requisite skills to the already burgeoning litany, so that our notion of comprehension has been enlarged to allow for an additional text type or more complex reading situation. To the contrary, there is growing evidence that what is required is *not* an expansion of existing models but rather a fundamental reconceptualization of the nature of text comprehension. Reflective of these expanding perspectives on text comprehension, there has been an array of boundary-testing studies. Foci of these boundary-testing studies include:

Table 10.3 Elements of Text Comprehension in Transitional Extensions

Element	Description
View of text	Fluid or static presentation in single or multiple modalities of single or multiple linked propositional networks
Typical text	Multiple informational texts, texts needing evaluation for credibility or accuracy, argumentative texts, non-static or non-linear texts, hypermedia, blogs, text messages
Reader's activity	Constructing meaning while connecting across texts; creating individual navigational path through links; considering author; responding interactively, building collaborative understanding
Reader's product	Mental representations of text/context – of text meaning, of topic, of text as product of author, of structure of intertext relations (for text networks like hypermedia), dialogic representation of text as ongoing conversation

- use of electronic books (De Jong & Bus, 2004);
- cohesion in hypertext (McNamara & Shapiro, 2005);
- strategies for navigating in hypertext (Salmerón, Cañas, Kintsch, & Fajardo, 2005);
- effects of structure and genre in an on-line newspaper (Vaughan & Dillon, 2006);
- computer text interface vs. traditional print (Kerr & Symons, 2006);
- signaling of hyperlinks (De Ridder, 2002);
- the role of text annotations (Wallen, Plass, & Brunken, 2005);
- hypermedia and cognitive flexibility (Spiro, Coulson, Feltovich, & Anderson 2004);
- author visibility (Nolen, 1995; Paxton, 1997, 2002); and,
- text believability (Horowitz, 1994).

Those studies relate aspects of text as more widely defined and in other than the typical reading situation to comprehension, pushing past a single, linear, "given" text, and together represent what we term "transitional extensions" of the current understanding of text comprehension (see Table 10.3).

FUTURE DIRECTIONS IN RESEARCH AND EMERGING CONCERNS FOR PRACTICE: PROSPECTIVE

Our intention in the final segment of this chapter is to project forward into the next decade of text research. As we transition into the prospective view, we build the case that we are at a turning point in reading, and that more than cosmetic adjustments in the models of text comprehension that have existed for many decades are needed. The question arises: If comprehension is the construction of mental representations of text, which itself has been more broadly configured, then what kinds of formation or reformation are occurring and how?

We may need now to restructure our understanding of text comprehension in light of the need to account for what's going on in these more varied reading situations. In essence, what makes them all reading? This perspective stands in contrast to a more balkanized understanding that involves a separate account of what comprehension means for each possible reading context. Do we go the direction of having more and more forms of mental representation that can be co-constructed, including textbase and situation model of text meaning, situation model of the topic, model of the text as product of author, model of structure of intertext relations (for text networks like hypermedia), or dialogic model of text as ongoing conversation? Or is there a way to reconceptualize reading comprehension that will avoid this splintering? Herein we consider the frameworks, dimensions, and processes that need to be carefully weighed as researchers move ahead to articulate this next generation of text comprehension models.

Conceptual and developmental frames

What has been seen in the studies based on a more expanded view of text and reading situations suggests some possible directions the field can go in rethinking the notion of comprehension. For example, the current trajectory suggests that moving comprehension up a level, to be viewed more as a connective activity and less as construction, may address the limitations of the one reader/one text models that have existed. By connective activity, we are referring to readers' attempts to form a more global, integrated representation of a topic or issue from multiple text sources be they written or oral; linguistic, graphic, or pictorial (i.e., a metatext).

There are both apparent strengths and potential limitations of this alternative conception of text comprehension intended to accommodate the shifting character of text and text comprehension. One potential benefit of this transitional model is that reader intention plays an explicit and significant role in the mental representation. However, a number of concerns with this orientation must be acknowledged. For one, as occurs in historical analysis, readers must be able to reconcile contradictory information and weigh the accuracy and credibility of sources in the course of deriving what they are accepting as their interpretation. For another, it would be essential that readers have some broader sense of the topic or domain within their situation model in order to gauge the relevance or centrality of propositions contributed by each text.

Another possibility of reframing the one reader/one text orientation would be to move away from focusing on the constructive aspect of reading comprehension back toward a more phenomenological view that would look at the experience of reading and the approach to reading as a gestalt. This would require a reintegration of the reader, the text, the activity, process, and product to consider how they might all be part of a holistic and indivisible experience. Such a phenomenological approach has typically been associated with explorations of readers' literary experience (e.g., Braun & Cupchik, 2001). Its application as well to the experience of readers studying or learning from text would require a shift away from externally-imposed explanations of readers' activity and toward the interesting and challenging question of how it is to be a reader engaged in learning (or struggling to learn) from a text.

Several obvious strengths and limitations with this phenomenological orientation merit discussion. What we gain from a more holistic view of text comprehension is the greater acknowledgment of the complexity of this process as readers navigate and integrate the multiple sources and forms of text for dynamic purposes and within ever changing contexts.

This more holistic and experience-oriented view can also serve as a form of validity check on our finer-grained explanations of components of the overall reading activity. If we can explain the role of, say, text structure in a reader's ability to recall unfamiliar text, but our explanation bears no relation to the reader's actual experience while reading, then we are missing something important. And although we can isolate and hierarchically order separate levels of cognitive processing that are active in reading, such as recognition, recall, comprehension, application, analysis, synthesis, and evaluation (RAND, 2002), the reader certainly does not experience them as separate and sequenced. Rather, they are more likely to occur simultaneously, in an overlapping and interactive fashion.

A critical limitation to the exclusive adoption of such a phenomenological approach, however, would be the loss of just those levels of granularity, isolation, and sequencing. The ability to identify the etiology of successes or difficulties and, subsequently, to structure meaningful learning environments that build on those contributory factors would become far more problematic.

Whether text comprehension is perceived as reconstructive, constructive, connective, or phenomenological has to do largely with the ontological frame brought to reading research and practice. That is to say, what do individuals believe the nature of text comprehension to be? There is another frame that we believe will be essential to any viable, alternative model of text comprehension to arise in the future—the developmental nature of comprehension (Alexander, 2003). It will not be enough to document the core processes and components indicative of meaningful reader-text-context interactions, but also to ascertain how those aspects of the phenomenon change over time, as individuals become more competent readers or as their knowledge of and interest in the topics or domains about which they are reading develops.

We need to begin to understand how text comprehension at age 6 is fundamentally different than at age 16 or 60 under any ontological frame, or how text comprehension for those reading about an unfamiliar topic is different than for those reading in areas of personal interest or expertise. Neither past nor contemporary models of comprehension allow for such phase-like and stage-like changes. We have been emphasizing the need for an overarching understanding of text comprehension that encompasses the variety of texts, readers, activities, contexts, and situations. At the same time, however, this understanding of text comprehension must facilitate the explanation of real and important differences in the experiences of readers at different developmental levels within a coherent developmental framework.

Motivational and sociocultural influences

In keeping with this reconceptualized view of text comprehension, we project that future models of text comprehension will need to more fully account for what readers are called upon to do or have chosen to do in response to all of these texts in all of these reading situations. Readers come to this variety of texts and reading situations with specific intentions in the form of task mastery goals, with expectations of what they will be able to accomplish, with beliefs about reading, and with both enduring interest related to reading as an activity and transient interest triggered by this particular reading situation (Guthrie & Wigfield, 1999). These motivational processes appear to be implicated in readers' level of engagement while reading and in the nature of the comprehension that results (Guthrie & Wigfield, 2005).

In addition, the growing trend in the psychological literature toward the synergy between cognitive and socioemotional forces in human learning and development suggests that this trend may find its way into the study of text comprehension in even more significant ways. Specifically, past and current models of text comprehension have remained for the most part "coldly cognitive," (Brown, Bransford, Ferrara, & Campione, 1983) in that the role of affective processes has remained outside their scope. In the future, by comparison, the emotional valences and the sociocontextual features that are parts of readers' mental formations and reformations about text will merit greater consideration.

There is little question that the context of schools has a powerful hand in the manner in which text comprehension comes to be viewed and enacted. But the long-term ramifications of *school reading* within models of text comprehension need to be more systematically instantiated. From the standpoint of educational practice, researchers may need to consider how current pedagogical programs or instructional models intended to support or enhance text comprehension may require realignment in terms of emerging models. In effect, it is not only the models that must undergo significant reconceptualization, but also the nature of reading programs that should work in concert with such emergent models.

Certainly assessment practices within schools and measurements within empirical research must also keep pace with the multiple texts/multiple representations models of comprehension we are envisioning (Duke, 2005). At a minimum, we hold that it will be necessary to build systems that allow for dynamic (real-time) assessment of the reader-texts-context interface and that permit the gauging of connectivity as well as construction from text. Further, such assessment systems must keep pace with development, examine emotional/affective dimensions as well as cognitive outcomes, and accommodate the social exchanges that occur during the comprehension process.

Although this prospective on text comprehension may seem daunting, if not impossible, there is already groundbreaking and relevant research underway, as noted. For this new conceptualization of text comprehension to take form, however, these pockets of theory and research must come together in a more integrated manner. We are hopeful that this will, in fact, come to fruition. We feel that it is essential for this to occur if we are to take models of text comprehension to the new level, commensurate with the rapid and real changes unfolding in the nature of texts and in the nature of reading contexts.

CONCLUDING REMARKS

At the outset of this chapter, we framed our guiding question as addressing the likelihood that changes in text forms, changes in theoretical orientations toward reading, variety in the outcomes of reading, and reformations of the character of reading instruction could take place without requiring also an alteration of our understanding of text comprehension. We think that these observed changes are indeed driving us again toward a necessary restructuring of what text comprehension means. Although we have described this change mechanism as being driven by forces somewhat external to the central conception of comprehension, such change can also be viewed as bidirectional in nature. Our modified understanding of text comprehension will in turn reshape our interpretations of what counts as text, and of how reading does and should occur. As with all scientific investigations, in our investigation of reading the nature of our observations and of the tools we choose to employ will be determined by how we define our constructs. The type of redefinition we are suggesting here will have important consequences, potentially opening up new avenues for furthering our understanding of the complex phenomenon of reading.

REFERENCES

Afflerbach, P. A., & VanSledright, B. (2001). Hath! Doth! What! The challenges middle school students face when they read innovative history text. *Journal of Adolescent and Adult Literacy, 44,* 696–707.

Alexander, P. A. (2003). Profiling the developing reader: The interplay of knowledge, interest, and strategic processing. In C. M. Fairbanks, J. Worthy, B. Maloch, J. V. Hoffman, & D. L. Schallert (Eds.), *The Fifty-first Yearbook of the National Reading Conference* (pp. 47–65). Oak Creek, WI: National Reading Conference.

Alexander, P. A., & Fox, E. (2004). Historical perspective on reading research and practice. In R. B. Ruddell & N. Unrau (Eds.), *Theoretical models and processes of reading* (5th ed., pp. 33–68). Newark, DE: International Reading Association.

Alexander, P. A., & Fox, E. (in press). Reading in perspective. In M. J. Fresch (Ed.), *Fifty years of reading research: A historic look at current practices.* Newark, DE: International Reading Association.

Alexander, P. A., & Jetton, T. L. (2003). Learning from traditional and alternative texts: New conceptualization for an information age. In A. Graesser, M. Gernsbacher, & S. Goldman (Eds.), *Handbook of discourse processes* (pp. 199–241). Mahwah, NJ: Erlbaum.

Anderson-Inman, L., & Reinking, D. (1998). Learning from text in a post-typographic world. In C. R. Hynd (Ed.), *Learning from text across conceptual domains* (pp. 165–181). Mahwah, NJ: Erlbaum.

Barr, R. (2002). Beginning reading instruction: From debate to reformation. In P. D. Pearson, R. Barr, M. L. Kamil, & P. Mosenthal (Eds.), *Handbook of reading research* (pp. 545–581). Mahwah, NJ: Erlbaum. (Original work published 1984)

Braun, I. K., & Cupchik, G. C. (2001). Phenomenological and quantitative analyses of absorption in literary passages. *Empirical Studies of the Arts, 19*, 85–109.

Britton, B. K., & Graesser, A. C. (Eds.). (1996). *Models of understanding text.* Mahwah, NJ: Erlbaum.

Brown, A. L., Bransford, J. D., Ferrara, R. A., & Campione, J. C. (1983). Learning, remembering, and understanding. In J. H. Flavell & E. M. Markman (Eds.), *Handbook of child psychology, Vol. II* (pp. 77–166). New York: Wiley.

Carrington, V. (2005). Txting: The end of civilization (again)? *Cambridge Journal of Education, 35*, 161–175.

Chambliss, M. (1995). Text cues and strategies successful readers use to construct the gist of lengthy written arguments. *Reading Research Quarterly, 30*, 778–807.

Coiro, J. (2003). Exploring literacy on the Internet. *The Reading Teacher, 56*, 458–464.

De Jong, M. T., & Bus, A. G. (2004). The efficacy of electronic books in fostering kindergarten children's emergent story understanding. *Reading Research Quarterly, 39*, 378–393.

De Ridder, I. (2002). Visible or invisible links: Does the highlighting of hyperlinks affect incidental vocabulary learning, text comprehension, and the reading process? *Language Learning & Technology, 6*, 123–146.

Duke, N. K. (2005). Comprehension of what for what: Comprehension as a nonunitary construct. In S. G. Paris & S. A. Stahl (Eds.), *Children's reading comprehension and assessment* (pp. 93–104). Mahwah, NJ: Erlbaum.

Gernsbacher, M. A., Robertson, R. R. W., Palladino, P., & Werner, N. K. (2004). Managing mental representations during narrative construction. *Discourse Processing, 17*, 145–164.

Gibson, E., & Levin, H. (1975). *The psychology of reading.* Cambridge, MA: The MIT Press.

Goldman, S. R., & Rakestraw, J. A. (2000). Structural aspects of constructing meaning from text. In M. L. Kamil, P. B. Mosenthal, P. D. Pearson, & R. Barr (Eds.), *Handbook of reading research: Vol. III* (pp. 311–335). Mahwah, NJ: Erlbaum.

Goldman, S. R., & van Oostendorp, H. (1999). Conclusions, conundrums, and challenges for the future. In H. van Oostendorp & S. R. Goldman (Eds.), *The construction of mental representations during reading* (pp. 367–376). Mahwah, NJ: Erlbaum.

Goldman, S. R., Varma, S., & Coté, N. (1996). Extending capacity-constrained construction integration: Toward 'smarter' and more flexible models of text comprehension. In B. K. Britton & A. C. Graesser (Eds.), *Models of text comprehension* (pp. 73–113). Hillsdale, NJ: Erlbaum.

Goodman, K. (1970). Reading: A psycholinguistic guessing game. In H. Singer & R. Ruddell (Eds.), *Theoretical models and processes of reading* (pp. 259–271). Newark, DE: International Reading Association.

Graesser, A. C., & Britton, B. K. (1996). Five metaphors for text understanding. In B. K. Britton & A. C. Graesser (Eds.), *Models of text comprehension* (pp. 341–351). Hillsdale, NJ: Erlbaum.

Graesser, A. C., Singer, M., & Trabasso, T. (1994). Constructing inferences during narrative text comprehension. *Psychological Review, 101*, 371–395.

Graesser, A. C., Swamer, S. S., Baggett, W. B., & Sell, M. A. (1996). New models of deep comprehension. In B. K. Britton & A. C. Graesser (Eds.), *Models of text comprehension* (pp. 1–32). Hillsdale, NJ: Erlbaum.

Greeno, J. G., & Moore, J. L. (1993). Situativity and symbols: Response to Vera and Simon. *Cognitive Science, 17*, 49–59.

Guthrie, J. T., & Wigfield, A. (1999). How motivation fits into a science of reading. *Scientific Studies of Reading, 3*, 199–205.

Guthrie, J. T., & Wigfield, A. (2005). Roles of motivation and engagement in reading. In S. G. Paris & S. A. Stahl (Eds.), *Children's reading comprehension and assessment* (pp. 187–213). Mahwah, NJ: Erlbaum.

Horowitz, R. (1994). Adolescent beliefs about oral and written language. In R. Garner & P. A. Alexander (Eds.), *Beliefs about text and instruction with text* (pp. 1–24). Hillsdale, NJ: Erlbaum.

Jenkins, J. J. (1974). Remember that old theory of memory? Well, forget it! *American Psychologist, 25*, 785–795.

Kardash, C. M., & Howell, K. L. (2000). Effects of epistemological beliefs and topic-specific beliefs on undergraduates' cognitive and strategic processing of dual-positional text. *Journal of Educational Psychology, 92*, 524–535.

Kardash, C. M., & Scholes, R. J. (1995). Effects of preexisting beliefs and repeated readings on belief change, comprehension, and recall of persuasive text. *Contemporary Educational Psychology, 20*, 201–221.

Kerr, M. A., & Symons, S. E. (2006). Computerized presentation of text: Effects on children's reading of informational material. *Reading and Writing: An Interdisciplinary Journal, 19*, 1–19.

Kintsch, W. (1986). Learning from text. *Cognition and Instruction, 3*(2), 87–108.

Kintsch, W. (1998). *Comprehension*. New York: Cambridge University Press.

LaBerge, D., & Samuels, H. (1974). Toward a theory of automatic information processing in reading. *Cognitive Psychology, 6*, 293–323.

Leu, D. J., Kinzer, C. K., Coiro, J. L., & Cammack, D. W. (2004). Toward a theory of new literacies emerging from the Internet and other information and communication technologies. In R. B. Ruddell & N. Unrau (Eds.), *Theoretical models and processes of reading* (5th ed., pp. 1570–1613). Newark, DE: International Reading Association.

Mathewson, G. C. (1976). The function of attitude in the reading process. In H. Singer & R. Ruddell (Eds.), *Theoretical models and processes of reading* (2nd ed., pp. 655–676). Newark, DE: International Reading Association.

McNamara, D. S., & Shapiro, A. M. (2005). Multimedia and hypermedia solutions for promoting metacognitive engagement, coherence, and learning. *Journal of Educational Computing Research, 33*, 1–29.

Mehan, H. (1979). *Learning lessons: Social organization in the classroom*. Cambridge: Harvard University Press.

Nolen, S. B. (1995). Effects of a visible author in statistical texts. *Journal of Educational Psychology, 87*, 47–65.

Osborn, J. (1968). Teaching a teaching language to disadvantaged children. *Monographs of the Society for Research in Child Development* [Language remediation for the disadvantaged preschool child], *33*(8), 36–48.

Paxton, R. J. (1997). "Someone with a life wrote it": The effects of a visible author on high school history students. *Journal of Educational Psychology, 89*, 235–250.

Paxton, R. J. (2002). The influence of author visibility on high school students solving a historical problem. *Cognition and Instruction, 20*, 197–248.

Pearson, P. D., & Gallagher, M, C. (1983). The instruction of reading comprehension. *Contemporary Educational Psychology, 8*, 317–344.

Pearson, P. D., & Hamm, D. N. (2005). The assessment of reading comprehension: A view of practices—past, present, and future. In S. G. Paris & S. A. Stahl (Eds.), *Children's reading comprehension and assessment* (pp. 13–69). Mahwah, NJ: Erlbaum.

Perfetti, C. A., Rouet, J., & Britt, M. A. (1999). Toward a theory of documents representation. In H. van Oostendorp & S. R. Goldman (Eds.), *The construction of mental representations during reading* (pp. 99–122). Mahwah, NJ: Erlbaum.

Pressley, M., & Allington, R. (1999). What should reading instructional research be the research of? *Issues in Education, 5*(1), 1–35.

RAND Reading Study Group (2002). *Reading for understanding: Toward an R&D program in reading comprehension*. Santa Monica, CA: RAND.

Rosenblatt, L. (1994). *The reader, the text, the poem: The transactional theory of the literary work*. Carbondale: Southern Illinois Press. (Original work published 1978)

Salmerón, L., Cañas, J. J., Kintsch, W., & Fajardo, I. (2005). Reading strategies and hypertext comprehension. *Discourse Processes, 40*, 171–191.

Samuels, S. J. (1983). A cognitive approach to factors influencing reading comprehension. *Journal of Educational Research, 75*, 261–266.

Samuels, S. J., & Kamil, M. L. (2002). Models of the reading process. In P. D. Pearson, R. Barr, M. L. Kamil, & P. Mosenthal (Eds.), *Handbook of reading research* (pp. 185–224). Mahwah, NJ: Erlbaum Associates. (Original work published 1984)

Shuy, R. W. (1981). Learning to talk like teachers. *Language Arts, 58*(2), 168–174.

Singer, H. (1969). Theoretical models of reading. *The Journal of Communication, 19*, 134–156.

Singer, H. (1970). Theoretical models of reading: Implications for teaching and research. In H. Singer & R. Ruddell (Eds.), *Theoretical models and processes of reading* (pp. 147–182). Newark, DE: International Reading Association.

Singer, H., & Ruddell, R. (Eds.) (1970). *Theoretical models and processes of reading*. Newark, DE: International Reading Association.

Singer, H., & Ruddell, R. (Eds.) (1976). *Theoretical models and processes of reading* (2nd ed.). Newark, DE: International Reading Association.

Spiro, R. J., Coulson, R. L., Feltovich, P. J., & Anderson, D. K. (2004). Cognitive flexibility theory: Advanced knowledge acquisition in ill-structured domains. In R. B. Ruddell & N. Unrau (Eds.), *Theoretical models and processes of reading* (5th ed., pp. 640–653). Newark, DE: International Reading Association.

van den Broek, P., Young, M., Tzeng, Y., & Linderholm, T. (1999). The landscape model of reading: Inferences and the online construction of memory representation. In H. van Oostendorp & S. R. Goldman (Eds.), *The construction of mental representations during reading* (pp. 71–98). Mahwah, NJ: Erlbaum.

van Oostendorp, H., & Goldman, S. R. (Eds.) (1999). *The construction of mental representations during reading.* Mahwah, NJ: Erlbaum.

Vaughan, M. W., & Dillon, A. (2006). Why structure and genre matter for users of digital information: A longitudinal experiment with readers of a web-based newspaper. *International Journal of Human-Computer Studies, 64,* 502–526.

Wade, S. E., & Moje, E. (2000). The role of text in classroom learning. In M. L. Kamil, P. B. Mosenthal, P. D. Pearson, & R. Barr (Eds.), *Handbook of reading research: Vol. III* (pp. 609–627). Mahwah, NJ: Erlbaum.

Wallen, E., Plass, J. L., & Brunken, R. (2005). The function of annotations in the comprehension of scientific texts: Cognitive load effects and the impact of verbal ability. *Educational Technology Research and Development, 53,* 59–72.

Wineburg, S. (1991). Historical problem solving: A study of the cognitive processes used in the evaluation of documentary and pictorial evidence. *Journal of Educational Psychology, 83,* 73–87.

Zwaan, R. A. (1996). Processing narrative time shifts. *Journal of Experimental Psychology, 22,* 1196–1207.

Zwaan, R. A., & Radvansky, G. A. (1998). Situation models in language comprehension and memory. *Psychological Bulletin, 123,* 162–185.

Zwaan, R. A., Magliano, J. P., & Graesser, A. C. (1995). Dimensions of situation model construction in narrative comprehension. *Journal of Experimental Psychology: Learning, Memory, and Cognition, 21,* 386–397.

11 Disciplinary Comprehension

Cynthia Shanahan

University of Illinois at Chicago

INTRODUCTION TO THE DOMAIN

Competent readers do not use a universal approach to reading. Depending upon the level of prior knowledge, the kind of text, and the purpose for reading, individuals alter their attention to different structural, rhetorical, and linguistic characteristics and think in varied ways about the elements they encounter. For example, a person reading for general enlightenment or pleasure might focus on a "My Turn" essay in *Newsweek* because of a catchy title. The individual might then look at the quote in bold in the center of the text, read a few lines at the beginning, and quickly skim through the text to see if it is something to read more carefully. If still interested, the person might read the essay closely, or, if time is of the essence—move to the conclusion. Since all of the "My Turn" essays have a common structure with which the reader is very familiar, she is able to be maximally effective in determining where the "meat" of the message lies, and because she is reading for pleasure she is under no obligation to think about the message in any particular way. The same individual, however, would not have the luxury of moving on if she were reading a textbook chapter for a course. Too, the structure of the textbook chapter would be more complex, the text longer, and the ideas more elaborated than in the essay. Study reading is very different from casual pleasure reading and a textbook chapter is very different from an essay.

But the differences do not end with just the purpose for reading and the text genre. Disciplines of study such as social science, mathematics, and science approach, represent, and critique information in unique ways. Too, even within those disciplines, there are differences among sub-disciplines. History reading is similar to political science reading but not identical; political science information is often included in history texts and visa versa, but the focus is different. Political science, as the study of governments and their political structures, will include how particular political structures were created (the history of those structures), but its main focus is on the structures themselves and how they operate within an overall political system. Political science texts are likely to include more technical vocabulary and rely more on classification and hierarchy than history texts. History texts may include explanations of particular governments and their political structures, but these explanations are embedded in the description of the chronological flow of events that is most often the structure of history texts. Biology and physics are both sciences, but the texts are structured differently, with physics texts including more math than the biology texts, for instance. These differences exist because the disciplines and sub-disciplines have unique traditions. Experts in a particular discipline understand this, and therefore, have a high degree of disciplinary knowledge. Experts approach texts in their discipline with familiarity because they are aware of their disciplinary traditions. Nonexperts are not. They know how to evaluate the quality and credibility of what they read because they understand the standards of their field. Nonexperts do not. They know how to interpret particular rhetorical moves because they have learned to make those moves themselves. Nonexperts have not.

Yet, we wonder why students have such difficulty learning from content area text. There are other chapters in this volume that clearly specify the range and depth of the problem of text reading in the content areas: Students have difficulty comprehending their science, math, and social science texts because of their difficulties with vocabulary, text structure, comprehension, and so on. These difficulties could be severe, affecting their comprehension of all texts, even in genres that should be familiar, or specific to texts in particular disciplines. Because of the difficulties, teachers often try to teach the concepts of their discipline in other ways—through lecture/discussion, hands-on demonstrations/experiments, and film—relieving students of the burden of difficult reading material (O'Brien, Stewart, & Moje, 1995; Muth, 1993; Shanahan, 2004; Stewart & O'Brien, 1989; Moje, Young, Readence, & Moore, 2000). Students who do not read do not become better readers and a cycle begins, so that, as an American College Testing (ACT) study reports (American College Testing, 2006), students do not leave high school with the ability to handle the more difficult text materials in college, nor (even if they do not attend college) do they leave with the ability to engage in the kind of informed decision making based upon reading called for in an optimally functioning democratic society. For example, if individuals cannot read scientific arguments, they will most likely rely on media "sound-bites" when determining their responses (personally, economically, and politically) to global warming.

Poor readers are poor readers for a variety of reasons, but even readers who are able to read fiction or materials with familiar content and structure can struggle with reading subject matter materials. Reading in the disciplines requires *disciplinary knowledge*—knowledge of the way information is created (e.g., with experimentation, document analysis, or case study) shared (e.g., structurally, rhetorically, linguistically, in journals, or books) and evaluated for quality. At a fundamental level, readers also struggle with the unique challenges in vocabulary and comprehension evident in disciplinary texts that are the result of the differences across disciplines. The purpose of this chapter, then, is to discuss those differences and their implications for teaching and learning.

BACKGROUND

Definitional issues

In this chapter, *disciplinary knowledge* is a term used to describe the kind of knowledge that experts in a particular discipline have, as noted above. It is similar to the term, *domain knowledge*, used by Patricia Alexander and her colleagues, but not identical. Alexander defines domain knowledge as "a more formal subset of content knowledge that broadly encompasses a field of study or thought" (Alexander, Schallert, & Hare, 1991). She places *disciplinary knowledge* within domain knowledge, with disciplinary knowledge having a set of more formal rules or generalizations and a history (referencing Foshay, 1962). Knowledge of a domain to Alexander is subsumed under content knowledge. The definition of disciplinary knowledge used in this chapter is different in that it is not encompassed within content knowledge, but focuses on the traditions that a discipline uses to define and study the range of topics typically taken up by that discipline. The assumption is that an individual with a high degree of disciplinary knowledge can bring that knowledge to bear in thinking about content in his field that is new to him. Wineburg (1991), for example, studied the reading of multiple texts by historians and high school students. The high school students knew something about the content of the readings, whereas the historians did not. And yet, the experts used reading processes that were very different from the high school students, even though the content was new. They read the materials as *historians*, engaging in a sophisticated critique of the materials rather than reading them as a mere collection of facts. In other words, they approached the reading with a particular mindset or interpretive lens that was a characteristic of their field of study.

So, what is the relationship between content knowledge and discipline knowledge? This chapter discusses content knowledge as interacting with disciplinary knowledge. Disciplinary knowledge includes knowledge of the range of disciplinary topics, but not knowledge of all of the topics themselves. For example, a chemist would know that chemistry has several branches and she would know what those branches study, even though she focused on only one of the branches—structural chemistry—and only did research in one aspect of structural chemistry. A historian would know that historians focus on different time periods and different aspects of history (such as economic or political history). A mathematician might be engaged in theoretical math even though he understands other foci. (As a theoretical mathematician said to me when I asked him to read statistics, "I can understand this, because the language is similar, but it takes me a little longer, because it's not identical.") Disciplinary knowledge is not an abstracted form of content knowledge, however. It includes knowledge of (1) how information is created, (2) standards of evidence and quality, (3) discourse modes and avenues used to communicate knowledge, and (4) power structures that exist to advance and restrict information. It is a knowledge of what counts and who counts. It is these other kinds of knowledge, rather than content knowledge, that is discussed in this chapter.

Disciplinary comprehension, the focus of this chapter, is the comprehension of texts that exist within a particular discipline. For history reading, it would include comprehension of history textbooks, popular and scholarly books written by historians, and primary source documents such as newspaper reports and editorials, interviews, letters, pictures, political cartoons, film, and the like. Comprehension in history is a critical experience that includes an evaluation of the source and context of the text and its corroboration with other texts. Comprehension in the fields of math and science are somewhat different, as will be discussed in this chapter.

Disciplinary comprehension requires more than basic reading achievement. Even students who read at grade level on standardized tests may struggle with comprehension of texts that are discipline specific.

Academic language is a term used to describe school-based discourse. It is considered different from everyday talk, in that there is a level of abstraction that takes the student out of ones' experiences in an attempt to generalize knowing and creates a specificity about the extent to which something is known. In addition, academic language is the language of expertise. That is, it asserts the authority of its authors. Academic language is especially evident as the written language in textbooks, research articles, research proposals, and the like, but is also engaged in by teachers when they provide subject matter instruction, especially as the grade level of instruction progresses. Academic registers are especially problematic for students who have few experiences with academic language in and outside of educational venues (Gee, 2001). Although there are similarities in the features of academic language across the disciplines, there are differences as well. This chapter will address those differences, especially regarding the written texts that students in secondary schools confront.

Theoretical/conceptual roots

The theoretical/conceptual roots for disciplinary comprehension come from various research traditions, three of which are reviewed here. Primarily using the methodology of think-aloud protocols, cognitive science has laid the groundwork for understanding how expert and novice readers in various disciplines approach texts in their fields, leading educators to understand that different disciplinary traditions are evident in the way experts read. The fields of functional linguistics and discourse analysis have engaged in a number of studies of the linguistic features of texts in science, the humanities, and the social sciences, showing that the way common linguistic features are used in various disciplines is, in part, a function of the discipline itself. And both cognitive scientists and educators have studied text structure and other textual features and its impact on student learning.

The impetus for bringing the work in these fields together is to understand more deeply how the task of reading changes when the discipline changes, so that educators can be more explicit in the way they teach students content area reading. There is some evidence that students can be taught to read in discipline-specific ways, such as reading like a historian (Hynd-Shanahan, Holschuh, & Hubbard, 2005; VanSledright, 2002; VanSledright & Frankes, 2002), and that this instruction is accompanied by more complex, critical reading. Too, my colleagues and I have been engaged in a study of disciplinary approaches to literacy, and this study helps to drive home the importance of taking a disciplinary stance when reading in the content areas (Shanahan, Shanahan, & Misischia, 2006). In this study, we sought to understand the way experts read in three disciplines—history, chemistry, and mathematics—in order to develop discipline-specific literacy strategies for high school students to use. We created three teams, one for each discipline, which consisted of two experts (practicing historians, chemists, and mathematicians), two teacher educators (pre-service teacher educators in history, chemistry, and mathematics), and two high school teachers. We conducted think-alouds with each of the discipline experts using a typical high-school level text and a higher-level text of the experts' choice (one they had considered reading or had started to read). The think-aloud protocols were audio taped and transcribed, and I engaged in constant comparison to distill key elements in the way experts read the discipline-based texts. We then used each team as member-checkers, using the think-aloud protocols and the key features as discussion starters. In addition, the team discussed the specific challenges of discipline-based high school texts, focusing the discussion on the challenges students faced with vocabulary, comprehension, fluency, and writing. These discussions were also audio taped and transcribed; the challenges they named were entered into a chart, and brought back to the next meeting for continued discussion. The result was a set of two documents for each of the disciplines—one focusing on the challenges students faced and the other focusing on the way experts approached reading.

The teams approached reading differently and suggested different kinds of challenges depending upon which discipline they represented. In terms of the challenges that students face, the teams suggested that technical vocabulary presented the biggest challenge for chemistry and mathematics. The mathematics team was much more insistent than the chemistry team, however, that discipline specific meanings of general terms were important. For example, "the" and "a" are important distinguishers in mathematics even though they are often glossed over in general reading. In addition, the mathematics team noted that meanings of symbols were important and that these meanings could change depending upon the context, if they are variables. The history team mentioned vocabulary challenges too, but their challenges focused on general terms (e.g., adversary), metaphorical terms (e.g., Black Sunday), and vocabulary that is not presently popular (e.g. The *Gilded* Age). The history team also noted the presence of specific vocabulary that was neither technical nor general, like The XYZ Affair Napoleon Bonaparte, and The Tonkin Gulf Resolution. For research regarding technical, general, and specific vocabulary, see Harman, Hedrick, and Fox (2000).

Regarding comprehension, the chemistry team and the mathematics teams both discussed the challenge of moving across different kinds of textual and informational displays such as traditional text, models, tables, figures, and alphabetic and numeric information expressed in formulas and equations. The chemists, however, were much more insistent than the mathematicians that it was essential for students to be able to transfer information from one form to another. That is, they insisted that students be able to explain a graph or a chart using text and visa-versa. The mathematics experts, moreover, did not exemplify this sort of transformation in their own reading. Rather, they read more linearly, regarding both narrative and symbolic information as sentences that carried meaning. The history team also mentioned the importance of moving across informational displays, adding paintings and audiovisual displays such as film to the mix. However, they differed in the central importance they placed on these other kinds of information—and expected students to be able to decide which were central to understanding the information and which might be superfluous or even misleading.

The chemists mentioned the challenge of moving from the particular (lab experiments, for example) to the general or abstract. The mathematicians mentioned the challenge of reading closely in order to reach convergence—to solve problems. The historians mentioned the challenge of reading multiple texts and documents about events in history and synthesizing these documents into an interpretation, especially when the documents might not all agree.

Regarding their approaches to reading, the teams differed the most in their stances towards critique. To the mathematicians, critique involved finding error in the argument itself, focusing on its precision, simplicity, and clarity. It did not matter *when* the text was written or *who* wrote it. To the chemists, critique also involved looking at some of the peripheral information in a text to evaluate trustworthiness (looking at the author and his expertise, the source of funding, if a research report, the prestige of the university, and so on), depending upon the type of text being used. The chemists discussed the need to read research and popular science articles differently from textbooks. They wanted students to be less critical in their reading of textbooks—to focus on understanding the concepts and procedures. The historians, on the other hand, believed that students should read *everything*, including textbooks, with a critical eye. To historians, it was essential that students understand that history is interpretive, that historians *construct* cause-effect claims based upon existing evidence. In textbooks and other documents, historians wanted students to understand who the author was, what stance she had, what time period she wrote in, what her politics were, what moral positions she took, and what kind of historian she was. They wanted students to be able to critique glorifications of either the past or the present, to see which viewpoints are left out, and so on.

To summarize, we found differences across the three disciplines in how they perceived their texts as challenging and in the way they approached the texts. The rest of this chapter will attempt to provide information from various lines of research that help explain those differences.

Historical perspectives

Perspectives on discourse differences in text   Olson (1977) was the first to coin the term *autonomous* to articulate the character of written language so that he could describe the "great divide" between orality and literacy. This characterization of the divide led many to believe that written language was monolithic in nature in its opposition to orality. Others (Vygotsky, 1986; Chafe, 1982) provided theoretical support to that notion; texts were generally thought of as monolithic in that they were different from spoken language in their use of decontextualized language. According to Geisler (1994), the notion of autonomous texts was challenged in the late 1950s. Toulmin (1958), among others, argued that the nature of the arguments used in texts varied from field to field, suggesting, for example, that an artist would not be convinced by the same kind of arguments as a scientist. Geisler (1994) writes, "People in Western literate societies have access to a range of discourse types, in both oral and written forms, which vary in their autonomy from context" (p. 9).

How did the various disciplines develop discourse traditions? There are at least three views regarding the reasons why academic language in each profession came to be distinguished from everyday language and from the language in other professions: One view is that it served to keep authority in the elite classes. Another is that it was a normal development as fields developed the ability to create generalized knowledge. Geisler (1994), a proponent of the first view, discusses the rise of the academic professions in America during the second half of the 19th century, (the Association of American Geologists, in 1840, the American Chemical Society in 1876, the American Mathematical Society in 1894, the American Physical Society in 1899, The American Social Science Association in 1865, the American Historical Association in 1884, the America Economic Association in 1885, and the Modern Language Association in 1883, and the American Philosophical Association in 1901). In Geisler's view, academic professional associations needed to guarantee expertise to secure the public confidence, and the professionals in the various associations instituted professional standards. The rise of the professions coincided with the rise of the academic university, which also instituted professional standards and guaranteed these through state and national credentials and licenses. According to Geisler, these standards were ostensibly used to hold "charlatanism" and other unethical practices at bay, but in reality served to keep the academic authority in the hands of the elite. The standards of each of these professions were instantiated in particular textual structures and discursive styles that distinguished the field from the general public and from other fields in order to maintain particular power structures.

Schleppegrell (2004), echoing the thinking of Halliday (1998), on the other hand, writes, "Academic Registers are not just pretentious ways of using language that only serve to exclude the uninitiated. The kinds of meanings that are created in academic contexts often cannot be expressed in the language of ordinary interaction" (p. 137). She discusses the need for scientists, for example, to develop the grammatical and lexical means of presenting scientific findings in order to share that information with other scientists and with those who needed to learn science. Historians, too, she argued, need language to place events as participants in cause-effect chains, and mathematicians need to develop a taxonomy of lexical terms and a set of relational processes to show the correspondences between terms and their equivalents. Thus, the disciplines developed different discourse styles and different kinds of texts as a function of the kinds of knowledge they were creating and sharing.

Bazerman's view (1998) encompasses both stances when he focuses on genre; he sees that discrete texts have expected forms within various disciplines, and that these forms are both created and embedded in sets of relations and transactions within fields that are influenced by social and epistemological affordances and constraints as well as by the nature of knowledge in the discipline. Traditions for codifying a field's knowledge are not merely a function of the way the knowledge itself is structured; rather the way the field constructs itself and its activities are, in some sense, about power relations and negotiations between both members of the field and those outside of it.

In order for a field to have an important impact, a range of discourses, sometimes outside of the field itself, needs to be used. For example, Bazerman (1998) discusses that, for Edison to ensure that his particular technology of incandescent lighting was utilized, he had to use the discourses required in the specific genres of the patent application, the newspaper, technical journals, legal briefs, and so on. The ability to use several genres well, to Bazerman, is an important part of expertise: "we have adjustments among many centres of discourse, accommodated through the semantic flexibility and pragmatic distances negotiated by skilled language users who know how to maintain social networks despite differences among themselves and who know how to take meanings from one domain and transform them appropriately for another domain" (p. 25).

These three views of the way differences in the disciplinary language have developed historically are important in our understanding of why texts differ and why it is important for students to not only know how to read, but to know something about the discipline itself. Specific fields of study have developed over many years and into the era of professionalism. Experts in these fields have generated new forms of knowledge, engaged in power struggles and alliances, and accommodated theoretical shifts. These elements converge in acts of written communication. It is no wonder that different fields have developed different kinds of text and discourse structures; the function of these texts is to both ideational and social. Texts serve to advance knowledge that can lead to improved conditions at the same time that they serve to maintain a field's hegemony.

STUDIES

Studies of discourse practices

The language in academic texts is more explicit, abstract, complex, and highly structured than oral language and the language in non-academic texts (Snow, 1987; Bazerman, 1997). Linguistically, then, academic texts are similar. But discourse analysts and linguistics also note that academic texts use different genres and forms of language based upon the discipline in which these texts are found. Wignell (1994) classified the discourses of science. Common discourse genres of science include (1) procedure (to provide instruction for experiments); (2) procedural recount (to record what has already been done in an experiment); (3) science report (to organize information by setting up taxonomies, parts, or steps, or by listing properties); and (4) and science explanation (describing how and why phenomena occur). Coffin (1997) classified common discourse genres of history to include (1) historical recount (to retell the events in a sequence); (2) historical account (to account for *why* things happened in a particular sequence); (3) historical explanation (to explain past events by examining cause/effect); and (4) historical argument (to advocate a particular interpretation). Marks and Mousley (1990) discuss that, in mathematics, (1) events are recounted (narrative genre), (2) methods described (procedural genre), (3) the nature of individual things and classes depicted (description and report), (4) judgments explained (explanatory genre), and (5) arguments developed (expository genre). Note that explanations and procedures are more frequent in science and mathematics and less frequent in history. Even through the genre descriptions are all depictions of academic texts and have some similarities, the fields also use distinct genres to provide information to readers reflecting their unique purposes. In addition, there are differences within each of the disciplines based upon the specific purpose and form of a particular text. Solomon and O'Neill (1998), for example, note that, even within the field of mathematics, different types of written text call for different temporal and pro-nominal structural features. Mathematicians, they explain, make fairly clear distinctions between the complementary informal or introductory material in text that include analogies, examples, motivations, and so on, and the formal structure of definitions, theorems, and proofs.

Grammatical resources are deployed differently in the disciplines. A characteristic of scientific writing is nominalization, and this is true, too, of mathematics writing (Pimm & Wagner, 2003). Scientists commonly change verbs to nouns. Thus, rather than write,

"They *distilled* it...." a scientist might write, "The distillation took place...." The verb *distilled* is changed to a technical noun, *distillation*. Nominalization functions to move information from the everyday and specific to the abstract and general (Martin, 1993; Halliday & Martin, 1993). *Distillation* becomes part of the technical vocabulary. There are not as many technical terms in history, so this process of creating technical terms is not as prevalent. However, nominalization does occur with general terms. For example, history texts are more likely to use nouns like *unemployment* than their verb forms.

Things and *processes* are the purview of science. Thus, science texts use technical vocabulary in ways that often suppress agency. The text becomes an authoritative account of *things*. Note that the subject in the previous science example regarding distillation, the actor who distilled is removed with nominalization. Scientists also classify. According to Halliday (1994), scientists use the processes of *identification* and *attribution* when classifying phenomena. In *identification,* the definition and the technical term are reversible: *solutions are mixtures; mixtures are solutions.* Attributions place the term within a particular complex of terms (*a neutron is part of an atom*) and cannot be reversed. Science texts have a high degree of lexical density, higher than that of either mathematics or history. Lexical density is marked by the number of content words embedded in clauses or by the number of content words or through the percentage of content words in relation to the total number of words (Fang, 2004). Many of these content words are technical terms, which must be deeply learned in order to learn the science behind them.

Problems and their logical solutions are the purview of mathematics. Mathematics texts engage in the process of *detemporalization.* "*What's happening,*" becomes "*What happens.*" When detemporalization is combined with nominalization, the explanation or solution that is being discussed appears both static and abstract—able to be applied to specific problems across time and space (Pimm & Wagner, 2003).

Actions and *events* are the purview of history. History text often provides background information and descriptions of those actions and events and discusses the verbal and mental processes that lead individuals to action (Schleppegrell, 2004). Classification is not a main function in the field, and verbs carry much of the meaning. Nominalization and resultant abstraction do exist, but for different purposes. Indeed, abstraction can be very challenging in history. Note the following sentence:

> The enlargement of the nation's industrial capacity, including the making of barbed wire and the advent of western train transportation, served the demands of the West.

In this sentence, the events (i.e., *enlargement of the nation's industrial capacity,* the *making of barbed wire,* the *advent of western train transportation*) are nominalized as participants (they are the subjects or agents in the sentence). The process, *served,* is realized as a verb. The three events are buried in the clauses of the sentence through nominalization, and so the reasoning is not overt. That is, you know after reading the sentence that the nation has more industry than it used to, it makes barbed wire, and it has created western train transportation, but those pieces of information are not the point of the sentence. Burying the reasoning in the clauses makes the sentence complicated, and this feature is more characteristic of history texts than of texts in science or mathematics.

Science texts are more explicit about the level of confidence individuals can have that a process will occur than other texts. Texts use phrases such as *it is likely* or *it is thought that* to temporize or hedge the extent to which something is true (Hyland, 1995), although in textbooks, hedging occurs less often (Fang, 2004). History texts, on the other hand, temporize much less and in different ways than do science texts. In the phrase, "*There were three major causes of World War II,*" the author doesn't let on that cause and effect relationships are actually the result of a historian's analysis of contiguous events and thus, only *may* be causes rather than a proven truth.

Science texts typically have a mixture of mathematical expressions, graphical displays, and written text (Lemke, 2001), which are all central to the interpretation of the text itself. The nature of these elements may not be so central in disciplines such as history. For example, history texts may include paintings of important historical events. These paintings provide supplemental rather than central information, and can even introduce misconceptions, if the painting has idealized depictions of what transpired.

Studies of experts and expert readers

Experts read and write in ways that draw upon disciplinary knowledge. In other words, most experts don't just read the page; they rely on the previous knowledge and beliefs (including biases) that are part and parcel of their expertise, and they approach the texts they are reading with particular mindsets. Latour and Woolgar (1979), for example, noted that scientists' reading processes changed if they were reading their own colleagues' texts and theorized that reading was a social, not just an intellectual pursuit.

A study of the reading of seven physicists (Bazerman, 1985) found that physicists' purposes for reading and their background knowledge were central in the way they approached texts. When finding important texts to read, all of the physicists seemed to use their sense of technical terminology and how it related to their specific area of interest in the field—that is, they knew the range of their discipline and the terminology to describe that range, and they searched for the terminology related to their own areas of focus, paying attention to the names of objects or phenomena, approaches or techniques, and individuals or research groups. All engaged in what Wineburg (1991) later called termed sourcing. That is, they were attracted to articles based upon the reputation of the authors or the research group. All refined their reading based upon their unique interests. They were attracted to texts describing phenomena they were studying, and once they began reading, they would stop if they felt like the text described research that was too far removed from their interests. The physicists were sensitive to how fast information in their specific area of research was created: they were not so concerned about timely searches for information if they were in areas (like remote sensing) in which new knowledge took time to create, but searched more often and with more timely methods in areas where knowledge creation was occurring quickly.

When reading, the physicists paid special attention to new information—to surprises, and they jumped around in the article to figure out where to spend their effort, with experimentalists focusing more on methods and theorists focused more on theory. When they had comprehension difficulties, and they did, they weighed the effort against the benefit. If they felt they could use the information in their own work, they were more likely to critique the text. If they believed the information they learned would help them build up their knowledge (but was not directly applicable to their work), they read uncritically, intending to learn the information. That is, they were most critical of the parts in which they had some knowledge, using the standards of quality in their field to make judgments about the work's merit, and the least critical when they lacked knowledge. This moving back and forth between learning and critiquing was a characteristic observed in all of the physicists as they read, except for one, whose broad knowledge of the field was seen as responsible for a constant critique.

In summary, the physicists' knowledge of the scope of the field, the content of the field, the quality of the sources of information, and the quality of the way that information was generated and reported was used in their reading. The physicists varied in the focus of their reading, whether they chose to read something or not, and how they read based upon their expertise, but all of this variation was within the scope of what it meant to be a physicist.

Expert historians exhibit their own disciplinary patterns while reading historical documents. A study comparing expert and high school readers as they read a set of documents about a single event in history (Wineburg, 1991) showed that the historians engaged in processes that were different (and much more sophisticated) from those of the high school students, even though the high school students had previously studied the topic and the historians had not. The high school students read each of the documents as if each were disconnected from the others for the purpose of fact collection. The historians, on the other hand, in addition to "learning" the information, engaged in three unique processes: sourcing, contextualization, and corroboration. That is, they paid attention to the author, what kind of document it was, and where it came from (sourcing). They thought about the time period in which it was written and considered what they knew about the political, social, economic, and/or cultural conditions of that time (contextualization). They looked for agreements and disagreements across the text and with their own views (corroboration). Like the physicists, they used their disciplinary knowledge to interpret the documents. Unlike the physicists, they did not adopt an uncritical learning mode when they read information about which they knew little.

Leinhardt and Young (1996) asked three historians to read two history texts—one that was close and one that was far from their areas of expertise. They analyzed the way the historians read by classifying them within two processes: identification and interpretation. When historians identify, they classify the genre they are reading (as letters, newspaper accounts, commentary, commission reports, and the like). They also engage in sourcing, contextualization, and corroboration, as discussed by Wineburg (1991). When historians interpret, they engage in a textual read and/or a historical read. A textual read involves word inspection, structural analysis, and summarization and is self-consciously responsive to the surface features of the text. A historian, for example, might make associations to specific words in the text, pay attention to the subtext, and note the tensions between the ostensible text and subtext. The historical read involves reading from a particular philosophical perspective. For example, a Marxist historian would be focusing on different aspects of the narrative than a feminist historian. A historian who is critical of "the great man in history" perspective would be wary of a text that touted the influence of a particular person above other elements. The researchers found that the historians used these same processes regardless of whether the texts they read were familiar or unfamiliar. However, with the unfamiliar document, they explicitly discussed when they lacked the information necessary to fully carry out identification and interpretation. They quite self-consciously accessed "specific knowledge of a relevant period, topic, figure, or theory from outside the text while engaged in a knowledgeable and purposive reading of structure and content inside the text" indicating a "dynamic interaction between historians' general document reading schemas and their specific topic expertise" (p. 476). When reading unfamiliar texts, the historians read from the text to the theory. When reading familiar ones, they read from the theory to the text. The historians they studied noted not only the immediate text situation, but also saw the text as "an artifact of history, as a product of a period, as an exemplar of a documentary set, as a piece of rhetoric, and as a collection of linguistic conventions that conveyed aspects of relationships between the writers and those they wrote about or to" (p. 478).

In a different take on expertise, Burton and Morgan (2000) studied the written work of mathematicians using 53 research papers: 23 pure, 20 applied, and 10 statistics papers. They noted the absence of author's presence in text, the ambiguous use of "we" ("we determine V_{10}") and the use of imperatives ("let us consider") as being prevalent in most of the publications they studied. They also noted that the authors both claimed authority by phrases such as "it is obvious that" and temporized authority by phrases such as "plausible though as yet unproved assumption," but claimed authority more than they temporized. They conclude that mathematicians, although they have some variability, have particularized ways of expressing themselves that are common in the community of mathematicians, regardless of whether they are from pure mathematics, applied mathematics, or statistics. In addition to nominalization such as that in scientific discourse, Pimm & Wagner, (2003) discuss the notion of *detemporalization* that takes place in mathematics writing.

These studies show that the disciplines of physics, history, and mathematics differ in the way information is represented in text and in the way experts approach text reading. However, these differences are not often shared with students who are attempting to read discipline-based texts. Students are taught to use general reading strategies and to approach content area texts as if they were monolithic purveyors of a generalized form of academic language.

Text studies

Researchers have engaged in studies of the effect of particular text structures and features on readers for a long time. Though some of this work is dated, it has specific application to the new work of theorizing disciplinary comprehension. Thus, this next section is a "re-look" at the work that has taken place within the last 30 or so years, with the idea this work, when combined with what it means to engage in disciplinary reading, can inform the field in thinking about new instructional directions.

The structure of text differs with genre differences. Newspaper articles, letters, novels, biographies, research proposals, research reports, trade magazine articles, and so on, all rely on unique structures. Theorists have classified text types across genres using different terminology: expository, narrative, descriptive, informational, and so on. Brewer (1980) suggested three basic discourse types: descriptive, which embodies a stationary perceptual scene; narrative, which embodies a series of events in time; and expository, which embodies abstract, logical processes. He also proposed four "discourse forces." These forces are meant to be an "interaction of the communicative intent of the author and the perception of the reader" (p. 224). In *informative* discourse, the author intends to provide information. In *entertaining* discourse, the author means to amuse, frighten, excite, or otherwise thrill the reader. In *persuasive* discourse, the author means to persuade the reader to adopt a particular set of ideas or take a particular action. In *literary-aesthetic* discourse, the author is providing an aesthetic experience. He also provided examples for each. For instance, a technical description of a plant in a botany text would be descriptive discourse for the purpose of informing, whereas a description of a house by a real estate agent would be a description for the purpose of persuading, and a description of an idyllic scene in a poem would be a description for literary-aesthetic purposes. These written discourse forces at times overlap. For example, there are times when an author's informational writing is so well written that it is deemed as having *aesthetic* value by readers. And a particular text may have several kinds of discourse types represented. History textbooks, for example, have description, narration, and exposition in them, all for the purpose of informing. Even though the main discourse type is narration, at times, historians depict certain scenes in great detail: a courtroom, a battlefield, or a factory. At other times, they explicitly discuss causes and effects or points of view, so that at those times, the passages are expository in nature. These different discourse structures evoke different responses from readers (Hynd & Chase, 1991). Science text, too, can be descriptive (e.g., in describing a cell) expository (e.g., in discussing the relation between an atom and a cell) and narrative (when discussing a sequence of activities that comprise a scientific process).

Within these discourse structures, authors can vary the rhetoric by varying the order (e.g., discussing the end result, then going back to the beginning of the procedure), varying the amount of detail, varying the visibility of the author, and varying the amount of information available to the narrator (as in literature). In informational texts in most disciplines, the author can employ several variants. An author can skip obvious steps in an argument, bring to bear every possible piece of evidence or be more judicious, present several sides of an argument or just one side, and be more or less visible. Although other classification schemes exist, these categories are useful in describing disciplinary texts. (For a more thorough review of the discourse of historical texts, see Berkhofer's (1995) "Beyond the Great Story: History as Text and Discourse" and White's (1978) "Tropics of Discourse.")

Generally, studies that aim to teach students about the structure of text have shown that students' comprehension and recall of texts improves with this instruction. (see, for example, Leon & Carretero, 1995; Mayer, 198; Meyer, 1984; Meyer & Rice, 1984). Most of these studies were conducted decade ago or more. The National Reading Report (NICHD, 2000) confirms, however, that teaching students to pay attention to the structure of texts increases the comprehension of those texts.

History texts

In many history textbooks, the author and the methods for creating the message are invisible. An author describes a series of events (narrative, with interspersed description) and discusses the cause and effect relationships among them. Even though these cause and effect relationships are read by historians as persuasive *arguments* about the events (Wineburg, 1991)—the idea that one event causes another or that an event has multiple outcomes is in the mind of the historian—the invisible author provides the typical reader with the perception that the causes are, indeed real. That is, because the author does not share his or her sources of information, analytic procedures, and determinations of reliability and validity, the cause and effect statements are not "checkable" and remain unquestioned (Paxton, 1999). The typical argument structure of expository texts is not explicitly represented in history textbooks either—the overarching structure is narrative and descriptive; the cause-effect arguments are embedded within this structure.

True, science textbooks also bury sources and procedures—an unknown author describes knowledge without explaining how the knowledge was created—but the lack of explanation may be more crucial in history. History relies on the compilation and analysis of data gathered after-the-fact; thus, reliability and validity are issues more than they are issues when controlled experiments are conducted. Also, historians choose evidence from a plethora of existing documents, so that the story they construct is by necessity a somewhat subjective one. As in the evaluation of qualitative research, a reader can only judge the quality of the analysis if he or she knows under what conditions and with what biases the research was conducted. If that information is hidden, then evaluation is difficult.

In history trade books such as biographies and in scholarly articles, more is available to the reader. Usually, the sources of information are noted in the form of footnotes and in citations, and differences in opinion about historians *may* be included in the discussions of a particular event or point in a person's life. For example, the assertion that Lincoln used cocaine may be openly refuted, with the evidence for that assertion laid out and then argued to be false or mistaken.

Primary documents in history present different challenges for readers. These documents represent various genres: newspaper articles and editorials, autobiographies, essays, scholarly and popular books, pictures, interviews, movies, newsreels, and so on. The discourse type and order, amount of detail, visibility of the author, and amount of information available to the narrator vary as well—in every document. It is the reader's job to determine the salience and creditability of each document, and variations within and across genres make this difficult.

To truly understand history from a historian's perspective, readers need to understand the interaction among these different genres, discourse types and modes, and the disciplinary tradition of history. Historians read these texts partly as persuasive arguments (Wineburg, 1991; Leinhardt & Young, 1996) that are open to critique. One area of research that is pertinent, then, is the research dealing with persuasive messages. The credibility of persuasive messages comes into play when readers perceive that a main task of reading is to determine what to believe, and this task does seem to be the task taken up by historians. Social scientists have engaged in research to determine the functions of persuasion for decades, concluding that the credibility of an argument exists not only in the argument itself but also in features of text that are peripheral to it (Chaiken, 1980, 1987; Petty & Cacioppo, 1986), such as a text's structural variants, the credibility of the author, and so on. For example, a reader might evaluate the length of the argument (a structural variant) with the idea that arguments that employ extensive evidence are more persuasive. Whereas historians use peripheral clues such as sourcing, contextualization, and corroboration to determine the credibility of the history texts they read (Wineburg, 1991; Leinhardt & Young, 1996), without instruction, students generally do not, perhaps because they do not perceive the task of reading history as that of deciding what to believe.

One question asked by social psychologists is whether one-sided or two-sided arguments are more persuasive (Karlins & Abelson, 1970). When an individual is already is predisposed towards a stance and when only one message is going to be heard, one-sided arguments are more persuasive. But if a message contradicts an individual's beliefs, or if it is probable that the individual will hear the other side from someone else, then a presentation of both sides of the argument is preferable. Buehl, Alexander, Murphy, and Sperl (2001) found that college students strengthened their already existing ideas when reading a one-sided argument with which they agreed. Furthermore, they either strengthened or changed their existing notions after reading a two-sided non-refutational text, but the direction of the change varied; their ideas did not always match the preferred ideas of the author. In history textbooks, not only is the argument usually one-sided, it is also embedded in a narrative structure. Thus, it is most likely to believed by naïve readers who lack the disciplinary knowledge that would orient them to the task of reading critically and who do not have the content knowledge to know that different interpretations of an event exist.

The research regarding the role of text structure in the reading of history texts without instruction is somewhat discouraging. In one study of fifth grade students reading of multiple documents, Vansledright and Kelly (1998) found that students did not notice genre and discourse differences across texts, and, with no record of the sources historians were using, they did not judge the validity of the texts they read. These findings are echoed in studies of older students as well (Wineburg, 1991; Stahl, Hynd, Britton, McNish, & Bosquet, 1996). Students fail to notice the differences across texts; rather they seem to approach each text as a collection of facts and read for the purpose of remembering the important ones and regard all texts as truth. Students also appear to have difficulty in writing about history. Even high school students in advanced placement classes have difficulty using rhetorical strategies to make historical explanations of arguments (Young & Leinhardt, 1998). Too, students seem to find that embedded cause-effect structure—that used in history textbooks—is more difficult to detect than other structures (Richgels, McGee, Lomax, & Sheard, 1987).

The picture changes with instruction, however. When cause-effect structure is made explicit, reader's comprehension of history text is facilitated, even under conditions of low prior knowledge (Voss & Silfies, 1996), and especially with difficult texts (Linderholm, Everson, van den Broek, Mischinski, Crittenden, & Samuels, 2001).

Improvements in comprehension also occur when the texts themselves are changed. Britton and Gulgoz (1991) studied the effect of changing expository historical text so that it is more explicit. They showed they could increase college students' free recall of text by identifying where inferences were called for in a text and repairing the text to make it explicit.

Finally, instruction that focuses on teaching students distinct disciplinary strategies seems to be effective. In one promising study, De La Paz (2005) found that instruction of middle school students in historical reasoning strategies helped them to write more accurate and persuasive historical essays than students who did not have such instruction. This study corroborates the findings of the Hynd-Shanahan, Holschuh and Hubbard (2005) study showing that students taught to source, contextualize, and corroborate were able to think critically about multiple texts about the Vietnam Conflict.

Science texts

Science texts vary by subdiscipline, with texts in chemistry and physics, for example, including more mathematics and tables of data than texts in biology or anatomy. That said, science textbooks have in common with history textbooks a hidden author, and they engage in description, narration (in describing a sequence of steps in a process), and exposition for informational purposes. Experimental articles in science have a fairly well-defined structure that begins with an abstract, and continues with an introduction, review of the literature, methods, findings, discussion, and conclusion. Other genres such as the popular science article, the lab report, or a proposal for funding, all have more or less identifiable structures as well.

The type of text one reads can affect the way that scientific information is processed. Baram-Tsabari and Yarden (2005) asked high school students to read scientific journal articles and popular science journal articles to determine the role of these two genres in the formation of scientific literacy. Those reading the scientific journals evidenced better inquiry skills, but those reading the popular science journal comprehended better and had better attitudes toward the reading.

Research regarding instruction about science text structure is mostly two-fold: (1) research on facilitative text structures for learning science and overcoming misconceptions, and (2) research in helping students use existing text structures to comprehend science texts. One area of research on facilitative text structures has focused on refutational text. Refutational text is text that identifies and acknowledges commonly held but scientifically invalidated ideas about the way the world works, then refutes those ideas, explaining the evidence for a scientifically valid explanation and showing how that scientifically valid explanation is more plausible and useful than the non-scientific explanation. For example, a science text would be refutational if it began something like, "Many people believe that a bullet that is fired from a gun will, if unimpeded, fall to the ground later than a bullet that is dropped straight down from the same height, but scientists have shown that this is not the case."

Literacy researchers, after years of studying conceptual change in science, have come to one fairly stable conclusion: students change their intuitive but non-scientific conceptions to more scientific ones by reading refutational text (e.g., Alverman, Hynd, & Qian, 1995). Not only is there experimental evidence that students move towards scientific theory after reading refutational text (Guzzetti, Snyder, Glass, & Gammas, 1993), there is also anecdotal evidence that students prefer refutational over non-refutational text (Guzzetti, Hynd, Williams, & Skeels, 1997). A number of studies and a meta-analysis (Guzzetti, Snyder, Glass, & Gammas, 1993) have concluded that refutational text is facilitative to comprehension if misconceptions are an issue.

Regarding instruction aimed at teaching students to use text structure and genre to improve comprehension of science text, Prain, Hand, and their colleagues engaged in a series of studies of models of writing in science, finding that students benefit from instruction that involves them writing for a variety of purposes to a variety of audiences, and in a variety of genres (Hand, 1999; Hand & Prain, 2002; Hand, Prain, & Wallace, 2002; Prain & Hand, 1999). They recommend that students are given writing assignments in science that include explanation, sets of instructions, letters, reports, diagrams, and so for the purpose of clarifying, applying, or persuading and to peers, younger students, a government agency, and others. Recall Bazerman's (1998) argument that scientists must often write across audiences in different genres when asking for funding in order to conduct research and in communicating to the public the findings and implications of their research. In addition, teaching students scientific discourse seems to improve performance in science (Veel, 1997).

The comprehension of scientific text also seems amenable to instruction that highlights particular text structures. Rossi (1990), for example, asked 10-year olds to read scientific texts in three conditions. In one version of the text, the macro-structural elements were underlined. In the second version, the researchers annotated the text with the nodes of a problem frame. A third version was unaltered. They found that good readers benefited from the macrostructure underlining and poor comprehenders benefited from both the annotation and the underlining.

Mathematics texts

The structure of mathematics texts has not been the focus of a good deal of study. Textbooks seem to have many of the same features as science texts. There is a need for readers to understand and synthesize different representations of information in charts, graphs, formulae, and linguistic explanations. The expert readers we studied, however, engaged in a more linear reading of text than scientists (Shanahan, Shanahan, & Misischia, 2006). Our perusal of textbooks indicated that the typical structure was similar to that explicated by Solomon and O'Neill (1998), who noted a distinction between informal and introductory materials and formal structures of definitions, theorems, and proofs. A chapter begins with a motivational or contextual introduction to the topic, introduces formal definitions that are necessary to understand the topic, *may* provide informal examples and analogies that explain the definitions, and moves to a formal explication of the topic that is a combination of prose and mathematical equations. All of these textual features are processed as sentences by expert readers.

Just as there are few explanations of the text structure of mathematics, there are few studies of comprehension of mathematics text that take these structural elements into account. One text-structure issue in mathematics (and some science) texts that has been studied is whether the "proof" or the "principle" is mentioned first. In the "proof-first" structure, after a brief introduction, the text begins with a hypothetical situation ("Consider that A equals....") in order to derive a principle or rule. In the "principle first" structure, the principle is stated, then proven. Dee-Lucas and Larkin (1990), among others, found that the "proof first structure" was more difficult for students to comprehend. Students reading a "proof first" structure had more difficulty determining important information, summarizing, and recalling the text. Dee-Lucas and Larkin (1991) also found that, for 40 undergraduates, if proofs were replaced by verbal equivalents, students were better able to solve similar verbal problems after reading. These findings suggest that students have difficulty engaging in reading of mathematics texts with traditional structures.

SYNTHESIS: WHERE ARE WE NOW IN THIS DOMAIN?

This chapter recognizes a strong historical, theoretical, and analytical foundation for the notion that reading is different among the various disciplines. Although reading comprehension entails similar processes regardless of the text (a reader must identify and understand words and engage in fluent reading and comprehension of connected text), there are significant differences in the texts themselves *depending upon the discipline* in which they exist, and expert readers in these disciplines read these texts within the frameworks of their discipline.

History texts use nominalization, but not necessarily to create technical vocabulary, whereas science and mathematics texts create technical vocabulary in that way. Science texts temporize or hedge more than history texts. Mathematics texts detemporalize (place information within the present), whereas temporalization is a key feature of history texts. In history texts, the graphic or visual information may or may not be central to understanding, but in science texts, it is of key importance. These and other differences exemplify the rhetorical moves that have been created as a result of the different structures of knowledge in the various disciplines and of the social and political realities of establishing a field of inquiry.

Expert readers read within in a disciplinary frame. It is not simply a matter of calling upon topic knowledge. Rather, expert readers use *disciplinary knowledge* to guide their reading—knowledge of the way individuals create, represent, and evaluate information, and this knowledge can guide reading even when topic knowledge is low. Historians, for example, engage in a critical reading of all texts in their field, regardless of the level of their topic knowledge; rather, they acknowledge that the topic is not one about which they are familiar and continue to speculate on the possibilities of a critique, moving from the text to the theory that guides their particular reading of the text. When a historian is familiar with the topic, he moves from theory to text. Note how one historian relies on a theoretical read of a text about Abraham Lincoln.

> Uh, and then, my response is first of all, I'm always kind of very suspicious and weary of the kind of "great man in history" approach, so I'm looking kind of carefully at how the author is embedding this argument. In other words, are they trying to undermine that great man in history, are they addressing the problem and dealing with the problem or are they letting the problem just kind of fester without addressing it. Uh, so I'm looking carefully at how they're kind of wording and locating the individual in history. (Shanahan, Shanahan, & Misischia, 2006, p. 25)

Scientists, on the other hand, move between reading in a critical mode and reading in a learning mode depending upon the level of their topic knowledge. When they do not know much about the topic, they read to understand, and they suspend the critique. When they know a lot about the topic, they engage in critique, much like the historians. That is, they evaluate the source of information, contextualize the reading within a time frame, and corroborate across sources. Note the attention paid to the source of information in this comment by a chemist as he reads an article in his field.

> An article in *Science* counts, because it's a premier journal and something you read here should be taken very seriously. Every field has its own journals. If you're in the field you know who the good people are. In the first one, the journal is obscure, and I don't think it's a first-ranked journal, and I don't know the authors. (Shanahan, Shanahan, & Misischia, 2006, p. 22)

Mathematicians engage in a different kind of critique than either the scientists or the historians. As they read, they differentiate the informal from the formal parts of the text and engage in a close reading, looking for error. The source and the context do not seem to matter.

> Sometimes, it takes about ten to 15 years to find a response to a problem. So, an article written in 1985 is just as important today as it was in 1985, and is not dated, like it is in other fields. (Shanahan, Shanahan, & Misischia, 2006, p. 25).

This chapter also recognizes a research direction showing that students who are taught to engage in strategies that orient them to disciplinary texts can improve in their comprehension of those texts. These studies have largely focused on the *structure* of the texts themselves; however, some studies in teaching history reading point to the possibility of teaching students to read text within a particular disciplinary frame.

IMPLICATIONS FOR FUTURE RESEARCH

Whereas linguistic and structural differences in the texts themselves and differences in the way expert readers read them have been fairly well documented, there is not yet a common language with which we can talk about these differences and what it means for instruction. Perhaps one of the clearest views of discipline-based reading was spawned by Wineburg's (1991) study of historians' reading. His codification of three distinct processes that historians use (corroboration, sourcing, and contextualization) has a great deal of utility. It is succinct and practical. Others, me included, have used it as a heuristic to teach students. These processes are somewhat peripheral to the processes involved in the actual reading of the text—they represent an *approach* to reading that presupposes particular kinds of textual understandings. It would be beneficial to the field if researchers could distill similar heuristics from their studies of expert/novice readers in other disciplines such chemistry and mathematics. Learning such approaches would mean that students would learn about what it means to engage in the processes of the discipline—they would gain disciplinary knowledge.

In addition to different approaches to reading, I believe it would be beneficial to the field to take a second look at using what we know about linguistic differences in texts to help students comprehend the texts they encounter in their content area classrooms. Linguistic differences among the disciplines are an aspect of disciplinary knowledge, and serve a disciplinary function. Those who study reading comprehension have shied away from the knowledge gained by linguistic analyses of texts in recent years. Yet, we do not know whether or not we can improve students' reading comprehension by laying bare the various rhetorical and linguistic moves one sees in disciplinary texts in high schools. For example, we have not studied what happens when we teach a biology student how verbs become nominalized and why. These types of studies need to take place.

Finally, the study of reading comprehension strategies is in need of change. So far, the field of reading has developed a wide array of reading comprehension strategies that can by applied "across the content areas." Although there is a body of research supporting their use (see the National Reading Panel Report, NICHD, 2000), these studies also suggest that they are most beneficial for poor readers who do not ordinarily use strategies. What is needed is the creation and experimental study of strategies that are truly discipline specific. In applying discipline-based strategies, a student would be learning something about the structure of knowledge in the field, the type of information that counts, the way knowledge is communicated, and/or how it is evaluated. Such strategies would remain context dependent. I can only speculate that these strategies would produce more sophisticated comprehension of texts in the same way that teaching students about sourcing, corroboration, and contextualization helped students to engage in more critical reading of their history texts.

IMPLICATIONS FOR PRACTITIONERS

An implication that has already been discussed in the field is that reading comprehension is more than just a general construct—it is context dependent and influenced in part by the kind of text that one reads. Instruction in disciplinary contexts, then, should include instruction in reading in the discipline. Reading is embedded in the practices of every discipline. The way a discipline creates, communicates, and evaluates knowledge is inextricably tied to reading. Reading in a discipline such as chemistry is vastly different than reading in another discipline such as history or literature in large part because their traditions for creating, communicating, and evaluating knowledge have developed somewhat independently. In addition, the kind of knowledge they create is based on different kinds of evidence. What that means instructionally is that secondary school teachers in the content areas need to work together with literacy specialists in joint efforts to improve reading comprehension. Content area teachers know more about their disciplines than do literacy specialists. Literacy specialists know more about reading than do disciplinary specialists. It means more than that, however. It also means that the institutions that train teachers need to help both literacy teachers and content area teachers understand the demands of disciplinary reading and provide teachers with the necessary knowledge to engage in the kind of reading comprehension instruction that would increase the likelihood that students could read and think deeply about their content area courses.

REFERENCES

Alexander, P.A., Schallert, D. L., & Hare, V. C. (1991). Coming to terms: How researchers in learning and literacy talk about knowledge. *Review of Educational Research, 61*(3) 315–343.

Alvermann, D., Hynd, C., & Qian, G. (1995). The effects of interactive discussion and text type on the learning of counter-intuitive science concepts. *Journal of Educational Research, 88*, 146–153.

American College Testing (2006). *Reading between the lines: What the ACT reveals about college readiness for reading.* http://act.org/path/policy/reports/reading.html

Baram-Tsabari, A., & Yarden, A. (2005). Text genre as a factor in the formation of scientific literacy. *Journal of Research in Science Teaching, 42*(4), 403–428.

Bazerman, C. (1985). Physicists reading physics: Schema-laden purposes and purpose-laden schema. *Written Communication, 2*(1), 3–23.

Bazerman, C. (1997). Discursively structured activities. *Mind, Culture, and Activity, 4*(4), 296–308.

Bazerman, C. (1998). *Shaping written knowledge: The genre and activity of the experimental article in science.* Madison: University of Wisconsin Press.

Berkhofer, R. F. (1995). *Beyond the great story: History as text and discourse.* Cambridge, MA: Harvard University Press.

Brewer, W. F. (1980). Literary theory, rhetoric, and stylistics. In. R. Spiro, B. C. Bruce, & W. F. Brewer (Eds.), *Theoretical issues in reading comprehension* (pp. 221–244). Hillsdale, NJ: Erlbaum.

Britton, B., & Gulgoz, S. (1991). Using Kintsch's computational model to improve instructional text: Effects of repairing inference calls on recall and cognitive structures. *Journal of Educational Psychology, 83*(3), 329–345.

Buehl, M. M., Alexander, P. A., Murphy, P. K., & Sperl, C. T. (2001). Profiling persuasion: The role of beliefs, knowledge, and interest in the processing of persuasive texts that vary by argument structure. *Journal of Literacy Research, 33*(2), 269–301.

Burton, L., & Morgan, C. (2000). Mathematicians writing. *Journal for Research in Mathematics Education, 31*(4), 429–453.

Chafe, W. (1982). Integration and involvement in speaking, writing, and oral literature. In D. Tannen (Ed.), *Spoken and written language: Exploring orality and literacy* (pp. 35 –53). Norwood, NJ: Ablex.

Chaiken, S. (1980). Heuristic versus systematic information processing and the use of source versus message cues in persuasion. *Journal of Personality and Social Psychology, 39*, 752–766.

Chaiken, S. (1987). The heuristic model of persuasion. In M.P. Zanna, J.M. Olson, & C.P. Herman (Eds.), *Social influence: The Ontario Symposium* (Vol. 5, pp. 3–39). Hillsdale, NJ: Erlbaum.

Coffin, C. (1997). Constructing and giving value to the past: an investigation into secondary school history. In F. Christie & J. R. Martin (Eds.), *Genre and institutions: Social processes in the workplace and school* (pp. 196–230). London: Cassell.

Dee-Lucas, D., & Larkin, J. H. (1990). Organization and comprehensibility in scientific proofs, or "Consider a particle p..." *Journal of Educational Psychology, 82*(4), 701–714.

Dee-Lucas, D., & Larkin, J. H. (1991). Equations in scientific proofs: Effects on comprehension. *American Educational research Journal, 28*(3), 661–682.

De La Paz, S. (2005). Effects of historical reasoning instruction and writing strategy mastery in culturally and academically diverse middle school classrooms. *Journal of Educational Psychology, 97*(2), 139–156.

Fang, Z. (2004). Scientific literacy: A functional linguistic perspective. *Science Education, 89*(2), 335–347.

Foshay, A. W. (1962). Discipline-centered curriculum. In A. H. Passow (Ed.), *Curriculum crossroads* (pp. 8–26). New York: Teachers College Press.

Gee, J. P. (2001). Language in the science classroom: Academic social languages as the heart of school-based literacy. In W. Saul (Ed.), *Crossing borders in literacy and science instruction: Perspectives on theory and practice* (pp. 13–32). Newark, DE: International Reading Association; Arlington, VA: National Science Teachers Association Press.

Geisler, C. (1994). *Academic literacy and the nature of expertise: Reading, writing, and knowing in academic philosophy.* Mahwah, NJ: Erlbaum.

Guzzetti, B., Hynd, C., Williams, W., & Skeels, S. (1997). What students have to say about their science texts. *Journal of Reading, 38*(8), 656–665.

Guzzetti, B., Snyder, T. E., Glass, G. V., & Gammas, W. S. (1993). Promoting conceptual change in science: A comparative meta-analysis of instructional interventions from reading education and science education. *Reading Research Quarterly, 28*(2), 116–159.

Halliday, M. A. K. (1994). *An introduction to functional grammar* (2nd ed.). London: Edward Arnold.

Halliday, M. A. K. (1998). Things and relations: Regrammaticising experience as technical knowledge. In J. R. Martin & R. Veel (Eds.), *Reading science: Critical and functional perspectives on discourses of science* (pp. 185–235). London: Routledge.

Halliday, M. A. K., & Martin, J. R. (1993). *Writing science: Literacy and discursive power.* Pittsburgh, PA: University of Pittsburgh Press.

Hand, B. (1999). A writing-in-science framework designed to enhance science literacy. *International Journal of Science Education, 21*(10), 1021–1035.

Hand, B., & Prain, V. (2002). Influences of writing tasks on students' answers to recall and higher-level test questions. *Research in Science Education, 32*(1), 19–34.

Hand, B., Prain, V., & Wallace, C. (2002). Influences of writing tasks on students' answers to recall and higher-level tests questions. *Research in Science Education, 32*(1), 19–34.

Harman, J .M., Hedrick, W. B., & Fox, E. A. (2000). A content analysis of vocabulary instruction in social studies textbooks for grades 4–8. *The Elementary School Journal, 100*(3) 253–271.

Hyland, K. (1995). The author in the text: Hedging scientific writing. *Hong Kong Papers in Linguistics and Language Teaching, 18*, 33–42.

Hynd, C., & Chase, N. (1991). The relation between text type, tone, and written response. *Journal of Reading Behavior, 23*, 281–306.

Hynd-Shanahan, C., Holschuh, J., & Hubbard, B. (2005). Thinking like a historian: College students' reading of multiple historical documents. *Journal of Literacy Research, 36*, 141–176.

Karlins, M., & Abelson, H.I. (1970). *How opinions and attitudes are changed* (2nd ed.). New York: Springer.

Latour, B., & Woolgar, S. (1979). *Laboratory Life: The social construction of scientific facts.* Thousand Oaks, CA: Sage.

Leinhardt, G. & Young, K. M. (1996). Two texts, three readers: Distance and expertise in reading history. *Cognition and Instruction, 14*(4), 441–486.

Lemke, J. L. (2001). The literacies of science. In W. Saul (Ed.), *Crossing borders in literacy and science instruction: Perspectives on theory and practice* (pp. 33–47). Newark, DE: International Reading Association; Arlington, VA: National Science Teachers Association Press.

Leon, J. A., & Carretero, M. (1995). Intervention in comprehension and memory strategies: Knowledge and use of text structure. *Learning and Instruction, 5,* 203–220.

Marks, G., & Mousley, J. (1990). Mathematics education and genre: Dare we make the same process-writing mistake again. *Language and Education, 4*(2), 117–135.

Martin, J. R. (1993). Life as a noun: Arresting the universe in science and humanities. In M. A. K. Halliday & J. R. Martin (Eds.), *Writing Science: Literacy and discursive power* (pp. 221–267). Pittsburgh: University of Pittsburgh Press.

Mayer, R. E. (1985). Structural analysis of Science prose: can we increase problem-solving performance? In B. K. Britton & J. B. Black (Eds.), *Understanding expository text* (pp. 65–87). Hillsdale, NJ: Erlbaum.

Meyer, B. J. F. (1984). Text dimensions and cognitive processing. In H. Mandl, N. L. Stein, & T. Trabasso (Eds.), *Learning and comprehension of text* (pp. 352). Hillsdale, NJ: Erlbaum.

Meyer, B. J. F., & Rice, C. E. (1984). The structure of text. In P. D. Pearson (Ed.), *Handbook of reading research* (pp. 319–351). New York: Longman.

Moje, E. B., Young, J. P., Readence, J. E., & Moore, D. W. (2000). Reinventing adolescent literacy for new times: Perennial and millennial issues. *Journal of Adolescent and Adult Literacy, 43,* 400–410.

Muth, K. D. (1993). Reading in mathematics: Middle school mathematics teachers' beliefs and practices. *Reading Research and Instruction, 32,* 76–83.

National Institute of Child Health and Human Development (NICHD). (2000). *Report of the National Reading Panel. Teaching children to read: An evidence-based assessment of the scientific research literature on reading and its implications for reading instruction: Reports of the subgroups* [NIH Publications No. 00-4754]. Washington, DC: U.S. Government Printing Office. Also available on-line: http://www.nichd.nih.gov/publications/nrp/report.htm

O'Brien, D. G., Stewart, R. A., & Moje, E. B. (1995). Why content literacy is difficult to infuse into the secondary school: Complexities of curriculum, pedagogy, and school culture. *Reading Research Quarterly, 30,* 442–463.

Olson, D. (1977). From utterance to text: The bias of language in speech and writing. *Harvard Educational Review, 47*(3), 257–281.

Paxton, R. J. (1999). A deafening silence: History textbooks and the students who read them. *Review of Educational Research, 69*(3), 315–339.

Petty, R. E., & Cacioppo, J. T. (1986). *Communication and persuasion: Central and peripheral routes to attitude change.* New York: Springer-Verlag.

Pimm, D., & Wagner, D. (2003). Investigation, mathematics education and genre: An essay review of Candia Morgan's "Writing mathematically: The discourse of investigation." *Educational Studies in Mathematics, 53*(2), 159–178.

Prain, V., & Hand, B. (1999). Students' perceptions of writing for learning in secondary school science. *Science Education, 83*(2), 151–162.

Richgels, D., McGee, L., Lomax, D. & Sheard, C. (1987). Awareness of four text structures: Effects on recall of expository text. *Reading Research Quarterly, 22*(2), 177–196.

Rossi, J. P. (1990). The function of frame in the comprehension of scientific text. *Journal of Educational Psychology, 82*(4), 727–732.

Shanahan, C. (2004). Teaching science through literacy. In T. Jetton & J. A. Dole (Eds.), *Adolescent literacy research and practice* (pp. 79–93). New York: Guilford.

Shanahan, C., Shanahan, T., & Misischia, C. (2006, December). *Frameworks for literacy in three disciplines.* Paper presented at the annual meeting of the National Reading Conference, Los Angeles, CA.

Snow, C. E. (1987). The development of definitional skill. *Journal of Child Language, 17,* 697–710.

Solomon, Y., & O'Neill, J. (1998). Mathematics and narrative. *Language and Education, 12*(3), 210–21.

Stahl, S., Hynd, C., Britton, B., McNish, M., & Bosquet, D. (1996). What happens when students read multiple source documents in history? *Reading Research Quarterly, 31,* 430–457.

Stewart, R. A., & O'Brien, D. G. (1989). Resistance to content area reading: A focus on pre-service teachers. *Journal for Reading, 33,* 396–401.

Toulmin, S. (1958). *The uses of argument.* Cambridge: Cambridge University Press.

VanSledright, B. (2002). Confronting history's interpretive paradox while teaching fifth graders to investigate the past. *American Educational Research Journal, 39,* 1089–1115.

VanSledright, B., & Frankes, L. (2002). Concept-and strategic-knowledge development in historical study: A comparative exploration in two fourth-grade classrooms. *Cognition and Instruction, 18,* 239–283.

VanSledright, B., & Kelly, C. (1998). Reading American history: The influence of multiple sources on six fifth graders. *Elementary School Journal, 98*(3), 239–265.

Veel, R. (1997). Learning how to mean—scientifically speaking: Apprenticeship into scientific discourse in the secondary school. In F. Christie & J. R. Martin (Eds.), *Genre and institutions: Social processes in the workplace and school* (pp. 161–195). London: Cassell.

Voss, J. F., & Silfies, L. N. (1996). Learning from history text: The interaction of knowledge and comprehension skill with text structure. *Cognition and Instruction, 14*(1), 45–68.

Vygotsky, L.S. (1986). *Thought and language.* Cambridge, MA: MIT Press.

White, H. (1978). *Tropics of discourse: Essays in cultural criticism.* Baltimore: The Johns Hopkins University Press.

Wignell, P. (1994). Genre across the curriculum. *Linguistics and Education, 6*(4), 355–372.

Wineburg, S. S. (1991). On the reading of historical texts: Notes on the breach between school and academy. *American Educational Research Journal, 28,* 495–519

Young, K. M., & Leinhardt, G. (1998). Wiring from primary documents: A way of knowing in history. *Written Communication, 15*(1), 25–68.

12 The Agency and Artistry of Meaning Makers within and across Digital Spaces

Robert J. Tierney

University of British Columbia

We seem to be approaching a confluence, verging on a zeitgeist,[1] as researchers, theorists and applied scholars encourage our rethinking the nature of literacy practices and meaning making, especially within and across new and changing digital environments. They include: social anthropologists interested in digital literacies as literacy practices and events (e.g., Barton, 1994; Barton & Hamilton, 1998; Street, 1984, 2003); cultural and critical theorists intent on studying the politics of individuals and group identities (Fairclough, 1992, 1995; Knobel & Lankshear, 2005; Lankshear & Knobel, 2003, Lambert,1993, Lanham, 2002), linguists including socio-semioticians interested in the advent of language systems, especially the shifts in signs via new media (e.g., Baudrillard, 1981; Lemke, 1998, 2001; Kress, 1997, 1998, 2003; Kress & van Leeuwen, 2001), cognitive psychologists interested in learning in the context of the new knowledge economies (e.g., Cognition and Technology Group at Vanderbilt, 2000; Spiro, 2006), literary theorists intrigued by discussions of author-reader-text relationships provoked by new forms of text (e.g., Landow, 1994 a, b; Miall & Kuiken, 1994; Miall 1999), and educators interested in the nature and role in learning (e.g., Cope & Kalantzy, 2000; Constanzo, 1994; Leu, 2006; Luke, 2005; New London Group, 1996; Pahl & Roswell, 2005; Reinking, 1997; Stein, 2004).

Some of these developments have their roots in technical breakthroughs and the realization of the impact that digital literacies are having in terms of meaning making, communication and other pursuits. The magnitude of these shifts should not be underestimated. As Gunther Kress (2003) stated:

> ... the broad move from the now centuries long dominance of writing to the new dominance of the image and ... the move from the dominance of the medium of the book to the dominance of the medium of the screen ... are producing a revolution in the uses and effects of literacy and of associated means for representing and communication at every level and every domain ... This in turn will have profound effects on human, cognitive/affective, cultural and bodily engagement with the world, and on the forms and shapes of knowledge. (p. 1)

As more and more people enlist digital literacies and growing numbers of homes, schools, community sites and offices access cellular technologies and have broadband connections, the use of digital literacies becomes increasingly ubiquitous in our everyday lives and contributes to shifts in what we can do, how, why, when, where, and with whom.[2]

This chapter attempts to braid together some of the threads or themes which seem to be informing our understanding of meaning making across and within digital spaces. The paper begins with a discussion of how we make meaning, including the influence of the architecture of digital spaces, the agency of the meaning making and, building upon the notion of agency, the social dimensions. The chapter closes with a brief discussion of the beginnings of a model of meaning making that attempts to braid together these threads.

WEAVING MEANINGS

How do individuals and groups weave meanings across composites of different engagements with the Internet, Web pages, blogs, videos, soundtracks, and other digital spaces? How do they transact meanings including explore, seek information, navigate, create, critique knowledge across multiple sources, Web sites, images, texts, video segments, sounds, etc.? How do they navigate, play, build, or participate within virtual worlds?

My view is that there is an artistry to meaning making that has more to do with the meaning maker than with the technologies, although the architectures supported by the technologies influence the expressions and approaches. As Bolter (2001), Douglas (1992), Gee (2003), Squire (2006), and others have discussed, these webs of images and texts, digital games or simulated environments are akin to scripts waiting to be enacted or scores to be played or dances to creatively pursue.

Our meaning making journeys may appear to follow, parallel or be inscribed by others, but we all have our own imprint, swagger or emerging meanings which ricochet or become compounded with one another as we wander through text. It is a mistake to believe that there is some kind of precise "mathematic" or "formulaic" rendering that is possible. Meaning making is never precise; it is not a form of exact mapping of sounds or meanings onto text. Meaning making involves approximation or a form of allowable band of interpretations or elasticity. It is befitting that meaning making has been compared with an orchestral rendition, dance or script that is enacted. There is always a certain elasticity to a score, script or choreography which is essential for the realization of the composition.

It has been suggested that the advent of digital spaces, especially with the advent of hypertext, represents a revolution in communication of a magnitude exceeding the printing press. Hypertext represents the basic architecture that undergirds the Internet as well as a host of interfaces that we now assume to be standard. Digital hypertext affords mutilayered and multimedia-based spaces to move across and within. As Spiro posits, hypertext makes a kind of nonlinearity and multidimensionality possible that could not be achieved with traditional linear media, refiguring thought from the ground up (Spiro, 2006, a b). Or, as Hull and Nelson (2006) stated:

> All about us, there are unmistakable signs that what counts as a text, and what constitutes reading and writing, are changing—indeed, have already changed and radically so—in this our age of digitally-afforded multimodality. To rehearse the obvious, it's possible now to easily integrate words with images and sound and music and movement in order to create digital artifacts that do not necessarily privilege linguistic forms of signification, but rather that draw upon a variety of modalities—speech, writing, image, gesture, sound—to create different forms of meaning. There are now web-based scholarly journals that illustrate and explore these possibilities ... there are community-based media organizations that promote a variety of forms of multimodal composing ... there are beginning to be empirical studies that examine multimodal practices in context ... theorizing about multimodality has begun.... Some scholars, it is true, recognized the advent and importance of multimodality as an aspect of literacy a long time ago, taking heed, for example, of the importance of multiple forms of representation (Witte, 1992). Yet, the full

import of this sea change in semiotic systems has, for most people, just begun to be felt.

Further, they suggested:

> these new multimodal spaces spurs a process of "braiding" or "orchestration" ... a multimodal text can create a different system of signification, one that transcends the collective contribution of its constituent parts. More simply put, multimodality can afford, not just a new way to make meaning, but a different kind of meaning.

The architecture of our engagement with these spaces provides for a juxtaposing of multiple texts that may achieve a crisscrossing of topics that Spiro, Coulson, Feltovich, and Anderson (1988)[3] have espoused to be powerful ways of knowing and learning complex knowledge. By using various microcosms, support can be gained for the acquisition of complex knowledge.

The intertextual and multilayered nature of hypertext (with the layering of texts, with image, and sound, etc., and linkages within and across layers) may expedite both the multiplier effects of making meaning and with the addition of multimedia active agents for transmediation, or what Forman (1998) has described as "the type of constructive conflict we deem to be the power of this multisymbolic approach to education" (p. 187). The multimedia nature of these forms of text being juxtaposed may afford a kind of semiotic engagement that provides students access to multiple symbol systems that allow an ongoing learning through analogies or metaphor. As Siegel (1995) suggested, these multimedia explorations have "a generative power that comes from juxtaposing different ways of knowing ... as a way of positioning students as knowledge makers and reflective inquirers" (p. 473). Or, as Witte (1992) suggested, "the influence of alternative intertexts on the constructive processes increases dramatically as the multiple voices of distinct constructive semioses mix on what might be called the battleground of the 'trace.' It is for this reason that ... all discourse ... is fundamentally dialogical" (pp. 287–288).

MEANING MAKING IN THE LABYRINTH
OF MULTILAYERED TEXT WORLDS

As one shifts from meaning making with single texts to multiple texts or sources, and sifts through ideas toward developing one's own constructions or remixing those of others, the active role of the meaning makers and the need for a different configuration of strategies and forms of self-direction seems apparent.[4] Based upon her work and that of her colleagues across a number of studies involving synthesizing from multiple print sources, Spivey (1997) argues that meaning makers pursue understandings across multiple texts using a rather consistent regimen. As she states, they

> ... shape their meanings with organizational patterns, make selections on the basis of some criteria of relevance, and generate inferences that integrate material that might seem inconsistent or even contradictory. In such acts writers not only read single text but also an intertext, as they perceive intertextual cues and make connections ... they also read the context ... (p. 191)

She also suggests that these same intertextual connections and these same processes parallel what meaning makers do in hypertext where similar constellations of multiple texts are visible with one possible exception. Whereas meaning makers using multiple print sources may need to pursue their own link, hypertext provides many of its own links.

As she suggests:

> People make across-text linkages and topical jumps, and they generate relations from one text to another as they do their transformation. The kind of intertextual connections that are so visible when people work in hypertext environments are the kinds of transformations that we have been considering.... A difference, of course, is that there has not been a programmer who built the interconnecting links into the database, and writers (readers) have to generate such links themselves ... making such inferences as "this supports...," "This adds to...," " This contradicts..." (pp. 209–210)

With hypertext, meaning makers may be constrained by a kind of labyrinth (Snyder, 1996) and proceed from one text to the next and one link to the next gingerly—lest they become lost, at a dead end, or miss what they perceive to be a key item. Indeed, meaning making within the labyrinth of some hypertexts maybe overly text driven. This was apparent in a study by Coiro and Dobler (2007), who examined the on-line comprehension strategies (via think alouds, responses to semistructured interview tasks and other responses) of successful sixth-grade comprehenders engaged with a preset Internet site dealing with the topic of tigers as an assignment prompting search engine usage. The architecture of on-line material, especially with hyperlinks and the use of thumbnails and annotations, seemed to prompt the use of such features to assist with the navigation of the texts.[5] Based upon their findings, the researchers suggested that one of the key distinctions between on-line and off-line comprehension is tied to the more frequent use of forward inferencing (vs. backward inferencing) which is aroused at the point of a hypertext link. They link this to a more multilayered inferential engagement of on-line meaning makers. As Coiro and Dobler stated:

> The skilled readers in our study engaged in a multi-layered inferential reading process that occurred across the three-dimensional spaces of Internet text ... combining traditionally conceived inferential reasoning strategies with a new understanding that the relevant information may be "hidden' beneath several layers of links on a website as opposed to one visible layer of information in a printed book. (p. 234)

They suggest that "... internet reading seems to demand more attempts to infer, predict and evaluate reading choices ... to require readers to orient themselves in a new and dynamic three-dimensional space ... to figure out how to get back to where they were" (p. 234). They suggest that the self-regulation of on-line comprehension seems tied to a similar set of recursive strategies of past models of composing (e.g., Tierney & Pearson, 1983). On-line comprehension involves planning within and across Web sites, predicting and following leads, monitoring how and where to proceed and evaluating relevance and judging merits. They noted that there were physical dimensions associated with these activities (e.g., scrolling, clicking) and speculated that the on-line environment might be more demanding and complex than off-line. In some ways, these results support the characterization of on-line comprehension as more likely to be aligned within the author(s) frame(s) or labyrinth(s) at the same time as it entails agility with being able to navigate, search, select and integrate across sources. As the authors state:

> Our findings suggest that the greater complexities in online reading comprehension may result largely from a process of self-directed text construction; that is, the pro-

cess online readers use to comprehend what they read as they search for the Internet text(s) most relevant to their reading needs.

> On one level, we observed skilled readers engaged in an ongoing "self-directed" planning process involving a series of inferences about what would best fit with their internal representation of the text's meaning. Simultaneously, on a second level, these readers constructed their own external texts. Each decision about which link was most relevant involved constructing the next element in the text they built. We observed readers actively anticipating and monitoring the relevancy of each new text unit, while quickly deciding whether to continue to add that text to their own external text by following deeper links within a page or to exclude that text and search elsewhere by clicking the back button as a fix-up strategy, for example. At the end of the reading session, it became clear that each reader had constructed not only his or her internal understanding of a certain text, but had also constructed a unique external representation of the Internet texts most applicable to their needs. (p. 241)

They contrast this with

> Readers who do not strategically plan and anticipate where they are headed within open Internet spaces may end up constructing a disjointed collection of random texts as opposed to a systematic compilation of carefully chosen texts from which to sift out a relevant point. Thus, an increased need to make forward inferences about text appeared to compound an already complex process of making bridging inferences about content in a manner that may prompt additional complexities to the process of reading online. (p. 242)

Again, the on-line demands of meaning making appear to prompt more use of what was labeled forward inferencing or a form of making predictions as meaning makers attempted to navigate the layers of text or information that the text template and on-line navigational tools might suggest. Forward inferencing seems to arise in conjunction with an interest in determining where links might lead and in assessing the possible saliency of what may be uncovered, especially by a hyperlink. When using search engines, they often relied on annotations offered with hyperlinks as a means of assessing the degree of relevance or the likelihood that an identified site would yield more or less relevant results. Coiro and Dobler (2007) conjectured that on-line comprehension could be differentiated from off-line comprehension in a number of ways. First, as meaning making proceeded on line, meaning making involved knowledge of topic and knowledge of print informational text structures akin to off line comprehension; in contrast, it involved knowledge of informational Web site structures as well as search engines.[6] Such influenced how they navigated the text including the physical nature of their approach (e.g., returns to the home page). Second, on-line comprehension involved to a degree similar and different inferential strategies. In response to questions that were set, the meaning makers made similar use of context and other text cues to what off-line comprehenders would use to explore the texts as they pursued answers to questions. But, as suggested, there was more forward inferencing as one chose what path to follow.

Teresa Dobson's research on reading hypertext novels suggests similar findings—especially the nature of the influence of hypertext architecture upon the approach and strategies that are prone to be employed depending upon the disposition of the meaning maker. She has done extensive probing of adolescents response to selected hypertext novels which are literary in nature (Dobson, in press; Dobson & Luce-Kapler, 2005;

Luce-Kapler, Dobson, Sumara, Davis, 2006). Her observations of and comments by her students suggest that hypertext novels provoke readers to be more self-consciousness and be text dependent or authorcentric.[7] Her analyses focused upon the comments of readers to their engagements; her findings tended to support that "… hypertext may encourage a particular level of meta-cognitive awareness among readers with respect to their reading processes, and, as well, as a level of critical awareness with respect to narrative structure and substance" (p. 14). Some of the students' comments were illustrative. In comparing the hypertext novel with a book, one student suggested "you can read it but you can't quite get into it as much" (p. 327). Students were not sure they had chosen the right links in the right order or that they had gotten what they needed to get from the text. Dobson argues that hypertext may lead to more physically localizing reading experiences tied to how the developers structure the plot. However she suggests, in her subsequent work with wikis, that meaning makers engaged in their own development of these structures seem to shift in their attitude (Dobson, 2004). As she stated:

> … in my current work with students reading hypertexts and writing collaboratively and individually) in malleable "wiki" writing spaces, I often find those who are exceedingly critical of hypertext structures as readers become wholly engaged as writers, often delighting in engaging the rhetorical ploys they previously eschewed. (pp. 17–18)

Dobson, together with her colleagues (e.g. Luce-Kapler, Dobson, Sumara, & Davis, 2006), has explored a range of engagements with other literature and other readers. Together this work begins to shift the focus to variations in meaning making by different readers in response to different hypertext novels. The work seems to stress the consciousness of the reader, which is raised by the hypermedia and the possibilities such might offer a diverse range of what they term "mindful" reading.

Indeed, intrigued by encountering a similar experience with the appeal of hypertext among students who were earlier users of animation and ways to link material, my colleagues and I explored various responses to hypertext construction in our observations of high schoolers, including a group of high school students set up to work on hypertext projects versus parallel forms of regular print-based projects (in science and literature) (Galindo, Tierney, & Stowell, 1989; Tierney, Kieffer, Whalin, Desai, Moss, Harris, & Hopper, 1997). We found a similar preoccupation and enamourment with form and the possibility of engaging the use of forms of special effects drawn from their exposure to pop culture. Our findings suggested that students appeared to approach hypertext with more questions and more interest but with more concern over form (e.g., the layering of material with links and interface with video) than the regular print-based projects. We found that the students viewed the advantages of the hypertext as allowing a way to "architecture" a space that affords a kind of edginess. When engaged with hypertext, students seemed more tied to the form and structure of the plot or presentation of the ideas than the ideas themselves. That is, hypertext prompted meaning makers to keep aligned with how the ideas might be structured or "architectured." Variations did occur but they were minimal depending upon a host of factors (digital architecture, the ideas, knowledge of the reader or writer, technical skills, and the nature of the collaboration). Again, a key factor seemed to be the novelty and an interest in impressing their peers with the special effects of the hypermedia.

The importance of how meaning makers position themselves (including goals, focus, perspective, authority) arises as salient from studies of meaning making from reading and writing multiple sources across a range of literacy settings. Indeed, the saliency of similar features come from un-mined (or at least underutilized) research on meaning making across texts and media—namely, research on reading and discourse syntheses studies (the process in which writers use multiple texts to develop their own texts), research on intertextuality, research on disciplinary expertise as well as studies of learning at a very young age where the amalgamation of image, sound and text is overt and commonplace or studies of adult learning in certain fields or occupations.

For example, the importance of the characteristics of the meaning maker is consistent with the findings emanating from the work of McGinley (1988, 1992) who engaged college students using multiple sources to develop essays. He noted that the shifts, search of, selection, and use of different sources was quite focused for the more able students but rather haphazard for those who were not. His findings of successful and less successful composers mirror the aforementioned findings of especially the linking that is required as well as the need for a focus to guide and assess the relevancy of sources and navigate efficiently and flexibly across sources toward integrated and coherent compositions or understandings. He relates his discussions of the findings of reading and writing from multiple sources to Wittgenstein's notion of crisscrossing the topical landscape as a metaphor for how meaning makers appear to engage with multiple sources or multiple texts (McGinley & Tierney, 1989). He stresses that meaning makers are engaged in a negotiation with self in the company of others (especially authors). He found that successful meaning making involved a kind of internal collaboration or dialectic as the meaning maker pursued agency as "a reader of the source articles, an essay writer, an essay reader, a note writer, and a note reader" (p. 241) and a reader of themselves.

The importance of agency and positionality within a community of others seems key for meaning makers at all ages as they explore their worlds and their relationship to these worlds through mixing, remixing, and networking with "snatches" of music, image, text, and so forth. Based upon her extensive ethnographic works in learning through a social-cultural lens, Dyson (1988, 1995) has suggested children's major developmental challenge is not simply to create a unified text world but to move among multiple worlds and coordinate multiple space/time structures toward defining self, including how one is placed in the company of others. As Dyson (1995) stated: "Children are not first and foremost learners; they are first and foremost people living the complexities of their day-to-day lives" (p. 36). Children seek to "imagine" relationships and situate themselves socioculturally and ideologically.

With older students, Mathison (1996) reached similar conclusions. In her examination of sociology students' abilities to offer substantive critique, she surmised that their development was based upon their ability to draw from their interactions with interpretative communities or disciplinary groups that can provide feedback on their meaning making in a fashion which might differ from what they might do on their own with other groups. Without such engagements, critiques remained unrefined and lacked the authority that comes with acquiring the agency. She surmised that success as a sociologist (insofar as critiques revealed) comes with exploring identity in a fashion that involves engagements with fellow sociologists.

In a similar vein, Sefton-Green (2006) and Rampton (2006) have observed that as youth interact with one another around games, music, and other exchanges, they use the "snatches" of music, phrases, etc., to rework, remix, adapt as they position themselves to assert their agency and to possibly explore their own identities.

AGENCY, ENACTMENT, AND EMBODIMENT

In some ways, these multiple engagements befit the view of meaning makers as a kind of multivocal and multiperspectival pursuer of understandings akin to what was suggested by Barthes, or other views of the social construction of multiple meanings. That is, the meaning maker is engaged in constructing selves or multiple personae in the company of others or a form of embodiment—a secondary engagement with or participation in the worlds constructed across, within or by layers of text and other media. The term embodiment is used to denote Csordas' (1999) use of embodiment—"an existential condition" (p. 143). At the same time, a meaning maker adopts one or more personae as he or she positions himself or herself with others and his or her worlds in a fashion growing out of their subjectivities, alliances, choices, and so forth.[8] In many ways, these studies suggest a link between meaning making and identity formation. As readers read they explore the world of the text for themselves relating to the imagined author and characters as well as events in certain ways.[9] In the aforementioned studies, the agency of the meaning maker (especially how the meaning maker positioned himself or herself, approached or navigated the text(s) (or digital space) was seen as key to his or her engagement with the ideas that were explored, the strategies that were employed as well as how the meaning maker wished to position himself or herself in the company of others.

In various digital spaces, the multiple embodiments of the meaning makers have been observed across a variety of literacy events. Several literacy scholars have noted that access to multimedia tools (e.g., digital video) enhances youths' explorations, expression and expansion of their sense of identity. By affording students access to these multimedia environments spaces, Rogers and Winters (2006), Alvermann, Hagood, and Williams (2001), Hull and Nelson (2006), and Hudak, Hull, and James (in press) have argued that students are afforded the possibility of having their literacy practices travel across spaces, in and out of schools, blurring traditional boundaries and forms of literate practices. These spaces also allow students to "juxtapose and transform genre practices for critical purposes, engage in the playful instability of genres, selves, and messages, and re-narrate their stories and identities in the process" (Rogers & Winters, 2006, p. 29). For example, as Rogers and Schofield (2005) indicate, the students mimic jackassing as well as hip-hop and various vignettes befitting their views of their cultures and their multiple identities within and outside of schools. Examined sociopolitically, these studies offer evidence of these engagements interfacing with emerging identities.

Observations of students engaged in the use of instant messaging suggest that the digital medium supports a fluid form of identity construction. In particular, Lewis and Fabos (2005) found that when adolescents instant message with one another they can shift identity almost simultaneously as they interact with one another in the context of others and so on. As Lewis and Fabos (2005) stated, "...they enact identities that depend upon a running analysis of the on-line and off-line contexts" (p. 494). They describe adolescents who shift their interactions to fit their relationship and stance with respect to one another as they instant message with each other with one another in the company of groups (e.g., from confidante to advisor to cynic to empathetic supporter with the different participants) and they do so in a fashion consistent with his or her overall sense of identity and understanding of the dynamics of the relationships. Lewis and Fabos described Amanda and other students being supportive with a fellow instant messenger, but terse with another as if Amanda (and others) were representing themselves as having multiple sides to whom they were during on-line exchanges.

Even more overtly, embodiment occurs in gaming. In the research on hypertext and gaming, observations of meaning makers suggest different alignments with authors or within the worlds in which gamers choose to position themselves. With the advent of interactive media, especially in the form of simulations and hands on virtual engagements, especially games, etc., meaning making as performance may be foregrounded and out of the shadows. At the same time, it may vary in how planned or contrived it may be. Certainly, as Squire (2006) and Gee (2003) suggest in the context of these digital spaces, knowing may go beyond moving from print to image to virtual or real environments interfaced with tools which offer opportunities to try on identities as one experiences and enters such worlds.

Again, such embodiments are not restricted to meaning making spurred by participation in a virtual reality environment; they are consistent with observations of meaning makers engaged in reading and their relationship to the text worlds with which they engage. As Enciso (1992) observed, meaning makers engage in a form of embodiment that may be culturally constructed and experience or direct affiliations with characters and events, adopting points of view, directing their emotional and visual attention—as they navigate their way within these worlds. Slatoff (1970) describes it as follows:

> As one reads one has the feeling one is moving into and through something and that there is movement in oneself — a succession of varied, complex, and rich mental and emotional states usually involving expectancy, tensions, and releases, sensations of anxiety, fear, and discovery, sadness, sudden excitements, spurts of hope, warmth, or affection, feelings of distance and closeness, and a multitude of motor and sensory responses to the movement, rhythm, and imagery of the work. (pp. 6–7)

As Rosenau (1992) suggests, a meaning maker "is an actor-receiver, participant observer, and an observing participant all at once" (p. 26). Again, observations of the complexity of such engagements can be found in many of the aforementioned accounts of meaning making within and across texts, text and images including classic cognitive accounts such as Bartlett's (1932) discussion of remembering or Rosenblatt (1983) and others discussion of how meaning making occurs.

Regardless of the context of the lived through experience (reading, writing, viewing, or gaming), one may be engaged in a world that is more akin to a form of process drama where the meaning making of others contribute to shifts in the direction and nature of one's engagement, or a form of theater where audience members are not fixed to a seat to enjoy the theatre as spectacle but are able to wander and position themselves in the plot, setting, or characters as they chose from a menu of possibilities and tools for so doing. And, adding to the complexity of any meaning making in such environments may be others which may vary from time to time—especially in some virtual environments. However, there may be ways that distinguish the participation spurred by a text and that offered by virtual reality. As one contemplates how meaning making occurs within virtual worlds from games to software environments (e.g., the Sim software construction spaces), the discussions of imaging and secondary world engagements may entail a physical response such as a guiding a cursor or clicking on a space.

The embodied engagements within and across these spaces occurs in a range of ways from quite broad and even global to quite narrow and intrapersonal. It can involve engagement across social worlds and involve exchanges of ideas done in a fashion akin to the exchange of goods or capital or forms of encroachment, absorption of adoption akin to colonization or hybridization. It can involve exchanges of thoughts or ideas for oneself or in the context of schooling. It may involve a form of mobility which offers individuals ways to locate or dislocate themselves as they relate to or interact within and across different spaces in different ways. An early theorist about "hyperreality," Jean Baudrillard, suggested that we live in a world drained of authenticity as a result of world full of illusions perpetuated by the media that surrounds and the mass-produced environments (e.g., malls, amusement parks, automobiles, etc.). The end result, he argued was an almost complete blurring of reality and unreality.

If meaning making is envisioned as a form of embodiment, then there may need to be a shift in how we view our meaning maker and the strategies that they employ whereas cognitive-based models of meaning making tend to suggest major phases such as planning, inferencing, connecting, and monitoring, perhaps our models should be reconsidered so that they are more aligned with the embodied engagement of meaning makers such as how people transact meanings with one another—engaging with, accessing, co-planning, co-authoring, searching and exploring, positioning, sharing, guiding, reflecting recycling and sustaining. In accordance with these notions and emanating from pragmatics (especially speech act theory) and its critique by Derrida (1988) and others, Judith Butler (1993) has delved into these issues in conjunction with bringing to the fore the notion of performativity with its antecedents in pragmatics including speech act theory and its critique by Derrida (1988).[10] Butler (1993), as Ruitenberg (in press) noted, suggests that performativity and agency are linked in complicated ways in a fashion more discursive and transactional than subservient than passive. As Butler suggests, meaning makers are not without agency, but their agency is not autonomous. As Ruitenberg (in press) noted, we should:

> conceive of students, and students of themselves, not as autonomous agents, nor as passive recipients of tradition, but rather as subjects whose actions and identities both depend on, and can make changes to, discourses that precede and exceed them. (p. 8)

Rather than perpetuate a within the head form of individualism, meaning makers are not alone. They move in and out of groups or operate in all manner of fashions—unified or dispersed, in concert or in disarray etc. Even in solitude, meaning makers may view themselves as operating in multiples, especially as they interact with texts of others and their own selves. We should recognize what some have termed the ensemble nature of meaning making—namely, the social nature of the meaning making—akin to a form of group co-authoring and enlist terms which represent a better fit with such engagements. For example, we might view meaning making through lens that recognize social nature of the processes and products of co-authorships involving shifting affiliations, negotiations, mediations, authorizing etc. (see Dyson, 1995; McEneaney, 2006).

WEAVING OUR WORLDS—SELF AND OTHERS

In his book *Literacy: An Introduction to the Ecology of Written Language*, David Barton (1994) suggested some key tenets about literacy based on explorations of everyday literacy in the United Kingdom (Barton & Hamilton, 1998). He proffered that literacy practices are situated in broader social relations "... It is a symbolic system used for communication and as such exists in relation to other systems of information exchange" (Barton, 1994, p. 34–35).[11] Purcell-Gates (2006) has argued in conjunction with her work in various sites that literacy "begins and ends in, or leads to, the social practices of literacy (actually ... never ends for many people) (Purcell-Gates, 2006, p. 44). Similarly, the work identified as "new literacy studies" with its antecedents in the sociosemiotic traditions (e.g., Halliday, 1973; Heath, 1980), represents, as Street (2006) and Kress (2003) have suggested, an interest in the history and social practices around the various symbol systems that are used.

Certainly literacy has, as its antecedents, a relationship to historical and cultural roots that inextricably define it as social and cultural practice that is interwoven with societal developments around issues of exchange. Literacies, including digital literacies, may offer ways of knowing and communicating, but they occur within a social fabric which involves the pragmatics of communication (who is doing what to whom and why) and matters of identity (construction of self, community, and others—especially tied to cultural as well as sociopolitical positioning). Whether we are operating with digital literacies or traditional print literacies, matters of identity, emerging status and various forms of participation of a sociopolitical nature occur.

Schmandt-Besserat (1978, 1986), who is credited with identifying the earliest uses of writing, was able to make such a discovery by uncovering the fabric associated with various tokens that she was able to link together across archeological digs as a result of understanding the cultural practices. For example, in her accounts of the earliest use of print, she discusses the use of print as a means of exchange—a means of engaging with trade including contractual arrangements between parties across time and space. As Schmandt-Besserat (1986) commented, the tokens carried with them forms of agency for groups and individuals: permitting estimation and computation of goods, means of exchange as well as reflection and as instruments of control and imagined possibilities.

In a similar fashion, Michael Taylor's (1987) account of the use of art of one of the oldest Australian aboriginal groups brings to the fore some of the parallels that exist between modern-day literacy practices (including digitally-based) and the deep-rooted traditions of a culture that has used art to explore world in the company of others for thousands of years. As Kunwinjka, for example, learn their art, they do so as apprentices in the company of mentors. As they progress, the art emerges amidst shared observations, conversations and advice across a range of situations. Their art serves to identify them—their place within community as well as across communities. At the same time, their art involves an exchange—it serves as both individual and community capital.

Literacy as the exchange of ideas or goods has historical roots, but the metaphor of literacy as capital has been heightened with the reference (and somewhat synonymous) use of the term knowledge economy,[11] or more recently knowledge society, to reference the advent of the information age, smart economies and the global Internet as the basis for the exchange of ideas. In terms of theory and research, notions of the new literacies have been linked to discussions of "culture capital" (Bourdieu, 1986) and the value given these literacies through a school reform lens as well as historical discussions of the impact of learning these literacies. Based upon her analysis of these new literacies in the lives of Americans who were born between 1895 and 1985 (Brandt, 2001), Brandt (2001) stated:

> Workers these days produce wealth not only by processing raw materials but by supplying those raw materials themselves in the form of knowledge and skills, including communication skills. (p. 6)

The argument undergirds the claims proffered by the New London group and others, and more recently the claim made by Cynthia Lewis and Bettina Fabos (2005) in *Instant messaging, literacies, and social identities*:

> If we mourn the loss of print literacy as we think we once knew it, then we may find ourselves schooling young people in literacy practices that dis-regard the vitality of their literate lives and the needs they will have for their literate and social futures at home, at work, and in their communities. (p. 498)

Or, as Selfe and Hawisher (2004) argued:

> If literacy educators continue to define literacy in terms of alphabetic practices only, in ways that ignore, exclude, or devalue new-media texts, they not only abdicate a professional responsibility to describe the ways in which humans are now communicating and making meaning, but they also run the risk of their curriculum no longer holding relevance for students who are communicating in increasingly expansive networked environments. (p. 233)

As our digital literacies expand and growing numbers of communities become wired or Internet wireless, it becomes well-nigh essential that individuals and groups neither be sidelined from participating nor constrained in ways that limit their ability to do so creatively and critically. In other words, it would seem limiting if they were not given (1) access which may carry with such certain technical requirements as well as (2) opportunities or the license to contribute creatively and critically as one pursues personal and group goals. Further, if students are to be participants and not spectators, they need opportunities to collaborate, communicate, acquire, sift through, create, and critique ideas as well as to solve problems.[12]

These notions of participation and the capital nature of these new literacies are consistent with the UN Geneva principles on building the information society that was the focus of the world summit on the informational society in 2003 (United Nations, 2003).[13] The summit began with:

> Principle 1: We, the representatives of the peoples of the world, assembled in Geneva from 10–12 December 2003 for the first phase of the World Summit on the Information Society, declare our common desire and commitment to build a people-centred, inclusive and development-oriented Information Society, where everyone can create, access, utilize and share information and knowledge, enabling individuals, communities and peoples to achieve their full potential in promoting their sustainable development and improving their quality of life, premised on the purposes and principles of the Charter of the United Nations and respecting fully and upholding the Universal Declaration of Human Rights.

The principles argued for participation "where human dignity is respected" and where we access these informational technologies to further development

> ... to reduce many traditional obstacles, especially those of time and distance, for the first time in history makes it possible to use the potential of these technologies for the benefit of millions of people in all corners of the world ... as tools and not as an end in themselves. Under favourable conditions, these technologies can be a powerful instrument, increasing productivity, generating economic growth, job creation and employability and improving the quality of life of all. They can also promote dialogue among people, nations and civilizations.

Taking one's place as a participant may not be as straightforward as the principles might suggest. Economic circumstances and/or social constructions of engagement with these technologies might preclude the possibility of access. Studies of intra-national differences within both developed and developing countries highlights that issues of access are limited for economically challenged groups and individuals. The United Nation's *Information Economy Report 2006: The Development Perspective* (United Nations, 2006)[14] analysis of trends in core ICT indicators, such as the use of Internet and mobile phones, as well as the role of broadband, suggests an expanded uptake of mobile phones but developing countries lag in Internet access and broadband expansion. Indeed, the uptake of mobile phones in developing countries exceeds that of developed countries, but the use of the Internet and the creation of Web-based resources in developing countries lags significantly behind developed countries.

Even within developed countries, such as the United States, participation seems tied to economic circumstances. As Cynthia Selfe and Gail Hawisher (2004) report, a U.S. study carried out over 5 to 6 years following various interviews of over 300 individuals and then the selection of subset of case studies (20) with a broad range of history of engagements with personal computers in ways that influenced their lives. From these case studies, they deduced a number of themes which brought to the fore the advantages afforded by these digital literacies, but how opportunities to participate were closely intermeshed with certain factors (race, gender, economic circumstances).

Certainly, critiques of these technologies have occurred in terms of the interests that they serve. On the one hand, critiques based upon postcolonial tenets decry the economic and cultural interests served by global spread of these new literacies. On the other hand, participation in these new literacies is heralded as democratizing and empowering with the view that these new literacies are also about us and how we position ourselves as meaning makers with respect to one another. A great deal has been written in the media and popular press about how digital literacies can contribute to cultural continuity or disruption, cultural expansion or erosion, cultural self determination or imperialism. But such discussions of technology range from expressions of concerns that engagement in digital literacies represents acquiescence to globalization and some form of technopoly that would undermine thinking and society (e.g., Neil Postman, 1993).

It has been argued that these new literacy spaces may be predisposed to certain ways to explore or define self during such exchanges—that is, certain literacy spaces may be predisposed to certain ideologies rather than others or forms of subordination to certain ideologies (Bruce & Hogan, 1998). For example, Omrod (1995) has examined the ways in which biology and culture come together in individual lives using the concept of performativity to emphasize gender, race, class and age as performance. As the sociological papers of Damarin (1995) and Grint and Gill (1995) indicate, certain ways of interacting with technologies define particular types of gender identity. For example, Michael Tierney (1995) (working with systems) and Hapnes and Sorenson (1995) (in studies of hacking) suggest that the behavior associated with computer usage and gaming may be aligned with ways of defining masculinarities. Further, as Squire (2006) and Gee (2003) suggest certain virtual environments (e.g., Sim worlds, civilization and games) may perpetuate certain political ideologies and ways of interacting with and constructing the world which may contribute to identity formations.[15] Squire (2006) for example suggests that "… games focus our attention and mold our experience of what is important in a world and what is to be ignored. The game designers' choices, particularly of what to strip away from a world, can be read as ideological when considered in relation to other systems" (pp. 21–22).

Wade and Fauske (2004), in their discussion of on-line discussions, suggest that individuals are "not passive reproducers in creating their identities their use of language and other social choices … language choices can be thought of as strategies designed to achieve particular goals in a particular context" (p. 140). Wade and Fauske (2004) argue that listservers, text messaging and other forms of exchanges may spur distinctiveness rather than sameness. Interestingly, the discussions of these developments in the media appear to have shifted from general discussions of these developments to a recognition of the sometimes more nuanced cultural dynamics at play.[16]

The complex nature of these spaces and how individuals and groups are located and displaced by them is apparent in studies of how historically marginalized groups form or find community via blogs, chatrooms, listserves or a combination of on-line or off-line spaces. For example, studies of a sense of community achieved for lesbians via e-mail listerves, blogs and other spaces, also may dislodge or serve to marginalize individuals depending upon their performances as members of these groups and the norms that are applied or develop across time (e.g., Wincapaw, 2000; Bryson, MacIntosh, Jordan & Un, 2006). Bryson et al. (2006) challenge the simple-minded, almost utopian, view that these digital environments serve as the foundation for a range of diverse spaces for all. As Bryson et al. suggest, one might find a haven or prison or have a sense of belonging or dislodgement in such spaces.

In contrast, studies of course-based online discussions suggests that on-line forms of interaction allow for a more fertile exchange across diverse student bodies. They have demonstrated that on-line interactions (e.g. threaded discussions) contribute to exchanges of ideas and community engagements which can enhance understanding of difference rather than dilute them. Further, that they might achieve greater understanding of diverse ideas than might occur in face to face interactions. For example, Merryfield (2003) found that students, especially students from different cultures with varying language skills, would more openly and respectfully discuss cultural and political issues—such as those involving terrorism and the war with Iraq—than they might be reluctant to do in a classroom. What is left unanswered is the extent to which sustained changes to community occur, whether or not such literacy practices contribute to changes in understanding that result in shifts in both attitude and behavior in cross-cultural situations, and how these literacy practices develop and become intertwined with other literacy developments. As Beach and Myer (2001) have argued and as various studies by Myer and his colleagues (Myer & Beach, 2001; Myer, Hammond, & McKillop, 1998; 2000) have demonstrated, selected digital literacies give meaning makers the tools for representing themselves and community as well as engaging with others and their communities. And, in so doing, they enhance understandings of self, one's own communities as well as others and their communities. However, such findings should be couched in the context of their situation and the frame undergirding the participations. As Levin (1996) and Turkle (1995) have noted, some on-line discussions perpetuate existing hierarchy, and may hide identifications in ways that contribute to silencing, alienating or marginalizing individuals and groups.

Traces of this debate can be seen in some of the exchanges that arose when *Time* magazine published a mirror on the cover of its magazine to herald the Person of the Year. As the desk editor suggested:

> … individuals are changing the nature of the informational age, that the creators and consumers of user-generated content are transforming art and politics an commerce, that they are the engaged citizens of a new digital democracy … this new global nervous system is changing the way we perceive the world. And the consequences of it are both hard to know and impossible to overestimate. (Stengel, Richard (2006) Now it's your turn. *Time*, December 25, 2006–January 1, 2007, p. 9.)

But, as Frank Rich noted in his *New York Times* editorial on December 24, 2006 (Week in Review, p. 8) entitled "Yes, you are the person of the year!" *Time* may have it right for perhaps for the wrong reasons. Frank Rich laments that Internet users seem to be more inclined to escapism than meaningful information exchange or learning. What neither Rich nor others seem to be contesting is that we are engaging with one another around ideas and shared experiences in ways that represent a shift in our literacy practices. In particular, the Internet with the advent of blogs, podcasting, text messaging, wikis, and other user-based initiatives represent sites which are transforming how, when, where, and why we interact with one another about what. The question arises from the claims: What is exchanged or from an educational perspective, what is learned when and how?

Admittedly, learning depends upon who is teaching what to whom and how. Studies of learning (digital or non-digital) may not lend themselves to overgeneralization across fields of study, the different possible architectures structures of any content, and the social dynamics involved. A number of studies have examined the use of digital sources as scaffolds to learning in a fashion consistent with the tradition of providing adjuncts (e.g., related text, various forms of representation, video, etc.) or engagements with ideas (e.g., problems, tasks etc.) or to provide feedback or motivation (e.g., Cognition and Technology Group at Vanderbilt, 1990; Kinzer & Leu, 1997). Some have studied and demonstrated the advantages of the use of selected digital tools as scaffolding for learning, as simulations or as ways to orchestrate case-based approaches via real world situations for complex knowledge acquisition such as teaching and medicine or developing reading strategies.[17] In studies of the use of digitally-based multiple cases by Spiro and others (e.g., Hughes, Packard, & Pearson, 2000a, b; Baker, 2006) suggest how important it may be to carefully plan cases and what may be revealed as well as the importance of the type of supports for delving into and across cases. The students' opportunity to control access to the cases may have some advantages as well as opportunities for teachers to provide well positioned support. For example, access to well-crafted cases focusing upon students across a range of sites, have been shown to support preservice teachers' knowledge and practices, but the transferability of these understandings to new knowledge domains and sites may be restricted without supple teacher support. In a similar vein, studies of the advent of animation, as a means of supporting complex learning in areas such as medicine, suggest variations in learning may be dependent upon how the animation is presented, probed and layered with text, audio etc. (e.g., Mayer & Moreno, 2002; Ruiz, Mintzer, & Leipzig, 2006).

As Bransford et al. (2000) summarized in his review of learning with technology for the National Research Council:

> In general, technology-based tools can enhance student performance when they are integrated into the curriculum and used in accordance with knowledge about learning. But the existence of these tools in the classroom provides no guarantee that student learning will improve, they have to be part of a coherent education approach (p. 216) … Much remains to be learned about these technologies. (p. 230)

Furthermore, implicit in all of the above is a theory of meaning making which guides why, when, how and why selected tools are enlisted. As mentioned, Mayer and Moreno (2002) have developed principles which might undergird the enlistment and juxtapositioning of animation and other modes of delivery in learning pursuits in some fields. In recent years, the work of Spiro and his colleagues (Spiro et al., 1987, 1990, 2003) has been notable as it has extended the study of knowledge acquisition with technology based upon what he suggests is the post-Gutenberg affordances of digital technologies and his theory of meaning making/ knowledge acquisition in what he suggests are ill-structured domains. In particular, Spiro and his colleagues have studied the use of hypermedia and video as the vehicle for achieving transferable problem-solving by mixing text and image across carefully constructed case-based learning in medicine and teaching. Spiro has had success in the pursuit of developing what he has termed "open and flexible knowledge structures to think with in context, not closed structures that tell you what to think across contexts" (Spiro, 2006b, p. 5). By using cases or video examples that "have been conceptually categorized is to show many variants from the same category. Learners with our systems quickly see variability in conceptual application across different clips as basic to understanding those ill-structured concepts" (p. 6). As Spiro argues, the medium affords the opportunity to craft cases toward achieving flexible knowledge:

> When one criss-crosses landscapes of knowledge in many directions (the main instructional metaphor of CFT, drawn from Wittgenstein; Spiro et al., 1988), a revisiting is not a repeating. The result is knowledge representations whose strength is determined not by a single conceptual thread running through all or most parts of the domain's representation, but rather from the overlapping of many shorter conceptual "fibers" (Wittgenstein, 1953), as befits an ill-structured domain. (p. 7)

Long-term and broader benefits have been recorded from such engagements. For example, longitudinal studies of students and adults (engaged in project-based work using multimedia platforms to explore and compose meaning) have been shown to have clear advantages related to achievement, identity, strategies and tools for learning, problem-solving, discovering and communicating. For example, in a 10-year study of the Apple Classroom of Tomorrow students, my colleagues and I (Tierney, Bond, & Bresler, 2006)[18] have claimed that access to call the resources and tools to engage in rich explorations with these new literacies afford the realization of personal, cognitive and social possibilities akin to "genres of power"—new texts, new ways of negotiating meaning, and ways of knowing. The literacies can be transformative in terms of lives—especially compared with peers without such opportunities. Indeed, students with high access to digital tools developed cutting edge uses of technology in ways that interfaced with the social fabric of their lives within and outside school and into the future.

Confirmation of similar impacts is apparent from other longitudinal examinations of the impact of digital literacies upon the lives of students and others over time. Cynthia Selfe and Gail Hawisher (2004) report a study carried out over 5 to 6 years following various interviews of over 300 individuals and then the selection of subset of case studies (20) with a broad range of history of engagements with personal computers in ways that influenced their lives. From these case studies, they deduced a number of themes. Their themes bring to the fore the extent to which the social fabric of life and the advent of these new literacies are closely intermeshed and how certain factors (race, gender, economic circumstances) can contribute to the circumstances that may be empowering to some and not others. As their first four themes suggest, literacy is interwoven into the social fabric in a manner which may stretch the life span.

Such studies support that sustained engagement in the productive use of digital technologies contributes in positive ways to various aspects of peoples lives including appearing to enhance their view of the possibilities and realities for a fuller participation in society in creative and a critical fashion which appears to personally, socially, educationally and economically advantageous. Certainly, such studies bring to the fore the premium placed upon economic advantage afforded by their skill at engaging in these spaces. They support the finding that power and literacy are inextricably linked and that the development of flexible and robust digital literacy practices may need to recognize and be built upon their multiple connections to social and cultural practices.

Unfortunately, such communities and learning envelopes may be more the exception than the rule. It seems paradoxical, but many schools may not support the transition of these new literacies to school settings in ways consistent with their potential, including the possible shifts in power dynamics that might occur (Sheehy, 2007). What may be accessible outside of school appears to have surpassed what most students in schools may have the opportunity to access. And, what may cross over to school may involve a mutation which may not have the same saliency or worth. As Street (2006) argued, outside of schools there is often an interest in global issues, networking, Webs, multimodality, flexibility, and so on, whereas inside schools there is often a tendency to stress stability and unity. Indeed, in some situations, these new literacies are framed as discrete skills such as programming, Internet access, or presentation skills rather than as learning tools with complex palates of possibilities for students to access in a myriad of ways. It is as if learning with technology is being perceived as "learning the technology" rather than using a range of multimodal literacy tools (supported by these technologies) in the pursuit of learning. Similarly, Squire (2006) has argued that the approach to learning within most schools falls short of what digital-based games are already achieving—most notably, situated learning with an array of imageful resources plus an accessible network of others and tied to developing expertise and understanding through performance.

As digital engagements with various media have been considered as literacies, there seems to be a crossing over of envelopes and potentially the beginnings of curricularizing these media as they are considered in terms of their learning benefits, the crossover to discussing the learning benefits of gaming, video making and other literacies which were predominately outside of school's purview (except perhaps in terms of possible negative effects—e.g., violence, wasted time) for learning about something and to individual and group empowerment through identity construction. Digital spaces are encased in a social context equivalent to what some have referred to as an envelope (Sefton-Green, 2006, Giaquinta, Bauer, & Levin, 1993).

Historically, we have tended to curricularizing of digital media as educators' attention has been drawn to these technologies as literacies. The curricularizing involves an advocacy for the crossing over of the use of different media use from informal settings (home, arcade etc.) to school settings. And, whereas the use of the media (e.g., games, video, digital cameras, mobile technologies, Internet, iPods, blogs, etc.) has been left to individuals and society to define and use, schools tend to redefine their use as they adopt a somewhat interventionist orientation. As one shifts from the real world to school, the orientation or theoretical perspective seems to shift from cultural anthropological and sociological accounts to studies of the media as educational approaches with learning outcomes as the goal. Lost in crossover to schools may be the social and culture possibilities—e.g., construction of identity, democratization, social interchanges, and so firth, and the use of the media from a semiotic perspective. These latter developments have arisen especially with the advent of new and increased usage of these digital tools—e.g., digital video and devices that allow for more interchanges or complex gaming or narratives.

Not surprisingly, the role of the teacher has emerged as key in most discussions of school improvement efforts around learning technology. Not surprisingly, the role of the teacher has emerged as key in most discussions of school improvement efforts around learning technology and also in the discussions of multimedia use for the advancement of new perspectives and understandings (see Baker, 2006). For instance, based upon his research in Los Angeles high schools with digital videos and his observations across various technology rich classrooms, Reilly (1996) suggested:

> The most important piece of hardware in the classroom isn't the multimedia computer, the video camera, or the network. It's the teacher's desk, where any innovation must pass in one form or another before it gets to students. The teacher isn't merely a gatekeeper, he or she is an orchestrator of activity and will greatly influence how technology fits into the classroom. (p. 207)

But, also not surprising, the potential and use in one setting may not be transferable to the other. In terms of schools, the transfer of students' engagements with these literacies outside of school may not fit well with in-school demands or norms.

Dwyer (1996), in his reflections of the Apple Classroom of Tomorrow (ACOT), suggested the importance of an approach to teaching which was authentic, interactive, collaborative, resource rich, inquiry driven and viewed knowledge transformation and its assessment in a fashion which was performance-based and afforded access to and support for multiple representations of ideas. It also demands a community which recognizes and supports the possibility of re-imaging selves across digital spaces and other literacy fields or spaces.

DISCUSSION

Within the advent of digital literacies, the embrace of the new and multiple literacies might be viewed as stating the obvious. However, it may not be—especially as one considers our history of research and theorizing about literacy. Several scholars have argued and shown that the literacy field has tended to maintain a tradition of theorizing literacy and studying texts in a fashion which is singular and separated from the growing fabric of digital literacies with which most of us most of the time engage as our primary sources. Further, the field has tended to focus upon the individual(s) versus group(s) as the meaning makers. While studies of digital literacy are beginning to embrace community dynamics and the ensemble style of engagements as well as multiple-text situations and their multilayeredness and linkages, our theories and models of meaning making tend to stick to the individual and one or a few threads rather than approach the study of literacy as requiring a consideration of the fabric and the composing processes of the ensembles.

To focus on the thread rather the fabric has the potential to inflate the trace while limiting (and perhaps distorting) its relationship to meaning making and to misrepresent reading as a monological experience. As Lemke (1998) posits, "Literacies are legion. Each one consists of interdependent social practices that link people, media objects, and strategies for meaning making." We are constantly navigating and building ever expanding and intermeshed webs of meaning as we engage with others and ourselves across face to face and other forms of communication, virtual and real, synchronized or not.

We are faced with a flood of web-like encounters involving arrays of different transactions (and co-constructions) daily as we engage with our colleagues, coworkers and others in various time zones. At times, one retreats and hopes for reprieve from the deluge and a quiet day in solitude without the onslaught, or perhaps wanting to keep it to a trickle.

The Webs and networks are rarely separate from one another although we do a form of selective engagement, sorting, etc. as we begin our day, perhaps checking and responding to e-mails, pursuing projects, relaxing as we peruse listserves, newspapers, etc. The multitasking with which we are engaging may involve a mix of direct and indirect or synchronized or non-synchronized developments—it may be that we are placing some matters on pause, but with an interest on moving ahead or connecting with others in various fashions with a form of joint advancement.

As we move across or within networks and web-like engagements, we are sifting, linking, sampling, following leads and paths at the same time as we are doing forms of layering and affiliating as we pursue for ourselves and others confirmations, understandings, plans, commitments, answers, directions or acknowledgements. Those researchers examining the cognitive strategies involved in meaning making on-line bring to the fore the importance of several strategies which may be somewhat nuanced in the networked environment—the importance of refining searches, forward inferencing (akin to predicting), making linkages and other integration in a fashion that coheres and is relevant, flexible and recursive. It suggests that the meaning maker(s) is/are engaged in simultaneous linking ideas together (texts, images, sounds) as the meaning maker(s) refine(s) or expand(s) understandings at the same time as they evaluate them and assess coherence.[19]

Spiro (1987, 2006) proposes an approach to meaning making which extends to the meaning makers' ability to navigate across multiple inputs with a great deal of speed and efficiency.[20] As he suggests, meaning making across digital material depends upon a fluidity and ability to discern relevance and glean meanings almost at a glance. For example, Spiro describes digital meaning makers as:

... being conductors (or jazz improvisers), rapidly bouncing excerpts from rich video clips off of each other. *He emphasizes that if the material is somewhat familiar and rich in content, meaning makers* ... capitalize on their affinity for this mode of "quick-cutting" across dense images (cf. Stephens, 1998) — and their accustomedness to nonlinear processing ... to criss-cross between many video excerpts to speed up and deepen the process of building interconnected knowledge from experience. (Spiro et al., 2006, p. 11)

To some extent, the agility and flexibility needed to do so involves meaning makers with some pre-existing knowledge of the topics, familiarity with the genres, and skill at efficiently discerning relevance across texts. [21] They are engaged as performative inquirers and with others in good haste, but in a fashion which is discerning of the relevance and discursive.

Perhaps our experience is informed by the same meaning making abilities that we have when we view art—especially impressionist art. We can savor the detail in relation to the composite. As we move from engagement to engagement or from one text to another or one Web site to another, we engage with the elements, but our view of their pertinence occurs via discerning composite(s) rather than a careful weighing of the separate elements. This is akin to a kind of gestalting, but in fashion that involves more of a leap in meaning making in a fashion akin to appreciating art as a whole rather than as a pile of threads or strokes or making one accountable for the pieces that might contribute to but do not define the meaning or coherence. The impressionistic discernment might be tied to seeing other composites of the same work. But the discernment of these composites may or may not be clearly interrelated. They may or may not be part of a search for the best fit. They may or may not be tied to crisscrossing a domain as Spiro has described meaning making in complex knowledge circumstances. They may be tied to a composite specific to a moment or a person or how or where the person is interested in proceeding or with which there is satisfaction—at least for now. [22]

As communication theorists indicate and research confirms, the engagement involves a relationship with the ideas which is personal and social rather than detached or individualistic. At one level (or perhaps across all levels), engagements involve conversations with one's self in the company of others. It involves, as Butler and others suggest, constructions which are performative and discursive. At another level, it is akin to conversation that may entail a form of reflective meaning making tied to negotiations across a set of e-mails or text messages or texts authored by others. At yet another level, it involves others—imagined or real. For example, it might entail trying to understand what the author wanted you to think or act. At yet another level, it might entail explore possible worlds and imagining or re-imagining possibilities for self. And, at a more macrolevel, it is tied to how we are networked and positioned with others in the context of exchanges locally and globally. It is consistent with a multivocal and multiple persona engagements both internal and external to the text or digital spaces including a set of virtual relationships with both imagined and real worlds and people. Plus these engagements occur in the context of navigating and journeying worlds—cultivating ideas and spurring meanings using range of texts where ideas are explored and mixed, created and critiqued, savored and digested, and used as fuel for expression of further considerations.

As one contemplates the nature of on-line meaning making within and across these spaces, one should be careful not to dichotomize the world as pre and post digital or processes as existing unique to meaning making within digital spaces or not. At the same time, one should not discount the affordances of technological developments. As many have noted, digital spaces bring to the fore affordances that should not be understated. However, as Owston (1997) emphasizes, "no medium, in and of itself, is likely to improve learning ... The key to the Web appears to lie in how effectively the medium is exploited" (p. 29). But certainly, these new spaces might heighten certain different dispositions over others as well as alternative ways to interact with ideas and others, including self. And, in terms of meanings, we seem to be on the frontier of a new form of public knowledge with the advent of citizen journalism and world less filtered and with shifts in notions of authorship, authority and copyright as well as ways of making texts, news, archives and access (see Willinsky, 2006).

Nor should one shy away from a theory or model of meaning making that captures how meanings are transacted within and among groups and individuals within these groups. As Lunsford and Ede (1990) noted, negotiations may proceed hierarchically or dialogically or both. In terms of the former, meaning making proceeds in a fashion which may be rigid and prescriptive. As Lunsford and Ede stated:

> ...rigidly, structured, driven by highly specific goals, and carried out by people playing clearly defined and delimited roles....the realities of multiple voices and shifting authority are seen as difficulties to be resolves. Knowledge ...is most often viewed as information to be found or a problem to be resolved. The activity of finding such information or solving such problems is closely tied to the efficient realization of a particular product end. (p. 133)

In terms of the latter, or dialogical, they suggest:

> The dialogical mode is loosely structured and the roles enacted within it are fluid; one person may occupy multiple and shifting roles as a project progresses. In this mode, the process of articulating goals is often as important as important as the goals themselves and sometimes even more important. Furthermore, those participating in dialogical collaboration generally value the creative tension inherent in multivoiced and multivalent ventures.... (p 133)

But, as you may have noted, there may be two forces in effect: the use of past models of meaning making and more in the way of old lens for examining what is emerging. Or, as Jonathan Sterne (2000) notes "... millennial narratives of universality, revolutionary character, radical otherness from social life, and the frontier mythos."

IN CLOSING

I hope my review spurs a mix of all of the above, but especially further ongoing enquiry across a wide range of literacy events and more deliberation about the nature of these occurrences from a variety of perspectives.[23] For myself, the review involved a great deal of search and reflection as well as a great deal of rethinking as I tried to anchor or connect disparate, but related research. This review has shifted direction several times as I encountered niche-like research that was important to mention or enlist. Gathering the resources for the chapter involved exploring a quite varied and wide range of studies from a diverse library of sources. For example, I gathered a massive set of materials that never seemed to stop growing. My search and navigational skills served were important antecedents, but did not suffice for the integration that a single piece demands. The mixing, at times, involved several different renderings, and I suspect that I will make shifts again and again as my thinking is adjusted or settles or is impacted by others. I wondered, at times, if a collaborative review would have been preferable as there are areas for which I yearned for input from knowledgeable others especially across some of the niches that I explored.

NOTES

1. Zeitgeist is used here to suggest a growing cultural ethos that prompts, in a Hegelian sense, the dialectical progression in thinking.
2. As Will Richardson (2006) details in his book for teachers, *Blogs, wikis and podcasts*, the Internet has contributed to a significant shift in the literacy demands and possibilities. With the number of blogs and other Web sites for exchanges of information growing by the millions with hits on Web sites in the millions every hour and over a million Web-log postings per day, he suggests:

   > Creating content of all shapes and sizes is getting easier and easier. High –bandwidth Internet access and expanding computer memory and storage continue to grow, and developers are creating tools to publish text or photos or video or whatever else easily to the Web. We're in the midst of an explosion of technologies that will continue to remake the Web into the community space...
   >
   > For most, however, the significance of these changes is still just starting to be realized. We are no longer limited to being independent readers or consumers of information...we can collaborate in the creation of large storehouses of information. In the process, we can learn much about ourselves and our world. (p. 2)

3. http://www.readingonline.org/research/impact/index.html#Spiro,R.J.,Coulson,R.L.
4. These notions might be extended (further as applications and cross-curriculum extensions in school or in out of school settings) to a form of what Kinder (1999) refers to as trans-media textuality which arises with the developing of a mix of various products (e.g., board games, trading cards, Web sites; see also Ito, in press).
5. While hyperlinks are different, they operate not unlike text cues that may or may not be available in printed versions of text which provide heads, sidebars, etc.
6. In a similar vein, Dwyer and Harrison (2006), building upon the work of Eagleton (2001, 2005) and Hargitai (2002) (especially in the area of search engine use), engaged students in workshops to improve their strategic engagement with Web-based resources and had some success in improving their skills and comprehension. Eagleton (2001) found middle school students without experience with Internet inquiry often making "hasty, random choices with little thought and evaluation" (p. 3). She coined the approach as a form of "snatch and grab." Hargitai (2002) found wide variability in search engine useage and success.
7. This contrasts with her discussion that hypertext reflects a shift from structuralist views of discrete, bounded, coherent, and linear meaning making to experiences which are more overtly fragmented, non-linear and intertextual consistent with poststructuralist view of meaning making. She has contended the instability, plurality of meaning tied to a somewhat endless network of connections afforded by hypertext.
8. There are several reviews of this research including studies of audience awareness of writers and sense of author by readers as well as studies of how meaning making occurs and develops (see Nelson & Calfee, 1998, Tierney & Shanahan, 1991). For discussions of persona, I would recommend Gibson (1969) as well as more recent discussion by Cherry (1998).
9. In biographic accounts, readers can recount their relationship with certain books and the authors in ways that was intimate and somewhat defining.
10. Rather than performativity being viewed as acting out one's identity, Butler (1993) suggested discourse(s) construct or are constructed by the nature of the identity forming participation of meaning makers. As Ruitenberg (in press) noted:

    > Discursive performativity means not that I, as autonomous subject, "perform" my identity the way an actor performs a role, but rather that I, as subject, *am performatively produced* by the discourse in which I participate. This perspective changes the ways in which the development of students' agency is regarded. (p. 6)

11. Peter Drucker, (1969). *The Age of Discontinuity; Guidelines to Our changing Society.* Harper and Row, New York, ch. 12.
12. I am drawing upon the notion of participation from the Nicaraguan literacy campaign discussions (Hirschon & Butler, 1983). Specifically, in discussing the campaign, Father Fernando Cardenal, S.J. (February, 1980) was questioned about the purpose of the campaign. He stated:

    > Literacy is fundamental in achieving progress and it is essential to the building of a democratic society where people can participate consciously and critically

in national decision-making. You learn to read and write so you can identify the reality in which you live, so that you can become a protagonist of history rather than a spectator.

In a similar vein, Alvin Toffler (1981) refers to the need for all of us to become productive consumers.

13. http://www.itu.int/wsis/docs/geneva/official/dop.html
14. http://www.unctad.org/en/docs/sdteecb20061_en.pdf
15. Some court rulings have addressed these issues.
16. In the *New York Times*, for example, a recent editorial discussed the phenomenon of text messaging from a cultural perspective. As Ken Nelson (2006) stated in his article "A parent's guide to teenspeak by text message. (*New York Times,* November 26, 2006, Week in Review, p. 4).

    Testing … is second nature to many teenagers and college students…children use the text-messaging function on their cellphones as a way to whisper to their friends out of earshot, so to speak, of parents and teachers, who are left to wonder what arcane language the children are speaking … what their children are doing today is not much different from what they did years ago; using new technology to create new ways of communicating.

17. The Voyage of the *Mimi* by the Bank Street Group was one of the earliest and engaged students in problem solving about whales and Mayan culture as they voyaged (Char & Hawkins, 1987). There are a large number of such examples—especially for science and mathematics (see Bransford et al., 2000).
18. The findings from this work highlight how digital literacies became woven in the social fabric of these students' lives—in and out of school—in ways that afforded them the opportunity to re-imagine themselves and explore educational and work related possibilities that enriched and enhanced their lives and many of those around them.
19. However, it is noteworthy that coherence may not be tied to completeness or stability, but may be tied to a sense of or desire for edginess, incompleteness and/or uncertainty. Indeed, different metaphors for understandings are tied to notions of situation-based, multiperspectival, layering, ill-structuredness, braiding or ongoing rather than fixed and definitive, comprehensive, singular or complete
20. In their work with video case studies, Spiro et al. (1987) draws heavily upon the work of Wittgenstein (1953) especially around crisscrossing the topical landscaping. As he stated:

    By criss-crossing the complex topical landscape, the twin goals of highlighting multifacetedness and establishing multiple connections are attained. Also, awareness of the variability and irregularity is heightened, alternative routes of traversal of the topic's complexity are illustrated, multiple routes for later information retrieval are established, and the general skill of working around that particular landscape is developed. (p. 8)

    Essentially his research informs a framework for thinking about the role of the architecture in a fashion similar to notions offered by semioticians. He provides evidence of the power of using these digital spaces for complex learning of transferable understandings and the importance of meaning makers engaging in a flexible fashion.

21. Again, one should not discount that the text may not match the learners' interests, backgrounds and prowesses. As Burbeles and Callister (1996) have speculated:

    …the desire to structure a hypertext in an open, dialogical fashion encounters a difficulty when we look at the concrete problems of the learner, and of the different types of readers who might encounter a hypertext. A form of organization that only allows a novice to search through direct and explicit connections may not facilitate the development of that novice into an independent and autonomous reader who can alter and add to what he or she finds in a hypertext. Conversely, a dialogical and flexible hypertext system, of much use to those who are prepared to be contributing co-authors of a text, might be too open-ended to be of much use to a novice or to a user who is simply interested in extracting specific and already-organized information from the textual source. ..many readers of hypertext end up browsing or performing the textual equivalent of "channel surfing": quickly scanning or surveying randomly accessed information, in very short snippets, with no overall sense of coherence or meaning for what they are exposed to.. A novice encountering a complex hypertext system for the first time cannot possibly know what information the system contains, without happening to come across it through searching or guesswork. (pp. 24–25)

22. It often extends beyond a single topic or engagement to a complex set of activities and an under-appreciated form of multitasking. For example, Steven Johnson (2006) for *Time* recently focused upon the multitasking and multiple use of these technologies by today's youth.

> Today's kids see the screen as an environment to be explored, inhabited, shared and shaped. They're blogging. They're building their MySpace pages. They're constructing elaborate fan sites for their favorite artists or TV shows. They're playing immensely complicated games, like Civilization IV—one of the most popular computer games in the world last autumn—in which players re-create the entire course of human economic and technological history.... The skills that they are developing are not trivial. They're learning to analyze complex systems with many interacting variables, to master new interfaces, to find and validate information in vast databases, to build and maintain extensive social networks cross both virtual and real-world environments, to adapt existing technologies to new uses... ("Don't fear the digital." *Time Magazine*, March 27, p. 42)

23. While representing the possibility for an agent-based model of literacy to begin to account for the demands of meaning making on-line, McEneaney (2006) called for a great deal more conceptualization if we are have a model with adequate explanatory or predictive value, Similarly, Kress (2003) in *Literacy in the New Media Age* closed with the following admonition.

> The major task is to imagine the characteristics of a theory which can account for the processes of making meaning in the environments of multimedia representation in multimediated communication, of cultural plurality and economic instability. Such a theory will represent a decisive move away from the assumptions of mainstream theories of the last century about language and learning. (p. 168)

REFERENCES

Alvermann, D. E., Hagood, M. C., & Williams, K. B. (2001). Image, language, and sound: Making meaning with popular cultural texts. Accessed June 2001 from: htyp://www.readingonline.org/newliteracies/lit_index.asp?HREF=/newliteracies/action/alvermann/index.html.

Barton, D. (1994). *Literacy: An introduction to the ecology of written language.* Oxford: Blackwell.

Barton, D., & Hamilton, M. (1998). *Local literacies: reading and writing in one community.* London: Routledge.

Bartlett, F. (1932). *Remembering: A study in experimental and social psychology.* Cambridge: Cambridge University Press.

Baudrillard, J. (1981). *Simulations.* New York: Semiotext(e).

Beach, R., & Myer, J. (2001). *Inquiry-based English instruction: Engaging students in life and literature.* New York: Teachers College Press.

Bourdieu, P (1986). The forms of capital. In J.G. Richardson (Ed.), *Handbook of theory and research for the sociology of education* (pp. 241–258). New York: Greenwood.

Bolter, J. D. (2001). *Writing spaces: The computer, hypertext, and the history of writing.* Hillsdale, NJ: Erlbaum.

Brandt, D. (2001). *Literacy in American lives.* Cambridge: Cambridge University Press.

Bransford, J. Brown, A. L., & Cocking, R. R. (Eds.). (2000). *How people learn; Brain, mind, experience and school.* National Academy Press.

Bruce, B. C., & Hogan. M. (1998). The disappearance of technology: Toward an ecological model of literacy. In D. Reinking, M., McKenna L., Labbo, & R. Kieffer (Eds.), *Handbook of literacy and technology: transformations in a post typographic world.* (pp. 269–281). Hillsdale, NJ: Erlbaum.

Burbules, N. C., & Callister, T. A., Jr., (1996). Knowledge at the crossroads: Alternative futures of hypertext environments for learning. *Educational Theory, 46*(1),: 23–50

Butler, J. (1993). *Bodies that matter: On the discursive limits of 'sex'.* New York: Routledge.

Butler, J (1997). *Excitable speech: A politics of the performative.* New York: Routledge.

Char, C., & Hawkins, J. (1987). Charting the course; involving teachers in the formative research and design of the Voyage of the Mimi. In R. Pea & K. Sheingold (Eds.) *Mirrors of minds: Patters of experience in educational computing* (pp. 141–167). Norwood, NJ: Ablex.

Cherry, R. (1998) , Self-representation in written discourse. *Written communication, 15*(3), 384–410.

Cognition and Technology Group at Vanderbilt. (1990). Anchored instruction and its relationship to situated cognition. *Educational Researcher, 19*(5), 2–10.

Coiro, J., & Dobler, B. (2007). Exploring the online comprehension strategies used by sixth-grade skilled readers to search for and locate information on the Internet. *Reading Research Quarterly, 42*(2), 214–257.

Cope, B., & Kalantzis, M. (Eds.) (2000). *Multiliteracies*. London: Routledge.

Costanzo, W. (1994). Reading, writing and thinking in an age of electronic literacy. In C. L. Selfe & S. Hilligosi (Eds.), *Literacy and computer: The complications of teaching and learning with technology* (pp. 195–219). New York: MLA.

Csordas, T. (1999). Embodiment. In G. Weiss & H. Haber (Eds.), *Perspectives on embodiment*. Routledge.

Damarin, S. (1995). Technologies of the individual: women and subjectivitiy in the age of information. *Research in Technology and Philosophy, 13*, 185–200.

Dobson, T. M., & Luce-Kapler, R. (2005). Stitching texts: Gender and geography in Frankenstein and Patchwork Girl. *Changing English, 12*(2), 265–277.

Dobson, T. M. (2004). Reading wikis: E-literature and the negotiation of reader/writer roles. Canadian Society for Studies in Education Annual Meeting, Winnipeg, MN, 27–30 May.

Dobson, T. M. (in press). Constructing (and deconstructing) reading through hypertext: Literature and the new media. In A. Adams & S. Brindley (Eds.), *Teaching Secondary English with ICT*. Maidenhead, UK: Open University Press.

Douglas, J. Y. (1992, Fall). What hypertexts can do that print narratives cannot. *Reader, 28*, 1–22.

Drucker, P. (1969). *The age of discontinuity; guidelines to our changing society*. New York: Harper and Row.

Dwyer, D. (1996). The imperative to change our schools. In C. Fisher, D. Dwyer, & K. Yocam. (Eds.), *Education and technology: reflections on computing in classrooms* (pp. 15–34). San Francisco: Jossey Bass.

Dyson, A. (1988). Negotiations among multiple worlds: The space/time dimensions of young children's composing. *Research in the Teaching of English, 22*(4), 355–390.

Dyson, A. (1995). Writing children: reinventing the development of childhood literacy. *Written Communication, 12*(1), 4–46.

Enciso, P. (1992). Creating the story world: A case study of a young reader's engagement strategies and stances. In J. Many & C. Cox (Eds.), *Reader stance and literary understanding: Exploring the theories, research, and practice* (pp. 75–102). Norwood, NJ: Ablex.

Fairclough, N. (1992). *Discourse and social power*. London: Polity Press.

Fairclough, N. (1995). *Critical discourse analysis*. London: Longman.

Forman, G. (1998) Multiple symbolization in the Long Jump Project. In C. Edwards, L. Gandini, & G. Forman (Eds.). *The hundred languages of children: The Reggio Emilia approach—Advanced reflections* (2nd ed., pp. 171–188). Greenwich, CT: Ablex.

Galindo, R., Tierney, R. J., & Stowell, L. (1989). Multi-media and multi-layers in multiple texts. In J. Zutell & S. McCormick (Eds.), *Cognitive and social perspectives for literacy research and instruction* (39th yearbook of the National Reading Conference). Chicago, IL: National Reading Conference.

Gee, J. P. (2003). *What video games have to teach us about learning and literacy*. New York: Palgrave MacMillan.

Giaquinta, J., Bauer, J., & Levin, J. (1993). *Beyond technology's promise*. Cambridge: Cambridge University Press.

Gibson, W. (1969). *Persona; a style study for readers and writers*. New York: Random House.

Grint, K., & Gill, R. (Eds.) (1995). *The gender technology relation: Contemporary theory and research*. London: Taylor and Francis.

Hapnes, T., & Sorenson, K. (1995). Competition and collaboration in the male shaping of computing. In K. Grint & R. Gill (Eds.), *The gender technology relation: Contemporary theory and research* (pp. 174–191). London: Taylor and Francis..

Halliday, M. A. K. (1973). *Explorations in the functions of language*. London: Edward Arnold.

Hawisher, G., & Selfe, C. (Eds.) (2000). *Global literacies and the World-Wide Web*. London: Routledge.

Heath, S. B. (1980). The functions and uses of language. *Journal of Communication, 30*, 123–133

Hirschon, S., & Butler, J. (1983). *And, Also Teach Them to Read*. Westport, CT: Lawrence Hill.

Hudak, G. M. Hull, G., & James, M. (in press). Geographies of hope: A study of urban landscapes and university-community collaborative. In P. O'Neill (Ed.), *Blurring boundaries: Developing writers, researchers, and teachers: A tribute to William L. Smith.*

Hull, G. A., & Nelson, M. A (2006). Locating the semiotic power of multimodality. University of California, Berkeley, available at http://www.dream.sdu.dk/uploads/files/hull-art3%5B1%5D.pdf

Ito, M. (in press). Technologies of the childhood imagination: Yugioh, media mixes, and everyday cultural production. In J. Karaganis & N . Jerimijenko (Eds.), *Structures of participation in digital culture.* Durham, NC: Duke University Press.

Johnson, S. (2006). Don't fear the digital *Time*, March 27, p. 42.

Kinder. M. (Ed.). (1999). *Kids' media culture.* Durham, NC: Duke University Press.

Kinzer, C., & Leu, D. (1997). The challenge of change: Exploring literacy and learning in electronic environments. *Language Arts, 74.*

Knobel, M., & Lankshear, C. (2005). New literacies: Research and social practice. In B. Maloch, J. M Hoffman, D. L. Schallert, C. M. Fairbanks, & J. Worthy (Eds.), *54th Yearbook of the National Reading Conference* (pp. 22–50). Oak Creek, WI: National Reading Conference.

Kress, G. (2003). *Literacy in the new media age.* London: Routledge

Kress, G. (1997). *Before writing: Rethinking paths into literacy.* London: Routledge.

Kress, G. (1998). Visual and verbal modes of representation in electronically mediated communication: The potentials of new forms of text. In I. Snyder (Ed.), *Page to screen: Taking literacy in the electronic era* (pp. **-**). Sydney: Allen & Unwin

Kress, G., & van Leeuwen, T. (2001). *Multimodal discourse. The modes and media of contemporary communication.* London: Arnold.

Lambert, J. (2002). *Digital storytelling: Capturing lives, creating community.* Berkeley, CA: Digital Diner Press.

Landow, G. P. (Ed.). (1994a). *Hyper/text/theory.* Baltimore: The Johns Hopkins University Press.

Landow, G. P. (Ed.). (1994b). *Hypertext 2.0: The convergence of contemporary critical theory and technology.* Baltimore: The Johns Hopkins University Press.

Lanham, R. (1993). *The electronic word: Democracy, technology, and the arts.* Chicago: The University of Chicago Press.

Lankshear, C., & Knobel, M. (2003) *New literacies: changing knowledge and classroom learning.* Berkshire and New York: Open University Press and McGraw Hill.

Lemke, J. (2001). Travels in hypermodality. *Visual Communication, 1*(3), 299–325.

Lemke, J. L. (1998) Metamedia literacy: Transforming meanings and media. In D. Reinking, M. McKenna L. Labbo, & R. Kieffer (Eds.), *Handbook of literacy and technology: transformations in a post typographic world* (pp. 283–301). Hillsdale, NJ: Erlbaum.

Leu, D. (2006). New literacies, reading research, and the challenge of change: a deictic perspective. In J.M. Hoffman, D. L. Schallert, C. M. Fairbanks, J. Worthy, & B. Maloch (Eds.), *55th Yearbook of the National Reading Conference* (pp. 1–20). Oak Creek, Wisconsin: National Reading Conference, Inc.

Levin, B. B. (1996). Learning from discussion; a comparison of computer-based versus face-to-face case discussions. Paper presented at the American Educational Research association Annual meeting, New York.

Lewis, C., & Fabos, B. (2005) Instant messaging, literacies, and social identities. *Reading Research Quarterly, 40*(4), 470–501.

Luce-Kapler, R., Dobson, T., Sumara, Iftody, T., & Davis, B. (2006). E-literature and the digital engagement of consciousness, In J. M. Hoffman, D. L. Schallert, C. M. Fairbanks, J. Worthy, & B. Maloch (Eds.), *55th Yearbook of the National Reading Conference* (pp. 171–181). Oak Creek, WI: National Reading Conference.

Luke, A. (2005) Foreword. In K. Pahl & J. Rowsell (Eds.), *Understanding literacy education: Using new literacy studies in the elementary classroom.* Thousand Oaks, CA: Sage.

Lunsford, A. & Ede, L. (1990). Singular texts/plusal authors. Carbondale: Southern Illinois University Press.

Mathison, M. (1996). Writing the critique, a text about a text. *Written Communication, 13*(3), 314–354.

Mayer, R., & Moreno, R. (2002). Animation as an aid to multimedia learning. *Educational Psychology Review, 14* (1), 87–99.

McEneaney, J. E. (2006) Agent-based literacy theory. *Reading Research Quarterly, 41*(3), 352–371

McGinley, W. (1988). The role of reading and writing in the acquisition of knowledge: A study of college students' reading and writing engagements in the development of a persuasive argument. Unpublished doctoral thesis, University of Illinois at Urbana-Champaign.

McGinley, W. (1992) The role of reading and writing while composing from sources. *Reading Research Quarterly, 27*(3), 226–249

McGinley, W., & Tierney, R. J. (1989). Traversing the topical landscape: Reading and writing as ways of knowing. *Written Communication, 6*(3), 243–269.

Merryfield, M. (2003) Using electronic discussions to enhance academic learning. Teaching Online, EOS Publishing.

Miall, D. S. (1999). Trivializing or liberating? The limitations of hypertext theorizing. *Mosaic, 32*(2), 157–171. Available at http://www.umanitoba.ca/publications/mosaic/backlist/1999/june/miall.pdf

Miall, D.S., & Kuiken, D. (1994). Beyond text theory: Understanding literary response. *Discourse processes, 17*, 337–352.

Myer, J. & Beach, R. (2001, March). Hypermedia authoring as critical literacy. *Journal of Adolescent & Adult Literacy, 44*(6). Available at http://www.readingonline.org/electronic/elec_index.asp?HREF=/electronic/jaal/3-01_Column/index.html

Myer, J., Hammond, R., & McKillop, A. M. (1998). Opportunities for critical literacy and pedagogy in student-authored hypermedia. In D. Reinking, M. McKenna, L. Labbo, & R. Kieffer (Eds.), *Literacy and technology: Transformations in a post-typographic world* (pp. 63–78). Mahwah, NJ: Erlbaum.

Myer, J., Hammond, R., & McKillop, A. M. (2000). Connecting, exploring, and exposing the self in hypermedia projects. In M. Gallego & S. Hollingsworth (Eds.), *What counts as literacy: Challenging the school standard* (pp. 85–105). New York: Teachers College Press.

Miall, D. S. (1999). Trivializing or liberating? The limitations of hypertext theorizing. Mosaic, 32(2), 157–171. Available at http://www.umanitoba.ca/publications/mosaic/backlist/1999/june/miall.pdf

Miall, D. S., & Kuiken, D. (1994). Beyond text theory: Understanding literary response. *Discourse processes, 17*, 337–352.

Nelson, N., & Calfee, R. (1998) The reading-writing connection. *7th yearbook of the National Society for the Study of Education.* Chicago; National Society for the Study of Education.

New London Group (1996). A pedagogy of multiliteracies: Designing social futures. *Harvard Educational Review, 66*(1), 60–92

Ormrod, S. (1995). Leaky black boxes in gender/technology relations. In K. Grint & R. Gill (Eds.), *The gender technology relation: Contemporary theory and research* (pp. 31–47). London: Taylor and Francis.

Owston, R. D. (1997). The World Wide Web: A technology to enhance teaching and learning? In *Educational Researcher, 26*(2), 27–33. Washington, DC: American Educational Research Association.

Pahl, K., & Rosell, J. (2005). *Understanding literacy education: Using new literacy studies in the elementary classroom.* Thousand Oaks, CA: Sage.

Postman, N. (1993). *Technopoly: The surrender of culture to technology.* New York: Vintage Press.

Purcell-Gates, V. (2006). What does culture have to do with it? In J. M. Hoffman, D. L. Schallert, C. M. Fairbanks, J. Worthy, & B. Maloch. (Eds.), *55th Yearbook of the National Reading Conference* (pp. 43–59). Oak Creek, WI: National Reading Conference.

Rampton, B. (2006). *Language in late modernity: Integration in an urban school.* Cambridge; Cambridge University Press,

Reilly, B. (1996). New technologies, new literacies, new problems. In C. Fisher, D. Dwyer, & K. Yocam (Eds.), *Education and technology: Reflections on computing in classrooms* (pp. 203–220).San Francisco: Jossey Bass.

Reinking, D. (1997). Me and my hypertext: A multiple digression analysis of technology and literacy (sic). *The Reading Teacher 50*(8).

Rich, F. (2006). Yes, you are the person of the year! *New York Times*, December 24, Week in Review, p. 8.

Richardson, W. (2006). *Blogs, wikis and podcasts.* Thousand Oaks, CA: Corwin Press

Rogers, T., & Schofield, A. (2005). Things thicker than words. Portraits of Multiple literacies in an alternative secondary program. In J. Anderson, M. Kendrick, T. Rogers, & S. Smythe (Eds.), *Portraits of literacy across families, communities and schools. Tensions and Intersections* (pp. 205–220). Mahwah, NJ: Erlbaum.

Rogers, T., & Winters, K. (2006). Using multimedia to support the literacies and lives of struggling youth. Paper presented at Canadian Society for Studies in Education. York University, Ontario, Canada, May, 2006.

Rosenau, P. M. (1992). *Postmodernism and the social sciences: Insights, inroads and intrusions.* Princeton, NJ: Princeton University Press.

Rosenblatt, L. M. (1983). *Literature as exploration* (4th ed.). New York: Modern Language Association. (Original work published 1938)

Ruitenberg, C. (in press). Discourse, theatrical performance, agency: The analytic force of 'performativity' in education. Yearbook *Philosophy of Education 2007.*

Ruiz, J., Mintzer, M., & Leipzig, R., (2006). The impact of E-learning in medical education. *Academic Medicine, 81*(3), 207–212

Schmandt-Besserat, D. (1978). The earliest precursor of writing. *Scientific American, 238,* 50–59.

Schmandt-Besserat, D. (1986). The origins of writing: An archeologist's perspective. *Written Communication, 3*(1), 31–46.

Sefton-Green, J. (2006) Youth, technology and media cultures. In J. Green & A. Luke (Eds.), Rethinking learning: What counts as learning and what learning counts. *Review of Research in Education* (pp. 279–306). Washington, D.C.: American Educational Research Association.

Selfe, C., & Hawisher, G. E. (2004). *Literacy lives in the informational age: Narratives of literacy from the United States.* Mahwah, NJ: Erlbaum.

Sheehy, M. (2007). Can the literacy practices in an after-school program be practiced in school? A study of literacies from a spatial perspective. Unpublished manuscript.

Siegel, M. (1995). More than words: the generative power of transmediation for learning. *Canadian journal of Education. 20*(4), 455–475.

Slatoff, W. (1970). *With respect to readers: Dimensions of literary response.* Ithaca, NY: Cornell University Press.

Snyder, I. (1996). *Hypertext: The electronic labyrinth.* New York: New York University Press.

Spiro, R. J. (2006a). The "New Gutenberg Revolution": Radical new learning, thinking, teaching, and training with Technology. *Educational Technology, 46*(1), 3–4.

Spiro, R. J. (2006b). The post-Gutenberg world of the mind: The shape of the new learning. *Educational Technology, 46*(2), 3–4.

Spiro, R. J., Collins, B. P. Thota, J. J., & Feltovich, P. J. (2003). Cognitive flexibility theory: Hypermedia for complex learning, adaptive knowledge application, and experience acceleration. *Educational technology 44*(5), 5–10.

Spiro, R. J., Coulson, R. L., Feltovich, P. J., & Anderson, D. (1988). Cognitive flexibility theory: Advanced knowledge acquisition in ill-structured domains. Tenth Annual Conference of the Cognitive Science Society. Hillsdale, NJ: Erlbaum,.

Spiro, R. J., & Jehng, J. C. (1990). Cognitive flexibility and hypertext: Theory and technology for the nonlinear and multidimensional traversal of complex subject matter. In D. Nix & R. J. Spiro (Eds.), *Cognition, education, and multimedia: Explorations in high technology* (pp. 163–205). Hillsdale, NJ: Erlbaum.

Spiro, R. J., Vispoel, W. L., Schmitz, J., Samarapungavan, A., & Boerger, A. (1987). Knowledge acquisition for application: Cognitive flexibility and transfer in complex content domains. In B.C. Britton & S. Glynn (Eds.), *Executive control processes* (pp. 177–200). Hillsdale, NJ: Erlbaum.

Spivey, N. N. (1997) *The constructivist metaphor: reading, writing and the making of meaning.* San Diego: Academic Press.

Squire, K. (2006) From content to context: Videogames as designed experiences. *Educational Researcher, 35*(8), 19–29.

Stein, P. (2004). Representation, rights, and resources: Multimodal pedagogies in the language and literacy classroom. In B. Norton & K. Toohey (Eds.), *Critical pedagogies and language learning.* Cambridge: Cambridge University Press.

Stengel, R. (2006). Now it's your turn. *Time,* December 25, 2006–January 1, 2007, p. 9.

Stephens, M. (1998). *The rise of the image the fall of the word.* Oxford University Press

Street, B. (1984). *Literacy in theory and practice.* Cambridge: Cambridge University Press.

Street, B. (2003). What's "new" in New Literacy Studies? Critical approaches to literacy in theory and practice. *Current Issues in Comparative Education. 5*(2). 1–14.

Street, B. V. (2006). New literacies, new times: How do we describe and teach forms of literacy knowledge, skills, and values people need for new times? In J. M Hoffman, D. L. Schallert, C. M. Fairbanks, J. Worthy, & B. Maloch (Eds.), *55th Yearbook of the National Reading Conference* (pp. 21–42). Oak Creek, WI: National Reading Conference, Inc.

Taylor, M. (1987). The same but different: social reproduction in innovation in the art of the Kunwinjka of western Srnhem land. Doctoral dissertation, The Australian national University.

Tierney, M. (1995) Negotiating a software career: Informal workplaces and the "lads" in a software installation. In K. Grint & R. Gill, R. (Eds.), *The gender technology relation: Contemporary theory and research* (pp. 192–209). London: Taylor and Francis.

Tierney, R. J., & Pearson, P. D. (1983). Towards a composing model of reading. *Language Arts, 60,* 568–580.

Tierney, R. J., & Shanahan, T. (1991). Research on the reading-writing relationship: Interactions, transactions, and outcomes. In R. Barr, M. L. Kamil, P. Mosenthal, & P. D. Pearson (Eds.), *Handbook of reading research, Volume II* (pp. 246–280). New York: Longman.

Tierney, R. J., Kieffer, R., Whalin, K., Desai, L., Moss, A. G., Harris, J. E, & Hopper, J. (1997). Assessing the impact of hypertext on learners' architecture of literacy learning spaces in different disciplines: Follow-up studies. Reading on-line, *Electronic Journal of the International Reading Association.*

Tierney, R. J., Bond, E., & Bresler, J. (2006). Examining literate lives as students engage with multiple literacies: the thread, the needle and the fabric. *Theory into Practice* issue on literacies of and for a diverse society: Curriculum, instruction and multiple literacies, *45*(4), 359–367.

Toffler, A. (1981). *The third wave.* London: Pan Books

Turkle, S (1995). *Life on the screen.* New York: Simon and Shuster

United Nations (2003). Declaration of principles: a common vision of the information society. World Summit on the information society; building the information society; a global challenge for a new millennium. Accessed December 12, 2003, from Geneva. http://www.itu.int/wsis/docs/geneva/official/dop.html.

United Nations (2006). *United Nations information economy report 2006: The development perspective.* Available at http://www.unctad.org/en/docs/sdteecb20061_en.pdf

Van Leeuwen, T. (1999). *Speech, music, sound.* London: Macmillan.

Wade, S. E., & Fauske, J. R. (2004). Dialogue online: Prospective teachers' discourse strategies in computer-mediated discussions. *Reading Research Quarterly, 39*(2), 134–160.

Wittgenstein, L. (1953). *Philosophical investigations.* New York: Macmillan.

Witte, S. P. (1992). Context, text, intertext: Toward a constructivist semiotic of writing, *Written Communication, 9*(2), 237–308.

13 Comprehension and Computer Technology

Past Results, Current Knowledge, and Future Promises

Michael L. Kamil and Helen Kim Chou

Stanford University

It is almost paradoxical to speak of reviewing the research on technology and comprehension. While technology is most often used to refer to computer technology, there are numerous other technologies that affect literacy and, more specifically, comprehension. Writing and printing are also technologies themselves, as Kamil, Intrator, and Kim (2000) have noted. This means that common usage favors some technologies over others. In the subsequent discussion, we will yield to common usage and focus primarily on the uses of computers for reading and instruction of reading, and most specifically on research that examines measures of comprehension. Despite the increasing emphasis on the use of computers in schools, there is a dearth of studies of the effects of computer technologies on literacy.

Kamil and Intrator (1998) analyzed the literature on computer technology and reading. They found that there were very few studies published in refereed journals and even fewer in mainline reading research journals. A similar finding is echoed in Murphy, Penuel, Means, Korbak, Whaley, and Allen (2002). These problems often complicate the synthesis of the findings, given that the research base is relatively thin. Despite the small number of studies, there is a high degree of consistency in the results. Almost all the research shows some advantage for computer use in instruction.

DEFINITION OF COMPREHENSION

In the review that follows, we adopt the usage and definitions of the National Reading Panel (NRP; NICHD, 2000). The NRP definition of comprehension included vocabulary as well as comprehension strategies. The definition is consistent with that of Whipple (1925), who believed that growth in reading is related to increases in vocabulary. It is also consistent with that of Davis (1942), who found that comprehension comprises two "skills": Word knowledge or vocabulary and reasoning. Excluded from this review are studies that focused on alphabetics—phonemic awareness and phonics. Studies of spelling or writing and composition that did not focus on reading comprehension were also beyond the scope of this review.

HISTORICAL REVIEWS OF EFFECTS OF TECHNOLOGY ON LITERACY

The invention of the printing press in the mid-15th century allowed the control of texts to move from clerical to commercial institutions. One result of this change was that many more persons had access to literacy over a much broader range of topics. By the end of the 15th century, books were widely available and the number of persons who needed or wanted to be literate was far greater than it had been at any time in history. Access to text on such a wide variety of secular topics required new skills in reading. It also created a need for instruction in reading for a far wider range of individuals than ever before.

In a similar fashion, the Internet has allowed control of texts and publishing to pass from commercial interests to the public. Anyone with a computer can publish text on the Internet. The range of text available to individuals has again expanded. Texts on many topics, even in many different languages, are immediately accessible. The discipline of publishers who, over the past 500 years, often guaranteed the accuracy and consistency of what was published is often absent. At the very least, this change has produced the need for much higher degrees of skill in what has been termed *critical reading*. More-over, research (Kamil & Lane, 1998) has found that the text on the Internet is often written at much higher levels than many popular reading materials, such as newspapers. This has also changed the definition of literacy by requiring more skill to be literate in one of the major electronic text environments. Each of these developments has led to greater demands for instruction in reading. Computer technology has accelerated those demands, but it has also held out another promise: That reading instruction could be moved to a computer-based model in which reading instruction would be individualized to meet student needs and relieve burdens on teachers, freeing them to provide other kinds of services to students.

There are other changes in the definition of literacy that result from computer technology. Foremost among them is the development of multimedia information in electronic text documents. Conventional texts can include pictures and illustrations, but electronic texts can include pictures, motion, and sound. The inclusion of multimedia information in documents, along with text, places added demands on the literacy skills of readers. Not only do readers of multimedia documents have to comprehend the text, but they have to be able to integrate the meaning of the multimedia information with the meaning of the text. Such multimedia documents push the boundaries of what it means to be literate.

Hypertext is a related development in computer technology that has expanded the definition of literacy. Hypertext is text that is linked electronically with other information outside the text being read. The links can provide the reader with additional information, elaboration of the current text, or support needed to read the text. For example, hypertext can provide links to definitions, to audio versions of the text, or to graphics that illustrate the text. The demands on the reader are both more complex and less. Readers must make decisions about whether or not to "interrupt" reading to explore the links. Readers must also know how to navigate the links and return to where they left the original text. Finally, readers must also be able to integrate the information contained in the links with the information from the current text, resolving any discrepancies. At the same time, hypertext may facilitate reading by enabling immediate access to additional information or reading support. However, many of the studies of hypertext do not measure reading variables but focus on learning and content outcomes. A review of research on hypertext, mostly with older readers, and mostly in the context of studying, is available (Chaomei & Rada, 1996).

All of the additional demands on reading have direct implications for how we define literacy. Some of these electronic text developments will eventually find their way into carefully crafted experimental work. For now, however, there are studies of multimedia text that do not involve computers. These studies suggest directions for research that do involve computers. Consequently, we have included them in a section on multimedia effects, even though they are, strictly speaking, not computer studies.

Shortly after the first demonstrations that reading could be taught by computer (Atkinson & Hansen, 1966–1967; Atkinson 1968–1969), Spache (1968–1969) voiced objections about the quality of that instruction. The dramatic improvements in the hardware capabilities of computers have encouraged the development of software that was far more capable. Kamil and Lane (1998) suggested that the difficulties in teaching reading by computer were rooted in certain limitations of computer hardware and software. Specifically, they pointed out that computers, at the time, could not listen to students read and correct their oral pronunciation, nor could they comprehend what students said in response to questions. Since then, there have been dramatic improvements in both areas for computer instruction. Many of these concerns have been addressed by the work of Mostow and his colleagues (Mostow & Aist, 2001; Beck, Jia, & Mostow, 2004; Mostow, Beck, Bey, Cuneo, Sison, Tobin, & Valeri, 2004; Mostow, Aist, Burkhead, Corbett, Cuneo, Eitelman, Huang, Junker, Sklar, & Tobin, 2003).

REVIEWS OF COMPUTERS AND LITERACY

A number of reviews have been conducted over the years to assess the general effects of computer technology on reading achievement. Among these are Kulik and Kulik (1991); Kulik (1994); Fletcher-Flinn and Gravatt (1995); Ryan (1991); Kamil (1982); Niemiec and Walberg (1985); Samson Niemiec, Weinstein, and Walberg (1986); Bangert-Drowns, Kulik, and Kulik (1985); and Reinking and Bridwell-Bowles (1991). All of these reviews suffer from being based on research with computers of an earlier generation that did not have the capabilities of today's hardware and software. They also suffer from attempting to analyze a very small research base, as noted earlier in this paper. However, the results from all of these studies are consistent. There has always been at least a moderate effect of computer technologies on reading outcomes.

One earlier review that focused exclusively on comprehension was conducted by Haller, Child, and Walberg (1988). They examined the effect of metacognitive instruction, delivered by computer, on reading comprehension. For the 20 studies, there were 115 effect sizes; the mean effect size was .71, indicating a rather large effect. Most of the effective studies were with seventh and eighth grade students. While this is highly suggestive, it was clearly done in an era of computer technology that was far less capable than current hardware and software.

More recent reviews of the effects of computer technology on reading have the advantage of having reviewed studies that involved newer technologies. In addition, many of these more recent reviews examine a broader base of reading outcomes, instead of focusing only on reading comprehension.

Murphy et al. (2002) analyzed 31 experimental studies of discrete education software implementations. They reached three conclusions. First, the research base is severely limited. This is consistent with the earlier findings of Kamil and Intrator (1998). However, they went further and noted that two-thirds of the studies found suffered from methodological flaws. Second, a positive association existed between the use of discrete educational software and achievement in reading. Again, this is consistent with other reviews, although adding the strict randomized design criterion to the analysis seems to attenuate the magnitude of the effects slightly. In this case, the effect size for reading was d = .35. The third conclusion is that research reports often do not report the effect sizes or results in a way that allows the calculation of those effects.

Waxman, Lin, and Michiko (2003) conducted a meta-analysis of 29 studies to see the effects of computer instruction on cognitive, behavioral, and affective outcomes. The overall effect size was .410. This result indicates that teaching and learning with technology has a small, positive, significant effect on student outcomes when compared to traditional instruction. The mean study-weighted effect size for the 29 studies containing cognitive outcomes was .448, and the mean study-weighted effect size for the 10 comparisons that focused on student affective outcomes was .464. On the other hand, the mean study-weighted effect size for the 3 studies that contained behavioral outcomes was −.091.

Pearson, Ferdig, Blomeyer, and Moran (2005) also reviewed 20 disparate studies of middle school applications and found an overall weighted effect size of .489.

Despite the methodological challenges in reviewing much of the research on computer instruction and reading, new generations of computers, software, learning theories, and new approaches to classroom instruction suggest that computers might have a different role to play than they did a decade or two ago. At the very least, it would be important to see how this is playing out, particularly in spite of such concerns as those of Cuban (2001) that implementation of computers has led to no real changes in classroom instruction.

THE CURRENT REVIEW

Search procedures

An electronic search was conducted using the ERIC and PsycInfo databases to locate studies that examined instructional issues pertaining to reading and computer technology. The same guidelines for the original NRP study were applied to the current search, and the computer reading instruction database was updated to include a total of 70 studies that met the NRP search criteria. In order to be included in the database, each study had to meet several established criteria. Only studies published in peer-reviewed journals were selected, which excluded popular articles, conference papers, and dissertation abstracts. Aside from a few meta-analyses included for reference, studies selected for inclusion in the database were experimental or quasi-experimental in nature. In addition, only studies conducted in English and with participants ranging in age from pre-school through secondary school were selected. Studies dealing exclusively with some distinct populations, such as second language learners or severely learning disabled students, were excluded from the primary analyses. On an individual basis, studies with students with mild to moderate learning difficulties were considered for inclusion based on the potential applicability of the study findings to the general student population.

This database was searched for studies that manipulated variables related to vocabulary and comprehension. This yielded a total of 25 studies, 8 of which examined vocabulary and 18 of which studies comprehension, with one study that examined BOTH vocabulary and comprehension. These 25 studies often included samples for multiple grade levels. A total of 46 different grade samples were specified. (Two of the studies were not specific about grade details and were not included in these totals.) Table 13.1 shows the distribution of grade samples across both vocabulary and comprehension studies.

What is important about these data is that there are more vocabulary grade samples at the elementary grades (preschool through Grade 4), 11 vs. 5. At middle school (Grades 5–8), there are more comprehension samples (15) than vocabulary (4). High school shows a similar pattern to middle school, with 9 comprehension samples compared to 2 for vocabulary.

In the current analysis, we have decided to use a narrative approach rather than a true meta-analysis, given both the small number of studies and the variations in methodological quality.

Table 13.1   Distribution of Grade Level Samples for Vocabulary and Comprehension Research Studies in the Database.

Grade	Vocabulary Sample	Comprehension Sample	Total
P	1	0	1
K	1	0	1
1	3	0	3
2	3	2	5
3	2	2	4
4	1	1	2
5	0	6	6
6	2	4	6
7	1	3	4
8	1	2	3
9	0	3	3
10	0	2	2
11	2	2	4
12	0	2	2
Total	17	29	46

VOCABULARY RESULTS

Most of the studies showing that computers have facilitated vocabulary learning have substantiated those results with informal, experimenter-designed tests. The difficulties in demonstrating vocabulary gains with standardized measures are serious (Pearson, Hiebert, & Kamil, 2007). For the more general analysis (mostly noncomputer) of vocabulary instruction in the NRP, only two of the studies in the National Reading Panel corpus demonstrated gains on standardized measures.

A total of 9 studies in the current database addressed the use of computers to teach vocabulary. Four of these dealt with sight vocabulary and are not central to the issue of meaning vocabulary which is most critical for comprehension. However, they do represent an important application of computer technology that is related to fluency, and consequently to comprehension, and they are included for that reason.

Davidson, Elcock, and Noyes (1996) found that giving voice prompts on demand increased reading ability on several measures of sight word knowledge. Pinkard (2001) found that a computer program that was based in culturally responsive instruction increased sight vocabulary for low SES African American students in grades 1–4.

Boling, Martin, and Martin (2002) demonstrated that first-grade students could improve significantly over a control group when allowed to use a computer-assisted program for meaning vocabulary. Heller, Sturner, Funk, and Feezor (1993) found that the type of input was an important variable for preschool students. However, students did benefit from computerized vocabulary instruction. Calvert, Watson, Brinkley, and Penny (1990) investigated the effect of computer presentation on word recall in a study with kindergarteners and second-grade students of high and low reading ability. The study found second graders recalled more words than kindergartners, and that older students with lower levels of reading ability could benefit from the computerized presentation of words with visual action.

A study which included remedial elementary and middle school students who were nonnative speakers was conducted by Heise, Papalweis, and Tanner (1991). This is one of the few studies that reports non-significant differences for the computer assisted instruction (CAI) group. However, the differences did show consistent improvement for the CAI group.

For sixth-grade students, Reinking and Rickman (1990) showed that students did improve in vocabulary learning when the definitions were presented on the screen with the text to be read. At the high school level two studies provide evidence on the effectiveness of computers in improving vocabulary knowledge. Feldman and Fish (1991) were primarily interested in studying the effects of computer supports on comprehension. However, they found that while comprehension did not improve with computer-supplied reading supports, poor readers became aware of the role that vocabulary played in comprehension. Kolich (1991) found that eleventh-grade students learned a list of vocabulary words presented by computer in rich contexts more efficiently than students who received definitional information only.

There is a thin body of evidence that suggests that students of all ages, from first grade through high school can be taught vocabulary by computers. Clearly, more research needs to be done. However, the direct instruction that is provided in most computer software for vocabulary offers a strong argument for the use of such programs. At the very least, the alignment with the NRP conclusion that direct instruction of vocabulary is effective in improving comprehension indicates that this type of computer instruction is a viable approach.

SUMMARY

It is clear that there is a small body of research that supports the use of computers in teaching vocabulary. The technologies did not involve new developments like speech synthesis and recognition. There is sufficient agreement in the findings to suggest that computer technology can provide instruction that will improve vocabulary performance.

Comprehension results

A total of 17 studies examined effects of comprehension instruction delivered by computer. These fall into several categories, but almost all of them involve either comprehension strategy instruction or metacognitive instruction. Nine of the studies involved some type of metacognitive or strategy instruction. This clearly reflects a continuation of the trend noted by Haller et al. (1988) to use computers to deliver strategy instruction. These studies also span the range from elementary through middle schools and the entire range of reading abilities.

MacGregor. (1988) suggests that third-grade students' use of a program that facilitated students ability to read text and ask questions results in gains in reading performance. While the effects were greater for average students than for good readers, there was improvement for all conditions. Answering questions is one of the strategies recommended by the National Reading Panel. This result suggests the need for more integration of computer instruction in comprehension strategy instruction.

Meyer and her colleagues (Meyer, Middlemiss, Theodorou, Brezinski, McDougall, & Bartlett, 2002) showed that strategy instruction that emphasizes the recognition of text structure could be effectively delivered by computer. The specific program involves a combination of computer presentation and live tutoring. This is also one of the few studies that involved a Web site as a primary delivery system. In addition to showing improvement in recall, there was an improvement in self-efficacy.

Another Web-based program for teaching metacognitive strategies for text comprehension to middle school students was reported by Johnson-Glenberg (2005). The texts were science-oriented and merged narrative and expository genres. Results showed that comprehension was significantly better in the intervention condition. These effects were greater for poor readers.

Rauenbusch and Bereiter (1991) investigated an educational microworld (MW) intended to provide opportunities for focused learning of reading comprehension strategies. The study used degraded texts where some letters were missing. However, the gifted seventh-grade students showed that they could learn meaning-based strategies and apply them, even in a transfer task.

One of the possibilities for computer instruction is that it could replace some of the functions of teachers. Salomon, Globerson, and Guterman (1989) used the computer to provide models, opportunity for higher level thinking, and metacognitivelike guidance (e.g., "Can I conjure up an image of the story?"). The study compared modeling higher versus lower level questions with a control condition. The study showed that there was significant improvement in comprehension, reinforcing the belief that well-designed computer tools can improve reading comprehension instruction.

Another of the National Reading Panel conclusions was that summarizing was an effective comprehension strategy. Franzke, Kintsch, Caccamise, Johnson, and Dooley (2005) showed that using the computer to support practice in summarizing was effective in raising comprehension scores for eighth-grade students. This program automates the assessment of summaries using Latent Semantic Analysis.

Tobias (1987, 1988) used a computer program to teach the value of text review. An experiment randomly assigned students to read a text passage displayed by computer with or without an explanation. A control group received no explanation. Another variable was whether the explanations were required or optional. Review groups learned more than those merely reading the text, and explanations facilitated the learning of students with little familiarity with the material, while slightly impairing knowledgeable students' performance.

Similarly, Reinking (1989) investigated whether computer presentations of texts would affect readers' estimation of their own learning and would contribute to comprehension differences. Students designated as good or poor readers in the fifth and sixth grade read printed expository passages and computer presentations that varied in the availability of computer assistance and whether the computer or the reader controlled the computer manipulations. Students' comprehension increased when they read computer-mediated texts and when their options for reading were controlled.

Gillingham, Garner, Guthrie, and Sawyer (1989) manipulated computer assistance in helping fifth grade students read science texts. A variety of assistance was provided, but not all students used the assistance. However, students in the prescribed assistance condition performed better than other conditions on answering synthesis questions. In a study with eighth- and nineth-grade students, McNamara, O'Reilly, Best, and Ozuru (2006) found improvements in reading comprehension by providing computerized reading strategy training with the assistance of animated agents. Benefits of the computerized training were found for students with both low and high prior knowledge of reading strategies, although gains were observed in different areas of comprehension.

A study that combined increased reading with self assessment was conducted by Vollands, Topping, and Evans (1999). The authors conducted a quasi-experimental action research evaluation of a program called *Accelerated Reader*. They found that sixth graders showed gains in reading achievement for at-risk readers that were superior to gains from regular classroom teaching. While this is a computer-based program, there is little instruction involved; the computer is used primarily as an assist in tracking reading and difficulty of reading.

Another set of studies examined the effects of various presentation conditions on reading processes. Gambrell, Bradley, and McLaughlin (1987) showed that students could read at the computer, but reported it was more difficult, despite the fact that they found it more interesting. This is another study in the line of studies about reading at the computer. Generally, reading at a computer screen is more difficult and less desirable. Gould and Grischkowsky (1984) showed better performance with hardcopy as did Grzeszkiewicz and Hawbaker (1996). Haas and Hayes (1985) showed how this effect could be ameliorated, as did Gould, Alfaro, Finn, Haupt, and Minuto (1987). There do appear to be some differences in recall, so care is needed with regard to the amount of reading at a computer screen that is required in software. Greenlee-Moore and Smith (1996), for example, found that there were no differences when students read short passages, but there were differences with longer passages.

Tancock and Segedy (2004) found that students who worked with offline texts outscored the treatment group on the comprehension questions for online texts and the response activities for every story, except one. In an interesting related issue, Kinzer, Sherwood, and Loofbourrow (1989) compared performance on a simulation with reading an expository text. What they found was that the reading of an expository text produced significantly greater performance over that following exposure to the simulation. They conclude that potential difficulties lie in reading for information from computer screens and in possibly detrimental effects of animation in computer simulations of knowledge acquisition.

SUMMARY

In general, computer software has been effective in teaching a variety of skills related to comprehension. Most of these skills cluster around strategies or metacognitive abilities. Few of these studies used what today are cutting edge technologies, like multimedia presentation, speech recognition, and the like. However, it is clear that this is a small but reliable base on which future efforts should build.

The National Evaluation of Educational Technology

Beginning in 2004, a randomized control research study was begun. This study was congressionally mandated as part of the No Child Left Behind Act. The study was designed to assess the effectiveness of learning technology in teaching reading in grade 1, reading comprehension in Grade 4, pre-algebra in Grade 6, and algebra in Grade 9. The research examined the effectiveness of educational technology in raising student achievement and also examined those conditions under which teachers employed technology. Of interest for this review are the results for the Grade 4 comprehension software.

The products in the study included a number of commercial products, which are not individually identified with specific results. The study was conducted over 2 years. The results indicate that simply none of the effect sizes, overall, were significantly different from zero for any of the products on standardized tests of comprehension. There were somewhat larger effects associated with the amount of software usage. There was no relationship of scores with problems getting access, technical difficulties, computer specialist in school, professional development on using technology, or poverty or urban variables (Dynarski et al., 2007).

While this might suggest that computer instruction is ineffective, another interpretation is much more likely. In the study, the programs replaced 10%–11% of instructional time. Given that there was no difference between live and computer instruction, it suggests that the computer replacement was as effective as the classroom instruction. This would represent a great improvement in computer capabilities over earlier software.

Multimedia text and reading comprehension

In texts where pictures, diagrams, graphs, and charts give supplementary information, the proficient reader must be able to integrate the verbal and visual information in a cohesive way. Adding carefully designed visual supports to augment text, such as illustrations and diagrams, can facilitate comprehension and the recall of text information (e.g., Levie & Lentz, 1982; Alesandrini, 1984; Peeck, 1993). Despite the potential instructional importance of visual support on text comprehension, the review of prior empirical research indicates that elementary school children typically demonstrate a tendency to interact with texts and visual information in a passive way and lack developed strategies for processing visual adjuncts and text information (e.g., Kirby, 1993; Moore, 1993; Moore & Scevack, 1997).

Considering the difficulty many readers encounter with synthesizing verbal and visual information in conventional texts, the challenges inherent in processing multimedia can be formidable. Multimedia processing requires unique demands for information synthesis and concentration. In some instances, multimedia applications can pose challenges to processing information in light of competing visual and verbal attentional demands, commonly referred to as the split-attention effect (e.g., Mayer & Moreno, 1998, 2002). Multimedia documents, or information that is provided in more than one modality are of specific interest because they often require the reader to integrate text with multiple modalities of information display such as audio, video, animation, and hyperlinks. Some studies suggest that difficulties with multimedia reading may be particularly salient when readers have low prior topic knowledge (e.g., Kozma, 1991; Shin, Schallert, & Savenye, 1994; Lawless & Kulikowich, 1996). Presently, there is a great need for additional research on the cognitive processes involved in multimedia reading and the optimal ways to design and evaluate multimedia texts for instruction.

NEW IDEAS FOR THE FUTURE IN COMPREHENSION AND TECHNOLOGY

In the following paragraphs, we discuss a few new developments in technology that are not yet researched, but seem to have great potential for expanding the role of technology in reading and reading instruction. An important development is the fact that federal regulations will require all textbooks to be available in electronic format. The National Instructional Materials Accessibility Standard (NIMAS) applies to all materials published on or after July 19, 2006. This effort applies primarily to issues of text accessibility. Given that all instructional materials will have to be available in electronic format suggests that far greater computer use in instructional materials is just on the horizon. More information can be found at the Web site for the Center for Applied Special Technology (http://www.cast.org/index.html).

The application of new technologies to reading instruction may provide unique opportunities to extend learning opportunities beyond the classroom. A few specific trends on the horizon that may have promising implications for reading instruction are adaptive agents, podcasts (or other portable audio files), online chats, "wikis" or collaboratively developed and edited content on Web sites, and computer games. Given the relatively recent application of these technologies to reading instruction, there is insufficient data available to assess their efficacy. In the absence of empirical research, we can currently only speculate on the potential benefits of these new technologies for enhancing comprehension. Some of the key benefits of these technologies appear to be cost-effectiveness, supporting social interactions around reading instruction, extending learning outside the classroom, and integrating reading and writing activities. While these new technologies may not have found their way into most mainstream classrooms at present, we mention them here as cutting-edge trends that may have a significant impact on the future development and delivery of reading instruction.

Adaptive agents as tools to provide strategic guidance during reading

Recent software developments have made the delivery of exceptionally interactive and individualized learning possible through the use of adaptive technology. Adaptive technology adjusts the instruction in computer lessons to the responses of the student. In conjunction with adaptive technology, *electronic agents* are sometimes developed to provide interactive tutoring and guidance. Electronic agents are electronic tools that accompany Web pages or software programs to offer assistance to readers of electronic text. That assistance can be of help in understanding a task, content, or, in the case of instruction, necessary background information. As the study of agents in learning contexts is a relatively new field, few peer-reviewed, published studies are available. There have been some studies using agents for instruction in other contexts. For example, Lester, Stone, and Stelling (1999) used an agent in the form of a bug character with middle school students working on problem solving tasks and found preliminary support for enhanced learning interactions. In a study with college students, Mayer, Dow, and Mayer (2003) found support for enhanced learning with a narrated agent in the science context.

In the context of reading instruction, an electronic agent may be an effective approach to providing consistent and timely reading support. By accompanying the reader through each text page and providing immediate feedback, an agent can be designed to provide relevant guidance at opportune moments. The capacity of the agent to ask questions and answer free form questions and dynamically interact with students is a hallmark of the technology. Students can learn new reading strategies and skills while engaged in the context of reading textbook materials, a design that is consistent with prior research that indicates that the learning of comprehension strategies is enhanced when strategies are presented in content materials (Wade & Moje, 2000). In an exploratory study, Kim and Kamil (2002) examined the use of an interactive agent to support reading comprehension among fourth- and fifth-grade students and found significant pre- to post-test increases in learning from the expository texts. Specific areas of reading support included in this study were the modeling of proficient reading strategies, encouraging the active processing of text and visual information, structural guidance for text processing, and vocabulary support.

NEW COLLABORATIVE TECHNOLOGIES
FOR READING AND INSTRUCTION

Podcasts can be described as audio or video files that are published on the Internet and available for download. Users can subscribe to podcasts on a variety of topics to periodically receive new files as the information is updated, much like a magazine subscription. Currently, subscriptions to most podcasts are available for free. Applied to the area of reading instruction, a podcast could be implemented in a wide range of applications, including audio podcasts of stories read aloud, vocabulary instruction, highlighting, extending, or reviewing key concepts for a lesson, and providing audio or video podcasts of classroom lectures and discussions. The steps involved with creating and publishing a podcast are relatively simple, and require little more than a computer, Internet connection, and widely available software, such as iTunes. An alternative to publishing on iTunes would be to publish the podcast onto a personal Web site or the school's Web site. To illustrate how a podcast could be implemented for reading instruction, here is an example of how a teacher could use a podcast as a tool to enhance vocabulary instruction. As a first step, the teacher would use software to create a podcast of key vocabulary terms and concepts, which could include a discussion of multiple word meanings, the relevance of the word, alternate pronunciations, and examples of the word being used in context. Podcasts can also contain slides, which enables teachers to further enhance vocabulary instruction by adding visuals to accompany the audio. Teachers could update these words as often as they wish and might find it useful to update on a weekly basis or to accompany each new lesson. Students would then subscribe to the podcast and download new words onto their computer or an MP3 player. The podcast could also be burned to compact discs for students who do not own MP3 players. In this example, students might be assigned to listen to the podcast before the lesson as the pre-instruction of difficult and key vocabulary words can enhance reading comprehension. Students can also periodically revisit the archived podcasts for additional vocabulary review. While this is an example of how podcasts could be used for vocabulary instruction for an older reader, a podcast that reads a storybook aloud with prompts and discussion of key vocabulary could be useful for younger readers.

Online chats have become increasingly popular among students as a way to communicate with friends. To participate in online chatting, students typically use a software program to send messages through the Internet. An advantage to online chats compared to using email is that messages can be sent and received instantly in rapid succession, which allows for more of an interactive and conversational format. While online chats are often seen as purely social interactions, it is not difficult to envision how they could be applied to enhance reading instruction. Online chats could be designed to provide opportunities for students to discuss readings, ask questions and receive feedback, and to connect students both in and out of the classroom. Teachers might choose to implement the online chat in a more formal way by scheduling an online chat at a particular time for the entire classroom or for smaller groups of students. Additional structure could be created by having teachers moderate the discussions, develop questions, specific prompts, and activities and giving time for students to prepare for the online chats. In a less structured way, students could use online chats to connect with their peers outside of the classroom, work on group projects, start discussion threads on topics that are of interest to particular students, and to provide or receive help from their classmates. As a supplement to regular classroom discussion, online chats can offer a way to extend reading comprehension through writing activities that involve collaborative discussion, formulating and presenting opinions, synthesizing multiple points of view, generating questions, and writing for an audience. The online chat format may also offer students who are shy or reluctant to speak in front of the class an alternative way to participate in classroom discussions. Because a computer with Internet connection is required to participate in the online chats, the availability of the technology could be a limiting factor for students who do not have access to a computer at home. If this presents a barrier to implementation, another option would be to schedule the online chat during school hours in locations where computers are typically available for all students, such as the classroom, library, or computer lab.

One way that new technologies may impact the delivery of group reading instruction is through the implementation of a collaboratively created and edited Web site. The Web site can be set up as a wiki or a Web site which allows the users to contribute and edit the content. A mainstream example of a wiki is the Web site Wikipedia (www. wikipedia.com), an online encyclopedia with information that is continually created, edited, and updated by the public. In the context of a more contained Web site, such as a classroom Web site, a collaborative format would enable students to share information about lesson concepts, utilize multimedia supports (i.e., hyperlinks, photos, Web resources), post questions and provide answers, engage in discussion and critique, and provide suggestions and feedback to peers. An advantage of having students participate in writing activities that connect with the course content is that it underscores the critical connection between reading and writing, an essential goal of comprehensive literacy instruction. Additionally, asking students to contribute content, as well as to critique and edit the content of others for accuracy and readability can encourage students to engage in reading comprehension strategies that involve critical thinking and review, clarifying inconsistencies in the text, presenting alternate view points, and summarizing information.

Computer games as tools for reading comprehension

One other trend that has become a focus of interest is the use of games and game technology in instructional contexts. While many of the current software titles are wrapped in a game format, even more seem to be on the way. These efforts will follow on the empirical and theoretical formulations that are becoming available. Among these are the work of Shaffer and Gee (2006) and Gee (2008). As development proceeds, we may see the melding of instruction and computer games that are designed to promote literacy and literacy instruction. To date, however, we have no real experimental confirmation of the efficacy of this approach.

While reading instruction has long been steeped in tradition, what these new technologies may offer is a way to make reading instruction more engaging and compelling for students. As a supplement to traditional reading instruction, agents, podcasts, online chats, wikis, and computer games could enhance comprehension by extending learning beyond the textbook, incorporating multimedia representations, and providing social opportunities to engage students in meaningful reading and writing activities. Further research is clearly needed to evaluate the efficacy of incorporating these and other new technologies for reading instruction. Although it is difficult to predict how new technologies will impact reading instruction and how it is conceptualized and delivered, the current movement towards using technology to support social interactions around reading and to engage students in authentic reading and writing activities may very well be telling indicators of what lies ahead in technology and comprehension instruction.

We can also hope that the future will show a serious reversal of the trends noted by Kamil and Intrator (1998) and see a serious increase in the number and quality of studies of the effects of computer technology used in the service of reading and learning to read. We can also hope that the technologies will provide richer and even more effective possibilities for instruction.

REFERENCES

Alesandrini, K. L. (1984). Pictures and adult learning. *Instructional Science, 13,* 63–77.

Atkinson, R. (1968–1969). A reply to A reaction to Computer-assisted instruction in initial reading: The Stanford project. *Reading Research Quarterly, 3,* 418–420

Atkinson, R, & Hansen, D. (1966–1967). Computer-assisted instruction in initial rea ding: The Stanford project. *Reading Research Quarterly, 2,* 5–26.

Bangert-Drowns, R.L., Kulik, J.A., & Kulik, C.C. (1985). Effectiveness of computer-based education in secondary schools. *Journal of Computer-Based Instruction, 12*(3), 59–68.

Beck, J. E., Jia, P., & Mostow, J. (2004). Automatically assessing oral reading fluency in a computer tutor that listens. *Technology, Instruction, Cognition and Learning, 2,* 61–81.

Chaomei, C., & Rada, R. (1996). Interacting with hypertext: a meta-analysis of experimental studies. *Human-Computer Interactions, 11*(2), 125–156.

Cuban, L. (2001). *Oversold and Underused: Computers in the Classroom.* Cambridge MA: Harvard University Press.

Davis, F. B. (1942). Two new measures of reading ability. *Journal of Educational Psychology, 33,* 365–372.

Dynarski, M., et al. (2007). Effectiveness of Reading and Mathematics Software Products: Findings from the First Student Cohort. Washington, DC: Department of Education Institute of Education Sciences (NCEE 2007-4005).

Fletcher-Flinn, C. M., & Gravatt, B. (1995). The efficacy of computer assisted instruction (CAI): A meta-analysis. *Journal of Educational Computing Research, 12*(3), 219–242.

Gee, J. P. A. (2008). *What video games have to teach us about learning and literacy.* New York: Palgrave Macmillan.

Gould, J., & Grischkowsky, N. (1984). Doing the same work with hardcopy and with CRT terminals. *Human Factors, 26,* 323–337.

Gould, J. D., Alfaro, L., Finn, R., Haupt, B., & Minuto, A. (1987). Reading from CRT displays can be as fast as reading from paper. *Human Factors, 29*(5).

Grzeszkiewicz, A., & Hawbaker, A. (1996). Investigating a full-test journal database: A case of detection. *Database, 19*(6), 59–62.

Haas, C., & Hayes, J. (1985). *Reading on the computer: A comparison of standard and advanced computer display and hardcopy.* (CDC Technical Report No. 7). Pittsburgh, PA: Carnegie-Mellon University, Communications Design Center.

Haller, E. P., Child, D. A., & Walberg, H. J. (1988). Can comprehension be taught? A quantitative synthesis of "metacognitive" studies. *Educational Researcher, 17*(9), 5–8.

Kamil, M. L. (1982). Technology and reading: A review of research and instruction. In J. Niles & L. Harris (Eds.), *New Inquiries In Reading Research And Instruction* (Thirty-first yearbook of the National Reading Conference). Rochester, NY: The National Reading Conference.

Kamil, M. L., & Intrator, S. (1998). Quantitative trends in publication of research on technology and reading, writing, and literacy. In T. Shanahan & F. Rodriguez-Brown (Eds.), *National Reading Conference Yearbook 47* (pp. 385–396). Chicago: The National Reading Conference.

Kamil, M. L., Intrator, S. M., & Kim, H. S. (2000). The effects of other technologies on literacy and literacy learning. In M. L. Kamil & P. B. Mosenthal (Eds.), *Handbook of reading research, Vol. III* (pp. 771–788). Mahwah, NJ: Erlbaum.

Kamil, M. L., & Lane, D. (1998). Researching the relationship between technology and literacy: An Agenda for the 21st century. In D. Reinking, M. McKenna, L. Labbo, & R. Kieffer (Eds.), *Handbook of literacy and technology: Transformations in a post-typographic world* (pp. 323–341). Mahwah, NJ: Erlbaum.

Kamil, M. L., & Lane, D. (1998, December). Information text, task demands for students, and readability of text on the Internet. Presented to the National Reading Conference, Austin, TX.

Kim, H. S., & Kamil, M. L. (2002). Adaptive learning guides in reading instruction. *51st Yearbook of the National Reading Conference* (pp. 253–262). Oak Creek, WI: National Reading Conference.

Kirby, J. (1993). Collaborative and competitive effects of verbal and spatial processes. *Learning and Instruction, 3,* 201–214.

Kozma, R. (1991). Learning with media. *Review of Educational Research, 61,* 179–211.

Kulik, C. C., & Kulik, J. A. (1991). Effectiveness of computer-based instruction: An updated analysis. *Computers in Human Behavior, 7,* 75–94.

Kulik, J. A. (1994). Meta-analytic studies of findings on computer-based instruction. In E. Baker & H. O'Neil (Eds.), *Technology assessment in education and training.* Hillsdale, NJ: Erlbaum.

Lawless, K., & Kulikowich, J. (1996). Understanding hypertext navigation through cluster analysis. *Journal of Educational Computing Research, 14,* 385–399.

Lester, J. C., Stone, B. A., & Stelling, G. D. (1999). Lifelike pedagogical agents for mixed-initiative problem solving in constructivist learning environments. *User Modeling and User-Adapted Interaction, 9,* 1–44.

Levie, W. H., & Lentz, R. (1982). Effects of text illustrations: A review of research. *Educational Communication and Technology Journal, 30,* 195–232.

Mayer, R., & Moreno, R. (1998). A split-attention effect in multimedia learning: Evidence for dual processing systems in working memory. *Journal of Educational Psychology, 90,* 312–320.

Mayer, R. E., Dow, G. T., & Mayer, S. (2003). Multimedia learning in an interactive self-explaining environment: What works in the design of agent-based microworlds? *Journal of Educational Psychology, 95,* 806–812.

Mayer. R. E., & Moreno, R. (2002). Aids to computer-based multimedia learning. *Learning and Instruction, 12,* 107–119.

Moore, P. J. (1993). Metacognitive processing of diagrams, maps and graphs. *Learning and Instruction, 3,* 215–226.

Moore, P. J., & Scevack, J. J. (1997). Learning from texts and visual aids: a developmental perspective. *Journal of Research in Reading, 20,* 205–223.

Mostow, J., & Aist, G. (2001). Evaluating tutors that listen: An overview of Project LISTEN. In K. D. Forbus & P. J. Feltovich (Eds.), *Smart machines in education: The coming revolution in educational technology.* Cambridge, MA: MIT Press.

Mostow, J., Aist, G., Burkhead, P., Corbett, A., Cuneo, A., Eitelman, S., Huang, C., Junker, B., Sklar, M. B., & Tobin, B. (2003). Evaluation of an automated Reading Tutor that listens: Comparison to human tutoring and classroom instruction. *Journal of Educational Computing Research, 29*(1), 61–117.

Mostow, J., Beck, J., Bey, J., Cuneo, A., Sison, J., Tobin, B., & Valeri, J. (2004). Using automated questions to assess reading comprehension, vocabulary, and effects of tutorial interventions. *Technology, Instruction, Cognition and Learning, 2,* 97–134.

Murphy, R., Penuel, W., Means, B., Korbak, C., Whaley, A., & Allen, J. (2002). E-DESK: *A review of recent evidence on the effectiveness of discrete educational software.* Planning and Valuation Service, U.S. Department of Education DHHS Contract #282-00-008-Task 3. Menlo Park, CA: SRI International. Available at http://ctl.sri.com/publications/downloads/Task3_FinalReport3.pdfNICHD. (2000). *Report of the National Reading Panel: Teaching children to read.* Bethesda, MD: National Institute of Child Health and Human Development.

Niemiec, R. P., & Walberg, H. J. (1985). Computers and Achievement in the Elementary Schools. *Journal Of Educational Computing Research, 1,* 435–440.

Pearson, P., Ferdig, R., Blomeyer, R., & Moran, J. (2005). *The effects of technology on reading performance in the middle school grades: A meta-analysis with recommendations for policy.* Naperville, IL: Learning Point Associates.

Pearson, P. D., Hiebert, E. H., & Kamil, M. L. (2007). Vocabulary assessment: What we know and what we need to learn. *Reading Research Quarterly, 42,* 282–296.

Peeck, J. (1993). Increasing picture effects in learning. *Learning and Instruction, 3,* 227–238.

Reinking, D., & Bridwell-Bowles, L. (1991). Computers in reading and writing. In R. Barr, M. L. Kamil, P. Mosenthal, & P. D. Pearson (Eds.), *Handbook of reading research* (Vol. 2, pp. 310–340). New York: Longman.

Ryan, A. W. (1991). Meta-analysis of achievement effects in microcomputer applications in elementary schools. *Educational Administration Quarterly, 27*(2), 161–184.

Samson, G. E., Niemiec, R., Weinstein, T., & Walberg, H. J. (1986). Effects of computer-based instruction on secondary school achievement: A quantitative synthesis. *AEDS Journal,* 312–326.

Shaffer, D. W., & Gee, J. P. (2006). *How computer games help children learn.* New York: Palgrave Macmillan.

Shin, E. C., Schallert, D. L., & Savenye, W. C. (1994). Effects of learner control, advisement, and prior knowledge on young students' learning in a hypertext environment. *Educational Technology Research and Development, 42,* 33–46.

Spache, G. (1968–1969). A reaction to Computer-assisted instruction in initial reading: The Stanford project. *Reading Research Quarterly, 3,* 101–109.

Tobias, S. (1987). Mandatory text review and interaction with student characteristics. *Journal of Educational Psychology, 79*(2), 154–161.

Tobias, S. (1988). Teaching strategic text review by computer and interaction with student characteristics. *Computers in Human Behavior, 4*(4), 299–310.

Wade, S. E., & Moje, E. B. (2000). The role of text in classroom learning. In M. Kamil, P. B. Mosenthal, P. D. Pearson, & R. Barr (Eds.), *Handbook of reading research* (Vol. 3, pp. 609–627). Mahwah, NJ: Erlbaum.

Waxman, H., Lin, M., & Michiko, G. (2003). A meta-analysis of the effectivenesss of teaching and learning with technology on student outcomes. Available at http://www.ncrel.org/tech/effects2/waxman.pdf

Whipple, G. (Ed.). (1925). *The Twenty-fourth Yearbook of the National Society for the Study of Education: Report of the National Committee on Reading.* Bloomington, IN: Public School Publishing Company.

STUDIES ANALYZED

Boling, C., Martin, S. H., & Martin, M. A. (2002). The effects of computer-assisted instruction on first grade students' vocabulary development. *Reading Improvement, 39,* 79–88.

Calvert, S. L., Watson, J.A., Brinkley, V., & Penny, J. (1990). Computer presentational features for poor readers' recall of information. *Journal of Educational Computing Research, 6,* 287–298.

Davidson, J., Elcock, J., & Noyes, P. (1996). A preliminary study of the effect of computer-assisted practice on reading attainment. *Journal of Research in Reading, 19,* 102–110.

Feldman, S. C., & Fish, M. C. (1991). Use of computer-mediated reading supports to enhance reading comprehension of high school students. *Journal of Educational Computing Research, 7,* 25–36.

Franzke, M., Kintsch, E., Caccamise, D., Johnson, N., & Dooley, S. (2005). Summary Street-Reg.: Computer support for comprehension and writing. *Journal of Educational Computing Research, 33,* 53–80.

Gambrell, L. B., Bradley, V. N., & McLaughlin, E. M. (1987). Young children's comprehension.

Gillingham, M. G., Garner, R., Guthrie, J. T., & Sawyer, R. (1989). Children's control of computer-based reading assistance in answering synthesis questions. *Computers in Human Behavior, 5,* 61–75.

Greenlee-Moore, M. E,, & Smith, L. L. (1996). Interactive computer software: The effects on young children's reading achievement. *Reading Psychology, 17,* 43–64.

Heise, B. L., Papalweis, R., & Tanner, D. E. (1991). Building base vocabulary with computer-assisted instruction. *Teacher Education Quarterly, 18,* 55–63.

Heller, J. H., Sturner, R. A., Funk, S. G., & Feezor, M. D. (1993). The effect of input mode on vocabulary identification performance at low intensity. *Journal of Educational Computing Research, 9,* 509–518.

Johnson-Glenberg, M. C. (2005). Web-based training of metacognitive strategies for text comprehension: Focus on poor comprehenders. *Reading and Writing, 18,* 755–786.

Kinzer, C. K., Sherwood, R. D., & Loofbourrow, M. C. (1989). Simulation software vs. expository text: A comparison of retention across two instructional tools. *Reading Research and Instruction, 28,* 41–49.

Kolich, E. (1991). Effects of computer-assisted vocabulary training on word knowledge. *Journal of Educational Research, 84,* 177–182.

MacGregor, S. K. (1988). Use of self-questioning with a computer-mediated text system and measures of reading performance. *Journal of Reading Behavior, 20,* 131–48.

McNamara, D. S., O'Reilly, T. P., Best, R. M., & Ozuru, Y. (2006). Improving adolescent students' reading comprehension with iSTART. *Journal of Educational Computing Research, 34,* 147–171.

Meyer, B. J. F., Middlemiss, W., Theodorou, E., Brezinski, K. L., McDougall, J., & Bartlett, B. J. (2002). Effects of structure strategy instruction delivered to fifth-grade children using the Internet with and without the aid of older adult tutors. *Journal of Educational Psychology, 94,* 486–519.

Pinkard, N. (2001). Rappin' Reader and Say Say Oh Playmate: Using children's songs as literacy scaffolds in computer-based learning environments. *Journal of Educational Computing Research, 25,* 17–34.

Rauenbusch, F., & Bereiter, C. (1991). Making reading more difficult: A degraded text microworld for teaching reading comprehension strategies. *Cognition & Instruction, 8,* 181–206.

Reinking, D. (1989). Computer-mediated text and comprehension differences: The role of reading time, reader preference, and estimation of learning. *Reading Research Quarterly, 23,* 484–98.

Reinking, D., & Rickman, S. (1990). The effects of computer-mediated texts on the vocabulary learning and comprehension of intermediate-grade readers. *Journal of Reading Behavior, 22,* 395–411.

Salomon, G., Globerson, T., & Guterman, E. (1989). The computer as a zone of proximal development: Internalizing reading-related metacognitions from a Reading Partner. *Journal of Educational Psychology, 81,* 620–627.

Shin, E. C., Schallert, D. L., & Savenye, W. C. (1994). Effects of learner control, advisement, and prior knowledge on young students' learning in a hypertext environment. *Educational Technology Research and Development, 42,* 33–46.

Tancock, S. M., & Segedy, J. (2004). A comparison of young children's technology-enhanced and traditional responses to texts: An action research project. *Journal of Research in Childhood Education, 19,* 58–65.

Tobias, S. (1988). Teaching strategic text review by computer and interaction with student characteristics. *Computers in Human Behavior, 4,* 299–310.

Vollands, S. R., Topping, K. J., & Evans, R. M. (1999). Computerized self-assessment of reading comprehension with the accelerated reader: Action research. *Reading and Writing Quarterly: Overcoming Learning Difficulties, 15,* 197–211.

Part IV

Elements of Reading Comprehension

14 Motivation and Reading Comprehension

Samuel D. Miller and Beverly S. Faircloth

University of North Carolina – Greensboro

INTRODUCTION

A student obligingly opens the text to the designated page and waits for a lesson to begin. Shortly thereafter, the teacher approaches the front of the room to start her instruction, intending to promote the student's understanding of today's text selection. This simple act, repeated daily across most grade levels in classrooms across the country, belies the complexity of factors that ultimately influence the nature of a teacher's instruction and a student's comprehension. Each factor has an influence, shaped across time by numerous members in the educational community—students, parents, teachers, administrators, district and state officials, researchers, and national politicians and policymakers. Judgments regarding a lesson's success and a student's comprehension are jointly determined by an interaction of these factors and their histories.

Student motivation also influences such judgments. Despite its own history, only recently has motivation moved a bit closer to center stage in literacy studies. Similar to comprehension, its studies are not immune from political influences in education. How we view motivation and promote its enactment are influenced by a variety of forces within society. The role motivation plays in promoting comprehension, whether explicitly or implicitly, across grade levels for students at different achievement levels and backgrounds, has yet to be determined. A number of factors are involved in addressing this question. Exploring the relationships among these factors, both historically and in today's educational climate, is the focus of this chapter.

Researchers adopt many lenses as they observe our student opening a text. Comprehension and motivation might vary as a function of gender, culture, socio-economic status, and grade level; a teacher's instructional practices, subject-matter expertise, and assignments; a school's accountability practices and funding levels; or state and federal accountability policies. Any change in the relative influence of any one of these factors affects how researchers study comprehension or motivation. In this review, we explore the role of these evolving influences and perspectives within each domain, as well as the intersection of these two fields.

We start our review by examining research from approximately the last 30 years. This time period represents a critical shift in how researchers studied reading and motivation as the field adopted a more cognitive perspective and started to apply its findings to public school classrooms (Bereiter & Scardamalia, 1987; Paris, 1986; Shulman, 1986; Resnick, 1981). To capture the energy of this time, we sought themed issues and research chapters on reading comprehension where many of today's most pressing issues were raised. For this review, intended to be more illustrative than exhaustive, we sought publications where authors focused on existing and possible relationships between reading comprehension and motivation. Our focus was first on reading comprehension, followed by a review of how motivation research might provide further insights. By conducting our review, we discovered that some early research questions were disregarded' thereby possibly limiting our understanding of what teachers might do to promote comprehension or motivation. Other research questions were reframed to reflect the latest insights. Finally, some of today's most pressing questions were not concerns 30 years ago.

The first two sections of this chapter look at what questions were raised 30 years ago by reading comprehension and motivation researchers. The last section looks at future directions by examining how our research questions were reframed with the introduction of the No Child Left Behind Act (NCLB). While we cannot confirm direct causality between future research efforts and NCLB, enough of a change in research focus has occurred to warrant such a discussion.

A LOOK BACK AT THE READING COMPREHENSION RESEARCH

The cognitive revolution in learning increased our insights into the nature of comprehension as researchers looked for ways to implement recent findings into classroom settings (Anderson & Pearson, 1984; Pearson, 1986). Paris, Lipson, and Wixson (1983) provided a framework for understanding the potential application of these insights by developing the idea of strategic reading. Strategic reading entailed more than simply learning a new reading strategy: strategic readers selected the most appropriate cognitive strategy, monitored whether their reading goals were met, and made changes along the way to insure their success. In addition to declarative and procedural knowledge, strategic readers possessed conditional knowledge, an understanding of *when* and *why* a particular strategy should be used.

To become strategic, students needed both skill and will. Will represented the motivational intent to become engaged with reading, to continue reading to reach goals, and to persist through difficulties. Motivation was no longer a simple incentive to energize a set of predetermined behaviors; instead, it resulted from learners' expectancies, values, and beliefs. Ultimately, motivation determined the extent to which students became engaged or disengaged in the learning process. Students would be unsuccessful if they acquired the necessary cognitive and metacognitive abilities yet lacked the motivation to become engaged (or vice versa). Paris et al.'s (1983) view of reading and motivation as complementary, multidimensional, and dynamic contrasted sharply with previous behavioral models (Gardner, 1985).

Winograd and Johnston (1987) examined how sociopolitical pressures could limit the extent to which comprehension instruction might reflect the multidimensionality and dynamism of a framework like strategic reading. The most obvious pressures related to requirements for teachers to present instruction within limited time frames, to implement prescribed curricula, and to direct their teaching towards certain accountability outcomes. The least obvious pressures related to the amount of time needed for teachers to develop higher levels of instructional expertise. Both sets of pressures determined the nature of students' learning and motivation by limiting the breadth and depth of teachers' instructional practices. For example, teachers might simplify instructional practices to focus mainly on test-defined content and skills; students then might pass mandated assessments without increasing their understanding of and motivation for reading. Next, teachers might focus on the development of socially shared knowledge by introducing students to different genres, critical ideas, or reading strategies. While such practices promoted interest and increased students' knowledge of the purposes and traditions of reading, they may not stretch far enough to allow reading to become personally meaningful to diverse students. Finally, teachers might encourage students to seek personal connections through reading, to develop an understanding of why certain types of texts are engaging at this point in their lives, and to see how their interests differ from classmates'.

To overcome the limiting effects of sociopolitical pressures, teachers needed to allow students to become more actively engaged in their learning. To provide such opportunities, teachers needed to promote Rosenblatt's (1978) concept of aesthetic versus efferent reading. By emphasizing concepts of play rather than work in their aesthetic instructional practices, reading would become a self-sustaining activity. The authors referred to Csikszentmihalyi's concept of flow (1977) and Nicholls' concept of task involvement (1984) to support their positions. This distinction between work and play (or aesthetic and efferent reading) underscored how sociopolitical pressures might influence a school's learning goals, which in turn, shaped teachers' instructional routines.

The next set of publications came from the first two handbooks of reading research (Pearson, Barr, Kamil, & Mosenthal, 1984; Barr, Kamil, Mosenthal, & Pearson, 1991), each of which had chapters related to reading comprehension and motivation. In the first handbook, Wigfield and Asher (1984) focused on attributions (Weiner, 1972) to explain differences in school performances among students of different racial or social class backgrounds. Despite this model's popularity, Wigfield and Asher viewed the attribution framework as too limited in focus to explain the complexities of classroom life. To understand the multidimensional nature of classroom learning and motivation, researchers needed a more comprehensive model.

In this second handbook, Tierney and Cunningham (1991) proceeded to document our growing understanding of the multiple dimensions of comprehension, the challenges of conducting classroom research, and the potential benefits of including motivation. They defined comprehension as understanding, recall, and the integration of information stated in or inferable from specific text passages (p. 610). While they acknowledged a dramatic increase in the number of comprehension studies, they could not identify any unifying instructional principles because most studies tended to focus on single strategies without paying adequate attention to the multidimensionality of reading comprehension. To capture this multidimensionality, they asked researchers to propose a vision of what it meant to be a reader in today's society.

Paris, Wasik, and Turner (1991) provided such a vision in the second handbook by expanding earlier notions of strategic reading. First, reading strategies differed from metacognitive strategies in that the latter were more developmental and complemented the former by enhancing a student's attention, memory, and overall learning. Second, metacognitive strategies, along with motivational tactics, mediated the investment of effort and promoted the acquisition of conditional knowledge. Third, conditional knowledge allowed readers to appreciate the importance or utility of using a particular strategy or set of strategies. It increased perceptions of competence, confidence, and expectations for success; thereby increasing the likelihood (or motivation) of students reading strategically. Studies by Paris, Cross, and Lipson (1984), Duffy, Roehler, and colleagues (Duffy & Roehler, 1986; Duffy, Roehler, & Putnam, 1987), and Schunk and Rice (1987) confirmed these benefits.

Even when students knew how to read strategically, however, they might avoid or resist becoming engaged because they lacked confidence in their abilities. Resistance or avoidance occurred when the cost of failure outweighed the probability of achieving success. To support this claim, the authors referred to Covington's research (1984) on self-handicapping strategies; such strategies promoted passive learning by allowing students to externalize the causes of their failures (Winograd & Johnston, 1987). While motivation received increased attention, recommendations for its promotion were quite general. Terms such as expectancies, values, goals, and personal significance were identified as its critical dimensions without specific references to how teachers might promote them in the classroom.

Two chapters in this handbook (Pearson & Fielding, 1991; Roehler & Duffy, 1991) attempted to identify instructional principles that promoted a vision of reading comprehension as a multidimensional, yet integrated, set of cognitive, metacognitive, and motivational processes. Such principles would provide teachers with the information they needed to promote motivation. Briefly, teachers needed to promote the active interpretation of prose by providing explicit explanations about the importance and utility of using a strategy or set of strategies, by modeling thought processes, by allowing for discussions of multiple viewpoints, and by using challenging, authentic tasks. Under such conditions, readers could make an author's ideas their own and share newly acquired knowledge with classmates. Teachers scaffolded their instruction to promote a gradual release of responsibility from teacher to students for reading independently while students concomitantly constructed a personal understanding of an author's ideas (Pearson & Gallagher, 1983). Such principles provided the framework for various models of reading instruction (cognitive apprenticeship: Brown, Collins, & Duguid, 1989; direct explanation model: Duffy et al., 1987; transactional strategies instruction: Pressley, Beard El-Dinary, Gaskins, Schuder, Bergman, Almasi, & Brown, 1992; active comprehension: Singer, 1978 and Singer & Donlan, 1982; assisted performance: Tharp & Gallimore, 1988; generative learning: Wittrock, 1974).

Reservations existed, however, regarding the potential of these models to promote engagement. Pearson and Fielding (1991) captured this concern by asking if it would be possible for "students to learn naturally what only can be taught artificially in a more conventional environment" (p. 852). To evaluate this hypothesis, researchers needed to expand their focus on the cognitive dimensions of reading to include the ways in which comprehension and learning in general are socially determined by more authentic reading tasks, activities, and purposes. This request to broaden the research perspective served as a harbinger of a growing interest in how various social and cultural factors affected students' cognitive performances.

In the next handbook of reading research (Kamil, Mosenthal, Pearson, & Barr, 2000), researchers turned their attention towards the social and cultural dimensions of reading comprehension (now referred to under the umbrella term "literacy"). Bean (2000) documented the changing nature of reading in the content areas by emphasizing the social nature of classroom learning, particularly as it related to the use of small-group discussions, multiple texts (including children's and multicultural texts), and technology. Alexander and Jetton (2000) pointed to the need for schools to adopt a more multidimensional and developmental view of text learning, sensitive to students' backgrounds and interests and to recent technological advancements. Wade and Moje (2000) discussed how participatory approaches to instruction expanded our notions of teaching and learning by including the use of traditional as well as unacknowledged and unsanctioned texts. As a result, what students read outside of school may have more powerful effects on their lives than what they've read in the classroom. Such social influences may be true particularly for those student populations who are traditionally marginalized by standard instructional approaches. These chapters and others in this handbook (Gadsen, 2000; Purcell-Gates, 2000; Wilkinson & Silliman, 2000) documented researchers' expanding vision of literacy beyond cognition to include various social and cultural factors (both within and outside the classroom).

Similar to Pearson and Fielding (1991) and Roehler and Duffy (1991), Au (2003) attempted to capture the instructional implications of this expanded vision. Learning no longer depended solely on the acquisition of cognitive abilities; instead, learning was situated within various social and historical contexts. To capture the multidimensional nature of this expanded vision, Au viewed students' ownership of literacy as the overarching goal of instruction. To promote ownership, teachers needed to promote cultural responsiveness by recognizing the importance of home languages; by using multicultural literature, authentic literacy tasks, and student-centered assessments; by conducting lessons and organizing peer study groups in culturally responsive manners; and by strengthening school-community relationships. Such practices helped students to make an author's (or authors') ideas their own. Instead of linking comprehension failures to a lack of acquiring a particular strategy or to confidence with applying a strategy or strategies, attention turned to issues of culture, language, and community.

While motivation still remained in the background, its importance increased as researchers acknowledged the need for students to understand the purposes for reading (the why vs. the how of reading). Guthrie and Wigfield's (2000) chapter underscored this importance and provided greater specificity regarding the promotion of motivation in classrooms. They presented a vision of engaged reading, in which, motivation played a more central role and social aspects of learning received greater attention. Accordingly, engaged readers "coordinated strategies and knowledge within a community of literacy to fulfill their personal goals, desires, and intentions" (p. 404). As demonstrated in the instructional program, Concept-Oriented Reading Instruction (CORI), teachers promoted engaged reading comprehension by using authentic activities to encourage students' adoption of knowledge and learning goals; by allowing students choices regarding the direction of their learning; by scaffolding strategy instruction with interesting texts, providing direct instruction when necessary; by emphasizing collaborative study; and by implementing student-centered assessment practices (Guthrie, Anderson, Alao, & Rinehart, 1999). Students read to meet personal goals, became strategic in their efforts to comprehend different texts, gained sophisticated knowledge of content disciplines, and valued socially interactive approaches to literacy (Guthrie, McGough, Bennett, & Rice, 1996; Guthrie, Wigfield, & VonSecker, 2000). Their vision of reading placed an equal emphasis on the motivational as well as the cognitive processes of reading.

Tierney and Cunningham (1991) could not have predicted how the complexity and scope of researchers' visions would change in the next 20 years. Researchers moved from the study of single strategies to considering the joint contributions of a variety of cognitive, social, and cultural influences. While motivation received increased attention, its focus still remained incomplete or perhaps one-sided. In the next section, we will discuss the nature of motivation from a broader perspective, particularly as it relates to whether our research efforts will lead to long-term engagement. Briefly, we want students to understand how they might make an author's (or authors') ideas their own, but we also want them to do so long after our interventions have ended.

CONTINUING THE LOOK BACK: MOTIVATIONAL RESEARCH

Like the field of reading, the concept of motivation has been shaped across its history by numerous forces (e.g., teachers, researchers, policy makers, and the like). With roots in the Latin word for *motor* or *to move*, the term has generally been understood to refer to the mechanisms that determine the direction (focus), the intensity (depth), and the persistence of an individual's behavior (Bandura, 1977, 1989; Kanfer, Ackerman, Murtha, Dugdale, & Nelson, 1994). Traditional motivational research has consistently demonstrated that whether or not students display these characteristics is determined by their expectations for success (Can I do this task?) and their valuing of the activity (Do I want to do this task? /Why do I want to do this task?) (Pintrich & Schunk, 2002). Reflecting insights from the cognitive revolution that also reshaped reading research, the integration of these two core issues (which has come to be referred to as the "expectancy-value model of motivation": Atkinson, 1964) provided a paradigm that continues to shape motivational research to the present day.

This expectancy-value framework incorporates many of the individual cognitive perspectives and processes considered influential determinants of achievement-related behavior and outcomes (Atkinson, 1964; see also Meece, Eccles, Kaczala, Goff, & Futterman, 1982). A wealth of studies has demonstrated that experiences related to students' expectancies of success are among the strongest predictors of their academic performance, particularly their grades or test scores (Eccles, Adler, Futterman, Goff, Kaczala, & Meece, 1983; Meece et al., 1982) as well as the types of cognitive, metacognitive, and self-regulatory strategies they employ (Pintrich & Schunk, 2002). In contrast, the beliefs students hold regarding reasons they might engage in academic endeavors have come to be recognized as predictive of intentional participation in those endeavors and are therefore crucial to an individual's choice to engage deeply as well as their continuing intention to learn (Meece et al., 1982; Pintrich & Schunk, 2002). So, while expectations of success have direct ramifications for strategy choice and current performance, valuing or finding personal significance in learning is crucial to the sort of intrinsic motivation that is central to sustained, long-term engagement, or engagement in learning outside of school settings.

Given the contrasting influence of these two dimensions of motivation, what seems clear is that the vision one adopts for learning shapes the facets of motivation considered important. If the aim is skill development or high grades and test scores, the motivational focus may reasonably center on strategies that develop skills, thereby supporting expectations of success and performance outcomes. If, on the other hand, comprehension is defined to involve personal significance and intrinsic commitment, anchoring learning in students' values becomes central. The vision for reading incorporated by reading researchers and scholars has driven the manner in which motivational research has been integrated with their work and, therefore, determined how the two domains have interacted to shape and define our understanding of comprehension.

A dichotomy of motivational focus can be seen in our review of reading comprehension research. The first experience (a focus on supporting expectancies) is consistent with strategic reading and related models (e.g., Paris, Lipson, & Wixson, 1983), whereas the second (a focus on the individual valuing of the learning process) relates more closely to Winograd and Johnston's (1987) focus on personal significance or Rosenblatt's (1978) concept of aesthetic versus efferent reading. However, it is not necessary to adopt an either/or position with regard to the two dimensions of motivation; an integration of skill development with intrinsic commitment may provide the most powerful support for reading comprehension. As will be seen, most instructional recommendations regarding reading comprehension have related to the question, Can I do this task (or demonstrate proficiency with this strategy)? as opposed to Why do I want to do this task? A thorough integration of both dimensions of motivation is missing in the reading comprehension literature.

Under the umbrella of student expectancies of success, many motivational researchers have demonstrated how student performance is undergirded by beliefs about their capacity to complete tasks successfully (e.g., self-efficacy according to Bandura, 1977, and expectancy of success as conceived by Eccles et al., 1983) as well as their interpretation of the causes of their success or failure (i.e., attribution theory by Weiner, 1990). Key aspects of these general expectancy frameworks have been explicitly integrated into many theoretical considerations of reading comprehension (e.g., the attribution theory model of Wigfield & Asher's 1984 handbook chapter). Insights from additional motivational research aimed at enhancing (rather than merely understanding) self-efficacy or expectancy of success through the acquisition of strategies and skills have been especially useful to reading researchers. While early attempts at cognitive strategy training focused on specific instruction or practice applying a particular strategy, continued research demonstrated the benefit of employing *combinations of strategies, general as well as specific strategies*, and *conditional knowledge* of the benefit of certain strategies and when and why to use them (Brown, Palinscar, & Armbruster, 1984). Paris, Lipson, and Wixson's (1983) early development of the notions of strategic reading, self-directed learners, and conditional knowledge reflects application of these principals, as did the work by Paris, Cross, and Lipson (1984), Duffy, Roehler, and colleagues (Duffy & Roehler, 1986; Duffy et al., 1987), and Schunk and Rice (1987). These motivational principles involving supporting expectancy also provided the framework for various strategic models of reading instruction outlined earlier (i.e., Brown, Collins, & Duguid, 1989; Duffy et al., 1987; Pressley, Beard El-Dinary, Gaskins, Schuder, Bergman, Almasi, & Brown, 1992; and others). A multidimensional understanding of strategic readers is reflected in the insights of Tierney and Cunningham (1991), Pearson and Fielding (1991), and Roehler and Duffy (1991), who placed emphasis on the use of multiple, integrated cognitive, metacognitive, and motivational processes and strategies.

This multidimensional perspective on reading comprehension (i.e., involving cognitive, metacognitive, and motivational processes and strategies) mirrors the growing understanding of the motivational ideal of self-regulation. Self-regulated learning refers to the processes whereby students activate, monitor, and sustain their own efforts toward learning. Developed through an interaction of environmental, cognitive, emotional, and behavioral factors, the experience is characterized by intense focus, depth of processing, persistence in the face of difficulty, and specifically higher achievement (Schunk & Zimmerman, 1996; Zimmerman, 2002). A contemporary examination of self-regulation offered by Paris, Byrnes, and Paris (2001) provides insight into this motivational mechanism at work. These authors suggest that efforts at self-regulation and experiences of competence are most valuable, not just for their own sake, but within the framework of individual efforts to achieve a personal sense of identity and agenda. That is, self-regulation and efficacy energize students' motivation by animating their efforts to clarify and achieve their preferred identity and follow their own agendas. Paris, Wasik, and Turner's (1991) expansion of the notion of strategic readers, incorporating metacognition, demonstrates the application of these insights to reading, as do Pearson and Fielding's (1991) and Roehler and Duffy's (1991) emphasis on multiple viewpoints and authentic tasks and Pearson and Gallagher's (1983) focus on students' personal connections with an author's ideas.

An important limitation of these applications of motivational research to reading comprehension studies must be noted. First, most reading comprehension research has incorporated the concept of expectancy only implicitly rather than directly investigating its role in reading comprehension. That is, while insights from expectancy research have been included widely in theoretical treatments of reading research, rarely are motivational constructs consciously defined and measured in reading literature. For example, Paris, Cross, and Lipson (1984) and Duffy, Roehler, and colleagues (1986, 1987) oriented their research to make use of ideas that emerge from motivational literature (such as metacognition), and eluded to the important role played by motivational constructs, but did not actually measure or examine those constructs. And although reading researchers explored what happened when expectancy of success was low or threatened (i.e., *self-handicapping*; Covington, 1984) in Paris, Wasik, and Turner's (1991) articulation of the impact of the high cost of failure on student engagement, the motivational construct was not measured or examined explicitly in relation to reading. Additionally, even when expectancy constructs provided insight to reading researchers, suggestions for concrete applications to classroom practice are often missing, as when researchers understood that motivation did not result from a single focus (Roehler & Duffy, 1991), but did not identify its dimensions nor specify the steps for its implementation in the classroom.

An important exception to the limited explicit application of motivational constructs appeared when Schunk and Rice (1987) demonstrated that when the benefit of reading comprehension strategies were made explicit (conditional knowledge), students were more aware of the importance of using strategies, and consequently were less likely to feel helpless, incompetent, or passive (because their expectancies for success were strengthened). Such specific investigation of motivational principles lends important support to the claims of reading researchers. Continued efforts to integrate the motivational and reading comprehension literature empirically would clearly further serve the efforts of comprehension researchers and practitioners. For example, closer examination of the skills required for implementation of self-regulation, such as forethought and self-reflection (Zimmerman, 2002), are not evident in reading comprehension research. Moreover, insights into the processes that support self-regulation (e.g., specific task analysis relative to the aims of reading comprehension, greater focus on learning than performance, and examination of factors that support attention to self-monitoring such as individual interest in the comprehension text) would have much to offer scholars and practitioners eager to support students' comprehension efforts.

While students' expectancies of success have been widely theorized (although tested on a much smaller scale) to support achievement and strategy acquisition, this has not necessarily led to enhancing student valuing of reading or to considerations of how such value may be related to comprehension. It is the second cornerstone of the expectancy-value model to which we turn for help. Student consideration of *whether (and why) they may or may not want to engage in a task* (i.e., their individual perceptions of their reasons for engagement) provides the dimension of motivation clearly linked with intentional, long-term, sustained, and volitional engagement (Pintrich & Schunk, 2002; for specific examples see Ames, 1992 and Dweck, 1999, for learning goals/mastery orientation as opposed to performance goals/ego orientation; Hidi & Renninger, 2006, for interest; Meece et al., 1982, on task value; and Turner, 1995, on intrinsic vs. extrinsic motivation). In the first reading handbook, Winograd and Johnston (1987) illustrated the important distinction between what is offered by skills and strategies and what is offered by valuing, making the argument that by focusing on content and skills, teachers may help students pass assessments without supporting their long term motivation, when focusing on personal connections to reading is likely to provide sustained, volitional engagement.

Several chapters reviewed from the second handbook of reading research (Paris, Wasik, & Turner, 1991; Pearson & Fielding, 1991; Roehler & Duffy, 1991) suggested *theoretical* connections between reading comprehension and students' valuing of that activity, including the use of meaningful examples of children's literature rather than traditional basal readers, promoting students' personal understanding of the author's ideas, and providing opportunities to share their thoughts in meaningful social discourse. Pearson and Fielding (1991) specifically suggested the necessity of finding personal significance in a reading experience. Winograd and Johnston's (1987) reference to Csikszentmihalyi's concept of the motivated state of *flow* (1977) and Rosenblatt's concept of *aesthetic reading* (1978) are also excellent examples of theoretical application of valuing to reading comprehension. These considerations of issues related to personal valuing suggest its importance to comprehension. However, as with the application of expectancy research, actual measurement or investigation of personal significance (or other experiences supporting valuing) has not been conducted. The primary focus of reading comprehension research remains application of strategy use to support student competency and expectancy of success. Explicit research supporting a vision for reading comprehension that involves deep engagement, continuing intention to learn, the finding of personal significance in reading, or reading outside of school settings, is practically nonexistent. This dearth of explicit investigations of these issues severely limits understanding and application of the construct of valuing.

In the third reading handbook, Guthrie and Wigfield (2000) offered a theoretical integration of motivation and comprehension, emphasizing the affective and intentional aspects of reading (i.e., those experiences associated with valuing according to motivation research) as well as the strategic and conceptual. Focusing on engagement in reading as an aim of instruction, these researchers outline practical suggestions for sustaining both expectancy of success and valuing of reading activities. As part of their CORI program, they suggest, in addition to strategic skill instruction, connecting to the affective aspects of reading comprehension via real-world (and therefore more meaningful and interesting) activities, student choice, interesting texts, collaboration, and assessment which involves culturally relevant self-expression. In order to actually investigate the relationship between motivation and comprehension, the authors generated the Motivation for Reading Questionnaire (MRQ; Wigfield & Guthrie, 1997) designed to assess general individual motivational orientation (re: self-efficacy, intrinsic motivation, extrinsic motivation) as well as employing teacher reports of student post-instruction motivation (Wigfield & Guthrie, 1997; Guthrie, Wigfield, Barbosa, Perencevich, Taboada, Davis, Scafiddi, & Tonks, 2004). Their ongoing study of these constructs has yet to specifically measure or report the degree to which the actual CORI settings or strategies supported student valuing of learning (e.g., whether specific activities were found interesting, meaningful, engaging) or to analyze concretely the relationship between that context-specific valuing and comprehension (e.g., through pre- vs. post-measures of comprehension or correlations between context-specific motivation and comprehension). Thus, our understanding of the relationship between students' valuing of specific learning experiences and their reading comprehension remains limited (more theoretical and implicit). Enlarging such investigations to explicitly explore these issues is a crucial next step.

Brophy (1999) recently articulated an explanation of the limited integration of valuing and reading comprehension research, arguing that across any area of study far less is known about values/interest/ appreciation than about expectancy of success; the facility that exists regarding skills and strategies that support expectancies of success is simply not yet mirrored in research or theory regarding student valuing of academic objectives. Although individuals have the potential to develop a great range of dispositions toward learning, these dispositions are actually developed within specific socialization experiences and learning opportunities (see also Alleman & Brophy, 2004). Because of the self-motivated choice, effort, and persistence necessary to sustain true engagement and comprehension, he argues that *scaffolding appreciation* for learning (including reading comprehension) is crucial. In order to support such appreciation, Brophy suggests research-based principles for providing naturally motivating, self-relevant context and activities (similar to the cognitive concept of *zone of proximal development*, Tharp & Gallimore, 1988).

First, Brophy argues that a supportive social context is an essential foundation for such affect regarding learning. Indeed, Eccles and Wigfield (2002) argue that it may be impossible to understand students' motivation without considering the context in which it is occurring. Specifically, many contemporary theoretical perspectives suggest that optimal achievement motivation is energized when students feel a sense of belonging, an interpersonal connection or sense of relatedness at school (Connell & Wellborn, 1991; Eccles, Lord, & Buchanan, 1996; Faircloth & Hamm, 2005; Juvonen & Wentzel, 1996; Wentzel, 1997, 1998). Faircloth and Hamm (2005) demonstrated that sense of belonging was an essential underlying factor in the relationship between the traditional dimensions of motivation and achievement (see also Goodenow, 1993; Kindermann, 1993; Roeser, Midgely, & Urdan, 1996). Specifically, students' self-reported sense of school belonging was essential to (i.e., it mediated, or statistically accounted for) much of the relationship between students' valuing of learning (as well as their expectancies of success) and their achievement. This demonstrated the crucial role played by a sense of belonging within the school milieu to the type of strategic reading and valuing that support reading comprehension.

Within a supportive context, Brophy argues that appreciation for learning can be supported though an optimal match between learning experiences and students' individual abilities, backgrounds, values, and interests, which fuels their ability to identify with learning activities. The work of Hidi (e.g., Hidi & Renninger, 2006), among others, demonstrates the pivotal role played by such appreciation of learning. They suggest the use of novelty, challenge, relevance, and student perspectives to trigger and maintain situational interest in order to support individual interests that are self-sustaining. Such carefully crafted self-relevance (e.g., through allowing students to generate curiosity questions, solve problems, and initiate their own strategies) has been shown to focus and sustain attention (Hidi, 1995; McDaniel, Waddill, Finstad, & Bourg, 2000), enhance learning (Schraw, Brunting & Svoboda, 1995), contribute to cognitive performance (Krapp, 2002), and support reading comprehension (Alexander & Jetton, 1996; Hidi, 1990).

Contemporary motivational research has also located important connections to such self-relevance within students' cultural and social backgrounds and experiences. Specifically, cross cultural investigations of motivation have demonstrated that motivational experiences can vary across cultures (Schunk & Zimmerman, 2006). Institutional practices often recognize and reward certain perspectives, while others are shamed or unsanctioned (Bartlett & Holland, 2002), suggesting that classroom practices may or may not be compatible with students' social or cultural perspectives (Gaines, 1997; Hemmings, 1996; Marin & Marin, 1991; Meece & Kurtz-Costes, 2001; Triandis, 1990). Students describe discordance between their culture and the world of school as a potentially prohibitive barrier to their engagement in learning (Phelan, Yu, & Davidson, 1994). Sensitivity to such issues provides an avenue for students to negotiate a place of attachment to school and learning tasks both culturally (Bourdieu, 1977) and socially (Lee & Croninger, 1999). These insights are nicely captured in the work of reading researchers such as Au (2003), Roehler and Duffy (1991), and Pearson and Fielding (1991), who make connections between reading and students' lived experiences including families, home life, language, and pop culture. Continued work in this area, explicitly exploring comprehension as a function of such insightful connections to students' lives and identities, can strengthen this important work.

According to Brophy (1999), such personal connection to learning can also be generated through educational content and tasks that students find worthwhile and authentic. Recent research supports the notion that multidimensional classrooms with open-ended or problem-based academic tasks that emphasize variety and complexity, prolonged engagement, meaningfulness, and cooperative group work, sustain an appreciation for learning, support achievement, and increase cognitive functioning, persistence, and affective involvement (Blumenfeld, Mergendollar, & Swarthout, 1987; Doyle, 1983; Fairbanks, 2000). Researchers have labeled such tasks as "high-challenge" (Miller, 2003), "open" (Turner, 1995), "dialogic" (Woodside-Jiron, Johnston, & Day, 2001), or "complex" (Perry, Phillips, & Dowler, 2004). Miller and Meece (1999) traced the development of strong personal connections to high-challenge tasks: the greater the number of opportunities students at every achievement level had to complete such tasks, the more they preferred them because they felt creative, experienced positive emotions, and worked hard (outcomes related to the value construct). Miller (1995) further linked the completion of such tasks to increased scores on standardized achievement measures and decreased retentions and referrals for special education services. Combined, these insights provide a compelling rationale for designing specific strategies and contexts that scaffold student appreciation for the value of learning, and for believing these strategies can animate and sustain academic choice, effort and persistence. As Brophy points out in making the case for the importance of his argument, however, the integration of these concepts is primarily implicit. Clearly, consideration of how these ideas inform the work of reading comprehension researchers and practitioners warrants concentrated and explicit research attention as they relate to reading comprehension.

As illustrated in this review, motivational theory and research have much to offer efforts to understand and support reading comprehension, and the vision adopted for reading comprehension will drive the manner in which motivational insights inform or empower those efforts. To date, integration of the two fields is reflected most directly in the work of reading researchers embracing a multidimensional and complex, strategic and self-regulated, and personally meaningful interpretation of comprehension. While these efforts are commendable, a continuing lack of concentrated integration of the two fields (i.e., motivation and reading comprehension) in research, coupled with lesser emphasis placed on students' valuing of the act of reading in favor of a focus on skill- and performance-enhancing strategies, imposes important limitations on the contribution of motivational insights to the work of reading comprehension researchers and practitioners.

FUTURE DIRECTIONS

Our research lens has widened from a focus of single strategies; to an evaluation of the complex interactions among cognitive, metacognitive, and motivational strategies; to a study of how various social and cultural dimensions influence learning (Decorte, Greer, & Verschaffel, 1996). Students' home life, peer groups, popular culture, and technology; the nature and types of their relationships within and outside of the classrooms; how they use reading, writing, and talking within and across different disciplines; and their families' historical and cultural backgrounds, either singularly or by interaction, all affect comprehension (Moje, Ciechanowski, Kramer, Ellis, Carrillo, & Collazo, 2004; Moll, 2000). While we need to celebrate the complexity of this growing understanding, we also need to be careful not to tie the ability to comprehend prose to any and every instructional practice or to any and every possible influence. Proclamations such as, "Everything is related" or "It depends on the student" provide minimal guidance to teachers as they attempt to promote comprehension within classroom settings. We therefore return to Tierney and Cunningham's (1991) call for researchers to state their vision of what it means to be a reader in today's society.

The concept of "third space" (Gutiérrez & Stone, 2000) offers another dominant vision. It recognizes the critical influences of students' social and cultural histories on their ability to interpret prose and provides guidance to teachers regarding their instructional responsibilities and roles. Moreover, it includes, yet extends, previous efforts to understand how comprehension develops in classroom settings (Au, 2003; Pearson & Fielding, 1991; Roehler & Duffy, 1991). Students' participation over time and the discourses they use and encounter in classrooms rather than simply an individual's level of expertise with reading strategies are the central unit of analysis. This juncture between students and teachers allows researchers to evaluate the extent to which learners are able to negotiate a position whereby they develop personally meaningful prose interpretations. The theoretical framework of a "third space" gives researchers the opportunity to understand the nature of students' interpretations, the tools and resources they need to discover significance within their studies, and the changing contributions of students and teachers across time within particular instructional activities (Gutiérrez & Stone, 2000; Lave & Wenger, 1991). The "third space" vision captures our growing understanding of how students' cultural and social histories influence their identities as learners within various classroom activities.

The No Child Left Behind Act provides an alternative vision. This legislation is our government's attempt to improve comprehension via the endorsement of scientifically based research (Reyna, 2004; Sweet, 2004). It has refocused attention on the identification of individual reading strategies, each of which was selected based on their potential for increasing achievement (Kamil, 2004). These strategies are expected to have positive effects for all students at every grade level, regardless of students' social or cultural backgrounds or experiences. Minimal attention, if any, is directed towards motivation, particularly as it relates to a student's disposition to engage voluntarily with an activity or study once the intervention is terminated. The No Child Left Behind vision provides a one-size-fits all solution to the complex and multidimensional problem of student comprehension.

We favor the "third space" framework because it captures our growing understanding of the multiple influences of students' social and cultural histories on their cognitive performances within and across classrooms. Despite this endorsement, however, we express caution regarding the potential of either vision to promote students' motivation to engage deeply in their academic studies while developing a continuing motivation to learn. As stated earlier, motivation can promote the acquisition of necessary reading strategies, which often lead to higher levels of classroom performance and it can support the discovery of personal significance and intrinsic commitment. Despite differences among theorists' conceptualizations of motivation (Kamberelis & Dimitriadis, 2005; Hickey, 2003), we believe this conceptual distinction has important implications for students and teachers.

We hope researchers attend to the dimensions associated with the motivational concept of value in their efforts to evaluate students' comprehension. The concept of *scaffolding appreciation* (Brophy, 1999) could have the same potential to help us understand motivation as the zone of proximal development has had on our understanding of learning and instruction. Given the constraints posed by present accountability pressures (Miller & Duffy, 2006), the goal of promoting students' intentional, long-term, sustained, and volitional engagement in classroom settings should be our primary goal for the next 20 years.

REFERENCES

Alexander, P., & Jetton, T. (1996). Instructional importance: What teachers value and what students learn. *Reading Research Quarterly, 32*(3), 290–308.

Alexander, P., & Jetton, T. (2000). Learning from text: A multidimensional and developmental perspective. In M. Kamil, P. Mosenthal, D. Pearson, & R. Barr (Eds.), *Handbook of reading research* (Vol. II, pp. 285–310). Mahwah, NJ: Erlbaum.

Alleman, J., & Brophy, J. (2004). Building a learning community and studying childhood. *Social Studies and the Young Learner, 17*(2), 16–18.

Ames, C. (1992). Classrooms: Goals, structures, and student motivation. *Journal of Educational Psychology, 84,* 261–271.

Anderson, R. C., & Pearson, P. D. (1984). A schematic-theoretic view of the basic processes in reading comprehension. In P. D. Pearson, R. Barr, M. L. Kamil, & P. Mosenthal (Eds.), *Handbook of reading research* (Vol. 1, pp. 255–291). White Plains, NY: Longman.

Atkinson, J. (1964). *An introduction to motivation.* Princeton, NJ: Van Nostrand.

Au, K. (2003). Literacy research and students of diverse backgrounds: What does it take to improve achievement? In C. Fairbanks, J. Worthy, B. Maloch, J. Hoffman, & D. Schallert (Eds.), *52nd yearbook of the National Reading Conference* (pp. 85–91). Oak Creek, WI: NRC.

Bandura, A. (1977). Self-efficacy: Toward a unifying theory of behavioral change. *Psychological Review, 84*(2), 191–215.

Bandura, A. (1989). Regulation of cognitive processes through perceived self-efficacy. *Developmental Psychology, 25*(5), 729–735.

Barr, R., Kamil, M., Mosenthal P., & Pearson, D. (Eds.). (1991). *Handbook of reading research* (Vol. II). Mahwah, NJ: Erlbaum.

Bartlett, L., & Holland, D. (2002). Theorizing the space of literacy practices. *Ways of Knowing, 2,* 10–22.

Bean. T. (2000). Reading in the content areas: Social constructivist dimensions. In M. Kamil, P. Mosenthal, D. Pearson, & R. Barr (Eds.), *Handbook of reading research* (Vol. III, pp. 629–644). Mahwah, NJ: Erlbaum.

Bereiter, C., & Scardamalia, M. (1987). An attainable version of high literacy: Approaches to teaching higher-order skills in reading and writing. *Curriculum & Inquiry, 17*(1), 9–30.

Blumenfeld, P. C., Mergendollar, J., & Swarthout, D. (1987). Task as a heuristic for understanding student learning and motivation. *Journal of Curriculum Studies, 19,* 135–148.

Bourdieu, P. (1977). *Outline of a theory of practice.* New York: Cambridge University.

Brophy, J. (1999). Toward a model of value aspects of motivation in education: Developing appreciation for particular learning domains and activities. *Educational Psychologist, 34,* 75–85.

Brown, J., Collins, A., & Duguid, P. (1989). Situated cognition and the culture of learning. *Educational Researcher, 18,* 32–42.

Brown, A. L., Palincsar, A. S., & Armbruster, B. B. (1984). Instructing comprehension fostering activities in interactive learning situations. In H. Mandl, N. Stein, & T. Trabasso (Eds.), *Learning from texts* (pp. 128–143). Hillsdale, NJ: Erlbaum.

Connell, J., & Wellborn, J. (1991). Competence, autonomy and relatedness: A motivational analysis of self-system processes. In M. R. Gunnar & L. A. Sroufe (Eds.), *Self-processes & development* (pp. 235–247). Hillsdale, NJ: Erlbaum.

Covington, M. V. (1984). The self-worth theory of achievement motivation: Findings and implications. *The Elementary School Journal, 85*(1), 7–37.

Csikszentmihalyi, M. (1977). *Beyond boredom and anxiety.* San Francisco: Jossey-Bass.

Decorte, E., Greer, B., & Verschaffel, L. (1996). Mathematics teaching and learning. In D. Berliner & R. C. Calfee (Eds.), *Handbook of educational psychology* (pp. 187–210). New York: Macmillan.

Doyle, W. (1983). Academic work. *Review of Educational Research, 53,* 159–199.

Duffy, G., & Roehler, L. (1986). The subtleties of instructional mediation. *Educational Leadership, 43,* 23–27.

Duffy, G., Roehler, L., & Putnam, J. (1987). Putting the teacher in control: basal reading textbooks and instructional decision making. *The Elementary School Journal, 87*(3), 357–366.

Dweck, C. (1999). Caution—Praise can be dangerous. *American Educator, 23*(1), 4–9.

Eccles, J. S., Adler, T. F., Futterman, R., Goff, S. B., Kaczala, C. M., & Meece, J. L. (1983). Expectancies, values and academic behaviors. In J. T. Spence (Ed.), *Achievement and achievement motives* (pp. 75–146). San Francisco: Freeman.

Eccles, J. S., Lord, S., & Buchanan, C. M. (1996). School transitions in early adolescence: What are we doing to our young people? In J. A. Graber, J. Brooks-Gunn, & A. C. Peterson (Eds.), *Transitions in adolescence* (pp. 143–162). Mahwah, NJ: Erlbaum.

Eccles, J. S., & Wigfield, A. (2002). Motivational beliefs, values, and goals. *Annual Review of Psychology, 53,* 109–132.

Fairbanks, C. M. (2000). Fostering adolescents' literacy engagements: "Kid's business" and critical inquiry. *Reading Research and Instruction, 40*(1), 35–50.

Faircloth, B. S., & Hamm, J. V. (2005). Sense of belonging among high school students representing four ethnic groups. *Journal of Youth and Adolescence, 34*(4), 293–309.

Gadsen, V. (2000). Intergenerational literacy within families. In M. Kamil, P. Mosenthal, D. Pearson, & R. Barr (Eds.), *Handbook of reading research* (Vol. 3, pp. 871–888). Mahwah, NJ: Erlbaum.

Gaines, S. O. (1997). *Culture, ethnicity, and personal relationship processes.* New York: Routledge.

Gardner, H. (1985). *The mind's new science: A history of the cognitive revolution.* New York: Basic Books.

Goodenow, C. (1993). Classroom belonging among early adolescent students: Relationships to motivation and achievement. *Journal of Early Adolescence, 13,* 21–43.

Guthrie, J., McGough, K., Bennett, L., & Rice, M. (1996). Concept-oriented reading instruction: An integrated curriculum to develop motivations and strategies for reaing. In L. Baker, P. Afflerback, & D. Reinking (Eds.), *Developing engaged readers in school and home communities* (pp. 165–190). Hillsdale, NJ: Erlbaum.

Guthrie, J. T., Anderson, E., Alao, S., & Rinehart, J. (1999). Influences of concept-oriented reading instruction on strategy use and conceptual learning from text. *The Elementary School Journal, 99*(4), 344–366.

Guthrie, J. T., & Wigfield, A. (2000). Engagement and motivation in reading. *Handbook of reading research* (Vol. II, pp. 403–422). Mahwah, NJ: Erlbaum.

Guthrie, J. T., Wigfield, A., Barbosa, P., Perencevich, K. C., Taboada, A., Davis, M. H., Scafiddi, N. T., & Tonks, S. (2004). Increasing reading comprehension and engagement through concept-oriented reading instruction. *Journal of Educational Psychology, 96*(3), 403–423.

Guthrie, J. T., Wigfield, A., & VonSecker, C. (2000). Effects of integrated instruction on motivation and strategy use in reading. *Journal of Educational Psychology, 92*(2), 331–341.

Gutiérrez, K. D., & Stone, L. D. (2000). Synchronic and diachronic dimensions of social practice: An emerging methodology for cultural-historical perspectives on literacy learning. In C. L. Lee & P. Smagorinsky (Eds.), *Vygotskian perspectives on literacy research: Constructing meaning through collaborative inquiry* (pp. 150–164). Cambridge: Cambridge University Press.

Hemmings, A. (1996). Conflicting images? Being black and a model high school student. *Anthropology & Educational Quarterly, 27*(1), 20–50.

Hickey, D. T. (2003). Engaged participation versus marginal nonparticipation: A stridently sociocultural approach to achievement motivation. *The Elementary School Journal, 103*(4), 402–429.

Hidi, S. (1990). Interest and its contribution as a mental resource for learning. *Review of Educational Research, 60*(4), 549–571.

Hidi, S. (1995). A re-examination of the role of attention in learning from text. *Educational Psychology Review, 7*, 323–350.

Hidi, S., & Renninger, K. (2006). The four-phase model of interest development. *Educational Psychologist, 41*(2), 111–127.

Juvonen, J., & Wentzel, K. R. (1996). *Social motivation: Understanding children's school adjustment.* New York: Cambridge University Press.

Kamberelis, G., & Dimitriadis, G. (2005). *Qualitative inquiry: Approaches to language and literacy research.* New York: Teachers College Press.

Kamil, M. L. (2004). Vocabulary and comprehension instruction: Summary and implications of the National Reading Panel findings. In P. McCardle & V. Chhabra (Eds.), *The voice of evidence in reading research* (pp. 213–234). Baltimore: Brookes Publishing.

Kamil, M., Mosenthal, P., Pearson, D., & Barr, R. (Eds.). (2000). *Handbook of reading research* (Vol. 3). Mahwah, NJ: Erlbaum.

Kanfer, R., Ackerman, P. L., Murtha, T. C., Dugdale, B., & Nelson, L. (1994). Goal setting, conditions of practice, and task performance: A resource allocation perspective. *Journal of Applied Psychology, 79*, 826–835.

Kindermann, T. A. (1993). Natural peer groups as contexts for individual development: The case of children's motivation in school. *Developmental Psychology, 29*(6), 970–977.

Krapp, A. (2002). An educational-psychological theory of interest and its relation to self-determination theory. In E. Deci & R. Ryan (Eds.), *The handbook of self-determination research* (pp. 405–427). Rochester, NY: University of Rochester Press.

Lave, J., & Wenger E. (1991). *Situated learning: Legitimate peripheral participation.* New York: Cambridge University Press.

Lee, V., & Croninger,R. (1999). *Elements of social capital in the context of six high schools.* Washington, DC: Office of Research and Improvement.

Marin, G., & Marin, B. V. (1991). *Research with Hispanic populations.* Newbury Park, CA: Sage.

McDaniel, M. A.,Waddill, P. J., Finstad, K., & Bourg, T. (2000). The effects of text-based interest on attention and recall. *Journal of Educational Psychology, 92*, 492–502.

Meece, J., & Kurtz-Costes, B. (2001). The schooling of ethnic minority children and youth. *Educational Psychologist, 36*(1), 1–7.

Meece, J. L., Eccles (Parsons), J. S., Kaczala, C., Goff, S. B., & Futterman, R. (1982). Sex differences in math achievement: Toward a model of academic choice. *Psychology Bulletin, 91*(2), 324–348.

Miller, S. (1995). Teachers' responses to test-driven accountability pressures: "If I change, will my scores drop?" *Reading Research and Instruction, 34*(4), 332–351.

Miller, S. D. (2003). How high- and low-challenge tasks affect motivation and learning: Implications for struggling learners. *Reading and Writing Quarterly: Overcoming Learning Difficulties, 19*(1), 39–57.

Miller, S. D., & Duffy, G. G. (2006). Are we crazy to keep doing this? *Reading Today, 24*(3), 18.

Miller, S. D., & Meece, J. L. (1999). Students' motivational preferences for different reading and writing tasks. *Elementary School Journal,* 19–36

Moje, E. B., Ciechanowski, K. M., Kramer, K., Ellis, L., Carrillo, R., & Collazo, T. (2004). Working toward a third space in content area literacy: An examination of everyday funds of knowledge and Discourse. *Reading Research Quarterly, 39,* 38–71.

Moll, L. (2000). Inspired by Vygotsky: Ethnographic experiments in education. In C. L. Lee & P. Smagorinsky (Eds.), *Vygotskian perspectives on literacy research: Constructing meaning through collaborative inquiry* (pp. 256–268). Cambridge: Cambridge University Press.

Nicholls, J. G. (1984). Achievement motivation: Conceptions of ability, subjective experience, task choice, and performance. *Psychological Review, 91,* 328–346.

Paris, S. G. (1986). Teaching children to guide their reading and learning. In T. E. Raphael (Ed.), *The contexts of school-based learning* (pp. 115–130). New York: Random House.

Paris, S., Byrnes, J., & Paris, A. (2001). Constructing theories, identities, and actions of self-regulated learners. In B. Zimmerman & D. Schunk (Eds.), *Self-regulated learning and academic achievement: Theoretical perspectives.* Mahwah, NJ: Erlbaum.

Paris, S., Cross, D., & Lipson, M. (1984). Informed strategies for learning: A program to improve children's reading awareness and comprehension. *Journal of Educational Psychology, 76* (6), 1239.

Paris, S., Lipson, M., & Wixson, K. (1983). Becoming a strategic reader. *Contemporary Educational Psychology 8,* 293–316.

Paris, S. C., Wasik, B. A., & Turner, J. C. (1991). The development of strategic readers. In R. Barr, M. Kamil, P. Mosenthal, & D. Pearson (Eds.), *Handbook of reading research* (Vol. II, pp. 609–640). Mahwah, NJ: Erlbaum.

Pearson, D., Barr, R., Kamil, M., & Mosenthal, P. (Eds.). (1984). *Handbook of reading research.* White Plains, NY: Longman.

Pearson, D., & Fielding, L. (1991). Comprehension instruction. In R. Barr, M. Kamil, P. Mosenthal, & D. Pearson, (Eds.), *Handbook of reading research* (Vol. II, pp. 815–60). Mahwah, NJ: Erlbaum.

Pearson, P. D. (1986). Twenty years of research in reading comprehension. In T. E. Raphael (Ed.), *The contexts of school-based literacy* (pp. 43–62). New York: Random House.

Pearson, P. D., & Gallagher, M. (1983). The instruction of reading comprehension. *Contemporary Educational Psychology, 8,* 317–344.

Perry, N., Phillips, L., & Dowler, J. (2004). Examining features of tasks and their potential to promote self-regulated learning. *Teachers College Record, 106*(9), 1854–1878.

Phelan, P., Yu, H. C., & Davidson, A. (1994). Navigating the psychosocial pressure of adolescence: The voices and experiences of high school youth. *American Educational Research Journal, 31*(2), 415–447.

Pintrich, P. R., & Schunk, D. H. (2002). *Motivation in education: Theory, research, and applications.* Columbus, OH: Merrill.

Pressley, M., Beard El-Dinary, P., Gaskins, I., Schuder, T., Bergman, J., Almasi, J., & Brown, R. (1992). Beyond direct explanation: Transactional instruction of reading comprehension strategies. *Elementary School Journal, 9*(5), 513–55.

Purcell-Gates, V. (2000). Family literacy. In M. Kamil, P. Mosenthal, D. Pearson, & R. Barr (Eds.), *Handbook of reading research* (Vol. III, pp. 853–870). Mahwah, NJ: Erlbaum.

Resnick, L. (1981). Instructional psychology. In M. R. Resenzweig & L. W. Porter (Eds.), *Annual review of psychology* (Vol. 32, pp. 659 – 704). Palo Alto, CA: Annual Reviews.

Reyna, V. F. (2004). Why scientific research? The importance of evidence in changing educational practice. In P. McCardle & V. Chhabra (Eds.), *The voice of evidence in reading research* (pp. 47–58). Baltimore: Brookes Publishing.

Roehler, L., & Duffy, G. (1991). Teacher's instructional actions. In R. Barr, M. Kamil, P. Mosenthal, & D. Pearson (Eds.), *Handbook of reading research* (Vol. II, pp. 861–884). Mahwah, NJ: Erlbaum.

Roeser, R. W., Midgley, C., & Urdan, T. C. (1996). Perceptions of the school psychological environment and early adolescents' psychological and behavioral functioning in school: The mediating role of goals and belonging. *Journal of Educational Psychology, 88*(3), 408–422.

Rosenblatt, L. (1978). *The reader, the text, the poem: The transactional theory of literary work.* Carbondale: Southern Illinois University Press.

Schraw, G., Brunting, R., & Svoboda, C. (1995). Sources of situational interest. *Journal of Reading Behavior, 27,* 1–17.

Schunk, D., & Rice, J. (1987). Enhancing comprehension skill and self-efficacy with strategy value information. *Journal of Reading Behavior, 3,* 285–302.

Schunk, D. H., & Zimmerman, B. J. (1996). Modeling and self-efficacy influences on children's development of self-regulation. In K. Wentzel & J. Juvonen (Eds.), *Social motivation: Understanding children's school adjustment* (pp. 154–180). New York: Cambridge University Press.

Schunk, D., & Zimmerman, B. (2006). Self-regulated learning. In P. Alexander & P. Winne (Eds.), *Handbook of educational psychology.* Mahwah, NJ: Erlbaum.

Shulman, L. (1986). Paradigms and research programs in the study of teaching: A contemporary perspective. In M. Wittrock (Ed.), *Handbook of research on teaching* (3rd ed., pp. 3–36). New York: Macmilan.

Singer, H. (1978). Active comprehension: From answering to asking questions. *The Reading Teacher, 31,* 901–908.

Singer, H., & Donlan, D. (1982). Active comprehension: Problem-solving schema with question generation for comprehension of complex short stories. *Reading Research Quarterly, 17*(2), 166–186.

Sweet, R. W. (2004). The big picture: Were we are nationally on the reading front and how we got here. In P. McCardle & V. Chhabra (Eds.), *The voice of evidence in reading research* (pp. 13–44). Baltimore: Brookes Publishing.

Tharp, R., & Gallimore, R. (1988). *Rousing minds to life: Teaching, learning, and schooling in social context.* Cambridge: Cambridge University Press.

Tierney, R. J., & Cunningham, J.W. (1991). Research on teaching reading and comprehension. In R. Barr, M. Kamil, P. Mosenthal, & D. Pearson (Eds.), *Handbook of reading research* (Vol. II, pp. 609–655). Mahwah, NJ: Erlbaum.

Triandis, H. C. (1990). Cross-cultural studies of individualism and collectivism. In J. J. Berman (Ed.), *Nebraska symposium on motivation 1989: Cross-cultural perspectives* (pp. 41–133). Lincoln: University of Nebraska Press.

Turner, J. (1995). The influence of classroom contexts on young children's motivation for literacy. *Reading Research Quarterly, 30*(3), 410–441.

Wade, S., & Moje, E. (2000). The role of text in classroom learning. In M. Kamil, P. Mosenthal, D. Pearson, & R. Barr (Eds.), *Handbook of reading research* (Vol. III, pp. 609–628). Mahwah, NJ: Erlbaum.

Weiner, B. (1972). Attribution theory, achievement motivation, and the educational process. *Educational Research, 42*(2), 203–215.

Weiner, B. (1990). History of motivational research in education. *Journal of Educational Psychology, 82,* 616–622.

Wentzel, K. R. (1997). Social motivational processes and interpersonal relationships: Implications for understanding motivation at school. *Journal of Educational Psychology, 91*(1), 76–97.

Wentzel, K. R. (1998). Social relationships and motivation in middle school: The role of parents, teachers, and peers. *Journal of Educational Psychology, 90*(2), 202–209.

Wigfield, A., & Asher, S. R. (1984). In Social and motivational influences on reading. In D. Pearson, R. Barr, M. Kamil, & P. Mosenthal, (Eds.), *Handbook of reading research.* White Plains, NY: Longman.

Wigfield, A., & Guthrie, J. (1997). Relations of children's motivation for reading to the amount and breadth of their reading. *Journal of Educational Psychology, 89*(3), 420–432.

Wilkinson, L., & Silliman, E. (2000). Classroom language and literacy learning. In M. Kamil, P. Mosenthal, D. Pearson, & R. Barr (Eds.), *Handbook of Reading Research* (Vol. III, pp. 337–360). Mahwah, NJ: Erlbaum.

Winograd, P., & Johnston, P. (1987). Some considerations for advancing the teaching of reading comprehension. *Educational Psychologist, 22*(3&4), 213–230.

Wittrock, M. C. (1974). Learning as a generative process. *Educational Psychologist, 11*(2), 87–95.

Woodside-Jiron, H. J., Johnston, P., & Day, J. (2001). Teaching and learning literate epistemologies. *Journal of Educational Psychology, 93*(1), 223–233.

Zimmerman, B. (2002). Achieving self-regulation: The trial and triumph of adolescence. In F. Pajares & T. Urdan (Eds.), *Academic motivation of adolescents.* Greenwich, CT: Information Age Publishing.

15 Vocabulary and Reading Comprehension
The Nexus of Meaning

James F. Baumann

University of Wyoming

In his classic 1944 article titled "Fundamental Factors in Reading Comprehension," Frederick B. Davis wrote, "It is clear that word knowledge plays a very important part in reading comprehension" (p. 191). Davis's statement has been used often, perhaps glibly, as a truism about the connection between vocabulary and reading comprehension. Indeed, there are various relationships between word knowledge and text understanding (Anderson & Freebody, 1981; Baumann, 2005; Nagy & Scott, 2000). Although it may be "clear" that vocabulary "plays a very important part in reading comprehension," the simplicity of the assertion belies its knottiness, as was acknowledged by the National Reading Panel (NRP) (2000): "Precisely separating the two processes is difficult, if not impossible" (pp. 4–15). Further, it may be conventional wisdom that vocabulary knowledge affects reading comprehension directly, but, as Baumann, Kame'enui, and Ash (2003) noted, "The evidence of a causal link between vocabulary and comprehension is historically long but empirically soft" (p. 758).

It is the purpose of this chapter to explore the nature of the complexities between vocabulary and reading comprehension, that is, to examine the nexus of meaning between understanding individual concepts and the broader comprehension of connected text. This chapter is organized into three sections. First is a presentation of theoretical and historical perspectives linking vocabulary and comprehension. Second is a review of significant research that examines if and how pedagogical attention to vocabulary influences reading comprehension. I close the chapter with a conclusion section that includes a summary and implications for research and practice.

THEORETICAL AND HISTORICAL PERSPECTIVES

Vocabulary and comprehension relationships

Evidence for the relationship between vocabulary knowledge and reading comprehension comes from several sources, including descriptive analyses, correlational studies, and examinations of readability and achievement test data.

Descriptive analyses   The first significant attention to connections between vocabulary knowledge and word comprehension was provided in the early 20th century in a series of works by E. L. Thorndike (1917a/1971, 1917b, 1917c). For example, in his oft-cited article titled "Reading as Reasoning" (1917a/1971), Thorndike analyzed readers' "mistakes" to comprehension questions after reading short paragraphs and concluded that understanding the meanings of words was prerequisite (although not necessarily sufficient) for readers to understand the overall passages.

Correlational studies   Several researchers explored vocabulary-comprehension associations several decades later using correlational and factor analytic methods. Davis (1944), in his "Fundamental Factors" study, examined relationships among nine indices of text understanding. He found that word knowledge correlated highly with various comprehension tasks, and a factor analysis revealed two key components: a broad comprehension measure he referred to as "reasoning in reading" and another he labeled "word knowledge" (p. 191). Several years later, Thurstone (1946) reanalyzed Davis's (1944) data using an alternate statistical procedure and challenged Davis's findings, reporting that there was only a single factor ("reading ability," p. 185). Thurstone did acknowledge, however, that one of Davis's tests—knowledge of word meanings—did demonstrate specific, unique variance.

About 20 years later, Davis (1968) returned to the issue of identifying components of reading comprehension and conducted a modified replication of his earlier work. He again reported that comprehension consisted of multiple components, with vocabulary being the most pronounced. Davis (1972) and Spearritt (1972) examined the 1968 Davis data further and, although they had somewhat different interpretations, they agreed about the centrality of vocabulary to comprehension. Rosenshine (1980) reviewed the same literature and concluded that *"different analyses yielded different unique skills, ...* [but] only one skill was consistent across the three analyses: remembering word meanings" (p. 543).

Examinations of readability and achievement test data   Measures of readability, or "ease of comprehension" (Harris & Hodges, 1995, p. 203), also provided insight into vocabulary-comprehension links. For example, Klare's (1974–1975) analyses of readability formulas revealed that a semantic factor (word knowledge) was the most powerful in predicting passage comprehension. Bloom (1976) noted that vocabulary and comprehension achievement tests correlated highly, and R. L. Thorndike's (1973) analysis of achievement test data in 15 different countries revealed strong relationships between vocabulary and comprehension tests.

In summary, on the basis of various analyses conducted over the first three quarters of the 20th century, it was generally accepted that vocabulary was indisputably linked to reading comprehension.

Explanations for vocabulary-comprehension relationships

In 1981, Anderson and Freebody wrote a highly influential chapter in which they sought to "summarize what is known about the role of vocabulary knowledge in reading comprehension" (p. 77). After documenting the strong vocabulary-reading comprehension association, Anderson and Freebody proposed three hypotheses, or positions, for the strong association: the instrumentalist, aptitude, and knowledge position.

1. *Instrumentalist*: This position posits that knowing word meanings is instrumental for, or enables, reading comprehension in a causal way. The implication of this perspective is that teaching word meanings should promote reading comprehension.
2. *Aptitude*: This position suggests that vocabulary is reflective of general aptitude, that is, persons with both a large vocabulary and strong reading comprehension are a function of them having "a quick mind" (Anderson & Freebody, 1981, p. 81). Thus, vocabulary and comprehension are both influenced by a third factor, overall verbal aptitude.
3. *Knowledge*: This view hypothesizes that vocabulary and comprehension are reflective of overall knowledge or schema. Therefore, a readers' general conceptual knowledge promotes or causes reading comprehension, not word knowledge per se.

Instead, vocabulary knowledge is indicative of a reader's broader knowledge base about a topic and the words used to describe it.

Other vocabulary researchers and theorists expanded upon or added to the three positions outlined by Anderson and Freebody (1981), providing additional views on vocabulary-comprehension relationships.

4. *Access*: Mezynski (1983) suggested that comprehension of text is a function of a reader's ability to efficiently locate and access word meanings when reading. Built on the theory of automaticity in reading (LaBerge & Samuels, 1974), this position suggests that the more quickly a reader can access semantic meanings (Stahl, 1991), the deeper the text comprehension.

5. *Input*: Krashen (1985) asserted that language acquisition is dependent on "comprehensible input," or connected text that is just beyond a language learner's current level of competence (Vygotsky, 1978). Although intended to explain vocabulary development in a second language, Krashen's position has been extended to first-language vocabulary development and has been used to argue for extensive independent reading (Krashen, 1989, 2004).

6. *Metalinguistic*: Nagy (2005) argued that one important dimension of the aptitude hypothesis involves a reader's metalinguistic awareness, or "the ability to reflect on and manipulate language" (p. 32) with respect to syntax, morphology, semantics, and other cues. Nagy (2007) asserted further that "some of the correlation between vocabulary knowledge and reading comprehension can be accounted for by appealing to the relationship of each of these with a third construct, metalinguistic awareness" (p. 54).

So, which of these hypotheses is "correct"? As will be obvious from the following review, this is the wrong question to ask. Given the complexity of vocabulary-comprehension relationships, there are instances in which each hypothesis (or a combination of several) has explanatory power and other instances in which one or more hypotheses do not. Working from the stance that all the hypotheses hold some ability to explain the vocabulary-comprehension nexus, I now turn to a review of the pedagogical literature.

PEDAGOGICAL ATTENTION TO VOCABULARY AND EFFECTS ON READING COMPREHENSION

For the purpose of this chapter, I view vocabulary instruction broadly, using the term *pedagogical attention* to denote that there are multiple direct and indirect ways to promote word knowledge. Likewise, I argue, that the research literature reveals that varying forms of pedagogical attention to vocabulary have different relationships to reading comprehension, and hence might be explained by different hypotheses. But first, I describe a structure for organizing the vocabulary-comprehension research.

A Framework for Effective Vocabulary Instruction

The research and theory on vocabulary instruction is long and rich (Beck & McKeown, 1991; Blachowicz & Fisher, 2000; Petty, Herold, & Stohl, 1967), and there has been considerable interest recently on theoretically based vocabulary instructional practices (Baumann & Kame'enui, 2004; Beck, McKeown, & Kucan, 2002; Block & Mangieri, 2006; Hiebert & Kamil, 2005; Stahl & Nagy, 2006; Wagner, Muse, & Tannenbum, 2007). One of the issues discussed in this literature has been the implementation of multi-faceted vocabulary instruction programs (Blackowicz & Fisher, 2000, 2006; Graves, 1987; Graves & Prenn, 1986; McKeown & Beck, 1988; Nagy, 1988). Graves

(2000, 2006) proposed a wide-ranging, theoretically based, four-component framework for comprehensive vocabulary instruction. These components are "(1) providing rich and varied language experiences; (2) teaching individual words; (3) teaching word-learning strategies; and (4) fostering word consciousness" (Graves, 2006, p. 5). Adopting Graves's framework, I address in the following subsections how vocabulary instructional actions related to each component may or may not promote reading comprehension.

Providing rich and varied language experiences

Graves (2006) stated that "one way to build students' vocabularies is to immerse them in a rich array of language experiences so that they learn words through listening, speaking, reading, and writing" (p. 5). There is considerable research examining how exposure to texts is associated with vocabulary enhancement, and there is some indication that this growth through exposure affects or mediates comprehension (Cunningham, 2005). Two related literatures are germane to this component: research on reading aloud to students and research on having students engage in independent reading.

Reading aloud to students   It has been argued that reading aloud to children is one of the most effective ways to promote their early literacy development (Adams, 1990; Anderson, Hiebert, Scott, & Wilkinson, 1985). Research reveals consistent associations between reading aloud and vocabulary development when preschool and elementary teachers read aloud to children (NRP, 2000; van Kleeck, Stahl, & Bauer, 2003) and when parents read to their preschoolers (Scarborough & Dobrich, 1994). For instance, a meta-analysis by Bus, van IJzendoorn, and Pellegrini (1995) revealed an overall effect size of .67 for the frequency of parent read-alouds to their preschool children and measures of oral language, which included vocabulary knowledge.

Simply reading books aloud to children is associated with vocabulary gains (e.g., Elley, 1989, Experiment 1), although multiple readings appear to be more facilitative than single readings (Senechal, 1997). Repetition of words within a text (Elley, 1989, Experiment 2; Robbins & Ehri, 1994) also enhances vocabulary acquisition from read-alouds.

Reader-listener interaction facilitates vocabulary acquisition during read-alouds (e.g., Dickinson & Smith, 1994; Lonigan & Whitehurst, 1998; Wasik & Bond, 2001). For instance, Wasik, Bond, and Hindman (2006) taught Head Start teachers to ask questions, build vocabulary, and make connections as they read aloud to their classes. Following a school year's implementation of the program, results revealed that children in the intervention classrooms outperformed children in control classrooms on vocabulary measures ($d = 0.73$ for receptive vocabulary; $d = .44$ for expressive vocabulary).

Researchers have evaluated various techniques for teaching vocabulary explicitly while reading aloud to young children (e.g., Beck & McKeown, 2001, 2007a; Coyne, Simmons, & Kame'enui, 2004; Juel & Deffes, 2004; Juel, Biancaross, Coker, & Deffes, 2003). For example, Biemiller and Boote (2006) explored the effects of kindergarten, first-grade, and second-grade teachers' word explanations when reading children's books aloud multiple times. In Study 1, children averaged a pretest/posttest gain of 12% for simply reading a book multiples times, with an added gain of 10% for words explained (22% gain total). In Study 2, the researchers increased the number of words taught and added daily and final reviews of word taught, reporting a pretest/posttest gain of 41%.

It should be noted, however, that even though the relationship between reading aloud and vocabulary is statistically reliable in many studies, the overall magnitude of the association between listening to books and children's language and literacy development is often modest in magnitude (Williams, 2007). For instance, on the basis of their review of studies examining the effects of parents reading aloud to their preschoolers, Scarborough and Dobrich (1994) reported that parent read-alouds accounted for no more than 8% of the variance in children's literacy and language abilities. Beck and McKeown (2007a) commented that studies examining the effects of "just reading aloud" on vocabulary revealed associations that ranged "from nonexistent to unimpressive" (p. 252).

What about possible relationships between and among reading aloud, vocabulary, and comprehension? Bus et al. (1995) reported an effect size of .55 for parent read-alouds on children's later reading achievement (which included comprehension). In another meta-analysis, Scarborough (1998, 2002) noted that the median correlation between kindergartners' expressive vocabulary and later reading performance (again including comprehension) was .49, with a correlation of .38 for receptive vocabulary. Morrow (1989) reported that kindergartners' comprehension of stories was enhanced by adult read-alouds, and there was some evidence that a small-group format (as opposed to one-on-one or large groups) was more effective in promoting story comprehension (Morrow & Smith, 1990).

In contrast, however, Meyer, Wardrop, Stahl, and Linn (1994) reported a negative relationship between the time kindergarten teachers spent reading to students and their reading achievement. Meyer et al. affirmed that there are benefits to reading aloud to children but that doing so is not "magical" in itself. Instead, they commented, that it is the quality of read-aloud events and the presence of other literacy activities that may relate to or influence young children's literacy achievement as much as simply reading aloud.

Senechal, Ouellette, and Rodney (2006) sought to tease out the relationship between vocabulary and later reading ability, referring to this association as "the misunderstood giant." They argued that reading aloud predicts children's language well but not children's early literacy abilities. Senechal et al. reanalyzed data from several longitudinal studies and found that children's vocabulary in kindergarten predicted reading comprehension in Grades 3 and 4 but not in Grade 1. The data, they argued, indicated that storybook reading has an indirect relationship to reading comprehension, with oral vocabulary being the mediating factor. Senechal (2006) suggested, therefore, that the dictum that there is no better way to prepare a child to learn to read than by reading aloud to her or him (Anderson et al., 1985) might be recast as "shared reading is an important activity because it can enhance children's vocabulary, which in turn, will be a strong predictor of children's comprehension in later grades" (p. 80).

Independent reading by students Some reading theorists have argued that children learn to read by reading (Smith, 1976). In other words, the more exposure learners have to written texts—at home or school—through independent, self-selected reading, the greater the reading development, including vocabulary acquisition (Krashen, 2004). A number of studies have demonstrated that students in the upper elementary and middle grades do learn word meanings just by reading (Anderson, 1996; Herman, Anderson, Pearson, & Nagy, 1987; Jenkins, Stein, & Wysocki, 1984; Nagy, Anderson, & Herman, 1987; Nagy, Herman, & Anderson, 1985; Schefelbine, 1990). There also is evidence that vocabulary can be acquired when reading electronic texts (Higgins & Cocks, 1999). Vocabulary-learning-by-reading also appears to be a cross-cultural phenomenon (Shu, Anderson, & Zhang, 1995) and applies to both first- and second-language acquisition (Krashen, 1989; Nagy, 1997).

Swanborn and de Glopper (1999) conducted a meta-analysis of 20 studies that explored incidental word learning during reading. Results demonstrated that, on average, "under natural reading circumstances students will spontaneously derive and learn the meaning of about 15 words of every 100 unknown words they encounter" (p. 279). This is three times as high as the commonly cited 5% chance of learning a word estimated by Nagy, Anderson, and Herman (1987). Swanborn and de Glopper explained this difference due to their use of an assessment approach sensitive to partial word knowledge.

Swanborn and de Glopper's (1999) analysis also suggested that students develop in ability to infer word meanings as they grow older. For example, students at Grade 4 demonstrated a .08 probability of learning a word, whereas a student at Grade 11 had about a .33 probability. Whether this growth in ability to use context is simply a maturational phenomenon or a function of intervening instruction, however, is a matter still unresolved.

Cunningham and Stanovich (1997, 1998, 2003) have provided longitudinal, correlational evidence for a wide-reading/vocabulary relationship. Employing hierarchical multiple regression procedures (see Stanovich & Cunningham, 2004), Cunningham and Stanovich (2003) documented that "avid readers excel in most domains of verbal learning" (p. 669) but vocabulary in particular. Drawing from the work of Hayes and Ahrens (1988)—which demonstrated that printed text is much more lexically complex than oral text—Cunningham and Stanovich argued that wide, independent reading, as measured by reading volume, "is the prime contributor to individual differences in children's vocabularies" (1998, p. 9).

Not all research, however, supports the notion that students learn words by simply reading (NRP, 2000). Several analyses suggest that written context may be not particularly rich and, in some instances, might be misleading (Baldwin & Schatz, 1986; Beck, McKeown, & McCaslin, 1983). Wilkinson, Wardrop, and Anderson's (1988) reanalysis of data by Leinhardt, Zigmond, and Cooley (1981) found little effect of silent reading on the reading achievement of elementary students with learning disabilities. Carver and Liebert (1995) found no evidence that students in Grades 3–5 who read relatively easy library books while enrolled in a summer reading program progressed in reading ability. Gardner's (2004) genre analysis of reading materials for children revealed that expository texts tended to have specialized vocabularies with much higher lexical density than narratives. Thus, she cautioned educators not to assume that incidental word learning when reading nonfiction will be as facile as when reading narratives.

In addition to the relationship between independent reading and vocabulary growth (e.g., Nagy, Anderson, & Herman, 1987; Nagy, Herman, & Anderson, 1985), and there is evidence of a link between independent reading and reading comprehension (e.g., Anderson, Wilson, & Fielding, 1988; Cipielewski & Stanovich 1992; Greaney, 1980; see Anderson, 1996). For instance, Jenkins et al. (1984) reported that fifth graders who were exposed to low-frequency words in passages they read independently not only learned those words but also were "better able to comprehend those parts of the stories involving key vocabulary when they had previously read the vocabulary in other passages" (p. 783). Taylor, Frye, and Maruyama (1990) examined the relationship between fifth-grade students' time spent reading at home and at school and their reading achievement as measured by a standardized reading comprehension measure. Even after controlling for prior reading achievement, Taylor et al. found that the volume of independent reading at school (but not at home) contributed to students' reading comprehension ability.

In summary, there is considerable evidence that providing children and adolescents rich and varied language experiences, particularly through exposure to texts read aloud and through their independent reading, positively affects vocabulary development. Anderson (1996) estimated that "at least one-third, and maybe as much as two-thirds, of the typical child's annual vocabulary growth comes as the natural consequence of reading books, magazines, and newspapers" (p. 64). In addition, there is some evidence that exposure to oral and written texts enhances students' understanding of the textual information.

Teaching individual words

Much of the research on vocabulary instruction addresses how one might teach students the meanings of specific words. This research is summarized in classic syntheses (e.g., Dale & Razik, 1963; Petty et al., 1967), influential reviews from the 1980s (e.g., Graves, 1986; Herman & Dole, 1988; Jenkins & Dixon, 1983; Mezinski, 1983), meta-analyses (e.g., Stahl & Fairbanks, 1986), and more contemporary reviews (e.g., Baumann et al., 2003; Blachowicz & Fisher, 2000; Jitendra, Edwards, Sacks, & Jacobson, 2004; Nagy & Scott, 2000; NRP, 2000). Although the literature on teaching word meanings is large, the RAND Reading study group (Snow, 2002) noted that "the number of studies that have directly examined the effects of vocabulary instruction on reading comprehension is still relatively small" (p. 36).

Overview of research What does the "relatively small" literature tell us about the effects of teaching individual words on text comprehension? Three reviews from the 1980s captured then, and still do now, some of the key principles (and limitations) of the extant research in this area. First, Mezynski (1983) provided a systematic analysis of research on vocabulary instruction and comprehension. She analyzed eight studies "that tested the premise that improving vocabulary would beneficially affect reading comprehension" (pp. 257–258). All studies demonstrated growth in word knowledge, but only four revealed a positive impact on comprehension. Mezynski noted that there were "methodological problems" and interpretation difficulties in that some studies were significantly underwritten in the methods sections and there was considerable variation across studies in the number of words taught, instructional procedures employed, and assessment tasks. In spite of these limitations, Mezynski identified three factors that were linked to enhanced comprehension: more practice of target words, breadth in instructional techniques, and encouragement of active processing.

Second, Graves (1986) identified 14 vocabulary intervention studies, 8 of which indicated some positive effect of vocabulary instruction on comprehension. Like Mezynski (1983), Graves noted limitations in methodology or detail in reports, leaving him to conclude that only the three studies by Beck, KcKeown, and colleagues (Beck, Perfetti, & McKeown, 1982; McKeown, Beck, Omanson, & Perfetti, 1983; McKeown, Beck, Omanson, & Pople, 1985) provided "convincing evidence that teaching vocabulary can increase comprehension of texts containing the words taught" (p. 61). From his analysis of these studies, Graves concluded that, in order for vocabulary instruction to affect comprehension, it needs to be multifaceted, of extended duration, require active processing, include multiple encounters with words, involve semantic associations among words, and promote automaticity in lexical access.

Third, Stahl and Fairbanks (1986) conducted a meta-analysis of 52 studies that explored the effects of vocabulary instruction on learning word meanings and reading comprehension. Results revealed a mean effect size of .97 for studies in which comprehension was assessed using passages that included words that were taught directly to the students. The effect size was more modest (.30) for studies whose assessments (typically standardized tests) did not include words that were taught. Stahl and Fairbanks concluded that three factors were most strongly linked to comprehension: "The most effective vocabulary teaching methods included both definitional and contextual information in the programs, involved the students in deeper processing, and gave the students more than one or two exposures to the to-be-learned words" (p. 72).

Illustrative studies It is a trio of studies by Beck, McKeown, and colleagues that are considered to be the seminal research demonstrating how vocabulary instruction in specific words can affect reading comprehension. In the first study (Beck et al., 1982), 27 fourth-grade students were taught the meanings of 108 low-frequency words presented in categories (e.g., the *moods* category included nine words such as *jovial, glum, placid, indignant*). Lessons spanned 5 months in weekly cycles totaling about 2.5 hours; each cycle focused on the 8–10 words within one category. The five lessons for each weekly cycle had students delve increasingly deeply into semantic associations by way of definitional and associational tasks. Games and an out-of-school "Word Wizard" activity were also aspects of the instruction. Students were exposed to 61 words 10–18 times across the lessons (i.e., words with *some* exposures), and students were exposed to the remaining 43 words between 24 and 40 times (i.e., words with *many* exposures). Students were pre- and postested only on a comparable set of 43 words (i.e., *none* words).

Students receiving the vocabulary instruction outperformed matched-paired students who received conventional language arts instruction only. This was true for a test of word definitions and a test for speed of lexical access (a reaction time measure). Results for a comprehension test that involved the prompted recall of narratives including a high proportion of target words (1 out of every 11) were somewhat equivocal. There was a slight advantage for a *many*-word story when compared to a *none*-word story, but there were no discernable effects for a *some*-word story. Beck et al. concluded that the instructional program was effective in teaching specific words (experimentals, on average, learned 85 new words) and that intensive vocabulary instruction held promise in enhancing students' comprehension of stories containing words so taught.

To explore vocabulary instruction and reading comprehension further, Beck, McKeown, and colleagues conducted a modified replication of their study (McKeown et al., 1983), again with fourth graders and using the same vocabulary and instructional program. The modifications involved revising the narrative comprehension measure such that the *many*, *some*, and *none* stories were more comparable in plot structure and overall readability. In addition, the comprehension assessment was changed from a prompted recall to a free recall task. The researchers also added a second comprehension measure consisting of a multiple-choice test for each of the three passages.

Results for the two vocabulary measures—the word definition and speed-of-lexical-access tests—replicated results from the first study: children in the experimental group outperformed control-group children on both measures for the *many* and *some* words. Results for the revised and new comprehension measures revealed that experimental-group children had greater recall and answered more comprehension questions correctly than students in the control group for both the *some* and *many* words.

In a third study with fourth graders, McKeown et al. (1985) sought to tease out how type of instruction and frequency of word encounters affected vocabulary learning and comprehension. Students received one of three treatments: *Traditional Instruction*, which primarily was teaching definitions; *Rich Instruction*, which was the kind of instruction employed in the previous two studies, but without the out-of-classroom component; or *Extended Rich Instruction*, instruction like the preceding but with the out-of-school component. Students were provided either 4 or 12 encounters with instructed words.

Results revealed that all three treatments exceeded a control group on a test of definitional knowledge, and 12 encounters resulted in better performance than 4 encounters on several vocabulary measures. However, special circumstances were required to enhance comprehension of texts containing taught words. Specifically, only *Rich Instruction* or *Extended Rich Instruction* in the high-encounter condition enhanced comprehension of texts containing taught words. In other words, definitional-only (*Tra-*

ditional) instruction, even at only the 4-encounter level, is sufficient for producing a basic level of understanding of new vocabulary. In order to enhance comprehension, however, a much more elaborate form of instruction that included many encounters with target vocabulary was needed.

As significant and influential as this research program was, several questions about it were posed. For example, Stahl, Burdge, Machuga, and Stecyk (1992) conducted a study that suggested that it was not necessary for words to be grouped in semantic clusters for effective vocabulary instruction. The RAND Reading Study Group (Snow, 2002) noted that the Beck and McKeown studies "used rather artificial texts heavily loaded with unfamiliar words" [that had been taught explicitly] and that "little, if any, research addresses the question of which conditions—the types of texts, words, readers, and outcomes—can actually improve comprehension" (p. 36). There also is little evidence (or exploration for that matter) as to whether the ambitious kind of instruction like that employed in the Beck and McKeown program (Beck et al., 2002) enhances students' general text comprehension, that is, on texts for which there was no instruction in specific embedded words.

In summary, the work of Beck, McKeown, and colleagues and other researchers supports the necessity of several key instructional conditions to be present if teaching word meanings is to promote comprehension. Stahl and Fairbanks (1986) documented three essential conditions through their meta-analysis: (a) provide both definitional and contextual information; (b) promote the deep processing of words and meanings; and (c) give learners multiple encounters with to-be-learned words. Several additional studies (e.g., Curtis & Longo, 2001; Medo & Ryder, 1993) support the efficacy of elaborate, deep, and multiple-exposure vocabulary instruction to promote reading comprehension. As Beck and McKeown (2007a) noted, "word learning does not occur easily" (p. 264), nor, I would argue, does enhancing comprehension of texts that contain instructed words.

Teaching word-learning strategies

Graves's (2006) third component of a comprehensive vocabulary program involves teaching students strategies for analyzing morphemic, or word-structure, clues (root words, prefixes, suffixes, Latin/Greek roots) and context clues as ways to enhance their ability derive or infer the meanings of unfamiliar words. Nagy and Anderson (1984) provided a rationale for teaching word-learning strategies, noting that "for every word known by a child who is able to apply morphology and context, an additional one to three words should be understandable" (p. 304).

Instruction in morphological analysis   Anglin's (1993) research documented that children grow significantly across Grades 1 to 5 in "morphological problem solving," or their ability to employ "tacit or explicit knowledge of the rules of morphological word formation" to derive word meanings (pp. 151–152). There is also evidence that instruction in morphemic elements and morphological analysis enhances this development and is particularly appropriate for students in the upper elementary grades and beyond (Nagy, Diakidoy, & Anderson, 1993; White, Power, & White, 1989).

Early research on teaching morphology (e.g., Hanson, 1966; Otterman, 1955; Thompson, 1958) was often methodologically limited and inconclusive (Baumann, Bradley, Edwards, Font, & Hruby, 2000). Subsequent research, however, demonstrated that instructional programs were effective in promoting students' knowledge of affixes and word roots and their ability to use that knowledge to infer the meanings of morphologically related novel words (e.g., Graves & Hammond, 1980; White, Sowell, & Yanagihara, 1989; Wysocki & Jenkins, 1987).

For example, in the Graves and Hammond (1980) study, seventh graders in an intervention group not only learned the meanings of prefixes but also outperformed controls in using that knowledge to determine the meanings of difficult transfer words that contained the prefixes they were taught. I could find only two morphemic analysis instructional studies that included a comprehension dependent measure (Hanson, 1966; Otterman, 1955), but neither study demonstrated transfer of word-learning instruction to a generalized measure of reading comprehension.

Instruction in contextual analysis Instruction in contextual analysis is not nearly as effective as direct instruction for acquiring the meaning of a *specific* word (Baumann et al., 2003; Sternberg, 1987), but there is considerable evidence that teaching students to develop their ability to use context clues holds promise for enhancing students' ability to acquire *many* word meanings through independent reading. The impact of such instruction on reading comprehension, however, remains somewhat obscure.

Early studies on context-clue instruction were inconclusive (cf., Askov & Kamm, 1976; Hafner, 1965), but later studies demonstrated that instruction in the identification and use of context clues promoted independent word learning to some degree. For example, Sternberg and colleagues (Sternberg & Powell, 1983; Sternberg, Powell, & Kaye, 1983) provided a theoretical perspective on contextual analysis and a set of context-clue types for instruction, which they then tested in two instructional studies with high school students and adults (see Sternberg, 1987, for brief descriptions of these studies). Results provided modest support for the efficacy of teaching specific context clue types to promote the ability to infer word meanings through context.

Other studies demonstrated that generalized instruction in context clues (e.g., Jenkins, Matlock, & Slocum, 1989) or instruction in specific context-clue types (e.g., Buikema & Graves, 1993; Carnine, Kame'enui, & Coyle, 1984; Patberg, Graves, & Stibbe, 1984) enhanced upper elementary and middle school students' ability to infer the meanings of novel, difficult words that were provided in reasonably rich contexts.

Goerss, Beck, and McKeown (1999) looked descriptively at the impact of a modeling and guided practice procedure for developing contextual analysis abilities of five fifth- and sixth-grade struggling readings. In a one-on-one setting, one of the investigators employed a five-component, interactive procedure to guide students through the use of context clues to infer word meanings. Goerss et al. reported that all participants improved on a word-meaning acquisition test (McKeown, 1985) following the intervention.

A meta-analysis by Fukkink and de Glopper (1998) of 21 intervention studies revealed a moderate effect size (mean $d = 0.43$) for teaching students to use context clues. After reviewing many of the same studies, however, Kuhn and Stahl (1998) cautioned that the effects might have been due at least as much to *practice* in contextual analysis as to explicit *instruction* in how to look for and apply context clues.

In summary, the research on teaching contextual analysis suggests that such efforts are worthwhile. However, like the research on morphemic analysis, the studies reviewed thus far provide little insight about the potential impact of contextual analysis instruction on text comprehension.

Multi-strategy instruction Several studies that explored the combination of teaching morphemic and contextual analysis provided some insight into the effects of such training on reading comprehension. Tomesen and Aarnoutse (1998) explored the impact of an intervention program in morphemic and contextual analysis on Grade 4 children in the Netherlands. Employing a direct instruction and reciprocal teaching model, children were provided twelve 45-minute, small-group lessons on morphemic and contextual analysis. Results indicated that experimental-group children outperformed uninstructed controls on two measures that evaluated students' ability to derive the meanings of unfamiliar words. Groups did not differ, however, on a general measure of reading comprehension: "A transfer effect to more general reading comprehension measures was not found to occur" (p. 123). Tomesen and Aarnoutse speculated that the intervention program was "probably too limited in length and breadth to produce a transfer effect on reading comprehension" (p. 124).

Colleagues and I also explored the effects of combined morphemic and contextual analysis instruction on word learning and the possible transfer of such instruction to reading comprehension in two intervention studies with fifth graders. We hypothesized that the instrumentalist hypothesis—word knowledge directly enables reading comprehension—might be extended such that enhancing morphemic and contextual analysis ability would lead to greater vocabulary knowledge which, in turn, would then lead to greater reading comprehension (see a later discussion of Nagy, Berninger, and Abbott's, 2006, study of morphological contributions to literacy abilities).

In the first study (Baumann, Edwards, Font, Tereshinski, Kame'enui, & Olejnik, 2002), we provided students twelve 50-minute explicit instruction lessons on morphemic and contextual analysis. Results revealed that intervention students' performance exceeded that of instructed controls on immediate posttests in ability to (a) derive the meanings of novel words that contained the morphological elements we taught, and (b) infer the meanings of novel words presented in rich contexts. We found no persistence in these effects on delayed posttests. Most relevant to this discussion, however, we found that experimentals did *not* outperform controls on questions about passages that included morphemically and contextually decipherable words. In other words, students' successful acquisition of word-learning strategies did not appear to enhance their text comprehension.

One of our explanations for the lack of a comprehension effect was the same as that of Tomesen and Aarnoutse (1998): We surmised that the intervention was too short in duration. We also considered measurement as a possible error source (limitations of a true/false comprehension question format we used). Of course, a plausible explanation was that our findings simply refuted the extended instrumentalist hypothesis: "Instruction in the generalizable linguistic cues from morphemic elements and context has insufficient transfer power alone to influence reading comprehension" (Baumann et al., 2002, p. 169).

Our second study (Baumann, Edwards, Boland, Olejnik, & Kame'enui, 2003) was more extensive and possessed enhanced external validity. We included more participants (157 students from 8 classrooms), classroom teachers provided the instruction, the study was longer in duration (33 lessons across 2 months), and morphemic and contextual analysis lessons were embedded in content lessons for a unit on the U.S. Civil War taught from the adopted social studies textbook. Our comparison group received the same content instruction but, rather than instruction word-learning strategies, students were provided explicit instruction in key vocabulary (Beck, McKeown, & Omanson, 1987) taken from the daily social studies lessons.

Results of this second study were similar to the first. There was a strong effect for morphemic analysis instruction. There were somewhat equivocal findings, however, for a measure sensitive to contextual analysis, with experimentals outperforming comparison group students on a delayed posttest but not on an immediate posttest. And, as in the first study, there were no group differences on a comprehension test, which was constructed from a slightly adapted social studies textbook excerpt the students had not read previously.

Given the lack of a comprehension effect in both of our studies—reinforced by the findings of Tomesen and Aarnoutse (1998) and several earlier studies (Hanson, 1966; Otterman, 1955) that included comprehension measures—one must conclude that there currently is no empirical evidence for enhanced reading comprehension as a function of word-learning strategy instruction. Perhaps it was simply naïve to expect an effect given the multiple factors that affect reading comprehension (Snow, 2002), as well as the relatively short duration of our intervention, which W. E. Nagy pointed out (personal communication, December 7, 2001), did not include other comprehension-enhancing factors such as wide reading.

In summary, there is evidence that word-learning strategy instruction—especially instruction in morphemic analysis—is a viable component of a broadly based vocabulary program. There exists no evidence as of yet, however, that word-learning strategy competence directly enhances text comprehension.

Fostering word consciousness

Graves (2006) defined *word consciousness* as "an awareness of and interest in words and their meanings" (p. 7). Nagy (2005) elaborated, stating that word consciousness includes "various aspects of words—their meanings, their histories, relationships with other words, word parts, and most importantly, the way writers use words effectively to communicate" (p. 30). Thus, word consciousness involves both a cognitive dimension (e.g., awareness of word choice; understanding that words have recurring common Latin and Greek roots) and an affective one (e.g., interest in word play; appreciation of figurative language) (Anderson & Nagy, 1992).

Word consciousness is often listed as a separate component of a vocabulary program, as is the case in this research review. However, most vocabulary researchers and theorists acknowledge that word consciousness ought to be integrated across all vocabulary teaching and learning processes. For instance, Graves and Watts-Taffe (2002) viewed word consciousness as "crucial to learners' success in expanding the breadth and depth of their word knowledge over the course of their lifetimes" (p. 145), and Stahl and Nagy (2006) argued that "word consciousness should permeate the vocabulary program" (p. 53).

Word consciousness is often placed within the domain of *metalinguistic awareness*, or "the ability to reflect on and manipulate structural features of language" (Nagy & Scott, 2000, p. 274). Metalinguistic awareness is usually thought of in terms of phonological or phonemic awareness (Adams, 1990), but it also applies to vocabulary in the form of (a) *syntactic awareness*: the ability to reflect on how word order affects meaning; (b) *metasemantic awareness*: the understating that words vary in meaning, as in polysemy (multiple meaning words), denotative/connotative meanings of words, and literal/figurative senses of words; and (c) *morphological awareness*: the realization that words may be made up of meaningful constituent parts (for elaboration on the various types of metalinguistic awareness, see Nagy & Scott, 2000; Nagy, 2007; Scott & Nagy, 2004).

The latter component—morphological awareness—has garnered particular attention with respect to its role and function in vocabulary learning (Carlisle, 2003, 2007; Nagy, 2007). For instance, Nagy et al. (2006) demonstrated through structural equation modeling that for students in Grades 4 to 8 morphological awareness contributed significantly to both students' (a) reading comprehension as mediated by their vocabulary knowledge (i.e., morphological awareness contributes to vocabulary knowledge, which then contributes to reading comprehension), and (b) reading comprehension directly (i.e., morphological awareness has a unique, independent relationship to reading comprehension). Nagy (2005) accounted for this complex relationship between meta-knowledge, vocabulary, and reading comprehension in his reciprocal model of vocabulary and reading comprehension, noting that "vocabulary contributes both directly and indirectly to reading comprehension" (p. 36).

There is no shortage of pedagogical advice for addressing word consciousness (e.g., Blachowicz & Fisher, 2004; Graves & Watts-Taffe, 2002; Scott & Nagy, 2004), but there is little indication that such practices are incorporated into day-to-day vocabulary instruction. Scott, Jamieson-Noel, and Asselin (2003) observed 23 upper-elementary teachers in Canada for over 300 hours and found that about half the instructional time was related to literacy. However, the time spent on vocabulary in either language arts or content subjects constituted only 6% of the total instructional time, and "most [vocabulary] instruction involved mentioning and assigning rather than teaching" (p. 269). Scott et al. also noted that there was a general absence of depth of vocabulary instruction and a "lack of instruction devoted to ... metalinguistic awareness" (p. 283).

Empirical evidence on the impact of instructional attention to word consciousness is scant. Lubliner and Smetana (2005) explored the effects of a 12-week-long, multi-faceted, metacognitive vocabulary program for fifth graders in low-performing Title I schools. Their program was designed "to help children monitor comprehension of words and internalize and implement word-learning strategies to increase comprehension of natural texts" (p. 166)—select aspects of metalinguistic awareness.

The classroom teachers modeled, coached, and provided guided practice in a series of vocabulary strategies that involved self-regulation, clarifying, and self-monitoring. The vocabulary strategies were integrated into social studies lessons based on the adopted social studies textbook. Results revealed that students in the intervention demonstrated significant pretest-to-posttest gains on measures of metacognitive skill, reading vocabulary, and reading comprehension. When comparing the intervention students to fifth-grade students in an above-average-performing school who did not receive the vocabulary intervention, Lubliner and Smetana (2005) reported that the "gap" between the two groups diminished, with "large, significant differences before the intervention [favoring students in the comparison school] and small, nonsignificant differences following the intervention" (p. 163).

Colleagues and I (Baumann, Ware, & Edwards, 2007) conducted a year-long formative experiment (Reinking & Bradley, 2008) in a fifth-grade classroom. We used Graves's (2006) four-part structure—which, of course, included word consciousness—to provide pedagogical attention to vocabulary within reading, language arts, and social studies classes. Students demonstrated growth on several cognitive measures of vocabulary knowledge. There also was evidence through analysis of students' dialogue and writing, parent questionnaires, and student surveys that students (a) grew in appreciation of words and their nuanced meanings; (b) recognized authors' and speakers' deliberate use of words to convey specific meanings; (c) acquired an interest in word and language play; and (d) developed diction such that they were conscious of how word choice affected their oral and written expressions.

In conclusion, there is a theoretical base and correlational evidence for a relationship between word consciousness and reading vocabulary and comprehension. There also is preliminary evidence that programs focusing on one or more dimensions of word consciousness may enhance students' vocabulary learning and appreciation as well as their comprehension.

CONCLUSION

Summary

It was the purpose of this to chapter to explore the nexus of meaning between vocabulary and comprehension. The relationship between word knowledge and text understanding has been demonstrated empirically in many ways and along multiple dimensions both historically and contemporarily. Theorists have attempted to explain this relationship by proposing various positions or hypotheses, six of which were articulated in this chapter. Research on pedagogical attention to vocabulary was then examined in relation to Graves's (2006) four-component framework for comprehensive vocabulary instruction. Following is a summary of those findings.

Providing rich and varied language experiences

- Reading aloud and independent reading are associated with vocabulary growth.
- Word repetition, multiple readings, reader-listener interactions, and attention to specific words enhance vocabulary development during read-alouds.
- There is some evidence that reading aloud and independent reading are associated with later reading achievement and comprehension, perhaps mediated by vocabulary growth.

Teaching individual words

- There is considerable evidence that specific words can be taught directly.
- There is some evidence that elaborate, rich instruction in specific words enhances reading comprehension.
- Basic, brief vocabulary instruction provides entry-level word knowledge, but it takes intensive vocabulary instruction to affect comprehension.
- To enhance comprehension, vocabulary instruction should provide definitional and contextual information, multiple exposures to words, and deep processing of words.

Teaching word-learning strategies

- There is strong evidence that instruction in morphemic analysis enhances students' ability to derive novel morphologically decipherable words.
- There is evidence that instruction in contextual analysis promotes students' ability to infer the meanings of novel words in text.
- There is no evidence that word-learning strategy instruction has a direct impact on reading comprehension.

Fostering word consciousness

- There is a relationship between various word consciousness, or metalinguistic, abilities and vocabulary knowledge.
- Morphological awareness, mediated by vocabulary knowledge, predicts reading comprehension.
- There is limited evidence that instructional attention to word consciousness promotes students' vocabulary and comprehension.

The six hypotheses

What do these findings suggest about the validity of the six hypotheses for vocabulary-comprehension associations? Which of them have explanatory power and under what circumstances? Nagy (2005) posited that "these hypotheses are all at least partly true" (p. 33), and Stahl (1991) noted that "the 'truth' captured by each of these hypotheses depends on the particular contexts in which a word is found, the way the task of comprehension is defined, and the amount and types of knowledge a person has about a word" (p. 183).

This review supports Stahl's (1991) relational view of vocabulary-comprehension associations. For instance, the enhanced comprehension of a text read aloud or read independently by a learner appears to be mediated by vocabulary knowledge and growth. Therefore, the input hypothesis (considerable exposure to decontextualized language) and the access hypothesis (fluency by the person reading aloud or the learner who is reading independently) are potential explanations for a vocabulary-comprehension relationship for Graves's component 1, rich and varied language experiences.

In contrast, the instrumentalist hypothesis (word knowledge enables comprehension) and the knowledge hypothesis (a learner's schema related to new words and textual material) would seem to support enhanced comprehension through the ambitious teaching of individual words, Graves's component 2. And there is support for the metalinguistic hypothesis (manipulating and reflecting on words and language) when it comes to word consciousness as a factor that enhances reading comprehension, component 4. As Nagy (2005) stated regarding the various hypotheses, "together they form a somewhat complex picture of the causal relationship between vocabulary knowledge and reading comprehension" (pp. 33–34).

Implications

For practice A critical instructional consideration is aligning one's vocabulary instructional goals with appropriate pedagogy (Beck & McKeown, 2007b). Graves and Prenn (1986, pp. 596–597) articulated this cogently: "Different methods of teaching words are appropriate in different circumstances.... there is no one best method of teaching words." Instead, they argued, that "various methods have both their costs and benefits and will be very appropriate and effective in some circumstances and less appropriate and effective in others."

This review reinforces a costs-and-benefit perspective. For instance, if one hopes to acquaint students with a general familiarity or a foot-in-the-door level of knowledge of many words, a teacher could either (a) expose students to many words through reading aloud or independent reading via Graves's "rich and varied language experiences" component, or (b) teach the basic meanings of a large set of words through brief instructional encounters as per Graves's "teaching individual words" component. These instructional actions would result in broad benefits at a relatively low cost.

We know, however, that exposure alone or brief instructions are not likely to result in improved text comprehension. For that to occur, vocabulary instruction must be of a more ambitious nature and involve elaborated instruction in passage-critical words as per Graves's "teaching individual words" component. This kind of instruction would result in a more specific benefit but at a relatively high cost. It is not as though one goal is more important than the other, but it is critical for educators to be aware of pedagogical costs and benefits when determining how to allocate precious time for vocabulary instruction.

A vocabulary program that enhances comprehension also must be multifaceted (Kamil & Hiebert, 2005; Nagy, 2005) and span an extended period of time. "Effective vocabulary instruction is a long-term proposition. Attention to vocabulary growth has to start early, in preschool, and continue throughout the school years" (Nagy, 2005, p. 28). Although the specific type of vocabulary instruction provided depends on the instructional goal and age of the student, there must be a persistent "focus on and commitment to vocabulary instruction" (Nagy, 2005, p. 28) throughout students' academic careers.

Thus, the admonition for teachers in preschool to postsecondary classrooms is to teach vocabulary often, well, and in appropriate curricular contexts. Practitioners also should realize that not all vocabulary instructional efforts will—or, for that matter, should—result in enhanced reading comprehension. Thoughtful cost/benefit awareness planning will inform the selection of specific vocabulary instructional approaches that align with particular instructional goals. Fortunately, there is a plethora of empirically grounded vocabulary instructional procedures and suggestions available in the applied literature from which teachers can draw (e.g., Baumann & Kame'enui, 2004; Beck et al., 2002; Blachowicz & Fisher, 2006; Block & Mangieri, 2006; Graves, 2006; Hiebert & Kamil, 2005; Johnson, 2001; Stahl & Nagy, 2006; Wagner et al., 2007).

For research   One theme of future research should be to explain further the intricacies of vocabulary-comprehension associations. The RAND Reading Study Group's (Snow, 2002) recommendations in this area are still germane today: "Research is called for that examines how the relationship between vocabulary knowledge and reading comprehension depends on specific conditions, including the type of reader, type of text, proportion of unfamiliar words, their role in the text, and the purpose for reading or the outcome being considered" (p. 88). In other words, descriptive and correlational studies are needed to examine the conflux of reader, text, task, and context factors related to if, how, and when word knowledge induces reading comprehension.

A second theme of future research should explore vocabulary interventions with the potential to enhance reading comprehension. Specifically, I see the need for (a) replication research and (b) extended, complex intervention studies.

Replication research is relatively infrequent in literacy education, perhaps because researchers consider it unnecessary, expensive in time or money, or unrewarded; or because journal editors may not view replication as worthy of journal space. The failure to conduct and report replication research promotes reliance one-shot vocabulary studies which, even if well conducted, are just that—unique investigations bound by the particular research sample, time, method, and context. Robinson and Levin (1997) argue that replication studies "provide *generalizability* encouragement by demonstrating the initial findings are not limited to the unique participant characteristics of a single sample" (p. 25).

It would behoove literacy researchers, funding agencies, journal editorial boards, and professional organizations, therefore, to value and encourage replications, as is typically the case in the physical, biological, and medical sciences. Robinson and Levin (1997) promote the conduct and publication of "multiple-experiment replication-and-extension studies" (p. 25). Unfortunately, this is uncommon in vocabulary instruction research, save for the triad of studies by Beck and colleagues (Beck et al., 1982; McKeown et al., 1983, 1985).

There is an important caveat to acknowledge here, however. *Replication* should not be construed as the conduct of multiple quantitative or experimental studies *only*. Berliner (2002) argued that the powerful context effects in education research ought to be embraced and explored by "replications" (my usage here) within and across other methodological frameworks that examine specific context effects, or "local knowledge." Berliner argued: "Therefore, ethnographic research is crucial, as are case studies, survey research, time series, design experiments, action research, and other means to collect reliable evidence" (p. 20). This is sage advice given the pressures to conduct and trust only "scientifically based research" as described by the No Child Left Behind Act of 2001.

By "extended, complex vocabulary intervention studies," I refer to Pressley, Disney, and Anderson's (2007) call for research that addresses "the big hypothesis" (p. 222). Pressley et al. argue that it is time to take what is known about quality classroom reading instruction (Gambrell, Morrow, & Pressley, 2007) and effective vocabulary instruction (Graves, 2006; Stahl & Nagy, 2006) and "move beyond the individual mechanisms of vocabulary teaching and learning" (p. 225). They propose instead exploring, the big hypothesis, or "the vocabulary instructional flooding hypothesis" (p. 225). Such studies would "flood" classrooms with research-based general pedagogy and specific vocabulary instructional practices so that researchers could explore complex, multifaceted, and long-term (at least an academic year) vocabulary interventions.

These kinds of studies would be particularly relevant to the issue of researching vocabulary-comprehension connections, for Pressley et al. (2007) argue that a "massive intervention over a long term has a better chance of producing discernable, more general effects [i.e., on reading comprehension] than the shorter term studies of the past" (p. 225). This type of messy research is needed in order to explore the complex contexts and interactions (Berliner, 2002) inherent in vocabulary instructional programs and to examine both commonalities and variation between and within them.

Finally, additional research is needed in two areas not addressed directly in this review: vocabulary assessment and vocabulary instruction for English learners. With regard to assessment, Pearson, Hiebert, and Kamil (2007) argued that vocabulary assessment is "grossly undernourished" (p. 282). Given the inadequacy of current assessment tools, Pearson et al. call for vocabulary assessment research so that the field might "develop and validate measures that will serve us in our quest to improve both vocabulary research and, ultimately, vocabulary instruction" (p. 283).

With regard to research on vocabulary learning and teaching for English learners, there has been some attention to this topic from the perspective of applied linguistics (e.g., Nation, 2001; Schmitt & McCarthy, 1997) and more recently from literacy educators (e.g., Bravo, Hiebert, & Pearson, 2007; Graves & Fitzgerald, 2006; Snow & Kim, 2007). However, the gaps in our knowledge are many (Blachowicz & Fisher, 2000) and there is urgency in exploring vocabulary instruction for English learners given the changing linguistic demographic in schools.

In conclusion, as Davis (1944) noted over 60 years ago, it is clear that word knowledge and reading comprehension are inextricably linked. Understanding in what ways they are linked and the nature of associational and causal links between the two, however, has been and remains a psycholinguistic-educational challenge. The RAND Reading Study Group (Snow, 2002) noted succinctly and understatedly that "the role of vocabulary instruction in enhancing comprehension is complex" (p. 35). I hope that this review has shed some light on this complexity and may guide researchers as they continue to unravel the enigmatic nexus of meaning between reading vocabulary and comprehension.

REFERENCES

Adams, M. (1990). *Beginning to read: Thinking and learning about print*. Cambridge, MA: MIT Press.

Anderson, R. C. (1996). Research foundations to support wide reading. In V. Greaney (Ed.), *Promoting reading in developing countries* (pp. 55–77). Newark, DE: International Reading Association.

Anderson, R. C., & Freebody, P. (1981). Vocabulary knowledge. In J. T. Guthrie (Ed.), *Comprehension and teaching: Research reviews* (pp. 77–117). Newark, DE: International Reading Association.

Anderson, R. C., Hiebert, E. H., Scott, J. A., & Wilkinson, I. A. G. (1985). *Becoming a nation of readers: The report of the Commission on Reading*. Washington, DC: The National Institute of Education.

Anderson, R. C., & Nagy, W. E. (1992, winter). The vocabulary conundrum. *American Educator*, 14–18, 44–47.

Anderson, R. C., Wilson, P., & Fielding, L. (1988). Growth in reading and how children spend their time outside of school. *Reading Research Quarterly, 23*, 285–303.

Anglin, J. M. (1993). Vocabulary development: A morphological analysis. *Monographs of the Society for Research in Child Development, 58* (10, Serial No. 238).

Askov, E. N., & Kamm, K. (1976). Context clues: Should we teach children to use a classification system in reading? *Journal of Educational Research, 69*, 341–344.

Baldwin, R. S., & Schatz, E. L. (1986). Context clues are ineffective with low frequency words in naturally occurring prose. In J. A. Niles & R. V. Lalik (Eds.), *Issues in literacy: A research perspective*. Thirty-fourth yearbook of the National Reading Conference (pp. 132–135). Rochester, NY: National Reading Conference.

Baumann, J. F. (2005). Vocabulary-comprehension relationships. In B. Maloch, J. V. Hoffman, D. L. Schallert, C. M. Fairbanks, & J. Worthy (Eds.), *Fifty-fourth yearbook of the National Reading Conference* (pp. 117–131). Oak Creek, WI: National Reading Conference.

Baumann, J. F., Bradley, B., Edwards, E. C., Font, G., & Hruby, G. (2000, December). *Teaching generalizable vocabulary-learning strategies: A critical review of the literature*. Paper presented at the annual meeting of the National Reading Conference, Scottsdale, AZ.

Baumann, J. F., Edwards, E. C., Boland, E., Olejnik, S., & Kame'enui, E. W. (2003). Vocabulary tricks: Effects of instruction in morphology and context on fifth-grade students' ability to derive and infer word meanings. *American Educational Research Journal, 40*, 447–494.

Baumann, J. F., Edwards, E. C., Font, G., Tereshinski, C. A., Kame'enui, E. J., & Olejnik, S. (2002). Teaching morphemic and contextual analysis to fifth-grade students. *Reading Research Quarterly, 37*, 150–176.

Baumann, J. F., & Kame'enui, E. J. (Eds.). (2004). *Vocabulary instruction: Research to practice*. New York: Guilford.

Baumann, J. F., Kame'enui, E. J., & Ash, G. (2003). Research on vocabulary instruction: Voltaire redux. In J. Flood, D. Lapp, J. R. Squire &, J. Jensen, (Eds.), *Handbook of research on teaching the English Language Arts* (2nd ed.) (pp. 752–785). Mahway, NJ: Erlbaum.

Baumann, J. F., Ware, D., & Edwards, E. C. (2007). "Bumping into spicy, tasty words that catch your tongue": A formative experiment on vocabulary instruction. *The Reading Teacher, 62*, 108–122.

Beck, I. L., & McKeown, M. G. (1991). Conditions of vocabulary acquisition. In R. Barr, M. Kamil, P. Mosenthal, & P. D. Pearson (Eds.), *Handbook of reading research*: Volume II (pp. 789–814). New York: Longman.

Beck, I. L., & McKeown, M. G. (2001). Text Talk: Capturing the benefits of read-aloud experiences for young children. *The Reading Teacher, 55*, 10–20.

Beck, I. L., & McKeown, M. G. (2007a). Increasing young low-income children's oral vocabulary repertoires through rich and focused instruction. *Elementary School Journal, 107*, 251–271.

Beck, I. L, & McKeown, M. G. (2007b). Different ways for different goals, but keep your eye on the higher verbal skills. In R. K. Wager, A. E. Muse, & K. R. Tannenbaum (Eds.), *Vocabulary acquisition: Implications for reading comprehension* (pp. 182–204). New York: Guilford.

Beck, I. L., McKeown, M. G., & Kucan, L. (2002). *Bringing words to life: Robust vocabulary instruction*. New York: Guilford.

Beck, I. L., McKeown, M. G., & McCaslin, E. S. (1983). Vocabulary development: All contexts are not created equal. *Elementary School Journal, 83*, 177–181.

Beck, I. L., McKeown, M. G., & Omanson, R. C. (1987). The effects and uses of diverse vocabulary instructional techniques. In M. G. McKeown & M. E. Curtis (Eds.), *The nature of vocabulary acquisition* (pp. 147–163). Hillsdale, NJ: Erlbaum.

Beck, I. L., Perfetti, C. A., & McKeown, M. G. (1982). Effects of long-term vocabulary instruction on lexical access and reading comprehension. *Journal of Educational Psychology, 74*, 506–521.

Berliner, D. C. (2002). Educational research: The hardest science of all. *Educational Researcher, 31*(8), 18–20.

Biemiller, A., & Boote, C. (2006). An effective method for building meaning vocabulary in primary grades. *Journal of Educational Psychology, 98*, 44–62.

Blachowicz, C. L. Z., & Fisher, P. (2000). Vocabulary instruction. In M. L. Kamil, P. B. Mosenthal, P. D. Pearson, & R. Barr (Eds.), *Handbook of reading research: Volume III* (pp. 503–523). Mahwah, NJ: Erlbaum.

Blachowicz, C. L. Z., & Fisher, P. (2004). Keep the "fun" in fundamental: Encouraging word awareness and incidental word learning in the classroom through word play. In J. F. Baumann & E. J. Kame'enui (Eds.). *Vocabulary instruction: Research to practice* (pp. 218–237). New York: Guilford.

Blachowicz, C. L. Z., & Fisher, P. (2006). *Teaching vocabulary in all classrooms* (3rd ed.). Englewood Cliffs, NJ: Merrill/Prentice Hall.

Block, C. C., & Mangieri, J. N. (Eds.). (2006). *The vocabulary-enriched classroom: Practices for improving the reading performance of all students in grades 3 and up.* New York: Scholastic.

Bloom, B. S. (1976). *Human characteristics and school learning.* New York: McGraw-Hill.

Bravo, M. A., Hiebert, E. H., & Pearson, P. D. (2007). Tapping the linguistic of Spanish-English bilinguals: The role of cognates in science. In R. K. Wager, A. E. Muse, & K. R. Tannenbaum (Eds.), *Vocabulary acquisition: Implications for reading comprehension* (pp. 140–156). New York: Guilford.

Buikema, J. L., & Graves, M. F. (1993). Teaching students to use context cues to infer word meanings. *Journal of Reading, 36,* 450–457.

Bus, A. G., van IJzendoorn, M. H., & Pellegrini, A. D. (1995). Joint book reading makes for success in learning to read: A meta-analysis on intergenerational transmission of literacy. *Review of Educational Research, 65,* 1–21.

Carlisle, J. F. (2003). Morphology matters in learning to read: A commentary. *Reading Psychology, 24,* 291–322.

Carlisle, J. F. (2007). Fostering morphological processing, vocabulary development, and reading comprehension. In R. K. Wager, A. E. Muse, & K. R. Tannenbaum (Eds.), *Vocabulary acquisition: Implications for reading comprehension* (pp. 78–103). New York: Guilford.

Carlo, M. S., August, D., & Snow, C. E. (2005). Sustained vocabulary-learning strategy instruction for English-language learners. In E. H. Hiebert & M. L. Kamil (Eds.), *Teaching and learning vocabulary: Bringing research to practice* (pp. 137–153). Mahwah, NJ: Erlbaum.

Carnine, D. W., Kame'enui, E., & Coyle. G. (1984). Utilization of contextual information in determining the meaning of unfamiliar words. *Reading Research Quarterly, 19,* 188–204.

Carver, R. P., & Liebert, R. E. (1995). The effect of reading library books at different levels of difficulty upon gain in reading ability. *Reading Research Quarterly, 30,* 26–48.

Cipielewski, J., & Stanovich, K. E. (1992). Predicting growth in reading ability from children's exposure to print. *Journal of Experimental Child Psychology, 54,* 74–89.

Coyne, M. D., Simmons, D. C., & Kame'enui, E. J. (2004). Vocabulary instruction for young children at risk of experiencing reading difficulties: Teaching word meanings during shared storybook readings. In J. F. Baumann & E. J. Kame'enui (Eds.), *Vocabulary instruction: Research to practice* (pp. 41–58). New York: Guilford.

Cunningham, A. E., & Stanovich, K. E. (1997). Early reading acquisition and its relation to reading experience and ability 10 years later. *Developmental Psychology, 33,* 934–945.

Cunningham, A. E. & Stanovich, K. E. (Spring/Summer, 1998). What reading does for the mind. *American Educator,* 8–15.

Cunningham, A. E., & Stanovich, K. E. (2003). Reading matters: How reading engagement influences cognition. In J. Flood, D. Lapp, J. R. Squire, &, J. Jensen (Eds.), *Handbook of research on teaching the English language arts* (2nd ed., pp. 666–674). Mahway, NJ: Erlbaum.

Cunningham, A. E. (2005). Vocabulary growth through independent reading and reading aloud to children. In E. H. Hiebert & M. L. Kamil (Eds.), *Teaching and learning vocabulary: Bringing research to practice* (pp. 45–68). Mahwah, NJ: Erlbaum.

Curtis, M. E., & Longo, A. M. (2001, November). Teaching vocabulary to adolescents to improve comprehension. *Reading Online, 5*(4). Available: http://www.readingonline.org/articles/art_index.asp?HREF=curtis/index.html.

Dale, E., & Razik, T. (1963). *Bibliography of vocabulary studies.* Columbus, OH: Ohio State University Bureau of Educational Research and Service.

Davis, F. B. (1944). Fundamental factors in reading comprehension. *Psychometrika, 9,* 185–197.

Davis, F. B. (1968). Research in comprehension in reading. *Reading Research Quarterly, 3,* 499–545.

Davis, F. B. (1972). Psychometric research on comprehension in reading. *Reading Research Quarterly, 7,* 628–678.

Dickinson, D. K., & Smith, M. W. (1994). Long-term effects of preschool teachers' book readings on low-income children's vocabulary and story comprehension. *Reading Research Quarterly, 29*(2), 104–122.

Elley, W. B. (1989). Vocabulary acquisition from listening to stories. *Reading Research Quarterly, 24,* 174–187.

Fukkink, R. G., & de Glopper, K. (1998). Effects of instruction in deriving word meaning from context: A meta-analysis. *Review of Educational Research, 68,* 450–469.

Gambrell, L. B., Morrow, L. M., & Pressley, M. (Eds.). (2007). *Best practices in literacy instruction* (3rd ed.). New York: Guilford.

Gardner, D. (2004). Vocabulary input through extensive reading: A comparison of words found in children's narrative and expository reading materials. *Applied Linguistics, 25,* 1–37.

Goerss, B. L., Beck, I. L., & McKeown, M. G. (1999). Increasing remedial students' ability to derive word meaning from context. *Reading Psychology, 20,* 151–175.

Graves, M. F. (1986). Vocabulary learning and instruction. In E. Z. Rothkopf (Ed.), *Review of research in education* (Vol. 13, pp. 49–89). Washington, DC: American Educational Research Association.

Graves, M. F. (1987). The roles of instruction in fostering vocabulary development. In M. G. McKeown & M. E. Curtis (Eds.), *The nature of vocabulary acquisition* (pp. 165–184). Hillsdale, NJ: Erlbaum.

Graves, M. F. (2000). A vocabulary program to complement and bolster a middle-grade comprehension program. In B. M. Taylor, M. F. Graves, & P. van den Broek (Eds.), *Reading for meaning: Fostering comprehension in the middle grades* (pp. 116–135). Newark, DE: International Reading Association.

Graves, M. F. (2006). *The vocabulary book: Learning and instruction.* New York: Teachers College Press.

Graves, M. F., & Fitzgerald, J. (2006). Effective vocabulary instruction for English-language learners. In C. C. Block & J. N. Mangieri (Eds.), *The vocabulary-enriched classroom: Practices for improving the reading performance of all students in grades 3 and up* (pp. 118–137). New York: Scholastic.

Graves, M. F., & Hammond, H. K. (1980). A validated procedure for teaching prefixes and its effect on students' ability to assign meaning to novel words. In M. L. Kamil & A. J. Moe (Eds.), *Perspectives on reading research and instruction.* Twenty-ninth yearbook of the National Reading Conference (pp. 184–188). Washington, DC: National Reading Conference.

Graves, M. F., & Prenn, M. C. (1986). Costs and benefits of various methods of teaching vocabulary. *Journal of Reading, 29,* 596–602.

Graves, M. F., & Watts-Taffe, S. M. (2002). The place of word consciousness in a research-based vocabulary program. In S. J. Samuels & A. E. Farstrup (Eds.), *What research has to say about reading instruction* (3rd ed., pp. 140–165). Newark, DE: International Reading Association.

Greaney, V. (1980). Factors related to amount and type of leisure time reading. *Reading Research Quarterly, 15,* 337–357.

Hafner, L. E. (1965). A one-month experiment in teaching context aids in fifth grade. *Journal of Educational Research, 58,* 471–474.

Hanson, I. W. (1966). First grade children work with variant word endings. *The Reading Teacher, 19,* 505–507, 511.

Harris, T. L., & Hodges R. E. (Eds.). (1995). *The literacy dictionary: The vocabulary of reading and writing.* Newark, DE: International Reading Association.

Hayes, D. P., & Ahrens, M. G. (1988). Vocabulary simplification for children: A special case of "motherese." *Journal of Child Language, 15,* 395–410.

Herman, P. A., Anderson, R. C., Pearson, P. D., & Nagy, W. E. (1987). Incidental acquisition of word meaning from expositions with varied text features. *Reading Research Quarterly, 22,* 263–284.

Herman, P. A., & Dole, J. (1988). Theory and practice in vocabulary learning and instruction. *Elementary School Journal, 89,* 43–54.

Hiebert, E. H., & Kamil, M. L. (Eds.). (2005). *Teaching and learning vocabulary: Bringing research to practice.* Mahwah, NJ: Erlbaum.

Higgins, N. C., & Cocks, P. (1999). The effects of animation cues on vocabulary development. *Reading Psychology, 20,* 1–10.

Jenkins, J. R., & Dixon, R. (1983). Learning vocabulary. *Contemporary Educational Psychology, 8,* 237–260.

Jenkins, J. R., Matlock, B., & Slocum, T. A. (1989). Approaches to vocabulary instruction: The teaching of individual word meanings and practice in deriving word meaning from context. *Reading Research Quarterly, 24,* 215–235.

Jenkins, J. R., Stein, M. L., & Wysocki, K. (1984). Learning vocabulary through reading. *American Educational Research Journal, 21,* 767–787.

Jitendra, A. K., Edwards, L. L., Sacks, G., & Jacobson, L. A. (2004). What research says about vocabulary instruction for students with learning disabilities. *Exceptional Children, 70,* 299–322.

Johnson, D. D. (2001). *Vocabulary in the elementary and middle school.* Needham Heights, MA: Allyn & Bacon.

Juel, C., Biancarosa, G., Coker, D., & Deffes, R. (2003). Walking with Rosie: A cautionary tale of early reading instruction. *Educational Leadership, 60*(7), 12–18.

Juel, C., & Deffes, R. (2004). Making words stick. *Educational Leadership, 61*(6), 30–34.

Kamil, M. L., & Hiebert, E. H. (2005). Teaching and learning vocabulary: Perspectives and persistent issues. In E. H. Hiebert & M. L. Kamil (Eds.), *Teaching and learning vocabulary: Bringing research to practice* (pp. 1–23). Mahwah, NJ: Erlbaum.

Klare, G. R. (1974–1975). Assessing readability. *Reading Research Quarterly, 10,* 62–102.

Krashen, S. (1985). *The input hypothesis: Issues and implications.* New York: Longman.

Krashen, S. (1989). We acquire vocabulary and spelling by reading: Additional evidence for the input hypothesis. *The Modern Language Journal, 73*(4), 440–464.

Krashen, S. D. (2004). *The power of reading: Insights from the research* (2nd ed.). Portsmouth, NH: Heinemann.

Kuhn, M. R., & Stahl, S. A. (1998). Teaching children to learn word meanings from context: A synthesis and some questions. *Journal of Literacy Research, 30,* 119–138.

LaBerge, D., & Samuels, S. J. (1974). Toward a theory of automatic information processing in reading. *Cognitive Psychology, 6,* 293–323.

Leinhardt, G., Zigmond, N., & Cooley, W. W. (1981). Reading instruction and its effects. *American Educational Research Journal, 18,* 343–361.

Lonigan, C. J., & Whitehurst, G. J. (1998). Relative efficacy of parent and teacher involvement in a shared-reading intervention for preschool children from low-income backgrounds. *Early Childhood Research Quarterly, 13,* 263–290.

Lubliner, S., & Smetana, L. (2005). The effects of comprehensive vocabulary instruction on Title I students' metacognitive word-learning skills and reading comprehension. *Journal of Literacy Research, 37,* 163–200.

McKeown, M. G. (1985). The acquisition of word meaning from context by children of high and low ability. *Reading Research Quarterly, 20,* 482–496.

McKeown, M. G., & Beck, I. L. (1988). Learning vocabulary: Different ways for different goals. *Remedial and Special Education, 9,* 42–46.

McKeown, M. G., Beck, I. L., Omanson, R., & Perfetti, C. A. (1983). The effects of long-term vocabulary instruction on reading comprehension: A replication. *Journal of Reading Behavior, 15,* 3–18.

McKeown, M. G., Beck, I. L., Omanson, R., & Pople, M. T. (1985). Some effects of the nature and frequency of vocabulary instruction on the knowledge and use of words. *Reading Research Quarterly, 20,* 522–535.

Medo, M. A., & Ryder, R. J. (1993). The effects of vocabulary instruction on readers' ability to make causal connections. *Reading Research and Instruction, 33*(2), 119–134.

Meyer, L. A., Wardrop, J. L., Stahl, S. A., & Linn, R. L. (1994). Effects of reading storybooks aloud to children. *Journal of Educational Research, 85,* 69–85.

Mezynski, K. (1983). Issues concerning the acquisition of knowledge: Effects of vocabulary training on reading comprehension. *Review of Educational Research, 53,* 253–279.

Morrow, L. M. (1989). The effect of small group story reading on children's questions and comments. In S. McCormick & J. Zuttell (Eds.), *Thirty-seventh yearbook of the National Reading Conference* (pp. 77–86). Chicago: National Reading Conference.

Morrow, L. M., & Smith, J. K. (1990). The effects of group size on interactive storybook reading. *Reading Research Quarterly, 25,* 214–231.

Nagy, W. E. (1988). *Teaching vocabulary to improve reading comprehension.* Newark, DE: International Reading Association.

Nagy, W. E. (1997). On the role of context in first- and second-language vocabulary learning. In N. Schmitt & M. McCarthy (Eds.), *Vocabulary: Description, acquisition and pedagogy* (pp. 64–83). Cambridge: Cambridge University Press.

Nagy, W. E. (2005). Why vocabulary instruction needs to be long-term and comprehensive. In E. H. Hiebert & M. L. Kamil (Eds.), *Teaching and learning vocabulary: Bringing research to practice* (pp. 27–44). Mahwah, NJ: Erlbaum.

Nagy, W. (2007). Metalinguistic awareness and the vocabulary-comprehension connection. In R. K. Wager, A. E. Muse, & K. R. Tannenbaum (Eds.), *Vocabulary acquisition: Implications for reading comprehension* (pp. 52–77). New York: Guilford.

Nagy, W. E., & Anderson, R. C. (1984). How many words are there in printed school English? *Reading Research Quarterly, 19,* 303–330.

Nagy, W. E., Anderson, R. C., & Herman, P. A. (1987). Learning word meanings from context during normal reading. *American Educational Research Journal, 24,* 237–270.

Nagy, W., Berninger, V. W., & Abbott, R. D. (2006). Contributions of morphology beyond phonology to literacy outcomes of upper elementary and middle-school students. *Journal of Educational Psychology, 98,* 134–147.

Nagy, W. E., Diakidoy, I. N., & Anderson, R. C. (1993). The acquisition of morphology: Learning the contribution of suffixes to the meanings of derivatives. *Journal of Reading Behavior, 25*, 155–170.

Nagy, W. E., Herman, P. A., & Anderson, R. C. (1985). Learning words from context. *Reading Research Quarterly, 20*, 233–253.

Nagy, W. E., & Scott, J. A. (2000). Vocabulary processes. In M. L. Kamil, P. B. Mosenthal, P. D. Pearson, & R. Barr (Eds.), *Handbook of reading research: Volume III* (pp. 269–284). Mahwah, NJ: Erlbaum.

Nation, I. S. P. (2001). *Learning vocabulary in another language.* Cambridge, UK: Cambridge University Press.

National Reading Panel. (2000). *Teaching children to read: An evidence-based assessment of the scientific research literature on reading and its implications for reading instruction: Reports of the subgroups* (NIH Publication Number 00-4769). Washington, DC: National Institute of Child Health and Human Development.

Otterman, L. M. (1955). The value of teaching prefixes and word-roots. *Journal of Educational Research, 48*, 611–616.

Patberg, J. P., Graves, M. F., & Stibbe, M. A. (1984). Effects of active teaching and practice in facilitating students' use of context clues. In J. A. Niles & L. A. Harris (Eds.), *Changing perspectives on research in reading/language processing and instruction.* Thirty-third yearbook of the National Reading Conference (pp. 146–151). Rochester, NY: National Reading Conference.

Pearson, P. D., Hiebert, E. H., & Kamil, M. L. (2007). Vocabulary assessment: What we know and what we need to learn. *Reading Research Quarterly, 42*, 282–296.

Petty, W., Herold, C., & Stohl, E. (1967). *The state of the knowledge about the teaching of vocabulary.* Cooperative Research Project No. 3128. Champaign, IL: National Council of Teachers of English. (ERIC Document Reproduction Service No. ED 012 395.)

Pressley, J., Disney, L., & Anderson, K. (2007). Landmark vocabulary instructional research and the vocabulary instructional research that makes sense. In R. K. Wager, A. E. Muse, & K. R. Tannenbaum (Eds.), *Vocabulary acquisition: Implications for reading comprehension* (pp. 205–232). New York: Guilford.

Reinking, D., & Bradley, B. A. (2004). *Formatiave and design experiments.* New York: Teachers College Press.

Robbins, C., & Ehri, L. C. (1994). Reading storybooks to kindergartners helps them learn new vocabulary words. *Journal of Educational Psychology, 86*(1), 54–64.

Robinson, D. H., & Levin, J. R. (1997). Reflections on statistical and substantive significance, with a slice of replication. *Educational Researcher, 26*(5), 21–26.

Rosenshine (1980). Skills hierarchies in reading comprehension. In R. J. Spiro, B. C. Bruce, & W. F. Brewer (Eds.), *Theoretical issues in reading comprehension* (pp. 535–554). Hillsdale, NJ: Erlbaum.

Scarborough, H. S. (1998). Early identification of children at risk for reading disabilities. Phonological awareness and some other promising predictors. In B. K. Shapiro, P. J. Accardo, & A. J. Capute (Eds.), *Specific reading disability: A view of the spectrum* (pp. 75–119). Timonium, MD: York Press.

Scarborough, H. S. (2002). Connecting early language and literacy to later reading (dis)abilities: Evidence, theory, and practice. In D. K. Dickinson & S. B. Neuman, *Handbook of early literacy research* (pp. 97–110). New York: Guilford.

Scarborough, H. S., & Dobrich, W. (1994). On the efficacy of reading to preschoolers. *Developmental Review, 14*, 245–302.

Schefelbine, J. L. (1990). Student factors related to variability in learning word meanings from context. *Journal of Reading Behavior, 22*, 71–97.

Schmitt, N., & McCarthy, J. (Eds.). (1997). *Vocabulary: Description, acquisition, and pedagogy.* Cambridge: Cambridge University Press.

Scott, J. A., Jamieson-Noel, D., & Asselin, M. (2003). Vocabulary instruction throughout the day in twenty-three Canadian upper-elementary classrooms. *Elementary School Journal, 103*, 269–268.

Scott, J. A., & Nagy, W. E. (2004). Developing word consciousness. In J. F. Baumann & E. J. Kame'enui (Eds.), *Vocabulary instruction: Research to practice* (pp. 201–217). New York: Guilford.

Senechal, M. (1997). The differential effects of storybook reading on preschoolers' acquisition of expressive and receptive vocabulary. *Journal of Child Language, 24*, 123–138.

Senechal, M. (2006). Testing the home literacy model: Parent involvement in kindergarten is differentially related to grade 4 reading comprehension, fluency, spelling, and reading for pleasure. *Scientific Studies of Reading, 10*, 59–87.

Senechal, M., Oiellette, G., & Rodney, D. (2006). The misunderstood giant: On the predictive role of early vocabulary to future reading. In D. K. Dickinson & S. B. Neuman, *Handbook of Early Literacy Research, vol. 2* (pp. 173–182). New York: Guilford.

Shu, H., Anderson, R. C., & Zhang, H. (1995). Incidental learning of word meanings while reading: A Chinese and American cross-cultural study. *Reading Research Quarterly, 30* (1), 76–95.

Smith, F. (1976). Learning to read by reading. *Language Arts, 53,* 297–299, 322.

Snow, C. E. (2002). *Reading for understanding: Toward an R & D program in reading comprehension.* Santa Monica, CA: RAND Corporation.

Snow, C. E., & Kim, Y. (2007). Large problem spaces: The challenge of vocabulary for English language learners. In R. K. Wager, A. E. Muse, & K. R. Tannenbaum (Eds.), *Vocabulary acquisition: Implications for reading comprehension* (pp. 123–139). New York: Guilford.

Spearritt, D. (1972). Identification of subskills of reading comprehension by maximum likelihood factor analysis. *Reading Research Quarterly, 8,* 92–111.

Stahl, S. A. (1991). Beyond the instrumentalist hypothesis: Some relationships between word meanings and comprehension. In. P. J. Schwanenflugel (Ed.), *The psychology of word meanings* (pp. 157–186). Hillsdale, NJ: Erlbaum.

Stahl, S. A., Burdge, J. L., Machuga, M. B., & Stecyk, S. (1992). The effects of semantic grouping on learning word meaning. *Reading Psychology, 13*(1), 19–35.

Stahl, S. A., & Fairbanks, M. M. (1986). The effects of vocabulary instruction: A model-based meta-analysis. *Review of Educational Research, 56,* 72–110.

Stahl, S. A., & Nagy, W. E. (2006). *Teaching word meanings.* Mahway, NJ: Erlbaum.

Stanovich, K. E., & Cunningham, A. E. (2004). Inferences from correlational data: Exploring associations with reading experience. In N. K. Duke & M. H. Mallette (Eds.), *Literacy research methodologies* (pp. 28–45). New York: Guilford.

Sternberg, R. B. (1987). Most vocabulary is learned from context. In M. G. McKeown & M. E. Curtis (Eds.), *The nature of vocabulary acquisition* (pp. 89–105). Hillsdale, NJ: Erlbaum.

Sternberg, R., & Powell, J. S. (1983). Comprehending verbal comprehension. *American Psychologist, 38,* 878–893.

Sternberg, R., Powell, J. S., & Kaye, D. B. (1983). The nature of verbal comprehension. In A. C. Wilkinson (Ed.), *Communicating with computers in classrooms: Prospects for applied cognitive science* (pp. 121–143). New York: Academic Press.

Swanborn, M. S. L., & de Glopper, K. (1999). Incidental word learning while reading: A meta-analysis. *Review of Educational Research, 69,* 261–285.

Taylor, B. M., Frye, B. J., & Maruyama, G. M. (1990). Time spent reading and reading growth. *American Educational Research Journal, 27,* 351–362.

Thompson, E. (1958). The "master word" approach to vocabulary training. *Journal of Developmental Reading, 2,* 62–66.

Thorndike, E. L. (1917a/1971). Reading as reasoning: A study of mistakes in paragraph reading. *Journal of Educational Psychology, 8,* 323–332. (Reprinted in *Reading Research Quarterly,* 1971, 6, 425–434).

Thorndike, E. L. (1917b). The psychology of thinking in the case of reading. *Psychological Review, 24,* 220–234.

Thorndike, E. L. (1917c). The understanding of sentences: A study of errors in reading. *Elementary School Journal, 18,* 98–114.

Thorndike, R. L. (1973). *Reading comprehension education in fifteen countries: An empirical study.* New York: Wiley.

Thurstone, L. L. (1946). A note on a reanalysis of Davis' reading tests. *Psychometrika, 11,* 185–188.

Tomesen, M., & Aarnoutse, C. (1998). Effects of an instructional programme for deriving word meanings. *Educational Studies, 24*(1), 107–128.

Van Kleeck, A., Stahl, S. A., & Bauer, E. B. (Eds.). (2003). *On reading books to children: Parents and teachers.* Mahwah, NJ: Erlbaum.

Vygotsky, L. S. (1978). *Mind in society: The development of higher psychological processes.* Cambridge, MA: Harvard University Press.

Wagner, K., Muse, A. E., & Tannenbaum, K. R. (Eds.). (2007). *Vocabulary acquisition: Implications for reading comprehension* (pp. 52–77). New York: Guilford.

Wasik, B. A., & Bond, M. A. (2001). Beyond the pages of a book: Interactive book reading and language development in preschool classrooms. *Journal of Educational Psychology, 93,* 243–250.

Wasik, B. A., Bond, M. A., & Hindman, A. (2006). The effects of a language and literacy intervention on Head Start children and teachers. *Journal of Educational Psychology, 98,* 63–74.

White, T. G., Power, M. A., & White, S. (1989). Morphological analysis: Implications for teaching and understanding vocabulary growth. *Reading Research Quarterly, 24,* 283–304.

White, T. G., Sowell, J., & Yanagihara, A. (1989). Teaching elementary students to use word-part clues. *The Reading Teacher, 42,* 302–308.

Wilkinson, I., Wardrop, J. L., & Anderson R. C. (1988). Silent reading reconsidered: Reinterpreting reading instruction and its effects. *American Educational Research Journal, 25,* 127–144.

Williams, T. L. (2007). *Re-examining the intuitive. Reading aloud and kindergartners' emergent literacy.* Unpublished manuscript, University of Georgia, Athens, GA.

Wysocki, K., & Jenkins, J. R. (1987). Deriving word meanings through morphological generalization. *Reading Research Quarterly, 22,* 66–81.

16 Cognitive Strategy Instruction

Janice A. Dole

University of Utah

Jeffery D. Nokes

Brigham Young University

Dina Drits

University of Utah

There was a time, and not that long ago, when few people knew what cognitive strategy instruction was. A relatively small group of educational psychologists and reading researchers had conducted two decades of research on cognitive strategies, but they were the only ones familiar with the work. Cognitive strategies and the instructional research behind them remained in rather esoteric research journals read by few other than the people who conducted the research.

Today, though, toward the end of the first decade in the 21st century, all reading educators have heard the term *strategy instruction,* and many of them incorporate strategy instruction into their literacy programs. In the translation from research to practice, strategy instruction has made its way into mainstream education. Teacher resource books about teaching strategies abound (Blanchowicz & Ogle, 2001; Harvey & Goudvis, 2000; Keene, 2006; Keene & Zimmerman, 1997; McLaughlin & Allen, 2001; Oczkus, 2004; Outsen & Yulga, 2002; Stebick & Dain, 2007; Tovani, 2004; Wilhelm, 2001; Zwiers, 2004), and practitioner journals frequently publish articles about teaching strategies to both elementary and secondary students (Clark & Graves, 2005; Fischer, 2003; Liang & Dole, 2006; Lloyd, 2004; Neufeld, 2005; Raphael & Au, 2005; Salembier, 1999; Samblis, 2006; Smith, 2006; Stahl, 2004; Wood & Endres, 1004–2005; Zygouris-Coe, Wiggins, & Smith, 2005). Some educators think that teaching comprehension means simply teaching strategies. In the transition from research to practice, strategy instruction has morphed into so many things that it no longer has a shared meaning.

The purpose of this chapter is to help researchers and educators understand cognitive strategy instruction from both research and practice perspectives. It could be argued that the literature is currently saturated with research, articles, and books about cognitive strategies. Nevertheless, there is still much to write about cognitive strategies—both in terms of more recent research and also in terms of how the construct has made its way into the reading instruction practitioner field.

This chapter first focuses on defining cognitive strategy instruction in terms of its genesis and on presenting the landmark studies that defined the field. Then, the chapter reviews several more recent sets of studies in which cognitive strategy instruction was embedded in conceptual and programmatic frameworks for comprehension instruction. Third, the chapter reviews more recent research in the content areas in which cognitive strategy instruction has been adapted for instructional purposes in secondary content areas, especially science and history. After this research has been reviewed, we take a more applied examination of cognitive strategy instruction as it has been conceptualized in practice. Here we make conceptual distinctions between strategies and the plethora of related constructs in the field today. We conclude with a discussion of the important distinction between the curriculum of cognitive strategies and the instructional delivery system used to teach strategies.

THE GENESIS OF AND KEY STUDIES IN COGNITIVE STRATEGY INSTRUCTION

We begin the chapter with a definition of cognitive strategies and the foundational body of theory and research in cognitive strategy instruction drawn from early cognitive psychological work conducted in the 1970s and 1980s.

Genesis

The genesis of cognitive strategies and cognitive strategy instruction lies in the field of psychology. From the ashes of behaviorism and after 50 years of denying the existence of the mind, cognitive psychologists began to focus on the mind exclusively, thinking about how humans process, organize, and store incoming information in memory. Many early cognitive researchers represented the mental processing that occurs in the mind as general activities or *cognitive strategies* for handling incoming information as well as *metacognitive strategies* for monitoring and evaluating the understanding of that information (Greeno, Collins, & Resnick, 1996; van Dijk & Kintsch, 1983). It is these constructs that form the foundation of cognitive strategy instruction.

Cognitive strategies   What is a strategy? At its simplest level, a strategy is a routine or procedure for accomplishing a goal. A *cognitive* strategy is a mental routine or procedure for accomplishing a cognitive goal. Van Dijk and Kintsch (1983) provide an excellent description of cognitive strategies:

> Thinking and problem solving are well-known examples: We have an explicit goal to be reached, the solution of a problem, and there may be specific operations, mental steps, to be performed to reach that goal. These steps are under our conscious control and we may be at least partly able to verbalize them, so that we can analyze the strategies followed in solving the problem. (p. 68)

Cognitive strategies, then, are mental routines or procedures for accomplishing cognitive goals like solving a problem, studying for a test, or understanding what is being read. While this definition may seem mundane, complications arise in the literature on cognitive strategies as different researchers have focused on different aspects of cognitive strategies over the last several decades. The earliest work using the term strategies focused on *general strategies* for solving problems (Newell & Simon, 1972). Some of these strategies include trial and error in which an individual randomly tries various ways of solving a problem, means-end analysis in which an individual examines the end and looks at the sequential steps to get to that end, and working backward to solve a problem. One of the hallmarks of these strategies is that they are transferable across many types of problems.

Van Dijk and Kintsch (1983) identified many types of strategies used for different cognitive tasks. These strategies include language strategies, grammatical strategies, discourse strategies, cultural strategies, social strategies, interactional strategies, pragmatic strategies, semantic strategies, schematic strategies, and stylistic and rhetorical strategies. They further delineated specific strategies involved in comprehension, including sociocultural strategies, communicative strategies, general reading strategies, local comprehension strategies, local coherence strategies, schematic strategies, and knowledge use strategies.

Weinstein and Mayer (1986), in their review of research on the teaching of learning strategies, conceptualized two main categories of strategies: 1) *teaching strategies*, such as the teacher presenting material in a certain way, and 2) *learning strategies*, such as the learner summarizing material in a certain way. They further differentiated eight categories of learning strategies, including basic and complex rehearsal strategies, basic and complex elaboration strategies, basic and complex organizational strategies, comprehension monitoring strategies and affective and motivational strategies.

As they reviewed the research, Pressley and Woloshyn (1995) identified a number of cognitive strategies for various tasks in different domains of knowledge. For example, they identified strategies for analyzing and solving problems (general strategies), memorizing a series of events or a timeline for a test (study strategies), planning, drafting, reviewing, and revising a critical essay (writing strategies), and self-questioning, constructing mental representational images, activating prior knowledge, rereading difficult-to-understand sections of texts, predicting or summarizing a text (reading strategies). What the strategies have in common is that they are cognitive procedures that aid in performance of specific cognitive tasks.

Metacognitive strategies   A specific set of general cognitive strategies is particularly relevant to comprehension; these are called *metacognitive strategies*. Metacognitive strategies are routines and procedures that allow individuals to monitor and assess their ongoing performance in accomplishing a cognitive task. For example, as students are studying for a test they might ask themselves: "Are things going well? Is there something I don't understand? Am I learning this material? Are there any gaps in my knowledge or understanding? If I do find a gap in my knowledge, do I know what to do about it? Can I repair the gap so that my understanding is complete?" Students who use metacognitive strategies are aware of the cognitive resources they have to accomplish a goal, they check the outcome of their attempts to solve problems, they monitor the effectiveness of their attempts, they test, revise and evaluate their strategies for learning, and they use compensatory strategies when comprehension breaks down. These compensatory strategies restore understanding and learning (Baker & Brown, 1984).

Metacognitive strategies have most often been conceptualized as comprehension monitoring (Weinstein & Mayer, 1986). Wagoner (1983) defined comprehension monitoring as "an executive function, essential for competent reading, which directs the reader's cognitive processes as he/she strives to make sense of incoming information" (p. 344). As students read, they often think about and monitor their ongoing understanding of a text. Baker and Brown (1984) reviewed an extensive body of work that demonstrated the kinds of metacognitive strategies or comprehension monitoring that good readers execute as they read. They found that good readers make hypotheses about the most likely interpretation of a text and then check that interpretation against the new, incoming information in a text. As they read, the original hypotheses are either confirmed or discarded for new hypotheses. Comprehension monitoring proceeds in this way until a breakdown occurs. Once a breakdown occurs, good readers must decide whether further action is necessary. If it is, then good readers must decide what type of compensatory strategy is most likely to repair the comprehension breakdown.

Another way to understand comprehension monitoring is to contrast good readers with young and less skilled readers who fail to use metacognitive strategies as they read. They proceed, instead, on "automatic pilot" (Duffy & Roehler, 1987), failing to notice when comprehension breaks down. Many young and less skilled readers have little awareness that they must make sense of text, they are often poor at evaluating their own performance, and they do not keep track of how their comprehension is proceeding (Baker & Brown, 1984). Further, they often do not know how to repair comprehension breakdowns.

A key issue in metacognitive strategies is the extent to which these strategies are under the conscious control of readers. Even though there is an assumption that meta-cognitive strategies are conscious processes, it is also understood that readers can proceed to read on automatic, and therefore, not conscious level. Paris, Wasik, and Turner (1991) refer to strategies as "actions selected deliberately to achieve particular goals" (p. 611). Strategies are conscious, deliberate and open to inspection. However, with time and practice, the use of both cognitive and metacognitive strategies can become less effortful and can be carried out efficiently and effectively at an automatic level (Pressley & Afflerbach, 1995; Schneider, Dumais, & Shiffrin, 1984).

Knowledge about cognitive and metacognitive strategies   Thus far, we have defined cognitive and metacognitive strategies. In their influential essay, Paris, Lipson, and Wixon (1983) applied the research on these strategies to reading comprehension and to students who become good, strategic comprehenders. They asked the question, "What would it take for students to become strategic in their reading?" They identified several of the factors necessary for students to become strategic readers, specifically the "inter-relations among awareness, motivation, instructional agents, and strategic behavior" (p. 294).

Paris et al. (1983) argued that strategies are deliberate actions, and they can often be difficult to learn and employ. Their value lies in their social nature, in that students and teachers can "publicly" share, evaluate, and understand the functions and the value of the strategies. This public nature of strategy understanding and application is especially important for beginning and low-achieving readers, because they are not aware of how to employ strategies or what purpose or function they serve.

To accept and use strategies, beginning and low-achieving readers must understand the purpose of the reading task and the different actions they can take to achieve their reading goals. Students must have the knowledge about strategies to choose to use them. A major contribution of the Paris et al. (1983) work was the researchers' addition to our understanding of the knowledge readers must have to become strategic readers. In addition to declarative and procedural knowledge, the authors added the idea of *conditional* knowledge. Declarative knowledge is the knowledge about what strategies are, and can "help in setting goals and adjusting actions to changing task conditions" (p. 303), and procedural knowledge is knowledge about how to employ strategies. Conditional knowledge adds the critical elements of "knowing when and why to apply various actions" (p. 303). Different strategies can be useful in different circumstances; not all strategies are useful all the time. Strategies must be used *flexibly* since different strategies are most effectively used in specific situations. By providing reasons to apply specific strategies in certain situations, conditional knowledge also gives value to these strategies.

To become strategic readers, however, these three kinds of knowledge are necessary, but not sufficient, the authors argued. *Motivation* is also necessary. Students must be persuaded to see that the goals of the strategies have personal relevance and meaning for them, that the various strategies have value and utility for them, and that self-managing their time and effort in using the strategies will aid them in achieving their reading goals.

The social context, including parents, peers, and teachers, assists students in acquiring both the motivation and the knowledge to employ strategies by helping them understand that the strategies they are learning are useful and necessary. To use strategies effectively in learning to read, the authors concluded, children must be told *when* and *why* to use strategies in order to become agents of their own strategy use, and "conditional knowledge is the glue that holds skill and will together" (pp. 310–312).

A further clarification of the nature of strategic reading comes from Alexander, Graham, and Harris (1998). They describe strategies as *procedural* in the sense that individuals must know specific procedures, whether these are algorithms or heuristics, in implementing a strategy. Strategies are *purposeful* in that readers have to make a choice in the use of a particular strategy. They are *effortful* in that strategy use is time-consuming and requires a certain amount of cognitive resources. Strategies are *willful* in that readers must have the motivation to actually use the strategy; knowing how to use it is not enough. Strategies are *facilitative* in that selecting and using strategies appropriately leads to better performance on cognitive tasks. Lastly, strategies are *essential* in that individuals are unlikely to achieve competence or proficiency in cognitive tasks without them.

Landmark studies

The facilitative and essential aspects of strategy use are the focus of this next section of the chapter. It is one thing to demonstrate that humans use cognitive and meta-cognitive strategies to process and monitor incoming information, to solve problems and to comprehend. It is quite another to demonstrate that these strategies can lead to improved performance. Yet, the cognitive research conducted during the 1970s and 1980s is replete with studies demonstrating that, in fact, cognitive and metacognitive strategies can be taught, and when taught, they can lead to increased performance. In this section, we highlight some of the key studies within this genre of research. We recognize that these are a very few among literally hundreds of studies demonstrating the effectiveness of strategy instruction.

We delimit our area of concern only to instructional studies in which groups of students were taught to use cognitive and metacognitive strategies, since this chapter concerns cognitive strategy *instruction*. As we do this, we do not differentiate cognitive from metacognitive studies, as many of the instructional studies we review did not make such a differentiation. Thus, even though we defined each separately for this chapter, throughout the rest of the chapter, cognitive and metacognitive studies will be discussed together as cognitive strategy instructional studies.

Single strategy studies   It is fitting to begin this review with an early study of Pressley (1976) since he was arguably the most influential proponent of cognitive strategy instruction and since his books remain among the seminal works of the practical application of cognitive strategy instruction (Gaskins & Elliot, 1991; Pressley & Woloshyn, 1995; Wood, Woloshyn, & Willoughby, 1995). In one of the first comprehension instructional studies, Pressley (1976) measured the effectiveness of training 86 third-grade students to use mental imagery on their reading comprehension scores. Students in the experimental condition were taught to create mental images of a text by being told that creating mental images was an effective way to remember, being shown pictures that contained the necessary elements for the text, and being given practice in this procedure. Students in the control condition were instructed to recall the text and "do whatever you can or have to in order to remember the story" (p. 257). Results showed that average and poor readers in the experimental groups correctly answered significantly more questions than did their counterparts in the control group. There was little difference in scores between good readers in the two conditions. Pressley (1976) concluded that when 8-year-olds are given training and practice in using mental imagery, consistently reading first and visualizing second, they showed improvements in their memory of a concrete and easy-to-understand story.

Another early seminal study was conducted by Singer and Donlan (1982) who tested whether high school students could be trained in generating specific types of questions about complex short stories, and whether this training increased their comprehension scores. Singer and Donlan's study was one of the first, if not the first, to determine whether students could generate their own questions, instead of answering questions the teacher had generated. Twenty-seven eleventh-grade students were divided into an experimental treatment group and a traditional instruction group, with both groups using the same six stories during the experiment and taking the same daily 10-point comprehension test. Instruction in the traditional group involved teacher-posed questions about the stories and student essay writing. The experimental group received instruction in five basic story elements (a problem-solving schema), one each day. Results indicated that knowing a problem-solution schema along with use of general and story-specific questions during reading helped students improve in their comprehension of short stories. The authors concluded that reading complex stories required training in these problem-solution strategies, and that high-school students were able to acquire this knowledge.

In a series of related studies, Brown and Day (1983) measured developmental growth in children's and adults' ability to use five basic "macrorules" of summarizing expository texts. The rules, some of which were taken from Kintsch & van Dijk (1978), are: a) deletion of unnecessary material, b) deletion of redundant information, c) superordination (i.e., substituting a superordinate term for instances of that term), d) selection of topic sentences, and e) invention, or creation of topic sentences that describe an implicit main idea.

Participants in Study 1 were 18 fifth graders, 16 seventh graders, 13 tenth graders, and 20 four-year college students. They were instructed to read a text three times, then write what they considered to be a good summary, followed by a constrained, 60-word summary. Findings revealed that even young children were able to perform certain rules of summarization. The probability of effectively using the superordination and selection rules increased with age. Use of the invention rule was infrequent by all groups, and use increased with age.

Next, two experts, who were college rhetoric teachers, performed a think-aloud while generating a summary. The experts performed perfectly on the deletion rules, and far superior to college students on the superordination and invention rules, and no differences between groups was found in the selection rules. Further, unlike the younger students, the experts combined ideas across paragraphs and wrote their summaries around topic sentences.

The final experiment was a repetition of the procedure from the first experiment; however, participants were 20 junior college students, a group considered less successful at using basic reading skills, and therefore, considered novice summarizers. Results showed that these students utilized the deletion rules at the same level as the 4-year college students. However, they performed at a level similar to seventh- and tenth-grade students on the remaining three rules.

In sum, the researchers found a clear developmental pattern for emergence of rule use: deletion emerges first, followed by superordination, then selection, and, much later, invention. The authors explained that, "we believe that the five rules differ in their ease of application because they demand different degrees of text manipulation on the part of the learner" (Brown & Day, 1983, p. 12).

Brown, Day, and Jones (1983) also looked developmentally at students' ability to summarize lengthy, complex stories. Participants were fifth-, seventh-, eleventh-grade, and first-year college students. Students were given stories to read and instructed to remember as much as possible all of the ideas in the story. A week later, they summarized the texts using unlimited words, a 40-word limit, and a 20-word limit.

Results again indicated developmental trends in students' ability to write summaries. College and eleventh-grade students were more likely than younger students to, a) plan ahead for efficiency and effectiveness of writing summaries, b) recognize the importance of higher-level words in writing summaries and, c) "condens[e] more idea units into the same number of words" (p. 977). The authors concluded that this process of using judgment, intention, knowledge and skill in succinctly summarizing lengthy texts was a "late-developing skill that continues to be refined throughout the school years" (p. 977).

Taylor and Beach (1984) studied the effects of training students to use a text structure strategy on their ability to comprehend and remember texts and to write essays. Participants were 114 seventh-grade students, who were divided into three groups: experimental instruction, conventional instruction, and no instruction. Students in the experimental condition received seven weeks of "instruction and practice in how to produce and study a hierarchical summary of social studies material that they read" (p. 139). This included making outlines that identified key passage ideas, generating main idea statements, and listing important supporting details. The conventional group received instruction in completing practice questions on main ideas and details from the text.

Results from this study indicated that the experimental group had significantly higher recall than other groups on an unfamiliar passage. However, on the recall of familiar texts, the experimental and conventional groups showed similar scores, which were significantly higher than the group that received no instruction. Results from the short answer and writing tests revealed no significant differences between the experimental and conventional groups, with both of these groups doing significantly better than the group that received no instruction. In sum, the hierarchical text structure training had the greatest effect on enhancing students' recall of unfamiliar, as opposed to familiar, text, which indicated that students were able to transfer the strategy to a new reading context.

Another pair of landmark studies was conducted by Idol and Croll (1987) and Idol (1987) who examined story mapping as a strategy in aiding reading comprehension. Students with learning disabilities and a heterogenous group of third- and fourth-grade students participated in two separate studies. A basic assumption in these studies was that all texts shared a basic organizational structure and that a link between students' knowledge structures (schemata) and text structure would facilitate comprehension. In the first study, results from responses to the reading comprehension questions indicated that all students improved through the intervention, a finding that suggests "mapping of story components is an effective way to build structural schemata" (p. 225). Additionally, four students who completed all phases of instruction maintained, on a significant level, the improved reading comprehension after the instruction was discontinued.

In the Idol (1987) study, 22 students were randomly assigned to one of two intervention groups, and 5 students were in a control group. A multiple-baseline design was used, where groups received the same intervention, begun on different days. The primary measure of comprehension was responses to the comprehension questions. Results showed a significant increase in the average scores of both intervention groups with story map use. Further, the low-achieving and learning disabled students showed a general and maintained improvement in comprehension scores. The author concluded that explicitly stating and explaining expectations in using the story mapping strategy created comprehension improvements in heterogeneous students' comprehension scores. Further, being grouped with mixed-ability students did not hinder high-achievers' performance, suggesting that grouping students by ability level may not be necessary.

The single strategy studies we have reviewed are exemplary of dozens of cognitive strategy instructional studies conducted during the 1980s. They each demonstrated that teaching students to use a single strategy—like using imagery (Pressley, 1976), self-questioning (Singer & Donlan, 1982), summarizing (Brown & Day, 1983), using text structure (Taylor & Beach, 1984), and using story maps (Idol, 1987)—can lead to significant improvement in reading comprehension. We now review multiple strategy studies in which researchers have taught several strategies in an effort to improve reading comprehension.

Multiple strategy studies   Arguably the single most important work on cognitive strategy instruction designed to improve reading comprehension was a set of landmark studies conducted and summarized by Palincsar and Brown (1984). These researchers developed an instructional intervention called reciprocal teaching. Reciprocal teaching involved instruction of a set of four cognitive and metacognitive strategies: summarizing, questioning, clarifying difficult parts of text, and predicting. The essential elements of reciprocal teaching included the initial modeling of the use of each the four strategies, small groups of students practicing the strategies with a peer acting as teacher, and the scaffolding of instruction toward independent use of the strategies by students.

In one study, seventh-grade struggling readers were divided into four groups in a laboratory setting: reciprocal teaching, another intervention, and two non-intervention groups. In the reciprocal teaching condition, the instructor assigned a passage of text and engaged students in a discussion of the four cognitive and metacognitive strategies. After reading the passage, either the student or teacher lead the dialogue with peers utilizing the four strategies to assist in comprehending the passage. Students worked in peer teaching groups practicing the use of the strategies until they could use the strategies independently. Throughout, instructors provided students with support as they learned the strategies and told students explicitly that these strategies were beneficial for understanding what they were reading. The measures of learning included dialogic changes, transfer tests, generalization tests, daily comprehension tests, and standardized reading tests. The second study was essentially a replication of the first except for one important difference. It was conducted in a naturalistic setting with classroom teachers and students in their regular reading groups. The results from both studies were similar, revealing that students in the reciprocal teaching groups outperformed the other groups. Palincsar and Brown's work led to a series of studies on reciprocal teaching in various settings (see Rosenshine & Meister, 1994 for a review of this work).

A second landmark study on cognitive strategy instruction was conducted by Paris, Cross, and Lipson (1984). Their study was, at the time, "one of the few experimental manipulations of metacognition and perhaps the only one to provide longitudinal, cross-sectional data from a classroom curriculum and intervention" (p. 1250). This study was key, in other words, in adding to the relatively new research base on training studies and to the overall understanding of strategy use and metacognition in reading. The researchers described metacognition as having two main components, a) declarative, procedural, and conditional knowledge about what strategies are, how to use them, and when and why various strategies should be used, and b) knowing how to "evaluate, plan, and regulate [one's] own comprehension in strategic ways" (p. 1241).

Participants were 87 third graders and 83 fifth graders from eight classrooms. Two classrooms from each grade were in the treatment group that received four months of the strategy curriculum, and two from each grade were control classrooms. In the ISL training, a researcher explained the strategies and their appropriate application to students, modeled strategy use, and providing guided and independent practice with feedback from the instructor and peers. Results showed that groups receiving the ISL training significantly outperformed control groups on the cloze and error detection tasks, which the authors concluded showed that the students were using the instructed strategies. The multiple-choice test results (of relative knowledge) indicated that almost all of the students from the treatment groups learned the strategies from the training rather than from a different source. However, no significant differences were found between the two groups on two standardized test measures.

The authors explained that the value of the study is that it shows convincingly that through direct instruction, group work, and open discussion about strategies, students in the classroom setting can be taught how, why and when to use reading strategies, and that they begin to use them on their own. Further, "we can infer from their increased performance on strategic tasks that they also learned how to evaluate, plan, and regulate their reading" (p. 1250). In sum, the study demonstrated that metacognition in reading can be taught to students.

Two studies conducted by Duffy and his colleagues (Duffy, Roehler, Meloth, Vavrus, Book, Putnam, & Wesselman, 1986; Duffy et al., 1987) were also pivotal in demonstrating the possibility and value of teaching cognitive strategies to students. The purpose of the studies was to examine whether teachers could be successfully taught to provide explicit instructions to students, whether these explanations improved students' awareness of the need to use strategies and how to apply them, and whether these explanations improved student achievement. Twenty-two fifth-grade teachers and their low reading group students participated in the first study and 20 third-grade teachers and their low reading group students participated in the second study. Trained teachers were compared to control group teaches who received no training.

In the first study, researchers taught teachers how to transform typical basal skills instruction into cognitive strategy instruction. Classroom teachers were instructed in how to explicitly discuss the mental processes and cognitive strategies involved in comprehension, focusing on the "reasoning" and problem-solving nature of strategy use instead of skill-based procedures. Specifically, teachers were trained to discuss openly with students the strategy (skill) they were learning, why they were learning it, why it was important, and how and when they could use it as they read.

The researchers found that, a) treatment group teachers were more explicit in their instruction than control group teachers and, b) this explicit instruction improved students' awareness of the need for strategy use and their metacognitive awareness of strategies. Additionally, results from the second study showed that treatment group students scored higher than controls on most parts of the nontraditional measures of reading achievement. Treatment students also scored higher on a maintenance test that was administered 5 months after the conclusion of the study.

ADVANCES IN COGNITIVE STRATEGY INSTRUCTION

Thus far, we have reviewed several landmark studies in cognitive strategy instruction. These included seminal works that laid the groundwork for understanding what strategies are and how to effectively teach them to students. We have not completed an exhaustive review, and we have limited our review mainly to studies that have influenced the field of reading. These studies were completed before 1990, and these and other studies have been reviewed extensively in several sets of research syntheses (Dole, Duffy, Roehler, & Pearson, 1991; Paris, Wasik, & Turner, 1991; Pearson & Fielding, 1991; Pressley, Johnson, Symons, McGoldrick, & Kurita, 1989; Pressley, Symons, Snyder, & Cariglia-Bull, 1989; Rosenshine & Meister, 1994).

To some in the educational research field, it would appear that all the major work on cognitive strategy instruction was conducted before 1990. Within the last 18 years, however, there has been additional research on cognitive strategy instruction. In particular, the next section of this chapter focuses in detail on four programs of research using cognitive strategy instruction. This research is significant because it demonstrates a focus on 1) ongoing, programmatic research where studies build on one another; 2) teaching cognitive and metacognitive strategies to groups of students in ecologically valid settings; and 3) embedding cognitive strategy instruction within texts students read.

Key cognitive strategy interventions

Collaborative Strategic Reading (CSR)   Vaughn, Klingner and their colleagues conducted a series of studies to examine the impact of a comprehension intervention program that teaches students to become strategic readers (Anderson & Roit, 1993; Kim, Vaughn, Klingner, Woodruff, Reutebuch, & Kouzekanani, 2006; Klingner & Vaughn, 1996, 1998, 1999; Klingner, Vaughn, Arguelles, Hughes, & Leftwich, 2004; Klingner, Vaughn, & Schumm, 1998; Vaughn, Chard, Bryant, Coleman, Tyler, Linan-Thompson, & Kouzekanani, 2000; Vaughn, Klingner, & Bryant, 2001). Collaborative Strategic Reading (CSR) was designed to meet three primary goals: 1) to provide cognitive strategy instruction to help students comprehend texts in the content areas, 2) to assist students, especially students with learning disabilities and English language learners, and 3) to provide opportunities for students to work in collaborative, peer-mediated environments. In CSR, students learn four cognitive and metacognitive strategies as they read texts, with the purpose of internalizing and routinizing the strategies so that the strategies could be applied to every text students read (Klingner & Vaughn, 1998). At the outset, teachers spend time teaching students to use the four strategies. Once the strategies have been taught, students work in small mixed-ability groups as they apply the strategies to their texts. A central feature of CSR is student collaboration in these groups. Each member of the team is assigned a different role. Each student takes a turn at one of the strategies, and over time, each student has an opportunity to use and practice each one.

In the Klingner, Vaughn, and Schumm (1998) study, researchers taught CSR in mixed-achievement level fourth-grade classrooms using a social studies text. They compared these students' achievement to students in two control classrooms that used researcher-led traditional instruction with the same text. Findings indicated that scores in the CSR classrooms showed improved gains in reading comprehension over the control classrooms, but the two conditions showed equal gains in content knowledge.

In a year-long, quasi-experimental study in 10 heterogeneous fourth-grade classrooms, Klingner, Vaughn, Arguelles, Hughes, and Leftwich (2004) trained teachers to implement CSR in their classrooms, stressing *how* to implement the intervention along with *why*, to foster understanding of its theoretical basis. They found that CSR classrooms showed gains over control classrooms in reading comprehension tests, although only gains made by high- and average-achieving students were different at a statistically significant level. Results from case studies of the teachers also revealed that teachers with higher levels of CSR implementation showed greater gains in student comprehension achievement than teachers with lower levels of implementation.

Finally, Kim, Vaughn, Klingner, Woodruff, Reutebuch, and Kouzekanani (2006) investigated the efficacy of a computer intervention model, Computer-Assisted Collaborative Strategic Reading (CACSR), on reading comprehension of middle school students with learning disabilities. Results showed that students improved their reading comprehension with CACSR more than did peers who used CSR. The researchers noted several advantages of CACSR over CSR, such as reduced teaching loads for teachers and enabling teachers to electronically track student performance.

Peer-Assisted Learning Strategies (PALS)   Another set of studies from the field of special education used Peer-Assisted Learning Strategies (PALS) to improve the reading fluency and comprehension of all students, but especially of low-achieving students with and without disabilities. PALS uses a peer-tutoring model to teach students to systematically apply a set of strategies, including summarizing, retelling, monitoring, elaborating, and predicting, to a variety of texts (Fuchs, Fuchs, & Burish, 2000; McMaster, Fuchs, & Fuchs, 2006). Initial teacher effort in teaching the strategies is extensive. This is followed by scaffolding and the gradual release of responsibility (Pearson & Gallagher, 1983) until students can work independently without teacher assistance.

The PALS intervention requires students to work in dyads of high- and low-achieving readers who alternate roles as "coach" and "reader." As these groups read passages using text appropriate to the lower reader, they follow a sequence of specific cognitive strategy activities that include prompting, correcting, and giving feedback to the reader when necessary (Mathes, Fuchs, Fuchs, Henley, & Sanders, 1994; Fuchs et al., 2000; Liang & Dole, 2006; McMaster et al., 2006).

In an early study during the developmental phase of PALS, Simmons, Fuchs, Fuchs, Hodge, and Mathes (1994) found that students in grades two through five who participated in a peer-tutoring program, Classwide Peer Tutoring (CWPT), improved over control students in comprehension. In a large-scale experimental study of general education classrooms in 12 schools, Fuchs, Fuchs, Mathes, and Simmons (1997) implemented PALS in classrooms during regularly scheduled reading instruction. Results showed that growth in comprehension, fluency, and accuracy in PALS classrooms was significantly higher than in non-PALS classrooms.

With the success of PALS, the program was modified and extended to kindergarten, first grade, and high school (Fuchs et al., 2001; Mathes, Howard, Allen, & Fuchs, 1998). Only first grade and high school PALS will be discussed here because they include comprehension measures.

First-grade PALS teaches decoding, word recognition, and fluency strategies. During the two main activities, *Sounds and Words* and *Partner Reading*, students work in dyads to make predictions about books, partner read, and summarize (Fuchs et al., 2001; Mathes et al., 1998). A 1998 study compared students receiving PALS reading instruction with those receiving their typical instruction. Results showed that all learner types in the PALS group showed improvement in measures such as word identification, oral reading rate, and phonological segmentation, but comprehension scores showed no significant increases. In another study, Mathes, Torgeson, and Allor (2001) found that low-achieving students in the PALS condition showed higher scores than students in the control condition in measures that included comprehension. Average- and high-achieving PALS students, however, did not show a significant difference from the control group, although the authors attribute this to a low sample size.

High-school PALS instruction is slightly modified from the original intervention, in that partner switching occurs more frequently and it almost exclusively uses expository texts. A 1999 study looked at reading comprehension and fluency of the students of 18 special education and remedial reading high school teachers. The PALS classrooms outperformed controls on comprehension scores (Fuchs, Fuchs, & Kazdan, 1999).

Transactional strategies instruction (TSI)   Unlike the CSR and PALS classroom interventions, which involve sequential sets of steps in strategy instruction, transactional strategies instruction (TSI) fosters the learning of how to appropriately select, coordinate, and apply cognitive strategies across content areas and across different texts. Pressley and colleagues (1992) coined the name to describe the combination of cognitive strategies that past research had shown to be effective individually, into a "wide repertoire" of strategies (Pressley, El-Dinary, Gaskins, Schuder, Bergman, Almasi, & Brown, 1992; Brown, Pressley, Van Meter, & Schuder, 1996; Schuder, 1993). Some of the strategies taught included making connections to prior knowledge, making and verifying predictions, summarizing, visualizing, using context clues, and rereading.

Several key principles underlie TSI instruction. These include that: a) readers link text with prior knowledge to construct meaning, b) meaning construction comes from transactions between group members, and c) students' reactions and interpretations during discussions about the text influences the teacher's instruction (Pressley et al., 1992; Brown, El-Dinary, Pressley, & Coy-Ogan, 1995). The small reading group and whole-class discussion format fosters cooperation and collaboration between peers and between teachers and students.

Results from several studies have shown TSI to be successful in improving comprehension in young readers. One program, Students Achieving Independent Learning (SAIL), considered to be a prototype of TSI, was developed to address the needs of at-risk students (Schuder, 1993). In a quasi-experimental mixed-method study, Brown et al. (1996) compared students receiving SAIL instruction to students receiving conventional reading instruction on a variety of measures. The 60 second graders participating in this year-long study were reading below grade level at the start of the school year. Findings revealed that SAIL students' comprehension scores were significantly higher, and students showed greater strategy awareness and use than control groups.

In a recent, mixed-method study, Reutzel, Smith, and Fawson (2005) compared 7- and 8-year-old students receiving TSI instruction with students receiving instruction in individual comprehension strategies, taught one-at-a-time. Findings indicated no differences between the two groups on standardized tests of reading comprehension, in recall of main ideas, or in survey results on motivation and strategy use. TSI students, however, significantly outperformed single strategy instruction (SSI) students on criterion or curriculum-based reading comprehension test scores, elaborated knowledge acquisition from science books, and retention of science content knowledge. Based on these results, the authors concluded that the considerably heavy time investment required for teachers to learn TSI is justified for its benefits.

Concept-Oriented Reading Instruction (CORI)   Concept-Oriented Reading Instruction (CORI) was designed to create "engaged" readers who are intrinsically motivated to build knowledge through a variety of texts and who are proficient in applying cognitive strategies for reading comprehension (Guthrie, Anderson, Alao, & Rinehart, 1999; Guthrie et al., 1996). The most important difference between this intervention and others reviewed here is that CORI combines strategy instruction with motivational features to teach students to learn from texts. The motivational features include providing hands-on activities, giving students choice and accountability, using interesting texts in multiple genres, and providing opportunities for collaboration and for using content goals during reading instruction. The strategy instruction includes teaching students to activate background knowledge, question, search for information in multiple texts, summarize, and organize information graphically (Guthrie et al., 1999; Guthrie, Van Meter, Hancock, Alao, Anderson, & McCann, 1998; Guthrie et al., 1996; Guthrie et al., 2004; Swan, 2003).

Empirical evidence for CORI in improving students' reading comprehension, use of comprehension strategies, and motivation for reading is substantial. In a key, quasi-experimental year-long study, Guthrie et al. (1998) compared four third- and fifth-grade classrooms receiving CORI instruction with peers receiving traditional basal and science instruction. Participants were from three schools with culturally diverse, and predominantly low-income and low-achieving populations. The major findings showed that, when adjusted for prior knowledge, CORI students were more likely than students in a control group to a) learn and use strategies for text comprehension, b) increase their ability to use a variety of strategies, c) increase their conceptual learning, and d) transfer conceptual knowledge.

In two connected studies, Guthrie et al. (2004) implemented two intervention conditions, standard CORI and CORI without the motivational component (Strategy Instruction alone) and compared these conditions to one another and to a control group that used traditional instruction. Results showed that standard CORI students scored higher than SI students on measures of reading comprehension, cognitive strategies, and motivation. These results indicate that the standard CORI model is most effective for producing motivated readers who use comprehension strategies.

Cognitive strategy instruction in content areas

In this section we consider cognitive strategy instruction in secondary content areas. Research in cognitive strategy instruction within secondary content areas is very limited and lags several years behind research on strategy instruction in general. Part of the reason for this is that there are several challenges of teaching discipline specific cognitive strategies to students and of researching such instruction. One challenge is that literacy researchers and language arts teachers are often unaware of the strategies that experts use within specialized disciplines. Because experts generally use cognitive strategies without conscious effort, it is sometimes difficult to understand the processes they engage in as they read within their disciplines. Language arts teachers may be unfamiliar with the types of texts and the cognitive strategies that are useful within these disciplines. Hence, they often teach general cognitive strategies that improve comprehension across disciplines rather than content-specific strategies.

On the other hand, teachers who have expertise in content areas may not have an understanding of common methods of providing strategy instruction. They may be familiar with the texts and strategies that are valued within the discipline, but they may not be familiar with cognitive strategy instruction. As a result of these challenges, there is a paucity of research on the teaching of domain-specific reading strategies.

However there is a small, but growing, body of research and an emerging research agenda in the disciplines of science and history. In this section we will contrast the research on cognitive strategy instruction in science with the research on cognitive strategy instruction in history. The purpose of doing so is to present two very different approaches to conducting research in cognitive strategy instruction within secondary content areas. The research agendas within the disciplines of science and history provide alternative models for those secondary content areas with little published research on the teaching of cognitive strategies.

Cognitive strategies in science Since the mid-1990s, many science educators have focused their attention on the concept of "science literacy" (Glynn & Muth, 1994, Kyle, 1995; Mayer, 1997; Norris & Phillips, 2003). Cognitive strategy instruction in secondary science classrooms originated with concerns about the challenges associated with reading difficult science texts, typically the textbook. Spence, Yore, and Williams (1995) suggested that

> science reading appears... to involve much greater conceptual demands than most narrative text. Readers must have knowledge about the scientific enterprise, the concept under consideration, the scientific language, the patterns of argumentation, the canons of evidence, the science reading process, the science text, and the *science reading strategies*." (p. 5, italics added)

Once the challenges of reading were identified, science teachers and/or researchers adapted or devised cognitive strategies that they hypothesized would help students deal with the complexities of scientific texts. There has been little research conducted on some of these strategies. For example, Spence, Yore, and Williams (1995) considered the effects of embedding multiple strategy instruction in a seventh-grade science classroom. Throughout one school year, explicit instruction was used to teach students strategies such as using the text structure, accessing prior knowledge, setting a purpose for reading, monitoring comprehension, using context to interpret the meaning of difficult vocabulary, identifying the main ideas, and summarizing. In addition, they promoted a general metacognitive awareness through open dialog about strategies with students. At the end of the school year, students' posttest scores showed a significant improvement in metacognitive awareness, self-management, and reading comprehension over their pretest scores. It is interesting to note that what these researchers label as "science reading strategies" are very similar to the cognitive strategies that have been shown to help students comprehend across disciplines.

Most of the cognitive comprehension strategies that have been specifically developed to help students comprehend science texts have not been investigated in published research. Fang (2006) proposed that middle school students should be taught to a) consider Greek and Latin roots of prefixes and suffixes in order to understand scientific words, b) recognize and deal with lengthy noun phrases, c) translate science language into ordinary language, and d) use an author's signposts to follow the author's logic and argumentation. Hofstein, Navon, Kipnis, and Mamlok-Naaman (2005) and Avraamidou and Zembal-Saul (2005) suggested that students would comprehend texts better if they applied elements of the scientific method to their reading. The former suggested that generating questions would improve comprehension. The latter suggested that learning to recognize the value of evidence was a key to comprehension. Like the science-specific cognitive strategies suggested by Fang (2006), there is no published research that demonstrates that these cognitive strategies indeed improve comprehension of scientific texts. Much research remains to be completed in this area.

Cognitive strategies in history

Researchers and history teachers have approached cognitive strategy instruction in history classes in a different and somewhat more systematic way. Early researchers attempted to identify reading strategies that historians used to construct meaning from the multiple, fragmentary, and contradictory texts that they read. Once these strategies had been identified, researchers observed students to see if and when they used the cognitive strategies that historians used. Recently researchers and teachers have investigated different ways of providing cognitive strategy instruction to students. The research on cognitive strategies in history is beginning to provide practical suggestions that history teachers can use in their classrooms.

Much of what we know about the strategies historians use to read multiple historical texts comes from a pioneering study conducted by Wineburg (1991). Using think-aloud protocols, he compared the reading strategies used by historians with those used by above average high school students. The historians and students were given eight documents and three pictures related to the Battle of Lexington from the American Revolutionary War. These documents included primary, secondary, tertiary, and fictional accounts of the battle. The documents included both the American and British points of view. Wineburg (1991) reported that historians employed three strategies to construct meaning from multiple texts, which he labeled *sourcing*, *corroboration*, and *contextualization*. Historians used sourcing when they looked at the document's source before reading it and used source information to make inferences about its content. Historians used corroboration when they made connections between information found in different texts, noticing both contradictions and similarities. Before accepting an important detail found in one text as plausible, it was checked against the information found in other texts. Historians used contextualization when they imagined the particular geographic, political, historical, and cultural context of the event and tried to comprehend documents with that context in mind.

In addition to exploring expert strategies in history, Wineburg (1991) also considered students' use of cognitive strategies. Eight academically gifted high school students thought aloud as they read the same documents the historians read. Without exception, these students read the documents in linear fashion, took the information at face value, made more effort to remember the facts than to understand the event, and became frustrated when the documents included contradictions. Texts represented information rather than evidence to them. Wineburg's pioneering study raised doubts about students' ability to use the cognitive comprehension strategies that historians used.

Stahl, Hynd, Britton, McNish, and Bosquet (1996) also found that high school students had a difficult time analyzing documents. They observed high school students' use of strategies while engaged in a writing activity after reading multiple historical texts. They found that most above-average tenth-grade students were able to learn the basic historical content while reading multiple texts. However, students did not employ sophisticated strategies as they read. Students did not use sourcing, contextualization, or corroboration. They failed to notice contradictions between sources. Other studies have also found that high school students do not regularly use expert strategies for reading multiple historical documents (Britt & Aglinskas, 2002), nor do undergraduate students employ sophisticated strategies like those used by historians (Perfetti, Britt, & Georgi, 1995).

Recently, several studies have investigated the effects of various types of cognitive strategy instruction on students' ability to analyze documents. Britt and Aglinskas (2002) investigated the use of a computer application called Sourcer's Apprentice to teach high school and undergraduate students the strategies of sourcing, corroboration and contextualization. Sourcer's Apprentice was designed to provide students with scaffolded learning experiences with multiple historical texts. Working on computers, students received training in the strategies followed by opportunities for guided practice. The computer program gradually removed support, and many students began to use expert strategies on their own. Students who had interacted with Sourcer's Apprentice for two days wrote essays that integrated and cited more information from primary and secondary sources than students who had not had exposure to Sourcer's Apprentice. Britt and Aglinskas (2002) concluded that the strategy of sourcing could be taught to students and that Sourcer's Apprentice was an effective tool for providing such instruction.

De La Paz (2005) was curious about combining instruction in historical reasoning with instruction in persuasive writing. She provided eighth-grade students with 12 days of explicit instruction in historical reasoning strategies followed by 10 days of explicit instruction on the composition of argumentative essays. Instruction included several opportunities to interact with multiple documents on controversial topics. Students were given mini-lessons on the target strategies that included detecting bias and corroboration. She found that students began to demonstrate an understanding of how historians reasoned with evidence. The students wrote longer, more persuasive argumentative essays with more specific arguments after having gone through the instruction.

Hynd-Shanahan, Holschuh, and Hubbard (2004) found that explicit cognitive strategy instruction yielded positive results with older students. They gave undergraduate students explicit instruction in the form of an essay on sourcing, context, and corroboration. They found that simply prompting these older students to think about the way historians analyzed documents helped the students discover historians' strategies. In addition, by talking about the work of historians, students began to develop a more mature understanding of historical inquiry. They seemed to become more aware of bias in historians' writings. The researchers believed that the reflective interviews that were intended to assess students' level of understanding may have influenced the students' understanding of historical reasoning as much as or more than the instructional intervention. The researchers concluded that the role of explicit instruction, combined with opportunities for reflection, were critical in the development of mature understanding of the discipline of history.

Much of the research on the teaching of strategies in history involve undergraduate students or above average high school students. However, in one recent study Nokes, Dole, and Hacker (2007) compared the use of different types of texts and different types of instruction on mainstream eleventh-grade students' development of content knowledge and use of historians' strategies. Students engaged in ten 1-hour reading lessons as part of a history unit. Eight classrooms of students participated in one of four treatment conditions using a) textbook accounts to study historical content, b) multiple texts to study historical content, c) textbook accounts to study cognitive strategies (i.e. sourcing, corroboration, and contextualization), or d) multiple texts to study cognitive strategies. Written and multiple choice posttest results indicated that both groups that used multiple texts learned historical content significantly better than their peers who studied with the textbook. However, only the group that used multiple texts to study cognitive strategies showed a significant increase in the use of sourcing and corroboration from pretest to posttest. Students in this study had a difficult time engaging in contextualization, even after explicit instruction.

Ferretti, MacArthur, and Okolo (2001) found that even younger students could begin to reason like historians. They provided fifth-graders with mini-lessons on the processes historians use to analyze and interpret historical evidence, including ways to evaluate bias in evidence, corroboration, and dealing with contradictions. There was no explicit instruction on sourcing or contextualization. Unlike all of the other studies on the reading of multiple texts, the students in this study produced a multi-media presentation that was shown to parents and peers at an after school open house. In addition, students took a multiple choice test to measure their content knowledge, and they were interviewed to assess their content knowledge and their understanding of the strategies associated with historical inquiry. The results of this study indicated that students with and without learning disabilities were able to learn the historical content and showed a more mature understanding of historical inquiry than their peers who had not been involved in such a unit. However, there was evidence that students did not spontaneously use the strategies of sourcing or contextualization when they had not been taught to do so explicitly.

History vs. science studies   Research on cognitive strategies that are specific to the domain of history is starting to provide practical suggestions for history teachers. Students need to have many opportunities to engage with multiple historical documents. Explicit cognitive strategy instruction helps students start to develop the strategies of sourcing and corroboration. Students have a difficult time engaging in contextualization. Future research should focus on how history students can be taught to use historians' strategies, including contextualization in a more sophisticated manner and, more importantly, how strategy use can lead to sophisticated historical inquiry like that conducted by historians.

Research on cognitive strategies that are specific to the domain of science and history is still in its infancy. Several strategies have been proposed, but little empirical research has been published about the results of instruction in these strategies. Moreover, little has been published on the cognitive strategies that scientists use as they read. Future research should seek to identify those strategies that experts use, and explore the effects of instructing secondary science students in those strategies.

Little research on cognitive strategies used in comprehension of other secondary content textbooks has been published. Discipline-related cognitive comprehension strategies might exist in math, health, music, or other subject areas that would help secondary students become better readers in those fields. Future research should investigate whether those strategies indeed exist, and what can be done to teach those strategies to secondary students in their content area classes.

CONCEPTUAL DISTINCTIONS BETWEEN COGNITIVE STRATEGIES AND RELATED CONSTRUCTS: UNDERSTANDING THE DOMAIN

Thus far, we have highlighted several key studies in cognitive strategy instruction, all conducted during the 1970s and 1980s. We also presented intervention programs of research conducted during the last two decades and discussed key studies in strategy instruction in content areas. During the last two decades, though, alongside the empirical research on cognitive strategy instruction, information about strategies has made its way into practice. In the translation from research to practice, cognitive strategy instruction has morphed into a number of different meanings.

In practice, the more general terms *comprehension strategies* or just *strategies* are used much more than the term *cognitive strategies*. We believe that the terms *strategies, cognitive strategies* and *comprehension strategies* have become confused in the educational field today. This confusion may well result in educators and researchers moving away from the use of the terms and the important ideas behind them. Such a movement would be unfortunate if the result is to ignore the significant body of research behind strategy use. In this section, we try to untangle some of the confusion around strategy instruction. This untangling can lead to a clarification in the field about what cognitive strategy instruction is and is not.

Cognitive strategies vs. comprehension strategies

Throughout this chapter we have used the term *cognitive strategy instruction* to delimit the strategies readers use to accomplish the goal of comprehension. However, researchers sometimes use the term *comprehension strategies* for these same strategies. There are many related constructs to untangle here. First, there is a distinction between cognitive strategies and comprehension strategies. Cognitive strategies can be *any* mental procedure used to reach a goal, such as solving a math or science problem. Using the term *comprehension strategies*, therefore, helps differentiate between any mental procedure to accomplish a goal and specific comprehension procedures to solve the specific goal of comprehension.

Second, some people differentiate cognitive strategies from comprehension strategies in a different way. Weinstein and Mayer (1986) differentiate between a *cognitive strategy* in the control of readers and a *comprehension strategy that teachers use* to accomplish the goal of assisting students in understanding texts they read. Comprehension strategies, then, are sometimes referred to as procedures *teachers* use to assist students in comprehension. Cognitive strategies, on the other hand, are procedures that *readers* use to help them comprehend better.

The distinction that Tierney and Cunningham (1984) made between instruction that helps students understand a given text and instruction that transfers to many texts is an important one. They argued that teachers instruct with comprehension strategies (also known as reading strategies), while students use cognitive strategies when they read. Further, comprehension strategies that teachers use help students understand a specific text they are reading, whereas cognitive strategies can be transferred across texts.

For example, the reading strategies in Tierney and Readence's popular book, *Reading Strategies and Practices* (2005), are all instructional practices that teachers use to improve their students' reading (the text includes decoding as well as comprehension practices). These include well-worn comprehension practices like the Directed Reading Thinking Activity (Stauffer, 1969) as well as newer practices like the Anticipation Guide (Readence, Bean, & Baldwin, 1989). These practices are meant to be used by teachers, not students. There is no assumption that these practices are to be used by students when they read texts on their own. There is no assumption that the practices transfer from one text to another. Tierney and Readence refer to them as "reading strategies."

Finally, the educational literature can use the term *comprehension strategies* as a superordinate term that includes strategies that readers use and strategies that teachers use. For example, the National Reading Panel (NRP, 2000) identifies cognitive strategies that readers use, like predicting and summarizing, and comprehension strategies that teachers use, like cooperative learning and graphic organizers, and uses the superordinate concept of comprehension strategies to define them both. Thus, the term *comprehension strategies* can be a superordinate term that includes cognitive strategies, but goes beyond what readers do to include what teachers do as well.

Learning strategies vs. teaching strategies

An understanding of the difference between cognitive and comprehension strategies leads to an understanding of the difference between learning strategies and teaching strategies. Basically, learning strategies is synonymous with cognitive strategies under the control of readers or learners. On the other hand, teaching strategies are strategies under the control of the teacher. The term *teaching strategies*, or comprehension strategies that teachers use, has become so commonplace that it has lost its meaning in the field. Often teaching strategies have included anything that teachers do to improve students' comprehension. Thus, *teaching strategies have become nothing more than activities and practices that teachers do with their students.*

Skills vs. strategies

Another set of constructs that have become confused in the educational literature and among teachers throughout the country is the difference between skills and strategies. During the 1980s, when so much research was being conducted on cognitive strategies, teachers taught reading comprehension as a sequence of separate *skills* that were identified in the basal reading programs that dominated American reading instruction during that time (Austin & Morrison, 1978). Paris et al. (1991) defined skills as automatic procedures that readers used but of which they were unaware. Comprehension skills were traditionally "taught" by having students complete workbook pages in which they chose "the main idea" of a paragraph from one of four alternatives, or they reorganized sentences in the correct "sequence" of a paragraph they just read. It was expected or assumed that through repeated practice, students would learn these skills and apply them to the new texts they read. It was believed that with repeated practice of using the skills, students would internalize them, and the skills would become a part of students' reading repertoire.

However, the classic study by Durkin (1978–79) demonstrated convincingly that practice using comprehension skills was not the same as actually teaching the skills. In fact, Durkin argued that teachers did no teaching; instead, students practiced the skills and teachers "tested" whether students could use them. In other words, when teachers directed students to "find the main idea" and to "create a summary of a story," there was no help or assistance for students who could not find the main idea or create a summary. Durkin found that teachers simply moved on to another student who was able to find the main idea or create a summary. Further, even if students did get the right answer to a main idea or summary question, it was often through unconscious awareness or luck rather than through conscious and deliberate planning and implementation of the skills. There was nothing intentional in either the teachers' instructions or the students' behaviors.

Durkin (1978–79) concluded that one of the big problems with the teaching of skills at the time was that there was no instruction in how to perform or use the skills. To Durkin, the *how to* was the missing element. Her work convinced a generation of reading researchers that many students were unlikely to learn comprehension skills well enough to apply them to their daily reading. Durkin concluded that the "mentioning" rather than teaching of skills was a major problem in comprehension instruction in American schools at that time.

One reason Durkin's study was so important was that the conclusions drawn from the study supported and led to the teaching of specific cognitive strategies with a focus on how to use the strategy when reading a text. In fact, two of the important landmark studies in cognitive strategies conducted by Duffy, Roehler, and their colleagues (Duffy et al., 1986, 1987) used Durkin's conclusions to transform the teaching of skills into the teaching of strategies for low readers. The hope was that by learning how to become strategic readers, students would learn *how to* use and apply the skills that heretofore had remained a mystery to them.

The curriculum of cognitive strategies vs. the instructional delivery system

A final distinction within the cognitive strategies research is the distinction between the curriculum of cognitive strategies and the instructional delivery system that researchers and teachers use to teach the strategies. Cognitive strategies themselves refer to the strategies that readers use—predicting, summarizing, visualizing, and so forth. Often, though, these strategies become entwined with the way they are taught. In the cognitive research literature, cognitive strategies have often been taught using a direct or explicit instructional delivery system. For example, in the work reviewed by Dole et al. (1991) and Pressley et al. (1989), much of the research on cognitive strategies used explicit instructional techniques to teach them. These include modeling of the strategy, guided practice with teacher feedback using the strategy, and independent practice using the strategy. There is a robust body of research to demonstrate the value of this explicit model of cognitive strategy instruction (see Rosenshine, 1997, for a review).

The explicit instructional delivery system, though, is only one way to teach cognitive strategies. A related, but distinct, instructional model is the direct or explicit explanation model (Duffy, 2002; Duffy & Roehler, 1987). Winograd and Hare (1988) identified five critical components of this instructional model. In the direct explanation model, instruction must help students: 1) understand the strategies in a meaningful way, 2) understand why they are learning the strategies and how the strategies can help them, 3) learn how to use the strategies step-by-step, 4) understand when and where the strategies can be used, and 5) evaluate their use of the strategies so they can monitor and improve their comprehension. In the Duffy et al. (1986, 1987) studies, teachers provided students with detailed explanations of reading strategies that included the declarative, procedural and conditional knowledge (Paris et al., 1983) identified as being critical to strategy use.

A third instructional delivery model for cognitive strategies is the cognitive apprenticeship model (Collins, Brown, & Newman, 1989; Stahl, 1997). In the reciprocal teaching studies (Palincsar & Brown, 1984), the primary delivery system used to teach the four strategies of predicting, summarizing, asking questions and clarifying was one in which a master-apprentice relationship was set up between teacher and student. The teacher taught the four strategies and how to use them through a scaffold system where the teacher modeled using the strategies and then scaffolded the instruction so that students gradually could take over responsibility for using the strategies on their own. Through peer collaboration, students help each other learn the strategies, and over time, students learn to use them independently. Thus, even though teachers taught four cognitive strategies to students, the instructional method for teaching them was different from the other cognitive strategy instructional studies.

A final instructional delivery system that is often used to teach strategies is has been labeled implicit or invisible strategy instruction (Dole, 2000; Vacca & Vacca, 2004). In the implicit strategy instruction model, teachers develop activities that require students to use cognitive strategies without making the students consciously aware of the strategy itself. So, for example, teachers may want their students to learn how to use a summarizing strategy. They may teach the strategy without any modeling, explanation or even discussion of the strategy itself. Another example of implicit strategy instruction would be when teachers ask students to use their background knowledge to think about what they might know about the topic of an upcoming text. In this case, teachers only ask students to use the strategy without any explanation of it. Durkin (1978–79) criticized this method of instruction because it did not show students how to use the strategy, but just asked students to use it. We would refer to this type of strategy instruction as implicit or invisible strategy instruction.

In sum, as studies of cognitive strategy instruction are examined, it is important to know not only what specific cognitive strategy or strategies were taught, but also the instructional model used to teach them. How strategies are taught can have as much of an impact on comprehension results as what was taught.

CONCLUSION

At the close of the first decade of the 21st century, where are we now in terms of our understanding of cognitive strategy instruction and its relationship and contribution to reading comprehension instruction? First, it seems as though cognitive strategy instruction has moved from its research origins into classroom practice. That move has been a rather bumpy one, and we believe that much of the fidelity of cognitive strategy implementation has been lost in the translation from research to practice. While there are a multitude of books, articles, and pamphlets about strategy instruction, we are not sure that those efforts have resulted in effective strategy instruction in current classrooms today (see also, Pressley, 2002).

Second, many researchers have worried that learning how to teach cognitive strategies effectively to students is a complex process, time intensive and fraught with difficulties (Pressley et al., 1989; Pressley & Woloshyn, 1995). The original landmark studies attest to many of the difficulties teachers face (see, particularly, Duffy et al., 1987; Pressley, Goodchild, Zajchowski, Fleet, & Evans, 1989), like the explicitness of the instruction, the difficulty of finding appropriate texts, and the balance between teaching the content of the text and teaching the strategies themselves. Professional development in cognitive strategy instruction is critical to its success.

Third, it is difficult for many teachers to understand the necessity of keeping the content of the text at the forefront while teaching strategies. Sometimes, in the rush to teach cognitive strategies, teachers work on the strategies without regard to the content of the text. This occurs, for example, when teachers only ask students questions about which strategies they used and why, instead of asking questions about the content of the selection. These teachers may forget that the goal of strategy instruction is improved understanding of a given text, and improving the ability to comprehend across texts, not learning the strategies.

Fourth, and finally, it is unclear what part cognitive strategy instruction plays in the total reading comprehension curriculum and how that plays out at different age and grade levels. No researcher we have ever read has proposed that the comprehension curriculum should *only* consist of cognitive strategies. But just what else should be taught and how it should be taught is another matter entirely. The answers to these questions remain for another generation of reading researchers.

REFERENCES

Alexander, P. A., Graham, S., & Harris, K. R. (1998). A perspective on strategy research: Progress and prospects. *Educational Psychology Review, 19,* 129–154.

Anderson, V., & Roit, M. (1993). Planning and implementing collaborative strategy instruction for delayed readers in grades 6–10. *The Elementary School Journal, 94,* 121–137.

Austin, M. C., & Morrison, C. (1978). *The first R: The Harvard report on reading in elementary schools.* Boston: Greenwood Press.

Avraamidou, L., & Zembal-Saul, C. (2005). Giving priority to evidence in science teaching: A first-year elementary teacher's specialized practices and knowledge. *Journal of Research in Science Teaching, 42,* 965–986.

Baker, L., & Brown, A. L. (1984). "Metacognitive skills and reading." In P. David Pearson (Ed.), *Handbook of reading research* (pp. 353–394). New York: Longman.

Blachowicz, C., & Ogle, D. (2001). *Reading comprehension: Strategies for independent learners.* New York: Guilford.

Britt, M. A., & Aglinskas, C. (2002). Improving students' ability to identify and use source information. *Cognition and Instruction, 20,* 485–522.

Brown, A. L., & Day, J. D. (1983). Macrorules for summarizing texts: The development of expertise. *Journal of verbal learning and verbal behavior, 22,* 1–14.

Brown, A. L., Day, J. D., & Jones, R.S. (1983). The development of plans for summarizing texts. *Child Development, 54,* 968–979.

Brown, R., El-Dinary, P.B., Pressley, M., & Coy-Ogan, L. (1995). A transactional strategies approach to reading instruction. *The Reading Teacher, 49,* 256–258.

Brown, R., Pressley, M., Van Meter, P., & Schuder, T. (1996). A quasi-experimental validation of transactional strategies instruction with low-achieving second-grade readers. *Journal of Educational Psychology, 88,* 18–37.

Clark, K. F., & Graves, M. F. (2005). Scaffolding students' comprehension of text. *The Reading Teacher, 58,* 570–580.

Collins, A., Brown, J. S., & Newman, S. E. (1989). Cognitive apprenticeship: Teaching the crafts of reading, writing and mathematics. In L. B. Resnick (Ed.), *Knowing, learning and instruction: Essays in honor of Robert Glaser* (pp. 453–493). Hillsdale, NJ: Erlbaum.

De La Paz, S. (2005). Effects of historical reasoning instruction and writing strategy mastery in culturally and academically diverse middle school classrooms. *Journal of Educational Psychology, 97,* 139–156.

Dole, J. A. (2000). Explicit and implicit instruction in comprehension. In B. M. Taylor, M. F. Graves, & P. Van Den Broek (Eds.), *Reading for meaning: Fostering comprehension in the middle grades.* New York: Teachers College Press.

Dole, J. A., Duffy, G. G., Roehler, L. R., & Pearson, P. D. (1991). Moving from the old to the new: Research on reading comprehension instruction. *Review of Educational Research, 61,* 239–264.

Duffy, G. G. (2002). The case for direct explanation of strategies. In C. C. Block & M. Pressley (Eds.), *Comprehension instruction* (pp. 28–41). New York: Guilford.

Duffy, G. G., & Roehler, L. (1987). Improving classroom reading instruction through the use of responsive elaboration. *The Reading Teacher, 40,* 514–521.

Duffy, G. G., Roehler, L. R., Meloth, M. S., Vavrus, L. G., Book, C., Putnam, J., & Wesselman, R. (1986). The relationship between explicit verbal explanations during reading skill instruction and student awareness and achievement: A study of teacher effects. *Reading Research Quarterly, 21,* 237–252.

Duffy, G. G., Roehler, L. R., Sivan, E., Rackliffe, G., Book, C., Meloth, M. S., Vavrus, L. G., Wesselman, R., Putnam, J., & Bassiri, D. (1987). Effects of explaining the reasoning associated with using reading strategies. *Reading Research Quarterly, 22,* 347–368.

Durkin, D. (1978–1979). What classroom observations reveal about reading comprehension instruction. *Reading Research Quarterly, 14,* 481–533.

Fang, Z. (2006). The language demands of science reading in middle school. *International Journal of Science Education, 28,* 491–520.

Ferretti R. P., MacArthur, C. D., & Okolo, C. M. (2001). Teaching for historical understanding in inclusive classrooms. *Learning Disabilities Quarterly, 24,* 59–71.

Fischer, C. (2003). Revisiting the Readers' Rudder: A comprehension strategy. *Journal of Adolescent & Adult Literacy, 47,* 248–256.

Fuchs, D., Fuchs, L.S., & Burish, P. (2000). Peer-Assisted Learning Strategies: An evidence-based practice to promote reading achievement. *Learning Disabilities Research & Practice, 15,* 85–91.

Fuchs, D., Fuchs, L. S., Mathes, P. G., & Simmons, D. C. (1997). Peer-Assisted Learning Strategies: Making classrooms more responsive to diversity. *American Educational Research Journal, 34,* 174–206.

Fuchs, D., Fuchs, L. S., Thompson, A., Svenson, E., Yen, L., Al Otaiba, S., Yang, N. McMaster, K.N., Prentice, K., Kazdan, S., & Saenz, L. (2001). Peer-Assisted Learning Strategies in reading: Extensions for kindergarten, first grade, and high school. *Remedial and Special Education, 22,* 15–21.

Fuchs, L.S., Fuchs, D., & Kazdan, S. (1999). Effects of Peer-Assisted Learning Strategies on high school students with serious reading problems. *Remedial and Special Education, 20,* 309–318.

Gaskins, I., & Elliot, T. (1991). *Implementing cognitive strategy instruction across the school: The benchmark manual for teachers.* Brookline, MA: Brookline Books.

Glynn, S. M., & Muth, D. (1994). Reading and writing to learn science: Achieving science literacy. *Journal of Research in Science Teaching, 31,* 1057–1073.

Greeno, J. G., Collins, A. M., & Resnick, L. (1996). Cognition and learning. In D. C. Berliner & R. C. Calfee (Eds.), *Handbook of educational psychology* (pp.15–46). New York: Macmillan.

Guthrie, J. T., Anderson, E., Alao, S., & Rinehart, J. (1999). Influences of Concept-Oriented Reading Instruction on strategy use and conceptual learning from text. *The Elementary School Journal, 99,* 343–366.

Guthrie, J. T., Van Meter, P. V., Hancock, G. R., Alao, S., Anderson, E., & McCann, A. (1998). Does Concept-Oriented Reading Instruction increase strategy use and conceptual learning from text? *Journal of Educational Psychology, 90,* 261–278.

Guthrie, J. T., Van Meter, P., McCann, A. D., Wigfield, A., Bennett, L., Poundstone, C. C., Rice, M. E., Faibisch, F.M., Hunt, B., & Mitchell, A. M. (1996). Growth of literacy engagement: Changes in motivations and strategies during Concept-Oriented Reading Instruction. *Reading Research Quarterly, 31,* 306–332.

Guthrie, J. T., Wigfield, A., Barbosa, P., Perencevich, K. C., Taboada, A., Davis, M. H., Scafiddi, N. T., & Tonks, S. (2004). Increasing reading comprehension and engagement through Concept-Oriented Reading Instruction. *Journal of Educational Psychology, 96,* 403–423.

Harvey, S., & Goudvis, A. (2000). *Strategies that work: Teaching comprehension to enhance understanding.* Portland, ME: Stenhouse Publishers.

Hofstein, A., Navon, O., Kipnis, M., & Mamlok-Naaman, R., (2005). Developing students ability to ask more and better questions resulting from inquiry-type chemistry laboratories. *Journal of Research in Science Teaching, 42,* 791–806.

Hynd-Shanahan, C., Holschuh, J. P., & Hubbard, B. P. (2004). Thinking like a historian: college students' reading of multiple historical documents. *Journal of Literacy Research, 36,* 141–176.

Idol, L. (1987). Group story mapping: A comprehension strategy for both skilled and unskilled readers. *Journal of Learning Disabilities, 20,* 196–205.

Idol, L., & Croll, V. J. (1987). Story-mapping training as a means of improving reading comprehension. *Learning Disability Quarterly, 10,* 214–229.

Keene, E. (2006). *Assessing comprehension thinking strategies.* Huntington Beach, CA: Shell Educational Publishing.

Keene, E. O., & Zimmerman, S. (1997). *Mosaic of thought: Teaching comprehension in a reader's workshop.* Portsmouth, NH: Heinemann.

Kim, A., Vaughn, S., Klingner, J. K., Woodruff, A. L., Reutebuch, C. K., & Kouzekanani, K. (2006). Improving the reading comprehension of middle school students with disabilities through computer-assisted Collaborative Strategic Reading. *Remedial and Special Education, 27,* 235–249.

Kintsch, W., & van Dijk, T. A. (1978). Toward a model of text comprehension and production. *Psychological Review, 85,* 363–394.

Klingner, J. K., & Vaughn, S. (1996). Reciprocal teaching of reading comprehension strategies for students with learning disabilities who use English as a second language. *The Elementary School Journal, 96,* 275–293.

Klingner, J. K., & Vaughn, S. (1998). Using Collaborative Strategic Reading. *Teaching Exceptional Children, 30,* 32–37.

Klingner, J. K., Vaughn, S., & Schumm, J. S. (1998). Collaborative Strategic Reading during social studies in heterogeneous fourth-grade classrooms. *The Elementary School Journal, 99,* 3–22.

Klingner, J. K., & Vaughn, S. (1999). Promoting reading comprehension, content learning, and English acquisition though Collaborative Strategic Reading (CSR). *The Reading Teacher, 52,* 738–747.

Klingner, J. K., Vaughn, S., Arguelles, M. E., Hughes, M. T., & Leftwich, S. A. (2004). Collaborative Strategic Reading: "Real-world" lessons from classroom teachers. *Remedial and Special Education, 25,* 291–302.

Kyle, W. C. (1995). Science literacy: Where do we go from here? *Journal of Research in Science Teaching, 32,* 1007–1009.

Liang, L. A., & Dole, J.A. (2006). Help with teaching reading comprehension: comprehension instructional frameworks. *The Reading Teacher, 59,* 742–753.

Lloyd, S.L. (2004). Using comprehension strategies as a springboard for student talk. *Journal of Adolescent and Adult Literacy, 48,* 114–124.

Mathes, P. G., Fuchs, D., Fuchs, L. S., Henley, A. M., & Sanders, A. (1994). Increasing strategic reading practice with Peabody classwide peer tutoring. *Learning Disabilities Research & Practice, 9,* 44–48.

Mathes, P. G., Howard, J. K., Allen, S. H., & Fuchs, D. (1998). Peer-Assisted Learning Strategies for first-grade readers: Responding to the needs of diverse learners. *Reading Research Quarterly, 33,* 62–83.

Mathes, P. G., Torgeson, J. K., & Allor, J. H. (2001). The effects of peer-assisted literacy strategies for first-grade readers with and without additional computer-assisted instruction in phonological awareness. *American Educational Research Journal, 38,* 371–410.

Mayer, V. J. (1997). Global science literacy: An earth system view. *Journal of Research in Science Teaching, 34,* 101–105.

McLaughlin, M., & Allen, M. B. (2001). *Guided comprehension: A teaching model for grades 3–8.* Newark: DE: International Reading Association.

McMaster, K. L., Fuchs, D., & Fuchs, L. S. (2006). Research on peer-assisted learning strategies: The promise and limitations of peer-mediated instruction. *Reading & Writing Quarterly, 22,* 5–25.

National Reading Panel (2000). *Report of the National Reading Panel: Teaching children to read. Report of the subgroups.* Washington, DC: National Institute of Child Health and Human Development.

Neufeld, P. (2005). Comprehension instruction in content area classes. *The Reading Teacher, 59,* 302–312.

Newell, A., & Simon, H. A. (1972). *Human problem solving.* Englewood Cliffs, NJ: Prentice-Hall.

Nokes, J. D., Dole, J. A., & Hacker, D. (2007). Teaching high school students to use heuristics while reading historical texts. *Journal of Educational Psychology, 99*(3), 492–504.

Norris, S. P., & Phillips, L. M. (2003). How literacy in its fundamental sense is central to scientific literacy. *Science Education, 87,* 224–240.

Oczkus, L. D. (2004). *Super six comprehension strategies: 35 lessons and more for reading success with CD-Rom.* Norwood, MA: Christopher-Gordon Publishers.

Outsen, N., & Yulga, S. (2002). *Teaching comprehension strategies all readers need: Mini-lessons that introduce, extend, and deepen reading skills and promote a lifelong love of literature.* New York: Scholastic Inc.

Palincsar, A. S., & Brown, A. L. (1984). Reciprocal teaching of comprehension-fostering and comprehension-monitoring activities. *Cognition and Instruction, 1,* 117–175.

Paris, S. G., Cross, D. R., & Lipson, M. Y. (1984). Informed strategies for learning: A program to improve children's reading awareness and comprehension. *Journal of Educational Psychology, 76,* 1239–1252.

Paris, S. G., Lipson, M. Y., & Wixon, K. K. (1983). Becoming a strategic reader. *Contemporary Educational Psychology, 8,* 293–316.

Paris, S. G., Wasik, B. A., & Turner, J. C. (1991). The development of strategic readers. In R. Barr, P. D. Pearson, M. Kamil, & P. Mosenthal (Eds.), *Handbook of reading research* (pp. 609–640). New York: Longman.

Pearson, P. D., & Fielding, L. (1991). Comprehension instruction. In R. Barr, M. L. Kamil, P. B. Mosenthal, & P. D. Pearson (Eds.), *Handbook of reading research,* Vol. II (pp. 815–860). New York: Longman.

Pearson, P. D., & Gallagher, M. C. (1983). The instruction of reading comprehension. *Contemporary Educational Psychology, 8,* 317–344.

Perfetti, C.A., Britt, M. A., & Georgi, M. C. (1995). *Text-based learning and reasoning: Studies in history.* Hillsdale, NJ: Erlbaum.

Pressley, G. M. (1976). Mental imagery helps eight-year-olds remember what they read. *Journal of Educational Psychology, 68,* 355–359.

Pressley, M. (2002). Comprehension strategies instruction: A turn-of-the-century status report. In C. C. Block & M. Pressley (Eds.), *Comprehension instruction: Research-based best practices* (pp. 11–27). New York: Guilford.

Pressley, M., & Afflerbach, P. (1995). *Verbal protocols in reading: The nature of constructively responsive reading.* Hillsdale, NJ: Erlbaum.

Pressley, M., El-Dinary, P. B., Gaskins, I., Schuder, T., Bergman, J. L., Almasi, J., & Brown, R. (1992). Beyond direct explanation: Transactional instruction of reading comprehension strategies. *The Elementary School Journal, 92,* 513–555.

Pressley, M., Goodchild, F., Zajchowski, R., Fleet, J., & Evans, E. D. (1989). The challenges of classroom strategy instruction. *The Elementary School Journal, 89,* 301–342.

Pressley, M., Johnson, C. J., Symons, S., McGoldrick, J. A., & Kurita, J. A. (1989). Strategies that improve children's memory and comprehension of text. *Elementary School Journal, 90,* 3–32.

Pressley, M., Schuder, T., Bergman, J.L., El-Dinary, P.B. (1992). A researcher-educator collaborative interview study of transactional comprehension strategies instruction. *Journal of Educational Psychology, 84,* 231–246.

Pressley, M., Symons, S., Snyder, B., & Cariglia-Bull, T. (1989). Strategy instruction research comes of age. *Learning Disability Quarterly, 12,* 16–30.

Pressley, M., & Woloshyn, V. (1995). *Cognitive strategy instruction that really improves children's academic performance.* Cambridge: Brookline Books.

Raphael, T. E., & Au, K. H. (2005). QAR: Enhancing comprehension and test taking across grade and content areas. *The Reading Teacher, 59,* 206–221.

Readence, J. E., Bean, T. W., & Baldwin, R. S. (1989). *Content area reading: An integrated approach.* Dubuque, IA: Kendall/Hunt.

Reutzel, D. R., Smith, J. A., & Fawson, P. C. (2005). An evaluation of two approaches for teaching reading comprehension strategies in the primary years using science information texts. *Early Childhood Research Quarterly, 20,* 276–305.

Rosenshine, B. (1997). *The case for explicit, teacher-led, cognitive strategy instruction.* Paper presented at the annual meeting of the American Educational Research Association, Chicago.

Rosenshine, B., & Meister, C. (1994). Reciprocal teaching: A review of the research. *Review of Educational Research, 64,* 479–530.

Salembier, G. B. (1999). Scan and Run: A reading comprehension strategy that works. *Journal of Adolescent & Adult Literacy, 42,* 386–394.

Samblis, K. (2006). Think-Tac-Toe, a motivating method of increasing comprehension. *The Reading Teacher, 59,* 691–694.

Schneider, W., Dumais, S. T., & Shiffrin, R. M. (1984). Automatic and control processing and attention. In R. Parasuraman & D. R. Davies (Eds.), *Varieties of attention* (pp. 1–27). Orlando, FL: Academic Press.

Schuder, T. (1993). The genesis of transactional strategies instruction in a reading program for at-risk students. *The Elementary School Journal, 94,* 183–200.

Simmons, D. C., Fuchs, D., Fuchs, L. S., Hodge, J. P., & Mathes, P. G. (1994). Importance of instructional complexity and role reciprocity to classwide peer tutoring. *Learning Disabilities Research and Practice, 9,* 203–212.

Singer, H., & Donlan, D. (1982). Active comprehension: Problem-solving schema with question generation for comprehension of complex short stories. *Reading Research Quarterly, 17,* 166–186.

Smith, L. A. (2006). Think-aloud mysteries: Using structured, sentence-by-sentence text passages to teach comprehension strategies. *The Reading Teacher, 59,* 764–773.

Spence, D. J., Yore, L. D., & Williams, R. L. (1995). Explicit science reading instruction in grade 7: Metacognitive awareness, metacognitive self-management, and science reading comprehension. Paper presented at the National Association for Research in Science Teaching Annual Meeting, San Francisco.

Stahl, K.A. (2004). Proof, practice, and promise: comprehension strategy instruction in the primary grades. *The Reading Teacher, 57,* 598–609.

Stahl, S.A.D. (1997). Instructional models in reading: An introduction. In S. A. Stahl & D.A. Hayes (Eds.), *Instructional models in reading.* Mahwah, NJ: Erlbaum.

Stahl, S. A., Hynd, C. R., Britton, B. K., McNish, M. M., & Bosquet, D. (1996). What happens when students read multiple source documents in history? *Reading Research Quarterly, 31,* 430–456.

Stauffer, R. G. (1969). *Directed reading maturity as a cognitive process.* New York: Harper and Row.

Stebick, D. M., & Dain, J. M. (2007). *Comprehension strategies for your K–6 literacy classroom: Thinking before, during, and after reading.* Thousand Oaks, CA: Corwin Press.

Swan, E. A. (2003). *Concept-Oriented Reading Instruction: Engaging classrooms, lifelong learners.* New York: Guilford.

Taylor, B. M., & Beach, R. W. (1984). The effects of text structure instruction on middle-grade students' comprehension and production of expository text. *Reading Research Quarterly, 19,* 134–136.

Tierney, R. J., & Cunningham, J. W. (1984). Research on teaching reading comprehension. In P. D. Pearson, R. Barr, M. L. Kamil, & P. Mosenthal (Eds.), *Handbook of reading research* Vol. 1, (pp. 609–655). New York: Longman.

Tierney, R. J., & Readence, J. E. (2005). *Reading strategies and practices* (6th ed.). Boston: Pearson.

Tovani, C. (2004). *Do I really have to teach reading?: Content comprehension, grades 6–12.* Portland, ME: Stenhouse Publishers.

Vacca, R. T., & Vacca, J. A. (2004). *Content area reading: Literacy and learning across the curriculum.* Boston: Allyn & Bacon.

Van Dijk, T. A., & Kintsch, W. (1983). *Strategies for discourse comprehension.* Orlando, FL: Academic Press.

Vaughn, S., Chard, D. J., Bryant, D. P., Coleman, M., Tyler, B., Linan-Thompson, S., & Kouzekanani, K. (2000). Fluency and comprehension interventions for third-grade students. *Remedial and Special Education, 21,* 325–335.

Vaughn, S., Klingner, J. K., & Bryant, D. P. (2001). Collaborative Strategic Reading as a means to enhance peer-mediated instruction for reading comprehension and content-area learning. *Remedial and Special Education, 22,* 66–74.

Wagoner, S. A. (1983). Comprehension monitoring: What it is and what we know about it. *Reading Research Quarterly, 18,* 328–346.

Weinstein, C. F., & Mayer, R. F. (1986). "The teaching of learning strategies." In M. C. Wittrock (Ed.), *Handbook of research on teaching* (pp. 315–327). New York: MacMillan.

Wilhelm, J. (2001). *Improving comprehension with think-aloud strategies: Modeling what good readers do.* New York: Scholastic.

Wineburg, S. S. (1991). Historical problem solving: A study of the cognitive processes used in the evaluation of documentary and pictorial evidence. *Journal of Educational Psychology, 83,* 73–87.

Winograd, P., & Hare, V. C. (1988). Direct instruction of reading comprehension strategies: The nature of teacher explanation. In C. E. Weinstein, E. T. Goetz, & P. A. Alexander (Eds.), *Learning and study strategies: Issues in assessment, instruction, and evaluation* (pp. 121–139). San Diego, CA: Academic Press.

Wood, K. D., & Endres, C. (2004–2005). Motivating student interest with the Imagine, Elaborate, Predict, and Confirm (IEPC) strategy. *The Reading Teacher, 58,* 346–357.

Wood, E., Woloshyn, V. E., & Willoughby, T. (1995). *Cognitive strategy instruction for middle and high schools.* Brookine, MA: Brookline Books.

Zwiers, J. (2004). *Building reading comprehension habits in grades 6–12: A toolkit of classroom activities.* Newark, DE: International Reading Association.

Zygouris-Coe, V., Wiggins, M. B., & Smith, L. H. (2005). Engaging students with text: The 3-2-1 strategy. *The Reading Teacher, 58*, 381–384.

17 Metacognitive Processes and Reading Comprehension

Linda Baker and Lisa Carter Beall

University of Maryland, Baltimore County

More than 30 years have passed since research on metacognition first got underway, with the onset of interest marked by the publication of the 1975 metamemory interview study of Kreutzer, Leonard, and Flavell and the seminal theoretical work of John Flavell (1976) and Ann Brown (1978). The early studies by developmental psychologists on age-related differences in children's metacognition captured the attention of researchers concerned with individual differences in reading achievement. The consistent finding that has held up over time is that students who are more successful readers exhibit higher levels of metacognitive knowledge about reading and are more skilled at evaluating and regulating their cognitive processes during reading.

Early researchers presented compelling evidence that metacognition played an important role in reading comprehension (e.g., Baker & Brown, 1984a, 1984b; Garner, 1987; Wagoner, 1983), a role that is now widely accepted (Hacker, Dunloskey, & Graesser, 1998; Israel, Block, & Bauserman, 2005). Two national committees determined, after careful review of existing empirical evidence, that metacognition and comprehension monitoring should be fostered in comprehension instruction (The National Reading Panel, 2000; Snow, Burns, & Griffin, writing for the National Research Council, 1998). Snow et al. concluded that children need to have control over procedures for monitoring comprehension and repairing comprehension in order to make adequate progress in learning to read beyond the initial level, and the National Reading Panel (2000) identified comprehension monitoring as a strategy shown through reliable and replicable research to affect comprehension.

The purpose of this chapter is to identify the multi-national historical roots of contemporary research on metacognition, to discuss landmark studies in the field, and to review some current directions in research on metacognitive processes in reading comprehension. Given the length constraints of this chapter, it is impossible to provide an exhaustive treatment of this literature. Rather, our goal is to present a selective overview, filtered through our own perspectives of what is important and what has not yet been discussed extensively elsewhere.

THEORETICAL AND HISTORICAL PERSPECTIVES

Research and theorizing germane to the topic of metacognitive processes in reading comprehension has a very long history, predating the coining of the term "metacognition" by more than three quarters of a century. We single out four prominent early psychologists, who happened to come from four different countries, whose contributions we view as significant: Edward L. Thorndike, Alfred Binet, Jean Piaget, and Lev Vygotsky.

The perspective that effective readers must have some awareness and control of the cognitive activities they engage in as they read that characterized the flurry of research on metacognition in the late 1970s and early 1980s was not new. Researchers, since at least the turn of the 20th century, were aware that reading involves the planning, checking, and evaluating activities now regarded as metacognitive skills (Dewey, 1910; Huey, 1908/1968; Thorndike, 1917). Edward L. Thorndike, a founding father of experimental and educational psychology, wrote that "The vice of the poor reader is to say the words to himself without actively making judgments concerning what they reveal" (Baker & Brown, 1984, p. 356).Thorndike found in his research that many sixth graders did not spontaneously test their understanding; although they often felt they understood, they in fact did not. Today, this would be referred to as poor comprehension monitoring. Thorndike's study of "reading as reasoning" was among the first to document the constructive nature of reading comprehension. The emphasis on the reader's own active role in sense-making is central to current research on metacognition, as will be discussed subsequently.

Another prominent figure in the early history of psychology also discussed processes that would now be regarded as metacognitive. French psychologist Alfred Binet is known primarily today for his development of what is now the Stanford-Binet Test of Intelligence. However, Binet did a great deal of other writing and reflection on issues of importance to developmental and educational psychology. Of most relevance here is his thinking about human judgment and one of its key components, criticism, sometimes referred to as auto-criticism. Criticism involves internally generated feedback used to evaluate potential solutions to a problem and to cull out ideas that are inadequate (Siegler, 1992). This evaluation and regulation would today be subsumed within the construct of metacognition. Like Thorndike, Binet also provided compelling evidence of constructive processing in reading comprehension (Binet & Henri, 1894, cited in Siegler, 1992).

Still a third individual to recognize the importance of skills now regarded as metacognitive was Swiss psychologist Jean Piaget. In one line of research, he provided early evidence that young children's comprehension monitoring was poor. When preschool children listened to a story or a technical description about how an object such as a faucet functioned, they often indicated that they had understood the message when in fact they had not. Moreover, the listeners seldom sought clarification or asked additional questions of the speaker (Piaget, 1926). Research conducted in the 1970s on referential communication corroborated Piaget's early observations and led directly to the seminal studies of Ellen Markman (1977, 1979) on comprehension monitoring while listening. Piaget also contributed to our understanding of self-regulation, a construct closely aligned with metacognition. He suggested that it proceeds through a developmental sequence of autonomous, active, and finally conscious regulation (Paris & Byrnes, 1989). Piaget, too, emphasized the active role of the child in constructing new understandings. And finally, Piaget's influence can be seen in today's research that puts peer collaboration at the center of metacognitively-oriented interventions.

The fourth prominent early influence is Soviet psychologist Lev Vygotsky. Although not widely known in the United States prior to the translation in 1972 of *Language and Thought* and in 1978 of *Mind in Society*, Vygotsky's original work was published in Russia in the 1930s. Social interaction is now recognized as an important mediator of metacognitive development. The theoretical underpinnings of this perspective are attributable to Vygotsky (1978), who argued that children develop the capacity for self-regulation through interaction with more knowledgeable others. These individuals initially assume responsibility for monitoring progress, setting goals, planning activities, allocating attention, and so on. Gradually, responsibility for these executive processes is given over to the child, who becomes increasingly capable of regulating his or her own cognitive activities. The transition from other-regulation to self-regulation that so occupied Vygotsky is at the heart of many conceptualizations of metacognitive development.

A more recent historical comment is also warranted. Research on metacognition has evolved over the past 30 years into two rather distinct lines of inquiry, undertaken within separate subdisciplines in psychology. The developmental work originated by John Flavell fueled the inquiry by developmental and educational researchers, as already discussed. It is this research tradition that is the focus of the present chapter. Another line of inquiry emerged from cognitive psychologists interested in judgments of learning and memory monitoring (e.g., Metcalfe & Shimamura, 1994); much of this research is of a more basic nature and involves adults as participants. Cognitive neuroscientists have recently begun to provide compelling evidence for the biological bases of metacognition through neural imaging studies (Fernandez-Duque, Baird, & Posner, 2000; see Baker, 2008, for further discussion). As yet, this research has not focused on metacognitive aspects of reading and still remains rooted in the cognitive science strand of inquiry.

DEFINITIONAL ISSUES

How metacognition is defined has important implications for how it is studied. The term initially was used by Flavell (1976) and Brown (1978) to refer to knowledge about cognition and regulation of cognition. This two-component conceptualization of metacognition has been widely but not exclusively used since that time. In this chapter we will continue to define metacognition in terms of knowledge and control components. Comprehension monitoring is the primary control component when the cognitive process in question is reading.

Two closely related constructs are associated with the control aspect of metacognition: self-regulation and executive functioning. Self-regulated learning is self-directed, intrinsically motivated, and under the deliberate, strategic control of the learner (Pintrich & Zusho, 2002). The term "self-regulation" is often used by educational psychologists to refer to the use of skills included within the regulatory component of metacognition, such as planning, monitoring, and evaluating. For example, Borkowski, Day, Saenz, Dietmeyer, Estrada, and Groteluschen (1992) asserted that self-regulation is the "heart" of metacognition. Executive function is a term with origins in cognitive psychology and neuroscience. It includes processes typically regarded as metacognitive in nature, such as planning, monitoring, and error correction and detection. Early childhood is an important period in the development of executive function, as is adolescence, and many developmental scientists are now studying this construct.

Whereas metacognition once was studied as a separate construct in relation to cognition, it is now recognized that one cannot understand how and why people perform as they do on cognitive tasks without an examination of motivational and affective as well as metacognitive factors. Borkowski and his colleagues (e.g., Borkowski, Carr, Rellinger, & Pressley, 1990; Borkowski et al., 1992) have argued that the "self-system" underlies the development of a metacognitive system. Paris and Winograd (1990) suggested expanding the scope of metacognition to include affective and motivational aspects of thinking. Although the suggestion to redefine metacognition in this way has not been taken up by other scholars, contemporary researchers examine the role of motivation, perceived competence, and attributional beliefs in the deployment of metacognitive strategies (Borkowski, Chan, & Muthukrishna, 2000; Pintrich & Zusho, 2002). We give special attention to some of this new research in the chapter.

LANDMARK STUDIES OF METACOGNITION AND COMPREHENSION

For the purposes of this review, our timeframe for "landmark" is that the study was conducted within the first 15 years of the "metacognitive era" (i.e., 1975–1989). The studies we selected for inclusion met one or more of the following criteria: (a) the study established research methods widely used in the subsequent study of metacognition; (b) the study generated a productive line of inquiry; and (c) the study established important findings that have stood the test of time. We restrict our population of readers to those in elementary, middle, and secondary schools. The landmark studies fall into several subgroups: those examining metacognitive knowledge about reading, those examining children's abilities to monitor their comprehension, and those examining the effects of instructional interventions to improve children's metacognitive knowledge and control.

Studies of metacognitive knowledge

One early study that satisfies all three landmark criteria was conducted by Myers and Paris (1978), who based their study on the original metamemory interview study of Kreutzer et al. (1975). Myers and Paris interviewed children about their metacognitive knowledge of reading. The pattern they found has been replicated consistently: younger readers have little awareness that they must attempt to make sense of text; they focus on reading as a decoding process, rather than as a meaning-getting process. In their study, Myers and Paris asked children in second and sixth grades a series of questions assessing their knowledge of person, task, and strategy variables involved in reading. Illustrative outcomes were that older students understood that the purpose of skimming was to pick out the informative words, whereas younger readers said they would skim by reading the easy words. In addition, the older students were more aware of strategies for dealing with words or sentences they did not understand. They were more likely to say they would use a dictionary, ask someone for help, or reread a paragraph to try to figure out the meaning from context.

A parallel line of inquiry that grew up alongside the developmental work focused on *individual* differences in metacognition, typically involving comparisons of better and poorer readers. Again, the pattern has been quite consistent, with better readers demonstrating more knowledge and control of reading than poorer readers. A landmark study that involved comparisons of the metacognitive knowledge of good and poor readers was conducted by Garner and Kraus (1981–82). Ability-related differences in knowledge about reading, like developmental differences, have been documented in countless studies, across age groups ranging from early childhood through later adulthood. Students' metacognitive knowledge about reading, whether assessed through interviews, questionnaires, or verbal reports, remains an active and important area of inquiry (Mokhtari & Reichard, 2002; Pressley & Gaskins, 2006).

Studies of comprehension monitoring

A number of studies that qualify for landmark status were conducted to examine children's comprehension monitoring. Many of these adapted the error detection paradigm, originally used in studies of comprehension monitoring while listening (Markman, 1977, 1979). In this paradigm, errors or problems are introduced into texts, and various indices are used to determine whether readers notice the problems and attempt to resolve them. Caution is needed in interpreting these studies because of students' propensity to believe texts are true and well-structured and because of their reluctance to acknowledge comprehension difficulties (see Baker, 1985). Nevertheless, the conclusion that remains valid today is that older and more skilled readers demonstrate better comprehension monitoring on these tasks.

In an illustrative early study, Baker (1984) asked good and poor readers in the fourth and sixth grades to read short expository passages that contained embedded errors—nonsense words, violations of prior knowledge, and contradictory information within the passage. Successful identification of these problems requires application of different standards of evaluation: lexical, external consistency, and internal consistency, respectively. Half of the children were specifically told that there would be problems, and examples of each type were provided. The remaining children were simply instructed to try to find things that made the text hard to understand. Children who received specific instructions identified more problems overall. Many children identified problems at the lexical level only, supporting the evidence from the early interview studies of a conception of reading as word understanding rather than meaning-getting. Other early studies that provided important and enduring insights about comprehension monitoring processes were conducted by Paris and Myers (1981); Garner (1981); Harris, Kruithof, Terwogt, and Visser (1981), and Winograd and Johnston (1982).

Studies aimed at fostering metacognitive skills

Synthesizing the early research on metacognition and reading, Baker and Brown (1984b) concluded:

> The evidence is clear that less experienced and less successful readers tend not to engage in the cognitive monitoring activities characteristic of more proficient readers. Though it is tempting to conclude that ineffective monitoring of one's cognitive processes during reading is the cause of poor comprehension, we caution against such a precipitous conclusion. The majority of the studies have shown that ineffective monitoring is associated with poor comprehension, but not that it is the cause. ... Further research is needed to establish more clearly the nature of the link between cognitive monitoring and reading comprehension. (p. 44)

At about the time those cautionary words were written, researchers were beginning to collect such evidence. Several training studies were implemented in the 1980s that provided solid evidence that the metacognitive knowledge and comprehension monitoring skills of good and poor readers alike could be enhanced through direct instruction. Some of these studies were more traditional controlled studies with training conducted by the researchers. Others were conducted within more ecologically valid classroom settings.

In several early studies, children were successfully taught to evaluate their understanding while reading (e.g., Baker and Zimlin, 1989; Miller, 1985, 1987). For example, Baker and Zimlin (1989) found that fourth graders could learn to evaluate their comprehension with respect to a variety of different standards, and that the training showed generalization and maintenance. In other studies, children were taught to regulate their comprehension once an obstacle arose. For example, Bereiter and Bird (1985) first identified strategies that expert readers use when they encounter comprehension difficulties. Then they taught seventh-grade students to use a set of fix-up strategies, including rereading and reading ahead in search of clarification. Not only did students show increased use of the strategies, they also showed improved comprehension. This study provided important early evidence of a causal link between comprehension monitoring and comprehension.

The general conclusion emerging from the training studies was that metacognitive knowledge and control of reading *could* be fostered. In view of such findings, classroom reading interventions began to be implemented that incorporated metacognitively-oriented instruction. Most of these efforts were based on the notion that the best way to promote metacognition is to discuss, model, and practice it explicitly (Duffy & Roehler, 1989). Many also incorporated Vygotsky's perspective that there should be a gradual transfer of responsibility for regulating performance from the adult to the child.

The classroom-based intervention efforts tended not to focus on metacognitive aspects of reading per se; rather, their goal was to promote children's reading comprehension by increasing children's metacognitive skills. A landmark instructional intervention was Paris, Cross, and Lipson's (1984) Informed Strategies for Learning (ISL). Third-grade children were given lessons in the classroom over a period of months on the use of various strategies for improving comprehension and comprehension monitoring. They were given opportunities to learn declarative, procedural, and conditional knowledge related to strategy use. The program was effective in promoting metacognitive knowledge about reading and comprehension monitoring.

A second landmark intervention study was conducted by Palincsar and Brown (1984), who developed an approach known as reciprocal teaching. Seventh-grade children working within small groups were taught to use the strategies of predicting, clarifying, summarizing, and questioning. These particular strategies were selected because they had the potential to promote comprehension as well as to provide information about how well comprehension was proceeding. The intervention was successful in promoting strategy use and reading comprehension. That the Palincsar and Brown (1984) study warrants landmark status for its generativity and educational significance was confirmed by Rosenshine and Meister (1994), who conducted a meta-analysis of the effectiveness of reciprocal teaching. Their analysis of 10 studies revealed a large median effect size of .88 on experimenter-developed comprehension assessments. This effect size, which represents the performance advantage of the experimental groups over the control groups, is a substantial one.

The final landmark study we offer is an empirical research synthesis. Haller, Child, and Walberg (1988) conducted a meta-analysis to determine the effects of metacognitive instruction on reading comprehension. The 20 studies included in their analysis yielded a mean effect size of .71, again a substantial one. The most effective metacognitive strategies were monitoring for textual consistency and self-questioning. The National Reading Panel's (2000) more recent synthesis of the literature confirmed the early evidence that metacognitive instruction can indeed be effective in enhancing comprehension.

CURRENT AND FUTURE RESEARCH

Early research on metacognition reinforced the perspectives of the historical forefathers—Thorndike, Binet, and Piaget, among them—that the learner plays an active role in the construction of meaning. Constructivism continues to be an underlying premise in the study of metacognition, with intervention studies providing evidence of students' ability to become more aware of the processes in which they engage during reading. Indeed, the momentum is shifting such that students may eventually have the opportunity to contribute as much to their own learning as do their teachers. The development of metacognition is a critical component of that process.

Programs that have demonstrated success in building metacognitive knowledge and control do so by making metacognition explicit. In order for students to lead the dialogue in a reciprocal teaching classroom, for example, they must first engage in self-review to ascertain their own level of understanding of the text (Greenway, 2002). Dialogue leaders begin to internalize teacher talk and think about questions the way teachers would ask them. Likewise, Questioning the Author (QtA, Beck & McKeown,

2001) encourages teachers to support students in a "dialogue with the author," one that promotes students' active construction of meaning from the text. One of the premises of QtA is that the author's ideas are fallible; knowing this can be very powerful for students because it purposefully invites them into the circle of meaning-makers rather than simply information-receivers. Reflecting on the truth or value of what has been written goes beyond merely understanding it and builds metacognitive awareness in the process.

Current researchers of metacognitive processes in reading comprehension take a constructivist approach and recognize the importance of motivation, self-efficacy, and collaboration among students and/or between students and teachers. Directly or indirectly, they also address students' beliefs about learning, including the source of knowledge, and whether students' believe they can influence their own learning. Our review of current metacognitive research will highlight the importance of the self-system (beliefs, attributions, motivation, and self-efficacy) and the programs and practices that have demonstrated success in building metacognitive awareness through their attention to the self-system and collaboration. Researchers today are not only examining influences of self-system factors in relation to metacognition and comprehension, but they are also examining the role of metacognition in conjunction with other cognitive skills such as word recognition and working memory. We include studies of this nature as well in this section of the chapter.

The self-system: Beliefs, attributions, motivation, and self-efficacy

Students approach a reading task with general beliefs about knowledge, goals for reading, and beliefs about their own capability for understanding the text. Schommer-Aikins, Mau, and Brookhart (2000) examined the epistemological beliefs of middle school students, testing the fit of a four-factor model identified in earlier work with college students (Schommer, 1990). The first factor, *Ability to Learn*, reflects students' beliefs about whether people can learn how to learn versus a belief that the ability to learn is fixed at birth. *Speed of Learning* refers to beliefs about whether concentrated effort is or is not useful. The *Structure of Knowledge* factor addresses students' beliefs about the certainty or ambiguity of knowledge, and *Stability of Knowledge* refers to whether knowledge is unchanging or evolving. All but the *Structure of Knowledge* factor fit the middle school data. Schommer-Aikens et al. found that belief in an incremental ability to learn and belief in the gradual nature of learning predicted a stronger grade point average among the middle school students, perhaps because the students were able to approach even a difficult task with confidence.

Beliefs about goals for reading affect students' approach to a text. Transaction beliefs give authority to the reader to learn in a personally meaningful way. In a study by Mason, Scirica, and Salvi (2006), eleventh-grade readers who saw their role as actively constructing meaning produced a more personal interpretation of text and generated a higher level of overall text interpretation than students whose beliefs about meaning construction limited them to understanding only what the author intended (transmission beliefs). Students in seventh through eleventh grades also demonstrated better text comprehension if they held transaction versus transmission beliefs about learning. On a writing task in the same study, middle school students who received specific instructions that not only invited them to consider the author's intent but also their own interpretation of the text produced more sophisticated overall interpretations. Although Mason et al. did not find an interaction between reading beliefs and writing task instructions, inviting students to participate in meaning construction may ultimately affect their beliefs about learning and subsequent academic attainment. As students progress through high school and college, demands on reading comprehension expand to include the integration of information from multiple texts. Students with sophisticated episte-mological beliefs, that is, belief in the tentative and personally-constructed nature of knowledge, demonstrate a deeper understanding of text, even after controlling for prior knowledge (Bråten & Strømsø, 2006).

Students' goals for reading can be considered a subset of their epistemological beliefs in that transaction beliefs should direct the reader's attention to a personally meaning-ful comprehension of the text. A good reader, then, should be one who questions what is read, re-reads confusing passages, and evaluates his or her understanding of what the author is trying to communicate. However, beliefs about the goals of reading are fre-quently more advanced than actual metacognitive control behaviors (Eme, Puustinen, & Coutelet, 2006). For example, fifth-grade readers questioned by Eme et al. were more likely than third graders to cite reading quickly and understanding as measures of a good reader, whereas the younger students indicated a good reader to be one who reads quickly without a mistake. Third- and fifth-grade students were equally likely to affirm the usefulness of rereading and underlining important passages as comprehension-enhancing strategies, whereas fifth graders placed more importance on visualization than did the younger students. On a reading task, fifth-grade students in the study did not attempt to correct comprehension difficulties by searching back through the text, even though students of that same age had identified re-reading as a useful strategy. The older students were no less likely than the younger students to classify comprehension difficulties at the lexical level only; in fact, only one student underlined a whole propo-sition as a source of misunderstanding (Eme et al., 2006). The behavior of these stu-dents may be a function of several different factors. First, it may reflect underdeveloped metacognitive control, including poor comprehension monitoring. Second, it may be evidence of naïve epistemological beliefs, where students characterize knowledge as iso-lated bits and pieces instead of understanding it to be comprised of highly interrelated concepts (Bråten & Strømsø, 2006). Third, it may demonstrate a lack of motivation to resolve comprehension difficulties because of the effort involved.

Interest also plays a role in whether or not students are motivated to monitor their comprehension effectively. In a study of eight- to nine-year-olds, De Sousa and Oakhill (1996) asked children to participate in two tasks where they had to read short passages, some of which contained embedded problems. One task was a more traditional school-like reading task, whereas the other was more game-like and rated as more interesting. In both cases, children were asked to identify the embedded problems. The children were similar in single-word reading and vocabulary skills, but differed in comprehen-sion skill. Poor comprehenders performed significantly better on the high interest task than on the traditional task, whereas good comprehenders' performance did not differ across tasks. The study provides a clear demonstration that comprehension monitoring involves not only skill, but will. If children who are poor readers are sufficiently moti-vated, they can demonstrate higher levels of competence than they otherwise would.

Over the years of schooling, relations among self-system factors, metacognition, and comprehension remain stable, at least in the absence of intervention. This stability was demonstrated in a study by Roeschl-Heils, Schneider, and van Kraayenoord (2003), who first examined children's metacognitive knowledge in Grades 3 or 4 in relation to reading motivation and reading comprehension and again in Grades 7 or 8. Students who scored higher on assessments of metacognitive knowledge in elementary school continued to do so in middle school. Similarly, relations among reading interest, self concept, reading ability, and metacognition were statistically significant at both time points. Metacognitive knowledge was a significant predictor of reading comprehension in elementary as well as middle school. Bouffard (1998) found similar interrelations among the self-system (e.g., children's beliefs about themselves as learners), metacog-nitive knowledge, and reading achievement in children who were assessed in Grade 4 and followed through to Grade 6. The self-system measures and reading measures were correlated at each time point, and they revealed similar patterns of relations over time. The strong and stable correlations among metacognition, motivation, self-concept, and comprehension in these studies suggest that interventions designed to enhance reading comprehension must target more than metacognition alone. Monitoring comprehension and deploying reading strategies is effortful, and students need to believe the effort is warranted and that the effort will be successful.

Building metacognitive awareness: The role of collaboration and motivation

Good readers tend to possess greater metacognitive strategy knowledge and tend to be more interested in reading than poorer readers (Roeschl-Heils et al., 2003). Recent efforts to facilitate students' reading comprehension have incorporated these "will and skill" components. DeCorte, Verschaffel, and Van De Ven (2001) demonstrated that highly interactive, collaborative instructional techniques for learning and applying comprehension and metacognitive strategies induced fifth-grade students to apply those strategies on a post-test more capably than students in a control group. A transfer test showed that the students were also able to apply the learned strategies spontaneously during a social studies lesson. Intervention group and control group students did not differ significantly on a post-test reading attitude scale. However, interviews with intervention group students suggested that they were focused on correctly applying the reading comprehension strategies in that they reported fewer irrelevant activities than control group students.

Student motivation has been successfully integrated with comprehension instruction in various reading programs, including Concept Oriented Reading Instruction (CORI; Guthrie, Wigfield, & Perencevich, 2004). A goal of CORI is to promote engaged reading, where students read frequently for interest, and learning is characterized by an investment of time, prior knowledge, and cognitive strategies. The use of strategies in this context builds metacognitive awareness because students are actively monitoring their comprehension and choosing strategies as a means of realizing their goals for reading. In a CORI classroom, motivated strategy use is supported by the rich context of real-world learning and guided multi-method strategy instruction that empowers students to use strategies as a means of exploring a subject or question of interest. Students provide the questions that guide teaching, and then participate in individual and small group opportunities for thinking, planning, writing, and revising in response to those questions.

Students in CORI classrooms develop skill in using strategies to identify important details from the text and to integrate information using multiple texts. It seems clear that developing and using these skills could promote beliefs about the contextual nature of knowledge and foster the adoption of transaction beliefs about learning. Third- through fifth-grade CORI students consistently demonstrate the characteristics of engaged readers: increased motivation, increased use of reading strategies, and gains in reading comprehension (Guthrie, Wigfield, Barbosa et al., 2004; Lutz, Guthrie, & Davis, 2006).

A basic premise of CORI is that students need to be taught multiple strategies that they can call upon during reading. The landmark work of Palincsar and Brown (1984) illustrated the value of instruction that focuses on more than one strategy at a time, and the National Reading Panel (2000) affirmed the effectiveness of a multiple strategies approach. In recent years, several other well-regarded approaches have been developed that combine multiple strategy instruction with peer collaboration. We focus here on just one, Collaborative Strategic Reading (Kim, Vaughn, Klingner, Woodruff, Reutebuch, & Kouzekanani, 2006; Klingner, Vaughn, & Schumm, 1998). (See other chapters in this volume for more discussion of strategies instruction.)

Collaborative Strategic Reading (CSR) teaches four strategies: preview (activate knowledge and predict what the passage will be about); click and clunk (monitor comprehension during reading by identifying difficult words and concepts and using fix-up strategies when the text does not make sense); get the gist (restate the most important ideas in sections or paragraphs during reading); and wrap-up (summarize after reading what has been learned and generate questions that a teacher might ask). The teacher uses direct explanation and modeling with the full class, and then students break into small groups where each student has a defined role. In an initial study with fourth graders, Klingner and Vaughn (1998) found greater improvement on a standardized reading comprehension test for students engaging in CSR relative to peers who did not use CSR.

Promising results have also been found for a computer-based application of collaborative strategic reading, particularly for students with reading difficulties. Computer-assisted instruction offers self-paced, individualized lessons that can be motivating to all students, but particularly so struggling students. In their study of Computer-Assisted Collaborative Strategic Reading (CACSR), Kim et al. (2006) reported gains in reading comprehension among middle school students who participated in this interactive learning environment. Students initially worked in pairs so as to promote dialogue about the text and encourage active meaning construction. At the beginning of each lesson, teachers provided explicit strategy instruction that was tailored to the identified needs of each student. The CACSR program consists of two parts: learning collaborative strategic reading (what each strategy is, when to use it, why it is important, and how to use it) and using collaborative strategic reading to learn (including computer-driven supports to learning). Students in the experimental condition outscored control group students in the quality of the main ideas they composed and in the questions they generated from the text. Overall, students and teachers expressed positive perceptions of CACSR, including the perception that reading skills had improved.

Metacognition and component skills of reading: Joint contributions to reading comprehension

Researchers today recognize that it is not sufficient to examine the contributions of metacognition to comprehension without also taking into account the variety of other factors that influence metacognition and comprehension. As already discussed, many studies incorporate self-system variables. For example, Roeschl-Heils et al. (2003) found that metacognitive knowledge accounted for more than 25% of the variance in reading comprehension among seventh and eighth graders, with reading self-concept accounting for an additional 5%.

Other studies examine the role of basic cognitive processes, such as word recognition and working memory, in relation to metacognition and comprehension. These modifications in research questions are fueled in part by new research methodologies. The current generation of data analytic techniques allows for more sophisticated analyses of contributions of multiple factors and examinations of pathways of possible influences.

It is very well documented that word recognition plays a critical role in reading comprehension. Zinar (2000) examined the extent to which comprehension monitoring skills contributed to the prediction of reading comprehension above and beyond word identification skills. Fourth-grade children's comprehension monitoring was measured online using the error detection paradigm. Students read passages containing embedded inconsistencies, and their reading times and lookbacks were assessed, as were verbalizations of problem detection. Word identification was a powerful predictor of reading comprehension, as expected, but the extent to which children slowed down their reading on encountering inconsistent information was also a significant predictor. In a supplementary analysis, Zinar determined that children who slowed down their reading when encountering the inconsistency and who looked back at the sentence that set up the inconsistency had the highest comprehension scores on a standardized test. In other words, those who showed evidence not only of evaluation but attempted regulation were better comprehenders.

The contribution of comprehension monitoring to comprehension was examined in conjunction with working memory and inference making by Cain, Oakhill, and Bryant (2004) in a longitudinal study of children aged 8 through 11. Comprehension monitoring was again assessed with error detection tasks, using age-appropriate materials in which students needed to find embedded inconsistencies. Working memory and comprehension monitoring were significant predictors of comprehension. Comprehension monitoring accounted for unique variance once working memory and other background variables (word reading skill, verbal ability) were controlled. Comprehension monitoring skill was significantly correlated with most measures at all three time points. The authors suggested that if working memory, comprehension monitoring, and inference making skills are inadequate, providing instruction in comprehension monitoring and inference making can help circumvent problems in reading comprehension that are associated with working memory limitations, which are generally regarded as less amenable to intervention.

This notion of compensation serves as the foundation of a line of research by Walczyk and his colleagues (e.g., Walczyk, Marsiglia, Johns, & Bryan, 2004). They proposed a model called the compensatory-encoding model (C-EM), in which readers whose decoding of words or verbal working memory capacities is inefficient can compensate so that literal comprehension of text is not disrupted. However, the use of compensations may draw cognitive resources away from higher level reading activities such as comprehension monitoring. The model was tested in third graders who were recorded as they read aloud texts containing embedded anomalies. Literal comprehension was assessed, as were the efficiency of word decoding, semantic encoding, and verbal working memory. Consistent with the model, inefficient readers compensated by pausing, looking back, rereading, and sounding out words more often than efficient readers, but they had literal comprehension scores as good as those of efficient readers.

These recent studies are all consistent with the view that metacognitive skill *influences* comprehension. However, better metacognitive control may be a *consequence* of better reading ability, as shown recently by Oakhill, Hartt, and Samols (2005). In two studies, children ages 9 and 10 were matched for reading vocabulary and word recognition skills. In one study, the better comprehenders identified more sentence level anomalies, but not word level problems, than the poorer comprehenders. In a second study, they were better at detecting inconsistencies in the text, especially when the inconsistent sentences were more widely spaced and so put a greater burden on working memory. Working memory ability was related to error detection, but comprehension ability was also a good, and sometimes better, predictor of comprehension monitoring. These results, then, are consistent with the view that comprehension influences metacognition. In reality, reciprocal causation is most likely; that is, improvements in metacognition contribute to improvements in comprehension, which in turn contribute to further improvements in metacognition. Research confirming the reciprocal nature of metacognition-comprehension links would be a fruitful direction for future research.

That beginning readers exhibit limited metacognitive awareness and control due to limited resources is now reflected in an updated model of automaticity in reading (Samuels, Ediger, Willcutt, & Palumbo, 2005). Whereas the original Laberge and Samuels (1974) model focused on the need to develop automaticity of decoding, so that attention could be directed at comprehension, the new model calls for developing automaticity in comprehension monitoring as well. Beginning readers have only enough processing capacity to focus on one component at a time. With repeated experience, readers learn to decode and to monitor their comprehension sufficiently well that they do not have to allocate attention to the processes; it is only when an obstacle is noted that attention is directed to the problem area. Empirical research is needed to test this new model.

IMPLICATIONS FOR PRACTICE

Other chapters in this volume address how the knowledge acquired through research is being translated into educational practice. Although an emphasis on metacognition in the classroom is warranted, it is important that metacognition not become an end in itself (Baker, 2002). When teachers provide instruction in comprehension monitoring, the process must of course take place on a conscious level. But the goal is for this "other regulation" to become internalized as "self-regulation." Reading proceeds automatically until a problem is detected; at that point metacognitive skills are deployed to resolve the difficulty. We have solid evidence that this characterization applies to good readers (Pressley & Gaskins, 2006), but we lack research demonstrating how the "automatic pilot" develops, and so teachers are still awaiting good guidance.

The role of the self-system in metacognitive awareness and control is an important one that teachers need to understand. Students' motivation to resolve comprehension difficulties prompts the use of metacognitive skills, as does a belief that the extra effort will be worthwhile. To some extent, student behavior may also be understood as a function of the type of tasks and assessments that take place in the classroom. Tests frequently measure "memory for text" rather than comprehension of text (Wiley, Griffin, & Thiede, 2005). Because students tend to overestimate their memory of what they have read, the need for reading strategies and comprehension monitoring strategies may not be apparent to them. Wiley et al. suggest that an emphasis on improving memory for text may even harm comprehension monitoring performance. Per Wiley et al., the implication for teachers and researchers is to match students' growing knowledge of strategies for learning and monitoring their comprehension with tasks that actually require those skills.

Many of the programs that have demonstrated success at building metacognitive awareness and reading comprehension allow students to actively construct an understanding of text, for example, by giving students tasks that require them to infer relations that are implied, but not explicitly stated, in the text. Reciprocal Teaching leads students to generate questions about the text and facilitate small group discussion. CORI uses students' prior knowledge as a basis for text comprehension, and meaning is built through interactive discussion in both CORI and QtA. When students are given permission to generate personally meaningful interpretations of text, the use of strategies for comprehending text might be seen as more worthwhile.

In light of evidence for the impact of epistemological beliefs on metacognitive control, a skilled teacher will legitimize students' different interpretations, and specifically, the process by which the student developed his or her interpretation. Helping students to develop transaction beliefs about learning leads them beyond a right or wrong approach to comprehension. Even well-meaning teachers, who report holding discussions in class where they encourage students to produce and respond to ideas, are sometimes surprised to find that most of the ideas actually come from themselves (Beck & McKeown, 2001). Becoming a discussion facilitator rather than being an information provider is perhaps as much of a challenge to the teacher as becoming a meaning maker is to the student.

CONCLUDING THOUGHTS

One of the charges to the authors of this volume was to provide a brief overview of classic research conducted when scholarly inquiry into the assigned topic was in its infancy. It was a welcome opportunity for the senior author to reread the early work on metacognitive skills of reading, including her own, and for the junior author to become acquainted with it. It was striking how extensively our current theory and research reflect issues and questions that were of concern at the outset, some 30 years ago.

Research findings also still look a great deal like they did originally, which is quite troubling. For example, Eme et al. (2006) found that third- and fifth-grade children relied almost exclusively on word-level criteria for evaluating their understanding, replicating the findings of Baker (1984) more than 20 years earlier. Similarly, Eme et al. found that third graders' conception of a good reader was one who reads quickly without making any mistakes, replicating the findings of Myers and Paris (1978) almost 30 years earlier. Other contemporary researchers, doing their work both within and outside of the United States, are also replicating the early evidence of limited metacognitive knowledge and control.

These patterns are troubling because they illustrate how slowly advances in research knowledge are translated into changes in classroom practice that in turn bring about changes in child outcomes. We now know more about how to foster metacognitive development than we did at the outset, and intervention studies now far outnumber more basic studies (see Israel et al., 2005), but the pace with which metacognitively-oriented instruction is incorporated into routine practice of classroom teachers is slow. Indeed, metacognition is still a term that needs to be defined to most audiences of educated adults.

Preparing for and writing this chapter also brought home to us that the field has lost three major pioneering leaders to untimely deaths. If it were not for Ann Brown, Ruth Garner, and Mike Pressley, this realm of inquiry may never have developed at all, let alone flourished. Their legacy lies in part in their substantive contributions to our understanding of metacognitive processes in reading comprehension, and we close the chapter by giving them tribute.

REFERENCES

Baker, L. (1984). Spontaneous versus instructed use of multiple standards for evaluating comprehension: Effects of age, reading proficiency and type of standard. *Journal of Experimental Child Psychology, 38,* 289–311.

Baker, L. (1985). How do we know when we don't understand? Standards for evaluating text comprehension. In D. L. Forrest-Pressley, G. E. MacKinnon, & T. G. Waller (Eds.), *Metacognition, cognition, and human performance* (pp. 155–206). New York: Academic Press.

Baker, L. (2002). Metacognition in comprehension instruction. In C. C. Block & M. Pressley (Eds.), *Comprehension instruction: Research based best practices* (pp. 77–95). New York: Guilford.

Baker, L. (2005). Developmental differences in metacognition: Implications for metacognitively-oriented reading instruction. In S. E. Israel, C. C. Block, K. L. Bauserman, & K. Kinnucan-Welsch (Eds.), *Metacognition in literacy learning: Theory, assessment, instruction, and professional development* (pp. 61–79). Mahwah, NJ: Erlbaum.

Baker, L. (2008). Metacognitive development in reading: Contributors and consequences. In K. Mokhtari & R. Sheorey (Eds.), *Reading strategies of first- and second-language learners: See how they read* (pp. 25–42). Norwood, MA: Christopher Gordon.

Baker, L., & Brown, A. L. (1984a). Metacognitive skills and reading. In P. D. Pearson, M. Kamil, R. Barr, & P. Mosenthal (Eds.), *Handbook of research in reading* (pp. 353–395). New York: Longman.

Baker, L., & Brown, A. L. (1984b). Cognitive monitoring in reading. In J. Flood (Ed.), *Understanding reading comprehension* (pp. 21–44). Newark, DE: International Reading Association.

Baker, L., & Zimlin, L. (1989). Instructional effects on children's use of two levels of standards for evaluating their comprehension. *Journal of Educational Psychology, 81,* 340–346.

Beck, I., & McKeown, M. (2001). Inviting students into the pursuit of meaning. *Educational Psychology Review, 13,* 225–241.

Bereiter, C., & Bird, M. (1985). Use of thinking aloud in identification and teaching of reading comprehension strategies. *Cognition and Instruction, 2,* 131–156.

Borkowski, J. G., Carr, M., Rellinger, E., & Pressley, M. (1990). Self-regulated cognition: Interdependence of metacognition, attributions, and self-esteem. In B. F. Jones & L. Idol (Eds.), *Dimensions of thinking and cognitive instruction* (pp. 53–92). Hillsdale, NJ: Erlbaum.

Borkowski, J. G., Chan, L. K. S., & Muthukrishna, N. (2000). A process-oriented model of metacognition: Links between motivation and executive functioning. In G. Schraw & J. Impara (Eds.), *Issues in the measurement of metacognition* (p. 42). Lincoln: Buros Institute of Mental Measurements, University of Nebraska.

Borkowski, J. G., Day, J. D., Saenz, D., Dietmeyer, D., Estrada T. M., & Groteluschen, A. (1992). Expanding the boundaries of cognitive interventions. In B. Wong (Ed.), *Intervention research with students with learning disabilities* (pp. 1–21). New York: Springer-Verlag.

Bouffard, T. (1998). A developmental study of the relationship between reading development and the self-system. *European Journal of Psychology of Education, 13,* 61–74.

Bråten, I., & Strømsø, H. (2006). Effects of personal epistemology on the understanding of multiple texts. *Reading Psychology, 27,* 457–484.

Brown, A. L. (1978). Knowing when, where, and how to remember: A problem of metacognition. In R. Glaser (Ed.), *Advances in instructional psychology* (pp. 7–165). Hillsdale, NJ: Erlbaum.

Cain, K., Oakhill, J., & Bryant, P. (2004). Children's reading comprehension ability: concurrent prediction by working memory, verbal ability, and component skills. *Journal of Educational Psychology, 96,* 31–42.

DeCorte, E., Verschaffel, L., & Van De Ven, A. (2001). Improving text comprehension strategies in upper primary school children: A design experiment. *British Journal of Educational Psychology, 71,* 531–559.

De Sousa, I., & Oakhill, J. (1996). Do levels of interest have an effect on children's comprehension monitoring performance? *British Journal of Educational Psychology, 66,* 471–482.

Dewey, J. (1910). *How we think.* Oxford: Heath.

Duffy, G. G., & Roehler, L. R. (1989). Why strategy instruction is so difficult and what we need to do about it. In C. B. McCormick, G. E. Miller, & M. Pressley (Eds.), *Cognitive strategy research: From basic research to educational applications* (pp. 133–154). New York: Springer-Verlag.

Eme, E., Puustinen, M., & Coutelet, B. (2006). Individual and developmental differences in reading monitoring: When and how do children evaluate their comprehension? *European Journal of Psychology of Education, 21,* 91–115.

Fernandez-Duque, D., Baird, J. A., & Posner, M. I. (2000). Executive attention and metacognitive regulation. *Consciousness and Cognition, 9,* 288–307.

Flavell, J. H. (1976). Metacognitive aspects of problem solving. In L. B. Resnick (Ed.), *The nature of intelligence* (pp. 231–235). Hillsdale, NJ: Erlbaum.

Garner, R. (1981). Monitoring of understanding: An investigation of good and poor readers' awareness of induced miscomprehension of text. *Journal of Reading Behavior, 12,* 55–64.

Garner, R. (1987). *Metacognition and reading comprehension.* Norwood, NJ: Ablex.

Garner, R., & Kraus, C. (1981–1982). Good and poor comprehender differences in knowing and regulating reading behaviors. *Educational Research Quarterly, 6,* 5–12.

Greenway, C. (2002). The process, pitfalls, and benefits of implementing a reciprocal teaching intervention to improve the reading comprehension of a group of year 6 pupils. *Educational Psychology in Practice, 18,* 113–13.

Guthrie, J., Wigfield, A., Barbosa, P., Perencevich, K.. Taboada, A., Davis, M., Scafiddi, N. T., & Tonks, S. (2004). Increasing reading comprehension and engagement through Concept-Oriented Reading Instruction. *Journal of Educational Psychology, 96,* 403–423.

Guthrie, J. T., Wigfield, A., & Perencevich, K. C. (2004). *Motivating reading comprehension: Concept-Oriented Reading Instruction.* Mahwah, NJ: Erlbaum.

Hacker, D. J., Dunloskey, J., & Graesser, A. C. (Eds.) (1998). *Metacognition in educational theory and practice.* Mahwah, NJ: Erlbaum.

Haller, E. P., Child, D. A., & Walberg, H. J. (1988). Can comprehension be taught? A quantitative synthesis of "metacognitive" studies. *Educational Researcher, 17(9),* 5–8.

Harris, P. L., Kruithof, A., Terwogt, M., & Visser, T. (1981). Children's detection and awareness of textual anomaly. *Journal of Experimental Child Psychology, 31,* 212–230.

Huey, E. B. (1968). *The psychology and pedagogy of reading.* Cambridge: MIT Press. (Original work published 1908)

Israel, S., Block, C., & Bauserman, K. (2005). *Metacognition in literacy learning: Theory, assessment, instruction, and professional development.* Mahwah, NJ: Erlbaum.

Kim, A., Vaughn, S., Klingner, J., Woodruff, A., Reutebuch, C., & Kouzekanani, K. (2006). Improving the reading comprehension of middle school students with disabilities through computer-assisted collaborative strategic reading. *Remedial and Special Education, 27,* 235–249.

Kinnunen, R., Vauras, M., & Niemi, P. (1998). Comprehension monitoring in beginning readers. *Scientific Studies of Reading, 2,* 353–375.

Klingner, J., Vaughn, S., & Schumm, J. (1998). Collaborative strategic reading during social studies in heterogeneous fourth-grade classrooms. *Elementary School Journal, 99,* 3–22.

Kreutzer, M., Leonard, C., & Flavell, J. (1975). An interview study of children's knowledge about memory. *Monographs of the Society for Research in Child Development, 40,* 1–60.

Laberge, D., & Samuels, S. (1974). Toward a theory of automatic information processing in reading. *Cognitive Psychology, 6,* 293–323.

Lutz, S., Guthrie, J., & Davis, M. (2006). Scaffolding for engagement in elementary school reading instruction. *The Journal of Educational Research, 100,* 3–20.

Markman, E. (1977). Realizing that you don't understand: A preliminary investigation. *Child Development, 48,* 986–992.

Markman, E. (1979). Realizing that you don't understand: Elementary school children's awareness of inconsistencies. *Child Development, 50,* 643–655.

Mason, L., Scirica, F., & Salvi, L. (2006). Effects of beliefs about meaning construction and task instructions on interpretation of narrative text. *Contemporary Educational Psychology, 31,* 411–437.

Metcalfe, J., & Shimamura, A. (1994). *Metacognition: Knowing about knowing.* Cambridge, MA: MIT Press.

Miller, G. (1985). The effects of general and specific self-instruction training on children's comprehension monitoring performances during reading. *Reading Research Quarterly, 20,* 616–628.

Miller, G. (1987). The influence of self-instruction on the comprehension monitoring performance of average and above average readers. *Journal of Reading Behavior, 19,* 303–317.

Mokhtari, K., & Reichard, C. A. (2002). Assessing students' metacognitive awareness of reading strategies. *Journal of Educational Psychology, 94,* 249–259.

Myers, M., & Paris, S. (1978). Children's metacognitive knowledge about reading. *Journal of Educational Psychology, 70,* 680–690.

National Reading Panel (2000). *Teaching children to read: An evidence-based assessment of the scientific research literature on reading and its implications for reading instruction.* Bethesda, MD: National Institute of Child Health and Human Development.

Oakhill, J., Hartt, J., & Samols, D. (2005). Levels of comprehension monitoring and working memory in good and poor comprehenders. *Reading and Writing, 18,* 657–686.

Palincsar, A., & Brown, A. (1984). Reciprocal teaching of comprehension-fostering and comprehension-monitoring activities. *Cognition and Instruction,* 117–175.

Paris, S. G., & Byrnes, J. P. (1989). The constructivist approach to self-regulation and learning in the classroom. In B. J. Zimmerman & D. H. Schunk (Eds.), *Self-regulated learning and academic achievement* (pp. 169–200). New York: Springer-Verlag.

Paris, S., Cross, D., & Lipson, M. (1984). Informed Strategies for Learning: A program to improve children's reading awareness and comprehension. *Journal of Educational Psychology, 76,* 1239–1252.

Paris, S. G., & Myers, M. (1981). Comprehension monitoring, memory, and study strategies of good and poor readers. *Journal of Reading Behavior, 13,* 5–22.

Paris, S., & Winograd, P. (1990). Promoting metacognition and motivation of exceptional children. *RASE: Remedial & Special Education, 11,* 7–15.

Piaget, J. (1926). *The language and thought of the child* (M. Gabain, trans.). London: Routledge & Kegan Paul.

Pintrich, P., & Zusho, A. (2002). The development of academic self-regulation: The role of cognitive and motivational factors. In A. Wigfield & J. Eccles (Eds.), *Development of achievement motivation.* San Diego, CA: Academic Press.

Pintrich, P. R., & Zusho, A. (2002). The development of academic self-regulation: The role of cognitive and motivational factors. In A. Wigfield & J. S. Eccles (Eds.), *Development of achievement motivation* (pp. 249–284). San Diego: Academic Press.

Pressley, M., & Gaskins, I. (2006). Metacognitively competent reading is constructively responsive reading comprehension: How can such reading be developed in students? *Metacognition and Learning, 1,* 99–113.

Roeschl-Heils, A., Schneider, W., & van Kraayenoord, C. E. (2003). Reading, metacognition and motivation: A follow-up study of German students 7 and 8. *European Journal of Psychology of Education, 18,* 75–86.

Rosenshine, B., & Meister, C. (1994). Reciprocal teaching: A review of the research. *Review of Educational Research, 64,* 479–530.

Samuels, S. J., Ediger, K. M., Willcutt, J. R., & Palumbo, T. J. (2005). Role of automaticity in metacognition and literacy instruction. In S. E. Israel, C. C. Block, K. L. Bauserman, & K Kinnucan-Welsch (Eds.), *Metacognition in literacy learning: Theory, assessment, instruction, and professional development* (pp. 41–59). Mahwah, NJ: Erlbaum.

Schommer, M. (1990). Effects of beliefs about the nature of knowledge on comprehension. *Journal of Educational Psychology, 82,* 498–504.

Schommer-Aikins, M., Mau, W-C., & Brookhart, S. (2000). Understanding middle students' beliefs about knowledge and learning using a multidimensional paradigm. *The Journal of Educational Research, 94,* 120–127.

Siegler, R. S. (1992). The other Alfred Binet. *Developmental Psychology, 28,* 179–190.

Snow, C. E., Burns, M. S., & Griffin, P. (Eds.) (1998). *Preventing reading difficulties in young children.* Washington, DC: National Academy Press.

Thorndike, E. (1917). The psychology of thinking in the case of reading. *Psychological Review, 24,* 220–234.

Vygotsky, L. S. (1978). *Mind in society.* Cambridge: Harvard University Press.

Wagoner, S. A. (1983). Comprehension monitoring: What it is and what we know about it. *Reading Research Quarterly, 28,* 328–346.

Walczyk, J. J., Marsiglia, C. S., Johns, A. K., & Bryan, K. S. (2004). Children's compensations for poorly automated reading skills. *Discourse Processes, 37,* 47–66.

Wiley, J., Griffin, T. D., & Thiede, K. W. (2005). Putting the comprehension in metacomprehension. *Journal of General Psychology, 132,* 408–428.

Winograd, P., & Johnston, P. (1982). Comprehension monitoring and the error detection paradigm. *Journal of Reading Behavior, 14,* 61–74.

Zinar, S. (2000). The relative contributions of word identification skill and comprehension-monitoring behavior to reading comprehension ability. *Contemporary Educational Psychology, 25,* 363–377.

18 Self-Regulated Comprehension

Dixie D. Massey

University of Puget Sound

This chapter discusses Self-Regulated Learning (SRL) as it is applied to reading comprehension. The goals of the chapter include: (a) establishing a definition of SRL, (b) presenting and challenging research supporting SRL in disciplines outside of reading as well as within the reading field, (c) describing and evaluating instructional approaches that have been associated with SRL within the reading field, and (d) reviewing the contributions of and work yet to be done in the field of SRL as applied to reading. This chapter poses questions regarding SRL as a way to challenge the status quo of research. Questions that the field of reading must address include how will we define SRL within the field of reading, what counts as evidence of SRL, how do we evaluate SRL, and finally, how do we implement SRL into reading classroom contexts.

SELF-REGULATION: DEFINITIONS, CONTEXTS, AND RESEARCH

Self-regulation is most frequently defined as "self-generated thoughts, feelings, and actions that are planned and cyclically adapted to the attainment of personal goals" (Zimmerman, 2000, p. 14). Theorists seem to make little distinction between self-regulation and self-regulated learning (SRL). Paris and Paris' (2001) description of self-regulated learning echoed Zimmerman's definition of self-regulation, with SRL defined as the individual's autonomy and control over monitoring, directing, and regulating "actions toward goals of information acquisition, expanding expertise, and self-improvement" (p. 89). Sungur and Tekkaya (2006) summarized SRL as "the degree to which students metacognitively, motivationally, and behaviorally participate in their learning process" (p. 307). Common to these definitions is the emphasis on individuals taking action to achieve self-established goals.

Zimmerman (1990) noted that self-regulated learners "are distinguished by (a) their awareness of strategic relations between regulatory processes or responses and learning outcomes and (b) their use of these strategies to achieve their academic goals" (p. 5). Though all learners may use regulatory processes to some extent, the self-regulated learner further distinguishes himself by monitoring the effectiveness of the strategies which he employs, what Zimmerman (1990) referred to as the feedback loop.

It should be noted that the research supports SRL as a domain-specific construct; that is, a learner may self-regulate in one particular area, such as problem-solving in math, but may not be equally self-regulated in another domain. According to Schunk (personal communication, 2006), "researchers gave up the idea that self-regulation processes generalize automatically across disciplines years ago because of evidence of poor transfer." Thus, much of the research supporting SLR must be approached cautiously as it applies to a specific field.

What is the purpose of SRL? Early academic self-regulated learning research began as a way to help individuals alter dysfunctional behaviors such as aggression or addictions (Schunk, 2005). By introducing goal setting and awareness of a feedback loop, participants were helped to change their observable behaviors. This was soon applied to such academic areas as study skills. Next, self-regulated learning for K–12 students in academic settings gained momentum with students showing a discrepancy between skills and abilities and academic achievement (Zimmerman, 2001). Currently, SRL has been applied to a variety of disciplines, including math, science, reading, music, and physical achievement.

For the purposes of this chapter and drawing from theorists' definitions, SRL is defined as an individual's ability to weave together knowledge and control components of metacognition independently and efficiently for the purpose of meeting a self-set goal, based on sufficient cognition, motivation, and desirable context (i.e., Baker, 2002; Griffith & Ruan, 2005; Sungur & Tekkaya, 2006; Wiley, Griffin, & Theide, 2005). The interaction is a crucial indicator that the person is able to combine knowledge and control aspects of metacognition and act on that combined knowledge. That is, the interaction assumes that a person is not just a receptacle of information, but is also an agent actively combining strategy and regulation.

Theory on Self-Regulation

As previously stated, early theories on SLR were linked to the behavioral domain of psychology. SLR was intended to help adults, and later students, control destructive or inappropriate behaviors. A person self-regulates in order to avoid punishment or gain a reward (see Mace, Belfiore, & Hutchinson, 2001, for a more detailed description). Bandura pioneered much of the early work in self-regulation, including identifying subprocesses of self-regulation, including self-observation, self-judgment, and self-reaction (Bandura, 1977, 1986). His early work was rooted in a behavioristic model, focusing on the reward, not the learning, which influences behavior. Based on Bandura's early theories, many researchers began to study self-regulation subprocesses and self-regulation strategies and how these affected self-regulation in specific contexts.

During the 1960s through the 1980s, the field of psychology experienced a revolution from a behavioristic stance to a more cognitive stance. SLR was adopted by cognitive psychologists. Rewards and punishment were viewed differently than they were under the strictly behavioristic camp. Zimmerman (1989) and Schunk (1984, 1989) theorized that instead of avoiding punishment, self-regulated learners self-initiated activities that promoted learning and a sense of self-efficacy. Their perception of self-efficacy was both a motivator to learn and a reward for learning.

The theoreticians continued to meld elements of a behavioral model with a more cognitive focus. Pintrich (see Schunk, 2005 for a summary description) proposed a four-phase model of self-regulation: forethought, monitoring, control, and reaction/reflection. Within each phase, there are four possible areas for self-regulation: cognition, motivation, behavior, and context. For example, in the first phase, forethought, cognition areas for self-regulation would include goal setting, prior content knowledge, and metacognitive knowledge. Motivational processes that might be self-regulated during the forethought phase include goal orientations, self-efficacy, perceived difficulty, task value, and interest. Behaviors that might be self-regulated during the forethought stage include planning behaviors related to time, effort, and self-observation. Finally, context self-regulation could include perceptions of the context (e.g., teacher support).

By the end of the 1980s, the cognitive camp developed what we currently recognize as the theory of social constructivism (Paris, Byrnes, & Paris, 2001). This theory emphasized the importance of social situations and cultural contexts. Paris, Byrnes, and Paris (2001) offered five principles of social cognition that form a framework for constructivist views of SRL:

1. Learning is situated in social and historical contexts that shape thinking.
2. Activities in local communities provide procedures, tools, values, and customs to newcomers trying to become a part of the local community.
3. Self is formed by the individual and the local community.
4. People understand themselves by looking back at their own history and forward to anticipated futures.
5. Thinking and learning can be both beneficial and lead to maladaptive thoughts and actions (pp. 255–258).

Paris, Byrnes, and Paris summarized the importance of these five principles by stating, "In the context of SRL, the actions that become regulated promote the person's status, success, or well-being" (p. 258). Notice the shift from the more behavioristic stance which included regulation of behaviors to avoid punishment or gain reward.

When discussing theories of self-regulation, it becomes difficult to separate theories of SRL from theories of motivation, theories of metacognition, and theories of learning. Self-regulation is most often situated as a subset of metacognition (Baker, 2002; Griffith & Ruan, 2005). Metacognition is generally thought to have two main categories: the knowledge component and the control component. The learner may have the entire knowledge component but be unable to control the use of that knowledge effectively. Alternately, the learner may be able to self-regulate, but still lack the comprehensive strategies needed to learn. Encompassing all are factors that influence metacognition, including cognition, motivation, and context (Baker 2002; Garner, 1987; Pressley & Afflerbach, 1995). For example, a student's cognition may not be developmentally advanced enough to think metacognitively. Context (e.g., social constraints and cultural norms) may influence a student's desire and ability to think metacognitively about their reading. The learners may have both the knowledge and control components and still lack the motivation to use either component. Conversely, "self-regulated learners plan, set goals, organize, self-monitor, and self-evaluate at various points during the process of acquisition" (Zimmerman, 2000, pp. 4-5). Table 18.1 offers a visual representation of self-regulated learning, as defined in this chapter.

Motivation and student learning are also important pieces of the theory underlying SRL. Zimmerman (1989) and Schunk (1984, 1989) offered one explanation, writing that "student learning and motivation are treated as interdependent processes that cannot be fully understood apart from each other" (Zimmerman, 1990, p. 6). Student

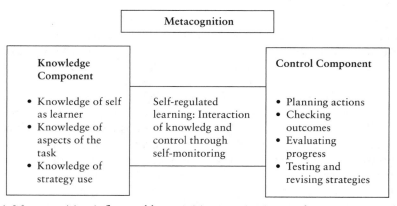

Figure 18.1 Metacognition influenced by cognition, motivation, and context.

learning and motivation, in turn, are influences on and influenced by metacognition. In a review of historical trends in SRL research, Paris and Paris (2001) pointed out that the body of knowledge about SRL is really a collection of wide-ranging topics, including social regulation, family influence on self-regulation, social and cultural influences on self-regulation, monitoring, and developmental issues influencing SRL. Paris and Paris reasoned that this was due to several factors, including the emphasis in the 1970s on isolating specific aspects of thinking for examination, an emphasis on cognitive dimensions, followed by a focus in the 1980s on strategy research—what kind of strategies do students use when approaching an academic task and what are the influences on strategy use. Strategy use research was later situated within classrooms, where individual teachers might give explicit directions about how to use one particular strategy. Eventually, this expanded to teachers giving instructions about how to use multiple strategies (e.g., Palinscar & Brown, 1984) and an awareness of the social and emotional factors influencing SRL.

Theory on self-regulation in reading

What exists as the theoretical basis for SRL in reading comprehension seems to be derived from (a) theories of SRL within the broader context of academic work, (b) theories and research of metacognition that have been appropriated to reading, and (c) strategy theory and research. There are several problems with this foundation. First, as previously stated, research on SRL in distinct fields is regarded as nongeneralizable by those most closely associated with the research. Second, our understanding of metacognition's relation to reading comprehension is incomplete, thus forming a faulty foundation for SRL's relation to reading comprehension. "It has been strongly suggested that metacognition is related to children's reading comprehension (Baker & Brown, 1984) although there is relatively little data on the relation" (Cross & Paris, 1988, p. 132). Third, following the definitions left by early theoreticians such as Zimmerman (1990) and Pintrich (2000), SRL is not the same thing as metacognition. As Zimmerman (1990) wrote, self-regulated learners use multiple metacognitive process at the same time. Thus, it is inappropriate to conclude that because a student can set goals, they are self-regulated learners. SRL involves more than strategy use, self-monitoring, and goal setting. It is each of those things working together. However, the search for landmark studies supporting SRL in reading comprehension does not show a solid background of research sustaining this complex view of SRL in our field.

LOOKING AT THE DATA: LANDMARK STUDIES AND RESEARCH BASE FOR SRL

Pintrich and Zusho (2002) pointed out that though self-regulation is recognized as an important construct in academic theory and practice, there has been little empirical research explicitly focused on self-regulation. The lack of research is certainly obvious when it comes to the use of SRL as a way to improve students' reading comprehension. Research in the broader educational field has examined individual components that may be part of SRL, including the influence of self-efficacy, goal setting, and strategy instruction. This research has generally been adopted as evidence supporting SRL for reading, specifically reading comprehension. However, as previously mentioned, there has been no evidence of generalizability of SLR processes across disciplines (Schunk, personal communication, 2006). "To foster self-regulation, one has to show students how specific strategies (e.g., goal setting, self-evaluation) apply in particular disciplines" (Schunk, personal communication, 2006). Thus, we cannot assume that research done in other areas will apply to reading comprehension, leaving us with a disturbing deficit in any research supporting SRL as a way to increase comprehension.

One of the most promising research studies specific to SRL and reading comprehension has occurred only recently, highlighting the fact that we have few landmark studies in this field. Souvignier and Mokhlesgerami (2006) asked if "the conclusions from the theoretical framework of self-regulated learning hold in an ecological setting such as a regular classroom" (p. 60). Twenty fifth-grade classes were compared on reading comprehension scores. Three classes received reading strategy lessons, five classes were taught with strategies and control aspects of self-regulation (including lessons on selecting which strategies were appropriate with certain texts, monitoring comprehension), and three classes received instruction with strategies, control aspects of self-regulation, and motivational aspects of self-regulation. These three groups were compared against nine classes serving as the control group receiving no special instruction. All groups receiving instruction outperformed the control group on measures of reading comprehension and reading strategy use. Differences between the three instructional models were minimal immediately following the implementation of the programs (September through January); however, long-term effects (defined as end of the same school year) showed that the group receiving instruction in reading strategies, knowledge aspects of self-regulation, and motivational aspects of self-regulation outperformed the other groups. In this study, we see an attempt to define SRL as knowledge and control and the measures were specific to reading comprehension. The same cannot be said of many of the studies that are often considered part of SRL research on reading comprehension.

There are some periphery studies that are often used to support SRL in reading. These studies are presented with extreme caution. While they are assumed to support SRL in reading comprehension, they are actually a collection of strategy studies or studies about the subprocesses of SRL, not SRL as a whole, leading us back to the difficulty in defining SRL. In fact, there are no SRL studies presenting direct evidence that SRL (not metacognition or the subprocesses of SRL) influences reading comprehension.

For example, the studies on Reciprocal Teaching are often taken as proof of the positive impact of SRL on comprehension. Palinscar and Brown (1984) conducted a series of studies evaluating the use of reciprocal teaching (summarizing, questioning, clarifying, and predicting) as a two pronged method for fostering comprehension and monitoring comprehension. Seventh graders reading two to three years below grade level were taught to use the four strategies. At the end of the study, students showed significant improvement in reading achievement. They also found that these gains generalized to the regular classroom settings.

Paris and colleagues (Paris, Cross, & Lipson, 1984; Paris & Jacobs, 1984) used Informed Strategies for Learning (ISL) "to stimulate greater awareness of declarative, procedural, and conditional knowledge, while also teaching children how to evaluate, plan, and regulate their own comprehension in strategic ways" (Cross & Paris, 1988, p. 133). ISL called for (a) modeling of the target strategies with discussion of rationales for each of the strategies, (b) guided practice, and (c) independent application of strategies. Paris and Jacobs (1984) reported significant correlations between comprehension and reading awareness for both the third and fifth graders in the study. The experimental group gained significantly more from pretest to posttest measures on reading awareness and strategic reading that those students in the control group.

Pressley, Levin, Ghatala, and colleagues did extensive work with monitoring (see Pressley & Ghatala, 1990, for a review of multiple studies). While one single study does not stand out as critical to the field, taken as a whole, these studies found that the nature of the test is an important determinant of student study regulation, regardless of the student age. They also found that many students were inefficient at monitoring their own reading; that is, the students were not able to select important sections of a text but relied on rehearsal and rereading strategies instead of selecting critical information.

Schunk and Rice (1989) worked with fourth- and fifth-grade students who had low comprehension. Each student received 35 minutes of strategy instruction over 15 consecutive school days. Each of the students was also placed into a treatment group. The first group, the product-goal group, was told to answer questions about what they read. The second group, the general-goal group, was told to try their best. The third group, the process-goal group, was asked to learn how to use the strategy. Posttest results determined that the children who were asked to learn to use the strategy performed higher reading comprehension achievement. Schunk and Zimmerman (2007) reflected that while this study provided evidenced emulative self-regulatory skill development, "this study did not explicitly address the self-regulated level" of skill development (p. 15). Further studies found that students who received strategy instruction with feedback on the value of strategy use (e.g., "You completed this successfully because you used the strategy.") increased their comprehension of texts more than students who received only one or the other types of instruction.

Schunk and Zimmerman (2007) summarized that their own studies and the studies of others such as those reviewed above show that (a) modeling strategies is an effective means of teaching reading strategies and (b) modeling strategies can raise student's self-efficacy, but that "moving to the self-regulated level requires that students internalize strategies" (p. 18). While these are certainly important studies, they serve to illustrate what Paris and Paris (2001) stated—that the body of knowledge about SRL is really a collection of topics on strategy use, self-efficacy, and monitoring.

The researchers do not claim that their studies support SRL; however, other theorists and researchers building literature reviews appropriate these studies as empirical evidence in support of SRL. It must be emphasized again that these topics in isolation do not fully support SRL as a way to improve comprehension. If we return to Zimmerman's (2001) frequently-cited definition, self-regulation encompasses the individual's ability to self-generate thoughts, feelings, *and* actions "that are planned and cyclically adapted to the attainment of personal goals" (p. 14). Only recently have studies begun trying to look at SRL as a complete framework instead of at individual components.

GUIDING PRINCIPLES AND READING MODELS OF SELF-REGULATED LEARNING

Because there is clearly a lack of solid research supporting SRL as a means for improving comprehension, it is premature to suggest guiding principles. Some believe that teaching comprehension strategies is the same or will substitute for self-regulation instruction.

> Rather than teaching students how to become self-regulated learners, the teachers seemed to expect that the behaviors would develop naturally if students were given enough assignments (e.g., workbook sheets) that prompted them to generate the kinds of thoughts generated by strategic readers as they read (i.e., that required them to report questions, images, or summaries that occurred to them as they read). There is, of course, no evidence that we are aware of that such prompting leads to anything like active, self-regulated use of comprehension strategies. (Pressley, 2006, p. 299)

Instructional models used to support SRL

Based on the research on SRL in other fields, the limited research on SRL and reading comprehension, and the theories proposed, it is commonly believed that in order for

SRL to affect comprehension, instruction should include three things: strategy instruction, self-directed learning opportunities, and self-assessment instruction. There are popular models of each. Strategy instruction has gained the most attention as it relates to reading, including Questioning the Author, (Beck, McKeown, & Kucan, 1997), Collaborative Strategic Reading (Klinger & Vaughn; 1999), Reciprocal Teaching (Palinscar & Brown, 1984), or Transactional Strategies Instruction (Pressley, El-Dinary, Gaskins, Schuder, Bergman, Almasi, Brown, et al., 2000). Problem-Based Learning is one popular approach to a self-directed learning model, while self-assessment is less focused on a specific model of instruction. Again, these are presented with caution, in acknowledgement of the fact that these models are often described as a way to develop self-regulated learners, but under careful examination we can see that they merely emphasize only one facet of SRL.

Questioning the Author   Questioning the Author (Beck, McKeown, & Kucan, 1997) helps students focus on understanding the text instead of finding one "correct" answer. They evaluate the point of view of the author and purpose. Initially, the teacher is the one modeling the asking of the questions. Eventually, students take over. Questions include initiating questions that focus on understanding what the text says. What is the author trying to say? What is the author's message? Next, students ask questions that evaluate the message of the author: Why does the author choose to include this particular information? Do you think the author's message is clear? This model assumes that students have knowledge of comprehension strategies and can make sense of the text. If a teacher finds that students are not able to answer the initiating questions, explicit teaching of comprehension strategies is necessary.

Collaborative Strategic Reading   Collaborative Strategic Reading (CSR) is a model for teaching that combines instruction in the use of multiple comprehension strategies with cooperative learning. Klinger and Vaughn (1999) used four strategies to help students understand a text: previewing, click and clunk (monitoring comprehension, then fixing comprehension break-downs through attention to word- and text-level strategies), get the gist (understanding the most important ideas in a text), and wrap-up (summarizing strategies). After modeling, teachers grouped students and assigned each member of the group one of the four strategies as primary responsibilities. After each student had sufficient practice with one of the four strategies, group roles might be switched.

Reciprocal Teaching   Reciprocal Teaching (RT) is one of the most consistently-referenced teaching models for fostering student self-regulation. Palinscar and Brown (1984) used four cognitive activities that were common to the majority of descriptions of critical reading: summarizing, questioning, clarifying, and predicting. Describing the process, Baker and Brown (1984) stated that each of the four activities was designed to serve the dual functions of comprehension-fostering and comprehension monitoring. Each of the four activities was taught explicitly and then modeled to the students. Students participated with the teacher and gradually were able to assume the role of teacher, coaching themselves and others through the four activities. First, students were assigned a segment of a text to be read. Next, the teacher or the student assumed the role of leader for the passage. After reading the assigned text silently, the leader summarized the content. If the summary indicated incomplete or inaccurate comprehension, clarification was sought. Then, the passage leader asked a question that a teacher might ask on a test about the passage. Finally, the leader predicted about future content.

Transactional Strategies Instruction   Transactional Strategies Instruction (TSI) (Pressley, El-Dinary, Gaskins, Schuder, Bergman, Almasi, & Brown, 1992) focuses on teaching practices as well as student comprehension strategies involved in literacy. Instruction involves extensive modeling, explanation, and coaching, with students gradually assuming responsibilities from the teachers for strategy use. Transactions occur between teachers and students, between readers and texts, and between students and students (El-Dinary, 2002). These transactions help shape the understandings of the text. TSI relies on reader response theory and psychological theories. Multiple transactions occur between the teacher and students, among the students within the reading group, and between the readers and the text. The teacher acts as a guide and model for comprehension strategies and interpretive processes. Pressley et al. emphasized the use of multiple strategies, stating, "Strategies is pluralized because students are taught to coordinate a repertoire of strategic processes" (p. 515). As the teacher leads a small group, she may begin modeling with a specific strategy, but she remains open to changing directions based on students' needs. "A long-term goal of this type of teaching is the students' self-regulated strategies the teacher encourages during reading group" (516).

Pressley et al. (1992) did not specify the comprehension strategies to be used, though they suggested that visualizing, accessing background knowledge, surveying, and asking for clarification were important strategies to be included in the repertoire of strategies taught. Though sharing some commonalities with RT, the researchers differentiated TSI from RT in several ways, including the use of more direct explanation of comprehension strategies, longer times given for instruction and introducing new strategies, and more focus on motivation of students.

These models do not necessarily include a regulatory approach. Paris and Paris (2001) were careful to point out that these approaches were designed to help students be more strategic readers. How much students use these strategies can be affected by the contexts that teachers provide. Problem-Based Learning (PBL) is one teaching approach aimed at providing opportunities for strategy-use within self-directed learning. Paris and Paris (2001) stated, "PBL promotes SRL because it places the responsibility on the students to find information, to coordinate actions and people, to reach goals, and to monitor understanding" (p. 94). Sungur and Tekkaya (2006) explored this connection between PBL and SRL. High school students were assigned to a treatment or control group. The control group received traditional biology instruction about the human respiratory and excretory systems. Students in the treatment group participated in a PBL experience. Results were mixed. The authors reported, "Although we showed that PBL had a positive influence on students' intrinsic goal orientation and task value, it did not affect control of learning beliefs, self-efficacy for learning and performance, and text anxiety" (p. 315). They did find that PBL enhanced students' use of strategies, effort regulation, peer learning, and their ability to apply existing knowledge to novel situation for problem solving purposes as opposed to the control group. The authors concluded that "PBL enhances the self-regulatory skills of 10th grade students" (p. 316). This was not applied to reading comprehension.

Paris and Paris (2001) proposed that self-assessment (sometimes described as self-monitoring) may be the link that combines strategy instruction and self-directed learning. "Learning depends on assessment of both product and process to know what is know, what requires additional effort, and what skills are effective" (p. 95). Thus, students are able to identify what strategies worked to bring about successful learning or unsuccessful attempts, monitor their progress, and regulate their efforts in additional attempts. When referring to reading, self-assessment includes using inner control to monitor reading behaviors (Clay, 1991; Joseph, 2005).

Black and Wiliam's (1998) extensive review of classroom assessment literature determined that self-assessment is part of the feedback loop that can raise students' academic performance as well as their self-esteem—what Afflerbach & Meuwissen (2005) described as the student's "sense of self as a reader" (p. 145). As students take responsibility for their own assessment, they are more likely to attribute success to their own effort, resulting in increased motivation to read. Traditional assessments often over-emphasize comparisons between students and lack substantive feedback for how students can improve, creating "a dependency for students; if they want to know how they are doing, they must rely on someone else to do the assessment" (Afflerbach & Meuissen, 2005, p. 147). Without a clear picture of what changes are needed, feedback (or lack of feedback) may reinforce learned helplessness or a defeatist attitude. In contrast, self-assessment includes comparisons to an individual goal or a specific standard and reinforces a student's perception of control.

Each of these instructional models is mentioned because they offer promise for future research on SRL; however the link between the models and SRL influencing reading comprehension remains theoretical. The field of reading comprehension has spent much time researching the first component of instruction suggested to influence SRL—strategy instruction. We have yet to offer definitive reading research to the collection of studies on self-directed learning and self-assessment instruction. These models are not equal to SRL. While SRL may become part of the models, we must be vigilant not to mistake one measure as a sign of SRL.

SIGNIFICANT CONTRIBUTION AND FUTURE DIRECTIONS

The topic of self-regulated learning has the potential to make a significant contribution to our knowledge base about teaching reading comprehension. First, it combines what we know about reading processes with metacognition and motivational research. These fields were long separated, even considered part of different departments in universities. Second, a focus on SRL moves us beyond the teacher as expert and students as repositories for content information. We center more fully on what it means to be a reader—complete with abilities to monitor one's own comprehension and regulate motivational factors. Third, SRL helps us consider more than just comprehension strategies. While the emphasis of comprehension strategy instruction has been useful for the field, merely teaching strategies does not ensure that our students know how and when to use them. Still, there is significant work to be done in order to better understand how to include SRL as a regular part of classroom reading instruction.

As researchers, we must be cautious about our enthusiasm for SRL. Zimmerman (1990) noted that assuming personal responsibility for learning and bettering oneself has long been a hallmark of the American dream. The sense of independence, efficiency, and "pulling ones' self up by the bootstraps" has shaped American democracy, economics, and certainly our education system. We must also consider students' interpretations of SRL. Paris, Byrnes, and Paris (2001) warned that while teachers and researchers view SRL as positive, students may not, or they may self-regulate those behaviors that allow them acceptance within their peer group:

> Too often, traditional accounts of SRL have assumed that students want to use effective strategies and want to be high achievers and they only lack knowledge about how to do so. Our account is decidedly different. We emphasize that students are regulated in their actions in order to enhance their social representation to others. . . If acting like X leads to positive acceptance, it is likely that students will direct their behavior and learning to become a better X. (p. 259)

The most obvious direction needed is a solid base of empirical studies on self-regulated comprehension. Contrary to what many believe, there is not a solid research base now. Looking at studies linked to SRL, we see a significant gap in time, with most of the studies conducted in the 1980s and then a long, quiet period with little to no research conducted. It is only recently, with such researchers as Souvignier and Mokhlesgerami (2006), that we are beginning to see studies applying SRL to reading comprehension. What we do have are collections and reviews of previously done studies of components of SRL in other fields, as if we can cite the benefits of SRL enough to make it valid in comprehension. We need to move beyond collections of studies on isolated components of self-regulation and rigorously study how SRL affects comprehension instruction. If we are to continue to build our understanding of SRL, we need (a) an agreed upon definition of SRL, (b) studies that combine strategy instruction, self-directed learning components, and self-assessment instruction, (c) common understandings about what counts as evidence of SRL, (d) ways of evaluating SRL, (e) further research about SRL specific to reading comprehension, and (f) specific methods of implementing SRL into classroom contexts. If we truly want to influence students' comprehension through SRL, then we must move beyond accepting theory for research, accepting strategy instruction for SRL, and assuming SRL will be viewed only as positive by our students.

REFERENCES

Afflerbach, P., & Meuwissen, K. (2005). Middle school self-assessment. In S. Israel, C. C. Block, K. Bauserman, & K. Kinnucan-Welsch (Eds.), *Metacognition in literacy learning* (pp. 141–164). Mahwah, NJ: Erlbaum.

Baker, L. (2002). Metacognition in comprehension instruction. In C.. Block & M. Pressley (Eds.), *Comprehension instruction* (pp. 77–95). New York: Guilford.

Baker, L., & Brown, A. L. (1984). Metacognitive skills and reading. In P. D. Pearson, R. Barr, M. Kamil, & P. Mosenthal (Eds.), *Handbook of Reading Research, Vol. I* (pp. 353–394). New York: Longman.

Bandura, A. (1977). Self-efficacy: Toward a unifying theory of behavioral change. *Psychological Review, 84,* 191–215.

Bandura, A. (1986). *Social foundations of thought and action: A social cognitive theory.* Englewood Cliffs, NJ: Prentice-Hall.

Beck, I., McKeown, M., & Kucan, L. (1997). *Questioning the author: An approach for enhancing student engagement with text.* Newark, DE: International Reading Association.

Black, P., & Wiliam, D. (1998). Inside the black box: Raising standards through classroom assessment. *Phi Delta Kappan,* 139–148.

Clay, M. (1991). *Becoming literate: The construction of inner control.* Portsmouth, NH: Heinemann.

Cross, D., & Paris, S. (1988). Developmental and instructional analyses of children's metacognition and reading comprehension [Electronic version]. *Journal of Educational Psychology, 80,* 131–142.

El-Dinary, P.B. (2002). Challenges of implementing Transactional Strategies Instruction for reading comprehension. In C. C. Block & M. Pressley (Eds.), *Comprehension instruction* (pp. 201–215). New York: Guilford.

Garner, R. (1987). *Metacognition and reading comprehension.* Norwood, NJ: Ablex Publishing Corporation.

Griffith, P., & Ruan, J. (2005). What is metacognition and what should be its role in literacy instruction. In S. Israel, C. C. Block, K. Bauswerman, K. Kinnucan-Welsch, *Metacognition in literacy learning* (pp. 3–18). Mahwah, NJ: Erlbaum.

Joseph, L. (2005). The role of self-monitoring in literacy learning. In S. Israel, C. C. Block, K. Bauswerman, & K. Kinnucan-Welsch, *Metacognition in literacy learning* (pp. 199–241). Mahwah, NJ: Erlbaum.

Klinger, J. K., & Vaughn, S. (1999). Promoting reading comprehension, content learning, and English acquisition through collaborative strategic reading (CSR). *Reading Teacher, 52,* 738–747.

Mace, F. C., Belfiore, P. J., & Hutchinson, J. M. (2001). Operant theory and research on self-regulation. In B. Zimmerman & D. Schunk (Eds.), *Self-regulated learning and academic achievement* (pp. 39–65). New York: Springer-Verlag.

Palinscar, A. S., & Brown, A. L. (1984). Reciprocal teaching of comprehension-monitoring activities. *Cognition and Instruction, 1,* 117–175.

Paris, S. G., Byrnes, J. P., & Paris, A. H. (2001). Constructing theories, identities, and actions of self-regulated learners. In B. Zimmerman & D. Schunk (Eds.), *Self-regulated learning and academic achievement* (pp. 253–287). New York: Springer-Verlag.

Paris, S. G., Cross, D. R., & Lipson, M. Y. (1984). Informed strategies for learning: A program to improve children's reading awareness and comprehension. *Journal of Educational Psychology, 76,* 1239–1252.

Paris, S. G., & Jacobs, J. E. (1984). The benefits of informed instruction for children's reading awareness and comprehension skills. *Child Development, 55,* 2083–2093.

Paris, S. G., & Paris, A. H. (2001). Classroom applications of research on self-regulated learning, *Educational Psychologist, 36*(2), 89–101.

Pintrich, P. (2000). The role of goal orientation in self-regulated learning. In M. Boekaerts, P. R. Pintrich, & M. Zeidner (Eds.), *Handbook of self-regulation* (pp. 451–502). San Diego, CA: Academic.

Pintrich, P., & Zusho, A. (2002). The development of academic self-regulation: The role of cognitive and motivational factors. In A. Wigfield & J. Eccles (Eds.), *Development of achievement motivation* (pp. 250–284). San Diego, CA: Academic.

Pressley, M. (2006). *Reading instruction that works.* New York: Guilford.

Pressley, M., & Afflerbach, P. (1995). *Verbal protocols of reading: The nature of constructively responsive reading.* Hillsdale, NJ: Erlbaum.

Pressley, M., El-Dinary, P. B., Gaskins, I., Schuder, T., Bergman, J. L., Almasi, J., Brown, Rheinberg, F., Vollmeyer, R., & Rollett, W. (2000). Motivation and action in self-regulated learning. In M. Boekaerts, P. R. Pintrich, & M. Zeidner (Eds.), *Handbook of self-regulation* (pp. 503–529). San Diego, CA: Academic.

Pressley, M., & Ghatala, E. S. (1990). Self-regulated learning: Monitoring learning from text. *Educational Psychologist, 25,* 19–33.

Pressley, M., Levin, J. R., Ghatala, E. S., & Ahmad, M. (1987). Test monitoring in young grade school children. *Journal of Experimental Child Psychology, 43,* 96–111.

Schunk, D. (1984). The self-efficacy perspective on achievement behavior. *Educational Psychologist, 19,* 199–218.

Schunk, D. (1989). Social cognitive theory and self-regulated learning. In B. J. Zimmerman & D. H. Schunk (Eds.), *Self-regulated learning and academic achievement: Theory, research, and practice* (pp. 83–110). New York: Springer-Verlag.

Schunk, D. (2005). Self-regulated learning: The educational legacy of Paul R. Pintrich. *Educational Psychologist, 40,* 85–94.

Schunk, D., & Rice, J. (1989). Learning goals and children's reading comprehension. *Journal of Reading Behavior, 21,* 279–293.

Schunk, D., & Zimmerman, B. (2007). Influencing children's self-efficacy and self-regulation of reading and writing through modeling. *Reading & Writing Quarterly, 23,* 7–25.

Souvignier, E., & Mokhlesgerami, J. (2006). Using self-regulation as a framework for implementing strategy instruction to foster reading comprehension. *Learning and Instruction, 16,* 57–71.

Sungur, S., & Tekkaya, C. (2006). Effects of problem-based learning and traditional instruction on self-regulated learning. *The Journal of Educational Research, 99,* 307–317.

Wiley, J., Griffin, T., & Theide, K. (2005). Putting the comprehension in metacomprehension. *The Journal of General Psychology, 132*(4), 408–428.

Zimmerman, B. J. (1989). Models of self-regulated learning and academic achievement. In B. J. Zimmerman & D. H. Schunk (Eds.), *Self-regulated learning and academic achievement: Theory, research, and practice* (pp. 1–25). New York: Springer-Verlag.

Zimmerman, B. J. (1990). Self-regulated learning and academic achievement: An overview. *Educational Psychologist, 25,* 3–17.

Zimmerman, B. J. (2000). Attaining self-regulation: A social cognitive perspective. In M. Boekaerts, P. Pintrich, & M. Zeidner (Eds.), *Self-regulation: Theory, research, and applications* (pp. 13–39). Orlando, FL: Academic.

Zimmerman, B. J. (2001). Theories of self-regulated learning and academic achievement: An overview and analysis. In B. J. Zimmerman & D. H. Schunk (Eds.), *Self-regulated learning and academic achievement: Theoretical perspectives* (2nd ed., pp. 1–38). Mahwah, NJ: Erlbaum.

Part V

Assessing and Teaching Reading Comprehension

19 Formal and Informal Measures of Reading Comprehension

Lauren Leslie

Marquette University

JoAnne Caldwell

Cardinal Stritch University

A review of research on assessments of reading comprehension should begin with a definition of the construct to be measured; in this case, reading comprehension. Although we considered beginning this chapter by presenting a theoretically based definition, we realized that in doing so we would necessarily restrict our review of assessments to those that fit the theory we had chosen, and therefore, our discussion would not be representative of the variety of assessments available to researchers and practitioners. Instead, we decided to review the research on assessments of reading comprehension and while doing so we would make explicit the theories that underlie each type of assessment.

THEORETICAL AND HISTORICAL PERSPECTIVES

A model of reading comprehension should be the foundation of the assessment development process. Unfortunately when assessments have been developed, the models of reading comprehension that serve as their foundation have rarely been explicitly defined. This problem and its results have been discussed by the Committee on the Foundations of Assessment, National Research Council (2001):

> To increase the chances of collecting evidence that supports the types of inferences one wants to draw, the design and selection of assessment tasks, along with the procedures for evaluating students' responses, should be guided jointly by the cognition and interpretation elements of the observations. The process of construct validation during test design should rest, in part, on evidence that the assessment tasks actually tap the cognitive content and processes intended. (p. 176)

A similar position was taken by Shepard (1993) when she stated that "logical analysis of test content and empirical confirmation of hypothesized relationships are both essential to defending the validity of test interpretations; however, neither is sufficient alone" (p. 443).

The main issue raised by the Committee and by Shepard is an old and central one: the process of construct validation. Over 30 years ago Cronbach stated: "One doesn't validate an assessment. Rather one validates the interpretation of data arising from a specific procedure" (1971, p. 447). Similarly, in his classic update of validity theory, Messick (1989) argued that construct validity is the one unifying conception of validity and it extends beyond the concept of test score meaning to include score utility and consequences. That is, evidence of construct validity requires not only that evidence supporting the meaning of the test score be provided, but also that the intended consequences of the test be examined. For example, what are the consequences of giving

403

a second-grade student a test of reading comprehension? The consequences could be many. The child could be evaluated for placement in a special education classroom. In this case, the consequence of the assessment could be placement or nonplacement and the benefits or disadvantages of the placement should be examined. Another second grader could be evaluated to determine the specific comprehension strategies that he or she needs in order to comprehend narrative text. In this case the stakes are not so high, but if the assessment indicated that the child was competent in retelling narrative text, yet it was not a valid measure of that ability, then the student would not receive the appropriate instruction. Although *all* the misuses of a test are not in the control of the test author or publisher, the test manual should describe the intended uses of the scores and potential misuses.

If in writing this chapter we only included reading comprehension assessments that were designed from a clearly defined theoretical model, were supported by research that validated the construct of reading comprehension being measured, and that specified the valid inferences to be made from the assessment, there would be no chapter to write. Although there are implicit models of reading comprehension at play whenever someone designs an assessment of it, few assessments have made their models explicit. Rather, we are left to infer the models based on the elements of reading that are measured. For example, some assessments of reading comprehension are quite general and implicitly define reading comprehension as some combination of vocabulary and passage comprehension. These instruments design assessments to measure students' understanding of words in context or in isolation, and also measure their understanding of short paragraphs of text. But there has been no systematic attempt to specify the processes used to understand the text. That is, there is no explicit description of how the reader constructs meaning in the text that is then measured by the assessment.

For example, when a student reads a paragraph and answers different types of questions, what is happening cognitively? What processes are being used to construct meaning sufficient for answering particular types of questions? These descriptions are missing on most assessments, particularly those of the formal variety. Because these processes are not described and verified we have little evidence that the items are in fact measuring the processes assumed to underlie the items. To put this another way, there is little evidence beyond logical analysis that scores on items purporting to measure inferential comprehension allow us to infer the conditions under which a student will be able to make valid inferences. Similarly, what do the scores on passages designed to measure explicit comprehension actually assess? Can we infer the process of reading comprehension just because it appears that items are measuring it? These are the validity issues that we will address when we examine formal standardized measures of reading comprehension.

On the other end of the specificity continuum are assessments developed in research laboratories that explicitly describe the theory that underlies them and designs measures of many subprocesses of comprehension (Kintsch & Kintsch, 2005). In addition, some researchers go so far as to suggest that to fully understand reading comprehension we must measure students' feelings about and engagement in the process of meaning construction (Guthrie & Wigfield, 2005). One example of such an approach would be to examine the motivation of students given the different types of assessment measures. For example, do students exert the same amount of mental effort when they answer a multiple-choice item as when they answer a constructed-response item? The description above illustrates that methods of assessing reading comprehension can be described along a continuum of the precision or specificity of the model assumed and the degree to which the measures are specified.

We have chosen to organize the formal assessments of reading comprehension section of this chapter around the complexity of the theory that underlies the assessments.

Therefore, we will begin with the most general models implied in the assessments of reading comprehension and end with more specific models. In addition, we will focus on the major issue of whether there is evidence for a unitary construct of reading comprehension or whether the conclusions made from a test of reading comprehension must be qualified by the reading of what, under what conditions, and for what purposes (Duke, 2005).

FORMAL ASSESSMENTS OF READING COMPREHENSION

Landmark studies

The measurement of reading comprehension using short paragraphs and multiple choice response options and constructed responses has a long research history. The classic study of the skills that comprise comprehension as measured by a standardized multiple-choice test was conducted by Davis (1944) who began by reviewing the literature on the skills describing reading comprehension and then conducted what Shepard (1993) would call a logical analysis. He categorized the skills into nine groups that he thought were conceptually distinct: "recalling word meanings, drawing inferences about the meaning of a word from the content, following the structure of a passage, formulating the main thought of a passage, finding answers to questions answered explicitly or merely in paraphrase in the content, weaving together ideas in the content, drawing inferences from the content, identifying a writer's techniques, literary devices, tone and mood, and recognizing the author's purpose, intent and point of view" (Davis, 1968, p. 504). Multiple choice items (with five choices) that he judged assessed these nine skills were developed and administered to over 400 college freshmen. The reliability coefficients of these nine tests varied considerably, in part, because the number of items used to measure the nine skills varied from 5 to 60. An additional weakness of Davis's earlier study was that items testing different skills were taken from the same passage; therefore, the correlations among the skills were inflated because of their interdependency upon the content of the passages. Five factors were identified that best explained the intercorrelations among items, but the first two accounted for more variance than the others: Knowledge of word meanings, verbal reasoning, sensitivity to implications, following the structure of a passage, and recognizing the literary techniques of a writer. Davis (1968) followed up his 1944 study by combining two of the nine item types, but this time he developed unique passages in which to embed items measuring different skills. Using many large samples he found that the largest percentages of unique comprehension variance were accounted for by items assessing memory for word meanings (32%) and drawing inferences from the content (20%), supporting the findings of Thorndike (1917). Davis's and Thorndike's findings formed the foundation of standardized tests of reading comprehensions for decades.

The first significant change in the assessment of reading comprehension occurred during the mastery learning movement of the 1970s and early 1980s. During this period educators were looking to find the particular reading subskills necessary for competent reading. The theory was that if they could divide the construct of reading comprehension, for example, into its discrete skills, then teaching those skills would result in improvement of comprehension. The curricula and tests of that era were replete with skills areas such as: sequencing, getting the main idea, and summarizing. The impact of curricula and tests adhering to such a theory was dramatic. In Wisconsin, for example, reading teachers were given the onerous task of managing the testing of these skills rather than teaching children to read. What practitioners learned during that era was that students might be able to score 80% on the skills test (the criterion chosen to represent mastery), but they were often unable to transfer that skill to a story or nonfiction text. In other words, teachers were unable to generalize the results of the assessments to students' reading in other contexts, or put another way, the tests were not valid indicators of the students' ability to reliably demonstrate the skill in a wide variety of contexts. This lack of generalizabiltiy and the simultaneous recognition that reading comprehension was a more complex construct than simply a set of skills led to challenges of the mastery learning approach to instruction and assessment.

Dissatisfaction with the mastery learning approach and the significant research on reading comprehension conducted in the 1980s by researchers at the Center for Reading Research (University of Illinois) led to a major shift in how reading comprehension was taught and ultimately assessed. The research studies that demonstrated that comprehension was influenced by the knowledge base of the reader and the structure of text as well as by students' understanding of reading strategies led the field to recognize that reading comprehension was not a unitary construct. It was argued that scores on standardized tests could not be generalized to situations where other passage types were used (e.g., narrative vs. expository) or to situations where the student's knowledge base was decidedly different (Johnston, 1984). Recognition of these influences on comprehension led several researchers to advocate that state level assessments of reading comprehension should include longer passages and measures of prior content and strategy knowledge, and simultaneously called for reporting separate scores for narrative and expository text. One data set that provided significant information about how the complex process of reading comprehension might be measured came from the Illinois Goal Assessment Program (1991). Several research questions were addressed using that data base. One question was whether reading comprehension was a unitary construct or whether the measurement of related constructs such as strategy knowledge and habits and attitudes toward reading represented different constructs. Factor analyses of data from over 2,700 Illinois students in Grades 3, 6, 8, and 10 found three factors to emerge. One factor was a combination of the prior knowledge and comprehension items, a second factor included the measure of metacognitive ability, and a third factor included the habits and attitudes measures (Pearson & Hamm, 2005). Additional research on how to best measure prior knowledge found that different methods illustrated different types of knowledge (Valencia, Stallman, Commeyras, Pearson, & Hartman, 1991).

Another focus of the Illinois research effort was to examine the effects of item formats on what was measured. The authors assumed that a relaxed, conversational interview would provide the most accurate representation of eighth-grade students' reading comprehension. The interview began with a prompt from which the students responded for as long as they wanted. Then the interviewer asked a series of questions that broke the topic down into more specific subtopics. They examined the ability of items written in four different formats to mimic the type of information gained from the interview. The item formats directed students to mark one correct answer, mark as many answers as they felt were correct, rate the choices of answers using a 0-1-2 scale, and select a set of questions that would best measure understanding of the passage they had just read. The results indicated that the "rate the choice of answers" format shared the most variance with the interview, followed in order by "select all plausible answers," the "single right answer" format, and the "select questions" format (Pearson & Hamm, 2005).

A separate study conducted using the third- through tenth-grade data set examined whether item formats judged to be more representative of deeper processes would cluster together and those judged to represent more superficial processes would do likewise. Unfortunately, the factor analyses found *that the passage from which the items were drawn* was the sole explanatory factor, not the cognitive process assumed to be assessed. These results support Shepard's (1993) claim that a logical analysis of items, even by experts in a field, cannot necessarily identify the underlying cognitive processes being measured.

A recent study of eighth and tenth graders replicated the impact of the passage from which items were written on reading comprehension. Lee (2002) analyzed the effects of passage, item, person, genre, and theme to determine if blocking on these variables would result in better generalizability coefficients and lower standard errors of measurement. Although the generalizability coefficients were somewhat greater when genre and content were considered as fixed factors, the coefficient was significantly improved when theme and passage were considered. Stated simply, the accuracy with which scores on a standardized test can be generalized is increased when the effects of theme and passage are considered separately. This finding suggests that tests should report scores separately across theme (three or four themes are recommended) and passage rather than the current practice of summing them and reporting a total score.

Reviews of current frequently used standardized measures of reading comprehension indicated that despite the calls for improved evidence of the validity of inferences made from the scores (see Cronbach, 1971; Messick, 1989; Shepard, 1993), research has not adequately addressed construct validity. An examination of the *Iowa Test of Basic Skills (ITBS) Guide to Research and Development* (2003) found that although the authors cited the writings of Cronbach and Messick, they decided that the most important aspect of validity to which an achievement test should be judged was content validity: the degree to which the content of the test appears to measure the curriculum of the district using the test. The ITBS authors suggest (p. 27) that "those responsible for making the content validity determination should either take the test and judge the appropriateness of the content given the district's curriculum, or answer three questions: 1) Are all of the cognitive processes considered important in the school represented on the test? 2) Are any desirable cognitive processes omitted? 3) Are any specific skills or abilities required for successful test performance unrelated to the goals of instruction?" Unfortunately, there was no effort to validate whether or not the items that appear to measure the cognitive processes were in fact doing so.

Similar results appeared when the California Achievement Test (CAT/5) was reviewed in the *Mental Measurements Yearbook* (McMorris, Liu, & Bringsjord, 2004). The CAT/5 developers used a thinking process framework to help balance the types of thought processes students would be required to use when responding to all items in the multiple-choice batteries. Items for all CAT/5 subtests were classified into six categories: gathering information, organizing information, analyzing information, generating ideas, synthesizing elements, and evaluating outcomes. Several tables of classified items were presented to allow school officials to evaluate the thinking process coverage against their local curricular emphasis. Again this is a logical analysis of content with no empirical verification. Carney and Schattgen (1994) noted in their critique of the CAT/5 that "issues of construct and criterion-related validity need more coverage" (p. 118) and that reviews of previous CAT editions have found "substantial" overlap between the CAT and its companion ability measure, the Test of Cognitive Skills. Therefore, although Carney and Schattgen (1994) called on the CAT/5 developers to discuss this issue, it does not appear from the 2004 review of the latest technical materials by McMorris, Liu, and Bringsjord, that CAT developers have done so.

Pearson and Hamm (2001) continued the research on item effects conducted within the Illinois Goal Assessment Program (1991) described earlier, but this time used a think-aloud procedure rather than an interview, and passages from the 1996 National Assessment of Educational Progress (NAEP). Rather than asking what item type best predicted another criterion, these studies focused on how item types affected both the cognitive processes in which students engaged and also how the items elicited effort or dispositions toward responding. They asked eighth graders to think aloud while responding to constructed response items or multiple-choice items and used a category scheme that indexed a wide array of cognitive behaviors. In their first examination of the data, few differences between item formats were found. However, after examining student responses to poetry and developing a category scheme based on cognitive flexibility theory, they reanalyzed the data from the first study and found marked differences in the types of responses elicited by constructed response versus multiple choice items.

Cognitive flexibility theory suggests that domains or cases that are "ill-structured" are best approached with a cognition that is "flexible." Flexible thinking is defined by three characteristics: that which avoids oversimplification and overregularization when reading a complex text, using multiple representations (many schemas, prototypes, analogies, etc.), and comparing multiple "sections" within a single text, such as stanzas in a poem, events in a narrative, or conceptual sections of an expository piece. Pearson and Hamm's (2001) case studies showed that short essay items elicited a greater proportion of cognitively engaging strategies. Furthermore, item format differences remained when they examined responses that exhibited linking across texts and using multiple representations. They concluded by stating that questions that are not *only* open-ended, but also ask students to make connections between and within texts, and questions that ask students to consider multiple aspects of theme, character, plot, conflict, or perspective can aid in increasing deeper engagement. However, they also found evidence that constructed response items may confuse a reader who is not used to or adept at thinking flexibly, and can cause confusion if students are acculturated into believing there *is only one right answer*.

Theoretically based measures of reading comprehension

The only other place where we found theoretically motivated research on the validity of formal measures of reading comprehension was in the laboratory at the University of Colorado. The assessments being examined in Kintsch's laboratory attempt to differentiate between three components of reading comprehension: processing of the text, inferencing, and knowledge use (Kintsch & Kintsch, 2005) measured through constructed responses (i.e., essays). The essays are judged by human raters and Latent Semantic Analysis (LSA), a machine learning method that constructs a representation of meaning that is similar to the structure of human knowledge of words and texts (Landauer & Dumais, 1997; Landauer, Foltz, & Laham, 1998). The system constructs this representation by observing how words are used in a large number of texts. Rather than examining the meaning of each word, it analyzes the relationship among all of the words and documents in a corpus. It handles words with multiple meanings by examining their inter-item correlations in the same context. The measure of their relation is the cosine between words or documents, and can be interpreted like a correlation coefficient. For example, Kintch and Kintch (2005) described how LSA addresses the word *mint* using its three meanings: mint leaves of a plant, a flavored candy, and to coin money. Although *mint* is related to each of these phrases (.20, .23, and .33, respectively), these phrases are not related to each other (.05); therefore, are not likely to be included in the same text sample.

Kintsch and Kintsch report the following correlations between LSA and two human raters on two measures of comprehension: recall of text (.77 for LSA vs. .76 for the human raters), and inference protocols (.51 for LSA vs. .81 for human raters). These results suggest that LSA has further to go to be as reliable in rating inferences as humans are. Their study comparing recall of text information and inference generation evident in the essays found that the recall and inference scores of 73 of the 102 college students were within 1.5 standard deviations of each other suggesting that the majority of the students were similarly able to recall the text and make inferences from it. However, they identified 23 students whose inference scores were 1.5 standard deviations lower than their recall scores, independent of whether their recall scores were high or low. That is, independent of whether their recall scores were high or low, their inference generation was significantly lower. There was only one student whose inference score was 1.5 SDs higher than his/her recall score. Kintsch and Kintsch concluded that the ability to recall text sets an upper limit to students' ability to answer inference questions.

Implications for practice

The implications of the results of this research review are significant. First, test producers cannot easily take the same content and make multiple-choice and constructed response items designed to tap understanding of it. Rather, if deep cognitive engagement is the goal of standardized achievement testing, then the format of such assessments will have to change. That is, they must require students to compare and contrast sections of text or several texts and ask them to examine texts using a variety of lenses. Second, we believe the progress in developing valid assessments of reading comprehension will require theoretical foundations. It is important to note that the only way that Pearson and Hamm found item format differences was to entertain a theoretical lens. Furthermore, the laboratory work of Kintsch and Kintsch (2005) provides a direction that future research should follow to understand whether or not their theory can guide the development of assessment of P–12 school based learning.

INFORMAL MEASURES OF READING COMPREHENSION

The same lack of connection between the theoretical foundations of assessment and the specific procedures used to measure reading comprehension that were discussed in the section on formal measures of reading comprehension apply to informal assessments as well. The Rand Reading Study Group (2002) identified three different types or outcomes of comprehension: knowledge, application and engagement. Knowledge includes successful comprehension of the text, integration of text information with prior knowledge, and critical evaluation of content. Application involves applying what was comprehended to new situations and tasks. Engagement represents the individual's involvement with the text. Most existing informal assessments of reading comprehension seldom address integration, evaluation, application or engagement (Francis, Fletcher, Catts, & Tomblin, 2005; National Research Council, 2001).

The absence of landmark studies involving informal assessment is disheartening. Articles on informal assessment tend to be general in nature focusing on the purposes of assessment (Carlisle & Rice, 2004; Glaser & Silver, 1994; Snyder, Caccamise, & Wise, 2005); descriptions of assessment techniques (Afflerbach, 2004; Black & Wiliam, 1998; Calfee & Miller, 2005; Carlisle & Rice, 2004; Paris & Paris, 2001); guidelines for assessment design (Afflerbach, 2004; National Research Council, 2001; Nichols, 1994; Tierney, 1998); clarification of terminology (Calfee & Miller, 2005); and new directions for assessment involving technology (Ercikan, 2006; Snyder, Caccamise, & Wise, 2005). Rarely is the theoretical base of informal assessments examined. Seldom are informal assessment techniques examined for their own sake with the validity and reliability of such measures compared, and evaluated. Similar to the formal measures of reading comprehension, correlational analyses are used to establish the test-retest reliability and concurrent and predictive validity of informal assessments. Yet, informal measures used in the classroom emphasize construct validity and diagnostic usefulness (Carpenter & Paris, 2005) and such instruments are often accused of being subjective, biased and unreliable. Any discussion of informal assessment measures must address these issues.

We define informal measures as assessments that do not interpret scores using comparative or normative data or employ standardized procedures for administration and scoring. Informal measures are primarily used by classroom teachers and assessment specialists to draw inferences about student performance and to inform instruction; that is, to make instructional modifications as suggested by student achievement. As such, they are closely related to curricular content and instructional strategies (Wixson & Carlisle, 2005). We include the following as examples of informal assessments of reading comprehension: questions, recall or retellings, informal reading inventories, think-alouds, sentence verification tasks, and a wide variety of assessments grouped under the general heading of performance or authentic assessments.

Classroom assessment

Most informal assessments of reading comprehension occur in the school or classroom as teachers and assessment specialists select or construct instruments to evaluate and summarize student performance. While external testing is often directed at program evaluation, internal or classroom assessments are used for making instructional adjustments, for evaluating student effort, performance and growth, and for assigning grades. As such, classroom assessment tends to be closely related to curricular content and instructional strategies (Wixson & Carlisle, 2005) and is closely aligned to the context of the instruction that preceded it (Brookhart, 2003). Such instruction often involves not just reading but listening and viewing visual aids and multimedia as well and it is impossible to identify the exact contributions of each to student performance. In addition to typical assessment options such as selected and constructed response items, a variety of performance and portfolio assessments have been recommended as options for assessing reading comprehension in the classroom (Afflerbach, 2004; Carlisle & Rice, 2004; National Research Council, 2001).

Most studies have not examined classroom testing and grading practices as specifically related to reading comprehension. However, in determining if students have understood a body of content such as language arts, social studies or science, it can be argued that reading comprehension is one key variable in such assessments. Also, examining classroom assessments in general offers insight into how teachers may use and evaluate assessments of reading comprehension. For these reasons, we believe that addressing classroom assessment in areas other than reading warrants inclusion in this chapter.

Teachers rely on a variety of assessments. While some are prepared by the teachers themselves, they also make substantial use of published assessment measures. Elementary reading teachers view a wide range of different comprehension assessments as being effective (Campbell, 2001) including informal reading inventories, literature response journals, conferences, critical thinking measures, rubric-based measures and essay/short answer assessments. Teachers value observation as an effective tool and feel that mandated building or district assessments are less helpful than examining students' written work, listening to retellings, asking questions, and taking anecdotal records (Deno, 1985; Taylor & Pearson, 2005).

The theoretical bases or assumptions that teachers have about what should be assessed have not been systematically studied. However, a review of classroom assessment finds that measures typically focus on superficial or rote learning and teachers usually do not analyze the questions they select from published materials such as teacher manuals (Black & Wiliam, 1998; Crooks, 1988). When teachers differentiate the level of their assessments as recall knowledge or higher order thinking, there is a tendency to consider understanding, reasoning and application as one kind of skill (McMillan, Myran, & Workman, 2002). This is unfortunate inasmuch as reasoning and application may represent different or higher levels of comprehension (Kintsch, 2005; National Research Council, 2001).

Classroom assessment practices tend to be highly individual and extremely idiosyncratic (Cizek, Fitzgerald, & Rachor, 1996; McMillan, 2003). Such assessments are shaped by internal factors such as individual teacher beliefs in the importance of helping students, promoting student understanding, and accommodating individual differences. External factors such as state mandated tests and school and district policies also influence classroom assessment practices (Black & Wiliam, 1998; McMillan, 2003). The highly individual nature of classroom assessment is a concern because it suggests that assessment of reading comprehension is similarly idiosyncratic to a specific teacher or classroom and has little theoretical foundation.

Much classroom assessment is formative in nature; that is, used to provide information and feedback to students and to modify instruction and learning activities. If used effectively, formative assessment can raise student achievement (Black & Wiliam, 1998). The power of classroom assessment lies in its direct connection to student work and the fact that it is interpreted in light of knowledge about individual students and classroom instructional conditions (National Research Council, 2001). However, this can also contribute to lack of validity and reliability in constructing assessments and evaluating student performance. Unfortunately, there is little research examining the validity and reliability of classroom assessments (Salinger, 2003). When teacher judgments of reading proficiency are correlated with standardized reading achievement tests, moderately strong correlations are reported with a median of .73 (Hamilton & Shinn, 2003) although teacher evaluation of student proficiency tends to be significantly higher than actual student performance in attaining lesson objectives (Deno, 1985).

A key issue is the lack of fit between measurement principles that are applied to large scale assessments and often taught in teacher education programs and those that fit classroom assessment practices (Moss, 2003). Brookhart (2003) believes that "the time has come to develop measurement theory for classroom assessment purposes and uses" (p. 5). Validity generally refers to evidence for the inferences that can be made from the assessment. Evidence for the validity of classroom assessments include the match between instructional objectives and classroom instruction as well as the extent to which an assessment contributes successfully to the teaching and learning process (Moss, 2003). Reliability generally refers to the degree to which an assessment produces consistent measurement across different scorers or contexts (Salinger, 2003). However, Smith (2003) suggests that reliability be conceptualized as a teacher having enough information "to make a reasonable decision about a student" (p. 30). Smith calls this sufficiency of evidence and defines it as the number of items on an assessment instrument or rubric or the number of assessments used to make a reliable or consistent judgment of student performance. Sufficiency, then, involves multiple outcomes, presentation formats and response formats with repeated assessments over many tasks helping to establish confidence in teachers' estimates of student abilities (Francis et al., 2005). Chester (2003) applied the concept of sufficiency of evidence to making high stakes decisions such as student promotion.

The use of questions in informal assessment

Question design that taps into the comprehension process is generally based upon systems of question categorization. An early example was Bloom's taxonomy of educational objectives (Bloom & Krathwohl, 1956) that included six categories of learning: knowledge, comprehension, application, analysis, synthesis and evaluation. This taxonomy was widely used to categorize different types of classroom questions with specific question words indicated for each category. At a more simplistic level, question content is broadly categorized as literal or explicit questions and inferential or implicit questions. The latter category is often termed higher-order thinking questions; however, this may represent a simplistic description (Applegate, Quinn, & Applegate, 2002; Bowyer-Crane & Snowling, 2005; Ciardiello, 1998; Graser & Person, 1994; Kintsch, 2005). Higher order questions encompass several variations. Low level inference questions demand some higher order thinking but have relatively obvious answers. For example, the answer is stated in the text but in different language or the question requires making connections between text segments that are not signaled by grammatical markers such as *because*. Higher order questions can also tap divergent thinking by asking students to move beyond the text to predict, hypothesize, or reconstruct. Evaluative thinking questions ask students to form opinions and offer rationales for the validity of their answers.

Questions that ask students to engage in divergent and evaluative reasoning tend to be indicative of deep comprehension (Grasser, Baggett, & Williams, 1996; Kintsch, 2005; McNamara, Kintsch, Songer, & Kintsch, 1996). However, such questions may have both inhibitory and facilitative effects on comprehension (van den Broek, Tzeng, Risden, Trabasso, & Basche, 2001) with the recall of older and better readers benefiting from inferential questions asked during reading as opposed to the significantly poorer recall of younger students. In addition, there is little uniformity to questions designated as inferential. Applegate, Quinn, and Applegate (2002) categorized questions as low and high level inferences and examined eight published informal reading inventories. Percentages for low level inference questions ranged from 6.6% through 36.6% while percentages for high level inferences ranged from 0.8% to 17.5%.

Teaching students to self-question has demonstrated positive effects on comprehension (Beck, McKeown, Hamilton, & Kucan, 1997; Mayer & Wittrock, 2006; Nokes & Dole, 2004; Rosenshine, Meister & Chapman, 1996) and the plausibility and specificity of questions asked by students during the reading process correlates with subject matter knowledge (Graesser & Olde, 2003). However, the prevailing model in classroom assessment is that questions emanate from the teacher or text and the role of the student is to answer them. The teacher then evaluates the answer to make judgments about the student's comprehension. Scoring selected response questions poses few problems; the answer is generally either right or wrong. However, it is extremely difficult to score open ended responses reliably and objectively (Francis et al., 2005; Kintsch, 2005).

Where do classroom questions come from? Some come from the textbooks that are used; some are no doubt constructed by the teacher. Little research has been done on the quality of questions that are constructed, chosen or asked in the classroom. While questions are probably the most frequent form of comprehension assessment, few studies of technical adequacy exist (Hamilton & Shinn, 2003) and these generally take the form of correlations with standardized measures (Fuchs, Fuchs, & Maxwell, 1988). A serious issue with using questions is their passage dependency; that is, whether they can be answered correctly without reading the passage. This generally occurs when students already know much of the text content prior to reading or can infer answers based upon extensive prior knowledge. Students can also engage in clever guessing of selected response items such as multiple choice questions (Paris, Carpenter, Paris, & Hamilton, 2005).

Another issue concerning question usage is whether students answer the questions from memory or have access to the text. In group standardized measures, students can look back in the text; however, much classroom assessment prohibits this. Looking back in the text to answer questions clearly changes the nature of the question-answering task (Johnston, 1984) and differentiates between understanding during reading and memory for what was read and understood (Leslie & Caldwell, 2006). Leslie and Caldwell (2001, 2006) determined that students with reading instructional levels at or above third grade were able to increase their ability to answer comprehension questions by looking back after reading, although look-backs were more effective for locating answers to explicit questions than answering implicit questions. At a high school level, only comprehension after look-backs correlated significantly with standardized test scores. Palincsar, Magnusson, Pesko, and Hamlin (2005) referred fourth graders to the text as an aid in answering questions and described the process as "one of constructing and revising coherent and sensible meaning" (p. 275). If looking back increases comprehension, this suggests that assessments that do not allow look-backs may actually underestimate a student's level of comprehension.

Retellings

The use of retelling to assess reading comprehension is based on various theoretical perspectives. Kintsch and Van Dyk's (1978) model of comprehension deconstructed a text base into semantic propositions (i.e., defined as a predicate and one or more arguments such as agent, object or goal) and measured recall as the percentage of propositions retold by the reader. Researchers interested in how students understood text structures such as narrative (Mandler & DeForest, 1979; Stein & Glenn, 1979) examined retellings using the elements of story (i.e., character, setting, goal, problem, events, and resolution). Other researchers interested in causal connections among segments of text have broken sentences into clauses consisting of a main verb (Kendeou & van den Broek, 2005; Magliano, Trabasso, & Graesser, 1999; van den Broek, Lorch, Linderholm, & Gustafson, 2001). Still others whose theoretical foundation is not clear have examined recall based on the total number of words retold (Fuchs, Fuchs, & Hamlett, 1989; Roberts, Good, & Corcoran, 2005), and the percentage of content words (exact matches or synonyms of text words) retold (Fuchs, Fuchs, & Maxwell, 1988). It is evident from these variations in the size of the unit used to evaluate recall that different theories are foundational to their use. So, when students are asked to retell text we cannot assume a common theoretical foundation. Rather, only by examining how retelling is scored can we begin to assess the validity of the assessment.

The common use of recall or retellings as a dependent variable in research and the inclusion of retelling formats into recently published informal reading inventories (Bader, 2002; Burns & Roe, 2002; Leslie & Caldwell, 2006; Stieglitz, 2002) suggest that asking students to recall and retell text is a valuable assessment tool. However, there is concern that retellings may underestimate the comprehension of some children because of linguistic production demands required by the retelling process (Francis et al., 2005; Palincsar, Magnussen, Pesko, & Hamlin, 2005). On the other hand, the difficulty of writing passage independent questions that are representative of the text and matching these to specific levels of comprehension may be a reason for preferring retelling to question responses (Fuchs, 1992; Roberts, Good, & Corcoran, 2005). Fuchs, Fuchs, and Maxwell (1988) found correlations between .76 and .82 for different forms of retelling scores (total number of words, percent of content words and percent of idea units) and a standardized reading comprehension test. Leslie and Caldwell (2006) found significant correlations between retelling and comprehension as measured by questions for upper middle school and high school text; no consistent patterns were evident for lower level texts. Similarly, they found significant correlations between the proportion of paraphrases in retelling and the ability to answer comprehension questions (Caldwell & Leslie, 2006).

Retellings are open-ended response formats and they are difficult and time-consuming to score. Scoring requires that the text must be broken into units and the student's responses matched to these. As indicated above, the particular unit of analysis may make this analysis more or less challenging. Matching what the student retells to each unit of analysis allows for a measure of the quantity of literal recall. Because narrative and expository text have different structures, the quality of literal recall is often measured using story maps for narratives and text maps for expository selections (Pearson & Hamm, 2005).

Scoring or analyzing retelling can involve more than just measuring literal recall. Students often offer a variety of different comments besides a literal retelling or paraphrase of the text. Students make inferences, they offer personal comments or observations, and they include unrelated or erroneous remarks. This suggests that limiting scoring of recall to literal components may provide an incomplete picture of the student's comprehension. To address this, retellings are often scored according to qualitative rubrics that match recall components to different elements such as gist/main idea, details/story elements, interpretive ideas, generalizations, supplementations, coherence, completeness, linguistic/language conventions, additional information not in the passage, and elicited feelings (Brown, Pressley, Van Meter, & Schuder, 1996; Hall, Markham, & Culatta, 2005; Irwin & Mitchell, 1983; Romero, Paris, & Brem, 2005).

Using retelling as an assessment tool demands attention to several issues: how to break the text into units, how to deal with extra-text comments such as inferences, and how to insure reliability of the scoring procedures. Research has not dealt with such issues at a classroom level. Teachers indicate that they find retelling helpful (Taylor & Pearson, 2005); however, there is no information on how they use it beyond a subjective or idiosyncratic level. If retelling is to become a viable classroom tool, uniform scoring guidelines and procedures must be designed. For example, Sudweeks, Glissmeyer, Morrison, Wilcox, and Tanner (2004) suggest that any judgments about a student's comprehension should be based on four to six passages in order to control as much as possible for specific passage effects and student by passage interactions. Reliability of scoring is another issue. In research studies, interscorer reliability for retellings is generally high; however, this would probably not occur in a regular classroom setting without extensive teacher training.

An additional concern is the time involved in listening, transcribing and scoring retellings. These may be too time consuming for regular classroom use and may limit assessment of retelling to the research context or to individual diagnosis of struggling readers. In addition to reliability issues, time for administration and scoring has been a major impetus to the development of curriculum-based measurement where questioning and inferential recall have been replaced by oral reading fluency, a maze task during silent reading where readers select which of four possible words best fits the text, and word recall, all of short passages, as measures of reading performance (Chidsey, Davis, & Maya, 2003; Deno, 1985; Fuchs, 1992; Fuchs, Fuchs, & Maxwell, 1988).

The informal reading inventory

The informal reading inventory (IRI) has a long history in informal comprehension assessment. Asking students to orally or silently read leveled passages and assessing comprehension through questions is a popular assessment. IRI administration is specifically matched to the needs of an individual and scores are derived from traditionally agreed upon percentages for acceptable word recognition and comprehension (Fuchs, Fuchs, & Deno, 1982). Paris and Carpenter (2003) describe IRIs as "authentic, daily, quick, immediate, flexible, teacher controlled, and student centered—all positive characteristics of classroom assessments" (p. 578). Informal reading inventories have changed immensely over the years because of advances in our understanding of reading comprehension, and now include a variety of assessment options: graded word lists, narrative and expository passages, interest inventories, measures of prior knowledge, retelling rubrics, and additional assessments that focus on early literacy, phonics knowledge and word identification (Bader, 2002; Burns & Roe, 2002; Ekwall & Shanker, 2000; Flynt & Cooter, 2004; Johns, 2005; Leslie & Caldwell, 2006; Silvaroli & Wheelock, 2001; Stieglitz, 2002).

An issue with the use of IRIs as measures of reading comprehension is the passage difficulty of the selections. To what extent are higher level passages more difficult than lower level ones? At the heart of this issue is the typical use of readability formulas to delineate IRI passage levels. Readability formulas are generally based on two factors: word difficulty and sentence complexity measured by the familiarity, frequency, and length of words and the number of words in a sentence with longer sentences presumed to be more difficult. Readability formulas have long been criticized as insufficient in describing passage difficulty (Klare, 1984) and the readability level of a single selection may vary depending upon the formula used. Such formulas are only rough indicators with most having a standard error of measurement that spans a full grade level (Stahl, 2003; Zakaluk & Samuels, 1988). Readability formulas do not address passage structure, the effect of reader prior knowledge upon comprehension, propositional and intersentential complexity or text coherence (Francis et al., 2005; Klare, 1984; Meyer, 2003). Because of these limitations, Leslie and Caldwell (2006) provided empirical validity of the increasing difficulty of their informal reading inventory passages. That is, they demonstrated that students who read passages that readability formulae rated more difficult scored lower than on passages rated easier.

Higher level IRI passages are generally more difficult than lower level ones; however, the difference between two different levels is probably not identical (Paris, 2002). That is, the differences between Grade 2 and Grade 3 passages might be less than between Grade 4 and Grade 5 passages. This poses a problem if the IRI is used to measure student growth in that pre and post test passages are seldom identical. Paris (2002) suggests several ways of dealing with this: use the same passages for pre and post assessment; report data in terms of categories as opposed to grade levels (i.e., percentage of questions answered correctly or number of ideas retold) or create scales of difficulty by multiplying raw scores (number of questions answered correctly) by the readability level of the text (Leslie & Allen, 1999).

Passage equivalency is another issue. IRIs typically provide several passages at a single grade level. Because of passage structure and topic content, these may not be equally difficult and a student may comprehend a narrative passage and evince difficulties with an expository selection at the same level (Caldwell & Leslie, 2003/2004; Leslie & Caldwell, 2006). Research has documented that narratives are easier for elementary children to comprehend than expository selections (Berkowitz & Taylor, 1981; Englert & Hiebert, 1984; Graesser, Golding, & Long, 1991; Grasser & Goodman, 1985; Leslie & Caldwell, 2006; Leslie & Cooper, 1993; Mulcahy & Samuels, 1987). Because of this, it is unrealistic to assume that an IRI level obtained in narrative text will carry over to expository material. Reading level should be qualified as narrative or expository and levels obtained through a mixture of narrative and expository selections may be suspect. Measurement of student progress using an IRI should involve pre- and post-testing of passages that are as similar as possible: same readability level, same structure and similar level of familiarity (Leslie & Caldwell, 2006).

Because IRIs primarily depend upon questions for comprehension assessment, the same issues that confront questioning in the classroom are present in IRIs. While most IRIs typically differentiate between literal or explicit questions and inferential or implicit ones, they do not differentiate between lower and higher inference levels. Applegate, Quinn, and Applegate (2002) classified IRI questions as text-based (literal and low-level inference questions) and response-based (high level inference and response items where the reader was asked to express or defend an idea). The majority of questions were text-based, a finding also noted by Calfee and Hiebert (1991) and there was much variation across the eight different IRIs examined with regard to inference levels. Duffelmeyer and Duffelmeyer (1989) found that less than half of the passages on three IRIs were suitable for measuring the ability to recognize an explicitly stated main idea or to generate a main idea statement where one was lacking in the text.

While IRIs demonstrate test-retest reliability (Paris, Pearson, Carpenter, Siebenthal, & Laier, 2002), this depends upon uniform administration and scoring procedures (Paris & Carpenter, 2003) as well as the quality of professional development offered to users (Calfee & Hiebert, 1991). Despite the difficulties associated with passage difficulty and passage equivalency in IRIs, a variety of studies have indicated that IRIs are sensitive to changes in a student's comprehension following instruction (Abbott & Beringer, 2000; Caldwell, Fromm, & O'Connor, 1997–1998; Dahl, Scharer, & Lawson, 1999; Duffy, 2001; Hoffman, Sailors, & Patterson, 2001; Johnson-Glenberg, 1999; Leslie & Allen, 1999; Millin & Rinehart, 1999; Montali & Lewandowski, 1996; Stahl, Pagnucco, & Stuttles, 1996; Worthy & Invernizzi, 1995).

Despite the enduring popularity of this instrument, little research exists that compares the validity, reliability and assessment accuracy of the latest published IRIs. There is little reason to believe that things are measurably different since Klesius and Homan (1985) found discrepancies across several inventories with regard to the readability estimates of individual passages, the passage dependency of questions, the scoring criteria for comprehension, and issues of interscorer reliability and concurrent validity. More recently, Spector (2005) examined the reliability of nine inventories and found that fewer than half reported any data on reliability in terms of alternate form reliability, score consistency, score agreement, internal consistency or interrater reliability.

Think-alouds

Asking readers to read a selection and think out loud as they do so has provided valuable information about the cognitive strategies that readers use as they attempt to comprehend text (Afflerbach & Johnston, 1984; Myers, 1988; Olson, Duffy, & Mack, 1984; Pressley & Afflerbach, 1995; Pritchard, 1990). The theoretical basis for think-alouds is the constructivist notion of learning. That is, as students read text they construct meaning and thinking aloud provides researchers the opportunity "to examine what the reader does to facilitate comprehension" (Myers & Lytle, 1986, p. 140). Numerous studies have examined the relationship between thinking aloud and comprehension (Bereiter & Bird, 1985; Chou-Hare & Smith, 1982; Cote, Goldman, & Saul, 1998; Crain-Thoreson, Lippman, & McClendon-Magnuson, 1997; Kavale & Schreiner, 1979; Kucan & Beck, 1997; Laing & Kambi, 2002; Leslie & Caldwell, 2006; Loxterman, Beck, & McKeown, 1994; Myers, Lytle, Palladino, Devenpeck, & Green, 1990; Zwaan & Brown, 1996) by asking students to answer questions or retell what they read. Such research suggests that thinking aloud may have a positive effect upon comprehension as measured by questions or retelling. However, the number and quality of think-aloud comments are closely tied to instructions given to students (i.e., to explain, predict, associate or understand; Magliano, Trabasso, & Graesser, 1999; van den Broek, Lorch, Linderholm, & Gustafson, 2001), reader purpose for entertainment or study (Narvaez, van den Broek, & Ruiz, 1999; van den Broek, Lorch, Linderholm, & Gustafson, 2001), the difficulty and coherence of the text (Cote, Goldman, & Saul, 1998; Caldwell & Leslie, 2003/2004; Leslie & Caldwell, 2006; Loxterman, Beck, & McKeown, 1994), and the structure of the text (Chou-Hare & Smith, 1982).

A variety of studies have focused on the use of think-alouds as an instructional tool, that is, as a teacher activity for increasing or improving student comprehension (e.g., Baumann, Seifert-Kessell, & Jones, 1992; Bereiter & Bird, 1985; Chi, De Leeuw, Chiu,

& LaVancher, 1994; Israel & Massey, 2005; Nist & Kirby, 1986; Silven & Vauras, 1992; Ward & Traweek, 1993). Fewer have addressed the possible use of think-alouds as an independent assessment tool (Myers, 1988; Myers & Lytle, 1986; Randall, Fairbanks, & Kennedy, 1986; Wade, 1990). In other words, can a student's comprehension be inferred from think-aloud comments apart from accompanying questions or retellings?

There are three issues with using think-alouds as an independent assessment tool: the reliability of the scoring, the validity of the system devised for coding or describing the comments, and the amount of text read before stopping to engage in a think-aloud. There is considerable variation across studies with regard to descriptions of think-aloud comments (Chou-Hare & Smith, 1982; Cote, Goldman, & Saul, 1998; Crain-Thoreson, Lippman, & McClendon-Magnuson, 1997; Israel & Massey, 2005; Myers, Lytle, Palladino, Devenpeck, & Green, 1990; Olshavsky, 1976). Part of this variation is due to the theoretical base underlying each study; however, despite the wide variety of coding systems, most include paraphrasing, inferencing, monitoring, and prediction.

In an attempt to devise a more uniform coding system, Leslie and Caldwell (2001) identified 11 categories of think-aloud comments common in the research literature and divided them into two groups: those that indicated understanding on the part of the students and those that indicated lack of understanding. They found significant negative correlations between these two classifications. They then limited the original list to eight think-aloud comments that were actually offered by eighth-grade students reading expository text: paraphrasing/summarizing; making new meaning or inferencing; questioning that indicates understanding; noting understanding; reporting prior knowledge; identifying personally; noting lack of understanding and questioning that indicates lack of understanding. Leslie and Caldwell (2006) found that the most frequent type of think-aloud statement was paraphrasing/summarizing which occurred from 40% to 75% of the time. The next most frequent was making new meaning (i.e., inferences) which ranged in frequency from 9% to 23%. Identifying personally and reporting prior knowledge had low percentages but were used consistently.

Trabasso and Magliano (1996a) recommended a more complex system for coding inferences made during thinking aloud and described inferences as causal explanations, predictions of future consequences, and associations that provide additional information and enrich or fill in detail. This coding of inferences has shown to be useful in understanding think-aloud statements during reading of narrative (Trabasso & Magliano, 1996b) and expository text (Caldwell & Leslie, 2006; Graesser & Bertus, 1998). Inferences can also be coded as knowledge-based or text-based; that is, the reader can make an inference using his or her prior knowledge or using information provided in the text (Kintsch & Kintsch, 2005). Caldwell and Leslie (2006) found that the source of inferences made by middle school students after reading expository text tended to be the text as opposed to the students' world knowledge.

In studies that have examined the think-aloud process, interrater reliability has been strong for identifying different think-aloud types. No studies have examined the extent to which such reliability would be present across different teachers or across different think-aloud sessions with the same teacher.

The majority of think-aloud studies asked readers to think out loud after each sentence. However, this may represent an unrealistic scenario for classroom assessment. Leslie and Caldwell (2006) placed STOP marks at the end of paragraphs unless the paragraphs contained so much new information that two stops were deemed necessary for a student to process the text effectively. Students experienced little difficulty in thinking aloud. Over 90% of their comments indicated they understood what they were reading and the total think-aloud scores correlated significantly with inferences made during retelling and question answering with and without look-backs.

Sentence verification task

Assessing reading comprehension through a sentence verification task is based on the assumption that comprehension involves retaining a memory representation that preserves meaning but not the exact words of the text. The Sentence Verification Task (SVT) involves developing four sentences based upon a short passage (Royer, 2001; Royer, Greene, & Sinatra, 1997). One sentence is an original copy of the sentence as it appeared in the text. A second sentence is a paraphrase of the original sentence with words changed but meaning retained. The third is a meaning-change sentence and the fourth is a distracter sentence which is syntactically similar to and consistent with passage meaning but is not related to the sentences in the passage. After reading a passage, the student labels a sentence as "yes" if the sentence means the same thing as the passage sentence (original and paraphrase sentences) and "no" if it does not (meaning-change and distracter sentences). The SVT test generally involves four to six short passages (approximately 12 sentences each) and can be constructed by teachers using any form of text. If passages are at an appropriate level for the population tested, average performance falls at 75%, with proficient readers scoring in the 80s and above and struggling readers scoring in the 70s and lower.

The SVT has been applied to technical text (Royer, Lynch, Hambleton, & Bulgarelli, 1984) and a variety of different populations: third through sixth graders (Rasool & Royer, 2001; Royer, Hastings, & Hook, 1979), college students (Royer, Abranovic, & Sinatra, 1987) and limited English proficient students (Royer & Carlo, 1991).

Reliability and validity data on the SVT technique were summarized by Royer (2001). Good comprehenders, as judged by teachers, scored higher on the SVT. Performance varies with the readability of the text and is positively correlated with other tests of comprehension. However, the technique is little used and this may be because it "just does not have the look and feel of what we mean by 'comprehension assessment'" (Pearson & Hamm, 2005, pp. 38–39). The fact that the technique is sensitive to variations in reading skill, can be used to track comprehension growth and diagnose reading problems, can be used with any form of text, and can be developed by teachers makes it worthy of more than a second glance.

Performance assessment

Performance assessment is a relatively generic term that encompasses a variety of assessment options. The National Research Council (2001) Committee on the Foundations of Assessment, defined performance assessment as "use of more open-ended tasks that call upon students to apply their knowledge and skills to create a product or solve a problem" (p. 30). Such tasks include but are not limited to open-ended problems, hands-on projects, essays, and portfolios of student work. Wiggins (1989) referred to such assessments as "authentic" because they are seen to have intrinsic task value.

Although the concept of performance assessment has been theoretically embraced by the educational field, little attention has been paid to criteria for assessing such measures and, because they are derived from actual performance, many just assume they possess validity (Linn, Baker, & Dunbar, 1991). The same issues that surround previously addressed informal assessments confront the evaluation of performance measures: the match of the task to comprehension levels; reliability of scoring; time involved in preparing, implementing and evaluating; the quality of the instrument; correlations with other measures of comprehension; and the need for teacher training and support. These same issues have faced states who implemented large-scale, high-stakes performance assessments (Pearson, DeStefano, & Garcia, 1998; Pearson, Spaulding, & Myers, 1998; Valencia, 2000). For example, Shapley and Bush (1999) investigated portfolio assessment in the primary grades and, despite 3 years of development, found poor interrater reliability related to lack of standardization of portfolio tasks, problems with scoring rubrics, and inadequate training. Similar issues were reported by Pearson, Calfee, Walker-Webb, and Fleischer (2002) when performance based assessments were used in large scale assessments.

Performance assessment has spawned an interest in rubrics resulting in the publication of sample rubrics in "how-to" texts and literacy textbooks. Unfortunately, the emphasis is upon choosing or constructing a rubric with little attention paid to suggestions for establishing content or concurrent validity and reliability (Miller & Calfee, 2004).

Synthesis

Formal standardized assessment will probably continue to hold a position of prominence due to the emphasis on accountability promulgated by the No Child Left Behind Act (2001). However, researchers and practitioners should continue to demand that such measures undergo stringent tests of construct validity. At the same time, most reading comprehension assessment takes the form of informal measures used in the classroom. Research addressing the validity and reliability of such assessments and guidelines for their implementation is unfortunately sparse and little research has focused on the design and use of informal measures. While educators agree that informal assessment is important, there is little agreement or specific information as to how it should be done (Deno, 1985). Hopefully, and perhaps in reaction to concerns about an over-emphasis on standardized high stakes assessment, researchers will turn their attention to informal assessment of reading comprehension. Such a direction would be aligned with the recommendations of the RAND Reading Study Group (2002) that called for research on comprehension assessment to address the needs, knowledge, and expertise of practitioners.

The National Research Council (2001) described the limitations of classroom assessment in terms of what is not presently addressed: "students' organization of knowledge, problem representations, use of strategies, self-monitoring skills and individual contributions to group problem-solving" (p. 29). This suggests that researchers and practitioners must not only examine current informal assessments but also design new ones to tap the variety and depth of student literacy performance. For example, Hannon and Daneman (2001) asked university students to read a short paragraph that described features of two types of terms: real (beaver) and artificial (jal) and then to answer true/false statements measuring text-based components (memory for explicit information and inferencing based on explicit information) and knowledge-based components (accessing prior knowledge and integration of prior knowledge with text information). Their most important finding was that the text-based and knowledge-based components were differentially correlated with a variety of diverse comprehension measures suggesting that the four components listed above assessed different aspects of comprehension and could be used to assess individual differences in comprehension processing. The ability of these measures to independently assess the components of *children's* comprehension is unknown.

Implications for future research

If research on classroom assessment is to be accepted by the profession, then researchers will need to question traditional views of validity and reliability and closely examine links between classroom instruction and assessment. Perhaps a first step is to accept that validity and reliability for classroom assessments must be re-conceptualized as suggested by Brookhart (2003), Francis et al. (2005), and Moss (2003). This would involve the recognition that no assessment is sufficient in itself and that guidelines for valid informal assessment must include attention to the purpose of instruction and the use of multiple measures over time. This calls for "aggregation across assessments, with the reliability of such an aggregation greater than the reliability of any of the individual indicators" (Pressley & Hilden, 2005, pp. 307–308). This approach would broaden the scope of research on classroom assessment to include the design, use and possible interaction of multiple instruments. An interesting line of research would be to compare multiple informal assessments to determine if and how they measure different kinds or levels of comprehension. For example, given a specific passage, would different results be obtained if students answered explicit or implicit questions, participated in thinking aloud, retold what they read, and engaged in a sentence verification task? How would these correlate with standardized measures of reading comprehension?

Questions used in informal assessment are extremely variable and may tap different levels of comprehension. A first step might be an extensive analysis of questions in classroom textbooks. To what extent do publishers differentiate questions? What type of question is more prevalent? What type of question correlates most strongly with standardized measures and with other informal assessments such as recall? This could suggest guidelines for constructing and choosing questions for evaluating reading comprehension. Research could also focus on teacher professional development in question analysis, formation, and usage.

Retelling is routinely used in research to measure comprehension and several IRIs have incorporated this method as well. However, research on adapting the retelling format to a classroom or diagnostic context is sorely needed and common guidelines for scoring retelling must be established. For example, how long should a passage be or how many passages should be read in order to generate a sensitive measure of comprehension? What is the relationship between amount of literal and inferential recall as indicators of comprehension? Could there be a way to assess retelling in a group format? Also, the effects of text structure upon recall need to be addressed. Unfortunately, given the context and time constraints of the classroom, retelling assessment may not be possible except in a written mode and this may well be confounded by a student's willingness to write as well as writing proficiency. Such questions have not been answered or seldom addressed.

At the present time, it is impossible to determine if published IRIs are more alike or different. While they all have similar components (passages, questions, word lists, etc.) and accept similar scoring guidelines, to what extent do they differ with regard to passage length, passage difficulty, passage content, passage coherence, question content, retelling guidelines, and so forth. To what extent and how do they address issues of validity and reliability? An in-depth analysis of current IRIs might help to determine more specific guidelines for IRI construction and usage.

Think-alouds have established a strong research base as mirroring the comprehension process during reading and as positively affecting comprehension measured through questions or retellings. There are indications that the think-aloud process can be an effective instructional tool. Less certain, however, is the role of the think-aloud process as an independent assessment of comprehension. No serious attempts have been made to transform think-alouds into such a tool (Pressley & Hilden, 2005) and specific guidelines for implementation need to be established before this can become a viable reality. The possibilities of the think-aloud process as an assessment tools was suggested by Brown, Pressley, Van Meter, and Schuder (1996) who used student interviews, retelling and think-alouds as assessment measures following implementation of strategies instruction and determined that the think-aloud data affirmed the effectiveness of instruction by providing important information regarding reader usage of the targeted strategies. Several other issues need to be addressed. How long should think-aloud passages be, and how many comments are needed for a valid assessment of comprehension? What do different types of comments indicate? Do think-alouds correlate with other measures of comprehension? Can the think-aloud process be adapted to a group format or to the context of the typical classroom?

Concluding thoughts

If informal assessment is to be responsive to the needs of instruction, it should be tied to the curriculum and the outcomes tested should be accepted as important instructional objectives (Glaser & Silver, 1994). The nature of the assessed performance and the criteria for judging it must become apparent to students as well as teachers with both becoming actively involved in judging their own performance. At this point in time, the educational and research community knows what to do. The prevailing question is how and where to begin. "We must step forward as advocates for assessments that foster better teaching practice, insist on curricular rigor, and value worthwhile student learning and engagement—all the while respecting the public mandate for accountability" (Valencia, 2000, p. 249).

REFERENCES

Abbott, S. P., & Beringer, V.W. (2000). It's never too late to remediate: Teaching word recognition skills to students with reading disability in Grades 4–7. *Annals of Dyslexia, 49,* 223–250.

Afflerbach, P. (2004). Assessing adolescent reading. In T. L. Jetton & J. A. Dole (Eds.), *Adolescent literacy research and practice* (pp. 369–391). New York: Guilford.

Afflerbach, P., & Johnston, P. (1984). Research methodology on the use of verbal reports in reading. *Journal of Reading Behavior, XVI,* 307–322.

Applegate, M. D., Quinn, K. B., & Applegate, A. (2002). Levels of thinking required by comprehension questions in informal reading inventories. *The Reading Teacher, 56,* 174–180.

Bader, L. (2002). *Bader reading and language inventory.* Englewood Cliffs, NJ: Prentice-Hall.

Baumann, J., Seifert-Kessell, N., & Jones, L. A. (1992). Effect of think-aloud instruction on elementary students' comprehension monitoring abilities. *Journal of Reading Behavior, 24,* 143–172.

Beck, I. L., McKeown, M. G., Hamilton, R. L., & Kucan, L. (1997). *Questioning the author: An approach for enhancing student engagement with text.* Newark, DE: International Reading Association.

Bereiter, C., & Bird, M. (1985). Use of thinking aloud in identification and teaching of reading comprehension strategies. *Cognition and Instruction, 2,* 131–156.

Berkowitz, S., & Taylor, B. M. (1981). The effects of text type and familiarity on the nature of information recalled by readers. In M. Kamil (Ed.), *Directions in reading: Research and instruction* (pp. 157–161). Washington, DC: National Reading Conference.

Black, P., & Wiliam, D. (1998). Assessment and classroom learning. *Assessment in Education: Principles, Policy and Practice, 5,* 7–74.

Bloom, B., & Krathwohl, D. (1956). *Taxonomy of educational objectives: The classification of educational goals.* New York: Longmans Green.

Bowyer-Crane, C., & Snowling, M. J. (2005). Assessing children's inference generation: What do tests of reading comprehension measure? *British Journal of Educational Psychology, 75,* 189–201.

Brookhart, S. M. (2003). Developing measurement theory for classroom assessment purposes and uses. *Educational Measurement, Issues and Practices, 22,* 5–12.

Brown, R., Pressley, M., Van Meter, P., & Schuder, T. (1996). A quasi-experimental validation of transactional strategies instruction with low-achieving second-grade readers. *Journal of Educational Psychology, 88,* 18–37.

Burns, B. D., & Roe, P. C. (2002). *Burns/Roe informal reading inventory.* Itasca, IL: Riverside Publishing.

Caldwell, J., Fromm, M., & O'Connor, V. (1997–1998). Designing an intervention for poor readers: Incorporating the best of all worlds. *Wisconsin State Reading Association Journal, 41*, 7–14.

Caldwell, J., & Leslie, L. (2003–2004). Does proficiency in middle school reading assure proficiency in high school reading? The possible role of think-alouds. *Journal of Adolescent and Adult Literacy, 47*, 324–335.

Caldwell, J., & Leslie, L. (2006). The effects of thinking aloud in expository text on recall and comprehension. Unpublished manuscript.

Calfee, R., & Hiebert, E. (1991). Classroom assessment of reading. In P. D. Pearson, R. Barr, M. Kamil, & P. Mosenthal (Eds.), *Handbook of reading research volume II* (pp. 281–309). New York: Longman.

Calfee, R. D., & Miller, R. G. (2005). Comprehending through composing: Reflections on reading assessment strategies. In S. G. Paris & S. A. Stahl (Eds.), *Children's reading comprehension and assessment* (pp. 215–236). Mahwah, NJ: Erlbaum.

Campbell, M.B. (2001). Inquiry into reading assessment: Teachers' perceptions of effective practices. *Reading Horizons, 42*, 1–20.

Carlisle, J. F., & Rice, M. S. (2004). Assessment of reading comprehension. In C. A. Stone, E. R. Silliman, B. J. Ehren, & K. Apel (Eds.), *Handbook of language and literacy* (pp. 521–540). New York: Guilford.

Carney, R. N., & Schattgen, S. F. (1994). [Review of] California Achievement Tests, 5th edition. In D. J. Keyser & R. C. Sweetland (Eds.), *Test critiques*, 10 (pp. 110–119). Austin, TX: PRO-ED.

Carpenter, R, D., & Paris, S. G. (2005). Issues of validity and reliability in early reading assessments. In S. G. Paris & S. A. Stahl (Eds.), *Children's reading comprehension and assessment* (pp. 279–304). Mahwah, NJ: Erlbaum.

Chester, M. D. (2003). Multiple measures and high stakes decisions: A framework for combining measures. *Educational Measurement: Issues and Practice, 22*, 32–41.

Chi, M. T., De Leeuw, N., Chiu, M., & LaVancher, C. (1994). Eliciting self explanations improves understanding. *Cognitive Science, 18*, 439–477.

Chidsey, R. B., Davis, L., & Maya, C. (2003). Sources of variance in curriculum-based measures of silent reading. *Psychology in the School, 40*, 363–377.

Chou-Hare, V., & Smith, D. C. (1982). Reading to remember: Studies of metacognitive reading skills in elementary school-aged children. *Journal of Educational Research, 75*, 157–164.

Ciardiello, A.V. (1998). Did you ask a good question today? Alternative cognitive and metacognitive strategies. *Journal of Adolescent and Adult Literacy, 42*, 210–219.

Cizek, G. J., Fitzgerald, S. M., & Rachor, R. E. (1996). Teacher assessment practices: Preparation, isolation, and the kitchen sink. *Educational Assessment, 3*, 159–179.

Cote, N., Goldman, S. R., & Saul, E. U. (1998). Students making sense of informational text: Relations between processing and representation. *Discourse Processes, 25*, 1–53.

Crain-Thoreson, C., Lippman, M. Z., & McClendon-Magnuson, D. (1997). Windows of comprehension: Reading comprehension processes as revealed by two think-alouds. *Journal of Educational Psychology, 89*, 579–591.

Crooks, T. J. (1988). The impact of classroom evaluation practices on students. *Review of Educational Research, 58*, 438–481.

Cronbach, L. J. (1971). Test validation. In R. L. Thorndike (Ed.), *Educational measurement* (2nd ed., pp. 443–507). Washington, DC: American Council on Education.

Dahl, K. L., Scharer, P. L., & Lawson, L. L. (1999). Phonics instruction and student achievement in whole language first-grade classrooms. *Reading Research Quarterly, 34*, 312–341.

Davis, F. B. (1944). Fundamental factors of comprehension in reading. *Psychometrika, 9*, 185–197.

Davis, F. B. (1968). Research in comprehension in reading. *Reading Research Quarterly, 3*, 499–545.

Deno, S. L. (1985). Curriculum-based measurement: The emerging alternative. *Exceptional Children, 52*, 219–232.

Duffelmeyer, F. A., & Duffelmeyer, B. B. (1989). Are IRI passages suitable for assessing main idea comprehension? *The Reading Teacher, 42*, 358–363.

Duffy, A. M. (2001). Balance, literacy acceleration, and responsive teaching in a summer school literacy program for elementary school struggling readers. *Reading Research and Instruction, 40*(2), 67–100.

Duke, N. K. (2005). Comprehension of what for what: Comprehension as a nonunitary construct. In S. G. Paris & S. A. Stahl (Eds.), *Children's reading comprehension and assessment* (pp. 93–106*)*. Mahwah, NJ: Erlbaum.

Ekwall, E., & Shanker, J. (2000). *Ekwall/Shanker reading inventory*. Boston: Allyn & Bacon.

Englert, C. S., & Hiebert, E. H. (1984). Children's developing awareness of text structures in expository material. *Journal of Educational Psychology, 76*, 65–74.

Ercikan, K. (2006). Development in assessment of student learning. In P. A. Alexander & P. H. Winne (Eds.), *Handbook of educational psychology* (pp. 929–952). Mahwah, NJ: Erlbaum.

Flynt, S. E. & Cooter, R. B. (2004). *Reading inventory for the classroom*. Englewood Cliffs, NJ: Prentice-Hall.

Francis, D. J., Fletcher, J. M., Catts, H. W., & Tomblin, J. B. (2005). Dimensions affecting the assessment of reading comprehension. In S. G. Paris & S. A. Stahl (Eds.), *Children's reading comprehension and assessment* (pp. 369–394). Mahwah, NJ: Erlbaum.

Fuchs, L. S. (1992). Identifying a measure for monitoring student reading progress. *School Psychology Review, 21*, 45–58.

Fuchs, L. S., Fuchs, D., & Deno, S. L. (1982). Reliability and validity of curriculum-based informal reading inventories. *Reading Research Quarterly, XVIII*, 6–25.

Fuchs, L. S., Fuchs, D., & Hamlett, C. L. (1989). Monitoring reading growth using student recalls: Effects of two teacher feedback systems. *Journal of Educational Research, 83*, 103–110.

Fuchs, L.S., Fuchs, D., & Maxwell, L. (1988). The validity of informal comprehension measures. *Remedial and Special Education, 9*, 20–27.

Glaser, R., & Silver, E. (1994). Assessment, testing and instruction: Retrospect and prospect. *National Center for Research on Evaluation, Standards, and Student Testing (CRESST)*. University of California, Los Angeles. Retrieved September, 2006, from http://www.cse. ucla.edu/Reports/TECH379.

Graesser, A. C., Baggett, W., & Williams, K. (1996) Question-driven explanatory reasoning, *Applied Cognitive Psychology, 10*, S17–S32.

Graesser, A. C., & Bertus, E. L. (1998). The construction of causal inferences while reading expository texts on science and technology. *Scientific Studies of Reading, 2*, 247–269.

Graesser, A. C., Golding, J. M., & Long, D. L. (1991). Narrative representation and comprehension. In R. Barr, M. L. Kamil, P. Mosenthal, & P. D. Pearson (Eds.), *Handbook of reading research* (vol. II, pp. 171–205). White Plains, NY: Longman.

Graesser, A. C., & Goodman, S. M. (1985). Implicit knowledge, question answering and the representation of expository text. In B. K. Britton & J. B. Black (Eds.), *Understanding expository text* (pp. 109–171). Hillsdale, NJ: Erlbaum.

Graesser, A. C., & Olde, B. A. (2003). How does one know whether a person understands a device? The quality of the questions the person asks when the device breaks down. *Journal of Educational Psychology, 95*, 524–536.

Graesser, A. C., & Person, N. K. (1994). Question asking during tutoring. *American Educational Research Journal, 31*, 104–137.

Guthrie, J. T., & Wigfield, A. (2005). Role of motivation and engagement in reading. In S. G. Paris & S. A. Stahl (Eds.), *Children's reading comprehension and assessment* (pp. 187–214). Mahwah, NJ: Erlbaum.

Hall, K. M., Markham, J. C., & Culatta, B. (2005). The development of the early expository comprehension assessment (EECA): A look at reliability. *Communication Disorders Quarterly, 26*, 195–206.

Hamilton, C., & Shinn, M. (2003). Characteristics of word callers: An investigation of the accuracy of teachers' judgments of reading comprehension and oral reading skill. *School Psychology Review, 32*, 228–240.

Hannon, B., & Daneman, M. (2001). A new tool for measuring and understanding individual difference in the component processes of reading comprehension. *Journal of Educational Psychology, 93*, 103–128.

Hoffman, J. V., Sailors, M., & Patterson, E. U. (2001). Text leveling and "little-books" in first-grade reading. *Journal of Literacy Research, 33*, 507–528.

Illinois Goal Assessment Program. (1991). *The Illinois reading assessment: Classroom connections*. Springfield, IL: Illinois State Board of Education.

The Iowa tests guide to research and development. (2003). Itasca, IL: Riverside Publishing.

Irwin, P. A., & Mitchell, K. N. (1983). A procedure for assessing the richness of retellings. *Journal of Reading, 28*, 391–396.

Israel, S. E., & Massey, D. (2005). Metacognitive think-alouds using a gradual release model with middle school students. In S. E. Israel, C. C. Block, L. Bauserman, & K. Kinnucan-Welsch (Eds.), *Metacognition in Literacy Learning* (pp. 183–198). Mahwah, NJ: Erlbaum.

Johns, J. J. (2005). *Basic reading inventory*. Dubuque, IA: Kendall-Hunt.

Johnson-Glenberg, M. C. (1999). Training reading comprehension in adequate decoders/poor comprehenders: Verbal vs. visual strategies. *Journal of Educational Psychology, 92,* 772–782.

Johnston, P. (1984). Prior knowledge and reading comprehension test bias. *Reading Research Quarterly, 19,* 219–239.

Kavale, K., & Schreiner, R. (1979). The reading process of above average and average readers: A comparison of the use of reasoning strategies in responding to standardized comprehension measures. *Reading Research Quarterly, XV,* 102–128.

Kendeou, P., & van den Broek, P. (2005). The effects of readers' misconceptions on comprehension of scientific text. *Journal of Educational Psychology, 97,* 235–245.

Kintsch, E. (2005). Comprehension theory as a guide for the design of thoughtful questions. *Topics in Language Disorders, 25,* 51–64.

Kintsch, W. (1998). *Comprehension: A paradigm for cognition.* New York: Cambridge University Press.

Kintsch, W., & Kintsch, E. (2005). Comprehension. In S. G. Paris & S. A. Stahl (Eds.), *Children's reading comprehension and assessment* (pp. 71–92). Mahwah, NJ: Erlbaum.

Kintsch, W., & van Dijk, T, A. (1978). Towards a model of text comprehension and production. *Psychological Review, 85,* 363–394.

Klare, G. (1984). Readability. In P. D. Pearson, R. Barr, M. Kamil, & P. Mosenthal (Eds.), *Handbook of reading research* (pp. 681–744). New York: Longman.

Klesius, J. P., & Homan, S. P. (1985). A validity and reliability update on the informal reading inventory with suggestions for improvement. *Journal of Learning Disabilities, 18,* 71–76.

Kucan, L., & Beck, I. L. (1997). Thinking aloud and reading comprehension research: Inquiry, instruction and social interaction. *Review of Educational Research, 67,* 271–299.

Laing, S. P., & Kambi, A. C. (2002). The use of think-aloud protocols to compare inferencing abilities in average and below-average readers. *Journal of Learning Disabilities, 35,* 436–447.

Landauer, T. K., & Dumais, S .T. (1997). A solution to Plato's problem: The Latent Semantic Analysis theory of acquisition, induction and representation of knowledge. *Psychological Review, 104,* 211–240.

Landauer, T. K., Foltz, P., & Laham, D. (1998). An introduction to Latent Semantic Analysis. *Discourse Processes, 25,* 259–284.

Lee, G. (2002). The influence of several factors on reliability for complex reading comprehension tests. *Journal of Educational Measurement, 39,* 149–164.

Leslie, L., & Allen, L. (1999). Factors that predict success in an early literacy intervention program. *Reading Research Quarterly, 34,* 404–424.

Leslie, L., & Caldwell, J. (2001). *Qualitative reading inventory — 3.* New York: Addison Wesley Longman.

Leslie, L., & Caldwell, J. (2006). *Qualitative reading inventory — 4.* Boston: Allyn and Bacon

Leslie, L., & Cooper, J. (1993). Assessing the predictive validity of prior-knowledge assessment. In D. J. Leu & C. K. Kinzer (Eds.), *Examining central issues in literacy research, theory and practice* (pp. 93–100). Chicago: National Reading Conference.

Linn, R. L., Baker, E. L., & Dunbar, S. B. (1991). Complex, performance-based assessment: Expectations and validation criteria. *Educational Researcher, 20,* 15–21.

Loxterman, J. A., Beck, I. L., & McKeown, M. G. (1994). The effects of thinking aloud during reading on students' comprehension of more or less coherent text. *Reading Research Quarterly, 29,* 353–368.

Magliano, J. P., Trabasso, T., & Graesser, A. C. (1999). Strategic processes during comprehension. *Journal of Educational Psychology, 91,* 615–629.

Mandler, J. M., & DeForest, M. G. (1979). Is there more than one way to recall a story? *Child Development, 50,* 886–889.

Mayer, R. E., & Wittrock, M. C. (2006). Problem solving. In P. A. Alexander & P. H. Winne (Eds.), *Handbook of educational psychology* (pp. 287–303). Mahwah, NJ: Erlbaum.

McMillan, J. H. (2003). Understanding and improving teachers' classroom assessment decision making: Implications for theory and practice. *Educational Measurement, Issues and Practices, 22,* 34–43.

McMillan, J. H., Myran, S., & Workman, D. (2002). Elementary teachers' classroom assessment and grading practices. *The Journal of Educational Research, 85,* 203–214.

McMorris, R. F., Liu, W. P., & Bringsjord, E. L. (2004). Review of the California Achievement Tests, Fifth Edition. In *Mental Measurements Yearbook,* Lincoln, NE: Buros Institute of Mental Measurements.

McNamara, D. S., Kintsch, E., Songer, N. B., & Kintsch, W. (1996). Are good texts always better? Interactions of text coherence, background knowledge, and levels of understanding in learning from text. *Cognition and Instruction, 14,* 1–43.

Messick, S. (1989). Validity. In R. L. Linn (Ed), *Educational measurement* (pp. 13–104). Washington, DC: American Council on Education.

Meyer, B. J. F. (2003). Text coherence and readability. *Topics in Language Disorders, 23,* 204–225.

Miller, R. G., & Calfee, R. C. (2004). Building a better reading-writing assessment: Bridging cognitive theory, instruction and assessment. *English Leadership Quarterly, 26,* 6–13.

Millin, S. K., & Rinehart, S. D. (1999). Some of the benefits of readers' theater participation for 2nd grade Title I-students. *Reading Research and Instruction, 39,* 71–88.

Montali, J., & Lewandowski, L. (1996). Benefits of a talking computer for average and less skilled readers. *Journal of Learning Disabilities, 29,* 271–279.

Moss, P. A. (2003). Reconceptualizing validity for classroom assessment. *Educational measurement, Issues and Practice, 22,* 13–25.

Mulcahy, P. I., & Samuels, S. J. (1987). Problem solving schemata for text types: A comparison of narrative and expository text structures. *Reading Psychology, 8,* 247–256.

Myers, J. (1988). Diagnosis diagnosed: Twenty years after. *Professional School Psychology, 3,* 123–134.

Myers, J., & Lytle, S. (1986). Assessment of the learning process. *Exceptional Children, 53,* 113–144.

Myers, J., Lytle, S., Palladino, D., Devenpeck, G., & Green, M. (1990). Think-aloud protocol analysis: An investigation of reading comprehension strategies in fourth and fifth grade students. *Journal of Psychoeducational Assessment, 8,* 112–127.

Narvaez, D., van den Broek, P., & Ruiz, A. B. (1999). The influence of reading purpose on inference generation and comprehension in reading. *Journal of Educational Psychology, 91,* 488–496.

National Research Council (2001). *Knowing what students know: The science and design of educational assessment.* J. Pelligrino, N. Chudowsky, & R. Glaser (Eds.), Washington, DC: National Academy Press.

Nichols, P. D. (1994). A framework for developing cognitively diagnostic assessments. *Review of Educational Research, 64,* 575–603.

Nist, S. L., & Kirby, K. (1986). Teaching comprehension and study strategies through modeling and thinking aloud. *Reading Research and Instruction, 25,* 254–264.

No Child Left Behind Act (2001). *Executive summary.* Retrieved September, 2006, from http://www.ed.gov/print/nclb/overview/intro/execsumm.html.

Nokes, J. D., & Dole, J. A. (2004). Helping adolescent readers through explicit strategy instruction. In T. L. Jetton & J. A. Dole (Eds.), *Adolescent literacy research and practice* (pp. 162–182). New York: Guilford.

Olshavsky, J. E. (1976) Reading as problem solving: An investigation of strategies. *Reading Research Quarterly, 4,* 654–674.

Olson, G. M., Duffy, S. A., & Mack, R. L. (1984). Thinking out loud as a method for studying real-time comprehension processes. In D. E. Kieras & M. A. Just (Eds.), *New methods in reading comprehension research* (pp. 245–278). Hillsdale, NJ: Erlbaum.

Palincsar, A. S., Magnusson, S. J., Pesko, S., & Hamlin, M. (2005). Attending to the nature of subject matter in text comprehension assessments. In S. G. Paris & S. A. Stahl (Eds.), *Children's reading comprehension and assessment* (pp. 257–278). Mahwah, NJ: Erlbaum.

Paris, S. G. (2002). Measuring children's reading development using leveled text. *The Reading Teacher, 56,* 168–170.

Paris, S. G., & Carpenter, R. G. (2003). FAQs about IRIs. *The Reading Teacher, 56,* 578–580.

Paris, S. G., Carpenter, R. G., Paris, A. H., & Hamilton, E. E. (2005). Spurious and genuine correlates of children's reading comprehension. In S. G. Paris & S. A. Stahl (Eds.), *Children's reading comprehension and assessment* (pp. 131–160). Mahwah, NJ: Erlbaum.

Paris, S. G., & Paris, A. H. (2001). Classroom applications of research on self-regulated learning. *Educational Psychologist, 36,* 89–101.

Paris, S. G., Pearson, P. D., Carpenter, R. D., Siebenthal, S., & Laier, B. (2002). *Evaluation of the Michigan Literacy Progress Profile (MLPP). Final Report Year 1.* Lansing, MI: Department of Education.

Pearson, P. D., Calfee, R., Walker-Webb, P. L., & Fleischer, S. (2002). *The role of performance-based assessments in large-scale accountability systems: Lessons learned from the inside.* Washington, DC: Council of Chief State School Officers.

Pearson, P. D., DeStefano, L., & Garcia, E. (1998). Ten dilemmas of performance assessment. In C. Harrison & T. Salinger (Eds.), *Assessing reading 1, the theory and practice* (pp. 21–49). London: Routledge.

Pearson, P. D., & Hamm, D. N. (2001). The cognitive demands of item formats on NAEP. Paper presented at the annual meeting of the American Educational Research Association, Seattle, WA.

Pearson, P. D., & Hamm, D. N. (2005). The assessment of reading comprehension: A review of practices- past, present, and future. In S. G. Paris & S. A. Stahl (Eds.), *Children's reading comprehension and assessment* (pp. 13–69). Mahwah, NJ: Erlbaum.

Pearson, P. D., Spaulding, E., & Myers, M. (1998). Literacy assessment in the New Standards Project. In M. Coles & R. Jenkins (Eds.), *Assessing reading to change practice in classrooms* (pp. 54–97). London: Routledge.

Pressley, M., & Afflerbach, P. (1995). *Verbal protocols in reading: The nature of constructively responsive reading.* Hillsdale, NJ: Erlbaum.

Pressley, M., & Hilden, K. R. (2005). Commentary on three important directions in comprehension assessment research. In S. G. Paris & S. A. Stahl (Eds.), *Children's reading comprehension and assessment* (pp. 305–315). Mahwah, NJ: Erlbaum.

Pritchard, R. (1990). The evolution of instropective methodology and its implication for studying the reading process. *Reading Psychology, 11*, 1–13.

RAND Reading Study Group. (2002). *Reading for understanding.* Santa Monica, CA: RAND Corporation.

Randall, A., Fairbanks, M. M., & Kennedy, M. L. (1986). Using think-aloud protocols diagnostically with college readers. *Reading Research and Instruction, 25*, 240–253.

Rasool, J. M., & Royer, J. M. (2001). Assessment of reading comprehension using the sentence verification technique: Evidence from narrative and descriptive texts. *Journal of Educational Research, 78*, 180–184.

Roberts, G., Good, R., & Corcoran, S. (2005). Story retell: A fluency-based indicator of reading comprehension. *School Psychology Quarterly, 20*, 304–318.

Romero, F., Paris, S. G., & Brem, S. K. (2005). Children's comprehension and local-to-global recall of narrative and expository texts [Electronic Version]. *Current Issues in Education, 8*(25).

Rosenshine, B., Meister, C., & Chapman, S. (1996). Teaching students to generate questions: A review of the intervention studies. *Review of Educational Research, 66*, 181–221.

Royer, J. M. (2001). Developing reading and listening comprehension tests based on the sentence verification technique (SVT). *Journal of Adolescent and Adult Literacy, 45*, 30–41.

Royer, J. M., Abranovic, W. A., & Sinatra, G. (1987). Using entering reading performance as a predictor of course performance in college classes. *Journal of Educational Psychology, 79*, 19–26.

Royer, J .M., & Carlo, M. S. (1991). Assessing the language acquisition progress of limited-English proficient students: Problems and a new alternative. *Applied Measurement in Education, 4*, 85–113.

Royer, J. M., Greene, B. A., & Sinatra, G. M. (1997). The Sentence Verification Technique: A practical procedure for testing comprehension. *Journal of Reading, 30*, 14–22.

Royer, J. M., Hastings, C. N., & Hook, C. (1979). A sentence verification technique for measuring reading comprehension. *Journal of Reading Behavior, 11*, 355–363.

Royer, J. M., Lynch, D. J., Hambleton, R. K., & Bulgareli, C. (1984). Using the sentence verification technique to assess the comprehension of technical text as a function of subject matter expertise. *American Education Research Journal, 21*, 839–869.

Salinger, T. (2003). Assessing the literacy of young children: The case for multiple forms of evidence. In S. B. Neuman & D. K. Dickinson (Eds.), *Handbook of early literacy research* (pp. 390–418). New York: Guilford.

Shapley, K. S., & Bush, M. J. (1999). Developing a valid and reliable portfolio assessment in the primary grades: Building on practical experience. *Applied Measurement in Education, 12*, 111–132.

Shepard, L. (1993). Evaluating validity. *Review of Educational Research, 19*, 405–450.

Silvaroli, N. J., & Wheelock, W. (2001). *Classroom reading inventory.* New York: McGraw-Hill.

Silven, M., & Vauras, M. (1992). Improving reading through thinking aloud. *Learning and Instruction, 2*, 69–88.

Smith, J. K. (2003). Reconsidering reliability in classroom assessment and grading. *Educational measurement, Issues and Practice, 22*, 26–33.

Snyder, L., Caccamise, D., & Wise, B. (2005). The assessment of reading comprehension: Considerations and cautions. *Topics in Language Disorders, 25*, 33–50.

Spector, J. E. (2005). How reliable are informal reading inventories? *Psychology in the Schools, 42*, 593–603.

Stahl, S. A. (2003). Vocabulary and readability: How knowing word meanings affects comprehension. *Topics in Language Disorders, 23*, 241–247.

Stahl, S. A., Pagnucco, J. R., & Stuttles, C. W. (1996). The effects of traditional and process literacy instruction on first graders' achievement and orientation toward reading. *Journal of Educational Research, 89*, 131–144.

Stein, N. L., & Glenn, C. (1979). An analysis of story comprehension in elementary school children. In R. O. Freedle (Ed.), *Advances in discourse processes (vol. 2): New directions in discourse processes* (pp 53–120). Norwood, NJ: Ablex.

Stieglitz, E. (2002). *Stieglitz informal reading inventory.* Boston, MA: Allyn & Bacon.

Sudweeks, R., Glissmeyer, C. B., Morrison, T. G., Wilcox, B. R., & Tanner, M. W. (2004). Establishing reliable procedures for rating ELL students' reading comprehension using oral retellings. *Reading Research and Instruction, 43*, 65–87.

Taylor, B. M., & Pearson, P. D. (2005). Using study groups and reading assessment data to improve reading instruction within a school. In S. G. Paris & S. A. Stahl (Eds.), *Children's reading comprehension and assessment* (pp. 237–255). Mahwah, NJ: Erlbaum.

Taylor, O. L., Payne, K. T., & Anderson, N. B. (1987). Distinguishing between communication disorders and communication differences. *Seminars in Speech and Language, 8*, 415–427.

Thorndike, R. L. (1917). Reading as reasoning. A study of mistakes in paragraph reading. *Journal of Educational Psychology, 8*, 323–332.

Tierney, R. J. (1998). Literacy assessment reform: Shifting beliefs, principled possibilities, and emerging practices. *The Reading Teacher, 51*, 374–390.

Trabasso, T., & Magliano, J. P. (1996a). Conscious understanding during reading. *Discourse Processes, 21*, 255–287.

Trabasso, T., & Magliano, J. P. (1996b). How do children understand what they read and what can we do to help them? In M. Graves, P. van den Broek, & B. Taylor (Eds.), *The first R: A right of all children* (pp. 158–181). New York: Teachers College, Columbia University Press.

Valencia, S.W. (2000). Snippets: How will literacy be assessed in the next millennium? *Reading Research Quarterly, 35*, 247–251.

Valencia, S. W., Stallman, A. C., Commeyras, M., Pearson, P. D., & Hartman, D. K. (1991). Four measures of topical knowledge: A study of construct validity. *Reading Research Quarterly, 26*, 204–233.

van den Broek, P., Lorch, R .F., Linderholm, T., & Gustafson, M. (2001). The effects of readers' goals on inference generation and memory for texts. *Memory and Cognition, 29*, 1081–1087.

van den Broek, P., Tzeng, Y., Risden, K., Trabasso, T., & Basche, P. (2001). Inferential questioning: Effects on comprehension of narrative texts as a function of grade and timing. *Journal of Educational Psychology, 93*, 521–529.

Wade, S. E. (1990). Using think alouds to assess comprehension. *The Reading Teacher, 43*, 442–451.

Ward, L., & Traweek, D. (1993). Application of a metacognitive strategy to assessment intervention and consultation: A think-aloud technique. *Journal of School Psychology, 31*, 469–485.

Wiggins, G. (1989). A true test: Toward more authentic and equitable assessment. *Phi Delta Kappan, 70*, 703–713.

Wixson, K. K., & Carlisle, J. F. (2005). The influence of large-scale assessment of reading comprehension on classroom practice: A commentary. In S. G. Paris & S. A. Stahl (Eds.), *Children's reading comprehension and assessment* (pp. 395–406). Mahwah, NJ: Erlbaum.

Worthy, J., & Invernizzi, M. A. (1995). Linking reading with meaning. *Journal of Reading Behavior, 27*, 585–603.

Zakaluk, B. L., & Samuels, S .J. (1988). *Readability: Its past, present and future.* Newark, DE: International Reading Association.

Zwaan, R. A., & Brown, C. M. (1996). The influence of language proficiency and comprehension skill on situation-model construction. *Discourse Processes, 21*, 289–327.

20 Assessing the Comprehension of Young Children

Katherine A. Dougherty Stahl

New York University

What measures of comprehension are most likely to be sensitive to the development of reading comprehension of young children, including emergent and novice readers? Emergent readers are in the process of learning how to handle a text, developing print concepts, and acquiring knowledge about the grapheme-phoneme system. Emergent reading may incorporate comprehension-related competencies such as labeling illustrations, story-telling in response to illustrations, and memorization of text. Novice readers are able to read in more conventional ways than emergent readers with a refined knowledge of word recognition that incorporates alphabetics, the orthographic system, and a bank of high-frequency vocabulary. However, novice readers have not achieved automaticity in these domains. As a result, recent research indicates a stronger relationship between fluency and comprehension for novice readers than for older readers in third and fourth grade (Paris, 2005; Paris, Carpenter, Paris, & Hamilton, 2005). Other developmental considerations in assessing the comprehension of young children include their lack of world experiences, vocabulary range, and attention spans.

THEORETICAL AND HISTORICAL PERSPECTIVES

Developmental differences make it necessary to carefully consider the appropriateness of tools that are used to assess young children. Sensitive measures can provide a window for viewing the development of reading comprehension competencies. Historically the instruction and assessment of reading comprehension have not begun until students enter the intermediate grades. However since comprehension is the essential purpose of reading, it is important to begin early to assess aspects of reading comprehension.

Generally, the assessment of comprehension is complex because comprehension can only be measured indirectly (Pearson & Johnson, 1978). As researchers and teachers, we must gather artifacts or evidence that is produced by the reader that coincides with our theory or definition of comprehension. This is exemplified in the wide variety of measures of comprehension used in the research reviewed throughout this handbook. The influence of theory can also be seen in the changes in assessment instruments historically.

In this chapter, I will review research that examines the comprehension assessment of young children. I will begin with a discussion of landmark studies that have contributed to our body of knowledge in this area. Then, I will describe particular assessment procedures and research related to those procedures, what researchers have learned about the development of comprehension from using each assessment, and classroom application issues. I have organized the assessment research to coincide with a few theoretical

Table 20.1 Theoretical Frame and Corresponding Assessments

Theoretical Points	*Assessments*
Comprehension is developmental, historical, and social. Changes over time in children's bio-sociocultural development and ever-increasing bank of experiences result in changes in reading comprehension capabilities (Kintsch, 1998; Nelson, 1996).	• Minimal reading/Nonreading Measures: Narrative Wordless Picture Books (Paris & Paris, 2003; van Kraayenoord & Paris, 1996); Sulzby's Classification Scheme (1985); Video measures • Retelling • Cued Recall • Verbal Protocols • Sentence Verification
Reading comprehension demands capable decoding, language processes and domain knowledge (Kintsch, 1998).	• Miscue analysis: Reading Miscue Inventory (Goodman, Watson, & Burke, 1987), running records, informal reading inventories • Curriculum-based Measures • Cloze and maze
Proficient readers tend to engage in some common strategies during the initiation of reading, during the act of reading, and after reading that enable them to integrate the material from the text with prior knowledge and experience. Strategies enable the reader to monitor, repair, and enhance comprehension (Kintsch, 1998; Paris, Lipson, & Wixson, 1983).	• Verbal Protocols • Strategy Scales: Index of Reading Awareness (Jacobs & Paris, 1987; Paris & Jacobs, 1984), Metacognitive Strategy Index (Schmitt, 1990), Major Point Interview (Keene & Zimmerman, 1997)
One role of school is to provide the instruction, experience, and the socio-cultural context that will promote student competency in utilizing external systems of knowledge for their own purposes and personal growth (Donald, 1991; Kintsch, 1998).	• Dynamic assessment • Common Instructional Passage Assessment (Stahl, Garcia, Bauer, Pearson, & Taylor, 2006)

points that apply to the assessment of comprehension of young children (see Table 20.1). Instruments that adhere to multiple aspects of the theory are described in the section where they have the strongest association.

LANDMARK STUDIES

Formal, standardized comprehension assessment measures have become more predominant in primary classrooms as a response to the accountability requirements of No Child Left Behind (2002). Leslie and Caldwell (see chapter 19, this volume) provide a thorough discussion of landmark studies related to formal, standardized assessments. Psychometrically, these tests tend to meet the traditional, empirically-based standards of reliability and validity required by policy makers and administrators. However, current theories of validity and reading comprehension have resulted in a fresh look at formative assessments and their ability to meet some of the needs identified in the Rand Report (Rand Reading Study Group, 2002; Snow, 2003). In particular, Snow (2003) notes that it is difficult for assessment measures

- To adequately reflect the complexity of reading comprehension;
- To identify why comprehension breaks down, separating "comprehension processes (inferencing, integrating new with existent knowledge) from lack of vocabulary, of domain-specific knowledge, of word reading ability, or of other reader capacities involved in comprehension;"
- To capture the "developmental nature of comprehension" and teachers' instructional emphases and effectiveness;
- To focus on "comprehension for engagement, for aesthetic response, for purposes of critiquing an argument or disagreeing with a position;"
- To capture instruction and to be psychometrically reliable and valid (pp. 193–195).

The Center for the Improvement of Early Reading Achievement (CIERA) was operational from 1997 until 2003. A series of CIERA studies, especially the center's dissemination of final reports synthesizing investigative outcomes, attempted to address these challenges. However, since much of the research had begun before the publication of the Rand Report (2002) or the report of the National Reading Panel (NICHHD, 2000), the CIERA researchers' investigations were much broader than the focus of these two reports. As a result, we have a collective body of research that provided some fundamental insights and advanced our knowledge about the comprehension assessment of young readers (see Paris & Hoffman, 2004; Paris & Stahl, 2005). CIERA researchers conducted surveys on the range of assessments available and investigated informal reading inventories. Several researchers were involved in the design of innovative assessments that had implications for comprehension as they incorporated considerations of classroom environment, varied instructional texts, and explored ways to measure children's emerging knowledge of narrative structure.

One of the culminating achievements of CIERA was to gather a large group of experts to discuss their research related to the assessment of reading comprehension with an emphasis on the young reader. Researchers addressed large-scale assessments and assessments in school contexts. Investigations that explored the influence of development, vocabulary, engagement and composition on reading comprehension and assessment were discussed. Although the published volume of research reported at this conference raises as many questions as it answers, an overview of the research reveals the necessity to balance reading theory, assessment principles, classroom practice, and policy in the development of a reading comprehension assessment system, rather than relying on one unitary tool (Paris & Stahl, 2005).

One insight derived from this body of assessment research, the importance of distinguishing between constrained and unconstrained reading skills, is quite specific to novice readers and has important implications for theories of reading development and assessment (Carpenter & Paris, 2005; Paris, 2005; Paris et al., 2005). Constrained skills (alphabet knowledge, phonological awareness, reading rate) achieve ceiling scores in a relatively short period of time. Alternatively, vocabulary and comprehension are more complex, develop continuously and have the potential for endless growth (Paris, 2005, p. 194). The lack of a normal distribution or the potential for floor and ceiling scores on constrained skills make parametric statistics, including Pearson correlations, inappropriate when incorporating constrained skills in statistical analyses. Certainly, a novice reader's ability level on constrained skills will influence comprehension before mastery or before growth reaches levels of asymptote. For example, high inaccuracy rates and disfluency are likely to affect the comprehension of a novice reader. However, mastery of constrained skills tends to have limited influence on the long-term reading achievement of unconstrained skills (Paris, 2005). As a result, Paris urges caution in using the assessment of constrained skills to make predictions and provide interventions with intimations for more general reading abilities. In this volume, Paris and Hamilton (chapter 2) discuss this body of research and its implications more thoroughly.

DEVELOPMENTAL MEASURES

Non-reading measures of comprehension

Multiple studies have been conducted using comprehension assessments that require little or no reading by novice readers, yet act as indicators of text comprehension during early reading acquisition. These assessments measure children's familiarity with text structures, their ability to approximate a sensible rereading of a text and their utilization of causal relationships in retelling (Lorch, Bellack, & Augsbach, 1987; Moss, 1997; Paris & Paris, 2003; Paris & van Kraayenoord, 1998; Sulzby, 1985; van den Broek, 2001; van den Broek, Lorch, & Thurlow, 1996; van Kraayenoord & Paris, 1996). Given a developmental and historical perspective, we must look at factors that develop over time, especially those that are displayed before traditional reading can be observed. There are several measures that can do this with validity and reliability. To date these measures have not been commonly used in classrooms. However, they can be powerful indicators of a child's meaning-making processes.

Narrative wordless picture book assessment   The construction of a narrative based on a wordless picture book predicts and correlates to other measures of reading comprehension (Paris & Paris, 2003; Paris & van Kraayenoord, 1998; van Kraayenoord & Paris, 1996). In these studies, children took a picture walk through a wordless picture book and performed a spontaneous oral telling of the story. Researchers asked the children questions about the narrative features of the text and to assess their explicit and implicit comprehension of the story. Van Kraayenoord and Paris (1996) conducted a longitudinal study with students in their first or second year of school and retested the same group of children 2 years later (at ages 7 or 8). Paris and Paris tested children ranging from kindergarten to second grade.

There were not any significant differences on the picture walk story construction due to grade level or reading ability (Paris & Paris, 2003; van Kraayenoord & Paris, 1996). However, van Kraayenoord and Paris found that the Story Total (aggregate of all the initial measures) administered to Year 1 and Year 2 students correlated significantly with a standardized cloze measure, think-aloud of text reading, and the Index of Reading Awareness (Jacobs & Paris, 1987) 2 years later.

Children's retellings (after the picture walk, without access to the pictures) and prompted recall displayed developmental trends with regular improvement from kindergarten through Grade 2 (Paris & Paris, 2003). Children who could read were also more successful at retelling than nonreaders. In prompted comprehension, explicit scores were significantly higher than implicit scores overall for first and second graders, but not kindergartners. The most difficult items related to setting, prediction, and theme. Easier items related to characters, problem, and outcome resolution. The picture walk score of readers was not correlated to the retelling or their comprehension score on an informal reading inventory. However, the retelling of the narrative comprehension task was significantly related to both the retelling and prompted comprehension on the informal reading inventory.

These results tend to support much of the reading research on the development of narrative comprehension in text (Mandler & Johnson, 1977; Stein & Glenn, 1979). The ability of readers to provide more complete retellings than nonreaders raises several questions. Did the more complete sense of narrative contribute to reading acquisition? Does exposure to stories over time result in an increased awareness of narrative? Because we have traditionally not administered assessments of narrative awareness and construction to young children, we do not have the answers to these questions. However, until kits are available that make the books easily accessible and the administration and scoring standardized, this kind of measure will remain unutilized.

This study also seems to suggest that the picture walk story construction has less developmental sensitivity than retelling or prompted comprehension. Kindergartners were as capable as older students in generating a story during a picture walk. During the picture walk, the majority of children demonstrated book-handling skills and created a cohesive story. However, the majority of children did not use strategies, such as prediction or questioning, during the picture walk. More research is needed to determine if children who use picture walks as a prereading activity on a regular basis change over time in story construction and strategy implementation.

Sulzby's classification scheme   Sulzby's (1985) classification scheme allows teachers to assess children's rereading of familiar storybooks. The classification scheme assesses how closely the reading approximation of an emergent reader matches the actual text. Features of story content, story structure and decoding precision are considered in scoring students on Sulzby's developmental scale. During this study, Sulzby asked children between 2- and 5-years of age to read or pretend read a favorite storybook. She consistently observed a progression of ten types of reading behavior that were developmental in nature. She found that very young children are "picture governed" and create each page in the present tense as a discrete unit with emphasis on the action. Pretend reading in the final stages of the picture driven classification would involve a story with mixed verb tenses and a sense of sequence but which is missing narrative ties (including the use of pronoun referents). At this stage, the child uses conceptual strategies to begin using wording and intonations that display a shift to an awareness of the differences in oral and written language forms. In the next stages, the reading becomes "governed by print." The subcategories in this stage reflect the child's increasing awareness of concepts about print and how words work. Aspectual reading (focusing on one or two aspects about print) and the imbalance of strategy use may make it appear that the child's reading is regressing, especially in regard to meaningfulness. Finally, due to increased self-regulation and the ability to self-correct, the child arrives at the stage of independence.

Like the narrative, wordless picture book assessment, this assessment allows us to view the child's ability to formulate a meaningful reconstruction of the text. This scale has important diagnostic value but is not commonly used in preschool or kindergarten settings. Professional development training is required for assessment procedures that examine the complex inherent processes of emergent reading.

Video measures   Studies involving memory and the reconstruction of televised stories may be used to assess many aspects of comprehension in nonreaders or novice readers. Studies involving memory for televised stories reflected that children as young as 4 years of age retrieved important events in free recall tasks and were able to recall nearly all the most important propositions in cued recall tasks (Lorch et al., 1987; van den Broek et al., 1996). The use of televised stories also was a vehicle for demonstrating systematic developmental differences in the comprehension and memory of story events (van den Broek et al., 1996). A comparison of 4- and 6-year-old children and adults revealed that the number of events recalled increases with age. The number of causal connections, followed by story grammar categories exerted the strongest effects on recall. All effects increased with the age of the subjects. The children were more likely to recall actions, but the adults were more likely to use the information about the goals and motives of the protagonist and the causal structure to propel their retelling. This is consistent with the work by Paris (Paris & Paris, 2003; van Kraayenoord & Paris, 1996) and Sulzby (1985) that demonstrated the developmental tendencies associated with awareness of text story grammar and recall of important text elements.

Van den Broek (2001) conducted a longitudinal study of children's narrative retelling and prompted recall. He found that the ability to retell and answer questions about a video positively correlated with scores on retelling and answering questions about a text the child read 2 years later.

The utilization of video or computer technology as a form of comprehension assessment may hold potential, especially for emergent readers and at-risk readers. It is a format that is familiar and engaging. It removes the child from burden of decoding, enabling him to use all resources to comprehend. It enables the examiner to tap into what the child is able to remember and views as important for retelling. It can provide important insights into what kinds of experiences need to be instructed, scaffolded and practiced before independent reading comprehension can be expected.

Retelling

Retelling tasks require the child to orally summarize the information that was seen, heard, or read. Retelling requires the reader to reconstruct the information from the text with varying degrees of integration with prior knowledge and links to other texts (Gambrell, Koskinen, & Kapinus, 1991). Retelling tasks often follow the reading of a text selection that is being used for some format of miscue analysis, such as a running record or reading inventory. For a more general discussion, see Leslie and Caldwell (chapter 19, this volume). The openness of the retelling task allows room for the observation of the child's thought processes, what is valued as important, and socio-cultural influences in story interpretation (Narvaez, 2002). Retellings have been used successfully with children in kindergarten and first grade (Geva & Olson, 1983; Morrow, 1984b, 1985; Moss, 1997).

Retellings demonstrate consequential validity. Consequential validity results in positive consequences for the examinee as a result of the experience (Messick, 1989). Studies have demonstrated that the practice of retelling narrative and expository texts, without specific instruction, results in improvements in adherence to story grammar, selection of high-level propositions, and cued recall (Gambrell et al., 1991; Gambrell, Pfeiffer, and Wilson, 1985; Morrow, 1984b, 1985).

Cameron, Hunt, and Linton (1985) determined that second graders produced very similar oral retellings, manually-written and computer-written retellings. This study supported many of the findings of Geva and Olson (1983) that investigated the oral retellings of first graders. Both studies found that young children were likely to include a prototypical opening, elaborated actions, and minimal, action-based endings. Second graders had less difficulty with verb tense decisions, less pronoun ambiguity and more complete story endings, although their retellings lacked the affective dimensions of emotion and moral judgment. Although paraphrasing predominated the retellings, better readers adjusted their retelling to the audience. They used more gist comments when retelling to the experimenter and more verbatim statements when retelling to a peer who was unfamiliar with the story (Geva & Olson, 1983). Evidence shows that retelling practice significantly improves the performance of proficient and less-proficient readers on a retelling task (Gambrell et al, 1991; Gambrell et al., 1985; Morrow, 1984b, 1985). Students with little experience in retelling or less verbal students may not reflect their reading comprehension on a retelling task. A study by Moss (1997) provided evidence that first graders constructed fairly complete and cohesive retellings of expository text that included key ideas.

There are some considerations in the use of retellings as an assessment measure. An oral retelling of a story places high cognitive demands on young children. "Especially for longer stories, the resource demands of producing an organized and sequentially and causally coherent story may exceed the resources available to children, especially young five- and six-year-olds" (Goldman, Varma, Sharp, & Cognition and Technology Group at Vanderbilt [CTGV] 1999, p. 139). As a result, a teacher or researcher would also want to ask the child questions to get a full representation of the child's understanding of a text.

Cued recall

Although retellings can provide the tester with valuable information about what the child perceives as important and the ability of the child to put together a sequence of events that is causally and logically propelled, research indicates that children understand much more than they are likely to include in a retelling (Mandler & Johnson, 1977; Stein & Glenn, 1979). Information relating to the goals, motives and feelings of the characters is commonly omitted from the retellings of young children (Cameron et al., 1985; Geva & Olson, 1983; Mandler & Johnson, 1977; Stein & Glenn, 1979). However, when asked questions about these areas, children have demonstrated insight and awarenesses that were not displayed in their retelling (Mandler & Johnson, 1977; Stein & Glenn, 1979).

Question-answering also reduces cognitive demands for young children. Wording of the question acts as an activation cue. The specificity of a question reduces the amount of information that needs to be held in working memory and organized for output. It also makes it clear to the child what information the adult is seeking, finds important, and is interested in hearing (Goldman et al., 1999). In order to get the broadest picture of a child's comprehension, it seems imperative to use both retelling and cued recall. Different types of information are reflected in each format.

The measures in this section require varying amounts of actual text reading. Retelling and cued recall measures may be conducted with reading, listening, or visual methods, such as a picture book or video. The evidence suggests that comprehension in nonreading contexts is consistent with understanding of texts (van den Broek, 2001). Children who experience difficulty comprehending stories presented in visual formats or as listening activities, without the burden of decoding, are likely to need additional comprehension support when they are also held accountable for reading text. These measures are useful for teachers and researchers in parsing out the reading comprehension difficulties of young readers. Children who encounter difficulties with particular aspects of narrative structures may need additional opportunities to use these structures orally and retelling personal experiences as a supplement to early text-based experiences.

Sentence verification

Sentence verification technique (SVT) is based on the assumption that when text is read and understood it is represented in memory in a way that preserves the meaning but not the exact wording of the text. The purpose of SVT is to establish whether or not the reader has formed that representation in memory. The sentence verification task produces results that meet high psychometric standards of reliability and validity (Royer, Greene, & Sinatra, 1987). A set of studies demonstrated that scores on the SVT are sensitive to other factors that affect and reflect comprehension. SVT tests are sensitive to text readability (Royer, Hastings, & Hook, 1979), reading skill (Rasool & Royer, 1986; Royer et al., 1979; Royer, Sinatra, & Schumer, 1990), and characteristics of text (Rasool & Royer, 1986). For a thorough discussion of SVT and its construction, see Leslie and Caldwell (chapter 19, this volume).

Basically, an SVT test consists of a set of passages, with each passage followed by a set of test sentences. The students read (or listen to) the passage and then, without looking back at the passage, they respond "Old" to indicate that a sentence with the same meaning was in the passage or "New" to indicate that the test item reflects a meaning change or distractor. "Yes" or "No" have been used, respectively, in more recent studies (Royer et al., 1990). These tests have been used with all age groups starting in third grade.

Despite the promise of SVT as a theoretically and psychometrically grounded comprehension assessment measure, it is rarely used. The simple "Yes" or "No" answer format could seemingly be incorporated in standardized, mass testing settings. The choice of "Yes" or "No" demands fewer cognitive resources than the multiple choice format, making it more developmentally appropriate for young children (Anderson & Freebody, 1983; Stahl, 2000). The increasing demand for high-stakes, standardized tests in the primary grades makes it more important than ever to examine alternative measures that have the potential to meet the developmental needs of young students.

MEASURES OF DECODING, LANGUAGE PROCESSING, AND DOMAIN KNOWLEDGE

Miscue analysis

Miscue analysis is an evaluation of oral reading errors. A miscue analysis may be conducted independently or as part of an informal reading inventory that includes questioning and retelling. This section of the chapter will focus only on miscue analysis as a lens for assessing comprehension. Some researchers (Clay, 1993a; Goodman, Watson, & Burke, 1987) advocate the use of error analysis as evidence of comprehension processes. According to Goodman et al. (1987), "the ability to produce semantically and syntactically acceptable structures or, if the structures are unacceptable, to correct them, provides evidence of a reader's predicting and confirming strategies" (p. 61).

The examinee is asked to read an unfamiliar passage aloud and the examiner records the examinee's reading of the text using a coding system. After the reading session, the examiner evaluates the reader's errors and self-corrections. Substitutions, omissions and teacher-assists are counted as errors. Typically, repetitions and self-corrections are recorded and evaluated but not counted as errors. Errors are analyzed for their syntactic and semantic acceptability in the sentence and passage, whether they resulted in changes in the meaning of the text, and grapho-phonetic similarity to the text. A coding form is used for the analysis with the consideration of syntactic and semantic acceptability always being given the highest priority. This emphasis on prediction, confirmation, meaning change, syntactic and semantic acceptability may justify the use of miscue analysis as a comprehension measure, especially when used with young children whose reading is often propelled by meaning (Clay, 1991, 1993a; Sulzby, 1985).

Reading Miscue Inventory (Goodman et al., 1987)   One distinction of Reading Miscue Inventory is the use of a lengthy piece of text (at least 500 words). For young readers this would involve using multiple books. Teachers and researchers are advised to compile a range of materials suitable for miscue analysis.

Reading Miscue Inventory in its purest form is extensive and time-consuming. A teacher would only be likely to do a Reading Miscue Inventory at the beginning and end of a year or with struggling readers that require specialized instruction. Miscues are analyzed by asking a series of questions about the miscues and self-corrections. The questions may be asked about acceptability at the passage level, sentence level, partial sentence level, and word level.

Running records   Running records have the same theoretical base and are very similar to one of the alternative abbreviated Reading Miscue Inventory procedures (Clay, 1993a; Goodman et el., 1987). Although the assessor may ask a few comprehension questions or request a retelling, the error analysis is the primary evaluation of the running record.

Two of the advantages of running records are the ease and flexibilty of administration. The coding format of running records enables them to be used without a typescript, easing the burden of preparation. Text length is not dictated. This enables running records to be conducted with a wide variety of texts. As a result, running records are likely to be administered with greater frequency than the Reading Miscue Inventory or an informal reading inventory. Clay (1993a; 1993b) recommends that running records be administered using any texts that children can read with 90%–95% accuracy. Typically, authentic texts are used. "Little books" that contain complete, cohesive stories or informational text that have been leveled using qualitative criteria (Peterson, 1991; Rhodes, 1981) are often selected as benchmark texts for systematic assessment. For novice readers, the content of these texts is likely to be within the realm of their experience and at or close to their instructional reading level. This increases the likelihood that the novice reader will be able to read the text with fluency, an important factor in the comprehension of novice readers.

Informal reading inventories   Informal reading inventories contain a collection of graded reading passages (See Leslie & Caldwell, chapter 19, this volume). The passages typically range from 100 to 300 words for primary level passages (Johns, 1997; Leslie & Caldwell, 2006). Multiple forms are provided for opportunities to pretest and posttest, determine listening comprehension levels, or to sample comprehension during silent reading with narrative and expository text. The availability of multiple, graded, reading passages with prepared questions and scoring guides with fairly standardized, prescribed procedures are the advantageous features of informal reading inventories. The grade level passages provided are designed to show yearly grade-level growth, but not intermittent progress. As a result, the growth of emergent readers and smaller intervals of growth may not be reflected.

There are several other disadvantages for novice readers. Comprehension and word recognition rates may be negatively affected by passages that are strictly governed by conventional notions of readability. The Dale-Chall readability formula (Chall & Dale, 1995), which has been extended from fourth to first grade, is based on an extrapolation. They caution that lower levels do not have the degree of confidence found in upper levels. This may be true for other readability formulas that are based on word difficulty and sentence length. Chall and Dale list physical features of text, the number of pictures and how they relate to text, language, organization, and cognitive complexity as important variables in the comprehensive nature of readability that have not been included in readability formulas and need to be judged separately. Repetitive pattern, familiar concepts, natural language, good match of illustrations and text, rhyme, rhythm alliteration, cumulative pattern, familiar story, and familiar sequence are features that seem to promote readability for early readers (Gourley, 1984; Peterson, 1991; Rhodes, 1981). Because of the reliance that early readers still have on meaning and language to facilitate decoding, these factors may more significantly impact their performance than the performance of older readers.

Finally, the required speficity of the match between beginning readers' knowledge and the IRI passage can be a limitation of commercial IRI use in the lower grades. Differences in vocabulary learned and tested may impact achievement levels on the IRI (Johns, 1997).

Additional considerations Miscue analysis of oral reading does provide a window for viewing the prediction, confirmation, and meaning-making process during reading. There is substantial evidence that demonstrates that poorer readers, younger readers, and readers with less prior knowledge make errors with less semantic acceptability and more graphic similarity (Chinn, Waggoner, Anderson, Schommer, & Wilkinson, 1993; Schlieper, 1977; Taft & Leslie, 1985; Wixson, 1979). Their errors are also more likely to be nonwords and left uncorrected. However, reading comprehension is dynamic and in many ways situated in the context (Chinn et al., 1993; Taft & Leslie, 1985; Wixson, 1979). Prior knowledge of the topic by the reader, instructional reading program, the type of teacher feedback in response to errors, and the difficulty of the material have all been found to influence student miscues and corrections (Chinn et al., 1993; Taft & Leslie, 1985; Wixson, 1979). These factors influence oral reading miscues and should always be considered in making an evaluation of reading comprehension based on miscue analysis. Additionally, all of these methods are highly reliant on the competence of the teacher in appropriate text selection, recording text reading, error analysis and interpretation. Extensive professional development is essential.

Curriculum–based measurement

Curriculum-based measurement (CBM) refers to a specific subset of curriculum-based assessment (CBA). CBA is typically an informal approach that uses observations and records of student performance on local curriculum as tools for instructional planning (Hasbrouck, Woldbeck, Ihnot, & Parker, 1999; Shinn, 1988). CBA tends to be hierarchical, non-normed, and have questionable validity and reliability. CBM, on the other hand, is a specific standardized set of procedures developed through the Institute for Research on Learning Disabilities as a formative evaluation system to help special educators assess student growth and plan instruction (Hasbrouck et al., 1999). CBM is now widely used by special educators, researchers, and classroom teachers as a valid and reliable measure of student growth.

In the area of reading, CBM usually consists of scoring the number of words correctly read per minute from a passage derived from a basal reader or literature anthology. Although this would seem to be purely a measure of reading fluency, studies have determined that passage reading CBM is highly correlated (.77 to .92) with standardized measures of comprehension (Fuchs & Fuchs, 1992; Kranzler, Miller, & Jordan, 1999; Madelaine & Wheldall, 1999; Shinn, Knutson, Good, Tilly, & Collins, 1992). Kranzler et al. (1999) determined that there was no evidence of gender or racial/ethnic bias of CBM in Grades 2 and 3.

CBM seems to be most sensitive and highly correlated to overall reading competence and reading comprehension before Grade 4 (Kranzler et al., 1999; Shinn, 1988; Shinn et al., 1992). This is consistent with a developmental theory of reading and the recent work by Paris (2005) on constrained and unconstrained abilities. The lack of automaticity of novice readers seems to contribute to difficulties in comprehension (Stanovich, 1980). Recent research indicates that fluency and comprehension may be dependent early in the process of reading acquisition, but they become independent after high levels of reading fluency are achieved (Paris, 2005). Correlations between fluency scores and comprehension scores diminish in the third and fourth grades (Paris et al., 2005). In other words, novice readers who struggle to decode words are less likely to understand the text, whereas an independent relation is evident among older students who read fluently but have poor comprehension. As readers become more automatic in word processing, comprehension difficulties are likely to be the result of unfamiliar content, idea density or some other source.

Teacher training and support are required for reliable application of CBM. As well as taking time away from instruction, the preparation of passages, administration and scoring are time intensive for teachers. Shinn (1988) has given explicit, procedural directions for the selection of reading passages and the development of local norms. Materials are to be randomly selected from the curriculum reading materials, tested for readability consistency and retyped to duplicate the grade-level text for the children and with word counts for the teachers.

The development of passage kits and widespread availability of Dynamic Indicators of Basic Early Literacy Skills has made CBM more accessible to teachers (Madelaine & Wheldall, 1999). Powell-Smith and Bradley-Klug (2001) found that students performed at more proficient levels on generic passages than passages derived from curriculum reading materials. Factors that may contribute to the attractiveness of generic passage kits are control of readability, consistent gradient levels of difficulty, and the inclusion of texts with complete, cohesive structures in their entirety. The compilation and utilization of this commercial packages increases time efficiency, standardization, reliability, and validity of CBM as a measure of student progress.

Cloze

Cloze was developed by Taylor (1953) as a mechanical approach to test item development and an alternative to the conventional standardized test of comprehension. In its original form, every nth word (usually every 5th word) in a passage is deleted. The examinee fills in each cloze blank. Only a precise replacement is scored as correct and higher scores indicate greater comprehension. One of the most serious criticisms of cloze is the lack of intersentential and intertextual comprehension. Shanahan, Kamil and Tobin (1982) demonstrated that the ability to fill in a cloze blank does not rely upon making sense of the total passage. This is in direct conflict with modern theories of comprehension.

Over the years, researchers have developed a variety of adaptations with modifications to address these criticisms and to moderate the difficulty of writing the precise word in the blank. Pearson and Hamm (2005, p. 23) list some of the variations in their review of comprehension assessments.

- Allow synonyms to serve as correct answers
- Delete only every 5th content word (leaving function words intact)
- Use an alternative to every 5th word deletion
- Delete words at the end of sentences and provide a set of choices from which examinees are to pick the best answer (this tack is employed in several standardized tests, including the Stanford Diagnostic Reading Test and Degrees of Power).

Cloze and modifications of cloze have been successfully used as a form of ESL and bilingual assessment (Bachman, 1985; Bachman, 2000; Francis, 1999). In an oral reading index, the L2 reader would need to direct attention to the oral production at the expense of comprehension. The cloze method allows the L2 reader to devote processing resources to comprehension (Francis, 1999). Francis (1999) also recommends using cloze passages as instructional tools for L2 learners. Small groups can discuss their response choices for developing language awareness and comprehension monitoring.

Maze

One of the modifications of cloze that has increased in popularity is the maze task. The maze task is a multiple-choice variation of the cloze task. The maze task is appealing because of its ease of administration and scoring. It can be administered in an individual or group setting, manually or on a computer program. The multiple-choice format makes it easy to score. Teachers value maze as an acceptable indicator of decoding, fluency and comprehension (Fuchs & Fuchs, 1992).

Timed maze tasks have been adopted as another form of CBM. Fuchs and Fuchs (1992) performed a preliminary study of several measures of reading comprehension to determine the potential for a computer-based measure. They evaluated oral and written recalls, oral and written cloze tasks, oral question-answering, and maze. In terms of validity, reliability, correlation with a standard measure, capacity to demonstrate student abilities and progress, and teacher satisfaction, the timed maze task showed the most promise. Since this study, the Fuchs have produced a technology-based CBM maze task series with 30 passages per grade level available commercially.

The preliminary maze work by Fuchs and Fuchs (1992) was conducted with middle school boys with mild to moderate disabilities. The investigation of maze as a valid, reliable, sensitive assessment of younger students was conducted by Shinn, Deno and Espin (2000). Results showed good alternate form reliability (.69–.90 for all monthly passages). Both group improvement and individual gain were reflected. Growth rates were correlated to the children's end-of-year standardized reading tests.

The variations in maze construction may cause variations in sensitivity, reliability, and validity. Care and deliberation in the selection of passages is crucial. The passages should be between 100 and 400 words long to allow for internal coherence (Parker & Hasbrouck, 1992). Passages for younger students would be likely to be at the lower end of this range. Since progress is reflected in gains, passages should have approximately the same readability, although this was not explicitly stated in any of the cited articles. Deletion strategies can also vary in number, ratio deletion, and content. The point at which deletions start in a passage can vary. Typically, they start in the second sentence. However, for younger children a longer lead-in may be desirable.

The greatest source of psychometric concern is the selection of distractors (Parker & Hasbrouck, 1992). The number, quality, and lexical characteristics of distractors can vary greatly. Parker and Hasbrouck (1992) recommend that test designers choose four

> ... distractors that are (a) the same part of speech as the deleted word, (b) meaningful and plausible within one sentence, (c) related in content to the passage (when possible), (d) as familiar to the reader as the deleted word, and (e) either clearly wrong or less appropriate, given broader passage content. (p. 216)

Evidence indicates that some maze tests are sensitive to the reading comprehension development of novice readers (Francis, 1999; Shinn et al., 1999). The minimal demand placed on working memory is advantageous for younger students. However, the text readability and the characteristics of the distractors would require deliberate consideration and evaluation in the selection or design of maze tasks for young readers.

Degrees of Reading Power and Lexile Measures of Comprehension

The Degrees of Reading Power (DRP; Touchstone Applied Science Associates, 1995) and Lexile Framework (Stenner, 1996) are two maze modifications that directly relate comprehension scores to readability scales. Student scores are norm-referenced, criterion-referenced, and indicate the level of books that a student ought to be able to read and understand with a predicted 75% comprehension rate. Both tests can be group administered and the multiple-choice format makes them easy to score. DRP passages are all nonfiction and Lexile passages are derived from authentic texts. Both are untimed. Both tests have the advantage of being developed by pschometric experts and have high correlations with standardized tests. The DRP has a deletion ratio of 1/46 to require comprehension of several consecutive sentences on longer passages. Below is one example of a primary DRP passage.

Years ago, there were no electric lamps. People had to _____ their homes differently. One way to do this was with candles.

     (a) paint   (b) shape   (c) light   (d) enter

The extensive sampling, norming, and standardization of these tests helps validate them as comprehension assessments.

MEASURES OF STRATEGY USE

Verbal protocols or think-alouds

During a think-aloud, a subject verbally reports his thinking as he does a particular activity. The use of verbal protocols as a valid research methodology has gained respect in several areas of research. Leslie and Caldwell (chapter 19, this volume) provide a general review of the literature on application of think-alouds as an assessment procedure. This chapter focuses on applying it with novice readers.

Think-alouds have not been commonly used as an assessment of reading comprehension with young children. However, they can be a valuable tool for observing and measuring student comprehension (Afflerbach & Johnston, 1984). Their validity is based on a different set of theoretical assumptions than most data sources. They provide insights into cognitive processes and affective aspects of reading that may not be fully represented by product measures and they provide a window that allows for historical analysis of mental processes.

Despite the potential of verbal protocols to reveal cognitive processes, there are still some concerns that require consideration (Afflerbach & Johnston, 1984; Pressley & Afflerbach, 1995). Training participants to engage in verbal reporting needs to be thorough enough that they understand the task, but not so rehearsed that it influences the validity of the report.

Stahl, Garcia, Bauer, Pearson, and Taylor (2006) reported that younger students (second and third graders) and older students (fourth and fifth graders) were able to engage in a think-aloud of an unfamiliar text after participating in a small group 10–15 minute training session. The training consisted of the assessor thinking-aloud about the cover and page 1 of the story *Wednesday Surprise* (Bunting, 1990). The assessor then invited the group of students to think-aloud about sections of text on pages 2 and 3. Stahl et al. used the think-aloud measure to study how age differences, instructional differences, and ability differences might affect children's text processing. For the better readers, the think-alouds did reveal how these young readers interacted metacognitively with the text. When the second graders missed decoding 30% of the words in the first three paragraphs, the assessor alternated reading the paragraphs aloud with the child. However, these children were typically unable to do little more than restate what they had read. In essence, this outcome was consistent with the growing body of research that indicates that labored decoding and a lack of fluency are factors that are likely to inhibit the comprehension of novice readers (Paris, 2005; Paris et al., 2005).

Strategy scales

A few quantitative measures exist that have been designed to assess children's awareness of their strategy use during reading (Jacobs & Paris, 1987; Keene & Zimmermann,

1997; Paris & Jacobs, 1984; Schmitt, 1990). These measures were also designed to evaluate the progress of instructional programs that focus on strategy instruction. The measures are sensitive to gains in metacognitive awareness that are fostered by strategy programs. The measures have been found to correlate with a variety of reading comprehension measures.

All of the measures are self-report measures. They all ask children about behaviors and thinking processes that they engage in before, during, and after reading. Two of the measures, the Index of Reading Awareness (Jacobs & Paris, 1987; Paris & Jacobs, 1984) and the Metacognitive Strategy Index (Schmitt, 1990) are multiple-choice tests that can be quickly administered and scored using a whole class setting. The multiple-choice format does not place less verbal, less articulate children at a disadvantage.

The Major Point Interview for Readers (Keene & Zimmerman, 1997) is an individually administered reading activity and interview that requires 20 to 45 minutes for each administration. The child reads a text selection and is asked to think-aloud as he reads. The text is then used as a springboard for an interview about the child's use of schema, question-generation, inference formation, mental imagery, and ability to summarize and synthesize the text. Quantitative values are assigned to each response. These researchers used the interview with second graders, but the think-aloud procedure and metacognitive awareness required for responses in the interview may be a stretch for many young readers. This measure would seem to work best for children who have had experience using think-alouds. Due to the duration of each administration and examiner expertise required, this may be a more useful tool for a clinic, rather than a classroom setting.

DYNAMIC ASSESSMENT

Dynamic assessment attempts to modify performance through examiner assistance to gain a better perspective on potential learning and change (Swanson & Lussier, 2001). It is based on the work of Vygotsky (1978) and his notion of the "zone of proximal development." The "zone of proximal development" (ZPD) involves, not what a child can currently do independently, but what he can do in a social interaction with assistance. Grigorenko and Sternberg (1998) discriminate between dynamic assessment and dynamic testing. They define dynamic assessment as being much broader, with greater emphasis on the intervention that is likely to facilitate the change. The goal of dynamic testing is to determine if alternative opportunities result in change. Compared to static forms of assessment, advocates of dynamic assessment claim that dynamic assessment provides a better estimate of ability, an opportunity to view nascent abilities, and results in improved abilities as a result of test procedures (Allal & Ducrey, 2000; Campione, 1989; Feuerstein, 1979). These claims have been made most frequently for particular populations whose capabilities have not traditionally been reflected on static intelligence and achievement tests. Most studies involving dynamic assessment have involved underachievers, students with low intelligence quotients, culturally different populations, or recent immigrants. Researchers believed that these populations might be more capable of learning than static tests indicated and that static measures did not always show the subtle increments of growth found in these populations (Grigorenko & Sternberg, 1998). Typically, a pretest is administered, feedback or organized, task-specific instruction is provided, and then the change is evaluated in a posttest.

Dynamic assessment takes many forms. It can be quantitative or qualitative. Quantitative dynamic assessment focuses on posttest scores, gain scores, or the number of assists needed before the task can be completed correctly or transferred to a novel situation (Allal & Ducrey, 2000; Campione, 1989). Qualitative dynamic assessment can be embedded in the instructional sequence. Observations of student behavior, interactions with students and student work samples can be used to organize learning and foster student growth (Allal & Ducrey, 2000). Studies of reciprocal teaching included both qualitative measures during the dialogues and quantitative data gathered as repeated measures (Palincsar & Brown, 1984).

Two meta-analyses are helpful in looking at the strengths and weaknesses of dynamic assessment. Swanson and Lussier's (2001) quantitative meta-analysis of 30 studies used effect size and a corrected effect size for pretest sensitivity and upward bias of within design studies to synthesize the research. Dynamic assessment was most effective with underachieving children under the age of ten. It was least effective with learning disabled students. Greater effect sizes were observed on visual/spatial measures than verbal. There was a larger effect size for between design studies, comparisons of dynamic assessment to a static condition, than within designs involving pre/post measures. Swanson and Lussier concluded that the positive effects of dynamic assessment are not simply the result of retesting, as some critics claim.

There are many problems with dynamic assessment. The nonstandardized procedures for feedback and intervention used in some models can only be applied to a laboratory setting (Campione, 1989; Feuerstein, 1979; Grigorenko & Sternberg, 1998). When feedback procedures have been made more standardized, they are so task-specific that transfer to other abilities is negligible and prediction value is compromised (Campione, 1989; Grigorenko & Sternberg, 1998). The time, effort and expertise required in constructing and administering dynamic assessment has hindered its popularity despite the alignment of researchers and teachers with its theoretical roots.

Alternatively, Stahl et al. (2006) describe the utilization of a common instructional passage, assessment of student comprehension of authentic literature specifically designed for use in the classroom instructional setting. The texts were fairly lengthy and complex in content because the teacher provided a scaffolded instructional experience. Instruction made the texts accessible to the students and provided a means of avoiding the decoding obstacles that often hinder the comprehension of novice or struggling readers. The three days of instruction were followed by a curriculum-linked assessment. Students engaged in a retelling and constructed response on Day 4. The common instructional passage assessment can be used to identify the processes that students use to comprehend a common text. Teachers can adapt this assessment format to a wide range of classroom texts. This is another assessment with consequential validity (Taylor, 2006).

The retelling task required the child to orally retell the story in Grade 2 or to provide a written retelling in Grade 4. Additionally, each question that required a constructed response was designed to tap the knowledge and comprehension processes emphasized in a theoretically-based comprehension instructional framework. The instructional framework incorporated vocabulary development, cognitive strategy instruction and responsive engagement (high-level discussion). An example of a question targeting each comprehension aspect and the targeted control for the book *Lazy Lion* is listed below.

Vocabulary/Prior Knowledge: Besides lazy, what other words would you use to describe the lion?
Cognitive strategy: Suppose the lion had asked a hippopotamus to build him a house. What do you predict would happen?
Responsive Engagement: If Lion were a person, is he the kind of person you would like for a friend? Why or why not?

The assessments discussed in this section reflect the social nature of learning and work. However, they raise new questions about issues of validity for individual scores, external accountability, reliability and generalizability (Linn, 1999; Pearson & Hamm, 2000/2005).

SYNTHESIS

Reading comprehension develops gradually over time and builds on competencies such as oral language, prior knowledge, sense of narrative, strategic processing and self-regulation. Summative assessments are formal, standardized measures designed to provide periodic progress reports to stakeholders. Modern theories of validity emphasize test consequences (Messick, 1989). Too often, the consequences of high-stakes tests are large amounts of instructional time spent teaching to the test, utilization of test preparation materials, and narrowing the curriculum. Particularly in the area of comprehension, high-level thinking and critical literacy are forfeited. Although the policy maker's goal is to encourage improvement in reading instruction and achievement, that is not the function of the summative test. The summative, standardized test is simply designed to provide a snapshot of large numbers of students on a particular day in order to detect trends. However, the pressure created by high-stakes tests is now influencing instruction in ways that are restrictive to comprehension development.

Despite the complexity of comprehension, many of the assessment tools described in this chapter have the potential to result in positive consequences for young readers. Most formative assessments are designed to inform the teacher of the examinee's strengths and weaknesses in specific areas of reading comprehension. As a result, the teacher can use formative test data to plan instruction rather than adhering to a script that may be developmentally inappropriate and unresponsive to specific student abilities. While being mindful of the need to incorporate explicit comprehension instruction, several of the assessments in this chapter can function instructionally. Using the gradual release of responsibility model as an instructional frame can ensure that teaching and coaching occur before the child is required to engage in the task independently (Pearson & Gallagher, 1983).

A teacher can use the wordless picture book instructionally and as an assessment tool (Paris & Paris, 2003; van Kraayenoord & Paris, 1996). Teaching children to construct a narrative with all of its component parts assists meaning-making and increases the likelihood of success when they are confronted with the wordless picture book narrative assessment. It also introduces the child to the important parts of a story that can be transferred to retellings of stories they hear and later read. Morrow's (1984a, 1984b) work with kindergartners is a successful demonstration of using questioning and guided retelling toward this end. Continuous instruction and practice in the utilization of story grammar enables the novice writer to know what to include in a written retelling or personal narrative compositions.

The teacher-student dynamic during and after the running record influences the way that early readers approach text. The running record procedure forces the child to be accountable for reading and self-monitoring. The child gradually assumes responsibility for more of the task in increasingly difficult texts and becomes an active problem-solver.

Many of the assessments addressed in this chapter can be formatted to help children become better readers (story maps, questioning, verbal protocols, cloze, dynamic assessment). The caveat is that teachers must have the professional knowledge that enables them to interpret assessment data and teach responsively. It increases the level of accountability of the teacher as a professional. For teachers to be able to do this successfully, a strong on-going, data-driven professional development effort must be in place.

IMPLICATIONS FOR FUTURE RESEARCH

The high-stakes tests that are used with increasing frequency in primary classrooms neglect recent definitions of validity that place value on data interpretation (Cronbach, 1971) and consequential validity (Messick, 1989; Salinger, 2005; Wixson & Carlisle, 2005). The vocationalization of teachers with mandated scripted programs, extensive test preparation, an underemphasis of process and project-based comprehension instruction, and an overemphasis on an out-dated model of skill-based comprehension instruction are a few of the consequences of the current high-stakes comprehension tests. Researchers need to examine ways to systematize and standardize assessment measures that allow for an expanded comprehension curriculum and the latest theoretical knowledge about the reading comprehension of novice readers. Unlike the linear assessments that are capable of measuring constrained skills, multiple measures are needed to view the complexities of unconstrained skills. Research is needed to find ways to formalize, legitimize, and aggregate a series of informal measures that portray a broad picture of reading comprehension. Carpenter and Paris's (2005) analysis of the Michigan Literacy Progress Profile provides a good example and starting point for this line of research.

Today, most theories of comprehension address the importance of the instructional or social context in comprehension. Young readers, in particular, require some form of scaffolding during their interactions with content-rich text. Decoding issues are more likely to confound comprehension assessment. Gathering and reporting information from text as opposed to narrating a contextualized experience is a novel expectation for most young children. However, few comprehension assessment procedures incorporate consideration of these factors. Using video and visual media technology to tap into comprehension competencies or to support text reading is an area that deserves further inquiry. Assessments like the common instructional passage that incorporate shared reading and instructional scaffolding need to be developed and formalized for novice readers.

These elements of comprehension assessment are specific to young children. However, they were addressed more broadly as assessment challenges in the Rand Report (2002). Concerns addressed in that report continue to be research priorities.

CONCLUDING THOUGHTS

The escalating demands for accountability are resulting in ever-increasing assessments for the youngest students. These demands are not going to disappear, nor are they totally unreasonable. Early intervention requires early diagnosis. Many of the comprehension problems that become evident in fourth grade have their roots in difficulties that began much earlier. If we use assessment as a teaching and learning tool, we can streamline instruction and do a better job of meeting individual student needs. Assessments need to be chosen systematically and deliberately, not added on to the existing assessment program as happens in many school districts. Effective assessment needs to be supported by sustained professional development. But primarily it needs to be a theoretically-driven system that is situated in instructional practice.

REFERENCES

Afflerbach, P., & Johnston, P. (1984). Research methodology on the use of verbal reports in reading. *Journal of Reading Behavior, XVI*, 307–322.

Allal, L., & Ducrey, G. P. (2000). Assessment of—or in—the zone of proximal development. *Learning and Instruction, 10,* 137–152.

Anderson, R. C., & Freebody, P. (1983). Reading comprehension and the assessment and acquisition of word knowledge. *Advances in Reading/Language Research, 2,* 231–256.

Bachman, L. F. (1985). Performance in cloze tests with fixed-ratio and rational deletions. *TESOL Quarterly, 19,* 535–555.

Bachman, L. F. (2000). Modern language testing at the turn of the century: Assuring that what we count counts. *Language Testing, 17,* 1–42.

Bunting, E. (1990). *Wednesday Surprise.* New York: Houghton Mifflin.

Cameron, C. A., Hunt, A. K., & Linton, M. J. (1985). Medium effects on children's story rewriting and story retelling. *First Language, 8,* 3–18.

Campione, J. C. (1989). Assisted assessment: A taxonomy of appproaches and an outline of strengths and weaknesses. *Journal of Learning Disabilities, 22,* 151–165.

Carpenter, R. D., & Paris, S. G. (2005). Issues of validity and reliability in early reading achievement. In S.G. Paris & S.A. Stahl (Eds.), *Children's reading comprehension and assessment* (pp. 279–304). Mahwah, NJ: Erlbaum.

Chall, J. S., & Dale, E. (1995). *Readability Revisited: The New Dale-Chall Readabilty Formula.* Cambridge, MA: Brookline Books.

Chinn, C. A., Waggoner, M. A., Anderson, R. C., Schommer, M., & Wilkinson, I. A. G. (1993). Situated actions during reading lessons: A microanalysis of oral reading error episodes. *American Educational Research Journal, 30,* 361–392.

Clay, M. M. (1991). Introducing a new storybook to young readers. *The Reading Teacher, 45,* 264–273.

Clay, M. M. (1993a). *An observation survey of early literacy achievement.* Portsmouth, NH: Heinemann.

Clay, M. M. (1993b). *Reading recovery: A guidebook for teachers in training.* Portsmouth, NH: Heinemann.

Cronbach, L. J. (1971). Test validation. In R. L. Thorndike (Ed.), *Educational measurement* (2nd ed.) (pp. 443–507). Washington, DC: American Council on Education.

Francis, N. (1999). Applications of cloze procedure to reading assessment in special circumstances of literacy development. *Reading Horizons, 40,* 23–44.

Fuchs, L. S., & Fuchs, D. (1992). Identifying a measure for monitoring student reading progress. *School Psychology Review, 21,* 45–58.

Gambrell, L. B., Koskinen, P. S., & Kapinus, B. A. (1991). Retelling and the reading comprehension of proficent and less-proficient readers. *Journal of Educational Research, 84,* 356–362.

Gambrell, L. B., Pfeiffer, W. R., & Wilson, R. M. (1985). The effects of retelling upon reading comprehension and recall of text information. *Journal of Educational Research, 78,* 216–220.

Geva, E., & Olson, D. (1983). Children's story retelling. *First Language, 4,* 85–109.

Goldman, S. R., Varma, K. O., Sharp, D., & Cognition and Technology Group at Vanderbilt (1999). Children's understanding of complex stories: Issues of representation and assessment. In S. R. Goldman, A. C. Graesser, & P. van den Broek (Eds.), *Narrative comprehension, causality, and coherence: Essays in honor of Tom Trabaso* (pp. 135–159). Mahwah, NJ: Erlbaum.

Goodman, Y. M., Watson, D. J., & Burke, C. L. (1987). *Reading miscue inventory: Alternative procedures.* New York: Richard C. Owen.

Gourley, J. W. (1984). Discourse structure: Expectations of beginning readers and readability of text. *Journal of Reading Behavior, 16,* 169–188.

Grigorenko, E. L., & Sternberg, R. J. (1998). Dynamic testing. *Psychological Bulletin, 124,* 75–111.

Hasbrouck, J. E., Woldbeck, T., Ihnot, C., & Parker, R. I. (1999). One teacher's use of curriculum-based measurement: A changed opinion. *Learning Disabilities Research and Practice, 14,* 118–126.

Jacobs, J. E., & Paris, S. G. (1987). Children's metacognition about reading: Issues in definition, measurement, and instruction. *Educational Psychologist, 22,* 255–278.

Johns, J. L. (1997). *Basic reading inventory: Pre-primer through grade twelve and early literacy assessments* (7th ed.). Dubuque, IA: Kendall/Hunt.

Keene, E. O., & Zimmermann, S. (1997). *Mosaic of thought.* Portsmouth, NH: Heinemann.

Leslie, L., & Caldwell, J. (2006). *Qualitative reading inventory 4.* Boston: Allyn and Bacon.

Linn, R. (1999). Assessments and accountability. *Educational Researcher, 29*(2), 4–16.

Lorch, E. P., Bellack, D. R., & Augsbach, L. H. (1987). Young children's memory for televised stories: Effects of importance. *Child Development, 58,* 453–463.

Madelaine, A., & Wheldall, K. (1999). Curriculum-based measurement of reading: A critical review. *International Journal of Disability, 46,* 71–85.

Mandler, J. M., & Johnson, N. S. (1977). Remembrance of things parsed: Story structure and recall. *Cognitive Psychology, 9,* 111–151.

Messick, S. (1989). Validity. In R. L. Linn (Ed.), *Educational measurement* (pp. 13–104). Washington, DC: American Council on Education.

Morrow, L. M. (1984a). Reading stories to young children: Effects of story structure and traditional questioning strategies on comprehension. *Journal of Reading Behavior, 16,* 273–288.

Morrow, L. M. (1984b). Effects of storyretelling on young children's comprehension and sense of story structure. In J. Niles (Ed.), *Yearbook of the National Reading Conference: Changing perspectives on research in reading/language processing and instruction* (Vol. 33, pp. 95–100). Rochester, NY: National Reading Conference.

Morrow, L. M. (1985). Retelling stories: A strategy for improving young children's comprehension concept of story structure, and oral language complexity. *The Elementary School Journal, 85,* 646–660.

Moss, B. (1997). A qualitative assessment of first graders' retelling of expository text. *Reading Research and Instruction, 37,* 1–13.

Narvaez, D. (2002). Individual differences that influence reading comprehension. In C. C. Block & M. Pressley (Eds.), *Comprehension instruction: Research-based practices* (pp. 158–175). New York: Guilford.

National Institute of Child Health and Human Development (NICHHD). (2000). *Report of the National Reading Panel. Teaching children to read: An evidence-based assessment of the scientific research literature on reading and its implications for reading instruction.* (NIH Publication No. 00-4769). Washington, DC: U. S. Government Printing Office. Available from: http://www.nationalreadingpanel.org

No Child Left Behind Act of 2001, Pub. L. No. 107-110, 115 Stat. 1425 (2002).

Paris, A. H., & Paris, S.G. (2003). Assessing narrative comprehension in young children. *Reading Research Quarterly, 38*(1), 36–76.

Paris, S. G. (2005). Re-interpreting the development of reading skills. *Reading Research Quarterly, 40,* 184–202.

Paris, S. G., Carpenter, R. D., Paris, A. H., & Hamilton, E. E. (2005). Spurious and genuine correlates of children's reading comprehension. In S.G. Paris & S.A. Stahl (Eds.), *Children's reading comprehension and assessment* (pp. 131–160). Mahwah, NJ: Erlbaum.

Paris, S. G., & Hoffman, J. V. (2004). Early reading assessments in kindergarten through third grade: Findings from the Center for the Improvement of Early Reading Achievement. *Elementary School Journal, 105*(2), 199–217.

Paris, S., & Jacobs, J. (1984). The benefits of informed instruction for children's reading awareness and comprehension skills. *Child Development, 55,* 2083–2093.

Paris, S. G., & Stahl, S. (2005). *Children's reading comprehension and assessment.* Mahwah, NJ: Erlbaum.

Paris, S. G., & van Kraayenoord, C.E. (1998). Assessing young children's literacy strategies and development. In S. Paris & H. Wellman (Eds.), *Global prospects for education: Development, culture, and schooling* (pp. 193–227). Washington, DC: American Psychological Association.

Parker, R. I., & Hasbrouck, J. E. (1992). The maze as a classroom-based reading measure: Construction methods, reliability, and validity. *The Journal of Special Education, 26,* 195–218.

Pearson, P. D., & Gallagher, M. C. (1983). The instruction of reading comprehension. *Contemporary Educational Psychology, 8,* 317–344.

Pearson, P. D., & Hamm, D. N. (2000/2005). The assessment of reading comprehension: A review of practices — Past, present, future. In S.G. Paris & S.A. Stahl (Eds.), *Children's reading comprehension and assessment* (pp. 13–69). Mahwah, NJ: Erlbaum.

Pearson, P. D., & Johnson, D. D. (1978). *Teaching reading comprehension.* Orlando, FL: Holt, Rinehart, Winston.

Peterson, B. (1991). Selecting books for beginning readers. In D. E. DeFord, C. A. Lyons, & G. S. Pinnell (Eds.), *Bridges to literacy: Learning from Reading Recovery* (pp. 119–147). Portsmouth, NH: Heinemann.

Powell-Smith, K. A., & Bradley-Klug, K. L. (2001). Another look at the "C" in CBM: Does it really matter if curriculum-based measurement reading probes are curriculum-based? *Psychology in the Schools, 38,* 299–312.

Pressley, M., & Afflerbach, P. (1995). *Verbal protocols of reading: The nature of constructively responsive reading.* Mahwah, NJ: Erlbaum.

RAND Reading Study Group (2002). *Reading for understanding: Toward an R & D program in reading comprehension.* Santa Monica, CA; Washington DC: RAND Corporation.

Rasool, J. M., & Royer, J. M. (1986). Assessment of reading comprehension using the sentence verification technique: Evidence from narrative and descriptive texts. *Journal of Educational Research, 79,* 180–184.

Rhodes, L. (1981). I can read: Predictable books as resources for reading and writing instruction. *The Reading Teacher, 34,* 511–518.

Royer, J. M., Greene, B. A., & Sinatra, G. M. (1987). The sentence-verification technique: A practical procedure for testing comprehension. *Journal of Reading, 30,* 414–422.

Royer, J. M., Hastings, C. N., & Hook, C. (1979). A sentence-verification technique for measuring reading comprehension. *Journal of Reading Behavior, 11,* 355–363.

Royer, J. M., Sinatra, G. M., & Schumer, H. (1990). Patterns of individual differences in the development of listening and reading comprehension. *Contemporary Educational Psychology, 15,* 183–196.

Salinger, T. (2005). Assessment of young children as they learn to read and write. In S. G. Paris & S. A. Stahl (Eds.), *Children's reading comprehension and assessment* (pp. 319–345). Mahwah, NJ: Erlbaum.

Schlieper, A. (1977). Oral reading errors in relation to grade and level of skill. *The Reading Teacher, 31,* 283–287.

Schmitt, M. C. (1990). A questionnaire to measure children's awareness of strategic reading processes. *The Reading Teacher, 43,* 454–461.

Shanahan, T., Kamil, M. L., & Tobin, A. W. (1982). Cloze as a measure of intersentential comprehension. *Reading Research Quarterly, 17,* 229–255.

Shin, J., Deno, S. L., & Espin, C. (2000). Technical adequacy of the maze task for curriculum-based measurement of reading growth. *The Journal of Special Education, 34,* 164–172.

Shinn, M. R. (1988). Development of curriculum-based local norms for use in special education decision-making. *School Psychology Review, 17,* 61–80.

Shinn, M. R., Knutson, N., Good, R. H., Tilly, W. D., & Collins, V. L. (1992). Curriculum-based measurement of oral reading fluency: A confirmatory analysis of its relation to reading. *School Psychology Review, 21,* 459–479.

Snow, C. E. (2003). Assessment of reading comprehension: Researchers and practitioners helping themselves and each other. In A. P. Sweet & C. E. Snow (Eds.), *Rethinking reading comprehension* (pp. 192–206). New York: Guilford.

Stahl, K. A. D. (2000, December). *The measurement of sequencing skill in primary grade readers.* Paper presented at the National Reading Conference, Scottsdale, AZ.

Stahl, K. A. D., Garcia, G. E., Bauer, E. B., Pearson, P. D., & Taylor, B. M. (2006). Making the invisible visible: The development of a comprehension assessment system. In K. A. D. Stahl & M. C. McKenna (Eds.), *Reading research at work: Foundations of effective practice* (pp. 169–184). New York: Guilford.

Stanovich, K. E. (1980). Toward an interactive-compensatory model of individual differences in the development of reading fluency. *Reading Research Quarterly, 16,* 32–71.

Stein, N. L., & Glenn, C. G. (1979). An analysis of story comprehension in elementary school children. In R. O. Freedle (Ed.), *New directions in discourse processing* (Vol. 2, pp. 53–120). Norwood, NJ: Ablex.

Stenner, A. J. (1996). Measuring reading comprehension with the Lexile Framework. Paper presented at the Fourth North American Conference on Adolescent/Adult Literacy, Washington, DC.

Sulzby, E. (1985). Children's emergent reading of favorite storybooks: A developmental study. *Reading Research Quarterly, 20,* 458–481.

Swanson, H. L., & Lussier, C. M. (2001). A selective synthesis of the experimental literature on dynamic assessment. *Review of Educational Research, 71,* 321–363.

Taft, M. L., & Leslie, L. (1985). The effects of prior knowledge and oral reading accuracy on miscues and comprehension. *Journal of Reading Behavior, 17,* 163–179.

Taylor, W. (1953). Cloze procedure: A new tool for measuring readability. *Journalism Quarterly, 9,* 206–223.

Taylor, B. (2006, November). Student assessments and preliminary student outcome data. In G. E. Garcia (Chair), Synthesizing three elements of reading comprehension instruction. Symposium conducted at the National Reading Conference, Los Angeles, CA.

Touchstone Applied Science Associates. (1995). *Degrees of reading power.* Benbrook, TX: Touchstone Applied Science Associates.

van den Broek, P. (2001). Fostering comprehension skills in preschool children. Paper presented at the Center for the Improvement of Early Reading Achievement Summer Institute, Ann Arbor, MI.

van den Broek, P., Lorch, E. P., & Thurlow, R. (1996). Children's and adults' memory for television stories: The role of causal factors, story-grammar categories, and hierarchical level. *Child Development, 67,* 3010–3028.

van Kraayenoord, C. E., & Paris, S. (1996). Story construction from a picture book: An assessment activity for young learners. *Early Childhood Research Quarterly, 11,* 41–61.

Vygotsky, L. (1978). *Mind in Society: The development of higher psychological processes.* (M. Cole, Ed.). Cambridge, MA: Harvard University Press.

Wixson, K. L. (1979). Miscue analysis: A critical review. *Journal of Reading Behavior, 11*(2), 163–175.

Wixson, K. K., & Carlisle, J. F. (2005). The influence of large-scale assessment of reading comprehension on classroom practice: A commentary. In S. G. Paris & S. A. Stahl (Eds.), *Children's reading comprehension and assessment* (pp. 395–406). Mahwah, NJ: Erlbaum.

21 Approaches to Teaching Reading Comprehension

Taffy E. Raphael, MariAnne George,
Catherine M. Weber, and Abigail Nies

University of Illinois at Chicago

How do we best teach our students to make sense of their reading? This question has been increasingly central to scholars and practitioners since the early 1980s. As a result, there is an extensive research base for making decisions about effective instruction for individual students, choices of frameworks to organize instruction within literacy and across school subjects, and processes for bringing coherence to school-wide comprehension instruction (Anderson, Hiebert, Scott, & Wilkinson, 1984; Tierney & Cunningham, 1984; Dole, Duffy, Roehler, & Pearson, 1991; Pearson & Fielding, 1991; Pressley, 2000, 2002; RAND Reading Study Group, 2002; Raphael, Highfield, & Au, 2006). In this chapter, we characterize the research base in terms of three waves that provide current bases for decisions about instructional approaches for improving diverse readers' comprehension and critical analyses of the wide array of text today. These three waves are:

- 1980s—*Individual Strategy Research*: Research focused on identifying strategies used by good readers, methods for teaching those strategies, and evaluating the impact or effectiveness of the strategy instruction on various measures of comprehension.
- 1990s—*Frameworks for Multiple Strategies*: Extending studies of strategy instruction to consider authenticity of activity settings, teacher-student interactions as students develop control over strategies (including use of multiple strategies over time), and where reading is used for a variety of purposes (e.g., inquiry, engagement, literature discussion).
- Current decade—*Bringing School-Wide Coherence to Comprehension Instruction*: Building on the body of research on comprehension instruction to support high-level instruction across grade level and school subject areas to create a coherent literacy curriculum. We focus on how students diverse in linguistic, economic, social, and cultural backgrounds, who depend on school for learning, can receive high-level, rigorous and coherent, comprehension instruction in each school year.

We conclude with a discussion of approaches that take into account new literacies that have begun to permeate classrooms, raising new questions and presenting new challenges in preparing students to understand the broad array of traditional and new forms of texts they will encounter.

FIRST WAVE: INDIVIDUAL STRATEGY RESEARCH

Current approaches to comprehension instruction have their roots in the explosion of research that took place in the 1980s and early 1990s, much of which can be traced to the research communities created with federal funding of the Center for the Study of Reading (CSR) at the University of Illinois at Urbana-Champaign and the Institute for Research on Teaching (IRT) at Michigan State University. These two organizations brought together cognitive psychologists, literacy educators, linguists, and teacher educators interested in improving our understandings of good readers and good instruction, respectively. Together, their researchers examined two sides of the coin related to comprehension instruction. At the CSR, the focus was on the content to be taught —what good readers do and what the less successful readers must learn to do. At the IRT, researchers examined teaching and teachers, how to effectively teach the content of the curriculum and develop teachers who are effective at doing so.

Scholars at the CSR and IRT, as well as others around the country interested in related issues, elaborated on theoretical understandings, specifically schema theory for understanding how information and texts are organized (e.g., Anderson & Pearson, 1984; Meyer, 1977; Stein & Trabasso, 1981), metacognitive lenses for understanding how readers control cognitive processes (Brown, Campione, & Day, 1981; Paris, Wasik, & Turner, 1991; Paris, Lipson, & Wixson, 1983), and the pedagogical content knowledge (Shulman, 1986) and cultural understandings (Au, 1980) teachers need to help their students achieve at high levels. Scholars examined the instructional practices of the times, documenting that comprehension instruction was largely absent from teachers' classroom practices (Durkin, 1978–79), guides to instruction in basal readers' manuals (Durkin, 1981), content area textbooks (Neilsen, Rennie, & Connell, 1982), and students' independent work (Anderson, Brubaker, Alleman-Brooks, & Duffy, 1985; Osborn, 1984).

By the end of the 1980s, an extensive body of research existed that identified (a) strategies good readers use, (b) the benefits of teaching those strategies to students across grade levels and abilities, and (c) effective teacher talk for developing good text comprehenders.

Identifying comprehension strategies of good readers

The question of how to teach students to comprehend is still being asked and with as much fervor today as it was earlier. Our answers are becoming more specific, effective, and personalized, however (Block & Pressley, 2002). Many of the specific, effective, and personalized answers to this question can trace their roots to the earliest studies that identified categories of individual strategies that, when taught, led to improved comprehension scores assessed by using retellings, short and extended question-answering, personal response, and so forth. While scholars may vary in the specific ways they carve up the comprehension pie (e.g., predicting as its own category or as a type of inference, questioning as its own category or as a strategy within monitoring), most scholars agree that comprehension instruction improves when readers have command of strategies for predicting, identifying important information, summarizing, making inferences, questioning, and monitoring (Raphael, Highfield, & Au, 2006; National Assessment Governing Board, 2004). Scholars' confidence in this set of categories is based in the extensive research characteristic of the 1980s, which focused on teaching and testing one strategy at a time (Pressley, 2002).

Looking at the area of summarization as an example, scholars such as Brown and Day (1983) began by exploring what is involved when readers summarize text, while others (e.g., Winograd, 1984) examined potential differences in successful and less successful readers' ability to construct summaries. Based on such studies, other researchers focused on the development of instructional approaches for teaching students to summarize and testing the effects of the instruction on the qualities of their summaries (e.g., Berkowitz, 1986; Taylor & Beach, 1984). Other scholars explored areas such as students' ability to make inferences (e.g., Hansen & Hubbard, 1984; Hansen & Pearson, 1983), to identify important information (Ogle, 1986; Schwartz & Raphael, 1985), to make predictions, to use questioning practices (e.g., Raphael & Pearson, 1985; Raphael & Wonnacott, 1985), and to monitor their reading (Paris, Saarnio, & Cross, 1986; also see reviews such as Tierney & Cunningham, 1984; Pearson & Fielding, 1991; Dole et al., 1991).

This body of research contributed not only to our understanding of how knowledge and use of individual strategies influences comprehension, but also raised important distinctions in what was being taught in the name of comprehension instruction. In their review in the first *Handbook of Reading Research*, Tierney and Cunningham (1984) noted a distinction between instruction which improved comprehension (i.e., understanding of a specific text or set of texts) and that which improved comprehension ability (i.e., the ability to apply strategy knowledge to new and different texts). Similarly, Paris, Lipson, and Wixson (1983) unpacked the knowledge that is necessary for strategic reading—what they referred to as both the skill and the will, when they detailed the differences among declarative, procedural, and conditional knowledge (i.e., knowing what a strategy is, how it works, and when and why it would be used, respectively). And, the research led scholars to examine effective means for helping students develop into independent, strategic readers.

Pearson (1985, 1986) described the importance of scaffolding students' learning, gradual releasing the responsibility for initiating, applying and controlling strategic activity from the teacher to the student. Initially, teachers explicitly teach students about the concept being introduced (vis à vis Duffy, Roehler, Sivan, Rackliffe, et al., 1987; Duffy 2002)—explaining what it is, why it is important, and how it works using instructional strategies such as thinking aloud and modeling. This is followed by sharing responsibility for its use with students through instructional strategies such as coaching until students are able to engage in independent, successful application of what they have learned in a variety of contexts. Au and Raphael (1998) describe the relative changes in activity level between teachers and students across this Gradual Release Model. They note that during the early phases, when the teacher explicitly teaches, thinks aloud, and models, teacher control is at its highest level while the students' activity levels are at their lowest. The students are actively observing—we hope—what the teacher is saying and doing, but they are not yet taking responsibility in a visible way in the use of the strategy. These levels of control and activity shift over the course of the Gradual Release Model, as teachers release control to the students and the students assume greater—and then total—responsibility for the strategy use in context (see Raphael, Highfield, & Au, 2006) (see Figure 21.1).

While the first wave of research focused primarily on defining comprehension, strategies, and instruction, the beginnings of research on how effective instructional talk varies across cultural groups took root. Sociolinguists (e.g., Cazden 1988, 2001) began unpacking the nature of language used in teaching, describing the prevalent use of a pattern of talk known as I-R-E (initiation, response, evaluation, or feedback) in which a teacher begins the exchange by asking a question, students bid for an opportunity to respond until one is called upon to provide the answer, and the teacher then evaluates the accuracy of the response.

While appropriate in some contexts (Wells, 1993), the I-R-E often derails learning for children who did not grow up in mainstream, white, middle class households. For example, Au (Au, 1980; Au & Mason, 1981) contrasted two teachers who differed in their understanding of and experience with Talk Story, a language pattern commonly used by native Hawaiians in co-constructing narratives about shared experiences and during story-telling. Both teachers conducted a guided reading lesson with the same group of primary grade students, one using the Talk Story participation structure, one

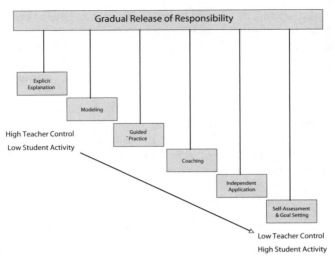

Figure 21.1 Steps in the gradual release of responsibility.

using the more conventional I-R-E. When Au analyzed the content of the discussion for proportion of time spent focused on comprehension and comprehension strategies relative to off-task (e.g., disciplinary) talk, she found that the students in the Talk Story participation structure had substantially greater interaction with the ideas of the text; those in the I-R-E structure spent the greatest amount of time in talk focused on discipline issues.

Taken together, the first wave of research on comprehension instruction established a critical base that identified important strategies to teach and methods for comprehension instruction, as well as introduced such complicating factors as changing patterns of talk over time and across cultures. The second wave of research built upon these concepts in important ways as the research moved from the laboratory setting and researcher-led strategy instruction contexts into the classroom.

THE SECOND WAVE: FRAMEWORKS USING MULTIPLE COMPREHENSION STRATEGIES

Au's work (Au, 1980; Au & Mason, 1981) set the stage for looking at constructivist classroom instructional settings that mesh the cognitive behaviors students engage in before, during, and after reading within a sociocultural perspective. In this context, knowledge is seen as the active relationship between the student and the environment, and learning takes place during the time the student is actively engaged with a complex, realistic instructional context. Thus learning involves the activity, concept, and culture, and all three are intertwined and interrelated (see Gavelek & Bresnahan, chapter 7, this volume).

Building on the first wave of what had been learned about comprehension strategy instruction, more sophisticated models of thinking showing the use of multiple strategies in sense making (e.g., Brown, Bransford, Ferrara, & Campione, 1983; Levin & Pressley, 1981) and the growing influence of sociocultural theory on learning and classroom practices led to frameworks that characterize the second wave using multiple strategies in authentic and meaningful classroom activity settings. Reciprocal Teaching, perhaps the landmark initial framework, was created and researched by Palinscar and Brown (1984, 1989; Palinscar, 1987). Building on Palinscar and Brown's research,

Pressley and colleagues (1992) developed and researched a similar framework—what they termed, Transactional Strategy Instruction or TSI. These frameworks, and others that follow, are grounded in Vygotsky's (1981) ideas about the social construction of knowledge and the dialogic and interactive nature of learning. In these frameworks, a set of ideas or principles provides the basis or outline that becomes more fully developed at a later stage (Liang & Dole, 2006).

Vygotsky's sociocultural theory provides a foundation for research into the roles played by teachers, students, and contexts in learning interactions (e.g., Bruner, 1986, 1996; Lee, 2000; Moll, 1990; Rogoff, Ellis, & Gardner, 1984; Wertsch, 1985). The importance of cultural and social influences and experiences for an individual's learning and development were described in two syntheses of general principles of learning (Bransford, Brown, & Cocking, 1999; Donovan, Bransford, & Pellegrino, 1999). Sociocultural theory explains the cognitive development of all individuals through their participation in sociocultural activities.

Activity Theories (Vygotsky, 1981; Leontiev, 1981; Rubinshtein, 1957) further contribute to the understanding of ongoing cognitive development. This view is grounded in the idea of sociocultural situatedness in which human thought emerges in the context of activities that are embedded in special social and cultural settings. Together, the collaborative interaction, intersubjectivity, and assisted performance comprise an "activity setting" (Tharp & Gallimore, 1988). An activity setting is a unit that transcends individuals and provides a meaningful way to integrate culture, local contexts, and individual function (Cole, 1985; Rogoff, 1982, 1990; Weisner & Gallimore, 1985). Examples of activity settings are explained in more detail later in this section. Within an activity setting, participation is both the goal and the means of learning (Dewey, 1916; Lave & Wenger, 1991; Rogoff et al., 1996). Learning and acting are indistinct, learning being a continuous, life-long process resulting from acting in situations. Learning then is a natural by-product of individuals engaged within authentic contexts in which knowledge is embedded naturally (Duffy & Jonassen, 1991; Brown, Collins, & Duguid, 1989).

Implementing multiple strategy instruction

This recognition of social and cultural factors in one's learning and development led to classroom settings being developed that encompassed activity settings within which comprehension strategy instruction is instantiated. Reciprocal Teaching, TSI, and other frameworks (e.g., SAIL) were constructed to integrate multiple strategy instruction and use within the before-during-after reading cycle, attempting to do so within more authentic and interactive classroom reading settings. Reciprocal Teaching incorporated authentic classroom activities to help students build a repertoire of comprehension strategies and learn how to coordinate the processes. Strategy instruction includes modeling, scaffolding, guided practice, and independent practice of the strategies all within the socially constructed nature of classroom discourse. Gradual release of responsibility is central to the flow of the activities that build students' metacognitive awareness about strategy application and self-regulation of reading.

In Reciprocal Teaching, the instructional framework is based on the principles of teaching students four representative comprehension strategies used before, during and after reading segments of text. The four strategies Palincsar put together were not designed to be the only potential strategies to use, but rather, illustrative of the importance of using strategies in combination across the reading cycle. The particular four associated with Reciprocal Teaching are summarizing, questioning, seeking clarification, and predicting upcoming text. Teaching occurs as students are working through the text, over a short period of time, with a set sequence of events which students follow after reading portions of text. The teacher models the strategies and, as students demonstrate their understanding of the strategy use, gradually turns increasing amounts of responsibility over to individual students who take turns leading the discussion. By participating in a number of lessons with the role of student leader rotated among small group members, the use of strategies is practiced and eventually internalized by students.

Transactional strategies instruction (TSI; Pressley et al., 1992) is an intervention framework designed to improve comprehension through the use of explicit strategy instruction, student practice with teacher feedback, and scaffolding about where and when to use the strategies. Instruction is transactional among group members, between the reader and text, and through socially constructed meaning. One of several transactional strategy instruction approaches is known as SAIL, (Students Achieving Independent Learning; Pressley et al., 1994). The SAIL framework was developed for elementary readers and focuses primarily on narrative text.

The SAIL framework begins with the teacher explicitly teaching several strategies (predicting, visualizing, questioning, clarifying, making associations, and summarizing). Think-alouds are modeled by the teacher and then practiced independently by the students. Students are encouraged to discuss their comprehension of texts, as well as the strategies they used to make meaning. The emphasis in this framework is on helping students learn when to use which comprehension strategy. Within this context, students develop metacognitive awareness about strategy application, discuss texts with the teacher and other students, build a broad base of knowledge, and are motivated to use reading strategies for pleasure reading.

Reciprocal Teaching and SAIL both integrate multiple strategies into the before, during and after reading cycle, drawing on research from single strategy instruction and the gradual release of responsibility. These two frameworks spawned the development of several similar frameworks as researchers recognized that highly skilled readers never use only one strategy, but rather fluidly coordinate a number of strategies to make sense of text (Pressley & Afflerbach, 1995). Examples of these multiple strategy frameworks include, Collaborative Strategic Reading (CSR), Scaffolded Reading Experience (SRE), Peer Assisted Learning Strategies (PALS), and Questioning the Author (QtA). All of these multi-strategy comprehension frameworks begin with teacher modeling, explicit instruction, guided practice, and independent use of multiple comprehension strategies (Liang & Dole, 2006).

Collaborative Strategic Reading (CSR) (Klingner, Vaughn, & Schumm, 1998, Klingner & Vaughn, 1999) is a framework that focuses on comprehending all types of text, including literature and content area material. CSR teaches four key comprehension strategies in the context of small cooperative groups. CSR borrows components from Reciprocal Teaching but elaborates on them. The four key strategies taught are: preview the text before reading, click and clunk to monitor while reading, getting the gist during reading, and wrap up after reading.

- Preview activates students' prior knowledge, through brainstorming, and has students make predictions about the text.
- Click and Clunk teaches students to monitor for understanding while they read. A "click" is defined as the moment when a student understands something s/he is reading and a "clunk" is defined as the moment when s/he gets stuck on a word and needs to use fix-up strategies to move on in the text.
- Getting the gist helps students to identify main ideas in the text that they are reading by asking themselves, "Who or what is this about?" and "What is most important about the who or what?"
- Wrap Up teaches students to review important ideas from what they've read and generate questions.

Like SAIL, CSR is implemented in two phases—first teaching and then using the strategies. CSR relies on cooperative learning activity (in groups or pairs of students) for the practice component. The teacher begins with a whole class introduction of a topic, followed by cooperative group activity, and ending with a whole class wrap up strategy in which the teacher discusses the passages read, key ideas, and questions that students have. During the cooperative group time, students are expected to implement the four key strategies that the teacher modeled. Students are assigned a specific role (leader, clunk expert, gist, announcer) within their group. The students work through the text together using clunk cards, cue cards, and learning logs as instructional supports to help them build comprehension throughout the reading cycle.

Scaffolded Reading Experience (SRE; Graves & Graves, 2003; Rothenberg & Watts, 1997; Tierney & Readence, 2005) frames reading for understanding before, during, and after reading. It can be implemented across all types of text, even those that are difficult for the reader. SRE has two phases—planning and implementation. During the planning phase, teachers consider students' instructional needs, select texts for students to read, and decide purpose for reading. During the implementation phase, strategies are used before, during, and after reading. Prereading is used to activate students' background knowledge, teaching vocabulary, and making predictions. During reading can include reading to students, silent reading, and assisted reading. Postreading activities give students opportunities to revisit the text through questioning, discussion, reteaching, and extension activities (such as drawing or graphic organizers).

Peer Assisted Learning Strategies (PALS; Fuchs, Fuchs, Mathes, & Simmons, 1997; Mathes, Howard, Allen, & Fuchs, 1998) empowers students to teach and learn from one another through focused peer interactions. PALS is a framework that students are able to apply to all areas of reading comprehension with a variety of texts. Teachers begin instruction in PALS by modeling and scaffolding students until they are able to engage in the activities independently. Once students are ready to engage in peer tutoring, the teacher pairs one higher reader, "the Coach," with one lower reader, "the Reader." Texts are chosen based on the instructional level of the lower reader. The students engage in a 10-minute reading session with the higher reader reading first so that s/he can model for the lower reader. The lower reader then reads the same passage and does a retelling of the story. After the 10-minute reading session, students continue to read through the text, alternating with each partner reading one paragraph and summarizing the main idea. The last planned activity in the PALS framework is a prediction relay in which students must make predictions, read the text, check predictions, and summarize important information. Peer assisted tutoring within the PALS framework takes approximately 30 minutes per day, 3 days per week.

While CSR, SRE, and PALS are very similar in design to Reciprocal Teaching and SAIL, Questioning the Author (QtA) (Beck, McKeown, Hamilton, & Kucan, 1997; Beck, McKeown, Worthy, Sandora, & Kucan, 1996) is the first framework in which students not only make meaning from the text but actually practice questioning the text and author in collaborative groups. There are four key concepts within the QtA framework—viewing the text and authors as a fallible, questioning students to make meaning of the text, dealing with text through questions focused on making meaning, and encouraging students to collaborate in constructing meaning. Teachers focus on questions to generate high-level conversations about text in their classrooms. Students engage in conversations around text with both the teacher and other students to broaden and deepen their understanding of the text. QtA discussions can be done whole-class or in small groups. Both contexts can be motivating for students, as well as develop higher levels of interaction with and comprehension of the text. QtA helps students take an evaluative stance when reading an essential aspect of critical reading.

Researchers started looking closely across curriculum and age levels to better understand more about how readers use multiple strategies in meaning making. Studies examined a variety of ways and aspects of how students use multiple strategies in such contexts as: reading and writing about topics (McGinley & Tierney 1989; Many, Fyfe, Lewis, & Mitchell, 1996); reading of content area text (i.e., Klingner & Vaughn, 1998, 1999; Guthrie & Cox, 1997); guided reading (i.e., Clay, 1991; Fountas & Pinnell, 1996); scaffolded instruction (i.e., Graves & Graves, 2003; Rothenberg & Watts, 1997); reading apprenticeship (Jordan, Jensen, & Greenleaf, 2001); linking literature and content area (Roser & Keehn, 2002); literature discussion groups (Kaser & Short, 1999; Kong & Pearson, 2005; Raphael, Pardo, Highfield, & McMahon, 1997); cooperative learning (i.e., Uttero, 1988; Stevens, Slavin, & Farnish, 1991); the level of motivation (Dole, Brown, & Trathen, 1996; Guthrie et al., 1996) and even developmental differences in comprehension (i.e., Oakhill, Cain, & Yuill, 1998; Smolkin & Donovan, 1993).

Multiple strategies in multiple activity settings

Classroom frameworks have been developed to incorporate multiple strategy instruction across content areas, as well as to meet the dual obligation of meeting students' needs with instructional level and grade-level texts (Florio-Ruane & Raphael, 2004; Raphael, Florio-Ruane, George, Hasty, & Highfield, 2001; Raphael, Pardo, Highfield, & McMahon, 1997). Thought, talk, and inquiry are woven throughout two such frameworks that integrate the instruction of multiple comprehension strategies across multiple activity settings. Both of these frameworks focus on student motivation, inquiry, peer-to-peer talk, and independent use of multiple strategies across a variety of texts.

Concept-Oriented Reading Instruction (CORI) is designed to assist teachers in motivating students to learn conceptual knowledge about content area subjects (Guthrie, Anderson, Aloa, & Rinehart, 1999; Guthrie & Cox, 1997; Guthrie et al., 2000; Guthrie et al., 1996) and Book Club *Plus* is a literature-based program in which students participate in reading, writing about, and discussing books (McMahon & Raphael, 1997; Raphael, Florio-Ruane, George, Hasty, & Highfield, 2004; Raphael, Pardo, Highfield, & McMahon, 1997).

Motivating students through CORI

Engagement and motivation are at the heart of the CORI framework. When teachers create conditions that enable reading engagement to be extensive and satisfying, students' reading comprehension and their measurable achievement increase (Guthrie & Cox, 2001; Guthrie et al., 1998). CORI is specifically designed to assist teachers in motivating students to learn conceptual knowledge about science and social studies content through the use of comprehension strategies. Units are built around a large knowledge goal with a unit lasting a few weeks to several months. Strategies taught in the CORI model are drawn from a body of knowledge on strategy learning and studies of searching for information (Guthrie, Anderson, Aloa, & Rinehart, 1999; Guthrie & Cox, 1997; Guthrie et al., 2000; Guthrie, Weber, & Kimmerly, 1993). The five strategies taught are activating background knowledge, questioning, searching for information, summarizing, and organizing graphically. Students use an inquiry stance reading many texts about a chosen topic with the goal being not only to learn the comprehension strategies but also to gain information through the use of the strategies.

To support strategy instruction, learning and knowledge goals are established, real world interactions take place, support is provided for being autonomous as well as for collaboration, and a wide choice of interesting texts is available. There are four phases or activity settings of the CORI framework:

- Phase 1. Students observe and personalize engaging in a subject area through direct observation and personalization. Background knowledge is activated and students are given the opportunity to formulate and ask questions from their observation. Building motivation is key in this phase.
- Phase 2. During search and retrieve, students gather texts pertinent to their inquiry. They read multiple expository texts and media to answer their questions. The teacher explicitly teaches various search strategies during this phase.
- Phase 3. Students start to learn and gain information about their topic from the texts they read. The teacher models comprehension strategies to students to help them comprehend what they read. Students express gist of information from texts and write summaries or organize graphically the several pieces they've read. In this phase, students take ownership of the ideas learned and relate the new knowledge to their personal topic questions.
- Phase 4. Students go public with sharing their information with their peers. This can be done in different ways such as team teaching to audience, multi-media presentation, etc.

The CORI framework has support for the cognitive strategies for knowledge construction during reading as well as support for the motivational development of learners. The framework has multiple group formats for instruction (whole class, small group, pairing, independent) with lots of opportunity for collaborative discussion-based learning. The choice of an interesting conceptual theme provides the valuable context for teaching the multiple comprehension strategies and for sustaining student motivation and engagement for long-term reading development.

Meeting the dual obligations through Book Club Plus

How students and teachers construct literacy communities is important to understanding how dynamic interactions between classroom contexts and activity shape literacy learning. Book Club *Plus* is grounded in four key principles of the sociocultural perspective:

- Emphasize the centrality of language for developing thinking and learners constructing meanings through their interactions with others;
- Recognition that learning is best facilitated by more knowledgeable others guiding the learner with appropriate tasks;
- Belief that individuals construct a sense of self as they participate in social contexts; and
- Belief that individuals construct meanings for language within their experiences and develop speech genres particular to given social contexts.

Teacher instruction is "contextualized to meet the particular needs of students' acquiring and developing literacy abilities (i.e., reading and writing) and oral language abilities (i.e., as speakers and listeners in meaningful discussion)" (McMahon & Raphael, 1997, p xii).

It is through different activity settings that teachers meet their dual obligations of insuring students have multiple and consistent opportunities to work with texts both at their instructional level as well as their grade level (Florio-Ruane & Raphael, 2004). During the settings that comprise Literacy Block, for example, students work with texts at their instructional level. The teacher's role is to explicitly teach and to scaffold in interactive sessions students' strategy learning and use. This instruction is critical for insuring that students develop their knowledge about how to read through work on comprehension, vocabulary, fluency, and so forth, under the direction of the teacher, and with texts designed to be appropriate to their instructional level. The pedagogical approach is sound, but students also need the opportunity to interact with and be challenged by the ideas within texts targeted for their age group—even if they cannot read this on their own. It is in the Book Club context that this second obligation is met.

The teacher's obligation in the Literacy Block setting is diagnostic—insuring that the appropriate texts are chosen to promote students' independence in reading. The teacher's obligation for the Book Club context is one of access—to insure that all students have access to the age-appropriate text used in that setting. Teachers use read-alouds, listening centers, buddy reading, advance reading at home, and so forth, to insure students are prepared to write in response to and talk about their book club books.

The Book Club *Plus* framework provides students time and opportunity to share their developing thoughts, ask each other questions, and collaboratively construct meanings of texts and of their own life experiences (Goatley, Brock, & Raphael, 1995; Highfield, 1998; McMahon & Raphael, 1997; Raphael & Brock, 1993). The teacher plays multiple roles and assumes multiple stances toward her students (Au & Raphael, 1998).

The literacy practices of the Book Club *Plus* framework are embedded within the activity settings of whole class instruction/discussion (opening, closing community share); independent work (reading, writing) and small group discussion (student led book clubs). The structure of these activities "link one social activity to another and thus organizes learning and cognition across activity contexts" (Rogoff, 1995, p. 129).

In opening and closing community share contexts, the entire class is involved. This is a setting for both instruction and/or discussion. Opening community share may involve the teacher providing instruction in skills and strategies associated with reading, writing, and talking about text; the teacher introducing ideas that support the theme of the unit; the teacher providing summaries of previous book content, or a theme related read aloud by the teacher. Topics for instruction are usually drawn from the four curricular areas: comprehension, literary aspects, composition, and language conventions. Closing community share is much more interactive between students and teacher and students and students. It provides a context in which the teacher and students can bring ideas and questions to the attention of the wider classroom community.

The second activity setting involves the independent work of reading and writing. During the Book Club cycle, reading is done in the assigned text students are reading in preparation for their book club discussion. The reading may be done alone, with a buddy, or with adult support (teacher, paraeducator, parent). This context is key for students gaining access to grade level text that will support their literature response logs and their book club discussions. During this reading time, students have the opportunity to apply reading skills and strategies.

Writing time follows the assigned reading. This context emphasizes the reading-writing connection. Writing here is used as a tool that can serve many functions: reflecting on reading, gathering and organizing information, practicing literary forms and sharing ideas with others. More formal, extended writing pieces can also be part of this time —writing into, through, and out of the unit.

The third activity setting centers around student led book clubs that follow writing time. Three to five students meet to discuss their common reading. These small groups engage in real conversation sharing personal, creative, and critical responses to literature. To maintain authenticity, students are not assigned roles; instead, they are charged with listening to peers' ideas and opinions—helping one another clarify confusing aspects of their reading, make interpretations and critiques of their texts, discuss authors' intent, and make important connections across text, to the theme, and to their own lives. The book clubs are the context at the crux of the program, from which the program takes its name, and to which all other components contribute. Book club discussions are guided by students' reading log entries but not constrained by them.

These activity settings in the multiple strategy frameworks hold the key to understanding how the social and discursive practices of thought, talk, and inquiry shape what gets learned, who gets to learn, and how that learning is organized (Gutiérrez & Stone, 2000). As we turn to the third wave of research, the bar is raised once again as researchers begin to tackle how the strategies and frameworks that research has demonstrated to be effective can be brought together to form a coherent, sustainable literacy curriculum to meet the needs of diverse learners.

THIRD WAVE: COHERENCE IN THE LITERACY CURRICULUM

The third wave of research on approaches to comprehension instruction focuses on initiatives that move beyond the level of the classroom(s) in a school or a network of teachers within a district or area to a focus on school-wide literacy reform. The need to consider the whole school for improving all students' literacy achievement stems from four critical areas of research. First, large-scale survey research has demonstrated the importance of coherence in the reading curriculum for reaching higher levels of student achievement, but that coherence cannot be defined simply by an adopted program (Newmann, Smith, Allenworth, & Bryk, 2001). Second, an extensive body of work on effective schools from the 1920s (e.g., Gray, 1925, cited in Hoffman, 1991) to current times (e.g., Datnow et al., 2002; Taylor, Pearson, Peterson, & Rodriguez, 2003, 2005) identifies characteristics distinguishing schools more successful in insuring students' high levels of literacy from those that are less so.

Researchers studying successful and unsuccessful approaches have discovered *factors*, *processes*, and *conditions* that are just as relevant today as they were over eight decades ago (Au, 2006; Austin & Morrison, 1961; Borman & Associates, 2005; Goldman, 2005; McNeil, 2000; Taylor, Pearson, Peterson, & Rodriguez, 2003, 2005). *Factors* that underlie successful reform include cooperation among teachers and administrators, clear definitions of roles and responsibilities, and clear criteria for evaluating success. *Processes* critical to school literacy reform include evaluating existing practices, identifying areas of need, and drawing on research relevant to making the needed changes. *Conditions* needed for school change include strong leadership, staff professionalism, cooperation among entities from state to district to local levels, and the need for adequate time to carry out the needed changes.

Third, schools today are under tremendous pressures to show improvement, based on the policies that are driven by the No Child Left Behind Act of 2001 (2002), a need which is even more pressing in schools serving high proportions of students from low-income families (Meier, Kohn, Darling-Hammond, Sizer, & Wood, 2004). Fourth, although teachers are essential in insuring that a coherent literacy curriculum that builds from grade level to grade level, they frequently have little buy-in to the school curricular approaches. Teachers often define the curriculum in terms of an adopted program imposed by outsiders, not something they construct with their colleagues to meet the needs of their specific children. Curriculum coherence across grades and sustainability is then limited because teachers have little to no ownership over something they had no part in creating (Au, 2005; Au, Hirata, & Raphael, 2005). Research on school change suggests the challenges schools face in beginning and sustaining a process that involves ongoing teacher collaboration to create a coherent, school-wide literacy curriculum that is focused on all students' learning (Cognition and Technology Group at Vanderbilt, 2000; Lipson et al., 2004; Taylor et al., 2005).

Researchers using the Standards-Based Change (SBC) Process, developed and tested in Hawaii—the 10th largest district in the United States—by Au (2005), then scaled to Chicago Public Schools, the country's 3rd largest district (Raphael et al., 2006), provide one illustration of a project designed to assist educators in creating supportive school contexts for enacting effective literacy instruction in classrooms (Au, 2005; Au, Raphael, & Mooney, in press). The SBC Process involves teachers in learning to make wise instructional decisions by aligning ongoing classroom assessments with end-of-year targets based in state standards, and aligning instructional decisions with students' needs relative to their current progress toward meeting their end-of-year goals. The process of unpacking or defining the "vision" of the literate student contributes to the development of a school-wide professional learning community (Dufour, 2004) with clear goals for student learning, a culture of collaboration, and a focus on results. Teachers understand that they are accountable for providing instructional activities that enable their students to achieve these learning goals, but the accountability is internally, rather than externally, imposed. Schools that have used this process have found that, while challenging, if sustained it leads to improvements in teachers' ownership of the curriculum, students' performance on classroom-based assessments, and achievement as measured by state tests (Au et al., in press).

Current issues and new directions

It is difficult to neatly characterize the current wave of reading comprehension research because we are just now dabbling in the surf. In this section, we build on the first three waves of research and discuss emerging themes and theories from current research. We also explore the connections between traditional reading comprehension research and new literacies, as well as possible directions for future research in approaches to teaching reading comprehension.

The invention of new technologies has provided us with many affordances, but has also introduced us to new challenges. It is no longer sufficient to simply discuss comprehension instruction within the context of culture and community, but to discuss it in terms of multiple cultures and multiple communities, including virtual. Schools today are comprised of increasingly diverse student populations that must learn to navigate new ways of making meaning while reading a wide-range of "texts." Because of this, researchers and educators must explore innovative strategies for teaching comprehension in order to equip students with the necessary tools for success in a global society.

New literacies build upon the foundation of reading comprehension research that has been laid over the past three decades. Traditional literacy theories, strategies, and activity settings are not obsolete, but more important than ever. We address key commonalities between new literacies and those examined in the first three waves: 1) motivation to learn, 2) construction of communities, and 3) importance of authentic tasks.

Motivation to learn

Technology can be highly motivating for students, enticing them to engage in literacy activities that they might not otherwise be interested in. Edutainment is big business in the United States, as companies capitalize on motivating students through the use of technologies with educative value. Unfortunately, much of the software marketed for educational purposes relies heavily on flashy pictures and sound effects rather than real literacy content. As literacy researchers and educators, it is our responsibility to build upon the motivating factors of technology while increasing the rigor of the tasks that students are asked to do with these technologies.

As the demands for reading comprehension change with the emergence of new technologies, we must find new ways of applying research-based strategies and frameworks such as CORI, QtA, and QAR to the new literacies. The value of technology does not lie in the tool itself, but in the literacies related to the tool. We must motivate students by teaching them the value of comprehension within the new literacies, not simply by handing exciting gadgets with bright colors and moving graphics.

CORI is a comprehension framework designed to motivate students while simultaneously engaging them in inquiry around science and social studies content. This framework can be applied to online reading as students engage in comprehension of texts across content areas. Teachers can scaffold students in transferring the five key strategies taught within the CORI framework to be able to engage in online inquiry.

QtA is another comprehension framework that has immense value as students develop strategies for comprehension within the new literacies. The premise of QtA is that the text and authors are fallible. This becomes increasingly important for students to understand as they find information on the Internet. Students must be able to question and make meaning from the text. Teachers can motivate students through the use of collaborative groups engaged in conversations about online texts.

Question Answer Relationships (QAR; Raphael et al., 2006) is a comprehension strategy that empowers students to find the information that they need in order to effectively respond to questions. The four key sources of information identified within QAR are: (1) Right There, (2) Think and Search, (3) Author and Me, and (4) On My Own. Students analyze questions to determine what the question is asking them to do and where they can locate information to do so. QAR can effectively be used when reading online, as students must be able to determine where to find information not only within a text, but across multiple sources of information and web sites.

Construction of communities

Classroom contexts must be constructed from a sociocultural perspective in which students work collaboratively on authentic new literacy tasks and teachers become facilitators, rather than deliverers of information. It is a shift from teacher-led discussions to communities of students constructing knowledge together. From this perspective, everyone in the classroom is viewed as integral in teaching one another. Social learning will influence teachers' and students' roles in new literacies classrooms. The knowledge about technology and it uses, that students bring to the classroom, will be embraced and shared, as well as used to construct new knowledge.

Effective instruction of online reading comprehension should be rooted in a sociocultural perspective and employ the gradual release of responsibility to develop strategic, critical readers who are able to independently apply strategies to authentic situations. Navigating results from a search engine, creating and publishing websites, and engaging in online conversations are examples of strategies in which students must become proficient.

Threaded discussion is an example of an activity designed to facilitate literature studies and build community by teaching students to comprehend online text and develop active, strategic, and critical reading skills (Grisham & Wolsey, 2006; Wolsey, 2004). Within the context of threaded discussions, students are connected online through e-mail, bulletin boards, listservs, or conference groups. They engage in conversations about common interests through asynchronous exchanges, which allow individuals to interact and exchange ideas at their convenience. Grisham and Wolsey studied middle school students who used First Class Client software to discuss *The Breadwinner* (Ellis, 2001). Students were required to use critical literacy strategies in their reading of the novel, as well as the postings in the threaded discussions, allowing them to constructively create knowledge and build a sense of community.

Threaded discussions allow students to interact in a variety of ways including, posting responses, reading responses, and responding to others' posts. The resulting text is nonlinear and comprehension of this text requires active navigation. Teachers begin instruction of threaded discussions by explicitly teaching how to navigate the texts, modeling, and scaffolding students toward independent use of the technology. Threaded discussions about literature require students to be critical, strategic readers as they find information in multiple sources, analyze, synthesize, and communicate their ideas of newly constructed knowledge. Within the context of threaded discussions, students engage in social interactions that enable them to gain a deeper understanding of complex problems and solutions, as well as an increased sense of responsibility. They are able to work within their Zones of Proximal Development to collaboratively produce written texts for real audiences that reflect students' own voices and perspectives, while using learned academic language (Grisham & Wolsey, 2006).

Authenticity of tasks

New technologies and tools have been influencing the definition and development of literacy for hundreds of years, including the inventions of paper, the printing press, and computers. The new technologies of today have a great impact on how people communicate, process information, and acquire new skills and strategies to negotiate within and across diverse communities of people. Leu, Kinzer, Coiro, and Cammack (2004) argue that the shift from an industrial age to an informational age requires people to be able to work in teams to identify problems, to locate information related to the problems, to critically evaluate and synthesize the information to problem-solve, and to quickly communicate solutions to others. Traditional approaches to teaching reading comprehension are limited in their scope and their effectiveness in helping students meet these requirements. Students must engage in tasks that enable them to apply these skills and strategies to authentic scenarios that encompass critical thinking and problem-solving skills. This becomes increasingly pertinent in this information age when anyone can publish anything on the Internet (Leu et al., 2004).

The 2009 National Assessment for Educational Progress reflects those expectations, as the test will require students to be able to engage in argumentation and scientific reasoning. They will need to look across several sources of information, including non-print sources; be able to synthesize information; and draw conclusions, based on the information that they have (National Assessment Governing Board, 2004).

In order to prepare students to meet these new demands and to be contributing citizens in a democratic society, we must think more broadly about what constitutes text and provide opportunities to interact with texts in authentic situations. Students will be greatly disadvantaged if teachers make only textbooks and trade books available to their students. In order to be truly literate in our society, teachers must equip students to navigate the Internet and negotiate across multimedia "texts," including pictures, graphics, videos, hypertext, use of color, hyperlinks, maps, and sound. Effective strategies for teaching online reading address the need for active engagement and monitoring for comprehension. The transactional nature of hypertext requires students to interact with text in new ways (McEneaney, 2000, 2002). The reader must read and comprehend text in a non-linear manner, as well as make decisions about what information to access and how to sequence it (Landow, 1992). These virtual and episodic text structures necessitate students to reason inferentially and make decisions about which hyperlinks will contribute to or deter from their quest for meaning. Another challenge with online reading is the lack of conventions; readers are required to devote attention to processes that are automatic in traditional print (McEneaney, 2000; Reinking, 1998).

Students often know a great deal about how to operate new technologies, but may not be equipped to employ the strategies required to comprehend the new literacies associated with the technology. Because of this, we must conceptualize what it means to teach reading comprehension in a new era. Reading on the Internet requires new skills and strategies, as well as employing traditional strategies in new ways. In addition to comprehending the written content of online texts, students must learn how to search for information, determine credibility of sources, make inferences, synthesize across texts, analyze the arguments being made, identify purpose for reading, skim, scan, read selectively, activate knowledge, discover new meanings of words, reread, take notes, and publish information (Coiro, 2006). Many of these strategies are employed by traditional texts, but the speed at which students are required to manage these tasks is exponentially faster and the amount of information available to them is exponentially more.

SEARCH (Henry, 2006) is one example of an online reading comprehension strategy that encompasses many of these important processes. The SEARCH acronym stands for:

1. Set a purpose for searching.
2. Employ effective strategies.
3. Analyze search-engine results.
4. Read critically and synthesize information.
5. Cite your sources.
6. How successful was your search?

SEARCH empowers students to strategically move through the process of online reading. Students must be taught explicit online navigational strategies and skills for metacognition while seeking information online. Think-alouds are one way for teachers to model strategic thinking about online navigation (Kymes, 2005).

New literacies provide greater opportunities for diverse knowledge gains, more personal applications to content, higher levels of engagement, opportunities to foster social justice and civic knowledge, and create more personal understanding of diverse world communities (Coiro, 2006). It is imperative for researchers to work in close collaboration with practitioners to develop new instructional strategies that will contribute to our understanding of reading comprehension development within new literacies.

CONCLUDING REMARKS

Students in the early years of the 21st century have grown up taking for granted such technologies as computers and the Internet, living in a global economy with instant access to ideas and images from throughout the world. At the same time, many students today face a future where without opportunities to develop the "habits of mind...that help students move from relatively passive absorption of information to habits in which they are able to form arguments, consider evidence, and apply judgments creatively" (Brunner & Tally, 1999, p. 461). Approaches to comprehension today must do more than solely develop strong readers of conventional text. Teachers must draw on the wealth of pedagogical knowledge to insure that they have created the kinds of communities in which students are engaged actively in their own learning, where they are taught and have opportunity to use in meaningful settings a broad array of strategies for comprehension and critical thinking, for organizing and analyzing information, and for questioning and evaluating a broad array of text. As Leu (2004, p. 1603) notes, we are now in an age in which "anyone may publish anything." Our approaches must not only insure that students of today may participate in such a world and have their voices heard, but that they are critical consumers of the texts they encounter.

REFERENCES

Anderson, L., Brubaker, N., Alleman-Brooks, J., & Duffy, G. G. (1985). A qualitative study of seatwork in first-grade classrooms. *The Elementary School Journal, 86*(2), 1–19.

Anderson, R. C., Hiebert, E. H., Scott, J. A., & Wilkinson, I. A. G. (1984). *Becoming a nation of readers: The report of the commission on reading.* Washington, DC: U. S. Department of Education.

Anderson, R. C., & Pearson, P. D. (1984). A schematic theoretic view of basic processes in reading comprehension. In P. D. Pearson (Ed.), *Handbook of Reading Research* (pp. 255–292). New York: Longman.

Au, K. H. (1980). Participation structures in a reading lesson with Hawaiian children. *Anthropology and Education Quarterly, 11*(2), 91–115.

Au, K. H. (2005). Negotiating the slippery slope: School change and literacy achievement. *Journal of Literacy Research, 37*(3), 267–288.

Au, K.H. (2006). *Multicultural issues and literacy achievement.* Mahwah, NJ: Erlbaum.

Au, K.H., Hirata, S.Y., & Raphael, T.E. (2005). Inspiring literacy achievement through standards. *The California Reader, 39*(1), 5–10.

Au, K. H., & Mason, J. (1981). Social organization factors in learning to read: The balance of rights hypothesis. *Reading Research Quarterly, 1*, 115–152.

Au, K. H., & Raphael, T. E. (Eds.). (1998). Curriculum and teaching in literature-based programs. *Literature-based instruction: Reshaping the curriculum* (pp. 123–138). Norwood, MA: Christopher-Gordon.

Au, K. H., Raphael, T. E., & Mooney, K. (in press). Improving reading achievement in elementary schools: Guiding change in a time of standards. In S. B. Wepner & D. S. Strickland (Eds.), *Supervison of reading programs* (4th ed.). New York: Teachers College Press.

Austin, M.C., & Morrison, C. (1961). *The torch lighters: Tomorrow's teachers of reading.* Cambridge, MA: Harvard University Press.

Beck, I. L., McKeown, M. G., Hamilton, R. L., & Kucan, L. (1997). *Questioning the author: An approach for enhancing student engagement with text.* Newark, DE: International Reading Association.

Berkowitz, S. J. (1986). Effects of instruction in text organization on sixth-grade students' memory for expository reading. *Reading Research Quarterly, 21*(2), 161–178.

Block, C. C., & Pressley, M. (Eds.). (2002). *Comprehension instruction: Research-based best practices.* New York: Guilford.

Borman, L. M., & Associates. (2005). *Meaningful urban educational reform: Confronting the learning crisis in mathematics and science.* Albany: State University of New York.

Bransford, J. D., Brown, A.L., & Cocking, R.R. (1999). *How people learn: Brain mind, experience, and school.* Washington, DC: National Academy Press.

Brown, A. L., Bransford, J. D., Ferrara, R. A., & Campione, J. C. (1983). Learning, remembering, and understanding. In J. H. Flavell & E. M. Markman (Eds.), *Handbook of child psychology, Vol. III. Cognitive development* (pp. 77–166). New York: Wiley.

Brown, A. L., Campione, J. C., & Day, J. D. (1981). Learning to learn: On training students to learn from texts. *Educational Researcher, 10*, 14–21.

Brown, A. L., & Day, J. D. (1983). Macrorules for summarizing texts: The development of expertise. *Journal of Verbal Learning and Verbal Behavior, 22*, 1–14.

Brown, J. S., Collins, A., & Duguid, P. (1989). Situated cognition and the culture of learning. *Educational Researcher, 18*(1), 32–42.

Bruner, J. (1986). *Actual minds, possible worlds.* Cambridge, MA: Harvard University Press.

Bruner, J. (1996). *The culture of education.* Cambridge, MA: Harvard University Press.

Brunner, W., & Tally, W. (1999). *The new media literacy handbook: An educator's guide to bringing new media into the classroom.* New York: Doubleday.

Cazden, C. (1988). *Classroom discourse: The language of teaching and learning.* Portsmouth, NH: Heinemann.

Cazden, C. B. (2001). *Classroom discourse: The Language of teaching and learning.* Portsmouth, ME: Heinemann.

Clay, M. (1991). *Becoming literate: the construction of inner control.* Portsmouth, NH: Heinemann.

Cognition and Technology Group at Vanderbilt. (2000). Adventures in anchored instruction: Lessons learned from beyond the ivory tower. In R. Glaser (Ed.), *Advances in instructional psychology* (Vol. 5, pp. 35–99). Mahwah, NJ: Erlbaum.

Coiro, J. L. (2006). Reading comprehension on the Internet: Expanding our understanding of reading comprehension to encompass new literacies. *The Reading Teacher, 56,* 458–464.

Cole, M. (1985). The zone of proximal development: Where culture and cognition create each other. In J. Wertsch (Ed.), *Culture, communication, and cognition: Vygotskian Perspectives* (pp. 146–161). Cambridge: Cambridge University Press.

Datnow, A., Hubbard, L., & Mehan, H. (2002). *Extending educational reform: From one school to many.* New York: RoutledgeFalmer.

Dewey, J. (1916). *Democracy and education.* New York: Free Press.

Dole, J. A., Duffy, G. G., Roehler, L. R., & Pearson, P. D. (1991). Moving from the old to the new: Research on reading comprehension instruction. *Review of Educational Research, 61*(2), 239–264.

Dole, J., Brown, K., & Trathen, W. (1996). The effects of strategy instruction on the comprehension performance of at-risk readers. *Reading Research Quarterly, 31,* 62–89.

Donovan, M. S., Bransford, J. D., & Pellegrino, J. W. (1999). *How people learn: Bridging research and practice.* Washington, DC: National Academy Press.

Dufour, R. (2004). What is a "professional learning community?" *Educational Leadership, 61*(8), 6–11.

Duffy, G. G. (2002). The case for direct explanation of strategies. In C. C. Block & M. Pressley (Eds.), *Comprehension instruction: Research-based best practices* (pp. 28–41). New York: Guilford.

Duffy, G. G., Roehler, L. R., Sivan, E., Rackliffe, G., Book, C., Meloth, M. S., et al. (1987). Effects of explaining the reasoning associated with using reading strategies. *Reading Research Quarterly, 22,* 347–268.

Duffy, T. M., & Jonassen, D. H. (1991). Constructivism: New implications for instructional technology? *Educational Technology, 31*(5), 7–12.

Durkin, D. (1978–1979). What classroom observations reveal about reading comprehension instruction. *Reading Research Quarterly, 15,* 481–533.

Durkin, D. (1981). Reading comprehension instruction in five basal reader series. *Reading Research Quarterly, 16,* 515–544.

Ellis, D. (2001). *The breadwinner.* New York: Oxford University Press.

Florio-Ruane, S., & Raphael, T. E. (2004). Reconsidering our research: Collaboration, complexity, design, and the problem of "scaling up what works." *National Reading Conference Yearbook, 54,* 170–189.

Fountas, I., & Pinnell, G. (1996). *Guided reading: Good first teaching for all children.* Portsmouth, NH: Heinemann.

Fuchs, D., Fuchs, L. S., Mathes, P. G., & Simmons, D. C. (1997). Peer-assisted learning strategies: Making classrooms more responsive to diversity. *American Educational Research Journal, 34,* 174–206.

Goatley, V. J., Brock, C. H., & Raphael, T. E. (1995). Diverse learners participating in regular education "Book Clubs." *Reading Research Quarterly, 30*(3), 352–380.

Goldman, S. R. (2005). Designing for scalable educational improvement: Process of inquiry in practice. In C. Dede, J. P. Honan, & L. C. Peters (Eds.), *Scaling up success: Lessons learned from technology-based educational improvement* (pp. 67–96). San Francisco: Josey Bass.

Graves, M. F., & Graves, B. (2003). *Scaffolding reading experiences: Designs for student success* (2nd ed.). Norwood, MA: Christopher Gordon.

Grisham, D. L., & Wolsey, T., D. (2006). Recentering the middle school classroom as a vibrant learning community: Students, literacy, and technology intersect. *Journal of Adolescent & Adult Literacy, 49*(8), 648–660.

Guthrie, J. T., Anderson, E., Aloa, S., & Rinehart, J. (1999). Influence of concept-oriented reading instruction on strategy use and conceptual learning from text. *The Elementary School Journal, 99,* 343–366.

Guthrie, J. T., & Cox, K. E. (1997). Portrait of an engaging classroom: Principles of concept-oriented reading instruction for diverse students. In K. R. Harris, S. Graham, & D. Deshler (Eds.), *Teaching every child every day: Learning in diverse schools and classrooms* (pp. 77–130). Cambridge, MA: Brookline Books.

Guthrie, J. T., & Cox, K. E. (2001). Classroom conditions for motivation and engagement. *Educational Psychology Review, 13*(3), 283–302.

Guthrie, J. T., Cox, K. E., Knowles, K. T., Buehl, M., Mazzoni, S. A., & Fasulo, L. (2000). Building toward coherent instruction. In L. Baker, J. T. Guthrie, & M. J. Dreher (Eds.), *Engaging young readers; Promoting achievement and motivation* (pp. 209–236). New York: Guilford.

Guthrie, J. T., Van Meter, P., Hancock, G. R., Alao, S., Anderson, E., & McCann, A. (1998). Does concept-oriented reading instruction increase strategy use and conceptual learning from text? *Journal of Educational Psychology, 90*, 261–278.

Guthrie, J. T., Van Meter, P., McCann, A. D., Wigfield, A., Bennett, L., Poundstone, C. C., Rice, M. E., Faibisch, F. M., Hunt, B., & Mitchell, A. M. (1996). Growth of literacy engagement: Changes in motivations and strategies during concept-oriented reading instruction. *Reading Research Quarterly, 31*, 306–332.

Guthrie, J. T., Weber, S., & Kimmerly, N. (1993). Searching documents: Cognitive processes and deficits in understanding graphs, tables, and illustrations. *Contemporary Educational Psychology, 18*, 186–211.

Gutiérrez, K., & Stone, L. (2000). Synchronic and diachronic dimensions of social practice: An emerging methodology for cultural-historical perspectives on literacy learning. In C. Lee & P. Smagorinsky (Eds.), *Vygotskian Perspectives on Literacy Research: Constructing Meaning through Collaborative Inquiry* (pp. 150–164). New York: Cambridge University Press.

Hansen, J., & Hubbard, R. (1984). Poor readers can draw inferences. *The Reading Teacher, 37*(7), 586–589.

Hansen, J., & Pearson, P. D. (1983). An instructional study: Improving the inferential comprehension of good and poor fourth-grade readers. *Journal of Educational Psychology, 75*, 821–829.

Henry, L. A. (2006). SEARCHing for an answer: The critical role of new literacies while reading on the internet. *The Reading Teacher, 59*(7), 614–627.

Highfield, K. (1998). Evidence of Literacy Learning in a Literature-Based Reading Program in T.E. Raphael & K.H. Au (Eds.), *Literature-Based Instruction: Reshaping the Curriculum*, (pp. 173–194). Norwood, MA: Christopher Gordon.

Hoffman, J. V. (1991). Teacher and schools effects in learning to read. In R. Barr, M. L. Kamil, P. B. Mosenthal, & P. D. Pearson (Eds.), *Handbook of reading research* (Vol. II, pp. 911–950). New York: Longman.

Jordan, M., Jensen, R., & Greenleaf, C. (2001). "Amidst familial gatherings": Reading apprenticeship in a middle school classroom. *Voices from the Middle, 8*, 15–24.

Kaser, S., & Short, K. G. (1999). Exploring culture through Children's Literature. *Language Arts, 75*(3), 185–192.

Klingner, J. K., & Vaughn, S. (1999). Promoting reading comprehension, content learning, and English acquisition through Colloarative Strategic Reading (CSR). *The Reading Teacher, 52*, 738–747.

Klingner, J. K., Vaughn, S., & Schumm, J. S. (1998). Collaborative strategic reading during social studies in heterogeneious fourth-grade classrooms. *Elementary School Journal, 99*, 3–21.

Kong, A., & Pearson, P. D. (2005). Learning: A process of enculturation into the community's practices. *Research in the Teaching of English, 39*(3), 226–232.

Kymes, A. (2005). Teaching online comprehension strategies using think-alouds. *Journal of Adolescent & Adult Literacy, 58*(6), 492–500.

Landow, G.P. (1992). *Hypertext: The convergence of contemporary literary theory and technology*. Baltimore: Johns Hopkins University Press.

Lave, J., & Wenger, E. (1991). *Situated learning: Legitimate peripheral participation*. Cambridge: Cambridge University Press.

Lee, C. D. (2000). Signifying in the zone of proximal development. In C. D. Lee & P. Smagorinsky (Eds.), *Vygotskian perspectives on literacy research: Constructing meaning through collaborative inquiry* (pp. 191–225). New York: Cambridge University Press.

Leontiev, A. N. (1981). The problem of activity in psychology. In J. V. Wertsch (Ed.), *The concept of activity in Soviet psychology*. Armonk, NY: Sharpe.

Leu, D. J., Jr., Kinzer, C. K., Coiro, J., & Cammack, D. W. (2004). Toward a theory of new literacies emerging from the Internet and other communication technologies. In R. Ruddell & N. Unrau (Eds.), *Theoretical models and processes of reading* (5th ed., pp. 1570–1613). Newark, DE: International Reading Association.

Levin, J. R., & Pressley, M. (1981). Improving childrens' prose comprehension: Selected strategies that seem to succeed. In C. M. Santa & B. L. Hayes (Eds.), *Childrens' prose comprehension: Research and practice* (pp. 44–71). Newark, DE: International Reading Association.

Liang, L. A., & Dole, J. A. (2006). Help with teaching reading compehension: Comprehension instructional frameworks. *The Reading Teacher, 59*(8), 742–752.

Lipson, M. Y., Mosenthal, J. H., Mekkelsen, J., & Russ, B. (2004). Building knowledge and fashioning success one school at a time. *The Reading Teacher, 57*(6), 534–542.

Many, J. E., Fyfe, R., Lewis, G., & Mitchell, E. (1996). Traversing the topical landscape: Exploring students' self-directed reading-writing processes. *Reading Research Quarterly, 31*(1), 12–35.

Mathes, P. G., Howard, J. K., Allen, S. H., & Fuchs, D. (1998). Peer-assisted learning strategies for first-grade readers: Responding to the needs of diverse learners. *Reading Research Quarterly, 33*, 62–94.

McEneaney, J. E. (2000). Learning on the web: A content literacy perspective. Retrieved March 1, 2007, from http://www.readingonline.org/articles/artindex.asp?HREmceneaney/index.html.

McEneaney, J. E. (2002, December). A transactional theory of hypertext structure. Paper presented at the National Reading Conference, Miami, FL.

McGinley, W., & Tierney, R. (1989). Traversing the topical landscape: Reading and writing as ways of knowing. *Written Communication, 6*, 243–269.

McMahon, S. I., Raphael, T. E., with Goatley, V. J., & Pardo, L. S. (Eds.). (1997). *The Book Club connection: Literacy learning and classroom talk.* New York: Teachers College Press.

McNeil, M. (2000). *Contradictions of school reform: Educational costs of standardized testing.* New York: Routledge.

Meier, D., Kohn, A., Darling-Hammond, L., Sizer, T. R., & Wood, G. (Eds.). (2004). *Many children left behind: How the No Child Left Behind Act is damaging our children and our schools.* Boston: Beacon Press.

Meyer, B. J. F. (1977). The structure of prose: Effects on learning and memory and implications for educational practice. In R. C. Anderson, R. Spiro & W. Montague (Eds.), *Schooling and the acquisition of knowledge* (pp. 179–200). Hillsdale, NJ: Erlbaum.

Moll, L. C. (1990). *Vygotsky and education: Instructional implications and applications of sociohistorical psychology.* New York: Cambridge University Press.

National Assessment Governing Board. (2004). Reading Framework for the 2009 National Assessment of Educational Progress (No. Contract No. ED-02-R-0007). Washington, D.C.: American Institutes for Research.

Neilsen, A. R., Rennie, B., & Connell, B. J. (1982). Allocation of instructional time to reading comprehension and study skills in intermediate social studies classrooms. In J. A. Niles & L. A. Harris (Eds.), *New Inquiries in reading research and instruction. Thirty-first yearbook of the National Reading Conference* (pp. 81–84). Rochester, NY: National Reading Conference.

Newmann, F. M., Smith, B. S., Allenworth, E., & Bryk, A. S. (2001). Instructional program coherence: What it is and why it should guide school improvement policy? *Education, Evaluation, and Policy Analysis, 23*(4), 297–321.

No Child Left Behind Act of 2001. Pub. L. No. 107-110, 115 Stat. 1425. (2002). Retrieved August 5, 2006, from http://www.ed.gov/policy/elsec/leg/esea02/107-110.pdf.

Oakhill, J., Cain, K., & Yuill, N. (1998). Individual differences in childrens' comprehension skill: Toward an integrated model. In C. Hulme and R. M. Joshi (Eds.), *Reading and spelling development and disorders* (pp. 343–367). London: Erlbaum.

Ogle, D. M. (1986). K-W-L: A teaching model that develops active reading of expository text. *The Reading Teacher, 39*(6), 564–570.

Osborn, J. (1984). Workbooks that accompany basal reading programs. In G. G. Duffy, L. Roehler, & J. Mason (Eds.), *Comprehension Instruction: Perspectives and Suggestions* (pp. 163–186). New York: Longman.

Palincsar, A. S. (1987). *Collaborating for collaborative learning of text comprehension.* Paper presented at the Annual Meeting of the American Educational Research Association, Washington, DC.

Palincsar, A. S., & Brown, A. L. (1984). Reciprocal teaching of comprehension-fostering and comprehension monitoring activities. *Cognition and Instruction, 2,* 117–175.

Palincsar, A. S., & Brown, A. L. (1989). Classroom dialogues to promote self-regulated comprehension. In J. Brophy (Ed.), *Advances in research on teaching* (Vol. 1, pp. 35–72). Greenwich, CT: JAI Press.

Paris, S. G., Lipson, M. Y., & Wixson, K. K. (1983). Becoming a strategic reader. *Contemporary Educational Psychology, 8*, 293–316.

Paris, S. G., Saarnio, D. A., & Cross, D. R. (1986). A metacognitive curriculum to promote children's reading and learning. *Australian Journal of Psychology, 38*(2), 107–123.

Paris, S., Wasik, B., & Turner, J. (1991). The development of strategic readers. In R. Barr, M. Kamil, P. Mosenthal, & P. D. Pearson (Eds.), *Handbook of reading research* (Vol. 2, pp. 609–640). New York: Longman.

Pearson, P. D. (1985). Changing the face of reading comprehension instruction. *The Reading Teacher, 38*(6), 724–738.

Pearson, P. D. (1986). Twenty years of research in reading comprehension. In T. E. Raphael (Ed.), *The contexts of school-based literacy* (pp. 43–62). New York: Random House.

Pearson, P. D., & Fielding, L. (1991). Comprehension Instruction. In R. Barr, M. L. Kamil, P. Mosenthal, & P. D. Pearson (Eds.), *Handbook of reading research* (Vol. II, pp. 819–860). New York: Longman.

Pressley, M. (2000). What should comprehension instruction be the instruction of? In M. Kamil, P. B. Mosenthal, P. D. Pearson, & R. Barr (Eds.), *Handbook of reading research* (Vol. 3, pp. 545–562). Mahwah, NJ: Erlbaum.

Pressley, M. (2002). Comprehension strategies instruction. In C. C. Block & M. Pressley (Eds.), *Comprehension instruction: Research based best practices* (pp. 11–27). New York: Guilford.

Pressley, M., & Afflerbach, P. (1995). *Verbal protocols of reading: The nature of constructively responsive reading.* Hillsdale, NJ: Erlbaum.

Pressley, M., Almasi, J., Scuder, T., Bergman, J., Hite, S., El-Dinary, P. B., & Brown, R. (1994). Transactional instruction of comprehension strategies: The Montgomery County, Maryland, SAIL Program. *Reading and Writing Quarterly: Overcoming Learning Difficulties, 10,* 5–19.

Pressley, M., El-Dinary, P. B., Gaskins, I., Scuder, T., Bergman, J., Almasi, J., & Brown, R. (1992). Beyond direct instruction: Transactional instruction of reading comprehension strategies. *Elementary School Journal, 92,* 513–555.

RAND Reading Study Group. (2002). *Reading for understanding: Toward an R&D program in reading comprehension.* Santa Monica, CA: RAND.

Raphael, T. E., & Brock, C. H. (1993). Mei: Learning the literacy culture in an urban elementary school. In D. J. Leu & C. K. Kinzer (Eds.), *Examining central issues in literacy research, theory, and practice* (Vol. 42, pp. 179–188). Chicago, IL: National Reading conference.

Raphael, T. E., Florio-Ruane, S., George, M., Hasty, N., & Highfield, K. (2001). Thinking for ourselves: Literacy learning in a diverse teacher inquiry network. *The Reading Teacher, 54*(6), 596–607.

Raphael, T. E., Florio-Ruane, S., George, M., Hasty, N., & Highfield, K. (2004). *Book club plus: A literacy framework for primary grades.* Lawrence, MA: Small Planet.

Raphael, T. E., Goldman, S. R., Au, K. H., Hirata, S., Weber, C. M., George, M., et al. (April, 2006). Toward second generation school reform models: A developmental model for literacy reform. Paper presented at the American Educational Research Association.

Raphael, T. E., Highfield, K., & Au, K. H. (2006). *QAR now: A powerful and practical framework that develops comprehension and higher-level thinking in all students.* New York: Scholastic.

Raphael, T. E., Pardo, L., Highfield, K., & McMahon, S. (1997). *Book club: A literature-based curriculum.* Littleton, MA: Small Planet.

Raphael, T. E., & Pearson, P. D. (1985). Increasing student's awareness of sources of information for answering questions. *American Educational Research Journal, 22,* 217–236.

Raphael, T. E., & Wonnacott, C. A. (1985). Heightening 4th grade students' sensitivity to sources of information for answering comprehension questions. *Reading Research Quarterly, 20,* 282–296.

Reinking, D. (1998). Synthesizing technological transformations of literacy in a post-typographic world. In D. Reinking, M. C. McKenna, L. D. Labbo, & R. D. Kieffer (Eds.), *Handbook of literacy and technology: Transforming in a post-typographic world* (pp. xi–xxx). Mahwah, NJ: Erlbaum.

Rogoff, B. (1982). Integrating context and cognitive development. In M. E. Lamb & A. L. Brown (Eds.), *Advances in developmental psychology* (Vol. 2). Hillsdale, NJ: Erlbaum.

Rogoff, B. (1990). *Apprenticeship in thinking.* New York: Oxford University Press.

Rogoff, B. (1995). Observing sociocultural activity on three planes: participatory appropriation, guided participation, and apprenticeship. In J. V. Wertsch, P. Delrio, & A. Alvarez (Eds.), *Sociocultural psychology: Theory and practice of doing and knowing* (pp. 139–164). New York: Cambridge University Press.

Rogoff, B., Ellis, S., & Gardner, W. (1984). Adjustment of adult-child instruction according to child's age and task. *Developmental Psychology, 20,* 193–199.

Rogoff, B., Matusov, E., & White, C. (1996). Models of teaching and learning: Participation in a community of learners. In D. R. Olson & N. Torrance (Eds.), *The handbook of education and human development: New models of learning, teaching and schooling* (pp. 388–414). Cambridge, MA: Blackwell.

Roser, N. L., & Keehn, S. (2002). Fostering thought, talk, and inquiry: Linking literature and social studies. *The Reading Teacher, 55*(5), 426–426.

Rothenberg, S. S., & Watts, S. M. (1997). Students with learning difficulties meet Shakespeare: Using a scaffolded reading experience. *Journal of Adolescent & Adult Literacy, 40,* 532–539.

Rubinshtein, S. L. (1957). *Bytie i soznanie [Being and consciousness].* Moscow: Izdatel'stvo Akademii Nauk, SSSR.

Schwartz, R. M., & Raphael, T. E. (1985). Concept of Definition: A key to improving students' vocabulary. *The Reading Teacher, 39*(2), 198–205.

Shulman, L. (1986). Those who understand: Knowledge growth in teaching. *Educational Researcher, 15*(2), 4–14.

Smolkin, L. B., & Donovan, C. (1993). Responses of first graders to information and picture storybooks within a classroom context. Paper presented at the annual meeting of the National Reading Conference, Charleston, SC.

Stein, N. L., & Trabasso, T. (1981). What's in a story: Critical issues in comprehension and instruction. In R. Glaser (Ed.), *Advances in the psychology of instruction* (Vol. 2). Hillsdale, NJ: Erlbaum.

Stevens, R. J., Slavin, R. E., & Farnish, A. M. (1991). The effects of cooperative learning and direct instruction in reading comprehension strategies on main idea identification. *Journal of Educational Psychology, 83,* 8–16.

Taylor, B.M., & Beach, R.W. (1984). The effects of text structure instruction on middle-grade students' comprehension and production of expository text. *Reading Research Quarterly, 19*(2), 134–146.

Taylor, B. M., Pearson, P. D., Peterson, D. P., & Rodriguez, M. C. (2003). Reading growth in high-poverty classrooms: The influence of teacher practices that encourage cognitive engagement in literacy learning. *The Elementary School Journal, 104,* 3–28.

Taylor, B. M., Pearson, P. D., Peterson, D. P., & Rodriguez, M. C. (2005). The CIERA School Change Framework: An evidenced-based approach to Professional Development and School Reading Improvement. *Reading Research Quarterly, 40*(1), 40–69.

Tharp, R., & Gallimore, R. (1988). *Rousing minds to life: Teaching, learning, and schooling in social context.* New York: Cambridge University Press.

Tierney, R. J., & Cunningham, J. W. (1984). Research on teaching comprehension. In P. D. Pearson, R. Barr, M. L. Kamil, & P. Mosenthal (Eds.), *Handbook of reading research* (Vol. I, pp. 609–655). New York: Longman.

Tierney, R. J., & Readence, J. E. (2005). *Reading strategies and practices: A compendium* (6th ed.). Boston: Allyn & Bacon.

Uttero, D. A. (1988). Activating Comprehension through Cooperative Learning. *Reading Teacher, 41*(4), 390–95.

Vygotsky, L. S. (1981). The genesis of higher mental functions. In J. V. Wertsch (Ed.), *The concept of activity in Soviet psychology* (pp. 144–188). Armonk, NY: Sharpe.

Weisner, T. S., & Gallimore, R. (1985). *The convergence of ecocultural and activity theory.* Paper presented at the American Anthropological Association, Washington, DC.

Wells, G. (1993). Reevaluating the IRF sequence: A proposal for the articulation of theories of activity and discourse for the anlaysis of teaching and learning in the classroom. *Linguistics and Education, 5*(1), 1–38.

Wertsch, J. V. (1985). *Vygotsky and the social formation of mind.* Cambridge, MA: Harvard University Press.

Winograd, P. W. (1984). Strategic difficulties in summarizing texts. *Reading Research Quarterly, 19*(4), 404–425.

Wolsey, T. D. (2004). *Literature discussion in cyberspace: Young adolescents using threaded discussion groups to talk about books.* Retrieved March 1, 2007, from http://www.readingonline.org/articles/art_index.asp?HREF=wolsey/index.html

22 Comprehension and Discussion of Text

Janice F. Almasi

University of Kentucky

Keli Garas-York

Buffalo State College

A mind, once stretched by a new idea, never regains its original dimensions.
Oliver Wendell Holmes

DEFINING DISCUSSION

Discussion has been a staple instructional activity used in classrooms for many years. However, its form and purpose have evolved considerably over time. In its typical, or traditional form, discussion occurs as a post-reading event in which the teacher assists and assesses students' comprehension of text (Barr & Dreeben, 1991). This type of discussion (alternatively referred to as recitations or teacher-led discussions) usually occurs with the whole class or with a small group of students. The teacher plays a central role by initiating topics for discussion, usually by asking questions, and soliciting student responses to those questions. Students typically assume the role of respondent, and the teacher evaluates their responses. Cazden (1986) and Mehan (1979) characterized the patterns of discourse in these classroom events as having an I-R-E (initiate, respond, evaluate) participant structure.

The types of questions asked during these more controlled teacher-led discussions of text tend to be literal, factual, and known-answer questions (Alpert, 1987; Skidmore, Perez-Parent, & Arnfield, 2003). Much of the research in the 1980s found that the type of teacher questioning found in traditional, teacher-led discussions diminished students' cognitive, affective, and expressive responses; stalled and interrupted student discourse; and led to decreased motivation, cognitive disengagement, and passivity (e.g., Alpert, 1987; Dillon, 1985).

Because traditional teacher-led discussions often consist of the teacher asking questions with known answers, there is actually little to discuss because the underlying theoretical assumption implies that there is a single, correct interpretation of text (Almasi, 2002). Thus, these classroom events take on an evaluative tone in which there are correct answers that lead to a particular interpretation of text.

The teacher is not only considered the interpretive authority, but also the authority in terms of how the interaction proceeds. That is, by asking questions the teacher not only determines the topics of conversation, but also who may talk, when they may talk, and for how long. Many teacher behaviors such as calling on some students less often, providing less wait time for some students, and providing evaluative feedback induce passivity among low achieving students in particular (Good, Slavings, Harel, & Emerson, 1987). These students often choose to remain passive to avoid making mistakes in public.

As well, when teachers persist in asking literal questions students adjust their expectations, values, and purposes for reading accordingly. In short, they learn that what is valued in terms of classroom expectations is a literal understanding of text, thus they focus on literal readings of texts rather than critical, higher level, or interpretive readings.

When the instructional context leads to student passivity and disengagement, comprehension suffers because proficient comprehension requires active cognitive engagement in which readers construct meaning and use metacognitive and self-regulatory strategies to make sense of texts (Baker & Brown, 1984; Garner, 1987; Meece, Blumenfeld, & Hoyle, 1988; Pressley, 2000). Thus, for the purpose of this chapter, traditional teacher-led forms of classroom discussion that feature a series of literal, known-answer questions and I-R-E participant structures will not be considered.

Instead, discussion is defined as a dialogic classroom event in which students and teachers are cognitively, socially, and affectively engaged in collaboratively constructing meaning or considering alternate interpretations of texts to arrive at new understandings (Almasi, 2002). In contrast to the notion of a single correct interpretation of text, this definition suggests theoretically that multiple and conflicting interpretations of text can co-exist (Fish, 1980; Rosenblatt, 1938/1976, 1978). Such discussion requires the type of critical and evaluative thinking that is essential to achieving higher levels of comprehension. It requires that participants have a questioning attitude, engage in logical analysis, make inferences, make evaluations, and make judgments about the texts they read and the ideas and interpretations of others (Almasi, 2007).

In dialogic discussions participants may enter the discussion with individual, temporary understandings or "envisionments" of text (Langer, 1995), but the discussion is a space in which all participants are open to the ideas, opinions, and interpretations of others (Bridges, 1979). Thus, the ideas contained in the text are contemplated, deliberated, and debated by respondents. This means individual interpretations may be shaped, reshaped, and altered by the discussion, but it also means that the discussion is shaped, reshaped, and altered by individual's contributions. In short, dialogic discussion is a recursive space that shapes and is shaped by its participants. It is a space where meaning resides (Fish, 1980; Rosenblatt, 1938/1976, 1978).

The goal of this chapter is to review research that examines the impact of such dialogic discussion on students' comprehension and understanding of text.

THEORETICAL ISSUES

Sociocultural theory

Sociocultural perspectives of learning assume learners actively construct knowledge in dialogic interactions with others (Vygotsky, 1978). From this perspective, learning involves a relationship between the learner's cognitive processes and the cultural, historical, and institutional settings in which the learner is situated (Wertsch, 1985). In contrast to traditional perspectives in which learning is viewed as the transmission of skills and knowledge to be applied later in authentic activities, sociocultural perspectives assume that learning develops through talk and interaction with others (Wells, 1986).

The guiding principles of dialogic discussion are rooted in sociocultural theories of development that maintain children learn the intellectual rules, procedural rules, and social conventions of discussion by observing and participating in them (Vygotsky, 1978). Social learning environments enable learners to observe and interact with more knowledgeable others as they engage in cognitive processes they may not be able to engage in independently. Learning in these social environments may occur incidentally as learners observe the cognitive and social processes of their peers, or learning may be more direct when teachers or peers function as more knowledgeable others to scaffold learning. Through scaffolding, learners become capable of achieving more than they could have independently (Rogoff, 1990; Vygotsky, 1978). As a result of incidental learning or scaffolded instruction, learners gradually internalize higher cognitive functions, such as interpreting literature or monitoring one's comprehension. Dialogic discussions provide a social environment in which students can observe the cognitive and social processes of their peers and begin to use the strategies they observe for interpreting literature and interacting with one another in a productive manner. Thus, learning occurs first on an interpersonal plane where language functions as a mediating tool. Over time, the learning appears on an intrapersonal plane where it is internalized for use by the learner (Vygotsky, 1978).

Instructional scaffolding for comprehension through discussion

Wood, Bruner, and Ross (1976) are credited with the original use of the scaffolding metaphor as it pertains to instructional contexts. In their study of the nature of the tutorial process as 3-, 4-, and 5-year-old children learned how to build a wooden structure while being tutored by an adult/expert, they noted that:

> Discussions of problem solving or skill acquisition are usually premised on the assumption that the learner is alone and unassisted. If the social context is taken into account, it is usually treated as an instance of modeling and imitation. But the intervention of a tutor may involve much more then this. More often than not, it involves a kind of "scaffolding" process that enables a child or novice to solve a problem, carry out a task or achieve a goal which would be beyond his unassisted efforts. (Wood, Bruner, & Ross, 1976, p. 90)

Their findings emphasized that a learner will not benefit from scaffolding unless they are able to "recognize a solution to a particular class of problems before he is himself able to produce the steps leading to it without assistance" (Wood, Bruner, & Ross, 1976, p. 90). That is, learners must be able to *recognize* the goal or what an appropriate end-product looks like before they can *produce* it on their own. In short, recognition and comprehension of the goal/task must precede production. The authors also stressed the importance of permitting children to do as much on their own as they are capable. That is, the adult, or more knowledgeable other, is a necessary, but temporary, part of the scaffolding process who cedes responsibility for completing parts of the task to the learner as quickly as they are able. Effective instruction requires the tutor to attend to two theoretical models: (1) a theory of how the task or problem may be completed and (2) a theory of the learner's performance characteristics that will enable the tutor to determine at what point responsibility can be handed over to the learner.

Wood, Bruner, and Ross (1976) concluded by offering a theory of instruction based on six scaffolding functions of the tutor. They noted that the tutor must: (a) *recruit* or enlist the learner's attention and interest in the task, (b) *reduce the degrees of freedom* in the task by simplifying it to make it manageable for a given learner until he or she can recognize the task's requirements, (c) *maintain direction* by regularly keeping the learner motivated to attain the goal, (d) *mark critical features* of the task to help the learner see the discrepancy between what they have produced and what is recognized as successful completion of the task, (e) *control frustration*, and (f) *demonstrate or model* solutions to the task. Meyer (1993) noted that this conceptualization of scaffolding not only included a component in which teacher scaffolding assisted cognition (i.e., reducing the degrees of freedom, marking critical features, demonstrating and modeling), but also a large motivational component related to student engagement (i.e., recruitment, maintaining direction, controlling frustration).

Extending Wood, Bruner, and Ross' (1976) conceptualization further, Meyer (1993) argued that scaffolding in practice often becomes an atheoretical metaphor in which the central tenets underlying it become forgotten. Using a social-constructivist perspective, she proposed three theoretical tenets underlying scaffolding: (a) knowledge is a constructive process in which meaning is negotiated among teachers and learners, (b) context influences this negotiation because one's interactions in a particular context influences the manner in which knowledge is constructed (i.e., some contexts are more supportive than others and some individuals are better at finding more supportive contexts), and (c) knowledge and context are unstable and co-evolve as a natural part of human interaction and development.

Meyer's (1993) third tenet accounts for changes in the context of negotiation. The ability to change with the context requires self-regulated learning. In terms of reading comprehension, self-regulated learners are metacognitively aware when something (e.g., an incongruity between the text and one's prior knowledge, an incongruity within the text itself) has disrupted their understanding and they know how to select and use a repair strategy to remedy their comprehension (Garner, 1987). Similar to Wood, Bruner, and Ross' (1976) notion of recognition preceding production, developing an internal monitoring system in which readers can recognize and resolve such incongruities is essential to proficient comprehension (Almasi, 1995; Baker & Brown, 1984; Paris, Wasik, & Turner, 1991; Pressley, Johnson, Symons, McGoldrick, & Kurita, 1989).

Although Wood, Bruner, and Ross (1976) never cited Vygotskian perspectives in their work, notions of the "zone of proximal development" (Vygotsky, 1978) are reflected in their finding that tutors must mark critical features of the task to highlight the discrepancy between what the learner is able to produce and their recognition of the ultimate goal. Echoing Pearson and Gallagher's (1983) model of explicit instruction in which, during guided practice, teachers gradually "release responsibility" for completing tasks to the students (p. 337), Meyer (1993) similarly emphasized the importance of gradually transferring responsibility for the learning from the adult, or more knowledgeable other, to the child so skills can be used independently. The child must develop the self-regulatory skills that will enable them to successfully complete tasks by actively participating in the process with adults, or more knowledgeable others, who gradually withdraw their support. Meyer (1993) stressed that adults must allow children to participate and regulate and children must know that the adult support is only temporary. These aspects of scaffolding, she argued, are often missing from instructional practice.

Like Wood, Bruner, and Ross (1976), Meyer (1993) also emphasized the importance of not only scaffolding for cognitive competence, but also for a child's motivational and social competence. Such scaffolding must occur from a non-evaluative stance in which the adult is present and available for social, cognitive, and motivational support as a "safety net" (Meyer, 1993, p. 44).

Meyer (1993) defined instructional scaffolding as "the temporary teacher support to the student in the ZPD" (pp. 45–46). Her definition included two processes: negotiation of meaning and transfer of responsibility for learning. Based on her review of literature, she identified six characteristics of instructional scaffolding: (1) teacher support (i.e., how the teacher helps students related new information to their prior knowledge), (2) transfer of responsibility to the learner, (3) dialogue between teachers and students to negotiate understanding, (4) non-evaluative collaboration as a type of formative feedback, (5) appropriateness of the instructional level (i.e., knowledge of the students' current competencies in order to provide guidance toward tasks that can be accomplished with assistance), and (6) co-participation (i.e., the importance of active student participation and engagement to become autonomous). From these six characteristics, Meyer (1993) concluded that scaffolded instruction is best explained by sociocultural theory:

> because it is collaborative, yet non-evaluative, and optimal for student participation and choice. The work of scaffolding is carried out through dialogue, reflecting a social plane of learning. Therefore the metaphor of scaffolding is not that the teacher provides the scaffold while the student builds knowledge, but the teacher and student jointly place the scaffold and construct the outer structure of shared meaning. The scaffolding is removed gradually, and the student completes the constructive process by assuming ownership and using the newly acquired knowledge. (p. 50)

It is through this lens of shared responsibility that scaffolding as an instructional component of discussion will be viewed in this review of literature. Similar to Liang and Dole (2006), we found two ways in which teachers scaffolded comprehension through discussion: microgenetic scaffolding and ontogenetic scaffolding.

Microgenetic scaffolding   Vygotsky's (1978) notion of genetic or developmental analysis is essential to understanding each type of scaffolding. Vygotsky (1978) aimed to study the development of higher mental functions (such as comprehension) by understanding its history. Wertsch (1985) noted that, for Vygotsky, the defining characteristics of higher mental functions as opposed to elementary mental functions were: (a) the emergence of voluntary regulation, (b) the emergence of conscious realization of mental processes, (c) the social nature of higher mental functions, and (d) the use of tools to mediate higher mental functions. In comprehension research, we often study the nature of voluntary regulation, or self-regulation, and recognize its importance. As well, we also recognize the importance of conscious realization of mental processes, or metacognition. However, when we begin to also examine the social nature of higher mental functions, such as comprehension and the use of tools such as language as a mediator of comprehension, the methods of examining such development become infinitely more complex.

Vygotsky (1978) believed that to study something historically did not mean studying past events. Instead, it meant to "study it in the process of change . . . to encompass in research the process of a given thing's development in all its phases and changes—from birth to death—fundamentally means to discover its nature, its essence, for 'it is only in movement that a body shows what it is'" (pp. 64–65). Thus, in examining how comprehension develops by participating in discussion, one must examine comprehension not as a product, but as a dynamic process that is continually changing.

Vygotsky's view of genetic or developmental analysis is essential to such study. Wertsch (1985, 1991) described Vygotsky's developmental analysis as consisting of four domains: (a) phylogenesis (i.e., biological evolutionary development), (b) sociocultural history, (c) ontogenesis, and (d) microgenesis. It is the latter two that coincide with the types of instructional scaffolding used to foster comprehension during discussion of text.

Wertsch (1991) described microgenesis as the "emergence of a mental process that occurs during a single training session" (p. 23) and as "the unfolding of a single psychological act (for instance, an act of perception), often over the course of milliseconds" (p. 23). In essence, microgenesis describes how thought develops on a moment-by-moment basis. This notion might be further defined as an act of cognition. Wortham (2006) used the term "'cognition' to describe the process of making sense of experience at the timescale of specific events" (p. 91). In this sense then, studying microgenetic development refers to the process by which thought or understanding develops in a specific event.

In a discussion, microgenetic scaffolding would seek to provide close support to assist comprehension of a particular text. Thus, we are introducing the term "microgenetic scaffolding" to describe scaffolding that is done on a moment-by-moment basis to assist comprehension. Liang and Dole (2006) explained that the ultimate goal of such scaffolding is to understand the content of a given text. They further explained that this type of scaffolding often features a high level of teacher involvement. Teachers in discussions that feature microgenetic scaffolding ask more open-ended questions, queries, and probes designed to help students think and comprehend at deeper levels. As well, teachers might assign roles during discussion as a means of scaffolding the interaction. Thus, the nature of discussions that feature microgenetic scaffolding will differ from those that feature ontogenetic scaffolding.

Ontogenetic scaffolding   Ontogenesis involves long-term development in which natural processes interact with cultural or social processes to create growth and change (Wertsch, 1985, 1991). The goal in ontogenetic development is to describe student growth and development over time. In terms of comprehension and discussion, this type of growth and development requires a different type of scaffolding because the immediate and long-term goals differ.

Wortham (2006) used the term "learning" to refer to the process of making sense of experiences on a longer timescale occurring across events. Wortham (2006) argued that learning cannot occur within a single event and that productive learning requires individuals to "systematically change the cognitive tools they use and how they react to affordances across events" (p. 101). Such change takes time because it involves gradual shifts and changes in cognitive processing.

Engeström (as cited in Wortham, 2006) noted that Vygotskian perspectives not only describe "the use of preexisting artifacts in cognition ('internalization'), but also the creation of artifacts that could subsequently be used ('externalization')" (p. 104). In this manner activities such as peer discussions of text are capable of "expanding" when students and teachers create new tools, artifacts, and ways of acting. As students move from one discussion event to another, over time they adopt different resources to adjust to different settings and circumstances. Through this gradual process they create new ways of interacting with one another and new ways of interpreting texts across time.

During this type of long-term, or ontogenetic, scaffolding the teacher's goal is not immediate cognitive development (i.e., comprehension of content) in a microgenetic sense, but ontogenetic development, in which students' abilities to interpret text and learn to sustain conversations about text are scaffolded longitudinally. This type of scaffolding requires teachers at times to relinquish comprehension of the immediate text in order to let children work through the social context and participate fully in the transaction. That is, rather than teachers guiding and scaffolding students' interpretations to deeper levels immediately, teachers foster long-term cognitive and social development.

This type of development is fostered more through discussions that have less teacher involvement, such as peer discussion. Almasi (2002) described peer discussion as an event in which:

> students gather to talk about, critique, and understand texts with minimal teacher assistance. Students determine their own topics of conversation and negotiate the procedural rules and social conventions that govern their discussion. Discourse is lively and focuses on personal reactions, responses, and interpretations of what has been read. Students also use a variety of strategic reading behaviors (e.g., comprehension monitoring, imagery, prediction, summarization) and higher levels of

abstract and critical thinking (e.g., making intertextual connections, critiquing author's craft) to participate meaningfully in discussions. (p. 420)

She further defined peer discussion as a sociocultural, dialogic, and democratic endeavor characterized by four features: (1) a moral dimension (i.e., students view themselves and others as worthy participants whose contributions are valued and respected and who are attentive and responsive to others), (2) student-centered, (3) collaborative, and (4) dynamic student roles that may vary from moment to moment. Almasi (2002) further noted that each feature is mutually dependent on the others for successful peer discussion to occur.

In this type of setting, teachers provide scaffolding in which they teach students about interpretive strategies and how to function in a peer discussion *prior to* and *following* peer discussion rather than *during* the discussion. Teachers scaffold in ways that help students learn to recognize features of the task (e.g., What went well in your discussion today? What might we work on to make the discussion better? What might we do to help one another understand the text better?). As well, they scaffold to help students learn to resolve issues on their own (e.g., You said that during your discussion some people tend to dominate, making it difficult for others to join in the conversation. What can we do next time so this is not a problem?)

The actual discussion is intended to be a pure, unimpeded transaction in which students come to their own interpretations rather than being guided in particular interpretive directions by the teacher. As such, reader response perspectives are also critical in framing peer discussion (Rosenblatt, 1938/1976, 1978).

RESEARCH SYNTHESIS

In gathering studies for this review, we found five ways in which researchers have examined discussion and comprehension. First, we examine studies in which the goal was to determine the impact of discussion on comprehension. Second, we examine studies of discussion in which microgenetic scaffolding was used to foster comprehension. Then the use of ontogenetic scaffolding during discussion is examined. This section is followed by a review of studies describing teacher change as they attempt move from microgenetic to ontogenetic scaffolding and studies describing ways to evaluate the quality of peer discussion. Finally, a review of studies from a critical perspective sought to understand student perceptions of discussion and highlight the cautions and limitations of student-centered discussions.

Impact of discussion on comprehension

Applebee, Langer, Nystrand, and Gamoran (2003) examined particular aspects of classroom discussions (e.g., dialogic interaction, envisionment building, extended curricular conversations) and related them to middle and high school students' literary performance on writing tasks (e.g., level of abstraction, level of elaboration). Nineteen schools and 974 students across the United States participated in the study. Data sources included four observations in each teacher's classroom, teacher questionnaires, student questionnaires, and written assessments of students' literacy performance, which were gathered in the fall and spring of one academic year. Results of principal components analysis suggested that dialogic interaction, envisionment building, and emphasis on curricular conversation are related elements that support student understanding of text. Results of hierarchical linear modeling analyses found that high academic demands and discussion-based approaches were significantly related to higher literacy performance across tracked levels.

Fall, Webb, and Chudowsky (2000) also found that discussion had a positive impact on comprehension in their study of over 500 tenth graders' performance on language arts tests in which they were either permitted to discuss stories with other peers for ten minutes or not permitted to discuss the text with others. The statewide language arts assessment measured students' ability to understand and interpret narrative text, make connections to their own lives, and assume a critical stance. Students were randomly assigned to one of three discussion conditions: discussion toward the beginning of the test, discussion toward the end of the test, and no discussion. Students were also asked to provide self-report evidence of changes in their understanding of text. Results showed that students who had the opportunity to discuss the story showed an increase in literal understanding of textual facts from the first part of the test to the second whereas students who did not have the opportunity to discuss showed a decrease in literal understanding. As well, students who participated in discussions showed more evidence of changes in their understanding of factual information throughout the test as a result of discussion. Finally, the study showed that even a small amount of discussion has the potential to produce significant increases in students' understanding of narrative text.

Van den Branden (2000) argued that comprehension problems have the most learning potential when they occur in natural, authentic reading situations and when learners negotiate the meaning of a text through social interaction. The quasi-experimental study examined the conditions under which negotiation of meaning promoted comprehension and the extent to which premodifying texts had an impact on first- and second-language learners' reading comprehension.

One hundred fifty-one Dutch fifth graders (61% native Dutch speakers; 39% non-native Dutch speakers) participated in the study and were assigned to one of four levels of Dutch proficiency based on their performance on an editing test administered prior to the start of the study: (a) very high proficiency, (b) moderately high proficiency, (c) moderately low proficiency, and (d) very low proficiency.

Students in each linguistically diverse group received all four treatment conditions as in a repeated measures design: (1) unmodified input condition (students read text and answer comprehension questions silently and independently), (2) premodified input condition (students read text in which vocabulary and syntax were simplified and repetition employed and then independently complete comprehension tests), (3) collective negotiation condition (students read the text silently and work with other students to determine the meaning of unfamiliar words and phrases and then independently complete comprehension tests), and (4) pair negotiation condition (students read the text and work with another students to determine the meaning of unknown words and phrases and then independently complete comprehension tests). The order of treatment condition was counterbalanced across each group. Students completed multiple-choice comprehension tests after they read each chapter of the text.

Analysis of variance with repeated measures showed statistically significant main effects. Post hoc analyses revealed that the collective negotiation and paired negotiation treatment conditions had a significant impact on student performance in several ways. First, students had significantly higher comprehension when they negotiated the meaning of the text via collective negotiation or paired negotiation than when they were exposed to both the unmodified and premodified versions of the text. Second, students at all levels of language proficiency had statistically significantly higher comprehension scores when involved in the two negotiation conditions than when in the unmodified condition. Further, the collective negotiation condition was statistically significantly superior to all other conditions at all levels of language proficiency. Finally, findings showed that both native and nonnative speakers scored significantly higher in the two negotiation conditions than in the premodified and unmodified conditions.

Van den Branden's (2000) findings suggest that for all students, particularly those with lower levels of language proficiency, collectively negotiating the meaning of text improved comprehension. For these students, the opportunity to work with peers to recognize and resolve their own comprehension problems provided more assistance with comprehension than modifying texts to make them easier to understand.

In summary, findings from these studies suggest that discussion, as a general instructional activity, fosters higher literacy performance in terms of level of abstraction and elaboration (Applebee, Langer, Nystrand, & Gamoran, 2003), significantly higher levels of literal understanding of text (Fall, Webb, & Chudowsky, 2000), and significantly higher levels of both literal and inferential comprehension for students at all levels of language proficiency (Van den Branden, 2000). When considering the impact of discussion on comprehension, it is not only important to understand its overall benefits as a general instructional activity, but also the impact of various types of scaffolding on comprehension.

Microgenetic scaffolding of comprehension during discussions

In this section, we examine the impact of two types of microgenetic scaffolding on comprehension: teacher scaffolding through role assignment and teacher scaffolding through teacher questioning, queries, and probing.

Teacher scaffolding through role assignment   Bond (2001) examined how her fifth-graders were able to use assigned roles to make sense of text during student-led discussions of text. Findings showed that students used the connector role most frequently as they made connections to past events, family, and relationships. These connections helped students understand and make sense of text by linking their lives to those of the characters in the texts they were reading.

Morocco and Hindin's (2002) qualitative study examined ways in which middle school students with disabilities contributed to peer-led discussions and how their participation enabled them to build textual understanding, social understanding, and understanding of text. Findings showed students were able to appropriate the discussion facilitation roles introduced by the teacher and they developed the ability to negotiate interpretations of literature through various discourse practices (e.g., stating claims, elaborating on others' claims, countering others' claims with alternate views, using argument to support claims). Like the students in Bond's (2001) study, these students also displayed the ability to deepen their understanding of text by making connections to knowledge from their own lives. Morocco and Hindin (2002) suggested that teacher scaffolding made the discussion task accessible to students. That is, the teacher's use of a sequence of activities that included establishing a purpose for the discussion, discussing and writing responses to text, and revisiting interpretations by reporting out the arguments in their discussions enabled students to meet with success.

In contrast, Almasi and Russell (1998, 1999) found teacher assignment of static roles during peer discussion of expository text to be limiting. Their 3-month descriptive case study followed a group of five third graders as they participated in discussions of expository texts as part of Concept-Oriented Reading Instruction (Guthrie, Van Meter, McCann, Wigfield, Bennett, Poundstone, Rice, Faibisch, Hunt, & Mitchell, 1996). Guthrie and McCann (1996) described these discussions as "Idea Circles," which are peer discussions fueled by multiple informational text sources. Similar to a peer discussion, the teacher is not physically present to guide students' understanding of text. However, the goal of idea circles is in contrast to the goal in discussions of narrative texts. Whereas discussions of narrative promote the possibility of diverse interpretation, idea circles seek to attain convergence of conceptual understanding. A particular concept (i.e., facts, relations among facts, and explanations) unites the students in dialogue as they build an abstract understanding from information, details, and data contained within the texts.

Almasi and Russell's (1998, 1999) findings revealed that, although the teacher was not physically present in the group, a "shared" culture emerged among students in the group in which the teacher (and her authority) were present semiotically in three ways. First, the teacher was present semiotically in that she assigned and sanctioned the roles that each student assumed. She was also present in the language of the tasks she used to focus student discourse. At times these tasks took on an "assignment status" that led to large amounts of task parameter metatalk focused on organization. Finally, the teacher was semiotically present through the language students used. Quite often the students appropriated the speech genre of the teacher to gain status and authority within the group.

This semiotic teacher presence led to anacretic discourse structures (i.e., one-way exchanges) rather than dialogic discourse. As well, student discourse was consumed by large amounts of metatalk (49.1% of all discourse) in which conversation focused more on who could talk and what they should be talking about rather than discourse related to content and meaning construction (38.4% of all discourse).

Overall, Almasi and Russell (1998, 1999) found students' voices lacked the procedural and declarative knowledge necessary to make them functionally dialogic. In order to make their voices heard and gain some semblance of respect within the group, students attempted to gain authority in four ways: (1) They used formulaic teacher language in an effort to "sound" like the teacher. (2) They used the language of the task in an attempt to force other students into compliance to complete the assigned task. (3) They identified with the teacher and often directly referred to the teacher and what "she said" to elicit authority. (4) They used the teacher-sanctioned authority of their assigned role to gain respect and force others to submit to them. Although the teacher's instructional moves (i.e., assigning roles, assigning a discussion task) were intended to scaffold student learning and comprehension, it led to power struggles among students and created fewer opportunities to construct meaning. These findings are in contrast to those of Bond (2001) and Morocco and Hindin (2002), who found role assignment during discussion enhanced comprehension.

Scaffolding through teacher questioning, queries, and probing   Many more studies have been conducted in which teachers engage in microgenetic scaffolding using teacher questions, queries, and probes. Wolf, Crosson, and Resnick (2005) examined the relationship between quality of classroom talk and the degree of academic rigor in reading comprehension lessons. Twenty-one reading comprehension lessons in grades one through eight were examined in 10 schools. Classroom talk consisted of whole class discussions of text in which the teacher asked questions. Stepwise regression analyses showed that student talk in the form of knowledge sharing and thinking were significant predictors of academic rigor during the lessons. Wolf, Crosson, and Resnick (2005) attributed the quality of student talk to high correlations with the types of questions teachers asked. When teachers probed using open-ended queries and follow-up probes such as "How did you know that?" students provided more elaborated responses.

Open-ended probes and queries are also essential to Beck, McKeown, Sandora, Kucan, and Worthy's (1996) examination of Questioning the Author. Questioning the Author is an instructional intervention in which students learn to grapple with the ideas in a text by suggesting that authors are fallible and that the ideas in a text may not be written as clearly as they could be (McKeown, Beck, & Worthy, 1993). In this way students can see that their need for active cognitive effort while reading may not be a result of their own inadequacies but the author's inability to clearly communicate. Teachers use a series of open-ended queries to initiate discussion, focus on the author's message, link information, identify difficulties with the way the author presented ideas, encourage students to use the text when they have misinterpreted it, recognize plot development and character thoughts/actions, and recognize author's technique (Beck, McKeown, Sandora, Kucan & Worthy, 1996). In their yearlong descriptive study of two teachers and their fourth graders, Beck et al. (1996) examined teacher questions and rejoinders, student-initiated discourse, and the relation between the amount of teacher and student talk. Findings showed teachers made significant changes in the types of questions they asked prior to implementing Questioning the Author and after implementation. Initially, teacher questions focused primarily on retrieving literal information from text. After implementing the Questioning the Author intervention, however, teachers asked more questions aimed at extending the discussion and constructing meaning. Teacher talk was also significantly reduced and student talk significantly increased as a result of participating in Questioning the Author. Prior to the intervention, teacher talk dominated about 80% of all discussion discourse, and dropped to about 60% while implementing Questioning the Author. Student comprehension showed significant increases as did their ability to successfully monitor their comprehension.

A more recent study aimed at investigating the effect of training six teachers to use Questioning the Author have shown similar findings in terms of shifts in teacher question-asking behaviors and amount of teacher and student talk (McKeown & Beck, 2004). Student comprehension and monitoring was not reported.

Sandora, Beck, and McKeown (1999) examined the effects of two discussion formats (Questioning the Author and Great Books) on sixth and seventh graders' comprehension and interpretation of literature. While both discussion formats afford students the opportunity to collaboratively construct meaning and examine text more closely while scaffolded by the teacher, Questioning the Author discussions occur as the text is being read and Great Books discussions occur after the text is read. Findings showed that student recall of text and their responses to open-ended questions was significantly higher for students who participated in Questioning the Author discussions than for those participating in Great Books discussions. As well, the length of students' recalls was significantly greater and their ability to recall complex story elements was greater for students who participated in Questioning the Author. Taken together, these findings suggest that Questioning the Author had a substantially positive impact on students' comprehension.

Like Questioning the Author, Instructional Conversations are discussions in which teachers promote analysis, reflection, and critical thinking among students. Students engage in dialogic conversation with each other and the teacher about textual ideas. Like Questioning the Author, Instructional Conversations are instructional and conversational and feature fewer literal or "known-answer" questions by the teacher. As well, they feature responsivity to student contributions, connected discourse, a challenging (but nonthreatening) atmosphere, and general participation (including self-selected turns; Goldenberg, 1993).

Saunders and Goldenberg (1999) examined the effects of using literature logs and instructional conversations with upper elementary limited-English-proficient and English-proficient students. Students in three fifth-grade and two fourth-grade classrooms were randomly assigned to one of four treatment conditions: (1) literature logs, (2) instructional conversation, (3) literature logs and instructional conversation, or (4) read and study (control). All four treatments were implemented in each classroom across a four day period of time to control for teacher effects. Results showed students who participated in the literature logs and instructional conversation condition and the instructional conversation only condition scored significantly higher on measures of factual and interpretive comprehension than their peers in the control and the literature log only conditions. Students in the three treatment conditions were significantly more likely to demonstrate an understanding of theme than students in the control condition.

Many (2002) conducted a seven-month naturalistic examination of the nature of instructional scaffolding that occurred as students and teachers constructed meaning of narrative and expository texts using instructional conversations. Fifty students and their teachers in multiage classrooms (third/fourth; fifth/sixth grades) participated in the year long study. Findings showed that scaffolding (by teachers and peers) served two purposes: (1) to help students attain more complex conceptual understanding of the texts (i.e., using outside sources for additional information, using text to support points, making intertextual connections); and (2) to help students develop a repertoire of strategies for reading, writing, and working from texts and strategies for socially constructing knowledge (i.e., presenting to an audience, participating in group discussion, working with peers). Teachers (and peers) also used a variety of scaffolding processes that ranged from scaffolding with more teacher/peer support (modeling, supplying information, clarifying, assisting) to support with student involvement (questioning, prompting, focusing attention) to scaffolding with the greatest amount of student involvement (self-monitoring, labeling effective processes). Overall, scaffolding did not reflect a traditional explanation, modeling, guided practice framework in which responsibility is gradually released to the student. Instead scaffolding reflected varying degrees of support for some students while others were using the same knowledge of strategy use on their own. Scaffolding was responsive to students' needs and was influenced by the classroom context.

McIntyre, Kyle, and Moore (2006) also examined the nature of teacher scaffolding during instructional conversations. Using grounded theory and collaborative teacher action research, they gathered and analyzed data over four days in one teacher's multi-age (grades 1–2) elementary classroom. Primary data sources included classroom observations, videotapes, interviews, student assessments, and home visits for family interviews. Findings revealed that "teacher-fronted" discourse that included telling, defining, and modeling at the beginning of lessons can lead to dialogic student interactions. As well, the teacher's use of non-evaluative responses, encouragement rather than praise, examples and suggestions, and linguistic and paralinguistic cues (e.g., pacing and hand gestures) facilitated students' participation and helped bring them into the discussion. In time the teacher became more spontaneous in her ability to scaffold.

Overall, the studies reviewed here found that microgenetic scaffolding, in particular those that use open-ended teacher questions, queries, and probes had a positive impact on student comprehension. Such scaffolding during discussion enhanced the quality of student talk and led to discussions with more academic rigor (Wolf, Crosson, & Resnick, 2005), led to significant gains in comprehension, recall, and ability to monitor their comprehension (Beck, McKeown, Sandora, Kucan, & Worthy, 1996; Sandora, Beck, & McKeown, 1999); led to significantly higher scores on literal and inferential comprehension and understanding of theme (Saunders & Goldenberg, 1999); and led to more complex conceptual understanding of the texts and the development of a repertoire of strategies for making sense of text (Many, 2002).

Ontogenetic scaffolding of comprehension: Peer discussion

As with microgenetic scaffolding, many research programs have examined the impact of ontogenetic scaffolding on comprehension within the framework of peer discussion. Those studies have examined the impact of peer discussion on comprehension of narrative text and expository text.

Peer discussion and narrative text   Goatley, Brock, and Raphael (1995) examined the nature of diverse learners' participation in student-led discussions of text as they assumed different roles, responsibilities, and means of negotiating the meaning of text. As well, they examined the manner in which these fifth graders developed the ability to interpret text. The study used the Book Club format (Raphael & McMahon, 1994) in which students first read the text, complete a written response to the reading, participate in a community share (i.e., discussion of text), and instruction. Findings revealed that culturally and linguistically diverse students and those who struggle with reading were capable of assuming varied roles in student-led discussions. Those roles varied from one moment to the next and suggested that assigned roles may not be conducive to the goals of student-led discussions. Students also assisted in negotiating and maintaining the topics of discussion and constructed meaning by using a variety of strategies to gather information from sources as they collaboratively constructed interpretations of text. In short, students were able to use the background knowledge available to them because of cultural differences as a way to help one another make sense of the text. This finding suggested that scaffolded assistance need not come solely from the teacher, but also from peers.

Like Goatley et al. (1995), Rice (2005) was interested in the impact of background on students' ability to construct meaning. Rice examined the responses of eight white sixth-graders as they discussed four realistic fiction Hispanic-American multicultural stories in peer-led discussion groups. In this qualitative investigation, the researcher met with students daily for four consecutive days to read and discuss the stories. Transcripts of the discussions were analyzed using constant comparative methods to determine the influence of students' class, race, and gender on their interpretation of multicultural stories. Findings revealed that students interpreted the plots and characters based on their own background experiences (i.e., socioeconomic status, race), which differed substantially from that of the characters. Socioeconomic status in particular had a large impact on students' interpretations of characters' actions in that students were often unable to relate to the characters and tended to "put down" the characters. Students' cultural norms for physical appearance, language, and food customs also influenced their interpretations to the extent that at times they were unable to identify with the universal themes present in the stories. Overall, Rice's analyses (2005) highlighted the importance of readers' sociocultural context and background on their responses to and interpretations of text.

McMahon and Goatley's (1995) naturalistic investigation examined how fifth graders with prior experience with student-led discussions acted as "knowledgeable others" for peers who had not participated in such discussions previously. The 4-week study examined the interactions of two students with experience in Book Clubs and three without experience. Transcripts of discussions and classroom activities, student interviews and students' written responses were analyzed inductively to identify emergent themes and patterns. Findings showed that initially students relied on an I-R-E pattern in which one student with prior experience in Book Clubs assumed the teacher-like role. Over time other students began to initiate topics of conversation and the group moved away from an I-R-E pattern to patterns with more dialogic interaction that included elaboration, clarification and debate. Findings from this study highlight the fact that students can serve as scaffolds for one another; however, their discourse can also revert back to more traditional patterns of classroom discourse without the support of teachers and peers to monitor and assist them as they adjust to new expectations and roles.

Collaborative Reasoning is a method of discussing texts that stimulates critical reading, critical thinking, and student engagement (Chinn & Anderson, 1998; Waggoner, Chinn, Yi, & Anderson, 1995) by asking students to reflect on central questions arising from their reading. Students take stances regarding their initial positions on the issue and look for textual evidence to support their stance. Students add reasons or provide challenges by suggesting alternate reasons. As in Book Clubs, an open participation structure is used to evoke more natural conversation. That is, students speak without raising their hands or being called upon, and students monitor their own participation and control their own topics of conversation. Through Collaborative Reasoning, students learn reasoning and argumentation skills and they learn how to respect diverse opinions.

In an examination of the effects of participation in Collaborative Reasoning on the development of individual reasoning, Reznitskaya, Anderson, McNurlen, Nguyen-Jahiel, Archodidou, and Kim's (2001) quasi-experimental study found that fourth and fifth graders who participated in Collaborative Reasoning discussions wrote persuasive essays containing significantly more arguments, counterarguments, rebuttals, uses of formal argument devices, and references to text information than the essays of students who did not participate in Collaborative Reasoning. Findings suggested that collaborative discussion formats such as Collaborative Reasoning provide an opportunity for students to learn how to retrieve argument-relevant information, construct and repair arguments, and anticipate flaws in arguments.

Anderson, Nguyen-Jahiel, McNurlen, Archodidou, Kim, Reznitskaya, Tillmanns, and Gilbert (2001) compared the impact of Collaborative Reasoning discussions and more traditional discussions on the reasoning and rhetorical strategies fourth graders used as they discussed narrative texts. All 104 students participated in both types of discussions, which were counterbalanced in terms of order. Results showed that once an argument stratagem was used for a rhetorical purpose (i.e., managing group participation, acknowledging uncertainty, personalizing the story, making argument explicit, and supporting arguments with evidence) the likelihood that it would be used again increased significantly. In essence, a "snowball phenomenon" occurred in which the use of argument stratagems spread to other children and to other groups once it was displayed. The diffusion of argument stratagems occurred more often in Collaborative Reasoning discussions than in traditional, teacher-controlled discussions.

Almasi (1995) also contrasted peer discussion with teacher-led discussion among 97 fourth graders. However, her major concern was with a particular event known as sociocognitive conflict that often occurs in peer discussion when students encounter incongruity. Using a quasi-experimental design, this study examined the nature of sociocognitive conflicts, the discourse associated with such conflicts, and how the cognitive processes associated with such conflicts were internalized by students in each condition. Findings revealed three different types of sociocognitive conflicts: conflicts with self (i.e., the metacognitive realization that some aspect of the text or one's interpretation was causing confusion), conflicts with others (i.e., realization that incongruent ideas were present among group members), and conflicts with text (i.e., realization that one's response was incongruent with information in the text). Students in peer discussions engaged in significantly more episodes in which there were conflicts with self, whereas students in teacher-led conditions engaged in substantially more conflicts with text. Such participation enabled students in peer discussions to recognize and resolve episodes of conflict significantly better than students in teacher-led discussions, suggesting that they had internalized this metacognitive ability as a result of their participation over time. As well, students in peer discussions were more actively engaged in their discussions in that they engaged in significantly more discourse, their discourse was significantly more complex, and they asked more questions than students in teacher-led discussions.

More recent studies have examined developmental differences between students who participate in peer discussion contexts and those who participate in teacher-led discussions and the impact on cognitive, social, and affective constructs (Almasi et al., 2004). This series of studies originated from a three-year longitudinal research initiative designed to understand students' ontogenetic and microgenetic development as they participated in peer discussions of text. The *process* and *products* of student learning through peer discussion was examined to understand how students' ability to talk about, interpret, and interact around text developed over time.

Almasi, Garas, Cho, Ma, Shanahan, and Augustino (2004) examined students' cognitive, social, and affective growth in grades K–3 in peer discussion and teacher-led discussion contexts. Participants included 26 teachers and the 412 students in their K–3 classrooms in suburban, urban, and rural contexts. Twelve of the teachers were in the peer discussion treatment condition, and 14 were in the control condition. Findings revealed that students in both conditions experienced significant growth in terms of word recognition and comprehension. However, significant differences did not exist between treatment conditions. More substantive findings were found related to social and affective measures of growth and development. Students in the peer discussion group valued reading significantly more than their counterparts in the control condition. Participation in peer discussions of text resulted in significant differences in the social relationships students built in their classrooms. The changes in social networks from the beginning of the year to the end of the year among peer discussion students exhibited an Egalitarian Pattern of social change. That is, their social networks homogenized over time—there were fewer social isolates and fewer social stars. In contrast, social networks among students in the control condition exhibited a Pattern of Inclusivity and Elitism over time where social ranks became more stratified. More students were labeled social stars creating a prominent, elite group of students. These findings suggest that peer discussion may assist children in becoming more tolerant of others and more accepting of diverse perspectives in terms of academics and play.

In a study of students' interpretive strategy use and language development, Almasi, Garas, Cho, Ma, Shanahan, Augustino, and Palmer (2005) used a time series, or panel, design to gain insight into the intra-individual and inter-individual changes that occurred across a three year time period as students progressed from first through third grade. The same cohort of students in one research site was measured repeatedly on a number of variables at successive points in time to understand the impact peer discussion had on individual students' interpretive strategy use and language development. Findings showed that when children had consistent opportunities to engage in peer discussions of text they were able to use interpretive strategies as tools to achieve deeper levels of comprehension as early as first grade, and with increasing frequency throughout third grade. As well, these findings showed that, with sustained exposure to peer discussion, young readers were able to learn how to cohere and sustain topics in conversations about text with sophistication. The ontogenetic scaffolding provided by the teachers in this study enabled this cohort of children to make substantive growth in terms of the way in which they interpreted literature and the way in which they learned to negotiate the social context in which they constructed their interpretations.

Peer discussion and expository text   Hogan, Nastasi, and Pressley (1999) examined the patterns of interaction within peer- and teacher-led discussions of scientific concepts. Over a 12-week period of time one eighth-grade teacher enacted peer-led discussions with six students in one class, and teacher-led discussions with six students in another class. Students were asked to construct an understanding of the nature of matter; use their model to explain the characteristics of solids, liquids, and gases; and present and defend their model to the whole class. Discussions as students engaged in these tasks were videotaped two to three times per week. Data analysis was inductive and included coding: modes of discourse, types of statements, discourse maps, interaction patterns, and response complexity. The goal in both types of discussion was to continually refine and work on weak or incomplete conceptions until they improved. Findings revealed, however, that the manner in which groups attained that goal differed in peer-led and teacher-led contexts. Peer discussions were more generative and elaborated than their discussions with teachers. Students were more apt to explore ideas through conceptual contributions, they asked more questions to clarify their understanding with one another, and they synthesized ideas more than students in teacher-led discussions. Overall, their responses grew increasingly complex and led to higher levels of reasoning the more they talked. Students in peer-led discussions developed the ability to persevere on their own until conceptual issues were resolved.

In teacher-led groups students talked less, asked substantially fewer questions, and their discourse consisted of more explanations. Discussion in teacher-led groups required fewer turns to arrive at higher levels of reasoning. This made the discussion more efficient, but attaining this level required progressive teacher questioning and probing.

Overall, studies using ontogenetic scaffolding have found a positive impact on students' comprehension. However, the depiction of this impact is more refined. Rather than general improvements on broad measures of literal and inferential comprehension, these studies showed the impact of peer discussion on specific aspects of comprehension and interpretation of text. Students are able to use background knowledge available to them because of cultural differences (Goatley, Brock, & Raphael, 1995) and sociocultural differences in terms of socioeconomic status and race (Rice, 2005) to make sense of and interpret text. Student in peer discussions were also able to internalize the ability to recognize and resolve conflicts significantly better than students in teacher-led discussions (Almasi, 1995). As well, these studies showed that students are capable of learning how to engage in dialogic conversations about text on their own (McMahon & Goatley, 1995) even as early as kindergarten and first grade (Almasi, Garas, Cho, Ma, Shanahan, Augustino, & Palmer, 2005). Students are also able to learn to think critically, retrieve argument-relevant information, construct and repair arguments, and anticipate flaws in arguments when they learn the principles of argumentative reasoning and enact them in peer discussions (Anderson, Nguyen-Jahiel, McNurlen, Archodidou, Kim, Reznitskaya, Tillmanns, & Gilbert, 2001; Reznitskaya, Anderson, McNurlen, Nguyen-Jahiel, Archodidou, & Kim, 2001). Finally, as implied by the theoretical discussion of instructional scaffolding by Wood, Bruner, and Ross (1976) and Meyer (1993), studies of peer discussion of text have shown that students show significant social and affective growth and development when compared to their peers in teacher-led contexts (Almasi, Garas, Cho, Ma, Shanahan, & Augustino, 2004).

Shifting to ontogenetic scaffolding

Research has shown that the open-ended nature of peer discussion has value, but teachers have difficulty learning how to successfully scaffold such conversations. Therefore, several lines of inquiry have examined the manner in which teachers learn to scaffold conversations, and have developed new means of assessing and evaluating the effectiveness of peer discussions.

Teacher movement toward peer discussions   Maloch (2002) explored the relationship between the teacher's role and students' participation in peer discussions of literature in third grade. Her 5-month qualitative study used constant comparative and discourse analysis to arrive at two themes. First, students had difficulty shifting from more passive roles in teacher-led discussion to more active roles in peer discussion. They often reverted to the more familiar routines of teacher-led discussions (i.e., raising hands, waiting for teacher leadership, looking for the teacher to help solve problems). Although the teacher supported students in this transition by providing explanations about student tasks and roles and her own, it took time for students to develop this awareness and their discussions were often unfocused and unproductive. A second theme examined the nature of the teacher's responsiveness to the students' difficulty and found that teachers can be effective as facilitators rather than in the more traditional role of leader. She found that effective scaffolding consisted of: metalinguistic interventions (or metatalk) in which the ground rules of discussion were highlighted, building a shared understanding of conversational strategies over time, and gradually handing over the responsibility for the discussion to students.

Like Maloch (2002), Scharer and Peters (1996) found teachers and students had difficulty learning to implement peer discussions. Their study examined the patterns of discourse and the relationship between teachers' perceptions of book discussions and the way in which students and teachers actually talked about books in their qualitative study of two upper elementary teachers. Transcripts of interviews and group discussions were primary data sources that were analyzed to identify patterns in the ways topics were initiated, sustained, and terminated. Findings revealed that although teachers felt that peer discussions were a valuable way to help children express their opinions, foster higher level thinking, and make personal connections to text, they had great difficulty shifting toward a more student-centered type of discussion. Topics for discussion were overwhelmingly controlled by the teacher and student responses tended to be directed to the teacher.

These studies, although few in number, suggest that developing classroom cultures in which more student-centered and dialogic conversations about text can occur is difficult for both students and teachers. Because of the difficult nature of such a shift, several researchers have attempted to analyze the quality of peer discussions to identify those features that lead to more productive discussions. The thinking here is that, if the qualities that make peer discussions successful can be identified, researchers will know which aspects to focus on while working with teachers and students.

Analyzing the quality of peer discussion Roller and Beed (1994) expressed concern about the quality of discussion in their examination of children's book sharing sessions. The Book Sharing Sessions occurred as part of a reading workshop in which struggling readers ranging in age from eight to 12 self-selected books, presented their book to the group, and other children and the teacher responded by offering questions and comments. Although Roller and Beed (1994) found sufficient evidence of exciting dialogue, there was also evidence that student dialogue was not always as rich as it might be. Three types of dialogue in particular raised concerns: (1) content-free enthusiastic dialogue, (2) substantive but lifeless dialogue, and (3) content-free and lifeless. Their reflection enabled them to come to the realization that teachers must build on children's enthusiasm and trust their oral culture as a legitimate means of constructing meaning—even if it might stand in contrast with adult oral culture.

Chinn and Anderson (1998) used argument network (i.e., interlocking sets of premises and conclusions) and causal network (i.e., discussion events linked in a causal sequence) approaches to represent the macrostructure of interactive argumentation during Collaborative Reasoning discussions. Their analyses of fourth graders' discussions of issues raised in narrative texts provided a means of evaluating the breadth, depth, and explicitness of students' arguments; the extent to which students communicated their perspectives (i.e., argument network); and it provided a means of evaluating students' ability to support and challenge causal links and their ability to compare value judgments and envisionments to one another (i.e., causal network).

Keefer, Zeitz, and Resnick (2000) also developed a means of evaluating the quality of literary discussions. In so doing they identified four dialogue types and contexts: critical discussion, explanatory inquiry, eristic discussion, and consensus dialogue. They contended that critical discussion was the most appropriate type of dialogue for discussions focused on literary content. They examined fourth graders' student-led discussions at the beginning and end of the year. Discussions focused on a question derived from texts that had been read aloud to students. Graphical coding analysis was developed to show the course of argumentation distributed among participants and then compared with content-based literary coding to assess the quality of discussion. The coding system permitted examination of the source of support for claims made (i.e., nontextual knowledge, facts from text, interpretation of textual information). The social distribution of argumentation was also charted by identifying attacks, challenges, and concessions. These analyses were used to determine the connection between discussion quality and arguments supported by premises based on interpretation of literary and textual issues.

Almasi, O'Flahavan, and Arya (2001) also developed a means of analyzing the quality of peer discussions. Their descriptive study examined the manner in which more and less proficient peer discussion groups managed topics and group process across four months. The microanalyses consisted of taxonomic analysis and contextual analysis of discourse and patterns of interaction. The contextual analysis determined how well conversations cohered in terms of whether topics were changed or sustained (e.g., topic shifts, linkages, returns) as students negotiated their discussions (Brinton & Fujiki, 1984; Schegloff, 1990). This was accomplished by considering the structure underlying the entire conversation, rather than simply local coherence (Agar & Hobbs, 1982; Reichman, 1978). As in many peer discussions, the groups deviated from talking about text at times. This talk was not off topic, as it facilitated how the group functioned. This type of talk is known as metatalk (Hobbs, 1990). Frequency data provided a description of the influence of metatalk on conversational growth and development. Thus, group management was examined by analyzing task parameter and group process metatalk. Task parameter metatalk consisted of talk about what can be discussed and the materials needed for discussion. Group process metatalk consisted of talk related to how the group functioned (e.g., turntaking, encouraging participation, interaction behaviors, topic shifts).

Results indicated coherence is key to conversational competence. Proficient peer discussion groups were able to sustain topics of conversation by revisiting old topics, making linkages between topics, and embedding topics within one another. These factors increased and developed gradually over time. Less proficient groups had substantially fewer linkages and embedded topics primarily because teachers and students initiated large amounts of metatalk. These findings suggest that large amounts of metatalk and teacher intrusion cause disjuncture to peer discussion and impair the group's ability to maintain topics.

Social/student perceptions of peer discussions

While a great deal of the research reviewed here has shown the positive effects of discussion on comprehension, it is also important to critically examine the social impact of more student-centered discussions on student perceptions and the social contexts they create. Using a multicase study approach, Alvermann, Young, Weaver, Hinchman, Moore, Phelps, Thrash, and Zalewski (1996) examined 95 middle and high school students' perceptions of class discussions of texts in five classes (English, language arts, gifted education, U. S. History, and Global Studies) across 1 academic year. Findings led to three assertions. First, students were aware of the conditions they believed to be conducive to discussion. In particular, students felt four conditions were important for good discussions: (1) working in small groups increased the degree to which each student could participate and decreased the potential for social risks, (2) knowing and liking group members contributed to student participation, but students also realized friendships could develop along the way, (3) contributing to group talk was every student's responsibility, and (4) staying focused on the topic contributed to creating quality discussions. The second assertion found the tasks teachers present and the topics or subject matter they assign for reading influence students' participation in discussion. Demanding tasks enabling students to reason and evaluate ideas were perceived as more interesting and worthy of discussion. Debatable topics students enjoyed and found interesting were more suitable for discussion. The third assertion found that students saw discussion as helpful in understanding what they read. As part of this assertion, students identified three ways discussions helped them understand text. First, students valued listening to one another and the opportunity to gain new ideas about a text from others' comments. Second, students found the opportunity to voice their opinions and persuade others as helpful. Finally, students found the opportunity to attend to vocabulary during discussions helpful as it provided the opportunity to identify and resolve the meanings of unknown words, which assisted comprehension of text.

Similar to Alvermann et al. (1996), Evans (2002) examined fifth-graders' perceptions of literature discussion groups and found similar results. Like the middle and high school students in Alvermann et al.'s (1996) study, these fifth-graders also had clear notions of the conditions that fostered effective discussion. They noted that basic requirements (i.e., reading the book, writing responses, and participating in the discussion), respect for one another's thoughts, having people with whom you can work in your group, the tasks, and the texts were all features that created productive discussions. Unlike the older students in Alvermann et al.'s (1996) study, the fifth-graders in Evans's (2002) study felt the gender makeup of their discussion group influenced how they participated in discussions. Students tended to have difficulty when in mixed-gender groups and preferred to work in same-gender groups. Likewise, these fifth-graders felt the presence of a bossy group member influenced their participation. Students who told others what to do had a negative influence on the group. These studies show that students of all ages have clear perceptions of what productive discussions look like.

Evans (1996) challenged the assumption that peer discussions provide "democratic" spaces where all students' voices are heard and valued equally. In her qualitative examination of the complexity in peer-led discussion contexts, she studied one group of five fifth graders as they engaged in six peer-led discussions of text across a two-week period of time. Constant comparative and content analyses were used to examine the manner in which students positioned and were positioned by one another. Findings revealed that students tended to assume particular roles. Initially students positioned one another based on leadership (i.e., verbal dominance and managing the discussion). In time, however, gender became a factor as the boys in the group began taunting one of the girls. Their efforts positioned the girls as powerless and led to the boys attaining power through teasing rather than through leadership skills.

In her year-long ethnographic study of literature discussions in a fifth/sixth grade classroom, Lewis (1997) also examined the ways social context and positioning shape peer-led discussions of text. Findings revealed that talk became a way for students to achieve social and interpretive power as they interpreted text. That is, in this classroom students who took learning and inquiry seriously had more power than those who did not. This created situations where students competed with one another to attain power. Such power often depended on the allegiances students formed in and out of school. Peer-led discussions also provided a means by which power relations were interrupted and possibly transformed when less powerful students challenged the ideas of those with more power. Overall, in the absence of an authority figure such as the teacher, findings showed that the peer-led discussion context often provided dominant students with a means of attaining a position of power as they interpreted literature.

Möller's (2005) interpretive case study examined the shifting roles one struggling reader experienced as she participated in literature discussions. Ashley was a student who struggled with decoding, comprehension, and acceptance in the group. She was a student who, in typical classrooms, might be singled out as "deficient," an "outsider to the literacy club" who might experience isolation and ostracism. However, her participation in 27 peer discussions as a learner, peer, and teacher enabled her to attain shifting positions ranging from less-capable member in need of support to capable peer working with peers to collaboratively construct meaning to more capable peer working at her developmental level and assisting others. Ashley moved fluidly in and out of these positions. She was able to help the group understand characters' situations, voice non-stereotypic and antiracist thinking, and connect emotionally to textual language in the process. Key to Ashley's growth was the teacher's support in terms of teaching comprehension and response strategies, valuing her contributions, and maintaining a classroom culture of acceptance and intolerance for taunting.

Möller and Allen (2000) also investigated struggling readers' responses to text as they engaged in literature discussions with their teacher. Their interpretive, inductive, and generative field study examined the discussions of four struggling readers as they responded to Mildred Taylor's *The Friendship*. The teacher (Möller) was present in the discussions to help students develop strategies for participating meaningfully in student-led literature discussions. She provided scaffolding by using supportive tones and gestures, creating a climate where students could explore uncomfortable aspects of the text, and asking questions and making statements to support students' inquiry. Categorical analysis found that the girls moved from spectators to actors in that they arrived at deep levels of interpretation in which they became personally involved. At varying times their responses and reactions to the text led them to engage by making connections to the author's craft, themselves, their families, their community, history, and present social issues. As well, their responses created a tension in which they were engaged but also resisted the meaning they were constructing. They resisted by critiquing the characters' actions, by rewriting themselves into the story, by predicting less negative outcomes for the characters, and by disengaging at times to create a safe space for themselves to rest from disturbing issues. The girls ultimately felt the need to create a safe space for the discussion in which they were willing to contribute. These struggling readers were able to use reading, writing, and discussion to construct meaning about the text and to develop an awareness of social justice issues related to historical racism.

In summary, these studies show mixed results in terms of the social and cultural impact of peer discussion. Whereas some students valued peer discussion and saw benefit in terms of assisting comprehension (Alvermann, Young, Weaver, Hinchman, Moore, Phelps, Thrash, & Zalewski, 1996), others felt gender and/or the presence of bossy or dominant group members influenced how they participated (Evans, 1996, 2002). Lewis (1997) found that talk in peer discussions became a way for students to exhibit and exert power. However, as Möller (2005) found, when teachers are able to create a classroom culture of respect, acceptance, and intolerance for taunting, even struggling students who are typically the victims of such taunting, can experience success.

IMPLICATIONS FOR PRACTICE

The studies reviewed here have several implications for practice. First, discussions that rely on a more student-centered, dialogic approach to discussion that moves beyond traditional, I-R-E participant formats lead to significant growth in comprehension. These findings are clear and consistent across all of the studies reviewed here and suggest that there is little value in traditional teacher-led discussions when compared with more student-centered dialogic discussions.

Findings also suggest that different types of teacher scaffolding foster distinct types of growth. Discussions featuring microgenetic scaffolding that uses open-ended teacher questions, queries, and probes foster general overall comprehension of the content of texts. Peer discussions featuring ontogenetic scaffolding over time tend to foster the development of comprehension and interpretive processes. This suggests that teachers should use both types of discussion; however, their use should be planful and deliberate. Teachers should not default to one particular type of discussion over the other. Instead, it would be helpful to assess the quality of student discussions and use such assessment to design a long-term developmentally appropriate plan for ontogenetically scaffolding students so they learn how to use interpretive and comprehension strategies to make sense of text and to learn how to interact with one another in a way that fosters respect, tolerance, and acceptance of others and of diverse perspectives. Along the way, other types of discussions should periodically have more teacher involvement by way of microgenetic scaffolding (e.g., using open-ended questions, queries, and probes and non-evaluative feedback) to teach students how to understand the content of particular texts. As Meyer (1993) reminded us, however, all scaffolding should be conducted as a joint, collaborative effort among teachers and students in which the teacher provides temporary support and then gradually releases responsibility for the task to students.

CURRENT AND FUTURE RESEARCH

While current research on discussion and its impact on comprehension is beginning to take on a more ecological approach in which social, cognitive, and affective constructs are examined across settings, we still know very little about the nature of instructional scaffolding, particularly ontogenetic scaffolding. Future research might begin to examine how teachers plan for and enact long-term scaffolding that leads to student learning. As well, research must take on the challenge of simultaneously studying teacher and student growth. Like complex ecological systems, classrooms are dynamic and in a constant state of flux. Researchers must begin to develop new designs that permit such study.

REFERENCES

Agar, M., & Hobbs, J. R. (1982). Interpreting discourse: Coherence and the analysis of ethnographic interviews. *Discourse Processes, 5*, 1–32.

Almasi, J. F. (1995). The nature of fourth graders' sociocognitive conflicts in peer-led and teacher-led discussions of literature. *Reading Research Quarterly, 30*(3), 314–351.

Almasi, J. F. (2002). Peer discussion. In B. Guzzetti (Ed.), *Literacy in America: An encyclopedia* (Vol. 2, pp. 420–424). New York: ABC.

Almasi, J. F. (2007). Using questioning strategies to promote students' active comprehension of content area material. In D. Lapp & J. Flood (Eds.), *Content area reading instruction* (5th ed. pp. 487–513). Mahwah, NJ: Erlbaum.

Almasi, J. F., Garas, K., Cho, H., Ma, W., Shanahan, L., & Augustino, A. (2004). The impact of peer discussion on social, cognitive, and affective growth in literacy. Paper presented at the 54th Annual Meeting of the National Reading Conference, San Antonio, TX.

Almasi, J. F., Garas, K., Cho, H., Ma, W., Shanahan, L., Augustino, A., & Palmer, B. M. (2005, November). A longitudinal study of development: Comprehension, interpretive strategy use, and language use among children in grades K–3. Paper presented at the 55th Annual Meeting of the National Reading Conference, Miami, FL.

Almasi, J. F., O'Flahavan, J. F., & Arya, P. (2001). A comparative analysis of student and teacher development in more proficient and less proficient peer discussions of literature. *Reading Research Quarterly, 36*(2), 96–120.

Almasi, J. F., Palmer, B. M., Garas, K., Cho, H., Ma, W., Shanahan, L., & Augustino, A. (2004). A longitudinal investigation of peer discussion of text on reading development in grades K–3. Final Report submitted to the Institute of Education Sciences.

Almasi, J. F., & Russell, W. (1998, December). Scaffold to nowhere? Appropriated voice, metatalk, and personal narrative in third graders' peer discussions of information text. Paper presented at the 48th Annual Meeting of the National Reading Conference, Austin, TX.

Almasi, J. F., & Russell, W. (1999, December). An ecology of communication: Peer discussions as semiotic systems. In L. Galda (Chair), Classroom talk about literature: The social dimensions of a solitary act. Symposium conducted at the 49th Annual Meeting of the National Reading Conference, Orlando, FL.

Alpert, B. R. (1987). Active, silent, and controlled discussions: Explaining variations in classroom conversation. *Teaching and Teacher Education, 3*(1), 29–40.

Alvermann, D. E., Young, J. P., Weaver, D., Hinchman, K. A., Moore, D. W., Phelps, S. F., Thrash, E. C., & Zalewski, P. (1996). Middle and high school students' perceptions of how they experience text-based discussions: A multicase study. *Reading Research Quarterly, 31*, 244–267.

Anderson, R. C., Nguyen-Jahiel, K., McNurlen, B., Archodidou, A., Kim, S., Reznitskaya, A., Tillmanns, M., & Gilbert, L. (2001). The snowball phenomenon: Spread of ways of talking and ways of thinking across groups of children. *Cognition and Instruction, 19*(1), 1–46.

Applebee, A. N., Langer, J. A., Nystrand, M., & Gamoran, A. (2003). Discussion-based approaches to developing understanding: Classroom instruction and student performance in middle and high school English. *American Educational Research Journal, 40*(3), 685–730.

Baker, L., & Brown, A. L. (1984). Metacognitive skills and reading. In P. D. Pearson, R. Barr, M. L. Kamil, & P. B. Mosenthal (Eds.), *Handbook of reading research* (Vol. 1, pp. 353–394). New York: Longman.

Barr, R., & Dreeben, R. (1991). Grouping students for reading instruction. In R. Barr, M. L. Kamil, P. B. Mosenthal, & P. D. Pearson (Eds.), *Handbook of reading research* (Vol. 2, pp. 885–910). New York: Longman.

Beck, I. L., McKeown, M. G., Sandora, C., Kucan, L., & Worthy, J. (1996). Questioning the author: A yearlong classroom implementation to engage students with text. *Elementary School Journal, 96*(4), 385–414.

Bond, T. F. (2001). Giving them free rein: Connections in student-led book groups. *Reading Teacher, 54*(6), 574–584.

Bridges, D. (1979). *Education, democracy, and discussion.* New York: University Press of America.

Brinton, B., & Fujiki, M. (1984). Development of topic manipulation skills in discourse. *Journal of Speech and Hearing Research, 27*, 350–358.

Cazden, C. B. (1986). Classroom discourse. In M. C. Wittrock (Ed.), *Handbook of research on teaching* (3rd ed., pp. 432–463). New York: Macmillan.

Chinn, C. A., & Anderson, R. C. (1998). The structure of discussions that promote reasoning. *Teachers College Record, 100*, 315–368.

Dillon, J. T. (1985). Using questions to foil discussion. *Teaching and Teacher Education, 1*, 109–121.

Dugan, J. (1997). Transactional literature discussions: Engaging students in the appreciation and understanding of literature. *Reading Teacher, 51*, 86–96.

Evans, K. S. (2002). Fifth-grade students' perceptions of how they experience literature discussion groups. *Reading Research Quarterly, 37*(1), 46–69.

Evans, K. S. (1996). Creating spaces for equity? The role of positioning in peer-led literature discussions. *Language Arts, 73*(3), 194–202.

Fall, R., Webb, N., & Chudowsky, N. (2000). Group discussion and large-scale language arts assessment: Effects on students' comprehension. *American Educational Research Journal, 37*(4), 911–941.

Fish, S. (1980). *Is there a text in this class? The authority of interpretive communities.* Cambridge: Cambridge University Press.

Garner, R. (1987). *Metacognition and reading comprehension.* Norwood, NJ: Ablex.

Goatley, V. J., Brock, C. H., & Raphael, T. E. (1995). Diverse learners participating in regular education "Book Clubs." *Reading Research Quarterly, 30*, 352–380.

Goldenberg, C. (1993). Instructional conversations: Promoting comprehension through discussion. *The Reading Teacher, 46*(4), 316–326.

Good, T. L., Slavings, R. L., Harel, K. H., & Emerson, H. (1987). Student passivity: A study of question asking in K–12 classrooms. *Sociology of Education, 60*, 181–199.

Guthrie, J. T., & McCann, A. D. (1996). Idea circles: Peer collaborations for conceptual learning. In L. B. Gambrell & J. F. Almasi (Eds.), *Lively discussions: Fostering engaged reading* (pp. 87–105). Newark, DE: International Reading Association.

Guthrie, J. T., Van Meter, P., McCann, A. D., Wigfield, A., Bennett, L., Poundstone, C. C., Rice, M. E., Faibisch, F. M., Hunt, B., & Mitchell, A. M. (1996). Growth of literacy engagement: Changes in motivations and strategies during concept-oriented reading instruction. *Reading Research Quarterly, 31*(3), 306–332.

Hobbs, J. R. (1990). Topic drift. In B. Dorval (Ed.), *Conversational organization and its development* (Vol. 38, pp. 3–22). Norwood, NJ: Ablex.

Hogan, K., Nastasi, B. K., & Pressley, M. (1999). Discourse patterns and collaborative scientific reasoning in peer and teacher-guided discussions. *Cognition and Instruction, 17*(4), 379–432.

Keefer, M. W., Zeitz, C. M., & Resnick, L. B. (2000). Judging the quality of peer-led student dialogues. *Cognition and Instruction, 18*(1), 53–81.

Langer, J. A. (1995). *Envisioning literature: Literary understanding and literature instruction.* New York: Teachers College Press and the International Reading Association.

Leal, D. J. (1993). The power of literacy peer-group discussions: How children collaboratively negotiate meaning. *Reading Teacher, 47*(2), 114–120.

Lewis, C. (1997). The social drama of literature discussions in a fifth/sixth grade classroom. *Research in the Teaching of English, 31*(2), 163–204.

Liang, L. A., & Dole, J. A. (2006). Help with teaching reading comprehension: Comprehension instructional frameworks. *Reading Teacher, 59*(8), 742–753.

Maloch, B. (2002). Scaffolding student talk: One teacher's role in literature discussion groups. *Reading Research Quarterly, 37*(1), 94–112.

Many, J. E. (2002). An exhibition and analysis of verbal tapestries: Understanding how scaffolding is woven into the fabric of instructional conversations. *Reading Research Quarterly, 37*(4), 376–407.

McIntyre, E., Kyle, D., & Moore, G. H. (2006). A primary-grade teacher's guidance toward small-group dialogue. *Reading Research Quarterly, 41*(1), 36–66.

McKeown, M. G., & Beck, I. L. (2004). Transforming knowledge into professional development resources: Six teachers implement a model of teaching for understanding text. *Elementary School Journal, 104*(5), 391–408.

McKeown, M. G., Beck, I. L., & Worthy, J. (1993). Grappling with text ideas: Questioning the author. *The Reading Teacher, 46*(7), 560–566.

McMahon, S. I., & Goatley, V. J. (1995). Fifth graders helping peers discuss texts in student-led groups. *Journal of Educational Research, 89*(1), 23–34.

Meece, J. L., Blumenfeld, P. C., & Hoyle, R. H. (1988). Student's goal orientations and cognitive engagement in classroom activities. *Journal of Educational Psychology, 80*, 514–523.

Mehan, H. (1979). *Learning lessons.* Cambridge, MA: Harvard University Press.

Meyer, D. K. (1993). What is scaffolded instruction? Definitions, distinguishing features, and misnomers. In D. J. Leu & C. K. Kinzer (Eds.), *Examining central issues in literacy research, theory, and practice: Forty-second yearbook of the National Reading Conference* (pp. 41–53). Chicago, IL: National Reading Conference.

Möller, K. J. (2005). Creating zones of possibility for struggling readers: A study of one fourth grader's shifting roles in literature. *Journal of Literacy Research, 36*(4), 419–460.

Möller, K. J., & Allen, J. (2000). Connecting, resisting, and searching for safer places: Students respond to Mildred Taylor's "The Friendship." *Journal of Literacy Research, 32*(2), 145–186.

Morocco, C. C., & Hindin, A. (2002). The role of conversation in a thematic understanding of literature. *Learning Disabilities: Research & Practice, 17*(3), 144–159.

Paris, S. G., Wasik, B. A., & Turner, J. C. (1991). The development of strategic readers. In R. Barr, M. L. Kamil, P. Mosenthal, & P. D. Pearson (Eds.), *Handbook of reading research* (Vol. II, pp. 609–640). New York: Longman.

Pearson, P. D., & Gallagher, M. C. (1983). The instruction of reading comprehension. *Contemporary Educational Psychology, 8*, 317–344.

Pressley, M. (2000). What should comprehension instruction be the instruction of? In M. L. Kamil, P. B. Mosenthal, P. D. Pearson, & R. Barr (Eds.), *Handbook of reading research* (Vol. 3, pp. 545–561). Mahwah, NJ: Erlbaum.

Pressley, M., Johnson, C. J., Symons, S., McGoldrick, J. A., & Kurita, J. A. (1989). Strategies that improve children's memory and comprehension of text. *Elementary School Journal, 90*(1), 3–32.

Raphael, T. E., & McMahon, S. I. (1994). Book club: An alternative framework for reading instruction. *Reading Teacher, 48,* 102–116.

Reichman, R. (1978). Conversational coherency. *Cognitive Science, 2,* 283–327.

Reznitskaya, A., Anderson, R. C., McNurlen, B., Nguyen-Jahiel, K., Archodidou, A., & Kim, S. (2001). Influence of oral discussion on written argument. *Discourse Processes, 32*(2& 3), 155–175.

Rice, P. S. (2005). It "ain't" always so: Sixth graders' interpretations of Hispanic-American stories with universal terms. *Children's Literature in Education, 36*(4), 343–362.

Roller, C., & Beed, P. (1994). Sometimes the conversations were grand and sometimes.... *Language Arts, 71,* 509–515.

Rogoff, B. (1990). *Apprenticeship in thinking: Cognitive development in social context.* New York: Oxford University Press.

Rosenblatt, L. M. (1938/1976). *Literature as exploration.* New York: Modern Language Association.

Rosenblatt, L. M. (1978). *The reader, the text, the poem: The transactional theory of the literary work.* Carbondale: Southern Illinois University Press.

Sandora, C., Beck, I., & McKeown, M. (1999). A comparison of two discussion strategies on students' comprehension and interpretation of complex literature. *Journal of Reading Psychology, 20,* 177–212.

Saunders, W. M., & Goldenberg, C. (1999). Effects of instructional conversations and literature logs on limited- and fluent-English-proficient students' story comprehension and thematic understanding. *Elementary School Journal, 99*(4), 277–301.

Scharer, P. L., & Peters, D. (1996). An exploration of literature discussions conducted by two teachers moving toward literature-based reading instruction. *Reading Research and Instruction, 36*(1), 33–50.

Schegloff, E. A. (1990). On the organization of sequences as a source of "coherence" in talk-in-action. In B. Dorval (Ed.), *Conversational organization and its development* (Vol. 38, pp. 51–77). Norwood, NJ: Ablex.

Skidmore, D., Perez-Parent, M., & Arnfield, S. (2003). Teacher-pupil dialogue in the guided reading session. *Reading: Literacy and Language, 37*(2), 47–53.

Van den Branden, K. (2000). Does negotiation of meaning promote reading comprehension? A study of multilingual primary school classes. *Reading Research Quarterly, 35*(3), 426–443.

Vygotsky, L. S. (1978). *Mind in society: The development of higher psychological processes.* Cambridge, MA: Harvard University Press.

Waggoner, M., Chinn, C., Yi, H., & Anderson, R. C. (1995). Collaborative reasoning about stories. *Language Arts, 72,* 582–589.

Wells, G. (1986). *The meaning makers: Children learning language and using language to learn.* Portsmouth, NH: Heinemann.

Wertsch, J. V. (1985). *Vygotsky and the social formation of mind.* Cambridge, MA: Harvard University Press.

Wertsch, J. V. (1991). *Voices of the mind: A sociocultural approach to mediated action.* Cambridge, MA: Harvard University Press.

Wolf, M. K., Crosson, A. C., & Resnick, L. B. (2005). Classroom talk for rigorous reading comprehension instruction. *Reading Psychology, 26,* 27–53.

Wood, D., Bruner, J. S., & Ross, G. (1976). The role of tutoring in problem solving. *Journal of Child Psychology and Psychiatry, 17*(2), 89–100.

Wortham, S. (2006). *Learning identity: The joint emergence of social identification and academic learning.* New York: Cambridge University Press.

23 Comprehension Instruction in Kindergarten through Grade Three

Cathy Collins Block and Jan Lacina

Texas Christian University

The purpose of this chapter is to report the diverse nature of research that supports comprehension instruction at the K–3 school level as well as the conceptual and theoretical roots from which this instruction arose. This chapter describes one of the most rapidly expanding bodies of knowledge in the field of reading education, and its long historical foundation. The largest portion of the discussion will focus on landmark studies that have changed and broadened the conceptualization of comprehension instruction at the primary grades. Before we describe the influence of these studies on today's instruction, we will review the theoretical tenets and evolving definition of comprehension instruction. We will closely describe comprehension instruction occurring in our schools today and promising directions for future research and practice.

HISTORICAL PERSPECTIVES CONCERNING COMPREHENSION INSTRUCTION IN K–3 SCHOOLS

As Pearl Buck said, "If you want to understand today, you have to search yesterday" (http://www.quotationsbook.com/quotes/40157/view). To understand comprehension practices in today's K–3 schools, it is important to review the long history of comprehension instruction in America's K–3 schools. Essentially, for the first 210 years (from 1678 to 1888), comprehension instruction did not exist. Our review of the literature found that students received direct instruction in alphabetic principles, phonological awareness, word analysis, vocabulary, fluency, dictation, articulation, and phrasing for 200 years before the very first lesson on comprehension instruction occurred. It was not until 1807 that a movement began to increase educators' awareness of the need for comprehension instruction. At that time, Webster published *The American Spelling Book* (1807–1827). *The American Spelling Book* (1829–1833) and Worchester's *Primer of the English Language* (1828–1841) followed. These books described how to teach syllabication and comprehension of simple, compound and complex sentences. Through this instruction from 1807 to 1898, educators became aware of the need to assess if students truly comprehended messages conveyed in sentences and paragraphs. From 1898 to 1920, new methods of comprehension instruction were created.

As city populations grew, people needed to communicate a wider variety of messages and ideas. Parents and community leaders demanded that students learn to read larger volumes of material in order to cultivate "the practice of reading to oneself without saying the words aloud" (Clews, 1899, p. 19). This new teaching method, silent reading, was far more than noiseless reading. It involved the complex process of getting thought from the printed page, and entirely new pedagogy. As practitioners of the time stated: "Silent reading objectives will never be obtained by oral reading methods" (Buswell &

Wheeler, 1923, p. 21). Thus, with this shift from oral to silent reading lessons, the first formal comprehension lessons to understand more than one sentence began. These lessons followed a similar pattern. For example, in one set of curricular materials teachers were asked to complete the following steps:

> The children are in their usual seats. Print on the blackboard. COME TO CLASS. Pointing to the words talking firmly to the pupils, Waste no words, say something like this. "What I have printed here means that all of you are to rise whenever you see this and come to this place where the little chairs are. I call this place the class." Before the children can comply with the request and COME TO CLASS, the teacher erases the request, says nothing, prints the words again, says nothing, looks at the class, asks the pupils to read the words, and then asks the pupils to do what the words say. (Watkins, 1922, p. 11)

With the advent of formal comprehension instruction, advancement in comprehension research occurred. One of the first findings was that context clues should be used as an instructional approach because they increased students' abilities to comprehend the books they read (Smith, 1940). As a result, K–3 school teachers' manuals from 1940 until the present include lessons designed to increase students' use of context clues. At the same time, comprehension lessons began to focus on meeting individual students' reading needs (McKee et al., 1950). As more and more teachers struggled to meet those needs, they found it practical to divide the class into smaller groups. By 1960 most comprehension materials provided lessons that could be used in small groups. At this time, however, regardless of the ability group level, teachers usually only asked questions to find out how much information students could remember from what they read. The Directed Reading Approach (DRA; Betts, 1946) was created to expand pedagogy and was used in more than 90% of the classrooms in North America (Smith, 1978; Stahl, 1999). By the mid-1950s, children read a text orally, discussed what they had read with their teacher, then read a portion of the text silently and answered questions over what they had read. In DRA lessons, teachers introduced new vocabulary terms, set the stage for reading, initiated external motivational techniques to build students' backgrounds and interest in a topic, supervised students' silent reading, and asked literal (and, more recently, interpretative and applied) questions about the information that students read. Still, DRA did not actually teach students how to comprehend when they were unable to do so.

Prior to 1970, in addition to the DRA approach, many teachers taught comprehension through giving directions to "read carefully," assigning workbook skill pages that covered a single comprehension skill, or orally asking questions after a text was read (Block & Israel, 2005a). From 1970 to the present, reading researchers have discovered a vivid array of metacognitive, multicultural, social linguistic, and constructivist principles that impact the way that we teach comprehension today. This body of research led us to discover that effective K–3 school lessons must (a) meet multiple students' pre-instructional levels of comprehension competence at the student's zone of proximal development; (b) include ample silent (but teacher monitored and assisted) reading practice in material that is of deep interest and challenge to students, and; (c) stimulate rich student generated questioning, high levels of thinking, much discussion of contrasting viewpoints, and students' application of the material read to real life situations. Regardless of the grade level at which K–3 reading comprehension instruction occurs today, the best lessons (according to the research we will report next), also provide teacher modeling and think-alouds, scaffolding, guided practice, direct instruction, and independent silent reading opportunities to use many comprehension skills, strategies, processes, and metacognitions independently (see Block & Pressley, 2002, for an extended review for the research in each of these fields).

As we reviewed this body of research and the numerous national studies calling for an increase in the amount of direct comprehension instruction occurring in schools today (National Reading Panel, 2000; RAND Reading Study Group, 2001; Sweet & Snow, 2003), we found consensus that the goal of comprehension instruction at the K–3 level is to produce students who not only:

> understand what they read but also know when they are not understanding what they read—that is, they monitor their comprehension. Comprehension monitoring is critical, for awareness of a failure to understand prompts the good reader to reread the text and try to make sense out of it. (Pressley, 2006, p. 322)

DEFINITIONAL ISSUES: THE EVOLUTION OF WHAT COMPREHENSION INSTRUCTION IS

The first definition of K–3 comprehension instruction occurred in the 1960s. Prior to that time, educators believed that comprehension was tied to intelligence and the ability to decode words. The ability to comprehend was viewed as merely a natural desirable outcome. As Duffy (2002) reported:

> In the early 1900s through 1960, comprehension was a desirable outcome, but we had no real understanding of how comprehension worked or how you taught it. We assumed comprehension was primarily a matter of intelligence: if your students were smart and could decode, they would comprehend. But you didn't teach it. (p. xiii)

Also, prior to 1960 it was a widespread belief that:

> it is not possible, or at least not wise to teach comprehension to young children who are still learning to decode text. This belief was to have stemmed from the assumption, so prevalent in many primary grade programs of the time, that phonics and word identification should be the sole priority in the primary grades. (Pearson & Duke, 2002, p. 247)

In 1978 Durkin changed this viewpoint. She defined comprehension as "the essence of reading" and as:

> the process in which [even young] readers construct meaning in interacting with text through a combination of prior knowledge and previous experience; information available in the text; the stance taken in relationship to the text; and an immediate, remembered or anticipated social interaction and communication. The meanings of words cannot be added up to give the meaning of the whole. The click of comprehension occurs when the reader evolves a schema that explains the whole message. (p. 482)

Today, the U. S. Department of Education defines K–3 comprehension instruction as "developing students' ability to (a) comprehend the literal meaning printed on a page; (b) interpret authors' intentions to report knowledge, show possession, implied meaning; and (c) evaluate and apply ideas in printed materials to their lives" (NRP, 2000, p. 76). This definition resulted from a critical review of comprehension research and analyzed

38 high quality studies that significantly increased young children's comprehension. Today, through the landmark studies we will cite, we know that teaching comprehension strategies early in children's lives can advance not only their ability to understand text but also their decoding and reading fluency skills (Block, 2006).

Recent research also finds that the ability to understand text is a complex process that develops over time (Block, 1999; Collins, 1991; Pearson & Fielding, 1991). Comprehension abilities differ from other major reading competencies such as phonemic awareness and phonics. Decoding skills can be mastered through highly effective teachers' instruction, and once their basic learning principles are known, most students can automatically use their basic skills to decode novel words. However, the ability to comprehend increasingly complex text can never occur by merely mastering a basic set of skills. Because every sentence is a uniquely new creation, comprehension requires that students continuously develop more and more advanced comprehension competencies and that students continuously apply their focused attention and self-guided thinking throughout every reading experience.

To develop these abilities, students must have instruction in (a) comprehension strategies and processes as well as how to independently select the ones that they will need to understand increasingly complex texts; (b) how to use textual features (e.g., subheadings, textbook organizational features, indexes, table of contents, and so forth) to follow an author's train of thought; and (c) how to think about their own thinking while they read. Thus, K–3 comprehension instruction today must help students learn how to *want* to correct confusions, tie new information to prior knowledge, and apply relevant information to their lives. Because of these complexities, it has been determined that primary educators should continuously and systematically add depth and breadth to the number of comprehension processes students learn. For example, a lesson that teaches students to use authorial clues to draw conclusions while they read should not look the same in first and third grades. As texts become more complex, teachers' modeling, direct instruction, and the number of processes that teachers ask students to independently apply in their reading should increase substantially.

Within the last few decades, researchers defined comprehension categories as: literal, inferential, and metacognitive comprehension (Block & Pressley, 2002). Research firmly established that many students cannot develop these three types of comprehension processes unaided (Block, Gambrell, & Pressley, 2004; Block, Rodgers, & Johnson, 2004; Durkin, 1978–1979). The NRP also found that to be most effective, comprehension instruction must contain (a) direct instruction, (b) expanded teacher explanations, and (c) transactional strategy instruction; that is, teachers' explanations of comprehension processes, with graphics to depict them, and highly effective monitoring of an individual student's applications of comprehension processes to text (NRP, 2000).

Moreover, to ensure that all primary-grade students receive the best comprehension instruction, students should experience three different types of comprehension lessons each year. When they do, their performances on measures of literal, inferential, and metacognitive comprehension increase as each type or strand of lesson systematically increases the number, depth, and breadth of comprehension processes students can independently apply while they read. These three types of comprehension lessons have also proven to increase students' vocabulary, decoding, problem solving, cooperative group skills, and self-esteem as determined by the Iowa Test of Basic Skills, the Harter Test of Self Concept, informal reading inventories, and standardized reasoning tests (Block, 1999; Block, Parris, & Whiteley, 2008; Collins, 1991). When three distinct types of comprehension lessons are included in K–3 school literacy programs, the instruction is referred to as Comprehension Process Instruction (CPI). CPI lessons combine direct, expanded teacher directions with transactional strategy instruction through the use of print-rich, developmentally appropriate textual experiences that actively engage students' independent thinking. In so doing, even the youngest readers can learn how to untangle confusions and overcome the complexities in print and technology that could have blocked their understanding.

In 2007, many researchers agreed that a highly effective comprehension instruction can be defined as including all of the above learning activities so students "can leave a reading experience with fresh perspectives, vital information, and new ideas. Through it, readers can also learn to use other important reading skills such as vocabulary, word analysis, phonetics, fluency, and oral language as they execute the complex comprehension processes needed to create meaning" (Block & Pressley, 2007, p. 220).

EMERGENT LITERACY AND PRIMARY GRADE COMPREHENSION

Our understanding of K–3 comprehension instruction is rooted in emergent literacy theory. Emergent literacy theory is based on the premise that listening, speaking, reading, and writing are interrelated domains of ability in a child's development (Morrow, 2005). Thus, young children who become proficient with listening comprehension and possess advanced speaking vocabularies will have a greater likelihood of success when developing their reading comprehension and writing skills (Snow, 1991).

Additionally, data shows that reading proficiency greatly improves if emergent readers have heard or read the text often and at early ages (Elster, 1994; Snow, 1991; Sulzby, 1985). There is ample evidence of the benefits of early exposure to book sharing, text being read aloud, and discussing texts with preschool teachers, peers and other adults, including an expanded vocabulary (Beck, McKeown, & Kucan, 2002; DeTemple & Snow, 2003; Brabham & Lynch-Brown, 2002); promotion of syntactic development (Chomsky, 1972); and, increased listening comprehension (Morrow & Gambrell, 2002). Evidence also exists that early exposure to oral reading of continuous text enables students to more effectively draw upon their prior memories of either hearing or seeing the text as young children for assistance in comprehending the first text that they read alone (Sulzby, 1985).

Unfortunately, significant data also exist relative to the negative effects of not having a strong emergent literacy background. We now know that those who do not develop good language skills before entering kindergarten (e.g., listening and speaking) have more difficulty acquiring literacy skills. For instance, Kaderavek and Sulzby (2002) found that preschool children with oral language impairment were less able than their normally developing peers to provide oral narratives or retell stories using discourse normally associated with written language. Those with less well-developed emergent literacy abilities and infrequent preschool literacy exposures had oral story retelling that contained significantly fewer past-tense verbs and refrained significantly less often to use personal pronouns. These infrequent uses limited these students' abilities to recognize referents and links to inferential comprehension that appear so often in text. Kaderavek & Sulzby (2002) concluded that emergent storybook reading can be a useful addition to oral language assessment because such experiences transfer to text comprehension and other types of higher-level language skills.

Additionally, Emergent Literacy Theory acknowledges that literacy development starts at birth and follows along a continuum, as opposed to "reading readiness" which presumes children are not ready to read until some predetermined point in time. As Teale and Sulzby (1986) aptly observed: "These behaviors and knowledge are not pre-anything. It is not reasonable to point to a time in a child's life when literacy begins. Rather ... we see children in the process of becoming literate, as the term emergent indicates" (p. xix).

Thus, from these ground-breaking studies, we have substantial evidence that comprehension abilities can develop from shortly after birth. At an early age (and throughout a person's life) exposure to rich language experiences in the home and other environments serve an important function in that person's ability to comprehend text (Morrow, 2005). During this period of emergent literacy, all children gain an increasing awareness of the relationship between spoken and written language (Teale & Sulzby, 1986). When literacy-rich home environments are present, other comprehension advantages emerge, including: (a) a large number of books being available for both children's and adult's reading; (b) parents that frequently read to children and frequently read themselves; (c) parents that read a wide variety of materials; (d) reading being associated by the child with pleasure; (e) parents that frequently take children to the library and to bookstores; (f) access to writing materials; and, (g) a social, emotional, and intellectual climate in the homes that is conducive to literacy growth (Morrow, 2005).

Such language-oriented environments have also shown to promote greater linguistic and cognitive development (Hart & Risely, 1995). They play a vital role in helping children develop concepts about print (e.g., words are made up of letters, sentences are made up of words, reading goes from left to right and top to bottom, sentences begin with capital letters, books have titles and authors, etc. [e.g., Gunning, 1996]).

In sum, emergent literacy experiences (from birth throughout the primary grades) enable rich, multi-modal language, comprehension, and literacy developments in the early years of a child's life. They also lay the foundation for these same students to progress fluidly from the beginning stages of phonemic awareness and decoding to proficiency with reading comprehension and composition throughout their school years.

LANDMARK STUDIES

In this section we will highlight several bodies of knowledge that expand not only our understanding of how children comprehend, but inform the methods we use in K–3 schools today to increase all aspects of students' comprehension. Among these was the first major critical review of research in reading comprehension (Scott, 1954). In this review of K–3 comprehension instruction prior to 1954, Scott characterized research as "fragmentary and unrelated, varied as to its underlining concepts, practical rather than theoretical, varied in quality and in importance, and inconclusive and limited" (1954, p. 19).

Researchers tried to overcome these limitations. Holmes and Singer's landmark work (1964) studied the effects of various programs on first grade reading and found:

> during the past 3 years, a review of research makes it clear that the profession is searching not only for ways for ordering the meanings behind objective data collection and relationships calculated in the past, but also for more fundamental data that searches for underlying meanings that aim to explain reading phenomena in smaller and smaller units. (p. 127)

At the same time, an additional landmark study of K–3 comprehension instruction was published by Barton and Wilder (1962). This study, entitled Columbia-Carnegie Study of Reading Research and its Communications, revealed that 90% of all schools provided basal instruction to all readers and that phonics and high interest reading material for less able readers were the two greatest needs in the classroom. No specific comprehension instructional methods were highlighted as being effective at that time.

In the next year, a "state of the union" of K–3 comprehension reading instruction was conducted by Austin and Morrison and published in the book entitled, *The First R* (Austin & Morrison, 1963). They found that in the 1960s various methods of teaching comprehension were being developed to respond to different socioeconomic backgrounds and ability levels of individual students:

> the teaching of comprehension skills is one of the most persistent [unaddressed] problems in K–3 schools today. Teachers and administrators alike indicate that more emphasis should be given to the development of comprehension and critical thinking in both the primary and intermediate grades. (p. 221)

While this review was followed by a 15-year gap in landmark studies, three major publications between 1978 and 1981 thrust K–3 comprehension instruction to the forefront of educators' minds once again. Teachers and researchers were riveted by Durkin's (1978–1979) findings that limited instructional time was devoted to improving any aspect of students' reading comprehension. In the same year, Pearson and Johnson (1978) wrote a "state of the union" on K–3 classroom methods. Their comprehensive review, a text that was less than 250 pages long, reported all research-based practices that were known at the time. Three years later the International Reading Association published the first book dedicated solely to research concerning comprehension instruction: *Comprehension and Teaching: Research Reviews* (Guthrie, 1981). This volume divided K–3 comprehension instruction into 12 components and contained chapters written by researchers who were conducting investigations in these 12 fields.

Three years later a major breakthrough occurred in the development of teaching comprehension strategies. Comprehension lessons evolved from teaching comprehension as single skills to learning skills in combination as strategies. Strategy instruction was defined as the use of more than one distinct skill as a means of unlocking meaning. Among the first researchers to teach a set of comprehension strategies in a single lesson were Palincsar and Brown (1984). Their work on reciprocal teaching instructed K–3 students on how to predict, question, clarify, and summarize in a single lesson. This instruction included teacher modeling and explanation with scaffolded transfer so that students led a reading group and used strategies without teacher prompting.

Building on this work, Duffy and his associates (Duffy et al., 1987) proposed that such instruction should be preceded with direct explanation and the explicit modeling of each strategy for students. This landmark work led to an important model of teaching that continues today. At the heart of its process, referred to as mental modeling or expanded explanations, teachers use think-alouds to describe what, how and when to apply strategies (Duffy, Roehler, & Herrmann, 1988). Their 1987 study of the effects of direct explanation strategy instruction on third-grade reading (with 10 groups of weak readers assigned randomly to the direct explanation treatment and 10 control groups receiving their usual instruction) was the first to prove that instruction should provide students with explanations and additional scaffolds whenever they needed assistance to become more proficient readers.

Meanwhile, Palincsar and Brown (1984) continued their research on the reciprocal teaching model. Their studies resulted in positive effects on students' reading achievement at the K–3 school level and demonstrated that students as young as 5 years old could learn to independently apply the four strategies that they were taught.

The next set of landmark studies were conducted by Pressley and others (see Pressley, 2006). These researchers took the work of direct instruction and reciprocal teaching and developed a series of K–3 school comprehension lessons that illuminated the transaction that occurs between teachers and students whenever they engage in comprehension instruction. These studies demonstrated in a classroom setting that students who are taught a small repertoire of comprehension strategies and how to use them can expand their own understanding. This research, transactional strategy instruction, taught K–3 students how to practice comprehension strategies without teachers' assistance and for the first time teachers modeled when and where to use strategies to correct information that was confusing to them. These findings as well as data from other researchers at this time sent the clear message that students' thinking about what they read truly mattered during an instructional lesson. Other researchers continued to document the significant qualitative and quantitative positive effects that teaching students more than one strategy in a single lesson had upon K–3 school achievement (Anderson, 1992; Anderson & Roit, 1993; Collins, 1991).

During this same period, Block (1993) and Collins (1991) conducted studies with K–3-aged children designed to increase students' thinking abilities and comprehension strategy use. Comprehension strategies that students learned included clarifying ideas, summarizing, making inferences, interpreting, evaluation, solving problems, and thinking creatively. In the comprehension-strategy instruction group, students participated in lessons twice weekly for 32 weeks in which: (1) the teacher explained and modeled a thinking and reading comprehension strategy (e.g., predicting, summarizing), and (2) the students selected literature and applied the strategy to it. In the control group, students received traditional instruction that did not emphasize these comprehension strategies. The experimental outperformed the control group on reading comprehension, vocabulary, and total battery sections of the Iowa Test of Basic Skills, in the ability to transfer cognitive strategies to applications outside school, measures of self-esteem, as well as critical and creative thinking. Dole, Brown, and Trathen (1996) investigated the effects of strategy instruction on the comprehension performance of at-risk fifth and sixth-graders. Similar significant positive effects were found.

Bauman and Bergeron (1993) posed a more specific study of the effects of very young children being taught to use story structure to enhance their ability to identify and recall central story elements. They compared four classes of Grade 1 students. Two classes were provided with explicit instruction in identifying key elements of stories: characters, setting (places and times), problem, events, and solutions. The other two classes listened to and read the same stories but were not taught specific comprehension strategies. Experimental students outperformed control students on all measures employed, including identifying the most important parts of a story and selecting a good summary of a story. A delayed assessment (2.5 weeks later) revealed a continuing effect for the story-structure instruction.

Three years later, Brown, Pressley, Van Meter, and Schuder (1996) examined the effectiveness of graphic organizers and visual symbols as aids to K–3 comprehension instruction. Known by the acronym SAIL (Students Achieving Independent Learning), experimental subjects significantly outperformed control subjects who did not receive explicit instruction, modeling, and dual-coded icons to teach comprehension strategies, particularly predicting, visualizing, questioning, clarifying, making associations (e.g., between the test and the students' experiences, between one test and another), and summarizing. Teachers modeled the use of these strategies by "thinking aloud" about their own use of comprehension strategies in the presence of students. Brown et al. (1996) studied the effectiveness of SAIL with low-achieving students and found that experimental subjects performed considerably better on standardized tests of reading comprehension and decoding. Today, SAIL is only one member of a larger family of approaches to K–3 comprehension instruction. These and other studies document that explicit comprehension instruction with dual-coded visual aids significantly improves children's decoding, fluency, comprehension and affective responses to literacy. Such methods do not detract from children's decoding development but rather demonstrate that comprehension and decoding appear to have a reciprocal, synergistic relationship (Block & Pressley, 2007).

During this same period, another group of scholars explored the effects of discussion and sociocultural theories in K–3 comprehension instruction. Using new types of discussion questions, prediction activities and how texts are read, a major step forward in comprehension instruction occurred. One such study is a classic. It is an evaluation of the KEEP (Kamehameha Early Education Program) program conducted by Tharp (1982). The KEEP curriculum, still in use in many Hawaiian schools, honored what students said about texts.

In 1998, a significant report was issued entitled *Preventing Reading Difficulties in Young Children* (Snow, Burns, & Griffin, 1998). It was followed by the National Reading Panel Report (NRP, 2000). These two landmark initiatives formed the foundation of The No Child Left Behind Act, federal legislation that required comprehension instruction to be one of five major components taught in all K–3 schools in the United States. The intensity of this focus is such that all students, regardless of their initial comprehension ability, are required to read on grade level by 2014. This is the climate in which comprehension instruction exists today. From 1678 to 2007, K–3 comprehension instruction evolved from not being taught at all in any K–3 school to being required by federal law to be taught in every U.S. public school.

By 2000, recommendations were made that K–3 school comprehension programs should include direct instruction (Duffy & Roehler, 1989) and be delivered through transactional strategy lessons, a method of teaching in which multiple comprehension abilities are learned, and applied to one's own cultural and experiential base (Pressley, Gaskins, Wile, Cunicelli, & Sheridan, 1991). Transactional strategies instruction is the teaching of self-regulated comprehension processes, "developing students who, on their own, use the comprehension strategies that excellent readers use [as identified by Pressly & Afflerbach, 1995]" (Pressley, 2006, p. 319).

Duke (2000) examined the types of materials that were used during instruction at the K–3 level and found that the instruction on how to read nonfictional texts was almost nonexistent. That study sparked a refocusing on new comprehension strategies that we should use to expand K–3 students' ability to comprehend nonfictional texts.

In recent years, contemporary researchers have engaged in numerous multiyear projects designed to (1) establish a clear and positive association between the need to advance a readers' vocabulary and his comprehension skills (Anderson & Freebody, 1981; Becker, 1977; Blachowicz & Fisher, 2000; Nagy, Anderson & Herman, 1987); (2) increase students' comprehension of nonfiction (Hiebert, Pearson, & Ayra, 2005; Pearson, 2005; Purcell & Duke, 2005); (3) build the metacognitive abilities of less able, young and adolescent readers (Afflerbach & Meuwissen, 2005; Baker, 2005; Schmitt, 2005); (4) assess more complex comprehension and metacomprehension processes (Block, 2005; Paris & Flukes, 2005); (5) enhance the effectiveness of teacher- and student-generated think-alouds (Block & Israel, 2005b; Duffy, 2005; Israel & Massey, 2005); (6) strengthen in-service and preservice teachers', literacy coaches' and reading specialists' abilities to advance students' comprehension of text and technology (Bean, 2004; Leu, 2005; Risko, Roskos, & Vukelich, 2005); and (7) identify developmental factors that effect students' abilities to internalize, automatize (LaBerge & Samuels, 1974), and transfer comprehension processes to new contexts without teacher prompting (Cummins, Stewart, & Block, 2005; Paris & Flukes, 2005). A synthesis of their findings appears in the next section of this chapter.

ONGOING RESEARCH THAT WILL IMPACT COMPREHENSION INSTRUCTION IN THE FUTURE

Research published from 2000–2008 is providing more specific answers into how comprehension instruction should be delivered in future K–3 school classrooms. For instance, a group of researchers found that certain comprehension strategies are easier to learn than others. This research is leading scholars to suspect that some modern scope and sequence practices can be altered to greatly advance less able readers' comprehension abilities (Block, Cummins, & Stewart, in press; Block, Paris, & Whiteley, 2008; Block & Reed, 2006). Other researchers have found that inferencing is a more difficult skill than imagery and predicting, (Kintsch, 2003; Yuill & Oakhill, 1991). These studies suggest that some comprehension abilities can be developed in as few as five lessons when they are taught at the most developmentally appropriate age level of K–3 student learners in the primary grades.

A second body of recent studies has made initial attempts to increase students' metacognitive strategic independent reading by teaching multiple strategies in single lessons. These methods help students learn comprehension processes that can work together to bring about meaning. For 25 years, K–3-aged students have been taught to find main ideas, predict based on pictures, and think about authorial writing patterns. Unfortunately, students were taught these comprehension processes as stand-alone procedures, making it difficult for them to understand when, where, and how to initiate these processes in conjunction with others while they read. By teaching them how to use more than one comprehension process in a single lesson, K–3 students may be shown how to view their comprehension and metacomprehension as a unified, self-controlled ability, and as a result comprehension increases significantly (Block, 2004). The research program that supports these lessons has found that even kindergarten students can use multiple strategies after 1 week of direct instruction and the results are significantly higher achievement than reported for treated control groups (Block, 2005; Block, Rodgers & Johnson, 2004; Cummins, Stewart, & Block, 2005; Stewart, 2004).

For years, researchers have also known that it usually takes longer to develop automaticity (Samuels, LaBerge, & Bremer, 1978; Samuels, 2002; Samuels, 2006) in comprehension than in decoding (e.g., Fielding & Pearson, 1994; National Reading Panel, 2000; Samuels, 2002; Stewart, 2004); however, we have not known exactly how long it takes to develop automaticity in specific comprehension processes in the K–3 grades. Prior to 2000, research suggested that students could transfer comprehension processes to standardized tests if they had direct instruction for eight months (Anderson & Pearson, 1984; Block, 1993; Collins, 1991). These studies found that various factors could prolong the time required for automaticity to develop. The most common reason was that students did not have a mechanism (such as a visual aid) to help them learn how to elicit more than one comprehension process during a single reading experience.

We now know that the internalization of comprehension process can take less time than previously believed when such aids are available. Studies demonstrate the value of delivering comprehension instruction in small groups when teachers and students describe how they comprehend (e.g., Block, Parris, & Whiteley, 2008). We also know that automaticity is developmentally sensitive. By first and second grade, for instance, students taught to use more than one comprehension process in a single lesson scored significantly higher on the Stanford 9 Vocabulary and Comprehension Subtests, enjoyed what they read more, compared what they read to other text more, and drew more conclusions as they read nonfiction than treated control groups (Block, Cummins, & Stewart, in press). Third graders also became significantly better at using nonfictional textual clues than control subjects. By fifth grade, experimental subjects were better able to predict from what they read in nonfictional texts (Block, 2005; Stewart, 2004). Teachers in each of these grades reported that teaching higher-level comprehension skills and more than one comprehension process in a single lesson was difficult to learn how to do (Cummins et al., 2005; Stewart, 2004).

Lastly, multiyear studies are demonstrating that by the end of 8 weeks experimental subjects can use more strategies continually, and apply 4.5 comprehension processes without teacher prompting as they read. In contrast, control subjects by week 8 were no higher in their abilities to independently apply comprehension processes than they had been in week 1, averaging only 2.5 strategies per book. These data have implications as to how many strategies we should teach per grade level, whether the comprehension strategies being taught should vary by grade level, and how long (on average) it takes for less able readers to master more than three of the comprehension processes employed by good readers (Cummins, Stewart, & Block, 2005).

SYNTHESIS: WHERE WE ARE NOW IN K–3 COMPREHENSION INSTRUCTION

Since 1990, we have learned more about the teaching of comprehension than at any point in history. Numerous research investigations reported herein have engaged diverse populations in innovative methods that build highly advanced levels of independent reading. They have yielded positive and consistent results relative to the efficacy of teaching comprehension processes at the K–3 school level. Thirty-six years of research, from 1970 to 2006, have created an exceptionally strong theoretical foundation upon which today's best practices rely. During the 1970s and 1980s many scientists determined that successful comprehension involved several cognitive and metacognitive abilities that enabled readers to interrelate numerous mental representations of meaning (Doctorow, Wittrock, & Marks, 1978; Taylor, 1982; van Dijk & Kintsch, 1983). These and other major advancements in our knowledge led to the important instructional advancements summarized below:

- Highly effective K–3 comprehension instruction must include highly effective instruction; teach think-alouds; modeling; scaffolding; guided practice; independent use of processes so that students develop an internalized self-regulation of comprehension processes; a time for students to tell teachers what they need and want to learn to comprehend better; ample reading, vocabulary and decoding development; and, rich shared experiences with fiction, nonfiction, and technologically based texts.
- Comprehension involves more than 30 cognitive and metacognitive processes, including making connections to background knowledge, interpreting text structures, questioning, clarifying meaning, comparing, contrasting, summarizing, imaging, setting purposes, using fix-up strategies, monitoring, cognizing, interpreting authors' intentions, pausing to reflect, paraphrasing, analyzing, recognizing personal perspectives, identifying gists, changing hypotheses, adding hypotheses, searching for meaning, being alert to main ideas, creating themes, determining importance, drawing inferences, corroborating congenial and non-congenial data, contextualizing, engaging in retrospection, generating, using mnemonic devices, predicting, organizing, and reorganizing text.
- At least 14 stand-alone K–3 curriculum programs were published to teach comprehension, including transactional strategies instruction; Comprehension Process Approach (CPA); reciprocal teaching; CORI; CSR; SAIL; QAR; K-W-L; explicit, elaborated instruction; informed strategies training; cognitive apprenticeships; imagery training; *Reason to Read*; and WebQuests.
- Helping students become self-regulated comprehenders is hard work. The quality of teacher-student interactions and collaborative talk can hasten students' development.
- Students can more quickly apply what they understand when teacher-student interactions include direct instruction, collaborative talk, teacher-reader groups (in which students teach comprehension processes) and student-led "think-alouds."

IMPLICATIONS FOR FUTURE RESEARCH AND PRACTICE

Contemporary researchers are benefiting from all of the landmark studies that occurred in our searches of "yesterday." They are seeking answers to more specific questions to help us "understand today" and lead us into a brighter tomorrow. We are confident that their work will have significant implications for the design of even more targeted and focused future K–3 comprehension practices. In the space available, we want to conclude the chapter by providing a glimpse into some of the issues that contemporary researchers are exploring.

As described in the next sentences, approximately half of the ongoing K–3 comprehension research studies in the United States are focused on new methods of improving classroom instruction. Specific questions being investigated by present research teams relate to these topics: (a) Why is rich research-based K–3 comprehension instruction not more common? (Graduate students of Michael Pressley); (b) How can we better teach metacognition? (Linda Baker); (c) How does children's comprehension change based on the demands of specific books? (Barbara Moss); (d) Is there a preferred order for introducing comprehension processes? (Cathy Block & Scott Paris); (e) How can we blend explicit, explanatory information smoothly and unobtrusively into an ongoing dialogue that continuously engages students with a text's content? (Janice Almasi); (e) How can we nudge students to synthesize knowledge from two sources of information as they create their own interpretation (James Flood, Diane Lapp, & Joanna P. Williams); (f) How can we better develop the comprehension abilities of young learners? (Gay Ivey, Lesley Mandel Morrow, Catherine Snow, & Katherine A. Dougherty Stahl); and (g) What instructional supports can we create so students of all levels of ability comprehend deeply and broadly? (Joanna P. Williams, John Guthrie, & D. Ray Reutzel).

Two other areas of research are receiving attention from several research teams. The first concerns how we can better assist K–3 grade students to transfer their reading comprehension abilities to listening comprehension and other content area texts (David Pearson & Nell Duke; Rachel Brown, Laura B. Smolkin, & Carol A Donovan). The second field of study is exploring how we can improve the professional development of teachers. The specific questions posed are: How can we teach teachers to explain well? How much support do teachers need to continue to teach comprehension effectively after their initial training has ended? (Peter Afflerbach, Gerald G. Duffy, Susan Israel, & Gail Sinatra), and how can we teach educators to teach comprehension as a series of unfolding, ebb-and-flow processes that enact interactive, strategic thinking, and not as a collection of strategies? (Irene Gaskins & Ann Marie Palincsar).

As a result of changing demographics within our nation's K–3 classrooms, new fields of study have also emerged. Among these are studies reporting how we can honor students' cultural and linguistic differences and simultaneously accelerate their comprehension of English (Kathy Au, Maria Carbo, & Jan Lacina). How can we help parents to improve their children's comprehension at home, how can we develop comprehension skills for this information technologically-driven age? (Donald Leu, David Rose, Bridget Dalton, Linda Labbo, & Michael Kamil), and how does the newest research on neurocognitive science impact our understanding of how K–3 students learn to comprehend (Eric R. Kandel, Cathy Collins Block, Sheri R. Parris, and Renate Nummela Caine).

CONCLUDING THOUGHTS

In this chapter, we described research that informed best-comprehension instructional practices in today's K–3 school. The message is clear—the most important recent discovery in reading research is how to teach comprehension at the K–3 school level. We also know much more about how to prevent reading comprehension failure for young children.

Comprehension tasks that students complete today are more informed by historically and contemporarily based comprehension research than was true in the past. These developments are noteworthy, especially when we realize how much progress comprehension instruction has made since 1946 (Block & Pressley, 2002). The theoretical and instructional practices of today are a monumental leap forward from the Horn Books and memorization exercises of 1678. Today, we are much closer to reaching the goal of helping students attain the sacred liberties that literacy and comprehension afford, so that all children can become expert readers.

REFERENCES

Afflerbach, P., & Meuwissen, K. (2005). Teaching and learning self-assessment strategies in middle school. In S. Israel, C. Block, K. Bauserman, & K. Kinnucan-Welsch (Eds.), *Metacognition in literacy learning: Theory assessment, instruction, and professional development* (pp. 157–160). Mahwah, NJ: Erlbaum.

Anderson, R. C., & Freebody, P. (1981). Vocabulary knowledge. In J. T. Guthrie (Ed.), *Comprehension and teaching: Research reviews* (pp. 77–117). Newark, DE: International Reading Association.

Anderson, V. (1992). A teacher development project in transactional strategy instruction for teachers of severely reading-disabled adolescents. *Teaching and Teacher Education, 8,* 391–403.

Anderson, R. C., & Pearson, P.D. (1984). A schema-theoretical view of basic processes in reading. In P. D. Pearson (Eds.), *Handbook of reading research* (pp. 255–291). New York: Longman.

Anderson, V., & Roit, M. (1993). Planning and implementing collaborative strategy instruction for delayed readers in grades 6–10. *Elementary School Journal, 94,* 121–137.

Austin, M. C., & Morrison, C. (with M. B. Marrison et al.). (1963). *The first R: The Harvard report on reading in elementary schools* (pp. 220–233). New York: Macmillan.

Baker, L. (2005, April). Multiple dimensions of reading achievement. Paper presented at the annual meeting of the American Educational Research Association, Chicago, IL.

Barton, A., & Wilder, D. (1962). Columbia-Carnegie study of reading research and its communication. In J. A. E. Figurel (Ed.), Challenge and experiment in reading. *International Reading Association Conference Proceedings, 7,* 170–176. New York: Scholastic Magazines.

Bauman, J. F., & Bergeron, B. S. (1993). Story map instruction using children's literature: Effects on first graders' comprehension of central narrative elements. *Journal of Reading Behavior, 25,* 407–437.

Bean, R. M. (2004). *The reading specialist: Leadership for the classroom, school, and community.* New York: Guilford.

Beck, I. L., McKeown, M. G., & Kucan, L. (2002). *Bringing words to life: Robust vocabulary instruction.* New York: Guilford.

Becker, W. C. (1977). Teaching reading and language to the disadvantaged: What we have learned from field research. *Harvard Educational Review, 47,* 518–543.

Betts, E. A. (1946). *Betts Basic Readers, Primer, Teacher Edition.* New York: American Book.

Blachowicz, C. L. Z., & Fisher, P. (2000). Vocabulary instruction. In M. L. Kamil, P. B. Mosenthal, P. D. Pearson, & R. Barr (Eds.), *Handbook of reading research* (Vol. 3, pp. 503–523). Mahwah, NJ: Lawrence Erlbaum.

Block, C. C. (1993). Strategy instruction in a student-centered classroom. *The Elementary School Journal, 94*(2), 137–153.

Block, C. C. (1999). The case for exemplary teaching, especially for students who begin first grade without the precursors for literacy success. In T. Shanahan (Ed.), *49th yearbook of the National Reading Conference* (pp. 71–85). Chicago: National Reading Conference.

Block, C. C. (2000). *How can we teach all students to comprehend well?* (Research paper No. 4). New York: Scholastic.

Block, C. C. (2004). *Teaching comprehension: The comprehension process approach.* Boston, MA: Pearson.

Block, C. C. (2005). What are metacognitive assessments? In S. E. Israel, C. C. Block, K. L. Bauserman, & K. Kennucan-Welsh (Eds.), *Metacognition in literacy learning: Theory, assessment, instruction, and professional development* (pp. 83–101). Mahwah, NJ: Erlbaum.

Block, C. C. (2006). Comprehension instruction: Research-based practices. In C. Cummins (Ed.), *Understanding and implementing reading first initiatives: The changing role of administrators* (pp. 72–89). Newark, DE: International Reading Association.

Block, C. C., & Israel, S. E. (2005a). The ABCs of performing highly-effective think-alouds. *The Reading Teacher, 58*(2), 154–167.

Block, C. C., & Israel, S. E. (2005b). *Reading first and beyond: The complete guide for teachers & literacy coaches.* Thousand Oaks, CT: Corwin Press.

Block, C. C., & Pressley, M. (Eds.). (2002). *Comprehension instruction: Research-based best practices.* New York: Guilford.

Block, C. C., & Pressley, M. (2007). Best practices in teaching comprehension. In L. B. Gambrell, L. M. Morrow, & M. Pressley (Eds.), *Best practices in literacy instruction* (3rd ed., pp. 220–243). New York: Guilford.

Block, C. C., & Reed, K. M. (2006). Trade books: How they significantly increase students' vocabulary, comprehension, fluency, and positive attitudes toward reading. Institute for Literacy Enhance Research Report 1739-004. Charlotte, NC: Institute for Literacy Enhancement.

Block, C. C., Caylor, N., & Whiteley, C. (2007). Teacher reader groups: Moving literature circles from discussing what we read to help each other how to read better. Manuscript in COE, TCU.

Block, C. C., Cummins, C., & Stewart, M. (in press). Internalization and transfer of comprehension processes: Effects on kindergarten to grade 5 students literacy achievement. Manuscript submitted for publication.

Block, C. C., Gambrell, L. B., & Pressley, M. (Eds.). (2004). *Improving comprehension instruction: Rethinking research, theory, and classroom practice.* San Francisco: Jossey-Bass.

Block, C. C., Paris, S. R., & Whiteley, C. S. (2008). CPMs: Helping primary grade students self-initiate comprehension processes through kinesthetic instruction. *The Reading Teacher, 61*(6), 440–448.

Block, C. C., Rodgers, L., & Johnson, R. (2004). *Comprehension process instruction: Creating reading success in grades K–3.* New York: Guilford.

Brabham, E. G., & Lynch-Brown, C. (2002). Effects of teachers' reading–aloud styles on vocabulary acquisition and comprehension of students in early elementary grades. *Journal of Educational Psychology, 94,* 465–473.

Brown, R., Pressley, M., Van Meter, P., & Schuder, T. (1996). A quasi-experimental validation of transactional strategies instruction with low-achieving second grade readers. *Journal of Educational Psychology, 88,* 18–37.

Buswell, G. T., & Wheeler, W. H. (1923). *The silent reading hour: Teachers' manual for the second reader.* Chicago, IL: Wheeler Publishing.

Chomsky, C. (1972). Stages in language development and reading exposure. *Harvard Educational Review, 42,* 1–33.

Clews, E. W. (1899). *Educational legislation and administration of the colonial governments.* New York: Columbia University Press.

Collins, C. (1991). Reading instruction that increases thinking abilities. *Journal of Reading, 34,* 510–516.

Cummins, C., Stewart, M. T., & Block, C. C. (2005). Teaching several metacognitive strategies together increases students' independent metacognition. In S. E. Israel, C. C. Block, K. L. Bauserman, & K. Kinnucan-Welsh (Eds.), *Metacognition in literacy learning: Theory, assessment, instruction, and professional development* (pp. 277–295). Mahwah, NJ: Erlbaum.

DeTemple, J., & Snow, C. E. (2003). Learning words from books. In A. van Kleeck, A. Stahl, & E. B. Bauer (Eds.). *On reading books to children: Parents and teachers* (pp. 95–113). Mahwah, NJ: Erlbaum.

Doctorow, M., Wittrock, M. C., & Marks, C. (1978). Generative processes in reading comprehension. *Journal of Educational Psychology, 70,* 109–118.

Dole, J., Brown, K., & Trathen, W. (1996). The effects of strategy instruction on the comprehension performance of at-risk students. *Reading Research Quarterly, 31,* 62–89.

Duffy, G. G. (2002). Foreward. In C. C. Block, L. B. Gambrell, & M. Pressley (Eds.), *Improving comprehension instruction: Rethinking theory and classroom practice.* San Francisco: Jossey-Bass.

Duffy, G. G. (2005). Developing metacognitive teachers: Visioning and the expert's changing role in teacher education and professional development. In S. E. Israel, C. C. Block, K.

L. Bauserman, & K. Kinnucan-Welsh (Eds.), *Metacognition in literacy learning: Theory, assessment, instruction, and professional development* (pp. 61–81). Mahwah, NJ: Erlbaum.

Duffy, G., Roehler, L., & Herman, G. (1988). Modeling mental processes helps poor readers become strategic readers. *Reading Teacher, 41*, 762–767.

Duffy, G. G., & Roehler, L. R. (1989). Why strategy instruction is so difficult and what we need to do about it. In C. B. McCormick, G. Miller, & M. Pressley (Eds.), *Cognitive strategy research: From basic research to educational applications* (pp. 133–154). New York: Springer-Verlag.

Duffy, G. G., Roehler, L. R., Sivan, E., Rackliffe, G., Book, C., Meloth, M., Vavrus, L.G., Wesselman, R., Putnam, J., & Bassiri, D. (1987). Effects of explaining the reasoning associated with using reading stratgies. *Reading Research Quarterly, 22*, 347–368.

Duke, N. K. (2000). 3.6 minutes per day: The scarcity of informational texts in first grade. *Reading Research Quarterly, 35*, 202–224.

Durkin, D. (1978–1979). What classroom observation reveals about reading comprehension instruction. *Reading Research Quarterly, 14*, 481–533.

Elster, C. A. (1994). "I guess they do listen": Young children's emergent readings after adult read-alouds. *Young Children, 49*(3), 27–31.

Fielding, L. G., & Pearson, P. D. (1994). Synthesis of research: Reading comprehension: What works? *Education Leadership, 51*(5), 62–67.

Gunning, T. G. (1996). *Creating reading instruction for all children* (2nd ed.). Needham Heights, MA: Allyn & Bacon.

Guthrie, J. (Ed.). (1981). *Comprehension and teaching: Research reviews*. Newark, DE: International Reading Association.

Hart, B., & Risely, T. R. (1995). *Meaningful differences in the everyday experience of young American children*. Baltimore: Brookes.

Hiebert, E. H., Pearson, D., & Ayra, D. J. (2005, December). Learning Complex Vocabulary in a science text. Paper presented at the annual meeting of the National Reading Conference, Miami, FL.

Holmes, J. A., & Singer, H. (1964). Theoretical models and trends toward more basic research in reading. *Review of Educational Research, 34*, 127–155.

Israel, S. E., & Massey, D. (2005). Metacognitive think-alouds: Using a gradual release model with middle school students. In S. E. Israel, C. C. Block, K. L., Bauserman, & K. Kinnucan-Welsch (Eds.), *Metacognition in literacy learning: Theory, assessment, instruction, and professional development* (pp. 183–198). Mahwah, NJ: Erlbaum.

Kaderavek, J. N., & Sulzby, E. (2002). Narrative production by children with and without specific language impairment: Oral narratives and emergent readings. *Journal of Speech, Language, & Hearing Research, 43*(1), 34–49.

Kintsch, W. (2003). *Comprehension: A paradigm for cognition*. New York: Cambridge University Press.

LaBerge, D., & Samuels, S. J. (1974). Toward a theory of automatic information processing in reading. *Cognitive Psychology, 6*, 293–323.

Leu, D. (2005, December). New advancements in instruction relative to technology comprehension. Presidential address presented at the annual meeting of the National Reading Conference, Miami.

McKee, P., et al. (1950). *Reading for meaning*. Boston: Houghton Mifflin. (Revised 1957, 1963).

Morrow, L. M. (2005). *Literacy development in the early years: Helping children read and write* (5th ed.). Pearson: Boston.

Morrow, L. M., & Gambrell, L. B. (2002). Literature-based instruction in the early years. In S. B. Neuman & D. K. Dickinson (Eds.), *Handbook of early literacy research* (pp. 348–360). New York: Guilford.

Nagy, W., Anderson, R., & Herman, P. (1987). Learning word meanings from context during normal reading. *American Educational Research Journal, 24*, 237–270.

National Reading Panel. (2000). *Report of the National Reading Panel Subgroups: Teaching children to read* (No. 00-4754). Washington, DC: Government Printing Office.

Palincsar, A. S., & Brown, A. L. (1984). Reciprocal teaching of comprehension-fostering and comprehension-monitoring activities. *Cognition and Instruction, 1*, 117–175.

Paris, S. G., & Flukes, J. (2005). Assessing children's metacognition about strategic reading. In S. E. Israel, C. C. Block, K. Bauserman, & K. Kinnucan-Welsh (Eds.), *Metacognition in literacy learning: Theory, assessment, instruction, and professional development* (pp. 121–141). Mahwah, NJ: Erlbaum.

Pearson, P. D. (2005, December). The impact of text genre on students' acquisition of science. Paper presented at the annual meeting of the National Reading Conference, Miami, FL.

Pearson, P. D., & Duke, N. K. (2002). Comprehension instruction in the primary grades. In C. C. Block & M. Pressley (Eds.), *Comprehension instruction: Research-based best practices* (pp. 247–258). New York: Guilford.

Pearson, P. D., & Fielding, L. (1991). Comprehension instruction. In R. Barr, M. L. Kamil, P. B. Mosenthal, & P. D. Pearson (Eds.), *Handbook of reading research* (Vol. 2, pp. 815–860). New York: Longman.

Pearson, P. D., & Johnson, D. (1978). *Teaching comprehension*. New York: Harcourt Brace College Publishers.

Pressley, M. (2006). *Reading instruction that works: The case for balanced teaching* (3rd ed.). New York: Guilford.

Pressley, M., Gaskins, I. W., Wile, D., Cunicelli, B., & Sheridan, J. (1991). Teaching literacy strategies across the curriculum: A case study at Benchmark School. In J. Zutell & S. McCormick (Eds.), *Learner factors/teacher factors: Issues in literacy research and instruction: Fortieth yearbook of the National Reading Conference* (pp. 219–228). Chicago: National Reading Conference.

Purcell, V., & Duke, N. (2005, December). Comprehending non-fictional text. Paper presented at the annual meeting of the National Reading Conference, Miami, FL.

RAND Reading Study Group. (2001). *Reading for understanding: Towards an R & D program in reading comprehension*. Washington, DC: RAND Education.

Risko, V. J., Roskos, K., & Vukelich, C. (2005). Reflection and the self-analytic turn of mind: Toward more robust instruction in teacher education. In S. E. Israel, C. C. Block, K. L. Bauserman, & K. Kinnucan-Welsh (Eds.), *Metacognition in literacy learning: Theory, assessment, instruction, and professional development* (pp. 315–335). Mahwah, NJ: Erlbaum.

Samuels, S. J. (2002). Fluency instruction. In A. Farstrup & J. Samuels (Eds.), *What research has to say about reading instruction* (2nd ed., pp. 347–369). Newark, DE: International Reading Association.

Samuels, S. J. (2006). Looking backward: Reflections on a career in reading. *Journal of Literacy Research, 38*(3), 327–344.

Samuels, S. J., LaBerge, D., & Bremer, C. (1978). Units of word recognition: Evidenced for developmental changes. *Journal of Verbal Learning and Verbal Behavior, 17*, 715–720.

Schmitt, M. C. (2005). Measuring students' awareness and control of strategic processes. In S. E. Israel, C. C. Block, K. L. Bauserman, & K. Kinnucan-Welsh (Eds.), *Metacognition in literacy learning: Theory, assessment, instruction, and professional development* (pp. 315–335). Mahwah, NJ: Erlbaum.

Scott, C. (1954, Spring). A 'forest' view of present research in reading. *Educational and Psychological Measurement, 14*, 208–214.

Smith, N. B. (1940). *Learning to read, primer 45*. New York: Silver Burdett.

Smith, N. (1978). *History of reading instruction*. New York: World Book.

Snow, C. E. (1991). The theoretical basis of the Home-School Study of Language and Literacy Development. *Journal of Research in Childhood Education, 6*, 1–8.

Snow, C. E., Burns, M. S., & Griffin, P. (Eds.). (1998). *Preventing reading difficulties*. Washington, DC: National Academy Press.

Stahl, S. (1999). Why innovations come and go (and mostly go): The case of whole language. *Educational Research, 28*(8), 13–22.

Stewart, M. T. (2004). Early literacy instruction in the climate of No Child Left Behind. *The Reading Teacher, 57*(8), 732–753.

Sulzby, E. (1985). Children's emergent reading of favorite storybooks: A developmental study. *Reading Research Quarterly, 20*, 458–479.

Sweet, A. P., & Snow, C. E. (2003). *Rethinking reading comprehension*. New York: Guilford.

Taylor, B. M. (1982). Text structure and children's comprehension and memory for expository material. *Journal of Educational Psychology, 74*, 323–340.

Teale, W. H., & Sulzby, E. (1986). *Emergent literacy: Writing and reading*. Norwood, NJ: Ablex.

Tharp, R. (1982). The effective instruction of comprehension: Results and description of the Kamehameha Early Education Program. *Reading Research Quarterly, 17*(4), 503–527.

Van Dijk, T., & Kintsch, W. (1983). *Strategies of discourse comprehension*. New York: Academic Press.

Watkins, E. (1922). *How to teach silent reading to beginners*. Chicago: J. B. Lippincott.

Yuill, N., & Oakhill, J. (1991). *Children's problems in reading comprehension*. Cambridge: Cambridge University Press.

24 Developing Higher Order Comprehension in the Middle Grades

Ruth Wharton-McDonald and Shannon Swiger

University of New Hampshire

According to the International Reading Association (1999), "adolescents entering the adult world in the 21st century will read and write more than at any other time in human history. They will need advanced levels of literacy to perform their jobs, run their households, act as citizens and conduct their personal lives" (p. 3). Despite these predictions, national assessment data suggest that few are prepared to take on these challenges. Fewer than one third of adolescents in the United States read proficiently, and overall reading performance among 12th-grade students actually declined between 1992 and 2005 (Perie, Grigg, & Donahue, 2005). According to the 1998 NAEP results, an even smaller percentage—less than 5%—could extend or elaborate the meanings of the materials they read (Donahue, Voelkl, Campbell, & Mazzeo, 1999).

While a great deal of attention has focused on early literacy development, the challenges of adolescent literacy have only more recently received attention. In 2007, adolescent literacy was rated as the "hottest" topic in literacy education by literacy leaders at the International Reading Association (Cassidy & Cassidy, 2007). Moreover, these same experts concurred that adolescent literacy *should* be a very hot issue. (This was in contrast, for example, to Direct/Explicit Instruction, which was judged to be very hot topic but one that the experts believed should not have been.) Thus, at the time this chapter is being written, there is a strong focus on early reading development and instruction and a growing focus on adolescent literacy.

The need for more attention to adolescent literacy is clear: By the time students reach high school, they are less likely to read on their own, less likely to be interested in reading, and as noted above, less likely to be proficient in reading than they were as primary students (e.g., Moje, Young, Readance, & Moore, 2000; Strommen & Mates, 2004). These declines in motivation and achievement seem to have their origins in the upper elementary grades and continue through middle school (International Reading Association, 1999; Chall & Jacobs, 2003; Wigfield, 1997).

The onset of these declines corresponds with the difficulty many students experience in reading as they transition from an emphasis on strategies for decoding and fluency ("learning to read") to an emphasis on using reading for understanding new concepts and ideas ("reading to learn"). Fluency, word meanings and prior knowledge are increasingly important in this stage of development. Students are expected to read and learn about unfamiliar topics where the vocabulary is unfamiliar and the linguistic structures are more complex. While comprehension has always been the objective in reading, it becomes a different sort of challenge at this stage.

The effects of the difficult transition some students experience in shifting from an emphasis on decoding and fluency to an emphasis on comprehension and information gathering have sometimes been described as "the fourth grade slump" (Chall, 1983; Chall & Jacobs, 2003; Chall, Jacobs, & Baldwin, 1990). Children who experience this "slump" in their reading skills and interests often fail to transition to the stage of reading development in which they can use reading as a tool for learning (Chall & Jacobs, 2003). Jeanne Chall (1983) hypothesized that this new stage of reading—the initial stage of "reading to learn" encompassed grades four through eight.

The need to support students in their efforts to master the more complex demands of middle school reading have been well recognized (e.g., Brown, 2002; Durkin, 1979; Chall & Jacobs, 2003; Pressley, 2002). Nearly three decades ago, Dolores Durkin (1979) set out to document the ways in which comprehension development was supported in classrooms. Despite the acknowledged need for comprehension instruction, Durkin found almost *no instruction* occurring in the classrooms she observed. In the 4,469 minutes of reading instruction she observed, Durkin documented exactly 10 minutes in which the teacher taught comprehension.

Instead, she observed that "teachers neglect[ed] comprehension because they [were] busy teaching phonics, structural analysis, or word meanings" (p. 481). With respect to comprehension, Durkin described teachers as mentioning information, interrogating students, assigning worksheets and assessment papers, and checking students' success. Thus, the students who comprehended well when they entered the classroom had some opportunities to practice their skills; those who struggled with comprehension received little or no instruction that would lead to improvement. Decades later, Michael Pressley and his colleagues (Pressley, Wharton-McDonald, Mistretta-Hampston, & Echevarria, 1998; Allington & Johnston, 2002) found essentially the same thing in grades four and five. And even more recently, Taylor and Pearson (2002) report that even in exemplary classrooms, there is very little comprehension instruction taking place.

Research conducted during the 1980s and 1990s demonstrated clearly that comprehension strategies could be taught (see in particular, chapters 18 and 22 in this volume)—and that when students learn to use strategies, their comprehension improves (see Pressley, 2002, 2006). Despite these well-understood findings, comprehension instruction continues to receive less attention in the classroom than other skills or content.

THE GOALS FOR READERS IN THE MIDDLE GRADES: WHAT READERS NEED IN ORDER TO COMPREHEND MIDDLE SCHOOL TEXTS

In recent years, there has been a concerted effort to introduce young readers to informational text much earlier than was the case when Jeanne Chall (1983, 1996) conceptualized the stages of reading development. As the inclusion of a wider range of texts becomes common practice in primary grade classrooms, one would expect students to be better prepared to take on these genres in the middle grades. Regardless of genre, however, the challenges of accessing text remain significant for readers in the middle grades. As readers make the transition from learning to read to becoming fluent readers of new information, they rely on proficiency in a number of areas of reading.

Skilled comprehenders recognize the words on the page automatically (Ehri & Snowling, 2004; Rasinski et al., 2005) and can decode unfamiliar words quickly; they read text fluently; they have a repertoire of comprehension strategies and they know when and how to combine them; they employ metacognition to monitor their reading processes. Moreover, skilled comprehenders know a lot of word meanings (vocabulary) and know a lot about the world (Anderson & Freebody, 1981).

Word recognition and fluency

In order to comprehend challenging text, the reader must first be able to access the words on the page—quickly and accurately. The typical middle school reader can hold approximately seven items in short-term memory at one time (Miller, 1956). This means that if the reader is focused on sounding out individual letters and combinations of letters and thinking about how to blend them together, there will be very little attentional capacity remaining for comprehension (LaBerge & Samuels, 1974; Rasinski et al., 2005; Tan & Nicholson, 1997). In a study of 303 ninth graders, Rasinski and his colleagues found a moderately strong correlation between reading fluency and reading comprehension (r = .53). Moreover, they argued that the 28% of the variance in comprehension explained by students' fluency likely underestimated the true contribution, since the students they studied represented a restricted sample: as a group, they performed below grade-level expectations for both fluency and comprehension. The authors suggest that if the sample had included more higher achieving students (increasing the range), the correlation would have been even higher.

When students lack fluency and automaticity, they tend to read less and avoid difficult materials (see Chall, 1983, 1996; Stanovich, 1986). Thus, not only is their comprehension affected directly, but one of their avenues to improvement (a lot of reading) is also restricted (Allington, 2006; Rasinski, & Hoffman, 2003). Given this potential outcome, it is important to recognize that fluency and automatic word recognition can be taught—with corresponding improvements in comprehension. In an experimental training study, Tan and Nicholson (1997) demonstrated that improving students' automatic recognition of words and phrases led to significant improvement in their reading comprehension. Rasinski and Hoffman (2003) describe numerous studies focused on improving students' fluency, in which comprehension also improved (e.g., Dowhower, 1989, 1994; Knapp & Winsor, 1998; Pinnell et al., 1995; Topping, 1987).

Comprehension strategies

Skilled readers are proficient decoders, recognize words quickly, and read fluently. But just getting the words off the page is not enough. The skilled reader actively constructs meaning from those words via a set of strategies such as predicting, imaging, questioning, summarizing, clarifying, inferring, and connecting to prior knowledge. Many of these strategies were documented by Pressley and Afflerbach (1995) in a series of verbal protocol analyses in which they had expert readers think aloud as they read texts in their fields. Good readers, as they documented, are extremely active, interacting with the text on both personal and intellectual levels as they read.

The comprehension strategies used by good readers do not always develop on their own—even among students who decode easily and read words quickly and accurately. Strategies *can* be taught, however, and studies consistently demonstrate positive effects of such instruction on reading comprehension (see, for example, Dole, Duffy, Roehler, & Pearson, 1991; Gambrell & Bales, 1986; Haller, Child, & Walberg, 1988; Palincsar & Brown, 1984; Pressley, 2002, 2006; Pressley et al., 1992; Trabasso & Bouchard, 2002).

In effective strategy instruction, the teacher explains the purpose of the strategy, how to use it, and when and where to use it. She models its use for students, and provides extensive opportunities for guided practice before expecting students to use the strategy independently. Strategies are taught just a few at a time and students learn to coordinate multiple strategies as they read. Strategies instruction is long-term and woven through the content areas so students learn to apply appropriate strategies to comprehend a wide range of genres (Pressley, 2000).

Metacognition

Metacognition is the awareness of one's own thinking processes that enables the learner to use strategies well. At the most basic level, the reader must be aware of whether or not he is understanding the text. As middle school students encounter more complex texts and must coordinate multiple strategies to comprehend them, the ability to monitor one's own processes and understanding becomes critical to success. Pressley (2002) suggests that in this context, metacognition, "develops most completely when students practice using comprehension strategies as they read" (p. 292). Thus, students not only need to learn the strategies, they need extended opportunities to practice them and opportunities to reflect on their use with others.

Vocabulary

A student's knowledge of vocabulary is strongly related to his or her ability to comprehend text (e.g., Anderson & Freebody, 1981; Beck, Perfetti, & McKeown, 1982; Graves, 2000; Nagy, Anderson, & Herman, 1987). Moreover, in a study examining the origins of the "fourth grade slump," Chall and Jacobs (2003) found that students' decline began not in overall comprehension, but with a slip in word meanings, evident in fourth grade. This was followed by a decline in word recognition and spelling and it was not until later—in middle school—that the students exhibited measurable difficulty in comprehension. Word knowledge is cumulative (Stahl & Nagy, 2006). The more words a student knows, the easier it is to learn new words. Thus, children who enter the intermediate grades with weak vocabularies are not able to take advantage of richer texts, and because they spend less time engaged with richer texts, they learn less about the world and fewer new words. And they fall further and further behind.

Causal evidence indicates that developing a student's vocabulary is one way to improve his comprehension (Beck, Perfetti, & McKeown, 1982; McKeown, Beck, Omanson, & Perfetti, 1983; McKeown, Beck, Omanson, & Pople, 1985). Chall and Jacobs (2003) urge educators not to be sanguine about students with limited word knowledge—even if the rest of their reading profile appears to be fine. Instructional practices that support vocabulary development are critical to comprehension development in the middle grades.

Prior knowledge

One of the reasons that vocabulary correlates with comprehension is that vocabulary can be a proxy for what a student knows about the world. If the student is familiar with terms such as *estuary, inlet, vegetation, wilderness, heron, tributary*, and *marine*, it is likely that she knows something about wetland ecosystems. Prior knowledge about a topic has a profound effect on comprehension. According to schema theory (e.g., Anderson, 1984; Anderson & Pearson, 1984; Rumelhart, 1980), knowledge is organized in complex, relational structures called *schemata*. Schemata constitute our knowledge about "objects, situations, events, sequences of events, actions, and sequences of actions" (Rumelhart, 1980, p. 34). Comprehension is a matter of activating or creating schemata that relate to the text and lead the reader to a meaningful interpretation. Readers' access of schemata allows them to make connections, predictions, and interpretations of what they are reading. For example, consider the following paragraph from a memoir my middle school son, Andrew, is currently reading:

> With the Red Sox, after I grounded out, I got back to the dugout and nobody said much. That wasn't a big deal. But when I went to the end of the dugout to put away my helmet, Grady Little [the manager] pulled me aside and told me: Swing away. Grady told me that the Red Sox wanted me to bring runners in, to drive the ball, because that's why they brought me there. I couldn't believe it, bro. I was so happy. Here I was doing what I thought the manager wanted me to do—make an out on purpose so we could move the runner—and the manager is telling me to take a hack

up there, to let it go. Can you believe that shit? I felt like I just got out of jail, bro. I felt like I could hit the way I wanted to hit. (Ortiz, 2007, p. 128)

Andrew has a well-developed schema for the game of baseball that enables him to easily make sense of terms like *grounded out, dugout, helmet, runners,* and *drive* in the current context. This includes understanding the distinction between a baseball player's helmet and a knight's helmet, and knowing that *runners* in this instance refers to base runners rather than track runners, numbers runners, or drug runners. His knowledge of the sequence of a game of baseball enables him to visualize the author hitting a ground ball, being thrown out at first base, returning to the dugout, and walking past his teammates to hang up his helmet. Andrew knows that baseball is strategic, so he understands that sometimes players make outs on purpose, but that normally, the objective is not to make outs. More specifically, he knows that the author, David Ortiz, is a champion home run hitter—which enables him to understand the player's frustration in holding back—and why he would be the right person to "bring runners in." On a linguistic level, Andrew knows that David Ortiz grew up in the Dominican Republic and sometimes uses familiar dialect in his talk. This helps him read right through the word "bro" without pausing—knowing that it is a form of the word "brother" and a familiar term for addressing someone. He can hear Ortiz's voice in his head as he reads it. He knows that adults in sports (and elsewhere) often use language that is not acceptable for children to use. This enables him to read right through the profanity, despite seeing it only rarely in print. He does all this without noticing, eager to get to the next page. Readers routinely draw upon their background knowledge in these ways when they encounter familiar topics and genres across the curriculum.

In the context of middle grades comprehension, students who know more about a topic or are more familiar with a particular text structure will be better able to comprehend a text. And the process of reading the text adds to their knowledge base, extends their schemata, and makes it easier to comprehend related text in the future. Students with limited prior knowledge have fewer schemata to draw upon, making comprehension more difficult. If it is too difficult, they may abandon the text altogether. So while those with prior knowledge continue to grow as readers and learners, those with limited background risk falling further and further behind. Stanovich (1986) referred to these cycles as the "Matthew Effect" because the rich get richer while the poor get poorer.

THE CONTEXT FOR LEARNING IN THE MIDDLE GRADES

The knowledge, skills, and strategies considered above are critical to the success of the intermediate level reader. But they do not tell the whole story. As students move out of the primary grades and into the middle school years, they not only encounter more complex texts and greater expectations for learning new content, they are also becoming more invested in their interests outside of school. It is during these years that academic motivation and achievement often begin to decline (Chall & Jacobs, 2003; International Reading Association, 1999; Wigfield, 1997). Middle school readers have been characterized as disinterested and unmotivated (e.g., Anderson, Wang, & Gaffney, 2006; McKenna & Kear, 1995). Despite documented declines, recent studies call such descriptions of disinterest into question by casting a wider net to try to understand young adolescent readers in a broader context.

Out-of-school literacies

Faulker (2005) makes the distinction between *public literacies*: The school-based literacies that highlight skills and knowledge necessary for school and allow students to function in the classroom and *private literacies,* which she defines as, "out-of-school literacies linked to literate practices that influence the personal, social and individual lives of students" (p. 109). She contends that the public literacies of school present too narrow a conception of what it means to be literate. Further, she attributes the alienation and disengagement that can characterize middle grades students to a failure to expand the conception of literacy in school.

Two major survey studies have documented the differences in students' public and private literacy practices (Ivey & Broaddus, 2001; Pitcher et al., 2007) and emphasized school practices that can help bridge the gap. Sharon Pitcher and her colleagues revised the Motivation to Read Profile (Gambrell, Palmer, Codling, & Mazzoni, 1996) to be more appropriate for adolescent readers and administered it to 384 students in the sixth to twelfth grades. In addition, they interviewed approximately 100 students in grades 6–11. The authors describe the main themes emerging from the interviews as "the discrepancies between students' views of themselves as readers in school and out of school, students' use of multiliteracies, the influence of family and friends on reading, the role of teachers and instructional methods and the importance of choice" (p. 391). Students who described themselves on the Adolescent MRP as "never" or "not very often" liking reading also listed the hunting and fishing magazines they read avidly at home. When they were on their own time (outside of school and school obligations), these same students reported spending many hours reading and writing on the Internet and in other flexible and varied formats. As noted by Darvin (2006), "It's amazing how important reading and writing can be when you use them for things that really matter to you" (p. 403). It seems that when asked, middle school students initially define "reading" as school reading, which they increasingly avoid. But when offered opportunities to elaborate, they reveal much more complex—and literate—profiles.

Whereas public (in-school) literacies remain focused on book-length texts and articles, the private (out-of-school) literacies of young adolescent readers are much more diverse, including many forms of electronic and popular media (Bean, Bean, & Bean, 1999). The materials that adolescents like to read are not easily available in school (Worthy, Moorman, & Turner, 1999). In addition, middle school students' reading engagement is influenced by their expectations for what they are required to *do* with a text. Janet Allen has referred to what she calls "the smell of the trap" (personal communication, September 16, 2005). Most often, the text is selected by the teacher and the assignment to read it is accompanied by an activity also designed by the teacher (e.g., book report, presentation, quiz). Allen suggests that by middle school, students have learned to anticipate these "traps" every time a new book (or other reading selection) is assigned. Under these circumstances, students often appear to be unmotivated and unengaged.

Ivey and Broaddus (2001) conducted a large-scale survey of middle school students in an effort to understand what materials and instructional practices motivated young adolescents to engage in literacy in school. Students in the study were very motivated by having opportunities to choose their own reading materials. Like most adult readers, they enjoyed "just plain reading," and they resisted reading opportunities in which the teacher chose the book, determined how it was to be read, and assigned a project at the end. The negative characterizations of middle school readers as disinterested non-readers seem closely linked with the instructional experiences they have and the disconnect they experience between the ways in which they are literate outside of school, and the expectations for literacies within the school walls.

Motivation and engagement

As the young adolescents in these studies demonstrate, a student will read and comprehend a piece of text not only because he *can* do it, but because he is *motivated* to do it. By the time students reach the intermediate grades, motivation is a significant factor influencing their comprehension development. According to Guthrie and Wigfield (2000), "motivation is what activates behavior. A less motivated reader spends less time reading, exerts lower cognitive effort, and is less dedicated to full comprehension than a more highly motivated reader" (p. 406). Since the development of higher order comprehension demands engagement in instruction and in reading, motivation is critical to students' progress. Guthrie and Wigfield (1997, 2000) suggest that motivation is the link between frequent reading and reading achievement at this level: Students who are motivated to read, read more and achieve more; their increasing competence motivates them to read more and the cycle continues (Guthrie, Wigfield, Metsala, & Cox, 1999; Stanovich, 1986).

During the middle childhood and early adolescent years, reading motivation shifts in important ways (see Eccles, Wigfield, & Schiefele, 1998, for a detailed discussion). Students' competence beliefs, values and intrinsic motivation for learning tend to decline across the elementary school years. Oldfather and her colleagues (Oldfather & Dahl, 1994; Oldfather & McLaughlin, 1993) have attributed the decline in motivation to changes in classroom conditions. In their studies, they noted that as students moved from "self-contained, responsive classrooms that honored students' voices and had no grades" to more teacher-centered learning environments in which students had little voice or choice in their learning options, their motivation to read declined. As some students leave the supportive environments of their primary grade classrooms, they may find reading and literacy activities to be unrewarding, too difficult or not worth the effort. When in-school reading is viewed as completely disconnected from private literacies, students risk becoming nonreaders (Strommen & Mates, 2004) or alliterate adolescents (Alvermann & Eakle, 2003) who are—at least initially—capable of reading but choose not to do so. Given the role of extensive reading in developing higher order comprehension, these choices are not insignificant.

Engagement follows from motivation. Guthrie, McGough, Bennett, and Rice (1996) describe engaged readers as "*motivated* to read for a variety of personal goals, *strategic* in using multiple approaches to comprehension, *knowledgeable* in their construction of new understanding from text, and socially *interactive* in their approach to literacy" (p. 403). Engagement is perhaps the central element in developing effective comprehension instruction in the middle grades. Strategies and knowledge are critical, but if the reader chooses not to use them, they are of little use. Likewise, motivation is necessary, but motivation does not exist in a vacuum. If the reader lacks the strategic knowledge or background to make sense of text or a learning environment that supports a socially interactive approach to literacy, motivation cannot support achievement, and, in fact, is largely unsustainable.

The relationship between engagement and achievement appears to be a reciprocal one (Guthrie & Wigfield, 2000). In a national sample of students, Campbell, Voelkl, and Donahue (1997) studied the relationship at three ages: 9, 13, and 17. They found that the more highly engaged readers had higher reading achievement than the less-engaged readers. In fact, the 13-year-old students who were highly engaged outperformed the 17-year-olds who were less reading-engaged. In addition, the engaged readers from families with low income and educational backgrounds were higher in achievement than less engaged readers from high income and educational backgrounds.

Summary

The development of higher order comprehension processes in the middle grades results from the complex interaction of a set of skills, strategies, and dispositions, all of which can be nurtured (or stifled) in the context of the school classroom. In order to create deep meaning from text, the student must first be able to access the text itself: She must have strong decoding and word recognition skills. She must be able to process the words, sentences and larger units of text fluently, so that words and phrases combine to make meaning. She relies on comprehension strategies to help her connect units within the text and units of text with her existing schemata. She must not only know how to use particular strategies, but she must know when and where and how to use them. Moreover, she needs the metacognitive knowledge to monitor her comprehension processes—so she is aware of when a new or different strategy is needed. The proficient reader also knows a lot of words: Her vocabulary knowledge enables her to grasp the concepts and contexts presented in the text. She is able to access background knowledge (schemata) related to the text content. This enables her to make predictions about what comes next, connect the new to the known, pose relevant questions, and form more complex interpretations of what she is reading. All of these skills, strategies, and understandings are important but remain essentially dormant unless the reader is also motivated to use them. In order for the learner to develop higher order comprehension, she must be interested, motivated to participate, and engaged in the literacy activity. It is only when instruction truly engages the student reader that learning can take place.

INSTRUCTIONAL FRAMEWORKS FOR DEVELOPING COMPREHENSION IN THE MIDDLE GRADES

In a detailed analysis of existing comprehension instruction, the authors of the RAND report on reading comprehension conclude that, "good instruction is the most powerful means of developing proficient comprehenders and preventing reading comprehension problems" (Snow, 2002, p.29). The sections that follow describe some examples of multidimensional instructional frameworks for developing comprehension in the middle grades. While the set chosen is certainly not complete, it represents a range of approaches which integrate the components reviewed in the first half of this chapter and which have adequate research evidence to support their use. There are many other promising methods that have been used to improve the comprehension of intermediate readers, but in most cases, they focus on a single strategy and/or they yet lack empirical evidence to support them.

Reciprocal teaching

Reciprocal teaching (Palincsar & Brown, 1984) is sometimes considered the grandfather (or, given its authors, the grand*mother*) of frameworks for comprehension instruction. It was the first empirically validated approach to the teaching of coordinated strategies instruction (Block & Pressley, 2002). Developed by Annmarie Palincsar and Ann Brown, reciprocal teaching focuses on four comprehension strategies: prediction, questioning, seeking clarification, and summarization. The strategies are taught through a fairly rigid sequence of instructional events, with a gradual release of responsibility from the teacher to the students. Together, the students and teacher read a passage of text, paragraph by paragraph. As they read, they learn and then practice the four strategies. Students first experience the strategies as modeled by the teacher; they then practice the strategies, supported by the teacher with specific feedback, coaching, hints, and explanation. The leadership role in the dialogue is gradually shifted from the teacher to the students, with the goal of developing independent, coordinated use of the four strategies.

Studies of the effects of reciprocal teaching have shown consistently positive results, with effect sizes ranging from weak to strong. In a review of 16 published and unpublished studies of reciprocal teaching, Rosenshine and Meister (1994) reported overall effect sizes of .32 when the outcomes were measured by standard tests of comprehension and

.88 when the outcome measures were teacher-developed. The most significant feature of reciprocal teaching is the interaction between the teacher and her students. The gradual release of responsibility—and the steps involving modeling and guided practice leading to independent strategy use—have been features of nearly all instructional frameworks in comprehension since.

Reciprocal teaching represented a major shift in approaches to comprehension instruction, and as such, has served as a model of sorts for all who came later. It has not been without its critics, however. The format is rigid and extremely time consuming. Ironically, despite its focus on the development of individual students, Brown and Campione (1998) have expressed concern that reciprocal teaching has been routinized by teacher and publishers: "The surface rituals of questioning, summarizing and so forth are engaged in, divorced from the goal of reading for understanding that they were designed to serve." In contrast to the way they were intended to be used, "these strategies are sometimes practiced out of context of reading authentic texts" (p. 177). Ultimately, reciprocal teaching laid the foundation for much of the coordinated strategies instruction that followed.

Transactional strategies instruction

Transactional Strategies Instruction (TSI) is an approach to teaching comprehension strategies with an emphasis on developing readers who are metacognitive and self-regulated. One of the most challenging aspects of teaching students to use comprehension strategies is that the strategies are not used one at a time, nor in a predetermined order. Rather, the effective reader selects the particular strategy needed from a collection of possible choices, combines strategies, and switches from one strategy to another when the first one is not working. The effective strategy user is flexible and self-regulated.

In TSI, readers are taught that the meaning of a text does not reside in the text alone; nor does it reside solely in the mind of the reader. Rather the meaning is created through the transaction between the text and the reader (Brown, El-Dinary, Pressley, & Coy-Ogan, 1995; Brown, Pressley, Van Meter, & Schuder, 1995; Pressley et al., 1992). Thus the reader is necessarily an active participant in the construction of comprehension. Moreover, readers learn that meaning emerges through transactions between members of the group. This is a far cry from the instructional setting in which students read passages in silence and respond to questions about the author's intended message. According to one of the principal architects of TSI (Michael Pressley), "... transactional strategies instruction is all about teaching students to choose active reading over passive reading and to decide for themselves which strategic process to use when they confront challenging texts" (Pressley & Wharton-McDonald, 2006, p. 320).

Students in the TSI classroom learn how, why, and when to use a set of comprehension strategies, most often including predicting, verifying predictions, visualizing, summarizing, restating, connecting information with background knowledge, and monitoring. Instruction typically takes place in small groups, but extends to whole class, read alouds and anywhere else in the curriculum where comprehension strategies would be helpful. Early in the instruction, the teacher assumes primary responsibility for explaining, modeling and providing guided practice in strategy use. However, over time, responsibility is gradually shifted to the students, first in a shared model, and then to one in which the students make decisions and assume responsibility for their strategic reading. During the transition process, the teacher serves as a coach, offering hints and other feedback to scaffold the process. Because the instruction is necessarily responsive to the discussions, interpretations, and needs of the students, instruction in this framework cannot be scripted in advance.

Three studies have investigated the effects of TSI directly. The first (Brown, Pressley, Van Meter, & Schuder, 1996) was a year-long quasi-experimental investigation of the effects of TSI on second-grade children's reading. The researchers compared reading performance in five classrooms where teachers used TSI to the performance of a comparable group of students in classrooms where teachers were well regarded as language-arts teachers but who were not using a TSI approach. By the spring of second grade, students in the TSI classrooms not only outperformed their peers in the comparison group in reading but they also learned more content over the course of the year. In addition, the teachers reported that TSI increased students' self confidence and enjoyment as readers.

The second study (Collins, 1991) described fifth- and sixth-grade students involved in comprehension instruction consistent with TSI, three days a week for a semester. At the end of the semester, students in the treatment group outperformed those in the control group by three standard deviations. Finally, Valerie Anderson (1992; Anderson & Roit, 1993) conducted a 3-month investigation of the effects of TSI on students with reading disabilities in grades 6–11. Although students in both the treatment and control groups made gains during the study, the students in the TSI group made larger gains. In addition, Anderson (1992) collected a range of qualitative data on the students that also supported the use of TSI. For example, students in the TSI group were more willing to read and attempt to understand difficult material, more willing to collaborate with classmates to understand text, and more likely to react to and elaborate upon text. Since one of the explicit goals of TSI is to develop more active, engaged readers, these qualitative outcomes are likely as important as the gains in test scores themselves.

The disadvantage to TSI has to do with its labor intensive nature (Brown, Pressley, Van Meter & Schuder, 1995; El-Dinary & Schuder, 1993). Teachers report that it demands a great deal of time, requires appropriate texts in multiple copies and requires teachers to relinquish some of the control they are accustomed to having in their classrooms.

Collaborative strategic reading

Like TSI, Collaborative Strategic Reading (CSR) was developed on the foundation of reciprocal teaching (Palincsar & Brown, 1984). Its authors combined their knowledge of cognitive strategies instruction with the findings from cooperative learning (e.g., Johnson & Johnson, 1989, 1999) to create a framework that was originally intended to support children with learning and/or behavioral disabilities in the regular education classroom (Klinger & Vaughn, 1999; Klinger, Vaughn, Dimino, Schumm, & Bryant, 2001; Klinger et al., 2004). Like TSI, it presents active strategy instruction in an engaging social (collaborative) learning environment.

CSR teaches four critical reading comprehension strategies with specific information about how and when to apply them to understand expository text (Klingner & Vaughn, 1999). Students are taught one strategy and its procedures at a time before they are taught to combine them. The four basic strategies include brainstorming and predicting (Previewing), monitoring understanding (Click and Clunk), finding the main idea (Get the Gist), and generating questions and reviewing key ideas (Wrap Up) (Klingner & Vaughn, 1999). Initially, the teacher defines and explains the strategy to the whole class, models its use, and role-plays its implementation with students. When the students are proficient with all four strategies, they are divided into heterogeneous groups with each student assigned a specific role. For example, students assume roles of leader, clunk expert (responsible for cuing problem-solving strategies), announcer, encourager, reporter, and timekeeper. Cue cards guide the group members through their assigned roles initially, providing structure and reminders, but as students become proficient in the procedures, the use of the cards is diminished. Students use learning logs to activate prior knowledge before reading and to record self-questions after reading.

Once the students are familiar with the strategies and the use of the roles, the teacher circulates among groups, providing assistance as needed. For example, he might need to clarify difficult words, model a strategy again, or encourage a student to participate. Like the TSI framework, CSR is designed to gradually shift the responsibility for learning from the teacher to the students.

A number of studies have investigated the effects of CSR on students' comprehension in upper elementary and middle school classrooms, with consistently positive results. Klingner, Vaughn, and Schumm (1998) provided CSR instruction in inclusive fourth-grade classrooms during social studies—with particular emphasis on helping students comprehend social studies texts. Students in the CSR group made significantly greater gains than students in the control group on the Gates-MacGinitie Reading Tests (MacGinitie & MacGinitie, 1989) and demonstrated equal proficiency in their knowledge of the social studies content. In another study (Bryant, Vaughn, Linan-Thompson, Ugel, & Hamff, 2000), CSR was implemented in an inclusive middle school program where students with and without disabilities made significant gains. In a year-long quasi-experimental study of fourth-grade classrooms, Klingner et al. (2004) provided professional development in the CSR framework to five intervention teachers and observed their instruction throughout the year, comparing their students' reading gains with those of students in five control classrooms. Students in CSR classrooms improved significantly in reading comprehension compared with the students in the control classrooms. However, when the gains in the two conditions were compared by achievement groups, only the gains made by the high/average-achieving group were statistically significant. Students in the CSR condition from the low-achieving and LD groups did improve more than their peers in the control classrooms, but the differences in gains did not reach statistical significance. Thus, although the framework was developed in an effort to support low-achieving students, it appears to be even more effective with their higher achieving peers. When CSR has been implemented to support English language learners, two other studies (Klingner & Vaughn, 1996, 2000) have documented significant gains for students who were learning English.

Like TSI, Collaborative Strategic Reasoning demands a high level of preparation and engagement on the part of the teachers. Klingner and her colleagues (Klingner, Vaughn, Arguelles, Hughes, & Leftwich, 2004) found that the teachers' implementation varied a great deal – even with the common professional development provided at the beginning of the study. Importantly, students' comprehension gains were associated with the quality of implementation of the CSR framework. The authors recognize that the implementation of a complicated framework of strategies instruction is both time consuming and challenging. It requires middle school teachers to "let go" of some of their control of their classroom and students. It demands a high level of intelligence to be able to respond to students' questions and difficulties in ways that support strategic thinking. Like Pressley and El-Dinary (1997), Klingner et al. (2004) question whether these types of instruction are "possible for only some teachers" (p. 293).

Concept oriented reading instruction

Concept Oriented Reading Instruction (CORI) differs from the other frameworks in its dual focus on comprehension strategies *and* student motivation to read. Based on Guthrie and Wigfield's theory of engaged reading (see Guthrie & Wigfield, 2000; Guthrie, Wigfield, & Perencevich, 2004), CORI merges explicit cognitive strategy instruction with motivational support practices in the context of content area (science) instruction.

The CORI model is based on a solid grounding in cognitive strategies instruction, including modeling, scaffolding, guided practice, and the conditional knowledge of when, where and how to use the strategies. What distinguishes it from other instructional frameworks are five additional contextual features: (1) *knowledge goals*: reading instruction takes place within the context of a content domain in which the knowledge goals are made clear to students; (2) *real-world experiences*: student experiences are prominently linked with the texts and instruction; (3) *autonomy support*: students learn to make meaningful choices and take control of their learning; (4) *collaboration*: students learn to work together; and (5) an abundance of diverse *interesting texts* in the content domain. These five features were developed for the explicit purpose of supporting students' motivation and engagement in the belief that "merging motivational and cognitive strategy support in reading comprehension instruction will increase engaged reading and reading comprehension" (Guthrie & Ozgungor, 2002; Guthrie, Wigfield, & Perencevich, 2004, p. 405).

A number of investigations support the effectiveness of this framework. In a year-long study in third and fifth grades, Guthrie and his colleagues (Guthrie, Anderson, Alao, & Rinehart, 1999; Guthrie et al., 1998) reported positive findings in both comprehension and motivation. Students in the classrooms where CORI was implemented improved in search and comprehension skills, writing, understanding of central concepts, comprehension of texts, and interpretation skills compared to comparable students in classrooms where they received more typical strategies instruction. Moreover, the majority of students reported greater motivation to read and participate in comprehension activities as the year progressed and more time spent reading.

In a subsequent study, Guthrie et al. (2004) compared CORI to two different third grade-classroom conditions— one in which students received essentially the same strategies instruction as provided in the CORI framework but without the motivational components (SI)—and one in which students received traditional instruction (TI). In each of the first two conditions—CORI and SI—students received similar instruction in the following reading comprehension strategies: (a) activating background knowledge, (b) questioning, (c) searching for information, (d) summarizing, (e) organizing graphically, and (f) identifying story structure.

After 12 weeks, the CORI students outperformed the SI and TI students on several measures of reading comprehension, though not all of the comparisons reached statistical significance. In addition, their self-reports indicated that they were more motivated and they read more than the students in the SI condition. Overall, students in the CORI condition were more motivated than SI and TI students and were more strategic readers than the SI students (Guthrie et al., 2004).

Like the frameworks described above, the effectiveness of CORI is highly dependent on well-trained, active teachers who truly understand (and support) the principles as well as the practices embodied by the model. Teachers must understand not only the content and the development of reading processes, but the motivational variables as well. Pressley (2006) suggests that one reason the students in the CORI condition (Guthrie et al., 2004) outperformed those in the Strategies Instruction (SI) condition may be a difference in the extent of training (10 days vs. 5) and the lack of expertise among teachers in the SI condition.

Concluding comment

The instructional frameworks described have demonstrated great potential for developing higher order comprehension among middle grades learners. In settings where the frameworks have been implemented, students have made significant gains in reading. That said, research continues to describe few classrooms where children are benefiting from these (or similar) approaches. In a year-long study of fourth- and fifth-grade classrooms, Pressley, Wharton-McDonald, Mistretta-Hampston, & Echevarria (1998) found that while teachers described comprehension as one of the most important goals in their literacy instruction, they provided almost no instruction that would help students reach that goal. Harkening back to the classic Durkin study of 1979, these teachers provided opportunities for students to *practice* comprehending text and they assessed how well students could do it, but they quite literally never taught it. Two years later, a larger, national study of fourth-grade classrooms replicated those findings (see Allington & Johnston, 2002 for a more complete description). More recently, in Taylor and Pearson's work with teachers and schools that "beat the odds," they report finding minimal (if any) comprehension instruction at the upper elementary level—even in exemplary classrooms and schools (Taylor & Pearson, 2002). Thus, while the research evidence in favor of comprehension instruction piles up, the gap between research and practice remains stubbornly wide.

GENERAL CLASSROOM PRACTICES WITH THE POTENTIAL TO SUPPORT COMPREHENSION DEVELOPMENT IN THE MIDDLE GRADES

There are some general classroom practices that, while less intense or focused than the frameworks described above, are observed more commonly in middle school classrooms, and when combined with explicit strategies instruction, have the potential to play a significant role in supporting higher order comprehension in middle grades students.

Extensive opportunities for reading

Educators often lament the "fact" that middle school students don't want to read. Yet when the sixth-grade students in Ivey and Broaddus' (2001) survey were asked what they enjoyed most in class, the highest number of them (63%) responded with free reading time. In interviews, students reported that having time to read in school actually gave them opportunities to think and comprehend. Moreover, adolescent readers—even those who are reluctant to read in school—indicate that they would do so given adequate time and access to personally engaging materials (Ivey & Broaddus, 2001; Worthy & McKool, 1996).

The International Reading Association's (IRA; 1999) position statement on adolescent reading states that time spent reading is related to reading success (Anderson, Wilson, & Fielding, 1988; Campbell, Kapinus, & Beatty, 1995; Campbell, Voelkl, & Donahue, 1998); that time spent reading is associated with attitudes toward additional reading (Cone, 1994); and that time spent reading is tied to knowledge of the world (Stanovich, 1986). Wide reading is further acknowledged to be one of the most powerful approaches to increasing students' vocabulary knowledge (Graves, 2000; Krashen, 2004; Stahl & Nagy, 2006). Given the roles played by vocabulary, world knowledge, and motivation in developing comprehension, it is clear that middle school instructional practices should include plentiful opportunities for students to read.

Available texts at an appropriate level of challenge

Providing opportunities for students to read can only support comprehension if students have access to books they can actually read (Allington, 2006). Too often at the middle school level, students are expected to read books that are well above their independent reading levels (e.g., Ivey & Fisher, 2005). If the student's cognitive energy is consumed by the process of decoding and interpreting vocabulary, there can be little remaining energy to devote to comprehending larger passages and deeper meanings. Moreover, if the available (or acceptable) materials are of little interest to students, they may choose to avoid reading—even when they are *able* to read. According to the IRA's position statement, "Adolescents deserve access to a wide variety of reading materials that they can and want to read" (IRA, 1999, p. 7). Effective instructional practices for middle school readers include the provision of easy access to materials that appeal to students. Unfortunately, the materials that appeal to middle school students can be difficult to find in school (Ivey & Broaddus, 2001; Worthy, Moorman, & Turner, 1999). If the goal is to develop motivated, engaged readers, then that needs to change.

Connections to Students' Out-of-School Lives

> *You build on what they know and what they care about.*
> (successful history teacher cited by Ivey & Fisher, 2005, p.10)

The evidence is clear that students (like adults) are more willing to read about things that interest them. Even those who appear to be among the most resistant to reading in school may yet be engaged, purposeful readers outside of school (Bintz, 1993; Ivey & Broaddus, 2001; Schraw, Bruning, & Svoboda, 1995; Worthy, 1998). Instructional practices that repair the disconnect between students' public and private literacies— practices that form connections between what is personally interesting to students and the materials they are asked to read in school will support the development of comprehension processes.

Opportunities for discussion

One of the common characteristics of reciprocal teaching, Transactional Strategies Instruction, Collaborative Strategic Reading and Concept-Oriented Reading Instruction is the emphasis on the socially constructive nature of comprehension. In each framework, discussion plays a key role in supporting the development of students' understanding of text. It is through the interaction—or the transaction—of ideas, language, and perspective that comprehension is developed. Students must have time for this discourse; however, by definition, that takes time. Again, discussion alone will not lead to the development of effective comprehension processes. However, when students have opportunities to discuss outcomes in science, debate issues in social studies or analyze literary themes with peers, they are forced to return to the texts for evidence to support their claims (Biancarosa, 2005). They model and practice the strategies of prediction, questioning, clarifying, summarizing, and synthesis. They are able to move their thinking forward in ways that enable them to return to text later with better developed ideas, new perspectives and more background knowledge.

Choice

> *It makes me want to read when I hear it's our choice and no one else's!*
> (sixth-grade student interviewed by Ivey & Broaddus, 2001, p. 350)

Teachers who offer students choices, challenging tasks, and collaborative learning environments increase their motivation to read and comprehend text (Snow, 2002). Indeed, adolescents like the student cited above clearly identify choice as a significant factor in motivating them to read (Guthrie & Wigfield, 2000; Ivey & Broaddus, 2001; Pitcher et al., 2007). Guthrie and Wigfield explain the power of choice in terms of the control it affords students. As students move from the primary grades into the intermediate years, there is more of an emphasis on teacher control and fewer opportunities for student decision making (Eccles & Midgley, 1989; Eccles, Wigfield, et al., 1993). Unfortunately, this shift takes place during the same time when students are striving to become more independent decision makers in their lives. Guthrie and his colleagues deliberately included student choice as a key feature of the CORI framework because they believed that choice plays a significant role in motivating engaged readers (Guthrie, Anderson, Alao, & Rinehart, 1999; Guthrie et al., 1998). Given the strength of student voices and the evidence that underlies engagement theory, choice appears to be a critical feature of effective comprehension instruction in the middle grades.

Read aloud

Read aloud is a daily practice in primary grade classrooms (e.g., Pressley, Wharton-McDonald, Mistretta, & Echevarria, 1998; Wharton-McDonald, Pressley, & Hampston, 1998), but as the pressure to cover content increases, fewer teachers make time for it as students move into the intermediate and secondary grades. Yet read aloud continues to provide valuable opportunities for modeling fluency and comprehension strategies, exploring complex ideas, building vocabulary, and increasing students' world knowledge. It provides a scaffold for supporting classroom discourse. Moreover, students describe read aloud as a tool for developing better conceptual understandings (Ivey, 2003) and they report that they value the experience in school (Ivey & Broaddus, 2001). When asked what they enjoyed most in class, 62% of sixth graders reported having their teacher read aloud. Again, the role of motivation must be acknowledged in considering an instructional framework for middle school students. Reading aloud to students—well beyond the point when they can read to themselves—provides a wide range of opportunities for modeling and supporting comprehension instruction in a format that students find highly engaging.

SUMMARY—WHAT IS KNOWN ABOUT SUPPORTING COMPREHENSION IN THE MIDDLE GRADES.

Comprehension instruction that supports the development of higher order processing of text at the middle school level demands a careful mix of strategies and skills instruction embedded within motivating, engaging environments. We know that many students struggle with the transition from the early challenges of "learning to read" to the later, more complex challenges of using reading as a tool for learning (Chall, 1983; Chall & Jacobs, 2003; Chall, Jacobs, & Baldwin, 1990; Perie, Grigg, & Donahue, 2005). We know that as students leave elementary school and move through middle school, their interest in school reading declines, while their interest in out-of-school literacy grows (Moje, Young, Readance, & Moore, 2000; Strommen & Mates, 2004; Wigfield, 1997; Worthy, 1998; Worthy, Moorman, & Turner, 1999). During the same period, we know that students' proficiency in reading is likely to decline (Chall & Jacobs, 1983; Chall Jacobs, & Baldwin, 1990).

As students make the transition from student-centered classrooms where the focus is on "learning to read" to more teacher-directed classrooms where they are expected to use reading to learn, they need instruction, opportunities and learning contexts that will support them through that process (e.g., Oldfather & Dahl, 1994; Oldfather & McLaughlin, 1993). Unfortunately, the limited research that has specifically targeted students and classrooms in grades four through eight—where student declines appear to take root—consistently reports an absence of comprehension instruction (Allington & Johnston, 2002; Pressley, Wharton-McDonald, Mistretta-Hampston & Echevarria,

1998) and an increase in the separation between in-school (public) literacies and out-of-school (private) literacies (Eccles & Midgley, 1989; Faulker, 2005; Pitcher et al., 2007).

In order for students in the middle grades to develop higher order comprehension, we know that they must be able to access the words accurately and fluently (LaBerge & Samuels, 1974; Rasinski et al., 2005; Tan & Nicholson, 1997). We know that they must be able to draw upon and coordinate comprehension strategies—and that strategies can be taught and learned with positive effects on comprehension (e.g., Pressley & Afflerbach, 1995; Dole, Duffy, Roehler, & Peterson, 1991; Palincsar & Brown, 1984; Pressley et al., 1992). We know that students with larger vocabularies and more extensive background knowledge have better comprehension—and that supporting these components through instruction helps improve comprehension (e.g., Anderson & Freebody, 1981; Beck, Perfetti, & McKeown, 1982; Graves, 2000; Stanovich, 1986).

In contrast to conventional wisdom, we know that young adolescents do, in fact, read—but that they prefer to read materials not often found in school (Ivey & Broaddus, 2001; Ivey & Fisher, 2005; Worthy, Moorman, & Turner, 1999). We know that by the intermediate grades, motivation and engagement are significant factors affecting students' comprehension development (Guthrie & Wigfield, 2000; Guthrie, Wigfield, Metsala, & Cox, 1999).

WHAT IS NOT KNOWN—DIRECTIONS FOR THE FUTURE

It has been nearly 25 years since researchers began to consider the unique needs of students making the transition from early conventional readers—those focused on "learning to read"—to intermediate readers, who must use conventional reading as a tool to explore new territory of ideas in print (Chall, 1983). It has been just as long since Durkin (1979) called attention to the utter lack of comprehension instruction for these students. Since that time, there have been remarkably few studies that have focused specifically on typically developing middle grades readers. Most of what we know about instructional supports for these students must be assembled from research with overlapping populations (e.g., primary-grades students, "adolescents," "struggling," or "reluctant" readers).

Most of the early efforts to address the well-recognized "slump" focused on strengthening instruction in the primary grades in an effort to prevent later difficulties. Despite a recent increase in attention to older readers, the focus of most large-scale research projects and intervention funding continues to be on instruction in the primary grades. For example, the proposed federal budget for 2006 included $1.1 billion budgeted for Reading First (for strengthening readers in grades K–3) and only $200 million proposed for Striving Readers (supporting instruction for students in high schools). Notice that students in the middle grades were left out completely. There is a profound need for more research that specifically investigates instructional approaches for students who fall between the primary grades and high school. Rather than drawing from studies targeting elementary or secondary students (as we have done in much of this chapter), we need studies that explicitly investigate teaching and learning experiences in middle schools.

Even in studies where comprehension instruction has been implemented with middle school students and positive effects, there is a need to better understand the circumstances under which such practices can be sustained. Researchers who have developed and studied instructional frameworks where students learn to coordinate multiple strategies and researchers consider motivation and engagement, there have been significant challenges to implementation—not from the perspective of the students, but rather from the perspectives of the *teachers* (e.g., Brown & Campione, 1998; Brown, Pressley, Van

Meter, & Schuder, 1995; Klinger et al., 2004; Pressley & El-Dinary, 1997). One explanation for the lack of coordinated comprehension instruction is that it demands a high level of training and expertise and tremendous commitment on the part of the classroom teacher. In many cases, in fact, it appears to be unsustainable in a "typical" classroom. The consistency of these findings raises the question of whether all teachers can learn to teach comprehension in these ways (e.g., El-Dinary & Schuder, 1993; Pressley & El-Dinary, 1997). This is a question that should be explored further.

Given the unique challenges presented by young adolescent readers and their teachers, there is a great deal of work to be done to further our understanding of these students as learners, including both their public and private literacies, the roles of motivation and engagement in their learning, and the challenges facing the teachers who work to implement effective instructional frameworks. These middle grades could well be the critical juncture for students and their literacy development. There is much work to be done to ensure that we guide them on a trajectory toward multiple literacies that connect them to the world and help them move forward in their lives.

REFERENCES

Allington, R. L. (2006). *What really matters for struggling readers: Designing research-based programs* (2nd ed.). Boston: Pearson Education.

Allington, R. L., & Johnston, P. H. (2002). *Reading to learn: Lessons from exemplary fourth-grade classrooms.* New York: Guilford Press.

Alvermann, D. E., & Eakle, A. J. (2003). Comprehension instruction: Adolescents and their multiple literacies. In C. Snow & A. Sweet (Eds.), *Rethinking reading comprehension* (pp. 12–29). New York: Guilford.

Anderson, R. C. (1984, November). Some reflections on the acquisition of knowledge. *Educational Researcher, 13*, 5–10.

Anderson, R. C., & Freebody, P. (1981). Vocabulary knowledge. In J. T. Guthrie (Ed.), *Comprehension and teaching: Research reviews.* Newark, DE: International Reading Association.

Anderson, R. C., & Pearson, P. D. (1984). A schema-theoretic view of basic processes in reading comprehension. In P. D. Pearon (Ed.), *Handbook of reading research* (pp. 255–292). New York: Longman.

Anderson, R. C., Wang, Q., & Gaffney, J. S. (2006). Comprehension research over the past three decades. In K. A. Dougherty Stahl & M. C. McKenna (Eds.), *Reading research at work: Foundations of effective practice.* New York: Guilford.

Anderson, R. C., Wilson, P. T., & Fielding, L. G. (1988). Growth in reading and how children spend their time outside school. *Reading Research Quarterly, 23*, 285–303.

Anderson, V. (1992). A teacher development project in transactional strategy instruction for teachers of severely reading-disabled adolescents. *Teaching and Teacher Education, 8*, 391-403.

Anderson, V., & Roit, M. (1993). Planning and implementing collaborative strategy instruction for delayed readers in grades 6–10. *Elementary School Journal, 94*, 121–137.

Bean, T. W., Bean, S. K., & Bean, K. F. (1999). Intergenerational conversations and two adolescents' multiple literacies: Implications for redefining content area literacy. *Journal of Adolescent and Adult Literacy, 42*, 438–448.

Beck, I. L., Perfetti, C. A., & McKeown, M. G. (1982). Effects of long-term vocabulary instruction on lexical access and reading comprehension. *Journal of Educational Psychology, 74*, 506-521.

Behrman, E. H. (2003). Reconciling content literacy with adolescent literacy: Expanding literacy opportunities in a community-focused biology class. *Reading Research & Instruction, 43*, 1–30.

Biancarosa, G. (2005). After third grade. *Educational Leadership, 63*(2), 16–22.

Bintz, W. P. (1993). Resistant readers in secondary education: Some insights and implications. *Journal of Reading, 36*, 604–615.

Block, C. C., & Pressley, M. (2002). Comprehension strategies instruction: A turn of the century status report. In C. C. Block & M. Pressley (Eds.), *Comprehension instruction: Research-based best Practices* (pp. 11–28). New York: Guilford.

Brown, A. L., & Campione, J. C. (1998). Designing a community of young learners: Theoretical and practical lessons. In N. M. Lambert & B. L. McCombs (Eds.), *How students learn: Reforming schools through learner-centered education* (pp. 153–186). Washington, DC: American Psychological Association.

Brown, R. (2002). Straddling two worlds: Self-directed comprehension instruction for middle schoolers. In C. C. Block & M. Pressley (Eds.), *Comprehension instruction: Research-based best practices* (pp. 337–350). New York: Guilford.

Brown, R., El-Dinary, P. B., Pressley, M., Coy-Ogan, L. (1995). A transactional strategies approach to reading instruction. *The Reading Teacher, 49*, 256–258.

Brown, R., Pressley, M., Van Meter, P., & Schuder, T. (1996). A quasi-experimental validation of transactional strategies instruction with low-achieving second-grade readers. *Journal of Educational Psychology, 88*, 18–37.

Brown, R., Pressley, M., Van Meter, P., & Schuder, T. (1995). *A quasi-experimental validation of transactional strategies instruction with previously low-achieving second-graders.* (Report No. 33). College Park, MD: National Reading Research Center.

Bryant, D. P., Vaughn, S., Linan-Thompson, S., Ugel, N., & Hamff, A. (2000). Reading outcomes for students with and without learning disabilities in general education middle school content area classes. *Learning Disability Quarterly, 23*, 24–38.

Campbell, J. R., Kapinus, B. A., & Beatty, A. S. (1995). *Interviewing Children About their Literacy Experiences.* Washington, DC: Office of Educational Research and Improvement.

Campbell, J. R., Voelkl, K. E., & Dohahue, P. L. (1997). NAEP 1996 trends in academic progress. (NCES Publication No. 97985r.) Washington, D.C.: U.S. Department of Education.

Cassidy, J., & Cassidy, D. (2007, February/March). What's hot, what's not for 2007. *Reading Today, 24*(4), 1, 10-11.

Chall, J. S. (1983). *Stages of reading development.* New York: McGraw-Hill.

Chall, J. S. (1996). *Stages of reading development* (2nd ed.). New York: McGraw-Hill.

Chall, J. S., & Jacobs, V. A. (2003, Spring). Poor children's fourth-grade slump. *American Educator: Research Round-Up.* Washington, DC: American Federation of Teachers.

Chall, J. S., Jacobs, V. A., & Baldwin, L. E. (1990). *The reading crisis: Why poor children fall behind.* Cambridge, MA: Harvard University Press.

Collins, C. (1991). Reading instruction that increases thinking abilities. *Journal of Reading, 34*, 510–516.

Cone, J. K. (1994). Appearing acts: Creating readers in a high school English class. *Harvard Educational Review, 64*, 450–473.

Darvin, J. (2006). "Real-world cognition doesn't end when the bell rings": Literacy instruction strategies derived from situated cognition research. *Journal of Adolescent & Adult Literacy, 49*(5), 398–407.

Dowhower, S. L. (1989). Repeated reading: Research into practice. *The Reading Teacher, 42*, 502–507.

Dowhower, S. L. (1994). Repeated reading revisited: Research into practice. *Reading and Writing Quarterly, 10*, 343–358.

Dole, J., Duffy, G., Roehler, L., & Peterson, P. D. (1991). Moving from the old to the new: Research on reading comprehension instruction. *Review of Educational Research, 61*, 239–264.

Durkin, D. (1979). What classroom observations reveal about reading comprehension instruction. *Reading Research Quarterly, 14*(4), 481–533.

Eccles, J. S., & Midgley, C. (1989). Stage-environment fit: Developmentally appropriate classrooms for young adolescents. In C. Ames & R. Ames (Eds.), *Research on motivation in education* (Vol. 3, pp. 139–186). San Diego, CA: Academic Press.

Eccles, J. S., Wigfield, A., et al. (1993). Negative effects of traditional middle schools on students' motivation. *The Elementary School Journal, 93*, 553–574.

Eccles, J. S., Wigfield, A., & Schiefele, U. (1998). Motivation to succeed. In W. Damon (Series Ed.) and N. Eisenberg (Ed.), *Handbook of child psychology (Vol. 3): Social, emotional, and personality development* (5th ed.). New York: Wiley.

Ehri, L. C., & Snowling, M. J. (2004). Developmental variation in word recognition. In C. A. Stone, E. R. Silliman, B. J. Ehren, & K. Apel (Eds.), *Handbook of language and literacy: Development and disorders* (pp. 433–460). New York: Guilford Press.

El-Dinary, P. B., & Schuder, T. (1993). Seven teachers' acceptance of transactional strategies instruction during their first year using it. *Elementary School Journal, 94*, 207–219.

Faulker, V. (2005). Adolescent literacies within the middle years of schooling: A case study of a year 8 homeroom. *Journal of Adolescent & Adult Literacy, 4*(2), 108–117.

Gambrell, L. B., & Bales, R. J. (1986). Mental imagery and the comprehension-monitoring performance of fourth- and fifth-grade poor readers. *Reading Research Quarterly, 21*(4), 454–464.

Gambrell, L. B., Palmer, B. M., Codling, R. M., & Mazzoni, S. A. (1996). Assessing motivation to read. *The Reading Teacher, 49,* 518–533.

Graves, M. F. (2000). A vocabulary program to complement and bolster a middle-grade comprehension program. In B. M. Taylor, M. F. Graves, & P. Van Den Broek (Eds.), *Reading for meaning: Fostering comprehension in the middle grades* (pp. 116–135). Newark, DE: International Reading Association and NY: Teachers College Press.

Graves, M. F., Juel, C., & Graves, B. B. (2001). *Teaching reading in the 21st century* (2nd ed.). Boston, MA: Allyn & Bacon.

Guthrie, J. T., Anderson, E., Alao, S., & Rinehart, J. (1999). Influences of concept-oriented reading instruction on strategy use and conceptual learning from text. *Elementary School Journal, 99,* 343–366.

Guthrie, J. T., McGough, K., Bennett, L., & Rice, M. E. (1996). Concept-oriented reading instruction: An integrated curriculum to develop motivations and strategies for reading. In L. Baker, P. Afflerbach, & D. Reinking (Eds.), *Developing engaged readers in school and home communities* (pp. 165–190). Hillsdale, NJ: Erlbaum.

Guthrie, J. T. & Ozgungor, S. (2002). Instructional contexts for reading engagement. In C. C. Block & M. Pressley (Eds.), *Comprehension instruction: Research-based best practices* (pp. 275–288). New York: Guilford.

Guthrie, J. T., Van Meter, P., Hancock, G., Alao, S., Anderson, E., & McCann, A. (1998). Does concept-oriented reading instruction increase strategy use and conceptual learning from text? *Journal of Educational Psychology, 90,* 261–278.

Guthrie, J. T., & Wigfield, A. (2000). Engagement and motivation in reading. In M. L. Kamil, P. B. Mosenthal, P. D. Pearson, & R. Barr (Eds.), *Handbook of reading research: Volume III* (pp. 403–422). New York: Erlbaum.

Guthrie, J. T., & Wigfield, A. (2005). Roles of motivation and engagement in reading comprehension assessment. In S. Paris & S. Stahl (Eds.), *Children's Reading Comprehension and Assessment* (pp. 187–213). Mahwah, NJ: Erlbaum.

Guthrie, J. T., Wigfield, A., Metsala, J. L., & Cox, K. E. (1999). Motivational and cognitive predictors of text comprehension and reading amount. *Scientific Studies of Reading, 3,* 231–256.

Guthrie, J. T., Wigfield, A., & Perencevich, K. C. (Eds.). (2004). *Motivating reading comprehension: Concept-oriented reading instruction.* Mahwah, NJ: Erlbaum

Haller, E. P., Child, D. A., & Walberg, H. J. (1988). Can comprehension be taught? A quantitative synthesis of "metacognitive" studies. *Educational Researcher, 17*(9), 5-8.

International Reading Association. (1999). *Adolescent literacy* (Position Statement). Newark, DE: Author.

International Reading Association & National Middle School Association. (2002). *Supporting young adolescents' literacy learning: A joint position statement of the International Reading Association and the National Middle School Association.* Newark, DE: International Reading Association.

Johnson, D. W., & Johnson, R. T. (1989). Cooperative learning: What special educators need to know. *The Pointer, 33,* 5–10.

Johnson, D. W., & Johnson, R. T. (1999). Making cooperative learning work. *Theory into Practice, 38*(2), 67–73.

Ivey, G. (2003). "The teacher makes it more explainable" and other reasons to read aloud in the intermediate grades. *The Reading Teacher, 56,* 812–814.

Ivey, G., & Broaddus, K. (2001). "Just plain reading": A survey of what makes students want to read in middle school classrooms. *Reading Research Quarterly, 36,* 350–377.

Ivey, G., & Fisher, D. (2005). Learning from what doesn't work. *Educational Leadership, 63*(2), 8–15.

Klinger, J. K., & Vaughn, S. (1996). Reciprocal teaching of reading comprehension strategies for students with learning disabilities who use English as a second language. *The Elementary School Journal, 96,* 275–293.

Klinger, J. K., & Vaughn, S. (1999). Promoting reading comprehension, content learning and English acquisition through collaborative strategic reading (CSR). *The Reading Teacher, 52,* 738–748.

Klinger, J. K., & Vaughn, S. (2000). The helping behaviors of fifth-graders while using collaborative strategic reading during ESL content classes. *TESOL Quarterly, 34,* 69–98.

Klinger, J. K., Vaughn, S., Arguelles, M. E., Hughes, M. T., Marie, T., & Leftwich, S. A. (2004). Collaborative strategic reading: Real world lessons from classroom teachers. *Remedial & Special Education, 25*, 291–302.

Klinger, J. K., Vaughn, S., Dimino, J., Schumm, J., & Bryant, D. (2001). *From clunk to click: Collaborative strategic reading.* Longmont, CO: Sopris West.

Klinger, J. K., Vaughn, S., & Schumm, J. (1998). Collaborative strategic reading during social studies in heterogeneous fourth-grade classrooms. *The Elementary School Journal, 99*, 3–22.

Knapp, N. F., & Winsor, A. P. (1998). A reading apprenticeship for delayed primary readers. *Reading Research & Instruction, 38*, 13–29.

Krashen, S. D. (2004). *The power of reading: Insights from the research* (2nd ed.). Portsmouth, NH: Heinemann.

LaBerge, D., & Samuels, S. J. (1974). Toward theory of automatic information processing in reading. *Cognitive Psychology, 6*, 293–323.

MacGinitie, W., & MacGinitie, R. (1989). *Gates-MacGinitie reading tests* (3rd ed.). Itsaca, IL: Riverside.

McKenna, M. C., Ellsworth, R. A., & Kear, D. J. (1995). Children's attitudes toward reading: A national survey. *Reading Research Quarterly, 30*, 934–956.

McKeown, M. G., & Beck, I. L. (1993). Grappling with text ideas: Questioning the author. *The Reading Teacher, 46*(7), 560–567.

McKeown, M. G., & Beck, I. L. (2004). Transforming knowledge into professional development resources. *Elementary School Journal, 104*, 391–408.

McKeown, M. G., Beck, I. L., Omanson, R. C., & Perfetti, C. A. (1983). The effects of long-term vocabulary instruction on reading comprehension: A replication. *Journal of Reading Behavior, 15*, 3–18.

McKeown, M. G., Beck, I. L., Omanson, R. C., & Pople, M. T. (1985). Some effects of the nature and frequency of vocabulary instruction on the knowledge and use of words. *Reading Research Quarterly, 20*, 522–535.

Miller, G. A. (1956). The magical number seven, plus-or-minus two: Some limits on our capacity for processing information. *Psychological Review, 63*, 81–97.

Moje, E. B., Young, J. P., Readance, J. E., & Moore, D. W. (2000). Reinventing adolescent literacy for new times: Perennial and millennial issues. *Journal of Adolescent and Adult Literacy, 43*, 400–410.

Nagy, W., Anderson, R., & Herman, P. (1987). Learning word meanings from context during normal reading. *American Educational Research Journal, 24*, 237–270.

Oldfather, P., & Dahl, K. (1994). Toward a social constructivist reconceptualization of intrinsic motivation for literacy learning. *Journal of Reading Behavior, 26*(2), 139–153.

Oldfather, P., & McLaughlin, H. J. (1993). Gaining and losing voice: a longitudinal study of students' continuing impulse to learn across elementary and middle school contexts. *Research in Middle Level Education, 3*, 1–25.

Ortiz, D., with Massarotti, T. (2007). *Big Papi: My story of big dreams and big hits.* New York: St. Martin's Press.

Palincsar, A. S., & Brown, A. (1984). The reciprocal teaching of comprehension-fostering and comprehension-monitoring activities. *Cognition and Instruction, 1*, 117–175.

Pinnell, G. S., Pikulski, J. J., Wixson, K. K., Campbell, J. R., Gough, P. B., & Beatty, A. S. (1995). *Listening to children read aloud.* Washington, DC: Office of Educational Research and Improvement, U.S. Department of Education.

Pitcher, S. M., Albright, L. K., DeLaney, C. J., et al. (2007). Assessing adolescents' motivation to read. *Journal of Adolescent and Adult Literacy, 50*, 378–396.

Pressley, M. (2000). Comprehension instruction in elementary school: A Quarter-century of research progress. In B. M. Taylor, M. F. Graves, & P. van den Broek (Eds.), *Reading for meaning: Fostering comprehension in the middle grades* (pp. 32–51). Newark, DE: International Reading Association.

Pressley, M. (2002). Metacognition and self-regulated comprehension. In A. E. Farstrup & S. J. Samuels (Eds.), *What research has to say about reading instruction* (pp. 291–309). Newark, DE: International Reading Association.

Pressley, M. (2006). *Reading instruction that WORKS: The case for balanced teaching* (3rd ed.). New York: Guilford.

Pressley, M., & Afflerbach, P. (1995). *Verbal protocols of reading: The nature of constructively responsive reading.* Hillsdale, NJ: Erlbaum.

Pressley, M., & El-Dinary, P. B. (1997). What we know about translating comprehension-strategies instruction research into practice. *Journal of Learning Disabilities, 30*, 486–488.

Pressley, M., El-Dinary, P. B., Gaskins, I., Schuder, T., Begman, J., Almasi, L., & Brown, R. (1992). Beyond direct explanation: Transactional instruction of reading comprehension strategies. *Elementary School Journal, 92*, 511–554.

Pressley, M., Johnson, C. J., Symons, S., McGoldrick, J. A., & Kurita, J. A. (1989). Strategies that improve memory and comprehension of what is read. *Elementary School Journal, 90*, 3–32.

Pressley, M., & Wharton-McDonald, R. M. (2006). The need for increased comprehension instruction. In M. Pressley (Ed.), *Reading instruction that works: the case for balanced teaching* (3rd ed., pp. 293–346). New York: Guilford Press.

Pressley, M., Wharton-McDonald, R. M., Mistretta-Hampston, J. M., & Echevarria, M. (1998). The nature of literacy instruction in ten grade-4 and -5 classrooms in upstate New York. *Scientific Studies of Reading, 2*, 159–191.

Rasinski, T. V., & Hoffman, J. V. (2003). Theory and research into practice: Oral reading in the school literacy curriculum. *Reading Research Quarterly, 38*, 510–522.

Rasinski, T. V., Padak, N. D., McKeon, C. A., Wilfong, L.G., Friedauer, J. A., & Heim, P. (2005). Is reading fluency a key for successful high school reading? *Journal of Adolescent & Adult Literacy, 4*(1), 22–27.

Rosenshine, B., & Meister, C. (1994). Reciprocal teaching: A review of the research. *Review of Educational Research, 42*, 479–530.

Rumelhart, D. E. (1980). Schemata: the building blocks of cognition. In R. J. Spiro, B. C. Bruce, & W. F. Brewer (Eds.), *Theoretical issues in reading comprehension* (pp. 33-58). Hillsdale, NJ: Erlbaum.

Snow, C. (2002). Reading for understanding: Toward an R&D program in reading comprehension. Santa Monica, CA: RAND.

Stahl, S. A., & Nagy, W. E. (2006). *Teaching word meanings*. Mahwah, NJ: Erlbaum.

Stanovich, K. E. (1986). Matthew effects in reading: Some consequences of individual differences in the acquisition of literacy. *Reading Research Quarterly, 21*, 360–407.

Strommen, L. T., & Mates, B. F. (2004). Learning to love reading: Interviews with older children and teens. *Journal of Adolescent & Adult Literacy, 48*, 188–200.

Tan, A., & Nicholson, T. (1997). Flashcards revisited: Training poor readers to read words faster improves their comprehension of text. *Journal of Educational Psychology, 89*(2), 276–288.

Taylor, B., & Pearson, P. D. (Eds.). (2002). *Teaching reading: Effective schools, accomplished teachers*. Mahwah, NJ: Erlbaum.

Topping, K. (1987). Paired reading: A powerful technique for parent use. *The Reading Teacher, 40*, 604–614.

Trabasso, T., & Bouchard, E. (2002). Teaching readers how to comprehend text strategically. In C. C. Block & M. Pressley (Eds.), *Comprehension instruction: Research-based best practices* (pp. 176–200). New York: Guilford.

Vaughn, S. (2001). Collaborative strategic reading as a means to enhance peer-mediated instruction for reading comprehension and content area learning. *Remedial & Special Education, 22*, 66–75.

Wharton-McDonald, R., Pressley, M., & Hampston, J. M. (1998). Outstanding literacy instruction in first grade: Teacher practices and student achievement. *Elementary School Journal, 99*, 101–128.

Wigfield, A. (1997). Children's motivations for reading and reading engagement. In J. T. Guthrie & A. Wigfield (Eds.), *Reading engagement: Motivating readers through integrated instruction* (pp. 14–33). Newark, DE: International Reading Association.

Worthy, J., Moorman, M., & Turner, M. (1999). What Johnny likes to read is hard to find in school. *Reading Research Quarterly, 34*, 12–27.

25 Improving Adolescent Comprehension

Developing Comprehension Strategies in the Content Areas

Mark W. Conley

Michigan State University

The field of adolescent literacy is engaged in a continual struggle with what it means to promote comprehension. Starting out as *content area reading*, the field was preoccupied with developing teaching activities for learning from texts. For nearly 20 years, from the early 1960s until the early 1990s, proponents of content area reading, and then *content area literacy*, recognizing the integrated roles of reading, writing, speaking and listening (McKenna & Robinson, 1990), churned out one teaching activity after another for fostering comprehension. The names of these activities are ubiquitous—semantic maps and graphic organizers, anticipation guides, three-level guides, journaling, I-searches, and the list goes on and on. A compendium of these activities is in its sixth edition (Tierney & Readance, 2004).

In the 1990s, the field turned its attention to adolescents. In an article documenting the shift, Lisa Patel Stevens argues for a reconceptualization of the field to include out of school literacies (Stevens, 2002). Critical of school-based approaches to comprehension, which, according to Stevens, focus on factual comprehension of texts, she promotes adolescent multiple literacies. This reframing poses a fundamental shift in views of comprehension to include the interaction of the learner, texts, contexts, and culture. In short, comprehension is no longer the oversimplified application of a teaching activity or task to a text, it is an ecological event characterized by the complexities of an "enactment of self" and the "interplay of multiple texts" (Moje Dillon, & O'Brien. 2000).

Despite these huge ideological and empirical swings—at one time for teaching activity and task and then toward a celebration of the adolescent—an important point is repeatedly ignored: comprehension, especially in the content areas, is about *learning* and, often, *doing* (Conley, 2007). Thorndike long ago recognized a very active and strategic role for readers and comprehension, including sorting and sifting, regarding some ideas as tentative and others as important, and organizing comprehension for some greater purpose, such as problem solving or communicating (Thorndike, 1917). Pressley and his colleagues have reinforced and elaborated this view with *comprehension strategies* as the engine that drives comprehension (Block, Gambrell, & Pressley, 2002; Pressley, 2000, 2006; Pressley & Hilden, 2006). Comprehension strategies are goal oriented processes that readers and writers use to construct meaning. What we know about comprehension strategies and comprehension comes mostly from studies of skilled reading (Pressley, 2006; Pressley & Afflerbach, 1995; Wyatt et al., 1993) and from studies of children who experience difficulties with reading (Cain & Oakhill, 2004). The message from this research is unequivocal: skilled readers know how to select and apply comprehension strategies where and when they need them to comprehend; struggling readers experience difficulties with comprehension because they know little about comprehension strategies or how to use them.

Research in content area literacy/adolescent literacy has rarely, if ever, addressed comprehension strategies, despite our growing understanding of their importance. Some critics of content area literacy have suggested that the research is overly restricted in its focus solely on teaching activities, tasks and text meanings, leaving the role of the reader out entirely (Moje et al., 2000). Adolescent literacy celebrates the uniqueness of adolescence combined with the potential of multiple literacies, yet leaves out any mention of comprehension strategies as a possible approach toward empowering adolescents (Conley, 2007). These omissions are important since both research perspectives—content area literacy and adolescent literacy—could benefit by considering the link between learning strategies and comprehension. For content area literacy, comprehension strategies provide a purpose for instruction—to teach students, for example, how to activate prior knowledge, summarize and question, and organize information for recall and/or writing. For adolescent literacy, comprehension strategies provide yet another form of literacy for constructing meaning within in-school and out-of-school contexts.

The purpose of this chapter is to explore comprehension strategies as a powerful foundation for adolescent comprehension in the content areas. Previous research on comprehension strategies has been limited by its focus on younger readers and writers with only very simple tasks, such as memory and recall (Pressley & Hilden, 2006). Much less is known about the potential for comprehension strategies that adolescents can employ to engage complex texts and tasks in the content areas. This chapter explores the potential for developing adolescents' understanding of comprehension strategies in the content areas.

THE FAILURE TO CONNECT TEACHING, LEARNING, AND ADOLESCENTS

Historically, content area reading was designed to "develop students' reading-to-learn strategies," including locating, comprehending, remembering, and retrieving information (Moore et al., 1983). A second stated purpose was to assist students in developing "reading-to-do" strategies, which include all of the tasks that accompany content area-specific work, such as "completing lab experiments, assembling mechanical devices and following recipes." The original notions of content area reading placed students at the center of instruction, with the goal of helping students develop understandings of reading strategies highly correlated with achievement in the content areas (Moore et al., 1983). Moore, Readance, and Rickelman's historical review pointed to methods textbooks devoted to content area reading as evidence of these views (Moore et al., 1983).

However, if we examine past or even current content area literacy textbooks, there is actually little, if any, evidence that content area literacy develops students' reading-to-learn strategies or that students are necessarily at the center of instruction. Table 25.1 represents a recent analysis of topics held in common among eight popular methods textbooks in content area literacy (Alvermann & Phelps, 2002; Brozo & Simpson, 2006; McKenna & Robinson, 2001; Readance, Bean, & Baldwin, 2001; Ruddell, 2007; Ryder & Graves, 1999; Unrau, 2003; Vacca & Vacca, 2004). To be sure, there are variations among the texts; some emphasize multiculturalism, English as a second language, technology, or No Child Left Behind policy more or less than others and in different ways. Table 25.1 represents the topics found most often among the texts.

As the table illustrates, these textbooks mostly depict instructional activities, often referred to as teaching or instructional strategies, such as graphic organizers, directed reading thinking activities, questioning (as instruction), K-W-L, Guided Reading Procedure, and text structure and other kinds of reading guides. While some activities reference comprehension strategies that students might use, such as summarizing or

Table 25.1

Chapter Topic

Chapter Topic	Subtopics within Chapters									
Introduction	classroom diversity, engagement	content literacy	teachers' roles	theoretical base	literacy strategies	social context	what it means to be literate	how students become at-risk, struggling readers	tracking, programmatic attempts at CAL	principles of Content Area Literacy
Students	struggling readers	students with disabilities, exceptional children	ESL/bilingual/ cultural diversity	Motivation and interest	social context	prior knowledge	reading process	what it means to be literate		
Texts	trade books	readability formulas	Internet	Selecting texts	readers theater	book clubs	literature in content area classes	readability checklists	friendly text scale, interestingness	Content Area Reading Inventory
		Fry	CLOZE	Raygor						
Unit and Lesson Planning	classroom organization	prereading	reader-text interactions	interweaving trade books	graphic organizer	accommodating individual differences	instructional models	grouping	assessing kids	Promoting independence
	standards based	collaborative culture	Directed reading activity, K-W-L, Explicit Teaching							
Vocabulary	List Group Label	semantic maps	graphic organizers	semantic feature analysis	categorization	context	decoding	dictionary	word association	word puzzles
	Vocabulary Self Collection	reinforcing vocabulary	context structure sound reference (CSSR)	word parts	PreP	Venn diagrams	time lines			

(continued)

Table 25.1 Continued

Chapter Topic	Subtopics within Chapters									
Comprehension	talking and discussion	questioning	PreP	prediction	anticipation guide	ReQuest	K-W-L	Guided Reading Procedure	Study Guides	Three-level guides
	text organization	Questioning the Author	Directed Reading Thinking Activity	graphic organizers	Options Guides	Integrating Other Language Processes	reaction guides	writing as reflection	learning logs	group mapping
	Predict Read Connect	reading response groups	Previews	summarizing	reciprocal teaching	problem solutions	point of view guides	teacher read-alouds	extending content knowledge	Text structure guides
	outlining	notetaking	teacher modeling	QARs						
Critical Thinking	IDEAL problem solving	Socratic questions	adjunct questions	knowledge as design	ReQuest					

Note: few books devote a single chapter to this topic.

Chapter Topic										
Writing	Writing Process	Exploratory Writing	Journal Writing	Essay Writing	Response Journals	Learning Logs	RAFT	Rubrics	composing and transcribing	quick writes
	possible sentences	guided writing	biography and auto-biography	I-search	responding to writing (teachers)	conferences	self and peer evaluation	responding to reading (students)	double entry journals	research
	websites	e-mail	mapping	using computers	summarizing	critical thinking	expressive writing	assigned writing	thesis support	
Studying	graphic organizers	summaries	text structure	semantic maps	problem solution outline	comparison contrast matrix	Venn Diagram	note taking	metacognition	test preparation
	essay writing	role of motivation	report writing	SQ3R	underlining	web quests	time management	studying from notes		

Note: few texts devote very much attention to this.

Chapter Topic

Subtopics within Chapters

Chapter Topic										
Discussion	collaborative learning	project based learning	cooperative groups	jigsaw	ReQuest	working in pairs	tutoring			
Assessment	high stakes observation oral retellings	standardized interviews group informal reading inventory	portfolio prior knowledge	readability prediction guide	text checklists grading	CLOZE standards	FLIP informal and authentic	purposes classroom assessment	CARI diagnostic decision making	naturalistic communication with parents
Technology	computers in the classroom	computer software	multimedia	Internet	locating and evaluating information					

Note: few of the texts deal with this. (Discussion)

Note: few texts devote a separate chapter to this. (Technology) questioning, the dominant representation within these textbooks is of teaching activities. Moreover, few methods texts deliberately connect teaching activities with the development of adolescents' comprehension strategies, particularly with different kinds of students (more vs. less able readers, for instance). Rather than making connections between teaching activities, learning strategies and different students, methods texts promote general teaching activities as serving the need only to develop knowledge in a content area. The texts do not demonstrate how teachers could use a graphic organizer or reading guide, for example, to help different students gain an understanding of how to activate prior knowledge or organize knowledge for later recall independently.

The research reviews for content area literacy and then adolescent literacy do not improve upon this picture, preferring to treat teaching activity and the development of comprehension strategies as distinct activities. Alvermann and Moore's (1991) review draws a distinction between "teaching strategies" which are content focused and teacher-initiated and "comprehension strategies" which are student directed and intended for building independence in reading and studying (Alvermann & Moore, 1991). Teaching strategies identified and reviewed include study guides, adjunct questions, graphic organizers, advance organizers, using text structure, and comprehending main ideas. Comprehension strategies include rehearsal (underlining, taking verbatim notes), elaborating (taking notes through paraphrasing), organizing (mapping) and comprehension monitoring (think-alouds, self-questioning). In Moore and Alvermann's review, teaching strategies and comprehension strategies are evaluated separately with regard to their efficacy with varying abilities of students and their comprehension. The review found that students who benefit the most from teaching strategies tend to be more able readers. An intriguing but untested hypothesis within this research is that more able readers are able to take greater advantage of teaching strategies compared with less able readers because more able readers already understand and know how to apply comprehension strategies. To the extent that teaching is recognized as a factor in developing comprehension strategies, Moore and Alvermann do acknowledge that comprehension strategies are best taught through direct instruction, explanation and modeling. Yet, none of the familiar content area reading teaching activities (maps, guides, etc.) is implicated for their effectiveness in promoting comprehension strategies. Again, as with Moore, Readance, and Rickelman's (1983) historical review, no connections are made between teachers' specific use of teaching strategies and students' development of comprehension strategies.

Bean's (2000) review reminds the field that students are at the center of literacy instruction, focusing on developing "reading and writing skill necessary to read, comprehend and react to appropriate instructional materials in a given subject area." Coming 17 years after Moore, Readance, and Rickelman's (1983) historical review, Bean reasserts that the students are central to the process of engaging with texts. Bean adds yet another twist by claiming that social contexts shape comprehension, including the content areas and out of school contexts. An implication of Bean's critique is that all of the previous work on teaching strategies and comprehension strategies needs to be reconsidered with regard to features of different social contexts, including the complexity of beliefs and practices within different disciplines and among teachers, variations in genre and task within and across content areas and differences in students' cultures, capabilities language, aspirations, and knowledge.

As expansive as this conceptualization is in comparison with previous research and reviews focusing on teaching activities and comprehension strategies, Bean's contextual perspective does not provide explicit connections between teaching and learning. While students are placed definitively at the center of socially constructed meaning making, Bean does not explain how learning could or should happen. As a result, just as much as the more cognitive-oriented views of the past do not connect teaching strategies and comprehension strategies, the social constructivist approach highlights adolescents' social milieu without providing insight about what teachers could or should do to help them (teaching strategies) or what students could or should do to help themselves (comprehension strategies). This ongoing omission—connecting teaching, learning, and adolescents—is responsible for severely limiting what the fields of content area literacy/adolescent literacy can recommend with regard to improving adolescent comprehension.

SEEKING BALANCE WITH THIRD SPACE

Moje et al.'s (2004) work with third space represents a groundbreaking attempt to return students to the center of comprehension, as envisioned by Bean, while connecting with the more cognitive point of view of strategies, promoted by Alvermann and Moore. One could argue that Moje's work finally delivers on Moore, Readance, and Rickelman's promise of placing adolescents at the center while teaching them how to comprehend.

Moje's notion of third space involves finding ways to build bridges between everyday knowledge and discourses (ways of reading, writing, and talking) and conventional academic knowledge and discourses. In comparison with earlier accounts, Moje acknowledges a much richer view of students' knowledge and discourse based on students' experiences with parents' work outside the home, work in the home, travel across countries, and engagement with environmental and health issues. Her assumption is that classroom teaching and learning often ignores the students' funds of knowledge and perspectives from home, peer groups and other networks of relationships.

Given the history of content area literacy and adolescent literacy research, it is relatively easy to see how students' knowledge, discourses and learning needs might be overlooked. If texts and text-driven teaching activities are the critical variables, dominating teachers' and their students' attention, as Alvermann and Moore claim, students' knowledge and literacies are often left out. If adolescents' multiple literacies are most important, the need for new literacy learning can be overlooked. Moje avoids both of these pitfalls by arguing that it is not enough just to celebrate what adolescents know and can currently do. They also need to become connected to conventional academic texts and discourses as a way of entry into disciplinary communities (such as mathematics and science) and the workplace.

But the story does not end here. It is not just about texts and tasks. Moje argues that teachers must find ways to help adolescents use their sometimes marginalized knowledge and ways of reading, writing and talking to engage themselves in conventional academic comprehension and learning. Moje documents how a science teacher teaching about the water quality fails to build on students' experiences with their families, including water pollution in the local community and community activism to address the problem. She also notes how students rarely volunteer what they know from home and family, because they do not see how the concepts under study are important to their lives, nor do they feel that the teacher will acknowledge what they know.

Adopting Moje's view means recognizing a much more complex picture of comprehension than depicted in the past research. In fact, it is not entirely clear what comprehension instruction might look like from a perspective balanced delicately between students' knowledge and literacies and academic texts and discourse. Moje offers several principles that might characterize comprehension instruction that bridges the home and the academic. For example, it is clear that teachers need to welcome different kinds of knowledge and discourses in the classroom. And comprehending academic texts and engaging in discourses about them requires knowing the structure, concepts, principles and discourses of a content area. What is less clear is how peer experiences, knowledge and discourses can be brought in alongside academic knowledge and discourses to develop students' capacity in the content areas. For instance, peer activities around music and popular culture equip students for critical analyses of texts. But how can teachers rally adolescents' critical discourses to critique classroom texts?

The view of teaching activities and strategies so prevalent in the research and reviews within content area literacy and adolescent literacy may not be adequate for the kind of bridging Moje describes. As Moje correctly notes, many teaching activities and comprehension strategies can be practiced in ways that are disconnected from the students or the disciplines in which they are used. There is often the assumption that infusing generic teaching and/or learning strategies into the disciplines is the key for developing content area or adolescent literacy. When the infusion doesn't "take" and teachers and students complain, the teachers are labeled "resistors" (Stewart & O'Brien, 1989). An alternative view might be that the teaching activities or comprehension strategies have not been carefully considered with regard to the disciplinary context—the structure, concepts and principles of the content area or the knowledge and discourses that students bring with them. In a complicated disciplinary context where, as Moje suggests, students have significant knowledge and discourses to apply yet fail to speak up about it, the teachers fail to invite and recognize students' knowledge, and the disciplines present their own unique challenges with respect to knowledge, genre and structure, the response from the field has been astonishingly simple, bordering on irrelevant. The prevailing wisdom has been to give teachers and students graphic organizers and comprehension guides. As Moje's research amply demonstrates, this prevailing wisdom is nowhere nearly enough and may even confuse an already complicated set of challenges for teachers and adolescents in the content areas.

DISCIPLINARY VIEWS OF COMPREHENSION STRATEGY INSTRUCTION

Yet another approach for adolescent comprehension is to consider disciplinary contexts—the content areas—and how learning strategies can be developed and applied appropriately. To a large extent, the content areas, including mathematics, science, social studies, and English, have been considered by content area literacy and adolescent literacy as monolithic. That is to say, the notion that there are multiple educational traditions, subdisciplines, multiple kinds of texts and tasks within subdisciplines, and multiple views of students and classroom discourse has rarely if ever been acknowledged. For instance, there is little recognition that mathematics consists of the subdisciplines of algebra, geometry, or trigonometry or that science consists of biology, chemistry, and physics. There is no acknowledgement that disciplines like English are comprised of different educational traditions or perspectives, often in tension with one another (Applebee, 1997). And there is little awareness that teaching social studies or history involves different assumptions about knowledge or pedagogy (Evans, 2006).

Treating the various disciplines as monolithic has made it easier for proponents of content area and adolescent literacy to promote generic comprehension strategies as a cure-all. As evidence, open up virtually any methods text for teachers and the same formats and templates for different comprehension activities are replicated from one content area to the next with little regard for the particular challenges of concepts, structure, genre or task within a content area or subdiscipline. In many teacher preparation courses, teachers are expected to make the necessary connections between content goals and teaching activities, often with very little guidance from a disciplinary point of view (Star, Strickland, & Hawkins, in press).

From the disciplinary side, there are numerous perspectives on what it means to learn. In the following sections, I review many of the predominant perspectives on learning within the disciplines of science, social studies, English and mathematics. This review is not meant to be exhaustive nor completely representative. Most, if not all of the perspectives on learning within the disciplines overlap as well as sometimes complement or conflict with one another. After each disciplinary review, I explore the implications of disciplinary, subtopic, and philosophical perspectives within each of the disciplines for comprehension strategies and strategy instruction. A key question for this review is: Given the multifaceted nature of disciplinary views of learning, what could our understanding of comprehension strategies have to offer?

DISCIPLINARY PERSPECTIVES ON SCIENCE LEARNING

There are several common goals in science teaching and learning (Anderson, 2007). These include including helping students develop *social agency*, defined as skills and discourses that will enable them to access science related jobs, and *agency in the material world*, defined as successful interaction (observing, measuring, predicting, explaining) with the world in ways that lead to responsible stewardship and action. Many researchers in science education also agree that most institutions of formal education do not help students learn science with understanding and that there is a persistent achievement gap in science learning that separates students by race, ethnicity, and social class (Lee & Luykx, 2007).

Beyond these common goals and beliefs, there are at least three distinct traditions within science teaching and learning (Anderson, 2007). Conceptual change research is the most prevalent of the research traditions. The conceptual change tradition characterizes learning problems as stemming from interactions between students' existing knowledge and scientific concepts. In some versions of this perspective, problems emerge from conflicts between what students have observed and come to know about the natural world and scientific discourse and understandings.

One recent study that illustrates conceptual change research is Scherz and Oren's (2006) intervention to change middle school students' images of science and technology (Scherz & Oren, 2006). The researchers are concerned about ways in which students' preconceptions and stereotypes of scientists and scientific work inhibit their choices about science careers. This problem is not helped and it is even exacerbated by the fact that school science takes place in classrooms far removed from the actual work of scientists in laboratories. The research intervention involves placing students in the role of journalists who explore a scientific subject that interests them. Students read up on background material on the subject and then go out into the field in laboratories or factories to observe and interview. Next, students process, analyze and communicate the information they have gathered to other students. As a result of this intervention, the researchers found that students changed their preconceptions and stereotypes of science in the workplace to reflect more informed conceptions. Moreover, students reported greater awareness for the different types of science oriented occupations available to them, as a result of their experiences in the study.

The sociocultural tradition is a second perspective within science education (Anderson, 2007). Whereas conceptual change researchers focus on developing understandings of scientific knowledge and practices, sociocultural researchers are interested in the culture and language of scientific communities. Put another way, conceptual change researchers investigate interactions with concepts about nature, while sociocultural researchers emphasize interactions among people about science. Sociocultural researchers confront the problem of conflicts among discourses, such as students' ways of knowing, doing, talking, reading, and writing scientific discourses. On the one hand, based on their experiences in their family and in the community, students can enter study of a topic already familiar with some of the discourses that communities of scientists employ to interact with nature. Challenging assumptions around issues of pollution is one example of the discourse students acquire through experiences in their community (Moje et al., 2004). On the other hand, students can enter a topic with little, if any, experience with the values, social norms and ways of using language used by scientific communities. How to acknowledge and transform students' discourses into scientists' language and practices, thus providing students agency in both the social and material worlds of science, is the learning problem undertaken by sociocultural science researchers.

A recent example from the sociocultural tradition involves an investigation of authoritative and dialogic discourse for making meaning in high school science lessons (Scott, Mortimer, & Aguiar, 2006). Within a unit on heat, cold and temperature, the researchers explore the tension between authoritarian discourse, in which teachers focus on the school science point of view, and dialogic discourse, in which students make sense of what the teacher is saying and interact with one another to entertain different points of view. The researchers document the complex interplay of authoritarian discourse, which is important for socializing students into scientific discourse, and dialogic discourse, which is important for students to practice and internalize the tools of scientific discourse. The researchers argue that a purposeful shifting from authoritative to dialogic discourse is necessary in order to introduce scientific discourse, problematize the content, uncover students' knowledge and discourses, and guide students' engagement.

A third tradition within science teaching and learning concerns critical research (Anderson, 2007). Critical researchers in science education assume that there is far too much emphasis placed on establishing and maintaining control over students, including their knowledge and discourse development. They emphasize that science knowledge and discourse are privileged and the product of dominant classes. Students who are not among the privileged—the economically disadvantaged, for example—are often marginalized. That many urban-based schools lack even the most basic materials or consistent curricula is evidence for this view (Ruby, 2006), though the exercise of power and privilege combined with the marginalization of others appears in many other forms as well.

A recent example of critical research in science education is Kenneth Tobin's study about teaching chemistry to migrant 10th graders (Tobin, 2005). Tobin notes that science, like other curricular areas, is guilty of engaging in social reproduction, producing "haves" and "have-nots" with regard to achievement. He indicts the existing social system in which teachers and students work as well as a lack of responsiveness to culture as reasons for the achievement gap in science education. Tobin's remedy for these problems involves teachers creating social capital and productive social networks with students. One teacher in Tobin's study became successful because she established a routine of meeting and informally interacting with students at the door, usually about family and social interests, guided students and encouraged them to participate, and engaged in informal conversations as she monitored their progress. The teacher continually demonstrated hope for her students and worked toward their success. Rather than focusing on a purely university-oriented view of science education, Tobin's teacher concentrated on helping her students develop a cultural toolkit containing "science facts and concepts, the ability to read and make sense of science-related texts, and a capacity to use science to make sense of experiences in critical events in the world" (p. 588). Tobin concludes that only by adopting these practices—inviting participation, engaging in responsive instruction and enjoyment of learning—issues of control are replaced by a focus on science learning and expanding possibilities in science for all students and not just a few.

COMPREHENSION STRATEGIES IN SCIENCE

Literacy researchers have sometimes acknowledged variations in perspective about science teaching and learning, differences are noted more often among teachers than within the discipline itself (Jetton & Anderson, 1997). The differences documented here between conceptual change, sociocultural and critical research pose the question: What are comprehension strategies that might be usefully applied from within each of these perspectives? What follows is an attempt to answer this question.

From a conceptual change point of view, comprehension centers on interactions between existing knowledge and new scientific knowledge. From a literacy perspective, this places a priority on at least four comprehension strategies: activating prior knowledge, predicting, questioning and summarizing. The conceptual change research concentrates on ways teachers, specialized curriculum materials and tasks can scaffold changes from naive conceptions to scientific understanding. There has been relatively little exploration in and outside the discipline about the benefit of empowering students for conceptual change through the use of comprehension strategies. Future research might productively explore the added value but also the added challenges of conceptual change that is not only teacher-directed but also supported by students' use of comprehension strategies. An important emphasis within this work must be finding ways for students to connect their use of these learning strategies with effective conceptual change as opposed to just encouraging students to lead themselves further into misconception.

From a sociocultural view of teaching and learning science, helping students connect their existing discourses with the discourses of the scientific community is important. Literacy researchers have only begun to understand the complexity of discourse within disciplinary contexts such as science. Moje's (2004) study is a good example of looking at discourse from a literacy perspective where it becomes clear that students' discourses from home and community are both essential and often ignored (Moje et al., 2004). The implication here is that comprehension strategies in science need to be considered with regard to discipline-specific conceptual goals, the discourse resources of students and the desired scientific discourses, in order to be successful. While it has been popular to recommend generic discussion activities for comprehension in content areas for a very long time (Alvermann, 1987), the sociocultural perspective in science illustrates that generic approaches run the risk of ignoring conceptual goals while failing to capitalize on and transform students' discourse into scientific discourse and understanding.

From a critical research point of view within science, acknowledging students' cultural capital, encouraging participation, and responsiveness to students are all important. And so, comprehension needs to be considered with regard to building rapport with students, inviting what they know and have experienced, and guiding them toward a greater potential for understanding and interacting with the material world. This perspective is grounded more in dispositions needed for effective comprehension than in concept or pedagogy. While literacy researchers have engaged themselves in critical research around comprehension, most often this research is concerned with identity formation or generic discussion practices, sometimes to the exclusion of disciplinary learning (Sutherland, 2005). As the critical research in science education traditions suggests, however, acknowledging students' identity and providing them with tools for understanding science can be the keys to empowering students in the classroom and beyond. As Pressley has noted, building motivation and positive dispositions toward learning are the best ways for creating conditions for learning strategy instruction (Pressley, 2006). The critical research view in science could provide a rich context for literacy researchers to connect adolescent identity and critical discourse with comprehension in the particular context of science teaching and learning.

DISCIPLINARY PERSPECTIVES ON LEARNING IN SOCIAL STUDIES

Disciplinary perspectives in social studies and history are as diverse as they are in science and have equally diverse implications for comprehension instruction. Evans (2006) documents the multiple traditions within social studies education as well as the swings in emphasis over the past century. There are the traditional historians who see the purpose of social studies as the acquisition of content knowledge about history, including mastery of chronologies and textbook-based learning (Leming, Ellington, & Porter, 2003). There are the social scientists who see social studies as teaching the social science disciplines, including sociology, economics, education, geography, and the law. Social efficiency educators focus on the world of tomorrow with an emphasis on business and industry. There are the social meliorists who seek to develop students' thinking about how to improve society. And finally, there are the social reconstructivists who teach students to critique the status quo and create a more just society.

More recently, there have been calls to bring all of these perspectives together to create more shared understandings (Wineburg, Stearns, & Seixas, 2007). However, these efforts have opened up even more complexity among these multiple perspectives with regard to teaching and learning. Rather than reducing this complexity and thereby selling short the potential of teaching and learning social studies, social studies educators are attempting to build productively on the tensions among the perspectives. So, for example, social studies educators embrace the insights from more student-centered perspectives that adolescents' experiences, ideas and understandings matter when it comes to historical thinking, while, at the same time, considering the thinking processes of working historians as well.

VanSledright (2004) compares the historical thinking of novices with the thinking of historians. The result is the identification of learning strategies unique to historical thinking. VanSledright proposes that one of the jobs of social studies education should be to close the gap between adolescent novices and expert historians. Doing this involves teaching novices the learning strategies practiced by historians. VanSledright focuses his efforts on the source work of historians as a form of critical literacy. Sources—documents, maps, historical accounts—all represent remnants of the past selected and organized from someone's perspective. Historians create their understanding of history based on sources and their own questions. Four strategies useful in learning from sources include: identification, or figuring out what a source is in the context of type, appearance, and timeframe; attribution, or recognizing that a source is constructed by a particular author for particular purposes in particular times and contexts; judging perspective, or judging an author's social, cultural, and political position; and judging reliability, or comparing one account with other accounts from a historical period.

COMPREHENSION STRATEGIES IN SOCIAL STUDIES

In the rare cases where comprehension in considered in the context of social studies, the approach is almost universally from the outside-in. Put another way, literacy researchers create their own assumptions about the kinds of comprehension that should be taught and learned and then examine social studies classrooms, teacher and student interactions and textbooks to determine whether desirable comprehension practices are occurring. In some cases, this approach leads to conclusions that little or no comprehension instruction is happening (Armbruster & Gudbrandsen, 1986). In other cases, a model for comprehension instruction is posited accompanied by claims that the model can be used "across the social studies genres—textbooks, primary sources, fictional texts or a combination" (Massey & Heafner, 2004). In either case, the multifaceted nature of social studies as a discipline and as a context for learning is overlooked.

And so, what are comprehension strategies from a social studies perspective? Answering this question requires acknowledging the multiple perspectives within social studies. If social studies is treated as a cognitive act of acquiring more knowledge, then the most important learning strategies might involve forming connections among various kinds of knowledge. If social studies is multidisciplinary, then there are probably different learning strategies appropriate to learning in sociology, economics, education, geography, and the law. As the social studies research suggests, each subdiscipline reflects different kinds of challenges and opportunities for learning. If social studies is about building worlds of tomorrow, then prediction might be most important for comprehension. If social studies is about improving or uprooting society, then comprehension strategies that represent a more critical edge, such as questioning, might be more effective.

The more compelling view, however, may be that, as social studies educators themselves have discovered, all of these views are collectively important. This translates into the challenging notion for literacy researchers that social studies represents a considerably more complex world for comprehension, in which comprehension strategies are *not* generalizable across all texts, tasks, and contexts. Selling generalized strategies in social studies poses two problems, (1) forcing social studies teachers to make their own specific instructional adaptations appropriate to already complicated contexts and (2) raising the possibility that retrofitting comprehension strategies to the discipline might neglect or gloss over some very important disciplinary dimensions. Contrary to the long-held assumption that teachers' abandonment of comprehension strategies implies their resistance (Stewart & O'Brien, 1989), for social studies teachers, it could just mean that they are confronting the complexity of the discipline while realizing that over-generalized approaches to comprehension in the social studies just won't work.

A possible way to proceed to connect literacy and social studies would be for literacy researchers to carefully examine the implications of multiple views of social studies and multiple views of historical thinking as a starting point for considering comprehension strategies. This means abandoning the assumption that comprehension is the same across all texts and contexts but also wading into the messy world of social studies teaching and learning.

DISCIPLINARY PERSPECTIVES ON LEARNING IN ENGLISH

There has been an ongoing tension in English education between those who want English to be about acquiring knowledge versus those who consider English education as acquiring ways of knowing. Put simply, the tension is between advocates of content and advocates of process (Applebee, 1997). There is a third position which attempts to balance concerns for content and concerns for process by considering significant content in the context of engaging activity both from a teaching and a learning perspective (Applebee, 1996).

Some of the most ardent proponents of content acquisition come from outside English education, such as E. D. Hirsh. Hirsch contends that there is a definite body of literacy knowledge that underlies what it means to be educated in American culture and society (Hirsch, 2006). There are also proponents of content acquisition from inside the profession when it comes to cognitive views of writing instruction, with research-based claims about what adolescents need to know and know how to do to write well (Graham & Perin, 2007; Hillocks, 2005). At the other end of the spectrum are those who question the cannon—privileged knowledge about literature and writing—in favor of, respectively, world literature (Power, 2003; Reese, 2002), literature reflecting diversity in human condition and experience (Blackburn, 2003; Goebel, 2004; Ressler, 2005), or literature produced for and by adolescents (Morrell, 2004; Schwarz, 2006).

The process perspective on English education offers up equally diverse points of view. There are those who advocate for English as a pathway toward more effective communication (Berger, 2005); those who see English as a way to promote active citizenship, democracy, and social justice (Mantle-Bromley & Foster, 2005); those who view English as a transaction between native language and culture and second language and culture (Cruz, 2004; Gutierrez & Orellana, 2006); and there are those who see English as the nexus for engaging in new literacies (Street, 2005). Attempts to balance content and process are evidenced by approaches which connect, for example, various kinds of literature with process goals (Whiten, 2005).

English education, like the other disciplines, also represents sociocultural and discourse perspectives. From the sociocultural side, there are studies of gender identity (Fairbanks & Ariail, 2006) and racial and cultural identity combined with concerns about marginalization in school and the need to acknowledge the intellectual and social capital that adolescents bring to the learning of English (Trainor, 2005). Starting out with concerns about literary interpretation, the discourse perspective explores tensions and conflicts among classroom participants as they struggle to shape understandings of literature and writing (Nystrand, 2006; Smagorinsky et al., 1994). Bridging the cognitive and the sociocultural, the discourse research has reported positive gains in achievement in discussion based classrooms with desirable features, including open exchange among students, authentic, open-ended questions, and follow-up questions (Applebee et al., 2003).

COMPREHENSION STRATEGIES IN ENGLISH

The diversity of theory, research and praxis within English education defies the application of any one or even a set of comprehension strategies. However, the content acquisition perspective might benefit from a focus on any one of a number of comprehension strategies, such as those identified by Deshler and his colleagues for students with learning disabilities (Bulgren, 2006; Bulgren & Scanlon, 1998; Deshler et al., 2001). Content enhancement and concept comparison strategies have been validated with students with learning disabilities and among students in inclusive classrooms in a range of content area disciplines. There are also proven strategies for improving adolescents' knowledge and performance with writing (Graham, 2006; Troia & Graham, 2002).

Comprehension strategies to enhance the various process perspectives within English are more difficult to identify, in part, because there can be little agreement about what it means for adolescents to learn how to "do" English differently or more effectively. Comprehension strategies that engage adolescents in asking and answering their own questions could prove useful when the mission is to encourage tools for democratic action and social justice. Activating prior knowledge might be important for helping adolescents connect their language and culture to understandings of new languages and cultures. The generic ways in which these comprehension strategies have been researched and promoted limits their utility without substantial extrapolation and adaptation to specific contexts and needs.

Identity, gender, social capital, power, and marginalization issues raised from a sociocultural perspective are not so easily addressed with a focus on comprehension strategies. The issues here are about who is asking the questions and for what purposes. Comprehension strategies within the sociocultural mix become very quickly enmeshed in concerns for who is teaching the students how to comprehend and for what agenda(s). The ultimate, desirable goal, from this point of view might be that all adolescents learn comprehension strategies in ways that help them in their quest for identity, aiding them in resisting marginalization, while promoting their assets among peers and adults.

The discourse perspective is already accompanied by a set of strategies, including question asking, following up on responses, and engaging in conversation. Research on comprehension strategies adds a concern that adolescents require specific kinds of explanation, modeling and feedback to productively engage in these strategies for discourse and comprehension (Pressley & Hilden, 2006).

DISCIPLINARY PERSPECTIVES ON LEARNING IN MATHEMATICS

Mathematics bears some resemblance to science in that there are cognitive perspectives, sociocultural perspectives, and critical discourse perspectives. All three perspectives in mathematics share a concern for students' ideas, experiences and interests, yet all three perspectives portray a different view of the nature and role of what student bring to mathematics learning.

From a cognitive point of view, the concern is for the types of mathematical knowledge children understand before and throughout their years of schooling (Siegler, 2003). Many children come to school already knowledgeable about numbers and mathematical concepts and principles. But many other children fail to understand concepts and principles that are basic to understanding more abstract ideas, and many confront problems when they are unable to make important connections among mathematical concepts. Even more problematic are ways in which children can generate flawed conceptions or mathematical procedures that can be very difficult to correct or unlearn. For instance, in a study of proportional reasoning, adolescents are provided with basic details of the amount of paint required to paint an irregular figure, a representation of Santa Claus. Next, they were asked to estimate the amount of paint required to paint the irregular figure, only now it is three times the size of an original figure. Most adolescents guessed the proportional answer, that it required three times the amount of paint, when, in reality, the answer is non-proportional, requiring just twice the amount of paint. In addition, students who engaged in the inappropriate reasoning indicated substantial certainty about the correctness of their answers.

The problems tackled within a sociocultural perspective on mathematics include creating classroom contexts for students to develop multiple mathematical literacies and connect mathematics to their developing identity (Cobb, 2004). This perspective is fueled in part by the realization that while many adolescents can be succeeding in mathematics, they choose not to continue their study because of conflicts between who they want to become and the expectations within the mathematics classroom. In one version of this work, adolescents were asked to make judgments about mathematical problems taken from in-school and out-of-school contexts (Jurdak, 2006). Adolescents addressed problems situated in school contexts by using in school mathematical tools, rules and norms while adolescents applied social and personal rules to problems situated in out-of-school contexts. This raises a dilemma about how to relate adolescents' problem solving models that are developed and applied in school to real world mathematical problems. Given the modern curriculum demands for more cognitively oriented mathematical achievement, the solution to this dilemma may not be as easy as inserting more real world mathematical problems into the curriculum. On the other hand, ignoring real world problems runs the risk of promoting a disconnect between in-school mathematics and adolescent identity and aspirations.

A third perspective within mathematics education concerns discourse. Like the concerns in science and literacy over discourse, this perspective focuses on engaging adolescents' existing discourses with mathematical discourses (Sfard, 2001). Sfard and others argue that discourse is the key to adolescent thinking, particularly with regard to building and using models of mathematical concepts and principles. Like the socioculturalists in mathematics, the discourse perspective advances the notion that the separation between school mathematics and real world mathematics is problematic. Where they differ is in the focus on context, as with the sociocultural view, versus communicative discourse, from the discourse view. And so the problem from the discourse perspective in mathematics concerns how to develop mathematical understandings and discourse through language. Sfard carefully documents adolescents' use of language to develop increasingly complex ways of thinking about mathematics, first with respect to labels and then on to abstract representations. It is often more comfortable for adolescents to use their everyday language to resolve conflicts. However, their use of everyday language can also become a pathway toward incomplete or flawed understandings.

COMPREHENSION STRATEGIES IN MATHEMATICS

In a recent review of content area literacy from a mathematics perspective, Star and his colleagues warn about the danger of literacy instruction in mathematics being devoid of mathematics learning (Star et al., in press). Star notes that many of the content area literacy textbooks prescribe activities for reading the mathematics textbook, something that "reflects a very limited understanding of mathematics texts as a unique genre." Mathematics texts are often referred to as containing worked examples with sentences sprinkled in. Mathematics educators all have something different to say about the problems posed by mathematics texts from a cognitive, sociocultural, or discourse perspective. However, it has never been clear how the teaching activities within content area or adolescent literacy would be in any way helpful with the problems in mathematical learning identified from within each of these perspectives. This leads us back to the question: What are comprehension strategies that might potentially be productive in mathematics?

Some mathematics education researchers go so far as to argue that comprehension is not a problem in mathematics learning (Mayer, 2004). Word problems, for example, require specific learning strategies, including translating, or converting individual sentences into internal mental representations; integrating, or building a model (selecting important information, making interpretations) of the problem situation represented by the problem; solution planning or monitoring, or devising a step by step plan for solving a word problem; and solution execution, or carrying out a plan for solving the problem. Many students are able to translate and integrate word problems, in effect, comprehending the problems. Yet, many students are unable to plan or carry out solutions to the problems either because they have little experience with the mathematics concepts or the word problems, or they haven't yet learned productive strategies for planning and executing solutions.

From a literacy point of view, two comprehension strategies would appear to be helpful with these mathematics strategies, summarizing and predicting. It might be productive for adolescents to ask periodically: What do I know now? What will happen if I try this solution? The history of content area literacy or adolescent literacy has not considered ways to relate comprehension strategies to the unique demands of mathematical problem solving. So, we know very little about what would happen by marrying concerns for mathematical learning with what we know about comprehension. On the other hand, the potential exists for finding a way to promote content area learning in mathematics and literacy together, rather than trading off one goal (disciplinary knowledge) for another (literacy).

The same kinds of concerns surround literacy and sociocultural and discourse perspectives in mathematics. While the content literacy/adolescent literacy perspectives promote the importance of context, multiple literacies and discourse, the research has neglected the particular challenges of mathematics contexts and discourses. The literacy research recognizes that activating prior knowledge is generally important, but says little, if anything, about the role of prior knowledge in mathematical model building, making connections between in school and out of school mathematics, or using discourse to build mathematical understandings and confront misconceptions.

IMPLICATIONS FOR RESEARCH AND PRACTICE

As this review demonstrates, content area literacy and adolescent literacy started out with good intentions - to place adolescents at the center of instruction and to build their capacity to study and learn in the content areas. However, as this review also demonstrates, the original mission very quickly went awry by generating compendia after cornucopia of general teaching activities, most of which are connected to gaining knowledge and only a very few of which have anything to do with comprehension strategy learning. The shift to adolescent literacy engaged the literacy profession in exploration and celebration of adolescence, but did little to address the problem of the ongoing disconnect between adolescents, literacy learning and the disciplines. Moje's research is the notable departure from tradition, at once bringing together insights about adolescents, multiple literacies and discourses in a content area context (Moje et al., 2004). Still, her work leaves us with many questions for how the literacy profession can deliberately proceed to strengthen our understanding of these connections.

Important clues for how adolescents might develop comprehension strategies productive in the content areas can be found in the diverse perspectives coming from within the content area disciplines. The history within content area literacy and adolescent literacy of offering up generic teaching activities for monolithic views of the disciplines has hindered our view of what might be possible. As this chapter illustrates, there are a number of potential connections but only if literacy researchers recognize the multifaceted nature of the content areas, including the subtopics and perspectives on learning.

When it comes to content area literacy and adolescent literacy, the research traditions are very familiar—do the comprehension research and then apply it to content area practice. This prevailing paradigm supports the flawed practice of researching comprehension and then infusing the findings into the content areas without considering what makes learning in content area contexts both diverse and often challenging. To understand comprehension strategies and how they might work in the content areas, researchers need to reverse this pattern and do what Herber called for many years ago—study disciplinary practice and research comprehension within disciplinary contexts (Herber & Nelson-Herber, 1981). Literacy researchers need to go from practice into research, rather than fitting isolated and decontexualized comprehension research into disciplinary practice, if we are ever to understand comprehension strategies in the disciplines.

For practice, this discussion raises a whole set of new possibilities for considering the contribution of comprehension strategies for learning in the content areas. The content areas pose many learning problems that literacy researchers have never envisioned or explored. Nuances of scientific understanding, purposes for and pitfalls in learning various science and mathematics concepts, issues of bias and point of view in source materials in social studies, and the multiple and sometimes conflicting goals of literature learning and writing instruction in English present a complex but fertile landscape for better understanding comprehension strategy instruction and learning.

In some cases, the existing milieu of teaching activities within content area literacy and adolescent literacy might be usefully applied in these contexts. In some cases, research and practice will need to be more inventive, developing new forms of comprehension teaching and learning. We need to consider the potential of any practice for teaching comprehension strategies at all. The all-too-typical pattern of rehearsing adolescents through questioning, summarization and predicting activities offers the illusion of comprehension instruction but does not build an understanding of comprehension strategies. Teaching comprehension strategies requires explanation, modeling, feedback and practice (Pressley, 2006). The future for improving adolescent comprehension requires a much better understanding for how teachers can help adolescents and adolescent can help themselves understand and apply comprehension strategies to learn successfully in the content areas.

REFERENCES

Alvermann, D. (1987). *Using discussion to promote reading comprehension.* Newark, DE: International Reading Association.

Alvermann, D., & Moore, D. (1991). Secondary school reading. In R. Barr, M. Kamil, P. Mosenthal, & P. D. Pearson (Eds.), *Handbook of reading research, Vol. II* (pp. 951–983). New York: Longman.

Alvermann, D., & Phelps, S. (2002). *Content reading and literacy: Succeeding in today's diverse classrooms* (3rd ed.). Boston: Allyn and Bacon.

Anderson, C. (2007). Perspectives on science learning. In S. Abell & N. Lederman (Eds.), *Handbook of research on science education* (pp. 3–30). Mahwah, NJ: Erlbaum.

Applebee, A. (1996). *Curriculum as conversation.* Chicago: University of Chicago Press.

Applebee, A. (1997). Rethinking curriculum in the English language arts. *English Journal, 86*(5), 25–31.

Applebee, A., Langer, J., Nystrand, M., & Gamoran, A. (2003). Discussion-based approaches to developing understanding: Classroom instruction and student performance in middle and high school. *American Educational Research Journal, 40,* 685–730.

Armbruster, B., & Gudbrandsen, B. (1986). Reading comprehension instruction in the social studies. *Reading Research Quarterly, 36*(1), 36–48.

Bean, T. (2000). Reading in the content areas: Social constructivist dimensions. In M. Kamil, P. Mosenthal, P. D. Pearson, & R. Barr (Eds.), *Handbook of reading research, Vol. III* (pp. 629–644). New York: Longman.

Berger, J. (2005). Transforming writers through grammar study. *English Journal, 95*(5), 53–60.

Blackburn, M. (2003). Exploring literacy performances and power dynamics at the loft: Queer youth reading the world and the word. *Research in the Teaching of English, 37*(4), 467–490.

Block, C., Gambrell, L., & Pressley, M. (2002). *Improving comprehension instruction: Rethinking research, theory and classroom practice.* San Francisco: Jossey-Bass.

Brozo, W., & Simpson, M. (2006). *Content literacy for today's adolescents.* New York: Prentice Hall.

Bulgren, J. (2006). Integrated content enhancement routines: Responding to the needs of adolescents with disabilities in rigorous inclusive secondary content classes. *Teaching Exceptional Children, 38*(6), 54–58.

Bulgren, J., & Scanlon, D. (1998). Instructional routines and learning strategies that promote understanding of content area concepts. *Journal of Adolescent and Adult Literacy, 41*(4), 292–302.

Cain, K., & Oakhill, J. (2004). Reading comprehension difficulties. In T. Nunes & P. Bryant (Eds.), *Handbook of children's literacy* (pp. 313–338). Dordrecht, the Netherlands: Kluwer Academic.

Cobb, P. (2004). Mathematics, literacies and identity. *Reading Research Quarterly, 39*(3), 333–337.

Conley, M. (2007). Reconsidering adolescent literacy: From competing agendas to shared commitment. In M. Pressley (Ed.), *Research we have, research we need.* New York: Guilford.

Cruz, M. (2004). Can English language learners acquire academic English? *English Journal, 93*(4), 14–19.

Deshler, D., Schumaker, B., Lenz, K., Bulgren, J., Hock, M., Knight, J., et al. (2001). Ensuring content-area learning by secondary students with learning disabilities. *Learning Disabilities Research and Practice, 16*(2), 96–108.

Evans, R. (2006). The social studies wars: Now and then. *Social Education, 70*(5), 317–322.

Fairbanks, C., & Ariail, M. (2006). The role of social and cultural resources in literacy: Three contrasting cases. *Research in the Teaching of English, 40*(3), 310–354.

Goebel, B. (2004). *An ethical approach to teaching Native American literature.* Urbana, IL: National Council of Teachers of English.

Graham, S. (2006). Strategy instruction and the teaching of writing. In C. MacArthur, S. Graham, & J. Fitzgerald (Eds.), *Handbook of writing research* (pp. 187–207). New York: Guilford.

Graham, S., & Perin, D. (2007). *Writing next: Effective strategies to improve writing of adolescents in middle and high schools.* Washington, DC: Alliance for Excellent Education.

Gutierrez, K., & Orellana, M. (2006). The 'problem' of english learners: Constructing genres of difference. *Research in the Teaching of English, 40*(4), 502–507.

Herber, H., & Nelson-Herber, J. (1981). *Practice into research: The other half of the formula.* Paper presented at the Second Annual Conference on Reading Research, New Orleans.

Hillocks, G. (2005). The focus of form vs. Content in teaching writing. *Research in the Teaching of English, 40*(2), 238–248.

Hirsch, E. D. (2006). *The knowledge deficit.* New York: Houghton Mifflin.

Jetton, T., & Anderson, P. (1997). Instructional importance: What teachers value and what students learn. *Reading Research Quarterly, 32*(3), 290–308.

Jurdak, M. (2006). Contrasting perspectives and performance of high school students on problem solving in real world, situated and school contexts. *Educational Studies in Mathematics, 63*(3), 238–301.

Lee, O., & Luykx, A. (2007). Science education and student diversity: Race/ethnicity, language, culture, and socioeconomic status. In S. Abell & N. Lederman (Eds.), *Handbook of research on science education.* Mahwah, NJ: Erlbaum.

Leming, J., Ellington, L., & Porter, K. (2003). *Where did social studies go wrong?* Washington, DC: Fordham Foundation.

Mantle-Bromley, C., & Foster, A. (2005). Educating for democracy: The vital role of the language arts teacher. *English Journal, 94*(5), 70–75.

Massey, D., & Heafner, T. (2004). Promoting reading comprehension in social studies. *Journal of Adolescent and Adult Literacy, 48*(1), 26–41.

Mayer, R. (2004). Teaching of subject matter. *Annual Review of Psychology, 55,* 715–744.

McKenna, M., & Robinson, R. (1990). Content literacy: A definition and implications. *Journal of Adolescent and Adult Literacy, 34*(3), 184–186.

McKenna, M., & Robinson, R. (2001). *Teaching through text: Reading and writing in the content areas.* New York: Allyn and Bacon.

Moje, E., Ciechanowski, K., Kramer, K., Ellis, L., Carrillo, R., & Collazo, T. (2004). Working toward third space in content area literacy: An examination of everyday funds of knowledge. *Reading Research Quarterly, 39*(1), 38–70.

Moje, E., Dillon, D., & O'Brien, D. (2000). Reexamining roles of learner, text, and context in secondary literacy. *The Journal of Educational Research, 93*(3), 165–180.

Moore, D., Readance, J., & Rickelman, R. (1983). An historical exploration of content area reading instruction. *Reading Research Quarterly, 18*(4), 419–438.

Morrell, E. (2004). *Linking literacy and popular culture.* Norwood, MA: Christopher Gordon.

Nystrand, M. (2006). Classroom discourse and reading comprehension. *Research in the Teaching of English, 40*(4), 392–412.

Power, C. (2003). Challenging the pluralism of our past: Presentism and the selective tradition in historical fiction written for young people. *Research in the Teaching of English, 37*(4), 425–466.

Pressley, M. (2000). What should comprehension instruction be the instruction of? In M. Kamil, P. Mosenthal, P. Pearson, & R. Barr (Eds.), *Handbook of reading research* (Vol. III, pp. 545–561). Mahwah, NJ: Erlbaum.

Pressley, M. (2006). *Reading instruction that works: The case for balanced teaching.* New York: Guilford.

Pressley, M., & Afflerbach, P. (1995). *Verbal protocols of reading: The nature of constructively responsive reading.* Hillsdale, NJ: Erlbaum.

Pressley, M., & Hilden, K. (2006). Cognitive strategies: Production deficiencies and successful strategy instruction everywhere. In D. Kuhn & R. Siegler (Eds.), *Handbook of child psychology* (Vol. 2). Hoboken, NJ: Wiley.

Readance, J., Bean, T., & Baldwin, S. (2001). *Content area literacy: An integrated approach.* Dubuque, IA: Kendall/Hunt.

Reese, J. (2002). Learning for understanding: The role of world literature. *English Journal, 91*(5), 63–69.

Ressler, P. (2005). Challenging normative sexual and gender identity beliefs through Romeo and Juliet. *English Journal, 95*(1), 52–58.

Ruby, A. (2006). Improving science achievement at high-poverty urban middle schools. *Science, 90*(6), 1005–1027.

Ruddell, M. (2007). *Teaching content area reading and writing.* New York: Wiley.

Ryder, R., & Graves, M. (1999). *Reading and learning in content areas.* New York: Wiley.

Scherz, Z., & Oren, M. (2006). How to change students' images of science and technology. *Science, 90*(6), 965–985.

Schwarz, G. (2006). Expanding literacies through graphic novels. *English Journal, 95*(6), 58–65.

Scott, P., Mortimer, E., & Aguiar, O. (2006). The tension between authoritative and dialogic discourse: A fundamental characteristic of meaning making interactions in high school science lessons. *Science, 90*(4), 605–631.

Sfard, A. (2001). Learning mathematics as developing a discourse. In R. Speiser & W. Maher (Eds.), *Proceedings of the 21st conference of PME-NA.* Columbus, Ohio: Clearinghouse for Science, Mathematics and Environmental Education.

Siegler, R. (2003). Implications of cognitive science research for mathematics education. In J. Kilpatrick, W. Martin, & D. Schifter (Eds.), *A research companion to principles and standards for school mathematics* (pp. 219–233). Reston, VA: National Council of Teachers of Mathematics.

Smagorinsky, P., Smith, M., & Marshall, J. (1994). *The language of interpretation: Patterns of discourse in discussions of literature.* Urbana, IL: National Council of Teachers of English.

Star, J., Strickland, S., & Hawkins, A. (in press). What is mathematical literacy? Exploring the relationship between literacy and content learning in middle and high school mathematics. In M. Conley, J. Freidhoff, M. Sherry, & S. Tuckey (Eds.), *Adolescent literacy policy and instruction: The research we have and the research we need.* New York: Guilford.

Stevens, L. (2002). Making the road by walking: The transition from content area literacy to adolescent literacy. *Reading Research and Instruction, 41*(3), 267–278.

Stewart, R., & O'Brien, D. (1989). Resistance to content area reading: A focus on preservice teachers. *Journal of Reading, 32*(5), 396–401.

Street, B. (2005). Recent applications to new literacy studies in educational contexts. *Research in the Teaching of English, 39*(4), 417–423.

Sutherland, L. (2005). Black adolescent girls' use of literacy practices to negotiate boundaries of ascribed identity. *Journal of Literacy Research, 37*(3), 365–406.

Thorndike, E. (1917). Reading as reasoning. *Journal of Educational Psychology, 8*(6), 323–330.

Tierney, R., & Readance, J. (2004). *Reading strategies and practices: A compendium.* New York: Allyn and Bacon.

Tobin, K. (2005). Building enacted science on the capital of learners. *Science, 89*(4), 577–594.

Trainor, J. (2005). 'My ancestors didn't own slaves': Understanding white talk about race. *Research in the Teaching of English, 40*(2), 140–167.

Troia, G., & Graham, S. (2002). The effectiveness of a highly explicit, teacher-directed strategy instruction routine: Changing the writing performance of students with learning disabilities. *Journal of Learning Disabilities, 35*(4), 290–305.

Unrau, N. (2003). *Content area reading and writing: Fostering literacies in middle and high school cultures.* New York: Prentice Hall.

Vacca, R., & Vacca, J. (2004). *Content area reading: Literacy and learning across the curriculum.* New York: Allyn and Bacon.

VanSledright, B. (2004). What does it mean to think historically and how do you teach it? *Social Education, 68*, 220–233.

Whiten, P. (2005). The interplay of text, talk and visual representation in expanding literary conversation. *Research in the Teaching of English, 39*(4), 365–397.

Wineburg, S., Stearns, P., & Seixas, P. (2007). *Knowing, teaching and learning history.* New York: New York University Press.

Wyatt, D., Pressley, M., El-Dinary, P., Stein, S., Evans, P., & Brown, R. (1993). Comprehension strategies, worth and credibility monitoring and evaluations: Cold and hot cognition when experts read professional articles that are important to them. *Learning and Individual Differences, 5*, 49–72.

26 Comprehension Difficulties among Struggling Readers

Richard L. Allington and Anne McGill-Franzen

University of Tennessee

The chapters in this volume illustrate the complexity of comprehension processes. They also illustrate how much is currently known about how understanding develops as readers read. At the same time, various chapter authors have acknowledged two things. First, while we know a lot, much remains to be learned about comprehension, particularly higher-order understandings. Second, while we can reasonably well describe what good comprehenders do and do not do before, during, and after reading, there are large numbers of children and adolescents who do not routinely do these things when they read. These readers, poor comprehenders, are the focus of this chapter.

We begin this chapter with a review of the evidence on the incidence of comprehension difficulties. Our emphasis is on studies that explore comprehension difficulties that arise even when adequate decoding skills are observed. The next section explores the nature of the reading instruction provided struggling readers both in general education classrooms and in remedial and special education settings. We consider the evidence in this area because it seems to us that only rarely has the field considered that reading instruction may be an important contributor to the proficiencies and inadequacies displayed by struggling readers.

The third, and final, section provides a summary of the research on interventions designed to ameliorate comprehension difficulties. We felt a review of extant analyses was an appropriate approach to summarizing the evidence thus far on interventions if only because of the large number of studies in this area that have been published.

HOW COMMON ARE COMPREHENSION DIFFICULTIES IN THE ABSENCE OF DECODING DIFFICULTIES?

Landmark studies and reviews

There is little research on the comprehension proficiencies of children in the initial stages of reading acquisition. In most cases, research on comprehension difficulties includes children in grades 3 or 4 or above. This is a significant limitation in the research. There are any number of questions to be answered concerning whether factors such as limited receptive vocabulary (e.g., Hart & Risley, 1995; White, Graves, & Slater, 1990), restricted world knowledge (e.g., Nation, 2005), basic memory processes (Vellutino, 2003), or instructional method (e.g., Dahl & Freppon, 1995; McIntyre & Freppon, 1994) influence the development of reading comprehension proficiencies.

Younger readers   Nation (2005) provides a comprehensive review of the psychological research on elementary school children with reading comprehension difficulties.

She notes that both decoding skill and linguistic proficiency are necessary but that neither are sufficient for reading comprehension to occur. Her review summarizes the research on the question: Are there children who are proficient decoders but poor comprehenders? Poor decoders but proficient comprehenders?

The answer is affirmative in both cases. As is demonstrated in Figure 26.1, from the Nation article, it seems more common to find good decoders who have comprehension difficulties (lower right quadrant) than it is to locate poor decoders who are good comprehenders (upper left quadrant). The data displayed in Figure 26.1 suggest the limited relationship of pseudo-word decoding and reading comprehension, something others have also reported (Carlisle, Schilling, Scott, & Zeng, 2004; Cunningham et al, 1999; Pressley, Hilden, & Shanklin, 2006; Walmsley, 1979). As these various studies suggest, poor decoders/good comprehenders do exist.

In a similar vein, Buly and Valencia (2002) assessed various reading proficiencies of 108 fourth-graders from 17 elementary schools who had failed to achieve the benchmark performance of the state reading assessment. They administered a battery of assessments including the Woodock-Johnson, Qualitative Reading Inventory-II, and the Peabody Picture Vocabulary Test. These data were analyzed using cluster analysis. Nearly 20% of the struggling fourth-graders they tested were accurate word callers but had comprehension problems and about 20% had problems with decoding but exhibited fewer problems with comprehension. Other clusters represented students who were slow, steady readers who comprehended well, deliberate decoders who were able to maintain comprehension and a small cluster (9%) that represented students with very poor performances on decoding and every other skills assessment.

Leach, Scarborough, and Rescorda (2003) studied the reading proficiencies of 66 fourth and fifth grade struggling readers, contrasting their skills development with that of 95 students who exhibited no reading difficulties. Each of the students was assessed on multiple measures to identify reading comprehension and decoding/word recognition proficiencies. The assessments included the comprehension component of the Peabody Individual Achievement Test-R, Woodcock-Johnson word reading and word attack sub-tests, the Lindamood Auditory Conceptualization Test, and assessments of

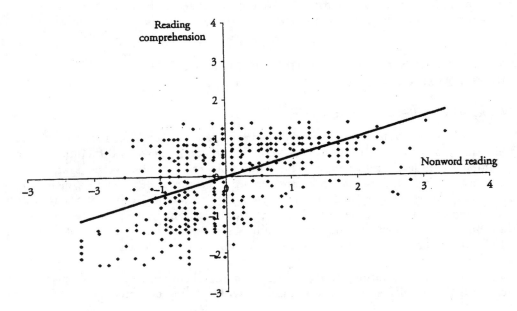

Figure 26.1 Scatterplot of the z-score relationship between non-word reading and reading comprehension for 7 to 10 year-old students.

sight word and nonsense syllable spelling, word and non-word reading automaticity and rapid automized naming measures.

Using a standard score of 90 as cutoff for adequate performance on all measures, 12 of the 66 struggling readers exhibited poor decoding/word reading but adequate comprehension, 28 demonstrated adequate decoding/word reading skills but failed to meet comprehension standard, and 26 failed to achieve the cutoff score on measures of either comprehension or decoding/word reading. In other words, roughly 42% of the struggling fourth- and fifth-grade readers in this sample had no difficulty with either word reading or non-word pronunciation.

Leach et al. (2003) report that an analysis of school records for students in this study indicated 40% of students had late-emerging reading disabilities—reading difficulties that appear after an initially successful start. They report that those students whose reading disability appeared later were better on all word and phonological measures but weaker on comprehension than students whose reading disability had appeared early. What was perhaps most troubling was that 10 of the 12 students exhibiting reading comprehension problems only had not been identified by their schools as experiencing reading difficulties.

While the Leach et al. (2003) study provides useful insights, the comprehension assessment (PIAT-R sentence reading task) limits our confidence in their incidence estimates. Had comprehension been assessed after reading more complex texts, such as those found in any upper-elementary classroom, it is possible that more students exhibiting comprehension difficulties would have been identified. Likewise, assessing higher-order comprehension—summarization, analysis, or synthesis tasks—might have tabbed more of the achieving readers as students exhibiting reading comprehension difficulties.

Nevertheless, we concur with their conclusion that:

> Reading disabilities in children beyond the primary grades appear to be heterogeneous with regard to the nature of their reading skill deficits...some children have comprehension problems only, some have just word-level difficulties, and some exhibit across the board weaknesses... Hence both assessment and instruction must be aligned with this reality. Most important, intervention programs need then to be selected on the basis of children's deficit type(s) rather than overall grade level. (Leach et al., 2003, p. 222)

Using a sample of 1,111 fourth-grade children from one Canadian school district, Rupp and Lesaux (2006) examined the relationship between performance on a provincial standards-based reading comprehension assessment and performance on a diagnostic assessment of reading comprehension (Stanford Diagnostic Reading Test) and several component skills measures (e.g., words correct per minute, Wide Range Achievement Test-3, word identification and word attack subtests on the Woodcock Reading Mastery Tests, one minute pseudo-word reading, WRAT-3 Spelling, Rosner Auditory Analysis Test, pseudo-word spelling, working memory for words).

Rupp and Lesaux found that scores on component measures did not reliably predict reader classifications on the standards-based assessment. While the proficient readers on the standards-based test performed well on all component skills, in the "below expectations" classification student performance was highly variable on component skills. They found that 40% of the students were high performers on both clusters (Word-level skills and Working-memory/Language Skills), 30% of students meeting expectations were low achievers on both clusters, and 30% were mixed achievers (high on one but not the other).

Rupp and Lesaux (2006) concurred with Leach and colleagues (2003):

The results further indicate that there is an important subgroup of children within the 'below expectations' group that has reading difficulties that are not primarily related to component skills of reading. This is a group for whom an intervention that targets foundational word-level and related cognitive and related linguistic skills would not be appropriate, yet these skills are often the target of remedial instruction in fourth grade. (p. 330)

Summary   Thus at least three groups of poor readers emerge: those with poor decoding skills, poor comprehension skills, or poor skills in both areas. However, we suspect the mix is more complicated than this. Too little comprehension-focused research, especially with developing readers, is available to adequately portray the heterogeneity (Rupp & Lesaux, 2006) within proficiency profiles of struggling readers. What is clear though, is that by fourth grade struggling readers exhibit a heterogeneity of development in component reading skills. Thus, the assumption that a single intervention will likely address the needs of all struggling readers is unsupported by the research.

Adolescent readers   Brasseur and Hock (2006) describe the reading development of 137 adolescent struggling readers from seven urban school systems. The typical student was entering ninth grade (CA = 14.9) and eligible for free or reduced-price meals (70%). The sample included 52%t African American, 29% Caucasian, and 15% Hispanic students. Each student was administered a series of standardized reading assessments and mean standard scores are reported on each. Roughly two of three (63%) struggling adolescent readers performed at low levels on each of the multiple measures. At the same time, these struggling readers scored significantly higher on measures of decoding and word reading than on fluency, vocabulary, or comprehension and scored significantly lower on all measures than readers judged proficient on the state reading assessment.

Brasseur and Hock (2006) do not report any further analyses of these data but one might reasonably expect, it seems, that a variety of patterns of proficiencies would be observed were these data analyzed using cluster or factor analysis techniques. However, the key finding was that these adolescent struggling readers had decoding proficiencies that were better developed than their reading comprehension proficiencies, further supporting the idea that struggling readers are not a homogeneous group, needing a single decoding intervention.

Adult readers   Fink (2006) reports on 66 high-achieving, high-education individuals who struggled with reading (sample included 6 MDs, 17 PhDs, 4 JDs, 19 Master's, 15 Bachelor's degree holders). One-third still had phonological/decoding problems, many were slow readers, all had begun to read later than typical, usually around age 10–11. Interest drove their reading. She reports that all of these adults had failed to respond to a variety of interventions, often interventions that had been validated in research with other struggling readers. All reported having difficulties developing decoding skills and in developing adequate reading skills at least until grade 3. The majority of subjects developed fluency in oral reading between ages 10 to 12 and became avid readers between ages 10 to 13. But over half needed extended time on standardized tests to achieve optimum scores.

Two thirds of these individuals never mastered spelling, and one third of them did not master spelling or other phonological decoding skills. Yet, they all became skilled readers—scoring at the highest levels in silent reading comprehension and vocabulary... (Fink, 2006, p. 137)

Further, Fink argues that deep knowledge on particular topics provided a scaffolding that allowed these readers to read with comprehension. Fink concludes that the design of interventions for such children has too often ignored both interest and the development of content knowledge, both critical factors in the success of her subjects. Additionally, an overemphasis on phonological skills and oral reading of words or passages would likely fail to show the strengths that these subjects exhibited on tests of silent reading comprehension.

Summary The evidence is quite clear that students can develop adequate decoding skills but lag in comprehension development. We agree with Duke, Pressley, and Hilden (2004) who note that the research suggests that 10–30% of poor readers have adequate decoding skills but impaired comprehension with the percentage of such cases increasing from the primary to the upper elementary grades.

Although there seems to be a larger group of students who lag in the development of both decoding and comprehension proficiencies, it is not clear that focusing on developing the decoding skills will necessarily result in these students then demonstrating effective text comprehension (Swanson, Hoskyn, & Lee, 1999). For some proportion of these delayed decoders it may be that resolving the decoding problems will lead to improved comprehension. But we fully expect that there will be others, perhaps many others, who develop effective decoding skills and still lag in comprehension development.

In fact, as Torgeson, Wagner, and Rashotte (1997) have noted, "We still do not have convincing evidence that the relative differences in growth on phonetic reading skills produced by certain instructional approaches led to corresponding advantages in orthographic reading skills and reading comprehension for children with phonologically-based reading disabilities" (p. 230).

The Nature of Instruction Offered Struggling Readers: Landmark Studies and Reviews

There is longstanding evidence that students who participated in remedial and special education interventions rarely exhibited accelerated growth in reading achievement (e.g., Carter, 1984; Kavale, 1988), particularly growth on assessments that primarily measured proficiency in reading comprehension. In other words, most struggling readers have not overcome the difficulties they experienced with reading as a result of participating in the typical remedial reading or special education intervention provided in American schools. Because the federal government provides substantial funds for remedial and special education, this failure, it could be argued, fueled the call for the program accountability reflected in the No Child Left Behind Act of 2001.

There have been few large-scale studies of the impact of special education services on the reading achievement of pupils with disabilities (Kavale, 1988). Instead, we have to rely on smaller scale impact studies but there have been few of even these. However, one good example is a recent study (Bentum & Aaron, 2003) that presented a post hoc longitudinal analysis of reading achievement of 394 students identified as pupils with learning disabilities and served in 27 special education resource rooms located in six school districts.

The researchers interviewed the teachers of these students to gather contextual data on the resource room reading instruction. The data on reading achievement were gathered for two cohorts (3 and 6 years of special education services) of students based on length of time they had received resource room services. Student achievement was measured on the Wide Range Achievement Test and the Wechsler Individual Achievement Test. The authors used standard scores from each test in exploring reading achievement gains across the two extended service periods.

Bentum and Aaron (2003) report no significant change in the status of word reading or reading comprehension proficiencies for either the 3 year or 6 year cohort. They found no significant difference in achievement growth of students who spent 5, 10, or 15 hours per week in resource room settings. They found no significant difference in achievement of students taught by teachers who emphasized a phonics approach and those whose teachers offered more eclectic intervention models. Thus the researchers concluded, "elementary students with LD, who are instructed in resource rooms, fail to make significant gains in the areas of word recognition [or] reading comprehension..." (Bentum & Aaron, p. 379). This finding of limited gains in reading for students receiving special education services echoes the findings of earlier studies (e.g., Kavale, 1988; Vaughn, Moody, & Schumm, 1998).

The research on the effects of remedial reading interventions is, unfortunately, similar. For instance, Carter (1984) analyzed national Title I remedial reading program data and concluded that there was little evidence that participation in remedial reading programs had any longer-term positive impact on reading achievement. An almost identical conclusion was reached two decades later by Borman and D'Agostino (2001) in their analysis of federally funded remedial reading programs. They also noted that any observed effects fade after 3 to 4 years so that any impact of early school interventions is typically unobservable by middle school. But they also argue that given the sporadic and typically limited support given struggling readers across the elementary grades it isn't surprising effects seem to fade over time.

So, why have typical school-based remedial and special education interventions failed to accelerate the development of reading proficiencies? It seems obvious to us that the notion that all children can achieve reading proficiency has little support in the trenches. Instead, children who struggle are too often seen as damaged or different in ways that obviate ever attaining normal levels of achievement. Instead of seeing powerful instruction matched to learners with different developmental needs as a way to interrupt the predicted outcomes, the field has generally blamed the children but not critically examined the nature of the instruction As McGill-Franzen (1994) noted: "When children fail to demonstrate requisite skills, it is usually the children, not the schools that are deemed at fault" (p. 21).

Available studies of the nature of instruction provided in remedial and special education interventions suggest that neither independent reading nor personalized comprehension instruction are typically the focus of these intervention programs. Based on the interviews they conducted, Bentum and Aaron (2003) reported that the majority of the LD teachers they studied reported that linking letters and sounds and decoding words were the major goals of their instruction. In other words, neither developing comprehension nor fostering independence were typically the focus of the interventions these LD teachers provided.

Vaughn, Moody, and Schumm (1998) observed instruction in special education resource rooms and found little tutoring or small group instruction, with groups of 8 to 9 students common. Most instruction was whole group with everyone reading the same book with little attention paid to the match between the books assigned and student reading levels, with students then working individually on seatwork with the teacher moving about providing assistance. There was much emphasis on decoding lessons but these lessons relied primarily on independent worksheet completion. While fewer comprehension lessons were observed, they primarily involved asking students to respond to literal questions after reading. The explicit teaching of comprehension strategies was largely absent from these resource room lessons. These findings are similar to those reported earlier researchers studying special education reading instruction (Morsink, Soar, Soar, & Thomas, 1986; Thurlow et al. 1983; Ysseldyke, Thurlow, Mecklenburg, & Graden, 1984; Zigmond, Vallecorsa, & Leinhardt, 1980).

In a unique study contrasting remedial and special education students reading instruction, Allington and McGill-Franzen (1989) reported on an observational study of 64 students from eight schools in six school districts. The districts represented rural, suburban and urban settings. Half of the subjects were identified as pupils with disabilities and half were receiving remedial reading funded by the federal Title 1 program. Equal numbers of students in each categorical program were observed for one full school day. The student observation instrument offered structured coding categories describing the instructional environment within a time recording system. The key contrast examined was the reading lessons that students from the two groups participated in, both classroom and pullout reading program participation.

One key finding was that pupils with disabilities received significantly less reading/language arts instruction than did remedial reading students (95 minutes per day vs. 110 minutes). Additionally, pupils with disabilities received less active teaching and more undifferentiated seatwork activity than remedial reading students, both in the classroom and resource room. In fact, the remedial student received roughly twice as much active teaching during their reading lessons. The authors concluded that the label a student is assigned does, in fact, make a difference in both the quantity and quality of reading instruction they receive.

McGill-Franzen and Allington (1990) reported on a qualitative study of 16 second-grade students, from three schools in two school districts. Each of the students was served in a supplemental reading program, half of the students were identified as having a reading disability and half as having a learning disability. The data gathered included a full-day observation of school experiences including observation of both classroom and supplemental reading lessons and interviews with classroom and specialists teachers and task analyses of the work these students were assigned during the day.

The findings indicated that an emphasis in decoding accuracy was the primary focus of both classroom and remedial and special education reading lessons. In addition, the supplemental reading instruction (delivered in either remedial reading classes or special education resource rooms) was typically not differentiated in ways that better met the needs of participating students than the classroom instruction. Instead, specialized reading instruction in both settings was "routinized" with individual specialist teachers electing to deliver reading instruction that was largely different from that offered in the classroom but with little attention to student needs or level of development and little attention to comprehension.

Shanklin (1990) reported similar results in her qualitative study of four remedial reading teachers. She describes the supplemental reading instruction offered 32 upper elementary grades struggling readers. The lessons did include a comprehension component but the activities described seem more appropriately viewed as assessment rather than instruction (e.g., teacher asks students questions after reading). In addition, the range of comprehension activities was quite restricted with a primary emphasis on asking students whether misread words "made sense" and asking them to retell the story that had been read. Little, if any, instruction in key comprehension strategies was reported.

While there is little evidence that most intervention programs have focused on fostering comprehension proficiencies there are two large-scale correlational research studies that suggest doing so might well alter the futures of the struggling readers these programs serve.

For instance, in their analyses of national Title I remedial program outcomes, Puma et al. (1997) found that the remedial teachers who placed a greater emphasis on comprehension and higher-order thinking skills were the teachers who produced higher student academic achievement. Puma and his colleagues (1997) concluded, "Instructional practices and content emphasis may also distinguish high-performing high-poverty schools. Schools where teachers adopted a balanced view of remedial skills and higher-order thinking had high-performing disadvantaged students. Rather than viewing instruction in basic skills as a prerequisite for higher-order and more challenging materials, teachers in these schools appeared to generally challenge their students with cognitively demanding material" (p.63). Unfortunately, as these researchers noted, there were few of the high-poverty schools in their national sample where this more balanced approach characterized the classroom and remedial instruction.

Nonetheless, their findings of a relationship between meaning-emphasis instruction and achievement echoes of an earlier study of the differences in the effectiveness of skills-emphasis and meaning-emphasis reading instruction in high-poverty schools. Knapp (1995) directed a 2-year study of 140 classrooms in 15 schools in 3 states. Classrooms were selected as representing skills- or meaning-emphasis reading and language arts instruction. His teams observed in classrooms and gathered teacher instructional logs. Achievement data were collected from a group standardized achievement test and an individually administered achievement test. These assessments provided measures of both reading comprehension and word identification. In addition, the author collected and evaluated writing samples from the children in these schools.

Differences in the observed classrooms were often large, particularly on lesson features related to comprehension gains. Discussion, for instance, was observed on 12% of the days (about once every 2 weeks) in skills-emphasis classrooms as compared to 66% of days in meaning-emphasis classrooms. Likewise, extended opportunities to read, especially silent reading activity, were far more common in the meaning-emphasis schools. On the other hand, low-level skills work, often in the form of workbook pages or skills sheets were far more common in the skills-emphasis classrooms.

In a comparison of the achievement outcomes from skills-emphasis and meaning emphasis classrooms Knapp reported that meaning emphasis instruction produced 5.6 NCE higher standardized achievement tests scores, which was statistically significant. In addition, writing was also significantly better in the meaning-emphasis classrooms. The observed gains in the meaning-emphasis classrooms for lower-achieving students were as large or larger than gains for higher-achieving students. The analyses controlled for both poverty and achievement differences. Knapp (1995) concluded, "Meaning-oriented practices do not impede the mastery of discrete skills and may facilitate it" (p. 136).

Summary   Thus, one longstanding concern remains, the availability and quality of comprehension focused reading instruction, in both the general education and the remedial and special education classrooms. While we have had research demonstrating the limited quantity and quality of such instruction for 20+ years, the most recent reports suggest that little has changed: Struggling readers remain unlikely to participate in many lessons that would improve their comprehension.

Reviews of Comprehension Interventions for Struggling Readers: Landmark Reviews of the Research

While the research indicates little emphasis on comprehension instruction in supplemental reading programs, there exists a trove of research investigating interventions to improve the reading comprehension of struggling readers. This is, perhaps, one good example of the failure of the research to practice progression that seems largely assumed though rarely achieved. These studies include both pupils identified as reading disabled and those struggling readers identified as learning disabled. We do not differentiate between these two populations if only because the only clear difference between these populations of struggling readers seems to the degree of lag in reading development (Jenkins, Pious, & Peterson, 1988; Ysseldyke, Algozzine, Shinn, & McGue, 1982). We begin this section with fluency interventions because dysfluency has been linked to poor comprehension. A summary of the reviews of research on comprehension interventions follows and we close this section with comments on what intervention issues remain largely unexplored.

Fluency The relationship between fluency and comprehension is not well understood (Schwanenflugel, Hamilton, Kuhn, Wisenbaker, & Stahl, 2004). Nevertheless, because the NRP identified fluency as one of the five primary components of scientific reading instruction, fluency and fluency interventions have garnered much attention in the past 5 years. We write "fluency," but there does seem to be confusion in the field currently about what that word means (Mathson, Solic, & Allington, 2006). In some cases, fluency is largely operationally defined as reading rate or a combination of rate and word reading accuracy. The proliferating use of the Dynamic Indicators of Basic Early Literacy Skills (DIBELS) in many schools is one indication of this confusion. While an increasing number of schools are measuring "fluency" with DIBELS, Kuhn and Stahl (2003) note that "There seems to be a consensus regarding the primary components of fluency: (a) accuracy in decoding, (b) automaticity in word recognition, (c) the appropriate use of prosodic features such as stress, pitch, and appropriate text phrasing" (p. 5). DIBELS produces proficiency estimates for the first two features but provides no evaluation of the final features of fluency. It may be this omission that has resulted in questions about whether DIBELS performances are much related to reading comprehension development or deficiencies.

Pressley, Hilden, and Shanklin (2006) studied the relationship between DIBELS proficiencies and comprehension and found that DIBELS explained only 20% of the variance in comprehension achievement as assessed on standardized assessments. Pressley (2006) notes that while the authors of the DIBELS reported a higher correlation between DIBELS performance on comprehension, even their studies indicate that the DIBELS assessment leaves much variance to be explained (these differences in the scope of the relationship between decoding and comprehension may result from the decisions on how comprehension is assessed (see Francis, Fletcher, Catts, & Tomblin, 2005 for a review). Pressley et al (2006) also found that the DIBELS comprehension measure produced scores that rarely reflected either recall or understanding of passage content. This suggests that DIBELS fails to meet the dual criteria proposed by Samuels (2006), "To be considered a fluent reader, the person should be able to decode and comprehend at the same time" (p. 340). In any event, Pressley (2006) concluded, "So, if you are interested in knowing about reading speed with low comprehension and memory of text, DIBELS is a great measure!"

Paris, Carpenter, Paris, and Hamilton (2005) provide an original critique of the research on the relationship between fluent oral reading and text comprehension and the limits of currents assessments of fluency. They note that any measure of reading fluency may simply be a proxy measure for other aspects of reading development (e.g., vocabulary, world knowledge, standard English language proficiency, motivation).

> This makes oral reading fluency a positive predictor of reading difficulties, but it does not mean that fluency is the cause of the difficulty. When causal status is erroneously inferred from a predictive relation, remedial intervention may be prescribed for the predictor variable. This reasoning is unscientific and inaccurate, but is evident in programs such as DIBELS that make oral reading fluency an instructional priority. (p. 139)

The authors note that while most studies find a positive statistical correlation between measures of fluency and comprehension, in many cases those correlations are largely spurious. This is because oral reading rate and accuracy are, by and large, constrained skills. That is, in most studies of fluency and comprehension, subjects read text at an accuracy rate between 90% and 100% and reading rate between 25 and 125 words per minute. This restricted variation creates ceiling effects that "threaten the validity of parametric statistics such as Pearson correlations" (p. 137). That is, neither accuracy nor rate scores are normally distributed.

Therefore, if reading accuracy is very low (e.g., 20%–50%), comprehension is unlikely simply because so much of the text was not accurately read and comparisons, in such cases, between accuracy and comprehension would "always reveal the obvious and spurious positive correlations" (p. 137). They note that such nonindependence among variables such as word recognition and comprehension "confounds and inflates the positive relation, and may invalidate correlational analyses" (p. 137).

In many studies of the relationship between fluency and comprehension, the positive correlations reported derive primarily from the outlier subjects, particularly the poorer readers because there is so little variance among the better readers, those with word reading accuracy above the 90% level. The substantial variance in accuracy for students with 0%–90% word reading accuracy produces positive correlations because performances on both word recognition and accuracy are low. Because of this, the available research, Paris et al. (2005) argue, may lead to "spurious interpretations of the correlations between the constructs [fluency and comprehension]" (p. 139).

Nonetheless, fluency is a hot topic in reading instruction currently, though seemingly a topic that is not well understood by either practitioners or researchers. Kuhn and Stahl (2003) note that successful emerging readers rather quickly acquire the ability to read with expression. That is, they read with appropriate phrasing and intonation. Once this is achieved "it is easier [for a young reader] to construct meaning from a text than when he or she struggles with word identification" (p. 3). In fact, they argue that the evidence suggests that when a reader is able to parse text into syntactically appropriate phrases it "signifies that the reader has an understanding of what is being read" (p. 6). In this, they agree with Schreiber (1980) who first outlined how fluency and comprehension might be linked.

We would note, however, that most students acquire the ability to read fluently with little, if any, explicit instruction focused on parsing sentences into phrases, assigning intonation values, and so on. However, some children experience difficulty developing as fluent, expressive readers (Allington, 2006, 2009). The NRP attempted to address this issue by examining classroom instructional activities that fostered fluency and, hopefully, comprehension. But as Kuhn and Stahl point out the NRP included a variety of instructional procedures (e.g., shared reading, repeated reading, and guided reading) that "were so wide ranging that one can draw only the broadest conclusions about the effectiveness of fluency-oriented instruction from their meta-analysis" (p. 6).

As for the NRP analysis of the repeated reading procedure as an intervention for struggling readers, Kuhn and Stahl (2003) indicate that it is not clear whether the improvements in fluency and comprehension the NRP found for repeated reading interventions can be solely attributed to the repeated reading activity. This is because few repeated reading intervention studies controlled for reading volume and in those cases where the control groups read comparable volume the advantages of repeated reading activities were minimized or eliminated.

Kuhn et al. (2007) report on a study designed to address at least some of the limitations in the research on the repeated reading procedure. They compared Fluency Oriented Reading Instruction (FORI) with a wide reading treatment (WR) and no treatment control in multiple second-grade classrooms in two states. The primary differences in the two treatment conditions were the weeklong repeated reading of a single text in FORI and the reading and rereading of multiple texts across each week in the WR classrooms. However, compared to the control classrooms both FORI and WR expanded students' opportunities to read connected text for comparable periods of time, between 20 to 40 minutes daily.

Both the FORI and the WR treatments produced significantly better achievement on all measures, including sight word reading, text reading rate, and passage comprehension, compared to the no treatment control condition. Nonetheless, the authors conclude: "The current study confirms that, not only did the Wide Reading approach do as well as the FORI approach, it was actually more effective for the participating students in two areas; first, improvements were seen sooner and, second, improvements were seen in connected text reading" (p. 27).

Thus, it seems that increasing the amount of actual reading practice, whether through repeated reading or wide reading, has the potential to improve reading comprehension of struggling readers. Given the evidence that these are the very children who typically read less both during planned instruction and voluntarily (e.g., Allington, 1983; Anderson, Wilson, & Fielding, 1988; Hiebert, 1983), enhancing reading volume seems to be a useful strategy for enhancing comprehension.

Summary The current focus on fluency has been set primarily as a factor involved in improving reading comprehension. In fact, virtually every argument made for focusing on fluency infers, at least, that reading in phrases with expression is necessary for comprehension (or an indication of comprehension).

Is there a link between fluency, as historically defined, and comprehension? We think the evidence suggests there is. Does training to improve fluency reliably result in improved comprehension? On this issue the research is less clear. We suppose the reason for this depends on several factors. The first is what sort of "training" is being offered. We have good evidence that training children to read words faster does not enhance comprehension and may not even enhance fluency (Dahl & Samuels, 1977). But studies using repeated reading methods have sometimes demonstrated general comprehension improvements. But then, so do studies that expand the volume of reading. The second factor is how both fluency and comprehension have been operationally defined by the researchers. The evidence indicates that students can achieve gains in speed of reading while not necessarily demonstrating improved comprehension. So, the precise role of fluent reading, that is, reading in phrases with expression and comprehension, still is not well understood. As Paris et al. (2005) noted,

> many people assert that a) fluency is correlated with good comprehension and therefore, b) children should develop fast, accurate, fluent reading in order to understand [the texts they read]. Both premise and implication are wrong. The data actually show that low fluency is correlated with low comprehension, a relation that is obvious and necessary, but it is certainly not causally true for high fluency and high comprehension. (p. 139)

Comprehension intervention research There are many summaries of the research on comprehension interventions available in the literature. If one wanted to summarize, generally, what each of these reviews concludes, one could use the short summary offered by Duke, Pressley, and Hilden (2004):

> One of the most certain conclusions from the literature on comprehension strategies instruction is that long-term teaching of a small repertoire of strategies, beginning with teacher explanation and modeling with gradual release of responsibility to the student is very effective in promoting students' reading comprehension. This conclusion holds true for students with learning disabilities as well... (p. 512)

But there are other conclusions that are also useful in considering what we know about effective comprehension instruction for struggling readers. For instance, Hiebert and Taylor (2000) described key features of grades 1 and 2 reading interventions. The majority of these interventions provided 1–1 or very small group intervention lessons (1–3), included writing activities, texts of appropriate difficulty, 30-minute periods, several were year-long, others one semester. Most of the interventions used tradebooks or leveled books, focused on fostering fluency, often through repeated readings, comprehension activities were common but seemed to have been mostly post-reading retellings, summarizing, discussion. In addition, word study/decoding was also common with word family or word categorization most common focus. Gains in comprehension were typically reported along with gains in other reading proficiencies. Thus, while these early interventions were not focused simply on improving reading comprehension, improvement in comprehension was a common outcome.

Other scholars have focused their attention on interventions designed specifically to advance the development of reading comprehension skills among populations of struggling readers. For instance, Gersten, Fuchs, Williams, and Baker (2001) reviewed interventions targeting the improvement of comprehension among pupils with learning disabilities. They concluded, "Use of story grammar elements to improve comprehension of narrative texts should be considered best practice for students with learning disabilities" (p. 296). They reported that modeling, demonstration, guided application are necessary facets based upon the comprehension interventions they reviewed. But they also found that little of the intervention research included longer-term evidence that pupils with learning disabilities ever gain autonomous control over strategy use. Most of the intervention studies were conducted over very limited periods of time with no measure of transfer or finding no transfer effects. All in all, they concluded that the evidence indicates that students with learning disabilities can learn comprehension strategies and use them to improve short-term comprehension outcomes but little evidence for longer-term independent use.

Mastropieri, Scruggs, Bakken, and Whedon (1996) reported that questioning students after reading or training students in the use of questioning strategies yielded a large overall effect size. The key features in all of these studies include teaching students to stop and question themselves before, during, or upon completion of reading to promote understanding of the printed material. They concluded that the "Strongest outcomes were observed for teacher-led questioning and self-questioning strategies, followed by text enhancement strategies, and finally, strategies involving basic skills instruction and reinforcement" (p. 197).

In a related review, Mastropieri and Scruggs (1997) summarize the comprehension intervention research by noting that teachers can improve the reading comprehension of pupils identified as learning disabled when they directly teach comprehension strategies that have been identified as effective in fostering comprehension development, provide modeling, guided instruction and practice, along with opportunities to practice strategy use in a variety of types of texts, and when they monitor student development and adjust instruction to students needs.

Oakhill and Yuill (1996) review the research in three areas: inference making, understanding text structure, and comprehension monitoring. They found inferences that required integration of information that was not adjacent in text was harder for students with specific comprehension disability (adequate decoding and vocabulary but poor comprehension). When testing global comprehension, better comprehenders did better than poor comprehenders when the passage was unavailable for review but that advantage over poor comprehenders was eliminated when passage was available for review. With inferences, however, the better comprehenders outperformed the poor comprehenders even when passage was available. "Even when a text is available for them to look over, the less skilled comprehenders are still unable to answer a high proportion of questions that require an inference" (p. 73).

They note that poor inferencing could be the result of (1) lack of background knowledge, (2) difficulty in integrating text information into a coherent whole, or 3) not realizing that inferences are necessary and permissible. The latter, for instance seems to have been the case with some of the students Wilhelm (1997) reported on. And if the poor readers cannot easily create a story structure in inventing or retelling, then one might expect that inferences that required recalling events, settings, or characters in a story might suffer. "The integration of information from different parts of a text is very much harder for poor comprehenders" (p. 80). Poor comprehenders benefited more from inference training than better comprehenders and more than the groups that engaged in decoding lessons. Imagery training produced the same result. Poor comprehenders improved with training while control subjects and better comprehenders did not.

Vaughn, Gersten, and Chard (2000) arranged effective comprehension interventions into two broad categories: Comprehension monitoring (repair) and text structuring (generating questions as they read using a story map, or other text structure guides). Both were considered comprehension strategy instruction because the students were taught to use a system to actively encourage them to think about what they were reading and the problems and solutions that they might use. Thinking aloud with support of peers is one newer promising approach, according to these researchers.

Vaughn et al. (2000) conclude that the evidence indicates that students with learning disabilities can be taught these strategies, but problems in transfering the strategies to independent application is apparent in the research. Teacher modeling, scaffolding, and support are critical in successful instruction. Peer tutoring and other opportunities to verbalize thinking seemed central to improvements in higher-order strategy use. Small group (n = 3) instruction with an expert teacher had greatest effect on improvement in reading achievement.

Walczyk and Griffith-Ross (2007) provide a review of the Compensatory-Encoding Theory (C-ET) which explains how struggling readers compensate for and overcome various difficulties they encounter as they read (word recognition, anaphora, syntactic complexity, vocabulary, inferencing, comprehension). They offer a list of seven compensatory strategies research has identified as compensations that both developing and struggling readers use when they encounter difficulties while reading. The strategies are listed from least to most disruptive.

1. *Slowing reading rate.* As reading proficiency develops, readers gain greater control over the rate at which they read. When difficulties are encountered, readers typically slow their rate of reading allowing them to sort out the difficulties the text imposes.
2. *Pausing.* A pause is an uncommonly long delay while reading. Pausing seems to provide the time needed for an inefficient subprocess to work. Pausing may be selected as the strategy when slowing reading rate fails to resolve the difficulty. Pausing may also signal that the reader is trying to work through the confusion or considering other strategic options.
3. *Look back.* Look backs occur when readers briefly glance back at a few words in that portion of the text that has been read. The compensation here seems to be one that restores information to working memory or assigns more attention to information already read. Look backs have been documented as useful in determining the meaning of an unknown word or concept or poorly written text.
4. *Read aloud.* Readers will often elect to read aloud when text is difficult or when the environment is noisy and distracting. This compensation seems to provide auditory feedback as well as slowing the rate of reading.

5. *Sounding out, analogizing to a known word, or contextual guessing.* When an unfamiliar word is encountered (one not recognized immediately) readers may use these strategies in an attempt to identify the word.

6. *Skip over a word.* At times readers decide not to work at figuring out an unknown word or they work at it and are unsuccessful. In these cases they may purposely skip the word and continue reading.

7. *Rereading text.* This strategy typically occurs when a reader finds the text is not making sense; rereading some portion of the text, perhaps returning to the beginning of a sentence and starting over or, at times, rereading a full paragraph or more. Rereading may resolve problems with syntax, phrasing, and prosody as well as disruptions caused by a lack of understanding of what was read.

Walczyk and Griffith-Ross (2007) conclude that struggling readers comprehend better in more relaxed settings that allow, even encourage, them to use any or all of these compensatory strategies. Allowing these students, for instance, to read aloud when they feel the need to do so, is one option that schools should consider. Likewise, allowing unrestricted time to read produces an environment where struggling readers can use the slower reading and rereading compensation strategies. They suggest also, that allowing struggling readers to select some of the texts they read is important because the use of compensatory strategies only seems to happen when readers are motivated to read for understanding. Likewise, working with struggling readers on setting purposes for reading, monitoring their own understanding, and familiarizing them with the seven compensatory strategies is both necessary and useful.

Summary   The research on comprehension interventions with struggling readers seems quite clear that improving performance is possible. However, as several of the authors of the landmark reviews noted, there is less evidence that comprehension-focused interventions produce either autonomous use of comprehension strategies or longer-term improvements in comprehension proficiencies. The lack of evidence stems from the heavy reliance on smaller sample sizes and shorter-term intervention designs as well as limited attention to a "gold standard" of transfer of training to autonomous use (Pearson, 2007).

And while this summary of the reviews of research on comprehension interventions must conclude, as did Pressley and his colleagues, that struggling readers can learn comprehension strategies, teaching those strategies is both a longer-term and more complicated process than is suggested by a review of the comprehension components of core reading programs (McGill-Franzen, Zmach, Solic, & Zeig, 2006).

In addition several contextual factors seem important when considering interventions to foster reading comprehension. These include providing expert instruction in very small groups, ensuring that the intervention provides substantial opportunity for wide reading of diverse texts, and focusing those texts, in large part, on topics of substantial interest to individual students. Complementing the findings of Kuhn et al. (2007) and Walczyk and Griffith-Ross (2007), Vellutino (2003) argues,

> One way to develop linguistic competencies is through extensive and diverse reading, because it is largely through reading that one encounters the more complex, the more abstract, and the more varied forms of language. Extensive and diverse reading is also the primary means by which children acquire discourses knowledge, that is, knowledge about the structural characteristics of different text types (e.g., narrative and informational) that is so important for interpreting and organizing the text. Extensive and diverse reading is also an important way to acquire world knowledge and domain specific knowledge and to increase reading fluency and pro-

ficiency (pp. 74–75). Obviously, instruction that capitalizes on children's inherent interests and surrounds them with high-interest reading materials at their level of proficiency is more effective than instruction that does less. (p. 77)

CONCLUSION

One problematic aspect of the research on reading comprehension difficulties is that it has been the rare study that assessed reading comprehension after students completed tasks that reflect the sort of reading assignments they must manage daily. By this we mean that few of the research studies had students read long passages of complex texts (e.g., a social studies textbook chapter, a multiple page article from a juvenile magazine). Such tasks would demand what we have dubbed "stamina," the ability to maintain strategy use across longer periods of time and larger amounts of information.

Likewise, few of the studies have clearly differentiated between comprehending narratives and comprehending informational texts. Few of the studies of struggling readers' comprehension have focused on higher-order comprehension (e.g., summarization, synthesis, analysis, literary response). And, finally, even fewer studies examined the sorts of reading comprehension that people regularly use outside of school settings. As Pressley (2002) noted,

> We know a great deal about how people comprehend text in anticipation of a short-answer test. Unfortunately, this is a task that matters only in school. For the most part, our purposes for reading in the real world are very different, from reading for pleasure, to reading to perform a particular task (to assemble a bicycle), to reading to find important information (such as the best time of year to vacation in Toronto), to reading to teach something to a child (perhaps reviewing the Bill of Rights to help a fifth-grader understand them). (p. 394)

A second problematic aspect of the research is that too few studies involved classroom or specialist teachers providing the comprehension instruction, especially over longer periods, such a school year. As Guthrie (2004) has noted, we have many, many studies involving a small number of children being taught a single skill or strategy over a few days or perhaps weeks by research assistants from the university sponsoring the project. But only one or two studies are available where public school teachers have provided instruction to large numbers of students on multiple comprehension strategies across 1 or more years.

Thus, in our view, while the research on the comprehension difficulties of struggling readers is vast and varied, there is too little research that provides useful guidance for developing the comprehension proficiencies of struggling readers in the context of actual classrooms across a school career. There is scant research, for instance, to guide the design of an effective 3-year-long intervention targeted to improving the comprehension of sixth-grade struggling readers such that they can enter secondary school with the proficiencies needed to manage the daily tasks of learning from grade level content area texts.

What the available research does provide is small bits of guidance as teachers approach the problem of providing useful comprehension strategy instruction. But the task of fitting all these small bits of guidance together falls to the teacher.

Practically speaking, good instruction of any sort emerges from a teacher's knowledge of the problem and of her students. The most powerful comprehension instruction cannot be simply sequenced, scripted and packaged. Effective comprehension instruction will be the result of a teacher using expert understanding of what the research says to design a lesson that seems likely to be useful and successful for a student, or group of students, that teacher knows well. Learning how to effectively develop reading comprehension proficiencies is complicated: it takes substantial time and support for teachers to become expert (Duffy, 2004). Teacher education programs and district professional development must make reading comprehension a priority, particularly comprehension instruction that supports struggling readers. The research studies reviewed here clearly demonstrate that students who are struggling, that is, below proficiency on important reading assessments, are not homogeneous in their development. Often, many, if not most struggling readers need instruction in comprehension strategies that will lead to independence, as well as, or instead of, instruction in fluency and other component skills. Teachers need access to the findings of successful research studies, such as those reviewed here, so that they might better adjust their instruction to fit the profiles of the struggling readers they teach.

REFERENCES

Allington, R. L. (1983). The reading instruction provided readers of differing abilities. *Elementary School Journal, 83*, 548–559.

Allington, R. L. (2006). Fluency: Still waiting after all these years. In S. J. Samuels & A. Farstrup (Eds.), *What research has to say about fluency instruction.* (pp. 94–105). Newark, DE: International Reading Association.

Allington, R. L. (2009). *What really matters in fluency: From research to practice.* New York: AllynBacon.

Allington, R. L., & McGill-Franzen, M. (1989). School response to reading failure: Chapter 1 and special education students in grades 2, 4, & 8. *Elementary School Journal, 89*, 529–542.

Anderson, R. C., Wilson, P., & Fielding, L. (1988). Growth in reading and how children spend their time outside of school. *Reading Research Quarterly, 23*, 285–303.

Bentum, K. E., & Aaron, P. G. (2003). Does reading instruction in learning disability rooms really work? *Reading Psychology, 24*, 361–382.

Borman, G. D., & D'Agostino, J. V. (2001). Title 1 and student achievement: A quantitative synthesis. In G. D. Borman, S. C. Stringfield, & R. E. Slavin (Eds.), *Title 1: Compensatory education at the crossroads.* (pp. 25–57). Mahwah, NJ: Erlbaum.

Brasseur, I., & Hock, M. (2006). What is the nature of adolescent struggling readers in urban schools? Unpublished paper, University of Kansas.

Buly, M. R., & Valencia, S. W. (2002). Below the bar: Profiles of students who fail state reading assessments. *Educational Evaluation and Policy Analysis, 24*(3), 219–239.

Carlisle, J. F., Schilling, S. G., Scott, S. E., & Zeng, J. (2004). *Do fluency measures predict reading achievement? Results from the 2002–2003 school year in Michigan's reading first schools.* (Technical report no. 1). Ann Arbor: University of Michigan.

Carter, L. (1984). The sustaining effects study of compensatory and elementary education. *Educational Researcher, 13*, 4–13.

Cunningham, J. W., Erickson, K., Spadorcia, S., Koppenhaver, D., Cunningham, P., Yoder, D., & McKenna, M. (1999). Assessing decoding from an onset-rime perspective. *Journal of Literacy Research, 31*(4), 391–414.

Dahl, K. L., & Freppon, P. A. (1995). A comparison of inner-city children's interpretations of reading and writing instruction in skills-based and whole language classrooms. *Reading Research Quarterly, 30*, 50–74.

Dahl, P. R., & Samuels, S. J. (1977). An experimental program for teaching high-speed word recognition and comprehension skills. In J. Button, T. Lovitt, & T. Rowland (Eds.), *Communications research in learning disabilities and mental retardation* (pp. 33–65). Baltimore: University Park Press.

Duffy, G. G. (2004). Teachers who improve reading achievement: What research says about what they do and how to develop them. In D. Strickland & M. Kamil (Eds.), *Improving reading achievement through professional development* (pp. 3–22). Norwood, MA: Christopher-Gordon.

Duke, N. K., Pressley, M., & Hilden, K. (2004). Difficulties with reading comprehension. In C. A. Stone, E. R. Silliman, B. J. Ehren, & K. Apel (Eds.), *Handbook of language and literacy: Development and disorders* (pp. 501–520). New York: Guilford.

Fink, R. (2006). *Why Jane and Johnny couldn't read — and how they learned.* Newark, DE: International Reading Association.

Francis, D. J., Fletcher, J., M, Catts, H. W., & Tomblin, J. B. (2005). Dimensions affecting the assessment of comprehension. In S. G. Paris & S. A. Stahl (Eds.), *Children's reading comprehension and assessment* (pp. 369–394). Mahwah, NJ: Erlbaum.

Gersten, R., Fuchs, L. S., Williams, J. P., & Baker, S. (2001). Teaching reading comprehension strategies to students with learning disabilities: A review of the research. *Review of Educational Research, 71*(2), 279–320.

Guthrie, J. T. (2004, May 1). Classroom practices promoting engagement and achievement in comprehension. Paper presented at the Reading Research 2004, International Reading Association, Reno, NV.

Hart, B. M., & Risley, T. R. (1995). *Meaningful differences in the everyday experiences of young children.* Baltimore: Paul Brookes.

Hiebert, E. H. (1983). An examination of ability grouping for reading instruction. *Reading Research Quarterly, 18*, 231–255.

Hiebert, E. H., & Taylor, B. M. (2000). Beginning reading instruction: Research on early intervention. In M. Kamil, P. Mosenthal, P. D. Pearson & R. Barr (Eds.), *Handbook of Reading Research, vol. III* (pp. 455–482). Mahwah, NJ: Erlbaum.

Jenkins, J. R., Pious, C., & Peterson, D. (1988). Categorical programs for remedial and handicapped students. *Exceptional Children, 55*(2), 147–158.

Kavale, K. A. (1988). The long-term consequences of learning disabilities. In M.C. Wang, M. Reynolds, & H. J. Walberg (Eds.), *Handbook of special education research and practice: Mildly handicapped conditions* (pp. 303–344). New York: Pergamon.

Knapp, M. S. (1995). *Teaching for meaning in high-poverty classrooms.* New York: Teachers College Press.

Kuhn, M. R., Schwanenflugel, P., Morris, R., Morrow, L., Woo, D., Meisinger, B., Sevick, R., Bradley, B. & Stahl, S. A. (2007). Teaching children to become fluent and automatic readers. *Journal of Literacy Research, 38*(4), 357–387.

Kuhn, M. R., & Stahl, S. A. (2003). Fluency: A review of developmental and remedial practices. *Journal of Educational Psychology, 95*(1), 3–21.

Leach, J. M., Scarborough, H. S., & Rescorda, L. (2003). Late-emerging reading disabilities. *Journal of Educational Psychology, 95*(2), 211–224.

Mathson, D., Solic, K., & Allington, R. L. (2006). Hijacking fluency and instructionally informative assessment. In T. Rasinski, C. Blachowicz, & K. Lems (Eds.), *Fluency instruction: Research-based best practice* (pp. 106–119). New York: Guilford.

Mastropieri, M. A., & Scruggs, T. E. (1997). Best practices in promoting reading comprehension in students with learning disabilities, 1976–1996. *Remedial and Special Education, 18*(4), 197–213.

Mastropieri, M. A., Scruggs, T. E., Bakken, J. P., & Whedon, C. (1996). Reading comprehension: A synthesis of research in learning disabilities. In T. E. Scruggs & M. A. Mastropieri (Eds.), *Advances in learning and behavioral disabilities* (Vol. 10, part B, pp. 201–227). Greenwich, CT: JAI Press.

McGill-Franzen, A. (1994). Is there accountability for learning and belief in children's potential? In E. Hiebert & B. Taylor (Eds.), *Getting reading right from the start: Effective early literacy interventions* (pp. 13–35). Boston: Allyn-Bacon.

McGill-Franzen, A., & Allington, R. L. (1990). Comprehension and coherence: Neglected elements of literacy instruction in remedial and resource room services. *Journal of Reading, Writing, and Learning Disabilities, 6* (2), 149–182.

McGill-Franzen, A., Zmach, C., Solic, K., & Zeig, J. L. (2006). The confluence of two policy mandates: Core reading programs and third-grade retention in Florida. *Elementary School Journal, 107*(1), 67–91.

McIntyre, E., & Freppon, P. A. (1994). A comparison of children's development of alphabetic knowledge in a skills-based and a whole language classroom. *Research in the Teaching of English, 28*(4), 391–417.

Morsink, C. V., Soar, R., Soar, R., & Thomas, R. (1986). Research on teaching: Opening the door to special education classrooms. *Exceptional Children, 53*, 32–40.

Nation, K. (2005). Children's reading comprehension difficulties. In M. Snowling & C. Hulme (Eds.), *The science of reading: A handbook.* (pp. 248–265). Oxford: Blackwell.

Oakhill, J., & Yuill, N. (1996). Higher order factors in comprehension disability: Processes and remediation. In C. Cornoldi & J. Oakhill (Eds.), *Reading comprehension difficulties: Processes and intervention* (pp. 69–92). Mahwah, NJ: Erlbaum.

Paris, S. G., Carpenter, R. D., Paris, A. H., & Hamilton, E. E. (2005). Spurious and genuine correlates of children's reading comprehension. In S. G. Paris & S. A. Stahl (Eds.), *Children's reading comprehension and assessment.* (pp. 131–160). Mahwah, NJ: Erlbaum.

Pearson, P. D. (2007). An endangered species act for literacy education. *Journal of Literacy Research, 39*(2), 145–162.

Pressley, M. (2002). Improving comprehension instruction: A path for the future. In C. C. Block, L. Gambrell, & M. Pressley (Eds.), *Improving comprehension instruction: Rethinking research, theory, and classroom practice* (pp. 385–399). San Francisco: JosseyBass.

Pressley, M., Hilden, K., & Shanklin, R. (2006). *An evaluation of end-of-grade 3 Dynamic Indicators of Basic Early Literacy Skills (DIBELS): Speed reading without comprehension, predicting little.* East Lansing: Literacy Achievement Research Center, Michigan State University.

Puma, M. J., Karweit, N., Price, C., Ricciuti, A., Thompson, W., & Vaden-Kiernan, M. (1997). *Prospects: Final report on student outcomes.* Washington, DC: U. S. Department of Education, Office of Planning and Evaluation Services.

Rupp, A. A., & Lesaux, N. K. (2006). Meeting expectations? An empirical investigation of a standards-based assessment of reading comprehension. *Educational Evaluation and Policy Analysis, 28*(4), 315–333.

Samuels, S. J. (2006). Looking backward: Reflections on a career. *Journal of Literacy Research, 38*(3), 327–341.

Schreiber, P. A. (1980). On the acquisition of reading fluency. *Journal of Reading Behavior, 12,* 177–186.

Schwanenflugel, P. J., Hamilton, A., Kuhn, M., Wisenbaker, J., & Stahl, S. A. (2004). Becoming a fluent reader: Reading skill and prosodic features in the oral reading of young readers. *Journal of Educational Psychology, 96*(1), 119–129.

Shanklin, N. L. (1990). Improving the comprehension of at-risk readers: An ethnographic study of four chapter 1 teachers, grades 4–6. *Journal of Reading, Writing, and Learning Disabilities, 6*(2), 137–148.

Swanson, H. L., Hoskyn, M., & Lee, C. (1999). *Interventions for students with learning disabilities.* New York: Guilford.

Thurlow, M. L., Ysseldyke, J. E., Graden, J. L., & Algozzine, B. (1983). What's "special" about the special education resource room for learning disabled students? *Learning Disability Quarterly, 6,* 283–288.

Torgeson, J. K., Wagner, R. K., & Rashotte, C. A. (1997). Prevention and remediation of severe reading disabilities: Keeping the end in mind. *Scientific Studies of Reading, 1*(3), 217–234.

Vaughn, S., Gersten, R., & Chard, D. J. (2000). The underlying message in LD intervention research: Findings from research syntheses. *Exceptional Children, 67*(1), 99–114.

Vaughn, S., Moody, S. W., & Schumm, J. S. (1998). Broken promises: Reading instruction in the resource room. *Exceptional Children, 64,* 211–225.

Vellutino, F. R. (2003). Individual differences as sources of variability in reading comprehension in elementary school children. In A. P. Sweet & C. E. Snow (Eds.), *Rethinking reading comprehension* (pp. 51–81). New York: Guilford.

Walczyk, J. A., & Griffith-Ross, D. A. (2007). How important is reading skill fluency for comprehension? *Reading Teacher, 60*(6), 560–569.

Walmsley, S. A. (1979). The criterion referenced measurement of an early reading behavior. *Reading Research Quarterly, 14*(4), 574–604.

White, T. G., Graves, M. F., & Slater, W. H. (1990). Growth of reading vocabulary in diverse elementary schools: Decoding and word meaning. *Journal of Educational Psychology, 82*(2), 281–290.

Wilhelm, J. D. (1997). *"You gotta be the book": Teaching engaged and reflective reading with adolescents.* New York: Teachers College Press.

Ysseldyke, J. E., Algozzine, R., Shinn, M. R., & McGue, M. (1982). Similarities and differences between low achievers and students classified as learning disabled. *Journal of Special Education, 16*(1), 73–85.

Ysseldyke, J. E., Thurlow, M. L., Mecklenburg, C., & Graden, J. (1984). Opportunity to learn for regular and special education students during reading instruction. *Remedial and Special Education, 5*(1), 29–37.

Zigmond, N., Vallecorsa, A., & Leinhardt, G. (1980). Reading instruction for students with learning disabilities. *Topics in Language Disorders, 1,* 89–98.

Part VI

Cultural Impact on Reading Comprehension

27 Reading Comprehension and Diversity in Historical Perspective
Literacy, Power, and Native Hawaiians

Kathryn H. Au and Julie Kaomea

University of Hawai'i

> If we think of education is an act of knowing, then reading has to do with knowing. The act of reading cannot be explained as merely reading words since every act of reading words implies a previous reading of the world and a subsequent re-reading of the world. There is a permanent movement back and forth between "reading" reality and reading words—the spoken word too is our reading of the world. We can go further, however, and say that reading the word is not only preceded by reading the world, but also by a certain form of writing it or rewriting it. In other words, of transforming it by means of conscious practical action. For me, this dynamic movement is central to literacy. (Freire, 1985, p. 18)

This quotation by the great Brazilian educator Paolo Freire highlights the view of reading comprehension taken in this chapter. We look at comprehension in terms of reading the world, understanding how literacy can be used to position individuals and cultural groups, to create narratives and counternarratives. Our goal in this chapter is to explore reading comprehension—as reading the world as well as the word—and issues of diversity from a historical perspective, highlighting insights gained from studies of the literacy and schooling of Native Hawaiians. The case of Native Hawaiians is of particular interest because of the traditional belief in the power of language. This belief is reflected in the saying, "I ka 'ōlelo no ke ola, i ka 'ōlelo no ka make" (Pukui, 1983, p. 129). The popular translation of this saying is, "In the language is life, in the language is death," and it reflects the conviction that language is so powerful that it can heal or destroy.

With respect to theoretical frameworks, the first author has conducted research primarily from a social constructivist perspective (Au, 1998), the second author from a critical perspective (e.g., Kaomea, 2003). Both of these perspectives have contributed to the framing of this chapter. To tell the story of the literacy of Native Hawaiians, as we have come to understand it, we took an eclectic view of methodology, seeking to incorporate histories of schooling, print materials, and audiences (Monaghan & Hartman, 2000). As might be expected, we consulted a variety of sources: primary, secondary, and original.

Our interpretive essay is intended to show how issues of power have played out over time in texts written by, for, and about Native Hawaiians. Publications such as newspapers and textbooks—or today's web pages—serve as a means by which diverse groups, such as Native Hawaiians, position themselves and are positioned by others. The content of widely distributed texts may exert a profound effect on a group's literacy rate and reading comprehension. We argue that a group's ready access to an abundance of texts that present its culture and worldview in an authentic and sympathetic manner contributes to increased rates of literacy and reading comprehension (Au, 1998). In contrast, when most popular texts promote misrepresentations and distortions of its culture and worldview, the result is likely to be lower rates of literacy and comprehension.

In the first part of this chapter, we look at the historical record. Not surprisingly, evidence indicates that literacy, in the forms of reading and writing introduced by Europeans, has from the outset held the potential to be both empowering and disempowering to Native Hawaiians. Literacy permitted Europeans to control the representations of Hawaiians to the outside world, while simultaneously justifying and enabling the political, economic, and social oppression of these indigenous inhabitants of the formerly sovereign Hawaiian nation. However, once literacy was mastered by Native Hawaiians, they claimed the power of print for themselves. Literacy thus provided Hawaiians with a means for preserving their history and culture as well as an avenue for taking political stances and expressing anticolonial resistance.

In the second part of this chapter, we move forward in time to look at how power relations evident in the past continue to exert a strong influence on the depiction of Native Hawaiian history and culture in current elementary school textbooks. The subtle and not-so-subtle uses of texts to position Native Hawaiians as inferior suggests the pervasiveness of an educational atmosphere in which some educators may (consciously or unconsciously) hold low expectations for the achievement of Native Hawaiian students. Many studies have shown how low expectations for students lead to lessons that emphasize low level skills and away from instruction in reading comprehension, including the critical evaluation of text (Au, 1998; Fitzgerald, 1995; Oakes & Guiton, 1995). Yet, as this chapter will suggest, reading comprehension—defined as the ability to evaluate texts critically and to provide counternarratives—has been an essential survival skill for Native Hawaiians since contact with Europeans and continues to hold cultural and educational significance.

Native Hawaiian leader and political scientist, Haunani-Kay Trask (1999), has described the contradictory narratives that pervaded her youth:

> When I was young the story of my people was told twice: once by my parents, then again by my school teachers. From my *'ohana* (family), I learned about the life of the old ones: how they fished and planted by the moon; shared all the fruits of their labors, especially their children; danced in great numbers for long hours; and honored the unity of their world in intricate genealogical chants. My mother said Hawaiians had sailed over thousands of miles to make their home in these sacred islands. And they had flourished, until the coming of the *haole* (whites).
>
> At school, I learned that the "pagan Hawaiians" did not read or write, were lustful cannibals, traded in slaves, and could not sing. Captain Cook had "discovered" Hawai'i, and the ungrateful Hawaiians had killed him. In revenge, the Christian god had cursed the Hawaiians with disease and death. (p. 113)

This quotation highlights the collisions between Native Hawaiian and Western narratives. We do not believe that there was ever a single Native Hawaiian viewpoint, or a single Western viewpoint, in any historical period. However, we think that it is possible to use documentary evidence to characterize the sentiments shared by many Native Hawaiians, or by many Westerners, and to highlight collisions in the literacy history of Native Hawaiians supported by such evidence.

LANGUAGE AND EDUCATION IN PRECONTACT HAWAI'I

Linguists place the Hawaiian language in the category known as Proto Central Eastern Polynesian that includes Maori, Rarotongan, and Tahitian, among others. From precontact times to the present, Native Hawaiians have enjoyed a rich oral tradition with legends, proverbs, poetical sayings, and lengthy chants memorized to preserve family history and genealogy (Pukui, 1983). The Hawaiian language is replete with subtleties, including *kaona* or hidden meanings and concealed references, which often cannot be inferred on the basis of logic and may only be understood by those who are intimately familiar with Hawaiian cultural codes. Thus, while reading and writing were unknown in precontact times, Native Hawaiians had a profound appreciation of many expressive and communicative functions of language.

Education in precontact times took place within the extended family, with children observing and working alongside their elders (Kelly, 1991; Pukui, Haertig, & Lee, 1972). Young people who showed special talents participated in courses of formal instruction lasting from 15 to 20 years, for example, to become healers, canoe builders, priests, and dancers of the hula (Dotts & Sikkema, 1994; Kamakau, 1968). Masters of the hula, for instance, had their own schools, called *hālau hula*, but schools in the Western sense, where students are sent for a general education, were unknown. Kelly (1991) writes, "If one had to summarize the essential characteristics of education in Hawaiian society, the terms that come to mind are: practical, skill-oriented, socially-useful, in tune with reality, environmentally-aware, conserver-cognizant" (p. 13). Kelly continues by noting that there appeared to be a combination of "on-the-job learning—together with memorization and rote" (p. 13).

EARLY CONTACT WITH EUROPEANS

Historical accounts bear witness to the devastating effects of contact with Europeans upon Hawaiian society. The Native Hawaiian population declined dramatically, from an estimated 300,000 or more in 1778,[1] to 124,449 in 1831–23, to 84,165 in 1850 (Schmitt, 1968, quoted in Benham & Heck, 1998). Many deaths occurred because Europeans brought with them diseases, such as venereal syphilis, influenza and tuberculosis, for which Native Hawaiians had no immunity. Moreover, the growing European influence also led to the disruption of all aspects of traditional life that had contributed to an orderly and productive Hawaiian society, including spiritual and religious beliefs, governance, and land tenure (Benham & Heck, 1998; Kameʻeleihiwa, 1992). Thus, Native Hawaiians who survived the physical threat still faced the psychic threat to their worldview and way of life.

Given this context, it is not surprising that literacy—as a form of expression introduced by Europeans—was used as a tool in the colonial subjugation of 19th-century Hawaiians. However, as this chapter will suggest, while the historical record reveals a repeated pattern of literacy being used against the interests of Native Hawaiians, it also shows many instances of Native Hawaiians using this newly acquired tool to secure their own national sovereignty and well-being.

Venezky (1991) asserts that literacy has a dual nature: a sociopolitical dimension tied to its role in society and deployment for cultural, economic, and political purposes; and a psychological dimension associated with cognitive and affective variables that contribute to, or detract from, an individual's motivation to gain proficiency in and make use of literacy. This dualism is evident in the historical relationship of Native Hawaiians to literacy, although we might argue for a closer connection between the two dimensions than Venezky implies. We find not only that literacy was both empowering and disempowering to Native Hawaiians, but that these beneficial and detrimental effects could be both sociopolitical and collectivist, as well as psychological and individualistic, in nature.

The beginnings of the literary disempowerment of Native Hawaiians can be traced back to the very start of contact between Native Hawaiians and Europeans, with the arrival of British explorer James Cook in 1778. While Western writers laud Cook's navigational prowess and credit him with the "discovery" of the Hawaiian Islands, Trask (1999), writing from a Native Hawaiian perspective, counters that Cook merely "stumbled upon this interdependent and wise society" (p. 5), nearly 1,000 years after ancient Polynesians had been negotiating these seafaring routes through their proficiency in noninstrument navigation. Archaeological evidence supports the Native Hawaiian view, indicating that the islands were settled around 800 A.D. by Polynesian voyagers, most likely from the Marquesas (Kirch, 2007). Voyaging, while infrequent, continued between Hawai'i and other groups to the south, especially the Society Islands, as indicated by Hawaiian chants in which voyagers are named, as well as by archaeological and linguistic evidence (Kirch, 2007).

The logs of Cook's voyages, along with subsequent missionary journals, began an extensive literary project of colonial representations that would help produce and maintain the European imagination of Polynesian people while simultaneously legitimizing England's imperial expedition and furthering their colonial aims. The narrative Trask absorbed in school, which draws from these early, colonial writings and continues as the dominant one to this day, casts Cook's arrival as a welcome event, a turning point for the better, providing the opportunity for Native Hawaiians to emerge from what Western missionaries and social scientists alike have characterized as a savage, feudal era. The misrepresentation of precontact Hawai'i as a violent and backward society can be seen in critically acclaimed modern volumes, such as *Shoal of Time: A History of the Hawaiian Islands* by Daws (1989), as well as in current day elementary Hawaiian studies textbooks. This image of the uncivilized, subservient Hawaiian and the honored European guest, which can be traced to Cook's arrival, and which continues to function as an essential selling point for the Hawai'i tourist industry, is an enduring colonial trope to which we return later in this chapter.

THE SPREAD OF LITERACY IN HAWAI'I

Venezky (1991) characterized the spread of literacy in the industrialized, Western nations as downward and outward. In its downward movement, literacy progressed from the church to the laity, within the laity from the nobility to the higher professions, and from the higher to the lower professions. In spreading outward, literacy moved from men to women and from the towns to the countryside. In the 19th century, Venezky noted, Western governments began to promote literacy in an effort to create an educated citizenry capable of participating productively in the civic, economic, and military affairs of the nation. The patterns described by Venezky are evident in the spread of literacy among Native Hawaiians.

The first party of Protestant Congregational missionaries from Boston, sponsored by the American Board of Commissioners for Foreign Missions, arrived in Hawai'i in 1820, bringing with them ideas about religion, literacy, and schooling prominent in that era in New England. These included a firm belief that native peoples must be converted to Christianity so that their souls could be redeemed; that they must learn to read and write to have direct access to the word of God through the Bible; and that universal schooling was the means by which literacy (and hence salvation) might best be achieved. While the Calvinist beliefs of these New England missionaries had evolved from the doctrine of predestination, a strict hierarchy remained in effect: the chosen class was to rule over others, and the unlearned were to submit to the leadership of the learned (Stueber, 1991). The missionaries saw literacy as a means both of saving the souls of Native Hawaiians, in keeping with the practices of Protestants since the Reformation, and of establishing dominion over them.

The missionaries continued with the earlier literary project of journal and letter writing, which, when sent back to the metropole, reinforced the colonial, Euro-American imagination of the savage state of the Hawaiian people while simultaneously legitimizing their evangelical mission. They also took on a second literary project, as they sought to reform these "heathens" by developing a Hawaiian-language orthography based on Roman characters and teaching the Hawaiian people to read the Bible and other religious texts. In 1822, the missionaries began translating the Bible into Hawaiian, using a system originally developed by missionaries in Tahiti (Wilson, 1991). In this way, Hawaiian became a written language. Literacy spread rapidly among Hawaiians, as the missionaries taught the king and the chiefs, then other adults. The missionaries converted the powerful queen regent, Ka'ahumanu, to Christianity in the early 1820s, and through her influence were able to enact the first educational laws in the Kingdom of Hawai'i in 1824.

Through the support of the chiefs, village schools cropped up nearly everywhere, staffed with Native Hawaiian men as teachers, hurriedly trained by the missionaries. The first Catholic priests arrived in the islands in 1827, and they succeeded in winning many Native Hawaiians to their religion, in part by establishing schools of their own. Records indicate that by 1831 an estimated 50,000 Hawaiian adults were attending more than 1,000 native schools, learning to read and write in the Hawaiian language (Stueber, 1991). Some schools may have been nothing more than a gathering place under a tree. Nevertheless, in only a decade, the majority of Hawaiian adults had become literate in their own language, albeit at a basic level.

After the early 1830s, when interest among adults began to wane and missionaries became disillusioned by the slow process of reforming Hawaiian adults (Grimshaw, 1989), the missionaries turned their attention to schools for children (Dotts & Sikkema, 1994). These common schools provided children with rudimentary instruction in reading and writing in the Hawaiian language, with Hawaiian adults, mostly men, doing the teaching. In 1840, Kamehameha III signed the general school laws, establishing a system of government schools reaching out to every village in the kingdom. The government common schools, staffed entirely by Native Hawaiians, taught reading and writing to tens of thousands of children with missionary primers as their texts. Tate (1962) explains that "through the printed word the missionaries gained access to the hearts and minds of their pupils; religious concepts and ideas were incorporated into the reading material; thus teachers converted as they taught" (p. 182).

Armstrong (1858), minister of public instruction in the Kingdom from 1848 to 1860, estimated that about three-fourths of the population could read the Hawaiian language, with most also being able to write. While studies of signature literacy would provide needed verification for the rate of literacy among Native Hawaiians, Armstrong's estimate compares favorably with the finding of a 75% rate of signature literacy for white males serving in the U.S. Army in the 1850s (Kaestle, Damon-Moore, Stedman, Tinsley, & Trollinger, 1991). In the Kingdom of Hawai'i, as in the United States, literacy rates for women in the 1820s through 1850s may have been somewhat lower than for men, judged by the greater presence of males in schools as both teachers and students during this period.

As suggested earlier, the missionaries' purpose in promoting literacy in the Hawaiian language was essentially conservative (cf. Lockridge, 1974), in the sense that they were seeking not just to convert Hawaiians to Christianity but to establish control over the social, political, and economic order of the Kingdom. The missionaries did not favor literacy in the Hawaiian language over literacy in English—far from it. Leaders such as Armstrong viewed English as a language far superior to Hawaiian and saw literacy in English as the ultimate goal. Armstrong (1858) wrote:

Were the means at our command, it would be an unspeakable blessing to have every native child placed in a good English school, and kept there until it had acquired a thorough knowledge of what is now, in fact, to a great extent, the business language of the Islands, and which would open to its mind new and exhaustless treasures of moral and intellectual wealth. (p. 11)

The scarcity of teachers able to teach in English, and the expense of hiring such teachers, was the reason Armstrong and other Americans promoted literacy in the Hawaiian language. American and European teachers in government English schools were paid salaries 10 times higher than those given to Native Hawaiian teachers in the common schools. Armstrong (1858) recommended a gradual shifting of funds to English-language schools as the only practical solution.

HAWAIIAN-LANGUAGE NEWSPAPERS

By the late 1800s, the literacy rate in Hawai'i compared favorably to that of any nation in the world (Wilson, 1991), an accomplishment much to the credit of the Native Hawaiian teachers in the common schools. The high literacy rate, along with the technology of the printing press, opened the way for the third prong of the colonial literary project—missionary controlled Hawaiian-language newspapers. An indication of a high level of newspaper readership among Native Hawaiians can be found in the fact that more than 100 different newspapers were published in the Hawaiian language. Issues of 75 different newspapers, published from 1834 to 1948, have survived and are currently being digitized; available issues may be seen at www.nupepa.org. Although it is not possible to determine the exact number or percentage of Native Hawaiians who read Hawaiian-language newspapers, circulation lists and oral histories indicate a widespread readership, with newspapers being delivered in rural areas as well as in the towns (Hori, undated).

Early newspapers in the Hawaiian language were directly or indirectly controlled by Calvinist missionaries who used the newspapers to proselytize, to civilize, and to assist in the progress of plantation-colonial capitalism. Silva's (2004) extensive analyses of *Ka Hae Hawaii* (The Hawaiian Flag) and *Ka Hoku Loa* (The Distant Star), for instance, demonstrate how the newspapers denigrated Hawaiians and other native people while asserting that every aspect of Western culture (and especially religion) was superior to native culture. The papers used the missionary dictate that labor equaled salvation to urge Hawaiians to work as laborers on the newly developed sugar plantations, and admonished Hawaiian men and women to conform to Euro-American gender behaviors.

An article in an 1856 issue of *Ka Hae Hawai'i*, for instance, begins with a list of the faults of Hawaiian women and provides a contrasting picture of "proper" womanly behavior:

Hawaiian women have many failings ... [When] I look at the woman, her body is dirty, her hair is not well-kept, and the dress, not clean. It is the same with the house, it is dirty, and everything in the house is mixed up ... The woman's work is to care for the house until it is clean. This is perhaps the greatest fault, *it is women just sitting*; not working with the hands, just lying on the mat ... Women in civilized countries, who are well-taught, are not like that ... The body and the house of the civilized woman is clean, and her husband likes her a lot. The mind of the husband is not on other women because he has a good woman. (quoted and translated in Silva, 2004)

In a similar vein, an 1861 issue of the Calvinist mission newspaper, *Ka Hoku Loa*, contained an editorial that reported on 383 Hawai'i church members who had been expelled from the church in the previous year for offenses including: not doing "real work" but "just sitting," which is a sin; not going to church; drinking; engaging in defiling and impure actions; not keeping the marriage laws; not keeping the Sabbath; and engaging in idol worship or traditional Hawaiian medicinal practices (Silva, 2004).

In October 1861, *Ka Hoku Loa* published a full-page condemnation of Native Hawaiian medicine, calling it "idolatry, falsehood, and murder." In November 1861, it attacked Native Hawaiian *mo'olelo* or traditional stories of "worthless" Hawaiian gods. In a scathing censure of Hawaiian mo'olelo, missionary John Emerson wrote: "If ignorant [and] uncivilized people wish to tell worthless things to their children to frighten them, that is their own business; but it is not right that they be published in the Newspapers" (quoted and translated in Silva, 2004).

The missionaries controlled the power of the printed word in Hawai'i for nearly 40 years. Then, in 1861, out of frustration with *Ka Hoku Loa* and *Ka Hae Hawaii*, and to the shock and outrage of the missionary establishment, a group of Native Hawaiian men formed an association to publish a newspaper for the expression of their own political opinions and the preservation of Hawaiian cultural traditions (Silva, 2004).

Ka Hoku o ka Pakipika (The Star of the Pacific) began a long tradition of nationalist, anticolonial resistance through the print media. The pages of *Ka Hoku o ka Pakipika* overtly and covertly talked back to the missionary discourse that denigrated Hawaiian culture and worked to disempower Hawaiians politically and economically. By demonstrating that they had mastered the technology of the printing press and the written language, and by displaying their skill in both traditional literature and modern political writing, the Hawaiian writers and editors of *Ka Hoku o ka Pakipika* countered the racist discourse that depicted them as uncivilized savages. For the first time, its authors and publishers dared to profess pride in Hawaiian traditions and culture in print. They spoke back to missionary efforts to domesticate Hawaiian women by printing traditional *mo'olelo* (stories) and *mele* (songs) in which Hawaiian women wielded tremendous power and lived adventurous lives. They challenged the repressive laws that prohibited the ancient religion along with traditional practices, such as hula and *la'au lapa'au* (Hawaiian medicine), by reproducing these traditional practices in print so that they could be communicated among the Hawaiians of the time and preserved for future generations. They also translated and published foreign news stories of world events, which had been withheld from Hawaiians by the missionary establishment, and which the Hawaiian editors viewed as essential to an informed and politically involved citizenry in a sovereign nation (Silva, 2004).

Ka Hoku o ka Pakipika may not have been radically antihegemonic. It did not urge its readers to take up arms and oust the foreigners who were controlling their lives in order to establish a more self-determining and self-governing Hawaiian society (Silva, 2004). Its editors were well aware of Hawai'i's vulnerable position as a small nation in the imperial century, and thus focused on the more plausible goals of strengthening their people's pride in their Hawaiian heritage, preserving valuable traditional knowledge, and providing a space for Hawaiians to contest the oppressive acts of the colonizers. As Silva writes:

> There was a "mental revolution" going on, a revolution meant to cast off the yoke of Puritan control over every aspect of Kanaka lives; a revolution where ink flowed rather than blood and that took place largely in the reflection and recreation of the oral tradition. (Silva, 2004, p. 83)

Ka Hoku o ka Pakipika was the first in a long series of Hawaiian nationalist newspapers. As Hawaiian nationalists learned to produce and distribute their own newspapers, the Hawaiian language became a threat to the colonial literary project. With the distri-bution of *Ka Hoku o ka Pakipika*, for the first time, Hawaiians in remote rural areas and on the neighbor islands were connected to anticolonial, nationalist thought on a weekly basis. For the colonizers, the potential for communication among this compara-tively large, and almost universally literate, Hawaiian community was dangerous in part because many of them could not understand Hawaiian, while those who did have a literal command of the language often could not grasp the *kaona* or veiled language and metaphorical subtleties that enabled Hawaiians to communicate political sentiments while escaping colonial surveillance.

THE ANTI-ANNEXATION PETITION

Armstrong and other Westerners, seeking to control the course of events in the Hawai-ian Kingdom during the 19th century, apparently failed to recognize that literacy was a sword that cut both ways. Literacy in the Hawaiian language gave Native Hawaiians a powerful political instrument, as well as a vehicle for cultural preservation and self-expression, which they put to excellent use. This legacy serves as a source of inspiration to contemporary Native Hawaiians seeking to bring the Hawaiian language back as a medium for everyday communication.

Recently, Silva (1999, 2004), a Native Hawaiian historian, has called Western histo-rians to task for interpreting events in 19th century Hawai'i, such as the overthrow of the monarchy, solely on the basis of English language sources. Silva argues persuasively that the neglect of Hawaiian-language sources, particularly Hawaiian-language news-papers, has contributed to misrepresentations of the actions and attitudes of Native Hawaiians towards these significant historical events. In the case of the 1893 over-throw, historians writing from a Western perspective have asserted that Native Hawai-ians showed little or no resistance to the imprisonment of Queen Lili'uokalani and the takeover of the Hawaiian government, engineered by American sugar planters and their allies (e.g., Daws, 1989).

The 1897 anti-annexation petition—a 556-page document containing the signatures of Native Hawaiians supporting a sovereign Hawaiian nation—created a sensation in the Hawaiian community when it was rediscovered and re-published by Silva and her colleagues in 1998. More than 21,000—more than half the population of 40,000 Native Hawaiians at the time—signed the petition (Silva, 1998), providing dramatic evidence of massive resistance to American annexation. Silva (1999) writes that the petition confirmed for present-day Native Hawaiians

> that their *kūpuna* [ancestors] had not stood idly, apathetically, by while their nation-hood was taken from them. Instead, contrary to every history book on the shelf, they learned that their ancestors had taken up the honorable field of struggle... (p. 4)

The anti-annexation petition provides further evidence that Native Hawaiians used literacy for the political purpose of supporting sovereignty, the continuation of their own nationhood, a stance directly opposed to that of many missionary descendants and their allies.

THE ELIMINATION OF HAWAIIAN-LANGUAGE SCHOOLS

Meanwhile, as the century proceeded and Hawaiian threatened to become a "language of power" (Anderson, 1991), demands for government, schools and other business to be conducted in English became more frequent and more forceful (Silva, 2004). These demands provided the context for a fourth prong of the missionary literary project, targeting the Hawaiian language schools, also known as the common schools of the Kingdom of Hawaiʻi. In 1880, the ministry of education began a determined effort to eliminate Hawaiian-language schools, replacing them with English-language schools. In 1878 the Board of Education reported that there were 169 Hawaiian-language schools, compared to 11 English-language schools. In 1888, English-language schools began to outnumber Hawaiian-language schools, 69 to 63. In 1897, following the 1893 overthrow of the Hawaiian monarchy and the outlawing of Hawaiian language from government activities and schools, the last Hawaiian-language school on the major islands closed, leaving only the tiny school on the remote and privately owned island of Niʻihau. Literacy in the Hawaiian language slowly faded away, along with the general status of the language as physical punishment and a sense of shame became associated with Hawaiian language use (Benham & Heck, 1998). Many Native Hawaiian families ceased to use their own language for everyday communication and did not teach the language to their children, but promoted the learning of English instead (Yamauchi & Wilhelm, 2001).

THE HAWAIIAN RENAISSANCE

According to Trask (1984), since the overthrow of the Hawaiian Kingdom, virtually every aspect of Hawaiian life has been determined and regulated by non-Hawaiians, first by the missionary-descended, European-American ruling class in power from 1893 to 1954, and by the Japanese settlers and their offspring, who have risen to political power since then. Over the past three decades, however, Native Hawaiians have made steady progress in regaining their footing in their own land.

Today, the Hawaiian language and culture are experiencing revitalization. In 1986, Native Hawaiian leaders succeeded in passing legislation that removed the 90-year ban on the Hawaiian language and led to the opening of Hawaiian immersion schools with instruction once again taking place in the Hawaiian language. With approximately 1,500 students currently enrolled in these schools, many children as well as elders are once again speaking, reading, and writing the Hawaiian language.

While the majority of Hawaiian students still attend English-language schools, these approximately 75,000 Hawaiian students are now studying Hawaiian history and culture in English-medium schools as well. Inspired by nationwide civil rights movements of the 1960s and 1970s, in 1978 the Hawaiian renaissance and sovereignty movement pushed through the state legislature a constitutional amendment demanding more Hawaiian courses of study in Hawaiʻi's state schools and colleges. During the 85 years between the United States' forcible overthrow of the Hawaiian monarchy in 1893 and the passing of this Hawaiian education mandate in 1978, the mention of Hawaiian language and culture in Hawaiʻi's public schools was virtually nonexistent. With this grassroots-inspired legislation, however, these colonial educational policies were finally reversed, and regular instruction in Native Hawaiian culture, history, and language has become a mandatory requirement for all of Hawaiʻi's public schools.

THE HAWAIIAN STUDIES CURRICULUM

The mandate for multicultural instruction in the indigenous culture of the native people of Hawaiʻi coincided with the emergence of political movements throughout the United States that aimed to increase the visibility of traditionally marginalized and underrepresented groups in museums, movie houses, mainstream broadcasting, and course syllabi (Phelan, 1993). During the 1970s and 1980s, curricula from kindergarten to college nationwide were undergoing revision to more adequately reflect non-European and nonwhite contributions to American history and culture. The Hawai'i state curriculum was no exception.

However, many of the Hawaiian studies textbooks (at least at the elementary school level), and the classroom instruction that accompanies these texts, leave much to be desired. As Kaomea (2000, 2003, 2005) argues, instead of departing from the colonial dynamics that have historically dominated the state, these largely non-Hawaiian authored Hawaiian studies texts simply extend the larger society's ongoing, colonial treatment of Native Hawaiians. The stereotypical depictions of Native Hawaiians that pervade the Hawaiian studies textbooks and curricula continue to serve the economic interests of the (neo)colonial state by fulfilling its need for docile Hawaiians and cheap, unskilled labor. As suggested in the earlier historical record, as the transported New Englanders began buying large plots of land and started massive sugar plantations requiring large numbers of native and imported laborers, the missionaries' religious aspirations gave way to more economic ones. With semiskilled and unskilled labor in high demand, Hawai'i's schools became less a means of religious conversion and more a site for socializing Hawaiian and immigrant children for work on the plantations. Consequently, the most serious task placed upon Hawai'i's schools during the plantation era was to make semiskilled agricultural pursuits acceptable to Hawai'i's youngsters—not to encourage or create avenues for social mobility, but to simply keep children of plantation laborers on the plantation (Kaomea, 2000).

Hawai'i's economic system has since "progressed" from a heavy reliance on the plantations to a similar dependence on the tourist industry. However, even as the face of Hawai'i's primary industry has changed, the need for a semiskilled or unskilled populace remains. Consequently, the level of social and economic mobility actually encouraged or granted by the present day school system continues to be suspect.

It would be a mistake to consider literacy as a means of disempowering Native Hawaiians to be a relic of the past, because modern day equivalents of the missionary literary project are readily found in schools today. Through a critical analysis of the state's elementary Hawaiian studies textbooks, Kaomea (2000) demonstrates how this largely Western-authored "Hawaiian" curriculum ultimately serves to perpetuate colonial stereotypes of Native Hawaiians—distorted, exoticized images which were first projected upon Hawai'i's native people by early European voyagers and which to this day remain essential to the allure of Hawai'i's tourist industry.

For instance, Kaomea's (2000) critical analysis of the elementary Hawaiian studies textbook chapter entitled *Captain Cook Finds the Hawaiian Islands* (Bauer, 1982) exposes the questionable origins of the familiar trope of the superior Caucasian and the naturally subservient native—a trope that, Kaomea argues, originated with Hawai'i's first tourist, Captain James Cook, and which continues to serve as a key selling point for Hawai'i's tourist industry.

The textbook chapter opens with a description of the Hawaiians' reception of Captain Cook upon his first arrival at Waimea, Kaua'i in 1778. Detailing the royal welcome given to Cook, it describes how the natives came out in their canoes to greet him, and that they were happy that he had come. The chapter goes on to explain that when Captain Cook came ashore, he was greeted by submissive Hawaiians who fell flat on their faces in reverence before him and remained in that posture until Cook gestured for them to rise. The textbook concludes that Captain Cook, because of his fair skin and light hair, was received by the Hawaiians as a god, or, if not a god, at least as royalty (Bauer, 1982). (Although the truth of this claim has recently been taken up for debate by scholars such as Marshall Sahlins (1995) and Gananath Obeyesekere (1992), it is rarely questioned in the general public and continues to be the pervasive message in elementary Hawaiian studies textbooks.)

Citing numerous hotel brochures that promise patrons the "royal treatment" and featuring photos of vacationing Caucasians lounging at poolside while dark-skinned waiters hover in the background ready to honor their every request, Kaomea (2000) argues that this familiar image of hospitable Hawaiian natives, ever-ready to be at the service of visiting foreigners, functions as an essential selling point for the Hawai'i visitor industry. She also demonstrates how these notions are circulated and reinforced throughout Hawai'i's public school system through an elementary school Hawaiian studies curriculum that drills students in the Hawaiian values associated with the aloha spirit and Hawaiian hospitality, and high school vocational programs that take teenagers on guided tours of hotel kitchens, gardens, and honeymoon suites in preparation for post-secondary jobs in this lowest-paid industry in the state.

Kaomea (2000) further estranges this familiar colonial trope by reading elementary Hawaiian studies textbooks alongside the journals and travelogues of Captain Cook and his men. Focusing her analysis on the *non dit* (Macherey, 1978), or that which remains unsaid in the children's textbooks, Kaomea demonstrates how the authors and publishers have omitted any mention of the litany of punishments that Cook and his men inflicted on the Polynesians in order to create an initial sense of terror among them and thereby assert their superiority over these "barbarians":

> What is left unsaid is how in his travels throughout the Polynesian islands Cook and his men regularly flogged Polynesian commoners and high ranking chiefs alike, with as many as six dozen lashes for the suspected theft of nails, hooks, and other small iron items (Edgar, 1778). What is left unsaid is how Cook made an example of one suspected thief by ordering a cross to be carved on both his shoulders, penetrating to the bone (Edgar, 1778), and how he had another clapped in irons, his head and beard shaved, and both ears cut off (Cook, 1784). What is left unsaid is how third Lieutenant Williamson shot a young Hawaiian chief to death just minutes before Cook first stepped ashore in Waimea, Kaua'i (Cook, 1967). (Kaomea, 2000, p. 337)

Through a detailed investigation of these historical silences, Kaomea offers a new perspective on this familiar colonial trope. As Kaomea argues, after this first fatal lesson in the power of firearms, it is no wonder that when Cook first stepped ashore in Hawai'i with Williamson at his side he was greeted by submissive Hawaiians who "fell flat on their faces, and remained in that humble posture till [Cook] made signs for them to rise" (Cook, 1967, p. 269). It is no wonder that Cook and his men found the Hawaiians to be polite, hospitable, fearful of giving offense, eager to please and sensible of their own inferiority (Cook, 1949). As they had done throughout the islands of Polynesia, Cook and his men used their military might to assert their superiority over Hawai'i's native people. As Kaomea (2000) writes, "They taught our Hawaiian ancestors the proper way to treat foreign visitors, and we learned our lesson well" (p. 337).

In her ensuing analyses, Kaomea juxtaposes the Hawaiian studies classroom texts and instructional materials with Hawaiian tour guide books and documents used for the training of Hawai'i's tourist industry workers, to explore how the material interests of the state's visitor industry continue to be expressed in this ostensibly Hawaiian curriculum.

With example after example, Kaomea (2000) reveals a disturbing, recurring link between the Hawaiian curriculum and the Hawai'i tourist industry—in Hawaiian studies textbooks that read like tour books, in the striking similarities between the Hawaiian studies curricular manuals and the state manuals for the training of professional tour guides, and in the curriculum's relentless indoctrination of Hawaiian values associated with the aloha spirit and "Hawaiian hospitality." By drawing upon and exploiting enduring colonial images of Hawaiians as hospitable natives who are naturally predisposed to serving and entertaining their honored guests, the "Hawaiian" curriculum subtly and not-so-subtly promotes a distorted notion of the Hawaiian culture as an exotic commodity to be consumed by visiting foreigners while simultaneously recruiting Native Hawaiian students as low paid, frontline tourist industry labor.

This inextricable link between the Hawaiian curriculum and Hawai'i's visitor industry points to an urgent need for Hawai'i's schools to question the suitability of this 30-year-old curriculum to modern Native Hawaiian concerns and affairs. However, given the state's dependence on the tourist industry as its primary economic mainstay, and its material interest in appropriating the Hawaiian culture for the industry's continued success, it is unlikely that Hawai'i's schools will see significant statewide changes in this area until Hawaiians gain more control over the Hawaiian curriculum and its implementation, and assume more power and influence in Hawai'i's educational system and the society at large (Kaomea, 2000).

In order for such changes to occur, various structural impediments will need to be overturned: Hawai'i will need larger numbers of Native Hawaiian teachers; Hawaiians, rather than outsiders, will need to write the "Hawaiian" textbooks and curricula; and all teachers, Hawaiian and non-Hawaiian alike, will need to go through a comprehensive course in using these Hawaiian materials in a culturally sensitive and appropriate manner. Until these structural changes are in place, the persistent colonial images of happy, hospitable, and naturally subservient natives that are perpetuated through this "Hawaiian" curriculum will continue to serve the economic interests of the state by fulfilling its need for cheap labor, docile Hawaiians, and willing and able "ambassadors of aloha."

By arguing that well-intended multicultural and indigenous studies texts that are put into place in advance of significant structural changes in school and community power relations can paradoxically reinscribe old colonial notions, Kaomea's (2000) research serves as a reminder that the "post" in postcolonialism doesn't mean colonialism is over. After centuries of distortion and appropriation of the Hawaiian culture, the colonialist economic, social, and political dynamics that have existed and continue to exist in Hawai'i's schools and the larger society make it difficult for Hawaiian studies texts to be conceived and received in truly progressive ways. Thus until the colonial dynamics of postcolonial Hawai'i are overthrown, the teaching of Hawaiian studies in Hawai'i schools may continue to be problematic.

TEXTS TO PROMOTE A NATIVE HAWAIIAN WORLDVIEW

In a paper entitled "Books are Dangerous," Maori writer Patricia Grace argues that there are four ways in which mainstream textbooks can be dangerous to indigenous readers and students from culturally diverse backgrounds: they do not reinforce our values, actions, customs, culture and identity; when they tell us only about others, they say that we do not exist; they may be writing about us but are writing things that are untrue; they are writing about us but saying negative and insensitive things that tell us that we are not good (cited in Smith, 1999). As the foregoing analysis suggests, an emphasis on reading comprehension as critical evaluation is essential preparation for students of diverse cultural backgrounds, who should be taught to unearth the underlying assumptions and distortions in "dangerous" mainstream textbooks and rewrite the world through texts that present their cultures and worldviews with greater accuracy, perception, and sensitivity.

As their ancestors have done in the past, Native Hawaiians, from *keiki* (children) to *kūpuna* (elders), are now beginning to claim the power of print for themselves as they begin to write and publish books in Hawaiian history and culture that tell stories about their local communities and privilege Native Hawaiian perspectives and concerns.

For instance, the bilingual book *The Fish and Their Gifts/Nā Makana a Nā Iʻa* (Stender, 2004), which won the Hawaiʻi Book Publishers Association's top Samuel M. Kamakau award for the 2005 Hawaiʻi Book of the Year, was written by a Native Hawaiian seventh-grade student and illustrated by his classmates. The book was part of an innovative book-publishing class project at the Kanu o ka ʻĀina Hawaiian-focused charter school, which is dedicated to perpetuating the Hawaiian language and culture through rigorous inquiry projects that incorporate native traditions such as *kalo* (taro) cultivation, outrigger-canoe sailing, and traditional Hawaiian protocol.

Another commendable set of Hawaiian-authored books are the *Hoʻulu Hou: Stories Told By Us* children's book series (Nā Kamalei Koʻolauloa Early Education Program, 2004, 2005, 2006). These bilingual English-Hawaiian picture books were written collaboratively by a committee of Hawaiian elders along with representatives of Native Hawaiian organizations in the Koʻolauloa community. The stories present the Native Hawaiian language and culture in an authentic and respectful manner, and feature people, places and stories that are unique to the Hawaiian community of Koʻolauloa.

Following in the tradition of the authors and editors of the Hawaiian resistance newspaper *Ka Hoku o ka Pakipika*, we anticipate that these will be the first in a long series of books through which Hawaiians young and old will begin to reclaim the Native Hawaiian right to talk back to the colonial discourses that pervade our school textbooks and retell the story of their people from the long silent *kanaka maoli* (indigenous Hawaiian) perspective.

CONCLUSION

We began this chapter with Freire's (1985) insight that reading the word involves not only reading the world but writing or rewriting it. We find this view of reading and reading comprehension to be particularly compelling in the case of Native Hawaiians and other diverse cultural groups whose status in society—including political, economic, social, psychological, educational, and even physical well being—are so often negatively impacted by the dominance of mainstream groups. We have argued that literacy may be both empowering and disempowering to diverse cultural groups. Literacy can be empowering when used by a group to position itself, for example, by asserting anticolonial political stances and preserving cultural traditions. But literacy can be disempowering to diverse cultural groups when used by the dominant group as a tool of colonialism, for example, by asserting colonialist political stances and advancing inaccurate and denigrating views of a diverse cultural group.

We illustrated the concept of literacy as disempowerment by discussing four prongs of the missionary literary project in Hawaiʻi. The first centered on logs and journals, dating back to first contact with the West, that advanced colonial representations of Native Hawaiians; the second, on a Hawaiian-language orthography and teaching the Hawaiian people to read the Bible and other Christian texts; the third, on popular texts such as newspapers that served to institutionalize colonial representations of Native Hawaiians and assert Western superiority; and the fourth, on elimination of the Hawaiian-language schools (also known as the common schools).

Other Native Hawaiian scholars have traced the missionary literary project in domains not addressed here. The disempowering uses of literacy in political and legal documents are extensively documented in Kame'eleihiwa's (1992) research on the 1848 *Māhele*, an event that stripped most Native Hawaiians of their lands, and in Osorio's (2002) research on the 19th century sumptuary laws and constitutions that destroyed the foundation of Native Hawaiian governance, traditionally rooted in relationships between the chiefs and the common people.

More importantly, we illustrated the concept of literacy as empowerment. This concept reflects Freire's (1985) observation that reading the word involves not just reading the world but writing or rewriting it, that literacy entails transforming the world through conscious practical action. Our first example dates from 1861 with the founding of the newspaper *Ka Hoku o ka Pakipika* by Native Hawaiians, initiating a long tradition of nationalist resistance to colonialism through popular texts. These texts advanced Hawaiian views of current events, provided access to accounts of world news withheld by missionary-influenced newspapers, and supplied a written record of traditional culture and practices for future generations. Our second example was the 1897 anti-annexation petition, signed by more than 21,000 Native Hawaiians in a dramatic demonstration of resistance to Western political domination.

Considerable historical research remains to be done, including studies of rates of literacy among Native Hawaiians during the 19th century and of 19th century Hawaiian language textbooks, such as primers. However, it is reasonable to expect the results of future work to reinforce the basic argument we have outlined.

In the second part of this chapter we showed how the legacy of the missionary literary project—literacy to disempower Native Hawaiians—continues to this day, offering elementary school Hawaiian studies textbooks as a prime example. These textbooks bear a striking resemblance to tourist industry documents depicting Western visitors as the honored guests of hospitable and subservient Native Hawaiians. Modern Hawaiian studies textbooks thus perpetuate a colonial trope that can be traced back to Cook's "discovery" of the islands.

In parallel fashion, the tradition of resistance to colonialism—literacy to empower Native Hawaiians—has been carried forward in the present day, with new force and sophistication. To show the continuation of this legacy we cited Kaomea's (2000) critique unveiling the colonial underpinnings of Hawaiian studies textbooks. We also highlighted examples of books written by Native Hawaiians, young people and adults, in both English and the Hawaiian language, that celebrate and perpetuate Hawaiian culture in the context of communities and with a sense of place.

We think that equally striking examples of literacy as empowerment and disempowerment could be presented by scholars studying other diverse cultural groups. We believe research along these lines to be vital in unpacking issues of school literacy achievement—or underachievement—among students of diverse cultural backgrounds. Drawing upon Freire's (1985) insights, we suggest that reading comprehension in the education of students of diverse backgrounds be defined as the ability to analyze texts critically and to use one's critical analysis as the basis for rewriting the world. One of the practical implications growing from our research is the vital importance of emphasizing instruction in reading comprehension, consistent with our definition, in contrast to limiting reading instruction to basic skills. In the modern "post" colonial era, where colonial influences still dominate, Native Hawaiians, as well as other diverse groups, must be prepared to position themselves—or suffer the continuing consequences of being positioned by others. Reading comprehension, as we have defined it, is a necessity for cultural survival. In this sense, as Native Hawaiians have long believed, words do hold the power of life and death.

NOTES

1. A compelling study by David Stannard (1989) challenges the conventional 1778 Hawaiian population estimates and suggests that the actual figure was 800,000 or more.

REFERENCES

Anderson, B. (1991). *Imagined communities: Reflections on the origin and spread of nationalism*. New York: Verso.

Armstrong, R. (1858). *Report of the president of the board of education to the Hawaiian legislature*. Honolulu, HI: Kingdom of Hawaii, Reign of Kamehameha IV, Fourth Year.

Au, K. H. (1998). Social constructivism and the school literacy learning of students of diverse cultural backgrounds. *Journal of Literacy Research, 30*, 297–319.

Bauer, H. (1982). *Hawaii the aloha state* (2nd ed.). Honolulu, HI: Bess Press.

Benham, M. A., & Heck, R. H. (1998). *Culture and educational policy in Hawai'i: The silencing of native voices*. Mahwah, NJ: Erlbaum.

Cook, J. (1784). *A voyage to the Pacific Ocean. Undertaken by the command of his majesty* (J. Douglas, Ed.) London: G. Nicol and T. Cadell.

Cook, J. (1949). *The voyages of Captain Cook round the world* (C. Lloyd, Ed.). London: Cresset Press.

Cook, J. (1967). *The journal of Captain James Cook. The voyage of the Resolution and Discovery* (J. C. Beaglehole, Ed.). London: The Hakluyt Society.

Daws, G. (1989). *Shoal of time: A history of the Hawaiian Islands*. Honolulu, HI: University of Hawaii Press.

Dotts, C. K., & Sikkema, M. (1994). *Challenging the status quo: Public education in Hawaii 1840–1980*. Honolulu, HI: Hawaii Education Association.

Edgar, T. (1778). *The Edgar journal of Captain Cook's third voyage 1776–1778*. London: Public Records Office.

Fitzgerald, J. (1995). English-as-a-second-language reading instruction in the United States: A research review. *Journal of Reading Behavior, 27*, 115–152.

Freire, P. (1985). Reading the world and reading the word: An interview with Paulo Freire. *Language Arts, 62*(1), 15–21.

Grimshaw, P. (1989). New England missionary wives, Hawaiian women and "the cult of true womanhood." In M. Jolly & M. Macintyre (Eds.), *Family and gender in the Pacific: Domestic contradictions and the colonial impact* (pp. 19–44). Cambridge: Cambridge University Press.

Hori, J. (undated). *Background and historical significance of Ka Nupepa Kuokoa*. Honolulu: Special Collections, Hamilton Library, University of Hawaii at Manoa.

Kaestle, C. F., Damon-Moore, H., Stedman, L. C., Tinsley, K., & W. V. Trollinger, J. (1991). *Literacy in the United States: Readers and reading since 1880*. New Haven, CT: Yale University Press.

Kamakau, S. M. (1968). *Ka po'e kahiko: The people of old*. Honolulu, HI: Bishop Museum Press.

Kame'eleihiwa, L. (1992). *Native land and foreign desires*. Honolulu, HI: Bishop Museum Press.

Kaomea, J. (2000). A curriculum of aloha? Colonialism and tourism in Hawai'i's elementary textbooks. *Curriculum Inquiry, 30*(3), 319–344.

Kaomea, J. (2003). Reading erasures and making the familiar strange: Defamiliarizing methods for research in formerly colonized and historically oppressed communities. *Educational Researcher, 32*(2), 14–25.

Kaomea, J. (2005). Indigenous studies in the elementary curriculum: A cautionary Hawaiian example. *Anthropology & Education Quarterly, 36*(1), 24–42.

Kelly, M. (1991). Some thoughts on education in traditional Hawaiian society. In *To teach the children: Historical aspects of education in Hawaii* (pp. 4–14). Honolulu: College of Education, University of Hawaii.

Kirch, P. V. (2007). Hawaii as a model system for human ecodynamics. *American Anthropologist, 109*(1), 8–26.

Lockridge, K. (1974). *Literacy in colonial New England: An enquiry into the social context of literacy in the early modern west*. New York: Norton.

Macherey, P. (1978). *A theory of literary production* (G. Wall, Trans.). London: Routledge and Kegan Paul.

Monaghan, E. J., & Hartman, D. K. (2000). Undertaking historical research in literacy. In M. L. Kamil, P. B. Mosenthal, P. D. Pearson, & R. Barr (Eds.), *Handbook of reading research* (Vol. III, pp. 109–121). Mahwah, NJ: Erlbaum.

Nā Kamalei Koʻolauloa Early Education Program. (2004, 2005, 2006). *Hoʻulu hou project: Stories told by us.* Hauʻula, HI: Na Kamalei.

Oakes, J., & Guiton, G. (1995). Matchmaking: The dynamics of high school tracking decisions. *American Educational Research Journal, 32*(1), 3–33.

Obeyesekere, G. (1992). *The apotheosis of Captain Cook: European mythmaking in the Pacific.* Princeton, NJ: Princeton University Press.

Osorio, J. K. K. (2002). *Dismembering Lahui: A history of the Hawaiian nation to 1887.* Honolulu: University of Hawaiʻi Press.

Phelan, P. (1993). *Unmarked: The politics of performance.* London: Routledge.

Pukui, M. K. (1983). *ʻOlelo Noʻeau: Hawaiian proverbs and poetical sayings.* Honolulu: Bishop Museum Press.

Pukui, M. K., Haertig, E. W., & Lee, C. A. (1972). *Nānā i ke kumu: Look to the source* (Vol. II). Honolulu, HI: Hui Hānai.

Sahlins, M. (1995). *How "natives" think: About Captain Cook, for example.* Chicago: University of Chicago Press.

Schmitt, R. C. (1968). *Demographic statistics of Hawaiʻi, 1778–1965.* Honolulu: University of Hawaiʻi Press.

Silva, N. K. (1998). *The 1897 petitions protesting annexation.* Honolulu: Special Collections, Hamilton Library, University of Hawaiʻi at Manoa.

Silva, N. K. (1999). Ke kūʻe kū ʻpaʻa loa nei mākou: Kanaka maoli resistance to colonization. Unpublished doctoral dissertation. University of Hawaiʻi.

Silva, N. (2004). *Aloha betrayed: Native Hawaiian resistance to American colonialism.* Durham, NC: Duke University Press.

Smith, L. T., (1999). *Decolonizing methodologies: Research and indigenous peoples.* London: Zed Books Ltd.

Stannard, D. E. (1989). *Before the horror: The population of Hawaiʻi on the eve of western contact.* Honolulu: Social Science Research Institute, University of Hawaiʻi.

Stender, J. K. (2004). *The fish and their gifts/Nā makana a nā iʻa.* Honolulu, HI: Kamehameha Schools Press.

Stueber, R. K. (1991). An informal history of schooling in Hawaiʻi. In *To teach the children: Historical aspects of education in Hawaiʻi* (pp. 16–36). Honolulu: College of Education, University of Hawaiʻi at Manoa and Bernice Pauahi Bishop Museum.

Tate, M. (1962). The Sandwich Islands missionaries create a literature. *Church History, 31*(2), 182–202.

Trask, H. K. (1984). Hawaiians, American colonization, and the quest for independence. *Social Process in Hawaiʻi, 31,* 101–136.

Trask, H. K. (1999). *From a native daughter: Colonialism and sovereignty in Hawaiʻi.* Honolulu: University of Hawaiʻi Press in association with the Center for Hawaiian Studies.

Venezky, R. L. (1991). The development of literacy in the industrialized nations of the west. In R. Barr, M. L. Kamil, P. B. Mosenthal, & P. D. Pearson (Eds.), *Handbook of reading research* (Vol. II, pp. 46–67). New York: Longman.

Wilson, W. H. (1991). Hawaiian language in DOE unique. *Ke Kuamoʻo, 1*(4), 4–6.

Yamauchi, L. A., & Wilhelm, P. (2001). E ola ka Hawaiʻi i kona ʻolelo: Hawaiians live in their language. In D. Christian & F. Genese (Eds.), *Case studies in bilingual education.* Alexandria, VA: TESOL.

28 Culturally Relevant Pedagogy and Reading Comprehension

Colleen M. Fairbanks and Jewell E. Cooper

University of North Carolina – Greensboro

Lynn Masterson

University of Texas – Austin

Sandra Webb

University of North Carolina – Greensboro

INTRODUCTION

In recent years, there has been, perhaps, more interest among literacy educators in supporting the reading development of diverse learners than any other area of reading research. Stemming from the politics of high-stakes assessment and the awareness that we have failed to provide students of color with the literacy skills society demands, literacy researchers have increasingly aimed their efforts at understanding the relationships between cultural diversity and literacy acquisition and the implications for literacy education. This work, begun more than 25 years ago, has been connected in more recent times to the understanding that students will learn to understand their reading better in classrooms that offer them culturally relevant and responsive instruction. It is the connection between these two—reading comprehension and culturally relevant/responsive—pedagogy that we take up in this chapter. We begin by defining culturally relevant and responsive pedagogy, making a somewhat artificial but useful distinction between the two. Then we examine studies that have been significant in clarifying both how enculturation and reading comprehension are intertwined and what we can do to ensure that the diverse students in the classroom learn to read effectively and critically.

CULTURALLY RELEVANT AND CULTURALLY RESPONSIVE PEDAGOGY

Culturally relevant or culturally responsive pedagogy has been supported in multicultural education for a quarter century. Though these specific terms have not always been used to describe such teaching/learning interactions, an overriding theme within both is the concept of culture (Goodenough, 1981) and the use of this concept to connect the home-community environment, the first place of learning for children, with the more structured academic environment—school. Culture can be defined in many ways. We use Goodenough's (1957, as cited in Bennett, 2003) definition of culture. As he explained, "Culture is not a material phenomenon; it does not consist of things, people, behavior, or emotions. It is rather an organization of perceiving, relating and otherwise interpreting them" (Bennett, p. 43). In addition, he concluded, "Culture, then, consists of standards for deciding what is, standards for deciding what can be, standards for deciding how one feels about it, and standards for deciding how to go about doing it" (Goodenough, 1981, p. 62). Consequently, Goodenough located culture in individuals but understood it was mediated by the contexts and practices of their communities and manifested by the ways in which individuals organize their experiences to give them structure and meaning. In other words, the organization of life experiences helps people comprehend the world around them, a complex world that includes the many communities in which individuals hold membership. With this in mind, Trueba (1990) believed "cultural knowledge is at the basis of competent reasoning, inferring, and identifying meaning from myriad competing interpretations" (pp. 1–2). Since learning is socially and culturally mediated, it follows that theories of culturally relevant/responsive pedagogy hold that schools cannot dismiss the learning that students bring with them to the teaching-learning environment.

Beginning in the 1980s, many researchers have advocated the explicit link to students' home-community cultures and the school culture in anthropological terms such as: (a) culturally appropriate (Au & Jordan, 1981); (b) culturally congruent (Mohatt & Erickson, 1981); (c) mitigating cultural discontinuity (Macias, 1987); (d) culturally responsive (Cazden & Legget, 1981; Erickson & Mohatt, 1982; Gay, 2000); (e) culturally compatible (Jordan, 1985, 3 as cited by Ladson-Billings, 1995, p. 159); (f) emancipatory (King, 1991); and (g) culturally relevant (Ladson-Billings, 1992a). For example, Au and Jordan (1981) distinguished between school learning and informal learning. They maintained that knowing the difference between these arenas is important in facilitating academic success for students and bringing the relevance of the text to the child's own experience to help the child make sense of the world. By doing so, the teacher facilitates a bridge between the home-community and school cultures. Further, Macias (1987), in an examination of the Papago early learning environment, found that when the home culture is radically different from that of the social mainstream, it is a still possible to introduce mainstream discourses in ways that do not erode the child's appreciation of his or her own culture. Nor is it necessary that the ethnicity, race, or culture of the teacher match the students, as Ladson-Billings (1994) illustrated. Rather, culturally competent teachers can learn enough of the child's home-community cultural context to be able to interpret behavior properly and adjust curriculum to the student's learning. Finally, King (1991) illustrated how responding to students through the incorporation of home-community cultures and encouraging teachers to assist students in critical reflection about social injustices can bridge students' home and school contexts.

These studies demonstrate the range and scope of interest in the relationships between children's learning and their cultural backgrounds. Yet, it was Ladson-Billings (1992a, 1992b) who initially defined the term *culturally relevant teaching* in terms of teachers' effectiveness in educating African American students. She later substituted pedagogy for teaching to acknowledge the critical, Freirian elements of her theory of education and to distinguish it from any specific instructional method. This shift can be seen in her 1995 definition of culturally relevant pedagogy:

> [A] pedagogy of oppression not unlike critical pedagogy but specifically committed to collective, not merely individual, empowerment. Culturally relevant pedagogy rests on three criteria or propositions: (a) students must experience academic success; (b) students must develop and/or maintain cultural competence; and (c) students must develop a critical consciousness though which they challenge the current status quo of the social order. (p. 160)

With these criteria in mind, Ladson-Billings (1992b) noted that culturally relevant teaching "is designed to *fit* the school culture to the students' culture but also to *use* student culture as the basis for helping students understand themselves and others, structure social interactions, and conceptualize knowledge" (p. 314, emphasis in the original). She urged teachers to attend to and to be in touch with the academic needs of their students and to *believe* that their students can achieve academic excellence not only because teachers want them to do so, but also because the students consciously choose for themselves to succeed academically. In addition to believing in students' abilities to succeed, teachers become actively involved in learning how students' cultures can be integrated in their day-to-day school learning experiences. For such an integration to occur, teachers may need to move beyond the architectures of their classrooms into the communities of their learners and families to discover the strengths of such settings (cf. Moll, 1990). By doing so, teachers explicitly demonstrate that they value students' home and community cultures, show students that they are accepted for who they are, and honor the education that occurs during the hours they are not at school. In other words, culturally relevant/responsive pedagogy insists that students' cultural competence is valued by their teachers and students are aware of it. Furthermore, culturally relevant teaching invites students to challenge the status quo, encouraging them to question how knowledge is created and through whose interpretations it is shared. In order for students to interrogate knowledge in this way, teachers must do so themselves. They must actively engage in what Ladson-Billings (1995) called "a fluid and equitable" mindset where they are both teachers and learners and they trust their students to teach them (p. 163).

Related to culturally relevant pedagogy but with a somewhat different focus is what Gay (2000) calls "culturally responsive teaching." Teaching, from Gay's perspective, not only relates to the various cultures of its students, but it also *responds* to their daily, lived experiences. It is a pedagogy that is active, directly connecting teachers with students individually and collectively. It is a pedagogy that actively "teaches *to and through* the strengths of students" (Gay, 2000, p. 29, emphasis in the original). Gay uses students' prior experiences, knowledge of culture, frames of reference, and styles of performance to make learning meaningful and relevant. In other words, teachers respond to students' cultural identities and how they perceive their places in their communities and the world. Teachers acknowledge, value, and teach the "legitimacy of cultural heritages," using this information in the formal curriculum. Multicultural resources, materials, and information are also used to teach students. Such pedagogy further employs a variety of instructional strategies that are delivered with attention to the learning styles of students.

Many research studies and conceptual writings have described how teachers make learning culturally relevant and responsive generally and in specific content areas (i.e., Alexander-Smith, 2004; Cook & Amatucci, 2006; Ensign, 2003; Gibson, 1996; Gutstein, Lipman, & Hernandez, 1997; Henry, 2001; Jones, Pang, & Rodriguez, 2001; Ladson-Billings, 1995; Lewis, Pitts, & Collins, 2002; Nelson-Barber & Estrin, 1995; Tate, 1995; Wiest, 2001). Yet, the connection between students' cultural backgrounds and reading comprehension has been most fully articulated theoretically. Galda and Beach (2001), for example, identified three aspects of social life that influence readers' interpretations of literary texts (i.e., their constructed meanings): (a) students' evolving class and cultural identities, (b) students' language practices, and (c) their prior historical or cultural knowledge—all of which are instantiated as students read and situate readers in the multi-layered contexts of their social worlds. Thus, textual interpretations differ based on the influence of these factors at the time an individual reads a text, creating the possibility that there may be as many readings as there are readers and that reading comprehension has become much more complicated.

This concept is not new to literary studies where the influence of postmodernism and reader response has challenged the notion of single, authoritative readings. Instead, reading is conceived as a social activity that entails a transaction between reader and text and takes place within the specific conventions of discourse or interpretive communities (Fish, 1980; Rosenblatt, 1978). Moreover, texts are written and constructed in dialogic relation to their writers and readers, and although this notion has applied most often to literary texts, it has its corollary with information texts (think of Native American readers' possible responses to historical texts about Manifest Destiny). Add to this the discomfort with reader responses based on either noncanonical, culturally derived responses or the anxiety that taking up issues of race, class, or gender (which children's personal responses often entail) instill in (predominantly White) teachers and the issues become even more complicated. For example, Copenhaver (2001) found that African American elementary students drew on their extensive understanding of race and race relations in small group discussion of *Malcolm X: A Fire Burning Brightly* (Myers, 2000). These responses displayed historical and cultural knowledge that students' teachers did not believe they had, that they did not generally encourage in whole class discussion, and that they often considered off topic. Similarly, Larson and Irvine (1999) described as "reciprocal distancing" those practices "in which teachers and students invoke existing sociohistorical and political distances between their communities in classroom interaction" (p. 394). Although both students and teachers engaged in reciprocal distancing, teachers' instantiation of it minimized the value of students' cultural resources as a means of meaning construction and impeded students' learning and their development as critical and competent readers.

These studies suggest that for researchers there is still much to do and that we might begin with an examination of our treatment of what and how texts mean and how students' voices might become a more valued part of comprehending texts, a topic we will return to later in this chapter. Suffice it to say that a quick ERIC search yields few studies that take up questions about the how and to what end readers' positions as raced, classed, and gendered people influence their text comprehension as it is more traditionally defined. For this chapter, however, we were charged with a review of literature that empirically tied culturally relevant/responsive pedagogy to students' reading comprehension. To accomplish this task, we organized our review of studies to those that focus on learners who are influenced by cultural experiences and knowledge (culturally relevant) that shape their reading and those that focus on the instructional implications that follow from these influences and illustrate how teachers and students use cultural knowledge to support academic learning (culturally responsive). Although there are many commonalities between conceptions of culturally relevant and culturally responsive pedagogy, it is the distinction—"fitting" the school to the student and *using* student culture in the curriculum—that has guided our examination of landmark studies of reading comprehension and by which we present the results of inquiries.

READING COMPREHENSION AND
CULTURALLY RESPONSIVE PEDAGOGY

Rather than a method comprising a collection of varied instructional strategies that are imposed on readers, culturally responsive pedagogy embodies an orientation toward literacy teaching and learning that draws from and builds upon the students' backgrounds and experiences with full acknowledgement of the available funds of knowledge they bring to the classroom. Thus, culturally responsive pedagogy becomes a way of connecting to the lived experiences of individual learners while considering the ways in which students are historically, socially, culturally, and linguistically situated. Responsive pedagogy is not only about the inclusion of a student's culture into the curriculum but also the belief that children from diverse backgrounds have the ability to participate in learning experiences that promote higher level thinking in response to text, such as participation in instructional conversations or book club discussions, rather than be relegated to skills-based and decontextualized exercises (Taylor, Pearson, Peterson, & Rodriguez, 2003, 2005). A number of educational scholars and researchers have described the nature of culturally responsive pedagogy (Au, 1993; Gay, 2000, 2002; Ladson-Billings, 2001); Gay (2002), however, offered the following characterization: "using the cultural characteristics, experiences, and perspectives of ethnically diverse students as conduits for teaching them more effectively" (p. 106). Therefore, culturally responsive pedagogy requires teachers to become knowledgeable about and sensitive to students' lives outside the school community and organize instruction around the principles of social constructivism that emphasize the importance and relevance of students' backgrounds (Au, 1993; Ladson-Billings, 2001).

In order to structure our discussion of landmark studies in culturally responsive instruction and its relationship to reading comprehension, we have organized our review using Wiley's (2005) framework. Based on ethnographic studies of children and adults' literacy practices in the context of social and cultural events, Wiley (2005) conceptualized culturally responsive literacy instruction by focusing on three primary processes: *adaptation, accommodation,* and *incorporation.* Adaptation involves processes that operate from a deficit theory. Children of diverse linguistic and ethnic backgrounds need to conform to the demands of school norms and standards. Although accommodation recognizes the real demands of standards, high-stakes testing, and mainstream discourses that dominate classroom interactions, the processes involved are sensitive to the cultural backgrounds, experiences, and needs of students. In this regard, teachers support students by focusing on differences and attempting "to meet learners halfway, working with them in an effort to change their language and literacy practices, to make them more compatible with schooled, middle-class norms" (Wiley, 2005, p. 151). In contrast, incorporation represents alternative processes that seek to integrate some of the cultural practices of students in an attempt to reduce the effect of the normalizing forces of White mainstream school cultures and provide an alternative to one-way acculturation practices.

Adaptation: Explicit instruction for assimilation and standardization

In recent history, the political climate of standardized testing has fueled interest in studies that focus on adaptation. The instructional climate of No Child Left Behind and its stated premise that *all* children must become competent readers has generated a new research focus on reading instruction aimed at closing the literacy gap between white, middle-class students and students from low-income families or students of color. School districts across the country, with awareness of and concern for this gap, scramble to find an answer that will fix the problem. Oftentimes, they turn to direct instruction programs such as SRA Corrective Reading (Marchand-Martella, Martella, & Martella, n.d.)—a scripted presentation of decoding that claims to "unlock the door to success" (Marchand-Martella, Martella, & Martella, n.d., p. 2) and includes "word attack skills and isolated sound-word practice, group reading activities to develop accuracy and oral reading fluency, workbook exercises, and opportunities to enrich reading with chapter books aligned with program levels" (p. 3). This program finds much of its support by citing gains in reading levels with children with learning disabilities or mental retardation or who were incarcerated as evidence of its effectiveness (Drakeford, 2002; Flores, Shippen, Alberto, & Crowe, 2004; Malmgren & Leone, 2000; Meese, 2001; Polloway, Epstein, Polloway, Patton, & Ball, 1986). Wiley's (2005) point is that adaptation is not genuinely culturally responsive because learners are expected to abandon their cultural history and adapt to new conditions. Inherently, not only the students but also their cultural backgrounds are considered deficient.

Studies focused on adaptation have been received with skepticism by those who argue that schools need to accept and value the language and learning practices of culturally diverse students (Willis & Harris, 2000). However, Barnitz (1998) argued, for example, that adaptive strategies to reading instruction are misguided. Rather, enhancing reading comprehension in culturally responsive ways needs to address the following conditions. First, students may experience difficulty with reading comprehension when the situational context does not support their reading. Second, effective instructional strategies include those that help learners connect texts with their own cultural and linguistic resources. Third, we know from many fields—education, psychology, linguistics, artificial intelligence, and philosophy—that many factors influence construction of meaning, especially prior social and cultural experiences and knowledge. Finally, comprehension instruction for all developing readers is "sensitive to orchestration of cognitive, linguistic, and cultural variables in order for literacy learners to construct meaning for the texts they are reading" and involves "strategies that access rich cultural background knowledge and native linguistic abilities as they (learners) read and write" (p. 92). Nonetheless, adaptive studies explore culturally responsive approaches to reading instruction that will help close the literacy gap. Contemporary studies are based on the belief that effective strategy instruction for students "particularly for those with language and learning disabilities, at a minimum will require much direct explanation and modeling of strategy use, as well as scaffolded student practice" (Whitaker, Gambrell, & Morrow, 2004, p. 148).

Accommodation: Culturally relevant instruction for achievement and school success

Much of the research exemplifying the construct of accommodation has emerged from studies that illustrate the need for explicit reading comprehension instruction. This research is based on the understanding that reading comprehension is an interactive process between reader, text, and context (Smagorinsky, 2001) and that text information in this process is related to prior knowledge and experiences. Thus, cultural and linguistic backgrounds are significant resources in constructing meaning from the text, a topic we explore in greater depth in the following section. Accommodation underscores the demands of the dominant Discourse (Gee, 1996) and works to build on students' cultural and linguistic knowledge through explicit instruction. Consistent with a sociocultural approach to learning, those who are more knowledgeable scaffold the learning by creating experiences and interactions within the zone of proximal development (Vygotsky, 1978), including the possibility that students, "given their individual social and cultural backgrounds, may also become the more knowledgeable other within the learning situation" (Goatley, Brock, & Raphael, 1995, p. 355). Accommodation perspectives recognize that students whose cultural backgrounds differ from the dominant culture are taught the language codes that will ensure successful participation in society (Delpit, 1995).

In the Center for the Improvement of Early Reading Achievement (CIERA) School Change Project, a study of 13 schools across the United States with student populations representing those from high poverty as well as diverse cultural backgrounds, Taylor et al. (2003, 2005) found that little time was actually spent in comprehension strategy instruction and that most often students were given comprehension practice in the form of worksheets on main ideas or a teacher-directed written response to the text. However, Taylor et al. (2003) also explored the types of comprehension instruction fostering students' reading growth and reported that when teachers asked higher level questions, including interpreting characters and making personal connections to the text, these practices challenged the students to think about what they had read and resulted in significant growth.

Given this finding, strategies such as Question Answer Relationship, (QAR; Raphael, 1986; Raphael & McKinney, 1983; Raphael & Pearson, 1985; Raphael & Wonnacott, 1985), consisting of explicit instruction in the use of questions to support reading, may be effective with diverse learners who are often thought to be less capable of higher level thinking and, therefore, rarely talk about texts. QAR provides students with common language and comprehension strategies to foster critical thinking abilities. As Raphael, Highfield, and Au (2006) note, "If students of diverse backgrounds do not receive the kind of comprehension instruction that can prepare them for assessments increasingly oriented toward higher-level thinking with text, we have little hope of being able to close the achievement gap" (p. 17).

While the CIERA project (Taylor et al., 2003, 2005) examined elementary reading instruction, Greenleaf, Schoenbach, Cziko, and Mueller (2001) focused on the adolescent learner and explored the use of an alternative instructional framework for remediation referred to as a "Reading Apprenticeship" (p. 81). Premised on the belief that isolated skills instruction—adaptive in nature—is limiting, this work provided a clear example of accommodation approaches and their impact on students' reading. In a high school established to provide "a college preparatory education for Latino, African-American, and immigrant students who had been historically deprived of such educational opportunities" (p. 93), the teachers and students formed a partnership as they engaged in collaborative inquiry about reading and the reading process. The course, Academic Literacy, created to meet the rigorous demands of reading content area texts, incorporated the instructional strategies of Reciprocal Teaching—questioning, summarizing, clarifying, and predicting (Palincsar & Brown, 1984), in addition to explicit, integrated instruction in self-monitoring, cognitive strategies, text analysis, teacher think alouds, modeling reading and problem solving with texts, and writing and discussing their own reading processes and confusion. Measured by the Degrees of Reading Power (DRP), this diverse student population gained 2 years of reading proficiency over the 7-month period.

These studies highlight the needs of students from culturally and linguistically diverse backgrounds, and their approaches were consistent with a practice of accommodation, since goals specifically address a need for closing the achievement gap. They further suggest creating a shared language of reading comprehension emphasizing higher level thinking for promoting student advancement on high stakes testing and enabling future opportunities in higher education, employment, and society (Raphael & Au, 2005). Students from diverse backgrounds do not require different reading comprehension strategies in this view; they need access to the strategies and opportunities that White middle class students have to engage in higher-level interactions with text for understanding of increasingly complex texts.

Incorporation: Designing instruction responsive to students' cultural identities

Research studies in this category illustrate how learning environments incorporate instruction that is responsive to the various cultural identities students bring with them to the classroom. These studies suggest that classrooms can be more culturally responsive by attending to the knowledge and practices of the local community. Such classrooms modify curriculum to address the needs of the local situation, bring students' backgrounds and experience to build on literacy traditions of families (Moll, Amanti, Neff, & Gonzalez, 1992; Moll & Gonzalez, 1994; Reyes & Halcon, 2001), support children's reading with quality literature that promotes learning about the diversity of the local setting (e.g., bilingual, multicultural literature), and attend to students' interests.

Fitzgerald and Graves (2004), for example, suggested a framework for improving reading comprehension with English Language Learners that focused on constructing meaning by engaging in before, during, and after reading strategies and modulating to learners' backgrounds, needs, and strengths to actively engage them in learning. With an emphasis on vocabulary development, Jimenez (2001) also demonstrated the importance of drawing on students' available cognate knowledge as a way to bridge home and school languages. He asserted that "such an omission is a waste of linguistic resources" (p. 157). In addition, the inclusion of culturally familiar topics makes it easier for culturally and linguistically diverse students to make personal connections with the text, thus enhancing the meaning making process. Gee (1996) believes it is critical for second language learners to learn the discourse practices of the mainstream community, an achievement less likely to occur if they are relegated to skills-based, pull-out programs "isolated from the mainstream discourse patterns" (p. 352).

Promoting such classroom interactions among students demonstrates a culturally responsive pedagogy and is readily evidenced in the following studies of book club discussions. In their study of a combined fourth and fifth-grade, culturally and linguistically diverse classroom, Kong and Fitch (2002–2003) found that when the teacher valued the students' experiences from home and community, she supported a learning environment in which the students felt safe to share personal stories and construct new knowledge. Through "guided participation" (p. 355), the teacher and more knowledgeable peers taught the others how to participate in the discussion. Students learned how to use contextual clues, make personal connections, and share thoughts and ideas while they engaged in the text both aesthetically and critically. These practices led to an increase of sight word vocabulary and the metacognitive ability to reflect upon and talk about their reading process. Similarly, Maloch (2005) reported the importance of the teacher in scaffolding students to norms and expectations for participation in peer-led conversations about text. In her study of two African-American boys in a third-grade classroom, the teacher was instrumental in the boys' increased success for participating in literature discussion groups. Congruent with culturally responsive teaching in which the teacher must care that the students achieve academically, Ms. P. mediated the interactions and, through encouraging comments and continual interaction, established the expectation for participation. This study did not directly measure comprehension but showed how students could gain cultural capital in order to participate in the conversation, leading to a deeper understanding of the text.

Literacy events, such as student-led discussions of text, illustrate the social nature of constructing meaning. It is in this context that students from diverse backgrounds have the opportunity to "construct discursive practices that shape interpretations of text" (Goatley, Brock, & Raphael, 1995, p. 355) while incorporating their lived experiences in the process. In their second analysis of the data, Goatley, Brock, and Raphael (1995) explored the comprehension strategies used by one group of diverse learners to construct meaning from the text. Like Kong and Fitch (2002–2003) and Maloch (2005) they, too, were interested in the degree to which the students scaffolded each others meaning making. Drawing on Duffy (1993), they found that students were using their ability to be strategic by taking the responsibility to apply known strategies to clarify information. The book club became a place of interdependence as the students worked together to make meaning of a difficult text.

Nystrand (2006) posited that classroom discussion is a critical element in the development of reading comprehension. Citing a study by Van den Branden (2000), he further noted that such text discussions were highly effective in supporting reading comprehension when students in multilingual classrooms are actively involved in solving problems that they identified in a text. Similarly, Saunders and Goldenberg (1999) reported fluent and limited English proficient students in fourth- and fifth-grade classrooms scored higher in factual and interpretive comprehension than the control group when involved in instructional conversations—"discussion-based lessons geared toward creating richly textured opportunities for students' conceptual and linguistic development" (Goldenberg, 1992–1993, p. 317). Explorations such as these demonstrate how conversations make a space for students to bring their own language and cultural knowledge to the meaning-making process and illustrate the means of incorporating culturally responsive reading pedagogy into diverse classroom settings. This structure stands in contrast to the transmission model of instruction that positions the teacher as the dispenser of knowledge without consideration of how the students are socially, culturally, or historically situated.

READING COMPREHENSION AND CULTURALLY RELEVANT PEDAGOGY

For our purposes, we include studies as culturally relevant when they examine how children's social and cultural contexts shape their worldviews and their learning and how students' ways of knowing drive instructional practices. This perspective draws upon sociohistorical learning theories based on Vygotsky and his followers and understands learning as a socially and culturally mediated activity through which learners acquire, appropriate, and transform knowledge within specific contexts (Cole, 1996; Moll, 2000; Vygotsky, 1986; Wells, 1999; Wertsch, 1991). Wells (1999) has argued that activities engage learners with the material and thinking world in specific contexts and help them develop and refine their use of semantic and material tools. For our purposes, the uses of language, as semiotic tools, are especially critical to our understanding of reading comprehension. It is through students' engagement with texts that students both learn new information and develop the higher order thinking skills necessary for further intellectual development and academic achievement. Wells (1999) based these arguments on the complementary nature of talk and texts, whereby students drawing on their everyday knowledge can be guided toward and can construct new understandings. This process extends not only to concepts or ideas (e.g., content) but also generic understandings of text that facilitate further (and more abstract) learning from text. This position suggests, then, a conception of reading comprehension tied closely to actual learners, the texts they read, and the contexts of their reading. As Moll (1998) has asserted, "Reading is understanding how a text works, how it gives rise to meaning, but also, it is understanding the reader's role in creating or mediating that meaning with text for particular purposes" (p. 67).

This sociocultural perspective has tended to treat culture broadly, focusing on the historical accumulation of tools and their uses across generations as a peculiarly human phenomenon. It represents thinking as a cognitive function of all humans but tells us less about reading and learning as it relates to the cultural differences that make up humanity. Other scholars, however, interested in the specific learning processes of students of color acquired within their cultural communities, have focused on how these students' worldviews shape their learning both in and out of school. As Moll (2000) argued, "People think in conjunction with the artifacts of culture, including, most prominently, the verbal and written interactions with other human beings" (p. 265). The language or dialect students speak, the funds of knowledge they acquire through their interactions with family and neighbors, and the tools they acquire in home contexts all contribute to the students' ways of making meaning and interacting in the social world (Moll, 1990). As a result, how learners interact with the texts they encounter in schools is not only mediated by the instruction they receive but also by the accumulation of their past histories with language and its uses as a tool for understanding.

This area of research has tended toward the theoretical, although some studies have, in fact, examined the complex interactions of students' linguistic or cultural practices and their developing abilities to construct meaning from text. These studies illustrate the means by which students' sociohistorical understandings can be used as resources supporting their text comprehension, in Ladson-Billings' (1992a) terms, fitting the school to the student. Specifically, this research focuses on cultural and linguistic knowledge or experiences as tools that students may exploit (when given authority and support to do so) to create increasingly rich and nuanced meanings from the text they read. Three areas of research have explored culturally relevant pedagogy and reading comprehension: (a) adapting classroom participant structures, (b) cultural modeling, and (c) creating hybrid spaces where home and school cultures can be transformed.

The work of three researchers and their colleagues has been of particular importance in this area: Au's (1980; Au & Jordon, 1981; Au & Mason, 1983) early work, along with Roland Tharp and others, with the Kemehameha Early Education Program (KEEP); Lee's (1993, 1995, 2000) work with cultural modeling as a means of adapting literature curriculum to students; and Gutierrez' (2000; Gutierrez, Baquedano-Lopez, & Tejeda, 1999; Gutierrez, Baquedano-Lopez, & Turner, 1997; Gutierrez, Rymes, & Larson, 1995) studies on hybridity and third space in classrooms. Underscoring all of this work is the understanding that cultural knowledge and practices are valuable forms of prior knowledge that shape students' reading but are often left untapped by most reading instruction. That readers rely on prior knowledge to make sense of text has been a bedrock principle of reading comprehension since the 1970s (Anderson, 1984). Moreover, the original conceptions of schema theory defined prior knowledge in its broadest social, cultural, and psychological terms (Alexander, Schallert, & Hare, 1991). However, much of the subsequent research and the vast majority of the instructional applications that followed focused on the topical content of texts, rather than the cultural or linguistic practices that might animate such knowledge.

More recently, however, literacy researchers have reasserted the importance of cultural knowledge as an essential element of students' reading comprehension (Gutierrez, Rymes, & Larson, 1995; Jimenez, Garcia, & Pearson, 1996; Meacham, 2001; Moll, 1998). Meacham (2001), for example, has contended, "Prior knowledge, an important concept within schema theory toward the enhancement of reading comprehension, has profound implications for the quantity of cultural information in the classroom" (p. 194). This cultural knowledge extends to not only knowledge of traditions and history but also to linguistic and cultural practices that constitute individuals' ways of knowing. No research effort has illustrated the importance of culturally based forms of prior knowledge more than Luis Moll and his colleagues (González, 1995; Moll, 1998, 2000). This research posited that students acquire funds of knowledge through their everyday practices with family and in their communities. This knowledge consists of the "historically accumulated bodies of knowledge and skills essential for household functioning and well-being" (González, 1995, p. 4). From these funds of knowledge, children learn to mediate their interactions in the social world and they are provided resources in both what and the how of social, cultural and, when afforded, of intellectual life (Moll, 2000). Through ethnographic studies in predominantly Latino communities, teachers and researchers explored funds of knowledge, and teachers connected with communities (and their cultural capital) in new ways, adapting instruction to the students who shared their classrooms. As González asserted, the funds of knowledge project aimed to "evaluate and weave elements of their own and their students' experiences into educational practice" (p. 6). Finally, funds of knowledge echoes culturally relevant pedagogy by illustrating the importance of improving instructional practice "by framing the curricula and pedagogy with familiar contextual cues" (González, 1995, p. 6). With respect to reading comprehension, this area of research points to reading instruction intended to "help children exploit the ample resources in their environment, to help children become, through literacy, conscious users of their funds of knowledge for their thinking and their development" (Moll, 1998, p. 74).

In one way or another, the bodies of work described below attend to these under-standings about students and their reading, broadening our understanding of prior knowledge and its relationship to reading comprehension. In addition, they all point to the impact of culturally relevant pedagogy on academic tasks, such as reading, demon-strating that such tasks are less straightforward, apolitical processes than sociocultural practices that provide or withhold access to students who have been traditionally mar-ginalized in academic settings.

Adapting classroom participation structures

During the 1970s and 1980s, teachers and researchers at KEEP, a demonstration school, sought to understand the most effective means of teaching Hawaiian children, who, as a group, had a history of school failure. The project was also one of the first literacy programs to take seriously the need to adapt school structures, specifically participa-tion structures, to the children the school served. A series of studies (Au, 1980; Au & Mason, 1983; Tharp, 1982) demonstrated the efficacy of this instruction for Hawaiian children. Specifically, Au's work (1980; Au & Jordon, 1981; Au & Mason, 1983) found that Hawaiian children spent more time engaged in academic tasks when they were taught in culturally appropriate and congruent ways and continued to outperform their peers even after they left the program at the end of the third grade.

With respect to reading comprehension, Tharp's (1982) study demonstrated the greater effectiveness of instruction that was "compatible with the culture of the stu-dents" (p. 23). This instruction followed a sociolinguistic pattern, known as E-T-R, in which teachers first drew on the children's experiences as a way to introduce the con-tent of the lesson, second introduced the reading material, and finally helped students examine the relationship between their experiences and the reading. According to Au (1980), the "constant interweaving of text-derived information with personal experi-ence and existing knowledge established the cultural congruence of the lesson at one level, that of content" (p. 94). In order for a reading lesson to use children's cultural practices, Au (1980) argued, it must also attend to the interactional patterns that the children learn at home and in their communities. In other words, it must attend to both what the children know from their experiences and how they typically relate to such knowledge through talk. Thus, Au looked specifically at the participation struc-tures the teachers intentionally established to resemble Hawaiian children's use of "talk-story," a conversational practice characterized by joint performance and turn-taking rules that involve more than one speaker. In the classroom, valuing talk-story entails speaking rights shared between children and the teacher and the acceptance of multiple speakers who volunteer to speak. Teachers effective in such participation structures were able to use their "authority to channel the talk-storylike participation structures toward academic goals" and to acquire this authority by permitting talk-storylike conversations in the classroom and sharing speaking rights with the children (p. 112).

The significance of the KEEP studies lies in their recognition that children par-ticipate in their learning in ways that are shaped by their cultural lives. Conducting the anthropological work to identify the participation structures students acquired at home and adapting instruction sensitive to these structures led teachers to adapt reading instruction to the children and helped them grow as readers. As Tharp (1982) noted at the time, "Comprehension is not wholly a function of intelligence and experi-ence; what teachers do during reading lessons affects what students learn" (p. 524). He meant not only that teachers should provide effective lessons in reading com-prehension but that they should also provide culturally relevant lessons in reading comprehension.

Cultural modeling

In her study with African American high school students, Lee (1993, 1995, 2000) illustrated how students developed their reading abilities by using specific linguistic practices, common to speakers of African American Vernacular English, as "heuristics and strategies for interpreting figurative language and literary tropes paralleling the work that more expert-like readers draw on to interpret rich literary texts" (Lee & Smagorinsky, 2000, p. 11). Lee's study focused on a two-pronged instructional intervention: (a) teaching African American students about the language practice of signifying that they already used in their everyday speech, and (b) helping them understand how this practice involved techniques and strategies also used in literary texts. Signifying is an art form within the African American community that encompasses "a rhetorical stance, and attitude toward language, and a means of cultural self-definition" (ibid.). It also shares certain properties with literary tropes and figurative language, specifically irony, metaphor, symbolism, and point of view. By examining students' use of signifying as a language practice and how it provided students with a set of tools for interpretation of signifying dialogues, Lee was also able to examine how this cultural resource could support students' development as readers in a school setting.

The focus on signifying is integral to our notions of cultural relevance and reading comprehension for several reasons. First, students' knowledge of this language practice was largely tacit, and studying it as a "metalinguistic activity" allowed students to "articulate the strategies they used to come to interpretation within signifying dialogues" (Lee, 1995, p. 197). In this respect, the practice of signifying could be used as a kind of prior knowledge that supported their reading of challenging literary texts. Second, enabled by this new understanding, students could apply these strategies to an academic task—reading literary texts—in a way that honored and drew upon the knowledge and skills the students acquired in their home settings. Results from the study further indicated:

> the students had appropriated the goals of the instruction intervention to: (a) begin to think about the act of interpreting fiction as expert readers do, (b) to develop a taste for tackling the language of literary texts, and (c) to support their responses to complex problems of interpretation with close textual analysis and by drawing on their knowledge of the social world of the text. (p. 625)

In other words, the students were able to draw on linguistic tools they already possessed (but which had, until then, remained unnamed) to mediate their understanding of written texts, and to link everyday concepts with academic (or, in Vygotsky's terms, scientific) concepts. This study also demonstrated an important part of our argument about cultural relevance. Specifically, Lee's research connects culturally and socially acquired tools to the academic task of reading comprehension, in this case to a specific kind of comprehension (literary interpretation) and exemplifies how these tools can become resources applied to other texts, thus advancing students' interpretive reading abilities. In short, her work suggests that effective teachers need to find ways to bring students' cultural practices into the classroom and use these rich resources to connect with the more traditional subject matter of mainstream schooling.

Hybridity and third space in the literacy classroom

Although research focused on hybridity and third space has become a contemporary research phenomenon, studies that address reading comprehension (in its most common forms) are scarce. Rather, studies of hybridity and third space in the classroom examine the intersection of students and their various discourses, classroom activities and texts, and their mutual transformation in activity systems (Gutierrez, 2000). The concept of hybridity, rooted in history, is a postcolonial term used to describe a recombination of existing cultures intertwined to form a hybrid culture (Bhabha, 1994). Hybrid cultures destabilize the hegemony of mainstream discourses through the creation of a space in which both cultures are valued and transformed (Pieterse, 2001). Kris Guitierrez and her colleagues (2000; Gutierrez, Baquedano-Lopez, & Tejeda, 1999; Gutierrez, Rymes, & Larson, 1995) have provided the most in-depth examinations of hybridity in the literacy classroom, focusing on the ways that instructional interactions foster, or fail to foster, the development of third space and hence the development of literacy among culturally and linguistically diverse students. Guteirrez (2000) defined third space as a "discursive space in which alternative and competing discourses and positionings transform conflict and difference into rich zones of mediational context and tools necessary for future development" (p. 157).

Within this framework, a study by Gutierrez, Rymes, and Larson (1995) illustrated the concept of hybridity through a nonexample, demonstrating how power relationships between teacher and student created missed opportunities to build on a student's prior (but faulty) knowledge about *Brown vs. the Board of Education*. The researchers identified teacher talk as the official script (facts about the landmark desegregation decision), student talk as the unofficial or counterscript (students' association of "Brown" with musician James Brown), and the place where these two intersected as "third space," a potentially productive place for learning that went unrealized. In a later study, Gutierrez, Baquedano-Lopez, and Tejada (1999) focused on the classroom culture and the ways in which hybrid language practices contributed to building a culture of collaboration that was "multi-voiced, polycontextual, and multi-scripted" (p. 287), where no one, including the teacher, was privileged. The study documented how the students' counterscript in the unofficial space of the classroom resulted in a student-initiated exploration of human reproduction. Sparked by one student calling another student "homo," the teacher engaged the students in a conversation first about name-calling. Another student, asking what the word "homo" meant, led to further conversation about men loving men and how a baby is made. In response, the teacher and the students, along with parental and school approval and participation, designed an age-appropriate unit of study. This topic was not a part of the official curriculum for second- and third-graders, nor was it a part of the students' home discourse. Yet, as Guteirrez et al. argue, this new "hybrid activity bridged the official and unofficial spaces of both home and school" (p. 292). In addition, throughout the six-week learning event, there were moments when the students' needs to share questions resulted in the teacher reorganizing the official script of a predefined task. Such moves, Guitierrez et al. (1999) noted, should be seen as "points of negotiation rather than disruption" (p. 294). The teacher built on the children's local knowledge and vocabulary by using both formal and colloquial language to make explicit the range of registers that can be used to make meaning. "This use of hybrid language was purposeful and not a random act and was used as mediating tools for language and content development" (p. 301).

Building on this seminal work, other literacy researchers have begun to examine hybridity in ways more clearly linked to the acquisition of skills, strategies, and resources associated with reading comprehension. For example, in a study of hybrid discourse practices, Kamberelis (2001) illustrated how a teacher's personal narrative, delivered in an animated conversational mode, disrupted the usual pattern of reading lessons by shifting students' focus from words within a specific text to their meanings in the broader world. At the same time, this event changed how teacher and students interacted and how students learned to read more strategically. Similarly, Solsken, Willet, and Wilson-Keenan (2000) demonstrated how Blanca, a first-grade, Puerto Rican girl, drew on a family story about her uncle's accident in response to a read aloud of *John Henry* (Keats, 1965). Although initially unrecognized, Blanca's story paralleled the tall tale genre under study as she imbued her oral account of her uncle's accident with elements of the genre and made connections to class discussion about the role of girls and women in tall tales. Although the researchers did not emphasize reading comprehension per se, it is clear from her hybrid story that Blanca understood Keats' story and its rhetorical elements. Finally, in a study of literacy practices in science instruction, Moje, Ciechanowski, Kramer, Ellis, Carrillo, and Collazo (2004) identified how Latino students connected everyday funds of knowledge from family, community, peer groups, and popular culture to mediate the discourses of science they encountered in texts and other classroom activities. The researchers noted that students drew upon their available funds without encouragement or validation and used them strategically both in their science literacy learning and in the maintenance and expression of their social and cultural identities. These studies illustrate an important tenet of hybridity theory, its relationship to new understandings of literacy practices, and the ways that students construct meanings from texts. Moreover, they illustrate, along with cultural modeling and the KEEP studies, the intimate connection between how students become literate in culturally relevant ways. As Gutierrez (2000) explained, "as students participate in literacy events, they are both creating and recreating situated practices during the construction of literacy knowledge. Framed in this way, cultural practices, learning, and development exist in a reciprocal relationship" (p. 159).

RETHINKING THE ROLE OF CULTURE, RETHINKING RESEARCH ON READING COMPREHENSION

As we conducted this review of research, we were struck by the paucity of studies explicitly examining reading comprehension. Despite the general belief that students' social and cultural practices are deeply intertwined with literacy learning, few studies categorically document the impact of culturally responsive or relevant pedagogy on students' reading comprehension. We have to come see this paucity as a reflection of two related issues. First, many researchers who are interested in cultural theory and its applications to literacy learning conduct qualitative and ethnographic forms of research that may not yield concrete or explicit links to reading comprehension as it has been traditionally measured with standardized tests, informal reading inventories, think alouds, or the like. More commonly, they examine practices and interactions that suggest the acquisition of new skills. In other words, they tend to focus on processes rather than outcomes. Second, framing studies of literacy classrooms in cultural theory has significant implications for the way literacy learning broadly and reading comprehension specifically are construed. These studies examine less the degree to which students understand a text and more the means by which they construct the meanings they do and how these meanings are shaped by cultural, historical, and situational contexts. In this concluding section, we explore what these findings, if you will, suggest for future research.

With respect to the first of these issues, the qualitative studies reported here have all broken new ground in reading comprehension and the practices by which it may be advanced. They have expanded our notions of prior knowledge, students' roles in reading processes, and the nature of the interactions between reader and text. Further, they renew and confirm the importance of the reader in the kinds of meanings that can be constructed from text as well as the value of these meanings. Whether by examining students' discussions of text in a book club or their ability to draw upon primary discourses as tools in the interpretation of literature, these studies shed light on the interplay between students' cultural and linguistic identities, the meanings they make from text, and the most effective ways to support their growth. This finding is consistent with Almasi, Garas-York, and Shanahan's (2006) conclusion about the contributions of qualitative research in the face of the scientifically based research favored by the National Reading Panel's (2000) report:

> The inclusion of the qualitative studies enables researchers, practitioners, and policy makers not only to see what activities need to be included to enhance text comprehension but also to see the conceptual and theoretical manner in which those activities relate to one another to create the conditions that foster text comprehension. (pp. 61–62)

Although the contributions of these studies have great value in constructing classrooms that are both culturally relevant and promote the development of reading abilities, there continues to be a need for more experimental research that documents the degree to and the manner in which culturally responsive and relevant pedagogical efforts contribute to increased reading comprehension abilities. As qualitative researchers ourselves, we were struck by the limited empirical evidence (quantitatively or qualitatively) generated that legitimated the claims we in this field have made for the impact of such pedagogy in teaching children to read. Reading study after study, we found ourselves asking, "How *do* we know that these strategies increase reading abilities specifically for marginalized students? What is the evidence in this study that relates directly to reading achievement?" These questions are essential, not only because of the current political climate but also because such evidence is the means by which a scholarly community makes its claims. As a consequence, our first recommendation concerns the need for more quantitative studies that explore the theories and principles we have generated through the qualitative research summarized here. We have fine examples of mixed methods studies that provide models for this new research (Goatley et al., 1995; Greenleaf et al., 2001; Lee, 1995).

The difficulty conducting such studies, however, brings us to our second issue. Much of the research in culturally relevant and responsive pedagogy argues that reading is a social practice influenced by cultural and historical contexts (Street, 1995). As such, how individuals come to their comprehension of texts is inextricably linked with their social and cultural identities. How then do we determine what constitutes a legitimate reading across multiple readers? And, how can we possibly measure it in a way that does not erase its cultural roots? Without adequate answers to such questions, we potentially become party to the same limitations leveled against standardized testing as a means of determining children's futures. The argument that accountability measures are a part of children's school futures does not mitigate against the dangers of measuring reading comprehension in ways that continue to privilege White ways of knowing and doing. Contemporary studies of cultural relevance and literacy learning remind us that marginalized students' knowledge is often ignored or dismissed as faulty. It also illustrates for us the overreliance on skills disconnected to meanings in their classrooms. In part, these practices stem from the power that teachers and others exert over what texts mean. The nuanced examinations of classroom interactions in work such as Gutierrez (2000; Gutierrez, Baquedano-Lopez, & Tejeda, 1999; Gutierrez, Rymes, & Larson, 1995), Kamberelis (2001), and Solsken et al. (2000) highlight how important the power over textual meanings can be for students' development as readers. Identifying ways students' meanings can count when we assess their comprehension, then, may be our most important task.

REFERENCES

Alexander, P., Schallert, D. L., & Hare, V. C. (1991). Coming to terms: How researchers in learning and literacy talk about knowledge. *Review of Educational Research, 61*, 315–343.

Alexander-Smith, A. C. (2004). Feeling rhythm of the critically conscious mind. *English Journal, 93*(3), 58–63.

Almasi, J. F., Garas-York, K., & Shanahan, L. (2006). Qualitative research on text comprehension and the report of the National Reading Panel. *The Elementary School Journal, 107*(1), 37–66.

Anderson, R. C. (1984). Some reflections on the acquisition of knowledge. *Educational Researcher, 13*(9), 5–10.

Au, K. (1980). Participation structures in a reading lesson with Hawaiian children: Analysis of a culturally appropriate instructional event. *Anthropology and Education Quarterly, 11*, 91–115.

Au, K. (1993). *Literacy in multicultural settings.* Fort Worth, TX: Harcourt Brace Jovanovich College Publishers.

Au, K., & Jordan, C. (1981). Teaching reasoning to Hawaiian children: Finding a culturally appropriate solution. In H. Trueba, G. Guthrie, & K. Au (Eds.), *Culture and the bilingual classroom: Studies in classroom ethnography* (pp. 139–152). Rowley, MA: Newbury House.

Au, K., & Mason, J. (1983). Cultural congruence in classroom participation structures: Achieving a balance of rights. *Discourse Processes, 6*, 145–167.

Barnitz, J. G. (1998). Enhancing reading comprehension. In M. F. Opitz (Ed.), *Literacy instruction for culturally and linguistically diverse students: A collection of articles and commentaries* (pp. 91–94). Mahwah, NJ: Erlbaum.

Bennett, C. I. (2003). *Comprehensive multicultural education: Theory and practice* (5th ed.). Boston: Allyn & Bacon.

Bhabha, H. K. (1994). *The location of culture.* London: Routledge.

Cazden, C., & Legget, E. (1981). Culturally responsive education: Recommendations for achieving Lau remedies. In H. Trueba, G. Guthrie, & K. Au (Eds.), *Culture and the bilingual classroom: Studies in classroom ethnography* (pp. 69–86). Rowley, MA: Newbury House.

Cole, M. (1996). *Cultural psychology: A once and future discipline.* Cambridge, MA: The Belknap Press of Harvard University Press.

Cook, L. S., & Amatucci, K. B. (2006). A high school English teacher's developing multicultural pedagogy. *English Education, 38*, 220–244.

Copenhaver, J. (2001). Listening to their voices connect literary and cultural understandings: Responses to small group read-alouds of *Malcolm X: A fire burning brightly. The New Advocate, 14*, 343–359.

Delpit, L. D. (1995). *Other people's children: Cultural conflict in the classroom.* New York: New Press.

Drakeford, W. (2002). The impact of an intensive program to increase the literacy skills of incarcerated youth. *Journal of Incarcerated Youth, 53*(4), 139–144.

Duffy, G. G. (1993). Teachers' progress toward becoming expert strategy teachers. *Elementary School Journal, 94*, 109–120.

Ensign, J. (2003). Including culturally relevant math in an urban school. *Educational Studies, 34*, 414–423.

Erickson, F., & Mohatt, C. (1982). Cultural organization and participation structures in two classrooms of Indian students. In G. Spindler (Ed.), *Doing the ethnography of schooling* (pp. 131–174). New York: Holt, Rineholt, & Winston.

Fish, S. (1980). *Is there a text in this class? The authority of interpretive communities.* Cambridge, MA: Harvard University Press.

Fitzgerald, J., & Graves, M. F. (2004). Reading supports for all. *Educational Leadership, 62*, 68–71.

Flores, M. M., Shippen, M. E., Alberto, P., & Crowe, L. (2004). Teaching letter-sound correspondence to students with moderate intellectual disabilities. *Journal of Direct Instruction, 4*, 173–188.

Galda, L., & Beach, R. (2001). Response to literature as a cultural activity. *Reading Research Quarterly, 36*, 64–73.

Gay, G. (2000). *Culturally responsive teaching: Theory, research, and practice.* New York: Teachers College Press.

Gay, G. (2002). Preparing for culturally responsive teaching. *Journal of Teacher Education, 53*, 106–116.

Gee, J. P. (1996). *Social linguistics and literacies: Ideology in discourses* (2nd ed.). New York: Routledge Falmer.

Gibson, S. E. (1996). Using culturally relevant approaches to teaching social studies. *Canadian Social Studies, 30,* 183–185.

Goatley, V. J., Brock, C. H., & Raphael, T. E. (1995). Diverse learners participating in regular education "book clubs." *Reading Research Quarterly, 30,* 352–380.

Goldenberg, C. (1992–1993). Instructional conversations: Promoting comprehension through discussion. *The Reading Teacher, 46,* 306–326.

Goodenough, W. H. (1981). *Culture, language, and society* (2nd ed.). Menlo Park, CA: Benjamin/Cummings.

González, N. E. (1995). The funds of knowledge for teaching project. *Practicing Anthropology, 17*(3), 3–6.

Greenleaf, C. L., Schoenbach, R., Cziko, C., & Mueller, F. L. (2001). Apprenticing adolescent readers to academic literacy. *Harvard Educational Review, 71,* 79–129.

Gutierrez, K. (2000). Synchronic and diachronic dimensions of social practice: An emerging methodology for cultural-historical perspectives on literacy learning. In C. D. Lee & P. Smagorinsky (Eds.), *Vygotskian perspectives on literary research: Constructing meaning through collaborative inquiry* (pp. 150–164). Cambridge, UK: Cambridge University Press.

Gutierrez, K. D., Baquedano-Lopez, P., & Tejeda, C. (1999). Rethinking diversity: Hybridity and hybrid language practices in the third space. *Mind, Culture, and Activity, 6,* 286–303.

Gutierrez, K., Baquedano-Lopez, P., & Turner, M. G. (1997). Putting language back into language arts: When the radical middle meets the third space. *Language Arts, 74,* 368–378.

Gutierrez, K., Rymes, B., & Larson, J. (1995). Script, counterscript, and underlife in the classroom: James Brown versus *Brown v. Board of Education. Harvard Educational Review, 65,* 445–471.

Gutstein, E., Lipman, P., & Hernandez, P. (1997). Culturally relevant mathematics teaching in a Mexican American context. *Journal for Research in Mathematics Education, 28,* 709–727.

Henry, A. (2001). The politics of unpredictability in a reading/writing/discussion group with girls from the Caribbean. *Theory into Practice, 40*(3), 184–189.

Jimenez, R. T. (2001). Strategic reading for language-related disabilities: The case of a bilingual Latina student. In M. de la Luz Reyes & J. J. Halcon (Eds.), *The best for our children: Critical perspectives on literacy for Latino students* (pp. 153–167). New York: Teachers College Press.

Jimenez, R. T., Garcia, G. E., & Pearson, P. D. (1996). Three children, two languages, and strategic reading: Case studies in bilingual/monolingual reading. *American Educational Research Journal, 32,* 67–97.

Jones, E. B., Pang, V. O., & Rodriguez, J. L. (2001). Social studies in the elementary classroom. Culture matters. *Theory into Practice, 40*(1), 35–41.

Jordan, C. (1985). Translating culture: From ethnographic information to educational program. *Anthropology and Education Quarterly, 16,* 105–123.

Kamberelis, G. (2001). Producing of heterglossic classroom (micro)cultures through hybrid discourse practice. *Linguistics and Education, 1,* 85–125.

Keats, E. J. (1965). *John Henry: An American legend.* New York: Knopf.

King, J. E. (1991). Unfinished business: Black student alienation and Black teachers' emancipatory pedagogy. In M. Foster (Ed.), *Readings on equal education: Vol. 11. Qualitative investigations into schools and schooling* (pp. 254–271). New York: AMS Press.

Kong, A., & Fitch, E. (2002–2003). Using book club to engage culturally and linguistically diverse learners in reading, writing, and talking about books. *The Reading Teacher, 56,* 352–362.

Ladson-Billings, G. (1992a). Culturally relevant teaching: The key to making multicultural education work. In C. A. Grant (Ed.), *Research and multicultural education* (pp. 106–121). London: Falmer Press.

Ladson-Billings, G. (1992b). Reading between the lines and beyond the pages: A culturally relevant approach to literacy teaching. *Theory into Practice, 31,* 312–320.

Ladson-Billings, G. (1994). *Dreamkeepers: Successful teachers of African American children.* San Francisco: Jossey-Bass.

Ladson-Billings, G. (1995). But that's just good teaching! The case for culturally relevant pedagogy. *Theory into Practice, 34*(3), 159–165.

Ladson-Billings, G. (2001). *Crossing over to Canaan: The journey of new teachers in diverse classroom.* New York: Wiley.

Larson, J., & Irvine, P. D. (1999). "We call him Dr. King": Reciprocal distancing in urban classrooms. *Language Arts, 76*, 393–400.

Lee, C. D. (1993). *Signifying as a scaffold to literary interpretation: The pedagogical implications of a form of African-American discourse genre.* Urbana, IL: National Council of Teachers of English.

Lee, C. D. (1995). A culturally based cognitive apprenticeship: Teaching African American high school students skill in literary interpretation. *Reading Research Quarterly, 30*, 608–631.

Lee, C. D. (2000). Signifying in the zone of proximal development. In C. D. Lee & P. Smagorinsky (Eds.), *Vygotskian perspectives on literary research: Constructing meaning through collaborative inquiry* (pp. 191–225). Cambridge: Cambridge University Press.

Lee, C. D., & Smagorinsky, P. (2000). Introduction: Constructing meaning through collaborative inquiry. In C. D. Lee & P. Smagorinsky (Eds.), *Vygotskian perspectives on literary research: Constructing meaning through collaborative inquiry* (pp. 1–15). Cambridge: Cambridge University Press.

Lewis, B. F., Pitts, V. R., & Collins, A. C. (2002). A descriptive study of pre-service teachers' perceptions of African-American students' ability to achieve in mathematics and science. *The Negro Educational Review, 53*(1/2), 31–42.

Macias, J. (1987). The hidden curriculum of Papago teachers: American Indian strategies for mitigating cultural discontinuity in early schooling. In G. Spindler & L. Spindler (Eds.), *Interpretive Ethnography at Home and Abroad* (pp. 363–380). Hillsdale, NJ: Erlbaum.

Malmgren, K. W., & Leone, P. E. (2000). Effects of short-term auxiliary reading program on the reading skills of incarcerated youth. *Education and Treatment of Children, 23*, 239–247.

Maloch, B. (2005). Moments by which change is made: A cross-case exploration of teacher mediation and student participation in literacy events. *Journal of Literacy Research, 37*, 95–142.

Marchand-Martella, N. E., Martella, R. C., & Martella, A. M. (n.d.). *SRA: The research base and validation of SRA's Corrective Reading Program* (brochure). New York: McGraw Hill. Retrieved May 5, 2007, from https://www.sraonline.com/////_CorrRead/_Brochure.pdf

Meacham, S. J. (2001). Vygotsky and the blues: Re-reading cultural connections and conceptual development. *Theory Into Practice, 40*, 190–197.

Meese, R. L. (2001). *Teaching learners with mild disabilities: Integrating research and practice* (2nd ed.). Belmont, CA: Wadsworth/Learning.

Mohatt, G., & Erickson, F. (1981). Cultural differences in teaching styles in an Odawa school: A sociolinguistics approach. In H. Trueba, G. Guthrie, & K. Au (Eds.), *Culture and the bilingual classroom: Studies in classroom ethnography* (pp. 105–119). Rowley, MA: Newbury House.

Moje, E. B., Ciechanowski, K. M., Kramer, K., Ellis, L., Carrillo, R., & Collazo, T. (2004). Working toward third space in content area literacy: An examination of everyday funds of knowledge and discourse. *Reading Research Quarterly, 39*, 38–70.

Moll, L. C. (Ed.). (1990). *Vygotsky and education: Instructional implications of sociohistorical psychology.* Cambridge: Cambridge University Press.

Moll, L. C. (1998). Turning to the world: Bilingual schooling, literacy, and the cultural mediation of thinking. In T. Shanahan & F. V. Rodriguez-Brown (Eds.), *Forty-seventh Yearbook of the National Reading Conference* (59–75). Chicago: National Reading Conference.

Moll, L. C. (2000). Inspired by Vygotsky: Ethnographic experiments in education. In C. D. Lee & P. Smagorinsky (Eds.), *Vygotskian perspectives on literary research: Constructing meaning through collaborative inquiry* (pp. 256–268). Cambridge, UK: Cambridge University Press.

Moll, L., Amanti, J., Neff, W., & Gonzalez, N. (1992). Funds of knowledge for teaching: Using a qualitative approach to connect homes and classrooms. *Theory into Practice, 31*(2), 132–141.

Moll, L. C., & Gonzalez, N. (1994). Lessons from research with language-minority children. *Journal of Reading Behavior, 26*, 439–456.

Myers, W. D. (2000). *Malcolm X: A fire burning brightly.* New York: HarperCollins.

National Reading Panel. (2000). *Teaching children to read: An evidence-based assessment of the scientific research literature on reading and its implications for reading instruction* (Report of the subgroups). Washington, DC: U.S. Department of Health and Human Services, Public Health Service, National Institutes of Health, and the National Institute of Child Health and Human Development.

Nelson-Barber, S., & Estrin, E. T. (1995). Bringing Native American perspectives to mathematics and science teaching, 34, 174–185.

Nystrand, M. (2006). Research on the role of classroom discourse as it affects reading comprehension. *Research in the Teaching of English, 40,* 392–412.

Palincsar, A. S., & Brown, A. L. (1984). Reciprocal teaching of comprehension-fostering and comprehension-monitoring activities. *Cognition and Instruction, 1,* 117–175.

Pieterse, J. N. (2001). Hybridity, so what? The anti-hybridity backlash and riddles of recognition. *Theory, Culture, & Society, 18,* 38–70.

Polloway, E. A., Epstein, M. H., Polloway, C. H., Patton, J. R., & Ball, D. W. (1986). Corrective Reading program: An analysis of effectiveness with learning disabled and mentally retarded students. *Remedial and Special Education, 7*(4), 41–47.

Raphael, T. E. (1986). Teaching question answer relationships, revisited. *The Reading Teacher, 39,* 516–522.

Raphael, T. E., & Au, K. H. (2005). QAR: Enhancing comprehension and test taking across grades and content areas. *The Reading Teacher, 59,* 206–221.

Raphael, T. E., Highfield, K., & Au, K. H. (2006). *QAR now: Question answer relationships.* New York: Scholastic.

Raphael, T. E., & McKinney, J. (1983). An examination of fifth- and eighth-grade children's question-answering behavior: An instructional study in metacognition. *Journal of Reading Behavior, 15,* 67–86.

Raphael, T. E., & Pearson, D. P. (1985). Increasing students' awareness of sources of information for answering questions. *American Educational Research Journal, 22,* 217–235

Raphael, T. E., & Wonnacott, C. A. (1985). Heightening fourth grade students' sensitivity to sources of information for answering comprehension questions. *Reading Research Quarterly, 20,* 282–296.

Reyes, M. de la Luz, & Halcon, J. J. (2001). *The best for our children: Critical perspectives on literacy for Latino Students.* New York: Teachers College Press.

Rosenblatt, L. (1978). *The reader, the text, the poem: The transactional theory of the literary work.* Carbondale, IL: Southern Illinois University Press.

Saunders, W. M., & Goldenberg, C. (1999). Effects of instructional conversations and literature logs on limited- and fluent-English-proficient students' story comprehension and thematic understanding. *The Elementary School Journal, 99,* 363–385.

Smagorinsky, P. (2001). If meaning is constructed, what's it made from? Toward a cultural theory of reading. *Review of Educational Research, 71,* 133–169.

Solsken, J., Willett, J., & Wilson-Keenan, J.-A. (2000). Cultivating hybrid texts in multicultural classrooms: Promise and challenge. *Research in the Teaching of English, 35,* 179–212.

Street, B. V. (1995) *Social literacies: Critical approaches to literacy in development, ethnography and education.* London: Longman.

Tate, W. F. (1995). Returning to the root: A culturally relevant approach to mathematics pedagogy. *Theory into Practice, 34,* 166–173.

Taylor, B. M., Pearson, P. D., Peterson, D. S., & Rodriguez, M. C. (2003). Reading growth in high-poverty classrooms: The influence of teacher practices that encourage cognitive engagement in literacy learning. *The Elementary School Journal, 104,* 3–28.

Taylor, B. M., Pearson, P. D., Peterson, D. S., & Rodriguez, M. C. (2005). The CIERA school change framework: An evidence-based approach to professional development and school reading improvement. *Reading Research Quarterly, 40,* 40–69.

Tharp, R. G. (1982). The effective instruction of comprehension: Results and description of the Kamehameha Early Education Program. *Reading Research Quarterly, 17,* 503–527.

Trueba, H. T. (1990). The role of culture in literacy acquisition: An interdisciplinary approach to qualitative research. *International Journal of Qualitative Studies in Education, 3*(1), 1–13.

Van den Branden, (2000). Does negotiation of meaning promote reading comprehension? A study of multilingual primary school classes. *Reading Research Quarterly, 35,* 426–443.

Vygotsky, L. S. (1978). *Mind in society: The development of higher psychological processes.* Cambridge, MA: Harvard University Press.

Vygotsky, L. S. (1986). *Thought and language.* Cambridge, MA: MIT Press.

Wells, G. (1999). *Dialogic inquiry: Towards a sociocultural practice and theory of education.* New York: Cambridge University Press.

Wertsch, J. V. (1991). *Voices of the mind: A sociocultural approach to mediated action.* Cambridge, MA: Harvard University Press.

Whitaker, C. P., Gambrell, L. B., & Morrow, L. M. (2004). Reading comprehension instruction for all students. In E. R. Silliman & L. C. Wilkinson (Eds.), *Language and literacy learning in schools* (pp. 130–150). New York: Guilford Press.

Wiest, L. R. (2001). Teaching mathematics from a multicultural perspective. *Equity and Excellence, 34*(1), 16–25.

Wiley, T. G. (2005). *Literacy and language diversity in the United States* (2nd ed.). Washington, DC: Center for Applied Linguistics.

Willis, A. I., & Harris, V. J. (2000). Political acts: Literacy learning and teaching. *Reading Research Quarterly, 35*, 72–88.

29 Reading Comprehension and English Language Learners

Kathryn Prater

The University of North Carolina at Greensboro

The purpose of this chapter is to review research focusing specifically on reading comprehension and students who are learning English as a second language. I identify two bodies of research and review landmark studies within each body. Finally, I discuss commonalities between the two research perspectives and suggest a way to use the information from both bodies of research to inform our understanding of the complex issues surrounding English language learners and reading comprehension. I explore studies related directly to reading comprehension and English language learners that are most likely to inform instructional practices in U. S. schools and suggest areas for further research. Specific parameters are set for each section of the review. In the Landmark Studies section, I include only research studies with empirical data related directly to reading comprehension. In subsequent sections of this chapter, I discuss research studies indirectly related to reading comprehension and reports by researchers on instructional practices.

INTRODUCTION

Data from the most recent U.S. Census indicate the number of people who speak a language other than English in the home doubled between 1980 and 2000 while the overall population grew by one quarter during that same time period (U.S. Census, 2007).

State education agencies reported more than 480 different languages were spoken in the homes of limited English proficient students in 2000–2001 (Kindler, 2002). The majority of these students spoke Spanish (79.2%) with Vietnamese, Hmong, Cantonese, and Korean speakers making up an additional 5.6%. All other languages reported comprised less than 1% of the limited English proficient student population (Kindler, 2002). During the 2003–2004 school year, 11% of the total enrollment in U.S. public schools, an estimated 3.8 million students, received English as a second language services. California, with 26% of all limited English proficient students and Texas, with 16% of all limited English proficient students, led the nation in reported number of students receiving English as a second language services (National Center for Educational Statistics, 2006). This increase is seen mostly in the elementary and middle school grades with 44% of all limited English proficient students enrolled in pre-Kindergarten through third grade and another 34% enrolled in fourth grade through eighth grade. Less than 20% of all limited English proficient students were enrolled in high school (Kindler, 2002). This increase in students learning English as a second language challenges state education agencies, local school agencies, and classroom teachers to adjust instructional practices to meet the needs of culturally and linguistically diverse students. Educators and policy makers look to research to suggest effective instructional strategies that will support students learning English as a second language. At this time, much of what we know about this particular student population and reading comprehension is based on research conducted with monolingual English speakers (Lesaux & Geva, 2006).

There are a number of ways to refer to students who speak languages other than English. Limited English proficient (LEP) is used in federal legislation and other official documents. For example, Kindler (2002), writing a report for the Office of English Language Acquisition, Language Enhancement and Academic Achievement for Limited English Proficient Students (OLEA), employed LEP to describe this student population. Students learning English in schools have also been labeled English as a Second Language (ESL) or English Speakers of Other Languages (ESOL). August and Shanahan (2006) use the term second-language learners to describe "individuals who come from language backgrounds other than a societal language (e.g., English in the U.S.) and whose second language proficiency is not yet developed to the point where they can profit fully from instruction solely in the second language" (p. 2). Individuals who live where the societal language is English are considered English language learners. I will use English language learners to refer to student participants who are learning English as a second language. In cases where a different term was used in the original research report (e.g., ESL), I continue with the language of the researchers.

BACKGROUND AND HISTORICAL PERSPECTIVES

English language learners have been a part of classrooms in America since the inception of compulsory public schooling (Crawford, 1989). Even with this long history, relatively little research has been conducted in the United States on the reading processes of English language learners reading in English. Much of what we know about second language (L2) reading is derived from research conducted on monolingual English speakers reading in English (L1) (Lesaux & Geva, 2006). Fitzgerald (1995) reviewed research centered on the cognitive reading processes used by second language learners reading in English in the United States. Findings from this synthesis suggest that English language learners use cognates to their advantage, monitor their comprehension, use metacognitive strategies, apply background knowledge and schema to assist in understanding texts, and comprehend differently depending on the text structure. Fitzgerald concludes that the studies "support the contention that the cognitive reading processes of ESL learners are *substantively* the same as those of native English speakers" (p. 180). Readers decode, or convert written symbols into spoken language, and apply background knowledge to construct an understanding of the author's message. In Bernhardt's (2000) synthesis of research on second language reading from across the world during the last decade of the 20th century the author is more skeptical. She asserts the "findings fall short of providing satisfying explanations of the second language process or of second-language reading instruction" and instead suggests "the vastness of the territory yet to be investigated" (p. 805).

In 2002, the Institute of Education Sciences convened a panel of experts and created the National Literacy Panel on Language-Minority Children and Youth. The panel's charge was to "identify, assess, and synthesize research on the education of language-minority children and youth with respect to their attainment of literacy, and to produce a comprehensive report evaluating and synthesizing this literature" (August & Shanahan, 2006, p. xiv). The panel identified specific areas of convergence between monolingual English reading and reading in English as a second language. For example, studies have shown that English language learners employ similar word-level skills as monolingual English readers when reading. According to Lesaux and Geva (2006), studies that focus on word-level skills demonstrate that "skills such as phonological processing and concepts of print that predict later literacy development in language-minority students are consistent with those identified in the studies conducted with English monolingual children" (p. 63). Lesaux (2006) found that after some instruction in the second language, English language learners' word reading skills "often matched those of native English speakers" (p. 89). In the area of reading comprehension, Lesaux concludes, "There is a lack of research examining the reading comprehension development of language-minority students. . . ." In a chapter that includes a review of studies focusing on reading comprehension, Shanahan and Beck (2006) offer a similar observation. "Given the small number of studies reviewed here [3], it is impossible to determine the best way to facilitate reading comprehension for English language learners" (p. 433). This lack of data led Lesaux to the following cautious statement based on the overall findings of the limited number of studies: "The second-language reading comprehension skills of language-minority children and youth do not appear to develop at the same extent as those of their language-majority peers" (p. 100).

Peregoy and Boyle (2000) identify several commonalities between monolingual English readers and English language learners reading in English. Good readers set a purpose for reading, apply various forms of background knowledge including knowledge of language (English and their heritage language), decode print, and use comprehension strategies to construct an understanding of the text. Several factors are unique to English language learners: English language proficiency, background knowledge, and literacy knowledge and experience in the heritage language (Peregoy & Boyle, 2000). It is necessary to attend to these differences, and Peregoy and Boyle caution that "teaching practices for native English speakers cannot simply be applied whole cloth to English language learners without modifications that consider, at the very least, students' English language proficiency and primary language literacy" (p. 243).

At this time, the findings drawn from research conducted on reading and reading comprehension in L2 are not conclusive. However, there is a general consensus regarding recommendations for effective reading instruction for English language learners. Gersten and Baker (2000) conducted focus groups with elementary- and middle-school educators and researchers across the country and identified five instructional variables that are "potentially critical" for effective instruction: (a) vocabulary development and using vocabulary as a "curricular anchor," (b) use of visuals to support concept and vocabulary development, (c) cooperative learning and peer-tutoring strategies, (d) strategic use of native language for support and clarification, and (e) adjusting language demand as cognitive demand increases. Gersten and Baker acknowledge that more research is needed on each of these variables to determine the impact individually and in concert with each other on student achievement.

LANDMARK STUDIES

This section will highlight studies that impacted the field upon publication and continue to inform research and practice regarding English language learners and reading comprehension. It is not an exhaustive review of literature. The following criteria were used to identify landmark studies:

- The studies include English language learners as participants.
- The age of the participants must range in age from 4 to 13 because most English language learners are enrolled in pre-kindergarten through eighth grade (Kindler, 2002).
- The data on the English language learners are disaggregated in the discussion of findings.

- The studies include at least one measure of reading comprehension.
- The studies were published in a peer-reviewed journal.
- The studies were conducted in the United States with English as the language of instruction. Studies where instruction is provided in two languages (English and the students' native language) are included if there are data related to reading comprehension in English.

When these criteria are applied, two distinct bodies of literature emerge based on the way the researchers defined reading comprehension.

The definition of reading comprehension varies according to the ways in which researchers view the act of reading. Reading may be viewed as a behavior that can be broken into its constituent parts and quantified. From this perspective, reading comprehension is an objective outcome of the act of reading and may be measured by answering questions (i.e., Woodcock Language Proficiency Battery-Revised passage comprehension subtest; Woodcock, 1991) or retelling after reading a passage. Alternatively, reading may be seen as a contextualized, social practice. If reading is considered a social practice, then the sociocultural situation and background experiences of the participants must be taken into account when measuring reading comprehension.

In the first studies reviewed in this section, researchers consider reading comprehension measures to be objective assessments of what a participant understands about a given text. The act of reading is divided into parts and each component is measured separately and then patterns or trends are noted among the constituent parts. In the second part of this section, researchers situate their work in a sociocultural perspective and endeavor to learn more about the social and individual influences that impact reading comprehension outcomes.

READING COMPREHENSION AS A COMPOSITE OF ABILITIES

When reading is defined as a decontextualized behavior, it can be divided into parts and these components can be studied and measured independently. For example, August, Francis, Hsu, and Snow (2006) state:

> Successful reading comprehension reflects the presence of many component capabilities. Comprehension relies on decoding skills (reading words accurately and fluently, accessing lexical representations), knowledge in several domains (vocabulary, linguistic structure, and discourse as well as world knowledge), and cognitive processing capacities (memory for text, accessing relevant background knowledge, drawing justified inferences). (p. 222)

Outcomes are generally reported as a quantitative value associated with a standard scale. Seven such studies will be discussed. All include comprehension instruction as one component of a reading intervention.

Vaughn, Mathes, et al. (2006) conducted a study that investigated the efficacy of a first grade intervention for Spanish-speaking English language learners whose core reading instruction was conducted in English. Trained teachers provided explicit instruction in phonological awareness, phonics, word reading, and text comprehension for first-grade students identified as at-risk for reading difficulties. The existing intervention used at each school for struggling readers was compared to the systematic, explicit intervention program in this quasi-experimental study. Reading comprehension was taught through explicit instruction in comprehension skills like sequencing, vocabulary development and story retell. The treatment group outperformed the comparison group on the Woodcock Language Proficiency Battery-Revised passage comprehension subtest (WLPB-R, Woodcock, 1991). The authors contend that, "without question, the most important outcome is the influence of the intervention on reading comprehension" (Vaughn et al., 2006, p. 176). Language support modifications (i.e., explicit explanation and teacher demonstration of tasks) and oracy and vocabulary development in the form of the story retell with vocabulary development component were added to the original intervention English intervention (Mathes, Torgeson, Wahl, Menchetti, & Grek, 1999) to support oral language development in English. In contrast to a study conducted by Mathes, Denton, Fletcher, Anthony, Francis, and Schatschneider (2005) with mono-lingual English speakers using the original version of the intervention that found no statistically significant gains in reading comprehension, this study did find significant differences between treatment and control groups. "We suspect that the addition of the story retell component may account for the difference [in the WLPB-R passage com-prehension subtest], particularly because this component was not included in the study with monolingual English at-risk readers" (p. 176). The authors also concluded that English language learners at risk for reading difficulties benefit from the same types of explicit, systematic interventions as monolingual students.

In a similar study, Vaughn, Cirino et al. (2006) utilized the same design, measures, and curricular materials including the addition of the oral language, vocabulary, and story retell components and no found significant differences between treatment and control groups on the WLPB-R passage comprehension subtest. Both groups made "meaningful progress" in comprehension. The researchers suggest that it is possible that the comparison group benefited from the presence of the treatment subgroup. "By iden-tifying all at-risk readers while simultaneously reducing the number of students requir-ing school-delivered intervention, we provided an opportunity for schools to focus more resources on a small group of students [the comparison group]" (p. 483). Vaughn et al. posit that differences in the initial English oral language standard scores for each treatment group (between 47 and 53 for this study compared to between 63 and 66 for the latter study) may have contributed to the variance in comprehension performance between the two studies.

Linan-Thompson, Vaughn, Hickman-Davis, and Kouzekanani (2003) conducted a study designed to "determine the effects of a supplemental reading intervention that included the elements of effective reading instruction and strategies for teaching English language learners on the reading outcomes of English language learners with read-ing problems" (p. 222). They identified the critical elements of reading instruction for English language learners as reading fluency, phonological awareness, comprehension and vocabulary development, and word study. The intervention incorporated effective instructional practices for English language learners such as explicit instruction and multiple opportunities for practice (August & Hakuta, 1997). The passage comprehen-sion subtest of the Woodcock Reading Mastery Test-Revised (WRM, American Guid-ance Services, 1987) was used to assess comprehension. The increases in scores on the passage comprehension subtest from pretest to posttest and at a four-week follow-up were significant. Scores continued to increase at a four-month follow-up, but the increases were not significant. According to Linan-Thompson et al., findings from this study suggest that English language learners at risk for reading problems benefit from the same types of intensive reading interventions as monolingual students provided the instruction incorporates effective English as a second language instructional practices.

Jitendra, Edwards, Starosta, Sacks, Jacobson, Choutka, et al. (2004) conducted a study of an intervention for children with severe reading difficulties using the *Read Well* (Sprick, Howard, & Fidanque, 1998) curriculum. This program is designed to provide explicit, systematic instruction in phonological awareness, phonics, fluency, vocabu-lary and reading comprehension in the context of thematic units. Jitendra et al. used a single-subject design not only to "provide information on the adequacy of the measures but also provide insights into factors that inhibit or enhance the implementation of the intervention for individual children" (2004, p. 422). One of the five participants was an English language learner. This second-grade student received special education services for all academic areas in a "learning support" classroom. A trained teacher provided the intervention in individual sessions four times a week for an average of 30 minutes per lesson. The passage comprehension subtest of the Woodcock Reading Mastery Test-Revised (WRMT-R; Woodcock, 1987) was used as the measure of reading comprehension. Two of the participants' comprehension scores improved following the *Read Well* intervention, including the English language learner. The researchers note that outcomes of reading fluency, phoneme segmentation and nonsense word reading fluency were more varied and less pronounced than those of passage comprehension and word attack, leading them to conclude, "These findings are noteworthy given the short duration of the intervention (2 to 7 weeks)" (p. 431).

Santoro, Jitendra, Starosta, and Sacks (2006) extended their research on *Read Well* (Sprick et al., 1998) to investigate the impact of the intervention on the reading comprehension of English language learners. In this study, four second-grade English language learners were selected to participate on the basis of an interview with the special education coordinator. One student qualified for special education services and a second student was referred for special education services during the study. The testing and intervention took place as a part of their ESL services. The passage comprehension subtest of the WRMT-R (Woodcock, 1987) was used to assess comprehension. Three of the four participants had both pretest and posttest data. For two of those participants, the passage comprehension scores increased; for the third student, the scores decreased. The authors concluded that the intervention did improve the decoding skills of the four students and that "the question of whether the *Read Well* intervention facilitated transfer of reading skills to comprehension skills was also evident for most children in the study" (p. 113).

Another study that investigated *Read Well* (Sprick et al., 1998) was conducted by Denton, Anthony, Parker, and Hasbrouck (2004). In this study, English language learners were tutored using either *Read Well*, a structured phonics program, or a revised version of *Read Naturally* (Hasbrouck, Ihnot, & Rogers, 1999), a program that provides comprehension and vocabulary instruction in the context of repeated readings. Subtests from the WRMT-R (Woodcock, 1987) were used to measure reading comprehension. Each tutoring treatment was compared to the untutored classmates' outcomes. Significant differences were found between the *Read Well* tutored group and the untutored students in word identification but no significant differences were found in other measures, including passage comprehension. There were no significant differences between the *Read Naturally* tutored group and the untutored students' outcomes.

The use of Peer-Assisted Learning Strategies (PALS; Fuchs, Fuchs, Mathes & Simmons, 1997) with English language learners with learning disabilities was investigated by Sáenz, Fuchs, and Fuchs (2005). PALS is a reciprocal classwide peer-tutoring strategy with three main components: partner reading with retell, paragraph shrinking, and prediction relay. These activities require students to collaborate with a peer to review, sequence, and summarize information as they read. PALS had been shown to be effective with monolingual English-speaking, learning-disabled students (Fuchs et al., 1997) and this was the first study to look at the impact of PALS on English language learners with and without learning disabilities. Comprehension was measured using the Comprehensive Reading Assessment Battery (CRAB; Fuchs, Fuchs, and Hamlett, 1989). This test utilizes comprehension questions, cloze passages, and number of words read correctly to assess comprehension of rewritten traditional folktales. One hundred thirty-two English language learners in 12 classrooms, grades three through six, participated in the study. Half of the classes were assigned to the treatment condition (PALS) and the remaining students received regular reading instruction for the duration of the 15-week study. Three PALS sessions were conducted during reading instruction each week. Sessions lasted 35 minutes. The main effect for treatment was statistically significant for the number of questions correct component of CRABS. None of the other main effects was statistically significant. The effect size for number of questions answered correctly was 1.02 across all student types. According to Sáenz et al. (2005), "The clearest conclusion to be drawn from study findings is that PALS improves the reading comprehension of English language learners with and without learning disabilities in transitional bilingual education classrooms" (p. 243).

These studies inform our understanding of reading interventions for struggling English language learners. The measures used to assess comprehension outcomes were *objective* and did not allow for further investigation of underlying factors that may have impacted the ability of the English language learners to construct meaning from the text.

COMPREHENSION AS SOCIALLY CONSTRUCTED MEANING MAKING ACTIVITY

From a sociocultural perspective, the act of reading is viewed as a socially constructed, meaning-making activity (Gee, 2003). Students' social worlds, cultural identities, and background knowledge are integral components of the reading process. According to sociocultural theories, reading—often referred to by the more encompassing term of literacy—is more than the sum of constituent parts. Literacy incorporates factors such as the type of text, the student's background knowledge of the content, and the ways in which students are expected to demonstrate understanding all impact reading comprehension according to this view of literacy. For the purposes of this chapter, knowledge of concepts and literacy skills in students' home language are considered background knowledge. In accordance with a sociocultural view of reading, reading comprehension is a complex interaction between text factors, including text structure and content, and reader factors such as background knowledge and strategy use. In the following section, I review research studies that are based in this perspective that investigate English language learners' text comprehension.

Langer, Bartolome, Vasquez, and Lucas (1990) investigated the ways that 12 bilingual fifth-grade students constructed meaning while reading fiction and nonfiction texts in English and in Spanish. All of the students had literacy abilities in Spanish and in English. The researchers used two types of questions to ascertain text comprehension and strategy use. Envisionment questions were designed to "provide as much access as possible to the unfolding of meaning as the students read" (Langer et al., 1990, p. 435), and probing questions provided opportunities for students to discuss their understanding of genre, organization, language and content. Students were also asked to recall what they remembered first orally and then in written form for each passage. Students read four passages (two in Spanish and two in English) in random order, completed the recall activities and then answered the questions. The envisionment questions were interspersed within each passage. Using both quantitative and qualitative data sources, case studies were developed for each student and then cross-case analyses were performed. Findings suggest that, "the students' abilities to use good meaning-making strategies made a difference in how well they comprehended—both in English and in Spanish" (Langer et al., 1990, p. 462). This meaning-making ability was more of a factor than language proficiency on text comprehension. Familiarity with text genre impacted students' ability to make meaning. The students reported knowing less about the genre of nonfiction reports and all students were able to comprehend and recall information from the stories more extensively than on the nonfiction reports. Finally, the question type affected how the students were able to demonstrate their understanding. "Open ended questions that tapped their own growing envisionments and understandings they developed allowed them to better reveal what and how well they understood than either display questions or questions that required a decontextualization of the referent or an objectification of the text" (Langer et al., 1990, p. 464).

García (1991) documented the factors that impact the reading test performance of 51 Hispanic students and 53 monolingual Anglo students in fifth and sixth grade. All of the Hispanic students were orally proficient in English and Spanish; not all of them were proficient in reading and writing in Spanish. The measures were researcher-developed and included a reading comprehension test based on commercial reading tests, a vocabulary test with words selected from standardized tests for grades five and six, and a prior-knowledge test based on the content of the six passages. A subgroup of 12 Hispanic and 6 Anglo students were selected to participate in "open-ended interviews in which they were asked how they determined their vocabulary and reading test answers" (García, 1991, p. 376). A representative sample including students with high, average, and low reading abilities formed the subgroup. The quantitative data analysis leaves the initial impression that the Anglo students clearly outperformed the Hispanic students on the comprehension measure. However, when background knowledge was controlled, there were no significant differences between the groups' scores, suggesting that it was lack of prior knowledge about the content of the passage that was the major obstacle. Interviews with a subsample of Hispanic students indicated that unfamiliar vocabulary in English had a considerable effect on the reading test performance. Using only test scores to evaluate the reading comprehension of these Hispanic students would not have provided a full account of their ability to understand the passages. García (1991) concludes that "Hispanic children's interview responses about how they had determined their answers as well as their responses to open-ended comprehension questions asked orally tended to provide more information about their passage comprehension than did their actual performance on the test" (p. 388).

Jiménez, García, and Pearson (1995) closely examined the cognitive and metacognitive knowledge of three female, sixth-grade students: a proficient Spanish bilingual reader, a proficient monolingual reader, and a less proficient Spanish bilingual reader, using case studies and cross case analysis. Students were selected based on teacher recommendation, correlating reading comprehension scores on standardized tests and the students' ability to think aloud while reading. Each participant completed a background questionnaire that included questions about age, language learning histories, and other relevant information. Researchers developed a prior knowledge assessment task for each passage that included a brief introduction to the topic and its genre and a request for students to write about something related to the topic. Then students read the passage and performed either a prompted or unprompted think aloud, depending on the passage. The two bilingual readers had opportunities to read and think aloud using texts in both English and Spanish. Each student was interviewed regarding "very general aspects of reading" (p. 74). Questions included, "What is reading?" and "Why do people read?" The bilingual students were asked an additional 11 questions specifically regarding bilingual reading. In compiling the individual profiles, "all data sources were drawn upon in an attempt to describe these students as completely as possible" (p. 76). The monolingual reader "possessed a sophisticated understanding of reading, a multistrategic approach to reading and a tendency toward global reflection concerning comprehension," (p. 88). The proficient bilingual reader attended carefully to vocabulary and used her understanding of words to help her construct meaning, including an understanding of cognates (i.e., species, *especies*). She employed a variety of strategies while reading in English and Spanish, demonstrating her ability to think across languages. The less proficient bilingual reader did not integrate her understanding of Spanish and English; instead, she viewed bilingualism as "confusing." Her strategy use was "fragmented" and she had difficulty coordinating strategies to solve comprehension problems. The researchers considered her view of reading "uninformed" because, "she described many different activities associated with reading, but she never implemented them in concert with one another" (p. 86). Jiménez et al. (1995) note that the "complex relationship between bilingualism and reading is revealed in several aspects of the reading process: How readers approach vocabulary, how they conceptualize the purpose of reading, how they interact with text, and how bilingual readers regard their two languages" (p. 88–89). They recommend teaching bilingual readers how to use their knowledge of words and strategies across languages. The profile of the proficient bilingual student reading in L2 (English) "demonstrates that bilingual students may possess untapped potential that is limited by models of reading based entirely on the thinking and behavior of monolingual Anglo readers" (p. 93).

Jiménez, García, and Pearson (1996) extended their work with bilingual readers to build "a broader and more general topology and explanation of bilingual reading strategies" (p. 94). Eight successful bilingual readers, three less successful bilingual readers, and three successful monolingual readers were selected using similar criteria to Jiménez, García, and Pearson (1995). In addition to the background questionnaire, prior knowledge assessment, think aloud assessment (prompted and unprompted), researchers added a retelling assessment to "double check comprehension problems that surfaced during the think alouds" (p. 97). Findings from this larger sample of monolingual and bilingual readers substantiated the findings of the smaller study. For example, "evidence from this study suggests that successful Latina/o readers possess an enhanced awareness of the relationship between Spanish and English, and that this awareness leads them to use successfully the bilingual strategies of searching for cognates, transferring, and translating" (p. 106). With respect to the less proficient bilingual readers, they continued to demonstrate the ability to monitor comprehension but lacked the strategy use to resolve comprehension problems. Both types of bilingual readers encountered problems with unknown vocabulary. The researchers suggest, "Learning efficient use of context, how to invoke prior knowledge, and how to make inferences could contribute to their comprehension abilities" (p. 106). Further research is needed on ways to facilitate cross-linguistic strategy use among bilingual readers.

A similar study was conducted by García (1998) with 13 bilingual students in fourth grade. Students were trained to conduct think alouds and then asked to read an expository and a narrative text in English and in Spanish (four total passages). Each student read a passage silently, participated in prompted and unprompted think alouds, and discussed their understanding of each passage in a retelling type interview. Students demonstrated similar bilingual strategies to those identified in Jiménez et al. (1996) including code-mixing, code switching, and translating although the use of these strategies was more frequent and varied reflecting "their language preference or dominance, reading experience in the particular language, reading ability and perceived text difficulty" (p. 259). Genre also played a role in students' ability to comprehend texts with some comprehension problems associated with reading a particular genre across English and Spanish.

COMPARING THE TWO INTERPRETATIONS
OF READING COMPREHENSION

Both of these bodies of research contribute important information to our understanding of the complexity of L2 reading and reading comprehension. In this section, I identify features of the studies that need further consideration, summarize the findings from each perspective, and suggest a pathway for future research that builds on the strengths of both bodies of research.

Most of the studies in the "Reading Comprehension as a Composite of Abilities" section meet the criteria for scientifically based reading research according to the National Reading Panel (National Institute of Child Health and Human Development, 2000). For this reason, the findings of these studies have been the foundation upon which reading programs and interventions that meet No Child Left Behind (NCLB) standards have been designed.

It is important to note several limitations of this body of research. First, the samples in the studies may not reflect the general English language learner student population. All of these studies included English language learners who were also identified through various criteria as at risk for reading difficulties or had already qualified for special education services. Several studies (Vaughn, Cirino, et al., 2006; Vaughn, Mathes, et al., 2006; Linan-Thompson et al., 2003) only included English language learners who were identified as at risk for reading difficulties. There are not standard criteria for defining at risk, so the definition varies across studies, making it difficult to generalize findings to the general English language learner population. According to Development Associates (2007), only 9% of all LEP students received special education services during the 2001–2002 school year. Findings from studies with English language learners who receive special education services need to be carefully considered before applying these findings to the general English language learner population since most English language learners do not need special education services.

Second, the samples were relatively small so it is difficult to make statistical inferences regarding the estimated 3.4 million English language learners in U. S. public schools (Kindler, 2002). For example, the largest sample was found in Fuchs et al. (1997), with 132 English language learner participants.

Third, there is a lack of consistency in the outcomes among the studies that investigated similar reading interventions. The series of studies conducted by Vaughn and her colleagues (Vaughn, Cirino, et al., 2006; Vaughn, Mathes et al., 2006) used the same instructional materials and procedures, but there was considerable variance in the comprehension outcomes of the two studies. Three studies (Denton et al., 2004; Jitandra et al., 2004; Santoro et al., 2006) investigated the efficacy on the *Read Well* reading intervention with varying outcomes.

Finally, the variability in grade levels, comprehension measures, and criteria for participation across the studies suggest that more evidence is required to make large-scale instructional program recommendations for English language learners in general education.

A key feature of the studies in the "Comprehension as Socially Constructed Meaning Making Activity" is that they provide opportunities for English language learners to demonstrate their understanding of texts through oral and written expression as well as objective measures. Concerns regarding this body of research include the small number of participants in the studies and the types of students who participated. The number of participants in these studies is limited due to the nature of the research methods. These studies involve individual interviews that provide detailed accounts of how English language learners engage with text to construct meaning. This information may be vital to gaining an understanding of how English language learners comprehend texts, but the generalizability of the findings is limited because of the small numbers. The participants were all considered bilingual, with some students being biliterate as well. The participants were in intermediate elementary grades and had already reached a level of proficiency in reading and speaking English. This does not reflect the general population of English language learners in U. S. public schools (Kindler, 2002).

Another limiting factor of this body of research includes the measures used to assess comprehension. Researcher-created measures do not have the reliability necessary to be applied to the general population of English language learners.

In sum—the number of participants, the varying criteria for identifying English language learners as at risk, the lack of consistent outcomes, and the variance in grade levels—biliteracy and bilingualism among the English language learner participants should cause consumers of both categories of research to be cautious in the ways the findings are used to inform future research and instructional practices.

With the previously mentioned cautions in mind, the findings from these two bodies of research do offer insights into the types of instruction that benefit English language learners' reading comprehension, and suggest ways of documenting comprehension that allow for a more complete disclosure of English language learners' text understanding.

For instance, the findings of the first category identify several key features of instruction that contribute to reading development for this group of learners. The findings suggest that English language learners who experience difficulty learning to read in English benefit from explicit instruction in phonological awareness, phonics, word reading, and text comprehension that has been modified to attend to specific language learning needs. For example, the interventions included structured experiences to develop oral language in English and multiple opportunities for practice.

In the second category, studies conducted with older students with knowledge of their heritage language produced findings that demonstrate unique qualities of bilingual readers. The qualitative data gathered through oral and written expression uncover processes that remain hidden when using only objective measures of comprehension. Proficient bilingual readers demonstrated how they were able to capitalize on their knowledge of Spanish and English to construct meaning from text while less proficient bilingual readers had difficulty integrating their understandings across languages. When allowed to retell and explain their meaning making strategies using English and Spanish, English language learners revealed more understanding of a text than standardized measures of comprehension in English suggest. The studies of reading comprehension with bilingual readers reveal that language development (L1 and L2) plays a role in bilingual students' abilities to construct meaning from text and express this understanding.

When considering findings from both categories, the complexity of reading comprehension in L2 is evident. Research suggests that a student's language proficiency in the heritage language and English, the student's control of basic reading skills such as word recognition, the student's ability to construct meaning from text, and the way in which the student is asked to demonstrate text understanding are all factors that impact English language learners' reading comprehension. New ways of understanding the multifaceted process of reading comprehension that take into account these factors are needed.

Some intriguing work has been done recently by Proctor, August, Carlo, and Snow (2005) in the area of developing a working model of L2 reading comprehension that builds on research conducted by Hoover and Gough (1990). Hoover and Gough applied the simple view of reading (Gough & Tunmer, 1986) to English language learners. According to the simple view of reading, reading comprehension results from the interaction between the reader's decoding ability and the reader's ability to understand language. In the Gough and Tunmer study, decoding was measured through nonsense word reading and listening comprehension was used to measure a reader's ability to understand language. Hoover and Gough found that decoding ability accounts for most of the variance in reading comprehension for young readers, and that linguistic knowledge accounts for more variance as decoding skills develop. Extending the work of Hoover and Gough, Proctor et al. (2005) developed a model that posits "listening comprehension maintains a proximal effect on reading comprehension, whereas vocabulary knowledge assumes a more dynamic relationship with reading comprehension as both a proximal and distal (through listening comprehension) predictor of reading comprehension" (p. 248). Multiple measures were used to assess decoding and linguistic ability in a study of 135 Spanish-English bilingual fourth graders designed to test the model. The Computer-Based Academic Assessment System (Sinatra & Royer, 1993) provided data regarding students' abilities to decode both nonsense and real words. The real word reading task also produced a fluency rate. Linguistic ability was measured using the Woodcock Language Proficiency Battery (Woodcock, 1991) subtests for English passage comprehension, English listening comprehension and English vocabulary knowledge. The researchers found that vocabulary and listening comprehension were more predictive of reading comprehension than automatic decoding and word recognition. In terms of the proposed model, "the interplay between vocabulary knowledge, listening comprehension, and reading comprehension was made clear through strong and significant relationships for all three pairs of variables" (p. 252). Proctor et al. (2005) concluded "positive changes in vocabulary knowledge had direct effects on reading comprehension but also on listening comprehension, through which reading comprehension was further affected" (p. 253). This model sheds more light on the individual components that contribute to L2 reading comprehension and suggests that vocabulary development impacts reading comprehension in multiple ways. However, the measures used for assessment require English language learners to demonstrate understanding by responding to multiple choice or short answer questions that do not allow for elaboration or further explanation. As discussed earlier, information gathered through these types of measures may not accurately reflect all that an English language learner understands about a text or word.

August et al. (2006) developed a new measure of reading comprehension that is designed to "reflect central comprehension processes while minimizing decoding and language demands" (p. 221). The Diagnostic Assessment of Reading Comprehension (DARC) alleviates some of the decoding and language demands of typical standardized comprehension measures and allows for the independent measurement of text memory, text inferencing, background knowledge, and knowledge integration. This assessment, according to August et al., uncovers the central comprehension processes used by English language learners when reading in English. However, there are other factors that raise concerns. The use of nonsense terms (i.e., Nan's tarp is like her culp) is used to reduce language demands, but nonsense terms may disallow the use genuine background knowledge. Also, ultimately, this is an objective measure of reading comprehension that attempts to simplify a very complex activity.

While these models and assessments may provide new ways of understanding L2 reading comprehension, the current ones available do not account for the complexity of assessing English language learners with respect to the sociocultural factors that impact text understanding and reading achievement. Key issues in both categories of research that impact validity and generalizability of the findings are the types of measures used to access English language learners' reading comprehension. In an attempt to identify a common ground between the two categories of research reviewed in this chapter, I offer two perspectives on the assessment of English language learners. These perspectives are aligned with the categories of research reviewed in this chapter and both acknowledge the central role of culture, language and context on student outcomes.

McCardle, Mele-McCarthy, and Leos (2005) in a special issue of *Learning Disabilities Research and Practice* on English language learners discuss the importance of cultural and contextual factors in assessment, instruction, and remediation for English language learners. They call for the identification of "salient variables" among specific subgroups (i.e., native Americans) and contend that understanding the affective and motivational factors that impact academic success are "especially important for ELLs who bring linguistic and cultural heritages that differ from those typically expected and accommodated within the educational setting" (McCardle et al., 2005, p. 71). Commenting on the current availability of assessments for English language learners, McCardle et al. note, "There is a clear need for effective methods to identify the social, cultural, emotional, instructional and linguistic factors that may impede normal language and academic development in ELLs without [learning disabilities]" (p. 70). This statement suggests that even within a scientifically based research paradigm there is recognition that English language learners bring a complex set of variables to the act of comprehending texts.

According to Gee (2003), reading and writing are inextricably linked to context in which these social practices are learned. Different contexts lead to varying opportunity to learn. Gee identified principles relevant to opportunity to learn and to the assessment of what is learned. Central to these principles are the equivalency of embodied, situated experiences; engagement in assessed social practices (i.e. reading expository texts and answering questions); and language learning opportunities. He asserts "an evaluative assessment is invalid and unjust if the people being assessed have not had, in terms of the sorts of principles I have developed here, equivalent opportunities to learn" (p. 44). Assessment must match not only what is taught. In order to be valid, assessment must incorporate the learning opportunity afforded the student and the social context in which the learning occurred.

Researchers who view reading comprehension as a composite of abilities such as McCardle et al. (2005), and researchers who view reading comprehensions as a socially constructed meaning-making activity such as Gee (2003), arrive at similar conclusions about assessment for English language learners from very different paths. A student's home language, culture, opportunity to learn, attitude, and aptitude combine in unique ways to impact achievement outcomes including reading comprehension. The complexity of reading comprehension in L2 cannot be captured by research methods that parse the composite abilities required to understand texts and do not account for the social, cultural, linguistic, and contextual variables that influence reading comprehension. We must develop research practices that untangle the intricate connections among the myriad of factors that impact academic achievement among English language learners while embracing the linguistic and sociocultural realities of English language learners.

REFERENCES

American Guidance Services. (1987). *Woodcock Reading Mastery.* Circle Pines, MN: Author.

August, D., Francis, D. J., Hsu, H. A., & Snow, C. E. (2006). Assessing reading comprehension in bilinguals. *The Elementary School Journal, 107,* 221–248.

August, D., & Hakuta, K. (1997). *Improving schooling for language-minority children: A research agenda.* Washington, DC: National Academy Press.

August, D., & Shanahan, T. (Eds.). (2006). *Developing literacy in second-language learners: Report of the National Literacy Panel on Language-Minority Children and Youth.* Mahwah, NJ: Erlbaum.

Bernhardt, E. (2000). Second-language reading as a case study of reading scholarship in the 20th century. In M. L. Kamil, P. B. Mosenthal, P. D. Pearson, & R. Barr (Eds.), *Handbook of reading research* (Vol. 3, pp. 791–812). Mahwah, NJ: Erlbaum.

Crawford, J. (1989). *Bilingual education: History, politics, theory, and practice.* Trenton, NJ: Crane.

Denton, C. A., Anthony, J. L., Parker, R., & Hasbrouck, J. (2004). Effects of two tutoring programs on the English reading development of Spanish-English bilingual students. *Elementary School Journal, 104,* 289–305.

Development Associates (2007). *Summary of Key LEP Findings.* Retrieved April 25, 2007, from http://www.devassoc.com/LEPkeyfind.asp

Fitzgerald, J. (1995). English as a second Language learners' cognitive reading processes: A review of research in the United States. *Review of Educational Research, 65*(2), 145–190.

Fuchs, L. S., Fuchs, D., & Hamlett, C. L. (1989). Monitoring reading growth using student recalls: Effects of informal reading comprehension measures. *Remedial and Special Education, 9,* 20–28.

Fuchs, D., Fuchs, L. S., Mathes, P. G., & Simmons, D. C. (1997). Peer-assisted learning strategies: Making classrooms more responsive to diversity. *American Educational Research Journal, 34,* 174–206.

García, G. E. (1991). Factors influencing the English reading test performance of Spanish speaking Hispanic children. *Reading Research Quarterly, 26,* 371–392.

García, G. E. (1998). Mexican-American bilingual students' metacognitive reading strategies: What's transferred, unique, problematic? *National Reading Conference Yearbook, 47,* 253–263.

Gee, J. P. (2003). Opportunity to learn: A language-based perspective on assessment. *Assessment in Education, 10,* 27–46.

Gersten, R., & Baker, S. (2000). What we know about effective instructional practices for English-language learners. *Exceptional Children, 66,* 454–470.

Gough, P. B., & Tunmer, W. E. (1986). Decoding, reading and reading disability. *Remedial and Special Education, 7,* 6–10.

Hasbrouck, J. E., Ihnot, C., & Rogers, G. (1999). Read Naturally: A strategy to increase oral reading fluency. *Reading Research and Instruction, 39,* 27–38.

Hoover, E., & Gough, J. (1990). The simple view of reading. *Reading and Writing: An Interdisciplinary Journal, 2,* 127–160.

Jiménez, R. T., García, E. G., & Pearson, P. D. (1995). Three children, two languages, and strategic reading: Case studies in bilingual/monolingual reading. *American Educational Research Journal, 32,* 67–97.

Jiménez, R. T., García, E. G., & Pearson, P. D. (1996). The reading strategies of bilingual Latina/o students who are successful English readers: Opportunities and obstacles. *Reading Research Quarterly, 31,* 90–112.

Jitendra, A. K., Edwards, L. L., Starosta, K., Sacks, G., Jacobson, L. A., & Choutka, C. M. (2004). Early reading instruction for children with learning disabilities: Meeting the needs of diverse learners. *Journal of Learning Disabilities, 37,* 421–439.

Kindler, A. L. (2002). *Survey of states' limited English proficient students and available educational programs and services. 2000–2001 summary report.* Washington, DC: National Clearinghouse for English Language Acquisition.

Langer, J. A., Bartolome, L., Vasquez, O., & Lucas, T. (1990). Meaning construction in school literacy tasks: A study of bilingual students. *American Educational Research Journal, 27,* 427–471.

Lesaux, N. K. (with Koda, K., Siegel, L. S., & Shanahan, T.). (2006). Development of Literacy. In D. August & T. Shanahan (Eds.), *Developing literacy in second-language learners: Report of the National Literacy Panel on Language-Minority Children and Youth* (pp. 75–122). Mahwah, NJ: Erlbaum.

Lesaux, N. K. & Geva, E. (2006). Synthesis: Development of literacy in language-minority students. In D. August & T. Shanahan (Eds.), *Developing literacy in second-language learners: Report of the National Literacy Panel on Language-Minority Children and Youth* (pp. 53–74). Mahwah, NJ: Erlbaum.

Linan-Thompson, S., Vaughn, S., Hickman-Davis, P., & Kouzekanani, K. (2003). Effectiveness of supplemental reading instruction for second-grade English language learners with reading difficulties. *The Elementary School Journal, 103,* 221–238.

Mathes, P. G., Denton, C. A., Fletcher, J. M., Anthony, J. L., Francis, D. J., & Schatschneider, C. (2005). An evaluation of two reading interventions derived from diverse models. *Reading Research Quarterly, 40,* 148–183.

Mathes, P. G., Torgeson, J. K., Wahl, M., Menchetti, M. C., & Grek, M. L. (1999). *Proactive beginning reading: Intensive small-group instruction form struggling readers.* Dallas, TX: Southern Methodist University.

McCardle, P., Mele-McCarthy, J., & Leos, K. (2005). English language learners and learning disabilities: Research agenda and implications for practice. *Learning Disabilities Research and Practice, 20,* 68–78.

National Center for Education Statistics (2006). *Participation in Education: Language Minority School-Age Children.* Retrieved March 20, 2007, from http://nces.ed.gov/programs/coe/2006/section1/indicator07.asp

National Institute of Child Health and Human Development. (2000). *Teaching children to read: An evidence-based assessment of scientific research literature and its implications for reading education: Reports of the subgroups* (NIH Publication No. 00-4754). Washington, DC: U.S. Government Printing Office.

Peregoy, S. F., & Boyle, O. F. (2000). English learners reading English: What we know, what we need to know. *Theory into Practice, 39,* 237–247.

Proctor, C. P., August, D., Carlo, M., & Snow, C. (2005). Native Spanish-speaking children reading in English: Toward a model of comprehension. *Journal of Educational Psychology, 97,* 246–256.

Sáenz, L. M., Fuchs, L. S., & Fuchs, D. (2005). Peer assisted learning strategies for ELLs with learning disabilities. *Exceptional Children, 71,* 231–247.

Santoro, L., Jitendra, A., Starosta, K., & Sacks, G. (2006). Read well with "Read Well": Enhancing the reading performance of English language learners. *Remedial and Special Education, 27,* 105–115.

Shanahan, T., & Beck, I. L. (2006). Effective literacy teaching for English language learners. In D. August & T. Shanahan (Eds.), *Developing literacy in second-language learners: Report of the National Literacy Panel on Language-Minority Children and Youth* (pp. 415–488). Mahwah, NJ: Erlbaum.

Sinatra, G. M., & Royer, J. M. (1993). Development of cognitive component processing skills that support skilled reading. *Journal of Educational Psychology, 85,* 509–519.

Sprick, M., Howard, L., & Fidanque, A. (1998). *Read Well: Critical foundations in primary reading.* Longmont, CO: Sopris West.

U. S. Census. (2007). *Characteristics of people who speak a language other than English at home.* Retrieved on March 10, 2007 from http://factfinder.census.gov/servlet/STTable?_bm=y&-geo_id=01000US&-qr_name=ACS_2005_EST_G00_S1603&-ds_name=ACS_2005_EST_G00_&-redoLog=false

Vaughn, S., Cirino, P. T., Linan-Thompson, S., Mathes, P.G., Carlson, C. D., Cardenas-Hagan, E., et al. (2006). Effectiveness of a Spanish intervention and an English intervention for English-language learners at risk for reading problems. *American Educational Research Journal, 43,* 449–487.

Vaughn, S., Mathes, P., Linan-Thompson, S., Cirino, P., Carlson, C., Pollard-Durodola, S., et al. (2006). Effectiveness of an English intervention for first grade ELLs at risk for reading problems. *Elementary School Journal, 107,* 153–181.

Woodcock, R. W. (1987). *Woodcock Reading Mastery Test-Revised.* Circle Pines, MN: American Guidance Service.

Woodcock, R. W. (1991). *Woodcock Language Proficiency Battery-Revised.* Chicago: Riverside.

30 Family Literacy and Reading Comprehension

Patricia A. Edwards

Michigan State University

Jennifer D. Turner

University of Maryland, College Park

Throughout history, the family has been the primary source for learning. Before the advent of schools, children were taught by their parents, older siblings, grandparents, and/or other relatives. And although schools now serve as sites for formal education, parents are still the child's "first and most important teacher" (Edwards, Pleasants, & Franklin, 1999). Because the family exists in a network of community, its members are continually communicating, negotiating, and otherwise interacting with schools, within the context of their cultural and community orientations (Bhola, 1996).

Family literacy is an important catalyst for consensus-building; teachers, administrators, parents, and communities acknowledge the critical role that families play in children's literacy lives, and these stakeholders often join together to create collaborative partnerships to improve children's literacy learning (Edwards, 2004; Risko & Bromley, 2001). It is ironic, then, that family literacy has also become center stage for conflicts and controversies around the role of parents in children's literacy education. The battle lines have been particularly drawn around families from culturally and linguistically diverse backgrounds. Current discussions related to the importance of family literacy have simultaneously raised concerns about the low literacy achievement of at-risk children, and the challenges associated with involving poor and/or culturally diverse parents in their children's educational lives have been raised. Over the past 10 years, there have been heated debates in academic and political circles about what constitutes good parenting, appropriate parent involvement, and acceptable literacy practices in homes and families (Arzubiaga et al., 2006; Edwards, 2004; Gadsden et al., 2006). These debates have especially impacted school-based and agency-based family literacy programs across the country, because most of these efforts are directed to people from poor, minority, and/or immigrant families who are learning English. As such, "parent involvement and parent-child literacy engagement, over time, have become a national priority, on the one hand, and the problems associated with both have been framed as unique to low-income and low-income minority families on the other hand" (Gadsden et al., p. 157).

Against this backdrop of conflict and controversy, our chapter explores the relationship between family literacy and comprehension. In particular, we highlight the recent scholarship conducted on culturally and linguistically diverse families, their home literacy practices, and their children's schooling experiences and literacy development. We begin with a discussion on family literacy from a historical perspective. Next we synthesize the current research on comprehension and its relationship to family literacy. Finally, we conclude with a summary of the critical research that is necessary for advancing our understanding of family literacy and comprehension.

FAMILY LITERACY: WHAT WE KNOW

Family literacy: Historical contexts and perspectives

The practice of family literacy has occurred for generations, but the two words were not unified as a concept until 1983, when Denny Taylor published her dissertation, *Family Literacy: Young Children Learning to Read and Write*. The purpose of her 1977 study was to "develop systematic ways of looking at reading and writing as activities that have consequences in and are affected by family life" (1983, p. xiii). Her groundbreaking ethnographic study carefully described the ways that families support the literacy development of their children and is considered to be the beginning of current research, practice, and interest in the area of family literacy.

Although family literacy has moved to center stage within the field of literacy education, there is much debate around the definition. Taylor (1997) revealed that "no single narrow definition of 'family literacy' can do justice to the richness and complexity of families, and the multiple literacies, including often unrecognized local literacies that are part of their everyday lives" (p. 4). Nevertheless, DeBruin-Parecki and Knol-Sinclair (2003) reported that "once the term *family literacy* was coined, its meaning became subject to broad interpretation to suit the context in which it was mentioned and implemented" (p. 1). Scholars have developed varying definitions of family literacy, because their theoretical and empirical orientations reflected different perspectives and disciplinary traditions, such as psychology, emergent literacy, beginning reading, anthropology, and sociology (Anderson, 1995; Burgess, 1997; Edwards, 1993, 2003; Heath, 1983; Morrow, 1983; Purcell-Gates & Dahl, 1991; Teale, 1984). Family programs also define family literacy is multiple ways, and according to Paratore (2001) "the field of family literacy is a complex and muddy arena—one in which there is wide disagreement about the goals, purposes, and potential effects on the lives of those the programs are intended to serve" (p. 100). She goes on to describe varying purposes and objectives for those involved with family literacy programs and interventions, ranging from preparing parents for well-paying jobs to enhance their economic independence to educating parents so they are most interested in and positive about their children's education. Clearly, the field is divided on how literacy and family literacy should be defined (Morrow, Paratore, Gaber, Harrison, & Tracey, 1993), on how interventions should be framed (Taylor, 1997), and on how program effects should be measured (Johnston, 1997; Murphy, 1997).

Family literacy programs: Reaching children by teaching parents

The lack of a universally accepted definition of family literacy has not curtailed family programs from emerging all over the world. Though such programs were not new in the late '80s, their growth and national prominence was enhanced by the development of the privately endowed National Center for Family Literacy and the federally funded Even Start Act (1988). Nearly 20 years later, there are thousands of family literacy programs serving thousands of families in a variety of ways.

Padak, Sapin, and Baycich (2002) define family literacy programs as "organized efforts to improve the literacy levels of educationally-disadvantaged parents and children" (p. 4). Currently, there are several types of family literacy programs which provide services to parents and their children. To categorize these varying levels of programmatic services, Nickse (1990) has developed a useful typology. Type 1 Programs (direct adult/direct children) provide literacy services for adults and children, and both attend the program. Type 2 Programs (indirect adult/indirect children), parents and children participate in family literacy activities, such as read aloud sessions. Type 3 Programs (direct adult/indirect children) deliver instruction only to adults, based upon the assumption that parents who enhance their own literacy skills will positively influence their children's literacy development. Finally, Type 4 Programs (indirect adult/direct children) deliver instruction to children only, with parent involvement encouraged but optional.

Family literacy programs are typically established by local and state agencies (Padak et al., 2002). Recently, however, local school districts and schools have been encouraged to organize family literacy programs as a way to build home-school partnerships. Paratore (2001) reported that elementary and secondary school teachers and administrators looking for solutions to assist low-achieving students have found family literacy programs to be a lifeline they can grab. In their work, Maiers, a first grade teacher, and Nistler, a university professor, initiated a family literacy program at an urban school (Nistler & Maiers, 2000). Together, they created a family literacy program which supported the literacy development of the children, strengthened home-school relationships, and enhanced communication between the parents and the teacher. Others (Morrow, 1995; Padak, Sapin, & Ackerman, 2001; Rodriguez-Brown, 2001; Shanahan, Mulhern, & Rodriguez-Brown, 1995) have affirmed the positive impact that school-organized family literacy programs have had on culturally and linguistically diverse children, teachers, parents, and communities.

While some herald the success of family literacy programs, others oppose these programs, particularly for diverse parents and children, because they appear to reflect a deficit perspective (Auerbach, 1989; Sigel, 1983). Gadsden (1994) summarized the disagreement and dissension that characterizes the work in family literacy as emerging from two seriously conflicting premises: one that perceives the family's lack of school-like literacy as a barrier to learning, and the other that sees the home literacy practices that are already present—however different they may be from school-based literacy—as a bridge to new learnings. Rather than choosing sides in the debate, however, Gadsden argues that both premises may be useful. She suggests that educators might adopt a reciprocal approach predicated on an understanding that teachers need to instruct parents in school-based literacy and also seek to learn about and integrate parents' existing knowledge and resources into school curricula.

Family literacy research: Contested ground

In her review of the research on the impact of the family on literacy development, Edwards (2003) documented three areas of convergence. First, norms, practices, and rules of participation differ in families (Heath, 1983; Morrow, 1993; Teale & Sulzby, 1986). Second, parents play varying roles in children's literacy development (Anderson, 1995; Burns & Collins, 1987; Mason, 1980; Purcell-Gates & Dahl, 1996; Rasinski, Burneau, & Ambrose, 1990). Third, transitions between the social context of the home and the school can present problems for some children (Bloome, 1983; Chall, Jacobs, & Baldwin, 1990; Tizard & Hughes, 1994; Wells, 1985).

While there is consistent convergence in these areas, Edwards found that scholars within the research community approached their work with families by employing very different courses of action, and these courses of action are the source of many hotly contested debates. Drawing on a framework proposed by Wiley (1996), Edwards identified three research-based courses of action:

- *Accommodation* requires teachers, supervisors, personnel officers and gatekeepers to have a better understanding of the communicative styles and literacy practices of their students;

- *Incorporation* requires researchers to study community practices that have not been valued previously by the schools, and to incorporate them into the curriculum. It also means surrendering a privileged position by acknowledging that something can be learned from other ethnic groups;
- *Adaptation* involves the expectation that children and adults who are held to have substandard knowledge and skills will acculturate or learn to match or measure up to the norms of those who control the schools, institutions and workplace. (Edwards, 2003, pp. 147–149)

There is strong research support for each of these courses of action. Supporters of accommodation argue that "literacy learning begins in the home, not the school, and that instruction should build on the foundation for literacy learning established in the home" (Au, 1993, p. 35). Research has shown that even in conditions of extreme poverty, homes are rich in print and family members engage in literacy activities of many kinds on a daily basis, including writing notes, cooking with recipes, writing grocery lists, reading magazines or newspapers, and reading religious materials (Anderson and Stokes, 1984; Heath, 1983; Purcell-Gates, 1996; Taylor & Dorsey-Gaines, 1988; Teale, 1986).

Accommodation has become an especially popular course of action in literacy teacher education. Over the past few years, teacher educators have developed strategies to prepare preservice teachers to accommodate students and families, including reading and responding to cultural autobiographies (Florio-Ruane, 2001); writing personal life stories (Fry & McKinney, 1997); engaging in cultural self-analysis (Schmidt, 1998); using photography to document local knowledge sources (Allen & Labbo, 2001); writing vision statements to develop powerful images of culturally responsive literacy pedagogy (Turner, 2006); and redesigning early field experiences to develop home-school relationships (Jones and Blendinger, 1994; Lazar & Weisberg, 1996). Although these strategies are important for developing cultural awareness and sensitivity in preservice teachers, the accommodation course of action may be too one-sided; it offers few resources to parents and is rooted within the naïve assumption that culturally sensitized teachers will be able to make up for learning experiences, opportunities, and resources that may be missing in the lives of some children. According to Edwards (2003), this may lead to early disillusionment for many new and experienced teachers, when they realize that, despite their sensitivity, their students still don't achieve at the level of middle-class counterparts.

The second course of action, incorporation, represents the perspective that "teachers and parents need to understand the way each defines, values and uses literacy as part of cultural practices. Such mutual understanding offers the potential for schooling to be adjusted to meet the needs of families" (Cairney, 1997, p. 70). Researchers who advocate for this course of action contend that "as educators we must not assume that we can only teach the families how to do school, but that we can learn valuable lessons by coming to know the families, and by taking the time to establish the social relationships necessary to create personal links between households and classrooms" (Moll, 1999, p. xiii).

Incorporation is a powerful course of action, yet several researchers have suggested this incorporation is too difficult to achieve, particularly in multicultural and/or multilingual classrooms because "in order for incorporation to occur, teachers need knowledge of the language, communication styles, and literacy practices of their students" (Wiley, 1996, p. 149). In essence, most teachers would have to become ethnographers to develop the kinds of deep "local knowledge" that the incorporation course of action requires, and although several researchers have proposed that very idea (Heath, 1983; Moll et al., 1992; Perez, 2001), others contend that it poses serious and complicated logistical problems for schools and teachers. For example, Wiley (1996) critiqued Heath's

(1983) suggestion of turning teachers into learners and students into ethnographers, noting that this "is no simple task; Heath's own efforts involved years of community and school ethnographic work" (p. 150). While schools and classroom teachers might agree that it would be beneficial to have knowledge of the language, communication styles and literacy practices of *all* their students, in reality it would be nearly impossible to gain this much needed knowledge during a nine-month school year.

The most intensive controversy and conflict has emerged from the last course of action, adaptation. Supporters of adaptation claim that many poor, minority, and immigrant parents want to give their children linguistic, social, and cultural capital to deal in the marketplace of schools (Gallimore, Weisner, Kaufman, & Bernheimer, 1989; Super & Harkness, 1986). They also have suggested "when schools fail to provide parents with factual, empowering information and strategies for supporting their child's learning, the parents are even more likely to feel ambivalence as educators [of their own children]" (Clark, 1988, p. 95). Essentially, the adaptive course of action resonates with Delpit's (1995) argument that African American and other students from diverse backgrounds must be explicitly taught the rules, norms, and conventions associated with the culture of power if they are to acquire school-based literacy and function productively in mainstream society.

Supporters of the adaptation approach do not lack cultural sensitivity or awareness; they recognize that there are multiple home-based activities, such as telling stories and singing songs (Glazer, 1989; Moss & Fawcett, 1995; National Education Goals Panel, 1997; Sonnenschein, Brody, & Munsterman, 1996) that support students' acquisition of literacy skills. Key adaptation studies, however, have focused on ways of showing parents how to read to their children or assist them with school-like literacy events (Darling & Hayes, 1989; Edwards, 1993; Handel, 1992; Rodriguez-Brown, Li, & Albom, 1999; Winter & Rouse, 1990). The idea of showing parents how to read aloud to their children is important, because while parent-child book reading is one of the most important home literacy practices that enhance children's literacy learning (Anderson, Hiebert, Scott & Wilkinson, 1985; Doake, 1986; Gallimore & Goldenberg, 1989; Huey, 1908; Teale, 1981), we know that diverse parents (e.g., lower socioeconomic status, minority parents) experience tremendous difficulties in sharing books with their young children (Farron, 1982; Heath, 1982a, 1982b, 1986; Heath, Branscombe, & Thomas, 1985; Heath & Thomas, 1984; McCormick and Mason, 1986; Ninio, 1980; Snow & Ninio, 1986). In her classic study and low socioeconomic (SES) mothers and book reading, Edwards (1989) explained that book reading is a very simple teacher directive, but a very complex and difficult task for some parents. She put forth the argument that to simply inform parents of the importance of reading to their children is not sufficient. Instead, scholars and practitioners must go beyond *telling* to *showing* lower socioeconomic parents how to participate in parent-child book-reading interactions with their children and support their attempts to do.

Thus, research within the adaptive course of action is committed to showing parents how to enact mainstream literacy practices (e.g., reading aloud to children) that are valued in schools and by teachers. In family literacy, the adaptation approach lead to the creation of family literacy programs that "train" parents how to read to their children. Controversy has sparked about the very nature of these programs, and the question "Should we be training parents to be more middle-class and White?" is at its core. Some researchers have warned that the adaptive approach is dangerous because it leads to "blaming the victim" (Cairney, 1997; Garcia, 1989; Nieto, 1993; Shockley, 1994; Street, 1995). Others claim that this approach communicates a deficit-model of learning development and ignores that literacy is embedded in home life (Anderson & Stokes, 1984; Erickson, 1989; Hearron, 1992; Taylor & Dorsey-Gaines, 1988). Critics of family literacy educational programs assert that the "training" approach to these programs suggest that the homes of poor, minority, and immigrant children are lacking in literacy (Anderson & Stokes, 1984; Auerbach, 1989; Chall & Snow, 1982; Delgado-Gaitan, 1987; Erickson, 1989; Goldenberg, 1984), or that these programs fail to recognize that "literacy is not something which can be pasted on to family life, it is deeply embedded within it" (MacLeod, 1996, p. 130). Others criticize family-parent training programs because they "have perpetuated the 'we know, you don't know' dichotomy" (Shockley, 1994, p. 500). Sigel (1983), for example, has argued that parent education and training programs are built upon on "interventionist" perspective which privileges the beliefs, practices, and attitudes of experts (e.g., educators, scholars) while marginalizing those held by and enacted in nonmainstream families. As the "experts," parent education programs presume that they must use their authority to help parents, thus they "directly intrude into the organization of families and attack their values, their language, and their practices of childrearing and household management" (Valdes, 1996, p. 198).

As an African American scholar who developed a family literacy program embedded within an adaptation perspective, and who has "trained" parents to read to their children, Edwards (1995) has been one of the few literacy researchers to challenge these criticisms. In response to the critics of the adaptive approach, she argues that parents, especially those from poor and/or minority backgrounds, want to know how school works and they want to understand how to help their children. She has raised very provocative questions, and we include them in our chapter because they illuminate the hegemonic structures of power and privilege that the adaptive course of action works to disrupt and dismantle:

- Where do these critics' fears, doubts, reservations come from?
- What do the critics think these parents are being "forced" to read?
- Does evidence exist where the critics have interviewed parents who have attended these family literacy programs?
- Is it fair for critics, as "privileged" scholars and practitioners, to insert their personal feelings about parent participation in family literacy programs, without also highlighting parent voices, perceptions and evaluations?
- Are critics' fears, doubts, and reservations about family literacy programs justified?

In her extensive work, Edwards has argued that these criticisms are not justified because the "authority is vested in those belonging to the mainstream culture, the literacy practices of the mainstream become the norm and have higher status in school contexts" (Auerbach, 1989, p. 173). According to Purcell-Gates (1996), children in academic families are familiar with cultural capital and the culture of literacy, which enables them to adapt to the literacy environment of school, because "they already know, or acquire implicitly as they develop, the varying registers of written language with the accompanying 'ways of meaning' and 'ways of saying,' the vocabulary, the syntax, the intentionality. This makes learning the 'new' so much easier" (pp. 182–183). Conversely, when children do not grow up in families who enact school-based literacy practices,

> Their social and cultural lives do not support this effort but rather exist separately and often compete with it. From the beginning they are challenged to learn a code that some of them may not even have realized existed before...The language and purposes for print encountered through formal education are foreign. The vocabulary is too hard and removed from their daily lives; the conventional syntax of exposition and complex fiction is unfathomable. Without a great deal of support and motivation, their level of literacy skill attainment is bound to be low compared with that of their peers who are natives of the educated literate world. (Purcell-Gates, 1996, p. 183)

Researchers who take the adaptive course of action understand that elementary and secondary schools cannot solve the problems of educating the nation's youngsters for the 21st century by themselves; the critical role of the home and family must be addressed to break the cycle of illiteracy and improve economic circumstances for youngsters. As former U. S. Secretary of Education Richard W. Riley stated at the 1996 International Reading Association Convention:

> My friends, it's time to get serious. The dumbing down of American education must end. If children need extra help to measure up, they should get it. Let's provide tutors, and call in the families, or keep the schools open late and open in the summer, too, if we must. But whatever we do, let's end this tyranny of low expectation once and for all. Illiteracy is the ball and chain that ties us to poverty. We must smash it forever.

Researchers have designed and implemented numerous adaptive-based interventions to "smash" illiteracy in culturally and/or linguistically diverse communities. For example, MOTHERREAD is a program that used books to create connections between mothers who are incarcerated and their children (Gaj, 1989). In the Mothers' Reading Program, Arrista (1989) taught adults to read through group creation of literature. Participants in this program would "read" the world (Friere, 1970), through dialogue about issues in the community—such as literacy, education, parenting, and the myriad of issues that affect mothers in present-day New York City. The dialogue was then transformed into written texts, and the resultant "community literature" became the core reading material used to build language skills. More recently, Project FLAME (Family Literacy: Apprendiendo, Mejorando, Educando [Learning, Improving, Educating]) was developed as a bilingual education program for Spanish-speaking parents. Studies of outcomes of Project FLAME (Rodriguez-Brown, Li, & Albom, 1999; Shanahan, Mulhern, & Rodriguez-Brown, 1995) indicate that it led to improved English proficiency for parents, improvements in children's knowledge of letter names and print awareness, more frequent visits by parents to school, more literacy materials in the home, and more confidence in helping with their children's homework. Finally, Paratore (2001) organized the Intergenerational Literacy Project (ILP) in 1989 to achieve three purposes: (a) to improve the English literacy of parents, (b) to support the literacy development and academic success of their children, and (c) to conduct research on the effectiveness of an intergenerational approach to literacy. To accomplish these goals, the Intergenerational Literacy Project offered literacy instruction to parents of preschool and school-age children. A fundamental premise of ILP is that parents who improve their own literacy skills and knowledge will promote literacy learning among their children.

In the next section, we highlight Edwards' work as an example of research from an adaptive approach specifically for African American students. Because this work has also served as the basis for national programs like Head Start and Even Start, we argue that this work offers important insights into the nature of adaptive-based research programs for parents and children.

A closer look at an adaptive family literacy program: The Donaldsonville example

Edwards (2004) contends that there are instances where the adaptive approach is highly appropriate for working with families and children around school literacy acquisition. Her work highlights one such instance: parent-child book reading. Elementary teachers across the country encourage parents to read to their children throughout the primary grades (Edwards, 2004). However, parents with poor reading skills cannot engage in book-reading interactions with their children because of their own reading deficiencies, and millions of others neither have the knowledge of its importance nor the skills to read to their children (Nickse, Speicher, & Bucheck, 1988). Chall, Heron, and Hilferty (1987) make this point even more compelling when they stated that "twenty-seven million Americans can't read a bedtime story to a child" (p. 190).

Even though Edwards was fully aware of the concerns about blaming parents for their children's school failures, she decided this should not prevent her from developing a book-reading program (*Parents as Partners in Reading*, see Edwards, 1993) for low-income African American parents and children. Her decision was based on the belief that these parents could learn to share books with their children, and that they could become active partners in their children's literacy development. Like W. E. B. Du Bois (1903/1990), Edwards believed that African American children needed to have "double-consciousness" to achieve in school. Put simply, African Americans need to know the literacy practices that are valued in their own homes and communities, but they also need to know those literacies that are related to school and society. This way, African American children will feel empowered because they can move successfully between the Black and White worlds. To support this sense of double consciousness, African American parents have struggled "to ensure that school provides their children with discourse patterns, interactional styles, and spoken and written languages codes that will allow them success in the larger society" (Delpit, 1995, p. 29).

The book reading program was designed to expose low-income parents and children to trade books as well as school-like interaction styles, such as labeling pictures and labeling letters. The program operated at Donaldsonville Elementary School in Donaldsonville, LA, a predominantly African American rural community. Despite the general misconception that low-income African American parents will not participate in school-based intervention programs because they are simply not interested in helping their children or they do not value education (Noguera, 2003), Edwards found that the African American parents in Donaldsonville were eager to participate in her book reading program. To help maintain their enthusiasm, Edwards asked for community support from a group of community leaders, including bus drivers, bar owners, family members (e.g., grandmothers), and the ministerial alliance. These community supporters encouraged parents to attend the book reading program and to become more involved at the elementary school.

The book reading program consisted of 23 two-hour sessions divided into three phases: *Coaching, Peer Modeling*, and *Parent-Child Interactions*. Each phase lasted for approximately 6 to 7 weeks. During phase one, Coaching, Edwards met with the mothers as a group. She modeled effective book reading behaviors and introduced a variety of teacher tapes, which highlighted specific book reading techniques. The tapes often began with the teacher providing a rationale for why a book was appropriate for accomplishing a particular objective. The objective could include such activities as pointing to pictures, labeling and describing pictures, and making text-to-life and life-to-text connections. The teacher, working with the child, would then model book reading, highlighting the particular objective they had selected. After parents viewed the teacher tape, Edwards involved them in a guided discussion of the applications of the strategy modeled by the teacher. The parents could stay on after the sessions to review tapes and interact with Edwards.

During the Peer Modeling phase, Edwards helped the parents to manage the book-reading sessions and strategies. This phase was specifically based on Vygotsky's (1978) work, which states, "The zone of proximal development defines those functions that have not yet matured but are in the process of maturation" (p. 86). Edwards assisted the parents by (a) guiding their participation in book-reading interactions with each other, (b) finding connections between what they already knew and what they needed to know, (c) modeling effective book-reading behaviors for them when such assistance was needed (encouraging them to review teacher tapes), and (d) providing praise and support for their attempts.

During the last phase, Parent-Child Interactions, Edwards released control to the parents and functioned primarily as a supportive and sympathetic audience: offering suggestions to the mothers as to what books to use in reading interactions with their children; evaluating the parent-child book-reading interactions; and providing feedback or modeling. In this final phase, the mothers shared books with their own children and implemented book-reading strategies they learned in the previous two phases (Coaching, Peer Modeling). From these interactions, the mothers learned the importance of involving their children in a book-reading interaction and recognized that "the parent holds the key to unlocking the meaning represented by the text" (Chapman, 1986, p. 12).

Edwards' work with Donaldsonville illuminates the conflict and controversy that plagues the field. On one hand, the program at Donaldsonville became a template for national programs with strong home-school components because this approach to showing African American parents how to engage in school-literacy practices with their children at home was extremely effective. However, Edwards met resistance from other researchers, who vehemently criticized her work because it implied that something was wrong, or deficient, with the ways in which African American parents socialize their children (Pellegrini, 1991).

Challenging these criticisms, Edwards has written several pieces (2003, 2004) that address researchers' strong reactions to her work. She contends that the adaptive approach was essential to her book reading program because it made visible to African American parents what the school meant by the phrase "read to your child." As an African American scholar, Edwards values and recognizes that many forms of literacy exist in families (Edwards & Danridge, 2001). Yet book reading remains one of the most frequently requested activities from teachers, and few take time to show parents what that literacy event should look like because they assume that families know how to read aloud to their children (Edwards, 2004). Consequently, low SES African American mothers, like those Edwards worked with, needed such an explicit program to acquire the skills and questioning strategies needed to help their children read at home.

FAMILY LITERACY AND COMPREHENSION: WHAT WE KNOW

Defining comprehension

Comprehension is a complex process that involves several facets. The Rand Report, *Reading for Understanding* (Snow & The Rand Reading Group, 2002), offers this definition of comprehension:

> We define reading comprehension as the process of simultaneously extracting and constructing meaning through interaction and involvement with written language. We use the words extracting and constructing to emphasize both the importance and the insufficiency of the text as a determinant of reading comprehension. Comprehension involves three elements: the reader who is doing the comprehending, the text that is to be comprehended, and the activity in which comprehension is a part. (p. 2)

For the sake of brevity, we focus our attention on readers and what they "do" to comprehend texts. Good readers comprehend because they have acquired, and can easily employ, basic reading skills. Pressley (2000) explains,

Reading is often thought of as a hierarchy of skills, from processing of individual letters and their associated sounds to word recognition to text-processing competencies. Skilled comprehension requires fluid articulation of all these processes, beginning with the sounding out and recognition of individual words to the understanding of sentences in paragraphs as part of much longer texts. (p. 2)

But readers with strong comprehension not only have good decoding and processing skills; they are also able to construct meaning from texts because they (a) have clear goals and purposes for reading; (b) read selectively and continuously make decision about how to read; (c) construct, revise, and question the meanings that they make while reading; and (d) make connections between the text and themselves, other texts, and the world (Block & Pressley, 2001; Duke & Pearson, 2002; Pressley, 2000). In other words, good readers comprehend the text because they use "their experience and knowledge of the world, their knowledge of vocabulary and language structure, and their knowledge of reading strategies (or plans)...to make sense of the text...and get the most out of it" (Armbruster, Lehr, & Osborn, 2003, p. 48).

Because good readers actively draw upon their prior knowledge, interests, attitudes, and expectations to the process of comprehending texts, it is important to recognize that "the cultural background of the readers exerts powerful influence on what is comprehended" (Irwin, 2007, p. 8). Students use their diverse cultural experiences, traditions, and knowledge as resources when they read texts, and they constantly attempt to make meaning of texts that are consistent with their multiple communities of practice, such as home, school, and peers (Hammerberg, 2004). Moreover, research in cultural psychology suggests that students from nonmainstream cultures may have different vocabularies and schema, and may have different attitudes towards language, approaches to school tasks, and varying interests in texts taught in school (Cole, 1996; Irwin, 2007; Nieto, 2001). From this social constructivist view, "the comprehension process is embedded in a complex socio-cultural context that makes each act of comprehension unique...the goal of reading is not inferring the intended message of the author but, rather, creating a message that is useful to the reader in that socio-cultural context" (Irwin, 2007, p. 10).

To summarize, comprehension results from an interaction among the reader, the strategies the reader employs, the material being read, and the context in which reading takes place. More specifically, readers with strong comprehension skills are able to make meaning from texts by purposefully drawing upon their prior knowledge, efficiently processing and decoding words, and actively employing strategies for understanding texts (e.g., metacognitive strategies, questioning, making predictions, summarizing). Equally important, comprehension is a process that is situated within a social and cultural context, and as a result, readers may construct meanings of texts that are in some ways different than their mainstream peers because they are drawing upon different interests, attitudes, schema, and prior knowledge.

Family literacy and its relationship to comprehension

Based on the research reports available to us, there is very little work that has explicitly studied the relationship between family literacy and comprehension. We speculate that this important relationship has not been addressed by the research community because it has been embroiled in the debates concerning the nature of family literacy, family literacy programs, and family literacy research. Lending support to this theory, Purcell-Gates (2000) asserts that "as we have begun to recognize and focus on the phenomenon of family literacy, its very definition remains elusive....there is real lack of agreement as to what family literacy is, [and] what it means for schooling" (p. 853).

Although comprehension has not been a specific focus of inquiry in family literacy research, a number of studies provide evidence of a positive relationship between family literacy and children's literacy skill development (Anderson et al., 1985; Chomsky, 1972; Haney & Hill, 2004; Laosa, 1982; Scarborough & Dobrich, 1994; Teale & Sulzby, 1986; Weigel, Martin, & Bennett, 2005). Because many of these skills and competencies are related to comprehension, it is very likely that family literacy practices may support children's meaning-making processes. In this section, we focus on several specific sets of foundational skills and knowledge that contribute to reading comprehension: early literacy concepts, phonological awareness and letter sound knowledge, world knowledge/prior knowledge, vocabulary/language knowledge, and motivation to read.

Early literacy concepts (print knowledge, uses of print)   Research on emergent literacy has clearly demonstrated that children begin to develop literacy and language skills before receiving informal reading instruction in school (e.g., Heath, 1983; Teale & Sulzby, 1986). Thus, children's literacy development and skill acquisition are greatly influenced by their parents and their home literacy environments. This early literacy and language development is highly significant because it is a strong predictor of children's success in school (Scarborough, 1991; Walker, Greenwood, Hart, & Carta, 1994; Werner & Smith, 1992). Children who have a limited vocabulary at age three because of limited experiences are already at-risk for literacy development and it is very difficult for them to catch up to their peers in school (Morrow, 2006).

Phonological awareness and letter-sound knowledge   According to Armbruster and her colleagues (2003), before children learn to read print, "they need to become aware of how the sounds in words work" (p. 2). Consequently, phonological knowledge, phonemic awareness, and alphabetic knowledge are considered to be important components of what parents "teach" at home. In their study of 47 children and their parents, Haney and Hill (2004) reported that the majority of the parents taught their children letter-names (71%) and sounds (65%), while fewer parents taught their children how to write letters (45%), and write and read words (26%). Although statistical significance was only found for direct teaching activities related to alphabet knowledge and writing words, children receiving any direct instruction from their parents tended to perform better on most emergent literacy tasks. Similarly, in her study of FLAME, an intervention program which taught bilingual parents to engage in school-based literacy events (e.g., reading books together, teaching letters, sounds, and words, playing rhymes and language games), Rodriguez-Brown (2001) reported that children whose parents attended the program made statistically significant gains on several early literacy measures, including a test of letter recognition and a test of print awareness.

World knowledge/prior knowledge   Based on cognitive models of reading that demonstrate how information is stored long-term memory in organized "knowledge structures," literacy researchers have established that the essence of learning is linking new information to prior knowledge about the topic, the text structure or genre (Anderson & Pearson, 1984). Consequently, "reading comprehension can be affected by world knowledge, with many demonstrations that readers who posses rich prior knowledge about the topic of a reading often understand the reading better than classmates with low prior knowledge" (Pressley, 2000, p. 3).

Vocabulary/language knowledge   Research has clearly shown that children who comprehend tend to have good vocabularies (Anderson & Freebody, 1991; Nagy, Anderson, & Herman, 1987). Pressley (2000) notes that children learn vocabulary both explicitly (through direct instruction) and incidentally (through everyday experiences in the real world). Although some words must be taught explicitly, most children learn vocabulary through conversations with people, listening to books and texts read to them, and independent reading (Armbruster, Lehr, & Osbourne, 2003). Consequently, family literacy plays an important role in children's vocabulary development, because their language skills are shaped by what parents say and do at home (Hart & Risley, 1995).

Shared reading is an especially important literacy practice which builds and enhances children's vocabulary knowledge (Crain-Thoreson & Dale, 1992; Payne, Whitehurst, & Angell, 1994; Senchal, Thomas, & Monker, 1995; Snow, 1991). In their meta-analysis of studies of early literacy development, Bus, va IJzendoorn, and Pelligrini (1995) found that the frequency of parent-child book reading had a positive effect on child literacy and language outcome measures among young children. Similarly, results from a study conducted by Lonigan and Whitehurst (1998) showed that the young children (ages 3 and 4) in the "parent reading" condition (e.g., parents received training and then read books according to the model provided) outperformed their counterparts in the "school reading condition" (e.g., teachers read books to children) and in the control group on measures of receptive and expressive language.

Motivation to read   Much of the research on the family's motivating influence on young readers has been conducted on parent-child book reading. Joint book reading, as a positive interaction between parents and children, is often assumed to be a prerequisite for success in school. As early as 1908, Huey revealed "the secret of it all lies in the parents reading aloud to and with their child" (p. 32). In *Becoming a Nation of Readers*, the authors state that: "Parents play roles of inestimable importance in laying the foundations for learning to read" (Anderson et al., 1985, p. 57). Mahoney and Wilcox (1985) concluded, "If a child comes from a reading family where books are a shared source of pleasure, he or she will have an understanding of the language of the literacy world and respond to the use of books in a classroom as a natural expansion of pleasant home experiences" (p. ix). Among families who routinely read stories to their children, Adams (1990) estimates that the children spend from 1,000 to 1, 700 hours in one-to-one literacy activities before entering school. Adams suggests that these children experiences another 2,000 hours of print "guidance" by watching *Sesame Street* and perhaps another 1,000 or 2,000 hours by playing with magnetic alphabet letters, participating in reading and writing activities in playgroup or preschool, exploring with paper and pencils and playing alphabet games on a computer (p. 85).

But for children in many families, there are no storybook routines, no magnetic letters on the refrigerator, no easy access to paper or pencils for creating messages, and no literacy games to play on a computer. Children from these homes may not even have access or exposure to *Sesame Street*. Thus, they will begin first grade without the "thousands of hours of school-like reading experience" (Adams, 1990, p. 90) that other families have the resources to provide. Adams' findings point to the fact that many preschool children who enter school each year have not been marinated or soaked in print, and these children may struggle with reading, which could eventually decrease their motivation to read in school (Edwards, 2004; Morrow, 2006).

Family literacy programs: Do they increase children's comprehension ability?

According to Purcell-Gates (2000), "evaluation of family literacy programs is extremely problematic and challenging" (p. 860). Yet some evaluative research has been conducted on family literacy programs, and by and large, this literature has reported that these programs have a positive impact on parents' and children's literacy skills, acquisition, and/or motivation. Padak and Rasinski (2003), for example, identify several important benefits for parents involved in family literacy programs, including (a) greater opportunities to learn literacy than in typical adult education programs, (b) increased reading achievement and writing ability, (c) greater knowledge about parenting options and child development, and (d) enhanced social awareness and self-advocacy. These benefits have been confirmed by other researchers. In Primavera's (2000) study of 100 adult participants in family literacy workshops, parents reported an increase in confidence, self-esteem, parental efficacy, literacy competence, and interest in educating themselves and their children. Fossen and Sticht (1991) found that 90% of the mothers participating in their Intergenerational Literacy Action Research Project, which involved basic-skills instruction and job training in community-based programs, had become more aware of the influence that they had on their children's educational achievements, and could articulate strategies that they used to work with their children, as a result of participating in the program.

Literacy researchers have also found that parents who participate in family literacy programs have greater capacity to support their children's literacy learning in school (Cook-Cottone, 2004; Edwards, 1995; Edwards & Danridge, 2001; Gadsden et al., 2006; Morrow & Young, 1997). Cook-Cottone (2004) posits that many effective family literacy programs have adopted sociocultural approaches to working with families and children. In these social constructivist-based programs, families are "mentored in the use of literacy tools and provided the necessary scaffolding for effective transmission of literacy knowledge from parent to child. In other words, the family literacy program functions as a Vygotskian mentor to the family…who in turn become mentors to the child" (p. 209). Cook-Cottone suggests that family literacy programs which utilize sociocultural approaches to educating parents capitalize on the power of the cultural, linguistic, and social practices that families enact with their children by utilizing home literacy as a bridge for apprenticing parents (and their children) into the mainstream literacy practices (e.g., reading to children, helping with homework, visiting libraries) valued in school. Similarly, studies conducted by Edwards and her colleagues (Edwards, 1995; Edwards & Danridge, 2001; Edwards, Danridge, McMillon, & Pleasants, 2001) and by Gadsden, Ray, Jacobs, and Gwak (2006), clearly demonstrate that parents, especially those from minority and/or poor backgrounds, place high value on literacy and education, and they often participate in family literacy workshops and programs because they *want* to learn specific strategies and techniques that they can use at home to support their children's literacy learning. Although these studies suggest that there is family literacy programs have a positive influence on the literacy lives and development of parents and children, it is important to remember that none of these studies directly or explicitly studied comprehension, most of these evaluative reports lacked appropriate controls, and were based upon favorable self-reports from participants (e.g., perceptions about literacy, attitudes towards literacy) rather than formal or informal literacy assessments.

FAMILY LITERACY AND COMPREHENSION: WHAT WE NEED TO KNOW

Research in the area of family literacy is lagging behind policy and practice. Public perceptions about its role in children's learning, public and private funding, and programs implementations are all outpacing empirically based knowledge about the conditions for its occurrence, the different forms family literacy can take, the actual impact of the practice of these different forms on children's school achievement, and the differential impacts of the various types of intervention on children's long-term success with schooling and academic tasks, and/or parents' increased agency and self-efficacy regarding their children's schooling. (Purcell-Gates, 2000, p. 853)

We begin this section with this quote from Purcell-Gates because it illuminates the paucity of family literacy research and underscores the dire need for work that will be beneficial for stakeholders interested in improving the literacy achievement of diverse students (e.g., children, families, teachers, scholars, family literacy professionals, policy-makers). In what follows, we discuss three areas that warrant further attention from literacy researchers: relationships between family literacy and comprehension, sociocultural influences on family literacy and comprehension, and combined effects of home and school environments on reading comprehension.

Relationships between family literacy and comprehension

Given the significant scholarly attention given to issues of comprehension over the past two decades, it is surprising that interest in comprehension within family literacy programs and scholarship seems extremely limited. We argue that it is time for researchers to move past their differences related to the various approaches to family literacy (e.g.,adaptation, incorporation, accommodation) and begin to expand their perspectives to consider more important questions such as: What are family literacy programs currently doing that might impact children's reading comprehension? And what intervention strategies and activities help parents to effectively support their children's reading comprehension? We may not entirely agree on the approach to facilitating family literacy, but these questions are critical to the literacy lives of our children and their families, and we must begin to address them. Perhaps, in working together, we will move beyond either/or approaches towards a pragmatic understanding of taking varying courses of action (i.e., accommodation, adaptation, incorporation) based upon the purposes of our family literacy work, the participants, and the tasks involved.

We agree with researchers like Purcell-Gates (2000) who call for more research in the field of family literacy, and particularly on the effectiveness of family literacy programs. In doing so, however, we also believe that multiple stakeholders (e.g., children, parents, schools), not just academicians, should benefit from the work that is conducted on family literacy and comprehension. As Edwards (2003) stated, "We must refrain from doing research where we, as a research community, are the only ones who learn from this research. We must commit ourselves to conducting research that has implications for practitioners, and we must do the work of disseminating that research" (p. 100). In reviewing this literature on family literacy and comprehension, it was clear to us that the implications for conducting work that makes a difference must be seriously considered if we are to make important advancements in the field. For example, is it ethical to place diverse families and children in "control groups" if we know that they would greatly benefit from the training and skills acquired in the intervention? Are we perpetuating deficit notions if we continue doing work comparing mainstream and non-mainstream children and families? As researchers, are we treating diverse families with respect, and taking time to build trusting relationships with them rather than simply viewing them as "subjects" in our studies? Responding to these types of questions may enable researchers to engage in family literacy research that will transform the lives of diverse families and children.

Sociocultural influences on family literacy and comprehension

In her review, Purcell-Gates (2000) argues that cultural issues in family literacy should be a top priority:

> Virtually unexplored by research is the issue of compatibility among the cultures of schools, homes, and family literacy programs. Studies...regarding the ways children

learn and the kinds of roles parents should be expected to play in this learning suggest a powerful cultural factor that needs to be directly addressed through inquiry. (p. 867)

As literacy researchers, then, we must be sensitive to and respectful of the cultural definitions of *family literacy* and *comprehension* within particular schools and communities. For example, in the Mexican-American families that Valdes (1996) studied, children were expected to "comprehend" *consejos*, brief homilies that were told by adults in the community. These consejos focused on numerous subjects, from working hard to getting along with siblings, and were used to communicate cultural values and expectations. According to Hammerberg (2004), these consejos, though not written, are still being "read" by the Mexican-American children in these families, which raises intriguing questions about comprehension and family literacy: How do these children "make meaning" of consejos? How do parents use different consejos to teach important life lessons and morals? And, how might the values and morals from these consejos shape Mexican-American students' comprehension when reading texts with strong ethical content, like fables? In other words, if these consejos become part of Mexican-American students' schema for certain texts, how might that impact their reading comprehension in school? These questions which emerge from Valdes' work, and from many other ethnographies of family literacy practices, remind us that as literacy researchers and educators, we can learn a great deal about the process of learning to read from diverse families and communities. From a sociocultural perspective, "family literacy and text comprehension" are practices which will be enacted in different ways and will represent varying meanings. We must remember that literacy is a social practice, and that for diverse students, family literacy practices and comprehension processes are deeply rooted within local definitions of what it means to be literate, because "ways of being literate change depending upon the cultural practice one is engaged in" (Hammerberg, 2004, p. 649).

Adopting a sociocultural perspective on family literacy and comprehension also requires an expanded image of "researcher." Literacy researchers and educational scholars at the university level have typically conducted research on the literacy practices of families (e.g., Heath, 1983; Li, 2002; Purcell-Gates, 1995;Taylor, 1997). However, we believe that expanding the image of researcher to include K–12 practitioners, culturally-diverse students and families, teacher education students, community leaders, and family literacy instructors, would advance the field in two important ways. First, literacy researchers who work collaboratively with practitioners and parents-children would have greater access to the local definitions of family literacy and reading comprehension enacted within specific communities. This type of insider knowledge is critical for understanding the role that culture plays in learning to comprehend texts (Hammerberg, 2004). Second, there is a gap between the research on home literacies and the practice and policy of such research (Purcell-Gates, 2000). However, literacy scholars may be able to bridge that gap by (a) working with K–12 practitioners to create programs and classrooms that successfully build upon diverse families' literacy practices, (b) working with community leaders to establish family literacy programs that give parents the training and skills that they need to support their children's literacy learning, and (c) working with parents to understand the benefits of participating in these programs for themselves and their children.

Combined effects of home and school literacy environments on reading comprehension

Literacy and language studies typically focus on children's skill acquisition and development within one isolated context (e.g., home *or* school). However, Weigel and his colleagues (2005) argue that more studies should focus on how aspects of home and school literacy environments combine to support children's skill development. For example, by taking an ecological approach within their study of preschoolers' home and child-care literacy environments, they found that while each context provided four important aspects of literacy and language development (i.e., demographics, literacy habits, attitudes and beliefs about children's literacy and language acquisition, literacy activities), several components (i.e., parents' and teachers' literacy-related beliefs, habits, and activities) combined to account for statistically significant variance in one or more of the children's literacy or language scores. From an ecological perspective, the Weigel et al. study affirms that children acquire literacy and language skills from multiple contexts (e.g., home *and* school) and it is important that future research investigate the interdependence between these environments. Such work may lead to interventions which strengthen cross-contextual "aspects that can be manipulated, such as parental and teacher attitudes; providing strategies that enhance development; and reminding parents and teachers to be cognizant of their own literacy habits in encouraging literacy and language in young children" (Weigel et al., 2005, p. 226).

CONCLUSION

Family literacy continues to be a controversial and complex issue for literacy researchers and practitioners. Conflicts and debates related to family literacy abound, from conceptual differences to varying courses of action for facilitating family literacy (i.e., accommodation, incorporation, adaptation). We believe that literacy researchers need to put aside their philosophical differences and work together in ways that support families' and schools' efforts to develop productive partnerships that improve students' literacy development. Children who live outside the mainstream of American life are precious humans and do not have time to wait until researchers find plausible answers about accommodating and incorporating their literacy practices into the school curriculum. While we patiently wait for answers from the research community, these families and children are constantly struggling to develop a "double consciousness" (Du Bois, 1903) of how to negotiate the borders between home and school. Double-consciousness does not only apply to African Americans; rather, it describes the tensions and conflicts that other ethnic minorities experience in the quest for school success and literacy acquisition (Delgado-Gaitain, 1987; Jimenez, Moll, Rodriguez-Brown, & Barrera, 1999; Purcell-Gates, 1996). And, as Purcell-Gates (1995) so eloquently describes in her research, White students from "invisible minority" groups like the urban Appalachians are also struggling to succeed in school and thus need to develop "double-consciousness." Consequently, the research and practitioner communities must become more sensitive to this sense of double-consciousness that many minorities hold: they want to connect with their cultural communities, but they also want to know the code of power (Delpit, 1995) so that they can be successful within mainstream society. If we are truly committed to improving diverse students' reading comprehension and literacy achievement, then we must come together to develop a family literacy agenda that empowers families and children to take ownership of mainstream and nonmainstream forms of literate practice.

REFERENCES

Allen, J., & Labbo, L. (2001). Giving it a second thought: Making culturally engaged teaching culturally engaging. *Language Arts, 79*(1), 40–52.

Anderson, A. B., & Stokes, S. J. (1984). Social and institutional influences on the development and practice of literacy. In H. Goelman, A. Oberg, & F. Smith (Eds.), *Awakening to literacy* (pp. 24–37). Exeter, NH: Heinemann.

Anderson, R. C., Hiebert, E., Scott, J. A., & Wilkinson, I. A. G. (1985). *Becoming a nation of readers: The report of the commission of reading.* Washington, DC: The National Institute of Education.

Anderson, R. C., & Pearson, P. D. (1984). A schema-theoretic view of basic processes in reading. In P. D. Pearson, R. Barr, M. L. Kamil, & P. Mosenthal (Eds.), *Handbook of reading research.* White Plains, NY: Longman.

Au, K. H. (1993). *Literacy instruction in multicultural settings.* Forth Worth, TX: Harcourt Brace Jovanovich College Publishers.

Auerbach, E. R. (1989). Toward a social-contextual approach to family literacy. *Harvard Educational Review, 59*(2), 165–181.

Block, C. C., & Pressley, M. (2001). *Comprehension instruction: Research-based practices.* New York: Guildford Press.

Burgess, S. (1997). The role of shared reading in the development of phonological awareness: A longitudinal study of middle- to upper-class children. *Early Childhood Development and Care, 127–128,* 191–199.

Bus, A. G., Van Ijzendoorn, M. H., & Pelligrini, A. D. (1995). Joint book reading makes for success in learning to read: A meta-analysis on intergenerational transmission of literacy. *Review of Educational Research, 65,* 1–21.

Cairney, T. H. (1997). Acknowledging diversity in home literacy practices: Moving towards partnership with parents. *Early Child Development and Care, 127–128,* 61–73.

Chall, J. S., Heron, E., & Hilferty, A. (1987). Adult literacy: New and enduring problems. *Phi Delta Kappan, 69,* 190–196.

Chall, J. S., & Snow, C. (1982). *Families and literacy: The contributions of out of school experiences to children's acquisition of literacy.* A final report to the National Institute of Education. Cambridge, MA: Harvard Graduate School of Education.

Chapman, D. L. (1986). Let's read another one. In D. R. Tovey & J. E. Kerber (Eds.), *Roles in literacy: A new perspective* (pp. 10–25). Newark, DE: International Reading Association.

Clark, R. M. (1988). Parents as providers of linguistic and social capital. *Educational Horizons, 66*(2), 93–95.

Cole, M. (1996). *Cultural psychology: A once and future discipline.* Cambridge, MA: Harvard University Press.

Darling, S. (1997). Opening session speech. Paper presented at the sixth annual Conference on Family Literacy, Louisville, KY.

Darling, S., & Hayes, A. (1988–1989). *Family literacy project final project report.* Louisville, KY: National Center for Family Literacy.

DeBruin-Parecki, A., & Knol-Sinclair, B. (2003). Introduction. In A. DeBruin-Parecki & B. Knol-Sinclair (Eds.), *Family literacy: From theory to practice* (pp. 1–6). Newark, DE: International Reading Association.

Delgado-Gaitan, C. (1987). Mexican adult literacy: New directions for immigrants. In S. R. Goldman & K. Trueba (Eds.), *Becoming literate as second language learners* (pp. 9–32). Norwood, NJ: Ablex.

Delpit, L. (1995). *Other people's children: Cultural conflict in the classroom.* New York: The New Press.

Delpit, L. (1988). The silenced dialogue: Power and pedagogy in educating other people's children. *Harvard Educational Review, 58,* 280–298.

Doake, D. B. (1986). Learning to read: It starts in the home. In D. R. Tovey & J. E. Kerber (Eds.), *Roles in literacy learning: A new perspective* (pp. 2–9). Newark, DE: International Reading Association.

Du Bois, W. E. (1903/1990). *The souls of black folk.* New York: Vintage Books/The Library of American.

Duke, N., & Pearson, P. D. (2002). Effective practices for developing reading comprehension. In A. E. Farstrup & S. J. Samuels (Eds.), *What research has to say about reading instruction* (3rd ed., pp. 205–242). Newark, DE: International Reading Association.

Edmondson, J., & Shannon, P. (1998). Reading education and poverty: Questioning the reading success equation. *Peabody Journal of Education, 73,* 104-126.

Edwards, P. A. (1989). Supporting lower SES mothers' attempts to provide scaffolding for bookreading. In J. Allen & J. Mason (Eds.), *Risk makers, risk takers, risk breakers: Reducing the risks for young literacy learners* (pp. 222–250). Portsmouth, NH: Heinemann.

Edwards, P. A. (1993). *Parents as Partners in Reading: A Family Literacy Training Program* (2nd ed.). Chicago: Children's Press.

Edwards, P. A. (1995). Empowering low-income mothers and fathers to share books with young children. *The Reading Teacher, 48*(7), 558–564.

Edwards, P. A. (2003). The impact of family on literacy development: Convergence, controversy, and instructional implications. NRC Annual Review of Research Address. In J. V. Hoffman, D. L. Shallert, C. M. Fairbanks, J. Worthy, & B. Maloch (Eds.), *52nd Yearbook of the National Reading Conference* (pp. 92–103). Milwaukee, WI: National Reading Conference.

Edwards, P. A. (2004). *Children's literacy development: Making it happen through home, school, and community connections.* New York: Allyn & Bacon.

Erickson, F. (1989). Forward. Literacy risks for students, parents, and teachers. In J. Allen and J. Mason (Eds.), *Risk makers, risk takers, risk breakers: Reducing the risks for your literacy learners* (pp. xiii–xvi). Portsmouth: NH: Heinemann.

Florio-Ruane, S. (2001). *Teacher education and the cultural imagination: Autobiography, conversation, and narrative.* Mahwah, NJ: Erlbaum.

Friere, P. (1970). *Pedagogy of the oppressed.* New York: Seabury Press.

Fry, P. G., & McKinney, L. J. (1997). A qualitative study of preservice teachers' early field experiences in an urban, culturally different school. *Urban Education, 32*(2), 184–201.

Gadsden, V. L. (1994). *Understanding family literacy: Conceptual issues facing the field.* Philadelphia: University of Pennsylvania National Center for Adult Literacy.

Gallimore, R., Weisner, R., Kaufman, S., & Bernheimer, L. P. (1989). The social construction of ecocultural niches: Family accommodation of developmentally delayed children. *American Journal of Mental Retardation, 94*(3), 216–230.

Glazer, S. (1989). Oral language and literacy. In D. S. Strickland & L. M. Morrow (Eds.), *Emerging literacy: Young children learn to read and write* (pp. 16–26). Newark, DE: International Reading Association.

Goldenberg, C. C. (1984, October). Low-income parents' contributions to the reading achievement of their first-grade children. Paper presented at the meeting of the Evaluation Network/Evaluation Research Society, San Francisco, CA.

Hammerberg, D. D. (2004). Comprehension instruction for socioculturally diverse classrooms: A review of what we know. *The Reading Teacher, 57*, 648–658.

Handel, R. E. (1992). The partnership for family reading: Benefits for families and schools. *The Reading Teacher, 46*(2), 117–126.

Haney, M., & Hill, J. (2004). Relationships between parent-teaching activities and emergent literacy in preschool children. *Early Child Development and Care, 174*, 215–228.

Hearron, P. F. (1992). *Kindergarten homework in nonmainstream families: The school-family interface in the ecology of emergent literacy.* Unpublished doctoral dissertation, Michigan State University, East Lansing, MI.

Heath, S. B. (1982a). Questioning at home and at school: A comparative study. In G. Spindler (Ed.), *Doing ethnography of schooling: Education anthropology in action* (pp. 102–129). New York: Hold, Rinehart & Winston.

Heath, S. B. (1982b). What no bedtime story means: Narrative skills at home and school. *Language in Society, 11*(2), 49–76.

Heath, S. B. (1983). *Ways with words. Language, life and work in communities and classrooms.* New York: Cambridge University Press.

Heath, S. B. (1986). Separating "things of the imagination" from life: Learning to read and write. In W. H. Teale & E. Sulzby (Eds.), *Emergent literacy: Writing and reading* (pp. 156–172). Norwood, NJ: Ablex.

Heath, S. B., Branscombe, A., & Thomas, C. (1985). The book as narrative prop in language acquisition. In B. Schieiffelin and P. Gilmore (Eds.), *The acquisition of literacy: Ethnographic perspective.* Norwood, NJ: Ablex.

Heath, S. B., & Thomas, C. (1984). The achievement of preschool literacy for mother and child. In H. Goelman, A. Oberg, and F. Smith (Eds.), *Awakening to literacy* (pp. 51–72). Portsmouth, NH: Heinemann.

Huey, E. B. (1908). *The psychology and pedagogy of reading.* New York: MacMillan.

Irwin, J. W. (2007). *Teaching reading comprehension processes.* New York: Pearson Education.

Jimenez, R. T., Moll, L., Rodriguez-Brown, F., & Barrera, R. (1999). Conversations: Latina and Latina researchers interact on issues related to literacy learning. *Reading Research Quarterly, 34*(2), 217–230.

Johnston, P., & Allington, R. (1991). Remediation. In R. Barr, M. L. Kamil, P. G. Mosenthal, & P. D. Pearson (Eds.), *Handbook of reading research* (Vol. 2, pp. 984–1012). New York: Longman.

Jones, L. T., & Blendinger, J. (1994). New beginnings: Preparing future teachers to work with diverse families. Action in Teacher Education: Celebrating Diversity in Teacher Education. *The Journal of the Association of Teacher Educators, XVI*(3), 79–86.

Lazar, A. M., & Weisberg, R. (1996). Inviting parents' perspectives: Building home-school partnerships to support children who struggle with literacy. *The Reading Teacher, 50*(3), 228–237.

Li, G. (2002). *East is east, west is west? Home literacy, culture, and schooling.* New York: Peter Lang.

Lonigan, C. J., & Whitehurst, G. J. (1998). Relative efficacy of parent and teacher involvement in a shared-reading intervention for preschool children from low-income backgrounds. *Early Childhood Research Quarterly, 13,* 262–290.

MacLeod, F. (1996). Integrating home and school resources to raise literacy levels of parents and children. *Early Child Development and Care, 117,* 123–132.

McCormick, C., & Mason, J. (1986). Intervention procedures for increasing preschool children's interest in and knowledge about reading. In W. H. Teale & E. Sulzby (Eds.), *Emergent literacy: Writing and reading* (pp. 90–115). Norwood, NJ: Ablex.

Moll, L. (1999). Forward. In J. Paratore, G. Melzei, & B. Krol-Sinclair (Eds.), What should we expect of family literacy? Experiences of Latino children whose parents participate in an intergenerational literacy project. Chicago: National Reading Conference; Newark, DE: International Reading Association.

Morrow, L. M. (1993). Home and school correlates of early interest in literature. *Journal of Educational Research, 76,* 221–230.

Morrow, L. M. (1995). Family literacy.

Morrow, L.M. (2006, December). Models affecting preschool programs over the years. Paper presented at the 56th Annual Meeting of the National Reading Conference, Los Angeles, CA.

Murphy, S. (1997). Who's reading whose reading? The National Center for Family Literacy evaluation process. In D. Taylor (Ed.), *Many families, many literacies* (pp. 149–151). Portsmouth, NH: Heinemann.

National Education Goals Panel. (1997). *Special early literacy report, 1997.* Washington, DC: U. S. Government Printing Office.

Nickse, R. (1991, April). A typology of family and intergenerational literacy programs: Implications for evaluation. Paper presented at the Annual Meeting of the American Educational Research Association, Chicago.

Nickse, R., Speicher, A. M., & Burcheck, P. (April, 1988). An intergenerational adult literacy project: A family intervention/prevention model. Paper presented at the annual meeting of the American Educational Research Association, New Orleans, LA.

Nieto, S. (1992). *Affirming diversity: The sociopolitical context of multicultural education.* New York: Longman.

Ninio, A. (1980). Ostensive definition in vocabulary teaching. *Journal of Child Language, 7,* 565–573.

Nistler, R. J., & Maiers, A. (2000). Stopping the silence: Hearing parents' voices in an urban first-grade family literacy program. *The Reading Teacher, 53,* 670–680.

Noguera, P. (2003). *City schools and the American dream: Reclaiming the promise of public education.* New York: Teachers College Press.

Padak, N., Sapin, C., & Ackerman, C. S. (2001). "Title 1 bought that coffee pot!": Family literacy professionals learn to collaborate. In V. Risko & K. Bromley (Eds.), *Collaboration for diverse learners: Viewpoints and practices* (pp. 87–104). Newark, DE: International Reading Association.

Padak, N., Sapin, C., & Baycich, D. (2002). *A decade of family literacy: Programs, outcomes, and future prospects.* ERIC Document Reproduction Service NO. ED 465 074.

Paratore, J. R. (2001). *Opening doors, opening opportunities: Family literacy in an urban community.* Boston: Allyn & Bacon.

Pellegrini, A. (1991). A critique of the concept of at risk as applied to the concept of emergent literacy. *Language Arts, 68,* 380–385.

Perez, B. (2001). Communicating and collaborating with linguistically diverse communities. In V. Risko & K. Bromley (Eds.), *Collaboration for diverse learners: Viewpoints and practices* (pp. 231–250). Newark, DE: International Reading Association.

Pressley, M. (2000). *Comprehension instruction: What makes sense now, what might make sense soon.* Retrieved on June 6, 2006 from http://www.readingonline.org.

Purcell-Gates, V. (1995). Other people's words: Breaking the cycle of low literacy.

Purcell-Gates, V. (1996). Stories, coupons, and the *TV Guide*: Relationships between home literacy experiences and emergent literacy knowledge. *Reading Research Quarterly, 31*(4), 406–428.

Purcell-Gates, V. (2000). Family literacy. In M. L. Kamil, P. B. Mosenthal, P. D. Pearson, & R. Barr (Eds.), *Handbook of reading research* (Vol. 3, pp. 853–870). Mahwah, NJ: Erlbaum.

Risko, V., & Bromley, K. (2001). (Eds.). *Collaboration for diverse learners: Viewpoints and practices*. Newark, DE: International Reading Association.

Rodriguez-Brown, F. (2001). Home-School connections in a community where English is the second language: Project FLAME. In V. Risko & K. Bromley (Eds.), *Collaboration for diverse learners: Viewpoints and practices* (pp. 273–288). Newark, DE: International Reading Association.

Scarborough, H. S., & Dobrich, W. (1994). On the efficacy of reading to preschoolers. *Developmental Review, 14,* 245–302.

Schmidt, P. R. (1998). The ABC's of cultural understanding and communication. *Equity & Excellence in Education, 31*(2), 28–38.

Shanahan, T., Mulhern, M., & Rodriguez-Brown, F. (1995). Project FLAME: Lessons learned from a family literacy programs for linguistic minority students. *The Reading Teacher, 48,* 2–9.

Shockley, B. (1994). Extending the literate community: Home-to-school and school-to-home. *The Reading Teacher, 47,* 500–502.

Sigel, I. E. (1983). The ethics of intervention. In I. E. Sigel & L. M. Laosa (Eds.), *Changing families* (pp. 1–21). New York: Plenum.

Snow, C. E., & Ninio, A. (1986). The contribution of reading books with children to their linguistic and cognitive development. In W. H. Teale & E. Sulzby (Eds.), *Emergent literacy: Writing and reading* (pp. 116–138). Norwood, NJ: Ablex.

Snow, C. E., & The RAND Reading Group. (2002). *Reading for Understanding: Toward and R&D Program in Reading Comprehension*. Santa Monica, CA: RAND.

Sonnenschein, S., Brody, G., & Munsterman, K. (1996). The influence of family beliefs and practices on children's early reading development. In L. Baker, P. Afflerbach, & D. Reinking (Eds.), *Developing engaged readers in school and home communities* (pp. 3–20). Mahwah, NJ: Erlbaum.

Street, B. V. (1995). *Social literacies: Critical approaches to literacy in development, ethnography and education*. London: Longman.

Super, C., & Harkness, S. (1986). The developmental niche: A conceptualization at the interface of child and culture. *International Journal of Behaviour Development, 9,* 1–25.

Taylor, D. (1983). *Family literacy: Young children learn to read and write*. Portsmouth, NH: Heinemann.

Taylor, D. (1997). *Many families, many literacies: An international declaration of principles*. Portsmouth, NH: Heinemann.

Taylor, D., & Dorsey-Gaines, C. (1988). *Growing up literate: Learning from inner-city families*. Portsmouth, NH: Heinemann.

Teale, W. H. (1981). Parents reading to their children: What we know and need to know. *Language Arts, 58,* 902–911.

Teale, W. H. (1986). Home background and literacy development. In W. H. Teale & E. Sulzby (Eds.), *Emergent literacy: Writing and reading*. Norwood, NJ: Ablex.

Turner, J. D. (2006). "I want to meet my students where they are!": Preservice teachers' visions of culturally responsive reading instruction. *National Reading Conference Yearbook, 55,* 309–323.

Turner, J. D., & Edwards, P. A. (in press). Old tensions, new visions: Implications of home literacies for teacher education programs, K–12 schools, and family literacy programs. In G. Li (Ed.), *Family literacy practices*.

Valdes, G. (1996). *Con respeto: Bridging the distances between culturally diverse families and schools*. New York: Teachers College Press.

Weigel, D. J., Martin, S. S., & Bennett, K. K. (2005). Ecological influences of the home and the child-care center on preschool-age children's literacy development. *Reading Research Quarterly, 40,* 204–233.

Wiley, T. G. (1996). Literacy and language diversity in sociocultural contexts. *Literacy and Language Diversity in the Unites States*. Center for Applied Linguistics and Delta Systems Co.

Part VII

Where to from Here?

31 Improving Comprehension Instruction through Quality Professional Development

Misty Sailors

The University of Texas at San Antonio

It should come as a relief to the field of reading research that a handbook of this caliber would have a chapter specifically focused on the professional development of teachers. For example, no longer is the field of reading research and policy interested in whether or not children can be taught to be more strategic in their thinking (Paris, Waskik, & Turner, 1991; Pressley, Borkowski, & Schneider, 1987; Pressley, 2000). Research has demonstrated that children can learn to do just that; it just takes time (Dole, Brown, & Trathen, 1996; Duffy, 2002; Pearson & Fielding, 1991; Pressley, Johnson, Symons, McGoldrick, & Kurita, 1990). Nor is this chapter focused on whether teachers are teaching comprehension or not. In fact, studies of the most accomplished teachers show them to be engaged in ongoing comprehension instruction (Knapp, 1995; Langer, 2000; Lipson, Mosenthal, Mekkelsen, & Russ, 2004; Metsala et al., 1997; Morrow, Tracey, Woo, & Pressley, 1999; Pressley, Rankin, & Yokoi, 1996; Taylor, Pearson, Clark, & Walpole, 2000). The fact is, teachers can improve their instructional comprehension practices and teach their children to be more strategic in their reading (Duffy, 1993a).

Rather, the significance lies in the fact that this handbook has dedicated space to the professional development of reading teachers (NICHD, 2000). While the government has recently dedicated millions of dollars to improving the educational literacy experiences of children who most deserve quality reading instruction (the No Child Left Behind Act), it is unclear under what conditions teachers best learn to improve their practices and those features of professional development that are helpful to children in improving their comprehension. Simply stated, the importance of the professional development of preservice and inservice teachers is evident in policy, but simply has not been addressed in the research.

In this chapter, I review the existing literature on the professional development of teachers in general, and then in the area of comprehension instruction specifically for both preservice and inservice teachers. I offer a description of two projects in which I have been engaged as a way of demonstrating the possibilities for the professional development of teachers and improvement of comprehension instruction. Finally, I offer discussion around issues that continue to plague teacher education, including what is not addressed in the field of research on comprehension instruction and the professional development of teachers.

PROFESSIONAL DEVELOPMENT AND TEACHER EDUCATION

Scholars have agreed for some time that teacher quality and expertise consistently and accurately predict student achievement (Darling-Hammond, 2000; Laczko-Kerr & Berliner, 2002; Snow, Burns, & Griffin, 1998). One approach to increasing student achievement is to improve the ability of teachers to effectively teach their students. It is through professional development activities that teachers improve their practices, a current focus of federally funded educational reform (the No Child Left Behind Act). Currently, 44 states in the United States require teachers to attend professional development activities (NCES, 2003, Overview). Thirty-two of these states require professional development in order for teachers to maintain their license and 33 require professional development for teachers to maintain their employment with the state. However, there are no clear directives for either the content or the context for what these professional development activities should look like (Lipson, Mosenthal, Mekkelsen, & Russ, 2004).

Consequently, it is no surprise that there are vast amounts of federal, state, and local monies devoted to professional development each year (Putnam & Borko, 2000). The literature that surrounds the professional development of teachers is filled with descriptions of those aspects of professional development that teachers describe as helpful. Drawn from the general teaching field, there seems to be a set of key qualities that produced positively-reported outcomes by teachers who responded to requests for descriptions of those aspects of professional development that they found helpful in improving their practices (Birman, Desimone, Porter, & Garet, 2000; Garet, Porter, Desimone, Birman, & Yoon, 2001; NCES, 1999; Porter, Garet, Desimone, & Birman, 2003). Included in these were features that centered on the structure of the professional development, including the form of, the duration in, and the collective participation of teachers at the same school, department or grade level in the professional development.

There also appears to be substantive features that have been described as having a positive association with reported outcomes by teachers. These features include specific content learning for teachers, the promotion of active learning, and the promotion of coherence, the alignment with the standards of districts, states, and professional organizations (Porter, Garet, Desimone, & Birman, 2003). Professional development that focused on specific instructional practices seemed to increase their use of those practices by teachers in their classrooms (Desimone, Porter, Garet, Yoon, & Birman, 2002). Further, teachers need proof that the topics and practices of professional development activities actually work with students (Butler, Lauscher, Jarvis-Selinger, & Beckingham, 2004; Stein, Schwan, & Silver, 1999).

Traditional "one shot" models of professional development rely primarily on direct instruction inside full-day inservice sessions presented by outside experts. Teachers are told about a recommended practice, it is demonstrated to them, and they are then expected to implement it in their classrooms. These professional workshops are not without fault. Teachers are not seen as active participants and the content is decontextualized and separate from teachers' daily work (Sandholtz, 2002). Besides, teachers describe these types of workshops as boring and irrelevant and report that they forget 90% of what was presented to them. Furthermore, they believe there is a lack of intensity and follow-up to these traditional workshops (NCES, 1999) and report that they want more and better inservice support (Anders, Hoffman, & Duffy, 2000).

Coupled with the lack of direction and the scant proof that the engagement of teachers in these "training models" of professional development has any significant impact on the learning of students (Cochran-Smith & Lytle, 1999; Duffy, 2004), it is no surprise that the topic of professional development has been the focus of many reports on teacher quality and education (Darling-Hammond, 2000; National Commission on Teaching and America's Future, 1996; NCES, 1999). Additionally, the political climate of today seems to support the professional development of classroom teachers, especially in the area of reading.

Inservice teacher education

Within the field of reading instruction, research has demonstrated that it is the quality of professional development offered to teachers that effects teacher knowledge, beliefs and practices, and student achievement (Anders et al., 2000; Duffy, 2004; Richardson, 1996), especially in the area of strategy instruction (Duffy, 2004; Duffy et al., 1987; Duffy, 1993a; Duffy, 1993b; Pressley et al., 1992). Studies have also shown that the professional development of teachers is a long-term process that requires careful monitoring and intensive follow-up support (Duffy, 1993a; Duffy, 1993b).

Synthesizing across studies of professional development, Anders, Hoffman, and Duffy (2000) outlined six features of "quality" reading teacher education efforts (p. 730). First, teachers must volunteer to participate and must have a choice in the content of the professional development and they must be personally invested in learning and implementing the new practice. Second, there must be intensive levels of support with sustained effort for the teachers. Third, teachers need support in the context of their practice and monitoring and coaching by a knowledgeable other. Fourth, teachers need opportunities and tools to reflect on their own practices systematically as they move toward change. Fifth, teachers should have opportunities to engage in conversations and discussions as they improve their practices. Finally, teachers must be part of a larger process of professional development, one that is inclusive of university-based researchers, school-based teacher educators, and teachers. That is, the professional development of teachers should be situated (Gee, 1990) and active (Garet et al., 2001).

As helpful as this work has been to the field of reading teacher education in thinking about the professional development of classroom reading teachers, this synthesis was not focused specifically on the professional development of comprehension instruction and classroom teachers. Most recently, the model of professional development that is active in reading teacher education has come from policy mandates, such as No Child Left Behind (NCLB). These policies have spurred numerous schools across the country to move toward the "coaching" of reading teachers as a model of professional development.

Professional organizations espouse the virtues of coaching, including the International Reading Association, the National Council of Teachers of English, National Council of Teachers of Mathematics, National Science Teachers Association, National Council for the Social Studies (IRA, 2006), and the Alliance for Excellent Education (Sturtevant, 2006). Several are beginning to describe the roles and responsibilities of reading coaches (Dole, 2004; Roller, 2006), the characteristics of coaches (Shanklin, 2006), the knowledge coaches must have in order to be effective, and the necessary qualifications of literacy coaches (IRA, 2004; IRA, 2006). Further, several are beginning to describe models of coaching (Bean, 2004; Toll, 2006; Walpole & McKenna, 2004). Theories of adult and higher education and cognitive coaching (Costa & Garmson, 2002) are driving this literature. In addition, the past few years has seen a plethora of texts emerge as a guide for coaches (Walpole & McKenna, 2004; Toll, 2006; Kise, 2006; Hasbrouck & Denton, 2005; Casey, 2006; Allen, 2006).

As with other aspects of professional development of which this chapter is concerned, the coaching literature is not empirically based and is not centered on comprehension instruction. The coaching literature tends to be focused on general reading instruction. This lack of attention to empirical studies around coaching led me to a research project designed to explore the impact of an intensive model of professional development and the impact the model had on the comprehension achievement of students. In the next section of this chapter, I briefly describe the project and the preliminary findings.

Teaching teachers to teach cognitive reading strategies

During the pilot year of this study, we worked in three low-income school districts in two large metropolitan areas in central and south Texas, working with 55 classroom teachers across the three participating school districts. These teachers represented self-contained classroom and content-area teachers, including reading, science, and social studies teachers. Across these classrooms, we worked with approximately 700 second to eighth graders from low-income backgrounds. We did not include students who were labeled as bilingual or special education in this study. The focus of the professional development centered on teaching the participating teachers the subroutines involved in strategic reading and how to explicate their own processes when working with their students (intentional instruction). These cognitive strategies included word recognition strategies, comprehension strategies, and fix-up strategies. Teachers in both the control and intervention groups participated in one 2-day summer workshops. Additionally, teachers in the intervention group received intensive support in their classrooms (a minimum of 2 days per month) from a highly qualified university-based reading mentor. The teachers in the control group received no additional support activities beyond the provided workshops.

This pretest-posttest control group research project was designed to test two professional models. Schools and teachers volunteered to participate; they were randomly assigned to condition groups at the school level. Demographic data were collected on all participants. An observation instrument that would document and describe the level of implementation of the professional development was designed and used to gather observational data (pre and post intervention). Student measures included results on the Wide Range Achievement Test (WRAT-3) to identify focus students in each classroom and the Group Reading Assessment Diagnostic Evaluation (GRADE) (American Guidance Services, 2001) as a pretest and posttest to monitor reading growth. Additionally, the use of cognitive reading strategies by focus students was monitored using an observational protocol. The data were analyzed to examine the variability in student change generated by the particular model of professional development (serving as the independent variable) as measured by GRADE achievement scores and use of instructional cognitive reading strategies (serving as the dependent variable). A factorial analysis of covariance (ANCOVA) served as the analytic strategy to investigate the effects of mentoring on the instructional practices of the teachers and the comprehension achievement of their students.

Findings from the pilot year of the study (Sailors, 2006) indicated there were statistically significant differences observed in the direction of the treatment group and the number of times they engaged their students in a comprehension strategy; there were no differences in engagement in word recognition or fix-up strategies. Although there were no statistically significant findings between the use of intentional instruction practices, the patterns were always in the direction of the treatment group. Further, the more times a mentor visited a treatment teacher, the more likely that teacher was to engage in intentional instruction ($F = 7.74$, df $= 1, 25$; $p < .05$). While we found no statistically significant differences in the qualitative aspects of the interactions between the mentors and participating teachers (conference only; demonstration lesson; critical feedback) to predict their behavior to engage in intentional instruction, in all instances, the practical effects were observed as being very large.

Furthermore, when I examined who initiated the interaction (who decided the conditions under which contact would take place, the mentor or the teacher), the data indicated that the practical effects for these variables were also very large. Finally, a statistically significant finding was observed in student performance on the GRADE from pretest to posttest by the treatment group ($F = 8.9$, df $= 1, 9.83$; $p < .05$). The multilevel regression equation yielded a between groups effect size of only .55 or 55%—providing a medium practical effect serving as evidence for meaningful change in student achievement as assessed by the GRADE.

These results support the importance of providing a teacher with professional development that is based on what the teacher needs to know at the time the teacher wants to know it and provided in ways that are active and connected to the teacher's daily work in the classroom.

Preservice teacher education

Just as quality inservice teacher education makes a difference in the literacy development of children, well-designed teacher education programs have a positive effect of reading instruction (Snow, 2002). Questions are often raised by groups concerned with teacher education regarding just how best to prepare beginning teachers to teach reading. While some groups are concerned with only the content and delivery systems of the programs (Snow, 2002; NICHD, 2000), other groups are beginning to explore and describe qualitative features of reading teacher preparation programs that are more difficult to capture and measure (Anders, Hoffman, & Duffy, 2000). Included in these features is attention to content, faculty and teaching, models of apprenticeship and early field experiences, diversity, candidate and program assessment, and governance and vision (IRA, 2007). Last, but not least, is the attention to the effects of teacher preparation on the learning of children in classrooms.

Contradictory to some reports that claim preservice teacher preparation programs are not teaching the "science" of reading (Walsh, Glaser, & Wilcox, 2006, p. 4), there is evidence that sites of exemplary reading teacher preparation do exist (IRA, 2003) and that graduates of these programs describe themselves as prepared to teach reading during their first years of teaching because of their preparation programs (Maloch et al., 2003). The Commission on Excellence in Elementary Teacher Preparation for Reading Instruction was commissioned by the International Reading Association to provide a state-of-affairs report in reading teacher education, identify characteristics of excellent reading teacher preparation programs, and to study the classroom effectiveness of the graduates of these sites of exemplary reading teacher preparation (IRA, 2003). Most interesting to the topic under discussion in this chapter are the findings of the IRA Commission related to the "effectiveness" of the programs on the instructional reading practices of their graduates.

Evidence from the work of the IRA Commission indicated that these teachers were quantifiably as prepared to teach reading as their more experienced colleagues in their schools during their first years of teaching. Based on observational data in the classrooms of graduates of the Sites of Excellence in Reading Teacher Education, which were located across seven states, the IRA Commission used quantitative data to explore the implementation of effective teaching practices by the graduates of these programs. Analysis of observational data indicated that graduates of these programs were more effective in using literacy instruction within a print-rich literacy environment (Hoffman, Sailors, Beretvas, & Duffy, 2004). Therefore, the findings of the IRA Commission study indicated that the teachers who attended high quality reading teacher preparation programs were well prepared to structure their classroom for comprehension instruction. The IRA Commission called for teacher educators to take a critical look at their practices and use the findings to inform their programs (Hoffman, Roller, et al., 2005; International Reading Association, 2003), as have others (Snow, 2002).

In this next section, I will use The University of Texas at San Antonio (UTSA) to illustrate just that: how one teacher preparation program engaged in ongoing reflective teacher preparation practices and piloted an innovative elementary reading teacher program. This project drew from the synthesized research on reading teacher preparation

(Anders, Hoffman, & Duffy, 2000; NICHD, 2000; Sailors, Keehn, Martinez, & Harmon, 2005; Snow, 2002) as a way of exploring the possibilities for the pragmatic application of the research with students who were being prepared to teach in inner-city schools.

While quantitative data do not exist to support the effectiveness of this project, I will present a description of the cohort and the anecdotal evidence of the effectiveness of the project. I collected observational data on the reading lessons of the university students four times (with a focus on their scaffolding of comprehension) and interviewed them twice during the three-semester cohort experience.

The literacy and technology learning cohort

Located at the UTSA, a large, Hispanic-serving institute that enrolls over 28,000 students, the Literacy and Technology Learning Cohort (LTLC) was housed inside the university's large teacher preparation program. Students seeking a degree in the standard Interdisciplinary Studies program at the UTSA can also seek a teaching certificate in one of three certification areas. Students enrolled in the standard EC-4 program are engaged in literacy and methods courses (in addition to standard courses) combined with 95 hours of early field experiences prior to their student teaching semester. Eighty percent of the courses in the standard EC-4 certification program are taught by adjunct instructors due to the large number of students and a lack of state funding. The LTLC were a group of 23 preservice teachers who were seeking an EC-4 certification within the degree plan.

The LTLC was designed to create a sense of community inside such a large program and to begin to study the strengths and challenges of creating and sustaining the type of reading teacher preparation program. To that end, the LTLC was committed to learning how to (a) employ culturally responsive literacy practices with a focus on comprehension instruction; (b) view literacy as a means of supporting learning in the content areas; and (c) employ the use of technology in the engagement of literacy with children. Most importantly, however, the group was committed to teaching in some of the poorest inner-city schools in Texas, such as those found in San Antonio. The model for the LTLC was a borrowed model—taking the strengths of each of the programs that participated in the IRA Commission and combining them in a way that was contextually sensitive to the San Antonio environment.

To that end, the students completed the final hours of their degree and certification requirements under the direction of two instructors, the author of this chapter and an adjunct instructor who held a Masters degree in Instructional Technology. These 27 hours of instruction included the required Principles of Learning and Classroom Organization and Management, two methods (Math/Science and Language Arts/Social Studies), and four literacy (Early Literacy Learning, Writing Processes and Development, Reading Comprehension, and Literacy Problems) courses, early field experiences and the requirements for student teaching as set forth by the state of Texas. All courses were taught at a local elementary school in San Antonio.

Rather than being taught by separate instructors under isolated conditions, these courses were aligned with each other in interdisciplinary ways, ensuring that the content of the courses, especially the literacy courses, focused first and foremost on teaching children to make meaning with text (traditional and otherwise). The five literacy-related courses drew from the construct of reading and writing as a recursive meaning-making system. Further, students learned to view reading as a system of cognitive strategies that readers employ as they interact with text. The content of the courses involved both word and text level strategies. The students learned to use assessments as a way of making instructional decisions for children. Finally, the students learned how to employ research-based comprehension practices inside the curriculum that their classroom teachers used.

Throughout the cohort experience, the preservice teachers completed 360 hours of early field experiences (not including student teaching) in a school district that supports children of low-income and minority backgrounds. For each student, these early field experiences spanned at least three grade levels over the course of the program (pre-kindergarten through Grade 4) in one of the three schools that supported the cohort's field experiences. The cohort began the year with the onset of the school's year, providing the university students the opportunity to set up, observe, and help the teacher implement instructional reading practices within a literacy-rich classroom. The students had many opportunities to practice that which they were learning in their university courses.

The classroom teachers who served as mentor teachers to the university students were selected by the university instructors based on their philosophical beliefs about teaching and learning, their views on childhood and children, and their instructional reading practices. These early field experiences were highly supervised by both the mentor teachers and the university instructors. The university students were very vocal about the experiences they were receiving from their mentor teachers. Many of them had friends in the traditional preparation program, and said they saw many differences in the experiences they were having when compared to the traditional experiences. Their classroom teachers, too, valued the opportunities to interact with the university students and the instructors.

Many of the teachers described the practices of the preservice teachers as "creative," "innovative," and "prepared to teach reading." These teachers attributed the success of the university students to the consistency within the cohort system. As one teacher reported, "The university students know the children, our classroom, and our curriculum because they have been with us for so long. It is a win-win situation for everyone." Additionally, the teachers reported that they were learning from their university students. Many innovative comprehension practices that the university students "tried out" in the classrooms were adopted by the mentor teachers. The teachers reportedly were excited about the ways the university students explained comprehension strategies to the class, during read alouds and small group instruction. These teachers reported that they, too, like their children, were learning how to be more metacognitively aware because of the presence of the university students in their classrooms.

In addition to the classroom experiences, these cohort students engaged in tutoring twice a week for two semesters. These tutoring experiences were based on learning to employ dynamic assessments (formal and informal) as a way of making instructional decisions for children. The structure for tutoring was based on research, and focused primarily on explaining cognitive strategies to children. Tutoring did not take place in the classroom; university students and their tutees met in the classroom assigned to the cohort. Although the tutoring was decontextualized from the classroom, the tutees were drawn from the classrooms in which the university students worked and the tutors were required to have ongoing contact with the classroom teacher concerning the ongoing analysis of and instruction for the tutoring lessons. This context also allowed for close supervising of the tutoring experience by the university instructors, who were able to model lessons for the university students.

The students described the content of the courses and their classroom-based and tutoring experiences in very positive ways. Several of the students told us at the end of the experience that they joined the cohort because of the draw to technology but that they quickly realized that it was the literacy aspects that was most important in their learning. One student admitted that teaching a child who struggled with reading to be much more difficult than she imagined, but that the work of the cohort made her feel confident that she would be able to do it. Others said that their classroom teachers that had the most impact on their learning to teach reading. In some of the classes, the mentor teachers were using a basal program that was scripted; students in these classrooms reported that they learned how to teach with the materials provided while adapting the materials (based on the content from their coursework under the careful direction of their mentor teacher) to the needs of the students on an individual basis. Other students found tutoring to be a safe place to try out new instructional practices before they were required to "do it with the whole class."

Their knowledge of reading instruction, especially in the area of comprehension was evident throughout the experience of the cohort. They began by integrating think alouds into their instructional practices during tutoring. They were "amazed" at how well their tutees picked up on the language of think alouds. They then began to move into the identification of the cognitive strategies needed by their students to engage in the types of reading in which they were requiring. They began to critically analyze the types of questions and think alouds in which they were engaging their tutees (and eventually, the students in their classrooms) with a move toward higher level forms of thinking. Finally, it was in tutoring (and, eventually in some classrooms) where the students began to take on the language of intentional instruction. That is, they learned to explain "how" readers do what they do when they engage in higher level thinking, especially critical thinking. Their knowledge was also evident in the professional talks they presented at state and international conferences (Sailors, Barerra, et al., 2005; Sailors, Leos, et al., 2005).

In short, although it was very focused on larger issues of educational equity and social justice, the LTLC was very much about providing preservice reading teachers with high quality experiences that connected their content learning about comprehension to their field experiences guided by committed faculty.

CONCLUDING THOUGHTS

Earlier, I championed the inclusion of this chapter in this book at this time. Given the political climate of education and the policies that surround teacher education, if ever there was a time, now is it. However, while I searched for studies on the professional development of teachers and comprehension instruction, I noticed two things. First, there is not any and, second, the field of reading research is still dichotomizing the professional development of preservice and inservice teachers.

First, while there is a growing body of research on reading teacher education (both preservice and inservice) and those aspects that are helpful to teachers and their students, including content, the delivery of professional development (issues of support and connectedness), and qualitative features (field-based and intensive), the information is focused on reading instruction in general, with scant attention to the specifics of comprehension instruction. There is simply too little attention paid to improving the professional development of teachers in the area of reading comprehension. If the call for research funded by the United States government is any indication, the field of reading research, with a focus on reading comprehension, is being prioritized. For example, opportunities for research have increased since the Teacher Quality Professional Development Reading Grants (Institute of Education Sciences) were introduced in 2003. Since then, 20 projects have been funded. Interestingly, only 5 of them center on comprehension as a focus; the others focus on reading and reading/writing in general (for example, teaching teachers to teach the five "pillars" as listed by the National Panel Report). Of these five, two are testing the efficacy of existing high school programs and three are developing models of professional development for elementary and middle school teachers. The one project that focuses on preservice teachers (out of the larger pool of 20) is focused on reading instruction, with no particular focus on comprehension. However, many of these were awarded in very recent years, long after the call for "high quality" instruction was issued. This appears to be yet another case of the placement of the horse before the cart.

Second, while there have been extensive reviews of the literature around reading teacher education (Anders, Hoffman, & Duffy, 2000; Darling-Hammond, 1999; Hoffman & Pearson, 2000; Snow, Burns & Griffin, 1998), scant attention has been paid to the ongoing professional development of teachers, beginning with preservice teacher education and following teachers into their first few years of teaching. That is, the field treats preservice and inservice teacher education as if they were different—one starts where the other ends.

A major issue is whether teacher learning is a developmental process. Some say it is (Snow, Griffin, & Burns, 2007) arguing that "it is crucial to conceptualize what teachers need to know to teach reading within a developmental framework: How much is needed so that novice teachers at a bare minimum do no harm?" (p. 10). This fosters a training model of teacher education, one in which teachers are taught basic skills of reading instruction and sent out to teach with the understanding that, in time, they will learn all that they need to know to support comprehension instruction. This is simply not true.

Research has demonstrated that the best teachers make instructional decisions "on the fly" and that they not be welded to following the prescriptions of commercial programs (Duffy & Kear, 2007). Hoffman and his colleagues (Hoffman et al., 1998) described these kinds of teachers as "principled"—those who make instructional decisions for their students based on the selection and adaptation of ideas from a variety of ideologies, methods, materials, and programs. Additionally, principled teachers employ "best practices" (Allington, 2002; Knapp, 1995; Langer, 2000; Metsala et al., 1997; Morrow et al., 1999; Pressley et al., 1996; Taylor et al., 2000) but also modify and adapt their practices in order to make instructional decisions based on the needs of their students and their vision for reading instruction (Duffy, 1998; Duffy & Hoffman, 1999). The National Reading Panel (NICHD, 2000) emphasized the adaptive aspect of good reading instruction in its summary of "Teacher Preparation and Comprehension Strategies Instruction" when they reiterated that reading comprehension is complex and so is teaching it. Teaching it, the Panel went on to say, does not mean that teachers have a specific set of instructional procedures that they can follow because comprehension instruction "cannot be routinized" (p. 4–125). Reading instruction focused on comprehension requires that teachers learn to be innovative, reflective, and responsive to the instructional needs of the children with whom they work (Duffy & Kear, 2007). Developmental training models lead to compliant teachers, not ones who can make instructional decisions for their children.

Having said that, perhaps it is time for the field of reading teacher education to rethink the way in which it conducts both teacher education itself and research on teacher education. For example, Bransford, Darling-Hammond, LePage, and Hammerness (2005) state, "We understand that teachers continually construct new knowledge and skills in practice throughout their careers rather than acquiring a finite set of knowledge and skills in their totality before entering the classroom" and that teachers should begin their preservice teacher programs being "prepared to learn throughout their lifetime" (p. 3). If this is the case, looking at specific practices within teacher education programs that promote high quality beginning teachers of comprehension, for examples, might be just part of the information needed to understand the process that reading teachers go through as they are learning to improve their instructional reading comprehension practices.

Preservice teachers enter into their programs with understandings of how to teach comprehension (usually it is read the story and ask them a lot of questions at the end) based on how they were taught to read. A solid preservice teacher education program will be the beginning of the "undoing" of this and a rebuilding of instructional practices in which children are engaged in active cognitive practices and strategies. This learning, for teachers, will continue long after they have left the halls of the university. Therefore, research is desperately needed that demonstrates under what conditions teachers continue to learn, what is helpful about those conditions, the developmental stages through which they progress, and what influence this learning has on student comprehension achievement. Research must reflect their learning not as dichotomized but as ongoing and long-term.

Because learning to teach cognitive reading strategies is a process that takes time (Duffy, 1993a), perhaps this is the most natural place to begin longitudinal research that tracks the learning of teachers, beginning in preservice teacher education programs and following the learning processes of these teachers as they continue to engage in professional development activities into their first years of teaching. Perhaps it is time to either cloth the emperor or simply replace him.

REFERENCES

Allen, J. (2006). *Becoming a literacy leader: Supporting learning and change.* Portland, ME: Steinhouse.

Allington, R. L. (2002). *Schools that work where all children read and write.* Boston, MA: Allyn and Bacon.

Anders, P. L., Hoffman, J. V., & Duffy, G. G. (2000). Teaching teachers to teach reading: Paradigm shifts, persistent problems, and challenges. In M. L. Kamil, P. B. Mosenthal, P. D. Pearson, & R. Barr (Eds.), *Handbook of Reading Research, Vol III.* Mahwah, NJ: Erlbaum.

Bean, R. (2004). *The reading specialist: Leadership for the classroom, school and community.* New York: Guilford.

Birman, B. F., Desimone, L., Porter, A. C., & Garet, M. S. (2000, May). Designing professional development that works. *Educational Leadership,* 28–33.

Bransford, J., Darling-Hammond, L., LePage, P., & Hammerness, K. (2005). *Preparing teachers for a changing world: What teachers should learn and be able to do.* New York: Jossey-Bass.

Butler, D. L., Lauscher, H. N., Jarvis-Selinger, S., & Beckingham, B. (2004). Collaboration and self-regulation in teachers' professional development. *Teaching and Teacher Education, 20,* 435–455.

Casey, K. (2006). *Literacy coaching: The essentials.* Portsmouth, NH: Heinemann.

Cochran-Smith, M., & Lytle, S. (1999). Relationship of knowledge and practice: Teacher learning in communities. In A. Iran-Nejad & C. D. Pearson (Eds.), *Review of research in education* (Vol. 24, pp. 249–306). Washington, DC: American Educational Research Association.

Costa, A. L., & Garmson, R. J. (2002). *Cognitive coaching: A foundation for renaissance schools.* Norwood, MA: Christoper-Gordon Publishers.

Darling-Hammond, L. (1999). *Teacher quality and student achievement: A review of state policy evidence.* Seattle, WA: Center for the Study of Teaching and Policy.

Darling-Hammond, L. (2000). Teacher quality and student achievement: A review of state policy evidence. *Education Policy Analysis Archives, 8.* Online article. Available at http://epaa.asu.edu/epaa/v8n1/. Retrieved November 6, 2004.

Desimone, L. M., Porter, A. C., Garet, M. S., Yoon, K. S., & Birman, B. F. (2002). Effects of professional development on teachers' instruction: Results from a three-year longitudinal study. *Educational Evaluation and Policy Analysis, 24,* 81–112.

Dole, J. (2004). The changing role of the reading specialist in school reform. *The Reading Teacher, 57,* 462–471.

Dole, J. A., & Osborn, J. (2004). Professional development for K-3 teachers: Content and process. In D. S. Stickland & M. L. Kamala (Eds.), *Improving reading achievement through professional development.* Norwood, MA: Christoper-Gordon Publishers.

Dole, J., Brown, K. J., & Trathen, W. (1996). The effects of strategy instruction on the comprehension performance of at-risk students. *Reading Research Quarterly, 31*(1), 62–88.

Duffy, G. G., & Kear, K. (2007). Adaptation or compliance: What is the real message about research-based practices? *Phi Delta Kappan, 88,* 579–581.

Duffy, G. G., Roehler, L. R., Sivan, E., Rackliffe, G., Book, C., Meloth, M. S., Vavrus, L. G., Wesselman, R., Putnam, J., & Bassiri, D. (1987). Effects of explaining the reasoning associated with using reading strategies. *Reading Research Quarterly, 23,* 347–368.

Duffy, G. G. (1993a). Rethinking strategy instruction: Four teachers' development and their low achievers' understandings. *The Elementary School Journal, 93,* 231–264.

Duffy, G. G. (1993b). Teachers' progress toward becoming expert strategy teachers. *Elementary School Journal, 94,* 109–120.

Duffy, G. (1998). Teaching and the balancing of round stones. *Phi Delta Kappan, 79,* 777–780.

Duffy, G. (2002). The case for direct explanation of strategies. In C. C. Block & M. Pressley (Eds.), *Comprehension instruction: Research-based best practices* (pp. 28–41). New York: Guilford.

Duffy, G. G. (2004). Teachers who improve reading achievement. In D. S. Stickland & M. L. Kamala (Eds.), *Improving reading achievement through professional development* (pp. 3–22). Norwood, MA: Christopher-Gordon Publishers.

Duffy, G. G., & Hoffman, J. V. (1999). In pursuit of an illusion: The flawed search for a perfect method. *Reading Teacher, 53,* 10–16.

Garet, M. S., Porter, A. C., Desimone, L., Birman, B. F., & Yoon, K. S. (2001). What makes professional development effective? Results from a national sample of teachers. *American Educational Research Journal, 38,* 915–945.

Gee, P. (1990). *Social linguistics and literacies: Ideology in discourses.* New York: Falmer.

Hasbrouck, J. & Denton, C. (2005). *The reading coach: A how to manual for success.* Longmont, CO: Sopris West.

Hoffman, J. V., & Pearson, P. D. (2000). Reading teacher education in the next millennium: What your grandmother's teacher didn't know that your granddaughter's teacher should. *Reading Research Quarterly, 35,* 28–44.

Hoffman, J. V., Roller, C. M., Maloch, B., Sailors, M., Duffy, G. G., Beretvas, S. N., & The National Commission on Excellence in Elementary Teacher Preparation for Reading (2005). Teachers' preparation to teach reading and their experiences and practices in the first three years of teaching. *The Elementary School Journal, 105*(3), 267–289.

Hoffman, J. V., Sailors, M., Beretvas, N., & Duffy, G. G. (2004). The Effective Elementary Classroom Literacy Environment: Examining the Validity of the TEX-IN3 Observation System. *Journal of Literacy Research, 36*(3), 289–320

International Reading Association (IRA) (2003). *Prepared to make a difference: An executive summary of the National Commission on Excellence in Elementary Teacher Preparation for Reading Instruction.* Newark, DE: Author.

International Reading Association (IRA) (2004). *The role and qualifications of the reading coach in the United States.* Newark, DE: Author.

International Reading Association (IRA) (2006). *Standards for middle and high school literacy coaches.* Newark, DE: Author.

International Reading Association (IRA) (2007). *Teaching reading well: A synthesis of the International Reading Association's research on teacher preparation for reading instruction.* Newark, DE: Author.

Kise, J. (2006). Differentiated coaching: *A framework for helping teachers change.* Thousand Oaks, CA: Corwin Press.

Knapp, M. S. (1995). *Teaching for meaning in high-poverty classrooms.* New York: Teachers College Press.

Laczko-Kerr, I., & Berliner, D. (2002). The effectiveness of "Teach for America" and other under-certified teachers on student academic achievement: A case of harmful public policy. *Education Policy Analysis Archives, 10.* Online article. Available at http://epaa.asu.edu/epaa/v10n37/. Retrieved November 6, 2004.

Langer, J. A. (2000). *Beating the odds: Teaching middle and high school students to read and write well.* (Report Series 12014). Albany: University at Albany State University of New York, National Research Center on English Language Learning and Achievement.

Lipson, M. Y., Mosenthal, J. H., Mekkelsen, J., & Russ, B. (2004). Building knowledge and fashioning success one school at a time. *The Reading Teacher, 57,* 534–542.

Maloch, B., Flint, A. S., Eldridge, D., Harmon, J., Loven, R., Fine, J. C., Bryant-Shanklin, M., & Martinez, M. (2003). Understandings, beliefs, and reported decision making of first-year teachers from different reading teacher preparation programs. *Elementary School Journal, 103,* 431–457.

Metsala, J. L., Wharton-McDonald, R., Pressley, M. J., Rankin, J., Mistretta, J., & Ettenberger, S. (1997). Effective primary-grades literacy instruction=Balanced literacy instruction. *The Reading Teacher, 50,* 518–521.

Morrow, L. M., Tracey, D. H., Woo, D. G., & Pressley, M. (1999). Characteristics of exemplary first-grade literacy instruction. *The Reading Teacher, 52,* 462–476.

National Center for Educational Statistics. (1999). *Teacher quality: A report on the preparation and qualifications of public school teachers.* Washington, DC: Office of Educational Research and Improvement.

National Center for Educational Statistics. (2003). *Overview and inventory of state education reforms: 1990–2000.* Washington, DC: Office of Educational Research and Improvement.

National Commission on Teaching and America's Future. (1996). *What matters most: Teaching for America's future.* New York: Author.

National Institute of Child Health and Human Development (NICHD). (2000). *Report of the National Reading Panel. Teaching children to read: An evidence-based assessment of the scientific research literature on reading and its implications for reading instruction.* (NIH Publication No. 00-4769). Washington, DC: U.S. Government Printing Office.

Paris, S., Waskik, B., & Turner, J. (1991). The development of strategic readers. In R. Barr, M. Kamala, P. Mosenthal, & P. D. Pearson (Eds.), *Handbook of reading research, Vol II* (pp. 609–640). New York: Longman.

Pearson, P.,D., & Fielding, L. (1991). Comprehension instruction. In R. Barr, M. L. Kamil, P. Mosenthal, & P. D. Pearson (Eds.), *Handbook of reading research* (vol. II, pp. 815–860). New York: Longman.

Porter, A. C., Garet, M. S., Desimone, L. M., & Birman, B. F. (2003). Providing effective professional development: Lessons from the Eisenhower Program. *Science Educator, 12,* 23–40.

Pressley, M. (2000). What should comprehension instruction be the instruction of? In M. L. Kamil, P. B. Mosenthal, P. D. Pearson, & R. Barr (Eds.), *Handbook of reading research, Vol. III* (pp. 545–562). Mahwah, NJ: Erlbaum.

Pressley, M., Borkowski, J., & Schneider, W. (1987). Cognitive strategies: Good strategy users coordinate metacognition and knowledge. In R. Vasta & G. Whitehurst (Eds.), *Annals of child development, Vol. X* (pp. 89–129). New York: JAI.

Pressley, M., El-Dinary, P., Gaskins, I., Schuder, T., Bergman, J., Almasi, L., & Brown, R. (1992). Beyond direct explanation: Transactional instruction of reading comprehension strategies. *Elementary School Journal, 92,* 511–554.

Pressley, M., Johnson, C. J., Symons, S., McGoldrick, J., & Kurita, J. (1990). Strategies that improve memory and comprehension of what is read. *Elementary School Journal, 90,* 3–32.

Pressley, M. J., Rankin, T., & Yokoi, L. (1996). A survey of instructional practices of primary teachers nominated as effective in promoting literacy. *The Elementary School Journal, 96,* 363–384.

Putnam, R. T., & Borko, H. (2000). What do new views of knowledge and thinking have to say about research on teacher learning? *Educational Researcher, 29,* 4–15.

Richardson, V. (1996). The role of attitudes and beliefs in learning to teach. In J. Sikula, T. Buttery, & E. Guyton (Eds.), *Handbook of research on teacher education* (pp. 102–119). New York: Simon & Schuster Macmillan.

Roller, C. (2006). *Reading and literacy coaches report on hiring requirements and duties survey.* Newark, DE: International Reading Association.

Sailors, M. (2006, November). "It's all about the kinds of questions I ask!": Supporting Reading Teacher Learning through a Model of Intensive Professional Development. Paper presented at the annual meeting of the National Reading Conference, Los Angeles, CA.

Sailors, M., Barerra, B., Gonzales, K., & Alexander, Y. (2005). Scaffolding reading instruction with struggling readers in an electronic environment. Paper presented at the annual meeting of the International Reading Association's Preservice Teacher Conference, San Antonio, TX.

Sailors, M., Keehn, S., Martinez, M., & Harmon, J. (2005). Early field experiences offered to and valued by preservice teachers at Sites of Excellence in Reading Teacher Education programs. *Teacher Education and Practice: Focus on Global Practices, 18,* 458–470.

Sailors, M., Leos, J., Escamilla, L., Palomino, J., Torres, K., Barrera, B., Gonzalez, K., Garcia, C., Hernandez, M., Cowey, L., & Callia, N. (2005). Using technology to enhance the literacy instruction of struggling readers. Paper presented at the annual meeting of the Texas Association for the Improvement of Reading, Round Rock, Texas.

Sandholtz, J. H. (2002). Inservice training or professional development: Contrasting opportunities in a school/university partnership. *Teaching and Teacher Education, 18,* 815–830.

Shanklin, N. L. (2006). What are the characteristics of effective literacy coaching? Literacy Coaching Clearinghouse. Available for download http://www.literacycoachingonline.org. Downloaded on March 1, 2007.

Snow, C. (2002). Reading for understanding: Toward a research and development program in reading comprehension. Santa Monica, CA: RAND.

Snow, C. E., Burns, S. M., & Griffin, P. (1998). *Preventing reading difficulties in young children.* Washington, DC: National Academy Press.

Snow, C., Griffin, P., & Burns, M. S. (Eds.). (2005). *Knowledge to support the teaching of reading: Preparing teachers for a changing world.* Hoboken, NJ: Josey-Bass Education.

Stein, M. K., Schwan, M. S., & Silver, E. A. (1999). The development of professional developers: Learning to assist teachers in new settings in new ways. *Harvard Educational Review, 69,* 237–269.

Sturtevant, E. G. (2006). *The literacy coach: A key to improving teaching and learning in secondary schools.* Washington, DC: Alliance for Excellent Education.

Taylor, B. M., Pearson, P. D., Clark, K. F., & Walpole, S. (2000). Effective schools and accomplished teachers: Lessons about primary-grade reading instruction in low-income schools. *The Elementary School Journal, 101,* 121–165.

Toll, C. (2006). Literacy coach's desk reference: The processes and perspective for effective coaching. Urbana, IL: National Council of Teachers of English.

Walpole, S., & McKenna, M. C. (2004). *The literacy coach's handbook: A guide to research-based practice.* New York: Guilford.

Walsh, K., Glaser, D., & Wilcox, D. D. (2006). What education school aren't teaching about reading and what elementary teachers aren't learning. Washington, DC: National Council on Teacher Quality.

32 Public Policy and the Future of Reading Comprehension Research

Cathy Roller
International Reading Association

The title of this article—as well as of my position at the International Reading Association (Director of Research and Policy)—assumes that there is a relationship between public policy and research on reading comprehension. The relationship is in both directions. Policy influences research and research influences policy. (Research and policy simultaneously influence each other and unidentified underlying variables influence both but these will not be addressed in this chapter.) This chapter will focus first on the influence of policy on research, then the reverse. Then it will examine the implications of the current policy-research situation, the position taken by the International Reading Association, and what we can expect in the future.

HOW POLICY HAS INFLUENCED RESEARCH

Since the largest funder of reading comprehension research is the federal government, there is clearly significant policy influence on research. The reading education community benefited immensely from the infusion of federal research money. This was particularly true during the period when the Office of Education Research and Improvement (OERI), the predecessor of the Institute for Education Sciences (IES) focused on funding a Research Center rather than individual researchers. For decades, government funding focused on reading achievement, including substantive funding for comprehension research. The Center for the Study of Reading at the University of Illinois was the first to be awarded the grant, followed by the Joint Center at the University of Maryland and the University of Georgia, and then the Center for the Investigation of Early Reading Achievement (CIERA) that was composed of multiple partner universities linked with the primary grantees, University of Michigan and Michigan State University. There continues to be a Center for the English Language Arts at SUNY, Albany.

The basic funding pattern for reading comprehension research has changed since the restructuring of the U. S. Education Department early in the current Bush administration. The reorganization placed all the research activities within the Institute of Education Sciences (IES) which now includes four centers:

1. The National Center for Education Research's (NCER) mission is similar to the old OERI, historically the funding sources for the Reading Research Centers, but now funding individual researchers.
2. The National Center for Education Evaluation (NCEE) funds the evaluations of federal programs such as Title I, Even Start, Reading First, Striving Readers, and the What Works Clearinghouse.

3. The National Center for Education Statistics (NCES) was established as independent of the Department, but now reports to Grover Whitehurst, the Director of IES, and continues to gather statistical data about education.

4. The National Center for Special Education Research (NCSER) was added to IES in 2004. Most of the funding by the former Office of Special Education and Rehabilitation Services (OSERS) has been transferred to this center.

It is no secret that one of Whitehurst's major objectives was to improve the quality of education research, which in general had a reputation of being weak and inconclusive, particularly when it came to answering questions related to policy. Whitehurst specifically changed strategies from funding research centers to direct funding of individual researchers. Despite the change in funding strategy, reading comprehension research has continued to receive significant funding. One of the most important factors contributing to sustained funding was the commitment, by Kent McGuire, acting director of OERI in 2001, to fund the Rand Corporation Study of Reading Comprehension and Mathematics (Snow, 2002). The Rand Corporation used the funding to convene a study group to lay out a research agenda in reading comprehension. The effects of the group's report are discernible in IES's current pattern of funding.

An analysis of funding makes other patterns apparent.[1] NCER has four major programs that can be used to fund reading comprehension research: Cognition and Student Learning, Interventions for Struggling Adolescent and Adult Readers (which has currently not awarded any grants), Reading and Writing Education Research, and Teacher Quality: Reading and Writing Research. One clear pattern is that researchers are required to follow a progression of funding reflected in five research goals adopted by IES. The goals first address projects at different stages of development and move from identification and description to development; then there are efficacy studies that include clinical trials and replication; and the fifth goal is the development of assessment tools. In sum, the five goals (stages) are: (1) to identify existing programs, practices, and policies that may have an impact on student outcomes and the factors that may mediate or moderate the effects of these programs, practices, and policies; (2) to develop programs, practices, and policies that are theoretically and empirically based and obtain preliminary (pilot) data on the relation (association) between implementation of the program, practice, or policy and the intended education outcomes; (3) to establish the efficacy of fully developed programs, practices, or policies that either have evidence of a positive correlation between implementation of the intervention and education outcomes or are widely used but have not been rigorously evaluated; (4) to provide evidence on the effectiveness of programs, practices, and policies implemented at scale; and (5) to develop or validate data and measurement systems and tools.

Another clear pattern is the increase since 2001 in the number of institutions where affiliated researchers have received grants. Between 2001 and 2006, researchers at 65 institutions received funding. Of those 65 institutions, 44 received single grants and 21 received multiple grants. Of the 21 institutions that received multiple grants:

- eight institutions had two grants awarded to a single principal investigator, usually at a two or three year interval, and often one addressed the development goal while the second addressed the efficacy or the efficacy and replication goals;
- five institutions were awarded two grants under different principal investigators;
- four institutions (UCLA, University of Wisconsin-Madison, Northern Illinois University, and Vanderbilt University) were awarded three grants under three different principal investigators;

- two institutions (The University of Pittsburgh and Florida State University) were awarded four grants under four different principal investigators;
- one institution (Columbia University, including Teachers College) was awarded five grants to four different principal investigators; and
- one institution (Carnegie Mellon) was awarded six grants with four different principal investigators.

While these data underline IES's move away from the large Center concept to funding individual researchers at their multiple institutions, they also demonstrate that some institutions have built strong research capacities that result in higher success rates than other institutions. It is noteworthy that none of the institutions that received multiple research grants previously housed a Reading Research Center.

Another clear pattern in funding is the focus on practices and materials that improve achievement. Thus, while the number of individual researchers who received grants includes scholars who were active in the Reading Research Centers, there has been a change in the institutions receiving the most awards. One hypothesis is that researchers from Cognitive Psychology and Special Education have been very successful in capturing reading comprehension research funds, while fewer grants have gone to the institutions that have historically housed the reading research centers.

Another discernible pattern of funding is the clear and specific focus on the effectiveness of educational interventions. IES specifically states that NCER research examine sthe effectiveness of educational programs, practices, and policies, including the application of technology to instruction and assessment. The goal of NCER research programs is to provide scientific evidence of what works, for whom, and under what conditions.

RESEARCH INFLUENCING POLICY

While it is clear that federal education policy influences the funding of educational research and research in reading, it is markedly less clear how education research influences policy related to reading instruction. The answer to the question of how reading research influences policy often necessarily focuses on whose research and what kinds of research.

In recent years, perhaps the most prominent example of research affecting policy is the influence of the National Reading Panel on the Reading First provisions of No Child Left Behind (NCLB) Act of 2001 [P.L. 107-110]. Prior to the passage of the NCLB, the government commissioned a panel to conduct meta-analyses of reading research. The National Reading Panel (2000) examined five areas of reading instruction: phonemic awareness, phonics, fluency, vocabulary, and comprehension strategies. The findings of the panel became part of the Reading First sections of the NCLB when the five areas investigated by the panel were dubbed the "essential components" of reading instruction in section 1208. The panel found that there were practices in each of the five areas that were supported by scientifically based reading research. The authors and implementers of the Reading First provisions of the Act would probably claim that the Act was a brilliant example of research influencing policy.

While Reading First called for the implementation of practices and materials supported by scientifically based research as defined in the NCLB Act, the basic problem is that, in fact, no programs and few practices have the kind of evidence behind them that the act requires. Critics of Reading First would argue that the scientifically-based reading research provisions of the law were in fact a subterfuge that resulted in the adoption of reading programs favored by the authors and implementers of the law. Indeed, the Inspector General of the Education Department documented that specific programs were favored and others excluded. He also documented that review panels were "stacked" with people who shared the ideological perspectives of the authors and implementers, including reviewers who appear to have financial interests in the products that they essentially mandated (http://www.ed.gov/about/offices/list/oig/aireports/i13f0017.pdf). Many educators view the implementation of Reading First as an example of opinion—masquerading as scientifically based reading research—influencing policy on a very large scale.

The issue of how research can influence policy is analyzed in *Influence: A Study of the Factors Shaping Education Policy*, prepared by Editorial Projects in Education Research Center (Swanson & Barlage, 2006). The document illuminates the Reading First experience. To explore factors that influence policy, Swanson and Barlage interviewed individuals knowledgeable about education policy and had them nominate Influential Studies, Influential Organizations, Influential People, and Influential Information Sources. They then listed the top 10 (and because of ties, 13 in some categories) nominees in each category and asked participants to rate their importance in influencing policy in the last 11 years. Table 32.1 is taken directly from their report.

In summarizing the findings the authors concluded:

1. The question of what influences educational policy can be a difficult problem to untangle. Certainly, numerous connections exist among the leading studies, organizations, people, and information sources receiving high marks in our expert surveys. However, several clusters of influence prove particularly noteworthy.
2. A major source of influence exists within the public sector, revolving around the U. S. Department of Education. Itself the second-ranked organization, the agency has conducted (through its statistical branch, NCES) or commissioned several of the most influential studies. The Department also has close connections to a substantial share of the highly influential figures in education policy and is responsible for a number of leading information sources (Swanson & Barlage, 2006, p. 5).

In the private sector, the Gates Foundation represents a major epicenter of influence, a highly ranked organization in its own right as well as a funder of other high-profile groups. The Education Trust and the Fordham Foundation can be found at the center of other nodes of influence, by virtue of their status as influential organizations and ties to highly-ranked persons, studies, and information sources.

Notably absent from this description of the sources of influence are reports issued by associations and university research centers. The reasons for this absence are clear in the report. In analyzing the source of the blockbuster studies, the researchers concluded that they are much more likely to be secondary analyses of existing data rather than original research, to have evaluation orientations, and to be produced by commissions and government agencies—and much less likely to be released by book publishers. None of the top ranked studies were released by associations or universities.

Influence (Swanson & Barlage, 2006) provides substantive insights to the type of work that researchers and associations will have to do if we want research to influence policy. *Influence* examined how the work of university researchers entered the influence ratings. For example, a group of studies by William L. Sanders—on value-added methodology and the Tennessee Value-Added Accountability System—were fourth on the list of influential studies. Studies on school reform by Richard F Elmore, on high school graduation rates by Jay P. Green, and on school choice and vouchers by Paul Peterson occupied positions 10 to 12 on the list of studies. On the list of influential people, Linda Darling-Hammond of Stanford University ranked 10th. In all cases the researchers are associated with a particular topic that they have pursued in considerable depth over a long period of time.

Table 32.1 Leading Influences in Education Policy (ranked by level of influence—high to low)

Studies	Organizations	People	Informaion sources
1. *National Assessment of Education Progress (NAEP)*. U.S. Department of Education	1. U.S. Congress	1. Bill Gates	1. National Assessment of Educational Progress (NAEP)
2. *Trends in International Mathematics and Science Study* (TIMSS). International Assocation for the Evaluation of Educational Achievment and National Center for Education Standards	2. U.S. Department of Education	2. George W. Bush	2. Education Week
3. *Teaching Children To Read: An Evidenced-Based Assessment of the Scientific Research Literature on Reading and Its Implications for Reading Instruction* (2000). The National Reading Panel	3. Bill and Melinda Gates Foundation	3. Kati Haycock	3. National Center for Educatton Statistics (NCES)
4. Tennessee Student/Teacher Achievement Ratio (STAR) experiment and related studies	4. Education Trust	4. G. Reid Lyon	4. New York Times
5. *Preventing Reading Difficulties in Young Children* (1998). National Academies' Commision on Behavioral and Social Sciences and Education (CBASSE)	5. National Governors Association (NGA)	5. Edward Kennedy	5. U.S. Department of Education
6. William L. Sanders on value-added methodology and the Tennessee Value-Added Accountability System	6. American Federation of Teachers (AFT)	6. Bill Clinton	6. Education Trust
7. Education Trust on teacher quality	7. Achieve, Inc.	7. James B. Hunt Jr.	7. Washington Post
7. *How People Learn: Brain, Mind, Experience, and School* (1999). National Academies' Commission on Behavioral and Social Sciences and Education(CBASSE)	7. National Education Association (NEA)	7. Richard W. Riley	8. Education Next
7. *What Matters Most: Teaching for America's Future* (1996). National Commission on Teaching and America's Future	9. Thomas B. Fordham Foundation	9. Marshal (Mike) Smith	8. Public Education Network (PEN) Weekly NewsBlast
10. Richard F. Elmore on school reform	10. Center on Education Policy (CEP)	10. Linda Darling Hammond	10. Education Gadfly
11. Jay P. Greene on high graduation rates		10. Margaret Spellings	11. Eduwork
12. Paul E. Peterson on school choice and vouchers		12. George Miller	
12. *Ready or Not: Creating a High School Diploma that Counts* (2004). American Diploma Project		13. Chester E. Finn Jr.	

Source: Swanson & Barlage, 2006, p. vi.

Even more important, these researchers are devoted to studying topics of interest to policy makers. This would seem a fairly obvious point, but it is much more important than it sounds. I remember making a policy-oriented presentation at a professional meeting. I suggested that policy makers have a right to hold educators responsible, and if researchers do not like using standardized achievement measures as accountability indices, the researchers needed to provide viable alternative measures. This requires proposing and studying those measures and making a case for their reliability, validity, and implementability. One researcher spoke to say, "but that's not what I'm interested in."

As researchers, and as a matter of academic freedom, we believe that we should study the questions we deem important. However, if we insist upon our own individual agendas, we cannot expect policy makers to be interested in our work. We are unlikely to influence policy makers with agendas that do not speak directly to current policy issues. Reading researchers tend to be more interested in research than in policy. They tend to become interested in policy only when policy inserts itself into their academic lives through legislation such as NCLB, which contained provisions that called for states to examine and determine whether university courses and syllabi were covering the five essential components.

WHERE DO WE STAND NOW?

Currently, much of the work being conducted in reading comprehension is heavily influenced by a skills-based tradition and much of it is the work from special educators and cognitive psychologists. However, this is more a matter of skilled grantsmanship than it is a bias against the topics of research and the underlying theories related to sociocultural perspectives that have predominated in this volume. I believe that reading comprehension researchers can redress the situation and capture more of the grant dollars by paying clear attention to the patterns of funding described in the earlier sections of this paper. The claim that the IES doesn't fund qualitative research or that it only funds clinical trials is false. However, IES clearly does expect the funded work to be moving through a research agenda that leads to a solid answer to the question, "Does this work?" As noted in the earlier section of this paper, they are quite clear and transparent about the focus of research funded by IES.

There are at least two clear examples of government-funded work of reading comprehension researchers. Elizabeth Birr Moje, University of Michigan, was funded by NICHD, OSERS, and OVAE, for The Study of Social and Cultural Influences on Adolescent Literacy Motivation and Development (as retrieved from http://www-personal. umich.edu/~moje/ald.htm, April 17, 2007). There were several aspects of this study that, I believe, made it attractive to NICHD. First, Elizabeth was connected to a network of researchers who had been studying motivation using a survey methodology and her work built on the previous work and extended it. Second, the grant proposal was thorough and extremely well written. Third, the grant included a mix of methodologies that ranged from surveys to ethnographies to the use of experimental tasks based on the outcome of earlier phases of the research. The methods chosen were appropriate for each of the phases of the proposed research.

Another successful emerging researcher, Misty Sailors, University of Texas, San Antonio, was successful in securing an IES funded Teacher Quality Professional Development Reading grant. This project is focused on studying the impact of mentoring on the instructional practices of classroom teachers, grades 2–8, in the area of cognitive reading strategies. There were several aspects of the proposal that made it appealing. First, the study was thorough in its design and was well written. That is, it identified the aspects of previous research that demonstrated that teachers could learn to teach comprehension in ways that were helpful to readers. Second, it identified the need to describe those conditions of the model that teachers found helpful in improving their instructional comprehension practices and it proposed to identify those aspects that were associated with gains in student outcomes. Third, it employed multilevel statistical models, including hierarchical linear modeling. Finally, although the reviewers recognized the primary investigator was a junior faculty, they were convinced that her doctoral program had prepared her for such a project as evident in her role in the IRA Commission study *Prepared to Make a Difference* (International Reading Association, 2003).

It is clear from both of these examples that it is possible to get government funding for work that addresses topics like motivation and based on sociocultural perspectives. It is a matter of selecting questions and framing the proposal in ways that are consistent with guidelines and policies that are clear and transparent and available to all. However, if researchers are unwilling to link theoretical questions to a research program that has as its major objective the practical questions about what works for improving literacy achievement, they should seek funding elsewhere. I can not emphasize enough that if research is to guide policy and practice, researchers must study questions that are of interest to policy makers. A wide range of methods and perspectives are possible as is a wide range of subquestions, but the commitment of the program to practical outcomes is essential.

INTERNATIONAL READING ASSOCIATION'S STATUS OF READING INSTRUCTION INSTITUTE

Given that most reading researchers are unlikely to conduct long term research programs on topics relevant to policy makers, and given that membership associations did not issue a single one of the blockbuster studies, how should the reading profession respond? In this section of the chapter I will share the International Reading Association's (IRA) response.

The IRA recently authorized the establishment of the Status of Reading Instruction Institute (SRII) that is charged with producing periodic descriptions of reading instruction in the U.S. based on information from nationally representative samples. Currently, no entity is collecting such data. While several government studies such as the National Assessment of Educational Progress (NAEP), the Schools and Staffing Survey (SASS), and the Early Childhood Longitudinal Study (ECLS) include teacher surveys of instructional practices, the data are self report and are connected neither to teacher logs of instructional practice nor to observations of teachers in classrooms.

There are occasional studies of practice, such as The First R (Bauman, Hoffman, Duffy-Hestor, & Ro, 2000) published in *Reading Research Quarterly* and a current study (Mesmer, 2007) published in *Journal of Literacy Research*. The samples these studies examine, however, are not representative in the same sense as NAEP and SASS and ECLS are. In one case, the study drew its samples from lists compiled by marketing firms that claim to include all teachers in the United States—but this claim is questionable. In the other case, the list was provided by IRA—clearly not a representative sample but a sample that is biased toward individuals who are interested enough in reading instruction to be members. It is also the case that individual researchers do not have the capacity to collect such data periodically into perpetuity.

Why did IRA establish SRII and charge it with producing periodic descriptions of reading based on nationally representative samples? First and foremost, IRA believes that progress and improvement in reading achievement requires accurate and detailed descriptions of the reading instruction actually occurring in schools and classrooms.

The descriptions are necessary because too many decisions about reading instruction are based on inference instead of data, and reading instruction has suffered from multiple, short-term fads. Periodically, groups of activists decide that reading is being taught badly. They raise a hue and cry, declaring that reading achievement is miserable because schools and teachers are teaching reading badly, and they publish documents and books, such as *Why Johnny Can't Read* (Flesch, 1955). In general their claims about instruction are merely inferences about how reading is being taught based on an inspection of curriculum materials and curriculum guides, or based on surveys and observations done with small samples of convenience. Because of these reports, many people believe there are wide swings in the methods used to teach reading. Others contend that these characterizations of reading instruction are exaggerations and that, in fact, there are few changes in the delivery of reading instruction.

Even legislative insistence on instruction based on scientifically-based reading research has not alleviated the problem. For example, Louisa Moats, in a recent Fordham Institute report entitled *Whole-Language High Jinks*, suggests in her subtitle that she knows *How to Tell When "Scientifically based Reading Instruction" Isn't* (Moats, 2007). She insists, based on her analysis of commercial reading materials, that children are not getting scientifically-based reading instruction. However, she provides absolutely no data on observations of instruction. Furthermore, her language is full of value-laden phrases that lack both the objectivity and precision of science. She refers to "deposing whole language offspring" and to the "whole language 'fig leaf' of balanced instruction"—language that is clearly intended to inflame rather than reflect or promote objective evaluation. The document raises ethical issues because, when providing examples of good practice, Moats refers readers to materials and professional development by Sopris West, a company in which Moats has substantial financial interest. When providing bad examples, she lists competitors.

It is difficult to refute such claims about the early reading instruction children receive when we literally have no reliable descriptions of reading instruction as it is delivered. The question of how reading is taught is an empirical one and research strategies exist for answering the question reliably and convincingly.

The second reason for SRII is that IRA is committed to evidence-based instruction and to making policy consistent with that goal. In a recent marketing survey, members indicated that advocacy for reading should be IRA's top priority. IRA determined that a biennial report describing instruction would be critical to influencing policy because: (1) it would provide a focus point for conversations about reading instruction at regular intervals; and (2) it would enable IRA to track trends. Both of these are features of the two most influential studies cited in the *Influence* study (Swanson & Barlage, 2006)—the NAEP assessment and TIMMS research programs. IRA believes it has a role to play in the research and policy equation because of its intensive focus on reading and its longevity as a player in the reading policy arena. The Board of Directors of IRA is committed to having reading research influence educational policy by providing good information about questions that interest policy makers. Hence, their commitment to establishing this policy research center within the organization.

WHAT DOES THE FUTURE HOLD?

I am optimistic that with efforts such as the one described above, the efforts of a number of seasoned reading comprehension researchers, and the efforts of talented emerging researchers, reading comprehension research will continue to move forward. I expect to see the topics and researchers represented in this volume gather an increasing share of the federal funds available for education research. My expectations are based on the belief that comprehension researchers are interested in the very practical question of what works in teaching and learning reading comprehension, and that the type of research agenda supported by IES and NICHD, essentially the careful building of research programs, is exactly what we need if we are to learn about comprehension.

Another reason for optimism is that many researchers who have previously focused on more basic reading skills from the perspective of special education or cognitive science are beginning to expand their focus to follow students into the development of many of the more complex cognitive and linguistic skills (and knowledge) that are related to reading comprehension. For example, Joseph Torgesen, from the Florida Center for Reading Research at Florida State University now, as a matter of routine, includes comprehension measures in his studies, as do many of his colleagues. He has also been focusing attention on the relationship between reading fluency and reading comprehension, with a view to understanding more about the way these two dimensions of reading proficiency interact with one another (personal communication, April 26, 2007). Another interesting development is the work of Carol Connor, also at FSU and the Florida Center for Reading Research, on interactions between the level of students' reading and vocabulary skills when they enter first grade, and the type and content of instruction that is most profitable for them during first grade. What she has shown so far is that students who enter first grade with strong basic reading skills and good vocabulary profit most if more of their instructional time is spent on self-directed reading and writing activities that focus on meaning and comprehension. In contrast, students who enter first grade with less well developed basic reading skills and lower vocabulary, reliably profit most if more of their time is spent in teacher directed explicit instruction focused on more basic skills like phonemic awareness, phonics, and vocabulary. This work shows promise of helping us learn how to respond more effectively to the individual needs of students during early reading instruction, and may also help to focus more work on methods that can be used to support the growth of reading comprehension much earlier than is often the case at present.

However, reading comprehension researchers and those who prepare these researchers will have to make several adjustments if they are to be successful. First of all, collaboration must be highly valued. The funding of research programs rather than Centers or individual studies means that a single researcher, working alone is not likely to have the resources, particularly intellectual resources, that such programs require. The stress on interdisciplinary work must become a major thrust in reading comprehension research. This will only happen if successful researchers, who win grants, find ways to incorporate emerging scholars and PhD candidates in the collaborative milieu that I believe is essential to successful research programs.

The second big issue is methods training. In the past 15 to 20 years, I believe we have seen the methods requirements for reading and literacy PhD programs diminish. It simply isn't possible to conduct collaborative, mixed-methods work if researchers do not know and understand the various methodologies that exist, their strengths and weakness, the types of questions they can answer, and how to interpret results. One or two or even three methods courses are not sufficient. The idea that doctoral candidates are prepared to do research, if they have one quantitative, one qualitative, and one methods course of their choosing, is simply not viable. Good researchers must know much more about methodology when they exit their programs, they must have had many opportunities to participate and conduct research, and they must continue to develop competence in methodology as the methods advance.

This is an exciting time in reading comprehension research. We are learning more each day and getting closer to understanding what we can do to help all children learn to read.

NOTE

1. All information related to IES is based on information taken from their Web site, http://www.ed.gov/about/offices/list/ies/index.html and retreived February 21, 2007.

REFERENCES

Bauman, J. F., Hoffman, J. V., Duffy-Hester, A. M., & Ro, J. M. (2000). The first r yesterday and today: U.S. elementary reading instruction practices reported by teachers and administrators. *Reading Research Quarterly, 35,* 338–377.

Flesch, R. (1955). *Why Johnny can't read: And what you can do about it.* San Francisco: Harper & Row.

Institute of Education Sciences. (2007). Retrieved February 21, 2007, from http://www.ed.gov/about/offices/list/ies/index.html

International Reading Association. (2003). *Prepared to make a difference: Research evidence on how some of America's best college programs prepare teachers of reading.* Newark, DE: Author.

Mesmer, H. A. E. (2007). Beginning reading materials: A national survey of primary teachers reported uses and beliefs. *Journal of Literacy Research, 38,* 389–485.

Moats, L. (2007). Whole language high jinks: How to tell when "scientifically-based reading instruction" isn't. Retrieved February 21, 2007, from http://www.edweek.org/media/influence_study.pdf

National Reading Panel. (2000). *Teaching children to read: An evidence-based assessment of the scientific research literature on reading and its implications for reading instruction.* Washington, DC: National Institute of Child Health and Human Development.

Snow, C. (2002). *Reading for understanding: Toward an R&D program in reading comprehension.* Washington, DC: Rand Corporation.

Swanson, C. B., & Barlage, J. (2006). Influence: A study of the factors shaping education policy retrieved from http://www.edweek.org/media/influence_study.pdf

33 Where to from Here?
Themes, Trends, and Questions

Gerald G. Duffy

University of North Carolina at Greensboro

Susan E. Israel

Author and Literacy Consultant

with

Stephanie G. Davis, Kathryn K. Doyle, Karen W. Gavigan, Erika Swarts Gray, Angela Jones, Kathryn A. Kear, Roya Qualls, Penny Mason, Seth A. Parsons, and Baxter Williams

> If it be true that good wine needs no bush, 'tis true that a good play needs no epilogue. Yet to good wine they do use good bushes; and good plays prove the better by the help of good epilogues.
>
> *Shakespeare, As You Like It, Rosalind's Epilogue*

With apologies to Lee Shulman (2004b), from whom we borrowed the idea for this opening, it is our hope that this volume of reading comprehension research will be "proved the better" by the help of an epilogue. And to extend our borrowing further, Shulman's title, *Calm Seas, Auspicious Gales*, which he borrowed from Shakespeare's *The Tempest*, will be our theme.

Shulman, and Shakespeare before him, note that human progress requires both gales and calm—gales to challenge our thinking and calm to reassure us. If such is truly the case, then this volume of reading comprehension research—providing as it does both gales and calm—will stimulate progress. In this final chapter, we use the "calm seas" and "auspicious gales" metaphor to close an ambitious project.

A GALE SKULKING AROUND THE EDGES

Every chapter in this volume has been rooted in a complex model of comprehension—a model that takes a nuanced and contextual view of what is involved in comprehension. It is predominately a sociocultural view, seen through a lens that emphasizes students' backgrounds and experiences, acknowledges the funds of knowledge they bring to the classroom, accommodates the idea that readers put their own imprint on what is written, rejects the idea of a single, correct text meaning, and argues that multiple and conflicting interpretations can co-exist. Consequently, comprehension is seen as multifaceted and contextualized with emphasis on individual stances and situational environments.

> Our meaning making journeys may appear to follow or parallel or be inscribed by
> others, but we all have our own imprint, swagger or emerging meanings ... as we
> wander through text. (Tierney, chapter 12)

But despite the theoretical, empirical, and pedagogical shifts reported in this volume,
there has lurked behind virtually every chapter the image of an earlier view called "a
simple model." As explicitly explained by several authors, and implicitly by others, the
simple model views comprehension as a matter of decoding plus language skill, and
views instructional practice as a matter of assessing and teaching discrete skills. In
virtually every chapter, the simple model lurks nearby.

> What students do on tests of reading comprehension or narrowly conceived responses
> to short readings and recall questions do little to reveal how students comprehend
> written texts in the real world. (Goodman & Goodman, chapter 5)

The reader feels the presence of the simple model because of a prevailing concern that
current efforts to improve reading instruction are driven by policy and accountability
testing based heavily on that model. Despite the fact that reports such as the National
Reading Panel (2000) describe comprehension as complex, current reading policy
emphasizes the "what" and "how" of reading—the declarative and procedural knowledge of basic skill processes—things that can be parsed, defined simply, measured in
standardized ways, and administered efficiently. Therefore, instead of a multidimensional view, there seems to be a unidimensional view.

> ... there is seemingly a growing disconnect between the nature of reading being
> espoused with the research community and the practice of reading being demanded
> by national mandates and carried out in classrooms. (Fox & Alexander, chapter
> 10)

The point is not that the simple model can be rejected completely. For both developmental and accountability reasons, many authors imply that the "simple view" *must* lurk
on the horizon. Decoding *is* an early emphasis, and accountability often comes down
to a matter of what can be measured in cost-efficient ways. Hence, the simple model
continues to play a role, despite chapter after chapter citing complexity rather than
simplicity.

> Decoding is necessary but not sufficient for comprehension. (Paris & Hamilton,
> chapter 2)

On the whole, the volume argues that a simple model may be necessary, but is clearly
not sufficient. When thinking was driven by behaviorism and cognitive information
processing, decoding, fluency, and more linear views of comprehension prevailed. Those
days are gone because, in a word, Vygotsky happened (or more specifically, we caught
up to his much earlier work). Then Rosenblatt was rediscovered (again, belatedly). As
is reflected in chapter after chapter, the Vygotskian understanding of the social cognitive framework of learning pushed the field toward a more complex view of comprehension by emphasizing the social situations that mediate learning, the role of active
action in learning, and the impact of cultural orientations. At the same time, the Rosenblatt understanding of the transactional relationship between reader and text forced
educators to accommodate the more complex idea that meaning is not universal but,

instead, varies by reader. To further complicate things, qualitative research methodology emerged, and with it we became still more aware of both the complexity and the common understandings associated with both learning and teaching comprehension.

> The issues of reading comprehension are complex. The field cannot be seduced into simple ways of thinking because the alternative is challenging. (Hoffman, chapter 3)

As a result, we are in the somewhat awkward position of living with measures reflecting the simple view, with policy reflecting that view, and with an apparent schism between that view and research reported in this volume.

> While it is clear that federal education policy influences the funding of educational research…, it is markedly less clear how education research influences policy related to reading instruction. (Roller, chapter 32)

CALM SEAS (OR RELATIVELY CALM)

Despite this apparent conflict, however, there are several areas where the seas feel calm. For instance, there has been little disagreement about what one teaches when teaching comprehension. Chapter after chapter make frequent reference to the importance of vocabulary, to the importance of strategies, to the importance of flexible thinking, and to the importance of being in conscious control of one's comprehension processes through self-regulation and metacognitive processes.

> … successful readers exhibit higher levels of metacognitive knowledge about reading and are more skilled at evaluating and regulating their cognitive processes during reading. (Baker & Beall, chapter 17)

But this is an area of *relative* calm. For instance, while strategies continue to be a centerpiece of comprehension instruction, and have received much emphasis in this volume, there is a growing concern that we must tighten definitional distinctions when we talk about strategies, cognitive strategies, metacognitive strategies, and comprehension strategies, when we talk about self-regulating and metacognitive aspects of comprehension, and when we use other "buzz words" associated with comprehension. Similarly, there appears to be a growing understanding that instruction should not focus on one strategy at a time but, instead, should focus on a more general notion of being strategic.

> In the transition from research to practice, strategy instruction has morphed into so many things that it no longer has a shared meaning. (Dole, Nokes, & Drits, chapter 16)

Similarly, this volume has conveyed a reassuring area of calm about instruction—what we should tell teachers about how to teach comprehension. In chapter after chapter, authors have agreed that instruction counts, that comprehension can be taught, and that intentional teaching of comprehension processes pays off for learners. Within the arena of intentional teaching, further, there has been strong agreement that explicit teaching and careful scaffolding are important.

> Learning and acting are indistinct, learning being a continuous, life-long process resulting from acting in situations. (Raphael et al., chapter 21)

But this too is an area of *relative* calm. There are several areas of concern. First, even though we have research that instructional interventions improve students' comprehension, instruction for struggling readers tends to emphasize decoding and fluency but not comprehension. Second, given that research substantiates the effectiveness of explicit teaching and careful scaffolding, the temptation is to package those research findings into highly prescriptive instructional programs and require teachers to follow them. Both examples, again, bring to mind the simple model lurking nearby. But throughout this volume, authors have reported research establishing that, while comprehension instruction helps all students, there are too many variations in texts, situations, and students to script instruction and that, instead, what is required is a teacher who makes the differential and responsive judgments.

> The most powerful comprehension instruction cannot be simply sequenced, scripted, and packaged. Effective comprehension instruction will be the result of a teacher using expert understanding of what the research says to design a lesson that seems likely to be useful and successful. (Allington & McGill-Franzen, chapter 26)

One of the major reasons instruction cannot be packaged and prescribed in advance is the growing understanding that "being explicit" does not mean students are passive recipients of explanations. Throughout the volume, repeated emphasis is placed on the importance of combining explicit teaching with dialogic approaches in which teachers and students, or students and students, engage in activity reminiscent more of a conversation than of a recitation. Such research also forces us to look differently at how established instructional techniques such as scaffolding, traditionally thought of in terms of a single lesson, must often be viewed as longitudinal. That is, because understandings about comprehension are seldom developed in single sessions, scaffolding becomes a technique that stretches over time.

> ... dialogic discussion is a recursive space that shapes and is shaped by it participants. (Almasi & Garas-York, chapter 22)

Related to this, many studies of student learning of comprehension have argued for more and more attention to the role of student engagement, student motivation, student sense of personal agency, and student valuing of comprehension tasks. In short, activity, attitude, and affective forces are increasingly recognized as impacting comprehension, and increasingly are becoming a focus of comprehension research, while simultaneously there is also a growing realization that passive and disengaged students seldom learn to comprehend well. Consequently, motivation is becoming more and more a focus of research on comprehension instruction.

> If the aim is skill development or high grades and test scores, the motivational focus may reasonably center on strategies that develop skills... If, on the other hand, comprehension is defined to involve personal significance and intrinsic commitment, anchoring learning in students' values becomes central. (Miller & Faircloth, chapter 14)

But, again, we see here the lurking shadow of the simple model. What is seductive about that model is that it charges us only with the relatively uncomplicated task of teaching skills. Our work becomes much more daunting when we must also determine and develop a student's will to comprehend.

In sum, these are provocative areas but, in general, they communicate a reassuring feeling of calm.

Approaching fronts

There were, however, issues and themes running through the volume that have potential to become auspicious gales. They lurk on the horizon, implied but seldom stated.

A major one in this regard is the developmental nature of reading comprehension. Is learning to comprehend a matter of going through stages? There seems to be the implicit understanding in some chapters that comprehension skill develops in a linear manner and, reminiscent of the simple view, that we should emphasize some things early on (e.g., decoding and fluency) and other things later in the school years (e.g., higher level comprehension). Others, however, imply a multicomponent process involving a variety of abilities working together to produce comprehension. Again, we see the tension between the simple view—in which linear, ordered progression is favored—and the complex view—which emphasizes a multidimensional view. This issue could develop into a gale.

The changing role of reading in content area disciplines is another approaching front. Several chapters reflect the growing understanding that varying textual demands require teachers to tailor strategies to text types and to content disciplines, and that decisions about what strategies to teach are situational rather than static and fixed.

> ... reading comprehension is more than just a general construct—it is context dependent and influenced in part by the kind of text that one reads. Instruction in disciplinary contexts, then, should include instruction in reading in the discipline. (Shanahan, chapter 11)

A problem with assessment is closely allied with this issue. Policy makers favor a simple view because we have tests to measure simple aspects of comprehension. But large-scale, easily administered tests of comprehension, for the most part, do not lend themselves to a complex view of comprehension with its focus on conditional knowledge questions of "why" and "when," on meaning making in particular times and places, on cultural and racial influences, on expanded versions of text, and on the deepening and increasingly complex understandings of the transactional nature of comprehension. Indeed, standardized tests of comprehension must insist on only one correct answer. Measuring a multidimensional view of comprehension will require different measures. These are not currently available, so this, too, is an approaching front.

> Formal, standardized ... tests tend to meet the traditional, empirically-based standards of reliability and validity required by policy makers and administrators. However, current theories of ... reading comprehension have resulted in a fresh look at formative assessments... (Stahl, chapter 20)

Similarly, the tension between research and policy has the feeling of an approaching storm. As this volume shows, potential research questions abound. Virtually every chapter ends with questions to pursue. We need to learn how to help culturally different and language different children, how to effectively teach children to comprehend in hypertext environments, how to teach students to comprehend in various content area disciplines, how to document the ways in which reading to learn and learning to read are reciprocal, and so on. The list goes on and on. However, two problems arise again and again. First, there is tension regarding the relative "goodness" of quantitative and qualitative methodologies, the degree to which we should base decisions on nonexperimental research, and the extent to which we can use large scale research designs to study a complex model of comprehension. Second, and closely related, is the question about the degree to which current research funding favors a simple model, thereby making it difficult to become smarter about the complex form of comprehension emphasized in this volume.

> Reading comprehension strategies are invisible, and methodologies to investigate them must be designed to give us appropriate information from which we make inferences and hypotheses about strategy use and development. (Afflerbach & Cho, chapter 4)

Closely allied to the issue of needed research is the question of what we do in the absence of clear evidence of what to do. One of the issues central to the complex view of comprehension is that it *is* complex and, as such, we do not have research evidence to guide us in every way. This, too, is an approaching storm.

> Children who live outside the mainstream of American life are precious human cargo and do not have time to wait until researchers find plausible answers... (Edwards & Turner, chapter 30)

These have been areas of concern, but have not yet reached the level of a gale. However, they contain the elements, and could grow.

Auspicious gales

While the volume has reported calm seas reassuring us and approaching storms to keep an eye on, it has also challenged us with auspicious gales. Two are pervasive throughout the book: cultural forces and technological forces. The contrast with the simple model of comprehension is implicit in these, because the challenges are rooted in complexity rather than simplicity.

A major challenge in coming years is the interaction between culture and comprehension. While current policy favors teaching culturally different and language different children using a simple model, various authors in this volume have made strong cases, based primarily on qualitative research findings, for the need to accommodate cultural differences in our teaching. The concept of a "third space"—a recombination of existing cultures intertwined to form a hybrid culture where both are valued, such as blending school patterns and home patterns, is a dominant theme in this area. Our definition of "background knowledge" becomes much more complex. As diversity increases, this challenge to our thinking will continue to grow. It will no longer be possible to ignore how cultural backgrounds cause students to process instruction differently while, at the same time, it will be difficult to conduct empirical research when comprehension is so heavily influenced by culture.

> Teachers need to find ways to bring students' cultural practices into the classroom and use these resources to connect with traditional subject matter. (Fairbanks et al., chapter 28)

A second and fast approaching auspicious gale is centered on the rapidly changing conception of text. This has been particularly evident in discussions of "new literacies" or "digital literacies" associated with technology, the Internet, hypertext, wikis, blogs, and associated advances emerging almost daily, but has also been evident in our growing understanding of how text is thought of differently in different disciplines. These understandings are driving us to consider alternative and sometimes uncertain ideas about how to develop comprehension in young people. The consensus is that specialized subject matter and new literacies require more sophisticated comprehension, that low-level reading processes will not suffice, and that higher-level processes involving inter-page, inter-site, and inter-textual skills will be required. This issue has a particularly overwhelming feel to it. While there is agreement that technology and growing understandings of textual differences have a potential to spur motivation to read, there is nonetheless a feeling that we are behind the curve. Technical breakthroughs are escalating and digital communication is pervasive, but we are still trying to figure out how to teach a process that many in the younger generation understand much better than do teachers.

> ... what these technologies may offer is a way to make reading instruction more engaging and compelling for students. (Kamil & Chou, chapter 13)

In sum, the volume has presented gales to challenge our thinking about comprehension and comprehension instruction. As with all aspects of this volume, the contrast to the simple model is startling.

SO WHAT DOES IT ALL PORTEND?

On the whole, this volume has communicated a sense of impending change. Sometimes these differences have a feeling of a gale, at other times one gets the feeling of storms fading out.

The lurking shadow of the simple model seems to be a storm fading out. The prevailing understanding is that a more complex, nuanced view of comprehension will ultimately dominate. Throughout the volume, research points to the complexity of how individuals comprehend and to the complexity associated with effectively teaching students to comprehend. While the simple view continues to skulk around, the message seems to be that its days are numbered.

But there seems to be a gale brewing regarding which of several theoretical positions will replace it. While all the theories discussed herein emphasize complexity in one way or another, all force us in different directions. Some are based in psychological perspectives, others push us toward cognitive processing, others toward authentic occasions for literacy, others toward sociocultural perspectives, others toward transactional perspectives, and still others toward biological explanations.

> ... theories serve as lenses drawing our attention to what to see. But if theories can direct us to what is important, they can also serve as a set of blinders leading us to ignore what would otherwise be important. (Gavelek & Bresnahan, chapter 7)

One gets the sense of impending change. Because we are learning so much about comprehension so quickly, there is also a sense that gaps exist. Consequently, yet another gale may be in the making, one having potential implications for both how we think about comprehension and how we think about studying comprehension. The root of the feeling lies with increased understanding of the many ways in which comprehension is mediated. Throughout the volume, there is the growing feeling—albeit, seldom explicitly stated—that seismic changes are coming. Changes in text, in technology, in the ways students are impacted by context, in the way institutions influence things, in the ways in which individuals are positioned within multiple cultural worlds, and in the roles played by issues of power and privilege in comprehension all point to change, and bring into question certain long-accepted notions about comprehension and comprehension instruction. It may become impossible, for instance, to confine comprehension to consistent and coherent models, or to think of comprehension in terms of stages of development, or to separate micro-level issues of in-classroom instruction from macro-level issues of institutions.

> ... we are reminded that students are not just consumers of text and they are not only positioned by texts ... [they] have their own perspectives, formulate principled opinions, and create new texts... (Damico, Campano, & Harste, chapter 8)

IN CONCLUSION

In sum, when reading chapters in this volume one cannot avoid a feeling that there are unreconciled issues and impending gales. But, to return to Shulman (2004a) once again, this is normal: "In disciplined inquiry in education, there is often lack of consensus about the ground, the starting points, for chains of reasoning" (p. 279).

Such is certainly the case in this volume. There *are* gales that challenge our thinking and push our understanding forward. But at the same time, comprehension research is, for all practical purposes, less than 50 years old. Given its youth, there is a significant foundation of agreed-upon knowledge.

Hopefully, then, this volume stimulates you with its gales, calms you with its unity, and promotes your understanding. Because, to return to Shulman (2004a) one last time, it is understanding that moves the field ahead:

> ... scholarship in all its forms becomes consequential only as it is understood by others — others who are engaged in related processes of discovery, invention, and investigation — and thus it becomes consequential as it stimulates, builds upon, critiques, or otherwise contributes to any community of scholars who depend on one another's discoveries, critical reviews, and inventive applications to move the work of the field ahead. (p. 303)

REFERENCES

Shulman, L. (2004). Disciplines of inquiry in education. In S. Wilson (Ed.), *The wisdom of practice: Essays on teaching, learning, and learning to teach* (pp. 273–308). San Francisco: Jossey-Bass.

Shulman, L. (2004). Calm Seas, Auspicious Gales. In S. Wilson (Ed.), *The wisdom of practice: Essays on teaching, learning, and learning to teach* (pp. 433–452). San Francisco: Jossey-Bass.

Index

eBooks – at www.eBookstore.tandf.co.uk

A library at your fingertips!

eBooks are electronic versions of printed books. You can store them on your PC/laptop or browse them online.

They have advantages for anyone needing rapid access to a wide variety of published, copyright information.

eBooks can help your research by enabling you to bookmark chapters, annotate text and use instant searches to find specific words or phrases. Several eBook files would fit on even a small laptop or PDA.

NEW: Save money by eSubscribing: cheap, online access to any eBook for as long as you need it.

Annual subscription packages

We now offer special low-cost bulk subscriptions to packages of eBooks in certain subject areas. These are available to libraries or to individuals.

For more information please contact webmaster.ebooks@tandf.co.uk

We're continually developing the eBook concept, so keep up to date by visiting the website.

www.eBookstore.tandf.co.uk